JN424121

The Korean Labor Law Bible

I would like to dedicate this book to my loving wife, Kim Jeongsook, who has quietly supported me throughout the long and sometimes arduous process of writing this new edition.

어려운 시절 묵묵히 남편을 믿고 내조하였던 사랑하는 아내(김정숙)에게 이 책을 바칩니다.

노동법 바이블

The Korean Labor Law Bible

초 판 발 행 | 2005년 2월 15일
개정7판 발행 | 2025년 3월 5일

지 은 이 | 정 봉 수
펴 낸 이 | 김 남 진

펴 낸 곳 | 중앙경제
디 자 인 | 이지훈, 최가영
마 케 팅 | 신석재, 김성울, 이소영, 윤지희, 김선혜
경 영 지 원 | 이상훈, 박세라, 조용환

주 소 | 서울시 중구 다산로 11길 19(신당동) 백석빌딩 신관 4층
전 화 | 02-2231-7293
팩 스 | 02-2235-5344
홈 페 이 지 | www.elabor.co.kr
출 판 등 록 | 80. 6. 21 제 2-66호

I S B N | 978-89-7017-569-0 (13320)
정 가 | 95,000원

: 개정증보 7판 :

ELABOR
HR CONTENT CREATOR

The Korean Labor Law Bible

Bongsoo Jung
Labor Attorney / Ph.D. in Law
법학박사/공인노무사 **정 봉 수**

<Bilingual in English and Korean>

노동법 바이블

중앙경제

Preface to the 7th edition

Climate change, digitalization, ultra-low birth rates and super-aging, polarization and inequality, the dual structure of the labor market, and job reductions have put the sustainability of the nation and society at risk. Amid these changes, I believe that labor law will provide universal standards for conflict resolution and the path toward a sustainable society.

Since publication of *The Korean Labor Law Bible* in January 2005, six more editions have been published: the 2nd Edition in September 2006, the 3rd Edition in March 2009, the 4th Edition in May 2011, the 5th Edition in June 2016 and the 6th Edition in January 2021. Now, three years later, this is the 7th and most expansive edition yet. As this and past editions have been made possible by my regular readers who have bought this book, I would like to express appreciation first to my customers.

I have been giving English lectures on labor law based on the editions of this book for more than 18 years, and for the last 18 years, have also contributed bilingual articles on labor issues to the monthly magazine, Labor Law . I hold an MA from Korea University Graduate School of Labor Studies and the PhD degree on Labor Law at the Graduate School of Ajoo University. This 7th Edition has been improved by including more practical cases and examples from my own work as a labor attorney. Also in the expansion are excerpts from my labor law lectures, previous formal studies of labor law, and bilingual article contributions.

The improvements in this 7th Edition can be seen in both content and structure. Firstly, the content has been updated to include the most recently established and revised labor laws, as well as the Supreme Court en banc rulings on ordinary wages, as of January 19, 2025. Secondly, I have inserted into each section labor issues from articles that I have contributed to the monthly magazine Labor Law. Thirdly, in the Korean version, I have attempted to update, supplement, and add contents on the advice of my academic advisor, professor Seung-gil Lee, chairman of the Korean Society of Labor Law, and to whom I am most grateful. Thanks also, Mr. Gavin C. Farrell, Professor in the Department of English Linguistics of Hankuk University of Foreign Studies, who reviewed the contents as an English language advisor. This edition has been reconstructed based upon the author's extended experience and consequently deeper knowledge, again grateful for my advisors' full support and direction.

Finally, I would like to thank those who have assisted me in revising and editing the 7th Edition. I would like to extend my special thanks specifically to Taeyoon Kim and Gayoung Choi of Jungang Publishing, Advisor Haesun Kim, Labor Attorneys Jihyun Ahn, Euikeun Park, Kemmy Kim, Daejoon Shin, Moonbae Park, and my longtime friend and proofreading editor, Dave Crofton. Without these people, this upgraded 7th Edition of the Korean Labor Law Bible would not have been possible.

January 20, 2025

Bongsoo Jung, Author

제7판을 내면서

기후 변화, 디지털화, 초저출산·초고령화의 변화, 양극화·불평등, 노동시장의 이중구조화, 일자리 감소 등에 따라 국가와 사회의 지속가능성이 위기에 직면해 있다. 이러한 변화 속에서 노동법이 갈등해결과 지속가능한 사회로 가기위한 보편적인 기준을 제공해줄 것이라 믿는다.

본서 저자는 '한국노동법 영문해설'을 2005년 1월에 최초 출간한 이래 2006년 9월개정판, 2009년 3월 3판, 2011년 5월 4판, 2016년 6월 5판, 2021년 1월 6판, 2025년 1월에 드디어 7판을 출간하게 되었다. 제6판이 나온 후 3년만이다. 꾸준히 이 책을 찾고 있는 독자들의 성원에 힘입어 계속적인 출간이 가능하였기에 무한한 감사의 인사를 드린다. 저자는 본서를 바탕으로 지난 18년 동안 영어로 노동법 강의를 진행해 오고 있으며, 18년 이상 월간지 '노동법률'에 노동 사례를 기고해 왔다. 또한 그 동안 고려대 노동대학원에서 노동법으로 석사학위를 취득했고, 아주대학교 법과대학원에서 노동법 전공으로 박사학위를 취득했다.

본서 7판은 내용면이나 구성면에서 좀 더 풍성해 졌고, 독자가 보다 쉽게 이 책에 접근할 수 있도록 세련된 편집 방식으로 다가가고자 노력하였다. 특히 독자가 7판을 눈여겨 살펴 볼 점들은 다음과 같다.

첫째, 2025년 1월을 기준으로 개정 또는 신설된 노동 관련법, 그리고 통상임금에 대한 대법원 합의체 반결 내용을 모두 반영하였다. 둘째, 저자가 월간 '노동법률'에 기고하였던 노동법 관련 사례나 해설들을 본서의 각 장에 배치하여 내용을 보다 충실하게 다듬었다. 셋째, 국문내용에서 아주대학교 법학 전문대학원 노동법 교수님이자 한국노동법학회 회장님이신 이승길 교수님의 감수를 통해 많은 부분이 수정, 보완, 추가 되었다. 또한 영문부분에서도 한국외국어대학교 영어학과 Gavin C. Farrell 교수님이 영어문장을 좀 더 영어 사용자에게 친숙할 수 있도록 철저한 감수를 해주셨다. 따라서 이번 7판은 저자의 폭넓은 실무 경험과 학계의 외부 전문가의 도움을 통해 훨씬 세련되고 전문화된 서적으로 재창조 되었다고 본다.

본서 출간에 도움을 주신 중앙경제사의 김태윤상무님, 최가영 대리님, 강남노무법인의 김해선 고문님, 안지현, 박의근, 김양경, 신대준, 박문배 노무사님, 끝으로 나의 오랜 친구이자 영문교정을 맡고 있는 Dave Crofton 님께 고개 숙여 감사를 드린다. 이러한 분들이 있어 본서의 7판 출간이 가능하였다고 생각한다.

2025년 1월 20일

저자 **정 봉 수**

Part I Introduction

Part Ⅱ Individual Labor Law

목 차

Part I 서 론

Part Ⅱ 개별적 근로관계법

Part Ⅳ Additional Sections

PartⅣ 노동법의 그 밖의 부문

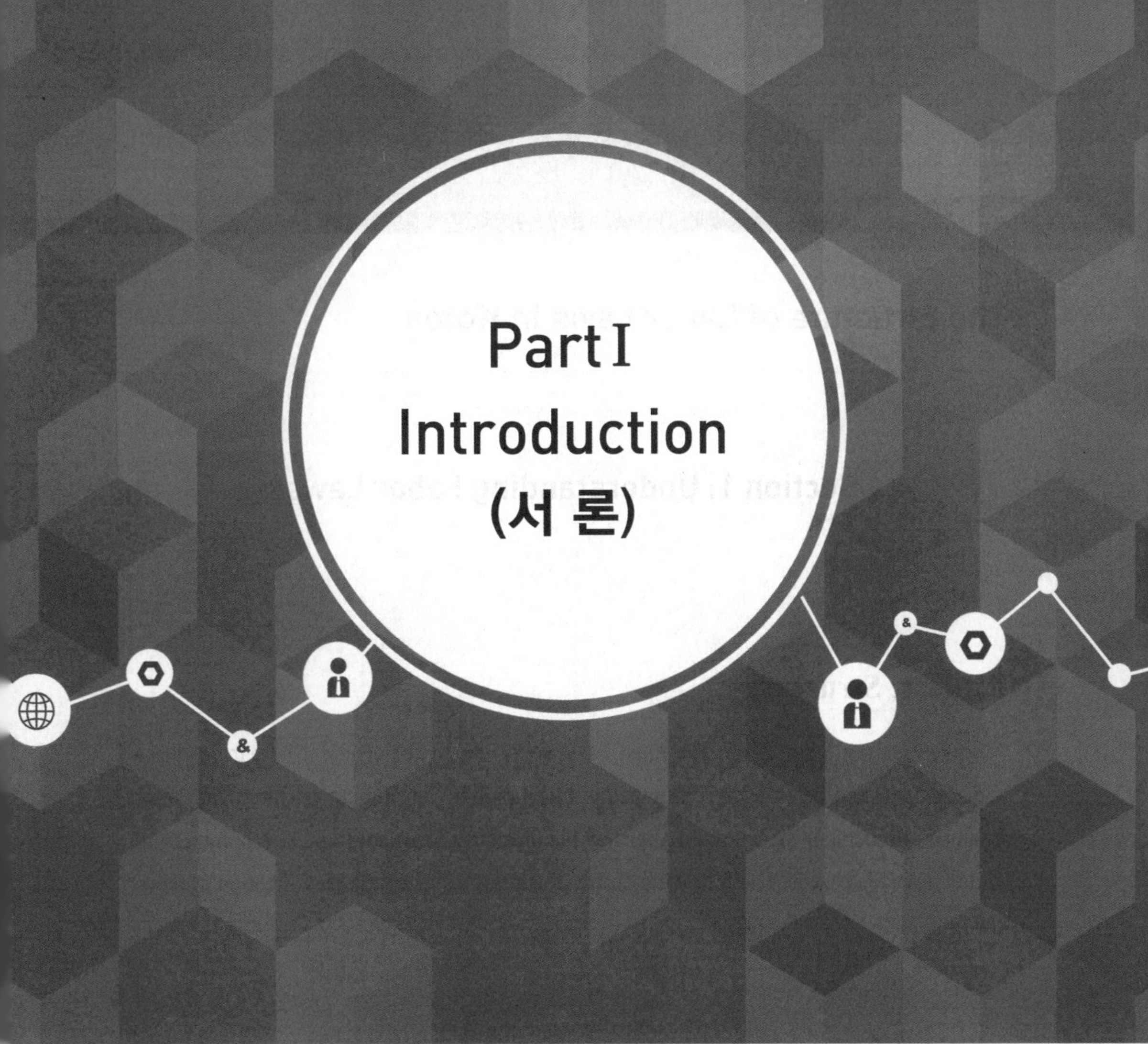

Part I Introduction (서 론)

Chapter 1. The Structure of Labor Laws in Korea

Chapter 1

The Structure of Labor Laws in Korea

Section 1: Understanding Labor Laws

I. Basic Structure

Understanding labor law is the most basic requirement for efficient human resource management, and it is on their knowledge of labor law that human resource and labor managers implement their tasks. Labor law is constantly being revised, so it is important to stay up-to-date on it. The following figure illustrates a systematic classification of labor law in Korea.

The Constitution of the ROK
Article 10 (Pursuit of Happiness, Human Dignity)

<Individual Employment Laws>	Working condition Article 32 of the Constitution	Labor Rights Article 33 of the Constitution	<Collective Labor Relations Laws>
- Equal Employment Act - Minimum Wage Act - Wage Claim Guarantee Act - Industrial Safety and Health Act - Industrial Accident Compensation Insurance Act - Dispatched Workers Act - Employment Insurance Act - Employment Security Act - Vocational Training Promotion Act - Disabled Employment Act - Seamen Act-Foreign Workers' Employment Act	Labor Standards Act Rules of Employment Labor Contract	Labor Union and Labor Relations Act Collective Agreement	- Labor Relations Commission Act - Labor-Management Council Act - Labor Union Act for Teachers - Labor Union Act for Public Employees - Public Service Men's Council Act- Tripartite Commission Act.

Additional Translation: Civil law

Punishment for Off Limit: Criminal Law

Chapter 1

한국 노동법의 체계

제1절 노동법의 이해

Ⅰ. 기본 구조

기업체에서 인사노무관리 실무를 원만히 수행하기 위해서 노동법 지식은 기본이다. 인사노무 담당자들은 노동법 지식을 바탕으로 여러 가지 인사노무관리 기법을 접목하여 인사노무관리를 수행하게 된다. 그런데 노동법에는 여러 가지 법률이 있고 법 자체도 자주 개정되고 있어 늘 주의를 요하는데 우선 그 법률들을 체계적으로 분류하여 정리해 보면 다음 도표와 같다.

헌 법
제10조-인간의 존엄성, 행복추구권

〈개별적노동법〉	헌법 제32조 근로조건	헌법 제33소 노동3권	〈집단적노동법〉
- 남녀고용평등법 - 최저임금법 - 임금채권보장법 - 산업안전보건법 - 산업재해보상보험법 - 파견법 - 고용보험법 - 직업안정법 - 근로자직업훈련촉진법 - 장애인고용촉진법 - 사내근로복지기금법 - 선원법 - 외국인근로자 노동법	근로기준법 취업규칙 근로계약	노동조합 및 노동관계조정법 단체협약	- 노동위원회법 - 근로자참여및협력증진에관한법률 - 교원의노동조합설립및운영에관한법률 - 공무원의노동조합설립및 운영에관한법률 - 공무원직장협의회설립및운영에관한법률 - 경제사회발전 노사정위원회법 등.

보충 해석 원리: 민법

한계 일탈 제재: 형법

Ⅱ. Categories of Labor Law

1. Individual labor relations laws

Individual labor relations laws define the relationship between individual employees and their employers. In other words, they provide legal criteria pertaining to a contract of employment between an employer and his/her employee, the details of the employment relationship, and the procedural requirements for modifying or terminating the employment relationship, thus protecting working conditions for individual employees.

2. Collective industrial relations laws

These laws govern labor relations between worker organizations, such as labor unions and employee representatives, and employers. They are intended to establish an autonomous problem-solving practice(labor-management autonomy) by guaranteeing the right to organize for all workers, particularly those who are underprivileged in social and economic terms, as compared to their employers, so that the former may be on an equal footing with the latter.

Ⅲ. Scope of Labor Law Application

Labor Standards Act		Companies with 5 employees or more	- Selected provisions apply to companies with 4 employees or fewer - The obligation to set the rules of employment applies to companies with10 employees or more
Industrial Safety and Health Act	General provision	All companies	- Companies in certain sectors and those with 4 employees or fewer are subject only to selected provisions.
	Appointment of personnel in charge of safety and health management	Companies with 100 employees or more	- In certain sectors, this provision applies only to companies with 50 employees or more.
	Appointment of a safety and health supervisor	Companies with 50 employees or more	- Certain sectors are exempted from this obligation
	Industrial safety and health committee	Companies with 100 employees or more	- In certain sectors, this provision applies only to companies with 50 employees or more.
Serious Accident Punishment Act		Companies with 5 employees or more	If a serious accident occurs when the employer has not taken safety measures, the employer will be punished.

Ⅱ. 노동법의 구성

1. 개별적 노동법

개별적 노동법은 근로자 개인과 사용자 간의 근로관계를 규율한다. 즉, 개별적 근로관계법은 사용자와 근로자 개인 간의 근로계약 체결, 근로관계의 체결, 근로관계의 내용 및 변경, 종료절차 등에 일정한 법적기준을 제시함으로써 근로자의 근로조건을 보호하는 것을 목적으로 한다.

2. 집단적 노동법

집단적 노동법은 노동조합 또는 근로자대표 등의 근로자집단과 사용자 간의 노사관계를 규율하는 법이다. 집단적 노동법은 사용자보다 경제, 사회적으로 열등한 지위에 있는 근로자들의 단결을 보장하여 사용자와 실질적으로 대등한 관계를 유지할 수 있도록 함으로써 노사 간의 자율적인 문제해결을 실현하는 것을 목적으로 하는 법이다.

Ⅲ. 노동법상의 적용범위

근로기순법		5인 이상 (제11조①)	– 5인 미만 사업자에도 일부 적용(제11조②) – 취업규칙은 10인 이상 작성의무(제93조)
산업안전보건법	일 반	전사업장 (제3조①)	– 일부 업종과 5인 미만 사업장은 일부조항만 적용
	안전보건관리 책임자선임	100인 이상 (제13조)	– 일부업종은 50인 이상
	안전·보건관리 등의 선임	50인 이상 (제14조, 16조)	– 일부업종은 제외
	산업안전보건위원회	100인 이상 (제19조①)	– 일부업종은 50인 이상
중대재해처벌법		5인 이상	사업주가 안전조치 하지 않은 상태에서 중대재해 발생 시 사업주 처벌함.

Minimum wage Act	All companies	
Equal Employment Act	All companies	- Companies with 4 employees or fewer are excluded.
Industrial Accident Compensation Insurance Act	All Companies	- Companies in certain sectors (including companies in agriculture, forestry and fishery with 4 employees or fewer) are excluded.
Act concerning the Promotion of Worker Participation and Cooperation	Companies with 30 employees or more	- All employers with the right to determine working conditions shall establish a labor-management council, whether there exists a labor union or not.
Trade Union and Labor Relations Adjustment Act	All Companies	
Act on Employment Promotion and Vocational Rehabilitation for the Disabled	Companies with 50 employees or more	- Persons with disabilities shall make up 2% or more of total permanent employees. - Employers who fail to meet the quota shall pay a levy, while those who exceed the 2% shall be granted a monetary reward. ※ Companies with fewer than 100 employees are exempted from the levy for not meeting the required quota.
Employment Insurance Act	All Companies	- Companies in certain sectors (including companies in agriculture, forestry and fishery with 4 employees or fewer) are excluded.

Ⅳ. The Sources of Labor Law and Order of Priority

1. Types of labor laws

The sources for labor laws are reference rules that judges use in court as the criteria for judgment in disputes related to labor law. These sources are: ① the Constitution, ② related labor laws, ③ common law, ④ self-governing rules, and ⑤ international labor law.

2. Conflicts in the sources of laws and their effects

(1) Principle of priority on higher laws

Higher laws are preferred to lower laws(e.g. the Constitution is higher than the Labor Standards Act).

(2) Principle of priority on special laws

Special laws are preferred to general laws(e.g. Labor Standards Act > Civil Law).

최저임금법	전사업장 (제3조)	
남녀고용평등법	전사업장 (제3조)	- 5인 미만 사업장에는 일부조항 적용제외
산업재해보상보험법	전사업장 (제6조)	- 5인 미만 농·임·어업 등 일부업종은 제외
근로자참여 및 협력증진에 관한 법률	30인 이상 (제4조)	- 노동조합 유무에 관계없이 근로조건의 결정권이 있는 30인 이상 모든 사업 또는사업장은 노사협의회 설치
노동조합 및 노동관계조정법	전사업장 (제5조)	
장애인고용촉진 및 직업재활법	50인 이상 (제28조)	- 상시근로자의 2% 이상을 장애인으로 고용 - 미고용시 부담금 납부, 초과고용시 장려금 ※100인 미만 사업장 부담금은 면제
고용보험법	전사업장 (제8조)	- 5인 미만 농·임·어업등 일부업종은 제외

Ⅳ. 노동법의 법원과 우선순위

1. 노동법의 법원

노동법의 법원이란 노동법과 관련된 분쟁에 있어 법관이 재판에서 판단기준으로 사용하는 규범이다. 노동법의 법원에는 ① 헌법, ② 노동관계법령, ③ 노동관습법, ④ 자율적 자치규범, ⑤ 국제노동법규가 있다.

2. 노동법의 우선순위

(1) 상위법 우선의 원칙

상위법이 하위법에 우선한다. 예) 헌법 〉 근로기준법

(2) 특별법 우선의 원칙

같은 순위의 법원 간에는 일반법보다 특별법이 먼저 적용된다. 예) 근로기준법 〉 민법

(3) Principle of priority on most recent laws

When two laws are applicable to the same situation, the law that has been most recently revised is preferred.

(4) Principle of priority on better conditions

Labor Laws promoting better working conditions are preferred over the 'principle of priority on higher laws.'

Ⅴ. The Principle of Priority on Favorable Conditions and Applciations

1. Principle

Recently, court rulings have emerged that have overturned existing practices, causing confusion in the workplace. Even if changing the rules of employment disadvantageously proceeds legally and with the consent of the majority of workers or consent of the union representing the majority, the labor contract with more favorable conditions continues to apply to workers who do not agree. In the past, when employers change rules of employment in a way that lowered working conditions to overcome internal and external difficulties, as long as they have gone through the procedures required to change the rules disadvantageously, the new rules apply to all workers in the entire company even if there are some opposed.[1)] However, recent Supreme Court rulings have overturned this practice by ruling that a labor contract with more favorable terms for even a small number of workers who disagree with changes to the rules of employment continues to apply. The background to these precedents is the principle that workers and employers must decide working conditions freely and on equal terms (Article 4 of the Labor Standards Act, or LSA), and when there is disagreement regarding the new rules and labor contracts, the labor contract with the more favorable conditions takes priority (Article 97 of the LSA).

1) Kim, Hyung-Bae, "Changing Employment Rules Disadvantageously and Advantageous Contents of Labor Contracts", 「Labor Law Forum」(29) Labor Law Theory Practical Society, Feb. 2020, P. 5; Park, Jong-hee, "Relationship between the Principle of Priority on Favorable Conditions between Employment Rules and Labor Contracts", 「Anam Law」 No. 56, Anam Law Society, 2018, p. 253.

(3) 신법 우선의 원칙

어떤 동위의 규정(법원)이 다른 동위의 규정 다음에 성립되어 두 개의 규정이 서로 충돌하면 나중에 성립한 규정이 우선한다.

(4) 유리조건 우선의 원칙

상위법 우선의 원칙에도 불구하고 그 내용이 근로자에게 유리한 경우에는 상위법원에 우선하여 하위법원이 적용된다.

V. 유리한 조건 우선의 원칙과 적용

1. 원 칙

최근 법원의 판결이 기존과 달라 실무에서 혼선을 주고 있다. 예를 들자면, 취업규칙의 불이익 변경 조항이 근로자의 과반수 동의나 과반수를 대표하는 노동조합의 동의를 얻어 적법하게 진행된 경우에도 이에 동의하지 않는 근로자는 계속해서 유리한 조건의 근로계약이 적용된다는 판결이다. 기존에는 사용자가 기업 대내외적으로 경영상 어려움을 극복하기 위해 취업규칙에 규정된 기존의 근로조건을 적법한 절차를 거쳐 저하시킬 경우에는 비록 소수의 반대자가 있다 하더라도 회사 전체에 적용되는 취업규칙이 근로자 모두에게 적용된다고 판단하였다.[1] 그러나, 최근에는 취업규칙 불이익 변경에 동의하지 않은 소수의 근로자들의 근로계약에 유리한 조건을 가진 조항이 있다면 그 조항이 적용된다는 판결을 하고 있다. 이러한 판례의 근거는 근로조건은 근로자와 사용자가 동등한 지위에서 자유롭게 결정하여야 하고(근기법 제4조), 취업규칙과 근로계약상 이견이 있을 때에는 근로계약의 유리한 조건이 우선적으로 적용된다는 기준이다(근기법 제97조).

---

1) 김형배, "취업규칙의불이익 변경과 근로계약의 유리한 규정", 「노동법포럼」(29) 노동법이론실무학회, 2020.2. 5면; 박종희, "취업규칙과 근로계약간의 유리한 조건 우선의 원칙과 근로조건의 집단적 결정법리와의 관계", 「안암법학」 제56호, 안암법학회, 2018, 253면.

2. Relations with labor contracts

(1) Labor contracts that are disadvantageous when compared to the Labor Standards Act

Parts of labor contracts that set working conditions below the standards set by the Labor Standards Act are null and void. The invalidated sections are to comply with the Labor Standards Act (Article 15 of the LSA). The labor contract outlines working conditions freely determined by the worker and the employer, but if such working conditions do not meet the mandatory regulations set forth in the Labor Standards Act, they will be invalidated, and that section of the labor contract will be changed to comply with the Labor Standards Act. Therefore, the working conditions specified in a labor contract should be the same or better than those outlined in the Labor Standards Act.

(2) Labor contracts that are disadvantageous when compared to the collective agreement

Any part of a labor contract that violates the working conditions and standards for treatment of workers stipulated in the collective agreement shall be invalid. The invalidated part(s) shall comply with the standards set by the collective agreement (Article 33 of the Trade Union Act: TUA). This regulation describes the normative effect of collective agreements, and explains that they have a compulsory and supplementary effect on the content of contracts. The compulsory effect is manifested by invalidating any part of a labor contract that violates the standards for working conditions and other treatment prescribed in the collective agreement. The supplementary effect is manifested by the fact that if there are no relevant provisions in the labor contract for handling a specific issue, the standards set in the collective agreement apply.[2)] If a labor contract is more favorable than a collective agreement, the question arises as to whether the more favorable section(s) of the labor contract will apply in accordance with the principle of preferential conditions. This section has a normative effect because the working conditions specified in the collective agreement are the product of the determination of working conditions concluded on an equal basis by labor and management. Therefore, within the scope of the general binding force of collective bargaining, the favorable conditions specified in the labor contract are excluded and

2) Labor Law Practical Research Society, 「Annotation of the Labor Standards Act (1)」, Park Youngsa, 2020, p. 391.

2. 근로계약과의 관계

(1) 법령보다 유리한 근로계약

근로기준법에서 정하는 기준에 미치지 못하는 근로조건을 정한 근로계약은 그 부분에 한하여 무효로 본다. 이 경우 무효로 된 부분은 근로기준법에 정한 기준에 따른다(근기법 제15조). 근로계약은 근로자와 사용자가 자유롭게 결정하는 근로조건이지만, 그러한 근로조건이 근로기준법에서 정한 규정에 미치지 못하는 경우에는 그 부분은 무효가 되고, 무효가 된 부분은 근로기준법에 정해진 기준을 따른다. 이 조항은 근로계약의 내용이 근로기준법에 정해진 근로조건을 위반한 경우, 그 내용은 무효가 되고 근로기준법의 기준이 근로계약의 내용이 된다는 것이다. 따라서 근로계약에서 정하는 근로조건은 근로기준법과 동일하거나 더 나은 조건이어야만 한다.

(2) 단체협약보다 유리한 근로계약

단체협약에서 정한 근로조건 기타 근로자 대우에 관한 기준에 위배되는 근로계약의 부분은 무효로 본다. 이 경우 무효로 된 부분은 단체협약에서 정한 기준에 의한다(노조법 제33조). 이 규정은 단체협약의 규범적 효력을 기술하고 있으며, 이는 강행적 효력과 보충적 효력을 동시에 가지고 있음을 말한다. 강행적 효력은 단체협약에서 정한 근로조건 기타 대우에 관한 기준을 위반하는 근로계약 부분을 무효로 하는 효력이다. 보충적 효력은 단체협약의 강행적 효력이 적용됨으로써 근로계약이 무효가 된 부분이 있거나 근로계약에 아무런 관련 규정이 없는 경우 단체협약에서 정한 기준이 적용된다.[2] 그러면, 단체협약보다 유리한 근로계약의 기준이 있는 경우에는 어떻게 적용될 것인가의 문제가 있다. 이 부분은 단체협약에 정해진 근로조건은 노사가 대등한 입장에서 체결한 근로조건에 대한 결정의 산물이므로 규범적 효력을 가진다. 따라서 단체교섭의 일반적 효력이 미치는 범위 내에서는 근로계약에서 정한 유리한 조건이 배제되고

---

2) 노동법실무연구회, 「근로기준법 주해(I)」, 박영사, 2020, 391면.

the contents of the collective agreement apply.[3)]

(3) Labor contracts that are more favorable than the rules of employment

Parts of labor contracts that set working conditions below the standards set by the rules of employment are invalid. Invalidated sections shall be changed so they comply with the rules of employment (Article 97 of the LSA). The labor contract should be maintained but with the same or more favorable conditions as the rules of employment. This also applies in the reverse situation. Therefore, if the rules of employment and the labor contract differ in terms of working conditions, the advantageous terms of the labor contract will apply first.[4)] There are some related court rulings: (1) Even if the revised rules of employment no longer require that a full-time allowance be paid, which had been required under the labor contract, for individual workers who do not agree to the change, the advantageous parts of the labor contract take precedence over the revised rules of employment.[5)] (2) In a case where a wage peak system was introduced as part of rules of employment that were revised with collective consent but after specifying the annual salary in an individual labor contract with a particular worker, the existing individual labor contract takes precedence over the rules of employment, despite the latter being revised with collective consent.[6)] (3) Even if the rules of employment are changed through legitimate procedures, they do not take precedence over existing advantageous employment contracts unless special circumstances dictate otherwise, such as the employee agreeing to the relevant change in the rules of employment.[7)]

Ⅵ. Labor Laws in Relation to Other Laws

1. In relation to Civil Law (Additional Translation)

Labor laws originating from the principles of civil law are generally applied under the

---

3) Lim, Jong-ryul, 「Labor Law」, Parkyoungsa, 2020, p. 162; Labor Law Practical Research Society, 「Annotation of the Labor Standards Act (1)」, Parkyoungsa, 2020, p. 393; Supreme Court ruling on Dec. 27, 2002, 2002Du9063.

4) Lim, Jong-ryul, 「Labor Law」, Parkyoungsa, 2020, p. 17.

5) Ulsan District Court ruling on June 14, 2017, 2016 Gahap 23102; Appellate Court ruling on Aug. 30, 2017, 2017 Na 53715; Supreme Court ruling on Dec. 13, 2017.

6) Supreme Court ruling on Nov. 14, 2019, 2018 Da 200709.

7) Supreme Court ruling on Apr. 9, 2020, 2019 Da 297083.

단체협약의 기준이 적용된다.[3)]

(3) 취업규칙보다 유리한 근로계약

취업규칙에서 정한 기준에 미달하는 근로조건을 정한 근로계약은 그 부분에 관하여 무효로 한다. 이 경우 무효로 되는 부분은 취업규칙에 정한 기준에 따른다(근기법 제97조). 그러므로, 근로계약의 기준은 취업규칙과 같거나 더 유리한 조건을 유지해야 한다고 해석된다. 따라서 이를 반대로 해석하면, 취업규칙과 근로계약의 근로조건이 서로 상이할 때는 근로계약의 유리한 조건이 우선 적용된다고 할 수 있다.[4)] 관련 판례로 (1) 근로계약에 의해 그동안 지급되었던 만근수당을 취업규칙을 통해 더 이상 지급되지 않도록 유효하게 변경하였다고 하더라도 그에 동의하지 않은 개별 근로자의 경우 취업규칙보다 유리한 근로계약이 우선하여 적용된다.[5)] (2) 근로자와 개별 근로계약에서 연봉을 특정한후 집단적 동의로 유효하게 변경된 취업규칙으로 임금피크제를 도입하면서 연봉을 대폭 삭감한 경우 기존의 개별 근로계약이 집단적 동의로 유효하게 변경된 취업규칙보다 우선하여 적용된다.[6)] (3) 취업규칙이 적법한 절차를 거쳐 변경되었다고 하더라도 해당 근로자가 그 취업규칙의 변경에 동의하는 등 특별한 행위가 존재하지 않는 한 취업규칙이 아닌 기존의 유리한 근로계약이 우선 적용된다.[7)]

Ⅵ. 다른 법률과의 관계

1. 민법과의 관계(보충 해석 원리)

노동법은 민법의 원리에 바탕을 두고 파생한 민법의 특별법으로서의 위치를

3) 임종률, 「노동법」 18판, 박영사, 2020, 162면; 노동법실무연구회, 「근로기준법 주해(I)」, 박영사, 2020, 393면; 대법원 2002.12.27, 2002두9063.

4) 임종률, 「노동법」, 18판, 박영사, 2020, 17면

5) 울산지법 2017.6.14, 2016가합23102; 항소심 부산고법 2017.8.30, 2017나53715; 상고심 대법원 2017.12.13, 자 2017다387(심리불속행 기각 판결임)

6) 대법원 2019.11.14, 2018다200709.

7) 대법원 2020.4.9, 2019다297083.

Civil Law . Though civil law is based upon principles such as the absolute principle of ownership, the principle of freedom to contract, and the principle of self-responsibility in accidents, this has only induced greater social inequality between people, and labor laws have been constituted to reform this inequality. Accordingly, principles under Civil Law have been applied to working conditions unregulated by labor law. These include the principle of good faith and sincerity and the principle of preventing the abuse of rights.

The employment section of the Civil Act has only 9 provisions in total, but is considered general law in labor law. In our capitalist economic system, as the Civil Act is based on the principle of freedom of contract, one party to the contract can freely terminate the contract on the premise of damages or a failure to meet certain requirements. However, if employment contracts allow employers, who are in a socially and economically superior position to employees in the labor contract relationship, to unilaterally dismiss employees, those employees whose ability to maintain a livelihood is based on earnings from employment are threatened with unemployment at any time, which places them in an unequal and oppressive relationship[8)]The Labor Standards Act was enacted under the Constitution to reduce the unequal nature of these relationships and to guarantee the basic right to human dignity and to pursue happiness.[9)]

2. In relation to criminal caw (Punishment for Off-limit)

Labor laws are regulations that must be strictly adhered to since punishment will result if violated. Given that working conditions regulated under the Labor Standards Act are mere minimum standards, violators are subject to criminal punishment in the event of any violation.

In cases where workers' rights disagree with the employer's ownership rights, a labor union's counteraction, such as a strike for the betterment of working conditions, is exempt from civil or criminal liability. However, any violence or destruction caused as a result of labor union activities will not be tolerated(Article 3 & 4 of the Trade Union Act).

---

8) Lim, Jongyul, 「Labor Law」, 18th ed., Park Young Sa, 2020, p.528;Kim,Allim,「The Labor Protection Law」, KNOU Press, 2013, p. 213.

9) Article 32 of the Constitution of Korea: (3) Standards of working conditions shall be determined by Act in such a way as to guarantee human dignity.

차지한다. 민법이 시민법 원칙인 소유권 절대의 원칙, 계약자유의 원칙, 과실책임의 원칙 등을 바탕으로 하고 있지만, 이러한 시민법 원칙은 사회적 불평등을 가져와 이에 대한 수정 원리로서 노동법이 탄생하였다. 따라서 노동법에 없는 근로기준에 관한 사항은 민법의 원리인'신의성실의 원칙','권리남용 금지의 원칙' 등이 적용된다.

민법상 고용에 관한 총 9개 조항은 노동법의 일반법적 효력을 가진다. 자본주의 경제체제에서 민법은 계약자유의 원칙을 기본원리로 하고 있기 때문에 계약당사자 일방은 일정한 요건이나 손해배상을 전제로 자유롭게 계약을 해지할 수 있다. 그러나 근로자와 사용자 사이의 근로계약 관계에서 사회적, 경제적으로 우월한 위치에 있는 사용자가 자유롭게 근로계약을 해지할 수 있도록 하면 취업을 해야 생계를 유지할 수 있는 근로자는 언제든지 실직될지 모르는 위험부담을 항상 안고 있으므로 불평등하고 억압적인 관계에 놓이게 된다.[8] 이러한 불평등 관계를 개선하고, 근로자의 기본 권리인 인간의 존엄성과 행복추구권을 보장해주기 위해 헌법에 따라 근로기준법이 만들어졌다.[9]

2. 형법과의 관계(한계 일탈 제재)

노동법은 강행규정으로 이의 위반 시 형사처벌의 대상이 된다. 노동법에 정하여진 기준은 최저 기준이므로 사용자가 이의 위반 시 근로기준 위반으로 형사처벌을 받게 된다.

근로자의 근로 3권 행사는 사용자의 재산권과 충돌한다. 그러나 노동조합의 근로조건 향상을 위한 쟁의행위 등 조합활동에 대해서는 민·형사상 면책이 된다. 다만, 어떠한 경우라도 폭력이나 파괴행위는 면책의 대상이 될 수 없다(노조법 제3조, 제4조).

---

8) 임종률, 「노동법」, 제18판, 박영사, 2020, 528면; 김엘림, 정봉수 「근로보호법」, 방송대 출판부, 2020, 213면.

9) 헌법 제32조 ③ 근로조건의 기준은 인간의 존엄성이 보장되도록 법률로서 정한다.

Section 2: Application of Labor Law

I. Limitations on Application of the Labor Standards Act

Some workers are not protected by Korean labor law, or there are limits to the protection offered. Representative examples include ① workers at workplaces ordinarily employing fewer than five people, and ② domestic workers. The Labor Standards Act(LSA) stipulates that the LSA shall apply to all businesses or workplaces in which five or more workers are ordinarily employed. This Act, however, shall not apply to any business or workplace which employs only relatives living together, or to workers hired for domestic work(Article 11 of the LSA).

1. Employees at workplaces ordinarily employing fewer than five people

(1) Introduction

In December 2010, employees at workplaces employing fewer than five people became eligible for severance pay. This has brought a lot of attention to those workers in inferior situations. Major articles of the LSA that are not applicable to such workers include, among others, ① restrictions on dismissal, ② suspension allowances, ③ restrictions on extended work, ④ extended work, night work and holiday work , and ⑤ annual paid leave. Due to their exclusion from these protections, such employees often work in inferior working environments. In the following pages, I would like to look at and explain situations where the LSA applies, and where it does not.

(2) Criteria for determining ordinary number of employees[10)]

1) The LSA applies to all businesses or workplaces in which five or more employees are ordinarily employed. Ordinarily employed means that, in objective estimation based upon socially accepted ideas, if the company employs five persons or more regularly

---

10) MOEL Guidelines: LS-8048, Nov 29, 2007; Kungi 01254-150, on Feb. 1, 1993.

제2절 노동법의 적용

Ⅰ. 근로기준법의 적용제한

근로자이지만 노동법 적용을 받지 못하거나 노동법의 보호를 제한적으로 받는 근로자들이 있다. 그 대표적 사례가 5인 미만 사업장의 근로자와 가사사용인이다. 근로기준법은 상시 5명 이상의 근로자를 사용하는 모든 사업 또는 사업장에 적용한다. 다만, 동거하는 친족만을 사용하는 사업 또는 사업장과 가사(家事)사용인에 대하여는 적용하지 아니한다(근기법 제11조)라고 명시하고 있다.

1. 5인 미만 사업의 근로자

(1) 의 의

2010년 12월부터 5인 미만 사업장의 근로자들도 퇴직금 규정을 적용받게 됨에 따라 이들 취약 근로자들에 대해 사회적 관심을 쏠리고 있다. 적용되지 않는 주요 규정으로는 ① 해고의 제한, ② 휴업수당, ③ 법 정근로시간의 제한, ④ 연장·야간·휴일 근로에 가산임금, ⑤ 연차유급휴가 등이 적용되지 않는다. 이러한 핵심 조항이 적용되지 않으므로 근로기본권의 보호를 받지 못하는 취약한 근로환경에서 근무하는 근로자들이라고 할 수 있다.

(2) 상시근로자 수 판단기준[10)]

1) 근로기준법은 상시 5인 이상의 근로자를 사용하는 사업 또는 사업장에 적용되는 바, 여기에서의 상시라 함은 사회통념에 의해 객관적으로 판단되어야 하는 것이므로 근로자 수가 때때로 5인 미만이 되더라도 상태적으로 보아 5인 이상이 되면 상시 5인 이상으로 보아야 할 것이다. 개별 근로조건 별로 근로기

10) 행정해석: 근로기준팀-8048, 2007.11.29; 근기 01254-150, 1993.2.1

on average, it is regarded that the company employs five persons or more, even though there are fewer than five employees at times. When evaluating violations of the LSA per separate working condition, the applicable period related to each case shall be considered. That is, as for dismissals, the number of employees shall be considered the ordinary number of employees working for the month prior to the dismissal date.

2) The Civil Law(Article 49) stipulates that the director shall register his/her name and address in the corporate registration certificate, while the Commercial Act(Article 382-(2)) regulates that relations between the company and the director comply with the rules concerning commissions. Therefore, the director, the representative of the corporate entity or labor union, or the executive directors are not employees in principle because they hold authority as business representatives or business executives without exclusive supervision from the employer. Even though a person holds one of these types of positions, if that person is supervised and managed by a person with authority as a business executive and is in reality engaged in provision of actual labor service for the purpose of earning money, such person shall be considered an employee.

3) In cases where the head office, branch office, local office, plant, etc. are located in the same place, they are deemed one business.

4) In cases where the head office, branch office, local office, plant, etc. are located in different locations, in principle, they are deemed separate businesses. However, even though their locations are different, if the branch office, local office to the branch office, local office, plant, etc. are separate from the head office, it is regarded as an independent business or workplace: ① If the business is different according to the Korean Standard Industrial Classification table; ② If separate collective agreements or rules of employment apply; and ③ If the labor office, plant, etc. cannot be operated independently, the office together with other higher offices shall be deemed one business.

5) In cases where the following management, accounting, etc. are operated independently.

(3) Major articles applicable to workplaces ordinarily employing fewer than five people

Topics related to major articles applicable to workplaces ordinarily employing fewer than five people include, among others, ① written statement of the employment contract,

준법 위반여부를 따질 경우에는 실익이 있는 대상 기간이다. 즉, 해고사건의 경우 사건 근로자의 법 적용 사유 발생일 전 1개월 동안 상시 근로자 수로 판단한다.

2) 민법 제49조는 이사의 성명, 주소를 법인의 등기사항으로 명시하고 있고, 상법 제382조 제2항은 회사와 이사의 관계는 위임에 관한 규정을 준용한다고 규정하고 있다. 이사, 법인단체 또는 조합 등의 대표자 또는 집행기관의 지위에 있는 자는 사업주와 사용종속 관계없이 업무대표권 또는 업무집행권을 가지고 있는 것으로 보아 원칙적으로 근로자로 보지 아니한다. 그러나 이와 같은 명칭을 사용하는 자라 하더라도 업무집행권을 가진 자의 지휘 · 감독을 받으면서 사실상 노무에 종사하고 그 대가로서 임금을 받고 있는 경우라면 근로자로 보아야 한다.

3) 본사, 지점, 출장소, 공장 등이 동일한 장소에 있는 경우에는 원칙적으로 분할하지 않고 1개의 사업으로 본다.

4) 본사, 지점, 출장소, 공장 등이 장소적으로 분산되어 있을 경우에는 원칙적으로 각각 별개의 사업으로 본다. 다만, 장소가 분산되어 있다 할지라도 지점, 출장소, 공장 등의 업무처리 능력을 고려할 때 하나의 사업이라고 말할 정도의 독립성이 없으면 상위 조직과 일괄하여 하나의 사업으로 본다.

5) 본사와 장소적으로 분산되어 있는 지점, 출장소, 공장 등이 다음 각 1호에 해당하는 경우는 독립성이 있는 것으로 보고 별개의 사업 또는 사업장으로 본다.

① 한국 표준산업 분류상 산업이 다른 경우, ② 서로 다른 단체협약 또는 취업규칙을 적용받는 경우, ③ 노무관리, 회계 등이 명확하게 독립적으로 운영되는 경우.

(3) 5인 미만 사업장에 적용되는 주요 규정

5인 미만 사업장에 적용되는 주요 규정으로는 ① 근로계약의 서면작성, ② 주휴일, ③ 휴게, ④ 재해보상, ⑤ 임금청산, ⑥ 임금지급, ⑦ 해고시기 제한, ⑧ 해고예고, ⑨ 출산휴가, ⑩ 퇴직금 등 관련 조항이 적용된다.

② weekly holidays, ③ recesses, ④ accident compensation, ⑤ payment of money or valuables, ⑥ payment of wage, ⑦ restrictions on dismissal timing, ⑧ advance notice of dismissal, and ⑨ maternity leave.

Even though the restrictions on dismissal are not applicable, advance notice of dismissal is required, which means that an employer shall give at least thirty days' advance notice to a worker the employer intends to dismiss. If notice is not given thirty days before the dismissal, ordinary wage of at least thirty days shall be paid to the worker. Most articles regarding wage to be paid for labor service are also applicable. That is, minimum wage applies, payment of wage shall be observed, and penal provisions for delayed payment of wage are applicable. Of particular note, severance pay became mandatory December 1, 2010. For the two years prior to December 1, 2012, the employer had to pay 50% of full severance pay to resigning employees, and 100% for the period beginning January 2013. Regardless of the length of service, severance pay only starts accruing from December 1, 2010. Also, according to Industrial Accident Compensation Insurance requirements, accident compensation for occupational injury, including medical treatment, suspension compensation, handicap compensation, etc. are applicable in the same way as for regular employees.

(4) Major articles not applicable to workplaces ordinarily employing fewer than five people

As many of the LSA provisions do not apply to workers at workplaces ordinarily employing fewer than five people, working conditions for such employees are quite inferior.

1) Restrictions on dismissal

① An employer can arbitrarily dismiss or discipline workers without justifiable reason; ② Even though a worker is unfairly dismissed, the worker cannot apply to the Labor Relations Commission for remedy; ③ An employer does not have to notify workers in writing of reasons for dismissal; ④ As the restrictions on dismissal for managerial reasons do not apply to such workers, an employer can dismiss workers at any time if business conditions deteriorate; ⑤ The two-year limitation on the use of temporary workers such as dispatch employees or short-term contract workers does not apply, and the employer can dismiss such workers at any time.

해고의 제한규정이 적용되지 않지만, 근로자를 해고하고자 할 경우에는 적어도 30일 전에 해고예고를 하여야 하고 이를 하지 못한 경우 적어도 30일분 1개월의 해고예고수당을 지급해야 한다. 그리고 근로의 대가인 임금에 대해서는 대부분 적용된다. 즉, 최저임금이 적용되고, 임금지급시기를 준수해야 하고, 임금체불에 대한 벌칙조항이 적용된다. 특히 퇴직금의 경우에는 2010.12.1부터 적용되어 최초 2년이 되는 2012.12.1까지는 법정퇴직금의 50%, 그 이후부터는 100% 지급해야 한다. 근로연수가 많은 경우라도 이 퇴직금규정 시행시기부터 계산하여 지급해야 한다. 그뿐만 아니라 업무상 재해를 당한 경우에는 일반근로자와 동일하게 산업재해보상보험법에 따른 요양보상, 휴업보상, 장해보상 등 보상규정 일체를 적용받는다.

(4) 5인 미만 사업장에 적용되지 않는 주요 규정

5인 미만의 사업장에 근로하는 근로자에게 아래의 규정이 적용되지 않기 때문에 근로기본권의 보호를 받지 못하고 열악한 근로환경에 처해 있다고 할 수 있다.

1) 해고 등의 제한

① 정당한 이유가 없어도 근로자들을 마음대로 해고하거나 징계할 수 있다. ② 근로자가 부당한 해고를 당했어도 노동위원회에 의한 구제를 받을 수 없다. ③ 사용자의 일방적인 해고에 대한 서면통지 의무가 없으며, ④ 경영상 해고 제한규정에도 적용되지 않으므로 회사 사정이 좋지 않을 때는 언제든지 해고할 수 있다. ⑤ 파견근로나 단기간 근로자를 사용할 경우에 자유롭게 언제든지 해고할 수 있기 때문에 2년의 사용기간 제한규정 적용 없이 계속 사용할 수 있다.

2) Allowances during suspension of business

When an employer suspends business operations, the workers cannot receive suspension allowances. Even though business operations are suspended for reasons attributable to the employer, the employer does not have to pay allowances to workers during such suspensions.

3) Restrictions on working hours

Workplaces ordinarily employing fewer than five people do not have to follow the 40 hours per week limitation or keep to a 5 day workweek. There are no restrictions on extending the work day beyond 8 hours, or even beyond 12 hours, nor does the employer have to pay additional allowances(50%) for overtime, night shift(10:00 pm to 06:00 am) or holiday work.

<Labor laws applicable to workplaces ordinarily employing fewer than five people>

Division		Applicable articles
Labor Standards Act	Chapter 1. General Provisions	Article 1~Article 13
	Chapter 2. Labor Contract	Article 15, Article 17, Article 19-(1), Article 20, Article 20~Article 22, Article 23-(2), Article 26, Article 35~Article 42
	Chapter 3. Wages	Article 43~Article 45, Article 47~Article 49
	Chapter 4. Working Hours and Recess	Article 54, Article 55, Article 63
	Chapter 5. Females and Minors	Article 64, Article 65-(1)&(3) (restricted to pregnant women and minors), Article 66~Article 69, Article 70-(2)&(3), Article 71, Article 72, Article 74
	Chapter 6. Safety and Health	Article 76
	Chapter 8. Accident Compensation	Article 78~Article 92
	Chapter 11. Labor Inspectors, etc.	Article 101~Article 106
	Chapter 12. Penal Provisions	Article 107~Article 116 (restricted to cases where an employer violates articles applying to businesses and workplaces ordinarily employing fewer than 5 people)
Minimum Wage Act		All employees
Equal Employment Act		All employees
Industrial Accident Compensation Insurance Act		All employees: Companies in certain sectors (including companies in agriculture, forestry and fisheries with 4 employees or fewer) are excluded.
Employment Insurance Act		All employees: Companies in certain sectors (including companies in agriculture, forestry and fisheries with 4 employees or fewer) are excluded.

2) 휴업수당

회사가 휴업해도 휴업수당을 받을 수 없다. 따라서 회사가 필요시 임의적으로 휴업을 하더라도 특별히 휴업수당을 지급하지 않기 때문에 사용자의 귀책사유로 휴업을 하여도 근로자들은 그 휴업기간 동안 임금이 지급되지 않는다.

3) 근로시간의 제한

5인 미만의 사업장은 주 40시간 근로자나 주5일제도 해당이 없고 하루 8시간을 초과해 무제한으로 연장근로를 시킬 수 있다. 연장근로도 주 12시간 한도에 대한 제한이 없고, 연장근로나 야간근로(22시~06시)에 근무 하거나 휴일에 근무해도 50%의 할증임금을 받지 못한다.

〈상시 5인 미만의 사업장에 적용하는 법규정〉

<table>
<tr><th colspan="2">구 분</th><th>적용법규정</th></tr>
<tr><td rowspan="10">근로기준법</td><td>제1장 총칙</td><td>제1조~13조까지의 규정</td></tr>
<tr><td>제2장 근로계약</td><td>제15조, 17조, 18조, 19조1항, 20조~22조까지의 규정, 23조2항, 26조, 35조~42조까지의 규정</td></tr>
<tr><td>제3장 임금</td><td>제43조~45조까지의 규정, 47조~49조까지의 규정</td></tr>
<tr><td>제4장 근로시간과 휴식</td><td>제54조, 55조, 63조</td></tr>
<tr><td>제5장 여성과 소년</td><td>제64조, 65조1항·3항(임산부와 18세 미만인 자로 한정한다), 제66조~69조까지의 규정, 제70조2항·3항, 71조, 72조, 74조</td></tr>
<tr><td>제6장 안전과 보건</td><td>제76조</td></tr>
<tr><td>제8장 재해보상</td><td>제78조~92조까지의 규정</td></tr>
<tr><td>제11장 근로감독관</td><td>제101조~106조까지의 규정</td></tr>
<tr><td>제12장 벌칙</td><td>제107조~116조까지의 규정(상시 5명 미만 근로자를 사용하는 사업 또는 사업장에 적용되는 규정을 위반한 경우로 한정한다)</td></tr>
<tr><td colspan="2">최저임금법</td><td>모든 근로자</td></tr>
<tr><td colspan="2">남녀고용평등과 일·가정 양립 지원에 관한 법률</td><td>모든 근로자</td></tr>
<tr><td colspan="2">산업재해보상보험법</td><td>모든 근로자(단, 5인 미만 농, 임, 어민 등 일부 업종은 제외)</td></tr>
<tr><td colspan="2">고용보험법</td><td>모든 근로자(단, 5인 미만 농, 임, 어민 등 일부 업종은 제외)</td></tr>
</table>

4) Annual paid leave

When a worker at a workplace employing at least five people has worked continuously for one year, 15 days of annual paid leave are ordinarily granted, but workers at workplaces ordinarily employing fewer than five people are not guaranteed any paid, non-statutory holidays. A worker at such workplaces must get permission to take a day off, and the employer can deduct one day's salary.

2. Domestic workers employed by a company

(1) Domestic worker not covered by the Labor Standards Act[11)]

This labor case involved an application for remedy for unfair dismissal, but was dropped as the domestic worker was not covered by the Labor Standards Act. The ruling stated: Even though this worker claimed he applied for a position posted by the company, his workplace was the summer house owned privately by the company president, and was employed by the president and her husband. Caretaking of the summer house was not related to the company's main business of construction. In addition, the worker had not done anything to contribute to the profit gaining activities of the company. In light of these facts, this worker, privately employed by the employer, is considered a domestic worker to which Article 11 of the LSA applies. It is therefore not necessary to review the facts of the dismissal or its justification.

(2) Domestic worker covered by the Labor Standards Act[12)]

In looking into the background of a worker beginning to work at the CEO's house, it was found that he had been employed by the company to work in the Management Department, and then was immediately assigned to work at the CEO's house. Since that time, the company had managed the worker's general matters regulated by labor law such as wage, service regulations, and payment of severance pay. The company had also handled the worker's social security insurance and other income deductions. Even though the type of work was at the discretion of the CEO, the worker still belonged to the

---

11) Gyunggi Labor Relations Commission: 2012Buhae1130

12) Industrial Accident Compensation Insurance Review Committee 2004-910, Sept. 14, 2004

4) 연차유급휴가

5인이상 사업장에 종사하는 근로자는 1년의 근무에 15일의 연차휴가를 유급으로 사용할 수 있으나, 5인 미만 사업장에 종사하는 근로자들은 유급휴가가 발생하지 않는다. 따라서 휴가를 사용하고자 할 경우에는 사용자의 승인을 얻어 무급으로 휴가를 사용할 수 있다.

2. 가사사용인의 근로기준법 적용여부

(1) 근로기준법이 적용되지 않는 가사사용인으로 각하 판정한 사례[11)]

근로자가 해고되어 부당해고 구제신청을 가져갔던 경우로서 이 사건 근로자들은 이 사건 사용자의 채용공고를 보고 채용되었다고 주장하나 근무장소가 이 사건 사용자의 대표이사가 개인적으로 소유한 별장이었다는 점, 별장에서 대표이사와 그의 남편에 의한 면접을 통하여 채용되었다는 점, 별장관리업무는 건설업을 주로 행하고 있는 이 사건 사용자의 사업내용과 직접적인 연관이 없고 이 사건 사용자에게 수익을 창출하는 업무를 하였다고 보기 어려운 점 등을 비추어 볼 때 이 사건 사용자가 채용한 근로자가 아닌 이 사건 사용자의 대표이사가 개인적으로 채용한 근로자로 근로기준법 제11조의 가사사용인에 해당하여 해고처분의 존재와 정당성 여부에 대하여는 별도로 논할 필요 없다 할 것이다라고 하여 근로기준법 적용을 배제하고 있다.

(2) 근로기준법이 적용된다고 본 사례[12)]

근로자가 대표이사의 자택에서 근무하게 된 경위를 살펴보면, 회사에서 채용하여 회사의 관리부로 소속을 두게 하고 대표이사의 자택에서 근무하도록 명령을 내린 것으로 확인되고, 이후 임금지급 관계, 복무관계, 퇴직금 지급 등 노동관계법에 따라 발생하는 제반 사항에 대하여 회사에서 일괄적으로 관리해온 것으로 확인되며, 제세공과금의 납부와 사회보장제도 등 대외적인 권리·의무관계에 있어서도 회사에 귀속되어 행하여진 점을 종합할 때 근로자를 대표이사가 사

11) 경기지노위, 2012부해1130 (주)건교산업 부당해고 구제신청 사건.
12) 행정해석: 산심위 2004-910, 2004.9.14.

company organization. This worker is clearly different from a worker hired independently by an individual as a private housekeeper, driver, or gardener. Accordingly, the decision by the Employee Welfare Corporation to reject the family's application for the survivors' pension because of the worker's supposed status as a domestic worker was inaccurate.

Ⅱ. Determining Applicability of the Labor Standards Act for Foreign Companies with Fewer than Five Employees

Foreign companies often have substantial headquarters, but their domestic branches or offices frequently employ fewer than five people. This situation has led to numerous disputes regarding whether the provisions of the Labor Standards Act (LSA) governing restrictions on dismissals and other protections apply to such workplaces. According to Article 11 of the LSA, the Act fully applies to businesses or workplaces employing at least five workers, while those employing fewer than five are excluded from the restrictions on dismissals under Article 23 and the remedies for unfair dismissal under Article 28.

Recently, the Supreme Court has delivered differing judgments on cases involving foreign companies with workplaces employing fewer than five people, adding to the confusion.

· **Case 1** (Supreme Court ruling on October 25, 2024, 2023Du37391): A German company established a Korean branch employing two workers and maintained independent legal and financial accounting systems. The Court determined that this branch constituted a workplace with fewer than five employees.

• **Case 2** (Supreme Court Ruling on October 25, 2024, 2023Du46074): An American company employed one worker in Korea, and assigned another Korean-based American company with more than five employees to handle this worker's salary and social insurance matters. The American company later dismissed the worker. The Court ruled that the workforce count for the purposes of the LSA could not include individuals employed outside Korea and thus deemed the branch to have fewer than five employees.

• **Case 3** (Supreme Court Ruling on October 25, 2024, 2023Du57876): An Australian travel company operated two separate legal entities in Korea but managed personnel, accounting, and other administrative tasks jointly in a single office. When one entity ceased operations, it dismissed its employee. The Court determined that while the two Korean entities were

적인 용도로 사용하였다 하나 법인인 회사 소속 근로자로 보는 것이 타당하며, 독립적인 지위에서 개인 가정에 고용되어 개인 가사서비스, 운전기사, 정원관리원 등의 산업활동을 행하는 가사사용인과는 달리 보아야 할 것이다. 따라서 원처분기관에서 근로자가 사업주의 자택에서 근무하였다는 이유로 가사사용인으로 잘못 판단하여 유족급여 및 장의비청구서를 반려 처분한 것은 부당하다.

Ⅱ. 5명 미만 외국계 기업의 근로기준법 적용여부

외국계 기업은 본사는 규모가 엄청 크지만, 국내에 투자하고 있는 영업소나 지점은 5명 미만인 경우가 많고, 이들에 대한 근로기준법 상 해고 등의 제한 규정의 적용 여부와 관련 하여 분쟁이 많이 발생하고 있다. 왜냐하면, 근로기준법 제11조는 상시 5명 이상의 근로자를 사용하는 사업 또는 사업장에 대해 근로기준법의 전부가 적용되며, 상시 4명 이하의 근로자를 사용하는 사업 또는 사업장은 근로기준법 제23조의 해고 등의 제한과 제28조의 부당해고 구제를 받을 수 없기 때문이다.

최근에 대법원은 외국계 기업의 5명 미만 사업장에 대해 사안별로 서로 다른 결론을 내고 있어 혼란을 주고 있다.

제1사건 (대법원 2024.10.25. 선고 2023두37391 판결)은 독일법인은 한국에서 2명의 근로자를 고용하여 한국법인을 설립하고 운영하였는데, 한국지점은 독립적인 법인격과 재무회계를 유지한다는 이유로 5명 미만 사업장으로 판단하였다.

제2사건 (대법원 2024.10.25. 선고 2023두46074 판결)은 미국법인은 근로자 1명을 한국에서 고용하여, 5명 이상의 다른 미국회사에 소속시켜 4대보험과 임금을 지급하도록 하였다. 미국법인은 그 1인 근로자를 해고하였다. 이 사건에서 대법원은 해당 1인 근로자에 대해 한국 노동법이 적용되지 않는 미국법인의 인원까지 합하여 5명 이상으로 볼 수 없다고 판단하였다.

제3사건 (대법원 2024.10.25. 선고 2023두57876 판결)은 여행업종의 호주법인은 한국에 서로 다른 2개의 법인을 운영하면서, 2개의 한국 법인을 하나의 사무실에서 인사, 회계관리 등을 같이 하였다. 두개의 법인 중 한 법인을 폐업하면서

legally distinct, they constituted a single workplace, making the entity that ceased operations a workplace with five or more employees.

• **Case 4** (Seoul High Court Ruling on February 3, 2023, 2022Nu50412): An American telecommunications company established a business office in Korea and employed two workers. The employees conducted business under the name of the headquarters, worked exclusively for it, and received additional incentives from the headquarters. Both the Administrative Court and Appellate Court ruled that the office was a workplace with five or more employees, considering its integration with the headquarters, and deemed a worker's dismissal unfair. The case was dismissed in the Supreme Court after the company withdrew its appeal.

This article will review the detailed circumstances of these four cases, analyze the criteria used in the judgments, and assess the applicability of those criteria to similar cases.

1. Cases Involving Foreign Companies with Fewer than Five Employees

(1) Case 1 (Supreme Court Ruling on October 25, 2024, 2023Du37391)

The German corporation in this case was a company manufacturing and selling construction flooring and road products. It established a Korean subsidiary on November 19, 2014. The employee concerned was hired as a business development manager at the Korean branch on October 15, 2019. The Korean branch consisted of two employees, including the employee concerned. Its duties included handling imports from the German corporation and quality assurance for its products. On April 17, 2020, the German corporation dismissed the employee concerned under the name of its Korean subsidiary but failed to provide written notice in accordance with Article 27 of the Labor Standards Act (LSA).

Although the Korean subsidiary operated independently with its own financial accounting and management systems, it reported transactions, sales performance, and accounting to the German corporation.

The worker filed a complaint with the Seoul Labor Commission on June 5, 2020, claiming the dismissal constituted unfair dismissal under the LSA. The Commission ruled on July 31, 2020, that the dismissal was unfair. The National Labor Relations Commission subsequently dismissed the appeal, upholding the initial decision on December 8, 2020.

여기에 소속된 근로자를 해고하였다. 대법원은 한국의 두개의 지점이 각각 독립된 법인이지만, 하나의 사업장으로 볼 수 있으므로 폐업한 법인을 5명 이상의 사업장으로 판단하였다.

제4사건 (서울고등법원 2023.2.3. 선고 2022두50412 판결)은 미국통신회사가 한국에 영업사무소를 설립하고 2명의 근로자를 고용하여 운영하였다. 이 한국영업소의 직원은 본사의 이름으로 영업을 하고, 본사를 위한 영업만 하고 그 영업의 대가로 추가 인센티브를 받았다. 1심과 2심 법원은 미국통신회사가 근로자를 해고한 사안에서 5인 이상 사업장으로 판단하여 부당해고로 인정하였다. 본 사건은 회사가 상고해 대법원에서 다투던 중 회사가 소를 취하해서 종결되었다.

위의 4가지 사건에 대해 구체적인 내용을 살펴보고 그 판단기준은 어디에 있었는지, 유사한 사안에 적용 가능한 지에 대해 검토하고자 한다.

1. 5명 미만 외국계 기업과 관련된 사례

(1) 제1사건 (대법원 2024.10.25. 선고 2023두37391 판결)

독일법인은 건설용 바닥재와 도로용 제품을 제작판매하는 회사로 2014. 11. 19. 한국법인을 설립하였다. 해당 근로자는 2019. 10. 15. 한국지사에 사업개발관리자로 채용되었고, 한국지사는 해당 근로자를 포함하여 2인으로 구성되어 있다. 한국지사의 업무는 독일 법인의 제품에 대한 수입을 담당하고 품질보증을 하는 업무를 수행하였다. 독일법인은 한국법인의 이름으로 2020. 4. 17. 해당 근로자를 해고하였다. 독일법인은 해당 근로자를 해고하면서 근로기준법 제27조에 의한 서면통지를 하지 않았다. 반면, 한국법인은 독립된 법인으로서 독자적인 재무회계를 유지하고 독자적으로 운영을 하였다. 하지만 한국법인은 독일법인에 거래처 관리, 매출보고, 회계관리 등을 보고하였다.

본 사건에 대해 해당 근로자는 2020. 6. 5. 서울지방노동위원회에 해고가 부당해고에 해당한다고 주장하면서 구제를 신청하였다. 이에 대해 서울지방노동위원회는 2020. 7. 31. 부당해고임을 인정하였다. 이에 대해 중앙노동위원회도 2020. 12. 8. 초심판정과 같은 취지로 재신신청을 기각하였다.

However, the Administrative Court overturned this decision, holding that the Korean subsidiary was an independent workplace with fewer than five employees under Article 11 of the LSA and was therefore not subject to the dismissal restrictions.[13)] The High Court, on the other hand, found that the worker should be regarded as part of a single workplace, considering the combined operations of the German and Korean entities, and recognized the dismissal as unfair.[14)]

The Supreme Court reversed this decision, stating,

In international labor relations where a foreign corporation establishes a legal entity or office in Korea and employs workers, the number of employees working domestically must be the standard for determining whether it qualifies as a workplace employing at least five workers under Article 11, Paragraph 1, of the LSA.

The Court further explained that only when the economic and social activities of the entities are substantively identical can they be considered as one workplace, nullifying the High Court's ruling.

(2) Case 2 (Supreme Court Decision, October 25, 2024, 2023Du46074)

Company 1 is a U.S. corporation specializing in optimization services for petroleum and gas machinery, with no domestic office in Korea. Company 2 is another U.S. corporation engaged in selling non-destructive testing equipment and operates a Korean sales office employing more than five workers. The two companies have no shareholder or business relationship.

The worker (plaintiff) entered into an employment contract with Company 1 on May 1, 2018, and performed duties in Korea while using business cards displaying Company 1's name, domain, and website address. The worker was the sole employee working in Korea under Company 1's supervision but worked at Company 2's office. Company 1 later notified the worker that their employment contract had been terminated.

The worker's social insurance and salary were managed by Company 2, which was reimbursed by Company 1.

---

13) Seoul Administrative Court Decision, Dec. 9, 2021, 2021GuHap53023.

14) Seoul High Court Decision, Feb. 3, 2023, 2022Nu32254.

그러나 행정법원은 해당 근로자의 소속인 한국법인이 독립성이 있는 사업장이므로 근로기준법 제11조에 의한 5명 미만 사업장에 해당되기 때문에 노동위원회의 판정을 취소하였다.[13] 이에 대해 고등법원은 한국법인의 해당 근로자는, 실질적으로 독일법인과 한국법인을 동일한 사업으로 간주하여야 하기 때문에 독일법인의 인원과 같이 고려하여야 판단하였고, 이 사건의 해당 근로자에 대해 부당한 해고로 인정하였다.[14]

그러나 대법원은 "외국기업이 국내에서 법인이나 영업소 등을 설립하여 사업 활동을 영위하며 근로자를 사용하는 국제근로관계에서는 원칙적으로 '국내에서 사용하는 근로자수'를 기준으로 '상시 5명 이상의 근로자를 사용하는 사업 또는 사업장'에 해당하는지 여부를 판단하여야 한다."고 판시하였다. 그 이유는 "근로관계의 각종 규율이 통일적으로 적용될 수 있는 실질적으로 동일한 경제적, 사회적 활동 단위라고 볼 수 있는 경우에 한하여 하나의 사업 또는 사업장을 구성할 수 있다."고 제시하면서 고등법원의 판결을 취소하였다.

(2) 제2사건(대법원 2024.10.25. 선고 2023두46074 판결)

참가인1은 미국법인으로 석유, 가스 관련 기계 최적화 서비스 사업을 하는 외국법인이고, 국내 사업장은 없다. 참가인2도 미국법인으로 비파괴 검사 장비 판매 사업을 영위하면서 한국 영업소를 두고 5명 이상을 고용하고 있다. 참가인1과 참가인2는 주주관계나 사업관계에 있지 않다.

원고(근로자)는 2018. 5. 1. 참가인1과 근로계약을 체결하여 근무하면서, 참가인1의 회사명, 도메인, 홈페이지 주소가 기재된 명함을 사용하였다. 원고는 참가인1 소속 근로자 중 유일하게 대한민국에서 근무하였는데, 참가인1의 지휘감독을 받으면서 참가인2의 사무실에서 근무하였다. 원고는 참가인1로부터 근로계약만료 통지를 받았다.

근로자는 참가인2를 통해 4대보험이 가입되었고, 급여도 참가인2로부터 받았다. 이러한 비용은 참가인1이 참가인2에게 차후 지급하였다.

---

13) 서울행정법원 2021. 12. 9. 선고 2021구합53023 판결

14) 서울고등법원 2023. 2. 3. 선고 2022누32254 판결

On June 9, 2020, the worker filed a complaint with the Seoul Labor Commission, arguing that the contract expiration notice constituted unfair dismissal. However, the Commission dismissed the complaint on August 5, 2020, reasoning that the worker's employer, Company 1, had no domestic office, and personnel management was conducted abroad, rendering the LSA inapplicable. The worker appealed to the National Labor Relations Commission on September 17, 2020, but the appeal was dismissed on April 24, 2020, for similar reasons.

The District Court ruled that the LSA did not apply because the governing law was Delaware state law.[15)]

The High Court (Appellate Court), however, determined that the number of employees should include both domestic and foreign workers employed by the foreign headquarters, reasoning that there was no justification for excluding foreign employees when assessing the number of regular employees. Since Company 1's global employee count exceeded five, the court ruled that the LSA applied and deemed the dismissal unfair.[16)]

The Supreme Court cancelled the High Court's ruling, stating:

In cases where a foreign corporation employs workers abroad, foreign labor laws apply unless there are special circumstances otherwise. Therefore, employees working abroad, to whom the LSA does not apply, cannot be included in determining whether the workplace constitutes a business or workplace employing at least five workers under Article 11, Paragraph 1, of the LSA.

(3) Case 3 (Supreme Court Ruling on October 25, 2024, 2023Du57876)

The plaintiff in this case was a domestic entity of a foreign corporation (a Dubai-based company, hereinafter "Company B/Plaintiff"), ultimately controlled by an Australian corporation ("Company A"). Similarly, another domestic entity ("Company C") was the Korean branch of another Dubai-based corporation ("Company D"), also controlled by the same Australian corporation (Company A). Both parties in this case, Company B/ Plaintiff and Company C, were companies engaged in the same business—overseas hotel reservations—but handled hotels in different regions. From March 2019 to October

15) Seoul Administrative Court Decision, May 12, 2022, 2021GuHap5281.

16) Seoul High Court Decision, June 8, 2023, 2022Nu44493.

원고는 2020. 6. 9. 서울지방노동위원회에 이 사건 기간만료통지가 부당해고라고 주장하며 부당해고 구제신청을 하였다. 서울지방노동위원회는 2020. 8. 5. "원고의 사용자는 참가인 본사인데 위 참가인은 국내에 사업장이 없고 근로자에 대한 인사노무관리를 외국에서 하여 근로기준법이 적용되지 않는다"는 이유로 원고의 구제신청을 각하하였다. 이에 원고가 불복하여 2020. 9. 17. 중앙노동위원회에 재심을 신청하였으나, 중앙노동위원회는 2020. 4. 24. "이 사건 초심판정과 같은 이유로 원고의 재심신청을 기각하였다.

제1심은 준거법이 미국 델라웨어주 법이기 때문에 근로기준법이 적용되지 않는다고 판단하였다.[15)]

제2심(원심)은 상시 근로자수를 판단할 때 국내 법인과 외국 법인을 달리 볼 이유가 없으므로 참가인 본사가 외국에서 사용하는 근로자 수까지 합산하여야 한다고 보고서, 참가인 본사의 외국 상시 근로자수를 합산하면 5명 이상이므로 근로기준법이 적용되고 부당해고에 해당한다고 판단하였다.[16)]

대법원은 "외국기업이 외국에서 사용하는 근로자에 대하여는 특별한 사정이 없는 한 외국의 노동관계법령이 적용될 뿐이므로, 대한민국 근로기준법이 적용되지 않는 외국에서 사용하는 근로자 수까지 합산하여 근로기준법 제11조 제1항의 '상시 5명 이상의 근로자를 사용하는 사업 또는 사업장'에 해당하는지 여부를 판단할 수 없다." 라고 원심판결을 번복하였다.

(3) 제3사건 (대법원 2024.10.25. 선고 2023두57876 판결)

원고는 A호주법인을 최상위 지배법인으로 둔 B외국법인(두바이)의 국내 법인이고, C는 A호주법인을 최상위 지배법인으로 둔 D외국법인(두바이)의 국내 영업소이다. 원고와 C는 동종 해외호텔예약업을 영위하면서 각자 다른 지역 호텔을 취급하였다. C는 2019. 3.경부터 2020. 10. 경까지 원고의 사무실을 함께 사용하였다. 특히, 원고와 C는 하나의 사업장에서 다음과 공동 운영되었다. ① 원고와 C의 인적·물적 조직과 재무회계가 서로 유기적으로 운영되었다. ②원

15) 서울행정법원 2022. 5. 12. 선고 2021구합52815 판결

16) 서울고등법원 2023. 6. 8. 선고 2022누44493 판결

2020, Company C shared Company B/Plaintiff's office space in Korea. The two entities operated as a single workplace, characterized by the following:

① The human and physical resources, as well as financial and accounting systems of Company B/Plaintiff and Company C, were interlinked and operated cohesively.

② Personnel and labor management for employees of both entities were centrally managed by Company D in Dubai.

③ By the time of the dismissal in question, Company B/Plaintiff and Company C had already consolidated their human and physical resources, functioning as a single economic and social unit for a significant period.

The employee in question ("the Employee") joined Company B/Plaintiff in October 2016 as an accountant. In October 2020, Company B/Plaintiff informed the Employee they were being dismissed due to closure of the business. The Seoul Labor Commission dismissed the Employee's request for remedy, ruling that Company B/Plaintiff and Company C were separate businesses. However, the National Labor Relations Commission overturned this decision, treating Company B/Plaintiff and Company C as a single workplace under the Labor Standards Act (LSA) and ruled the dismissal was unfair.

The District Court held that while Company B/Plaintiff and Company C were formally distinct and independent legal entities, they functioned operationally as a single workplace. Combining the number of employees from both entities exceeded five, making the LSA applicable, and the dismissal was deemed unfair.[17)]

The Appellate Court upheld this ruling, emphasizing that the core criterion should be the substantive uniformity and integration of business operations, including production, sales, management, personnel, labor, and accounting, rather than merely focusing on legal structures.[18)]

The Supreme Court affirmed the lower court's decision, establishing criteria for assessing the integration of workplaces under the LSA. The Court ruled:

The term "business or workplace" under Article 11, Paragraph 1, of the Labor Standards Act refers to a unit of economic and social activity that is cohesively and organically managed. The separation of corporate legal entities is a key criterion for

---

17) Seoul Administrative Court Decision, Sept. 23, 2022, 2021GuHap68704.

18) Seoul High Court Decision, Sept. 22, 2023, 2022Nu65919.

고 직원들과 C 직원들에 대한 인사 및 노무관리가 D외국법인(두바이) 측에 의하여 통일적으로 이루어졌다. ③원고와 C는 이 사건 해고 무렵 이미 인적·물적 조직이 통합되어 실질적으로 동일한 경제적, 사회적 활동단위로서 상당한 기간 동안 운영되어 온 상태였다.

참가인(근로자)은 2016. 10. 원고회사에 입사하여 회계 업무를 담당하였는데, 원고는 2020. 10. 사업 폐지에 따라 참가인에게 통상해고를 통보를 하였다. 서울지방노동위원회는 원고와 C를 별개의 사업(장)으로 판단해 구제신청을 각하하였다. 그러나 중앙노동위원회는 원고와 C를 사실상 하나의 사업(장)으로 판단하고 근로기준법 적용하여 부당해고로 판정하였다.

제1심은 원고와 C는 별개의 독립된 법인의 형태를 취하고 있으나, 실질적으로는 경영상의 일체를 이루는 '하나의 사업장'으로 운영되었다. 원고와 C의 상시 근로자수를 합산하면 5명 이상이므로 근로기준법이 적용되고, 부당해고에 해당한다고 판단하였다.[17)]

제2심(원심)도 제1심 판결을 그대로 인용하면서, 법적 형식에 기초한 사업의 외형적 조직이나 구성뿐만 아니라, 생산, 판매, 관리, 인사, 노무, 회계를 망라하는 사업 경영활동의 실질적 동일성 내지 단일성 여부가 핵심적 기준이 되어야 한다고 판단하였다.[18)]

대법원도 원심의 판결을 유지하면서 두 법인 간 동일성 판단기준을 제시하였다. "근로기준법의 적용 단위가 되는 같은 법 제11조 제1항의 '사업 또는 사업장'이라 함은 경영상의 일체를 이루면서 유기적으로 운영되는 경제적, 사회적 활동 단위를 의미한다. 법인격의 분리 여부가 독립된 사업 또는 사업장에 해당하는지를 판단하는 우선적인 기준이 되므로 법인격이 다른 조직은 특별한 사정이 없는 한 하나의 사업 또는 사업장을 구성할 수 없음이 원칙이다. 다만, 별개의 법인격을 가진 여러 개의 조직 사이에 단순한 법인간의 협력관계나, 계열회사, 모자회사 사이의 일반적인 지배종속관계를 넘어 실질적으로 동일한 경제적, 사회적 활동단위로 볼 수 있을 정도의 경영상 일체성과 유기적 관련성이 인

17) 서울행정법원 2022. 9. 23. 선고 2021구합68704 판결
18) 서울고능법원 2023. 9. 22. 선고 2022누65919 판결

determining whether they constitute separate businesses or workplaces. As a rule, organizations with separate legal personalities cannot constitute a single workplace absent special circumstances. However, when multiple legally distinct entities exhibit operational and economic integration to the extent that they function as a single unit, they may be considered a single business or workplace. Factors to consider include the nature, purpose, and method of operations; uniformity in directives, employment, dismissal, and labor management; and the degree of interdependence in human, physical, and organizational resources, as well as financial and accounting integration.

(4) Case 4: Appeal (Seoul High Court Decision, February 3, 2023, 2022Nu 50412), Withdrawn during Supreme Court Proceedings

An American telecommunications company established a Korean subsidiary ("Corporation A") on November 22, 2007, employing three regular workers. The employee in question ("the Employee") joined Corporation A on January 4, 2016, as a sales director and was dismissed on October 12, 2020. The Employee filed a complaint with the Seoul Labor Commission on December 17, 2020, seeking remedy for unfair dismissal.

The Korean subsidiary served as a local office for marketing and customer support on behalf of the U.S. headquarters. The following facts were relevant:

① Recruitment and salary negotiations for the Employee were conducted directly by an executive of the U.S. headquarters via video interview;

② The Employee conducted sales activities in Korea, signing contracts using templates provided by the U.S. headquarters, and received performance-based incentives;

③ Contracts were executed in the name of the U.S. headquarters, not the Korean subsidiary;

④ A manager from the U.S. headquarters supervised the Employee, reviewed weekly reports, and approved leave and expenses;

⑤ Organizational charts listed the U.S. headquarters executive as the Employee's superior;

⑥ Daily reporting and expense approvals were directed to the U.S. headquarters;

⑦ The Employee received HR-related emails directly from the U.S. headquarters;

⑧ The Employee did not receive any direction or supervision from the Korean subsidiary's representative director.

The Seoul Labor Commission ruled on February 10, 2021, that the U.S. headquarters and Corporation A together constituted a single workplace forming an operational unit. It

정되는 특별한 사정이 있는 경우에는 이들을 하나의 사업 또는 사업장으로 볼 수 있다. 이때 복수의 조직이 하나의 사업 또는 사업장에 해당하는 특별한 사정이 있는지 여부는 업무의 종류, 성질, 목적, 수행방식 및 장소가 동일한지, 업무지시와 근로자의 채용, 근로조건의 결정, 해고 등 인사 및 노무관리가 조직별로 구분되지 않고 동일한 사업주체 내지 경영진에 의하여 통일적으로 행사되었는지, 각 단위별 사업활동이 내용이 하나의 사업목적을 위하여 결합되어 인적, 물적, 조직과 재무, 회계가 서로 밀접하게 관련되어 운영되는지 등과 같은 사정을 종합적으로 고려하여 신중하게 판단하여야 한다."고 판시하였다.

(4) 제4사건 : 대법원 상고 중 취하됨. (고등법원 2023.2.3. 선고 2022두 50412 판결)

미국통신회사는 2007. 11. 22. 한국에 A법인을 설립하고 상시근로자 3명을 사용하여 통신업을 하고 있다. 해당 근로자는 A법인에 2016. 1. 4. 입사하여, 영업이사로 근무하던 중 2020. 10. 12. 해고되었다. 해당 근로자는 2020. 12. 17. 서울지방노동위원회에 부당해고 구제신청을 하였다.

한국지점은 미국본사를 대신해서 마케팅과 고객지원을 하고 있었다. 본사의 이사가 한국 A법인의 이사로 등재되어 있고, 한국법인은 인사규정이 없으며 인사관리를 본사에서 직접하였다. 구체적인 내용은 다음과 같다. ①해당 근로자에 대한 채용은 미국본사의 임원이 직접 화상면접을 통해서 이루어졌다. 연봉협상은 본사의 임원과 직접 하였다. ②해당 근로자는 국내에서 영업활동을 하고, 계약이 성사되는 경우 미국 본사 매니저가 제공한 계약서를 가지고 고객과 계약을 체결한다. 그리고 그 영업의 대가로 성과급을 지급 받았다. ③한국법인은 고객과의 당사자가 되지 않았고, 법인 본사의 이름으로 계약서를 작성하였다. ④본사 매니저는 해당 근로자에게 업무지시를 하고, 매주 주간보고를 받았다. 해당 근로자는 연차휴가에 대한 승인과 비용지출에 대한 승인을 사전에 받았다. ⑤조직도에 해당 근로자의 상급자는 본사의 임원으로 표시되어 있었다. ⑥일상적인 업무에 대해 본사의 상급자에게 보고하였고, 비용지출에 대해서도 사전승인을 받고 사용하였다. ⑦본사의 인사담당자로부터 휴가사용을 촉진하라는 요청 메

determined that the company, with at least five regular employees, was subject to the LSA's dismissal restrictions. This ruling was upheld by the National Labor Relations Commission on May 17, 2021, and by the Administrative Court, which dismissed the company's appeal.

The Seoul High Court cited precedent in its judgment:

A workplace is defined as an operationally cohesive unit of economic and social activity. The determination of whether a workplace constitutes an independent economic unit must consider factors such as the nature of the business, employee interactions, the integration of physical and organizational resources, and unified managerial oversight. Spatial separation does not necessarily imply operational independence; even geographically distinct entities, like foreign headquarters and domestic offices, may be considered a single workplace if integration exists.[19)]

The Seoul High Court, in adjudicating this case, cited the following legal precedent:

A workplace refers to an economic and social activity unit that operates cohesively and organically as a single management entity. The determination is based on whether the unit satisfies the conditions of being a substantively independent economic entity, regardless of the separation of corporate legal personality. A workplace can consist of either a single location or multiple locations, and this must be assessed by comprehensively considering specific facts.20) Furthermore, whether an employer has acted as a "single operational entity" should be judged not by formalities but based on the substantive employment relationship. Therefore, the determination of whether a unit qualifies as a single workplace under the criteria for applying the Labor Standards Act must take into account factors such as the uniformity of work locations, the use of provided facilities, the business's purpose and operational methods, the organizational structure, personnel exchanges, and the specific directions and supervisory relationships in the course of work execution.

The Court further stated:

The managerial separation and independence of multiple "businesses or workplaces" should be judged comprehensively by examining factors such as the organic interconnection or distinction between their purposes, personnel exchanges involving executives or employees, the separation of finances and accounting, the physical independence of work locations, the

---

19) Seoul Administrative Court Decision, June 1, 2022, 2021GuHap69752.

20) Supreme Court Decision, Oct. 26, 2007, 2005Do9218.

일을 받았다. ⑧해당 근로자는 한국법인 대표의 지휘, 감독을 받은 적이 없다.

서울지방노동위원회는 2021. 2. 10. "미국본사와 한국 A법인은 사실상 하나의 영업조직으로서 경영상 일체를 이루는 하나의 사업 또는 사업장에 해당한다. 미국본사 뿐만 아니라 A법인도 해당근로자의 실질적 사용자이고, 회사가 사용하는 상시 근로자가 5인 이상이므로 근로기준법 제23조의 해고제한 규정에 적용된다."고 판단하였다. 회사는 재심을 신청하였으나, 중앙노동위원회는 2021. 5. 17. 초심판정과 같은 취지로 회사의 재심신청을 기각하였다. 행정법원도 동일한 판단을 하고 본 사건을 기각하는 판결을 하였다.[19]

서울고등법원은 본 사건을 판단하면서 다음과 같은 판례논리를 인용하였다. "사업장이라 함은 경영상 일체를 이루며 유기적으로 운영되는 경제적, 사회적 활동 단위를 의미하며, 법인격의 분리 여부와 무관하게 실질적으로 독립된 경제 단위로서의 요건을 충족하는지를 기준으로 판단한다. 단일 장소와 복수의 장소를 구분하여 사업장이 구성될 수 있는 경우도 있으며, 이는 구체적인 사실관계를 종합적으로 고려하여 판단한다.[20] 다만 사업주가 '하나의 활동주체'로서 활동한 것인지 여부는 형식이 아닌 실질적인 근로관계를 기준으로 판단하여야 한다. 따라서 근로기준법 적용 기준이 되는 하나의 사업장인지 여부는 근로장소의 동일성과 더불어 제공된 설비의 사용관계, 사업의 목적 및 수행방법, 조직체계, 인사교류, 업무 수행 과정에서의 구체적인 지휘, 감독관계 등을 종합적으로 고려하여 판단하여야 한다."

그리고 "여러 '사업 또는 사업장'의 경영상 분리 독립성은 각 목적 사업 사이의 유기적 연관성이나 차별성, 임원이나 근로자 등의 인적 교류 여부, 재정이나 회계의 분리 여부, 업무 장소의 분리 독립 여부, 경영상 의사결정 조직의 분리 여부, 업무상 지휘감독이나 근태관리의 분리 여부 등을 전체적으로 살펴 판단하여야 한다. 여기서 장소적 독립성은 '사업 또는 사업장'의 독립성을 판단하는 하나의 요소일 뿐, 장소적으로 독립되어 있다고 하여 반드시 경영상 독립된 '사업 또는 사업장'으로 인정할 것은 아니다. 이는 외국에 위치한 본사와 국내 영업소와 같이 장소

19) 서울행정법원 2022. 6. 1. 선고 2021구합69752 판결
20) 대법원 2007. 10. 26. 선고 2005도9218 판결

organizational independence of managerial decision-making structures, and the separation of work supervision and attendance management. In this context, spatial independence is only one factor in determining the independence of a "business or workplace." Spatial independence alone does not necessarily imply managerial independence as a "business or workplace." This principle applies equally to cases where foreign headquarters and domestic offices are spatially independent.

After reviewing the precedent and factual relationships in this case, the Seoul High Court concluded: "Although the plaintiffs present themselves as separate and independent legal entities, they have, in practice, been operated as a single workplace forming an integrated management unit."

The case was finalized on October 16, 2024, as the company withdrew its appeal to the Supreme Court, affirming the High Court's decision.

2. Judgments and Applicability of Each Case

(1) Case 1: Supreme Court ruling on October 25, 2024, 2023Du37391

The Supreme Court recognized the Korean branch of a German corporation, consisting of two employees, as an independent entity with financial autonomy. It ruled that, as an independent workplace, the employee count for the purposes of the Labor Standards Act (LSA) should consider only the employees of the Korean branch, and exclude those of the foreign corporation.

The Court emphasized that the term "business or workplace" in Article 11 of the LSA refers to workplaces located within South Korea. It further stated: *"A business or workplace is deemed to exist only when the economic and social activities are so integrated and cohesive that the regulations governing employment relationships can be uniformly applied."*

In this case, the German corporation's Korean branch operated independently in the South Korean market, generating its own revenue and conducting its own operations. Although the Korean subsidiary was subject to the German corporation's management as a subsidiary, the Court found this to be characteristic of a multinational corporation and not grounds to negate the branch's independence.

This judgment affirms the independence of a Korean branch if it operates its own accounting and business activities, even under the control of a foreign parent company.

적으로 독립성이 인정되는 경우에도 마찬가지로 보아야 한다"고 판시하였다.

서울고등법원은 위 판례 기준과 사실관계를 확인한 후, 본 사건에 대해 "원고들은 별개의 독립된 법인의 형태를 취하고 있기는 하나, 실질적으로는 경영상의 일체를 이루는 하나의 사업장으로 운영되었다"고 판단하였다. 대법원에서 상고 진행 중 회사가 취하하여 고등법원 판결이 확정되었다(2024년 10월 16일).

2. 각 사례별 판단 및 적용 가능성

(1) 제1사건 : 대법원 2024.10.25. 선고 2023두37391 판결

대법원은 국내의 사업장이 2명으로 구성되어 있는 독일법인의 한국지사는 독립법인이고, 재무적 독립성을 인정하였다. 이는 독립된 사업장으로 상시 근로자수 산정에서 외국법인을 제외한 한국법인의 인원만 고려해야 한다고 판단하였다. 대법원은 상시 근로자 산정에 있어 "근로관계의 각종 규율이 통일적으로 적용될 수 있는 실질적으로 동일한 경제적, 사회적 활동 단위라고 볼 수 있는 경우에 한하여 하나의 사업 또는 사업장을 구성할 수 있으므로, 근로기준법 제11조의 사업 또는 사업장은 대한민국 내에 위치한 사업 또는 사업장을 말한다."라고 판정하였다.

이 사건의 전제가 된 독일법인과 이 법인이 설립한 한국법인은 독일제품에 대해 한국시장에서 독자적으로 영업하고 독자적인 수익을 창출하는 한국법인의 역할을 수행하였다. 비록 한국법인이 독일법인의 자회사 형태로 운용되어 관리 운영에서 지배를 받았다고 하더라도 이는 다국적 기업의 한국지사로서 특징에 기인한 것으로 판단하였다.

이번 판결에서 보면, 비록 한국법인의 모기업인 독일법인에 종속되어 운용되고 있지만, 독자적인 회계결산, 사업운영을 하고 있다는 점에서 한국 사업장의 독립성을 인정하고 있다.

(2) 제2사건 : 대법원 2024.10.25. 선고 2023두46074 판결

미국법인이 한국지사 설립도 하지 않고, 1명의 근로자를 고용하여 한국에 위치한 제3의 외국법인에 근로자를 소속시키고, 4대보험과 급여를 지급해 오던

(2) Case 2: Supreme Court Ruling on October 25, 2024, 2023Du46074

In this case, a U.S. corporation did not establish a Korean branch but employed one worker in Korea and assigned that worker to a third foreign corporation's office. The third corporation handled the worker's payroll and social insurance. The U.S. corporation later dismissed the worker. The Supreme Court ruled that the employment relationship existed only between the worker and the U.S. corporation that signed the employment contract and issued work instructions. It dismissed the argument that the worker's payroll and insurance arrangements through the third corporation established an employment relationship between the employee and that third corporation.

The High Court had previously ruled that the employee count should include the foreign corporation's global workforce, deeming the business a workplace with five or more employees. However, the Supreme Court rejected this, stating that the LSA applies only to workplaces located within South Korea. Since the U.S. corporation had no legal presence in South Korea, it was not subject to the LSA.

This decision establishes that foreign corporations without a legal entity or office in Korea are not subject to South Korean labor laws, even if they employ individuals within Korea

(3) Case 3: Supreme Court Ruling on October 25, 2024, 2023Du57876

In this case, the Korean branches of two foreign subsidiaries of the same Australian parent corporation shared office space and integrated their operations. The two entities exchanged personnel and operated their financial systems as a single unit. When one branch closed, the employee of that branch was dismissed. The Supreme Court ruled that the two entities functioned as a single workplace, given their integration of human and physical resources, financial systems, and unified management. Consequently, the dismissal was deemed unfair under the LSA. The Court distinguished this case as one involving two separate legal entities that, in practice, operated as a single business unit. It ruled that the closure of the branch was more akin to the dissolution of a department rather than the closure of an entire business. This decision highlights that multiple entities with operational, financial, and personnel integration can be deemed a single workplace for the purposes of the LSA.

(4) Case 4: High Court Ruling on February 3, 2023, 2022Nu50412

An American telecommunications company established a Korean subsidiary ("Corporation A")

중, 이 근로자를 해고한 사건이다. 여기서 해당 근로자가 제3의 미국법인으로부터 비록 급여를 지급받았고 4대보험이 가입되었다고 하더라도 근로관계는 없다고 판단하였다. 따라서 근로관계에 있어 실제 해당 근로자와 근로계약을 체결하고 업무를 지시하는 미국법인이 실제로 사용자로 인정하였다. 원심(고등법원)은 비록 1명 사업장이라고 하더라도 본사의 인원까지 합쳐서 판단하여야 하기 때문에 5명 이상 사업장이라고 판단하였다. 그러나 대법원은 상시 근로자 산정에 있어 한국노동법이 적용이 되는 대한민국 내에 위치한 사업 또는 사업장을 말한다고 판단하였다. 따라서 한국에 어떠한 법인도 없기 때문에 근로기준법의 적용대상이 아니라고 판단을 하였다.

사실상 한국 내 영업소나 법인이 없이 1명을 고용한 외국기업이 한국노동법을 적용할 수 없다는 것은 타당한 판단이다. 하지만 한국에 법인이 있고, 2명 이상 5명 미만을 고용한 경우에는 한국노동법이 적용되는지 여부는 업무의 구체적인 내용을 가지고 판단하여야 할 것이다.

(3) 제3사건 : 대법원 2024.10.25. 선고 2023두57876 판결

외국 모기업이 설립한 각기 다른 자회사의 한국지사와 한국영업소가 하나의 장소에서 영업을 하였다. 한국지사와 영업소는 인사교류도 하였고, 회계적으로도 하나의 기업처럼 운용되었다. 그러던 중 한국영업소가 폐업을 하면서 거기에 소속된 근로자가 해고되었다. 대법원은 모기업이 같은 한국지사와 한국영업소는 동일한 사업장으로 판단하여, 영업소 폐업으로 인한 해고는 부당한 해고라고 판정하였다. 이 사례는 형식상 두개의 다른 사업체이지만, 유기적으로 동일한 사업장에서 유사한 업무를 수행하였기 때문에 하나의 사업장으로 판단하였다. 즉, 영업소 폐업은 일정규모의 한 부서가 폐지 되는 것으로 판단해서 실제 기업이 폐업하는 것과 구분하였다. 외국 모기업이 세운 한 한국내 2개의 다른 회사는 사실상 인적, 물적, 회계적으로 동일하게 운영되었기 때문에 하나의 사업장으로 본 사례이다.

(4) 제4사건 : 고등법원 2023.2.3. 선고 2022두50412 판결

미국통신회사는 한국에 독자 법인을 설립하고 통신업을 하고 있다. 한국에서

to engage in telecommunications services. The employee concerned ("the Employee") was hired by the U.S. headquarters through an interview conducted by a U.S. executive. The Employee conducted business in Korea in the U.S. headquarters' name and used its contracts and systems.

The Seoul Labor Commission ruled that the U.S. headquarters and Corporation A constituted a single workplace. It found that the U.S. headquarters effectively managed recruitment, work instructions, and compensation, and thus the combined workforce exceeded five employees, making the LSA applicable.

Both the first and second instances upheld this judgment, rejecting Corporation A's claim that only the Korean subsidiary's employees should be considered. The case was closed after the company withdrew its Supreme Court appeal, finalizing the High Court's decision. This case reinforces that foreign headquarters and a Korean subsidiary may be treated as a single workplace if there is substantial integration in personnel, operations, and decision-making.

3. Conclusion

Case 1 affirms the independence of a Korean subsidiary if it operates independently, while **Case 2** clarifies that foreign corporations without a legal presence in Korea cannot be subject to the LSA. However, **Case 3** and **Case 4** establish that operational and managerial integration can lead to multiple entities being treated as a single workplace under the LSA. The key precedent established in Case 1 and Case 2 is:

A business or workplace is deemed to exist only when the economic and social activities are so integrated and cohesive that the regulations governing employment relationships can be uniformly applied. The term "business or workplace" in Article 11 of the Labor Standards Act refers to workplaces located within South Korea.

At the same time, **Case 4** highlights the importance of examining the substantive and practical relationships governing employment to determine whether the LSA is applicable. Courts appear to be moving toward recognizing the independence of Korean subsidiaries in some cases while emphasizing the importance of operational and managerial integration in others. Foreign corporations operating in Korea must carefully evaluate the criteria for determining employee counts under the LSA to ensure compliance.

근무하는 해당 직원은 본사 임원의 면접을 통해서 채용되었고, 본사의 이메일과 홈페이지를 사용하였고, 본사의 계약서를 가지고 본사의 이름으로 한국 고객 회사와 계약을 체결하였다. 본사 매니저가 해당 직원에게 업무를 지시하였고, 직원 또한 업무 보고를 하였다. 해당 근로자의 연차휴가 사용이나 비용지출도 본사 상급자의 사전 승인을 받고 업무를 수행하였다. 비록 한국법인에서 업무를 수행하지만, 채용부터 업무수행 일체, 그리고 급여와 인센티브도 본사에서 결정하였다. 이러한 경우 비록 한국직원이 3명이지만, 본사와 한국지점은 동일한 사업이나 사업장으로 간주하여 5인 이상의 사업장으로 판단하였다. 반면 회사는 국내 사업장 근로자 만을 상시 근로자 수로 판단하여야 한다는 주장을 하였는데, 1심과 2심은 이에 동의하지 않았다. 회사가 상고하여 대법원에서 다투던 중 회사가 상소를 취하하여 고등법원의 판결이 확정된 사안이다.

3. 시사점

제1사건은 한국의 독립법인을 인정한 사건이고, 제2사건은 한국사업에서 1명만 고용하고 있었기 때문에 예상할 수 있었던 판례였다. 하지만, 여기서 인용한 판례는 앞으로 5명 미만 외국기업의 판단에 있어 기준을 제시한 것이라 본다. 그 내용은 "근로관계의 각종 규율이 통일적으로 적용될 수 있는 실질적으로 동일한 경제적, 사회적 활동단위라고 볼 수 있는 경우에 한하여 하나의 사업 또는 사업장을 구성할 수 있으므로, 근로기준법 제11조의 사업 또는 사업장은 대한민국 내에 위치한 사업 또는 사업장을 말한다."고 판시하고 있다. 그러나 제3사건과 제4사건에서 보면, 비록 한국내 외국기업의 독립법인이 있다고 하더라도 근로관계의 실질적이고 구체적인 관계에서 사업장 규모를 판단하여야 한다고 판시하고 있다. 따라서 하나의 사업 또는 사업장에 해당하는지 여부는 구체적인 사실관계를 검토한 후 판단해야 한다. 아울러 법원은 제1사건에서 인용된 내용과 같이 외국 본사와 한국지사 관계에 있어, 한국법인의 독립성을 확대하는 방향으로 판단하고 있는 점에서 국내에서 활동중인 외국기업은 상시 근로자수 판단 유의해야 할 것이다.

Section 3: Employee and Employer

I. Concept of Employee

1. Definition

Article 2(1) of the Labor Standards Act stipulates that the term “worker” in this Act refers to a person who offers work to a business or workplace to earn wage, regardless of the kind of job(s) he/she is engaged in. Whether someone is an employee or not is dependent on the following factors: ① it is not determined by the kind of job(s) he/she is engaged in; ② the person works at a business or workplace; ③ the person offers work to earn wage. In understanding this concept, wage are at the center, while the key point to consider is whether a subordinate relationship exists between the work provider and the work user.[21)]

2. Scholarly views

(1) Interpretational

This view claims that the current judicial ruling regarding the criteria for determination of employee status has some difficulty in understanding because its criteria are enumerated with factual evidence in parallel order. To overcome this problem, the criteria can be categorized into substantial signs and formal signs from which employee status can be determined as existing or not.[22)] Such substantial signs include whether there is command and control, the relationship between the work offered and the current business, and the work provider's situation. The formal signs refer to items whose existence depends on the employer's decisions, which include whether income tax and social security insurance premiums are paid, whether personnel evaluations for the person are performed, and whether the person

21) Lim, Jongryul, 「Labor Law」, 13th edition, 2015, Parkyoung sa, page 32.

22) Kang, Sungtae, Different types of employment, and judgment of employee status under the Labor Standards Act†「Labor Law Study」No. 11 ho, 2000, p. 35.

제3절 근로자와 사용자

Ⅰ. 근로자 개념

1. 개 념

근로기준법 제2조 제1항은 '근로자'란 직업의 종류와 관계없이 임금을 목적으로 사업이나 사업장에 근로를 제공하는 자를 말한다.라고 정의하고 있다. 근로자의 개념 요소를 '직업의 종류를 불문하고', '사업 또는 사업장에', '임금을 목적으로 근로를 제공하는 자'라고 설명하고 있다. 근로자의 개념 설정에서 임금을 그중심 개념으로 두고 있으며, 또한 노무 제공자와 노무 이용자 사이에 사용종속관계를 근로자의 핵심적인 요소로 파악하고 있다.[21)]

2. 학설의 검토

(1) 해석론적 이론

이 학설은, 현재 판례가 취하고 있는 문제점, 즉 사용종속관계를 바탕으로 근로자성 판단 논리의 사실적 징표들을 병렬적으로 나열하는 데서 발생하는 문제점을 극복하기 위하여 근로자성을 실질적 징표와 형식적 징표를 구별하여 판단하여야 한다고 주장한다.[22)] 이 학설은 실질적 징표로서 '지휘·감독의 존재여부',' 제공된 노무와 당해 사업과의 관계' 및' 노무공급자의 사정', 반면 형식적 징표로 사용자의 선택에 의하여 그 운영실태의 변경이 가능한 사항과 결부된 요소가 되는 항목으로써' 보수액',' 보수의 종류',' 지급의 방법',' 사용자에 의한 세금 · 사회보험료의 지급여부', '취업자에 관한 인사고과서류의 작성여부' 및

21) 임종률,『 노동법』, 제18판, 2020, 박영사, 32면.
22) 강성태, 특수고용관계와 근로기준법상 근로자성 판단, 『노동법학』제11호, 2000, 35면.

has a contractual duty to receive permission before getting a second job.[23)] That is, this view holds that employee status can be determined through the substantial signs, and formal signs can be excluded from the factors that determine a subordinate relationship.

(2) Law-based[24)]

This view holds that the concept of 'employee' should be interpreted in accordance with the related legal provisions. Korean labor law has the definition of employee in Article 2(1) of the Labor Standards Act(the LSA), and any judgment of employee status should begin with interpretation of this provision. The LSA definition of 'employee' contains four determining factors: ① the status can be determined regardless of the kind of job; ② the person offers work to earn wage; ③ the person offers work at a business or workplace; and ④ the person offers work. Of these four factors, status can be determined regardless if the kind of job is not directly related to establishing employee status, and so will not be included for consideration.

3. Judicial ruling

The Supreme Court gave clear criteria for determination of employee status in a lawsuit case involving a full-time instructor at a private institute: first, employee status may exist regardless of the type of contract; second, the criteria for determination of a subordinate relationship are enumerated to 12 items; third, the conditions suggested as signs of employee status shall be determined as decisive or not by considering whether the employer can unilaterally decide whether those conditions exist. These criteria are used to determine employee status, and they are stipulated in the following paragraph.

The Supreme Court[25)] ruled that whether a person is considered an employee under the Labor Standards Act shall be determined by whether, in actual practice, that person offers work to the employer as a subordinate of the employer in a business or workplace to earn wage, regardless of the contract type such as an employment contract or a service

---

23) Yoo, Sungjae, 「Legal arrangement according to the variety of employment types: employee status in non-traditional employment」, Korea Legislation Research Institute, 2003.

24) Park, Jonghee, Employee concept according to the Labor Standards Act, 「Labor Law Study」, No. 16 ho, 2003, pp. 74-76.

25) Supreme Court ruling on Dec. 7, 2006: 2004Da29736 Full-time instructors' employee status

'부업에 관해 허가를 받아야 할 계약상의 의무'를 들고 있다.[23] 즉, 이러한 구분을 통해 근로자성의 판단기준에서 사용종속관계의 요소 중 형식적 징표는 배제하고, 실질적 징표를 가지고 판단하여 한다고 주장한다.

(2) 실정법상 이론[24]

실정법상 정의규정에 충실하게 근로자 개념을 형성하자는 주장이다. 이 학설은 우리나라의 경우 근로기준법 제2조 제1항에 근로자에 대한 정의규정을 두고 있으므로, 근로자성 판단은 이러한 정의규정에서 출발하여야 한다고 주장한다. '근로자'의 정의에 포함된 항목으로 "직업의 종류와 관계없이", "임금을 목적으로", "사업이나 사업장에", "근로를 제공하는 자"여야 한다는 네 가지 요소가 있다. 위의 네 가지 기준 중 "직업의 종류와 관계없이"는 근로자성과는 무관하므로, 이를 제외한 나머지 세 가지를 가지고 판단할 수 있다.

3. 판례법리

종합반 강사에 대한 근로자성 판단 사례에 있어서 대법원은 근로자 여부를 판단하는 명확한 기준을 제시하고 있다. 첫째는 계약의 형식과 무관하다. 둘째, 사용종속관계 기준을 12가지로 나열하고 있다. 셋째, 사용종속관계 판단기준으로 제시된 항목에 있어 사용자가 일방적으로 결정할 수 있는 부분인지 아닌지 판단하여야 한다고 설명하고 있다. 이 판례는 근로자성 판단에 대한 기준으로 사용되고 있으며, 그 판단기준은 다음과 같다.

판례[25]는 근로기준법상 근로자에 해당하는지 여부는 계약의 형식이 고용계약인지 도급 계약인지보다 그 실질에 있어 근로자가 사업 또는 사업장에 임금을 목적으로 종속적인 관계에서 사용자에게 근로를 제공하였는지 여부에 따라 판단하여야 한다고 보고 있다. 여기서 말하는 종속적인 관계가 있는지 여부는 ①

23) 유성재, 『취업형태의 다양화에 따른 법제정비방안(II)–특수고용직 종사자의 노동법적 지위를 중심으로』, 한국법제연구원, 2003.

24) 박종희, 근로기준법상의 근로개념, 『노동법학』, 제16호, 2003, 74~76면.

25) 대법원 2006.12.7, 2004다29736, 종합반 입시 강사의 근로자성.

contract. Whether or not a subordinate relationship with the employer exists shall be determined by collectively considering: ① whether the rules of employment or other service regulations apply to a person; ② whether that person's duties are decided by the employer, ③ whether the person has been significantly supervised or directed during his/her work performance by the employer; ④ whether his/her working hours and workplaces were designated and restricted by the employer; ⑤ who owns the equipment, raw materials or working tools; ⑥ whether the person can be substituted by a third party hired by the person; ⑦ whether the person's service is directly related to business profit or loss as is the case in one's own business; ⑧ whether payment is remuneration for work performed or ⑨ whether a basic or fixed wage is determined in advance; ⑩ whether income tax is deducted for withholding purposes; ⑪ whether work provision is continuous and exclusive to the employer; ⑫ whether the person is registered as an employee by the Social Security Insurance Act or other laws, and the economic and social conditions of both sides. Provided, that as whether basic wage or fixed wage is determined, whether income tax is deducted for withholding, and whether the person is registered for social security insurances could be determined at the employer's discretion by taking advantage of his/her superior position, the characteristics of employee cannot be denied because of the absence of these mentioned items.

The above criteria are not applied formally or uniformly, but in the event facts equivalent to the above items exist, it should be determined after reviewing whether these facts were decided by the employer's superior position or required naturally by such job characteristics.[26)]

4. MOEL Guidelines: Criteria for determining "employee" status[27)]

Whether a person is considered an employee under the LSA shall be decided by whether that person offers work to the employer as a subordinate of the employer in a business or workplace to earn wage in actual practice, regardless of whether the type of contract is an employment contract or service agreement under Civil Law.[28)]

---

26) Supreme Court ruling on May 11, 2006, 2005Da20910: Ready-mix truck driver case

27) MOEL Guidelines: LSA team-5241, on Dec. 9, 2009; LSA team-1333, on Feb. 2, 2016.

28) Supreme Court ruling on Sept. 11, 2008, 2008Da27035.

업무 내용을 사용자가 정하고, ② 취업규칙 또는 복무(인사)규정 등의 적용을 받으며 ③ 업무수행 과정에서 사용자가 상당한 지휘·감독을 하는지, ④ 사용자가 근무시간과 근무장소를 지정하고 근로자가 이에 구속을 받는지, ⑤ 노무제공자가 스스로 비품·원자재나 작업도구 등을 소유하거나 ⑥ 제3자를 고용하여 업무를 대행하게 하는 등 독립하여 자신의 재산으로 사업을 영위할 수 있는지, ⑦ 노무제공을 통한 이윤의 창출과 손실의 초래 등 위험을 스스로 안고 있는지와 ⑧ 보수의 성격이 근로 자체의 대상적(對償的) 성격인지, ⑨ 기본급이나 고정급이 정하여졌는지 및 ⑩ 근로소득세의 원천징수 여부 등 보수에 관한 사항, ⑪근로제공 관계의 계속성과 사용자에 대한 전속성의 유무와 그 정도, ⑫ 사회보장제도에 관한 법령에서 근로자로서 지위를 인정받는지 등의 경제적·사회적 여러 조건을 종합하여 판단하여야 한다. 다만, 기본급이나 고정급이 정하여졌는지, 근로소득세를 원천징수하였는지, 사회보장제도에 관하여 근로자로 인정받는지 등의 사정은 사용자가 경제적으로 우월한 지위를 이용하여 임의로 정할 여지가 크기 때문에, 그러한 점들이 인정되지 않는다는 것만으로 근로자성을 쉽게 부정하여서는 안 된다.

상기 기준은 형식적·획일적으로 적용되는 것이 아니라, 상기 기준에 부합되는 사실관계가 존재하는 경우에도 이것이 사용자의 우월한 지위에 기인하는 것인지 아니면 업무의 특수성상 당연히 존재하는 것인지의 여부를 판단하여야 할 것이다.[26]

4. 근로자성의 구체적 판단기준(행정해석)[27]

근로기준법상 근로자에 해당하는지를 판단함에 있어서는 그 계약의 형식이 민법상 고용계약인지 또는 도급계약인지에 관계없이 그 실질에 있어 근로자가 사업 또는 사업장에 임금을 목적으로 종속적인 관계에서 근로를 제공하였는지 여부에 따라 판단한다.[28]

---

26) 대법원 2006.5.11, 2005다20910(레미콘 운송업자 사건).
27) 행정해석: 근로기준과-5241, 2009.12.9; 근로개선정책과-1333, 2012.2.16.
28) 대법원 2008.9.11, 2008다27035.

The MOEL determines whether the contractor has employee or freelancer status when considering collectively the seven items suggested below by the aforementioned Supreme Court ruling.

(1) Whether the rules of employment or service regulations apply to a person whose duties are decided by the employer, and whether the person has been supervised or directed during his/her work performance specifically and individually by the employer

Supervision and direction mean that the person implements the work that the employer wants him/her to do under the employer's direction and command. Whether the work is performed under the direction and supervision of the employer shall be determined by considering the following criteria collectively:

1) Whether such things as employment, training, retirement, etc. apply to said person;

2) Whether said person can decide what work he/she will do, or whether said person has freedom to obey or reject work instructions.

(2) Whether his/her working hours, working days and workplaces are designated and restricted by the employer

1) Whether his/her working hours or working days are designated: falls under Restrictions in working hours;

2) Whether his/her workplaces are designated or the times determined when said person shall provide labor service in the directed workplaces: falls under Restrictions in workplaces

(3) Whether a third party hired by said person can be a substitute for him/her

The inability to substitute someone for oneself to do the labor service is not a basic criterion in determining whether a subordinate relationship exists or not, but when a substitute is possible, this becomes a significant indicator that a relationship of direction and supervision may not exist.

(4) Whether said person owns the equipment, raw material, or working tools he/she uses

If the machine or tools owned by the work performer are very expensive, and if the person shall be responsible for his/her own workplace injuries, he/she is closer to being a business owner who judges and takes on risk at his/her own discretion, and indications that he/she is an employee are weak.

노동부는 이러한 대법원 판례의 기준에 따라 아래의 7가지의 세부기준을 종합적으로 고려하여 근로자인지 프리랜서인지 판단하려고 한다.

(1) 업무의 내용이 사용자에 의하여 정하여지고 취업규칙 또는 복무(인사)규정 등의 적용을 받으며 업무수행과정에 있어서도 사용자로부터 구체적이고 직접적인 지휘·감독을 받는지 여부

지휘·감독이란 사용자의 지휘·감독을 받아 사용자가 원하는 내용의 일을 하는 것을 말하는 것으로서 다음과 같은 기준들을 종합적으로 고려하여 판단한다.

1) 채용·교육·퇴직 등 노무관리의 수행 여부
2) 업무내용의 결정과 업무지시에 대한 승낙·거절 자유의 여부

(2) 사용자에 의하여 근무시간과 근무장소가 지정되고 이에 구속을 받는지 여부

1) 사용자가 출퇴근 시간이나 출근일을 정하는 경우 등은 시간적 구속에 해당한다.
2) 작업장소가 정해져 있거나 사용자가 지시한 장소에서 근로하는 경우 등은 장소적 구속에 해당한다.

(3) 근로자 스스로가 제3자를 고용하여 업무를 대행케 하는 등 업무의 대체성 유무

노무제공의 비대체성은 사용종속관계에 대한 기본적인 판단기준은 아니나, 대체성이 인정되는 경우에는 지휘·감독 관계가 부인되는 요인의 하나이다.

(4) 비품, 원자재나 작업도구 등의 소유관계

업무수행자가 소유하고 있는 기계·기구가 매우 비싸거나, 업무상 손해를 본인이 부담한다면 스스로의 계산과 위험부담으로 행하는 사업자의 성격이 강하고 근로자성을 약하게 하는 요소가 된다.

(5) Whether payment is remuneration for work and whether a basic wage or fixed wage is determined in advance:

1) If remuneration is a fixed amount regardless of work performance and paid at a fixed rate for work, and if the fixed amount is designed to provide a living for the person, this can be described as characteristics of being an employee;

2) If the person's level of remuneration is remarkably higher than other employees who do the same or a similar job in a corresponding company, this can be remuneration for a business assignment with individual responsibility and risk and not a characteristic of being an employee.

(6) Whether work provision is continuous and exclusive to the employer

If the person is restricted from simultaneous employment with another company by company regulations, or if the person cannot work for two or more companies at the same time due to his/her unavailability in reality, said person's provision of labor service can be regarded as exclusive to the employer.

(7) Whether the person is registered as an employee under the Social Security Insurance Acts or other laws

In cases where the person pays income tax on his/her remuneration, this is a supplementary fact that can be positively determined as an employee characteristic. However, simply because remuneration has not been subject to income tax is not a clear indication that this remuneration isn't a wage.

5. Comments

The scholarly view and judicial view are consistent in the following criteria: ①In employment relations, employee status shall be determined by whether there is a subordinate relationship between the parties or not(judgment by subordinate relations); ② whether there is a subordinate relationship between the parties or not shall not be determined by the type of contract or title, but by actual facts of the labor provision relations(judgment based upon actual relations); and ③ the actual facts of the labor provision relations shall be determined in consideration of an overall collective evaluation of all items(overall consideration).

(5) 보수가 근로자체의 대상적 성격을 가지고 있는지 여부와 기본급이나 고정급이 정하여져 있는지 여부 등 보수에 관한 사항

1) 보수가 일의 성과와 관계없이 고정급 부분이 있고, 업무의 배분 등에 의해 사실상 고정급으로 되어 있으며, 그 금액이 생계유지 기능 등 생활 보장적인 요소가 강하다고 인정되는 경우에는 근로자성이 인정된다.

2) 보수 수준이 당해 기업에서 같거나 비슷한 업무를 하는 종업원에 비해 현저히 높다고 하면, 이는 스스로의 계산과 위험으로 사업경영을 행하는 사업자에 대해 지불하는 대가로 인정될 수 있어 근로자성이 약해진다.

(6) 근로제공 관계에 계속성과 사용자에의 전속성 유무와 정도

전속성은 제도적으로 타사의 업무에 종사하는 것이 금지 되거나 또는 현실적으로 근로자가 시간적 여유가 없어서 2개 이상의 사업장에 동시에 근로를 제공할 수 없다면 전속성이 있다.

(7) 사회보장제도에 관한 법령 등 다른 법령에 의하여 근로자로서의 지위를 인정 받는지 여부

보수에 대해 근로소득세를 납부할 경우에는 근로자성을 긍정적으로 판단하는 보강요소가 되며 단, 근로소득세 부과대상이 아니라는 이유만으로 임금이 아니라고 할 수는 없다.

5. 코멘트

학설과 판례는 다음과 같은 기준을 가지고 일관성 있게 판단하고 있다. 고용관계에 있어 ① 사용종속관계의 존재여부에 따라 근로자성을 인정할 수 있고(종속성에 의한 판단), ② 사용종속관계의 존재여부는 계약의 형식이나 명칭이 아니라 노무공급 관계의 실질적 사실관계에 따라 판단하며(실질적 판단), 또한 ③ 노무공급 관계의 실질적 사실관계는 그것을 둘러싼 제반 요소를 종합적으로 고려하여 판단한다(종합적 고려). 따라서 사용종속관계에 대한 판단은 근로관계

Accordingly, employee status according to subordinate relations shall be determined after considering practical facts of the employment and reviewing them overall. Judicial ruling states that the criteria for ruling on employee status shall not be determined by the format of employment relations, and shall not consider as important in judgment whether the person paid corporate tax or was registered for the social security insurances, which can easily be decided by the employer due to his/her superior position. These points emphasize that employee status shall be determined by employment relations in actuality.

Ⅱ. Related labor cases

1. Employees

(1) In cases where a person works for an employer in a subordinate relationship which takes the form of subcontracting, the person is an employee under the LSA.

If a person agrees to provide only a certain type of labor to a business or workplace of a contractor-employer while remaining in a subordinate employment relationship, and to receive payment according to results of the work done, or performance, the person also becomes an employee as defined in Article 2 of the LSA, even when the contract has taken the form of subcontracting .[29)]

(2) When a director of a company is engaged in a given type of work and gets paid for such work by the employer, as well as performing the mandated job of handling business management, it is possible to classify him/her as an employee under the LSA.

The LSA defines an employee as a person who provides labor for an employer and receives payment in return for the work done. Accordingly, in cases where a director is engaged in a certain type of work and gets paid for such work, in addition to performing the mandated executive job, the director can be deemed an employee as defined in the LSA.[30)]

---

29) Supreme Court ruling on May 26, 1987, 87Do604

30) Supreme Court ruling on May 12, 1992, 91Nu11490

의 실질적 관계를 가지고 종합적으로 판단하여야 할 것이다. 판례는 근로자성 판단기준에서 고용계약의 형식에 구애됨이 없이 판단하여야 하고, 사용자의 경제적 우위에 의하여 쉽게 결정될 수 있는 사업소득세 납부여부, 4대보험 가입여부 등은 근로자성 판단에서 중요한 부분이 될 수 없다고 보고 있다. 이는 실질적인 근로관계를 파악하여 근로자성 여부를 판단한다는 점을 강조하고 있는 부분이라 할 수 있다.

Ⅱ. 관련 판례

1. 근로자로 인정한 판례

(1) 도급계약의 형식을 빌린 종속 노동관계의 근로자도 근로기준법상의 근로자에 해당된다.

도급계약의 형식을 빌렸다 하더라도 그 계약내용이 사용자와의 사이에 사용종속관계를 유지하면서 도급인의 사업 또는 사업장에 특정한 노무제공만을 목적으로 하고 있고 그 노무제공에 대하여 능률적 급여 내지 성과급을 지급받기로 하는 것이라면 이에 따라 노무를 제공한 자는 근로기준법 제2조 소정의 "근로자"에 해당한다.[29]

(2) 회사의 이사가 회사로부터 위임받은 사무를 처리하는 것 이외에 일정한 노무를 담당하고 그 대가로 일정한 보수를 지급받는 경우에는 근로기준법상의 근로자이다.

근로기준법의 적용을 받는 근로자란 사용자로부터 근로의 대가를 받고 사용자에 근로를 제공하는 자를 말하는 것이므로, 회사의 이사가 회사로부터 위임받은 사무를 처리하는 이외에 일정한 노무를 담당하고 그 대가로 일정한 보수를 지급받아 왔다면 근로기준법상의 근로자라고 볼 수 있다.[30]

29) 대법원 1987.5.26, 87도604.

30) 대법원 1992.5.12, 91누11490.

(3) A person who provides a specific service under the direction and supervision of others, such as directors, and who receives fixed pay as remuneration can be regarded as an employee defined by the Labor Standards Act.[31)]

Whether it is appropriate to regard a director as an employee defined by the Labor Standards Act has nothing to do with the manner in which the contract is made but whether the director was paid to provide a service that requires him to be subordinate to another. Such a director can be regarded as an employee regardless of whether he/she is holding the position or title of a company director or auditor, in the real sense or just in name, as long as he/she receives remuneration as compensation for providing a specific labor service under the direction and supervision of the employer or he/she receives remuneration as compensation for taking charge of a specific labor service under the direction and supervision of persons such as the representative director in addition to the duties assigned to him/her by the company.

(4) The Supreme Court ruled that native English instructors working for "C" Language Institute are employees rather than freelancers, and are entitled to severance pay, annual paid leave allowance, and weekly holiday allowance.

The main point of this case was whether native instructors are employees or freelancers. The courts used the legal criteria for determining whether someone is an employee or not in their judgment. However, the Defendant claimed that the Plaintiffs ① signed an 'Agreement for Teaching Services' voluntarily, not an employment agreement, and also paid business taxes; ② that the Defendant paid remarkably high benefits in consideration of there being no severance pay; and ③ that, as the Plaintiffs agreed that this agreement would not include severance pay, if the Plaintiffs requested additional severance pay, it would be a violation of the good-faith principle.[32)]

(5) Election offices and election campaign staff for a lawmaker are respectively considered workplaces and employees under the Labor Standards Act

The scope of application in the Labor Standards Act(Article 11) regulates, "This Act shall apply to all businesses or workplaces in which five or more workers are ordinarily employed." Workplace refers to designated workplaces or parts of a business implemented to do all kinds of continuous work as activities under a systematically organized body. The

---

31) Supreme Court ruling on Sept. 26, 2003, 2002Da64681

32) Supreme Court ruling on June 11, 2015, 2014Da88161

(3) 대표이사 등의 지휘·감독 아래 일정한 노무를 담당하고 그 대가로 일정한 보수를 지급받아 왔다면 그러한 임원은 근로기준법상의 근로자에 해당한다.

근로기준법의 적용을 받는 근로자에 해당하는지 여부는 계약의 형식에 관계없이 그 실질에 있어서 임금을 목적으로 종속적 관계에서 사용자에게 근로를 제공하였는지 여부에 따라 판단하여야 할 것이므로, 회사의 이사 또는 감사 등 임원이라고 하더라도 그 지위 또는 명칭이 형식적·명목적인 것이고 사용자의 지휘·감독 아래 일정한 근로를 제공하면서 그 대가로 보수를 받는 관계에 있다거나 또는 회사로부터 위임받은 사무를 처리하는 외에 대표이사 등의 지휘·감독 아래 일정한 노무를 담당하고 그 대가로 일정한 보수를 지급받아 왔다면 그러한 임원은 근로기준법상의 근로자에 해당한다.[31)]

(4) 대법원은 C 어학원의 원어민 강사들이 프리랜서가 아닌 근로자임을 인정하고, 피고에게 원고의 근로자신분으로 발생하는 퇴직금, 연차휴가 수당, 주휴수당에 대해 지급의무가 있다고 판결하였다.

사건의 주요 쟁점은 원고의 신분이 근로자인지 프리랜서인지에 달려있다. 피고는 원고가 근로계약이 아닌 강의서비스 계약을 체결하였고, 원고의 사업소득세를 납부하였으며, 퇴직금이 없음을 고려하여 현저히 많은 보수를 지급했고, 원고들도 이에 동의하여 (퇴직금이 없다는 것) 계약을 하였기 때문에, 추가적으로 이를 청구하는 것은 신의칙에 반한다고 주장하였다. 하지만, 법원은 근로자성 판례법리를 사용하고 있다.[32)]

(5) 국회의원 선거사무소와 선거사무원은 각각 근로기준법상의 사업장과 근로자에 해당한다.

근로기준법의 적용범위를 규정한 근로기준법 제11조는 상시 5인 이상의 근로자를 사용하는 모든 사업 또는 사업장에 적용한다고 규정하고 있는바, 여기서 말하는 사업장인지 여부는 하나의 활동주체가 유기적 관련 아래 사회적 활

31) 대법원 2003.9.26, 2002다64681.
32) 대법원 2015.6.11, 2014다88161

Labor Standards Act applies to this kind of workplace, even though it is a one-time business or operates only temporarily, without limitations to the type of business nor whether it is for profit or a non-profit organization. As Article 2 of the Labor Standards Act does not stipulate the specific kinds of work an employee is engaged in, work for a political body belongs to a business, workplace, or a job, as defined by the Labor Standards Act.

A candidate set up an election office to organize his campaign, hired people to be paid on a daily basis, had them participate in election campaigning under his command and supervision, and required their work for a period of time(13 days). In this case, this operation shall be considered as a workplace as stipulated by the Labor Standards Act(Article 11). Although the election campaign staff were designated for and registered with the National Election Commission, if they had an agreement with the candidate to be paid a daily wage and they provided contractual labor service under the candidate's direction and supervision, they are considered employees under the Labor Standards Act.[33)]

2. Employer

(1) Executive officials are not employees as defined in the LSA.

Executive officials, including directors, are mandated by their employer to deal with a certain scope of business management. In general, they are not in an employment relationship that requires them to provide a given type of work under the supervision and control of the employer and receive a given amount of wage in return. In this sense, executive officials shall not be considered employees under the LSA, unless under some exceptional circumstances.[34)]

(2) Even though the person has provided labor service, if he was not in an employment relationship, he cannot be regarded as an employee under the Labor Standards Act.

In a ruling in Busan, a plaintiff could not be an employee when considering the following items collectively: Even though the employee's place of work was restricted to company premises and the company could not substitute him with other employees, the service provider was not limited to specific working hours when his coming to and

33) Supreme Court ruling on Oct. 26, 2007, 2005Do9218.

34) Supreme Court ruling on Dec. 22, 1992, 92Da28228

동으로서 계속적으로 행하는 모든 작업이 이루어지는 단위 장소 또는 장소적으로 구획된 사업체 일부분에 해당되는지에 달려있으므로, 그 사업의 종류를 한정하지 아니하고 영리사업인지 여부도 불문하며, 1회적이거나 그 사업기간이 일시적이라 하여 근로기준법의 적용대상이 아니라 할 수 없고, 근로자를 정의한 같은 법 제2조 1항에서도 직업의 종류를 한정하고 있지 아니하므로, 정치단체도 위 각 조문의 사업이나 사업장 또는 직업에 해당된다 할 것이다.

국회의원 입후보자가 선거활동을 하기 위하여 일정한 장소에서 선거사무소를 두고, 사람을 일급제로 고용하여 자신의 지휘·감독하에 선거홍보를 하게 하면서 일정기간(13일) 동안 계속해서 운영하여 온 경우, 위 선거사무소는 적어도 그 범위 내에서는 근로기준법 제11조에서 정한 사업장에 해당한다고 보는것이 타당하고, 선거사무소에서 선임되어 관할 선거관리위원회에 신고를 마친 선거사무원이라고 하더라도 선거후보자와 사이에 일급제로 금원을 지급받기로 약정하고 선거후보자의 지시·감독을 받아 소정의 근로를 제공하였을 경우 근로기준법상의 근로자에 해당한다.[33)]

2. 사용자로 인정한 판례

(1) 회사의 이사 등 임원은 근로기준법상의 근로자가 아니다.

회사의 업무집행권을 가진 이사 등 임원은 그가 회사의 주주가 아니라 하더라도 회사로부터 일정한 사무 처리의 위임을 받고 있는 것이므로 특별한 사정이없는 한 사용자의 지휘·감독 아래 일정한 근로를 제공하고 소정의 임금을 받는 고용관계에 있는 것이 아니어서 근로기준법상의 근로자라고 할 수 없다.[34)]

(2) 노무제공자가 노무를 제공하였다고 하더라도 사용종속관계가 인정되지 않을 경우 근로기준법상 근로자로 볼 수 없다.

근무 장소가 당해 사업장으로 제한되어 있고, 노무제공자들이 제3자를 고용하여 업무를 대행하게 할 수 없어 업무의 대체성이 없다고 하더라도 노무제공 자들

---

33) 대법원 2007.10.26, 2005도9218.
34) 대법원 1992.12.22, 92다28228.

leaving the office was controlled. The company did not have any authority to discipline the person for violation of service regulations, even though the company exercised some rights to direct and supervise in the course of work performance. His earnings were not remuneration for his labor service, and he did not receive fixed or basic pay. The establishment or termination of the labor service contract was up to the service provider.[35)]

Ⅲ. Judgment of Employee Status, with a Checklist

1. Introduction

With the arrival of the Fourth Industrial Revolution, various new occupations have been created, and while a number of intermediate occupations for both workers and the self-employed have surfaced, the criteria for determining employee status have also expanded. There has been a tendency for companies to reduce direct employment by outsourcing marginalized tasks in order to reduce labor costs and generate more profit. These outsourced services include owner-operated truck drivers, onsite after-service technicians, delivery people, shop operators, call center employees, debt collectors, commissioned delivery contractors, car sales personnel, and freelancers. Companies are directly involved in the performance of their outsourced and subcontracted tasks in order to gradually expand their operating profit. The main characteristic of subcontracting or of individual business owners is that they accomplish their tasks independently. If the employer directly manages and supervises them, this can be considered a form of illegal contract or dispatch. In such cases, the company would immediately bear additional labor costs such as employment obligations, severance pay and social insurances premiums.

Judgment on the characteristics of employee status is based on a 2006 court ruling, although it can be difficult to judge employee status because issues have to be considered on a case-by-case basis and judgments vary depending on the intuition and inclination of the judges. Therefore, it could be said that it is necessary to establish a quantification standard that will take into consideration the characteristics of the work involved and the relevant issues for various individual situations, within the standard principles of the judgment. In the following paragraphs, a checklist for the determination of employee status is presented to assist in the understanding of employee status.

---

35) Busan District Court ruling on May 17, 2006, 2005Gudan1293.

에게 기본적으로 출·퇴근에 대한 제한이 없어 근무시간의 제한을 받지 않고 있는 점, 업무수행과정에서 어느 정도의 지휘·감독권을 행사하였으나 근무 위반 등 행위에 대한 징계권이 없는 점, 작업의 대가가 근로 자체의 대상적 성격을 가진다고 볼 수 없고, 기본급, 고정급이 정해져 있지 않는 점, 노무공급관계의 성립과 종료가 노무제공자 측에게 있다고 보이는 점 등을 종합하면, 근로자로 보기 어렵다.[35)]

Ⅲ. 근로자성 판단기준과 체크리스트

1. 개 념

제 4차 산업혁명의 도래로 직업의 종류가 다양해지고, 그 중에는 근로자성과 사용자성을 동시에 가지고 있는 직업이 존재함에 따라 점점 근로기준법상 '근로사성' 판단이 모호해지고 있다. 기업은 더 많은 이윤 창출과 서비스의 전문성 등을 이유로 근로자를 직접 고용하는 대신 외주화와 같이 간접고용을 선호하고 있다. 이러한 예로 지입차주, 서비스 기사, 배달기사, 매점운영자, 콜센터직원, 채권추심원, 도급운송기사, 카마스터, 프리랜서 등이 등장하였다. 원칙적으로 상기 직업 종류는 각자의 업무를 자신의 책임하에 자율적으로 수행해야 함에도 불구하고 기업은 업무의 효율성 증대를 위하여 이들의 업무수행에 직접적, 간접적으로 관여하게 된다. 즉, 도급업무나 개인사업자 업무의 특징이 독립적으로 업무를 완수를 하는 것인데, 사업주가 이들을 직접 관리 감독하게 되면 그 시점부터 진정 도급의 형태가 아닌 불법파견의 리스크를 갖게 된다. 이러한 경우 기업은 당장 이들에 대한 고용의무와 퇴직금, 사회보험료 등 추가 인건비를 부담해야 한다.

원칙적으로 근로기준법상 근로자성 판단은 2006년 대법원 판례를 기준으로 삼고 있지만, 직업의 특성 및 업무 성격에 따라 별적으로 판단되어져야 하고 판례에 따라 다소 법관의 성향이 일부 포함된 경우가 있어 근로자성 판단 기준을 만드는데 어려움이 있다. 이러한 이유로 아래에서는 2006년 대법원 판례를 바탕으로 각 사례별 판단 기준을 정립하고자 한다.

35) 부산지방법원 2006.5.17, 2005구난1293.

2. Criteria for Determining Employee Status

(1) Employee status in the Labor Standards Act

First of all, I would like to look at employee status as it relates to the standard court ruling on this issue, concentrating on the definition of "employee" in the Labor Standards Act.

Article 2 (1) of the Labor Standards Act stipulates that the term "worker" refers to a person who offers work to a business or workplace to earn wages, regardless of the type(s) of job he/she is engaged in. The concept of "employee" includes the following factors: ① it is not determined by the type(s) of job he/she is engaged in; ② the person works at a business or workplace[36]; ③ the person offers work to earn wages. Under this definition, wages are put at the center, while the key point to be considered is whether a subordinate relationship exists between the work provider and the party who authorizes the work. That is, "employee" means "a person who offers work to earn money through a subordinate relationship."[37]

A subordinate relationship is one where a person hired by an employer provides work under the employer's direction and orders, and carries out tasks as required by the employer. In other words, an employee who offers work to earn wages can be considered as "a person offering work under a subordinate relationship with an employer."[38]

(2) Understanding subordinate relations

When judging worker status, the case is judged based on the above-mentioned "Substantial criteria for determining employee status," and the method of judging is to evaluate the worker under the Labor Standards Act if a large number of these criteria are met, by reviewing each case individually and comprehensively. The criteria can be divided into human subordinate relations, economic subordinate relations, and the dual judgment factors.[39]

1) Human subordinate relations

Human subordinate relation factors are the degree to which an employer manages and supervises workers in the course of their work. In recent years, this situation has been judged

---

36) Lim, Jongryul, 「Labor Law」, 18th Ed., 2019, Parkyoungsa, 2020, p. 29.

37) Ha, Kaprae, 「Labor Standards Act」, 33rd Ed., Joongang Economy, 2020, p. 102.

38) Supreme Court ruling on Dec. 7, 2006, 2004da29736 .

39) Kang, Sung-Tae, "Judgment Determination in Special Employment Relations and Labor Standards Act," Labor Law, No. 11, 2000, p. 35.

2. 근로자성 판단기준

(1) 근로기준법상의 근로자성

근로자성 판단기준으로 근로기준법의 근로자 개념을 바탕으로 한 기준판례를 구체적으로 살펴보고자 한다.

근로기준법은 근로자란 "직업의 종류와 관계없이 임금을 목적으로 사업이나 사업장에 근로를 제공하는 자를 말한다"(제2조 제1항 제1호). 이 정의에 포함된 사항은 ① 근로자는 사용자와 근로계약을 형성하고 근로자를 제공하는 것이고, ② 근로자는 임금, 즉 근로자가 사용자에게 근로를 제공하고 이에 대한 대가(임금)를 받아 생활하는 자이다.[36] ③ 근로자는 특정 사업 또는 사업장에서 그 사업 또는 사업장의 사용자와 사용종속관계를 형성하고 있다.[37]

근로자에 대한 개념을 이해하는데 대표적인 판례가 2006년 학원강사에 대한 근로자성 판단기준이다. 이 판례는 근로자에 대한 개념을 사용종속관계로 표시하는 징표를 열거하면서 사용자의 우월한 지위에서 정해지는 판단잣대는 제한적으로 해석되어져야 한다고 명시하고 있다.[38]

(2) 판례의 사용종속관계의 이해

판례는 근로자성을 판단할 때, 위에서 제시된 '사용종속관계의 구체적 판단기준'을 가지고 판단하며, 판단방법은 특정한 사안에 대해 개별적이고 종합적으로 검토하여 이러한 기준을 다수 충족하게 되면 근로기준법상 근로지라고 본다. 이 기준을 인적종속, 경제적 종속성 그리고 이중적판단요소로 구분할 수 있다.[39]

1) 인적종속관계

인적종속요소는 사용자가 근로자를 업무수행과정에서 관리 감독하는 정도이다. 최근 판례는 다양한 직업의 발생과 업무의 독립적인 수행 등을 고려하여 인

---

36) 임종률, 『노동법』, 제18판, 박영사, 2020, 29면

37) 하갑래, 『근로기준법』, 제33판, 중앙경제사, 2020, 102면

38) 대법원 2006.12.7, 2004다29736(종합반 강사의 근로자성 판단)

39) 강성태, "특수고용관계와 근로기준법상 근로자성 판단", 『노동법학』, 제11호, 2000, 35면 이하

by reducing the employer's work instructions from "specific and individual command and supervision" to "significant command supervision" in determining human subordinate relations in consideration of the occurrence of various jobs and the related independent contractors.[40)] Specifically, such items include ① the type of contract; ② the exercise of disciplinary authority such as hiring, firing, disciplinary action etc., ③ control over situations such as commutes or leave; ④ supervision and control during work performance; ⑤ whether working hours and place of work are controlled.

2) Economic subordinate relations

Economic subordinate relations depend on whether workers can make a profit on their own. In the case of part-time instructors, a performance-based pay system was used to apportion tuition fees with an employer according to the number of students who attended an academy. In this case, part-time instructors were not considered workers.[41)] Specifically, consideration of such items includes ① whether the company owns the necessary supplies, raw material work tools, etc.; ② whether the company is responsible for expenses incurred in the work; ③ whether a third party can perform the work for the person on his behalf and whether it is possible to engage in other tasks simultaneously; ④ whether or not the intent is to generate profit and manage their own business; ⑤ whether it is possible to engage in other business during working hours; ⑥ whether business risks are compensated for; ⑦ whether remuneration is paid for the work; and ⑧ whether long-term work is possible and whether there is any reference to exclusiveness (whether work is prohibited from other companies while performing the business).

3) Dual judgment factors

The dual judgment factors are whether a basic or fixed salary has been established: matters concerning remuneration, such as whether income tax is withheld, and whether the relationship is recognized as a worker in the social security system. If this is recognized, it can be a factor in affirming a judgment of employee status. If it is not recognized, the situation should not be denied employee status solely on this basis.[42)]

Specifically, related items include ① whether there is a fixed salary for the performer, and ② the burden of earned income tax, and whether or not four social insurances are insured.

---

40) Supreme Court ruling 2004da29736, on Dec. 7, 2006: Full-time instructors' employee status.

41) Supreme Court ruling on July 30, 1996: 98do732.

42) Supreme Court ruling on Sept. 7, 2007.

적 종속성 판단에 있어 사용자의 업무지시를 '구체적이고 개별적인 지휘·감독'에서 '상당한 지휘감독'으로 완화하여 판단하고 있다.[40] 구체적으로 ① 계약의 종류, ② 근로자의 채용, 해고, 징계 등 징계 권한 행사 여부, ③ 출퇴근, 휴가 등 통제를 받는지 여부, ④ 업무지휘 감독을 받는지 여부, ⑤ 근로시간과 근무장소 구속 여부를 가지고 판단한다.

2) 경제적 종속관계

경제적 종속요소는 근로자가 스스로 이윤을 창출할 수 있는지의 여부에 따라 결정된다. 시간제 강사의 경우에는 학원에서 수강한 학생의 수에 따라 수강료를 사용자와 나누어 가지는 성과급제를 사용하였고, 이 경우 시간제 강사의 경우에는 근로자로 보지 않았다.[41] 구체적으로 ① 비품, 원자재 작업도구 소유여부, ② 업무 중 발생 비용을 회사가 처리해주는 지의 여부, ③제3자 대한 대행가능여부와 타 업무 종사 가능 여부, ④ 이윤창출 가능여부와 개인의 수익사업 가능여부, ⑤ 독립사업으로 회사에 복무 중 타 사업에 종사여부, ⑥ 사업위험 부담여부, ⑦ 보수가 근로의 대가인지 여부, ⑧ 장기근속이 가능한 업무인지의 여부와 근로의 전속성(업무수행 중 타사에 취업금지) 여부를 말한다.

3) 이중적 요소

이중적 판단요소는 "기본급이나 고정급이 정하여졌는지; 근로소득세의 원천징수 여부 등 보수에 관한 사항; 사회보장제도에 관한 법령에서 근로자로서 지위를 인정받는지" 의 여부인데 사용자가 경제적으로 우월한 지위를 이용하여 임의로 정할 여지가 크다는 점에서 이것이 인정 된 경우에는 근로자성 판단을 긍정하는 요소가 될 수 있지만, 이것이 부정된다고 해서 이 기준만을 이유로 근로자성을 부인해서는 안될 것이다.[42]

구체적으로 ① 업무수행자에 대해 고정급이 있는지의 여부, ② 근로소득세 부담과 4대보험의 가입여부가 이에 해당한다.

---

40) 대법원 2006.12.7, 2004다29736(종합반 강사에 대한 근로자성 인정)

41) 대법원 1996.7.30, 98도732, 입시학원 단과반 강사 근로자성 부인 사건

42) 대법원 2007.9.7, 2006도777, 미용학원 강사의 근로자성 인정사건

(3) The court's judgment of subordinate relations

<Checklist for evaluating employee status[43)]>

Supreme Court Ruling (Items: details for judgment)		Factual Grounds for Employee Status	Weight	Judgment	
				Employee	Contractor
1) Human subordinate relations (weighting: 2 points for each item = 10 points in total)	① Type of contract	Type of contract (employment contract or service contract)	2		
	② Application of Rules of Employment; Right to manage personnel	Whether rules of employment were applied; Right to hire, dismiss, and discipline employees	2		
	③ Arrival/departure from work, annual leave	No control over arrival/departure time, no annual leave granted	2		
	④ Supervision during work performance	Supervision and control during work performance	2		
	⑤ Working hours; Work place	Whether working hours are controlled; Whether the workplace is mandated	2		
2) Economic subordinate relations (weighting: 1 point for each item = 8 points in total)	① Ownership of equipment, working tools	Who owns the equipment, tools, etc.; Whether damage claims are possible or not	1		
	② Expenses	Whether operating costs are subsidized, expenses reimbursed, corporate credit card usage, etc.	1		
	③ Substitution by a 3rd party	Whether work is exclusive or if another person can be substituted in the event of absence	1		
	④ Pursuit of profit; Independent business	Whether pursuit of profit through individual effort is possible; Whether the individual can generate his own profit	1		
	⑤ Independent business	Whether independent business is possible	1		
	⑥ Liability for damages	Whether the director is responsible for losses	1		
	⑦ Remuneration for labor	Whether wage is decided by evaluation of total sales, or paid at a fixed amount in return for work provided	1		
	⑧ Continuous work; Exclusive work	Work is continuous; Whether the work is exclusive	1		
3) Dual judgment factors (if positive, score 1 point for each item)	① Whether basic pay is fixed	Majority of pay is based on basic wage or incentive pay	1/0		
	② Income tax and social security insurances	Whether corporate tax or income tax is deducted; Whether premiums for social security insurances are deducted	1/0		
Evaluation (20 points in total)		<Only judged when related items are engaged.>		0	0

* In the review, weighting is divided into two stages: employee status and employer status. The more checks that are calculated in the total sums, the stronger the considered status.

---

43) Jung, Bongsoo, "A Study on the Employee Status of Native English Teachers", Master's Thesis, Korean University graduate school, 2013, p. 79.

(3) 판례의 사용종속관계 기준을 이용한 판단

〈근로자성 파악을 위한 체크리스트 및 판단[43]〉

대법원 판례 기준 (판단 잣대)		근로자성 분석 세부 내용	점수	판 단	
				근로자	사용자
1) 인적 종속성 (가중치 각 항목 2점 = 총 10점)	① 계약 종류	계약의 종류(근로계약 또는 위임계약)	2		
	② 취업규칙 적용 및 인사권 행사	취업규칙, 사규 적용여부 판단, 근로자 채용, 해고, 징계 권한 행사	2		
	③ 출퇴근, 휴가 통제	사용자 출퇴근 및 휴가사용 통제여부	2		
	④ 업무수행 중 지휘, 감독 여부	업무수행 중 상당한 지휘감독 여부	2		
	⑤ 근로시간, 근로 장소 구속	근로시간이 정해져 있거나 근로장소 제한 여부	2		
2) 경제적 종속성 (가중치 각 항목 1점 = 총 8점)	① 비품, 원자재, 작업도구소유	작업도구 소유여부, 업무상 손해 책임여부	1		
	② 비용처리	운영비 지원여부, 업무수행 발생비용 처리, 법인카드 제한 없이 사용여부	1		
	③ 제3자대행가능, 타업무 종사	전속적 사용여부, 부재시 제3자에 대체 가능여부	1		
	④ 이윤창출, 개인사업성	본인의 노력으로 이윤창출 가능여부, 개인이 수익사업을 할 수 있는지 여부	1		
	⑤ 독립사업	회사에 복무 중 타사업에 종사 가능여부	1		
	⑥ 사업실패 책임	사업실패에 대한 책임	1		
	⑦ 보수 근로대가	임금이 매출에 대한 평가인지, 매월 근로의 대가로 받는 고정급인지여부	1		
	⑧ 근로의 계속성, 전속성 여부	계속적 근로여부(장기근속 여부), 업무수행중 타사에 취업금지 여부	1		
3) 2중적 요소 (긍정일 때만 항목 당1점)	① 고정급여부	주요 급여의 구성항목이 기본급인지 성과급인지 여부	1/0		
	② 근로소득세, 4대보험	사업소득세 부담, 4대보험 적용 및 4대보험료 납부여부	1/0		
평가점수 (20점 만점)		〈해당되는 사항만 판단하고 점수 반영〉		0점	0점

* 검토의견에 있어 가중치를 나누어 근로자성이 강한 경우 근로자 부분에, 독립사업자성이 강한 경우 사용자 부분에 표시한 그 개수를 합하여 근로자성 여부를 판단한다.

43) 정봉수, "원어민 강사의 노동법적 지위에 관한 연구", 고려대학교 석사논문, 2013, 79면: '근로자성 판단기준 가중치 산정'을 가지고 재편집하여 작성.

Judgment of employee status should be centered on subordinate relations, and each case should be analyzed individually and comprehensively. In other words, human subordinate relations (10 points), economic subordinate relations (8 points), and dual judgment factors (reflected only when positive - 2 points), are judged for a total of 20 points. If there is no relevant item to be determined, that part is not reflected.

Judgment criteria for workers should be characterized differently according to the type of job; such judgement also depends on the degree of involvement of the employer in evaluating the employee status. In evaluating employee status at each job, it is necessary to supplement economic subordinate relations with human subordinate relations. Therefore, it is necessary to analyze, concretely and comprehensively, each individual case in order to accurately determine whether we are dealing with an employee or an independent contractor.

근로자성 판단은 사용종속관계를 중심으로, 각 사안별 해당 판단항목을 개별적으로 분석하고 종합적으로 판단하여야 한다. 즉 1) 인적종속성(10점), 2) 경제적 종속성(8점), 3) 이중적 요소(긍정일때만 점수 반영, 2점)으로 총 20점을 기준으로 판단하였다. 판단지표가 되는 해당항목이 없을 경우 그 부분은 반영하지 않는다.

근로자성 판단기준은 업종별로 특징적 판단 잣대를 적용해야 하며, 해당 업종도 사용자의 관여 정도가 어느 정도인지에 따라 달라진다. 따라서 사실관계에 따라 사용자의 인적종속관계를 중심으로 경제적 종속관계를 보충하는 차원에서 해당 사안별로 구체적이고 종합적으로 판단하여야 근로자인지 개인사업자인지에 대한 정확한 구분이 가능할 것이다.

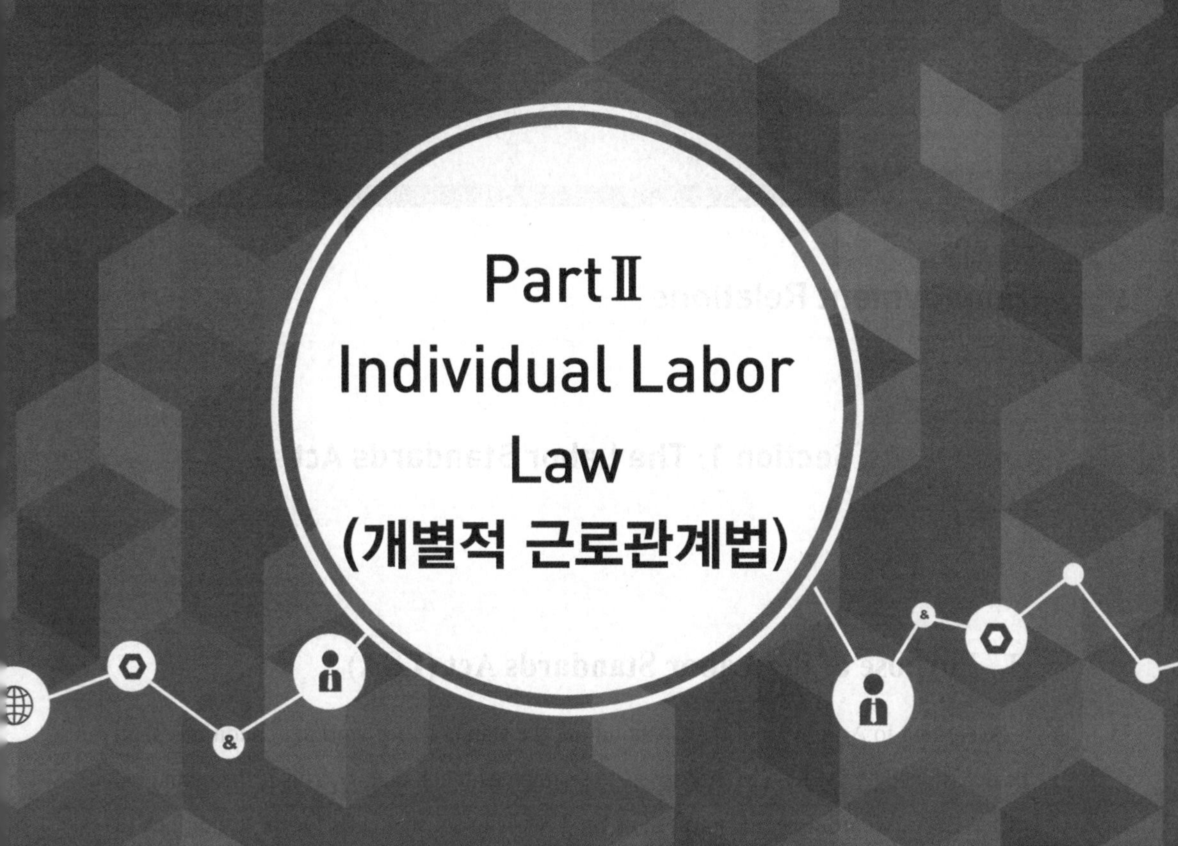

Part Ⅱ Individual Labor Law (개별적 근로관계법)

Chapter 2

Employment Relations

Section 1: The Labor Standards Act

I. Purpose of the Labor Standards Act (LSA)

According to Article 32 of the Constitution, the standards for working conditions shall be determined by the LSA in ways so as to guarantee human dignity. This is the main goal of the LSA. Accordingly, the purpose of the LSA is to set standards for the conditions of employment in accordance with the Korean Constitution, thereby securing and improving the living standards of workers and developing a well-balanced economy.

II. Characteristics of the LSA

The LSA not only stipulates regulations on public law that deal with labor management and opinion, but also specifies regulations on private law that requires compensation for damages resulting from an employer's violation of the LSA which causes the worker to terminate his/her labor contract.

근로관계

제1절 근로기준법

Ⅰ. 근로기준법의 의의

헌법 제32조 제3항은 '근로조건의 기준은 인간의 존엄성이 보장되도록 법률로써 정한다.'라고 하여 근로조건을 국가의 강행 법률로 정할 것을 규정하고 있으며 이를 근거로 하여 제정된 것이 근로기준법이다. 따라서 근로기준법은 헌법에 의거하여 근로조건의 기준을 정함으로써 근로자의 기본적 생활을 보장, 향상시키며 균형 있는 국민경제의 발전을 도모함을 목적으로 한다(근기법 제1조).

Ⅱ. 근로기준법의 법적 성격

노사 쌍방의 의사 여하를 불문하고 실현되는 점에서는 공법적 성격뿐만 아니라 사용자의 근로기준법 위반에 대하여는 그로 인한 손해배상 청구나 근로계약을 해지할 수 있는 권한을 근로자에게 부여하고 있는 점(근기법 제19조)에서는 사법(私法)적 성격도 아울러 지니고 있다.

Ⅲ. Basic Principles of the LSA

1. Prohibition against lowering working conditions

The conditions of employment provided herein cannot be lowered, thus the parties of employment shall not depress working conditions under the pretext of complying with the LSA(Article 2 of the LSA).

The minimum wage system guarantees the minimum amount of hourly wage for employees. An employer can pay more than the minimum wage, but the part of an employment contract stipulating a wage which is less than the minimum wage shall be invalid, and any missing amount from the minimum wage must be paid additionally. For violations, the employer shall be punished by imprisonment for up to three years or a fine not exceeding KRW 20 million(Articles 6 and 28 of the Minimum Wage Act).

2. Labor and management's equal decision power

The conditions of employment shall be determined through mutual agreement between employers and their workers on an equal footing(Article 4 of the LSA).

The Labor Standards Act requires written agreement from or consultation with the employee representative for matters such as changes in working hours, managerial dismissals, etc. "This employee representative refers to the labor union, where there is an organized labor union representing more than half the employees at a business or workplace; or this shall refer to a person who represents more than half the employees, where there is no such organized labor union."(Article 24(3) of the LSA).

3. Thorough fulfillment of working conditions

Both employers and workers shall comply with the collective agreement, the rules of employment, and the terms of the labor contract, and both parties are obliged to do so in good faith(Article 5 of the LSA).

The Minister of Employment and Labor has the authority to order amendment to the rules of employment where they are deemed to conflict with laws or decrees or the collective agreement(Article 96 of the LSA). If a labor contract includes employment conditions which

Ⅲ. 근로기준법의 기본 원리

1. 근로조건의 저하 금지

근로기준법의 근로조건은 최저기준이므로 근로관계 당사자는 이 기준을 이유로 근로조건을 저하시킬 수 없다(근기법 제3조).

최저임금은 근로자에 대하여 임금의 최저수준을 보장하는 제도이므로 사용자는 최저임금액 이상을 지급하여야 하고, 최저임금액에 미달하는 임금을 정한 근로계약은 그 부분에 한하여 무효로 하며, 무효로 된 부분에 있어 최저임금액과의 차액의 임금을 추가적으로 지급하여야 한다. 이를 위반한 경우 3년 이하의 징역 또는 2천만원 이하의 벌금에 처한다(최임법 제6조, 28조).

2. 노사대등의 결정

근로조건은 근로자와 사용자가 동등한 지위에서 자유의사에 의하여 결정되어야 한다(근기법 제4조).

근로기준법은 사용자가 근로시간제도의 변경, 경영상 해고 등에 있어 일정한 사항에 대하여 근로자대표와 서면합의 또는 협의를 하도록 하고 있다. 이 경우 근로자대표는 "당해 사업 또는 사업장에 근로자의 과반수로 조직된 노동조합이 있는 경우에는 그 노동조합, 근로자의 과반수로 조직된 노동조합이 없는 경우에는 근로자의 과반수를 대표하는 자"를 의미한다(근기법 제24조 제3항).

3. 근로조건의 성실이행

근로자와 사용자는 단체협약·취업규칙과 근로계약을 준수하여야 하며, 각자가 성실하게 이행할 의무가 있다(근기법 제5조).

고용노동부 장관은 법령이나 단체협약에 어긋나는 취업규칙의 변경을 명할 수 있다(근기법 제96조). 취업규칙에서 정한 기준에 미달하는 근로조건을 정한 근로계약은 그 부분에 관하여는 무효로 한다. 이 경우 무효로 된 부분은 취업규

are below the standards stipulated in the rules of employment, such nonconformity shall be null and void. In this case, the invalidated provisions shall be governed by the standards provided for in the rules of employment(Article 97 of the LSA). A labor contract which establishes working conditions which do not meet the standards provided for in the Labor Standards Act shall be null and void to that extent. In this case, those conditions invalidated shall be governed by the standards provided in this Act(Article 15 of the LSA).

4. Equal treatment

The Constitution of the Republic of Korea(Article 11-①) stipulates, "...there shall be no discrimination in political, economic, social or cultural life on account of sex, religion or social status." In aligning with this, the Labor Standards Act contains a provision on equal treatment which includes the additional item of 'nationality', stipulating, "No employer shall discriminate against employees on the basis of gender, or give discriminatory treatment in relation to working conditions on the basis of nationality, religion or social status." Other provisions on equal treatment are gradually being introduced in other Acts as social need arises to do so, regarding irregular employment status, age, disability, and foreign workers, etc.

There are two principles the Court uses in identifying the criteria for determining whether discriminative treatment, which it defines as "the same thing treated in a different way, or different things treated in the same way", is justifiable or not. First, in order for a situation/action to be considered discriminative treatment, the primary requisite is that the employees claiming discrimination should be basically in the same working group with the target comparison employees. Gender discrimination refers to discrimination simply based on gender without justifiable reason.[1] Second, even though employees claiming discrimination and the target comparison employees are working in the same workplace and at the same kind of job, if the employer discriminates in their working conditions based upon reasonable criteria in consideration of the detail and type of work and other conditions, this discrimination can be considered justifiable.[2]

---

1) Supreme Court ruling on Oct. 29, 2015: 2013da1051.

2) Supreme Court ruling on Feb. 26, 2002: 2000da39064.

칙에 정한 기준에 따른다(근기법 제97조). 근로기준법에서 정하는 기준에 미치지 못하는 근로조건을 정한 근로계약은 그 부분에 한하여 무효로 한다. 이 경우 무효로 된 부분은 근로기준법에서 정한 기준에 따른다(근기법 제15조).

4. 균등대우

우리나라 헌법 제11조 1항은 "... 누구든지 성별·종교 또는 사회적 신분에 의하여 ... 모든 영역에서 차별을 아니 한다"라고 규정하고 있다. 이와 관련하여 근로기준법도 균등처우 규정을 두고 '국적'을 추가하여 "성별, 국적, 신앙과 사회적 신분을 이유로 근로조건에 대한 차별적 처우를 하지 못한다"라고 규정하고 있다. 근로기준법 외에도 사회적 변화에 따른 차별금지 조항이 계속해서 추가되어 현재는 비정규직, 연령, 장애인, 외국인 등에 대한 차별금지 규정을 개별 법률로써 도입하고 있다.

그러면 차별금지에 대한 판단기준을 어떻게 보아야 하는가? 에 있어 법원은 차별적 처우란 '같은 것을 다르게, 다른 것을 같게 취급하는 것'이라 정의하면서 다음의 두 가지 원칙을 제시하고 있다. 첫째, 차별적 처우에 해당하기 위해서는 우선 그 전제로써 차별을 받았다고 주장하는 사람과 그가 비교대상자로 지목하는 사람이 본질적으로 동일한 업무집단에 속해 있어야 한다.[1] 둘째, 같은 사업장에서 같은 직종에 근무하는 근로자집단이라고 하더라도 근로의 내용, 근무형태 등 제반 여건을 고려하여 합리적인 기준을 정하여 차별하는 경우에는 정당한 차별로 인정하고 있다.[2]

---

1) 대법원 2015.10.29, 2013다1051.
2) 대법원 2002.2.26, 2000다39063.

(1) Gender discrimination

Gender discrimination is prohibited under Article 11(1) of the Constitution, with a more detailed explanation given in Article 32(4): "Special protection shall be accorded to working women, and they shall not be subjected to unjust discrimination in terms of employment, wage and working conditions." Article 6 of the Labor Standards Act prohibits gender discrimination and includes penalties for violations. In particular, the Equal Employment Act enacted in 1987 defines gender discrimination(Article 2) as follows:

First, it means that an employer applies different hiring and working conditions to employees, or takes other disadvantageous measures against them without justifiable reason on account of gender, marriage, status within the family, and whether or not they are pregnant or have had a child, etc.

Second, it is discrimination even if an employer applies the same hiring or working conditions, but the number of one gender to whom the conditions apply is considerably less than that of the opposite gender, thus causing a disadvantageous result to one gender. This reflects the fact that indirect discrimination due to corporate culture can be deemed gender discrimination.

Third, provided that this shall not apply to cases involving any of the following items: ① Where a specific gender is inevitably required in view of the nature of the duties; ② Where measures are taken to protect maternity, such as during pregnancy, childbirth or nursing by female employees, etc.; or ③ Other cases where affirmative action measures are taken under this Act or other Acts. These exceptions are designed to avoid any reverse discrimination.[3)]

Concrete provisions regarding gender discrimination in the Equal Employment Act can be summarized as follows: ① An employer shall not discriminate on grounds of gender in recruitment and hiring of employees. When recruiting and hiring female employees, an employer shall not present nor demand certain physical conditions, such as related to appearance, height, weight, etc., and marital status not required for performance of the relevant duties(Article 7). ② An employer shall provide equal pay for work of equal value in the same business. The criteria for work of equal value shall be skills, efforts, responsibility and working conditions, etc. required to perform the work(Article 8). "Work of equal value" in judicial rulings means the same work when comparing men and women

---

3) Lim, Jongryul, 「Labor Law」, 14thed.,2016.Parkyoungsa,p.374.

(1) 남녀 성차별

성차별금지는 헌법 제11조 1항에 명시되어 있으며, 헌법 제32조 4항에서 "여자의 근로는 특별한 보호를 받으며, 고용·임금 및 근로조건에 있어서 부당한 차별을 받지 아니한다"라고 구체적으로 기술하고 있다. 이를 현실적으로 반영하는 근로기준법 제6조에서는 성차별을 금지하고, 위반한 자에 대해 벌칙조항을 두고 있다. 특히 1987년에 제정된 남녀고용평등법에서는 성차별(제2조)을 아래와 같이 규정하고 있다.

첫째, '차별'이란 사업주가 근로자에게 성별, 혼인, 가족 안에서의 지위, 임신 또는 출산 등의 사유로 합리적인 이유 없이 채용 또는 근로의 조건을 다르게 하거나 그 밖의 불리한 조치를 하는 경우이다.

둘째, 사업주가 채용조건이나 근로조건은 동일하게 적용하더라도 그 조건을 충족할 수 있는 남성 또는 여성이 다른 한 성(性)에 비하여 현저히 적고 그에 따라 특정 성에게 불리한 결과를 초래하며 그 조건이 정당한 것임을 증명할 수 없는 경우를 포함한다. 즉, 기업문화에서 간접적인 차별도 성차별로 인정할 수 있다.

셋째, 차별에 대한 예외로서 ① 직무의 성격에 비추어 특정 성이 불가피하게 요구되는 경우, ② 여성 근로자의 임신·출산·수유 등 모성보호를 위한 조치를 하는 경우, ③ 그밖에 이 법 또는 다른 법률에 따라 적극적 고용개선조치를 하는 경우를 두고 있다. 이는 다른 성에 대한 역차별 문제를 사전에 배제하기 위한 것이다.[3)]

남녀고용평등법에서 성차별에 관한 구체적인 규정은 다음과 같이 요약된다. ① 모집과 채용에서 차별을 금지하고(제7조), 특히 사업주가 여성 근로자의 모집과 채용에서 그 직무에 필요하지 아니한 용모, 키, 체중 등의 신체적 조건, 미혼 조건 등을 제시하거나 요구하여서는 아니 된다. ② 임금에서 동일한 사업 내의 동일 가치 노동에 대하여는 동일한 임금을 지급하여야 한다(제8조). 동일 가치 노동의 기준은 직무 수행에서 요구되는 기술, 노력, 책임 및 작업조건 등

3) 임종률, 「노동법」, 제18판, 2020. 박영사, 374면.

in the corresponding workplace and nearly the same work in practical terms, or the work of basically the same value as evaluated through objective job evaluations in spite of slightly different jobs. Whether the work is of equal value or not shall be estimated in comprehensive consideration of technology, working conditions, education, career, working period, etc.[4] ③ An employer shall not discriminate on grounds of gender in providing benefits, such as money, goods or loans, etc., in order to compensate his/her employees aside from wage(Article 9). ④ An employer shall not discriminate on grounds of gender in education, assignment and promotion of his/her workers(Article 10). ⑤ An employer shall not discriminate on grounds of gender in retirement age or whether certain workers are dismissed or designated to retire. No employer shall make a labor contract that stipulates marriage, pregnancy or childbirth of female workers as grounds for resignation(Article 11).

(2) Nationality

Nationality refers to the status according to the Nationality Act, and discrimination can exist for certain employees such as foreigners without Korean nationality, overseas Koreans, and illegal migrant workers, etc. Recently, discrimination due to nationality has caused significant social issues due to the increased number of foreign workers. Article 22 of the Foreign Workers Employment Act enacted in August 2003 stipulates, "No employer shall discriminate or unfairly treat any person on the grounds that he/she is a foreign worker." However, this article does not include any penal provisions and only applies to non-professional workers in relation to the employment permit system. Accordingly, the prohibition of discrimination based on nationality follows Article 6 of the Labor Standards Act that "No employer shall give discriminatory treatment in relation to the working conditions on the basis of nationality," and the penal provisions therein. However, justifiable discrimination is allowed, with the related MOEL Guideliness explaining, "Determining whether discrimination based on nationality exists or not shall require consideration of all related items collectively: whether the discrimination in working conditions was only based on nationality or not; other entire factors regarding the working conditions such as wage and working hours; and in addition, whether

---

4) Supreme Court ruling on Mar. 14, 2003: 2002do3883; Supreme Court ruling on Mar. 14, 2013: 2010da101011.

으로 한다. 여기서 판례가 말하는 '동일 가치 노동'이란 해당 사업 내의 서로 비교되는 남녀의 노동이 동일하거나 실질적으로 거의 같은 성질의 노동 또는 그 직무가 다소 다르더라도 객관적인 직무평가 등을 통하여 본질적으로 동일한 가치가 있다고 인정되는 노동에 해당하는 것을 말하고 동일 가치의 노동인지 여부는 직무 수행에서 요구되는 기술, 작업조건, 학력·경력·근속기간 등의 기준을 종합적으로 고려하여 판단하여야 한다.[4] ③ 임금 외의 금품으로 근로자의 생활을 보조하기 위한 금품의 지급 또는 자금의 융자 등 복리후생에서 남녀를 차별하여서는 아니 된다(제9조). ④ 교육·배치 및 승진에서 남녀를 차별 하여서는 아니 된다(제10조). ⑤ 정년·퇴직 및 해고에서 남녀의 차별을 하여서는 아니 된다. 특히 여성 근로자의 혼인, 임신 또는 출산을 퇴직 사유로 예정하는 근로계약을 체결하여서는 아니 된다(제11조).

(2) 국 적

국적은 국적법상 지위를 말하며, 대한민국의 국적을 소유하지 않은 외국인근로자, 해외동포, 불법체류자 등을 대상으로 한 차별이 발생할 수 있다. 최근에 외국인근로자가 증가하면서 국적에 의한 차별이 주요 사회적 이슈가 되고 있다. 2003년도 8월에 제정된 '외국인 근로자고용법'에서 "사용자는 외국인근로자라는 이유로 부당하게 차별하여 처우하여서는 아니 된다"라고 규정하고 있지만(제22조), 이에 대해 처벌규정이 없고, 적용범위도 고용허가제와 관련된 비전문직 외국인 근로자에게만 적용되어 한계가 있다. 따라서 국적에 의한 차별은 근로기준법 제6조"...국적을 이유로 근로조건에 대한 차별적 처우를 하지 못한다"는 규정과 위반 시 관련 벌칙규정에 따른다고 할 수 있다. 다만, 차별에 합리적인 이유가 있는 경우에는 그 예외가 인정된다. 관련 행정해석은 "국적을 이유로 근로조건을 차별하는 것에 해당하는지의 판단은 근로조건에 대한 차별이 단순히 국적만을 이유로 한 것인지 여부와 차별의 대상인 근로조건에 대하여 임금, 근로시간 등 근로자 대우에 관한 일체의 요소를 전반적으로 고려하여 합리적인 기준에서 벗어난 차별이 있었는지 여부 등을 종합적으로 판단하여야

---

4) 대법원 2003.3.14, 2002도3883; 대법원 2013.3.14, 2010다101011.

discrimination exists that exceeds reasonable criteria for the work."[5)]

There are many cases related to discrimination due to nationality.

① A Constitutional Court ruling in 2007, "Even though industrial trainees with a trainee's contract provided labor service under the employer's direction and supervision, they then received wage. In actual relations, as only foreign industrial trainees were excluded from the application of major labor laws without justifiable reason, we find this unreasonable." The fact that industrial trainees are excluded from some parts of the Labor Standards Act, unlike ordinary employees, is arbitrary discrimination.[6)] ② Supreme Court ruling in 1995: Foreign worker "A" from Thailand, who came to Korea under a trainee working visa, was seriously injured while working beyond the permitted sojourn period. Foreign worker A applied for compensation from the Employee Welfare Corporation for medical treatment, but was rejected by the Corporation as foreign worker A was an illegal migrant worker working illegally. However, the Supreme Court ruled that even though illegal employment is clearly an act warranting punishment, the work already provided is actual performance that makes the worker subject to the protection of labor law. Accordingly, illegal foreign workers may apply for and receive Industrial Accident Compensation Insurance.[7)] ③ Supreme Court ruling in 2015: Some illegal foreign workers living in Seoul and Gyeonggi Province submitted a report of their establishment of a labor union to the Seoul Regional Labor Office on May 3, 2005, but their application was rejected due to their illegal status. Even in the courts there have been disputes on whether a labor union of illegal foreign workers is permissible or not, but the Supreme Court ruled on June 25, 2015 that it was.[8)]

(3) Religion

The Labor Standards Act regulates that no employer shall give discriminatory treatment in relation to working conditions on the basis of religion, which includes specific religions, religious beliefs, world view, socialist creed, or political line of a particular political party, etc.[9)] However,

---

5) MOEL Guidelines: May 25, 1994, Gungi 68207-585.

6) Constitutional Court (Industrial trainee system): Aug. 30, 2007 2004hnma670.

7) Supreme Court ruling: Sept. 15, 1995: 94nu12067 (Rejection of occupational injury application

8) Supreme Court ruling on June 25, 2015: 2007do4995 (Rejection of labor union's report of establishment)

9) Kim, Hyungbae, 「Labor Law 」, 24thed.,2015,Parkyoungsa,p.239.

한다"는 입장이다.[5)]

국적에 의한 차별의 사례로 ① 헌법재판소는 "산업연수생이 연수라는 명목하에 사업주의 지시·감독을 받으면서 사실상 노무를 제공하고 수당 명목의 금품을 수령하는 등 실질적인 근로관계에 있는 경우에는, 근로기준법이 보장한 근로기준 중 주요사항을 외국인 산업연수생에 대하여만 적용되지 않도록 하는 것은 합리적인 근거를 찾기 어렵다"라고 하여 근로기준법을 일부 적용하지 않는 것은 위헌이라고 판단하였다.[6)] ② A는 태국국적 외국인으로 산업연수 체류자격으로 입국하였으나, 체류기간을 초과하여 불법체류자로 근무하던 중에 부상을 입었다. A는 요양신청을 하였으나 공단은 A가 불법 취업한 외국인이라는 이유로 산재불승인을 하였다. 그러나 대법원은 불법체류는 단속의 대상임을 명백히 하고 있으나, 이미 제공된 사실적 행위의 노동에 대해서는 노동법의 보호가 있어야 한다는 취지에서 불법체류자도 산재보험이 적용된다고 판결하였다.[7)] ③ 서울과 경기도의 불법체류자로 구성된 외국인근로자들이 2005년 5월 3일 서울지방노동청에 노동조합 설립신고를 제출하였으나 불법체류자라는 이유로 거부당하였다. 이 노동조합 인정 여부에 대해 장기간 법원에서 다툼이 있었으나 2015년 6월 25일 결국 대법원 합의체 판결에서 불법체류자들로 구성된 노동조합의 설립을 인정하였다.[8)]

(3) 신앙

근로기준법은 신앙을 이유로 근로조건에 대한 차별적 처우를 하지 못한다고 규정하고 있다. 신앙을 이유로 한 차별은 특정의 종교, 종교적 신념, 정치적 세계관, 사회주의적 신조, 특정정당의 정치노선 등을 이유로 해당 근로자를 차별하는 것이다.[9)] 다만, 특정의 사상과 직접적으로 연결된 목적으로 수행하는 사업인 경향사업에 있어서는 그 사업목적에 반하여 행동하는 경우에는 차별적 처

5) 행정해석 근지 68207-585, 1994.5.25.

6) 헌법소원 사건(산업연수생제도): 2007.8.30, 헌재 2004헌마670.

7) 대법원 1995.9.15, 94누12067(요양불승인처분취소).

8) 대법원 2015.6.25, 2007두4995 전원합의체 판결(노동조합설립신고서 반려처분취소).

9) 김형배, 「노동법」, 제24판, 2015, 박영사, 239면.

with the exception of purpose-based companies organized to carry out business directly connected to specific ideas, it is not deemed a violation if there is discrimination regarding an employee whose behavior is in conflict with the purpose of the company he or she works for. ① In 2005, the Constitutional Court ruled as justifiable dismissal in cases where the employee behaved in violation of the purpose of his/her employing company. "Whether there is justifiable reason or not when an employer intends to dismiss an employee shall be considered concretely for each individual case. Such general reasons are that the employee's violations should be serious enough to make it very difficult to maintain continuous employment relations with the employer, which means that the employer cannot expect any further work from the employee concerned due to the serious violation. Justifiable reasons for dismissal include: the employee's work performance was seriously inferior to his/her occupational abilities; the employee cannot work due to some illness; exclusively for purpose-based companies organized to carry out business directly connected to specific ideas, the employee disagrees with the purpose of his/her employing company; and others.[10)] ② In 1994, the Supreme Court ruled that an employee's behavior that violates the purpose of his/her employing company is deemed a justifiable reason for dismissal. "Even though the employee's real estate speculation, which was the reason for disciplinary dismissal, seemed like some minor misconduct in his personal life, in comprehensive consideration of the purpose of his employer, the Urban Development Corporation, which was established to create for citizens housing security and improve welfare through residential land development and supply, housing construction, etc., and the work scope of the employee engaged in real estate-related compensation, this real estate speculation by the employee could cause very negative effects of the social evaluation of the Urban Development Corporation."[11)]

(4) Social status

'Social status' is a position formed over a considerable time and part of social evaluation, and refers to a social position that one cannot adjust through one's intention or performance.[12)] A judicial ruling on June 19, 2016 explained, "Social status is a position formed over a long time in society and part of social evaluation, and refers to the social classification that a

10) Constitutional Court decision on Mar. 31, 2005: 2003hunba12 (Justifiable reasons for dismissal).

11) Supreme Court ruling on December 13, 1994: 93nu23275 (ruling related to a purpose-based company)

12) Lim, Jongryul, p. 376; Kim, Hyungbae, p. 240; Kaprae Ha, 「The Labor Standards Act」28thed,JoongangEconomy,p.79.

우를 허용하고 있다.

관련 사례로 헌법재판소는 경향사업에 저촉되는 경우를 정당한 해고의 사유로 인정하고 있다. ①"사용자가 근로자를 해고함에 있어서 정당한 이유의 유무는 개별적 사안에 따라 구체적으로 결정될 일이지만 그 일반적 내용은 해당 근로자와 사용자 사이의 근로관계를 계속 유지할 수 없을 정도의 이유, 즉 해당 근로자와의 근로관계의 유지를 사용자에게 더 이상 기대할 수 없을 정도의 것이 되어야 하는 것이다. 여기에는 업무에 대한 적성에 흠이 있거나 직무능력이 부족한 경우, 계약상의 노무급부를 곤란하게 하는 질병, ... 특정 신조나 사상과 밀접히 연관된 소위 경향사업(傾向事業)에 있어서 근로자가 이러한 경향성을 상실한 경우 등이 일반적으로 이러한 정당한 이유에 해당하는 것으로 인정되고 있다."[10]

대법원도 경향사업에 반하는 근로자의 행위에 대해 정당한 해고로 인정하고 있다. ②"근로자에 대한 징계 사유인 부동산투기행위가 근로자의 사생활에서의 비행에 불과하다고 할지라도, 택지의 개발과 공급, 주택의 건설 등을 통하여 시민의 주거생활의 안정과 복지향상을 목적으로 설립한 도시개발공사의 설립목적, 부동산보상 관련 업무를 담당하는 근로자의 업무내용 등의 여러 사정을 종합적으로 고려하면, 도시개발공사 소속 근로자의 부동산투기행위는 객관적으로 그 공사의 사회적 평가에 심히 중대한 악영향을 미치는 것으로 평가될 수 있는 경우라고 할 것이다."[11]

(4) 사회적 신분

'사회적 신분'이란 상당한 기간이 지나면서 형성된 지위로서 사회적 평가가 수반되고, 자신의 의사나 능력으로 피할 수 없는 사회적 위치를 말한다.[12] 판례는 "사회적 신분이란 사회에서 장기간 점하는 지위로서 일정한 사회적 평가를

10) 헌법재판소 2005.3.31, 헌재2003헌바12(해고에 대한 정당한 이유의 해석).

11) 대법원 1994.12.13, 93누23275(경향사업 관련 판결).

12) 임종률, 「노동법」, 제18판, 2020, 박영사, 376면; 김형배, 240면; 하갑래, 「근로기준법」 제33판, 2020, 중앙경제, 79면.

specific group of employees cannot adjust through their intention or performance."[13)]

Recently, there has been some headline news on a judicial ruling regarding a case of discrimination owing to social status. The employees concerned were transferred to non-fixed term employment and then placed in their own group after being hired for temporary positions. Unlike regular employees, the workers in this group were not eligible for title promotions. Different salary regulations were applied, and they were also ineligible for housing or family allowances, or meal expenses. The employees concerned took legal action for the unpaid allowances, stating that this discrimination was null and void due to it being a violation of equal treatment according to Article 6 of the Labor Standards Act. The court ruled, "Besides job, the type of work and position can be part of social status if they require social evaluation or are social classifications that an employee cannot change through intention or performance." The court judged that being part of a group of workers with non-fixed employment status was part of social status, adding, "With the exception of salary regulations, the same rules of employment and personnel regulations apply to non-fixed term employees. The quantity, quality and difficulty of their work and their contribution to the company were not less than their regular employee counterparts, so this discrimination amounts to a violation of Article 6 of the Labor Standards Act."

5. Prohibition against forced labor

An employer shall not force a worker to work against his/her own free will through the use of violence, threats, confinement or by any other means that unjustly restrict mental or physical freedom(Article 7 of the LSA). A person who violates the provisions of the prohibition against forced labor shall be punished by imprisonment of up to five years or by a fine not exceeding fifty million won(Article 107 of the LSA).

6. Prohibition against violence

Accidents or any other mishaps caused by the worker shall not be a legitimate reason for physical or verbal abuse(Article 8 of the LSA). A person who violates the provisions of

---

13) Seoul Southern Court ruling on June 19, 2016: 2015kahap3505.

수반하는 것으로서, 사업장 내에서 근로자 자신의 의사나 능력 발휘에 의해서 회피할 수 없는 사회적 분류를 말한다"라고[13] 판시하고 있다.

최근에 사회적 신분으로 인한 차별사건에 대한 판결이 나와 화제가 되고 있다. 그 내용은 다음과 같다. 해당 근로자들은 계약직 근로자로 입사해 업무직(무기계약직) 근로자로 전환이 됐다. 이들은 회사에서 일반직 근로자들과 달리 직급 승진도 적용받지 못했다. 또 일반직 근로자들과 보수규정도 다르게 적용받으며 주택수당, 가족수당, 식대 등 수당도 지급받지 못했다. 이에 근로자들은 이러한 차별은 근로기준법 제6조의 균등처우 규정을 위반해 차별적 대우는 무효'라며 수당 지급을 청구했다. 이에 법원은 "직업뿐 아니라 사업장 내의 직종, 직위도 사회적 평가를 수반하거나, 근로자 스스로의 의사나 능력으로 벗어날 수 없는 사회적 분류라면 사회적 신분이라 할 수 있다"고 판단하며 무기계약직을 '사회적 신분'으로 판단했다. 법원은 "보수규정만 달리 적용하고 있을 뿐, 무기계약직 근로자와 일반직 근로자들은 동일한 취업규칙, 인사규정을 적용받고 있으며, ... 업무의 양과 질, 난이도나 회사에 대한 기여도가 무기계약직 근로자가 적다고 보기 어려운 점 등을 들어 ... 근로기준법 제6조를 위반했다"고 판단했다.

5. 강제근로의 금지

사용자는 폭행·협박·감금 기타 정신상 또는 육체상의 자유를 부당하게 구속하는 수단으로써 근로자의 자유의사에 반하는 근로를 강요하지 못한다(근기법 제7조). 강제근로의 금지 규정을 위반한 자는 5년 이하의 징역 또는 5천만원 이하의 벌금에 처한다(근기법 제107조).

6. 폭행의 금지

사용자는 사고 발생 기타 어떠한 이유로도 근로자에게 폭행·구타 행위를 하지 못한다(근기법 제8조). 폭행의 금지 규정을 위반한 자는 5년 이하의 징역 또

13) 서울남부지법 2016.6.10, 2014가합3505(사회적 신분과 관련 판결).

'prohibition of violence' shall be punished by imprisonment of up to five years or by a fine not exceeding fifty million won(Article 107 of the LSA).

7. Elimination of intermediary exploitation

No one shall intervene in the employment of another person for the purpose of making a profit, nor shall anyone gain benefit as an intermediary unless otherwise provided by law(Article 9 of the LSA). 'Gaining benefit as an intermediary' is any act to introduce or intervene in the employment of another person for the purpose of making a profit, or to influence establishment or renewal of an employment contract, and includes receiving money in return for introducing the employment opportunity to a person looking for employment. This does not require a direct act of introducing or intervening in gaining or renewing employment.[14)]

8. Guarantee of exercising civil rights

An employer shall not reject a request from a worker to grant the time necessary to exercise his/her right to suffrage or other civil rights, or to perform official duties during his/her working hours; however, the time requested may be changed, unless such alteration impedes the exercise of those rights or the performance of those civil duties(Article 10 of the LSA). When an employee leaves his/her workplace during working hours to exercise civil rights or perform civil duties, he/she shall be paid for the hours spent for that purpose(e.g. reserve forces training, civil defense drills or training, voting, etc.).

---

14) Supreme Court ruling on Sept. 25, 2008, 2006do7660 "Violation of the LSA".

는 5천만원 이하의 벌금에 처한다(근기법 제107조).

7. 중간착취의 배제

누구든지 법률에 의하지 아니하고는 영리로 타인의 취업에 개입하거나 중간인으로서 이익을 취득할 수 없다(근기법 제9조). 「영리로 타인의 취업에 개입」하는 행위, 즉 제3자가 영리로 타인의 취업을 소개 또는 알선하는 등 근로관계의 성립 또는 갱신에 영향을 주는 행위에는 취업을 원하는 사람에게 취업을 알선해 주기로 하면서 그 대가로 금품을 수령하는 정도의 행위도 포함되고, 반드시 근로관계 성립 또는 갱신에 직접적인 영향을 미칠 정도로 구체적인 소개 또는 알선행위에까지 나아가야만 하는 것은 아니다.[14)]

8. 공민권 행사의 보장

사용자는 근로자가 근무시간 중에 선거권 기타 공민권의 행사 또는 공의 직무를 집행하기 위하여 필요한 시간을 청구하는 경우에는 거부하지 못한다. 다만, 그 권리행사 또는 공의 직무를 집행함에 지장이 없는 한 청구한 시각을 변경할 수 있다(근기법 제10조). 공민권 행사가 소정근로시간 중에 이루어질 경우에 임금을 지급하여야 한다(예시: 예비군 훈련, 민방위 교육훈련, 투표 등).

---

14) 대법원 2008.9.25, 2006도7660【근기법 위반】.

Section 2: Labor Contracts

I. Signing a Labor Contract, Effective Period and its Effects

1. Signing a labor contract

A labor contract can become effective by means of oral agreement, present practices, or precedents when an employee begins work, even if no contract has been drafted. A labor contract does not demand a specific type of form.[15)]

When a contract of employment is concluded, the employer shall clearly state to the employee concerned the wage, given hours of work, holidays, paid annual leave, and other working conditions, and shall specify in writing the components of his/her wage, and the methods of calculation and payment(Article 17 of the LSA). Given that general working conditions are provided for in the rules of employment, etc., it is possible that a contract of employment may only contain specific conditions for the particular employee, such as his/her job description and location of work, along with the clause 'other working conditions shall be the same as prescribed in the rules of employment.' However, a contract of employment may not provide for any estimated amount of penalty or damages or any compulsory deposit in case the employee breaches the agreement.

2. Effective period of a labor contract

The effective period of a labor contract is generally initiated as soon as the contract is signed, but the actual time considered in the calculation of severance pay or annual leave starts from the first day the employee provides his/her work.

---

15) MOEL Guidelines: Nosa 1451-4133.

제2절 근로계약

Ⅰ. 근로계약의 작성, 성립시기와 효력

1. 근로계약의 작성

근로계약은 특별한 형식을 요구하지 않으므로 일반적으로 사용종속관계 아래서 근로가 개시되면 서면계약이 체결되어 있지 않더라도 구두계약이나 관행·관습에 의하여 근로관계는 성립된 것으로 본다.[15)]

근로계약 시 근로자에 대하여 임금, 소정근로시간, 휴일, 연차유급휴가, 기타의 근로조건을 명시하고 임금의 구성항목, 계산방법 및 지급방법, 소정근로시간, 휴일, 연차 유급휴가에 관한 사항에 대하여는 서면으로 명시하여야 한다(근기법 제17조). 근로조건은 취업규칙 등에 통일적으로 규정되므로 근로계약서에는 종사업무, 작업장소 등 개인적인 사항만 명시하고 나머지 근로조건은 취업규칙에 정한 바에 따른다고 기록할 수 있다. 그러나 근로자가 근로계약을 이행하지 못한 데 대한 위약금 또는 손해배상액을 예정하거나 강제저축을 하도록 정할 수 없다.

2. 근로계약의 성립 시기

근로계약의 성립 시기는 일반적으로 근로계약 체결 시이지만 퇴직금, 연차휴가 산정을 위한 기산일의 확정을 위해서는 실제로 노무제공을 개시한 날부터 판단한다.

---

15) 행정해석: 협력1451-4133.

3. Labor contract effect and duties of the parties

(1) Legal effect of a labor contract

A labor contract that fails to meet the standards of employment shall be null and void to that extent. The conditions invalidated shall be governed by the Labor Standards Act(Article 15 of the LSA). The Court ruled that an employer attempting to restrict the basic rights of an employee guaranteed by compulsory provisions such as the right to claim severance payment by applying the principle of good faith goes against the constitutional value and nature of compulsory provisions of the Labor Standards Act.[16)]

(2) Duties of the parties in a labor contract

1) Primary duty

The employment contract is a legal agreement entered into for a worker to offer work and for an employer to pay wages for that work. Here, the main obligations of workers is to provide work, and employers to pay wages in return. Workers must faithfully provide the work specified in the employment contract at a fixed time and place. If the worker fails to do so for reasons attributable to the worker, the employer may claim compensation for damages or terminate the employment contract (Article 390 of the Civil Act). Even if the employer fails to receive the worker's work, the entire wage must be paid for work already performed (Article 538 of the Civil Act).

2) Secondary duty

In addition to the main obligations in these employment contracts, workers are obligated to be faithful and employers are obligated to protect, both on the “good faith” principle between contracting parties.[17)] Workers are obligated to protect the interests of the employer without engaging in acts that violate that employer’s interests. Employers also have a duty to protect the workers with whom working relations have been established.[18)]

Even if there are no such provisions in the employment contract, workers are obligated to be faithful in accordance with the principle of good faith in the Civil Act. Such integrity obligations

---

16) Supreme Court ruling 2012da89399 on Dec. 18, 2013.

17) Lim, Jongryul, 「Labor Law」 18th Ed., Parkyoungsa, 2020, p. 360; Supreme Court ruling on Nov. 28, 2013: 2011da60247.

18) Ha, Kaprae,「The Labor Standards Act」 33rd Ed., Joongang Economy, 2020, pp. 149-165.

3. 근로계약의 효력 및 당사자 의무

(1) 근로계약의 법적 효력

근로기준법에 정한 기준에 미달하는 근로기준을 정한 근로계약은 그 부분에 관하여는 무효이고 무효로 된 부분은 근로기준법이 정한 기준으로 보충된다(근기법 제15조). 판례는 사용자가 "신의칙의 적용을 통하여 퇴직금청구권과 같은 법률상 강행규정으로 보장된 근로자의 기본적 권리를 제약하려 시도하는 것은 헌법적 가치나 근로기준법의 강행 규정성에 정면으로 반하는 것으로 보아, 허용될 수 없다"고 보았다.[16)]

(2) 근로계약의 당사자 의무

1) 주된 의무

근로계약은 근로자가 사용자에게 근로를 제공하고 사용자는 이에 대하여 임금을 지급하는 것을 목적으로 체결된 계약이다. 여기서 근로자와 사용자의 주된 의무는 근로제공과 임금 지급이다. 근로자는 근로계약서에 기재된 업무를 정해진 시간과 장소에서 성실하게 제공해야 하는데 근로자의 귀책사유로 근로제공 의무를 이행하지 못하게 되면, 사용자는 근로자에게 손해배상을 청구하거나 근로계약을 해지할 수 있다(민법 제390조). 또한 사용자가 근로자의 근로를 수렴하지 못한 경우에도 임금 전액을 지급해야 한다(민법 제538조).

2) 부수적 의무

이러한 근로계약의 주된 의무와 함께 계약당사자의 신의성실 원칙에 따른 의무로 근로자는 성실의무, 사용자는 보호의무를 부담한다.[17)] 근로자는 근로관계에 있어 사용자의 이익을 침해하는 행위를 하지 않고 그 이익을 보호해야 하는 성실의무를 진다. 사용자도 근로관계에 있어 근로자의 이익을 보호해야 하는 보호의무를 진다.[18)]

---

16) 대법원 2013.12.18, 2012다89399.

17) 임종률, 「노동법」 18판, 박영사, 2020, 360면; 대법원 2013.11.28, 2011다60247.

18) 하갑래, 「근로기준법」 제33판, 중앙경제, 2020, 149-165면.

include the duty to maintain trade secrets, to be faithful, to avoid engaging in concurrent business with the employer's competitors, and to comply with regulations. Employers are also obligated to protect workers in accordance with the principle of good faith inherent in the employment contract. Typical examples are the duty to consider safety, the using employer's duty to dispatched workers, and the duty to prevent sexual harassment in the workplace.

Ⅱ. Terms of Contract

1. Principle

The term of a labor contract shall not exceed two years, except in cases where no term is fixed or the term is fixed as a necessary measure for the completion of a certain project. When a fixed-term contract is made, the employment relationship under the contract shall be automatically terminated upon maturity of the fixed term. If an employee has been employed for a term exceeding 2 years, the employee shall be treated as if he/she had signed a contract of employment for an indefinite term. However, in cases where an employee is employed for longer than 2 years for the work required to complete a particular project or task, the employee may not be treated as working under a contract of employment for an indefinite term.

2. Exception[19)]

Employment contracts for fixed-term employees and the right to anticipate automatic renewal of the employment contract If an employee signs an employment contract for a fixed period, it is a principle that the employment is naturally terminated when the fixed period expires, and if not renewed, the employment contract is complete without the employer's expression of intent to reject renewal. However, in cases where there is a conditional provision in the employment contract, the rules of employment or the collective agreement that the current employment contract will be renewed if certain conditions are satisfied, despite expiration of the contract period, and those conditions are satisfied, this shall exceptionally apply. In the event there is no such conditional provision, but in

---

19) Supreme Court ruling on Apr. 14, 2011, 2007doo1729 "Unfair Dismissal & Unfair Labor Practice".

근로자는 근로계약에 규정이 없어도 민법상 신의성실원칙에 따른 성실의무를 진다. 그러한 성실의무에는 영업비밀 유지업무, 충실의무, 경쟁업체에 대한 겸업금지 규정, 청렴의무 등을 진다. 사용자도 근로계약에 내재된 신의성실원칙에 따른 근로자를 보호해야 하는 의무를 진다. 대표적인 것이 안전을 배려할 의무, 파견근로자에 대한 사용사업주의 의무, 직장내 성희롱예방 의무 등이다.

Ⅱ. 근로계약기간

1. 원 칙

근로계약은 기간의 정함이 없는 것과 일정한 사업완료에 필요한 기간을 제외하고는 그 기간은 2년을 초과하지 못한다. 기간을 정하여 채용한 후 그 기간이 만료되면 근로관계는 자동으로 종료된다. 2년을 초과하여 사용할 때는 기간의 정함이 없는 근로계약을 체결한 근로자로 간주된다. 다만, 사업의 완료 또는 특정업무 완성에 필요한 기간 등 사용기간제한의 예외가 인정되는 경우에는 2년을 초과하여 사용하더라도 무기근로계약으로 간주되지 않는다.

2. 예외: 기간제 근로계약과 갱신기대권[19)]

기간을 정하여 근로계약을 체결한 근로자의 경우 그 기간이 만료됨으로써 근로자로서의 신분관계는 당연히 종료되고 근로계약을 갱신하지 못하면 갱신 거절의 의사표시가 없어도 당연 퇴직되는 것이 원칙이다. 그러나 근로계약, 취업규칙, 단체협약 등에서 기간만료에도 불구하고 일정한 요건이 충족되면 당해 근로계약이 갱신된다는 취지의 규정을 두고 있는 경우 예외가 될 수 있다. 그러한 규정이 없더라도 근로계약의 내용과 근로계약이 이루어지게 된 동기 및 경위, 계약 갱신의 기준 등 갱신에 관한 요건이나 절차의 설정 여부 및 그 실태, 근로자가 수행하는 업무의 내용 등 당해 근로관계를 둘러싼 여러 사정을 종합하여 볼 때 근로계약 당사자 사이에 일정한 요건이 충족되면 근로계약이 갱신

19) 대법원 2011.4.14, 2007두1729【부당해고, 부당노동행위】.

collectively considering various situations around the employment relations related to the employment contract and the intention and procedures, the criteria and requirements for renewing the contract, and employee duty types, in cases where the employee could reasonably anticipate having his/her employment contract renewed with the belief of both parties(employee and employer) that the employee would have the employment contract renewed if certain conditions were satisfied, and those conditions were satisfied, it can be accepted as unfair dismissal if his/her employment contract were not renewed.

Ⅲ. Considerations when Writing a Labor Contract

1. Application of the principle of priority on favorable conditions

In application of the legal source that determines working conditions, higher-level rules take precedence over lower ones. The principle of application means that the order of hierarchy of effectiveness begins with laws like the Labor Standards Act, then collective agreements, then rules of employment, then individual labor contracts. If a lower rule violates a higher rule, the lower rule is invalidated (Articles 15 and 97 of the LSA and Article 33 of the TUA). Nevertheless, the principle of priority on favorable conditions applies to rules of employment and labor contracts.

As stated in Article 97 of the Labor Standards Act, the principle of priority on favorable conditions applies to rules of employment and labor contracts. In order to legally change rules of employment disadvantageously pursuant to Article 94 of the Labor Standards Act, the consent of a labor union representing a majority of workers, or if there is no such union, the consent of a majority of the workers, must be obtained. However, the employment contract of any workers who oppose the unfavorable rules of employment changes remains in effect even if the disadvantageous change to the rules is legal.

In general, it is desirable that only items particular to the relevant worker are stipulated, and that overall working conditions that apply to all workers are in accordance with the rules of employment.

Even though the conditions for changing rules of employment disadvantageously are met, the principle of priority on favorable conditions in labor contracts is applicable

된다는 신뢰관계가 형성되어 있어 근로자에게 근로계약이 갱신될 수 있으리라는 정당한 기대권이 인정되는 경우에는, 사용자가 이를 위반하여 부당하게 근로계약의 갱신을 거절하는 것은 부당해고와 마찬가지로 아무런 효력이 없다.

Ⅲ. 근로계약 작성시 고려사항

1. 유리한 조건 우선원칙의 적용

근로조건을 결정하는 법원의 적용에 있어 상위규범 우선 적용원칙에 따라 근로기준법의 강행법, 단체협약, 취업규칙, 근로계약 순서대로 적용된다. 하위규범이 상위규범 위반을 위반하는 경우 그 하위규범은 무효가 되고, 무효가 된 부분에는 상위규범이 적용된다(근기법 제15조, 제97조, 노조법 제33조). 그러나 취업규칙과 근로계약 사이에서는 유리한 조건 우선의 원칙이 적용된다.

취업규칙과 근로계약 사이의 유리한 조건 우선의 원칙은 근로기준법 제97조에 명시된 바와 같이 유리한 근로조건을 가진 근로계약이 취업규칙 보다 우선적으로 적용된다.

그러면, 근로기준법 제94조에 따른 취업규칙 불이익 변경을 적법하게 하기 위해서는 근로자 과반수를 대표하는 노동조합이 있는 경우에는 그 노동조합의 동의, 그러한 노동조합이 없는 경우에는 근로자의 과반수의 동의를 받아 불이익한 근로조건을 변경할 수 있다. 그러나 근로자 개별 근로자의 근로계약서에 명시된 부분이 있는 경우에는 취업규칙의 불이익 변경조건이 적법하게 변경되었다고 하더라도 불리하게 변경된 취업규칙에 반대하는 소수 근로자의 근로계약은 계속적으로 유효하게 유지된다.

따라서 일반적으로 근로계약서의 기재사항은 해당 근로자에 대한 특별한 내용만 기재하고, "나머지 다른 근로자들과 동일하게 적용되는 근로조건은 취업규칙의 내용에 따른다" 라고 명시하는 것이 바람직하다.

취업규칙 불이익 변경요건을 갖추었음에도 불구하고 근로계약의 유리한 조건 우선의 원칙이 적용되어 반대하는 근로자의 근로조건이 계속 효력을 갖는 사례가

and the working conditions of workers opposed to the change continue in effect.[20] This is justified by the purpose of labor law to prevent the unilateral reduction of working conditions by employers, emphasizing the principle of mutually determining the working conditions in accordance with Article 4 of the Labor Standards Act. Employers wishing to adapt to changes in the business environment and maintain flexible employment relations will find it desirable to state in the labor contract that special matters for the worker are written therein and all other conditions are in the rules of employment.

2. Prohibition against Predetermined Non-observance[21]

In cases where an employee promises to pay a fixed amount of money in the event that he/she breaks an agreement to work for a certain period of time, if the employee has to pay this penalty immediately upon resigning ahead of the mandatory service period regardless of whether the company will suffer damages due to the early resignation, this is a clear violation of Article 20(Prohibition against Predetermination of Non-observance) of the Labor Standards Act. In addition, in cases where the employee has to return his/her wage that would have been paid to the employee simply because the employee resigns prior to the previously agreed end-of-service date, such provision of the employment contract violates the purpose of the above Article and will not be deemed valid.

However, in cases where there is an agreement that the employer will subsidize the cost of a training course for the employee and the employee promises to reimburse the entire or partial costs if he/she resigns early, such an agreement can be considered justifiable. In this case, the employer not only subsidized the training for occupational necessity and benefits, but also completely paid(or partially paid considering the employee's individual desire to take the training) the expenses for the employee. If such a mandatory service period and reimbursement amount are determined to be within a reasonable and acceptable range, and the employee does not have to continue to work against the employee's will, such agreement will not violate Article 20 of the Labor Standards Act.

---

20) Supreme Court ruling on Apr. 9, 2020, 2019 Da 297083, Supreme Court ruling on Nov. 14, 2019, 2018 Da 200709, Supreme Court ruling on Dec. 13, 2017 2017 da 26138.

21) Supreme Court ruling of Oct. 23, 2008, 2006da37274 "Cancellation Fees".

나오고 있다.[20] 이는 근로기준법 제4조의 근로조건의 대등한 결정원칙을 강조하면서, 사용자의 일방적 근로조건의 저하조치를 예방하기 위한 노동법적 특성이라고 할 수 있다. 사용자가 시장환경변화에 적응하고 유연한 고용관계를 유지하기 위해서는 근로계약 작성시 해당 근로자에 대한 특별한 사항은 근로계약서에 기재하고 나머지는 취업규칙에 일임한다고 명시하는 것이 곤란에서 벗어나는 길이다.

2. 위약 예정의 금지[21]

근로자가 일정 기간 동안 근무하기로 하면서 이를 위반할 경우 소정 금원을 사용자에게 지급하기로 약정하는 경우, 그 약정의 취지가 약정한 근무기간 이전에 퇴직하면 그로 인하여 사용자에게 어떤 손해가 어느 정도 발생하였는지 묻지 않고 바로 소정 금액을 사용자에게 지급하기로 하는 것이라면 이는 명백히 근로기준법 제20조(위약 예정의 금지)에 반하는 것이어서 효력을 인정할 수 없다. 또, 그 약정이 미리 정한 근무기간 이전에 퇴직하였다는 이유로 마땅히 근로자에게 지급되어야 할 임금을 반환하기로 하는 취지일 때에도, 결과적으로 위 조항의 입법 목적에 반하는 것이어서 역시 그 효력을 인정할 수 없다.

다만, 그 약정이 사용자가 근로자의 교육훈련 또는 연수를 위한 비용을 우선 지출하고 근로자는 실제 지출된 비용의 전부 또는 일부를 상환하는 의무를 부담하기로 하되 장차 일정 기간 동안 근무하는 경우에는 그 상환의무를 면제해 주기로 하는 취지인 경우에는, 그러한 약정의 필요성이 인정된다. 이때 주로 사용자의 업무상 필요와 이익을 위하여 원래 사용자가 부담하여야 할 성질의 비용을 지출한 것에 불과한 정도가 아니라 근로자의 자발적 희망과 이익까지 고려하여 근로자가 전적으로 또는 공동으로 부담하여야 할 비용을 사용자가 대신 지출한 것으로 평가되며, 약정 근무기간 및 상환해야 할 비용이 합리적이고 타당한 범위 내에서 정해져 있는 등 위와 같은 약정으로 인하여 근로자의 의사에 반하는 계속 근로를 부당하게 강제하는 것으로 평가되지 않는다면, 그러한 약정까지 근로기준법 제20조에 반하는 것은 아니다.

---

20) 대법원 2020.4.9, 2019다297083; 대법원 2019.11.14, 2018다200709; 대법원 2017.12.13. 2017다26138.

21) 대법원 2008.10.23, 2006다37274【약정금】.

Ⅳ. Items to be Considered When Writing an Employment Contract

1. Introduction

Recently, an important court ruling was made on the validity of an employment contract. A certain company unfavorably changed its employment rules to reduce bonuses, although with the consent of a majority of workers. However, according to the principle of preferential conditions, it was judged that the company could not reduce the bonus of opposing workers unless their employment contracts were also changed.[22)] Therefore, it is necessary to revise the written employment contract when working conditions are changed unfavorably.

When an employer hires someone, the first thing that must be done is to create an employment contract, which outlines the responsibilities of both parties to the contract—the worker provides work to the employer and the employer pays wages in return (Article 2 of the Labor Standards Act, or "LSA").[23)] Preparing a written employment contract is to clarify working conditions between workers and employers, and to prevent disputes. The employer is obligated to prepare one, and failure to do so can result in a fine of not more than 5 million won for each worker who does not have a written contract. In labor disputes, the burden of proof is on the employer. I will outline the essential items in an employment contract, with these items examined through standard employment contracts for each employment type.

2. Required Information to be Stipulated in a Written Employment Contract

(1) Items required to protect workers

Article 17 of the Labor Standards Act requires employers to specify certain items in employment contracts(Including electronic documents pursuant to Article 2 (1) of the「Framework Act on Electronic Documents and Transactions」) and hand them out to new hires to sign. It should be issued again when changes are made. Such items include ① wages, ② contractual working hours, ③ holidays under Article 55, ④ annual paid leave under Article

22) Supreme Court ruling on Apr. 9, 2020: 2019da297803.

23) Ha, Kaprae,「The Labor Standards Act」33rd Ed., Joongang Economy, 2020, p. 127.

Ⅳ. 근로계약 작성시 유의사항

1. 근로계약서의 이해

최근 근로계약서의 효력에 관한 중요한 판결이 나왔다. 회사는 근로자 과반수의 동의를 받아 상여금을 삭감하는 내용으로 취업규칙을 불리하게 변경하였다. 그러나 반대한 근로자의 근로계약서를 변경하지 않은 이상 유리한 조건 우선의 원칙에 따라 반대 근로자의 상여금은 삭감할 수 없다고 판시하였다.[22] 이와 같은 상황에 대비하여 근로계약서의 서면 작성과 함께 근로조건이 불리하게 변경될 때는 근로계약서의 수정이 불가피하다.

사용자가 근로자를 채용할 경우 제일 먼저 해야 할 일은 근로계약서의 작성이다. 근로계약은 근로자가 사용자에게 근로를 제공하고 사용자는 그 대가로 임금을 지급하는 쌍방의 의무를 가진 계약이다(근기법 제2조).[23] 근로계약을 서면으로 작성하는 것은 근로조건을 근로자와 사용자가 명확히 하자는 것이고, 차후 분쟁이 발생할 것을 예방하기 위함이다. 그러한 취지에서 근로계약의 서면 작성은 사용자의 의무사항이고, 이를 위반할 경우 사용자에게 미작성 근로계약 건당 500만원 이하의 벌금(과태료)를 부과한다. 노동분쟁에 있어 입증책임은 사용자가 지기 때문에 사용자 스스로를 보호하기 위해서도 근로계약의 서면 작성은 반드시 필요하다. 이에, 다음에서 근로계약서의 필수 기재사항을 설명하고, 각 고용형태별 실제 표준 근로계약서와 각각의 유의사항에 대해서도 살펴보고자 한다.

2. 근로계약 작성시 필수기재사항

(1) 근로자 보호를 위해 필요한 기재사항

근로기준법 제17조를 살펴보면 사용자가 근로계약서를 서면(「전자문서 및 전자거래 기본법 제2조1호에 따른 전자문서를 포함한다)으로 작성하면서 필수 기재사항을 명시하고 동일 서류를 근로자에게도 교부해야 한다고 명시하고 있다. 이를 변경할 때에도

22) 대법원 2020.4.9. 선고 2019다297803 판결.
23) 하갑례, 「근로기준법」 제33판, 중앙경제, 2020, 127면.

60, and ⑤ matters concerning the place of employment and the work expected. When entering into an employment contract with a worker under the age of 18, a parental consent form must be attached (Article 66 of the LSA).

When entering into an employment contract with a fixed-term or part-time worker, the following essential items must be specified in writing: ① Matters concerning the period of the work contract, ② Matters on working hours and breaks, ③ Matters on the composition of wages and methods of calculation and payment, ④ Matters on holidays and leave, and ⑤ the place of employment and the work expected. In particular, ⑥ working days and working hours per working day are only required for part-time workers (Article 17 of the Fixed-Term and Part-time Employment Act).

(2) Items to protect employers

Employment contracts should be drawn up based on mutual agreement between labor and management and on equal terms, but in reality, since the employer selects and hires the most desirable worker from a number of applicants, the employment contract is concluded with the working conditions dictated by the employer. Since the employer decides the details of the contract from a superior position, the Labor Standards Act places restrictions on contract details.

Despite these restrictions, employers can take steps to protect themselves and take actions, such as dismissal, with unqualified or poor workers. First, workers unsuitable for the job can be dismissed within the probation period, which is usually set at 3 months, but can be extended if necessary. Workers on probation may be dismissed without prior notice, unless the probationary period exceeds three months, then a notice of dismissal must be made 30 days before dismissal. Second, if it is difficult to evaluate whether a worker is eligible for work through the probation period, a one-year fixed-term working condition can be set together with the probation period. Third, it is necessary to obtain a pledge to comply with the service regulations (security), and prepare grounds for disciplinary action for workers who violate them. Fourth is related to employees' personal information, which, in general, employers can use in personnel management, but only upon gaining the employee's consent for areas not already permitted by law. Essentially, a letter of consent signed by the employee is necessary before using that employee's personal information.

동일하게 교부해야 한다. 작성해야 할 조건은 ① 임금, ② 소정근로시간, ③ 제55조에 따른 휴일, ④ 제60조에 따른 연차 유급휴가, ⑤ 취업의 장소와 종사하여야 할 업무에 관한 사항 등이다. 18세 미만인 근로자와 근로계약을 체결하는 경우에는 "친권자의 동의서"를 반드시 첨부해야 한다(근기법 제66조).

기간제근로자나 단시간근로자와 근로계약을 체결하는 때에는 다음과 같은 필수 기재사항을 서면으로 명시하고 교부해야 한다. ① 근로계약기간에 관한 사항, ② 근로시간·휴게에 관한 사항, ③ 임금의 구성항목·계산방법과 지불방법에 관한 사항, ④ 휴일·휴가에 관한 사항과 ⑤ 취업의 장소와 종사하여야 할 업무에 관한 사항이다. 특히, ⑥ 근로일과 근로일별 근로시간은 단시간근로자에만 해당된다(기간제법 제17조).

(2) 사용자 보호를 위해 필요한 기재사항

근로계약은 노사가 대등하고 동등한 입장에서 작성되어져야 하지만, 실제는 사용자가 다수의 지원자 중에 가장 바람직한 근로자를 선발하여 고용하기 때문에 사용자가 제시한 근로조건 위주로 근로계약이 체결된다. 사용자가 사회적 강자의 입장에서 계약 내용을 결정하기 때문에 근로기준법은 근로계약 작성시 일정 제한을 두고 있다.

이러한 제한 조치에도 불구하고, 사용자는 스스로 보호할 수 있는 조항을 두어 부적격한 근로자나 불성실한 근로자에 대해 해고 등의 필요한 조치를 할 수 있다. 그 조항은 다음과 같다. 첫째, 수습기간을 정하여 업무에 적합하지 않은 근로자를 수습기간 내에 해고할 수 있다. 수습기간은 보통 3개월로 정해지지만, 필요시 연장할 수 있다. 이 경우 최초 3개월 내의 수습근로자에게는 사전예고 없이 해고할 수 있으나, 3개월 초과하여 수습기간을 둔 경우에는 해고 30일 전에 해고예고를 하여야 한다.

둘째, 수습기간을 통해 근로자의 업무 적격여부를 평가하기 어려운 경우에는 수습기간과 함께 1년의 기간제 근로조건을 설정할 수 있다. 셋째, 복무규정 (보안) 준수 서약서를 받아서, 근로자가 복무규정 위반시 징계할 수 있도록 근거를 마련해야 한다. 넷째, 개인 정보 사용동의서이다. 일반적으로 사용자는 고용된 근로자의 개인정보를 인사관리 목적상 사용할 수 있지만, 인사업무상 법령과 관련 없는 업무에는 사용할 수 없기 때문에 미리 개인정보 사용동의서를 받아 두어야 한다.

3. Details Not to Include in Employment Contracts

The Labor Standards Act specifies invalid details in employment contracts. These include: ① Working conditions that do not meet the standards of the Labor Standards Act, with such invalid section(s) to be judged as in accordance with the Labor Standards Act (Article 15); ② If any of the working conditions set forth in an employment contract is found to be inconsistent with actual conditions, the worker concerned shall be entitled to claim damages from the employer resulting from breach of the working conditions (Article 19); ③ Employers shall not prescribe penalties or damages for failure to fulfill the employment contract (Article 20); ④ No employer shall offset wages against an advance or other credits given in advance on the condition of a worker's labor (Article 21); and ⑤ No employer shall enter into a contract with a worker, in addition to a labor contract, which stipulates compulsory savings or the management of savings (Article 22).

3. 기재해서는 안 되는 근로계약 내용

사용자가 근로계약서에 기재하면 안 되는 내용은 다음과 같이 근로기준법에 명시되어 있다. ① 우선 근로기준법의 기준에 미치지 못하는 근로조건을 정한 근로계약은 무효이고, 그 무효가 된 부분은 근로기준법에 따른다(제15조). ② 근로계약에 명시된 근로조건이 사실과 다를 경우에는 사용자가 근로조건 위반을 원인으로 근로자에게 손해배상을 해야 한다(제19조). ③ 사용자가 근로계약 불이행에 대한 위약금 또는 손해배상액을 예정하는 근로계약을 체결할 수 없다(제20조). ④ 전차금이나 그 밖에 근로할 것을 조건으로 하는 전대채권과 임금을 상계하는 계약을 체결하지 못한다(제21조). ⑤ 사용자는 근로계약에 덧붙여 강제 저축과 또는 저축금의 관리를 규정하는 계약을 체결하지 못한다(제22조).

Section 3 : Rules of Employment

I . Korean labor law: Rules of Employment and the Employer's Legal Responsibilities

1. Introduction

Rules of employment set up an important system so that employers can systematically and uniformly manage their workers in a business or workplace. These rules refer to the employer determining the regulations needed to maintain corporate order and work efficiency at the workplace and the working conditions that will apply to all workers.[24] These rules of employment must be observed by the workers in the process of providing work, and also outline consequences for violating these rules. "Working conditions" refer to the conditions stipulated in the rules of employment in relation to worker wages, working hours, procedures for dismissal, and other treatment.[25]

Rules of employment can be written and enforced unilaterally by the employer, but once they are written, the employer and employees are bound to them and consequences for breaking those rules will apply to the applicable party, whether worker or employer. Employers cannot unilaterally change working conditions that have already been established. Any unfavorable changes are of no legal effect without the consent of a majority of the workers to whom the changes apply. In addition, the employer has both a legal obligation to prepare and report the rules to the Ministry of Employment and Labor, and a legal obligation to notify the workers of those rules in a public way. This is to ensure that the minimum standards set by the Labor Standards Act apply, through the rules of employment, to workplaces.[26]

---

24) Supreme Court ruling on Nov. 28, 1997: 97da24511.

25) Supreme Court ruling on June 23, 1992: 91da19210.

26) Lee, Seonggil, "A Legislative Review of the Employment Rules System," Labor Law Research (8) 69-119, Seoul National University Labor Law Research Society, June 1999, p. 78.

제3절 취업규칙

Ⅰ. 취업규칙과 사업주의 법적의무

1. 의의

사용자가 사업 또는 사업장에서 근로자를 체계적이고 통일적으로 관리할 수 있도록 중요한 시스템을 설정하는 것이 취업규칙이다. 취업규칙은 사용자가 사업장에서 기업의 질서유지와 효율적 업무수행을 위하여 필요한 복무규정과 근로자 전체에 적용될 근로조건을 정한 규정을 말한다.[24] 여기서 복무규율이라고 하면 근로자가 근로를 제공하는 과정에서 지켜야 할 작업질서에 관한 규칙과 이를 위반한 경우에 대한 제재를 말한다. 그리고 근로조건이라고 하면 근로자의 임금, 근로시간, 해고 그 밖에 근로자의 대우에 관하여 정한 조건을 말한다.[25]

취업규칙은 사용자가 일방적으로 작성하여 시행할 수 있지만, 일단 작성된 규정은 사용자와 근로자가 이에 구속되어 이를 위반한 경우에는 각각 제재가 가해진다. 그리고 사용자는 이미 확정된 근로조건에 대해 일방적으로 변경할 수 없다. 사용자가 취업규칙을 불이익 하게 변경할 때에는 그 적용 근로자의 과반수 동의를 얻어야 법적 효력을 가진다. 또한 사용자는 취업규칙을 작성하여 이를 고용노동부에 신고해야 하는 법적 의무와, 그 내용을 근로자들에게 게시하고 주지시켜야 하는 법적의무를 동시에 가지고 있다. 이렇게 하는 이유는 취업규칙을 통해서 근로기준법이 정한 최저 기준이 사업장에 적용될 수 있도록 하는 입법적 배려라고 할 수 있다.[26]

---

24) 대법원 1997. 11. 28. 선고 97다24511 판결.

25) 대법원 1992. 6. 23. 선고 91다19210 판결.

26) 이승길, "취업규칙법제에 관한 입법론적 고찰", 노동법 연구(8) 69-119, 서울대학교 노동법연구회, 1999. 6. 78면.

2. Legal Nature of Rules of Employment

Rules of employment enforce legal regulations that must be observed in the workplace (legal effect), while providing the principle of equal decision-making between labor and management in determining working conditions (contractual effect).[27] The courts have ruled, "Rules of employment are written by the employer, based on the employer's corporate management rights, in order to unify the service rules and working conditions of workers at the workplace. This is because the purpose of the Labor Standards Act is to protect and strengthen the position of workers in their reality of subordinate labor relations to protect and improve their basic livelihoods. This compels that rules of employment be drafted and become the legal norm."[28]

"Contractual effect" refers to the effect that arises from the relationship between the employer and the worker in the employment contract. Although working conditions are stipulated in rules of employment, any unfavorable changes are of no legal effect without the consent of the majority of the target workers (proviso to Article 94 of the Act). This is in accordance with the principle of protecting workers' vested rights and determining equal working conditions (Article 4 of the Act).

3. Specific Legal Obligations of the Employer in Relation to the Rules of Employment

Rules of employment are legal obligations that must be prepared by employers who employ at least a certain number of workers. Their specific details and effect are described in the Labor Standards Act.

---

27) Kim, Hyungbae, 「Labor Law」 24th ed., Parkyoungsa, Feb. 2015. p. 297; Lim, Jong-ryul, 「Labor Law」, 24th ed., Parkyoungsa, p. 366.

28) Supreme Court ruling on July 26, 1977: 77da355.

2. 취업규칙의 법적 성질

취업규칙은 사업장에서 준수해야 하는 법규적 규정을 강제하면서도 근로조건의 결정에 있어서는 노사 대등결정원칙을 제공하고 있다. 이는 법규범적 효력과 계약적 효력을 동시에 가지고 있다고 할 수 있다.[27] 판례도 "취업규칙은 사용자가 기업경영권을 바탕으로 사업장에 있어서의 근로자의 복무규율이나 근로조건을 획일적이고 통일적으로 정립하기 위하여 작성하는 것이다. 이는 근로기준법이 종속적 노동관계의 현실에서 불평등한 근로자의 입장을 보호하고 강화하여 그들의 기본적 생활을 보호하고 향상시키려는 목적으로 그 작성을 강제하고 이에 법규범성을 부여하고 있다"[28] 고 설명하고 있다.

계약적 효력은 사용자와 근로자 간의 근로계약 관계에서 발생하는 효력을 말한다. 취업규칙에 정해진 근로조건에 따라 근로자들의 근로조건이 구속되지만, 취업규칙에 정한 근로조건을 불이익 하게 변경할 경우에는 그 대상 근로자 과반수의 동의를 전제로 법적 효력이 발생한다(법 제94조의 단서). 이는 근로자의 기득권 보호, 근로조건 대등결정의 원칙에 따른 것이다(법 제4조).

3. 취업규칙과 관련된 사용자의 구체적 법적의무

취업규칙은 일정규모 이상의 근로자를 고용한 사용자가 의무적으로 작성해야 하는 법적 의무사항이다. 근로기준법은 취업규칙에 관한 구체적 내용과 효력을 기술하고 있다.

27) 김형배, 「노동법」 제24판, 박영사, 2015.2. 297면; 임종률, 「노동법」 제24판, 박영사, 366면.
28) 대법원 1977. 7. 26. 선고 77다355 판결.

1. Size of workplaces obligated to draw up rules of employment rules

(1) Legal requirements

Employers who employ "10 or more ordinarily-employed workers" must prepare rules of employment and report them to the Minister of Employment and Labor (Article 93 of the Act). It is much more difficult for smaller workplaces to have rules of employment in place, so their preparation is left to the discretion of the employer and is not a legal obligation.

(2) Practical application

The number of "ordinarily-employed workers" is determined by dividing the number of total employees by the number of working days in the one month prior to the date of occurrence of the reason for application of the law (the time when it is necessary to determine whether the rules of employment have been drawn up and the duty to report) (Enforcement Decree to the Labor Standards Act, Article 7-2). While employers employing fewer than 10 workers are not obligated to prepare or report establishment of rules of employment, if they are drawn up, all regulations stipulated by law related to those rules apply.[29)] Here, employers obliged to prepare and report establishment of rules of employment refer to those who have substantial authority and responsibility for matters that constitute the details of those rules, such as workplace rules and working conditions.[30)]

2. Items to be stated in the rules of employment

(1) Legal requirements

Article 93 of the Labor Standards Act lists the items to be written in the rules of employment as it relates to working conditions and employment regulations to be uniformly applied to a business or workplace. Article 93 consists of 13 items and applies to all workers in the relevant business or workplace, and can be divided into mandatory and optional items.

---

29) Seoul High Court ruling on Sep. 15, 2005: 2004nu23621.

30) Supreme Court ruling on Dec. 24, 1992: 92do2341.

1. 취업규칙의 작성의무가 있는 사업장 규모

(1) 법적 요구사항

'상시 10명 이상'의 근로자를 사용하는 사용자는 취업규칙을 작성하여 고용노동부장관에게 신고하여야 한다(법 제93조). 10인 이상의 사업장에 법적의무를 주고 있는 것은 10인 미만의 영세규모의 사업장은 회사의 체계가 갖추어 졌다고 보기 어렵기 때문에 일정규모 이상의 사용자에게 법적의무를 두고 있다. 10인 미만 사업장의 경우에는 취업규칙의 작성이 법적의무가 아닌 사업주의 재량에 맡겨져 있다.

(2) 실무적용

상시근로자 수는 법 적용 사유(취업규칙 작성과 신고 의무 적용여부를 판단해야 하는 시점) 발생일 전 1개월 동안 사용한 근로자의 연인원을 가동일수로 나누어 판단한다(시행령 제7조의2). 10인 미만을 고용한 사업주는 취업규칙의 작성과 신고의무는 없으나 일단 작성된 경우에는 법에서 정한 취업규칙에 관한 모든 규정이 적용된다.[29] 여기서 취업규칙을 작성하고 신고해야 할 의무가 있는 사용자는 직장규율이나 근로조건의 결정 등 취업규칙의 내용을 이루는 사항에 관해서 실질적인 권한과 책임을 갖는 자를 의미한다.[30]

2. 취업규칙의 기재사항

(1) 법적 요구사항

작성 내용은 사업 또는 사업장에 통일적으로 적용할 근로조건과 복무규율에 관한 내용으로 근로기준법 제93조에서 취업규칙의 기재사항을 열거하고 있다. 모두 13가지의 사항으로 구성되어 해당 사업 또는 사업장의 근로자 전체에 대해 적용되는 사항으로 필수적 기재사항과 임의적 기재사항으로 구분할 수 있다.

29) 서울고등법원 2005. 9. 15. 선고 2004누23621 판결.
30) 대법원 1992. 12. 24. 선고 92도2341 판결.

(2) Practical application

Of the matters listed in Article 93 of the Labor Standards Act, rules of employment must stipulate essential working conditions such as wages, working hours, recess hours, and holidays. Since there are no standards required by law in a number of areas related to shift work, family allowance, and others, including these items in rules of employment is optional. However, any wage reductions in the rules of employment (as part of the employer's disciplinary options) are limited to no more than 10% of one pay period. Finally, nothing in the rules of employment can be of a lower standard than in the Labor Standards Act or the applicable workplace collective agreement (Articles 95 and 96).

3. Procedures for drafting and changing rules of employment

(1) Legal requirements

The law defines how rules of employment are to be drafted and changed. The employer shall hear the views of the labor union organized by a majority of workers, or if there is no union organized by a majority of workers, the employer shall hear the views of a majority of workers in the relevant business or workplace. However, if the rules of employment are to be changed unfavorably for workers, their consent must be obtained before such change will have any effect (Article 94 of the Act). If the employer does not hear the views of applicable workers or obtain their consent before changing the rules unfavorably, a fine of not more than 5 million won shall be imposed (Article 114 of the Act). This is to protect the principle of equality between labor and management in determining working conditions and to ensure decent working conditions for the workers.

(2) Practical application

In general, if the already-existing working conditions or employment regulations are written into rules of employment, it is sufficient to inform the workers that rules of employment have been created and reflect the already-existing working conditions/ employment regulations. When introducing any new regulations into the rules, the views of a majority of the workers must be heard. If there are any changes that will be unfavorable to the workers, the consent of the affected workers must be obtained.

(2) 실무적용

근로기준법 제93조에 열거된 사항 중 임금, 근로시간, 휴게시간, 휴일 등과 같이 근로자 보호를 위하여 지켜야 하는 필수적인 근로조건은 반드시 그 내용을 취업규칙에 기재하여야 한다(필수적 기재사항). 그러나 교대근로, 가족수당 등에 관한 사항 등은 법에서 정한 기준이 없고 그 시행이 강제되는 것이 아니므로 해당 사업 또는 사업장에서 이를 도입하거나 시행하는 경우에만 취업규칙에 기재하여야 할 의무가 있다(임의적 기재사항). 다만, 취업규칙에 감급(減給)의 제재를 정한 경우에는 그 감액의 총액이 1임금지급시기의 10%를 초과할 수 없고 취업규칙의 내용이 근로기준법이나 해당 사업장의 단체협약 보다 더 낮아서는 안된다(법 제95조, 제96조).

3. 취업규칙의 작성과 변경절차

(1) 법적 요구사항

취업규칙을 어떻게 작성할 것인가와 어떻게 변경할 것인지는 법으로 정해져 있다. 사용자는 취업규칙의 작성 또는 변경에 관하여 해당 사업 또는 사업장에 근로자의 과반수로 조직된 노동조합이 있는 경우에는 그 노동조합, 근로자의 과반수로 조직된 노동조합이 없는 경우에는 근로자 과반수의 의견을 들어야 한다. 다만, 취업규칙을 근로자에게 불리하게 변경하는 경우에는 그들의 동의를 받아야 한다(법 제94조). 사용자가 취업규칙 변경과정에서 의견청취 또는 동의를 얻지 않는 경우 500만원 이하의 벌금에 처한다(법 제114조). 이는 근로조건의 결정에 있어 노사 대등의 원칙을 반영하고 근로자의 근로조건 보호를 위한 것이다.

(2) 실무적용

취업규칙의 작성과 변경 절차에 있어 근로자 과반수의 의견청취인지 그 동의를 받아야 하는지에 대해서는 새로운 취업규칙의 작성인지 아니면 기존 취업규칙의 변경인지에 따라 달라 질 수 있다. 일반적으로 기존의 근로조건 또는 복무규정에 관한 사항을 취업규칙에 기재한 경우에는 근로자들에게 취업규칙의 작

Changes to rules of employment that are considered unfavorable to workers generally include lowering the working conditions or removing the existing rules on working conditions and introducing new rules that are less favorable. There are three categories of criteria for judging whether changes to the rules of employment are disadvantageous. First, if there are multiple changes to the rules, a decision will be made for each individual working condition, but if there is an interactive relationship or linkage between factors that determine one working condition, it shall be decided comprehensively. For example, even if the severance pay rate is adjusted downward, it is not considered a disadvantage if the total amount of severance pay does not decrease because the number of wage items included in the average wage increases.[31)] Second, if a change to the rules of employment is beneficial to some workers and unfavorable to others, it is deemed unfavorable if the benefits resulting from the favorable and unfavorable are mixed with each other.[32)] Third, if the change subdivides and materializes the contents conceptually because the existing regulations are unclear or comprehensive, and therefore are intended to resolve controversies in interpretation, it cannot be regarded as a disadvantageous change.[33)]

4. Reporting rules of employment

(1) Legal requirements

Employers who regularly employ 10 or more workers must prepare rules of employment and report them to the Minister of Employment and Labor after hearing the views of their affected workers (Articles 93 and 94 of the Act). Before reporting the establishment or changes to the rules of employment, the employer must submit ① the employment rules and ② documents proving that the views of the labor union representing the majority of the workers, or the majority of the workers themselves, have been heard. If changes to the rules are unfavorable, documents must be submitted proving that consent has been obtained from the labor union representing the majority of workers, or from the majority of workers themselves (Article 15 of the Enforcement Regulation).

31) Supreme Court ruling on Aug. 28, 1997: 96da1726.

32) Supreme Court ruling on May 14, 1993: 93da1893.

33) Supreme Court ruling on Aug. 25, 2011: 2010guhap42263.

성이나 변경에 대해 주지시키는 정도로 충분하다. 취업규칙에 기존에 없던 복무규정을 도입하는 경우에는 근로자의 과반수의 의견을 들어야 한다. 그리고 변경되는 취업규칙이 근로자들에게 불이익한 변경인 경우에는 그 대상 근로자들의 동의를 얻어야 한다.

취업규칙의 불이익한 변경은 기존의 규정을 변경하여 근로조건을 낮추는 것이 일반적이지만, 기존의 근로조건에 관한 규정을 삭제하는 경우, 이전의 근로조건보다 불리한 규정을 신설하는 경우도 포함된다. 취업규칙 불이익 변경의 판단기준은 다음의 세가지로 구분할 수 있다. 첫째, 취업규칙 변경사항이 여러 개인 경우에는 개별 근로조건별로 판단하되, 하나의 근로조건을 결정짓는 여러 요소 사이에 서로 대가관계나 연계성이 있는 경우에는 종합적으로 판단한다. 예를 들어 퇴직금 지급률이 하향 조정되더라도 평균임금에 포함되는 임금 항목이 많아져서 전체적으로 퇴직금액이 감소되지 않는다면 불이익으로 보지 않는다.[31] 둘째, 취업규칙의 내용 변경이 일부 근로자에게는 유리하고, 일부 근로자에게는 불리한 경우와 같이 유불리에 따른 이익이 근로자 상호간에 충돌되는 경우에는 불이익한 변경으로 판단한다.[32] 세번째로 종래의 규정이 불명확하거나 포괄적이어서 그 내용을 개념적으로 세분화하여 구체화하는 차원에서 취업규칙 내용을 변경하는 경우에는 해석상 논란을 해소하기 위한 것으로써 불이익한 변경으로 볼 수 없다.[33]

4. 취업규칙의 신고

(1) 법적 요구 사항

상시 10인 이상의 근로자를 사용하는 사용자는 취업규칙을 작성하고 그에 대한 의견청취를 거친 뒤에 고용노동부장관에게 신고하여야 한다(법 제93조, 제94조). 취업규칙을 신고하거나 변경하려면 ①취업규칙과 ②근로자의 과반수를 대표하는 노

31) 대법원 1997. 8. 26. 선고 96다1726 판결.
32) 대법원 1993. 5. 14. 선고 93다1893 판결.
33) 대법원 2011. 8. 25. 선고 2010구합42263 판결.

(2) Practical application

When a report of establishment of or changes to the rules of employment is received, the labor inspector shall check whether the necessary information pursuant to Article 93 of the Labor Standards Act is included and whether documents have been attached that prove that the views have been heard/consent has been obtained from a labor union representing the majority of workers, or a majority of the workers themselves. After that, a review is made by the labor inspector within 20 days of receiving the report, to ensure the details of the rules of employment do not conflict with relevant laws or regulations or the relevant collective agreement, and that any changes to the rules of employment, without proof of worker consent, are not unfavorable. If the procedural requirements for the rules of employment are not met, or if the details are in violation of law or collective agreements, a period of up to 25 days shall be given to comply with an order for correction.[34] Here, if the employer submits a "Report on Establishment of/Changes to Rules of Employment" certified by a licensed labor attorney, along with a report of that labor attorney's review of the rules of employment or changes to those rules, an additional examination of the relevant rules by the labor inspector will be waived.[35]

5. Obligation to notify workers of the rules of employment

(1) Legal requirements

Employers must post or retain the rules of employment in a place where workers can read them at any time, and make them widely known to workers (Article 14 of the Act). The rules must not be seen by the workers as merely internal documents of the employer and of no effect. Since rules of employment are the norms within the company as determined by the employer, it is not necessary to follow the method stipulated in Article 14 of the Labor Standards Act for new or changed rules to take effect, but the rules of employment must be made widely known to the workers by any suitable method.[36]

---

34) Ministry of Employment and Labor, Regulation No. 48, "Guidelines for Examination of Rules of Employment."

35) Labor Standards Team-8048, Nov. 29, 2007, "Guidelines for Waiving Examination of Workplace Rules of Employment upon Confirmation of Examination by Certified Labor Attorney."

36) Supreme Court ruling on Feb. 12, 2004: 2001da63599.

동조합 또는 근로자 과반수의의견을 들었음을 증명하는 자료를 첨부하여 제출하여야 한다. 취업규칙을 불이익하게 변경하는 경우에는 과반수 노동조합이나 근로자의 과반수의 동의를 받았음을 증명하는 자료를 제출하여야 한다(시행규칙 제15조).

(2) 실무적용

근로감독관은 취업규칙 신고가 들어온 경우 근로기준법 제93조에 따른 필수기재사항 포함 여부와 근로자 과반수를 대표하는 노동조합 또는 근로자 과반수 의견이 첨부되어 있는지를 확인한다. 그후 내용 심사를 통해 취업규칙의 내용 법령 저촉 여부, 당해 단체협약 저촉 여부, 변경된 취업규칙의 근로자 불리 여부 등을 심사한다. 근로감독관은 신고 접수 후 20일 이내 심사한후, 취업규칙의 절차적 구비요건을 갖추지 못한 경우나 내용이 법령이나 단체협약에 위반된 경우 25일 이내의 시정기간을 부여하여 변경을 명한다.[34] 여기서 취업규칙 심사 시 사용자가 신고서와 함께 공인노무사의 「취업규칙 작성(변경) 신고 확인 보고서」를 제출하는 경우에는 해당 취업규칙에 대한 심사를 면제한다.[35]

5. 취업규칙 주지의무

(1) 법적 요구사항

사용자는 취업규칙을 근로자가 자유롭게 열람할 수 있는 장소에 항상 게시하거나 갖추어 두어 이를 근로자에게 널리 알려야 한다(법 제14조). 주지할 수 없는 취업규칙은 사용자의 내부문서에 불과하고 취업규칙으로써 효력이 없기 때문이다. 취업규칙은 사용자가 정하는 기업 내의 규범이기 때문에 신설 또는 변경된 취업규칙의 효력이 생기기 위해서는 근로기준법 제14조에 정한 방법에 의할 필요는 없지만 적어도 법령의 공포에 준하는 절차로 그것이 새로운 기업 내 규범인 것을 널리 종업원 일반으로 하여금 알게 하는 절차 즉, 어떠한 방법이든지 적당한 방법에 의한 주지가 필요하다.[36]

---

34) 고용노동부예규 제48호, "취업규칙 심사요령"
35) 근로기준팀-8048, 2007.11.29. "공인노무사 심사확인시 사업장 취업규칙 심사 면제에 관한 지침"
36) 대법원 2004. 2. 12. 선고 2001다63599 판결.

(2) Practical application

The workers must be notified by the employer for the drafted or changed rules of employment to have any effect. Although the method of posting is not described in detail by law, if the right of access is guaranteed so that workers can read them at any time, it can be considered that the duty of disclosure has been fulfilled by the employer, even if the rules are posted on the internal computer network.[37)]

6. Representation of a majority of workers

(1) Legal requirements

When reporting the rules of employment, the views of the labor union shall be heard if there is a labor union organized by a majority of workers in the relevant business or workplace, or the opinion of a majority of workers shall be heard if no such labor union exists. Consent must be obtained from this union, or the majority of workers if no such union exists, if changes are unfavorable (Article 94 of the Act). "A majority of workers" refers to the majority of the workers who are subject to the change(s) in the rules of employment.[38)]

(2) Practical application

1) When the rules of employment are applied uniformly: In order to unilaterally make changes to existing working conditions in a way that is unfavorable to workers, consent from the group of workers to whom the previous rules of employment apply must be obtained through a collective decision-making method. In addition, if the changes to the rules are to apply only to a specific group of workers at the time of the change, but application to other groups of workers is expected in the future, consent from all workers expected to be affected now or in the future shall be obtained. In other words, even if only company executives are directly disadvantaged in the immediate changes to the salary system for executives, if the rules shall apply to any general employee in the future

---

37) Supreme Court ruling on June 23, 1992: 92nu4253.

38) Supreme Court ruling on Feb. 29, 2008: 2007da85997.

(2) 실무적용

작성 또는 변경한 취업규칙의 효력이 발생하려면 사용자가 이 내용을 근로자들에게 알려야 한다. 게시방법에 대해 구체적으로 기술하고 있지 않으나, 예를 들면, 근로자가 언제든지 쉽게 열람할 수 있도록 접근권이 보장된다면 사내 전산망에 게시한 경우 주지의무를 이행하였다고 볼 수 있다.[37)]

6. 과반수 근로자의 대표

(1) 법적 요구사항

취업규칙을 신고할 때 해당 사업 또는 사업장에 근로자의 과반수로 조직된 노동조합이 있는 경우에는 그 노동조합, 근로자의 과반수로 조직된 노동조합이 없는 경우에는 근로자의 과반수의 의견을 들어야 한다. 그리고 불이익한 변경인 경우에는 그 동의를 받아야 한다(법 제94조). 그 동의방법은 근로자 과반수로 조직된 노동조합이 있는 경우에는 노동조합의, 그와 같은 노동조합이 없는 경우에는 근로자들의 회의방식에 의한 과반수의 동의가 있어야 하고 여기서 말하는 근로자의 과반수라 함은 기존 취업규칙의 적용을 받는 근로자집단의 과반수를 뜻한다.[38)]

(2) 실무적용

1) 취업규칙이 동일하게 적용되는 경우: 취업규칙의 변경에 의하여 기존 근로조건의 내용을 일방적으로 근로자에게 불이익하게 변경하려면 종전 취업규칙의 적용을 받고 있던 근로자 집단의 집단적 의사결정방법에 의한 동의를 요한다. 그리고 취업규칙의 변경 시점에는 특정 근로자 집단만이 직접적인 적용대상이지만 다른 근로자집단에게도 변경된 취업규칙의 적용이 예상되는 경우에는 해당 집단을 포함한 근로자집단을 기준으로 판단한다. 즉, 간부사원 급여체계 변경은 당장에는 간부사원만이 직접적인 불이익을 받더라도 일반 사원도

---

37) 대법원 1992. 6. 23. 선고 92누4253 판결.

38) 대법원 2008. 2. 29. 선고 2007다85997 판결.

through promotion, the consent of a majority of all employees—executives and general employees—is required.[39)]

2) When working conditions differ between worker groups and separate employment rules apply: There are no personnel transfers between worker groups, and workers in the two groups have different working conditions at the time of hiring. Under such circumstances, if the rules of employment are changed for a specific group, "the majority of workers" is deemed to be the majority of workers in the affected group, not the entire workforce. This would apply, for example, in a workplace where personnel are divided into production and management according to business necessity.[40)]

3) Labor union organized by a majority of workers: A labor union organized by a majority of workers refers to a union organized by a majority of all workers for whom the existing rules of employment apply, regardless of whether or not they are members of a union: i.e., it does not mean a labor union organized by a majority of only workers eligible to join a labor union. Even if changes are made disadvantageously only towards executives who are not eligible for union membership, if the changed working conditions will likely apply to ordinary workers in the future, consent from the union organized by a majority of workers shall include those for whom the changed working conditions are expected to apply in the future.[41)]

II. Disadvantageous Changes in the Rules of Employment and Exceptions

1. Effect of disadvantageous changes to the rules of employment

When changing rules of employment in a way that is unfavorable to workers, consent from the labor union is required if there is a labor union organized by a majority of workers. If there is no such union, consent from the majority of workers is required (Article 94 of the LSA). If the employer unilaterally changes the rules of employment

39) Supreme Court ruling on May 28, 2009: 2009doo2238.

40) Supreme Court ruling on Dec. 7, 1990: 90daka19647.

41) Supreme Court ruling on Nov. 12, 2009: 2009da49377.

승진에 따라 장래에는 변경된 간부사원 급여체계의 적용이 예상되므로 이때는 간부사원과 일반사원을 포함한 전체근로자 과반수의 동의가 필요하다.[39)]

2) 근로자집단 간 근로조건이 다르고 각각 별개의 취업규칙을 적용받는 경우: 근로자집단 사이에 인사이동에 의한 교류가 없고 입사 시부터 별도의 근로조건을 적용받는 근로조건이 이원화 되어 둘 이상의 집단으로 구분되는 상황에서 특정 집단을 대상으로 취업규칙이 변경되는 경우 전체 근로자가 아닌 해당 집단의 근로자를 대상으로 과반수 여부를 판단한다. 예를 들면, 한 사업장에서 경영상 필요에 따라 생산직과 관리직으로 나누어 인사노무관리를 별도로 하고 있는데 이 중 관리직만을 대상으로 취업규칙을 변경하는 경우라 할 수 있다.[40)]

3) 근로자 과반수로 조직된 노동조합: 근로자 과반수로 조직된 노동조합은 조합원 자격 유무에 관계 없이 기존 취업규칙의 적용을 받고 있던 전체 근로자 과반수로 조직된 노동조합을 의미한다. 노동조합에 가입할 수 있는 자격을 가진 근로자의 과반수로 조직된 노동조합을 의미하는 것은 아니다. 이는 조합원 자격이 인정되지 않는 간부 직원에게만 불이익하게 변경하는 경우라 하더라도 일반 근로자에게도 장래에 변경된 근로조건의 적용이 예상된다면 변경된 근로조건의 적용이 예상되는 근로자를 포함한 전체 근로자의 과반수로 조직된 노동조합이 동의의 주체가 된다.[41)]

Ⅱ. 취업규칙 불이익 변경과 예외

1. 취업규칙 불이익 변경의 효력

취업규칙을 근로자에게 불리하게 변경하는 경우에는 근로자 과반수로 조직된 노동조합이 있는 경우에는 그 노동조합, 그러한 노동조합이 없는 경우에는 근로자 과반수의 동의를 필요로 한다(근기법 제94조). 이러한 동의를 구하지 않

39) 대법원 2009. 5. 28. 선고 2009두2238 판결.
40) 대법원 1990. 12. 7. 선고 90다카19647 판결.
41) 대법원 2009. 11. 12. 선고 2009다49377 판결.

without obtaining such consent, the change(s) have no effect on workers who have been subject to the existing rules, and shall only apply to new workers hired after the rules were changed.[42] Even in court rulings, if the employer wishes to lower the existing working conditions for specific workers due to disadvantageous changes in the rules of employment, consent from the workers subject to the previous working conditions or rules is required. If such consent is not obtained, changes to the rules of employment are of no effect. If no such labor union exists, the consent of a majority of workers, according to meeting procedures for business or other units, is required. It is also acceptable to gather opinions of each worker in each department and then the workers discussing among themselves in a setting where there is no intervention or interference from the employer.[43]

In spite of previous court rulings changing the employment rules disadvantageously, recent court rulings have determined that the working conditions stated in the labor contract of a few workers who oppose the collective consent continue to apply in accordance with the principle of priority on favorable conditions.

2. Related cases

(1) Supreme Court ruling on Nov. 14, 2019 (2018 Da 200709)

1) Background

An employer and worker signed a contract with a basic annual salary of 70,900,000 won in March 2014. The monthly salary was 5,908,330 won. On June 25, 2014, the employer introduced and announced a wage peak system as part of the rules of employment, with the consent of the labor union organized by a majority of the employees. This wage peak system stipulated that the basic salary in an annual salary contract would be 60% of the 'standard wage peak' for workers with less than two years before reaching retirement age, and 40% for workers with less than one year remaining. From October 1, 2014 to June 30, 2015, the employee in this case received 3,545,000 won per month, which is 60% of

42) Supreme Court ruling on June 24, 2011, 2009 Da 58364.

43) Supreme Court ruling on May 14, 2004, 2002 Da 23185, 23192.

고 사용자가 일방적으로 변경한 경우에는 기존의 취업규칙의 적용을 받던 근로자들에게는 변경 효력이 없고, 변경된 취업규칙 이후 입사한 신규근로자에 대해서만 변경된 취업규칙이 적용된다.[42] 판례에서도 사용자가 취업규칙의 변경에 의하여 기존의 근로조건을 근로자에게 불리하게 변경하려면 종전 근로조건 또는 취업규칙의 적용을 받고 있던 근로자의 집단적 의사결정방법에 의한 동의를 필요로 하고, 이러한 동의를 얻지 못한 취업규칙의 변경은 효력이 없으며, 그 동의방법은 노동조합이 없는 경우에는 근로자들의 회의방식에 의해 과반수의 동의를 얻어야 하고, 여기서 회의방식에 의한 동의라 함은 사업 또는 한 사업장의 기구별 또는 단위 부서별로 사용자측의 개입이나 간섭이 배제된 상태에서 근로자간 의견을 교환하여 찬반을 논한 후 이를 전체적으로 취합하는 방식도 허용된다고 판시하고 있다.[43]

취업규칙을 불이익하게 변경하는 조건에 대해 기본적인 입장에서 불구하고, 최근 판례는 집단 동의방식을 거부한 소수 근로자의 근로계약서에 기재된 근로조건의 내용은 근로조건에 유리한 조건 우선의 원칙에 따라 계속 적용된다고 판시하고 있다.

2. 관련 사례

(1) 대상판결: 대법원 2019.11.14, 2018다200709

1) 사실관계

이 사건 사용자와 근로자는 2014년 3월경 기본연봉을 70,900,000원으로 정한 연봉계약을 체결하였다. 위 기본연봉을 월로 환산하면, 5,908,330원이 된다. 사용자는 2014년 6월 25일 소속 근로자의 과반수로 조직된 노동조합의 동의를 받아 취업규칙인 “임금피크제 운용세칙”을 제정, 공고하였다. 이 세칙은 연봉계약에 따른 기본연봉을 정하고, 정년이 2년 미만 남아 있는 근로자에게

42) 대법원 2011.6.24, 2009다58364.

43) 대법원 2004.5.14, 2002다23185, 23192.

his monthly basic wage, because less than two years remained for the employee before the employee reached retirement age, while 40% of the monthly basic wage or 2,363,330 won would be paid for the final year before reaching retirement age When the employer in this case notified the employee of the details due to the application of the wage peak system on September 23, 2014, the employee expressed his objection to application of the wage peak system.

2) Summary of the court ruling

Article 97 of the Labor Standards Act protects workers, who are in subordinate positions, preventing them from being subject to working conditions that do not meet the standards set in the employment rules. If Article 97 of the Labor Standards Act is interpreted for opposite situations, taking into account the content of these regulations and their legislative purpose, individual labor contracts that stipulate working conditions more favorable than the standards stipulated in the rules of employment are valid and take priority over the standards stipulated in the rules, since the collective consent stipulated in Article 94 of the Labor Standards Act is only a requirement for effective change of the rules. Even if there is collective consent for unfavorable changes to the rules of employment, the principle of free determination of working conditions stipulated in Article 4 of the Labor Standards Act is still observed. Therefore, rules revised unfavorably cannot be regarded to take precedence over existing individual labor contracts that set more favorable working conditions even if collective consent is obtained. The labor contract details remain valid, and cannot be changed according to the revised rules of employment, without the worker's individual consent.

는 '임금피크 기준연봉'의 60%, 정년이 1년 미만 남아 있는 근로자에게는 '임금피크 기준연봉'의 40%를 지급하도록 규정하고 있다. 이 사건 사용자는 2014년 10월 1일 부터 2015년 6월 30일 까지는 이 사건 근로자의 정년이 2년 미만 남아 있다는 이유로 월 기본급의 60%인 3,545,000원을, 2015년 7월 1일 부터 2016년 6월 30일(원고의 정년퇴직일)까지는 월 기본급의 40%인 2,363,330원을 지급하였다. 이 사건 사용자가 2014년 9월 23일 임금피크제 적용에 따른 임금 내역을 통지하자, 이 사건 근로자는 사용자에게 임금피크제의 적용에 동의하지 아니한다는 의사를 표시하였다.

2) 판결요지

근로기준법 제97조는 개별적 노사 간의 합의라는 형식을 빌려 근로자로 하여금 취업규칙에서 정한 기준에 미달하는 근로조건을 따르게 하도록 하는 것을 막아 종속적 지위에 있는 근로자를 보호하기 위한 규정이다. 이러한 규정 내용과 입법 취지를 고려하여 근로기준법 제97조를 다시 해석하면, 취업규칙에서 정한 기준보다 유리한 근로조건을 제시한 개별 근로계약 부분은 유효하고 취업규칙에서 정한 기준에 우선하여 적용된다. 근로기준법 제94조가 정하는 집단적 동의는 취업규칙의 유효한 변경을 위한 요건에 불과하므로, 취업규칙이 집단의 동의를 받아 근로자에게 불리하게 변경된 경우에도 근로기준법 제4조가 정하는 근로조건 자유결정의 원칙은 여전히 지켜져야 한다. 따라서 근로자에게 불리한 내용으로 변경된 취업규칙은 집단적 동의를 받았다고 하더라도 그보다 유리한 근로조건을 정한 기존의 개별 근로계약 부분에 우선하는 효력을 갖는다고 할 수 없다. 이 경우에도 근로계약의 내용은 유효하게 존속하고, 변경된 취업규칙의 기준에 의해 유리하게 근로계약의 내용을 변경할 수 없으며, 근로자의 개별 동의가 없는 한 취업규칙보다 유리한 근로계약의 내용이 우선하여 적용된다.

(2) Supreme Court ruling on Dec. 13, 2017 (2017 Da 26138)

1) Background

An employer and employee signed a labor contract for a full-attendance allowance of 600,000 won when actual working days numbered at least 20 days per month. As the company's financial situation deteriorated, the employer held a labor-management council meeting on April 26, 2016 to decide on a "self-reliance plan." That same day, 144 (69.9%) of the 206 employees agreed that all contract allowances besides basic wage would be rescinded, to be effective from May 1, 2016. The employee in question received the self-reliance plan, but did not agree to the plans to rescind allowances, so did not sign or place his seal on the labor contract with working conditions that followed the self-reliance plan. The employer determined that it was not necessary to pay the contracted allowance to the worker since the majority of workers agreed to the rescinding, and the employee did not receive the full-time allowance in his original labor contract.

2) Summary of the court ruling[44)]

The standards in rules of employment invalidate the part(s) of labor contracts with poorer working conditions. However, better working conditions in a labor contract take precedence over the rules of employment. As long as rules of employment only set the workplace's minimum standards, if they have been changed unfavorably for the employees, even through legitimate procedures, they are not more applicable than the individually-signed employment contract.

---

44) The original trial was in the Ulsan District Court, which ruled on June 14, 2017 (2016 Gahap 23102). The Appellate Court gave the same ruling, to which the employer appealed. The Supreme Court dismissed the employer's appeal without any additional review.

(2) 대상판결: 대법원 2017.12.13,2017다26138

1) 사실관계

이 사건 사용자와 근로자는 실제 근무한 날짜가 월 20일 이상인 경우 60만원의 만근수당을 지급하기로 하는 근로계약을 체결하였다. 사용자는 자금상황이 악화되자 2016년 4월 노사협의회를 개최하여 자구계획안을 의결하고, 2016년 4월 26일에 소속 근로자 206명 중 144명(69.9%)의 근로자들로부터 "기본임금 외에 모든 약정수당을 폐지한다. 〈중략〉 본 합의사항은 2016년 5월 1일 부터 시행한다"는 내용의 자구계획안에 동의한다는 취지의 동의서를 제출받았다. 사건 근로자는 변경안에 대하여 동의를 하지 않았고, 자구계획안에 의해 근로조건이 변경된 근로계약서에 서명하거나 날인하지도 않았다. 사용자는 자구계획안에 대하여 근로자들 과반수가 동의한 이상 근로자에게 약정수당을 지급할 필요가 없다고 판단하고, 변경된 근로계약 조건에 근거하여 이 사건 근로자에게 지급해오던 만근수당을 지급하지 않았다.

2) 판결요지[44)]

취업규칙은 그것이 정한 기준에 미달하는 근로조건을 정한 근로계약을 그 부분에 한해서만 무효로 하는 효력을 가질 뿐이고, 취업규칙에서 정한 내용보다 근로계약에서 정한 근로조건이 근로자에게 유리한 것일 때에는 당연히 근로계약에서 정한 근로조건이 취업규칙보다 우선하여 유효하게 적용된다. 또한 취업규칙이 근로계약과의 관계에서 최저 기준을 설정하는 효력만 가지는 이상, 근로계약을 체결한 이후 시점에 취업규칙이 적법한 절차를 거쳐 근로자에게 불리하게 변경되었다고 하여 유리한 근로계약에 우선하여 불리하게 변경된 취업규칙이 적용된다고 볼 수 없다.

---

44) 원심은 울산지방법원 2017. 6. 14. 선고 2016가합23102 판결, 항소심도 동일한 판단을 하고, 사용자의 항소를 기각하였다. 대법원은 심리불속행으로 이 사건 사용자의 상고를 기각하였다.

Ⅲ. Rules of Employment and Other Rules

1. Relations

If a labor contract includes employment conditions below the standards stipulated in the rules of employment, such nonconformity shall be null and void. In this case, the invalidated provisions shall be governed by the standards in the rules of employment(Article 97 of the LSA).

2. Rules of employment, law, and collective agreement

Even though an employer may prepare or amend the rules of employment, the amendment shall not conflict with any law or decree or collective agreement applicable to the workplace concerned(Article 96 of the LSA).

(1) Differences between the collective agreement and the rules of employment

The collective agreement concerns working conditions and other standards on the treatment of employees, and should be in writing and signed by both parties, that is, the employer and the employee representative. Besides, the collective agreement is, in principle, effective only for unionized employees for a limited period of time. By contrast, the rules of employment are drawn up unilaterally by the employer and contain general rules and regulations on the employees' service and working conditions applicable to all employees at the workplace.[45)]

(2) ROE amendments that infringe on the collective agreement have no legal effect, regardless of justifiable procedure in their amendment[46)]

As Article 96(1) of the Labor Standards Act regulates, "Rules of employment shall not conflict with any Act, subordinate statute, or a collective agreement applicable to the business or workplace concerned," amendments to the rules of employment that infringe on the collective agreement have no legal effect, regardless if justifiable procedures were

---

45) Supreme Court ruling on Apr. 25, 1997, 96Nu5421.

46) Seoul District Court ruling on Mar. 18, 2003, 2002Guhap31671.

Ⅲ. 취업규칙과 근로계약·법령·단체협약과의 관계

1. 취업규칙과 근로계약의 관계

취업규칙에 정한 기준에 미달하는 근로조건을 정한 근로계약은 그 부분에 관하여는 무효로 하며 무효로 된 부분은 취업규칙에 정한 기준에 의한다(근기법 제97조).

2. 취업규칙과 법령 · 단체협약의 관계

취업규칙은 사용자가 작성·변경할 수 있지만 법령 또는 당해 사업장에 적용되는 단체협약에 반할 수 없다(동법 제96조 제1항).

(1) 단체협약과 취업규칙의 차이

단체협약은 근로조건 기타 근로자의 대우에 관한 기준 등에 관한 사항을 정하는 협정으로서 서면으로 작성하여 노사 쌍방이 서명날인 하여야 하고, 유효기간에 있어서 일정한 제약이 따르며, 원칙적으로 노동조합원 이외의 자에 대하여는 그 규범적 효력이 미치지 아니하는 것이고, 이에 비하여 취업규칙은 사용자가 근로자의 복무규율과 임금 등 당해 사업의 근로자 전체에 적용될 근로조건에 관한 준칙을 규정한 것을 말한다.[45]

(2) 단체협약에 반하는 취업규칙의 변경은 절차의 적법 여부에 관계없이 그 효력이 없다.[46]

근로기준법 제96조 제1항은 '취업규칙은 법령 또는 당해 사업 또는 사업장에 대하여 적용되는 단체협약에 반할 수 없다'고 규정되어 있으므로 단체협약에 반하는 취업규칙의 변경은 절차의 적법여부와 관계없이 그 효력이 없다 할 것이어서 결국 무효인 취업규칙에서 정한 정년에 근거하여 참가인에 대하여 한

45) 대법원 1997.4.25, 96누5421.

46) 행정법원 2003.3.18, 2002구합31671.

followed in their amendment. Accordingly, it is definitely unfair dismissal if the employer notifies an employee of his/her dismissal on the basis of a regulation of 'retirement age' as stipulated in the ineffective rules of employment.

(3) Procedures for revision of rules of employment concerning working conditions after a collective agreement becomes ineffective.[47)]

Although the collective agreement may become ineffective, portions concerning working conditions will continue to be applied as before. A revision procedure is required, as stipulated in Article 94 of the Labor Standards Act, in order to revise the rules of employment unfavorably to employees about portions related to working conditions. On the other hand, an employer shall, with regard to disadvantageous amendment of the rules, receive the consent of a labor union, if there is a labor union composed of the majority of the workers in the business or workplace concerned, or otherwise the consent of the majority of said employees. Accordingly, the sole approval of the employee representative cannot be seen to be evidence that procedures were followed prior to disadvantageous revision of the rules.

(4) Retroactive application of the collective agreement[48)]

The collective agreement refers to the agreement made between the labor union and employer or employers' association concerning the determination of terms and conditions of employment. In cases where the labor union and the employer have agreed or approved the criteria for retroactively determining working conditions such as previous wage, working hours, and retirement pay, such agreement or approval applies to the labor union members or employees who have worked after implementation of the collective agreement. Even though the payment rate for severance pay in the rules of employment are changed disadvantageously, in cases where the labor union and the employer agree on the collective agreement regarding a revised severance pay rate, such agreement applies to those existing employees to whom the collective agreement applies, regardless of whether those employees knew the disadvantageous revision to their severance pay.

---

47) MOEL Guidelines: on Aug. 26, 2003, Kungi 68207-1087.

48) Supreme Court ruling of August 22, 1997, 96da6967【Severance Pay】

퇴직통보는 사실상 부당한 해고에 해당한다고 할 것이다.

(3) 단체협약이 실효된 후 근로조건에 관한 취업규칙의 변경절차[47)]

단체협약이 실효되었음에도 불구하고 실효된 단체협약 내용 중 근로조건에 관한 부분은 실효 이전과 같이 계속 적용하여 온 경우, 이러한 근로조건에 관한 부분은 취업규칙의 개정으로 불이익하게 변경하기 위해서는 근로기준법 제94조에 규정된 변경절차를 거쳐야 할 것이다. 한편, 취업규칙을 불이익하게 변경하는 경우에는 당해 사업 또는 사업장에 근로자의 과반수로 조직된 노동조합이 있을 경우에는 그 노동조합, 근로자의 과반수로 조직된 노동조합이 없을 경우에는 근로자 과반수의 동의를 얻어야 하며 근로자대표의 동의만으로는 불이익변경의 절차를 이행한 것으로 볼 수 없다.

(4) 단체협약에 의한 소급적 적용[48)]

단체협약은 노동조합이 사용자 또는 사용자 단체와 근로조건 기타 노사관계에서 발생하는 사항에 관하여 체결하는 협정이다. 노동조합이 사용자 측과 기존의 임금, 근로시간, 퇴직금 등 근로조건을 결정하는 기준에 관하여 소급적으로 동의하거나 이를 승인하는 내용의 단체협약을 체결한 경우에 그 동의나 승인의 효력은 단체협약이 시행된 이후에 그 사업체에 종사하며 그 협약의 적용을 받게 될 노동조합원이나 근로자들에 대하여 생긴다. 취업규칙 중 퇴직금 지급률에 관한 규정의 변경이 근로자에게 불이익함에도 불구하고 노동조합이 사용자 측과 변경된 퇴직금 지급률을 따르기로 하는 내용의 단체협약을 체결한 경우에는, 기득이익을 침해하게 되는 기존의 근로자에 대하여 종전의 퇴직금 지급률이 적용되어야 함을 알았는지 여부에 관계없이 원칙적으로 그 협약의 적용을 받게 되는 기존의 근로자에 대하여도 변경된 퇴직금 지급률이 적용된다.

47) 행정해석: 근기 68207-1087, 2003.8.26.
48) 대법원 1997.8.22, 96다6967【퇴직금】.

Chapter 3

wage

Section 1: Wages and Labor Law

Ⅰ. Wage Requisites and Standards for Judgment

> **Article 2 (5) of the LSA. Definition of wage**
> The term "wage" means wage, salary, and any other money or valuables, regardless of its title, which the employer pays to a worker as remuneration for work.

1. Wage Requisites

(1) Paid by the employer

Given that wage are what the employer pays to the employee, the service charge that a worker receives from customers in a hotel or restaurant cannot be considered as wage in principle.

(2) Remuneration for work

As wage are paid as remuneration for work, they cannot be deemed to be wage if the employer renders payment under friendly and favorable terms outside of work, or if the employer provides pay as part of welfare, or if the employee receives reimbursement for actual expenses.

(3) Any payment regardless of label

wage are paid in forms of salary or allowance in general. If the employer is paying remuneration for work to the subordinate employee, it is considered wage, regardless of what

Chapter 3

임 금

제1절 노동법상 임금

Ⅰ. 임금의 개념

근로기준법 제2조 제5항【임금의 정의】
"임금"이란 사용자가 근로의 대가로 근로자에게 임금, 봉급, 그밖에 어떠한 명칭으로든지 지급하는 일체의 금품을 말한다.

1. 임금의 요건

(1) 사용자가 지급할 것

임금은 사용자가 근로자에게 지급한 것이므로 호텔, 식당 등에서 손님이 직접 근로자에게 지급하는 봉사료는 원칙적으로 임금이라고 할 수 없다.

(2) 근로의 대상일 것

임금은 근로의 대가로 지급하는 것이므로 근로의 제공과는 상관없이 사용자가 호의적·은혜적으로 지급하는 경우나 복지후생의 목적으로 제공하는 경우 또는 실비변상적으로 지급하는 경우 등은 임금으로 볼 수 없다.

(3) 명칭을 불문한 일체의 금품

임금은 봉급 또는 수당이라는 명칭으로 지급되는 것이 보통인데, 사용자가

label the payment is given. Accordingly, we shall not estimate information allowance and welfare fees as wage just by their titles, because wage are differentiated by payment conditions.

2. Concrete Criteria for Wage

(1) Money paid under friendly and favorable terms is not considered to be wage

Money is not considered wage if paid for optional, courteous, and friendly reasons including congratulatory and consolation allowances, awards for quality control activities, or money paid favorably to celebrate special occasions such as the company's foundation day.

(2) Money paid for actual expenses is not considered wage

Money paid to reimburse actual expenses for the purchase of production instruments such as security equipment is not wage. Reimbursements for purchase of work uniforms, tools and materials, business trip expenses, travelling expenses, account expenses, confidential expenses, and information fees are also not considered wage.

(3) Welfare allowances are not considered wage (in principle)

The welfare allowance in its true meaning is not a wage because it cannot be treated as remuneration for work. However, if paid regularly to all workers in accordance with the collective agreement, rules of employment, or a repeated precedent, it is considered wage under the Labor Standards Act.

Wages	Non-wages
• Regular and continual bonuses and grants • Severance pay (post-paid wage) • Benefits paid for paid holidays or paid monthly/annual leave • Allowance for suspended work • Monetary payment for employee benefit, such as price-linked allowance, commuter allowance, and family allowance whose payment is a general and established practice.	• Monetary payment made as a token of courtesy, goodwill, or favor, such as allowance for congratulations or condolence • Monetary payment made to reimburse the already-paid expenses for business trips • Dismissal allowance • Compensation for damage, such as suspended work compensation

사용종속관계 아래에 있는 근로자에게 근로에 대한 대가로 지급하면 그 명칭과 관계없이 임금으로 간주된다. 따라서 정보비, 복리후생비 등 명칭만을 가지고 임금의 해당 여부를 판단하여서는 안 되며 지급실태에 따라 달라진다.

2. 임금의 판단기준

(1) 은혜적·호의적으로 지급되는 금품은 임금이 아니다.

경조금, 위문금 등 임의적, 의례적, 호의적 의미에서 지급되는 금품, QC 활동 등에 대한 포상금이나 회사 창립일 등 경축일에 호의적으로 특별히 지급되는 금품과 같이 은혜적으로 지급되는 금품은 임금이 아니다.

(2) 실비변상적인 금품은 임금이 아니다.

보안장비 구입비 등과 같이 생산수단 구입을 위한 실비변상적인 금품은 임금이 아니다. 작업복구입비, 작업용품 대금, 출장비, 여비, 판공비, 기밀비, 정보비 등도 마찬가지이다.

(3) 복리후생비는 임금이 아니다(원칙적).

순수한 의미의 복리후생비는 근로의 대가로 볼 수 없으므로 임금이 아니나, 수당의 이름이 복리후생비라 하더라도 단체협약, 취업규칙 등에 의하거나 또는 관례나 관행에 따라 정기적으로 전 근로자에게 같은 금액을 지급하는 경우에는 순수한 의미에서 복리후생비로 볼 수 없으므로 근로기준법상 임금이다.

임금에 해당하는 경우	임금에 해당하지 않는 경우
· 정기적·계속적으로 지급하는 상여금, 생산장려금, 능률수당 · 퇴직금(후불성 임금) · 유급휴일, 연월차휴가 미사용 수당 · 휴업수당 · 정기적·일률적으로 지급하도록 명시되어 있거나 관례적으로 지급되는 물가수당·통근수당·가족수당·월동수당 등의 복리후생적 성격의 금품	· 경조금·위로금 등의 의례적 호의적으로 지급되는 금품 · 여비·출장비 등의 실비변상조로 지급되는 금품 · 해고예고수당 · 휴업보상등의 재해보상금

Ⅱ. Employee Incentives

Many companies still incorrectly include employee incentives in calculating the total amount of wage. The following analyzes reviews whether employee incentives should be included when calculating wage under administrative guidelines, MOEL Guidelines, and/or judicial rulings.[49]

1. Characteristics of Bonuses in the Wage System

(1) Calculation rules for wage: Whether bonuses are included when calculating wage[50]

1) Bonuses to be included as wage

In cases where payment conditions, amounts, and payment rates are regulated in the rules of employment, or where employees are paid habitually and naturally expect to get paid: regular bonuses, exercise subsidies, etc.

2) Bonuses not included as wage

In cases where payments are not paid habitually, but paid temporarily or definitely based on company profits at the employer's discretion: employee incentives, production bonuses, reward bonuses, incentive allowances, etc.

(2) Bonuses/benefits paid temporarily or indefinitely are excluded when calculating the total wage.[51]

Of the incentives based on business performance, bonuses/benefits which have never been paid annually but have been paid temporarily based on corporate profits(or where the purpose is not specific) shall be excluded when calculating total wage for determining the Industrial Accident Compensation Insurance premium.

(3) Criteria for business performance bonuses[52]

The Employee Welfare Corporation has regulated the "Criteria for Business Performance

---

49) Jung, Bongsoo, 「Major Labor Issues and Related Cases」, 3rd ed., 2014. Jungang, p. 212.

50) Article 476 of Regulations of the Ministry of Employment and Labor.

51) MOEL (MOEL) Guidelines: Jingsu 68607-285, on Jun. 9, 1994.

52) MOEL Guidelines: Kongdan Jingsu 6510-52, on Jan. 23, 2003.

Ⅱ. 인센티브 보너스(상여금)

많은 기업에서는 아직도 경영성과금을 임금으로 판단하여 임금총액에 삽입하고 있는바, 여기에 대하여 행정지침, 판례, 행정해석을 살펴보고자 한다.[49)]

1. 상여금의 임금성 여부

(1) 임금산정지침에 따라 상여금의 임금 여부[50)]

1) 상여금이 임금인 경우

취업규칙 등에 지급조건, 금액, 지급시기가 정해져 있거나 전 근로자에게 관례적으로 지급하여 사회통념상 근로자가 당연히 지급받을 수 있다는 기대를 갖게 되는 경우: 정기상여금, 체력단련비 등

2) 상여금이 임금이 아닌 경우

관례적으로 지급한 사례가 없고, 기업이윤에 따라 일시적, 불확정적으로 사용자의 재량이나 호의에 의해 지급하는 경우: 경영성과배분금, 격려금, 생산장려금, 포상금, 인센티브 등

(2) 일시적으로 지급되거나 불확정적인 금품[51)]

경영성과에 따른 성과금 중 관례적으로 지급한 예가 없고 기업이윤에 따라 일시적으로 지급되거나 그 지급사유의 발생이 불확정적인 금품은 평균임금 산정의 기초가 되는 임금총액에서 제외된다.

(3) 근로복지공단의 경영성과 배분금의 판단지침[52)]

지급조건이 경영성과와 연계되어 있다면 임금으로 보기 어려울 것이다. 이때

49) 정봉수, 「노사문제별 사례별 대응방안」, 제3판, 중앙경제사, 2014, p.212.

50) 노동부예규 제476호, 2002.1.22.

51) 행정해석: 1994.6.9, 징수 68607-285.

52) 근로복지공단의 경영성과배분금의 판단지침, 공단징수 6510-52, 2003.1.23.

Bonuses" as follows: ① if the condition for payment is related to business performance, the bonus is not to be considered wage; ② business performance is acceptable in various areas such as corporate profits, output, total sales, cost-saving measures, quality assurance targets, accident ratio, market share, labor disputes, and so on; and ③ if the payment was decided by the results of business performance(such as sales, profits, etc.), even though the bonus has been paid regularly for a certain period due to good business performance, payment is not usually recognized as a general practice regulated as remuneration for work. Even though the company has included the business performance bonus into average wage to calculate severance pay, or the company has stipulated in the rules of employment, 'the bonus is paid according to the results of company business,' a business performance bonus whose payment and amount is determined by business results is not wage regardless of whether or not there is repeated payment. However, regular bonuses with no connection to business performance shall be included in total wage.

2. Cases where Incentives are Included when Calculating wages

1) If employee incentives and production promotion bonuses of the same amount are paid periodically and given to all employees pursuant to the collective bargaining agreement(CBA), they are characterized as wage.[53)]

A certain company claimed that employee incentives and production promotion bonuses were not calculated as wage because they had been an indefinite amount of money paid at the discretion of the employer for the purpose of preventing labor disputes or bringing about early termination of wage negotiations with employees. However, although there had been slight changes in bonuses since 1996, the above bonuses/benefits had been paid uniformly in regards to payment amount, payment period, etc. It was a burden for the employer to pay employee incentives and production promotion bonuses to all employees uniformly according to the wage CBA. In terms of formal items such as payment rules, purpose, etc., the payment was also definite and scheduled, so these bonuses were not paid annually and were temporary in nature. When the above incentives and promotion bonuses are analyzed totally and substantively, they were wage determined to be as remuneration for work.

53) Seoul Appellate Court ruling on Sep. 18, 2003, 2002Na18697.

경영성과라 함은 기업이윤, 매출액, 비용절감, 불량률, 재해율, 시장점유율, 노사분규상황 등이 폭넓게 인정된다. 경영성적(매출액, 이익금 등)의 평가결과에 따라 지급여부가 결정되었다면 결과적으로 경영성적이 좋아 일정기간 계속 지급하였다 하더라도 근로의 대상이라고 볼 수 없다. 회사가 퇴직금 기초인 평균임금에 포함시켰다던가, 취업규칙에'경영성과에 따라 지급한다'고 규정하더라도, 경영성과와 무관하게 주기적으로 지급한 정기상여금 등은 임금총액에 포함되나, 경영성과에 따라 지급액이 결정되는 배분금은 비록 반복 지급되었다 하더라도 임금이 아니다.

2. 경영성과금이 임금인 경우

1) 경영성과금과 생산장려격려금이 지급액과 지급시기가 일정하고 협약에 의해 모든 근로자에게 일률적으로 지급되도록 규정되어 있다면 임금의 성질을 갖는다.[53]

피고회사는 경영성과금 및 생산장려격려금이 노동쟁의를 방지하거나 임금협상을 신속하게 마무리하기 위한 목적으로 무쟁의 내지 임금협상의 조기타결을 조건 삼아 근로자들에게 은혜적으로 지급하는 불확정적인 금원이어서 임금에 포함되지 않는다고 주장하나, 위 금품은 1996년 이후에는 그 명칭만 조금 달리할 뿐 그 지급액, 지급시기 등이 일정한 점에 비추어 보면, 경영성과금 및 생산장려격려금은 임금협약에 의하여 피고회사가 모든 근로자에게 일률적으로 의무적으로 지급하도록 규정한 것으로 그 지급규정이나 명목 등 형식적인 사항만을 고려하여 그 지급 사유의 발생이 불확정적이고 일시적으로 지급되는 것이라거나 의례적, 은혜적 급부라고 볼 수 없고, 위 성과금 및 격려금을 전체적, 실질적으로 파악해 보면 근로의 대가로 지급되는 임금의 성질을 갖는다고 할 것이다.

53) 서울고등법원 2003.9.18, 200218697.

2) Individual sales incentives that have been paid regularly and periodically shall be included in average wage.[54)]

A company's salary system consists of the basic annual salary and annual incentives. The basic annual salary is paid monthly, and the annual incentive is paid in January as a lump sum payment based upon the valuation of sales targets and outcomes for the fiscal year. The amount of severance pay the company gives reflects the basic annual salary without including the annual incentive. An employee requested that the company re-calculate his severance pay, insisting that the annual incentive be included in the calculation of average wage because the annual incentive belongs to the wage concept. When his request was rejected, he filed a suit against the company. In determining whether individual items of pay may be identified as wage reflected in the calculation of average wage, the following criteria is considered: ① the items are paid regularly and periodically; ② they are mandated by the employer according to collective bargaining agreement, rules of employment, salary regulations, the labor contract, or habitual practice; or ③ employees identified under general conditions are paid uniformly. If individual items of pay meet any of these criteria, the items of pay shall be considered wage regardless of their titles. The annual incentive was ruled as wage.

3. Cases Where Incentives are Not Calculated as wages

(1) Whether profit-sharing bonuses paid on the basis of business performance are considered wage.[55)]

According to Article 2 of the Labor Standards Act, the term "wage" means wage, salary, and any other kind of money or valuables(regardless of title), which the employer pays to a worker as remuneration for work. In cases where employee incentives were previously determined in regards to the method of payment, amount, and payment period in the rules of employment, the employee incentives were paid customarily to all employees. This repeated payment led employees to expect a bonus. Accordingly, these bonuses shall be regarded as a part of wage.

54) Seoul District Court ruling on Jun. 21, 2007, 2006Na20978.

55) MOEL Guidelines: wage 68207-134, on Feb. 28, 2002.

2) 근로의 대가로 정기적으로 지급된 개인 영업성과 연봉은 평균임금에 포함한다.[54]

이에 대한 사례를 살펴보면, 회사의 임금체계는 기본연봉과 성과연봉으로 구성되어 있고 기본연봉은 매월 기본급으로 지급하고, 성과연봉은 해당 연도 영업목표 및 경영성과를 평가해 이듬해 1월에 일괄해 지급했다. 회사는 갑에게 퇴직금을 지급하면서 위 성과연봉을 포함시키지 않고 기본연봉을 기초로 평균임금을 산정해 퇴직금을 지급했으나, 갑은 위 성과연봉이 임금이기 때문에 평균임금 산정 시 포함해야 한다면서 퇴직금 재산정을 요구했고 회사가 이를 받아들이지 않자 소송을 제기했다. 어떤 금품이 평균임금 산정의 기초가 되는 임금에 해당하는지 여부를 가늠할 수 있는 구체적인 사안으로 근로자에게 계속적·정기적으로 지급되며 단체협약, 취업규칙, 급여규정, 근로계약, 노동관행 등에 의해 사용자에게 그 지급의무가 지워져 있고, 또한 일정한 요건에 해당하는 근로자에게 일률적으로 지급하는 것이라면, 그 명칭 여하를 불문하고 임금이라고 볼 수 있을 것이라면서 영업 성과연봉을 임금으로 판단했다.

3. 경영성과금이 임금이 아닌 경우

(1) 경영성과를 기초로 지급하는 이익분배금[55]

근로기준법 제2조의 규정에 의거 임금이라 함은 사용자가 [근로의 대상]으로 근로자에게 임금, 봉급 기타 어떠한 명칭으로든지 지급하는 일체의 금품을 말하는 것으로, 성과금이 취업규칙 등에 지급조건·금액·지급시기가 정해져 있거나, 모든 근로자에게 관례적으로 지급하여 사회통념상 근로자가 당연히 지급받을 수 있다는 기대를 갖게 되는 경우라면 임금성을 인정할 수 있다.

그러나 취업규칙에 근로조건을 미리 명시하지 않고 노사합의를 통해 경영목표를 정해놓고, 목표에 도달할 경우 일정액 또는 일정비율의 성과급 또는 일시

54) 서울중앙지방법원 2007.6.21, 2006나20978.

55) 행정해석: 임금 68207-134, 2002.2.28.

However, without regulating this working condition, which was previously provided in the rules of employment, the company management and labor determined the business profit target. In the event that the employer makes a decision to pay a fixed amount(e. g., a certain incentive rate or a one-time bonus), then if that target is achieved, such bonuses will not be treated as wage, because what they received is dependent upon the result of business performance. Whether a payment condition is met or not determines the actual payment, that is, the amount being disbursed based on an evaluation of the company's performance. Therefore, since the condition for the payment is variable, temporary, and based on the company's performance, this payment cannot be regarded as part of wage.

That company's rules of employment stipulate that "the bonus can be paid in consideration of yearly corporate performance. If business performance is good, as in the case of company profit, the company may, through internal decision-making, determine whether to pay special incentives, the amount and conditions required for payment for each department." Accordingly, this type of profit-sharing bonus is paid according to whether a business surplus is achieved or not. Therefore, in consideration of the payment conditions and purpose, it is difficult to deem this payment as wage according to Article 2 of the Labor Standards Act.

(2) Determination of whether employee incentives are included as wage[56)]

The characteristics of valuables that a company pays to its employees: A certain labor union requested that the company pay employee incentives, which the company discussed with the labor union, but actual payment and method of payment of the incentives could not be agreed upon. The company decided to pay an incentive based on business performance and paid an actual incentive on March 4, 1999, December 23, 1999, and December 29, 2000, only to incumbent employees, and with different payment criteria and payment rate per employee.

Ruling: The company regulated the employee incentives and general criteria for payment in the internal wage rules, but there were no other rules related to payment, period, or concrete rate for incentives in the rules of employment or collective bargaining agreement. Employee incentives were paid irregularly, with no fixed rate and at different amounts per employee. The company determined payment and method according to

56) Daegu District Court ruling on Feb. 21, 2014, 2013Gahap8360.

금 등을 지급하기로 정한 경우라면, 이는 그 지급조건의 충족여부가 경영실적 평가결과에 따라 결정되고, 평가결과에 따라 지급조건과 금액을 달리하게 되거나 또는 지급하지 않을 수도 있게 되는 등 그 지급사유의 발생이 불확정적이고 일시적이므로 이를 기왕의 근로인 - 그 지급이 확정되어 사용자에게 지급의무가 부과되어지는 - 근로기준법에 의한 임금으로 볼 수는 없을 것이다.

취업규칙에 의거 연간 기업업무실적을 참작하여 상여금을 지급할 수 있다고 명시하고, 연간 경영실적, 즉 경영이익이 발생되는 경우에는 내부품의 절차를 거쳐 이를 각 사업부서별로 평가하여 동 금품의 지급기준, 지급금액 등을 확정, 지급하고 있는 것으로 보인다. 따라서 이와 같은 이익분배금은 경영이익의 발생이라는 요건의 충족여부에 따라 비로소 지급기준이나 금액이 확정되는 것이므로 이는 그 지급조건이나 목적 등에 비추어 볼 때 기왕의 근로에 대상으로 지급이 확정되는 근로기준법 제2조의 규정에 의한 임금성격을 가진다고 보기는 어려울 것이다.

(2) 특별상여금[56)]

원고 회사가 근로자에게 지급된 금품의 성격은 노동조합이 회사에 특별상여금의 지급을 요구하거나 회사가 노동조합의 의견을 청취한 적은 있었으나, 회사와 노동조합 사이의 합의에 의하여 특별상여금의 지급여부나 그 방법이 정해진 것은 아니었으며, 회사의 경영성과에 따라 그 경영진의 판단에 의하여 지급여부 및 방법이 결정되어, 특별상여금이란 명목으로 1999년 3월 4일, 1999년 12월 23일, 2000년 12월 29일 재직 중인 근로자들을 대상으로 지급기준, 지급률을 달리하여 지급하였다.

판결 내용은「원고 회사가 급여규정에 특별상여금의 일반적인 지급기준이 규정되어 있을 뿐, 그밖에 취업규칙, 단체협약 등에 특별상여금의 지급여부, 지급시기 및 구체적인 지급률 등에 관하여 아무런 규정이 없는 점, 지급시기가 부정기적이고 지급률도 일정하지 아니하였으며, 근로자별로 그 액수를 달리 정해 지급된 점, 노동조합과의 합의 없이 회사의 경영성과에 따라 경영진의 판단에

56) 대구지방법원 2014.2.21, 2013가합8360.

company performance. In consideration of this situation, it is hard to deem that employee incentives were paid continuously and periodically as remuneration for work or that such a customary practice was established. As the employer has no obligation to pay incentives in the rules of employment, collective agreement, or wage regulations, the employee incentives shall not be interpreted as wage.

(3) Whether profit-sharing bonuses are included as wage.[57)]

The characteristics of valuables that a certain company pays to its employees: There were no regulations for profit-sharing bonuses in the collective bargaining agreement. Since the company exceeded its production target by more than 100% from December 1996 to 2000, it paid 100% profit-sharing bonuses on average.

Ruling: The wage regulated in the company's collective bargaining agreement(CBA) consist of base pay, bonuses, and allowances, but there are no regulations for employee incentives. According to the wage CBA concluded every year, profit-sharing bonuses are to be paid according to whether a production target scheduled in a given year was achieved. Therefore, the payment method and amount of profit-sharing bonuses were the same each year and these bonuses were paid irregularly. Accordingly, the Company does not have a legal duty to pay profit-sharing bonuses. This means that these bonuses are not considered wage.[58)]

(4) Determination of whether performance bonuses for each company section are to be included as wage.[59)]

The characteristics of remuneration that a certain company paid to its employees: "The Company stipulates in its rules of employment that it can pay employee incentives once a year in consideration of business performance for each company division; the payment, method, criteria, and size of incentive shall be determined according to business performance every year." Since establishment of the employee incentive regulations in 1995, payment rates and payment subjects were applied differently in the second half of

57) Changwon District Court ruling on May 17, 2001, 2000Gu3242.

58) Changwon District Court ruling on May 17, 2001, 2000Gu3242.

59) MOEL Guidelines 02-03886, on Dec. 14, 2002.

의해 지급여부 및 방법이 결정된 점 등의 제반 사정을 고려하여 보면, 회사와 소속 근로자들 사이에 특별상여금이 근로의 대상으로서 계속적·정기적으로 지급되고 있다거나 그러한 관례가 성립되었다고 할 수 없을 뿐만 아니라, 특별상여금의 지급에 관한 취업규칙, 단체협약, 급여규정 등에 의하여 지급의무가 있다고 할 수도 없으므로 임금으로 볼 수 없다.」

(3) 성과배분 상여금[57)]

관련사례를 살펴보면, 원고에게 지급된 금품의 성격은 성과배분상여금에 대해 단체협약에 별도로 그 지급근거가 명시되어 있지 않고, 1996~2000년까지 매년 12월에 생산목표 달성률이 100%를 초과하여 성과 배분상여금으로 그 지급 기준금액의 100%를 지급 받았다.

판결 내용은 원고 회사의 단체협약 규정상 근로자의 임금은 기본급, 상여금 및 수당으로 구성되어 있고, 특별상여금에 관하여는 아무런 규정이 없는 점, 또한 매년 체결되는 임금협약서의 규정에 의하더라도 성과배분상여금은 당해연도 초에 계획한 생산목표의 달성여부에 따라 지급여부가 결정되므로 그 지급이 확정되어 있다고 보기 어렵고, 그 지급방법과 금액이 매년 동일하며 위 성과배분상여금이 계획적·정기적으로 지급되고 그 지급에 관하여 단체협약 등에 의하여 회사에 지급의무가 지워져 있다거나 그러한 관계가 성립되었다고 보기 어렵다 할 것이므로 위 성과배분 상여금은 임금이 아니다.[58)]

(4) 사업부별 성과급[59)]

원고 회사가 근로자에게 지급된 금품의 성격은 회사의 취업규칙에 "회사는 각 사업부별 업적을 참작하여 연 1회 이상 성과급을 지급할 수 있다. 단, 성과급의 지급여부, 지급방법, 지급기준 및 지급액에 대해서는 당해연도의 경영실적에 따라 정한다"라고 되어 있으며, 1995년 성과급 제도가 생긴 이래 1995년

57) 창원지방법원 2001.5.17, 2000구3242.
58) 창원지방법원 2001.5.17, 2000구3242.
59) 행정해석: 국행심 02-03886, 2002.2.14.

1995, in the first half and second half of 1996, in the first half and second half of 1999, and in the first half and second half of 2000. Bonuses were not paid in 1997 and 1998.

Ruling: "Employee incentives were not fixed amounts each time and the rules of employment stipulate that 'the Company can pay incentives once a year in consideration of business performance for each company section; the method, criteria, and size of incentive shall be determined according to annual business performance." Since the reason for the incentive, concrete payment criteria, amount, and time are unfixed, it is difficult for employee incentives to be definitely determined and paid. In consideration of the fact that employee incentives in 1997 and in 1998 were not paid, the employee incentives shall be included as remuneration granted temporarily and irregularly according to the company's business performance."

(5) Whether variable employee incentives are included as wage.[60)]

A certain company paid variable employee incentives in appreciation of employee efforts in smoothly implementing the core business. There were no regulations for variable incentives in the rules of employment. Even though they had been paid a few times temporarily in 1999 and 2000, these bonuses were not paid uniformly and varied individually in payment.

Ruling: "There are no regulations concretely stipulated in the rules of employment related to variable or regular incentives. There is also no agreement for variable incentives in the CBA. These bonuses were only paid once each year, in 1999 and 2000, so it is difficult to regard the variable incentives as a repeated practice to be paid to all employees uniformly and regularly. In consideration of these facts, variable employee incentives cannot be regarded as wage, but remuneration to be paid to employees under friendly and favorable terms according to each employee's business performance."

60) MOEL Guidelines 02-03729, on Nov. 18, 2002.

하반기, 1996년 상·하반기, 1999년 상·하반기 및 2000년 상·하반기에 지급 시기별로 지급률, 지급대상 등을 조금씩 달리하여 지급하고 1997년과 1998년에는 미지급하였다.

재결 내용은 성과급의 지급액이나 지급대상이 매회 일정하지 아니한 점, 회사의 취업규칙에 의하더라도 "회사는 각 사업부별 업적을 참작하여 연 1회 이상 성과급을 지급할 수 있다. 단, 성과급의 지급여부, 지급방법, 지급기준 및 지급액에 대해서는 당해연도의 경영실적에 따라 정한다"라고 되어 있어 지급사유의 발생 여부, 구체적인 지급기준·금액·시기 등이 불확정적이므로 성과급의 지급이 확정되어 있다고 보기 어렵다 할 것이고 이는 1997년과 1998년에는 성과급이 지급되지 않은 것에 의해서도 확인되는 점 등에 비추어 볼 때 회사가 근로자들에게 지급한 성과급은 회사의 경영실적에 따라 일시적·불확정적으로 지급한 시혜적 성격의 금품이다.

(5) 변동성과급[60]

관련사례를 보면, 핵심사업의 순조로운 진행에 대해 근로자들의 노고를 위로하고자 변동성과급이라는 명목으로 금전이 지급되었고, 취업규칙 등에 그 지급이 명시되어 있지 않았으며, 1999년과 2000년에 한시적으로 몇 차례 지급되었을 뿐 지급액도 일률적이지 않고 액수의 차이도 상당하며, 개인 근로자별 지급액에도 차이가 있다.

재결 내용은 「변동성과급 또는 그 밖의 다른 명목으로 성과급 지급에 관한 사항이 취업규칙 등에 구체적으로 명시되어 있지 아니하며, 단체협약을 통해서도 변동성과급의 지급에 관한 합의를 한 사실을 확인할 수 없고, 지급횟수도 1999년과 2000년에 각 1회에 그치고 있어 위 변동성과급이 모든 직원에게 일률적·정기적으로 지급되는 관행이 성립되었다고 보기도 어렵다는 점을 고려하여, 위 변동성과급은 임금이라기보다는 사업주가 경영실태 등을 고려하여 그 직원에게 호의적·은혜적으로 지급한 것」에 불과하다.

---

60) 행정해석: 국행심 02-03729, 2002.11.18.

Ⅲ. Ordinary Wage

1. Understanding Ordinary Wage[61)]

(1) Concept of ordinary wage

The term 'ordinary wage' means hourly wage, daily wage, weekly wage, monthly wage, or subcontract wage determined to be paid in periodic or lump sums to the worker for prescribed or whole labor.[62)] That is, 'ordinary wage' means the wage determined to be paid periodically and uniformly regardless of the number of actual work provisions or the amount received as remuneration for quality or quantity of the labor.

(2) Reasons for calculating ordinary wage

Ordinary wage applies to ① dismissal allowances replacing advance notices of dismissal, ② wage added for overtime, night, or off-day work, ③ ordinary wage stipulated in the rules of employment to calculate annual paid leave, and ④ in cases where the pay is under 'paid allowance,' not under average wage according to the Labor Standards Act.

(3) Methods of calculating ordinary wage

When calculating ordinary wage, the hourly wage rate is applied in principle. Daily wage, weekly wage, monthly wage, or subcontract wage can be calculated at the hourly wage rate as in the following:

1) Hourly wage rate of daily wage

With respect to wage determined by the daily wage rate, the amount is calculated by dividing the daily wage rate by the contractual working hours per day. Contractual working hours represent those working hours which the workers and employers have agreed upon within the limit of the legal standard working hours(Article 2(7) of the LSA).

---

61) It has been revised to reflect the intent of the Supreme Court en banc ruling on ordinary wages issued in December 2024.

62) Article 6(1) of the Enforcement Decree to the Labor Standards Act

Ⅲ. 통상임금

1. 통상임금의 이해[61)]

(1) 통상임금의 개념

'통상임금'이란 근로자에게 정기적·일률적으로 소정근로 또는 총 근로에 대하여 지급하기로 정해진 시급금액·일급금액·주급금액·월급금액 또는 도급금액을 말한다.[62)] 즉, 근로의 질 또는 양의 대가로 실제 근로일수나 수령액에 구애됨이 없이 정기적·일률적으로 지급하기로 정해진 임금을 의미한다.

(2) 통상임금의 산정 사유

통상임금으로 산정해야 하는 경우로는 ① 해고예고에 갈음하는 해고수당, ② 시간외근로, 야간 및 휴일근로에 대한 가산임금, ③ 연차 유급휴가 수당의 경우 취업규칙 등의 정함에 따라 통상임금으로 산정하는 경우, ④ 기타 근로기준법에서 '유급'으로 지급하기로 한 임금이다.

(3) 통상임금의 산정방법

통상임금은 시간급으로 산정함이 원칙이다. 일급·주급·월급·도급금액을 시간급 통상임금으로 환산하는 방법은 다음과 같다.

1) 일급의 시간급 통상임금

일급금액으로 정해진 임금에 대하여는 그 금액을 1일의 소정근로시간수로 나눈 금액이 시간급 통상임금이 된다. 소정근로시간이란 법정근로시간의 범위 안에서 근로자와 사용자 간에 정한 근로시간으로 정의하고 있다(근로기준법의 제2조 제7항).

---

61) 2024년 12월 통상임금에 대한 대법원 전원합의체 판결 취지를 반영하여 재 작성 되었음.
62) 근로기준법시행령 제6조 제1항.

2) Hourly wage rate of weekly wage

With respect to wage determined by the weekly wage rate, the amount is calculated by dividing the weekly wage rate by the contractual working hours per week. Weekly wage refers to ordinary wage that are to be paid on a weekly basis.

3) Hourly wage rate of monthly wage

With respect to wage determined by the monthly wage rate, the amount is calculated by dividing the monthly wage rate by the contractual working hours per month. Monthly wage refers to ordinary wage that are to be paid on a monthly basis.

In cases where legal standard hours are regulated to the same as contractual working hours, the calculation is as follows:

⇒ Where legal standard hours mean 40 hours weekly, excluding rest hours

Standard hours calculated for monthly ordinary wage = (40 hours + 8 hours) x 4.345 weeks ≒ 209 hours

4) Hourly wage rate of subcontract wage

With respect to wage determined by the subcontract wage system, the amount is calculated by dividing the total sum of wage under the subcontract wage system for the period of wage calculation by the whole number of working hours during that period.

 **Ministry of Employment and Labor Guidelines**

1) As long as the welfare allowance is paid periodically and uniformly, it shall be included in the realm of ordinary wage.[63]

In cases where the welfare allowance has been paid to all employees periodically and uniformly for the contractual working hours or legal standard working hours for the purpose of supplementing the low wage level of employees working in social welfare facilities, this allowance shall be included in the realm of ordinary wage. Here, the term "periodic" means that the employer shall pay wage for contractual working hours or legal standard working hours. The term "uniform" means that the employer shall not only pay all employees, but also pay all employees who meet a certain condition or reach a certain level of working conditions.

---

63) MOEL Guidelines: on Oct. 4, 2002, Wage 68207-730

2) 주급의 시간급 통상임금

주급금액으로 정하여진 임금에 대하여는 그 금액을 주의 통상임금 산정기준 시간 수로 나눈 금액이 시간급 통상임금이다. 주급 금액이란 1주를 단위로 하여 지급하기로 정해진 통상임금을 말한다.

3) 월급의 시간급 통상임금

월급금액으로 정하여진 임금에 대하여는 그 금액을 월의 통상임금 산정기준 시간 수로 나눈 금액이 시간급 통상임금이 된다. 월급 금액이란 1월을 단위로 하여 지급하기로 정하여진 통상임금을 말한다.

법정기준 근로시간을 소정근로시간으로 정한 경우의 계산례는 다음과 같다.
⇒ 주 법정근로시간이 휴게시간을 제외하고 40시간인 경우

월의 통상임금 산정기준 시간수 = (40시간+8시간) × 4.345주 ≒ 209시간

4) 도급임금의 시간급 통상임금

도급금액으로 정하여진 임금에 대하여는 그 임금산정기간에 있어서 도급제에 의하여 계산된 임금의 총액을 당해 임금산정 기간의 총 근로시간 수로 나누어 시간급 통상임금을 산정한다.

행정해석

1) 복지수당이 정기적·일률적으로 지급되는 경우 통상임금의 범위에 포함되는 것으로 보아야 한다.[63]

복지수당이 사회복지시설 종사자들의 열악한 임금수준을 보전해주기 위한 목적으로 전 근로자를 대상으로 소정근로시간 또는 법정근로시간에 대하여 정기적·일률적으로 지급하는 경우라면 이는 통상임금의 범위에 포함되는 것으로 보아야 할 것이다. 여기서 "정기적"이라 함은 소정근로시간 또는 법정근로시간에 대하여 지급을, "일률적"이라 함은 모든 근로자에게 지급되는 것뿐만 아니라 '일정한 조건 또는 기준에 달한 모든 근로자'에게 지급하는 것도 포함되는 것이다.

63) 행정해석: 임금 68207-730, 2002.10.4.

2) Even though the company and the labor union agree in a collective bargaining agreement to include into ordinary wage those wage and valuables which are exclusive in the realm of ordinary wage according to the LSA guidelines, it is not possible to deem that they are converted to ordinary wage by the law.[64]

If a company decides by collective bargaining agreement (CBA) and the rules of employment to include into the realm of ordinary wage valuables which are not included in the realm of ordinary wage according to LSA regulation, the company shall follow the promised rules. However, even though the company and the labor union agree in the CBA and rules of employment to include into ordinary wage those wage and valuables which are exclusive in the realm of ordinary wage according to LSA guidelines, it is not possible to deem that they are converted to ordinary wage according to Article 6 of the Enforcement Decree to the LSA.

2. Substantial Criteria for Determining Ordinary Wage

(1) Concept of ordinary wage

Recent judicial rulings concerning rules for calculation and scope of ordinary wage have differed from MOEL Guidelines to MOEL Guidelines, something which has caused much confusion for corporate management. However, the Supreme Court, with all judges in attendance, offered clarification on December 18, 2013 and December 19, 2024: 'Ordinary wage' means wage which are determined to be paid periodically or in a lump sum to an employee for their prescribed work or whole work. This ordinary wage is used as the standard wage to calculate added allowance for overtime, night and holiday work, annual paid leave allowance, dismissal pay, and for paid leaves that employers have to provide under the Labor Standards Act. If this ordinary wage has not been calculated properly, it is not as simple as re-calculating and paying the correct amount from now on, but the employer shall recalculate all kinds of allowances such as overtime, night and holiday work, and other allowances that were paid over the past three years. Furthermore, the employer shall recalculate the severance pay for resigned or dismissed employees and pay the difference.[65]

(2) Legal criteria for determining ordinary wage

1) Ordinary wage means wage that an employer pays to an employee as remuneration for their prescribed work or whole work, and those which are paid regularly and

---

64) MOEL Guidelines: on Oct. 8, 2002, Wage 68207-735

65) Supreme Court ruling on Dec. 19, 2013: 2012Da89399; 2024. 12. 19. 2020da247190

2) 근로기준법 규정에 의한 통상임금에서 제외되는 임금 및 금품을 노사관계자 간에 통상임금의 범위에 포함하기로 정하였더라도 법 규정에 의한 통상임금으로 전환되었다고 볼 수는 없다.[64)]

근로기준법의 규정에 의한 통상임금의 범위에 포함되지 않는 금품을 노사관계자 간에 단체협약, 취업규칙 등으로 통상임금의 범위에 포함시켜 제 수당의 지급기준으로 삼기로 정하였다면 그에 따라야 할 것이다. 그러나 근로기준법 규정에 의한 통상임금에서 제외되는 임금 및 금품을 노사관계자 간에 단체협약·취업규칙 등으로 통상임금의 범위에 포함하기로 정하였더라도 이를 근로기준법시행령 제6조의 규정에 의한 통상임금으로 전환되었다고 볼 수는 없을 것이다.

2. 통상임금의 구체적 판단기준

(1) 통상임금의 의의

최근 판례가 통상임금의 산정 및 범위와 관련하여 고용노동부의 기존 행정해석과 차이가 있어 기업운영에 많은 혼란을 주어 왔으나, 2013년 12월 18일과 2024년 12월 19일 대법원 합의체 판결에서 명확한 내용을 제시하였다. 통상임금은 근로자에게 정기적·일률적으로 소정근로 또는 총 근로에 대하여 지급하기로 정해진 금액을 말한다. 이 통상임금은 근로기준법상 사용자에게 부여된 연장·야간·휴일 근로에 대한 가산임금, 연차유급휴가 수당, 해고예고수당, 기타 법령에 유급으로 명시된 기준금액으로 사용된다. 이 통상임금이 잘못 계산되었다면 앞으로 가산수당 등 임금산정을 제대로 하면 되는 것으로만 끝나는 것이 아니라 지난 3년간에 지급된 연장·야간·휴일근로수당, 기타 각종 유급으로 지급된 수당에 대해 재정산되어야 하고, 심지어 퇴직자에 대한 퇴직금 계산도 다시 정산하여 지급해야 한다.[65)]

(2) 법원의 판단법리

1) 소정 근로 또는 총 근로의 대가로 근로자에게 지급되는 금품으로서 그것이 정기적·일률적으로 지급되는 것이면 원칙적으로 모두 통상임금에 속하는 임금이다. 근로기준법의 입법 취지와 통상임금의 기능 및 필요성에 비추어 볼 때 어떤 임금이

---

64) 행정해석: 임금 68207-735, 2002.10.8.

65) 대법원 2013.12.19, 2012다89399; 2024. 12. 19. 2020다247190

uniformly are considered ordinary wage in principle. For legislating the Labor Standards Act and the function and necessity of ordinary wage, what should be included as ordinary wage shall be fixed wage paid regularly and uniformly. This means non-fixed wage are not ordinary wage, as they are not paid regularly and uniformly and may or may not be paid. Here, being paid 'uniformly' not only means that payment is made to all employees, but also to all employees qualified according to certain conditions or criteria. Here, 'certain criteria' refers to 'fixed conditions' in considering the concept of ordinary wage, because the ordinary wage is used to calculate 'fixed and generally accepted regular wage.'[66)]

2) Even though a particular allowance or bonus, etc., may be paid for a period exceeding one month, if these are paid regularly and uniformly, these components can be included in ordinary wage.[67)]

3) Mutual agreements between employer and employees that exclude a particular allowance from consideration as ordinary wage according to the Labor Standards Act are null and void because such an agreement sets conditions lower than that of the Labor Standards Act.[68)]

(3) Application of ordinary wage

1) Bonuses

Bonuses are included into the realm of ordinary wage even if they are not paid regularly every month. Rules for calculating ordinary wage explain the bonus as follows[69)](The Supreme Court en banc rulings on ordinary wages from 2013 and 2024 have been applied.).

Name of payment made to employees	Ord. Wage	Avg. Wage	Other Paymt
Bonuses A. In cases where payment conditions, amounts, and payment rates are regulated in the rules of employment, or where employees are paid habitually and naturally expect to get paid: regular bonuses, exercise subsidies, etc.	○	○	
B. In cases where payment is not made habitually, but paid temporarily or definitely in accordance with company profits according to the employer's discretion and favor			○

66) Supreme Court ruling on Jan. 29, 2010:2009Da74144

67) Supreme Court ruling on Feb. 9, 1996: 94Da19501; Supreme Court ruling on Jun. 13, 2003: 2002Da74282

68) Supreme Court ruling on Nov. 29, 2007: 2006Da81523

69) MOEL Regulation 476, Jan. 22, 2002; Supreme Court ruling

통상임금에 해당하려면 그것이 정기적·일률적으로 지급되는 고정적인 임금에 속하여야 하므로, 정기적·일률적으로 지급되는 것이 아니거나 실제 근무성적에 따라 지급 여부 및 지급액이 달라지는 것과 같이 고정적인 임금이 아닌 것은 통상임금에 해당하지 않는다. 여기서 「일률적」으로 지급되는 것이라 함은 「모든 근로자」에게 지급되는 것뿐만 아니라 「일정한 조건 또는 기준에 달한 모든 근로자」에게 지급되는 것도 포함되고, 여기서 말하는 「일정한 조건」이란 「고정적이고 평균적인 임금」을 산출하려는 통상임금의 개념에 비추어 볼 때 「고정적인 조건」이어야 한다.[66)]

2) 근로자에 대한 임금이 1개월을 초과하는 기간마다 지급되는 것이라도 그것이 정기적·일률적으로 지급되는 것이면 통상임금에 포함될 수 있다.[67)]

3) 성질상 근로기준법에 정한 통상임금에 포함될 수당을 통상임금에서 제외하기로 하는 노사 간 합의는 같은 법이 정한 기준에 미치지 못하는 근로조건을 정한 계약으로서 무효이다.[68)]

(3) 통상임금의 적용

1) 상여금

상여금을 매월 정기적으로 지급하는 방식을 취하고 있다면 통상임금의 범위에서 포함된다. 「통상임금 산정지침에 따른 상여금」은 다음과 같다[69)](2013년과 2024년 통상임금에 대한 대법원 전원합의체 판결 반경).

근로자에게 지급되는 금품의 명칭	통상 임금	평균 임금	기타 금품
상여금 가. 취업규칙 등에 지급조건, 금액, 지급시기가 정해져 있거나 전 근로자에게 관례적으로 지급하여 사회통념상 근로자가 당연히 지급 받을 수 있다는 기대를 갖게 되는 경우: 정기상여금, 체력단련비 등	○	○	
나. 관례적으로 지급한 사례가 없고, 기업이윤에 따라 일시적, 불확정적으로 사용자의 재량이나 호의에 의해 지급하는 경우 경영성과배분금, 격려금, 생산장려금, 포상금, 인센티브 등			○

66) 대법원 2010.1.28, 2009다74144.
67) 대법원 1996.2.9, 94다19501; 대법원 2003.6.13, 2002다74282.
68) 대법원 2007.11.29, 2006다 81523 등 참조.
69) 노동부예규 제476호, 2002.1.22에 대법원 판결 반영한 내용.

1) As the regular bonus is paid regularly and uniformly(e.g. 100% paid every even month) as fixed wage for labor service, it shall be considered ordinary wage as stipulated in the Labor Standards Act.[70)]

2) The bonus in this case is only applicable to employees working for six months or more with a certain amount paid quarterly, and calculated according to the number of years of service. This bonus is paid every quarter, distinguishing it from annual salary divided into monthly payments, but this difference in payment time does not preclude it from being considered as ordinary wage. As the bonus in this case has been previously fixed, it shall be considered ordinary wage as it is a fixed wage paid regularly and uniformly.[71)]

2) Payments made for an employee's living costs or welfare, regardless of working hours

Name of payment made to employees	Ord. Wage	Avg. Wage	Other Paymt
① Commuting allowances, vehicle maintenance subsidies			
A. If rendered periodically and uniformly to all employees	O	O	
B. If rendered variably according to the number of days in attendance or to a few employees			O
② Company housing allowances, winter fuel allowances, kimchi allowances			
A. If rendered periodically and uniformly to all employees	O	O	
B. If rendered temporarily or to a few employees			O
③ Family allowances, education allowances			
A. If rendered uniformly to all employees regardless of marital status	O	O	
B. If rendered only according to the number of family members or to a few employees (paid as child education allowances, employee training allowances, etc.)			O
④ Meals or meal allowances			
A. If rendered uniformly to all employees by means of a labor contract, employment rules, or etc.	O	O	
B. Actual meals paid in accordance with the number of days in attendance			O

1) A certain company has paid all cleaning workers a fixed meal allowance, household subsidy, transportation subsidy, morning meal costs, sanitation allowance, and snack allowances as fixed amounts every month, all of which shall be considered ordinary wage to be paid

70) Incheon District Court ruling on Feb. 23, 2012: 2011Gahap6096; Seoul Appellate Court ruling on Oct. 1, 2010: 2010na34618

71) Supreme Court ruling on Mar. 29, 2012: 2010Da91046

1) 정기상여금(매월 짝수달 100%지급)은 근로의 대가로서 정기적·일률적으로 지급되는 고정적 임금이라고 봄이 타당하므로 근로기준법상 통상임금에 해당된다.[70]

2) 이 사건 상여금은 6개월을 초과하여 계속 근무한 근로자에게 근속연수의 증가에 따라 미리 정해놓은 각 비율을 적용하여 산정한 금액을 분기별로 지급하는 것으로서, 매월 월급형태로 지급되는 근속수당과 달리 분기별로 지급되기는 하지만 그러한 사정만으로 통상임금이 아니라고 단정할 수 없다. 이 사건 상여금은 그 금액이 확정된 것이어서 정기적·일률적으로 지급되는 고정적인 임금인 통상임금에 해당한다.[71]

2) 근로시간과 관계없이 근로자의 생활보조적, 복리후생적으로 지급되는 금품

근로자에게 지급되는 금품의 명칭	통상 임금	평균 임금	기타 금품
① 통근수당, 차량유지비			
가. 전 근로자에게 정기적, 일률적으로 지급하는 경우	○	○	
나. 출근일수에 따라 변동적으로 지급하거나 일부 근로자에게 지급 경우			○
② 사택수당, 월동연료수당, 김장수당			
가. 전 근로자에게 정기적·일률적으로 지급하는 경우	○	○	
나. 일시적으로 지급하거나 일부 근로자에게 지급 하는 경우			○
③ 가족수당, 교육수당			
가. 독신자를 포함하여 전 근로자에게 일률적으로 지급하는 경우	○	○	
나. 가족 수에 따라 차등 지급되거나 일부 근로자 에게만 지급하는 경우(학자보조금, 근로자 교육비 지원 등의 명칭으로 지급)			○
④ 급식 및 급식비			
가. 근로계약, 취업규칙 등에 규정된 급식비로써 근무일 수와 관계없이 전 근로자에게 일률적으로 지급하는 경우	○	○	
나. 출근일수에 따라 차등 지급하는 경우			○

1) 모든 환경미화원에게 정액급식비, 가계보조비, 교통보조비, 급량비(조식대), 위생비, 간식대로 매월 일정금액을 지급하였으므로, 이는 근로의 대상으로

70) 인천지방법원 2012.2.23, 2011가합6096; 서울고등법원 2010.10.1, 2010나34618.

71) 대법원 2012.3.29, 2010다91046.

regularly and uniformly as reward for labor service.[72)]

2) If a welfare allowance has been paid uniformly, regularly, and at a fixed rate to all employees of the same business according to the collective wage agreement, this is not money paid temporarily and according to favor for welfare, but wage paid as remuneration for labor service according to employment relations. In addition, this is not wage paid individually or at a variable rate, but fixed wage for ordinary working days and working hours, so shall be considered ordinary wage.[73)]

3) Even though some employees with lower work attendance rates have been paid transportation and meal allowances differently than other workers, these allowances have been paid to all employees and shall be considered ordinary wage.[74)]

4) Even though a company enters into an agreement with employees that it will not calculate into ordinary wage the meal allowances that have been paid at a fixed rate to all employees, this shall be considered an illegal employment contract.[75)]

5) Service allowances have accumulated according to the length of service for all cleaning workers employed for at least one year; meal, transportation, sanitation, and hazard allowances have been paid at a fixed rate every month to all cleaning workers. Quarterly, attendance, exercise, and traditional holiday allowances have been paid to all cleaning workers regularly and at a fixed rate if they meet certain criteria. As these allowances are fixed wage paid regularly and uniformly as reward for labor service, they shall be considered ordinary wage.[76)]

III-2. Supreme Court Decisions on Ordinary Wage

Ordinary wages refer to predetermined compensation agreed upon for the hours an employee is contractually obligated to work. It is mandated that the employment contract explicitly specify both ordinary wages and contractual working hours (Article 17 of the Labor Standards Act). Ordinary wages serve as the basis for calculating additional compensation for overtime work, holiday work, night work, and similar categories. To maintain ordinary wages at the lowest

---

72) Ulsan District Court ruling on Feb. 3, 2006: 2005Gadan8384.

73) Busan Appellate Court ruling on Sep. 25, 1996: 96Gu2583.

74) Seoul District Court ruling on May 18, 2006: 2005Gahap57290.

75) Supreme Court ruling on Feb. 22, 1994: 93Da9620.

76) Supreme Court ruling on Sep. 8, 2011: 2011Da22061.

서 정기적·일률적으로 지급되는 고정적인 임금으로 통상임금에 포함된다.[72)]

2) 복지수당이 임금협약에 따라 동일직종 근로자 모두에게 일률적, 정기적, 고정적으로 지급되는 것이라면, 이는 복지후생을 위한 임의적, 은혜적 금품이 아니라 사용종속관계에서 행하는 근로의 대상으로서 지급되는 금품, 즉 임금에 해당되고, 또 개인적, 비 고정적 임금이 아니라 통상의 근로일, 근로시간에 대한 고정적 임금이어서 통상임금에 속한다고 본다.[73)]

3) 모든 근로자에게 지급하되 예외적으로 출근비율이 낮은 근로자에게는 다른 방식으로 지급하겠다는 취지의 교통비 및 중식대도 통상임금에 포함된다.[74)]

4) 전 근로자에게 일정액으로 지급하는 식대보조비는 통상임금산정 시 포함시키지 않기로 노사 간 합의가 있었어도 이는 위법한 근로계약이다.[75)]

5) 1년을 초과하여 계속 근무한 환경미화원들에게 근속연수가 증가함에 따라 일정 금액을 가산하여 1년 근속 당 일정금액을 지급한 근속가산금과 모든 환경미화원에게 매월 정액으로 지급한 급량비, 교통보조비, 위생수당, 위험수당 및 모든 환경미화원에게 일정한 기준에 따라 정기적·고정적으로 지급한 기말수당, 정근수당, 체력단련비, 명절휴가비는 모두 근로의 대가로 정기적·일률적으로 지급되는 고정적인 임금이므로 통상임금에 포함된다.[76)]

Ⅲ-2. 통상임금 관련 대법원 합의체 판결

통상임금은 근로자가 소정근로시간에 근무한 대가로 받기로 한 사전적으로 약속된 임금이다. 근로계약 체결 시에도 반드시 통상임금과 소정근로시간을 명시하도록 되어 있다(근로기준법 제17조). 이는, 사전에 지급하기로 정해진 임금뿐만 아니라 연장근로, 휴일근로, 야간근로 등에 대한 가산 임금을 계산하기 위한

72) 울산 지법 2006.2.3, 2005가단8384.
73) 부산고등법원 1996.9.25, 96구2583.
74) 서울지방법원 2006.5.18, 2005가합57290.
75) 대법원 1994.2.22, 93다9620.
76) 대법원 2011.9.8, 2011다22061.

possible level, employers have introduced a system of annual regular bonuses. Consequently, the wage structure in our country consisted of 50% ordinary wages and 50% non-ordinary wages. The groundbreaking decision that significantly rectified this distorted wage structure was a unanimous Supreme Court ruling in 2013. The core meaning of this decision can be summarized into two key points. Firstly, the decision established that regular bonuses paid at certain intervals exceeding one month as remuneration for work are considered part of ordinary wages. Secondly, any consensus reached among employers and employees to exclude certain wages, falling under ordinary wages according to the Labor Standards Act, from ordinary wages, is invalid.

1. First Case[77]

(1) Background

The defendant company(hereinafter, referred to as "the Company") paid bonuses every even month, in accordance with the Company's Bonus Payment Regulation, with the full amount paid to employees with at least two months of service. However, a different amount calculated by application of a pre-determined rate, according to the corresponding period of the bonus payment, is paid to new employees with less than two months of service, those who have just returned after taking at least two months of leave, and those who are on leave. As for those who resigned during the corresponding period of bonus payment, the company pays the pro-rated amount according to the number of days worked. When determining the amount of wage to be included in ordinary wage in the collective agreement concluded on October 8, 2008, the Company and the labor union excluded the bonuses from calculation of ordinary wage, assuming that the bonuses in this case were not included in ordinary wage in the Labor Standards Act.

(2) Legal issues considered

1) Whether or not the bonuses in this case are included in ordinary wage;

2) Although the Company and the union agreed to exclude the bonuses from calculation of ordinary wage, if an employee applied for additional wage, claiming that the agreement was invalid, whether or not this claim violated the good-faith principle.

---

77) Supreme Court ruling on Dec. 18, 2013, 2012Da89399 En Banc Unanimous Decision.

기준으로 삼고 있으므로 사용자는 통상임금의 최대한 낮은 수준을 유지하기 위해서 연단위로 지급하는 정기 상여금제도를 도입하였다. 그 결과 우리나라 임금은 50%의 통상임금과 50%의 비통상임금으로 구성되어 있다. 이렇게 왜곡된 임금 구조를 획기적으로 바로잡은 판결이 2013년 대법원 합의체 판결이다. 이 판결의 핵심은 두 가지이다. 첫째, 근로의 대가로 1개월을 초과하는 일정기간마다 지급하는 정기상여금은 통상임금에 해당된다. 둘째, 근로기준법 상 통상임금에 속하는 임금을 통상임금에서 제외하기로 한 합의는 효력이 없다.

1. 제1판결 임금사건[77)]

(1) 주요 사실관계

피고회사는 상여금지급규칙에 따라, 이 사건 상여금을 짝수 달에 지급하되, 근속기간이 2개월을 초과한 근로자에게는 전액을, 근속기간이 2개월을 초과하지 않는 신규 입사자나 2개월 이상 장기 휴직 후 복직한 자, 휴직자에 대하여는 상여금 지급대상기간 중 해당 구간에 따라 미리 정해 놓은 비율을 적용하여 산정한 금액을 각기 다르게 지급하였다. 상여금 지급대상기간 중에 퇴직한 근로자에 대해서는 근무일 수에 따라 일할계산하여 지급하였다. 피고와 노동조합은 2008년 10월 8일 체결한 단체협약에서 통상임금에 포함될 임금의 범위를 정하면서, 이 사건 상여금이 근로기준법 소정의 통상임금에 해당하지 않는다는 전제하에 이 사건 상여금을 통상임금 산입에서 제외하였다.

(2) 이 사건의 쟁점

1) 피고회사의 상여금이 통상임금에 해당하는지 여부

2) 노사가 상여금을 통상임금 산정에서 제외하기로 합의하였음에도, 근로자인 원고가 그 합의의 무효를 주장하며 추가임금을 청구하는 것이 신의칙에 반하는지 여부

77) 대법원 2013. 12. 18. 선고 2012다89399 전원합의체 판결.

(3) Court ruling

1) Even though the Company paid the bonus for a period exceeding one month(every two months during each period of wage payment), this amount has satisfied the requirement of periodic payment, as it was paid periodically. Also, since whether or not the payment was made, and the amount had already been determined uniformly for all employees, the bonus qualifies as uniform and fixed. As the bonus payment varies according to the particular service period(as of two months), it could be misunderstood that there is no uniformity or it could incorrectly be regarded as money not previously determined. However, in considering it in the situation of overtime work(when the ordinary wage needs to be calculated), whether the employees concerned had served two months or not was already determined. As those who resigned received their bonus in proportion to the number of days they worked, the bonus is recognized as uniform and fixed. As explained above, those on leave were treated differently, due to their extraordinary situations, and so it is not an obstacle to consider that payment ordinary wage. Accordingly, the regular bonus in this case shall be included in ordinary wage.

2) A labor contract which establishes working conditions that do not meet the standards provided for in the Labor Standards Act shall be null(Article 15 of the Labor Standards Act). Accordingly, even though the employer and the union agreed to exclude the regular bonus as legally included in ordinary wage, this mutual agreement is invalid as it is in violation of the Labor Standards Act. As the above agreement is invalid, it is a principle that the employer shall recalculate the overtime work allowance, adding the wage included in legal ordinary wage, and that the employee can apply for retroactive payment for the variance from the amount already paid. However, the additional wage claim based on the regular bonus can be restricted due to the good-faith principle. In those workplaces where there were no agreements on the exclusion of ordinary wage, additional wage for different amounts recalculated by including the regular bonus in the ordinary wage can be claimed, provided, that this retroactive claim can be valid only for the amount payable for the past three years.

(3) 판 결

1) 이 사건 회사의 임금산정 기간인 1개월을 초과한 2개월마다 지급되더라도 정기적으로 지급되었기 때문에 정기성 요건 충족한다. 또한, 그 지급여부 및 지급액이 이미 모든 근로자에게 일률적으로 확정되어 있기 때문에 일률성과 고정성 인정된다. 근속기간에 따라 달리 지급되므로(2개월 기준) 일률성이 없거나 사전에 확정되어 있지 않은 임금으로 오인할 수 있으나, 초과근로를 하는 시점(통상임금 산정이 필요한 시점)에서 볼 때, 해당 근로자가 2개월의 근속기간을 채우고 있는지 여부는 이미 확정되어 있는 사실이고, 중간퇴직자에게도 근무일수에 비례하여 상여금을 지급하므로, 일률성과 고정성이 인정된다. 위에서 설명한 바와 같이, 휴직자에 대한 특별한 취급도 해당 개인의 특수한 사정을 고려한 것에 불과하므로, 통상임금 인정에 장애사유가 되지 않는다. 따라서 이 사건 정기상여금은 통상임금에 해당한다.

2) 근로기준법이 정한 기준보다 낮은 임금 등 불리한 근로조건 계약은 무효(근로기준법 제15조 참조)이다. 따라서 법률상 통상임금에 해당하는 정기상여금 등의 임금을 통상임금에서 제외하기로 노사가 합의하였다 하더라도 위 합의는 근로기준법에 위반되어 무효이다. 위와 같은 합의가 무효이므로, 법률상 통상임금에 해당하는 임금을 통상임금 산정에 포함시켜 다시 초과근로수당을 계산한 다음, 소급하여 이미 지급받은 것과의 차액을 추가임금으로 청구할 수 있는 것이 원칙이나, 정기상여금에 기초한 추가임금 청구는 신의칙에 의해 제한되는 경우가 있다. 통상임금 제외 합의가 아예 없었던 사업장의 경우에는 당연히 통상임금으로 산정되지 아니한 정기상여금 등을 포함시켜 계산한 차액을 추가임금으로 청구할 수 있다. 다만, 사용자가 소멸시효 항변을 할 경우 최종 3년분만 인정 가능하다.

2. Second Case[78)]

(1) Background

Whether the amount of kimchi bonus should be determined based on whether it is part of ordinary wage; Whether Lunar New Year and Chuseok(Korean Thanksgiving) bonuses, summer leave bonuses, gift allowances, birthday allowances, individual pension premium subsidies, group insurance, etc., which were paid to incumbent employees as of a particular time period, are included in ordinary wage.

(2) Judgment Criteria for Determining Ordinary wage

Ordinary wage is the wage determined to be paid uniformly when contractual labor service is provided. All allowances which legally qualify as ordinary wage shall be included in ordinary wage regardless of the title of the allowance. It is recognized as the basic wage when calculating additional wage for extended work, night-time and holiday work, allowance replacing advance notice of dismissal, and the unused annual leave allowance. Additional wage under the Labor Standards Act shall be 150%, calculated by adding 50% of ordinary wage.

1) Requirements of ordinary wage

Since ordinary wage becomes the basic wage used to calculate additional wage, it should be considered financial remuneration reflecting the value of labor service provided ordinarily for contractual working hours in accordance with the employment contract(remuneration for labor). Accordingly, the additional wage paid for special work provided, and not for assigned work as per the employment contract, shall not be considered ordinary wage. In addition, this ordinary wage must have been determined before providing actual overtime work. The reason for this is that the previously determined ordinary wage calculation shall be used immediately when the overtime work is actually provided. Requirements of the ordinary wage shall be comprised of all two components: ① periodicity and ② uniformity.

---

78) Supreme Court ruling on December 18, 2013, 2012Da94643: The explanation has been revised by removing the fixed nature portion, reflecting the amended ruling on ordinary wages issued on December 19, 2024 (2020Da247190).

2. 제2판결 임금사건[78)]

(1) 주요 사실관계

지급 직전 노사협의를 통해 액수를 정하기로 한 김장보너스의 통상임금 해당 여부. 특정 시점에 재직 중인 근로자에게만 지급하기로 한 것으로 볼 여지가 있는 설·추석 상여금, 하계휴가비, 선물비, 생일자지원금, 개인연금지원금, 단체보험료 등의 통상임금 해당 여부

(2) 통상임금의 판단기준

통상임금이란 근로계약에서 정한 근로를 제공하면 확정적으로 지급되는 임금이다. 명칭과 관계없이 통상임금의 법적인 요건을 갖추면 모두 통상임금에 해당한다. 통상임금은 연장·야간·휴일 근로에 대한 가산임금, 해고예고수당 및 연차휴가수당 등을 산정하는 기준임금이 된다. 근로기준법상 초과근로수당은 통상임금에 50%를 가산한 150%이다.

1) 통상임금의 개념적 징표와 요건

통상임금은 초과근로수당 산정 등을 위한 기초임금이므로, 근로자가 근로계약에 따른 정상적인 근로시간에 통상적으로 제공하는 근로의 가치를 금전적으로 평가한 것이어야 한다(소정근로의 대가). 따라서 근로계약에서 정한 근로가 아닌 특별한 근로를 제공하고 추가로 지급받은 임금은 통상임금 아니다. 또한, 근로자가 실제로 초과근로를 제공하기 전에 미리 확정되어 있어야 한다. 그래야만 실제 초과근로가 제공될 때 사전에 확정된 통상임금을 기초로 하여 가산임금을 곧바로 산정할 수 있기 때문이다. 통상임금의 요건 → 근로의 대가로서의 임금이 ① 정기성, ② 일률성을 모두 갖추고 있어야 통상임금에 해당한다.

---

78) 대법원 2013.12.18, 2012다94643: 기본의 판례에서 2024. 12. 19. 통상임금 수정 판결(2020다247190)을 반영한 고정성 부분 삭제하여 다시 설명함.

2) Requirement of periodicity

[Regular bonuses] Employees are paid their regular wage once a month in return for work, but their regular bonus is paid either every two months, once per quarter, or once a year, depending on the company. These bonuses are regarded as having a character of periodicity if they are paid periodically, despite being paid every two months, every quarter, every half year or each year. Accordingly, the regular bonus normally paid for a period exceeding one month can be included into the ordinary wage.

This is a wage which is paid periodically for a previously-determined period. Even if it is paid for a period exceeding one month, if it is paid periodically for a regular period, it is included in ordinary wage.

3) Requirement of uniformity

It is considered ordinary wage only when it is paid to all employees or all employees meeting identical conditions or criteria. Even though the bonus is not paid to all employees, but only to those who meet the identical conditions or criteria, it is considered to have a characteristic of uniformity. Accordingly, identical condition here means that it is not changeable from time to time, but is fixed. Even though there may be some restrictions concerning payment of a particular wage to an employee on leave, returning from leave, or under disciplinary measures, these restrictions are designed to consider the individual special circumstances, but cannot deny the uniformity of wage to normal employees maintaining a regular employment relationship. Therefore, this wage is included in ordinary wage.

As ordinary wage includes the concept evaluating the value of contractual work, the identical conditions or criteria shall be conditions related to work. Accordingly, the family allowance paid only to those employees with dependent family cannot be considered ordinary wage, as the payment condition is not related to work performed. Provided, that in cases where the company pays a fixed allowance under the description of family allowance to all employees, and then pays an additional amount to employees with a dependent family, the fixed amount that is paid to all employees uniformly as remuneration of work shall be included in ordinary wage, but the additionally-paid family allowance shall not.

2) 정기성 요건

> **[정기상여금의 경우]** 보통 근로의 대가를 1개월에 한 번씩 월급으로 받지만, 정기상여금은 월급과 달리 2개월마다 지급하는 회사도 있고, 분기마다 지급하는 회사도 있고, 1년마다 지급하는 회사도 있을 수 있다. 이처럼 상여금이 월급과는 달리 2개월마다, 3개월마다, 6개월마다, 1년마다 등으로 지급이 되더라도 정기적으로만 지급이 되면 정기성을 갖춘 것이다. 따라서 1개월을 초과하는 기간마다 지급되는 것이 일반적인 정기상여금도 통상임금이 될 수 있다.

미리 정해진 일정한 기간마다 정기적으로 지급되는 임금이어야 한다. 어떤 임금이 1개월을 초과하는 기간마다 지급이 되더라도, 일정한 기간마다 정기적으로 지급되는 것이면 통상임금에 포함될 수 있다.

3) 일률성 요건

「모든 근로자」 또는 「일정한 조건이나 기준에 달한 모든 근로자」에게 일률적으로 지급되어야 통상임금이 될 수 있다. 모든 근로자에게 지급되는 것은 아니더라도 일정한 조건이나 기준에 달한 근로자들에게는 모두 지급되는 것이면 일률성이 인정된다. 여기서 「일정한 조건」이란 시시때때로 변동되지 않는 고정적인 조건이어야 한다. 휴직자나 복직자 또는 징계대상자 등에 대하여 특정한 임금의 지급이 제한되어 있더라도, 이는 해당 근로자의 개인적인 특수성을 고려한 것일 뿐이므로, 정상적인 근로관계를 유지하고 있는 근로자에 대하여 그 해당 임금의 일률성이 부정되지는 아니한다. 즉 그 해당 임금도 통상임금이다. 통상임금이 소정근로의 가치를 평가한 개념이므로 일정한 조건 또는 기준은 근로와 관련된 조건이어야 한다. 따라서 부양가족이 있는 근로자에게만 지급되는 가족수당은 그 조건이 근로와 무관하므로 통상임금 아니다. 다만, 모든 근로자에게 기본금액을 가족수당 명목으로 지급하면서, 실제로 부양가족이 있는 근로자에게는 일정액을 추가로 지급하는 경우, 그 기본금액은 모든 근로자에게 일률적으로 지급되는 근로의 대가와 같으므로 통상임금에 해당한다. 그러나 추가지급되는 가족수당은 통상임금 아니다.

(3) Criteria for judgment

In order to become ordinary wage for calculating additional wage for night-time, holiday, and extended work, in its evaluation for overtime work, the wage to be paid for the work stipulated in the employment contract shall be paid periodically for a certain time frame(periodicity), and be paid uniformly to all employees or all employees corresponding to the identical conditions or criteria related to work(uniformity). When the above conditions are satisfied, it is ordinary wage regardless of what it may be called.

(4) Substantial Applications

1) Wage changed according to the length of service period (long-service allowance)

Service period is related to employee proficiency(long experience) and so corresponds to identical conditions or criteria related to work, and all employees meeting these conditions and criteria shall be paid uniformly. In considering overtime work, the employees' service period is not an unclear condition for either its period or its fulfillment. Therefore, as there is uniformity, this is ordinary wage.

2) Wage paid according to special skills, experience, etc. (technology, qualifications, license allowances, etc.)

These allowances are paid to employees with special skills and experience related to work, corresponding to the identical conditions or criteria, which satisfies the requirement of uniformity. When considering it while the employee is providing overtime work, as the corresponding technology and particular experience are already determined, this can be considered as fixedness, and so is included in ordinary wage.

3) wage depending on performance results

Incentives are the bonuses payable upon favorable evaluation of the performance results for the specific period worked, and by determining whether or not payment is due and the amount to be paid. At the time of providing overtime work, performance evaluation and follow-up incentive, plus the amount of payment, are not yet determined. Accordingly, as this payment has a condition that cannot be determined in advance and thereby not admissible as fixed, it is not ordinary wage. However, even if an employee receives the lowest scores in their work performance evaluation, and if a minimum is still paid, this minimum amount can be determined as the amount to be paid regardless of their lowest scores, and so this amount is included in ordinary wage, as it is fixed. In cases where the

(3) 판단기준

야간, 휴일, 연장근무 등 초과근로수당 산정 등의 기준이 되는 통상임금이 되기 위해서는, 초과근무를 하는 시점에서 판단해 보았을 때, 근로계약에서 정한 근로의 대가로 지급될 어떤 항목의 임금이, 일정한 주기에 따라 정기적으로 지급이 되고(정기성), 「모든 근로자」나 「근로와 관련된 일정한 조건 또는 기준에 해당하는 모든 근로자」에게 일률적으로 지급이 되며(일률성), 이러한 요건을 갖추면 그 명칭과 관계없이 통상임금에 해당한다.

(4) 구체적인 내용

1) 근속기간에 따라 달라지는 임금(근속수당 등)

근속기간은 근로자의 숙련도와 밀접하게 관련되므로 일률성에 있어서「근로와 관련된 일정한 조건 또는 기준」에 해당하고 그 조건 또는 기준을 충족한 모든 근로자에게 지급되는 임금이므로 일률성이 인정된다. 초과근로를 하는 시점에서 보았을 때, 그 근로자의 근속기간이 얼마나 되는지는 이미 확정되어 있는 사실이지, 성취 여부가 불확실한 조건이 아니다. 따라서 고정성 인정되므로 통상임금이다.

2) 특수한 기술, 경력 등을 조건으로 하는 임금(기술수당, 자격수당, 면허수당 등)

특수한 기술이나 경력이라는 「근로와 관련된 일정한 조건 또는 기준에 해당하는 모든 근로자」에게 일률적으로 지급이 되므로 일률성 요건 충족된다. 근로자가 초과근로를 제공하는 시점에서 보았을 때, 해당 기술의 보유나 특정한 경력의 구비 여부가 이미 확정되어 있기 때문에 고정성이 인정된다. 따라서 통상임금에 해당한다.

3) 근무실적에 좌우되는 임금

성과급은 특정기간 근무실적을 평가하여 이를 토대로 지급여부나 지급액이 결정되는 임금이다. 초과근로를 제공하는 시점에서 근무실적에 대한 평가와 그에 따른 성과급 지급여부 및 지급액이 확정되어 있지 아니하다. 따라서 사전에 확정될 수 없는 사실을 조건으로 하기 때문에 고정성이 인정되지 않아 통상임금이 아니다. 다만, 근무실적에서 최하등급을 받더라도 최소한의 일정액은 보장되는 경우라면, 그 최소한도의 금액만큼은 받는 것이 확정되어 있기 때문에 고정적인 임금으

incentive is already determined to be paid this year based on the performance results of last year, as the payment and amount are already guaranteed at the time of working overtime, this incentive is fixed and belongs to the ordinary wage. Provided, that if the incentive that should have been paid last year was delayed only in its payment, this is not a fixed amount and is not included in ordinary wage.

[Examples]
(1) Work performance was scored as A, B, or C: those receiving the lowest grade, C, were paid 1 million won, those receiving a B were paid 2 million won, and those receiving an A were paid 3 million won. Therefore, a minimum of 1 million won was guaranteed, and this 1 million won shall be included in ordinary wage. The additional money paid for the higher grades are not ordinary wage.
(2) Work performance was scored as A, B, or C: those receiving the lowest grade, C, were paid nothing, those receiving a B were paid 2 million won, and those receiving an A were paid 3 million won. In this case, as those receiving a C will not be paid at all, the incentive bonuses are not included in ordinary wage.

4) Amount of Kimchi bonus not confirmed

The collective agreement stipulates that ‘a kimchi bonus is paid during Kimjang(the kimchi-making period), with the amount determined through labor-management consultation.’ The amount was determined in this way just prior to the payment date. In this case, the amount to be paid cannot be confirmed at the time of overtime work performance, and therefore cannot be regarded as a fixed payment or included in ordinary wage.

Type of Wage	Characteristics of Wage	Ordinary Wage or Not
Technology Allowance	Allowance paid to employees with technological or other qualifications (qualification, license allowances, etc.)	Ordinary wage
Length of Service Allowance	Wage which varies according to length of service	Ordinary wage
Family Allowance	Varies by the number of dependents	Not ordinary wage (not related to work)
Family Allowance	Paid regardless of the number of dependents	Ordinary wage (described as family allowance, but it is paid uniformly)
Incentive Bonus	Both payment and amount are determined by work performance	Not ordinary wage (Condition is variable; not considered fixed)
Incentive Bonus	Minimum amount guaranteed	The lowest fixed amount is ordinary wage (paid uniformly and in a fixed amount)
Regular Bonus	Bonus (regular bonus) paid periodically	Ordinary wage
Regular Bonus	Temporary and/or irregular bonus paid at the employer’s discretion (Incentive/Performance-based incentive)	Not ordinary wage (not determined in advance or paid in a non-fixed amount)

로 통상임금에 해당한다. 전년도 근무실적에 따라 당해 연도에 성과급의 지급 여부나 지급액을 정하는 경우에도, 초과근무를 제공하는 시점인 당해 연도에 그 성과급의 지급 여부나 지급액수가 확정되어 있으므로 고정성이 있어 통상임금에 해당한다. 단, 전년도에 지급해야 할 것을 그 지급시기만 늦춘 것에 불과한 것일 경우에는 일반적인 성과급과 마찬가지이므로, 고정성이 없어 통상임금이 아니다.

[구체적인 사례]

(1) 근무실적을 A, B, C로 평가하여 최하 C등급은 100만원, B등급은 200만원, A등급은 300만원의 성과급을 지급하기로 하였다면 최소 100만원은 보장되므로 100만원만큼만 통상임금, 나머지는 통상임금이 아니다.

(2) 근무실적을 A, B, C로 평가하여 최하 C등급은 0원, B등급은 200만원, A등급은 300만원의 성과급을 지급하기로 하였다면, C등급을 받을 경우 성과급이 없기 때문에 위 회사의 성과급은 전부 통상임금이 아니다.

4) 지급액수가 확정되어 있지 않은 김장보너스

단체협약상 「김장철에 김장보너스를 지급하며, 지급금액은 노사 협의하여 지급한다」라고 되어 있고, 매년 김장보너스 지급 직전에 노사협의를 통해 그 금액이 정해졌는데, 금액이 일정하지 않았던 경우 초과근로를 제공하는 시점에서, 노사협의에 따른 그 지급액수를 확정할 수 없으므로, 사전에 이미 확정되어 있는 임금이 아니다. 따라서 고정성 없으므로, 통상임금이 아니다.

임금명목	임금의 특징	통상임금 해당 여부
기술수당	기술이나 자격보유자에게 지급되는 수당(자격수당, 면허수당 등)	통상임금○
근속수당	근속기간에 따라 지급여부나 지급액이 달라지는 임금	통상임금○
가족수당	부양가족 수에 따라 달라지는 가족수당	통상임금× (근로와 무관한 조건)
	부양가족 수와 관계없이 모든 근로자에게 지급되는 가족수당 분	통상임금○ (명목만 가족수당, 일률성 인정)
성과급	근무실적을 평가하여 지급여부나 지급액이 결정되는 임금	통상임금× (조건에 좌우됨, 고정성 인정×)
	최소한도가 보장되는 성과급	그 최소한도 만큼만 통상임금○ (그 만큼은 일률적, 고정적 지급)
상여금	정기적인 지급이 확정되어 있는 상여금(정기상여금)	통상임금○
	기업실적에 따라 일시적, 부정기적, 사용자 재량에 따른 상여금(경영성과분배금, 격려금, 인센티브)	통상임금× (사전 미확정, 고정성 인정×)

Ⅲ-3. Implications of the Supreme Court En Banc Rulings on Ordinary Wages (2013 and 2024)

1. Introduction

In Korea, wages are classified into two key concepts: ordinary wages, a pre-determined notion, and average wages, a retrospective one. Average wages represent the total amount of actual wages received and are used in calculating severance pay and industrial accident compensation. Ordinary wages, on the other hand, refer to a pre-determined hypothetical wage stipulated in the employment contract for contractual working hours. This wage is used to calculate additional pay for overtime, night shift work, and holiday work.

Before the Supreme Court's December 2013 ruling, ordinary wages were defined as wages regularly and uniformly paid in a fixed manner within a single wage payment period. Consequently, many companies introduced bonuses and various allowances to limit ordinary wages to approximately 50% of total wages. However, the Supreme Court's en banc decision in December 2013 expanded the definition of the wage payment period from monthly to yearly, recognizing all annual bonus payments as ordinary wages. This ruling brought significant simplification and transformation to Korea's wage system. Nevertheless, the 2013 decision maintained the criterion of "fixedness" by defining ordinary wages as compensation for contractual work that is regularly, uniformly, and paid in a fixed manner.

The 2013 ruling excluded conditional bonuses tied to the employee's presence on the payroll as of the final day of the wage payment period or contingent upon the number of days worked in the final month of employment. Even when such bonuses had been paid regularly and uniformly for decades, their conditional nature upon retirement excluded them from being classified as ordinary wages. As a result, many companies continued to implement bonuses contingent upon employment status or working days, leading to ongoing disputes over whether such bonuses should be included in ordinary wages. In December 2024, the Supreme Court issued another en banc ruling, removing "fixedness" from the definition of ordinary wages being compensation that is regularly and uniformly paid in a pre-determined amount for contractual work. This shift resulted in the inclusion of bonuses tied to employment status or working days within the scope of ordinary wages.

Ⅲ-3. 노동법상 '통상임금'개념에 대한 대법원(전원합의체) 판결 변화

1. 의의

우리나라의 임금은 사후적 개념인 평균임금과 사전적 개념인 통상임금으로 구성되어 있다. 평균임금은 실제로 수령한 임금총액으로 퇴직금과 산업재해 보상금에서 사용되고, 통상임금은 근로계약서에서 소정근로에 대해 받기로 한 사전적 가상임금으로 연장, 야간, 휴일근로 등을 계산하기 위한 기본임금으로 사용된다.

2013년 12월 대법원(전원합의체) 판례 이전에는 통상임금이 되기 위해서는 정기적이고 일률적으로 1임금지급시기 내에 고정적으로 지급하는 임금을 분류되었다. 이에 많은 기업들이 상여금과 각종 수당을 도입하여 통상임금을 총 임금의 50% 정도로 설정하였다. 이에 대해 2013년 12월 대법원은 통상임금에 대한 전원합의체 판결을 통해 1임금 지급시기인 월간을 연간으로 확대하여 연간 단위로 지급되는 상여금을 모두 통상임금으로 인정하였다. 이로 인하여 우리나라의 임금체계가 단순화되는 대대적인 변화를 가져왔다. 하지만 2013년 대법원 판결은 통상임금을 소정 근로의 대가로 정기적, 일률적, 고정적으로 지급하는 임금이라고 정의하여 '고정성'을 유지하였다.

2013년 대법원 판결은 마지막 달에 급여 지급일 현재 재직자 조건부 상여금이나 퇴직하는 달의 근무일수 조건부 정기상여금을 통상임금에서 제외시켰다. 이는 수십년 정기적이고 일률적으로 상여금을 지급하다가 마지막 달 퇴직 시점에서 딱 한번 재직 조건부로 지급하였다고 하여 해당 상여금을 통상임금에서 제외시켰다. 이로 인하여 여전히 많은 기업들이 '재직 조건부 상여금'을 계속 유지하면서 상여금의 통상임금 분쟁이 계속 발생하였다. 그리고 최근 대법원은 2024년 12월 전원합의체 판결을 통하여 2013년 대법원 판결과 달리, 통상임금의 판단기준인 소정근로에 대한 정기적이고 일률적으로 지급하기로 한 임금의 정의에서 '고정성'을 삭제하였다. 그 결과 재직 조건부와 근무일 수 조건부 상여금에 대해서도 통상임금을 인정하게 되었다.

This paper seeks to understand the concept of ordinary wages and explore its application through analysis of the landmark Supreme Court en banc rulings of December 2013 and December 2024, which represent significant milestones in Korea's history of wage-related jurisprudence.

2. Facts and Content of the Rulings

(1) Supreme Court En Banc Ruling of December 2013[79)]

Gab-eul Autotech paid bonuses bi-monthly according to its bonus payment regulations. For employees who resigned during the bonus payment period, bonuses were calculated on a pro-rata basis based on the number of days worked. However, bonuses such as Chuseok (Korean Thanksgiving), Lunar New Year, and vacation allowances were only paid to employees who were actively employed on the payment date.

The Supreme Court en banc ruling stated that: (1) Even though bonuses were paid every two months—exceeding the one-month wage payment period, the regularity requirement was satisfied because payments were made consistently; (2) Since the eligibility and amounts of the bonuses were uniformly determined for all employees, the criteria of uniformity and fixedness were also met. The Court expanded the wage payment period applicable to determining ordinary wage from one month to one year, establishing that such bonuses fell under the category of ordinary wages.

However, the Court excluded Chuseok, Lunar New Year bonuses, and vacation allowances from ordinary wages because they were payable only to employees actively employed on the payment date. Bonuses that could not be received upon retirement, even if paid regularly and uniformly, were excluded from ordinary wages.

(2) Supreme Court En Banc Ruling of December 2024[80)]

Hanwha Life paid annual bonuses equivalent to 850% of monthly base pay, divided into nine installments, including regular bi-monthly bonuses, Chuseok and Lunar New

---

79) Supreme Court ruling on Dec. 18, 2013, Cases 2012Da89399 / 2012Da94643 (Supreme Court En Banc Ruling on Ordinary Wages).

80) Supreme Court En Banc ruling on Dec. 19, 2024, Case 2020Da247190 (Hanwha Life Insurance Case) / Case 2013Da302838 (Hyundai Motor Case).

우리나라의 임금구조에서 역사적인 획을 긋는 2013년 12월과 2024년 12월 대법원 전원합의체의 두개 판결의 변경된 주요 내용을 통해서 통상임금의 개념을 이해하고, 통상임금에 대한 적용에 대해 알아보고자 한다.

2. 두개의 대상판결의 내용

(1) 2013년 12월 대법원 전원합의체 판결(갑을오토텍)[79]

갑을오토텍은 상여금지급규칙에 따라 상여금을 짝수 달에 지급하였고, 상여금 지급대상기간 중에 퇴직한 근로자에 대해서는 근무일수에 따라 일할 계산하여 지급하였다. 그러나 추석과 설상여금이나 휴가비 등은 지급일 현재 재직 근로자에게만 지급하였다.

대법원 전원합의체는 "이 사건 회사의 1임금지급 산정 기간인 1개월을 초과한 2개월 마다 지급되더라도 정기적으로 지급되었기 때문에 정기성 요건이 충족된다. 또한 지급 여부와 지급액이 모든 근로자에게 일률적으로 확정이 되었기 때문에 일률성과 고정성이 인정이 된다"고 판결하였다. 임금의 지급시기를 1월에서 1년으로 기간을 확정하여 판결한 것이다.

그러나 당시 대법원 전원합의체는 이 사건 회사의 설과 추석 상여금, 하기 휴가비 등은 특정 시점에 재직 중인 근로자에게만 지급하기로 한 것이기 때문에 통상임금으로 볼 수 없다고 판결하였다. 즉, 정기적이고 일률적으로 지급하더라도 퇴직 시에 임금수령일에 재직하지 않으면 받을 수 없는 상여금은 통상임금으로 보지 않았다.

(2) 2024년 12월 대법원 전원합의체 판결(한화생명보험 및 현대자동차)[80]

'한화생명보험'은 월 기준급여의 850%를 상여금으로 지급하면서, 정기상여금 짝수 월, 설과 추석상여금, 하계상여금으로 나누어 연간 총9회에 걸쳐 분할

79) 대법원 2013. 12. 18. 선고, 2012다89399 / 2012다94643 판결 (통상임금 대법원 전원합의체 판결)
80) 대법원 합의체 판결 2024. 12. 19. 선고, 2020다247190 판결 (한화생명보험 사건) / 2013다302838 판결(현대자동차 사건)

Year bonuses, and summer bonuses. These bonuses were only paid to employees who were actively employed on the payment date, therefore excluding those who had resigned prior to the payment date. Similarly, Hyundai Motor paid annual bonuses equivalent to 750% of ordinary wages, distributed bi-monthly and during Chuseok, Lunar New Year, and summer vacation. Employees who worked less than 15 days in the applicable month did not receive the bonuses.

In its December 2024 ruling, the Supreme Court redefined the concept of ordinary wages by removing "fixedness" from the definition of ordinary wages being compensation paid regularly and uniformly in a pre-determined amount. The Court emphasized that the essence of ordinary wages lies in compensation for contractual work. Therefore, bonuses tied to employment status on the payment date or contingent upon the number of days worked were also recognized as ordinary wages. To ensure legal stability and protect trust, the Court ruled that the new legal interpretation would only apply to ordinary wage calculations made after the ruling's announcement date.

3. Concept and Functions of Ordinary Wages as Interpreted by the Supreme Court En Banc Rulings

(1) The Concept of Ordinary Wages

The Supreme Court emphasized the compensatory nature of ordinary wages for contractual work and removed the requirement for fixedness. In 2024, the Court ruled:

"Article 6, Paragraph 1 of the Enforcement Decree of the Labor Standards Act defines ordinary wages as the amount paid to employees for contractual work or total work on a regular and uniform basis, including hourly, daily, weekly, monthly, or contractual amounts. In accordance with the purpose and definition in the regulations, ordinary wages refer to wages paid regularly and uniformly as compensation for contractual work. As ordinary wages serve as the basis for calculating various other wages under the Labor Standards Act, their essence lies in evaluating the value of work provided during contractual work hours. Regularity and uniformity are conceptual markers supporting the idea that the wage is compensation for contractual work. Wages paid regularly and uniformly, as agreed upon, are considered ordinary wages, regardless of any conditions

지급하였다. 상여금은 지급일 현재 재직 중인 직원에 한하여 지급하며 지급일 이전에 퇴직한 직원에게는 지급하지 않았다.

'현대자동차'는 통상임금의 750%를 격월, 설과 추석, 하기휴가에 분할하여 지급하였다. 격월 상여금은 각 100%, 설-추석 상여와 하기휴가는 각각 50%씩 지급하면서, 지급일에 해당하는 월에 15일 미만 근무한 자는 상여금 지급대상에서 제외하였다.

대법원 전원합의체는 통상임금의 개념을 재정립하면서, 정기적, 일률적, 고정적으로 지급하는 금품의 개념에서 '고정성'을 삭제하였다. 통상임금의 본질인 소정 근로의 대가성을 중심으로 판단하기 때문에 재직 조건부 상여금과 근무일수 조건부 상여금도 통상임금으로 포함시켰다. 다만, 법적 안정성과 신뢰 보호를 위해 새로운 법리의 효력을 이 판결 선고일 이후의 통상임금 산정부터 적용하기로 하였다.

3. 대법원 전원합의체 판결을 통해 본 통상임금의 개념과 기능

(1) 통상임금의 개념

2024년 12월 대법원 전원합의체 판결은 종전과 달리 통상임금의 개념을 소정근로에 대한 대가성을 강조하고 있으며, '고정성'을 삭제하였다. 대법원은 "근로기준법 시행령 제6조 제1항은 통상임금을 근로자에게 정기적이고 일률적으로 소정근로 또는 총 근로에 대하여 지급하기로 정한 시간급 금액, 일급 금액, 주급 금액, 월급 금액 또는 도급 금액 이라고 규정한다. 법령의 정의와 취지에 충실하게 통상임금 개념을 해석하면, 통상임금은 소정근로의 대가로서 정기적, 일률적으로 지급하기로 정한 임금을 말한다. 통상임금은 근로기준법이 규정한 여러 임금을 산정하는 기준이 되므로, 그 본질은 근로자가 소정근로시간에 제공하기로 정한 근로의 가치를 평가한 기준임금이라는 데에 있다. 정기성과 일률성은 그 임금이 소정근로의 대가인 임금임을 뒷받침하는 개념적 징표이다. 근로자가 소정근로를 온전하게 제공하면 그 대가로서 정기적, 일률적으로 지급하도록 정해진 임금은 그에 부가된 조건의 존부나 성취 가능성과 관계

attached to their payment or the likelihood of fulfilling those conditions. While conditions attached to wages can be considered when determining whether the wage truly compensates for contractual work, the mere uncertainty of condition fulfillment does not negate the wage's status as ordinary wages. The concept of ordinary wages implicitly carries the meaning of 'pre-determined regulation regarding wage payment,' so any payments made on a temporary or fluctuating basis, regardless of contractual work, remain excluded from ordinary wages."[81]

(2) The Functions of Ordinary Wages

The Court provided five reasons for excluding the requirement of fixedness from ordinary wages, which can also be understood as the functions of ordinary wages:

First, ordinary wages are based on legal provisions. Article 6, Paragraph 1 of the Enforcement Decree of the Labor Standards Act defines ordinary wages as amounts paid regularly and uniformly for contractual or total work. Ordinary wages represent the value of contractual work converted into wages, with the fundamental criterion for determining ordinary wages being the "compensatory nature of contractual work." Regularity and uniformity are typical characteristics of wages paid for contractual work, ensuring that the scope of ordinary wages is determined in advance in a reasonable manner by setting clear payment terms and conditions.

Second, ordinary wages are a pre-determined concept used to calculate statutory allowances. Ordinary wages are linked to mandatory legal provisions that ensure appropriate compensation for overtime, etc. Therefore, ordinary wages are an obligatory concept that cannot be arbitrarily altered by the parties involved.

Third, ordinary wages reflect contractual work, regardless of actual work performed. In this regard, ordinary wages differ from average wages, which are determined after the fact based on the total wages actually received. Ordinary wages, as a theoretical construct, are based on the idea of "an employee providing the full contractual work." When this condition is met, the hypothetical wage paid for it constitutes the ordinary wage.

Fourth, ordinary wages are determined before overtime work or additional work is

---

81) Supreme Court En Banc ruling on Dec. 19, 2024, Case 2020Da247190 (Hanwha Life Insurance Case).

없이 통상임금에 해당한다. 임금에 부가된 조건은 해당 임금의 객관적 성질을 실질적으로 판단하는 과정에서 소정근로 대가성이나 정기성, 일률성을 부정하는 요소 중 하나로 고려될 수는 있지만, 단지 조건의 성취 여부가 불확실하다는 사정만으로 통상임금성이 부정된다고 볼 수는 없다. 이러한 통상임금을 이루는 개념에는 '임금 지급에 관한 일정한 사전적 규율'의 의미가 내포되어 있으므로, 소정근로의 제공과 관계없이 일시적이거나 변동적으로 지급되는 금품은 여전히 통상임금에서 제외된다"라고 판시하였다.[81)]

(2) 통상임금의 기능

이번 대법원 판결에서는 통상임금에서 '고정성'을 제외하는 이유로 5가지를 설명하고 있는데, 이는 '통상임금의 기능'과 같다고 볼 수 있다.

첫째, 통상임금은 법령에 근거하고 있다. 근로기준법 시행령 제6조 제1항은 통상임금을 근로자에게 정기적이고 일률적으로 소정근로 또는 총 근로에 대하여 지급하기로 정한 금액이라고 정의한다. 통상임금은 소정근로의 가치를 임금으로 전환한 개념으로, 법령상 정의된 통상임금의 본질적인 판단 기준은 '소정근로 대가성'이다. '정기성'과 '일률성'은 이러한 '소정근로 대가성' 있는 임금의 전형적 속성으로서, 임금의 지급 시기와 지급 대상이 미리 일정하게 정해지도록 요구함으로써 통상임금의 범위를 사전에 합리적으로 결정하도록 하는 역할을 담당한다.

둘째, 통상임금은 법정 수당을 계산을 위한 사전적 확정개념이다. 통상임금은 법정수당 산정의 도구로서 연장근로 등에 대하여 법이 정한 합당한 보상을 하도록 한 강행법규와 관련되어 있다. 따라서 통상임금은 당사자가 그 의미나 범위를 임의로 변경할 수 없는 강행적 개념이다.

셋째, 통상임금은 실근로와 무관하게 소정근로를 반영한 것이다. 이 점에서 통상임금은 법정시간내에서 근로자에게 실제 지급된 임금의 총액을 기초로 하기 때문에 사후적으로 산정되는 평균임금과 구별된다. 통상임금은 가상의 도구개념이고 그 개념이 전제하는 근로자는 '소정근로를 온전하게 제공하는 근로자'

---

81) 대법원 합의체 판결 2024. 12. 19. 선고, 2020다247190 판결 (한화생명보험 사건)

provided. This is necessary so that both employers and employees can predict the costs or compensation associated with overtime work and make decisions regarding the provision of such work. When overtime is actually performed, additional pay can be immediately calculated. The key consideration for ordinary wages is the amount determined for the contractual work. The "likelihood of meeting the conditions to receive that wage" is not a factor in determining ordinary wages.

Fifth, the concept of ordinary wages aligns with the policy goal of the Labor Standards Act to discourage overtime work. According to the Act, employers must specify the "contractual working hours" when entering into employment contracts (Article 17, Paragraph 1, Item 2), and the total weekly working hours, excluding break times, must not exceed 40 (Article 50, Paragraph 1). Since overtime work causes greater fatigue and restricts employees' free time, the Labor Standards Act limits overtime and provides for additional pay of at least 50% of the ordinary wage for overtime work (Article 56), along with penalties for violations related to overtime (Articles 109 and 110). The purpose of these provisions is to reduce overtime, ensuring that workers have a dignified life and are compensated appropriately for working overtime.[82)]

4. Implications of the Supreme Court En Banc Rulings on Ordinary Wages

The Supreme Court en banc rulings on ordinary wages in 2013 and 2024 have reformed Korea's wage system significantly and clarified the compensatory nature of wages for contractual work. These rulings played, and are playing, a pivotal role in improving employee quality of life by increasing ordinary wages and restricting excessive overtime.

First, the rulings brought groundbreaking improvements to the wage system. Before 2013, most companies defined ordinary wages as fixed payments made during a single wage payment period. This led to an abnormal salary structure where bonuses accounted for over 50% of annual salary. The 2013 ruling simplified the wage system by redefining the wage payment period from a monthly to an annual basis.

---

82) Supreme Court ruling on Dec. 7, 2023, Case 2020Do15393.

이다. '소정근로의 온전한 제공'이라는 요건이 충족되면 이를 이유로 지급되는 가상의 임금이 통상임금이다.

넷째, 통상임금은 연장근로 등을 제공하기 전에 산정된다. 그래야 사용자와 근로자는 연장근로 등에 대한 비용 또는 보상의 정도를 예측하여 연장근로 등의 제공 여부에 관한 의사결정을 할 수 있고, 연장근로 등이 실제 제공된 때에 가산임금을 곧바로 산정할 수 있다. 통상임금에서 고려할 것은 소정근로를 온전하게 제공한 경우에 지급되는 임금이 얼마로 정해져 있는가이다. '실제로 조건을 충족하여 그 임금을 지급받을 가능성'은 통상임금에서 고려할 필요가 없다.

다섯째, 통상임금 개념은 연장근로 등의 억제라는 근로기준법의 정책 목표에 부합하고 있다. 근로기준법에 따르면 사용자는 근로계약을 체결할 때 '소정근로시간'을 명시하여야 하고(제17조 제1항 제2호), 1주 간의 근로시간은 휴게시간을 제외하고 40시간을 초과할 수 없다(제50조 제1항). 연장근로 등은 근로자에게 더 큰 피로와 긴장을 주고 근로자가 누릴 수 있는 생활상의 자유시간을 제한하므로, 근로기준법은 연장근로를 제한하는 규정을 두면서(제53조) 연장근로 등에 대해 통상임금의 50% 이상을 가산한 임금을 지급하도록 하는 한편(제56조), 연장근로 등 관련 규정 위반에 관한 처벌 조항도 두고 있다(제109조, 제110조). 통상임금의 취지는 근로자의 인간다운 생활을 보장하기 위하여 연장근로 등을 억제하고 연장근로 등의 가치에 상응하는 금전적 보상을 해 주려는 데에 있다.[82]

4. 통상임금에 대한 대법원 전원합의체 판결 변경의 시사점

2013년과 2024년에 있었던 두개의 통상임금에 대한 대법원의 합의체 판결은 우리나라의 임금체계를 획기적으로 개선했고, 소정근로에 대한 대가성 임금의 성격을 명확히 하였다. 이를 통해서 높아진 통상임금을 통해서 연장근로 등을 제한함으로써 근로자의 생활의 질을 향상시킨 역할을 할 것으로 예상된다.

첫째, 임금체계의 획기적인 개선이다. 2013년 이전만 해도 대부분의 기업들

82) 대법원 2023. 12. 7. 선고 2020도15393 판결.

Second, the rulings established that ordinary wages are compensation for contractual work. Article 17 of the Labor Standards Act explicitly states that ordinary wages are those paid as compensation for contractual working hours, emphasizing their role as pre-determined wages regularly and uniformly paid for contractual work.

Third, the rulings resulted in an increase in ordinary wages. When ordinary wages are correctly reflected, additional allowances for overtime and holiday work—calculated at 50% of actual wages—substantially increase employers' labor costs. This financial burden incentivized employers to limit overtime and holiday work, thereby contributing to the improvement of overall quality of life for their employees.

이 통상임금을 1임금지급시기에 고정적으로 지급하는 임금으로 설정함으로써 각종 상여금제도가 연봉급여의 50% 이상을 차지하는 비정상적인 급여구조를 가지고 있었는데, 2024년의 통상임금 판결은 1임금지급시기를 월 단위가 아닌 연단위로 확정함으로써 임금구조를 간단히 하는데 기여를 하였다.

둘째, 소정근로에 대한 대가로 받는 것이 통상임금임을 명확히 하였다. 근로기준법 제17조에서 근로계약서를 작성할 경우에 소정근로시간의 대가로 받는 것이 통상임금임을 명시하고 있다. 즉, 통상임금은 소정근로에 대한 대가로 받는 것이라는 사실을 설명하고 있다. 이에 통상임금은 근로자에게 정기적이고 일률적으로 소정근로에 대해 지급하기로 정해진 임금임을 분명히 하고 있다.

셋째, 통상임금에 대한 2024년 대법원 전원합의체 판결로 인해 통상임금이 높아졌고, 통상임금을 반영해 연장근로 등에 대해 실제 받는 임금의 50%를 가산해 지급하면 사용자의 인건비 부담이 커졌다. 이를 통해 사용자는 연장근로나 휴일근로를 스스로 제한해 실제로 근로자의 삶의 질을 향상시켰다.

Ⅳ. Average Wage

1. Concept

Article 2 of the LSA (Definition of Average Wage)

① The term "average wage" means the amount calculated by dividing the total amount of wage paid to the relevant worker during three calendar months prior to the date of calculation by the total number of calendar days during those three calendar months. This shall apply to all employment including that of less than three months.
② If the amount calculated pursuant to the provisions of paragraph (1) is lower than the ordinary wage of the worker concerned, the amount of the ordinary wage shall be deemed average wage.

Enforcement Decree to the LSA, Article 2 (Period and wage Excluded from the Calculation of Average Wage)

① In cases where the period of calculating average wage, as provided in Article 2 of the Act, includes the period falling under any of the following subparagraphs, the period and wage paid for that period shall be deducted respectively from a basis period for the calculation of average wage and the total amount of average wage:

1. A probationary period within 3 months;
2. A period of shutdown due to a cause attributable to the employer as prescribed in Article 46 of the Act;
3. A period of maternity leave as prescribed in Article 74 of the Act;
4. A period of suspension of work for medical treatment due to occupational injury or disease as prescribed in Article 78 of the Act;
5. A period of childcare leave as prescribed in Article 19 of the Act on Equal Employment for Worker-Family Reconciliation;
6. A period of strike as prescribed in subparagraph 6 of Article 2 of the Trade Union and Labor Relations Adjustment Act;
7. A period of suspension of service or of non-work owing to performance of duties as prescribed in the Military Service Act, the Reserve Forces Act, or the Framework Act on Civil Defense; provided that the same shall not apply in cases where wage are paid during that period; and
8. A period of suspension of work with approval from the employer caused by non- occupational injury, disease, or other reasons.

2. Methods for Calculating Average Wage

(1) General calculation

Average wage mean the actual wage paid for actual work provided and calculated into the daily wage rate. Average wage is the amount calculated by dividing the total amount of wage paid to the relevant worker during three calendar months prior to the date of calculation by the total number of calendar days during those three calendar months.

$$\text{Average Wage} = \frac{\text{Total amount of wage paid for the last three calendar months}}{\text{Total number of calendar days in the last three calendar months(89–92 days)}}$$

Ⅳ. 평균임금

1. 평균임금의 개념

근로기준법 제2조【평균임금의 정의】

① 제6항 평균임금이라 함은 이를 산정하여야 할 사유가 발생한 날 이전 3월간에 그 근로자에 대하여 지급된 임금의 총액을 그 기간의 총 일수로 나눈 금액을 말한다. 취업 후 3월 미만도 이에 준한다.

② 제1조 제6항의 규정에 의하여 산출된 금액이 당해 근로자의 통상 임금보다 저액일 경우에는 그 통상임금액을 평균임금으로 한다.

시행령 제2조【평균임금의 계산에서 제외되는 기간과 임금】

① 법 제2조 제1항 제6호에 따른 평균임금 산정기간 중에 다음 각 호의 어느 하나에 해당하는 기간이 있는 경우에는 그 기간과 그 기간 중에 지급된 임금은 평균임금 산정기준이 되는 기간과 임금의 총액에서 각각 뺀다.

1. 근로계약을 체결하고 수습 중에 있는 근로자가 수습을 시작한 날부터 3개월 이내의 기간
2. 법 제46조에 따른 사용자의 귀책사유로 휴업한 기간
3. 법 제74조에 따른 산전후휴가 기간
4. 법 제78조에 따라 업무상 부상 또는 질병으로 요양하기 위하여 휴업한 기간
5. 「남녀고용평등과 일·가정 양립지원에 관한법률」 제19조에 따른 육아휴직 기간
6. 「노동조합 및 노동관계조정법」 제2조 제6호에 따른 쟁의행위기간
7. 「병역법」, 「예비군법」 또는 「민방위기본법」에 따른 의무를 이행하기 위하여 휴직하거나 근로하지 못한 기간. 다만, 그 기간 중 임금을 지급받은 경우에는 그러하지 아니하다.
8. 업무 외 부상이나 질병, 그 밖의 사유로 사용자의 승인을 받아 휴업한 기간

2. 평균임금의 산정방법

(1) 일반적인 계산

평균임금은 실제로 제공된 근로에 대해 실제로 지급받은 임금을 의미하며 일급 개념으로 산출된다. 평균임금 산정은 이를 산정해야 할 사유가 발생한 날 이전 3월간에 그 근로자에 대하여 지급된 임금의 총액을 그 기간의 총 일수로 나눈 금액을 말한다.

$$\text{평균임금} = \frac{\text{사유가 발생한 날 이전 3월간의 인금총액}}{\text{사유가 발생한 날 이전 3월간의 총일수(89일}\sim\text{92일)}}$$

1) The total amount of wage paid for the last three calendar months

The total amount of wage includes all wage under the Labor Standards Act excluding other forms of payment. In determining whether individual items of pay may be identified as wage reflected into the calculation of average wage, the following criteria shall be considered: ① the items are paid regularly and periodically; ② they are mandated by the employer according to collective bargaining, rules of employment, salary regulations, the labor contract, or habitual practice; or ③ employees identified under general conditions are paid uniformly. If individual items of pay meet any of these criteria, the items of pay shall be considered wage regardless of their titles.[83)]

In cases where bonuses are paid once per annum and paid for periods exceeding one month, the total monetary value of the bonus paid for a certain month shall not be included into the calculation of average wage. The bonuses shall be calculated by dividing the total monetary value of bonuses paid to a relevant employee(during the twelve calendar months before the day on which cause for calculating their average wage occurs) by the total number of calendar months, which is 3/12 times the total monetary value of bonuses paid per year.[84)]

2) Total number of calendar days in the last three calendar months prior to the occurrence date

The date on which the event occurred or the incident which necessitates such calculation means, in the event of resignation, the day in which the employer accepts the letter of resignation submitted by the employee. In the event of an industrial accident, it is the day on which the injury occurred, or the day when the disease is confirmed by diagnosis. However, the periods excluded from calculation are periods of shutdown on account of the employer, periods of maternity leave, periods of suspension from work for medical treatment owing to occupational injury or disease, periods of childcare leave, periods of strike, periods of approved suspension from work, and periods of suspension of service owing to performance of duties.

The period of three months does not signify 90 days, but three(3) calendar months(89~92 days) from the occurrence date. For employment of less than three months, the actual period served is calculated.

---

83) Seoul Central District Court ruling on Jun. 21, 2007, 2006Na20978.

84) MOEL Guidelines: on Feb. 24, 2003, wage 68207-120.

1) 3월간 임금 총액

임금 총액에는 기타 금품을 제외한 근로기준법상 임금 모두가 포함된다(아래 표 참조: 임금의 성질에 따른 분류). 어떤 금품이 평균임금 산정의 기초가 되는 임금에 해당하는지 여부를 가늠할 수 있는 구체적인 사정으로서 근로자에게 계속적·정기적으로 지급되며 그 지급에 관해 단체협약, 취업규칙, 급여규정, 근로계약, 노동관행 등에 의해 사용자에게 그 지급의무가 있고, 또한 일정한 요건에 해당하는 근로자에게 일률적으로 지급하는 것이라면, 그 명칭 여하를 불문하고 임금이라고 볼 수 있다.[83)]

상여금의 지급률을 연간단위로 설정하여 1개월을 넘는 단위로 지급하고 있는 경우에는 이를 지급받은 그 월의 임금으로 취급하여 일시에 전액을 평균임금에 산입하는 것이 아니며, 평균임금을 산정하여야 할 사유가 발생한 날 이전 12개월의 기간 동안에 지급받은 상여금 전액을 그 기간 동안의 근로월수로 분할 계산하여 즉, 3/12을 평균임금산정 기준 임금총액에 산입한다.[84)]

2) 사유발생일 이전 3월간의 총일수 계산

사유가 발생한 날과 그 지급사유가 발생한 때라 함은 사직서를 제출한 경우 사용자가 이를 수리한 날을 말한다. 재해보상의 경우에는 사상의 원인이 되는 사고가 발생한 날 또는 진단에 의해 질병이 발생 되었다고 확정된 날을 말한다. 다만, 평균임금 산정대상 기간에서 제외되는 기간은 사용자 귀책사유로 인한 휴업기간, 산전·산후 휴가기간, 업무상 질병·부상 기간, 육아휴직기간, 쟁의행위기간, 업무 외 질병 휴직기간, 공의직무 수행기간 등이다.

3월간은 90일을 말하는 것이 아니고 기산일로부터 소급하여 역월 3개월간 포함된 일수(89~92일)를 말한다. 취업 후 3월 미만인 경우에는 그 기간만을 대상으로 평균임금을 산정한다.

---

83) 서울지방법원 2007.6.21. 2006나20978.

84) 행정해석: 임금 68207-120, 2003.2.24.

(2) Exceptional case: Calculation of average wages during periods of leave

1) "Average wage" where an employee came to resign after a period of leave from work that the employee took with approval from the employer due to non-occupational injury, illness or other reason shall be calculated as follows: "average wage" to calculate severance pay refer to the amount calculated by dividing the total amount of wage paid to the relevant employee during three calendar months prior to the date of calculation by the total number of calendar days during those three calendar months(Article 2 of the LSA). If the amount calculated by this method is lower than the ordinary wage of the employee concerned, the ordinary wage shall be deemed as average wage.

2) In cases where the period of calculating average wage includes the period falling under a period of leave from work with approval from the employer caused by nonoccupational injury, illness, or other reason, the period and wage paid for that period shall be deducted respectively from a basis period for the calculation of average wage and the total amount of average wage(Article 2 of the Enforcement Decree to the LSA). Therefore, in cases where an employee took a leave of absence for non-occupational injury, illness or other reason in accordance with Article 2(8) of the Enforcement Decree to the LSA(with approval from the employer), the remaining period and wage excluding the period mentioned above shall be used for the calculation of average wage. If the leave of absence exceeds three months, the first day of the leave of absence shall be the date for calculating average wage based on the previous three months. In any case, if the amount calculated above is lower than the ordinary wage of the employee concerned, the amount of the ordinary wage shall be deemed as average wage.[85)]

3) In cases where leave of absence is due to the employee's choice or actions, this period shall be included in the standard period in calculating average wage.[86)] In cases where an employee could not provide labor service during the period required for calculating average wage due to the employee's choice or actions, this period shall be included in the standard period in calculating average wage. On the other hand, in cases where an employee took a leave of absence with approval from the employer, caused by non-occupational injury, diseases or other reasons according to Article 2(8) of the Enforcement Decree to the LSA, the remaining period and wage excluding the period mentioned above shall be used for the calculation of average

85) MOEL Guidelines: Retirement Pension Dept-518, Oct. 21, 2008

86) MOEL Guidelines: Wage 68207-132, Feb. 27, 2003.

(2) 예외적인 경우: 휴직기간의 평균임금 산정방법

1) 업무 외 부상이나 질병, 그 밖의 사유로 사용자의 승인을 받아 휴업한 후 퇴직하게 된 경우에 평균임금을 다음과 같이 계산한다. 퇴직금 산정을 위한 평균임금은 이를 산정하여야 할 사유가 발생한 날 이전 3개월 동안에 그 근로자에게 지급된 임금의 총액을 그 기간의 총 일수로 나눈 금액을 말하며 (「근로기준법」제2조), 이러한 방법으로 산출된 평균임금액이 당해 근로자의 통상임금보다 금액이 적을 경우에는 그 통상임금을 평균임금으로 하도록 정하고 있다.

2) 평균임금 산정기간 중에 업무 외 부상 또는 질병으로 사용자의 승인을 받아 휴업한 경우에는 그 기간과 그 기간에 지불된 임금은 평균임금 산정기준이 되는 기간과 임금의 총액에서 각각 공제하도록 규정하고 있다(근로기준법시행령 제2조). 따라서 근로자가 업무 외 부상이나 질병, 그 밖의 사유로 사용자의 승인을 받아 휴업한 기간일 경우에는 동 기간을 제외한 나머지 일수 및 임금을 대상으로 평균임금으로 산정하여야 하며, 휴직한 기간이 3개월을 초과하여 평균임금 산정기준 기간이 없게 되는 경우에는 휴직한 첫날을 평균임금산정 사유발생일로 보아 이전 3월간을 대상으로 평균임금을 산정하여야 한다. 아울러, 위와 같은 방법으로 산출된 평균임금액이 당해 근로자의 통상임금보다 저액일 경우에는 그 통상임금액을 평균임금으로 하여야 한다.[85]

3) 휴직기간이 근로자 귀책사유에 해당되는 경우 평균임금산정 기준기간에 포함하여 평균임금을 산정하여야 한다.[86] 만일 평균임금 산정기준이 되는 기간에 근로를 제공하지 못한 사유가 결근 등 근로자 귀책사유에 해당되는 경우에는 동기간도 평균임금산정 기준기간에 포함하여 평균임금을 산정하여야 한다. 반면에 휴직기간이 같은 법 시행령 제2조 제1항 제8호의 규정에 의한 업무 외 부상·질병 기타의 사유로 인하여 사용자의 승인을 얻어 휴업한 기간으로 볼 수 있는 경우에는 동기간을 제외한 나머지 일수 및 임금을 대상으로 평균임금을 산정하여야 하며, 휴직한 기간이 3개월을 초과하여 평균임금 산정기준기간이

---

85) 행정해석: 퇴직연금복지과-518, 2008.10.21.

86) 행정해석: 임금 68207-132, 2003.2.27.

wage. If the leave of absence exceeded three months, the first day of the leave of absence shall be the date for calculating average wage based on the previous three months. In any case, if the amount calculated above is lower than the ordinary wage of the employee concerned, the ordinary wage shall be deemed average wage.

3. Adjustment of Average Wage

(1) Average wage in special cases (When to use special case for calculation of average wage)[87)]

1) When the period excluded from the calculation of average wage is 3 months or longer (Article 1)

If the period of time excluded from the calculation of average wage is at least three months(Article 2(1) of the Enforcement Decree to the LSA), the average wage shall be calculated based on the date on which the cause for calculating average wage occurs. The same shall apply mutatis mutandis to adjustment of average wage(Article 5 of the Enforcement Decree to the LSA). In this case, "the month when the injury or illness occurred" shall be deemed to be "the month of the first day of the period excluded from the calculation of average wage".

2) If the reason for calculating the average wage occurred on the first day work is provided (Article 2)

If the reason for calculating the average wage occurs on the first day work is provided, the average wage is calculated from the average daily wage that was supposed to be paid to the worker.

3) When wage are paid collectively by two or more workers (Article 3)

In the event wage are paid collectively with two or more workers in one pair, the employee's career, production performance, working days, technical skills, responsibilities, and distribution practices shall be taken into account, unless a pre-determined payment method is provided for individual workers. We estimate the wage per worker and use the amount to estimate the average wage.

---

87) Enforcement Decree to the Labor Standards Act, Article 4 (Average Wage in Special Cases) Where it is impossible to calculate an average wage in accordance with Article 2 (1) 6 of the Act and Articles 2 and 3 of this Decree, such an average wage shall be as determined by the Minister of Employment and Labor; [Special Case Notice for Calculation of Average Wages by the Minister of Ministry of Employment and Labor (No. 2015-77, notice released on October 14, 2015)].

없게 되는 경우에는 휴직한 첫날을 평균임금산정 사유발생일로 보아 이전 3월간을 대상으로 평균임금을 산정하여야 한다. 아울러 위와 같은 방법으로 산출된 평균임금액이 당해 근로자의 통상임금보다 저액일 경우에는 그 통상임금액을 평균임금으로 하여야 한다.

3. 평균임금 조정

(1) 특별한 경우의 평균임금(평균임금산정 특례고시)[87)]

1) 평균임금의 계산에서 제외되는 기간이 3개월 이상인 경우(제1조)

평균임금의 계산에서 제외되는 기간이 3개월 이상인 경우(근기법 시행령 제2조 제1항) 제외되는 기간의 최초일을 평균임금의 산정사유가 발생한 날로 보아 평균임금을 산정한다. 평균임금의 조정(근기법 시행령 제5조)의 경우에도 이를 준용한다. 이 경우 "부상 또는 질병이 발생한 달"은 "평균임금의 계산에서 제외되는 기간의 최초일이 속한 달"로 본다.

2) 근로제공의 첫날에 평균임금 산정사유가 발생한 경우(제2조)

근로를 제공한 첫날에 평균임금 산정사유가 발생한 경우에는 그 근로자에게 지급하기로 한 임금의 1일 평균액으로 평균임금을 추산한다.

3) 임금이 근로자 2명 이상 일괄하여 지급되는 경우(제3조)

근로자 2명 이상을 1개조로 하여 임금을 일괄하여 지급하는 경우 개별 근로자에 대한 배분방법을 미리 정하지 않았다면 근로자의 경력, 생산실적, 실근로일수, 기술·기능, 책임, 배분에 관한 관행 등을 감안하여 근로자 1명당 임금액을 추정하여 그 금액으로 평균임금을 추산한다.

---

87) 근로기준법 시행령 제4조【특별한 경우의 평균임금】 법 제2조 제1항 제6호, 이 영 제2조 및 제3조에 따라 평균임금을 산정할 수 없는 경우에는 고용노동부 장관이 정하는 바에 따른다. [고용노동부 평균임금산정 특례 고시(제2015-77호, 2015.10.14)]

4) If part of the total wage is not clear (Article 4)

If the period in which the average wage is included includes payment of an additional portion in the average wage, the average wage shall be deducted from the total amount of wage paid out of the extra period from the total number of days.

5) When the total amount of wage is not clear (Article 5)

If the average wage cannot be calculated in accordance with the provisions of Article 1 through Article 4 of the Special Notice on Calculation of Average Wage, the head of the regional Employment and Labor Office shall consider the average wage of the worker as deemed appropriate in consideration of the following:

1) Matters concerning wage level and inflation assessment in the area where the workplace is located;

2) Matters concerning the monthly salary, monthly income, and monthly average salary reported under the Income Tax Act, the National Pension Act, the National Health Insurance Act, and the Employment Insurance Act;

3) Matters concerning wage of workers engaged in the same occupation as the worker at workplaces of the same or similar size as the type of business in the area where the workplace is located;

4) Matters concerning documentary evidence, such as records held by the person or his / her family, etc.(in this case, only if the employer approves) of the money received during the period providing work at the workplace;

5) Matters concerning employment labor statistics, such as the "Report on Labor Status by Employment Type" and the "Labor Work Survey Report", which are surveyed and published by the Minister of Employment and Labor.

(2) Adjustment of average wage in special cases (Article 5 of the Enforcement Decree to the LSA)

1) The average wage applicable to the calculation of compensation, etc. for the employee pursuant to accident compensation under the Labor Standards Act shall, when the average amount of monthly ordinary wage per employee(hereinafter referred to as the "average amount") paid to employees in the same business category in the same business or workplace to which the relevant employee belongs has changed by at least five percent from the average amount paid in the month when an injury or a disease occurs, be such amount increased or decreased

4) 임금총액의 일부가 명확하지 아니한 경우(제4조)

평균임금의 산정기간 중에 지급된 임금의 일부를 확인할 수 없는 기간이 포함된 경우에는 그 기간을 빼고 남은 기간에 지급된 임금의 총액을 남은 기간의 총 일수로 나눈 금액을 평균임금으로 본다.

5) 임금총액의 전부가 명확하지 아니한 경우 등(제5조)

평균임금산정 특례고시 제1조부터 제4조까지의 규정에 따라 평균임금을 산정할 수 없는 경우에는 지방고용노동관서장이 다음 각 호의 사항을 감안하여 적정하다고 결정한 금액을 해당 근로자의 평균임금으로 본다.

1) 해당 사업장이 있는 지역의 임금수준과 물가사정에 관한 사항

2) 해당 근로자에 대한 「소득세법」과 관련 법령에 따라 기재된 소득자별 근로소득원천징수부, 「국민연금법」·「국민건강보험법」·「고용보험법」에 따라 신고된 보수월액·소득월액·월평균임금 등에 관한 사항

3) 해당 사업장이 있는 지역의 업종과 규모가 동일하거나 유사한 사업장에서 해당 근로자와 동일한 직종에 종사한 근로자의 임금에 관한 사항

4) 해당 사업장의 근로제공기간 중에 받은 금품에 대하여 본인 또는 그 가족 등이 보유하고 있는 기록(이 경우 사업주가 인정하는 경우에만 한정한다) 등 증빙서류에 관한 사항

5) 고용노동부 장관이 조사·발간하는 "고용형태별 근로실태 조사보고서" 및 "사업체 노동력 조사보고서" 등 고용노동통계에 관한 사항

(2) 특별한 경우의 평균임금이 조정(근기법 시행령 제5조)

1) 근로기준법 재해보상 규정에 따른 보상금 등을 산정할 때 적용할 평균임금은 그 근로자가 소속한 사업 또는 사업장에서 같은 직종의 근로자에게 지급된 통상임금의 1명당 1개월평균액(이하 "평균액"이라 한다)이 그 부상 또는 질병이 발생한 달에 지급된 평균액보다 100분의 5 이상 변동된 경우에는 그 변동비율에 따라 인상되거나 인하된 금액으로 하되, 그 변동 사유가 발생한 달의 다음 달부터 적용한다. 다만, 제2회 이후의 평균임금을 조정하는 때는 직

at the aforesaid rate of change, but such rate shall apply to the month immediately following the month of occurrence of grounds for change and the months subsequent thereto. Provided, that the second or latter adjustment of average wage shall be calculated based on the average amount of the month in which a cause for immediately preceding change occurred.

2) Where the business or workplace to which the relevant employee belongs is permanently closed down, the adjustment of average wage under paragraph(1) shall be based on a business or workplace of the same business type and scale as at the time when the employee received the occupational injury or was diagnosed with the occupational disease.

3) If there is no employee engaged in the same occupational category as the relevant worker, the adjustment of average wage under paragraph(1) or(2) shall be based on employees engaged in the occupation of similar category.

4) The average wage applicable to computation of retirement benefits under Article 8 of the Act on the Guarantee of Employees' Retirement Benefits, which shall be paid to an employee who suffers from an occupational injury or disease, shall be the average wage adjusted in accordance with paragraphs(1) through(3).

4. Items to be included in average wage

1) As long as a meal allowance is paid periodically and uniformly, this cannot be pure welfare or a bonus expressing favor, but shall be regarded as money characteristic of wage paid as remuneration for labor service.[88)]

2) As the total wage calculated for average wage are any money and valuable goods an employer pays to a worker for their work, what the worker receives continuously and regularly, and what the employer has to pay according to the collective agreement and rules of employment, regardless of how such payments are termed, a holiday work allowance shall be included [in calculation of severance pay].[89)]

3) As overtime allowance is not money paid under friendly and favorable conditions, but rather, is remuneration the employer has to pay for an employee's work, regardless of its label, overtime allowance shall be included into average wage when calculating severance pay.[90)]

---

88) Supreme Court ruling on May 15, 2001, 2001Do1186.

89) Supreme Court ruling on Apr. 14, 1992, 91Da5587

90) Seoul District Court ruling on May 26, 2005, 2005Na175.

전 회의 변동 사유가 발생한 달의 평균액을 산정기준으로 한다.

2) 제1항에 따라 평균임금을 조정하는 경우 그 근로자가 소속한 사업 또는 사업장이 폐지된 때는 그 근로자가 업무상 부상 또는 질병이 발생한 당시에 그 사업 또는 사업장과 같은 종류, 같은 규모의 사업 또는 사업장을 기준으로 한다.

3) 제1항이나 제2항에 따라 평균임금을 조정하는 경우 그 근로자의 직종과 같은 직종의 근로자가 없는 때는 그 직종과 유사한 직종의 근로자를 기준으로 한다.

4) 업무상 부상을 당하거나 질병에 걸린 근로자에게 지급할 「근로자퇴직급여 보장법」 제8조에 따른 퇴직금을 산정할 때 적용할 평균임금은 제1항부터 제3항까지의 규정에 따라 조정된 평균임금으로 한다.

4. 평균임금 포함여부

1) 식대가 정기적 일률적으로 지급되는 한, 그것을 근로제공과 무관한 단순한 복지후생이거나 은혜적인 급부라 할 수 없으므로 근로 대가로서의 임금의 성질을 지닌 것으로 보아야 할 것이다.[88)]

2) 평균임금의 산정기초인 임금총액에는 사용자가 근로의 대상으로 근로자에게 지급하는 일체의 금품으로서 근로자에게 계속적·정기적으로 지급되고 단체협약, 취업규칙 등에 의하여 사용자에게 그 지급의무가 지워져 있는 것이면 그 명칭이 어떠하든 모두 포함된다 할 것이므로, 휴일근로수당이 이에 포함됨은 당연하다.[89)]

3) 연장근로수당은 임의적·은혜적으로 지급된 급여라 할 수 없고 그 명칭을 불문하고 근로의 대상으로서 사용자에게 지급의무가 발생하는 임금이라고 할 것이므로, 퇴직금 산정의 기초인 평균임금에 연장근로수당도 포함된다.[90)]

---

88) 대법원 2001.5.15, 2001도1186.

89) 대법원 1992.4.14, 91다 5587.

90) 서울중앙지법 2005.5.26, 2005나175.

4) As incentive bonuses, special bonuses, or production incentives have been determined at the discretion of the employer for their payment, payment rate, and payment period, they are not designated average wage.[91)] In cases where an incentive bonus satisfies some specific conditions, it can be admitted as wage and shall also be included into the calculation of average wage. Otherwise, it shall be considered as a form of the employer's praise or favorable reward, which then denies it the character of wage and therefore excluding it from the calculation of average wage. If the company did not regulate in the CBA or rules of employment any payment of incentive bonuses, special bonuses or production incentives, but determined them at the employer's discretion according to business performance, then, unless the habitual practice for payment was settled, such remuneration shall be denied as having the character of wage.

However, if the incentive bonuses were to be included in the average wage, according to the CBA or rules of employment, in cases where the company calculates average wage for severance pay and an unused annual leave allowance or, despite the absence of specific regulation, if the company has repeatedly included incentive bonuses in the calculation of average wage for severance pay for a long time, this common business practice may be deemed working conditions. In cases where the employer wishes to unfavorably change the working conditions admitted as habitual practice, the company must go through the proper procedure required to unfavorably revise the rules of employment.

5. wage paid irregularly for periods exceeding 3 months

(1) Bonuses

There are no regulations stipulated in labor law about matters concerning payment of bonuses, but bonuses shall be deemed wage as remuneration for work when they are stipulated in the rules of employment for payment conditions, amount, and payment period, or when they have been paid so habitually to all employees that the employee may have natural expectations to receive a bonus as a matter of course. On the other hand, in cases where the payment rate of bonuses was established per year-unit and paid for the period exceeding one month, the total amount of bonus paid for a certain month shall not be included into calculation of average wage. The bonuses shall be calculated by dividing the

91) MOEL Guidelines: Labor Standard 1758, Mar. 25, 2005.

4) 경영성과급, 특별상여금 및 생산장려금 등의 지급여부·지급률·지급시기 등이 대표이사에 의해 임의적으로 결정되어 왔다면 평균임금에 해당되지 않는다.[91] 성과급적 특별상여금의 경우에도 요건이 충족될 때에 임금성이 인정될 수 있으며, 평균임금 산정 시에도 포함되어야 할 것이나, 그렇지 못한 경우에는 이는 사업주의 포상적·은혜적 급부로 보아야 할 것으로 임금성이 부인되므로 평균임금 산정 시 제외될 수 있을 것이다.

회사가 경영성과급, 특별상여금 및 생산장려금 등의 지급에 대하여 단체협약이나 취업규칙 등에 전혀 정한 바가 없고, 지급여부·지급률·지급시기 등이 경영성과에 따라 대표이사에 의해 임의적으로 결정되어 왔으며, 지급관행이 생겼다고 보기도 어려운 경우에는 임금성이 부인될 수 있을 것이다. 그러나 회사의 단체협약 및 취업규칙 등에 퇴직금 및 연차휴가수당 지급을 위한 평균임금 산정 시 이러한 경영성과급 등을 포함하여 산정한다고 규정되어 있거나, 명시적인 규정은 없더라도 경영성과급 등을 포함하여 산정한 퇴직금 등의 지급이 장기간 반복됨으로써 노사 당사자 간에 관행으로 형성되어 사용자에게 지급의무가 있다고 여겨질 수 있을 경우에는 이러한 관행은 근로조건화 되었다고 할 수 있을 것이며, 관행화된 근로조건을 불이익하게 변경하고자 할 경우에는 취업규칙 불이익 변경절차를 거쳐야 할 것으로 사료된다.

5. 3개월의 초과하는 기간에 지급한 임금

(1) 상여금

상여금의 지급 등에 대하여는 노동관계법에 별도 규정되어 있지 아니하나, 취업규칙 등에 지급조건, 금액, 지급시기가 정해져 있거나 전 근로자에게 관례적으로 지급하여 사회통념상 근로자가 당연히 지급 받을 수 있다는 기대를 갖게 되는 경우에는 근로의 대상성을 갖는 임금으로 보고 있다. 한편 상여금의 지급률을 연간단위로 설정하여 1개월을 넘는 단위로 지급하고 있는 경우에

91) 행정해석: 근로기준과-1758, 2005.3.25.

total amount of bonuses paid to a relevant employee during the twelve calendar months before the day on which a cause for calculating his average wage occurred by the total number of calendar months, which is 3/12 times the total amount of bonuses paid per year.[92)]

(2) Whether to include annual paid leave allowance into average wage to calculate severance pay

1) Unused annual paid leave allowance already occurring before retirement

By the criteria of attendance rate during the year prior to the retirement year, 3/12 of the unused annual paid leave allowance of annual paid leave occurring the year prior to the retirement year shall be included into "the basic wage items to calculate average wage for severance pay."

2) Unused annual paid leave allowance occurring only because of retirement

The unused annual paid leave allowance that the employee is granted just because of retirement in the retirement year according to attendance rate of the year before the retirement year shall not be included into "the basic wage items to calculate average wage for severance pay," because the unused annual paid leave allowance is not wages paid during the calculation of average wage.

6. The period for calculation of average wage

(1) Calculation of average wage during periods of leave[93)]

Average wage where an employee resigned after a period of leave from work that the employee took with approval from the employer due to non-occupational injury, illness or other reason shall be calculated as follows: average wage to calculate severance pay refers to the amount calculated by dividing the total amount of wages paid to the relevant employee during three calendar months prior to the date of calculation by the total number of calendar days during those three calendar months(Article 2 of the LSA). If the amount calculated by this method is lower than the ordinary wage of the employee concerned, the ordinary wage shall be deemed as average wage. In cases where the period of calculating average wage includes the period falling

---

92) MOEL Guidelines: wage 68207-120, on Feb. 24, 2006.

93) MOEL Guidelines: Retirement Pension Dept-518, on Oct. 21, 2008.

는 이를 지급 받은 그 월의 임금으로 취급하여 일시에 전액을 평균임금에 산입하는 것이 아니며, 평균임금을 산정하여야 할 사유가 발생한 날 이전 12개월의 기간 동안에 지급 받은 상여금 전액을 그 기간 동안의 근로월수로 분할계산하여 즉, 3/12을 평균임금산정 기준 임금총액에 산입한다.[92)]

(2) 연차유급휴가수당의 퇴직금 산정을 위한 평균임금 포함여부

1) 퇴직하기 전 이미 발생한 연차유급휴가 미사용수당

퇴직 전전년도 출근율에 의하여 퇴직 전년도에 발생한 연차유급휴가 중 미사용하고 근로한 일수에 대한 연차유급휴가 미사용수당액의 3/12을 "퇴직금 산정을 위한 평균임금 산정 기준임금"에 포함한다.

2) 퇴직으로 인해 비로소 지급사유가 발생한 연차유급휴가 미사용수당

퇴직 전년도 출근율에 의하여 퇴직년도에 발생한 연차유급휴가를 미사용하고 퇴직함으로써 비로소 지급사유가 발생한 연차유급휴가 미사용수당은 평균임금의 정의상 산정사유 발생일 이전에 그 근로자에 대하여 지급된 임금이 아니므로 "퇴직금 산정을 위한 평균임금 산정 기준임금"에 포함되지 아니한다.

6. 평균임금 산정대상기간

(1) 휴직기간의 평균임금 산정[93)]

업무 외 부상이나 질병, 그 밖의 사유로 사용자의 승인을 받아 휴업한 후 퇴직하게 된 경우에 평균임금을 다음과 같이 계산한다. 퇴직금 산정을 위한 평균임금은 이를 산정하여야 할 사유가 발생한 날 이전 3개월 동안에 그 근로자에게 지급된 임금의 총액을 그 기간의 총 일수로 나눈 금액을 말하며(「근로기준법」 제2조), 이러한 방법으로 산출된 평균임금액이 당해 근로자의 통상임금보다 적은 금액일 경우에는 그 통상임금을 평균임금으로 하도록 정하고 있다. 평균임

92) 행정해석: 임금 68207-120, 2006. 2. 24.

93) 행정해석: 퇴직연금복지과-518, 2008.10.21.

under a period of leave from work with approval from the employer caused by non-occupational injury, illness, or other reason, the period and wages paid for that period shall be deducted respectively from a basis period for the calculation of average wage and the total amount of average wage(Article 2 of the Enforcement Decree to the LSA).

Therefore, in cases where an employee took a leave of absence for non-occupational injury, illness or other reason in accordance with Article 2(8) of the Enforcement Decree to the LSA(with approval from the employer), the remaining period and wages excluding the leave of absence shall be used for the calculation of average wages. If the leave of absence exceeds three months, the first day of the leave of absence shall be the date for calculating average wages based on the previous three months. In any case, if the amount calculated above is lower than the ordinary wage of the employee concerned, the ordinary wage shall be deemed as average wage.

(2) A period of suspension from office in calculating average wage[94)]

In this case, the criteria for calculating average wages shall be decided upon whether the suspension from office is justifiable or not. If the suspension from office is justifiable, the suspension period and the wages paid during the suspension period shall be included in the total period and amount of wages respectively in calculating average wages, provided that, when the amount calculated for average wage is lower than the ordinary wage of the employee concerned, the ordinary wage shall be deemed average wage. If the suspension from office is unjustifiable, it is legitimate that the suspension period and the wages paid for the suspension period shall be deducted respectively from a basis period for the calculation of average wage and the total amount of average wage according to Article 2(8) of the Enforcement Decree to the LSA.

(3) Calculation of average wage for a full-time officer in the labor union.[95)]

In cases where a full-time union officer, who is engaged exclusively in affairs of the labor union and does not provide labor service, resigns from the company at the same time as his union service period expires, the initial day(last day of wage payment) of the labor union's full-time officer for calculating average wages shall be considered the "date on which a cause for calculating his average wage occurred," unless there is a special agreement to the contrary.[96)]

94) MOEL Guidelines: Wage 68207-562, Jul. 16, 2003

95) MOEL Guidelines: Wage 68207-317.

96) MOEL Guidelines: Wage 68207-545.

금 산정기간 중에 업무상외 부상 또는 질병으로 사용자의 승인을 받아 휴업한 경우에는 그 기간과 그 기간에 지불된 임금은 평균임금 산정기준이 되는 기간과 임금의 총액에서 각각 공제하도록 규정하고 있다(근로기준법시행령 제2조).

따라서 근로자가 업무 외 부상이나 질병, 그 밖의 사유로 사용자의 승인을 받아 휴업한 기간일 경우에는 동기간을 제외한 나머지 일수 및 임금을 대상으로 평균임금으로 산정하여야 하며, 휴직한 기간이 3개월을 초과하여 평균임금 산정기준기간이 없게 되는 경우에는 휴직한 첫날을 평균임금산정 사유발생일로 보아 이전 3월간을 대상으로 평균임금을 산정하여야 한다. 아울러, 위와 같은 방법으로 산출된 평균임금액이 당해 근로자의 통상임금보다 작은 액수일 경우에는 그 통상임금액을 평균임금으로 하여야 한다.

(2) 대기발령 기간의 평균임금 산정[94)]

평균임금 산정기준은 대기발령의 정당성 여부에 따라 달리 보아야 한다. 대기발령이 정당한 처분이라면 그 기간과 그 기간 중에 지불된 임금은 평균임금 산정기준이 되는 기간과 임금의 총액에 각각 포함하여 평균임금을 산정하고, 다만, 평균임금이 통상임금보다 저액일 경우에는 그 통상임금액을 평균임금으로 보아야 한다. 부당한 처분이라면 이를 근로기준법 시행령 제2조 제1항 제8호에 준하는 것으로 보아 그 기간과 그 기간 동안에 지급받은 임금을 평균임금 산정기준이 되는 기간과 임금의 총액에서 각각 공제하는 것이 타당하다.

(3) 노조 전임자의 평균임금 산정[95)]

먼저 사업장에 근로를 제공하지 않고 노동조합업무만을 수행한 노동조합 전임자가 전임기간 만료와 동시에 퇴직하는 경우에 있어서 평균임금은 이에 대한 노사 간의 정함이 없는 한 노동조합 전임을 개시한 날(최종 임금지급일)을 “평균임금을 산정하여야 할 사유가 발생한 날”로 본다.[96)]

---

94) 행정해석: 2003.7.16, 임금 68207-562.

95) 행정해석: 2001.5.3, 임금 68207-317.

96) 행정해석: 1994.9.7, 임금 68207-545.

V. Minimum Wage

1. Concept

The minimum wage system is the nation intervening in the decision-making process between employer and employee, designed to protect employees earning low wage by stipulating and legally requiring employers to pay minimum wage levels or higher. The minimum wage is determined annually on the 5th of August by the Minimum Wage Council, which is composed of 9 representatives from each of the following groups: labor, management, and government. The minimum wage they determine is effective from January 1 to December 31 of the following year. The minimum wage mainly influences small and medium-sized companies who employ low-income workers such as guards, janitors, migrant workers, etc., and this directly affects the process of making decisions on salary.[97)]

The increase in minimum wage is the most desirable way to reduce the difference in wage between regular and irregular employees, but a great change is expected for SMEs and small-scale service companies that are unable to pay the minimum wage. According to the current minimum wage system in Korea, one minimum wage is applied at all workplaces, without distinction as to the type of industry or region, and all employers are obligated to pay at least the minimum wage.

Employers can pay more than the minimum wage, but parts of employment contracts that stipulate a wage lower than the minimum wage shall be invalid, with the difference to be paid additionally. Employers shall be punished for violations with imprisonment of up to three years or a fine not exceeding KRW 20 million.[98)]

In the following, I will explain the employer's obligations, the criteria for determining violations of minimum wage, calculation of hourly wage for minimum wage, and the practical applications thereof.

---

97) Jung, Bongsoo, "Minimum Wage and the Employer's Obligations", 「Labor Law」, Jungang, December 2013.

98) The Minimum Wage Act, Article 6 and 28.

Ⅴ. 최저임금

1. 최저임금의 의의[97)]

최저임금제란 국가가 노사 간의 임금결정 과정에 개입하여 임금의 최저수준을 정하고, 사용자에게 이 수준 이상의 임금을 지급하도록 법으로 강제하여 저임금 근로자를 보호하는 제도이다. 최저임금은 각 9인의 노·사·공익 대표로 구성(총 27인)된 최저임금위원회에서 매년 8월 5일까지 결정하고, 다음 연도 1월 1일부터 12월 31일까지 적용된다. 최저임금은 주로 저임금 근로자를 사용하는 중소기업 사업장에 많은 영향을 가져오며, 저임금 근로자인 경비원, 청소원, 외국인 노동자 등의 임금결정에 직접적인 결과를 가져온다.

최저임금의 인상은 정규직과 비정규직의 임금수준 차이를 줄일 수 있는 가장 바람직한 방법이지만, 최저임금을 지급하기 어려운 중소기업이나 소규모 서비스업의 경우에 매우 큰 변화가 예상되고 있다. 우리나라의 현행 최저임금제도에 의하면 모든 사업장에서 업종이나 지역의 구분 없이 하나의 최저임금만 적용되고, 사용자는 최저임금액 이상 지급해야 할 의무를 진다.

우리나라의 현행 최저임금제도에 의하면 모든 사업장에서 업종이나 지역의 구분 없이 하나의 최저임금만 적용되고, 사용자는 최저임금액 이상 지급해야 할 의무를 진다. 최저임금은 근로자에 대하여 임금의 최저수준을 보장하는 제도이므로 사용자는 최저임금액 이상을 지급하여야 하고, 최저임금액에 미달하는 임금을 정한 근로계약은 그 부분에 한하여 무효로 하며, 무효로 된 부분에 있어 최저임금을 지급하여야 한다. 이를 위반한 경우 3년 이하의 징역 또는 2천만원 이하의 벌금에 처한다.[98)]

아래에서는 최저임금의 적용에서 사업주의 의무, 최저임금의 위반여부, 판단기준, 최저임금의 시간급 계산을 살펴보고, 구체적 최저임금 적용사례를 살펴보고자 한다.

---

97) 정봉수, “최저임금과 사업주의 의무”, 「월간 노동법률」, 중앙경제사, 2017.8.
98) 최저임금법 제6조, 28조.

(1) Scope of application

The minimum wage shall apply to all businesses or workplaces.

1) Deduction from application of minimum wage: a 10% deduction is applicable for a person who is still in a probationary employment period and three months have not passed from the beginning of employment.

2) Exclusion from application of minimum wage: ① a person who has remarkably low abilities to work due to a mental or physical handicap and for whom the employer has obtained approval from the Ministry of Employment & Labor; ② any business using only relatives living together, ③ those hired for household work, and ④ seamen who are subject to the Seaman Act, or ship owners employing such seamen.

(2) Minimum wage and employer obligations

The minimum wage system guarantees the minimum amount of hourly wage for employees. An employer can pay more than the minimum wage, but the part of an employment contract stipulating a wage which is less than the minimum wage shall be invalid, and any missing amount from the minimum wage must be paid additionally. For violations, the employer shall be punished by imprisonment for up to three years or a fine not exceeding KRW 20 million(Articles 6 and 28 of the Minimum Wage Act). In addition, when a minimum wage is announced, the employer shall inform employees of ① the new minimum wage rate, ② the scope of wages excluded from application of minimum wage, and ③ the effective date. This notice must be posted in places where it can easily be seen by all employees, or through other appropriate methods. For violations of this, the employer shall be punished by a fine up to KRW 1 million(Articles 11 and 31 of the Act). Exceptions to the application of minimum wage are those to whom any of the following subparagraphs apply and for whom the employer obtains permission from the Minister of Employment and Labor: ① A person who has remarkably low abilities to work due to a mental or physical handicap and ② Other people as deemed inappropriate for application of the minimum wage.[99)]

1) Obligation to give notice

When the minimum wage is announced, the employer shall inform employees of ① the minimum wage rate, ② scope of wage excluded from application of minimum wage, and ③

---

99) The Minimum Wage Act, Article 7 (Exclusion from Application of Minimum Wage)

(1) 최저임금 적용범위

근로자를 사용하는 모든 사업 또는 사업장에 적용된다.

1) 감액적용대상은 수습사용 중에 있는 자로서 수습사용 한날부터 3월 이내인 자는 10% 감액 적용이 가능하다.

2) 적용제외 대상은 ① 정신 또는 신체의 장애로 근로능력이 현저히 낮은 자로서 사용자가 고용노동부 장관 인가를 받은 자, ② 동거하는 친족만을 사용하는 사업의 종사자, ③ 가사사용인, ④ 선원법의 적용을 받는 선원 및 선원을 사용하는 선박의 소유자

(2) 최저임금과 관련 사업주 의무

최저임금은 근로자에 대하여 임금의 최저수준을 보장하는 제도이므로 사용자는 최저임금액 이상을 지급하여야 하고, 최저임금액에 미달하는 임금을 정한 근로계약은 그 부분에 한하여 무효로 하며, 무효로 된 부분에 있어 최저임금액과의 차액의 임금을 추가적으로 지급하여야 한다. 이를 위반한 경우 3년 이하의 징역 또는 2천만원 이하의 벌금에 처한다(최저임금법 제6조, 28조). 또한, 사용자는 최저임금이 고시되면 최저임금액, 최저임금에 산입하지 않는 임금의 범위, 효력발생일 등에 관하여 근로자들이 쉽게 볼 수 있는 장소에 게시하거나 그 외의 적당한 방법으로 근로자에게 주지시켜야 한다. 이를 위반한 경우 100만원 이하의 과태료가 부과된다(동법 제11조, 31조). 최저임금의 적용에 예외는 ① 정신장애나 신체장애로 근로능력이 현저히 낮은 자와 ② 그밖에 최저임금을 적용하는 것이 적당하지 아니하다고 인정되는 자로 고용노동부 장관의 승인을 받은 자이다.[99)]

1) 사용자의 주지의무

사용자는 최저임금이 고시되면 ① 최저임금액, ② 최저임금에 산입하지 않는 임금의 범위, ③ 효력발생일 등에 관하여 근로자들이 쉽게 볼 수 있는 장소에 게시하거나 그 외의 적당한 방법으로 근로자에게 주지시켜야 한다.

---

99) 최저임금법 제7조(최저임금의 적용제외).

effective date. This notice must be posted in places where it can easily be seen by employees, or through other appropriate methods.

2) Obligation to pay minimum wage

An employer shall pay the minimum wage in full to employees covered by the minimum wage rules. If a labor contract between an employer and employee provides for a wage that is less than the minimum wage rate, such provision shall be null and void and the invalidated provision regarded as stipulating that the same wage as the minimum wage rate shall be paid.

3) Joint liability for contractor

In the event that a project is carried out under contract, if the contractee has paid its employees wages lower than the minimum wage rate for reasons for which the contractor is liable, the contractor, along with the contractee, shall take joint liability. The reasons a contractor will be considered liable are ① a contractor's act of determining unit labor costs lower than the minimum wage rate at the time of contract signing; and 2) a contractor's act of lowering unit labor costs to below the minimum wage rate in the middle of the contract period.

4) Supplement allowance due to reduced contractual working hours

Even though the contractual working hours are reduced due to the Labor Standards Act(Article 50), the employer cannot lower the previously paid wage subject to the minimum wage without justifiable reason. If the salary paid after reducing contractual working hours is less than the amount paid before working hours were reduced, a supplemental allowance shall be paid.

5) Penal provisions for violation of the minimum wage level

① Imprisonment of up to three years or a fine not exceeding 20 million won

- paying lower than the minimum wage rate
- lowering the previous wages on grounds of the minimum wage, according to the Minimum Wage Act
- failure to pay the required supplement allowance if reduced contractual working hours result in reduced wages

② Fine not exceeding 1 million won

- failure to inform employees of the minimum wage announced by decision of the Minister of Employment and Labor

2) 최저임금의 지급의무

사용자는 최저임금의 적용을 받는 근로자에 대하여 최저임금액 이상을 지급하여야 한다. 최저임금액에 미달하는 임금을 정한 근로계약은 그 부분에 한하여 이를 무효로 하며, 무효로 된 부분은 최저임금액과 동일한 임금을 지급하기로 한 것으로 간주된다.

3) 도급사업자의 연대책임

도급으로 사업을 행하는 경우 수급인이 도급인의 책임 있는 사유로 근로자에게 최저임금액에 미달하는 임금을 지급한 때는 도급인은 해당 수급인과 연대하여 책임을 진다. 그 책임있는 사유의 범위는 ① 도급인이 도급계약의 체결 당시 인건비 단가를 최저임금액에 미치지 못하는 금액으로 결정하는 행위, ② 도급인이 도급계약 기간 중 인건비 단가를 최저임금액에 미치지 못하는 금액으로 결정하는 행위

4) 근로시간 단축에 따른 임금보전

사용자는 강행규정에 의해 근로시간(근로기준법 제50조)의 소정근로시간이 단축되는 경우라도 정당한 사유 없이 최저임금의 적용대상이 되는 임금을 단축 전 금액보다 낮출 수 없다. 이 경우, 단축 전 소정근로시간으로 산정한 최저임금액과 단축 후의 소정근로시간으로 산정한 최저임금액(최저임금액 인상분 포함)을 비교하여 적은 경우에만 임금보전을 한다.

5) 최저임금법 위반의 벌칙

① 3년 이하의 징역 또는 2천만 이하의 벌금
- 근로자에 대하여 최저임금액 이상의 임금을 지급하지 아니한 경우
- '최저임금법'에 의한 최저임금을 이유로 종전의 임금수준을 저하시키는 경우
- 근로시간 단축에 따른 임금보전을 행하지 않는 경우

② 100만원 이하의 과태료
- 노동부장관이 결정 고시한 최저임금액 등을 근로자에게 주지시키지 않은 경우

2. Criteria for Determining Violations of Minimum Wage Law

To determine whether the wage paid by a workplace are less than the minimum wage, ① the total wage included in the minimum wage from the wage paid monthly ② will be divided by the monthly contractual working hours, and then hourly minimum wage calculated, and ③ then the amount will be compared with the current minimum wage.[100)]

The scope of wage to be included in calculation of minimum wage according to the Minimum Wage Act includes ① wage or allowances to be paid according to wage items stipulated in a collective agreement, the rules of employment, and/or an employment contract, or repeated regular payments; and ② wage or allowances to be paid periodically or in a lump sum once or more every month for contractual labor according to previously agreed-upon payment conditions and payment rate(Article 2 of the Enforcement Decree to the Act(Table 2)).

The range of wages not included in the minimum wage (as specified in Appendix 1, Article 2 of the Enforcement Rules of the Minimum Wage Act) is as follows.

(1) wage, other than those paid regularly once or more every month

1) Diligence allowances paid for superior attendance over periods exceeding one month;

2) Length of service allowances paid for continuous work over periods exceeding one month;

3) Incentives, efficiency allowances, or bonuses presented for various reasons over periods exceeding one month; and

4) Other allowances paid temporarily or incidentally, such as marriage allowances, winter fuel allowances, kimchi allowances, exercise subsidies, etc., and which have no fixed payment date or are irregularly paid, even though payment conditions were determined in advance.

(2) wage, other than those paid for contractual working hours or contractual working days

1) Annual or monthly paid allowances, work allowance on paid leave, work allowance on paid holidays;

2) wage and additional allowances for extended work or holiday work;

3) Additional allowances for night work;

4) Day & night-duty allowances; and

---

100) Supreme Court ruling on Jun. 29, 2007 2004 da 48836 (Calculation of minimum wage).

2. 최저임금의 위반여부 판단기준

사업장에서 지급하는 임금이 최저임금 위반인지 여부를 판단하기 위해서는 ① 월 단위로 지급받는 임금에서 최저임금에 포함되는 임금 총액을, ② 월 소정 근로시간으로 나누어 시간당 임금으로 환산해, ③ 고시된 최저임금과 비교하여야 한다.[100)]

최저임금 산정 시 포함되는 임금 범위는 ① 단체협약·취업규칙 또는 근로계약에 임금항목으로서 지급근거가 명시되어 있거나 관례에 따라 지급하는 임금 또는 수당 ② 미리 정해진 지급조건과 지급률에 따라 소정근로에 대하여 매월 1회 이상 정기적·일률적으로 지급하는 임금 또는 수당이다(동법 시행규칙 제2조 별표2).

최저임금에 포함되지 않는 임금의 범위(동법 시행규칙 제2조 별표1)는 다음과 같다.

(1) 매월 1회 이상 정기적으로 지급하는 임금 외의 임금

1) 1월을 초과하는 기간의 출근성적에 의하여 지급하는 정근수당,

2) 1월을 초과하는 일정기간의 계속근무에 대하여 지급하는 근속수당,

3) 1월을 초과하는 기간에 걸친 사유에 의하여 산정하는 장려수당, 능률수당 또는 상여금,

4) 기타 결혼수당, 월동수당, 김장수당, 체력단련비 등 임시 또는 돌발적인 사유에 따라 지급하거나, 지급조건이 사전에 정해진 경우에도 그 사유 발생일이 확정되지 아니하거나 불규칙적인 임금·수당이 이에 해당된다.

(2) 소정의 근로시간 또는 소정의 근로일에 대하여 지급하는 임금외의 임금

1) 연·월차휴가 근로수당, 유급휴가 근로수당, 유급휴일 근로수당,

2) 연장시간 근로, 휴일근로에 대한 임금 및 가산임금,

3) 야간근로에 대한 가산임금,

4) 일·숙직수당,

---

100) 대법원 2007.6.29, 2004다48836(최저임금 계산).

5) wage not admitted to be paid for a contractual working day, regardless of how such payments are termed.

(3) Other wage deemed inappropriate to be included in the minimum wage

Actual or similar expenses to support employee welfare such as meals, dormitory accommodation or other housing, company shuttle buses, etc.

3. Hourly Wage Calculation for the Minimum Wage

The minimum wage shall be determined in units of hours, days, weeks, or months. When determining the minimum wage in units of days, weeks or months, the hourly wage shall also be indicated. The hourly wage determined for a month shall be the monthly amount divided by the number of contractual working hours in one month. In order to calculate the hourly wage of the monthly wage, the amount of the wage divided by the number of working hours per month becomes the hourly minimum wage(Article 5 of the Act, Article 5 of its Enforcement Decree). The prescribed working time of one month includes paid weekly holiday allowances(Article 55 of the Labor Standards Act) and paid allowances on off-days according to a collective agreement. The related court ruling and administrative interpretations are as follows:

(1) Court ruling

The court ruling for the contractual working hours per month is that "Article 5 of the Enforcement Decree to the Minimum Wage Act stipulates that the wage paid on a weekly or monthly basis shall be wage divided by the number of contractual working hours per week or month. The so-called 'weekly holiday allowance', which is a wage for a paid holiday, is regularly paid at least once a month for given work. Therefore, this regularly paid weekly holiday allowance shall be included in the wage calculation."[101] In a sample case of 40 hours per week, there are 209 contractual working hours for the month, including the weekly holiday allowance.

---

101) Supreme Court ruling on Jan. 11, 2007, 2006 da 64245 (Case related to minimum wage)

5) 기타 명칭여하에 관계없이 소정근로에 대하여 지급하는 임금이라고 인정할 수 없는 임금이 이에 해당된다.

(3) 기타 최저임금액에 산입하는 것이 적당하지 아니한 임금

식사, 기숙사, 주택제공, 통근차 운행 등 현물이나 이와 유사한 형태로 지급되는 급여 등 근로자의 복리후생을 위한 성질의 것이 이에 해당된다.

3. 최저임금의 시간급 계산

최저임금액은 시간·일(日)·주(週) 또는 월(月)을 단위로 하여 정한다. 이 경우 일·주 또는 월을 단위로 하여 최저임금액을 정할 때는 시간급으로도 표시하여야 한다. 월(月) 단위로 정해진 임금은 그 금액을 1개월의 소정근로시간 수로 나눈 금액으로 한다. 월 임금의 최저임금을 계산하기 위해서는 월 단위의 최저임금에 포함되는 임금을 1개월의 소정근로시간 수로 나눈 금액이 시간급 최저임금이 된다(최저임금법 제5조, 시행령 제5조). 1개월의 소정근로시간은 유급주휴수당(근로기준법 제55조)과 단체협약 등에서 유급으로 처리된 유급수당도 포함한다. 관련한 판례와 행정해석은 다음과 같다.

(1) 판 례

1개월의 소정근로시간 수에 대해 판례는 “최저임금법 시행령 제5조는 주 단위 또는 월 단위로 지급된 임금에 대하여 ‘1주 또는 1월의 소정근로시간 수’로 나눈 금액을 시급으로 규정하고 있는바, 주급제 혹은 월급제에서 지급되는 유급휴일에 대한 임금인 이른바 주휴수당은 소정근로에 대해 매월 1회 이상 정기적으로 지급되는 임금이라 할 것이어서 비교대상 임금을 산정함에 있어 주휴수당을 가산하여야 한다”고 판시하고 있다.[101] 이 경우 주 40시간의 경우 주휴수당을 포함하여 월의 소정근로시간은 209시간이 된다.

---

101) 대법원 2007.1.11, 2006다64245(최저임금 관련 사건).

(2) MOEL Guidelines

According to Article 5-2 of the Minimum Wage Act and Article 5 of the Enforcement Decree to the same Act regarding wage for application of the minimum wage, the monthly wage prescribed for a monthly period shall be the wage divided by the number of contractual working hours per month. In a workplace that conducts a 40-hour workweek each month, "if 8 hours of Saturday work are treated as paid working hours" even though there is no work duty provided on this Saturday, the number of hours worked in a month for the application of the minimum wage is calculated as 243 hours including paid weekly holiday allowance [{40 hours + 8 hours(Saturday paid work) + 8 hours(paid weekly holiday)} × 365/7 ÷ 12 ≒ 243 hours].[102)]

(3) Practical applications of the minimum wage

1) Quarterly incentives, meal charges and vehicle maintenance expenses

① Quarterly incentives shall not be considered part of the minimum wage.

② The "meal charge(food expenses)" is paid regularly and uniformly to all employees on a monthly basis in accordance with the collective agreement and the rules of employment, and so it is decided to include these in the ordinary wage in the rules of employment. Meal charges are included as wage for the application of minimum wage. A "vehicle management fee" is paid to the driving worker at least once a month in accordance with predetermined payment conditions and is understood as a duty or service allowance for the specific worker, and can therefore be included as wage for the application of minimum wage.[103)]

2) Bonuses and sales bonuses

① Bonuses calculated on a yearly basis and regular bonuses

In cases where a bonus is paid equally each month, after it is calculated and fixed for the yearly period, this monthly bonus is included in the minimum wage.

② Sales bonus (based on results)

The sales bonus, for which the monthly amount varies according to the sales results of the individual salesperson, is equivalent to a wage, in accordance with the sales incentive bonus

---

102) MOEL Guidelines on Aug. 21, 2004, Wage Policy-3074; Dec. 21, 2009, Labor Standards-5970.

103) MOEL Guidelines on Dec. 15, 2010 Wage Welfare-2356

(2) 행정해석

최저임금의 적용을 위한 임금의 환산방법에 대하여 「최저임금법」 제5조의2 및 같은 법 시행령 제5조의 규정에 의하면 월 단위로 정해진 임금에 대하여는 그 금액을 1월의 소정근로시간수로 나눈 금액을 시간에 대한 임금으로 환산하고 있다. 1주 40시간제를 실시하는 사업장에서 당초 근로제공 의무가 없는 '토요일의 8시간을 유급처리하는 경우'에 최저임금 적용을 위한 1월의 환산 근로시간 수는 매주 유급처리되는 8시간을 합하여 월 243시간[{40시간+8시간(토요일 유급처리분) + 8시간 (유급 주휴)} × 365/7÷12 ≒ 243시간]을 적용한다.[102]

(3) 구체적 최저임금 적용사례

1) 분기성과급, 식대, 차량관리비

① 분기성과급은 최저임금 산입을 위한 임금에 포함되지 않는다.

② "식비(식대)"는 단체협약 및 취업규칙에 따라 전 근로자에게 매월 정기적·일률적으로 지급하면서 취업규칙에서 통상임금으로 포함하기로 정하였다면 최저임금에 산입되는 임금이다. "차량관리비"는 운전근로자에 한하여 미리 정하여진 지급조건에 따라 일률적으로 매월 1회 이상 정기적으로 지급하고 있다면 이는 특정 업무 종사자에 대한 직무수당 또는 운행수당 등의 성격으로 이해되므로 최저임금 산입을 위한 임금에 포함된다.[103]

2) 상여금 및 판매수당(생산고)

① 1년 단위 산정 상여금, 정기상여금

상여금의 산정기간이 연간단위로 계산하여 월로 분할하여 균등하게 지급되는 경우에는 최저임금에 포함된다.

② 판매수당(실적에 의한 수당)

영업사원의 판매실적에 따라 매월 금액이 달라지는 판매수당은 「최저임금법

102) 행정해석: 임금정책과-3074, 2004.8.21; 근로기준과-5970, 2009.12.28.
103) 행정해석: 임금복지과-2356, 2010.12.15.

set forth in Article 5(2) of the Enforcement Decree to the Minimum Wage Act. Therefore, Article 5-2 of the Minimum Wage Act stipulates that the sum of the monthly sales bonus divided by the total number of working hours per month and the monthly salary divided by the number of working hours per month shall be included in the minimum wage.[104)]

In cases where a fitness trainer carries out individual fitness training for a member, if the trainer receives an additional fee according to a predetermined payment condition and payment rate, such fee can be considered equivalent to a sales bonus and included in the minimum wage. Such sales bonus is calculated into hourly wage after it is divided by monthly contractual working hours; the wage determined in monthly units, such as the basic wage, is also divided by monthly contractual working hours. The sum of both wage should be evaluated to determine whether it exceeds the minimum wage.[105)]

3) Welfare benefits

1) It is reasonable that a improvement bonus corresponding to money for welfare, such as an allowance which helps to improve the life of an employee is money which does not count in the minimum wage.[106)]

2) Even if a “welfare allowance” is included in regular wage, if it is explicitly stated in the collective agreement as a subsidy for living expenses or a benefit for welfare, according to Table 1 of Article 2 of the Enforcement Decree to the Minimum Wage Act, it shall be seen as a wage not included in application of the minimum wage in terms of welfare benefits.[107)]

4. Minimum Wage and Ordinary Wage

(1) Understanding the difference between minimum wage and ordinary wage

Calculation of the minimum wage is based upon the hourly minimum wage just like ordinary wage. The minimum wage includes all items inclusive of ordinary wage

104) MOEL Guidelines on Feb. 14, 2004 Wage Policy-501; Apr. 3, 1990 Wage 32240-4770; Oct. 2, 2005 Wage Policy-801; Jun. 20, 2003 Wage 68200-471

105) MOEL Guidelines on Oct. 2, 2015 Labor Standards-4782

106) MOEL Guidelines on Feb. 7, 2014 Labor Improvement-659

107) MOEL Guidelines on May 17, 1989 Wage 32240-7146

시행령」 제5조 제2항에서 정하고 있는 생산고에 따른 임금에 해당된다 할 것이므로「최저임금법」 제5조의2 및「최저임금법 시행령」 제5조 제3항에 의거 당해 월 총 근로시간수로 나눈 금액과 월 기본급을 월 소정근로 시간수로 나눈 금액을 합산한 후 당해 연도 최저임금과 비교하여 위반 여부를 판단해야 한다.[104)]

헬스 트레이너가 회원별 개인수업(PT) 업무를 맡아 수행할 경우, 미리 정하여진 지급조건과 지급률에 따라 추가적으로 수업료를 지급받고 있다면 이는 최저임금에 산입되는 생산고 임금에 해당된다고 볼 수 있으므로, 수업료는 총 근로시간으로 나눠 시간당 임금으로 환산한 뒤, 기본급 등 월 단위로 정해진 임금을 소정근로시간(유급으로 지급되는 주휴수당 등 포함)으로 나누어 환산한 시간당 임금과 합산하여 시간급 최저임금 미달 여부를 판단하여 한다.[105)]

3) 복리후생 수당

1) 근로자의 생활을 보조하는 수당 등 복리후생을 위한 금품에 해당하는 처우개선비는 최저임금에 산입하지 않는 임금으로 봄이 타당하다.[106)]

2) "복지수당"이 비록 통상임금에 포함되어 지급되고 있다 하더라도 단체협약 등에 명백하게 생계비보조 또는 복리후생적인 성격의 수당임을 명시하고 있다고 한다면 이는 최저임금법시행규칙 제2조 별표 1에서 규정하고 있는 복리후생적인 수당으로 보아 최저임금의 적용을 위한 임금에 산입하지 아니하는 임금으로 보아야 한다.[107)]

4. 최저임금과 통상임금

(1) 최저임금과 통상임금의 차이 이해

최저임금은 통상임금과 같이 시간급 최저임금을 기준으로 계산된다. 최저임금은

104) 행정해석: 임금정책과-501, 2004.2.14; 임금 32240-4770, 1990.4.3; 임금정책과-801, 2005.10.2; 임금 68200-471, 2003.6.20.

105) 행정해석: 근로기준정책과-4782, 2015.10.2.

106) 행정해석: 근로개선정책과-659, 2014.2.7.

107) 행정해석: 임금 32240-7146, 1989.5.17.

and is evaluated according to actual payments, but ordinary wage shall be the amount determined to be paid in the beginning as it is a base from which to calculate the overtime wage rate. This ordinary wage means wage determined to be paid periodically or in lump sums to the employee for contractual or whole labor. For a related example, an incentive wage due to production volume shall be included in minimum wage, but not included in ordinary wage.

(2) Differences from ordinary wage[108)]

Item	Ordinary wage	Minimum wage
Definition/ Purpose	Ordinary wage refers to hourly wage, daily wage, weekly wage, monthly wage, or contract wage which are determined to be paid periodically or in lump sum to a worker for their prescribed work or whole work (Article 6 of the Enforcement Decree to the Labor Standards Act).	The purpose of this Act is to bring stability to workers and improve labor force quality by guaranteeing a minimum level of wage (Article 1 of the Minimum Wage Act).
Calculation method	Calculated into hourly wage rate (Monthly ordinary wage ÷ monthly contractual working hours).	Calculated into hourly wage rate (Monthly minimum wage ÷ monthly contractual working hours).
Legal enforcement	No legal enforcement.	Legal enforcement, with cases of violation rendered invalid.
Usage	wage determined to be paid in advance; used for paid leave allowances.	wage actually paid; used for guaranteeing employee livelihood.
(i) Regular meal charge	Included in ordinary wage.	Included in minimum wage.
(ii) Performance bonus	1) Fixed bonuses are included in ordinary wage. 2) Performance bonuses are recognized as ordinary wage to the extent they are guaranteed to a minimum. 3) Sales bonuses are excluded.	1) Annual bonus payments are excluded. 2) Monthly bonuses are included in minimum wage. 3) Monthly performance bonuses are included in the minimum wage. 4) Sales bonuses are included in minimum wage.
(iii) Welfare allowance	Regular, uniform, and fixed welfare allowances are included.	Monthly regular, uniform, and fixed welfare allowances are included.

108) Supreme Court ruling on Jan. 11, 2007: 2006 da 64245; MOEL Guidelines on Jun 29, 2006 Wage and Working Hours 1539; MOEL Guidelines on Dec. 20, 2006 Wage and Working Hours 3848

통상임금이 포함되는 모든 항목이 포함되며, 사후적으로 지급하는 임금으로 평가되지만, 통상임금은 연장근로수당 등의 기초가 되므로 사전적으로 지급이 확정된 임금만을 말한다. 이 통상임금은 근로자에게 정기적이고 일률적으로 소정근로 또는 총 근로에 대하여 지급하기로 정하여진 금액을 말한다. 관련된 예로, 생산량에 따른 성과 임금은 최저임금의 산입범위에는 포함되나, 통상임금에는 포함되지 않는다.

(2) 통상임금과의 차이[108]

구 분	통상임금	최저임금
목 적	근로자에게 정기적이고 일률적으로 소정근로 또는 총 근로에 대하여 지급하기로 정한 시간급 금액, 일급 금액, 주급 금액, 월급 금액 또는 도급 금액을 말한다(근기법 시행령 제6조).	근로자에 대하여 임금의 최저수준을 보장하여 근로자의 생활안정과 노동력의 질적 향상을 꾀함을 목적으로 한다(최임법 제1조).
계산방법	시간급으로 계산 (월 통상임금 ÷ 월 소정근로시간)	시간급으로 계산 (월 최저임금 ÷ 월 소정근로시간)
법적강제여부	법적강제 없음	법적 강제 및 위반시 무효
사용용도	사전적 임금으로 유급수당 계산근거	사후적 임금으로 근로자의 생활보장
(i) 정기식대	통상임금 포함	최저임금 포함
(ii) 성과급	1) 고정상여금은 통상임금에 포함 2) 성과상여금은 최저한도로 보장되는 한도 내에서 통상임금 인정 3) 판매수당 미포함	1) 연단위 산정하여 매월 지급하는 상여금 제외됨. 2) 매월 산정단위 상여금 최저임금 포함. 3) 매월 단위 성과상여금 최저임금 포함 4) 생산고(판매수당)에 따른 임금 포함
(iii) 복지수당	정기적 일률적 고정적 복지수당 포함	월 단위 정기적 일률적 복지수당 포함

108) 대법원 2007.1.11, 2006다64245; 행정해석: 임금근로시간정책팀-1539, 2006.6.29; 임금근로시간정책팀-3848, 2006.12.20.

Ⅵ. Shutdown Allowances

1. Legal Standards for shutdown Allowances

(1) Concept

Article 46 of the LSA (Pay for Suspension of Business)

① If a business is suspended for reasons attributable to an employer, the employer shall pay the workers concerned a payment of seventy percent or more of average remuneration during the period of suspension. If the amount equivalent to seventy percent of average remuneration exceeds normal remuneration, then normal remuneration may be paid.
② An employer who cannot continue business operations for unavoidable reasons may, upon approval from the Labor Relations Commission, pay remuneration lower than the standards stipulated in paragraph ① for the suspension of business.

LSA Enforcement Decree, Article 26 (Calculation of Suspension Allowance)

Where an employee has received a part of wage during a period of suspension due to any reason attributable to the employer, the employer shall, in compliance with the main sentence of Article 46 (1) of the Act, pay him/her an allowance equivalent to at least 70 percent of the difference calculated by subtracting that part of wage already paid to the said employee from the average wage: Provided, That where ordinary wage are paid as suspension allowance in accordance with the proviso to Article 46 (1) of the Act, the difference between the ordinary wage and the part already paid during the period of suspension shall be paid.

LSA, Article 109 (Penal Provisions) Employers shall be punished for violations of the above Article 46 (Pay for Suspension of Business) with imprisonment of not more than 3 years or a fine of not more than KRW 30 million.

According to the Labor Standards Act, when a worker is suspended for reasons attributable to the employer, the employer is required to pay at least 70% of the average wage(or 100% of the ordinary wage)(Article 46(1)). However, if it is impossible to continue the business for unavoidable reasons, an amount that is less than the legal shutdown allowance may be paid if this is approved by the Labor Commission(Article 46(1)). In order to guarantee the effectiveness of the shutdown compensation system, an employer who violates the provisions of shutdown compensation shall be sentenced to imprisonment of not more than three years or fined not more than KRW 30 million(Article 109).

Shutdown allowances are intended to guarantee the right of workers to live by providing certain allowances when they are unable to work for reasons not attributable to them. On

Ⅵ. 휴업수당

1. 휴업수당의 법적 기준

(1) 의 의

근로기준법 제46조【휴업수당】
① 사용자의 귀책사유로 휴업하는 경우에 사용자는 휴업기간 동안 그 근로자에게 평균임금의 100분의 70 이상의 수당을 지급하여야 한다. 다만, 평균임금의 100분의 70에 해당하는 금액이 통상임금을 초과하는 경우에는 통상임금을 휴업수당으로 지급할 수 있다.
② 제1항에도 불구하고 부득이한 사유로 사업을 계속하는 것이 불가능하여 노동위원회의 승인을 받은 경우에는 제1항의 기준에 못 미치는 휴업수당을 지급할 수 있다.

근로기준법 시행령 제26조【휴업수당의 산출】
사용자의 귀책사유로 휴업한 기간 중에 근로자가 임금의 일부를 지급받은 경우에는 사용자는 법 제46조 제1항 본문에 따라 그 근로자에게 평균임금에서 그 지급받은 임금을 뺀 금액을 계산하여 그 금액의 100분의 70 이상에 해당하는 수당을 지급하여야 한다. 다만, 법 제46조 제1항 단서에 따라 통상임금을 휴업수당으로 지급하는 경우에는 통상임금에서 휴업한 기간 중에 지급받은 임금을 뺀 금액을 지급하여야 한다.

제109조【벌칙】 휴업수당 규정을 위반한 자(법 제46조)는 3년 이하의 징역 또는 3천만원 이하의 벌금에 처한다.

근로기준법에서는 사용자의 귀책사유로 휴업하는 경우에는 그 근로자에게 평균임금의 100분의 70% 이상의 수당(또는 통상임금의 100%)을 지급하여야 한다(제46조 제1항). 다만, 부득이한 사유로 사업을 계속하는 것이 불가능하여 노동위원회의 승인을 받은 경우에는 법정휴업수당에 미달하는 수당을 지급할 수 있다고 규정하고 있다(제46조 제1항). 휴업보상제도의 실효성을 보장하기 위하여 휴업보상 지급규정을 위반한 자는 3년 이하의 징역 또는 3천만원 이하의 벌금에 처한다고 규정하고 있다(제109조).

휴업수당은 근로자의 귀책사유가 아닌 이유로 근로를 할 수 없게 된 경우에 일정한 수당을 근로자에게 지급하여 근로자의 생존권을 보장하는데 그 취지가

the other hand, if an employer is forced, for unavoidable reasons, to pay legal shutdown allowances until the business can no longer continue, this will cause excessive burden on the employer and will severely hinder operations, which may result in insolvency of the company. This is why an exemption for shutdown compensation is stipulated.[109)]

"Shutdown" refers to a situation in which a worker is unable to provide work against his/her will despite being willing to provide the work under the employment contract.[110)] Civil Act provisions relating to the shutdown of a business provide exemption of employer fault in case of a force majeure beyond the employer's responsibility.[111)] However, if an employee fails to receive work due to the employer's fault, it is possible to claim the full amount of wage, and not just the shutdown allowance.[112)] In cases like this, the Civil Act provisions have difficulty in proving the employer's intention or negligence, so the Labor Standards Act provides a shutdown allowance system to guarantee the minimum life standards of workers without relying on the Civil Act's risk-bearing principle.[113)]

(2) Requirements for shutdown allowance

As a requirement for shutdown, first, there must be fault attributable to the employer. Employer's fault is any reason that may arise within the employer's managerial influence.

Second, the business should not be closed due to force majeure. Force majeure means that the reason for the shutdown of a business should occur from outside and the employer could do nothing to control it. Typical examples would be natural disasters, war, and large regional blackouts.

---

109) Lim Jong-Ryul, Labor Law, 17th ed. Park Young-sa, 2019, p. 422; Jung Myung-hyun, Duality of Legal Characteristics for shutdown Allowance, Justice Magazine (147), Korea Law Institute, April 2015, p. 253.

110) Supreme Court ruling on Oct. 11, 2012: 2012da12870.

111) Civil Act: Article 537 (Obligor's Burden to Bear Risk)
If the performance of an obligation of one of the parties to a bilateral contract becomes impossible by any cause for which neither of the parties is responsible, the obligor may not be entitled to counter-performance.

112) Article 538 (Impossibility of Performance due to Cause for Which Obligee is Responsible)
(1) If the performance of an obligation of one of the parties to a bilateral contract becomes impossible by any cause for which the obligee is responsible, the obligor may demand counter-performance. The same applies to cases where performance becomes impossible by any cause for which neither of the parties is responsible in the case of *mora creditoris*. (2) In cases in the preceding paragraph, if the obligor has received any benefit by being relieved of his own obligation, he shall return such benefit to the obligee.

113) Labor Law Case Study Group, Interpretation of the Labor Standards Act (III), 2nd ed. Parkyoungsa, 2020, p. 121.

있다. 이와 함께 사용자가 부득이한 사유로 사업계속이 불가능한 경우까지 법정휴업수당 지급을 강제한다면 사용자에게 지나친 부담을 주어 기업의 운영에 막대한 지장을 초래하여 기업의 파산을 촉진하는 결과까지 초래할 수 있다는 점을 고려한 휴업보상에의 감면규정을 두고 있다.[109)]

'휴업'이란 근로자가 근로계약에 따라 근로를 제공할 의사가 있음에도 불구하고 그 의사에 반하여 근로를 제공하지 못하는 경우를 말한다.[110)] 휴업과 관련된 민법 조항은 사용자의 귀책사유가 없는 불가항력적인 사항으로 근로를 수령하지 못한 경우에 책임을 면한다고 규정하고 있다.[111)] 그러나 사용자의 책임있는 사유로 근로를 이행하지 못한 경우에는 휴업수당이 아니라 사용자에게 임금 전액을 청구할 수 있다고 규정하고 있다.[112)] 이 경우 민법 조항은 사용자의 고의나 과실 등을 증명해야 하는 어려움이 있기 때문에 민법상 위험 부담 법리에 의존하지 않고도 근로기준법은 근로자의 최저 생활을 보장하려는 취지에서 휴업보상제도를 두고 있다.[113)]

(2) 휴업수당의 지급요건

휴업의 요건으로

첫째, 사용자의 귀책사유가 있어야 한다. 사용자의 귀책사유는 사용자의 세력권 내에서 발생할 수 있는 모든 사유를 말한다.

둘째, 불가항력으로 인한 휴업이 아니어야 한다. 불가항력이란 휴업의 사유가 외부로부터 발생하여 사용자의 권한 범위 밖에서 발생한 사유를 말한다. 대

---

109) 임종률, 노동법 제18판, 박영사, 2020, 422면; 정명현, 휴업수당의 법적 성질의 이중성, 저스티스 147, 한국법학원, 2015.4, 253면.

110) 대법원 2012.10.11, 2012다12870.

111) 민법 제537조【채무자위험부담주의】쌍무계약의 당사자 일방의 채무가 당사자쌍방의 책임없는 사유로 이행할 수 없게 된 때는 채무자는 상대방의 이행을 청구하지 못한다.

112) 민법 제538조【채권자귀책사유로 인한 이행불능】① 쌍무계약의 당사자일방의 채무가 채권자의 책임있는 사유로 이행할 수 없게 된 때는 채무자는 상대방의 이행을 청구할 수 있다. 채권자의 수령지체중에 당사자 쌍방의 책임없는 사유로 이행할 수 없게 된 때에도 같다. ② 전항의 경우에 채무자는 자기의 채무를 면함으로써 이익을 얻은 때는 이를 채권자에게 상환하여야 한다.

113) 노동법실무연구회, 근로기준법 주해(Ⅲ), 제2판, 박영사, 2020, 121면.

Third, it is assumed that shutdown(full or partial closure) has taken place.

(3) Amount of suspension allowances

1) Full payment of wage

In case of a shutdown due to an employer's intention or negligence, the full wage shall be paid. This includes suspension without legitimate reason, forced leave, and unfair dismissal. In accordance with Article 538(1) of the Civil Act, the employer shall pay 100% of wage, not shutdown allowances, when workers are suspended due to illegal activity by the employer. However, an interim benefit obtained during the same period may be deducted pursuant to paragraph 2 of Article 538 of the Civil Act.[114)]

2) Shutdown allowances

In case of shutdown due to an employer's fault, an allowance shall be paid of at least 70% of the average wage.[115)] In principle, employer's fault is a management obstacle that occurs within the scope of the employer's power and will include situations such as being closed due to shortage of funds, shortage of raw materials, decrease in order volume, reduction of market and output, shortage of raw materials in subcontracted factories due to the parent company's poor management, or shortage of operations due to insufficient funds.[116)] A partial shutdown allowance shall be paid when only part of the workplace is closed or when working hours are reduced.[117)]

---

114) Supreme Court ruling on June 28, 1991: 90daka25277 (Damage compensation).

115) Judgment of reasons attributable to an employer

(1) Reasons attributable to an employer: ① Closure of business due to economic reasons; ② Shortage of raw material, reduction of orders; ③ Electricity failure, stagnant sale of products, or capital shortage; ④ Plant transfer, destruction by fire, machinery damage, or reduction of work volume; and ⑤ Subsidiary plant's shortage of raw materials and funds owing to the head company's financial difficulties.

(2) Reasons not attributable to an employer: ① Flooding of the entire plant; ② Closure due to illegal political strike; ③ Legal plant lockout; ④ Incendiary fire by a third party (arson); and ⑤ Plant closure due to natural disasters.

116) MOEL Guidelines: Gungi 68207-106, Sep. 21, 1999; Wage Policy Team - 711, Mar. 29, 2006

117) MOEL Guidelines: The shutdown Allowance System, Labor Standards - 387, Feb. 13, 2000.

표적인 사례가 자연재해, 전쟁, 지역의 대규모 정전사태 등이다.

셋째, 휴업을 할 것을 전제로 한다. 휴업은 전면적 휴업도 될 수 있고, 부분적 휴업도 될 수 있다.

(3) 휴업수당의 규모

1) 임금 전액지급

사용자의 자신의 고의나 과실로 인해 휴업하는 경우 임금 전액을 지급해야 한다. 여기에는 정당한 사유없는 대기발령, 강제휴직, 부당해고 등이 해당된다. 이는 민법 제538조 제1항에 의거하여 사용자의 불법행위로 인하여 근로자가 휴업하는 경우의 휴업수당이 아니라 임금 100%를 지급해야 한다. 다만, 민법 제538조의 제2항에 의거하여 중간이익을 공제할 수 있다.[114)]

2) 휴업수당 지급

사용자의 귀책사유로 인하여 휴업하는 경우 평균임금의 70% 이상의 휴업수당을 지급해야 한다.[115)] 사용자의 귀책사유란 원칙적으로 사용자의 세력범위 안에서 생긴 경영장애로 자금난, 원자재 부족, 주문량 감소, 시장불황과 생산량 감축, 모회사의 경영난에 따른 하청공장의 자재부족이나 자금난에 의한 조업단축 등으로 인한 휴업을 말한다.[116)] 사업장의 일부만 휴업하는 경우나 1일 근로시간 중 일부 근로시간을 단축하는 경우에 부분휴업 수당을 지급한다.[117)]

---

114) 대법원 1991.6.28, 90다카25277(손해배상).

115) 사용자 귀책사유 유무 판단

(1) 사용자의 귀책사유 인정: ① 불황 등으로 인한 경영상 휴업, ② 원료 부족, 주문 감소 ③ 정전, 제품판매 부진, 자금난, ④ 공장 이전·소실, 기계 파손, 작업량 감소, ⑤ 모회사 경영난에 따른 하청공장의 자재·자금난

(2) 사용자의 귀책사유 불인정: ① 전체 공장의 침수, ② 불법정치파업으로 휴업, ③ 정당한 직장폐쇄, ④ 제3자의 방화로 인한 화재, ⑤ 천재 기타 자연현상 등에 의한 휴업.

116) 행정해석: 근기 68207-106, 1999.9.21; 임금근로시간정책팀-711, 2006.3.29.

117) 고용노동부 행정해석: 휴업수당제도 기준, 근로기준과-387, 2009.2.13.

3) Reduction of shutdown allowances

In order to reduce shutdown allowances, an employer may have urgent cause to not continue business operations for unavoidable reasons, and will need to get approval from the Labor Relations Commission(Article 46(2) of the LSA).[118] This means that if a company expects to go bankrupt, even if the employer is at fault, it may pay less than the legal shutdown allowance if so approved by the Labor Relations Commission.[119]

Conditions for the reduction of shutdown allowance require ① as a substantial requirement, the inability to continue business operations for unavoidable reasons and ② as a procedural requirement, the approval of the Labor Relations Commission. Even if it is impossible to operate the business for unavoidable reasons, it is not possible to avoid or reduce shutdown allowances without obtaining approval from the Labor Commission.[120]

Shutdown allowances can be paid at less than 70% of the average wage, and can even be avoided.[121]

4) Unpaid leave

Employer's fault under Article 46 of the Labor Standards Act refers to managerial obstacles that occur within the scope of the employer's power and includes situations such as financial shortages, shortage of raw materials, and market recession. If it is impossible to continue the business due to force majeure circumstances, such as a natural disaster, this cannot be regarded as the fault of the employer[122] because it is impossible for the employer to manage and control such occurrences. There is no obligation to pay shutdown allowances, regardless of whether the Labor Relations Commission has approved them.[123]

---

118) MOEL Guide: Gungi 68207-598, Feb. 28, 2000.

119) MOEL Guidelines: Standards of the Shutdown Allowance System, Labor Standards Team - 387, Feb. 13, 2009: Approval Process of Labor Commission Decision on Shutdown Allowance (by Employer) → Submission of Application for Approval of Reduced Shutdown Allowance (to the Labor Relations Commission) → Confirmation and Review (by related official) → Deliberation & Resolution (Judgement Committee, within 30 days) → Notification.

120) Supreme Court ruling on Sep. 17, 1968: 68nu151.

121) Supreme Court ruling on Nov. 24, 2000: 99doo4280.

122) MOEL Guidelines: Labor Standards Team - 802, Feb. 16, 2010

123) MOEL Guidelines: Gungi 68207-598, Feb. 28, 2000

3) 휴업수당의 감액

휴업수당을 감액하여 지급할 수 있는 경우는 사용자의 귀책사유에도 불구하고 부득이한 사유로 사업계속이 불가능하여 노동위원회의 승인을 얻은 경우이다(근기법 제46조 제2항).[118] 이는 기업의 도산이 예상될 정도의 피해가 발생할 경우 사용자의 귀책사유가 있다고 하더라도 노동위원회의 승인을 받은 경우 법정 휴업수당에 못 미치는 휴업수당을 지급할 수 있다.[119]

휴업수당 감액요건에는 ① 실질적 요건으로 부득이한 사유로 사업계속이 불가능할 것을 요하며, ② 절차적 요건으로 노동위원회의 승인으로 요한다. 부득이한 사유로 인해 사업계속이 불가능하다 할지라도, 노동위원회로부터 승인을 받지 못해 절차적 요건을 충족하지 못한다면 휴업수당의 지급을 면하거나 감액할 수 없다.[120]

휴업수당 감액수준은 평균임금의 100분의 70 이하의 휴업수당을 지급할 수 있으며, 전액 감액도 가능하다.[121]

4) 무급휴업

근로기준법 제46조에 의한 '사용자의 귀책사유'는 원칙적으로 사용자의 세력범위 안에서 생긴 경영장애로서 자금난, 원자재 부족, 시장불황 등으로 인한 경우를 말하며 천재지변이나 재난과 같이 사용자에게 책임을 물을 수 없는 불가항력적인 사정으로 사업 계속이 불가능하게 된 경우에는 사용자의 귀책사유로 볼 수 없나.[122] 천재지변 등 불가항력적인 사유는 사용자의 지배관리가 불가능하므로 사용자의 귀책사유로 볼 수 없다. 이때 노동위원회의 승인 여부와 관계없이 휴업수당 지급의 의무가 없다.[123]

---

118) 행정해석: 근기 68207-598, 2000.2.28.

119) 고용노동부 행정해석: 휴업수당제도 기준, 근로기준과-387, 2009.2.13: 노동위원회의 승인 절차 휴업결정(사용자) → 기준미달 휴업수당 지급승인 신청서 제출(관할 지방노동위원회) → 확인.검토(심사담당) → 심의.의결(심판위원회, 30일 이내) → 통보.

120) 대법원 1968.9.17, 68누151.

121) 대법원 200.11.24, 99두4280.

122) 행정해석: 근로기준과-802, 2010.2.16.

123) 행정해석: 근기 68207-598, 2000.2.28.

2. Cases of Shutdown Allowances

(1) Full payment

1) If an employee's(unfair) dismissal was invalidated or canceled, the employee's status as a worker would still be in existence, and it would be considered that the worker's failure to provide work was attributable to the employer. Article 538(1) of the Civil Act may request the payment of all wage available for the dismissed period.[124)]

2) If suspension of vehicle driving(discontinuance) measures against a worker was found to be unreasonable, in which case the employee was not able to provide work due to the employer's fault, the employer shall pay a shutdown allowance as prescribed by Article 46 of the Labor Standards Act. If, however, the employee is deemed unable to provide work due to intention or negligence of the employer, a claim for the full amount of wage under Article 538(1) of the Civil Act shall also occur.[125)]

(2) Payment of shutdown allowances

1) If a contractor was given an order to suspend operations by the government, if subcontractors also had to shut down their operations(which cannot be translated as force majeure), the subcontractors should pay shutdown allowances to their workers.[126)]

2) If a contractor's removal of hazardous chemicals restricts access to a subcontractor's workers and if they fail to provide work, this is hardly considered to be force majeure beyond the scope of the employer.[127)]

(3) Reduction of suspension allowances

1) A Bupyeong plant closed for more than three months due to a sharp drop in sales after an incident with contaminated dumplings, and the inventory increased during this period. As a result, managerial difficulties can be understood as about 80 workers were dismissed for business reasons. Unless consumer confidence was restored in the near future, normal operation would be difficult. Therefore, it is possible to reduce the shutdown allowance if it is impossible to continue the business for unavoidable

---

124) Supreme Court ruling on Dec. 22, 1981: 81da626.

125) MOEL Guidelines: Wage/Working Hour Team - 711, Mar. 29, 2006.

126) Supreme Court ruling Sep. 10, 2019: 2019do9604.

127) MOEL Guidelines: Labor Standards Team - 3535, May 30, 2018

2. 휴업수당의 적용사례

(1) 임금전액 지급

1) 사용자의 부당한 해고처분이 무효이거나 취소된 때는 그동안 해고당사자의 근로자 지위는 계속되고 있었던 것이 되고, 근로자가 그간 근로 제공을 하지 못한 것은 사용자의 귀책사유로 인한 것이라 할 것이니 근로자는 민법 제538조 제1항에 의하여 계속 근로하였을 경우 받을 수 있는 임금의 전부 지급을 청구할 수 있다.[124)]

2) 사용자의 근로자에 대한 차량승무정지(배차중단) 조치가 부당한 것으로 판명된 경우라면 사용자의 귀책사유로 인해 근로를 제공할 수 없게 된 경우 근로기준법 제46조 소정의 휴업수당을 지급하여야 할 것이나, 사용자의 고의나 과실로 인하여 근로를 제공하지 못한 것으로 인정되는 경우에는 민법 제538조 제1항의 규정에 의한 임금전액에 대한 청구권도 동시에 발생한다.[125)]

(2) 휴업수당 지급

1) 원청업체에 대한 작업중지명령으로 인한 하청회사의 휴업은 불가항력이라고 주장할 수 없는 사유로 휴업한 것으로 근로자에게 휴업수당을 지급할 의무가 있다.[126)]

2) 원청업체의 유해화학 물질 제거 작업에 따라 하도급업체 소속 근로자의 출입이 제한되어 근로를 제공하지 못한 경우라면, 이는 사용자의 세력범위를 벗어난 불가항력적인 사유로 보기 어렵다.[127)]

(3) 휴업수당의 감액

1) 만두파동 이후 3개월 이상 회사 매출이 제로에 가까운 급감, 재고량 증가로 부평공장을 폐쇄하였다. 이로 인하여 약 80명의 근로자를 정리한 사실 등의 경영상 어려움이 인정된다. 앞으로도 소비자의 신뢰가 회복되지 않는 한 정상조업이 어려운 사업계속이 불가능한 경우에 해당하므로 휴업수당 감액에 해당

---

124) 대법원 1981.12.22, 81다626.

125) 행정해석: 임금근로시간정책팀-711, 2006.3.29

126) 대법원 2019.9.10, 2019도9604.

127) 행정해석: 근로기준정책과-3535, 2018.5.30.

reasons(Incheon LRC 2004 shutdown 1).

2) Due to bankruptcy, deficits accumulated even after the company liquidation procedure began, and there was no alternative for normalization as attempts to sell the company were unsuccessful. In this case, unavoidable shutdown is a valid reason for the reduction of shutdown allowances(Incheon LRC 2000 shutdown 1).

3) A situation in which a company goes to the brink of bankruptcy due to an unforeseen fire is considered an unavoidable reason for the employer(NLRC 89 Shutdown 1).

(4) Unpaid leave

1) An employer is not obliged to pay any shutdown allowance for a period of suspension due to interruption of work by a third party.[128)]

2) Absence or leave of absence due to natural disaster or other similar instances, and disciplinary actions such as suspension from work, temporary suspension of work, illness, etc., shall not be regarded as a case of employer fault and shall not be reason for payment of a shutdown allowance.[129)]

(5) Deduction of interim income

Even if an employee whose employer declared a business suspension found another paying job during the period of business suspension or acquired an "interim income," the employer shall provide the employee business suspension pay.[130)]

Business suspension pay is intended to provide a minimum living for the employees affected by business discontinuance for a reason attributable to the employer. The notion of business suspension includes cases where an individual employee, although they intend to provide work as specified in the labor contract, finds it impossible to do the work. In short, the provision on business suspension pay applies to the employee in question. Therefore, within the range of 70% of the ordinary wage(that is, the business suspension pay rate), interim wage(earned during the suspended period) may not be deducted from shutdown allowance. In other words, only the amount in excess of the business suspension pay rate may be deducted.

---

128) Guidelines: Labor Standards Team - 2855, June 9, 2004

129) Lim Jong-Ryul, Labor Law, 17th edition, Park Young-sa, 2019, p. 423

130) Supreme Court ruling on Jun. 28, 1991, 90DaKa25277.

된다(인천지노위 04휴업1).

2) 부도에 따라 회사정리절차가 개시된 이후에도 적자가 누적되고 있고, 경영정상화를 위한 대안이 존재하지 않아 회사매각을 추진하고 있으나 회사매각도 성과를 거두지 못하고 있다. 이 경우에는 부득이한 휴업상태가 휴업수당의 감액 사유에 해당된다(인천지노위 00휴업1).

3) 원인 미상의 화재발생으로 인한 기업이 부도 직전까지 가는 경영상 긴박한 상태의 도래는 사용자로서도 어쩔 수 없는 불가항력적인 사유로 휴업수당을 감할 수밖에 없는 경우에 해당된다(중노위 89휴업1).

(4) 무급휴업

1) 제3자의 출근방해로 인한 피치 못할 휴업기간에 대하여 사용자가 휴업수당을 지급하여야 할 의무는 없다.[128)]

2) 천재지변이나 그밖에 이에 준하는 사유, 징계처분으로서 정직, 출근정지, 질병 등에 따른 결근이나 휴직은 사용자의 귀책사유로 볼 수 없고 이는 휴업수당 지급사유가 되지 않는다.[129)]

(5) 중간수입 공제

휴업기간 중에 근로자가 다른 기업에 취업하여 임금을 받는 등 중간수입이 있는 경우에도 휴업수당을 지급해야 한다.[130)]

휴업수당은 근로자의 최저생활을 보장하려는 취지에서 사용자의 귀책사유로 인하여 휴업하는 경우에는 사용자는 휴업기간 중 당해 근로자에게 그 평균임금의 100분의 70이상의 수당을 지급하는 것인바, 여기서의 휴업이란 개개의 근로자가 근로계약에 따라 근로를 제공할 의사가 있음에도 불구하고 그 의사에 반하여 취업이 거부되거나 불가능하게 된 경우도 포함된다고 할 것이므로, 근로자가 지급받을 수 있는 임금액 중 휴업수당(평균임금 70%)의 한도에서는 이를 이익공제의 대상으로 삼을 수 없고, 그 휴업수당을 초과하는 금액에서 중간수입을 공제하여야 한다.

---

128) 행정해석: 근로기준과-2855, 2004.6.9

129) 임종률, 노동법, 제18판, 박영사, 2020, 423면.

130) 대법원 1991.6.28, 90다카25277.

Section 2: Payment of wage

Ⅰ. How to Pay Wages

Article 43 of the LSA (Payment of Wages)

① Payment of wages shall be directly made in full sum to the worker in cash; however, if otherwise stipulated in special provisions of laws or decrees or in collective agreement, wages may be partially deducted or paid in other forms.

② Wages shall be paid at least once a month on a fixed day; however, this shall not apply to extraordinary wages, allowances, or any other similar payments, nor to those wages provided for byPresidentialDecree.

LSA Enforcement Decree, Article 23 (Exception to Wages to be Paid at Least Once Monthly)

The term "extraordinary wages, allowances, or other similar payments, or the wages prescribed by Presidential Decree" in the proviso to Article 43 (2) of the Act means those falling under the following subparagraphs:

1. Allowance for good attendance payable on the basis of the attendance record for a period exceeding one month
2. Seniority allowance payable for consecutive service for a fixed period exceeding one month
3. Incentive, proficiency allowance, or bonus calculated on a ground sustaining for a period exceeding one month
4. Other various allowances paid on an irregular basis.

Article 109 of the LSA (Penal Provisions) Employers shall be punished for violations of the above Article 43 (Payment of wage) with imprisonment of not more than 3 years or a fine of not more than KRW 30 million.

The Labor Standards Act states that payment of wage shall be directly made in full sum to the worker in cash and paid at least once per month on a fixed day, thereby including the principles of cash payment, direct payment, total payment, and fixed-day payment.

1. The Principle of Cash Payment

wage shall be paid in cash, not in kind. Accordingly, wage shall be paid in convertible

제2절 임금지급

Ⅰ. 임금 지급원칙

근로기준법 제43조【임금지불】

① 임금은 통화로 직접 근로자에게 그 전액을 지급하여야 한다. 다만, 법령 또는 단체협약에 특별한 규정이 있는 경우에는 임금의 일부를 공제하거나 통화 이외의 것으로 지급할 수 있다.

② 임금은 매월 1회 이상 일정한 기일을 정하여 지급하여야 한다. 다만, 임시로 지급하는 임금, 수당 기타 이에 준하는 것 또는 대통령령이 정하는 임금에 대하여는 그러하지 아니하다.

근로기준법 시행령 제23조【매월 1회 이상 지급하여야 할 임금의 예외】

법 제43조 제2항 단서에서 "임시로 지급하는 임금, 수당, 그밖에 이에 준하는 것 또는 대통령령으로 정하는 임금"이란 다음 각 호의 것을 말한다.

1. 1개월을 초과하는 기간의 출근 성적에 따라 지급하는 정근수당
2. 1개월을 초과하는 일정 기간을 계속하여 근무한 경우에 지급되는 근속수당
3. 1개월을 초과하는 기간에 걸친 사유에 따라 산정되는 장려금, 능률수당 또는 상여금
4. 그밖에 부정기적으로 지급되는 모든 수당

제109조【벌칙】 임금지불 규정을 위반한 자(법 제43조)는 3년 이하의 징역 또는 3천만원 이하의 벌금에 처한다.

근로기준법은 임금의 지급에 관하여 임금은 통화로 직접 근로자에게 그 전액을 지불하여야 하며 매월 1회 이상 일정한 기일을 정하여 지급하여야 한다고 규정하여 통화불, 직접불, 전액불, 정기불의 원칙을 정하고 있다.

1. 통화지급

사용자는 근로자에게 통화로서 임금을 지급하여야 하며, 근로자에게 불리한

cash(i.e. bank notes or coins) except for special cases prescribed in law or collective agreement. A cashier's check issued by the bank, however, does not violate the principle of cash payment, though bill payment is treated as an agreed extended payment.

1) **Legal cases**: ① Payment by certified check; ② Payment by shares for incentive pay
2) **Illegal cases**: ① Payment of a check not guaranteed by the bank; ② Company shares, bills, or goods

2. The Principle of Direct Payment

wage shall be paid directly to the employees. This rule does not allow exceptions by law or collective agreement, and also does not permit any delegation or proxy. However, the principle is not violated if a family member serves as a messenger in case of any illness affecting the recipient. The family member can collect the payment or it can be transferred into a designated bank account upon the employee's request. However, this excludes seamen, who are exempt from direct payments due to the different working conditions at sea.

1) **Legal cases**: ① Payment to the wife for inevitable cases, ② Payment to seamen's families, ③ Deduction in cases of seizure for wage credit, ④ Unclear address of the employee
2) **Illegal cases**: ① Payment to the labor union, ② Payment to parental authority or proxy, ③ Payment to the grantee for wage credit

3. The Principle of Total Payment

wage shall be paid in total amounts to all employees after applicable deductions according to the law or collective agreement. Legal deductions include income tax, resident tax, medical insurance, national pension, etc. collective agreement deductions include union membership fees(check-off system).

현물급여는 금지된다. 따라서 법령이나 단체협약에 의한 예외를 제외하고는 임금은 강제 통용력이 있는 화폐(은행권과 주화)로 지급되어야 한다. 다만, 은행에서 발행하는 자기앞수표는 통화지급의 원칙에 위배되지 않으며 어음으로 지급한 것은 당사자 간의 기일연장 합의에 불과한 것으로 본다.

1) **합법사례**: ① 보증수표의 지불 ② 성과급으로 주식의 지급

2) **불법사례**: ① 은행의 지급 보증이 없는 당좌 수표 지불 ② 회사 주식이나 어음 또는 현물 지급

2. 직접지급

임금은 직접 근로자 본인에게 지급되어야 한다. 이에는 법령이나 단체협약에 의한 예외가 인정되지 않으며, 위임이나 대리에 의한 임금 수령도 인정되지 않는다. 그러나 근로자가 질병 등으로 인해 그 가족이 사자(심부름꾼)로서 임금을 수령하거나 근로자의 희망에 의해 지정된 은행 계좌에 이체하는 경우는 직접불의 원칙에 위배되지 않는다. 다만, 선원인 근로자는 해상근로의 특성으로 직접지급의 예외가 허용된다.

1) **합법사례**: ① 불가피한 경우 부인에게 지급 ② 선원의 가족에게 지급 ③ 임금채권의 압류 시 사용자가 이를 공제하여 납부 ④ 근로자의 주거불명인 경우

2) **불법사례**: ① 노동조합에 지급 ② 친권자 또는 대리인에 지급 ③ 임금채권을 양수인에게 지급

3. 전액지급

법령 또는 단체협약에 의해 임금의 공제가 인정되는 경우를 제외하고는 임금은 그 전액을 근로자에게 지불하여야 한다. 법령에 의해 공제가 인정되는 것은 갑종근로소득세, 주민세, 건강보험료, 국민연금 등이 있으며, 단체협약에 의하여 인정되는 경우는 조합비 일괄공제(check-off system)가 있다.

1) **Legal cases**: ① Deductions for advance payment, ② Replacement of a taxi driver's insufficient daily deposit by wage, ③ Deductions due to disciplinary action; ④ No wage for no work during strikes

2) **Illegal cases**: ① Prohibition of pre-determination of non-observance, offsetting wage against advances, and compulsory saving; ② Replacement of compensation for damage due to illegal acts or default

4. The Principle of Fixed-day Payment

wage shall be paid on a fixed day, one or more times in a month, to promote stability for employees. wage or allowances paid temporarily to be admitted as exceptions shall include, ① Diligence allowances paid for superior attendance during the period exceeding one month, ② Service allowances paid for continuous work during the period exceeding one month, ③ Incentives, efficiency allowances or bonuses presented for various reasons during the period exceeding one month; and ④ Other allowances paid irregularly.

1) **Legal cases**: Change of payment date

2) **Illegal cases**: Delayed payment of wage

 **MOEL Guidelines**

1. Unless there is a special agreement, an employee who quits his or her job before the selected day of wage increase may not receive the increased wage.[131)]
2. Upon indictment of unfair labor practice by the Labor Relations Commission, the employer shall pay entire wage during the period of dismissal.[132)]
3. An employee who terminates employment for personal reasons shall be paid all severance pay and wage owed him or her.[133)]
4. If bonus pay is guaranteed every year, an employee resigning before the bonus pay day will be able to receive it in an amount pro-rated to their service days.[134)]
5. Although Chuseok bonus is fixed yearly, the amount shall be paid to those who resign before the payment day.[135)]

---

131) MOEL Guidelines: Kungi 680207-1877

132) MOEL Guidelines: Nojunggun 1455.9-2721

133) MOEL Guidelines: Kungi 1455-8121, Mar. 24, 1982

134) MOEL Guidelines: Bubmoo 811-9256

135) MOEL Guidelines: Bubmoo 811-18993, Sep. 1, 1978.

1) **합법사례**: ① 가불임금의 공제 ② 택시기사의 사납금부족액과 임금상계 ③ 징계로 인한 감봉 ④ 쟁의기간 중의 무노동 무임금
2) **불법사례**: ① 위약금 예약, 전차금, 강제저축 ② 불법행위, 채무불이행으로 인한 손해배상과 임금의 상계

4. 정기지급

근로자의 생활안정을 위하여 임금은 매월 일정한 날에 1회 이상 지급하여야 한다. 매월 1회 이상이라 함은 매월 1일부터 말일까지 적어도 1회 이상 지급하여야 한다는 의미이다. 다만, 임시로 지급되는 다음의 임금·수당은 예외가 인정된다. ① 1월을 초과하는 기간의 출근 성적에 의하여 지급하는 정근수당, ② 1월을 초과하는 일정 기간의 계속 근무에 대하여 지급되는 근속수당, ③ 1월을 초과하는 기간에 걸친 사유에 의하여 산정되는 장려금·능률수당 또는 상여금, ④ 기타 부정기적으로 지급되는 제 수당

1) **합법사례**: 임금 지급기일의 변경
2) **불법사례**: 체불임금

행정해석

1. 특약이 없는 한 임금인상 결정 이전 퇴직자에게 임금인상분이 소급 지급되지 않는다.[131]
2. 노동위원회로부터 부당노동행위 판정을 받았다면 해고기간 중 임금 전액을 지급해야 한다.[132]
3. 근로자의 귀책 사유에 의한 징계퇴직자라 하더라도 퇴직금과 임금은 전액 직접 지급해야 한다.[133]
4. 상여금의 지급기일 이전에 퇴직한 근로자에게도 1년간의 보장된 상여금은 월할계산하여 해당분 만큼을 지급하여야 한다.[134]
5. 매년 일정률의 중추절 상여금을 지급한 관례가 있다면 지급일 이전에 퇴직자에게도 지급하여야 한다.[135]

---

131) 행정해석: 근기 680207-1877, 1995.11.21.
132) 행정해석: 노정근 1455.9-2721, 1965.7.5,
133) 행정해석: 근기 1455-8121, 1982.3.24,
134) 행정해석: 법무 811-9256, 1978.5.4,
135) 행정해석: 법무 811-18993, 1978.9.1.

6. If the employer tries their best to pay wage on time but fails to do so due to financial difficulties from stagnant business, then the employer shall not be punished for delayed payment.[136)]
7. An employee dismissed as disciplinary punishment shall be paid severance pay and wage covering service days.[137)]
8. Whether an industrial trainee causes actual damage intentionally or by mistake, it is a violation of the Labor Standards Act if the employer deducts their wage for the loss.[138)]
9. If a subcontractor fails to pay wage to employees without contributory cause by the immediate preceding contractor, the immediate preceding contractor shall not bear the burden with the subcontractor concerned.[139)]

II. The Principle of Complete Payment of Wage & Exceptions[140)]

Company A gives a 20 percent discount to its employees when they buy company products, up to a maximum of KRW 2 million per year. Only employees and their direct family members living together may receive this discount when they purchase products. However, it was confirmed that one employee violated this company regulation, so the company issued a written warning and deducted, with the employee's agreement, KRW 500,000 from his salary: the amount involved in the violation. This type of situation has occurred frequently in business, and deals directly with whether a company can recover claimed damages by deducting employee wage.

As the wage paid in return for work provided directly support the employee's ability to sustain him or herself, deducting wage to pay for claims is strictly regulated. Article 43(Payment of wage) of the Labor Standards Act stipulates, "(1) Payment of wage shall be made in full to workers; however, if otherwise stipulated by special provisions of laws or decrees or a collective agreement, wage may be partially deducted or may be paid by other means than cash." Other provisions that deal with this subject include Article 20(Prohibition of Predetermination of Nonobservance),[141)] Article 21(Prohibition of Offsetting

136) Supreme Court ruling on May 10, 1985, 87Do2098

137) MOEL Guidelines: Kungi 1455-3680, May 2, 1981

138) MOEL Guidelines: Kungi 68207-2907, Sep. 28, 2000

139) MOEL Guidelines: Haeji 125-12829, Aug. 26, 1983

140) Jung, Bongsoo, "The Principle of Complete Payment of wage", 「Labor Law」, Jungang, Aug 2016.

141) Article 20 (Prohibition of Predetermination of Nonobservance): No employer shall enter into a contract by which a penalty or indemnity for possible damages incurred from breach of a labor contract is predetermined.

6. 사용자가 임금지급을 위하여 최선의 노력을 다하였으나 경영부진으로 인한 자금사정 악화로 도저히 임금지급기일을 지킬 수 없었던 경우라면 임금체불의 죄책을 물을 수 없다.[136)]
7. 업무상 과실로 징계해고된 자에게도 퇴직금과 해당 근로기간에 대한 임금은 지급하여야 한다.[137)]
8. 산업연수생의 고의 또는 과실로 인하여 현실적으로 손해가 발생한 경우 그 손해액을 당해 근로자의 임금에서 공제하는 것은 근로기준법 위반이다.[138)]
9. 직상수급자의 귀책사유 없이 하수급인이 임금을 체불하였을 시는 직상수급자는 임금지불에 대한 연대책임은 없다.[139)]

Ⅱ. 임금 전액 지급의 원칙과 예외[140)]

A 회사는 자사제품에 대해 직원에게 연간 200만원 한도 내에서 20%를 할인해주고 있다. 그 수혜대상은 직원 본인과 동거 직계가족에 한한다. 한 직원이 이 규정을 위반하여 회사의 물품을 구입한 것이 확인되어 회사는 해당 근로자에게 서면 경고를 하면서, 본인의 동의를 얻어 급여에서 부당이익금 50만원을 공제하였다. 이와 같은 사례는 일반적으로 많이 발생하는 사례로서 임금채권과 손해배상 채권을 상계할 수 있는 지 여부에 대한 문제와 밀접한 관련이 있다.

근로의 대가로 받는 임금은 근로자의 생존권 보장에 직결되기 때문에 임금에서 채권의 공제를 엄격히 제한하고 있다. 근로기준법 제43조 제1항에서 "임금은 전액을 지급하여야 하며, 임금의 일부 공제는 법령 또는 단체협약에 특별한 규정이 있는 경우에 한한다"고 명시하고 있다. 그밖에도 '위약 예정의 금지',[141)]

136) 대법원 1985.5.10, 87도2098.
137) 행정해석: 근기 1455-3680, 1981.5.2,
138) 행정해석: 근기 68207-2907, 2000.9.28.
139) 행정해석: 해지 125-12829, 1983.8.26.
140) 정봉수, "임금 전액지급의 원칙과 예외", 「월간 노동법률」, 중앙경제사, 2016.8.
141) 제20조【위약 예정의 금지】사용자는 근로계약 불이행에 대한 위약금 또는 손해배상액을 예정하는 계약을 체결하지 못한다.

wage against Advances),[142] Article 22(Prohibition of Compulsory Saving),[143] and Article 95(Limitation on Punitive Provisions).[144] Despite the principle of complete payment, there are a few exceptions. Some legitimate reasons for deductions include: ① deductions allowed by law or decrees(court rulings); ② deductions allowed by the collective agreement; ③ deductions made to correct miscalculation of wage.[145] Also, even though an exception for wage claims has the employee's consent, this needs to be handled in a strictly regulated manner. Here I would like to take a substantial look into exceptions to complete payment of wage.

1. The Principle of Complete Payment & Exceptions

(1) The principle of complete payment

The purpose of complete payment of wage is designed to protect employees and provide stability in their earning of a living by means of prohibiting employers from unilaterally deducting wage and requiring their complete payment of wage. Some exceptions exist, but these are strictly regulated in special provisions of laws or decrees or in collective agreements.[146] The courts have ruled, "In cases where an employer reduces personnel and at the same time unilaterally cuts bonuses, if the employees continue to work without any particular claims, this deduction of wage still amounts to a unilateral decision by the employer and the employees' rights to claim these unilaterally-reduced bonuses shall not be considered waived."[147]

---

142) Article 21 (Prohibition of Offsetting wage against Advances): No employer shall offset wage against an advance or other credits given in advance on the condition of worker's labor.

143) Article 22 (Prohibition of Compulsory Saving): (1) No employer shall enter into a contract with a worker, in addition to a labor contract, which stipulates compulsory savings or the management of savings.

144) Article 95 (Limitation on Punitive Provisions): If a punitive reduction in wage for a worker is stipulated in the rules of employment, the amount of reduction for each infraction shall not exceed half of one day's average wage, and the total amount of reduction shall not exceed one-tenth of the total amount of wage during each period of wage payment.

145) Lim, Jongyul, 「Labor Law」, 18th ed., Park Young Sa, 2020, Park-young-sa, p. 417.

146) Article 109 (Penal Provisions): (1) Persons who violate the provisions of Article 43 shall be punished by imprisonment of up to three years or by a fine not exceeding twenty million won.

147) Supreme Court on Jun. 11, 1999, 98 Da 22185

'전차금 상계의 금지',[142] '강제저축의 금지',[143] '제재 규정(감급)의 제한'[144] 등의 명시적 규정이 있다. 또한, 임금 전액지급을 원칙으로 하면서 최소한의 예외를 두고 있다. 임금 공제가 합법적으로 가능한 것으로는 ① 법령(법원의 판결문), ② 단체협약, ③ 임금착오 지급에 의한 공제가 있다.[145] 다만, 임금채권에 대해 근로자의 동의를 전제로 전액 지급의 예외, 즉 상계에 대한 예외를 인정하지만 엄격히 규제하고 있다. 이러한 전액 지급의 예외에 대해 살펴보고자 한다.

1. 전액 지급 원칙과 예외

(1) 전액 지급의 원칙

임금 전액지급의 취지는 사용자가 일방적으로 임금을 공제하는 것을 금지하여 근로자에게 임금 전액을 확실하게 지급받게 함으로써 근로자의 경제생활을 위협하는 일이 없도록 그 보호를 도모하려는 데 있다. 임금의 전액 지불에 대한 예외는 법령이나 단체협약으로 가능하다고 명시하여 엄격하게 제한하고 있다.[146] 법원은 "경영위기로 인하여 인원을 감축하면서 상여금을 일방적으로 삭감하고 이에 대해 근로자들이 별다른 이의 없이 근무하고 있는 경우에도 이는 사용자의 일방적인 임금삭감으로 근로자가 상여금 청구권을 포기하였다고 볼 수 없다."고 판시하고 있다.[147]

---

142) 제21조【전차금 상계의 금지】사용자는 전차금이나 그밖에 근로할 것을 조건으로 하는 전대(前貸)채권과 임금을 상계하지 못한다.

143) 제22조【강제 저금의 금지】① 사용자는 근로계약에 덧붙여 강제 저축 또는 저축금의 관리를 규정하는 계약을 체결하지 못한다.

144) 제95조【제재 규정의 제한】취업규칙에서 근로자에 대하여 감급(減給)의 제재를 정할 경우에 그 감액은 1회의 금액이 평균임금의 1일분의 2분의1을, 총액이 1임금지급기의 임금 총액의 10분의 1을 초과하지 못한다.

145) 김형배, 『노동법』 제24판, 박영사, 2015년, 364면; 임종률, 『노동법』, 제18판, 박영사, 2020, 417면.

146) 제109조【벌칙】(1) 43조를 위반한 자는 3년 이하의 징역 또는 2천만원 이하의 벌금에 처한다.

147) 대법원 1999.6.11, 98다 22185.

(2) Exceptions

1) Deductions allowed by law or decree

Laws and decrees which allow deductions are limited to income tax law, social security insurance laws, and other stipulated laws. In addition, a court decision to allow seizure of wage can be implemented by seizing one-half of wage exceeding the minimum cost of living(KRW 1.85 million).[148)]

A particularly remarkable judicial ruling was recently made which ruled that deductions can be made from monthly wage, but not from severance pay or retirement pension. "Since Article 7(Protection of Right to Receive Benefits) of the Employee Retirement Benefit Security Act(ERBSA) stipulates that the right to receive benefits under a retirement pension plan shall neither be transferred to others nor offered as collateral, such provision prohibiting transferring the retirement benefits as collateral is part of statutory law. Accordingly, a court ruling to allow seizure of benefits under a retirement pension plan is null and void, and a third-party debtor can refuse the payment, by quoting the above, from an employee's benefits, even if ordered by a court. On the other hand, Article 246(Claims Subject to Prohibition of Seizure) of the Civil Execution Act(CEA) regulates that an amount equivalent to a maximum of 1/2 of wage, retirement pension or other wage claims of similar nature can be deducted. Since Article 7(Protection of Right to Receive Benefits) of the ERBSA and Article 246(Claims Subject to Prohibition of Seizure) of the CEA are affected by the relationship between general law and special law, it is translated that all benefits under retirement pensions shall not be transferred as collateral.[149)] This means that because the ERBSA is a special law, it takes precedence over the CEA, which is a general law.

2) Deductions allowed by a collective agreement

Deductions of union dues(or dues checkoff) are typical deductions allowed by a collective agreement. In cases where the labor union requests that the company deduct 10

---

148) Supreme Court on Mar. 16, 1994, 94 Ma 1882; Civil Execution Act: Article 246 (Claims Subject to Prohibition of Seizure) (1) None of the following claims shall be seized: 4. Amount equivalent to 1/2 of wage, pension, salary, bonus, retirement pension, or other wage claims of similar nature: Provided, that where the amount falls short of the amount prescribed by Presidential Decree in consideration of the minimum cost of living under the National Basic Living Security Act or exceeds the amount prescribed by Presidential Decree in consideration of the cost of living for a standard family, such amount (1.85 million won) prescribed by Presidential Decree shall apply respectively;

149) Supreme Court ruling on Jan. 23, 2014, 2013 Da 71180

(2) 전액 지급원칙의 예외

1) 법령에 의한 예외

법령에 의해 공제가 인정되는 경우는 소득세법, 4대 보험징수법 등으로 명시된 경우에 한해서 가능하다. 또한 채권자가 법원에서 임금채권에 대한 압류 판결을 받은 경우에는 월 지급되는 임금에 한해서 최저생계비 185만원을 초과하는 임금의 2분의 1 상당액을 압류할 수 있다.[148)]

특히 주목해야 할 최근 판례는 임금채권 압류는 월 임금에서는 가능하지만, 퇴직금이나 퇴직연금에 대해서는 압류할 수 없다고 명확히 판결하고 있다. "근로자퇴직급여 보장법 제7조에서 퇴직연금제도의 급여를 받을 권리에 대하여 양도를 금지하고 있으므로 위 양도금지 규정은 강행법규에 해당한다고 볼 것이다. 따라서 퇴직연금제도의 급여를 받을 권리에 대한 압류명령은 실체법상 무효이고, 제3채무자는 그 압류채권의 추심금 청구에 대하여 위 무효를 들어 지급을 거절할 수 있다. 한편 민사집행법은 제246조 제1항 제4호에서 퇴직연금 그밖에 이와 비슷한 성질을 가진 급여채권은 그 1/2에 해당하는 금액만 압류하지 못하는 것으로 규정하고 있으나, 이는 위 퇴직급여법상의 양도금지 규정과의 사이에서 일반법과 특별법의 관계에 있으므로, 퇴직급여법상의 퇴직연금채권은 그 전액에 관하여 압류가 금지된다고 보아야 한다."[149)]

2) 단체협약에 의한 공제

단체협약에 의한 공제는 조합비 공제(check-off)가 대표적인 내용이다. 이와 관련하여 노동조합에서 매월 공제되는 조합원 조합비의 10배에 상당하는 조합원 1인당 50만원의 쟁의기금의 공제를 요구하는 경우에 회사는 이에 대해 협조해야 하는 문제가 있다. 이에 대해 고용노동부는 개인의 동의가 없더라도 노동조합의 적법한 결의 절차[조합원의 총회(대의원)의 의결이나 노조 규약상 관

---

148) 대법원 1994.3.16, 94마1822. 민사집행법 제246조(압류금지채권) 제1항 제4호에서 급료·연금·봉급·상여금·퇴직연금, 그밖에 이와 비슷한 성질을 가진 급여채권의 2분의 1에 해당하는 금액. 다만 단서에서 근로자의 급여 중 최저생계비(4인 가족 기준 185만원)에 해당하는 금액의 압류금지.

149) 대법원 2014.1.23, 2013다71180.

times the usual monthly union dues(such as KRW 500,000 from each union member towards preparations for a strike), the company will need to decide whether to cooperate or not. For its part, the MOEL(MOEL) expressed its official opinion that if the labor union decides to raise funds to prepare for a strike by means of a legitimate decision-making process such as by resolution at a general meeting of all union members(or union representatives), the company shall cooperate by deducting the special union fees from employee monthly wage even though there is no individual consent to do so.[150] This means that, according to MOEL, it would be considered unfair labor practice for an employer to refuse to deduct the amount requested by the labor union to prepare for a strike.

3) Deductions to correct miscalculation of wage

In cases where an employer overpaid an employee by mistake, equivalent deductions from wage would be to correct the miscalculation, making it possible to adjust wage or severance pay, regardless of the principle of complete payment of wage. Provided, even in this case, the courts have ruled that the amount of retirement benefits deducted to retrieve overpaid wage shall be a maximum of 1/2 of the retirement benefits.[151]

2. Criteria for Judgment & Related Cases regarding Other Deductions

(1) Criteria for judgment

The principle of complete payment of wage strictly prohibits, in accordance with Article 43 of the Labor Standards Act, related judicial rulings and MOEL Guidelines, an employer deducting an employee's wage to cover damage claims against the employee.[152] This is because such a deduction is determined unilaterally by the employer.

Regarding the justification for this, judicial ruling has stipulated the following criteria for judgment[153] "It is prohibited for an employer to unilaterally deduct an employee's wage to cover claims against the employee by the employer, but in cases where the employer deducts or replaces the employee's wage after obtaining the employee's consent, as this consent can be regarded as the employee voluntarily agreeing to this deduction,

150) MOEL Guidelines: Jun. 6, 2004, labor union – 1501

151) Supreme Court ruling on May 20, 2010, 2007 Da 90760

152) Supreme Court ruling on Sep. 28, 1976, 73 Da 1768

153) Supreme Court ruling on Oct. 23, 2001, 2001 Da 25184

련이 있는 경우]를 통해 결정한 쟁의기금에 대해서도 조합비 공제로서 공제해 주어야 하며, 이 경우에 조합원 개별 동의가 필요하지 않다는 입장이다.[150] 즉, 사용자가 노동조합이 회사를 상대로 투쟁하기 위한 조합비 특별공제를 거부하는 경우에는 부당노동행위에 해당된다고 볼 수 있다.

3) 임금계산 착오 지급에 의한 공제

사용자가 임금계산의 착오 등으로 인하여 임금을 더 많이 지급한 경우에는 급여 계산상의 문제이므로 임금 전액지급 원칙과 상관없이 급여나 퇴직금에서 정산이 가능하다. 다만, 이 경우에도 법원은 사용자가 근로자에게 부당이득반환채권을 자동채권으로 하여 근로자의 퇴직금 채권을 상계하는 것은 퇴직금 채권의 2분의 1을 초과하는 부분에 해당하는 금액에 관하여만 허용된다고 보고 있다.[151]

2. 기타 공제(상계)의 가능 여부에 대한 판단기준 및 관련 사례

(1) 판단기준

근로자의 임금이 사용자가 가지는 근로자의 불법행위를 원인으로 하는 채권과 상계(공제)가 가능한지에 대해 근로기준법 제43조 제1항의 임금의 전액지급 원칙과 판례와 행정해석에서도 이를 금지하고 있다.[152] 이것은 상계(공제)라는 것이 사용자의 일방적인 의사표시에 의해서 행해지기 때문이다.

이에 대해 상계의 가능 여부에 대한 판단기준을 판례[153]는 다음과 같이 판시하고 있다. "사용자가 근로자에 대하여 가지는 채권을 가지고 일방적으로 근로자의 임금채권을 상계(공제)하는 것은 금지된다고 할 것이지만, 사용자가 근로자의 동의를 얻어 근로자의 임금채권에 대하여 공제(상계)하는 경우에 그 동의가 근로자의 자유로운 의사에 터 잡아 이루어진 것이라고 인정할 만한 합리적인 이유가 객관적으로 존재하는 때는 근로기준법 제43조 제1항 본문에 위반하

150) 고용노동부 행정해석: 노동조합과-1501, 2004.6.5.

151) 대법원 2010.5.20, 2007다90760 전원합의체.

152) 대법원 1976.9.28, 75다1768.

153) 대법원 2001.10.23, 2001다25184.

this would not be a violation of Article 43 of the Labor Standards Act. Provided, in view of considering the purpose of the principle of complete payment of wage, determination of whether the employee actually voluntarily agreed to this deduction shall be strictly and carefully made."

(2) Related cases

1) Reimbursement of training expenses

In cases where an employer assigns an employee overseas and subsidizes all training expenses for the employee to attend a training program, and that employee does not serve the compulsory employment period after completing the training, the employer can legitimately require that the employee to reimburse part or all of the training expenses covered by the company. Accordingly, a training regulation that exempts an employee from the duty of reimbursement if that employee serves the compulsory employment period after completing the commissioned overseas training is not equivalent to a contract by which a penalty or indemnity is predetermined for damages incurred from a breach of the labor contract. Neither does such a training regulation violate Article 7 of the LSA(Prohibition of Forced Labor: No employer shall force a worker to work against his own free will through any means which unlawfully restrict mental or physical freedom) nor Article 21(Prohibition of Offsetting wage against Advances: No employer shall offset wage against an advance or other credits given in advance on the condition of a worker's labor).[154]

2) Deductions from bonuses

Sometimes an employer reduces or does not pay bonuses, with labor union consent, in the process of coping with the company's business difficulties. The MOEL has released guidelines for two different cases: bonuses already incurred and bonuses expected to be incurred. In cases where the employer intends to deduct from bonuses already incurred, which were paid in return for employee labor service, this is null and void even with labor union agreement or revision of company rules. In such cases, individual employee consent must be received. However, the employer reducing or deducting from bonuses expected in the near future is possible through revision of the collective agreement with labor union consent, or revision of

154) Supreme Court ruling on Feb. 25, 1992, 91 Da 26232 (Korean Air)

지 아니한다고 보아야 할 것이다. 다만 임금 전액지급의 원칙의 취지에 비추어 볼 때 그 동의가 근로자의 자유로운 의사에 기한 것이라는 판단은 엄격하고 신중하게 이루어져야 한다."라고 판시하고 있다.

(2) 관련사례

1) 연수비 상환의 경우

기업체에서 비용을 부담 지출하여 직원을 해외에 파견하여 위탁 교육을 시키고 이를 이수한 직원이 교육 수료 일자로부터 일정한 의무재직기간 이상 근무하지 아니할 때는 「기업체가 부담한 해당 교육비용의 전부 또는 일부를 상환하도록 할 수 있다. 따라서 해외 위탁교육을 받은 후 의무재직기간 동안 근무하는 경우에는 이를 면제하기로 한 기업체의 교육훈련규정」은 근로기준법 제20조에서 금지된 위약금 또는 손해배상예정의 약정은 아니다. 근로기준법 제7조가 금지하는 사용자가 정신 또는 신체상의 자유를 부당하게 구속하는 수단으로써 근로자의 자유의사에 반하는 근로를 강요하는 것이거나 같은 법 제21조가 금지하는 전차금 기타 근로할 것을 조건으로 하는 전대채권과 임금을 상계하기로 하는 내용의 것이 아니라고 볼 수 있다.[154)]

2) 상여금의 삭감

기업의 경영상 어려움을 타개하기 위해서 노동조합과 합의를 통해서 상여금을 삭감하거나 반납하는 경우가 있다. 이에 대해 고용노동부는 이미 발생한 근로에 대한 상여금과 앞으로 발생할 상여금을 구분하여 판단하고 있다. 이미 발생한 근로의 대가로서의 상여금을 삭감(반납)하는 경우에는 노동조합과의 합의 또는 회사규정의 개정만으로는 무효이고, 개별 근로자들의 동의가 있어야 한다. 그러나 앞으로의 근로조건으로서의 상여금을 삭감(하향조정)하는 경우에는 노동조합과의 합의를 거쳐 단체협약을 개정하거나 회사규정을 노조 또는 근로자 과반수의 동의를 얻어 변경하는 것으로 가능하며, 개별근로자들의 동의는

---

154) 대법원 1992.2.25, 91다26232(대한항공).

the company rules after obtaining consent from the labor union or the majority of employees. In such cases, receiving individual employee consent is not necessary.[155)]

The courts have made rulings that align with this guideline. The wage(including bonuses) or severance benefits already incurred are considered the employee's private property, so unless the labor union receives an individual employee agreement, it is not possible to deduct or delay those payments through a collective agreement. Accordingly, a collective agreement cannot require employees to reimburse payments already received, unless there is agreement from each individual employee.[156)]

3) Housing loans from the company

In cases where an employee resigns before they have reimbursed the company for a housing loan received from the company, and the employer deducts all unpaid debt in a lump sum from the severance benefits, this may be considered a violation of the principle of complete payment of wage. However, the courts have ruled in favor of lump sum deductions from severance benefits for the following reason: "Since the collective agreement is the agreement to determine items occurring in labor and management relations, it can be a real expression of the intentions of both parties. It can also be admitted that the individual employee's voluntary decision and agreement make it possible to deduct wage instead of entering a formal claim for repayment of debts owed to the company by that employee. In view of these points, if the collective agreement was made justifiably and contains items permitting the requirement to reimburse unpaid loans, such a collective agreement does not violate the principle of complete payment of wage."[157)]

Ⅲ. Inclusive Wage Systems[158)]

When designing a labor contract, the employer determines the base pay for the employee. Then, the employer generally calculates wage and added allowances with the

155) MOEL Guidelines: Apr. 15, 1999, LSA 68207-587

156) Supreme Court ruling on Jan. 28, 2010, 2009 Da 76317

157) Supreme Court ruling on Jun. 27, 2003, 2003 Da 7623

158) Jung, Bongsoo, "Inclusive Wage System and its Limits", 「Labor Law」, Jungang, August 2012.

필요하지 않다.[155)]

법원에서도 동일하게 판단하고 있다. 이미 지급 청구권이 발생한 임금(상여금 포함)이나 퇴직금은 근로자의 사적 재산영역으로 옮겨져 근로자의 처분에 맡겨진 것이어서, 노동조합이 근로자들로부터 개별적인 동의를 받지 않는 이상 사용자와 사이의 단체협약만으로 이에 대한 포기나 지급유예와 같은 처분행위를 할 수 없으므로, 단체협약으로 근로자에게 이미 지급한 임금을 반환하도록 하는 것은 그에 관하여 근로자들의 개별적인 동의가 없는 한 효력이 없다.[156)]

3) 주택자금 등 대출금의 경우

회사가 주택자금을 근로자에게 대여해주고, 일정액을 급여에서 상환하다가 중도에 퇴직하는 경우에는 사용자가 퇴직금에서 주택자금이 미 상환된 전체금액에 대해 공제하는 경우에 전액지급의 원칙에 위배되는지에 대한 문제가 있을 수 있다. 이에 대해 판례는 "단체협약은 노동조합이 사용자 또는 사용자 단체와 근로조건 기타 노사관계에서 발생하는 사항에 관하여 체결하는 협정으로 체결과정에서도 그 진정성과 명확성이 담보되어 있다는 점과, 개별 근로자의 자유로운 의사에 터 잡아 이루어진 동의가 있는 경우 사용자는 근로자에 대한 자동채권과 근로자의 임금채권을 상계할 수 있다는 점 등에 비추어 볼 때, 적법하게 체결된 단체협약이 사용자의 근로자에 대한 대출 원리금 등 채권 등을 공제할 수 있도록 규정하고 있도록 한 단체협약이 임금 전액지급의 원칙에 위배되어 무효라고 볼 수 없다."라고 판시하면서 퇴직금에서 주택자금 대출금 공제를 인정하고 있다.[157)]

Ⅲ. 포괄임금제[158)]

근로계약을 체결함에 있어서 사용자는 근로자에 대하여 기본임금을 결정하고

155) 고용노동부 행정해석: 근기 68207-587, 1999.4.15.

156) 대법원 2010.1.28, 2009다76317.

157) 대법원 2003.6.27, 2003다7623.

158) 성봉수, "포괄임금제의 제한사항", 「월간 노동법률」, 중앙경제사, 2012.8.

base pay for overtime, off-days, and night work. However, in order to consider working structure and job characteristics, efficiency of calculation, or to encourage a strong work ethic, an employer can include general allowances such as overtime allowance, etc. in the base pay and also pay a certain amount of allowance every month under the inclusive wage system. In this case, as long as the conditions are not deemed disadvantageous to the employee, it does not violate the law.

An inclusive wage system where an employer pays a fixed monthly salary is convenient for management, but can only be applied in some situations, as it can easily violate the Labor Standards Act. An inclusive wage system is a salary payment system where the employer determines the total wage, which include statutory allowances such as overtime, night, and holiday work allowances in consideration of job characteristics and convenience in calculating wage, and then pays a fixed wage every month. This system is often designed for use at workplaces where it is hard to measure working hours due to the job characteristics or for the convenience of calculating working hours even though those working hours are measurable. However, this inclusive wage system is also commonly used to avoid paying various allowances required under the Labor Standards Act. Originally, statutory allowances under the Labor Standards Act were meant to be paid for actual work provided. If an employer pays wage that include statutory allowances in advance, this could violate the Labor Standards Act, but is allowed, albeit with strict limitations as determined in judicial rulings and administrative guidelines.

There are two generally-accepted types of inclusive wage systems. The first is for special work where it is difficult to measure working hours. The second is for convenience of calculation.

1. Inclusive Wage Systems and related Judicial Principles[159)]

Article 17 of the Labor Standards Act stipulates that an employer shall clearly state wages, contractual working hours, and other working conditions in the employment contract. Other matters such as constituent items of wages and the calculation and payment methods of wages shall be specified in writing. Article 56 of the LSA regulates

---

159) Supreme Court ruling on Aug. 19, 2005, 2003Da66523.

이를 기초로 연장·휴일·야간근로 등에 대한 임금 또는 가산수당을 합산하여 지급함이 원칙이라 할 것이다. 그러나 근로형태, 업무의 성질 등을 참작하거나 계산의 편의와 직원의 근무의욕을 고취한다는 뜻에서 기본임금에 연장근로수당 등 제 수당이 포함되어 있다거나 매월 일정액을 제 수당으로 지급하는 내용의 계약을 체결하였다고 하더라도 근로자에게 불이익이 없고 제반 사정에 비추어 정당하다고 인정될 때는 이를 무효라 할 수 없는데 이러한 임금 계산방법을 포괄산정임금제라고 한다.

매월 고정적인 임금을 지급하는 포괄임금제는 관리의 편리성이 있지만, 근로기준법에 저촉될 수 있기 때문에 예외적인 경우에만 허용된다. 포괄임금제는 업무의 특수성 또는 계산의 편의를 고려하여 연장·야간·휴일근로 수당 등 법정 수당을 포함하여 임금총액을 결정하고 이에 따라 매월 고정적 급여를 지급하는 제도를 말한다. 이 제도는 업무의 성격 또는 근로형태의 특수성으로 인하여 근로시간 산정이 어려운 경우나 근로시간 산정이 가능하더라도 실무상 계산의 편의를 위해 사용되고 있다. 그런데 근로기준법상 발생하는 각종 법정수당을 지급하지 않기 위해 포괄임금제를 악용하는 경우도 많이 있다. 근로기준법상 법정수당은 원래 실제 근로제공을 통해서 발생하는 수당인데, 포괄임금제는 미리 법정 수당을 모두 포함하고 지급하는 것이어서 근로기준법 위반의 소지가 크므로 이에 대한 판례나 행정해석에서는 엄격한 제한을 두고 허용하고 있다.

포괄임금제를 인정하는 경우는 두 가지로 분류할 수 있다. 첫째는 업무가 근로시간 산정이 어려운 특수한 형태의 근로이고, 둘째는 근로시간 계산이 가능하지만, 계산의 편의를 위해 고정연장근로수당을 신설하여 포괄임금제로 하고 있는 경우이다.

1. 포괄임금제와 관련된 판례법리[159)]

근로기준법 제17조는「사용자는 근로자에 대하여 임금, 소정근로시간 기타의 근로조건을 명시하여야 한다. 이 경우 임금의 구성항목, 계산방법 및 지불방법

159) 대법원 2005.8.19, 2003다66523 정리요약.

that an employer shall pay an additional 50% or more of the ordinary wage for extended work, night work, or holiday work. Based on these regulations and the rules stipulated concerning ordinary wage, in making an employment contract, the employer shall first determine basic pay, and then from this basic pay, shall calculate the statutory allowances such as overtime, night work, and holiday work allowances according to actual working hours.

In principle, the payment of wage is according to the number of working hours. There are exceptional cases where working hours cannot be measured when considering actual hours worked, employment types and job characteristics like surveillance and intermittent work. In this case, the employer can make a wage payment contract that follows an inclusive wage system where the employer and employee can determine a monthly or daily wage that reflects all allowances, including statutory allowances, without deciding the basic pay in advance, or the employer can make an employment contract with fixed amounts inclusive of all statutory allowances, based only on the previously determined basic pay, without considering the actual number of hours worked. This inclusive wage system is permissible when there is no disadvantage to the related workers or as a justifiable method in view of special situations related to those jobs.

However, if working hours of a specific job are measurable, the principle is to pay wage according to working hours as reflected in the Labor Standards Act, unless a special situation exists where the LSA requirements do not apply. Therefore, for an employer to create a wage payment contract that uses an inclusive wage system(paying a fixed amount for statutory allowances) regardless of the number of working hours, is to violate the Labor Standards Act in principle and is not allowable by law.

2. Inclusive Wage System by Job Characteristics

(1) Requirements

1) Job characteristics and working structure

The inclusive wage system can be adopted when working structures, working hours, or rest hours in the working area are irregular, and when overtime and night work are

에 관한 사항에 대하여는 서면으로 명시하여야 한다.」고 규정하고 있다. 동법 제56조는 「기준근로시간을 초과하여 근로한 연장근로와 야간근로 또는 휴일근로에 대하여는 통상임금의 100분의 50 이상을 가산한 임금을 지급하여야 한다.」고 규정하고 있다. 이러한 규정들과 통상임금에 관한 정하고 있는 규정에 의하면, 사용자는 근로계약을 체결함에 있어서 기본임금을 결정하고 이를 기초로 하여 근로자가 실제로 근무한 근로시간에 따라 연장근로, 야간근로, 휴일근로 등이 있으면 그에 상응하는 연장, 야간, 휴일근로수당 등의 법정수당을 산정하여야 한다. 이러한 원칙적인 임금 지급방법은 근로시간 수의 산정을 전제로 한 것인데, 예외적으로 감시·단속적 근로 등과 같이 근로시간, 근로형태와 업무의 성질을 고려할 때 근로시간의 산정이 어려운 경우가 있을 수 있다. 이러한 경우에는 사용자와 근로자 사이에 기본임금을 미리 산정하지 아니한 채 법정수당까지 포함된 금액을 월 급여액이나 일당임금으로 정하거나, 기본임금을 미리 산정하면서도 법정 제 수당을 구분하지 아니한 채 일정액을 정하여 이를 근로시간 수에 상관없이 지급하기로 약정하는 내용의 포괄임금제에 의한 임금 지급계약을 체결할 수 있다. 이러한 포괄임금은 그 근로자에게 불이익이 없고 여러 사정에 비추어 정당하다고 인정될 때는 유효하다.

그러나 위와 같이 근로시간의 산정이 어려운 경우가 아니라면, 달리 근로기준법상 근로시간에 관한 규정을 그대로 적용할 수 없다고 볼만한 특별한 사정이 없는 한, 상기한 바와 같은 근로기준법상의 근로시간에 따른 임금 지급의 원칙이 적용되어야 할 것이다. 따라서 근로시간 수에 상관없이 일정액을 법정수당으로 지급하는 내용의 포괄임금제방식의 임금지급 계약을 체결하는 것은 근로기준법에 명백히 위반되므로 허용될 수 없다고 하겠다.

2. 업무의 성격에 따른 포괄산정

(1) 요 건

1) 업무의 성격 또는 근로형태

근로형태나 업무의 성질상 근로시간과 휴게시간이 불규칙하거나, 근로자가

naturally included in the working structure, even though the employee can decide on the working hours at their own discretion.

If the calculation of working hours is difficult, an inclusive wage system can be introduced. The following types of work to which this system is applicable are presented in the Labor Standards Act.

1) Supervisory/intermittent work: The working hours, rest and holiday regulations in the Labor Standards Act shall not apply to workers engaged in supervisory/intermittent work once the employer has received approval from the Minister of Employment and Labor (Article 63 (3) of the LSA).

2) Work outside the workplace: If a worker is unable to calculate working time due to working all or part of the working time outside the workplace (or other reasons), they shall be deemed to have worked the contractual working hours (Article 58 (1)).

3) Discretionary work: The discretionary work in Article 58 (3) of the Labor Standards Act refers to tasks where it is difficult to calculate working time because of the characteristics or performance rather than the amount of work. Written consent is required from the employee representative in order to qualify the work as within the contractual working hours. Specific tasks include designing and analyzing research and development and information processing systems, organizing articles for newspapers and broadcasts, designing and designing-related job, and producing and supervising broadcasting and film production (Article 58, Clause 3).

2) Employee consent

Under circumstances in which the inclusive wage system is accepted as an exception to the payment structure for added wage in the Labor Standards Act, the system shall be specified concretely in a labor contract or rules of employment, or at least by a clear verbal agreement in principle. However, the inclusive wage can be admitted by two parties if it has already been habitually used in wage calculation for work such as surveillance, work that is intermittent, work that is every other day, and shift work, or if the employees have complied without disagreement to the work that requires regular overtime work and night work at measurable working hours.

재량을 가지고 근로시간 등을 결정할 수 있어 근로시간 측정이 가능하더라도 근로형태상 연장·야간근로 등이 당연히 포함되어 있는 경우에는 포괄산정 임금제가 인정될 수 있다.

근로시간의 산정이 어려운 경우에 대해서는 포괄임금제를 도입할 수 있으며, 이러한 업무는 근로기준법상 제시된 다음과 같은 업무이다.

① 감시 단속적 근로: 감시 단속적 근로자로서 사용자가 고용노동부장관의 적용제외 인가를 받은 경우 근로기준법의 근로시간, 휴게, 휴일 규정을 적용하지 아니한다. 이는 고용노동부장관의 승인을 전제로 근로시간의 적용이 제외된다(근기법 제63조 제3항).

② 사업장 밖 근로: 근로자가 출장 및 기타 사유로 근로시간의 전부 또는 일부를 사업장 밖에서 근로하여 근로시간을 산정하기 어려운 경우, 소정근로시간을 근로한 것으로 본다(제58조 제1항).

③ 재량근로: 근로기준법 제58조 제3항의 재량근로업무는 전문적 업무로 근로의 양보다는 질이나 성과가 중시되어 근로시간 산정이 어려운 업무를 말한다. 해당업무를 소정근로시간으로 인정받기 위해서는 근로자대표와의 서면합의가 필요하다. 구체적 업무로는 연구개발이나 정보처리시스템의 설계나 분석 업무, 신문이나 방송 등 기사의 취재 편성 업무, 디자인이나 고안업무, 방송이나 영화 제작의 프로듀서나 감독 업무 등이 있다(제58조 제3항).

2) 근로자의 동의

포괄산정 임금제는 근로기준법의 가산임금 지급체계에 대한 예외를 인정하는 것이라는 점에서 명시적으로 근로계약서를 작성하였거나 취업규칙 등에 구체적으로 명시하였거나, 적어도 구두라도 포괄산정 내역에 관해 구체적이고 명시적인 합의가 있어야 하는 것이 원칙이다. 다만, 감시·단속적 근로, 격일제근로, 교대제근로 등 업무의 성격상 근로시간 구속이 약하거나, 근로시간 구속이 명확하다 하더라도 연장근로, 야간근로 등이 규칙적으로 발생하는 업무로서 근로자의 이의 없이 관행으로 포괄산정 계산을 해왔다면 묵시적인 합의가 인정된다.

(2) Effect

In cases where the inclusive wage system is introduced legally and properly through mutual agreement due to the difficulty of measuring working hours, the employee cannot request additional wage for overtime or night hours. Thus, even if the inclusive wage is less than the wage calculated by actual working hours, the employer does not have to pay the difference.

(3) Related cases

1) Judicial rulings allow inclusive wage systems due to the special nature of work for cargo truck drivers whose working hours are difficult to measure, guards engaged in surveillance and intermittent work, workers contracted on a daily basis, part-timers with remarkably short contractual working hours, shift workers on 24-hour shifts, and other similar jobs. As for other jobs where the working hours cannot be measured in reality, if the employer and employees agree to fixed overtime and holiday work allowances for a certain number of working hours each month, and if the employees have received those fixed allowances without complaint for a certain period of time, this inclusive wage system is allowed unless there is disadvantage to the employees when considering all circumstances.[160)]

2) In cases where an inclusive wage payment system has been agreed upon in the employment contract, the inclusive wage that the employee receives for overtime work allowance and other allowances equivalent to overtime, night, and holiday allowances(in accordance with the Labor Standards Act) is an acceptable inclusion of overtime allowance, night work allowance and holiday work allowance. In cases where the inclusive wage payment system has been agreed upon at a workplace, the employer does not pay the difference in allowances for overtime.[161)]

3) The labor service that the employees provided to Construction Company S was to guard and patrol workplaces for 24 hours straight every second day: surveillance work with lower mental and physical stress. This work naturally included overtime, night, and holiday work exceeding standard working hours under the Labor Standards Act. The

---

160) MOEL Guidelines: Wage Team - 2534, on Sep. 1, 2006.

161) Supreme Court ruling on June 14, 2002, 2002Da16958.

(2) 효 과

실근로시간의 측정이 어려워 당사자 합의로 포괄산정 임금제를 적법·타당하게 도입한 경우, 근로자는 따로 연장·야간 등의 가산임금을 청구할 수 없다. 이 경우 포괄산정 임금이 실제근로에 따라 산정된 임금보다 적을지라도 사용자는 그 차액을 지급하지 않을 수 있다.

(3) 관련 사례

1) 판례는 근로시간 파악이 어려운 화물운송 운전자, 감시 단속적 근로자에 해당하는 경비원, 근로계약이 하루 단위로 이루어지는 일용직 근로자, 소정근로시간이 현저히 적은 단시간 근로자, 격일제근로자 등에 대해서 근로형태의 특수성에 따른 포괄임금제를 인정하고 있다. 이들 업무는 현실적으로 근로시간 측정이 곤란하여 노사 간 근로계약에 의하여 실제 연장 휴일근로 시간과 관계없이 월별로 일정 시간 분 또는 일정액의 연장휴일 근로수당 등을 지급받기로 하고 당해 근로자가 일정기간 동안 아무런 이의 없이 동 수당을 수령해 온 경우, 제반 사정에 비추어 근로자에게 불이익이 없다고 인정될 때는 포괄임금제를 인정하고 있다.[160)]

2) 포괄임금제에 의한 임금지급 계약이 체결된 경우, 근로자가 포괄임금으로 지급받은 연장근로수당 또는 이에 갈음한 연장수당, 야간수당, 휴일수당 등에는 근로기준법의 규정에 의한 연장근로수당, 야간근로수당, 휴일근로수당이 모두 포함되어 있다. 사업장에 포괄임금제에 의한 임금지급 계약이 체결된 경우에는 연장 근로에 대한 수당과의 차액을 지급할 필요가 없다.[161)]

3) 원고들이 피고 S건설에게 제공한 근로는 신체 또는 정신적 긴장이 적은 감시적 업무로서 1일 24시간 경비·순찰이라는 근로형태의 특수성으로 인하여 근로기준법상의 기준 근로시간을 초과한 연장근로, 야간근로, 휴일근로가 당연히 예상된다 할 것이어서, 원고들과 피고 S건설 사이에 체결된 근로계약은 기본임

---

160) 행정해석: 임금근로시간정책팀-2534, 2006.9.1.

161) 대법원 2002.6.14, 2002다16958.

employment contract made between the employees and the company was not one with an ordinary type of wage payment(basic pay plus various allowances), but an inclusive wage system that paid a fixed amount monthly that included various allowances, as it is difficult to measure the employees' working hours in terms of overtime, night, and holiday work due to the specific job characteristics. When they were initially hired, the employees agreed on such an inclusive wage system in consideration of the specific type of work, and had never complained about the validity of this system until their employment at Apartment G was terminated. Considering the aforementioned items, the inclusive wage system in this case shall not be determined null and void.[162)]

4) In the cases where the inclusive wage system can be deemed justifiable, it is necessary to consider the type and nature of the work (such as whether it involves surveillance and intermittent work), and the difficulty of calculating the working hours when considering the working time. The amount of allowance included in the statutory allowance is set as a monthly benefit or daily wage, or the basic wage calculated in advance, but if the statutory allowance is not classified and a fixed amount is set as the statutory benefit allowance, it is valid when a wage contract under the inclusive wage system is concluded. However, it should not be disadvantageous to the workers. Therefore, it is justified in light of the various circumstances mentioned above. In addition, the rulings also reject the inclusive wage system if calculation of the working hours is not difficult, unless there is a special situation where the working hours regulation in the Labor Standards Act cannot be applied. In this case, if a contract is concluded in advance under the inclusive wage system, it is judged whether the inclusive wage contract is legal or not after reviewing if the statutory allowance included in the inclusive wage is correct. If the wages paid under the inclusive wage system fall short of the statutory allowance calculated according to the standards established by the LSA, and if it will be disadvantageous to the employees, it will be null and void. In such a case, the company shall compensate the employee(s) equal to the amount to be paid in legal standard allowances.[163)]

---

162) Seoul Appellate Court ruling on Jul. 23, 2004, 2004Na2740.

163) Supreme Court ruling on June 26, 2014, Decision 2011 do 12114.

금을 정하고 이를 기초로 각종 수당을 가산하여 지급하는 통상적인 임금지급방식이 아니라, 근로시간, 근로형태와 업무의 특성상 시간 외, 야간, 휴일에 근로자가 실제로 근무한 시간을 확정하기 어려운 점 등을 참작하여 각종 수당을 모두 포함한 일정액을 매월 지급하기로 하는 이른바 포괄임금제에 의한 임금지급방식을 취하고 있었던 것으로 보는 것이 타당하고, 원고들이 피고 S건설에 입사할 당시 위와 같은 근로형태의 특수성을 고려하여 포괄임금제 약정을 하였고, 각 입사 후부터 G아파트 경비업무를 종료한 때까지 단체협약을 내세워 위 포괄임금제 약정의 효력을 다투지 아니한 점에 비추어 보면, 위 포괄임금제 약정이 무효라고 볼 수는 없다.[162)]

4) 감시 단속적 근로 등과 같이 근로시간, 근로형태와 업무의 성질을 고려할 때 근로시간의 산정이 어려운 것으로 판단되는 경우에는 사용자와 근로자 사이에 기본임금을 미리 산정하지 아니한 채 법정수당까지 포함된 금액을 월급여액이나 일당임금으로 정하거나 기본임금을 미리 산정하면서도 법정 제 수당을 구분하지 아니한 채 일정액을 법정 제수당으로 정하여 이를 근로시간에 상관없이 지급하기로 약정하는 내용의 이른바 포괄임금제에 의한 임금지급계약으로 체결하더라도 그것이 달리 근로자에게 불이익이 없고 여러 사정에 비추어 정당하다고 인정될 때에는 유효하다. 그러나 위와 같이 근로시간의 산정이 어려운 경우가 아니라면 근로기준법상의 근로시간에 관한 규정을 그대로 적용할 수 없다고 볼 만한 특별한 사정이 없는 한 근로기준법상의 근로시간에 따른 임금지급의 원칙이 적용되어야 하므로, 이러한 경우에 앞서 본 포괄임금제 방식의 임금 지급계약을 체결한 때에는 그것이 근로기준법이 정한 근로계약에 관한 규제를 위반하는지를 따져 포괄임금에 포함된 법정수당이 근로기준법이 정한 기준에 따라 산정된 법정 수당에 미달한다면 그에 해당하는 포괄임금제에 의한 임금 지급계약 부분은 근로자에게 불이익하여 무효라 할 것이고 사용자는 근로기준법의 강행성과 보충성 원칙에 의하여 근로자에게 그 미달하는 법정수당을 지급할 의무가 있다."고 판시하고 있다.[163)]

162) 서울고등법원 2004.7.23, 2004나2740.
163) 대법원 2014.6.26. 선고 2011노12114 판결

3. Inclusive Wage System for Convenient Calculation

(1) Requirement

When working hours are measurable, but overtime and night hours are not included in the working conditions, job description or job characteristics, the inclusive wage system does not apply to the job. However, it is valid to pay a fixed amount for overtime as an added allowance according to the rules of employment, labor contract, or mutual agreement to make calculation convenient and encourage people to work those hours.

For example, employees who work more than a certain number of working days can be paid a fixed allowance previously described as per the position, while those who work less than a fixed number of working days can be paid the fixed working allowance deducted in proportion to the days missed. A typical example is a fixed overtime allowance. In this case, if an employee works more overtime than previously determined for the fixed overtime allowance, the employer shall pay an extra statutory allowance. However, if the employee has worked less overtime than previously determined for the fixed overtime allowance, the employer shall still pay the fixed overtime allowance. For an example, if the inclusive wage incorporates overtime allowance for 10 hours per week, the employment contract shall specify basic pay and the fixed overtime allowance in the salary details. The payroll data should have a separate item for fixed overtime allowance in the constituent items of wage.

(2) Effect

Even though an employer designs a contract that includes a fixed allowance for overtime, to make calculation convenient, the employee can request the difference if the number of actual working hours served is more than the fixed number specified in advance, provided, however, that an employer shall not be required to pay the difference for jobs such as security, where it is difficult to measure actual working hours.

(3) Related cases

1) Even though an inclusive wage system was agreed upon, such agreement is not valid in cases where the fixed overtime allowance is significantly lower than the amount calculated in accordance with the Labor Standards Act. In reviewing employment type and job characteristics, this wage structure was designed as an inclusive wage system that paid a certain fixed amount for overtime allowance, even though measuring the

3. 계산의 편의 등을 위한 포괄산정

(1) 요 건

근로시간 측정이 가능하면서 연장·야간근로가 근로의 내용에 당연히 내재되어 있지는 않아, 근로형태나 업무의 성격이 포괄산정 임금제에 해당되지 않는다 하더라도 계산의 편의와 근무의욕 고취를 목적으로 취업규칙, 근로계약 또는 당사자 합의를 통해 일정액을 연장근로 가산수당 등 제 수당으로 지급하더라도 근로자에게 불이익하지 않는 한 이를 무효로 볼 수 없다.

일정 일수 이상의 근무실적이 있는 자에 대하여 시간외·야간·휴일근무의 수당조로 직급별 금액을 정하여 지급하고 정하여진 근무일수에 미달한 직원 대하여 미달일수에 비례하여 일정액을 감하도록 된 근무수당을 예로 들 수 있다. 그 대표적인 것이 고정연장 근로수당이라 할 수 있다. 이 경우, 실제로 정해진 고정연장근로보다 더 연장근로를 한 경우에는 별도의 법정수당을 지급해야 하며, 고정연장 근로시간을 채우지 못한 경우에도 고정연장근로수당을 공제할 수 없다. 예를 들어, 주 10시간의 연장고정수당을 포함한 포괄임금인 경우에는 근로계약서에 기본급과 연장근로수당을 명확하게 기재하여야 하고, 또한 급여지급대장에서도 별도의 임금구성 항목인 고정연장수당이 구분되어 있어야 한다.

(2) 효 과

계산의 편의 등을 위해 연장근로수당 등을 일정액으로 정하는 계약을 체결하더라도 개개 근로자가 실제로 계산한 근로시간에 따라 산정된 금액의 합계가 이미 지급된 일정액의 합계액보다 많다면 근로자는 그 차액의 지급을 요구할 수 있을 것이다. 다만, 야간 순찰업무 등과 같이 실근로시간 측정이 어려운 업무에 대해서는 차액을 지급치 않을 수 있다.

(3) 관련 사례

1) 포괄임금 약정을 체결하였더라도 근로기준법에 의하여 계산한 연장근로수당에 현저히 모자란 경우에는 해당 약정은 무효이다. 근로형태와 내용 등에 비추어 이 사건은 근로시간의 산정이 어려운 경우 등이 아님을 전제로 하여, 임금

number of hours worked is not difficult in this case. After a service allowance ceased to be paid(since May 1, 2004), the fixed overtime allowance became noticeably lower than the overtime allowance calculated in accordance with the Labor Standards Act. Accordingly, the agreement to pay a lower amount under the inclusive wage system is null and void, and the company shall pay back a suitable amount that was not paid.[164)]

2) Judging whether the inclusive wage system is violated: There have been two judicial precedents for determining whether an inclusive wage system is possible for white-collar workers. The first involved a white collar worker employed by a foreign life insurance company. In this case, the court deemed it difficult to calculate working hours, unlike production workers, because the business culture common to this company centered on performance tasks due to the nature of the company's insurance sales work. In such cases, the inclusive wage system is recognized.[165)] The second involved white-collar workers who concluded an inclusive wage contract by signing a collective agreement offering a fixed overtime allowance of 10 hours per week for 40 hours of work per week. Workers did not receive any extended allowance for up to 10 hours a week even if overtime was performed that week. The Supreme Court concluded that such a wage system cannot be regarded as monthly remuneration based on an hourly wage or as a legitimate inclusive wage system in light of the fact that workers can calculate their hours easily.[166)]

IV. Procedures for Wage Adjustments (Increases, Reductions, Freezes, Returns)

I. Introduction

Labor and management together can freely determine and adjust wages through labor contracts, employment rules, and collective agreements. An employer unilaterally cutting wages has no effect. Reductions, freezes, or wage returns are unfavorable changes to working conditions, so legal procedures must be adhered to by the labor and management before taking such steps.

164) Supreme Court ruling on May 13, 2010, 2008Da6052.

165) Seoul Central District Court ruling on February 13, 2018

166) Supreme Court ruling on December 10, 2009

체계가 일정금액의 연장근로수당을 지급하기로 하는 포괄임금제인데, '봉사료' 지급이 중단된 날 (2004.5.1 경) 이후에는 원고들이 지급 받은 연장근로수당이 근로기준법의 기준에 의하여 계산한 연장근로수당에 현저하게 미치지 못하였고, 그 미달되는 부분의 포괄임금약정은 무효라고 보아 피고가 원고들에게 그 부분 임금을 지급할 의무가 있다.[164)]

2) 포괄임금제의 위반 여부 판단: 위의 사무직 근로자에 대한 포괄임금제가 가능한지 여부에 대해 판례는 2가지의 기준을 가지고 있다. 첫 번째는 외국계 생명보험회사의 사무직 근로자로 월 20시간의 연장근로에 대한 고정연장수당을 정하여 급여 지급이 이루어졌다. 이 경우 법원은 회사업무 특성상 과업 중심의 업무 문화가 일상화 되어 생산직 근로자와 달리 근로시간 산정이 어렵다고 판단하였다. 이와 같은 경우에는 포괄임금제를 인정하고 있다.[165)] 두 번째는 사무직 근로자의 경우로 1주 40시간 근무에 대해 주당 10시간의 고정연장근로수당을 정한 단체협약을 체결하여 포괄임금제를 실시하였다. 근로자가 1주에 연장근로가 이루어지더라도 주10시간 까지는 연장근로수당을 지급하지 않았다. 이에 대해 대법원은 임금체계를 월별 보수액을 기준으로한 시간급 금액이 산정되었다고 볼 수 없고, 근로시간 산정이 가능한 근로자에 대한 포괄임금제 제한 법리에 비추어 볼 때, 정당한 포괄임금제로 볼 수 없다고 판단하였다.[166)]

Ⅳ. 임금조정 (인상, 삭감, 동결, 반납) 절차

임금은 노사가 근로계약, 취업규칙, 단체협약을 통해 자유로운 의사로 결정하고, 조정할 수 있다. 근로조건의 핵심인 임금은 노사가 협의하여 자유로이 결정하는 것으로 회사가 일방적으로 삭감하면 이는 무효가 된다. 임금인상이 아닌 임금의 삭감, 동결, 반납은 근로자에게 불리한 변경조건 이기에 노사의 적법한 절차를 거쳐야 한다.

164) 대법원 2010.5.13, 2008다6052.
165) 서울중앙지법 2018.2.13. 선고 2017가단5061696 판결.
166) 대법원 2009.12.10. 선고 2008다57852 판결.

1. Wage Increases and Wage Reductions

Wage increases are decided through collective bargaining if there is a labor union. Wages have generally been raised every year through collective bargaining between labor and management, and if negotiations do not result in wage increases, the labor union increases the pressure through strikes. Employers generally increase their workers' wages to the minimum extent acceptable to the labor union. Wages can also be reduced through collective bargaining if the economy is bad or the company is in trouble. In this case, if the union consists of a majority of the workers concerned, non-union members are also affected by the wage adjustment concluded by the labor union due to the general binding force of the workplace (Article 35 of the Labor Union Act). In workplaces without a labor union, wage increases are determined unilaterally by the company within an appropriate range through changes to the employment rules or labor contract. However, since wage reductions are regarded as an unfavorable change working conditions, an agreement between labor and management is necessary.

Wage reductions refer to a lower wage than before being paid at a certain point in the future. The total wages paid is lowered by reducing or abolishing the basic wage and/or various allowances, with the process carried out in a manner decided in collective decision-making. If there is a majority union, this is done through a collective agreement, but if there is no majority union, it is necessary to go through the procedures required to make unfavorable changes to the employment rules. Even if labor and management have agreed, wages cannot be reduced below the minimum wage level, and additional rates or legal allowances (such as overtime/night/holiday work allowances, weekly holiday allowance, annual paid allowance, etc.) are not subject to reductions, in accordance with the Labor Standards Act.[167] Also, the reduced wage is not included in the calculation of average wage.

2. Wage Freezes

Freezing wages refers to keeping wages the same for future work as was paid for past work of the same type. In cases where a company regularly increases regular wage, ceasing or additionally restricting this regular increase in wage is an unfavorable change to working conditions. The company can freeze wages through amendment of

167) Ministry Guidelines: Labor Standards Team-797, Mar. 26, 2009.

1. 임금인상 및 임금삭감

임금인상은 노동조합이 있는 경우 집단적 교섭을 통해 이루어진다. 노사협상을 통해 매년 임금을 인상해왔고, 원만하게 인상되지 않는 경우 노동조합은 파업을 통해 협상력을 높여 임금인상을 한다. 사용자는 노동조합의 임금인상 요구에 수용가능한 만큼 임금인상을 하게 된다. 노동조합과 교섭을 통해 경기가 좋지 않거나 회사가 어려움에 처한 경우에는 임금삭감도 가능하다. 노동조합이 당해 사업장의 과반수로 구성되어 있는 경우에는 비조합원도 사업장 단위의 일반적 구속력(노동조합법 제35조)에 의해 임금인상이나 삭감도 당해 노동조합이 체결한 임금조정안을 적용 받는다. 노동조합이 없는 사업장의 경우에는 임금인상은 취업규칙이나 근로계약을 변경하는 방법으로 회사가 적정한 범위에서 일방적으로 결정한다. 다만, 임금삭감은 불이익한 근로조건으로의 변경이므로 노사간 협상을 통한 합의가 필요하다.

임금삭감은 종전보다 장래 일정시점 이후로 임금을 낮추어 지급하는 것이다. 기본급이나 각종 수당을 축소 또는 폐지하면서 임금지급 총액을 낮추게 된다. 임금삭감 절차는 집단적 의사결정 방식에 의해 이루어진다. 과반수의 노동조합이 있는 경우에는 단체협약을 통해서 이루어지지만, 과반수 노동조합이 없는 경우에는 취업규칙 불이익 변경절차를 거쳐야 한다. 노사가 합의하였다고 하더라도 최저임금 수준 이하로 삭감할 수 없고, 근로기준법에서 정한 할증률이나 지급의무를 규정하고 있는 법정수당 (연장/야간/휴일근로수당, 주휴수당, 연차수당 등)은 감액대상으로 할 수 없다.[167] 또한 삭감된 임금은 평균임금 산정시 포함되지 않는다.

2. 임금동결

임금동결은 동일한 내용의 근로제공에 대해 종전과 같은 임금을 지급하는 것을 말한다. 임금인상을 하지 않더라도 정기호봉승급이 있는 회사에서 승급을 제한하는 경우에는 근로조건의 불이익 변경으로 단체협약의 수정이나 취업규

167) 행정해석: 근로기준과-797, 2009.3.26

the collective agreement or following the procedures for changing the employment rules disadvantageously. However, it is not a disadvantageous change to working conditions if wages are frozen when there is no regular salary increase.

3. Wage Returns

Wage returns refer to the return of wage bonds (wages, bonuses, etc.) already incurred for previous work based on the free-will consent of the individual worker. Due to the waiver of the right to claim wages that occurred legally, wages can only be returned through due process. Since a unilaterally-determined wage deduction by the employer violates the principle of paying full wages, individual workers' written consent is required.[168] However, even in this case, any waiver of the right to claim severance pay is invalid because it violates the Labor Standards Act.[169]

For procedures to be deemed reasonable, individual workers' consent is required. Since the return of wages is effective only if it is the individual workers' voluntary decision, individual workers must recognize the purpose of wage returns and sign a return consent form in their own name.[170] While the court holds that it is desirable to obtain consent for each individual worker when returning wages, it is also possible to obtain individual consent by having workers sign a name list of workers if the company has sufficiently explained the difficult situation to the workers.[171] An agreement to return wages in the collective agreement has no effect. This is because the return of wages involves wages that already belong to individual workers, and the union cannot be forced to abandon individual member property rights. Wages returned by workers come from the workers' income and are returned voluntarily, and the employer is not obligated to return them again to the worker.[172] Returned wages are included in the calculation of average wages as they are wage bonds that were given to the employee and then returned to the employer by the employee.[173]

---

168) Article 43 of the Labor Standards Act (Wage Payment) and Supreme Court ruling June 11, 1996: 98da22185 Waiver of wage claims is recognized as a clear expression of the employee's intention.

169) Supreme Court ruling July 26, 2002: 2000da27671.

170) Labor Ministry Guidelines: Labor Standards Team 68207-843, Dec. 13, 1999.

171) Supreme Court ruling on Sep. 29, 2000: 99da67536.

172) Seoul District Court ruling on Apr. 16, 2003: 2002na 20291.

173) Supreme Court ruling on Apr. 10, 2001: 99da39531.

칙의 불이익 변경을 통해서 임금동결을 할 수 있다. 그러나 정기호봉승급이 없는 경우 임금을 동결하더라도 이는 근로조건의 불이익한 변경이 아니다.

3. 임금반납

임금반납은 기왕의 근로에 의해 이미 발생된 임금채권 (임금, 상여금 등)을 개별근로자의 자유의사에 따른 동의를 바탕으로 반납하는 것을 말한다. 적법하게 발생한 임금청구권의 포기로써 적법 절차를 통해서만 임금반납은 가능하다. 사용자의 일방적 임금공제는 임금의 전액 부지급원칙을 위반하기 때문에 개별 근로자의 서면동의가 필요하다.[168] 특히, 퇴직금 청구권의 포기는 근로기준법 위반이 되어 무효이다.[169]

합당한 절차를 밟기 위해서는 개별 근로자의 동의서가 필요하다. 임금반납은 개별 근로자의 자유의사에 기초할 때만 유효하므로 반드시 개별 근로자들이 임금 반납의 취지를 인식하고 반납동의서를 개별 명의로 작성해야 한다.[170] 다만, 법원은 임금반납 시 개별 근로자 각각의 동의서를 받는 것이 바람직하나 회사가 어려운 사정을 근로자에게 충분히 설명했다면 회람 형식으로 동의여부를 표시하도록 하는 방식을 취하는 것도 가능하다는 입장이다.[171] 단체협약에 의한 임금반납 합의는 효력이 없다. 임금반납은 이미 조합원 개인에게 귀속된 임금에 대한 것이므로 노동조합이 조합원 개인 재산권을 포기하도록 할 수 없기 때문이다. 근로자가 반납한 임금은 근로자의 소득으로 귀속되었다가 자진 반납한 것으로써 사용자는 반환할 의무가 없다.[172] 다만, 반납된 임금도 평균임금 산정에 포함된다. 반납된 임금은 일단 근로자의 소득으로 귀속되었다가 반납한 임금채권이기에 평균임금 산정에 포함해야 한다.[173]

---

168) 근로기준법 제43조(임금지급 원칙)과 대법원 1996.6.11. 선고 98다22185 판결: 근로자의 명백한 의사표시로서 임금채권포기는 인정된다.

169) 대법원 2002.7.26 선고 2000다27671 판결.

170) 행정해석, 근기68207-843, 1999.12.13.

171) 대법원 2000.9.29. 선고 99다67536 판결.

172) 서울지방법원 2003.4.16. 선고 2002나20291 판결.

173) 대법원 2001.4.10. 선고 99다39531 판결.

Section 3: The Protection of wage

Ⅰ. Preventive Measures against Delayed Payment of wages[174)]

Providing work not meant to be on a voluntary basis and not receiving wage is slave labor. Thus, delaying payment of wage is a serious offense and subject to imprisonment for up to three years or a fine of up to 30 million won.[175)] Delayed payment of wage is punishable for each violation towards individual workers, so if the employer delays payment of wage to a large number of workers, that employer will face heavy penalties. Despite these strong penalties, it is not easy to settle problems related to unpaid wage. Even if a worker who was not paid complains to the local Employment Labor Office(hereinafter referred to as "Labor Office"), and the Labor Office confirms that the wage remain unpaid and the employer is punished, the worker still has to take separate legal action to receive the unpaid wage. If the employer does not have any property, the employer can receive a certain amount of money for the most preferential wage from the Wage Bond Guarantee Fund. Receiving unpaid wage through civil litigation and the Insolvency Payment Claim System is a complex process and takes a long time, which is not helpful in practical terms.

1. High Interest Levied

In order to prevent delayed payment of wage and early liquidation of unpaid wage, the Labor Standards Act was amended in 2005 to create a "Late Payment Interest System for Unpaid wage." If an employer fails to pay all or part of wage and retirement benefits owed within 14 days of the required date of payment, the employer shall pay the late payment interest rate prescribed by Presidential Decree(currently 20% per year) for the number of days payment was delayed, starting from the day following the required date of

174) Jung, Bongsoo, "Preventive Measures for Delayed Wage 「Labor Law」, Jungang, Oct. 2019.

175) The Labor Standards Act (LSA): Article 109 (paragraph 1).

제3절 임금채권의 보호

Ⅰ. 임금체불 예방조치[174)]

근로를 제공하고 임금을 받지 못하는 것은 노예노동에 해당된다. 따라서 임금체불은 중대범죄에 해당하므로 3년 이하의 징역 또는 3천만 이하의 벌금을 처벌받는다.[175)] 이 벌칙과 벌금은 체불된 근로자 개인에 해당되므로 다수의 근로자에게 임금을 체불하게 되면 가중처벌을 받는다. 이러한 강력한 처벌조항에도 불구하고 임금체불을 해결하는 방법은 쉽지가 않다. 체불된 근로자가 노동청에 진정하여 임금체불확인을 받고 사용자를 형사처벌하더라도 사용자가 임금을 지급하지 않는 경우에는 근로자는 별도의 민사소송을 통해서만 체불된 임금을 받을 수 있다. 사업주가 재산이 없는 경우 임금채권보장기금의 대지급금제도를 통해서 최우선변제 임금을 일정한 한도 내에서 지급받을 수 있다. 이러한 민사소송과 대지급금제도를 통해 체불임금을 받는 것은 복잡한 과정과 오랜 시간이 소요되므로 실질적인 도움은 되지 않는다.

1. 지연이자제도

임금체불의 예방 및 체불임금의 조기청산을 유도하기 위하여 2005년 근로기준법 개정을 통해 '미지급 임금에 대한 지연이자 지급제도'가 마련되었다. 사용자는 임금 및 퇴직급여의 전부 또는 일부를 그 지급사유가 발생한 날로부터 14일 이내에 지급하지 아니하는 경우 그다음 날부터 지급하는 날까지의 지연 일수에 대하여 대통령령이 정하는 이율(현행 연20%)에 따른 지연이자를 지급하여야 한다(재직근로자에게 지연이자(100분의 20)가 적용된다. - 2025년 10월부터 적용).

---

174) 정봉수, "임금체불예방제도", 「월간 노동법률」, 중앙경제사, 2019.10.
175) 근로기준법 제109조 제1항.

payment(Delayed interest (20%) will be applied to current employees. – Effective from October 2025.). This high interest rate helps to prevent an employer from intentionally paying back wages only when he or she is forced to, and without consequences for delaying payment. If an employer delays payment of wages due to a natural disaster, armed conflict or other reasons such as legal or actual bankruptcy, this provision shall not apply to the period during which such reasons continue to exist.

The Labor Standards Act: Article 37 (Late Payment Interest on Unpaid wage)

① An employer who fails to pay all or part of the wage or benefits (only those paid in a lump sum) pursuant to Article 36 or subparagraph 5 of Article 2 of the Employee Retirement Benefit Security Act, respectively, within fourteen days from the day when the cause for payment occurs, shall pay late payment interest for the number of days from the date following expiry of the fourteen day period until the payment is made, at a rate up to 20/100 and as prescribed by Presidential Decree in consideration of financial conditions, including the late payment interest rate applicable among banks under the Banking Act.

② If an employer delays payment of wage due to a natural disaster, armed conflicts or other reasons prescribed by Presidential Decree, the provisions of paragraph (1) shall not apply to the period during which such reasons continue to exist.

The late payment interest system levies a much higher rate of interest(20% annually) than the statutory interest of 6% a year, as a way to induce quick payment. However, if the employers do not have any money or assets to effect payment, there is no way to protect the affected workers' rights, no matter how high the interest rate.[176] The reasons why 20% annual interest payment is not used well on unpaid wage is as follows. First, there is no penalty for failing to pay the late payment interest, unless the worker takes the employer to civil court.[177] Second, workers tend to agree to withdraw their complaints if they simply receive their unpaid wage. Third, the Labor Inspector only considers whether the unpaid wage have been paid when determining punishment, and not the interest for delaying payment, since there are no items related to delayed payment interest in the "Official Document on Details of Unpaid wage". Delayed payment interest is only considered in civil lawsuits for unpaid wage, meaning there is very limited effectiveness in preventing wage payment delays.

---

176) Park, Keun-hoo et al., MOEL, "A Study on Expansion of the Wage Bond Guarantee System", Dec. 23, 2016, p. 17.

177) Ha, Kap-rae, 「The Labor Standards Act」 32nd Ed., 2019, p. 296.

지연이자제도는 사용자가 불가피한 사정없이 의도적으로 임금을 체불하는 것을 막기 위해 고율의 이자를 부가하는 제도로 사용자가 천재지변, 법률상 또는 사실상 도산 등으로 임금을 지급할 수 없는 경우에는 적용이 면제된다.

근로기준법 제37조【미지급 임금에 대한 지연이자】

① 사용자는 제36조에 따라 지급하여야 하는 임금 및 「근로자퇴직급여 보장법」 제2조 제5호에 따른 급여(일시금만 해당된다)의 전부 또는 일부를 그 지급 사유가 발생한 날부터 14일 이내에 지급하지 아니한 경우 그다음 날부터 지급하는 날까지의 지연 일수에 대하여 연 100분의 40 이내의 범위에서 「은행법」에 따른 은행이 적용하는 연체금리 등 경제 여건을 고려하여 대통령령으로 정하는 이율 (연 20%)에 따른 지연이자를 지급하여야 한다.

② 제1항은 사용자가 천재·사변, 그밖에 대통령령으로 정하는 사유에 따라 임금 지급을 지연하는 경우 그 사유가 존속하는 기간에 대하여는 적용하지 아니한다.

지연이자제도는 체불사업주로 하여금 법정이자(상법 연6%)보다 높은 연 20%의 이율을 부담하게 하여 신속한 체불청산을 유도하기 위하여 도입되었으나, 체불사업주가 사실상 무자력자가 되어 근로자가 임금채권 자체를 지급받지 못할 경우에는 임금에 대하여 아무리 높은 이율의 이자가 붙더라도 근로자의 권리보장에 실질적인 기여를 하지 못한다는 근본적인 한계점이 있다.[176] 체불임금에 대한 연 20%의 지연이자 지급이 현실적으로 강제되지 않고 있는 이유는 첫째, 지연이자를 지급하지 않은데 대한 벌칙규정이 없고, 근로자의 민사상 청구권만 인정되기 때문이다.[177] 둘째, 근로자들이 체불임금만 받으면 진정 또는 고소사건 취하해주려는 경향이 있기 때문이다. 셋째, 노동청이 사법처리 단계에서도 처벌수위 결정시 체불임금 원금 지급여부만 고려될 뿐 지연이자 지급 여부까지는 고려되지 않는다는 점이 작용하고 있기 때문이다. 특히, 체불금품확인원에 기재되는 '체불임금 등 내역'에도 따로 지연이자에 관한 항목이 마련되어 있지 않아 현재 체불 진정사건 조사과정에서 체불금액에 대한 지연이자 조사가 별도로 이루어지기 어려운 상황이다. 따라서 지연이자 적용은 임금체불 민사소송에서만 활용되고 있으므로 사실상 임금체불을 예방하는데 한계가 있다.

---

176) 박근후 외 4명, 고용노동부 용역자료, "임금채권보장제도 확대방안 연구", 2016.12.23, 17면.
177) 하갑례, 「근로기준법」, 제32판, 2019, 296면.

2. Punishment for Offenses against One's Intention

The Labor Standards Act: Article 109 (Penal Provisions)

① Any person who violates the provisions of Article 36, 43 (Payment of wage), 44 (Payment of wage in Subcontract Businesses), 44-2 (Joint Responsibility for Paying wage in the Construction Industry), 46 (Allowances during Business Suspension), or 56 (Extended Work, Night Work and Holiday Work) shall be punished by imprisonment of up to three years or by a fine not exceeding 30 million won.

② Prosecution against a person who violates the provisions of Article 36, 43, 44, 44-2, 46 or 56 shall not take place against the clearly expressed wishes of the victim.

No-punishment offenses are a system where imprisonment of up to three years or a fine of up to 30 million won is imposed on employers who have delayed payment of wages in principle, but the Ministry of Employment and Labor(MOEL) does not prosecute if it is against the clearly expressed wishes of the related worker(s). Employers are forced to solve voluntary liquidation of unpaid wages through agreement with workers by paying unpaid wages instead of suffering criminal penalties. However, if there is a large number of workers whose wage remain unpaid, the employer shall be deemed to have committed the same offense against each unpaid worker.[178] Accordingly, in order to avoid penalties according to the no-punishment offenses system, written consent from all unpaid workers must be obtained.[179]

To facilitate the swift repayment of overdue wages, employers are exempt from criminal punishment at the employee's request. However, this exemption does not apply to employers who, after being listed due to two or more criminal convictions for wage arrears, default on wage payments again. Additionally, employees who suffer damages from habitual wage arrears may now claim compensation in court for up to three times the amount owed. In such cases, the court will consider various factors, including the duration, circumstances, and scale of the arrears, the employer's efforts to resolve the issue, and the employer's financial status, in accordance with legal principles governing compensation for unlawful acts. Habitual arrears are defined as ① deliberate wage arrears, ② arrears persisting for more than three months within a year, or ③ amounts exceeding three months of average wages.[180]

---

178) Supreme Court ruling on Apr. 14, 94da1724.

179) Labor Inspector's Practical Guide, MOEL, "Handling of Unpaid wage", 2016, p. 33.

180) MOEL Press Release, September 26, 2024: Bill to Eradicate Habitual Wage Arrears Passes National Assembly Plenary Session. The law will take effect one year after its promulgation.

2. 처벌과 반의사불벌죄 제도

근로기준법 제109조【벌칙】
① 제36조(퇴직후 14일 이내 임금지급), 제43조(임금지급의 원칙), 제44조 (도급사업의 임금지급), 제44조의2(건설업의 임금지급 연대책임), 제46조 (휴업수당) 또는 제56조(가산임금)를 위반한 자는 3년 이하의 징역 또는 3천만원 이하의 벌금에 처한다.
② 제36조, 제43조, 제44조, 제44조의2, 제46조 또는 제56조를 위반한 자에 대하여는 피해자의 명시적인 의사와 다르게 공소를 제기할 수 없다.

반의사불벌죄는 임금지급을 지체한 사용자에 대하여 원칙적으로 3년 이하의 징역 또는 3000만원 이하의 벌금을 처하도록 하되, 해당 근로자가 처벌을 원하지 않는 경우에는 공소를 제기할 수 없도록 하는 제도이다. 사용자가 형사처벌을 받지 않는 대신에 체불된 임금을 지급함으로써 근로자와의 합의를 통한 자율적인 임금체불청산을 강제하기 위하여 도입되었다. 다만, 임금체불이 다수인 경우 그 범죄가 단일한 것이라고 인정하기 어려울 때는 지급을 받을 수 없었던 근로자 각자에 대하여 같은 범죄가 있다고 인정하여야 한다.[178] 따라서 반의사불벌죄에 의거하여 처벌을 면하려면 체불된 개별 근로자들의 전원 서면 동의를 얻어야 한다.[179]

사업주의 신속한 체불임금 변제를 위해 근로자가 원하면 사업주를 형사처벌하지 않았으나, 2회 이상 형사처벌을 받는 명단공개 사업주가 다시 임금을 체불하는 경우는 '반의사 불벌죄'를 적용하지 않는다. 그리고 상습적인 체불 등으로 손해를 입은 근로자는 법원에 손해배상 3배 이내의 금액을 청구할 수 있게 된다. 이에 대해 법원은 불법행위에 대한 손해배상 법리에 따라 체불 기간이나 경위, 규모, 사업주의 해결 노력, 재산상태 등을 고려하여 판단하게 된다. 상습적인 체불이라 함은 ① 명백한 공의로 체불, ② 1년 동안 3개월 이상 체불, ③ 체불액이 3개월 통상임금 초과하는 경우를 말한다.[180]

178) 대법원 1995.4.14, 94도1724.
179) 고용노동부 근로감독관 실무지침서, "체불사건 업무처리요령", 2016, 33면.
180) 고용노동부 보도자료, 2024. 9. 26.: 상습체불 근절법 등 국회 본회의 통과. 시행시기는 이법 공포후 1년 후 시행된다.

Ⅱ. The Insolvency Payment Claim[181)]

When a company goes bankrupt, its employees cannot receive wage or severance pay in cases where the employer is not able to make such payments. In cases where the employer is able to pay, there are some institutional mechanisms such as "preferential reimbursement" or "most preferential reimbursement" by which employees can receive their overdue wage and severance pay through lawsuits and forced auction. Because this process requires considerable time and expense, it is necessary for society to assist these employees and their dependents with living expenses during this period. Accordingly, the government introduced the Wage Claim Guarantee(WCG) on July 1, 1998. The WCG guarantees basic financial security for employees by paying unpaid wage and severance pay on behalf of an employer if employees cannot receive them due to bankruptcy or insolvency of the company.

1. Eligibility for Insolvency Payment and Amount

(1) Reasons for insolvency payment

Insolvency payment is money that the government pays on behalf of the employer for overdue wage, etc. of employees whose employment has ended due to company bankruptcy on the condition that the government is reimbursed later by the employer.

1) 'Declaration of bankruptcy' and 'decision on the commencement of rehabilitation procedures' under the Debtor Rehabilitation and Bankruptcy Act: This is judicial bankruptcy determined by court ruling.

2) 'Recognition of facts such as bankruptcy' by the Minister of Employment and Labor under Article 5 of the Presidential Decree of the WCG Act: In cases where an employer becomes bankrupt due to deterioration of business or for other reasons, upon request by an employee the head of the regional Labor Office will recognize the employer as being bankrupt. The criteria for a declaration of being deemed bankrupt are ① the business has been closed in reality, ② there is no prospect of resuming business, and

3) the employer is incapable of paying wage or severance pay. As most bankruptcies

181) Jung, Bongsoo, 「Wage Manual」, KangNam labor law firm, Dec. 2019, pp. 119~126; Legislative Research Institute, Living Law Information(https://easylaw.go.kr), 'Advance Payment for the Protection of Wage Claims', April 15, 2024

Ⅱ. 대지급금제도[181)]

근로자가 취업했던 기업이 도산했을 때, 사업주의 변제능력이 없는 경우에는 근로자가 받아야 할 임금이나 퇴직금을 받을 수 없게 된다. 사업주가 변제능력이 있는 경우 향후에 소송과 경매절차 등을 통해 근로자들이 지급받지 못한 임금과 퇴직금을 우선변제 혹은 최우선변제 받을 수 있는 제도적 장치가 있지만, 이 같은 절차는 상당한 시간과 비용이 필요하므로 그 기간 동안 이들과 그 가족을 위한 생계를 사회가 보호해 줄 필요성이 있다. 이에 따라 정부는 1998.7.1부터 임금채권보장제도를 실시하고 있다. 임금채권보장제도란 기업의 도산 또는 지불불능으로 인하여 퇴직한 근로자가 임금 및 퇴직금을 지급받지 못한 경우 정부가 사업주를 대신하여 일정 범위의 체불임금과 퇴직금을 지급해 줌으로써 근로자의 기본적인 생활안정을 도모하고자 하는 제도이다.

1. 도산대지급금의 지급요건과 지급액

(1) 도산대지급금의 지급사유

도산대지급금은 사업주가 파산 등 사유로 인하여 퇴직한 근로자의 임금 등을 지급 받지 못 할 경우 정부가 나중에 사업주로부터 변제받기로 하고 사업주를 대신하여 지급하는 금액을 말한다.

1) 「채무자 회생 및 파산에 관한 법률」에 의한 '파산의 선고' 및 '회생절차개시의 결정': 재판상 도산으로 법원의 재판으로 결정된다.

2) 「임금채권보장법 시행령 제5조」에 의한 고용노동부 장관의 도산 등 사실인정: 사업주가 경영악화 등으로 인해 사실상 도산 상태에 빠져 있는 경우 퇴직근로자의 청구에 의해 지방노동관서장이 도산으로 인정한다. 이는 ① 사업주가 사실상 사업활동을 중단하여야 하며, ② 사업을 재개할 전망이 없어야 하며,

3) 임금 및 퇴직금 지급할 수 없어 사실상 도산 인정을 받는 등 모든 요건을 충족해야 한다. 중소규모에서 발생하는 도산의 다수가 법률상의 절차를 거치지

181) 정봉수,「임금 매뉴얼」, 강남노무법인, 2019.12, pp. 119~126면; 법제처, 생활법령정보(https://easylaw.go.kr), "임금채권보장을 위한 대지급금", 2024. 4. 15.

in small and medium companies occur without judicial procedures, recognition of facts such as bankruptcy becomes reason for insolvency payment. Accordingly, it is stipulated that companies ordinarily employing up to 300 persons can be recognized as actually bankrupt by the head of the regional Labor Office because judicial bankruptcy for such small companies is not easy to obtain.

(2) Eligibility for claim

1) Criteria for employers

An employer who wishes for insolvency payment to be made on his behalf shall satisfy the following conditions:

1) The employer shall be an employer of a company recognized as a business to which Industrial Accident Compensation Insurance applies.(A business or workplace that ordinarily employs one employee or more. For agriculture, forestry, fisheries, and hunting, companies that employ five employees or more; and construction projects whose contract fees are 20 million won or more);

2) The employer to which this law applies shall have carried out business for six months or more; and

3) The company shall be legally declared bankrupt by a court or recognized as bankrupt by a regional Labor Office.

2) Employees entitled to insolvency payment

Criteria for employees to be entitled to insolvency payment: ① At the time of termination of employment, the employer satisfies the above "employer criteria," and ② employees shall cease working for the business or workplace concerned one year prior to three years after the declaration of bankruptcy or the recognition of facts such as bankruptcy, etc.

(3) Amount of insolvency payment

Insolvency payment shall constitute unpaid wage or allowances for suspension of business for the final three months of employment and unpaid severance pay for the final three years of employment.

The Wage Claim Guarantee system is designed to provide a minimum level of financial security for employees of bankrupt companies, and so the amount paid by the government is not equal to total normal wage but within limited maximums. Even within the wage

않는 사실상 도산의 형태로 일어나고 있으므로 도산 등 사실인정을 도산대지급금의 지급사유로 인정하고 있다. 이에 따라 재판상 도산을 인정받기가 어려운 상시근로자 300인 이하의 일정규모 기업은 지방노동관서의 장이 사실상 도산을 인정할 수 있도록 규정하고 있다.

(2) 도산대지급금의 청구요건

1) 사업주 요건

사업주가 임금채권보장의 대상이 되는 사업주가 되기 위해서는 다음과 같은 요건을 모두 갖추고 있어야 한다.

1) 산재보험 당연적용 사업에 해당하는 사업의 사업주이어야 한다.(상시근로자 1인 이상의 사업 또는 사업장, 단 농업, 임업, 어업, 수렵업은 상시 5인 이상: 총 공사금액 2천만원 이상 건설공사)

2) 법의 적용대상 사업주가 된 후 6개월 이상의 기간 동안 당해 사업을 행한 사업주여야 한다.

3) 도산대지급금 지급사유인 파산선고 등을 받았거나 도산 등 사실인정을 받아야 한다.

2) 근로자의 요건

근로자가 도산대지급금을 지급받을 수 있는 요건은 다음과 같다. 첫째, 퇴직 당시의 사업주가 상기의 사업주 요건을 갖추고 있어야 한다. 둘째, 이러한 요건을 갖추고 있는 사업주의 사업에서 파산선고나 도산 등 사실인정을 신청한 일로부터 1년 전이 되는 날 이후부터 3년 이내에 당해 사업에서 퇴직했어야 한다.

(3) 도산대지급금의 지급액

체당금으로 지급이 보장되는 체불임금의 범위는 최종 3월분의 임금 (또는 휴업수당) 및 최종 3년간의 퇴직금이다.

임금채권보장제도는 도산기업에서 퇴직한 근로자들의 최소한의 생활안정에 기여하고자 하므로, 국가에 의해 대신 지급되는 임금의 수준은 미지급된 임금 등의 전액이 아니라 일정한 상한액의 범위 내의 금액이다. 지급이 보장되는 임

claim to be guaranteed, individual employee wage level is not completely covered but is limited according to age.

<Limits for insolvency payment according to age>

Employee Age	~30 years	30~40 years	40~50 years	50~60 years	60+ years
Wage & severance pay	2.2 mil. won	3.1 mil. won	3.5 mil. won	3.3 mil. won	2.3 mil. won
Suspension allowance	1.54 mil. won	2.17 mil. won	2.45 mil. won	2.31 mil. won	1.61 mil. won

※ Note: Amounts in the table above are for each month's wage or suspension allowance, and severance pay for each year of service.

※ How much is the insolvency payment? Employee A's salary was 4 million won and he was 45 at the time of employment termination. wage was not paid for his final five months, and neither was severance pay for his five service years.

- wage for final three months: 3.5 million won x 3 months = 10.5 million won
- Severance pay for final three years: 3.5 million won (one month's average wage) x 3 years = 10.5 million won

The total insolvency payment amount is 21 million won.

2. Procedures for Requesting an Insolvency Payment

(1) Judicial bankruptcy

1) Request for confirmation and insolvency payment amount(employee→Labor Office)

Applicants for insolvency payment shall submit a request for the insolvency payment amount and confirmation of causes for insolvency payment to the head of the regional Labor Office. The period of effective application is within two years from the date of judicial bankruptcy(date of bankruptcy, commencement date of rehabilitation procedures). The request for payment and application for confirmation shall be submitted to the head of the regional Labor Office with jurisdiction over the workplace at the time of employment termination. As each retired employee shall confirm their unpaid wage, all employees shall submit their own requests for payment and application for confirmation.

2) Report of occurrence of judicial bankruptcy(employee→Labor Office)

3) Notification of confirmation of facts(Labor Office→employee)

4) Forwarding of application for payment(Labor Office→Employee Welfare Corporation [EWC])

5) Remittance of insolvency payment(EWC→bank→employee)

6) Exercise of subrogation right(EWC→employer)

금채권에도 개별근로자의 임금수준을 모두 보장해주는 것이 아니라, 연령에 따른 상한액을 두고 있다.

〈연령에 따른 체당금 상한액〉

	30세 미만	30~40세 미만	40~50세 미만	50~60세 미만	60세 이상
임금 및 퇴직금	220만원	310만원	350만원	330만원	230만원
휴업수당	154만원	217만원	245만원	231만원	161만원

※ 비고: 임금과 휴업수당은 1월분, 퇴직금은 1년분을 기준으로 한다.

※ 월 400만원을 받던 근로자의 퇴직 당시 연령이 45세이고 최종 5월분의 임금과 최근 5년간의 퇴직금이 체불되었다면, 체불금은?
- 최종 3월분의 임금: 350만원 x 3개월 = 1050만원;
- 최종 3년간의 퇴직금: 350만원 (1월의 평균임금은 400만원이나 월정상한액 350만원) x 3년 = 1050만원 따라서 체당금은 2100만원

2. 도산대지급금의 청구절차

(1) 재판상 도산의 경우

1) 도산대지급금 확인신청 및 지급청구(근로자→노동관서)

도산대지급금 청구인은 지방노동관서의 장에게 도산대지급금지급청구서와 도산대지급금의 지급요건에 대한 확인신청서를 제출한다. 신청기간은 재판상 도산의 인정일(파산일, 회생절차 개시일)부터 2년 이내이다. 지급청구서 및 확인신청서는 퇴직 당시의 사업장을 관할하는 지방노동관서의 장에게 제출한다. 퇴직근로자 개개인에 대한 미지급임금 등을 확인해야 하므로 지급청구서와 확인신청서는 개별근로자 모두가 제출하여야 한다.

2) 재판상 도산발생 현황보고서(사업주→노동관서)

3) 사실 확인결과 통지(노동관서→근로자)

4) 지급청구서 송부(노동부→근로복지공단)

5) 도산대지급금 입금(근로복지공단→금융기관→근로자)

6) 대위권 행사(근로복지공단→사업주)

(2) Recognition of facts such as bankruptcy

1) Request for confirmation and application for payment(employee→Labor Office)

Employees who wish to receive recognition of facts such as bankruptcy shall submit an application for such recognition of facts to the head of the regional Labor Office. The period for application shall be within one year from the termination date. Applications for recognition shall be submitted to the head of the regional Labor Office with jurisdiction over the workplace. In cases where there are two employees or more terminated due to closure of the identified business or workplace, it is acceptable for only one to submit the application for recognition.

2) Notification of the decision on confirmation(Labor Office→employee)

The criterion for recognition of facts such as bankruptcy is that the employer is incapable of paying wage or has remarkable difficulty in paying. "Employer incapable of paying wage or having remarkable difficulty paying" refers to conditions where the employer does not have any property to reimburse wage, where it is impossible to change the property into cash within three months, and where it is impossible for the employer to pay wage by borrowing or other means.

3) Application for confirmation of causes for insolvency payment(employee→Labor Office)

4) Notification of decision on the confirmation of facts(Labor Office→ employee)

5) Forwarding of the application for insolvency payment and remittance of insolvency payment(Labor Office→EWC→employee)

6) Exercise of subrogation right(EWC→employer)

3. Charges Imposed on Employer and Exercise of Subrogation Right

(1) Charges imposed on employer

The Minister of Employment and Labor shall impose on an employer charges equivalent to "an amount less than 2/1000ths of the total wage" in order to cover the expenses required to make insolvency payment. The rate of charges shall be determined and announced by the Minister of Employment and Labor via review process of the Deliberation Commission on the Wage Claim Guarantee Fund. Charges to the employer shall be collected along with the Industrial Accident Compensation Insurance premium.

(2) 도산 등 사실인정의 경우

1) 확인신청 및 지급청구(근로자→노동관서)

도산 등 사실인정을 받고자 하는 퇴직근로자는 지방노동관서의 장에게 도산 등 사실인정신청서를 제출한다. 신청기간은 퇴직한 날의 다음 날부터 1년 이내이다. 인정신청서는 당해 사업주의 주된 사업장의 소재지를 관할하는 지방노동관서의 장에게 제출한다. 동일사업 또는 사업장에서 퇴직한 근로자가 2인 이상인 경우에는 그중 1인의 퇴직근로자가 인정신청서를 제출하면 된다.

2) 확인결과 통지(노동관서→근로자)

도산 등 사실에 대한 인정을 받기 위한 요건은 사용자가 "임금 등을 지급할 능력이 없거나 지급이 현저히 곤란"하여야 한다. 임금 등을 지불할 능력이 없거나 지급이 현저히 곤란한 경우란 일반적으로 사업주에게 임금지급에 충당할 수 있는 자산이 없거나 있어도 환가에 3월 이상의 시간이 소요될 것으로 확인되는 경우, 차입금이나 기타 방법에 의해서도 임금을 지급할 가능성이 없는 경우를 말한다.

3) 도산대지급금 지급요건의 확인신청(근로자→노동관서)

4) 사실 확인결과 통지(노동관서→근로자)

5) 도산대지급금 지급청구서 송부 및 체당금 송금(노동관서→근로복지공단→근로자)

6) 대위권 행사(근로복지공단→사업주)

3. 사업주의 부담과 대위권 행사

(1) 사업주의 부담

고용노동부 장관은 도산대지급금의 지급에 소용되는 비용을 충당하기 위해 사업주로부터 "임금총액의 1천분의 2 범위 내"에서 부담금을 징수한다. 부담금 비율은 고용노동부 장관이 임금채권보장기금 심의위원회 심의를 거쳐 결정, 고시하게 된다. 사업주의 부담금은 산재보험료에 통합하여 징수하고 있다.

(2) Exercise of subrogation right

When making insolvency payment to an employee from the Wage Claim Guarantee Fund, the Minister of Employment and Labor does so as the substitute for the employer so that the employee can receive unpaid wage and severance pay against their employer within the insolvency payment limit.

Ⅲ. The Small Amount Insolvency Payment Claim[182)]

To resolve these problems, a new payment solution has been proposed in addition to legal preventive measures. A high rate of 20% interest is placed on employers to facilitate their payment of delayed wage. This is to preclude employers avoiding punishment if they do not pay the unpaid wage until they are prosecuted. In addition, the unpaid workers, regardless of their employer's ability to pay their wage, can receive up to 10 million won in unpaid wage from the Wage Claim Guarantee Fund, after the Labor Office confirms that wage were not paid, and issued the confirmation of unpaid wages. This is called the Small Amount Insolvency Claim System. The maximum payout was increased from 4 million won to 10 million won on July 1, 2019, which will assist greatly with resolving financial problems related to unpaid wage. Herein, the following are the related legal preventive systems for unpaid wage and the Small Amount Insolvency Claim System in detail.

1. Purpose for Introduction

The existing insolvency payment claim system is limited to those who were employed by companies declared legally bankrupt, but does not apply to employees who have not received their wage from a company that is still operating. To better implement the basic purpose of the Wage Claim Guarantee System and improve the livelihoods of unpaid workers, the Small Amount Insolvency Payment Claim System(Small Amount IPC System) was introduced on January 20, 2015. For those unpaid workers whose employment ended with companies still in operation, a certain amount of the insolvency payment can be paid when the when the labor

182) Jung, Bongsoo, "The Insolvency Payment Claim", 「Labor Law」, Jungang, Oct. 2019.

(2) 대위권의 행사

임금채권보장기금에서 사업주를 대신하여 도산대지급금을 지급한 경우, 고용노동부 장관은 사업주에 대하여 체당금 지급 범위 내에서 근로자의 임금 및 퇴직금청구권을 대위하여 행사하게 된다.

Ⅲ. 간이대지급금제도[182)]

임금체불을 해결하기 위해 법적인 예방조치와 함께 새로운 임금체불 해결책이 제시되고 있다. 그 예방책으로 체불된 임금의 지급을 촉진하기 위해 연 20%의 고율의 지연이자제도와 사업주가 체불된 임금을 지급하면 형사처벌을 면해주는 반의사불벌죄가 있다. 이와 함께, 체불된 근로자는 사용자의 임금지급 능력과 상관없이 노동청에서 임금체불 확인서를 발급 받으면, 1000만원 한도내에서 체불된 임금을 임금채권기금에서 수령할 수 있다. 이를 간이대지급금제도라 하며 기존의 400만원 한도에서 2019년 7월 1일부터 1000만원으로 한도가 확대되어 임금체불 해결에 획기적으로 도움이 될 것이다. 이에 관련된 임금체불 예방제도와 간이대지급금제도에 대해 구체적으로 살펴보고자 한다.

1. 도입 취지

기존 도산대지급금제도는 지급대상을 사실상, 법률상 도산한 사업장에서 퇴직한 근로자로만 한정하여, 체불근로자의 대다수를 차지하는 가동 중인 사업장에서 퇴직한 근로자는 보호대상에서 제외된다는 문제점이 있었다. 체불근로자의 생계안정을 지원하는 임금채권보장제도의 기본취지가 더욱 충실히 구현될 수 있도록 2015년 1월 20일 임금채권보장법 개정을 통해 '간이대지급금 제도'가 도입되었고, 도산하지 않은 사업장의 재직근로자에 대하여도 미지급임금에 임금체불확인서를 받으면, 일정 범위의 간이대지급금 지급이 이루어지게 되었

182) 정봉수, "간이대지급금제도", 「월간 노동법률」, 중앙경제사, 2019.10.

inspector confirmed the unpaid wage and issued the certificate of unpaid wages.[183] The Small Amount IPC System is simpler than the existing general IPC System, which helps to protect, in actual terms, the rights of unpaid workers. While the general IPC system requires that the company has gone bankrupt, compensation through the Small Amount IPC System only requires confirmation from the court that a worker's wage remain unpaid.

2. Process of Making a Small Amount IPC

(1) Petitioning the Labor Office for unpaid wages

When a worker complains to the Labor Office about failing to receive wage owed, an investigation begins. The labor inspector begins by requesting attendance of the relevant parties to a hearing. If a settlement agreement is concluded between the parties or the unpaid wage are paid, the case is closed. If the unpaid wage are not paid, despite an order to do so from the labor inspector, the criminal punishment process begins, and the worker can also obtain a confirmation certificate of the unpaid wage from the labor inspector.

(2) Applying for an insolvency payment claim

If a worker applies for a Small Amount IPC with a Confirmation Certificate of Unpaid wage attached, the Labor Welfare Corporation shall decide whether to pay the Small Amount IPC within 14 days of receiving the claim.194).[184]

(3) Scope of payment

Both general and Small Amount IPCs are paid on behalf of the employer for the final three months' wage(including suspension allowances) and the final three years' retirement allowances. However, 2.2 million won to 3.5 million won per month(up to 2 million won) can be paid out under the general IPC, depending on age. The Small Amount IPC is based on the criteria of the general IPC as well, but the maximum payout is 10 million won, while the maximum amount per wage item(including suspension allowance) and retirement benefits is separated and shall not exceed 7 million won each.

---

183) Ji, Hee-jung, "The Protection of Workers Eligible to Make a Small Amount Insolvency Payment Claim", 「Legal Issues and Discussion」, May 2017, p. 43.

184) WCGA Implementation Rule: Article 5, paragraph 2.

다.[183] 간이대지급금제도는 기존의 도산대지급금 제도보다 지급요건이 간소하여 체불 근로자들의 실질적인 권리보장에 도움이 된다. 도산대지급금은 도산여부를 조사하는 과정에서 사업주의 재산조사도 함께 이루어지지만, 간이대지급금제도는 임금체불확인서서만 확보하면 체당금이 지급된다.

2. 간이대지급금 처리절차

(1) 노동청 체불임금 진정

임금체불이 발생하여 근로자가 노동청에 진정을 접수하면 임금체불사건이 진행된다. 근로감독관은 관계자 출석요구 등으로 사실관계를 파악하고, 그 과정에서 당사자 사이에 합의가 되거나 체불임금이 지급되면 종결처리가 이루어진다. 근로감독관의 시정지시에도 불구하고, 체불임금 청산이 이루어지지 않으면 형사처벌절차가 진행되고, 이러한 절차와 별도로 근로자는 체불금품확인원을 발급받아 진행된다.

(2) 근로복지공단에 체당금 신청

근로자가 체불금품확인원이 첨부된 간이대지급금 지급청구서를 제출하면 근로복지공단은 청구서를 제출받은 날부터 14일 이내에 간이대지급금 지급여부를 결정하고 청구인에게 지급할 소액도산대지급금을 지급하여야 한다.[184]

(3) 지급액 범위

도산대지급금과 간이대지급금은 모두 최종 3개월 치 임금(휴업수당 포함)과 최종 3 년 치 퇴직금을 사업주 대신 지급하는 것으로 그 지급액 내역은 동일하다. 그러나 도산대지급금은 연령에 따라 월 220만원에서 350만원까지(최대 2100만원) 차 등 지급한다. 간이대지급금은 지급기준에 따라, 최대 1000만원으로 하고 임금(휴업수당)과 퇴직급여를 구분하여 그 상한액을 각각 700만원으로 한다.

---

183) 지희정, “간이대지급금 지급대상이 되는 근로자의 보호방안”, 「법제논단」, 2017.5, 43면.
184) 임금채권보장법 시행규칙 제5조 제2호.

Ⅳ. Statute of Limitations

1. Purpose of the Statute of Limitations

Wage claims are valid for a maximum of 3 years according to the statute of limitations. The term 'wage' refers to payment that includes bonuses, overtime work pay, monthly/annual leave pay, and severance pay, as defined in the Labor Standards Act. When an employer fails to pay wage or severance pay to an employee whose employment relationship is discontinued by reason of retirement, etc., the employer shall pay deferral interest at a rate of 20% per year in addition to the unpaid wage or severance pay. However, the deferral interest will not apply to periods during which there exist certain reasons specified in the relevant legislation, such as natural disaster, war, or legal or de facto bankruptcy.

1) The right to request payment for unused annual leave has a three-year statute of limitation. The date of calculation starts on the day after the leave expires, provided that it has not been redeemed for the past one-year period after being granted.[185)]

2) A labor contract which establishes working conditions that do not meet the standards provided for in the Labor Standards Act shall be null(Article 15 of the Labor Standards Act). Accordingly, even though the employer and the union agreed to exclude the regular bonus from ordinary wage, this mutual agreement is invalid as being in violation of the Labor Standards Act. As the above agreement was invalid, it is a principle that the employer shall recalculate the overtime work allowance, adding the wages included in legal ordinary wage, and that the employee can apply for retroactive payment for the variance from the amount already paid. However, this retroactive claim can be valid only for the amount payable for the past three years.[186)]

The statute of limitations system recognizes the time-sensitive status of rights or claims that have not been exercised for a certain period of time, even if that status does not conform to a true rights relationship.[187)] In other words, if people do not exercise specific rights for a certain period of time, they can no longer exercise those rights due to the statute of limitations. The reason for this is to limit rights that have not been exercised,

---

185) Supreme Court ruling on Jun. 30, 1995, 94Da47155.

186) Supreme Court ruling on Dec.18, 2013, 2012Da89399.

187) Oh, Young-hwan, Lee, Ro-moon, 「General Provisions of the Civil Code」, 2009, MJ Media, p. 350.

Ⅳ. 소멸시효제도

1. 소멸시효 목적

임금채권의 소멸시효 기간은 3년이다. 여기서 '임금'은 근로기준법상의 임금으로 상여금, 시간외근로수당, 연·월차 유급휴가수당, 퇴직금 등이 모두 포함된다. 사용자가 퇴직 등으로 근로관계가 종료된 근로자에게 임금·퇴직금을 체불했을 경우 연 20%의 지연이자 지급의무가 부과된다(근로기준법 제37조). 단, 천재·사변, 법률상·사실상 도산 등 법령에 규정된 사유가 존속하는 기간에는 지연이자율의 적용이 제외된다.

1) 연차휴가근로수당의 지급청구권은 3년의 소멸시효가 적용되고, 그 기산점은 취득한 날부터 1년의 경과로 휴가 불실시가 확정된 다음 날이 된다.[185)]

2) 근로기준법이 정한 기준보다 낮은 임금 등 불리한 근로조건 계약은 무효(근로기준법 제15조 참조)이다. 따라서 법률상 통상임금에 해당하는 정기상여금 등의 임금을 통상임금에서 제외하기로 노사가 합의하였다 하더라도 위 합의는 근로기준법에 위반되어 무효이다. 위와 같은 합의가 무효이므로, 법률상 통상임금에 해당하는 임금을 통상임금 산정에 포함시켜 다시 초과근로수당을 계산한 다음, 소급하여 이미 지급받은 것과의 차액을 추가임금으로 청구할 수 있다. 다만, 사용자가 소멸시효 항변을 할 경우 최종 3년 치만 인정 가능하다.[186)]

소멸시효란 일정한 기간 동안 권리를 행사하지 않는 사실상태가 계속되는 경우에 그 상태가 진실한 권리관계에 합치되지 않더라도 그 사실상태를 인정하려는 제도이다.[187)] 즉, 일정한 기간 동안 권리행사를 하지 않는 경우에 시효의 완료로 인하여 더 이상 권리행사를 할 수 없는 것이다. 이러한 소멸시효를 두는 이유는 행사하지 않는 권리를 제한하여 법적 안정을 꾀하고 신속한 권리관계 설정을 촉진하기 위함이다. 근로기준법도 근로자 보호를 위하여 권리행사 불이

---

185) 대법원 1995.6.30, 94다47155.

186) 대법원 2013.12.18, 2012다89399.

187) 오영환, 이로문, 「민법총칙」, 2009, MJ미디어, 350면.

and to promote the establishment of legal security and expedite claims or the use of rights. The Labor Standards Act(LSA) also attaches a statute of limitations to non-performance of rights to promote their exercise and thereby protect workers.

Since the statute of limitations for deferred wages is only three years, the amount of claimable wages is gradually reduced as the period passes before the three years expire. In particular, at the stage of petitions and accusations filed with the Ministry of Employment and Labor, suspensions of the statute of limitations on deferred wages are not allowed, and so action in a civil court is required. In other words, as labor inspectors handle investigations of complaints regarding deferred wages, and determine the facts behind the delay by examining the workers affected and their employers, these legal actions have no effect on the statute of limitations. On the other hand, claims for compensation for occupational accidents are recognized as filing for work compensation with the court. The statute of limitations is suspended and claims for industrial accident compensation can be extended to 5 years.

Since they are both special laws designed to protect workers, the LSA and the Industrial Accident Compensation Insurance Act(IACI) differ from other laws in terms of suspensions and duration before the statute of limitations kicks in. I will look into the overall statute of limitations in the LSA.

2. Statute of Limitations[188)]

(1) Concept

"Statute of limitations" refers to expiration of a right that has not been exercised. The principle is that the law does not protect those who "sleep" on it. This means that if people have a right they can exercise but do not for a certain period of time, they will not be able to exercise it, so that the state of legal tranquility already established will be maintained. Most statute of limitations in labor law start at three years. A concept similar to the statute of limitations under the LSA is "exclusive period." After expiration of an exclusive period, no further legal appeal can be made. Since it aims at the rapid establishment of legal relations, exclusive period differs from statute of limitations.[189)]

---

188) Jung, Bongsoo, "Statute of Limitations", 「Labor Law」, Jungang, Apr. 2013.

189) Supreme Court ruling on Sep. 20, 1996 96da25371

행에 대한 소멸시효제도를 두고 있다.

임금채권 소멸시효는 3년으로 짧기 때문에 소멸시효 만료로 인해 청구 가능한 임금 체불금이 점점 줄어든다. 특히, 고용노동부의 진정 및 고소 단계에서는 임금체불에 대한 시효의 중단이 인정되지 않기 때문에 이를 해결하는데 있어 민사적 절차인 재판상 청구를 하여야 한다. 다시 말해, 근로감독관이 임금이 체불된 근로자와 해당 사용자를 확정하는 노동청의 진정 또는 고소단계에서는 소멸시효에 전혀 영향을 주지 않는다. 이에 반해 산재보상의 청구는 업무상 재해 보상에 있어 재판상 청구로 인정받기 때문에 소멸시효가 중단되고, 이에 따른 청구권의 소멸시효도 5년으로 연장된다.

근로자 보호를 위한 동일한 특별법임에도 불구하고 근로기준법과 산업재해보상법은 소멸시효의 중단과 기간에 차이를 두고 있다. 이와 관련된 근로기준법상의 전반적인 시효에 대해 구체적으로 살펴보고자 한다.

2. 소멸시효[188)]

(1) 소멸시효 개념

소멸시효는 권리행사를 할 수 있음에도 해당기간 동안 그 권리를 행사하지 않아 시효가 경과하여 더 이상 권리행사를 할 수 없는 상태를 말한다. 법은 권리 위에 잠자는 자를 보호하지 않는다는 원칙이 적용된다. 이는 행사할 수 있는 권리는 있지만, 일정 기간 동안 권리행사를 하지 않는 경우 이를 못하게 함으로써 이미 형성된 법적 평온 상태를 유지하게 한다는 것이다. 노동법상 대부분 소멸시효는 3년을 기준으로 한다. 근로기준법상 소멸시효와 유사한 개념이 제척기간이다. 제척기간이 지나면 더 이상 법적 이의를 제기할 수 없다. 제척기간은 법률관계의 신속한 확정을 목적으로 하므로 소멸시효와 그 기간에 있어 차이가 있다.[189)]

188) 정봉수, "근로기준법상 소멸시효제도", 「월간 노동법률」, 중앙경제사, 2019.4.
189) 대법원 1996.9.20, 96다25371.

(2) Details of the statute of limitations

1) Wage bonds under the Labor Standards Act

Wage bonds will expire unless the claims for deferred wage are exercised within three years(Article 49 of the LSA). Wage bonds can be categorized as monthly salary, retirement allowance, unused annual allowance and so on. Monthly wage(base salary, overtime allowance, holiday work allowance, etc.) are paid on the salary payment date and rights can be exercised from the time when they are not paid, so salary calculation will begin from the regular payment date. Bonuses shall be calculated when the right to receive the bonus is incurred, while severance pay shall be calculated from the date of retirement due to the obligation to pay the employee on that day.

Annual paid leave is calculated from the date of conversion to a wage claim after using one year for granted annual leave.[190)] In other words, if annual paid leave is managed on a yearly basis, if an employee enters 2018, his annual paid leave from January 1, 2019 to December 31, 2019 will be granted on the first day of 2020, 15 days' annual leave if he works at 80 percent or more for the period. During 2020, annual leave shall be used. The starting point for a claim for unused annual leave shall be 2021, and this right shall exist for three years(Article 36, Article 60 of the LSA).

2) Benefits under the Industrial Accident Compensation Insurance Act (IACI Act)

Rights protected by the IACI Act shall extinguish unless they are exercised within 3 years of when the right to claim compensation for a work injury or disease begins. However, the right to receive disability benefits, survivor benefits, funeral expenses benefit, compensation pensions for pneumoconiosis, and survivor's pensions for pneumoconiosis will expire within five years if not exercised(enacted Dec. 13, 2018, Law No. 15665). The insurance benefits of the IACI Act can be divided into the following three categories: ① Claims for continuous insurance benefits, ② Claims for lump sum insurance benefits, and ③ Claims for pension benefits. Each type of pension insurance benefit has a different point when the statute of limitations kicks in.

1) Claims of continuous insurance benefits include claims to medical care benefits and work suspension benefits. Medical care benefits are paid when a worker is injured or becomes sick in relation to work, and in principle is paid as reimbursement of actual medical

190) Supreme Court ruling on Sep. 14, 1992 92da17754

(2) 소멸시효 내용

1) 근로기준법상 임금채권

임금채권은 3년간 행사하지 않으면 시효로 소멸한다(근기법 제49조). 임금채권은 월 급여, 퇴직금, 미사용 연차수당 등으로 분류할 수 있으며 유형별 소멸시효 기산점이 다르다. 매월 지급되는 월 임금(기본급, 연장근로수당, 휴일근로수당 등)은 임금 지급일에 지급의무가 발생하고 이때부터 권리를 행사할 수 있으므로 기산점은 정기지급일부터 진행된다. 상여금은 상여금에 관한 권리가 발생한 때 지급의무가 발생하며, 퇴직금은 근로자가 퇴직한 날 다음 날에 지급의무가 발생하므로 퇴직일 다음 날부터 기산한다. 연차유급휴가는 휴가 사용기간인 1년 완료 후 15일이 임금청구권으로 전환되는 시점부터 기산된다.[190] 즉, 연도별 관리로 판단할 경우 2018년 입사자의 경우, 2019년 1월 1일부터 2019년 12월 31일까지 80퍼센트 이상 출근한 경우에 한해 15일의 연차휴가가 발생한다. 다음 연도인 2020년 1년 동안 연차휴가를 사용하여야 한다. 2021년 1월 1일부터 미사용 연차휴가에 대한 임금청구권의 기산점이 되며, 이는 3년간 청구가 가능하다(근기법 제36조, 제60조).

2) 산재법상 보상급여

산재법은 업무상 부상 또는 질병에 대해 권리를 3년간 행사하지 아니하면 시효로 말미암아 소멸한다. 다만, 장해급여, 유족급여, 장의비, 진폐보상연금 및 진폐유족연금을 받을 권리는 5년간 행사하지 아니하면 시효의 완성으로 보아 소멸한다(시행 2018.12.13, 법률 제15665호, 2018.6.12, 일부개정). 산재법의 보험급여는 다음의 세 가지로 나누어 볼 수 있다. ① 계속적 보험급여의 청구, ② 일시금 보험급여의 청구, 그리고 ③ 연금보험급여 이렇게 세 가지의 형태로 청구하며 각각 소멸시효의 기산점이 다르다.

1) 계속적 보험급여의 청구에는 요양급여, 휴업급여 등이 있다. 요양급여는 근로자가 업무상의 사유로 부상을 당하거나 질병에 걸린 경우 지급하며 현물급여가 원칙이다(산재법 제40조). 즉 보험금을 받을 권리의 소멸시효 기산일은 근

190) 대법원 1992.9.14, 92다17754.

expenses(Article 40 of the Act). That is, the period before the statute of limitations for the right to claim this insurance benefit kicks in begins the day after the cost of medical treatment is paid, not when a worker's occupational injury or illness first occurs.[191] Since the work suspension benefit is paid for a period that a worker who has been injured or sick cannot work, the period before the statute of limitations kicks in begins the day after the worker first becomes unable to work so they can receive medical treatment(Article 52 of the Act).

2) Claims for lump-sum insurance benefits include claims to lump sum payments of disability compensation, survivor compensation, or an allowance of some sort. A lump sum disability compensation payment shall be paid to a worker who has been injured on the job or suffered from a work-related illness, and whose disability continues after recovery. A disability benefit is provided when a worker has completed their treatment and the disability is fixed(Article 57 of the Act). Survivors' compensation is paid in the form of a pension in principle, but if there is no legal beneficiary, a lump sum compensation is possible. The period before the statute of limitations kicks in begins on the day after the relevant worker has died(Article 62 of the Act). Funeral expenses are only paid when they have actually occurred(Article 71).

3) Pension insurance benefits include pensions for disabilities and survivors, with payment beginning the first month after the month in which the reason for payment occurred.

In the case of noise-induced hearing loss, the Labor Welfare Corporation's Guidelines for Work Disabilities previously claimed that the 3 years' limitation begins "when leaving the noisy workplace," but the court ruled that it could be considered to have begun at the time of "healing" instead.[192] As a result, in 2016, the MOEL changed the statute of limitations for noise-induced hearing loss so that the calculation date begins from diagnosis. Therefore, in recent cases, the court has ruled that "the statute of limitations for a person diagnosed with noise-induced hearing loss after a long absence from the noisy workplace cannot be considered to have come into effect even if they have applied for a disability benefit after three years have passed from the time of diagnosis." [193]

---

191) Hwang, Won-hee, "Calculating when the statute of limitations occurs for work-related accident benefits", Labor Law Review, 27, Apr. 2013, Korean Comparative Labor Law Association, p. 382; Supreme Court ruling on Dec. 17, 2008, 2006da35865

192) Supreme Court ruling Sep. 4, 2014: 2014doo7374; Park, Jong-Tae, "Review of Standards for Recognition of Occupational Hearing Impairment," Monthly Labor Law, May 2017.

193) Seoul Administrative Court ruling on Apr. 20, 2017: 2017goodan 50655.

로자가 업무상 부상 또는 질병에 걸린 날이 아니라 요양에 필요한 비용이 발생한 다음 날이 된다.[191] 휴업급여는 업무상 사유로 부상을 당하거나 질병에 걸린 근로자에게 요양으로 인해 취업하지 못한 기간에 대해 지급하므로, 취업하지 못한 다음 날부터 소멸시효 기산일이 시작된다(산재법 제52조).

2) 일시금 보험급여의 청구에는 장해보상일시금, 유족보상일시금, 장의비 등이 있다. 장해보상일시금은 근로자가 업무상 부상을 당하거나 질병에 걸려 완치 후에도 장해가 남은 근로자에게 지급한다. 장해급여는 재해근로자가 치료가 종결되어 장해가 고정된 시점에서 진행된다(산재법 제57조). 유족보상일시금은 연금수급권자가 없는 경우에 한해 지급하며, 소멸시효 기산일은 재해근로자가 사망한 다음 날이 된다(산재법 제62조). 장의비는 실제로 장제를 지낸 경우에 한해 지급한다(산재법 제71조).

3) 연금보험급여에는 장해보상연금, 유족보상연금 등이 있으며, 지급시기는 그 사유가 발생한 달의 다음 달 초일부터 시작된다.

특히, 소음성 난청의 경우 종전의 근로복지공단 업무지침에는 장해급여청구권에서'소음작업장을 떠났을 때'를 기준으로 3년의 소멸시효가 완성된다고 판단하였으나, 대법원은 소음성 난청과 관련하여 장해보상청구권은'치유'시점으로 본다고 판결하였다.[192] 이에 따라 2016년 고용노동부는 소음성 난청 소멸시효를 '진단일로부터 기산한다'는 내용으로 변경하였다. 이로 인하여 최근 판례에서는"소음작업장에서 퇴사한 지 한참 후에 소음성 난청 진단을 받은 사람이 -그 진단을 받은 때로부터 청구기간이 3년이 경과한 때 - 장해급여를 신청하였어도 소멸시효가 완성되었다고 볼 수 없다."[193]고 판시하고 있다.

---

191) 황운희, "산재보험급여의 소멸시효 기산일", 「노동법논총」 제27집, 한국비교노동법학회, 2013.4, 382면; 대법원 2008.4.17, 2006다35865 전원합의체 판결.

192) 대법원 2014.9.4, 2014두7374, 박종태, "소음성 난청의 업무상 재해 인정기준 검토,「월간 노동법률」, 중앙경제사, 2017.5.

193) 서울행정법원 2017.4.20, 2017구단50655.

(3) The statute of limitations for wage bonds and the statute of limitations for prosecution

"Statute of limitations refers to expiration of the period during which an employee who has the right to receive compensation may exercise a claim against the employer in the event of a delay in the payment of wage or severance pay. The statute of limitations for prosecution refers to expiration of the period when prosecution can occur for violating labor law, such as delaying the payment of wage, and begins either on the date the violation occurred or the date a continuing violation ends.

The period before the statute of limitations kicks in for prosecution of violation of labor-related Acts in terms of delayed payment of wage was extended from 3 years to 5 years in 2007(Article 249, Paragraph 1, Item 5 of the Criminal Procedure Act). The period before the statute of limitations for prosecution kicks in shall be deemed to have started 14 days from the date the wage should have been paid or the date the violations terminate(Article 252 of the Criminal Procedure Act). According to Article 49 of the LSA, the statute of limitations for a wage bond kicks in after three years. However, since the statute of limitations for prosecution is now 5 years, prosecution for delayed payment of wage will continue to be possible.194) Thus, an employee may file a claim for unpaid wage for a period of five years.

3. Suspension of Statute of Limitations

(1) Concept

Termination of a statute of limitations is occurrence of the factual condition on which the statute of limitations is based. The reasons for termination of the statute of limitations are: ① A request for trial(Article 170 of the Civil Act); ② Participation in bankruptcy proceedings(Article 171); ③ Issuance of a payment order from the court(Article 172); ④ A summons for reconciliation(Article 173); ⑤ Unilateral attendance at the court(Article 173); ⑥ Notification by registered mail(Article 174): claim for money in the case of monetary bonds, if the request is made based upon registered mail, it is only valid for 6 months if

194) MOEL Guide, 「Guide on Handling Unpaid wage」, 2016, pp. 31-32.

(3) 임금채권 소멸시효와 공소시효

소멸시효는 돈 받을 권리가 있는 근로자가 사용자를 상대로 임금이나 퇴직금의 체불이 있는 경우에 청구권을 행사할 수 있는 기간을 말한다. 이에 대해 공소시효는 임금체불 등 노동법 위반 사용자를 법 위반행위가 있는 날 또는 법 위반행위가 계속되는 경우 종료일로부터 형벌권을 행사할 수 있는 기간을 말한다.

임금체불로 인한 노동관계법령 위반 범죄의 공소시효 기간은 2007년에 기존 3년에서 5년으로 연장되었다(형사소송법 제249조 제1항 제5호). 공소시효 기산점은"범죄행위가 종료된 때부터(형소법 제252조) 임금지급일 또는 퇴직일로부터 14일이 경과한 때"까지를 말한다. 이에 반해 임금채권의 소멸시효는 3년이다(근기법 제49조). 임금채권의 소멸시효 3년이 완성되었다 하더라도 공소시효가 아직 남아 있으므로 임금체불사업주에 대한 형사처벌이 가능하다.[194] 따라서 공소시효를 근거로 하여 근로자는 체불된 임금에 대해 5년간 청구가 가능하다.

3. 소멸시효 중단

(1) 소멸시효 중단의 개념

소멸시효의 중단은 시효의 기초가 되는 사실상태를 발생하는 것으로 시효가 중단하게 되는 내용이다. 소멸시효의 중단사유는 ① 재판상 청구(민법 제170조): 소의 각하 또는 취하가 있으면 시효중단 효력이 없음, ② 파산절차 참가(제171조), ③ 지급명령(제172조): 법원에 지급명령을 신청한 경우, ④ 화해를 위한 소환(제173조), ⑤ 임의출석(제173조), ⑥ 최고(제174조): 금전채권의 경우 금전청구, 다만 최고를 한 경우 6월 내에 재판상 청구, 파산절차 참가 등을 하지 않는 경우 시효중단 효력 없음, ⑦ 압류, 가압류, 가처분(제176조), ⑧ 승인(제177조): 채무자가 채권자에게 채무가 있음을 인정한다는 의미이고 보편적으

194) 고용노동부 근로기준정책과, 「체불사건 업무처리 요령」, 2016, 31~32면.

a court filing or application for bankruptcy was not made; ⑦ Foreclosures, provisional attachment, provisional dispositions(Article 176) ⑧ Approval(Article 177): meaning that the debtor has confirmed a debt to the creditor.

(2) Details

1) Details of reasons for suspension

Since wage bonds have a 3-year statute of limitations, if an employee has not filed a claim during the 3-year period leading up to statute of limitations, the claim can no longer be made. However, in the event of a trial claim, seizure of the wage bond, or provisional attachment, if the employer agrees to the wage bond, the statute of limitations shall not occur. If the employer writes a memorandum on the unpaid wage and pays part of those unpaid wage, the statute of limitations shall be suspended.[195)]

If the worker informs their employer of the unpaid wage by means of registered mail, this shall be the reason for a six-month suspension of the statute of limitations(Article 174 of the Civil Act). However, the notification letter shall have the effect of ceasing the statute of limitations for six months, unless the worker requests a trial, participates in bankruptcy proceedings, responses to reconciliation, has seizure or accepts a provisional disposition.[196)]

2) Relationship to delayed payment of wage

1) Whether an employee's claim for unpaid wage can be a reason for suspending the statute of limitations: A criminal or civil complaint filed against a judicial authority, such as a labor inspector, is not accepted as a trial claim.[197)] However, in the event of unfair dismissal, when the related workers are involved in the administrative court's proceedings as auxiliary participants while the National Labor Relations Commission is working as the defendant, the statute of limitations is suspended.[198)]

2) Whether issuance of a labor supervisor's confirmation of unpaid wage can be

---

195) Supreme Court ruling on Jun. 10, 2010: 2010da8266.

196) Ha, Kap-rae, 「Labor Standards Act」, 28th Ed., 2016, Jongang Kyungjaesa, p. 315.

197) Supreme Court ruling on Mar. 12, 1999: 98da 18214, Kumho construction company

198) Supreme Court ruling on Feb. 9, 2012: 2011da20034

로 지불각서 등이 해당된다.

(2) 소멸시효 중단 내용

1) 중단사유

임금채권은 3년간의 소멸시효를 가지므로, 이를 근로자가 3년 동안 청구하지 않았을 때는 소멸시효의 만료로 인해 더 이상 다툴 수 없다. 다만, 재판상 청구, 임금채권에 대한 압류 또는 가압류를 한 경우, 사용자가 임금채무에 대해 동의한 경우 소멸시효는 중단이 된다. 사용자가 임금체불에 대해 각서를 써주고 체불금의 일부를 변제한 경우에도 소멸시효는 중단이 된다.[195]

임금채권에 있어 미지급한 부분에 대해 사용자에게 내용증명으로 최고를 할 경우에는 6개월간 소멸시효의 중단 사유가 된다(민법 제174조). 다만, 최고는 시효 중단의 효과가 있으나 6개월 내에 재판상의 청구, 파산절차참가, 화해를 위한 소환, 압류 또는 가처분을 하지 않으면 소급하여 시효중단의 효력이 없어진다.[196]

2) 임금체불과의 관계

1) 근로자가 체불 임금 진정 제기가 시효중단 사유가 되는지 여부: 근로감독관 등 사법당국에 형사고발이나 고소를 하는 경우에는 재판상 청구로 인정되지 않아 시효중단효력이 없다.[197] 다만, 부당해고사건에 있어 중앙노동위원회를 피고로 하고 근로자를 보조참가인으로 하여 진행된 행정소송에서는 임금채권에 대한 시효의 중단을 인정하였다.[198]

2) 근로감독관의 임금체불확인서 발급이 시효의 중단에 해당하는지 여부: 임금체불이 된 근로자가 회사를 상대로 고용노동부에 진정하여 임금체불을 확정하는 과정에서 사용자의 임금체불에 대해 확인하는 경우에는 소멸시효의 중단으로 볼 수 없으나, 사용자가 임금체불에 대해 변제하겠다는 확인서를 작성해

195) 대법원 2010.6.10, 2010다8266.
196) 하갑래, 「근로기준법」, 제28판, 2016년, 중앙경제사, 315면.
197) 대법원 1999.3.12, 98다18214 금호건설사건.
198) 대법원 2012.2.9, 2011다20034.

termination of the statute of limitations: In cases where a worker who has taken a petition for unpaid wage to the MOEL, if the employer simply confirms the amount of unpaid wage, this will not be regarded as statute of limitations. However, if the employer has made a written confirmation of payment of the delayed wage, this can be regarded as a suspension of the statute of limitations.[199]

3) Relationship to the IACI Act

In accordance with the IACI Act, a worker's filing of a claim that they have an occupational injury or illness can terminate the statute of limitations, which will affect all claims related to Industrial Accident Compensation Insurance benefits(Article 113 of the IACI Act). In general, submitting a complaint to the MOEL regarding unpaid wage will not be considered a trial claim. However, if an industrial accident application is filed with the Labor Welfare Corporation, it shall be regarded as a trial claim which can terminate statute of limitations. As a precedent, a worker filed an application for occupational accident compensation benefits, but was rejected. Then after he did not apply for review within 90 days after the rejection, the corporation dismissed his late claims due to the statute of limitations. However, the Supreme Court recognized that the claim for insurance benefits pursuant to Article 36(1) of the IACI Act as a reason for termination of the statute of limitations, separate from the reason for the statute of limitations under the Civil Act.[200]

199) Kang, Ji-hyeon, "Issues Regarding statute of limitations on Wage Bonds", 「Attorneys」 Vol. 49, 2016, p. 216; Seoul District Court ruling on Jan. 21, 2016: 2015na42147

200) Supreme Court ruling on Jun. 15, 2018: 2017da9119

준 경우에는 소멸시효의 중단으로 볼 수 있다.[199]

3) 산재법과의 관계

산재법상 업무상 부상 또는 질병에 대한 산재보험 청구는 소멸시효를 중단시키고, 산재보험 급여 관련 모든 청구권에도 소멸시효의 중단을 가져온다(산재법 제113조). 일반적으로 임금채권에 대해서 고용노동부에 진정, 고소 등을 제기하는 것을 재판상 청구로 볼 수 없지만, 산재업무의 특성에 따라 근로복지공단에 산재신청을 하는 경우 재판상 청구로 보아 소멸시효의 중단사유가 된다. 이와 관련된 판례로 산재보험급여 수급권자가 보험급여를 신청하였으나, 불승인을 받아 90일 이내에 소를 제기하여야 한다는 처분을 받았음에도 소를 제기하지 않고 있다가 3년 내 다시 보험 급여를 청구한 사안에 대해 근로복지공단은 소멸시효가 완성되었다고 부지급 처분을 내렸다. 이에 대해 대법원은 산재보험법 제36조 제1항에 따른 보험급여 청구는 이를 민법상의 시효 중단 사유와는 별도의 고유한 시효 중단 사유로 인정하여 소멸시효의 중단 사유로 인정하였다.[200]

---

199) 강지현, "임금채권의 소멸시효 관련 실무상 쟁점", 「변호사」제49집, 2016, 216면. 서울중앙지법 2016.1.21, 2015나42147.

200) 대법원 2018.6.15, 2017다9119.

Chapter 4

Working Hours, Recess, Off-Days and Leave

Section 1: Working Hours

I. Concept of Working Hours

1. Scope of Working Hours

(1) Concept

Working hours refer to the actual working hours during which the employee provides labor service prescribed by the employment contract under the employer's direction and supervision. Even if an employee is not actively engaged in work during working hours, such as during waiting, rest, or sleep time, if it is effectively under the control and supervision of the employer, it is considered part of the working hours, not as rest time with guaranteed freedom of use.[201)] Article 50 of the Labor Standards Act regulates that working hours shall not exceed 8 hours per day and 40 hours per week, excluding recess hours. The employer shall pay an additional fifty percent(50%) of the ordinary wage for each working hour exceeding the legal standard working hours(or contractual working hours per part-time workers). Working hours are usually implemented within contractual working hours that the employer and the employee have agreed upon, but there have been some disputes in recognizing working hours in cases where the employee conducted work before or after contractual working hours, or in cases of waiting time for work, training hours, traveling hours, company events, etc.

---

201) Supreme Court ruling on Nov. 23, 2006, 2006da41990.

근로시간, 휴게, 휴일, 휴가

제1절 근로시간

Ⅰ. 근로시간의 개념

1. 근로시간의 범위

(1) 근로시간의 의의

근로시간이란 근로자가 사용자의 지휘·감독 아래 근로계약상의 근로를 제공하는 시간, 실 근로시간을 말한다. 근로자가 작업시간 도중에 현실로 작업에 종사하지 않은 대기시간이나 휴식, 수면시간 등이라도 하더라도 그것이 휴게시간으로서 근로자에게 자유로운 이용이 보장된 것이 아니고 실질적으로 사용자의 지휘, 감독하에 놓여있는 시간이라면 이는 근로시간에 포함된다.[201] 근로기준법 제50조에서 근로시간은 휴게시간을 제하고 1일에 8시간 1주일에 40시간을 초과할 수 없다고 규정하고 있다. 이 법정근로시간(단시간 근로자의 경우 '소정근로시간')을 초과하는 근로시간에 대해 통상임금의 50%를 가산하여 지급하여야 한다. 근로시간은 대게 당사자 간에 근로하기로 합의한 소정근로시간 이내에 이루어지지만, 근로자가 사업주의 지시에 의해 시업시간 전 또는 종업시간 후에 업무를 수행한 경우, 또는 그 외 대기시간, 교육시간, 출장시간, 행사시간 등에 대해 근로시간 인정여부에 대한 다툼이 생기는 경우가 많다. 이에 대해 근로시간에 대한 판단 기준을 명확히 하고, 그 구체적 사례에 대해 검토해보고자 한다.

---

201) 대법원 2006. 11. 23. 선고 2006다41990 판결.

(2) Criteria used in calculating working hours

1) Whether working hours are stipulated in the labor contract, rules of employment, or the collective agreement

Working hours shall be the total working hours from when the employee starts to provide contractual work to the employer to when the employee finishes his/her work, excluding recess hours. The Labor Standards Act regulates that the employment contract shall include the starting and finishing times for work, and the rules of employment shall contain statutory items that must be included.

2) Whether the employee is under the employer's direction and supervision.

Working hours mean the time during which the employee provides labor service described by the employment contract under the employer's direction and supervision. Even though waiting time or recess and sleeping time are times that the employee is not engaged in actual work in the middle of working hours, if these times are not allowed to be used freely by employees, but are, in practice, under the employer's direction and supervision, those times belong to working hours.[202)]

Whether the subsidiary time required in actual working hours belongs to working hours or not shall be judged by whether those times are implemented under the employer's direction and supervision. Such subsidiary times include the time needed to change into the work uniform and gather necessary tools, waiting time, conferences prior to work, shift-changes, wash-up time after finishing the work day, organizing things for the next day's work after finishing the workday, travel time during business trips, etc.[203)]

3) Whether work characteristics under the employment contract are acceptable or not.

The type of work described under the employment contract is not limited to the work tasks themselves, but actual working hours shall include those times essentially required to prepare for work and to arrange things after finishing the work day in relation to actual work performance. It is regarded as working hours in cases where those activities besides actual working hours are stipulated as the employee's mandatory duties according to related laws, collective agreements, rules of employment, labor practices, and employment contracts, or in cases where non-implementation charges disadvantage the employees concerned.

---

202) Supreme Court ruling on May 27, 1993, 92Da24509.

203) Supreme Court ruling on Mar. 9, 1993, 92Da22770.

(2) 근로시간의 판단기준

1) 근로계약, 취업규칙, 단체협약 등에 규정되어 있는지 여부

근로시간의 계산은 근로자가 사용자에게 소정의 근로를 제공하기 시작한 시간부터 그 제공을 종료한 시각까지의 총 시간에서 휴게시간을 공제한 시간으로 산출하는데, 근로기준법에서는 시업과 종업시간을 근로계약에 명시토록 하고 취업규칙에서 반드시 기재하여야 할 필요적 기재사항으로 정하고 있다(근기법 제17조, 제93조).

2) 사용자의 지휘·감독 하에 있는지 여부

근로시간이라 함은 사용자의 지휘·감독 아래 근로계약상의 근로를 제공하는 시간을 말하는 것으로, 작업시간 도중에 현실로 작업에 종사하지 않은 대기시간이나 휴식·수면시간이라 하더라도 그것이 휴게시간으로서 근로자에게 자유로운 이용이 보장된 것이 아니고 실질적으로 사용자의 지휘·감독 아래 놓여있는 시간이라면 당연히 근로시간에 포함시켜야 한다.[202)]

작업복을 갈아입는 시간, 작업도구 준비시간, 대기시간, 작업 전 회의, 교대시간, 작업 후 목욕시간, 작업종료 후 정돈 시간, 출장 중 이동시간 등 실제근로에 부속되는 시간이 근로시간 인지 여부도 사용자의 지휘·명령 아래서 이루어지는지에 따라 판단된다.[203)]

3) 근로계약상 업무성이 인정되는지 여부

근로계약에서 정하여진 근로의 종류는 반드시 그 근로자체만을 뜻하지 않고 그 근로에서 실작업에 필요불가결한 준비행위나 작업종료 후 뒷정리를 위한 시간도 실근로시간에 포함된다. 실 근로시간외의 활동으로 법령, 단체협약, 취업규칙, 노사관행 또는 근로계약에서 근로자의 의무로 명백히 정하거나 그 불이행에 대한 일정한 불이익이 과해진 경우에는 근로시간에 포함된다.

---

202) 대법원 1993.5.27, 92다24509.
203) 대법원 1993.3.9, 92다22770.

2. Concrete Judgments of Working Hours

(1) Time worked before the workday starts

1) In cases where the employee arrives at the workplace earlier than the official starting hour

Whether the company shall pay wage for working hours when the employee comes earlier to the workplace to ensure normal operations shall be dependent upon the following: If the employee did not come to work earlier than the official starting hour, his wage could be reduced or he might be punished for a violation of service regulations. If this situation does not exist, then the time before the official starting hour does not belong to working hours.[204)]

2) Conferences held before working hours

Conferences held before working hours to deal with safety training for underground mine workers, work directions, and organization of working groups. These meetings shall be held essentially for the purpose of underground shift work and be implemented under the employer's direction and supervision. Therefore, these meetings shall be included in actual working hours.[205)]

(2) Time worked after the workday is over

The end of the workday is the time for the employee to be free from the employer's direction and supervision. When the employee continues to be under the employer's direction and supervision after he finishes his regular work time, actual working hours end when the employee is actually free from the employer's direction and supervision. Such examples of the end of the workday not being the end of actual working hours are workplace repairs, examinations, organization, and cleaning conducted after completing work under the employer's direction and supervision.[206)]

(3) Waiting time

Recess hours under the Labor Standards Act mean the time that employees can use freely, away from the employer's direction and supervision, regardless of the name

---

204) MOEL Guidelines: Kungi 01254-13305, on Aug. 30, 1988.

205) Supreme Court ruling on Sept. 28, 1993, 93Da3363.

206) Supreme Court ruling on Mar. 9, 1993, 92Da2270.

2. 구체적 판단사례

(1) 시업 전 시간

1) 조기 출근한 경우 근로시간

시업시간 이전에 조기 출근토록 하여 시업에 지장이 없도록 하는 것을 근로시간으로 인정하여 임금이 지급되어야 할 것인가 여부는 조기출근을 하지 않을 경우 임금을 감액하거나 복무 위반으로 제재를 가하는 권리의무관계라면 근로시간에 해당될 것이나 그렇지 않다면 근로시간에 해당되지 않는다.[204)]

2) 작업시간 전 취업회의 시간

작업시간 전에 갖는 취업회의 내용인 갱내 근무자에 대한 보안교육이나 작업지시 및 작업조의 편성은 갱내 교대근무를 위한 필요불가결한 것으로서 사용자의 지휘 감독에 의한 구속하에 행해질 수밖에 없으므로 실근로시간에 포함시키는 것이 타당하다.[205)]

(2) 종업 후 시간

근로시간이 끝나는 종업시각은 근로자가 사용자의 지휘 감독으로부터 벗어났다고 인정되는 작업종료 시각이다. 그러나 작업이 끝나도 계속하여 사용자의 지휘 감독아래 있을 때는 시업시각의 경우처럼 그 구속으로부터 벗어난 시각이 종업시각이 된다. 사용자의 지휘 감독아래 하는 작업 후 기계 기구의 정비 점검 정돈과 사업장의 청소 등 이에 속한다.[206)]

(3) 대기시간

근로기준법상의 휴게시간이란 휴게시간·대기시간 등 명칭여하에 불구하고 근로자가 사용자의 지휘·감독으로부터 벗어나 자유로이 사용할 수 있는 시간을 말한다. 따라서 취업규칙상 근로형태는 아니지만, 사업주의 묵시적인 동의

---

204) 행정해석: 근기 01254-13305, 1988.8.30.
205) 대법원 1993.9.28, 93다3363.
206) 대법원 1993.3.9, 92다22770.

given for such times, such as waiting time, etc. In this case, unlike the working structure stipulated by the rules of employment, under the employer's implied agreement, the employees work every two hours in repeated practices and off-time employees take recess hours, playing chess or baduk, or watching TV. There is a clear division of waiting time and working hours. The employees cannot go out of the workplace during this waiting time, but they can use it freely, away from the employer's direction and supervision. In this case, the waiting time shall be recognized as recess hours.[207]

In cases where an employee drives a company car as necessary from time to time, just like a regular driver of a company car, if the employee cannot use the waiting time freely, this shall be regarded as working hours; but, if such time is free for the employee to use as he/she wishes, it is considered part of recess hours and cannot be included in working hours.[208]

(4) Education and training time

It is working hours when the employer implements job training during working hours in relation to work, concerning work safety and work efficiency to improve productivity, and it is also working hours when the employer gives compulsory training outside of working hours or during a holiday. However, it is not working hours when the employee attends compulsory individual training like driver's education, regardless of the company's business, or when moral or safety training etc. is recommended to employees and provided by the nation due to major national policies outside of working hours or during a holiday.[209]

(5) Company picnics or events

In cases where the company hosts a picnic party, athletic event, etc., if the employee needs to attend the picnic party, athletic event, etc., the participating time shall be deemed as working hours. Conversely, if the employer hosts a picnic party, athletic event, etc. for the purpose of welfare, and if employees are free to participate in the event at their own

---

207) MOEL Guidelines: Kungi 68207-3298, on Oct. 25, 2000.

208) Supreme Court ruling on July 28, 1992, 92Da14007.

209) MOEL Guidelines: Kungi 01254-14835, on Sept. 29, 1988.

하에 관례적으로 근로자들 스스로 2시간 단위로 작업을 하고 작업을 하지 않는 근로자들은 대기실에서 장기, 바둑, TV 시청 등을 하는 형태로서, 대기시간과 근무시간의 구분이 명백하고, 근로자가 사전에 대기시간을 알고 있으며, 그 대기시간 중에는 사업장 밖으로 나갈 수는 없지만, 사용자의 지휘·감독을 벗어나 자유로이 이용할 수 있다면 이는 휴게시간으로 인정할 수 있다고 판단된다.[207)]

업무용 자동차 운전자와 같이, 필요할 때마다 간헐적으로 운전업무를 하는 경우 다음 운전업무까지 대기하는 시간은 그 시간을 자유롭게 이용할 수 없는 한 이를 근로시간으로 보는 것이 원칙이나 자유로운 이용이 보장되면 휴게시간으로서 근로시간에 포함되지 않을 수 있다.[208)]

(4) 교육시간

사용자가 근로시간 중에 작업안전, 작업능률 등 생산성 향상 즉 업무와 관련하여 실시하는 직무교육과 근로시간 종료 후 또는 휴일에 근로자에게 의무적으로 소집하여 실시하는 교육은 근로시간에 포함되어야 할 것이다. 그러나 근로자가 회사와는 관계없는 운전면허증 소지자에 대한 소양교육과 같은 법적 이행 개인의무사항 교육이나 국가기관 등의 시책사업으로 사용자에게 협조를 요구하여 근무시간외 또는 휴일에 회사에서 단체로 근로자에게 의무사항이 아닌 권고사항으로 시행하는 국민정신교육, 안전관계교육 등은 근로시간에 포함된다고 볼 수 없을 것이다.[209)]

(5) 야유회 등의 행사

일반적으로 사용자가 근로자의 야유회, 체육대회 등의 행사를 행하는 경우, 그 야유회, 체육대회 등의 참가자가 근로자의 의무로서 강제되는 경우에는 그 참가시간은 근로시간으로 보아야 할 것이고, 반대로 이러한 야유회, 체육대회 등을 사용자가 복리후생적인 의미에서 행하고 근로자가 이에 참가하는 여부가

207) 행정해석: 근기 68207-3298 2000.10.25.
208) 대법원 1992.7.28, 92다14007.
209) 행정해석: 근기 01254-14835, 1988.9.29.

discretion, it shall not be deemed as working hours even though employees attend such an event.[210)]

If the company hosts a picnic party on a working day according to the company's operation rules, the wage for that day shall be paid accordingly. If the picnic party was held on a holiday, the wage payable on that holiday and ordinary wage to compensate for holiday work(i.e. the picnic party) shall be paid.[211)]

(6) Business travel

1) Travel time between employee accommodations and the appointed workplace

In calculating working hours for business travel, travel time to the workplace shall be included in working hours in principle, but when the workplace is on the way to the regular office, such travel time can be excluded from working hours. However, for long-distance business travel, travel time from the company workplace to the workplace on business travel shall be included in the working hours.[212)]

2) When the employee is required to engage in business travel at night or during a holiday by order of the employer, such time shall be regarded as night or holiday work.

In cases where the employee carries out his duties in whole or in part outside the workplace for business travel or for other reasons, the calculation of working hours shall follow Paragraphs 1 and 2 of Article 57 of the Labor Standards Act. In consideration of the concept of the same Article, if it is evident that the employee conducts business travel at night or during holidays by order of the employer, the night work and holiday work shall be considered working hours. However, if the employee only travels to the workplace during the night or holiday and does not engage in any business, it is difficult to deem such travel time night work or holiday work.[213)]

---

210) MOEL Guidelines: Kungi 01254-554, on Jan. 10, 1989.

211) MOEL Guidelines: Kungi 1455-7105, on July 12, 1979.

212) MOEL Guidelines: Kungi 68207-1909, on June 14, 2001.

213) MOEL Guidelines: Kungi 68207-2650, on Aug. 5, 2002.

그의 자유에 맡겨진 때는 근로자가 임의로 이에 참가하더라도 그 시간은 근로시간이 아니라고 보아야 할 것이다.[210)]

회사운영방침에 따라 근로하여야 할 날에 야유회를 실시하는 경우라면 임금은 당연히 지급되어야 하며, 유급휴일에 야유회를 실시하는 경우라면 휴일에 당연히 지급되는 임금과 당해 유급휴일의 근로(야유회)에 대한 소정의 통상임금을 지급하면 되는 것이다.[211)]

(6) 출 장

1) 출장업무 수행을 위해 이동하는 시간

출장에 있어 통상 필요한 시간을 산정할 경우 출장지로의 이동에 필요한 시간은 근로시간에 포함시키는 것이 원칙이나 출퇴근에 갈음하여 출장지로 출근 또는 출장지에서 퇴근하는 경우는 제외할 수 있을 것이다. 다만, 장거리 출장의 경우 사업장이 소재하는 지역에서 출장지가 소재하는 지역까지의 이동시간은 근로시간에 포함시키는 것이 타당하다.[212)]

2) 사용자의 지시에 의해 야간 또는 휴일에 출장업무상 이동이 명확한 때는 야간·휴일근로로 볼 수 있다

출장근무 등 사업장 밖에서 근로하는 경우에 있어서의 근로시간 산정에 관하여는 근로기준법 제57조 제1항 및 제2항에서 특례를 규정하고 있는바, 동조의 취지로 볼 때 사용자의 지시에 의해 야간 또는 휴일에 출징업무를 수행하는 것이 명확한 때는 야간, 휴일근로로 볼 수 있으나 단순히 야간 또는 휴일에 이동하는 때는 야간, 휴일근로를 한 것으로 보기 어렵다.[213)]

---

210) 행정해석: 근기 01254-554, 1989.1.10.
211) 행정해석: 근기 1455-7105, 1979.7.12.
212) 행정해석: 근기 68207-1909, 2001.6.14.
213) 행정해석: 근기 68207-2650, 2002.8.5.

Ⅱ. Recess Periods

The purpose of a recess is to relieve worker fatigue and reduce the boredom caused by continual work, thereby enabling them to continue to work feeling refreshed and willing to work.[214)]

A "recess period" is the period of time during which a worker is free to rest without being directed or supervised by an employer.[215)]

The Labor Standards Act states, "Working hours per week shall not exceed 40 hours excluding recess hours. Working hours per day shall not exceed 8 hours excluding recess hours. In calculating working hours, waiting hours the worker spends while under the employer's direction and supervision for work shall be regarded as working hours."(Article 50 of the Labor Standards Act). The recess period in the Labor Standards Act is excluded from working time, but time waiting for work is determined to be working time, not a recess period. Although the relationship between working time and recess period is clear, there is a vague distinction between "waiting time" and "recess period". In designating working hours, it is possible to secure optimal working hours even within statutory working hours if the proper recess period is used in consideration of the characteristics of the work. In order to design a suitable working time system, the concept of recess periods, and the criteria for distinguishing between "waiting time" and "recess period" is explained, along with examples of some working time systems using relevant recess periods.

1. Concept of a Recess Period and its Practical Use

Recess hours are free hours and excluded from and occur after a certain number of working hours. According to the Labor Standards Act, "An employer shall allow a recess period of 30 minutes or more for every 4 working hours and at least 1 hour for every 8 working hours during working hours"(Article 54 of the Labor Standards Act). "Any person

---

214) Ha, Kaprae, Labor Standards Act」, 33rd ed., Joongang Economy, 2020, p. 323; Lim Jongyul, Labor Act 17th ed., 2019, p. 460.

215) Government Guide: Bubmoo 811-28682, issued on May 15, 1980.

Ⅱ. 휴게시간

휴게제도는 근로자가 계속해서 근로할 경우 육체적·정신적 피로가 쌓이게 되므로 근로자의 피로를 회복시키고 권태감을 감소시켜 노동력의 재생산과 작업 의욕을 확보 유지하는 데 그 목적이 있다.[214] 휴게시간은 근로시간 중간에 사용자의 지휘와 감독을 받지 않고 근로자가 자유로이 휴식을 가지는 시간을 말한다.[215]

근로기준법에서는 1주 근로시간은 휴게시간을 제외하고 40시간을 초과할 수 없고, 1일의 근로시간은 휴게시간을 제외하고 8시간을 초과할 수 없다고 기술하고 있다. 근로를 제공하지는 않지만, 작업을 위하여 근로자가 사용자의 지휘와 감독 아래에 있는 대기시간은 근로시간으로 보고 있다(법 제50조). 근로기준법상 휴게시간은 근로시간에서 제외되지만, 근로를 위해 대기하는 시간은 휴게시간이 아닌 근로시간으로 판단하고 있다. 이 경우 근로시간과 휴게시간의 관계가 명확하지만, 대기시간과 휴게시간은 구분이 모호한 면이 있다. 근로시간을 설계함에 있어서 업무의 특성을 고려하여 적절한 휴게시간을 잘 이용한다면, 법정근로시간 내에도 최적의 근로시간 확보가 가능하다. 이하에서는 적합한 근로시간제도의 설계를 위하여 휴게시간의 개념, 대기시간과 휴게시간을 구분하는 기준을 이해하고, 휴게시간을 이용한 근로시간제도 사례를 검토해 보고자 한다.

1. 휴게시간의 개념과 사용

휴게시간은 일을 하고 다음 일을 원활히 하기 위해 근로의무가 면제된 쉬는 시간이다. 근로기준법에서 근로시간이 4시간인 경우에는 30분 이상, 8시간인 경우에는 1시간 이상의 휴게시간을 근로시간 도중에 주어야 한다(근기법 제54조). 이 휴게규정을 위반한 자는 2년 이하의 징역 또는 1천만원 이하의 벌금에

---

214) 하갑래, 「근로기준법」 제33판, 2020년, 323면; 임종률, 「노동법」, 제18판, 2020년, 460면.

215) 법무 811-28682, 선고일자: 1980.5.15

who violates the provision of 'recess period' shall be punished with imprisonment of up to 2 years or a fine not exceeding 20 million won"(Article 110). "Working hours per week shall not exceed 40 hours excluding recess hours, and working hours per day shall not exceed 8 hours excluding recess hours. Waiting hours that the worker spends while under the employer's direction and supervision for work shall be regarded as working hours"(Article 50).

(1) Free use of recess periods

"Recess period" means time which a worker is free to use away from the supervision and command of an employer during working hours.[216] Here, the term "working hours" refers to the time when a worker provides work in a labor contract under the direction and supervision of an employer. Even if a worker is not actively working(i.e. waiting time, rest time, sleeping time, etc.), if it is a period of time when that free use is not guaranteed to the worker and is actually time under the control and supervision of an employer, this time is included in working hours.[217]

A recess period is part of the working hours from the start to the end of work, so even during a recess period it is unavoidable that a worker may still be subject to a certain level of restriction, such as the command and supervision of an employer to continue to carry out work. In other words, workers can be given free breaks, but at the same time there may be some restricted recess periods, depending on the nature of the work, when it is necessary to maintain continuity of work and efficiently respond to emergency situations. In this case, if workers are free to use the recess period beyond the command and supervision of the employer, even though they are restricted within the workplace or are not allowed to leave the workplace during the break without permission, these limitations, which may be required in order to meet objective criteria recognized in advance, can be accepted as a reasonable limitation as to where and how breaks are used.[218]

---

216) Supreme Court ruling on Apr. 14, 1992: 91da20548.

217) Supreme Court ruling on Nov. 23, 2006: 2006da41990; Supreme Court ruling on Dec. 5, 2017: 2014da74254.

218) Government Guide: The Legislative Office 16-0239, issued on Aug. 19, 2016.

처한다(법 제110조). 또한, 법정근로시간은 휴게시간을 제외하고 주 40시간, 1일 8시간으로 제한하고, 작업을 위한 대기시간은 휴게시간이 아닌 근로시간으로 규정하고 있다(법 제50조).

(1) 휴게시간의 자유이용

휴게시간이란 근로자가 근로시간 도중에 사용자의 지휘·명령으로부터 완전히 벗어나 자유로운 이용이 보장된 시간을 의미한다.[216] 여기서 근로시간이라 함은 근로자가 사용자의 지휘·감독 아래 근로계약상의 근로를 제공하는 시간을 말한다. 근로자가 작업시간 도중에 실제로 작업에 종사하지 않은 대기시간이나 휴식·수면시간 등이라 하더라도 그것이 휴게시간으로서 근로자에게 자유로운 이용이 보장된 것이 아니고 실질적으로 사용자의 지휘·감독하에 놓여있는 시간이라면 이는 근로시간에 포함된다.[217]

휴게시간은 작업의 시작으로부터 종료 시까지로 제한된 시간 중의 일부이므로, 휴게시간 중이라고 하더라도 다음 작업의 계속을 위하여 사용자의 지휘·감독 등 일정 수준의 제약을 받는 것은 부득이하다. 즉, 근로자에게 그 종사하는 업무의 특성에 따라 자유로운 휴게시간을 부여하면서도 업무의 연속성을 유지하고 업무와 관련한 긴급 상황에 효율적으로 대응할 수 있도록 하는 등 최소한의 질서유지를 위하여 휴게시간의 이용에 관한 제한이 이루어질 수 있다. 이 경우 근로자로 하여금 사용자의 지휘·감독을 벗어나 휴게시간을 자유롭게 이용할 수 있도록 하고 그 장소를 사입장 안으로 제한하거나 휴게시간에 사업장 밖에 나갈 수 있도록 하면서도 이를 사전에 마련된 객관적 기준에 합치되는 경우에만 허가하는 등의 제한은 휴게시간의 이용 장소와 방법에 관한 합리적인 제한이다.[218]

---

216) 대법원 1992.4.14, 91다20548.

217) 대법원 2006.11.23, 2006다41990; 대법원 2017.12.5, 2014다74254.

218) 법제처 16-0239, 회시일자: 2016.8.19

(2) Scope and use of recess periods

1) Principle

Article 54(1) of the Labor Standards Act stipulates that an employer shall provide a recess period of 30 minutes or more for 4-hour periods of work, or 1 hour or more for 8-hour periods of work. This is the minimum standard for recess periods that employers must provide for workers who work continuously for specific periods of time.[219)] Even if the recess period is provided and given in divided portions distinct from working hours, as long as such recess periods are reasonable in view of the nature of the work and the working conditions, this cannot be regarded as a violation of the recess regulation.[220)]

2) Working hours of fewer than 8 hours

Employers shall provide 30 minutes or more of recess period during the working hours to workers whose working time is more than 4 hours and fewer than 8 hours.[221)] However, since this is the lowest standard, it is not a problem to provide more recess time.

3) Divided recess periods

The Labor Standards Act does not include any provision for dividing a recess period into 10 minutes for every hour or 20 minutes for every two hours. A breakdown of subdivided hours is not permitted, as the purpose of a recess period is to provide relief from fatigue, promote work efficiency, prevent work accidents, provide eating time and meet other socio-cultural requirements.[222)]

4) Working hours exceeding 8 hours

When working more than 8 hours per day, a recess period of 30 minutes or more per 4 hours of overtime and 1 hour or more for 8 hours of overtime or more shall be provided to employees pursuant to Article 54 of the Labor Standards Act.[223)]

---

219) Government Guide: The Legislative Office 15-0847, issued on Dec. 24, 2015.

220) Government Guide: Gungi 68207-3307, Dec. 2, 2002.

221) Government Guide: The Legislative Office 15-0847, issued on Dec. 24, 2015.

222) Government Guide: Gungi 0125-884, June 25, 1992.

223) Government Guide: Working condition guide team-722, Feb. 6, 2009.

(2) 휴게시간의 범위와 부여방법

1) 원 칙

사용자는 근로시간이 4시간인 경우에는 30분 이상, 8시간인 경우에는 1시간 이상의 휴게시간을 근로시간 도중에 주어야 한다고 규정하고 있다(근기법 제54조 제1항). 이는 문헌상 일정 시간 동안 계속적으로 근로하는 근로자에게 사업주가 부여하여야 하는 휴게시간의 최저기준을 정한 것이다.[219] 근무시간과 명백히 구분하여 휴게시간을 분할하여 부여하더라도 작업의 성질, 근로여건 등에 비추어 사회통념상 합리성이 있고 휴게제도의 취지를 벗어나지 않는 한 이를 법 위반으로 보기 어렵다.[220]

2) 8시간 미만의 근로시간

사용자는 근로시간이 4시간 이상 8시간 미만인 근로자에게 30분 이상의 휴게시간을 근로시간 도중에 주어야 한다.[221] 다만, 이는 최저 기준이므로 더 많은 시간을 주는 것은 문제가 없다.

3) 분할부여

휴게시간을 분할해 1시간마다 10분, 2시간마다 20분 등과 같이 세분화해 부여할 수 있는지에 대해 근로기준법에는 이에 관한 규정이 없으나 피로해소, 작업능률증진, 재해발생예방, 식사 기타 및 사회적-문화적 욕구의 실현 등이 휴게의 목적인 만큼 지나치게 세분화된 휴게시간은 인정되지 않을 수 있나.[222]

4) 8시간을 초과하는 근로시간

하루 8시간을 초과하여 연장 근로를 하는 경우, 연장 근로 4시간에 대하여 30분 이상, 8시간 이상 근로 시 1시간 이상의 휴게 시간을 근로기준법 제54조에 의거하여 부여할 법적 의무가 있다.[223]

219) 법제처 15-0847, 회시일자: 2015.12.24.
220) 근기 68207-3307, 회시일자: 2002.12.2.
221) 법제처 15-0847, 회시일자: 2015.12.24.
222) 근기 0125-884, 1992.6.25.
223) 근로조건지도과-722, 회시일자: 2009.2.6.

2. Classification of Waiting Time and Recess Period

(1) Standard for determination

"Working time" refers to the time during which an employee provides work under the direction and supervision of an employer. Any waiting time is under the direction and supervision of the employer, and so shall be regarded as working time(Article 53(3) of the Labor Standards Act). On the other hand, "recess period" refers to the time in which a worker is free to use away from the command and supervision of an employer during working hours.[224)]

Both "waiting time" and "recess period" are common, in terms of occurrence during working hours. The difference is that "waiting time" is the time preparatory to engaging in work as soon as the employer instructs and is therefore under the direction and supervision of the employer. "Recess period" on the other hand, is time which workers are free to use separate from the direction and supervision of an employer. Therefore, distinction between the two is made according to whether the worker can freely use the time available.[225)] If the worker can clearly distinguish the recess period before starting work, and can freely use it with no direction or supervision of an employer, it must be regarded as a recess period, but if it is not known when there will be work-related instruction from the employer while the worker is waiting, the time cannot be considered a recess period, but as working time.[226)]

1) Drivers for transportation companies

When transportation company workers, such as tour bus drivers, go to work and are certain of the time they will be dispatched for work, and freely wait at the workplace, that waiting time is considered a recess period. However, when workers wait without knowing when they will be requested to work for the employer, such waiting time is not considered a recess period. However if, due to the nature of the work, it is not possible to uniformly set a certain recess period in advance, if the dispatch time of the day is clearly defined so

224) Guidelines on Working Hours and Recess Period for Surveillance or Intermittent Work, Oct. 2016.

225) Lee, Seonggil. "Recess Periods According to Labor Law", Labor Law, Apr. 2004, Vol. 155, Joongang Kyungjae.

226) Government Guide: Gungi 01254-12495, Aug. 5, 1987.

2. 대기시간과 휴게시간의 구분

(1) 판단기준

근로시간은 근로자가 사용자의 지휘·감독 아래 근로계약상의 근로를 제공하는 시간을 말한다. 그 명칭 여하를 불문하고 근로자가 그 노동력을 사용자의 처분 아래에 두고 있는 경우에는 근로시간으로 인정한다. 작업을 위하여 근로자가 사용자의 지휘·감독 아래에 있는 대기시간 등은 근로시간으로 본다(근기법 제53조 제3항). 이에 반해 휴게시간은 근로자가 근로시간의 도중에 사용자의 지휘·명령으로부터 완전히 벗어나 자유로운 이용이 보장된 시간을 말한다.[224)]

대기시간과 휴게시간은 모두 출근한 상태에서 근로시간 중간에 부여한다는 공통점이 있다. 그러나 대기시간은 사용자의 지시가 있으면 바로 작업에 종사해야 하는 시간으로 작업상 지휘·감독 하에 놓여 있다. 반면에 휴게시간은 사용자의 지휘·감독에서 이탈하여 근로자가 자유로이 이용할 수 있는 시간이다. 따라서 양자의 구별은 그 시간을 근로자가 자유롭게 이용할 수 있는지의 여부에 따라 판단한다.[225)] 작업의 진행 상황에 따라 근로자가 미리 작업개시 전에 휴게시간을 명백히 구분할 수 있는 상황에 있고, 그 시간 중에 사용자의 지휘·감독을 벗어나 자유로이 시간을 활용할 수 있다면 휴게시간으로 보아야 할 것이다. 다만 사용자로부터 언제 업무지시가 있을지 불분명한 상태에서 대기하는 시간은 휴게시간으로 볼 수 없고 근로시간으로 본다.[226)]

1) 운수회사의 버스기사

관광버스 운수회사의 근로자가 출근 시간에 출근하여 퇴근 시까지 어느 시간에 배차가 될지 불확실하여 사업장 내에서 어느 정도 자유롭게 대기는 하고 있으나 사용자로부터 언제 운행 요구가 있을지 모르는 상태에서 대기 중 일 경우에는 그 대기 중의 시간은 휴게시간 이라고는 볼 수 없다. 그러나 업무의 성질상 일정 시간의 휴게시간을 미리 일률적으로 정할 수는 없으나 근무 전일 혹은 근무 당일에 출근과 동

---

224) 감시, 단속적 근로자의 근로시간과 휴게시간 구분에 대한 가이드라인, 2016.10.
225) 이승길, "노동법상의 휴게시간", 월간 노동법률, 2004.4, Vol.155. 중앙경제.
226) 근기 01254-12495, 회시일자: 1987.8.5.

that the distinction between dispatch time(vehicle operation time) and waiting time is clear before work or on the day of work, and if the worker knows the waiting time in advance and if such waiting time is available freely beyond the direction and supervision of the employer, this is a recess period.[227)]

2) Apartment security guards

In this instance, apartment security guards worked 24 hours from 07:00 to 07:00 the next day, and then rested. Of these 24 hours of duty, the recess period consisted of 6 hours, and was divided into 1 hour for lunch, 1 hour for dinner, and 4 hours for a night break(from 24:00 to 04:00). They were required to respond immediately if something urgent happened, even if it occurred during the night recess period. Although guards were wearing their work uniforms and allowed to take a nap during the night recess period, they were ready to react immediately in case of emergency, and therefore such night rest periods shall be regarded as working time.[228)]

3) Goshiwon (long-stay inn) receptionists

Goshiwon receptionists do not have predetermined times set aside for recess periods. As visitors or new tenants do not have fixed arrival times, the receptionists must remain in place without leaving the Goshiwon house. The owner provides the necessary work instructions without special time constraints, and receptionists must also fulfill unscheduled instructions. Although the receptionists did not have any special work to do, and although they took long breaks or studied during many of the waiting hours, such time is considered to be a waiting time for work, not a recess period completely free from direction and supervision.[229)]

4) Postal vehicle drivers

Drivers working in the postal logistics service have often taken breaks(such as eating or sleeping) at work, while working every other day. However, these breaks were taken during gaps in time while waiting to provide labor between the time of going to work and

---

227) Government Guide: Bubmoo 811-28682, issued on May 15, 1980.

228) Supreme Court ruling on Dec. 13, 2017: 2016da243078.

229) Seoul Central District Court ruling on June 23, 2017: 2017no922.

시에 당일의 배차시간이 명백히 정해져서 배차시간(차량운행시간)과 대기시간의 구분이 명백하고, 근로자가 사전에 대기시간을 알고 있으며, 그 대기시간 중에는 사용자의 지휘·감독을 벗어나 자유로이 이용할 수 있다면 이는 휴게시간이다.[227)]

2) 아파트 야간 경비원

한 아파트의 경비원들은 아침 7시부터 다음 날까지 24시간을 근무하고, 그다음 날은 쉬는 격일제 근무를 해왔다. 24시간 중 휴게시간은 총 6시간 – 점심 1시간, 저녁 1시간, 야간휴게시간(자정 12시부터 새벽 4시까지) 4시간 – 으로 구성됐다. 입주민들은 경비원들에게 야간휴게시간에 가수면상태라도 급한 일이 발생하면 즉각 반응할 것을 서면으로 지시했다. 경비원들이 야간휴게시간에 근무복을 입고 가수면상태로 휴식을 취하면서 급한 일이 발생하면 즉각 반응할 수 있는 상태로 일했다면, 이러한 야간휴게시간은 근로시간으로 본다.[228)]

3) 고시원 총무

고시원 총무들에게는 휴게시간으로 사용할 수 있는 구체적 시간이 미리 정해져 있지 않았다. 방문자나 새로운 세입자가 찾아오는 것은 정해진 시간이 있는 것이 아니므로 고시원을 벗어나지 않고 항상 자리를 지키고 있어야 했다. 고시원 주인은 특별한 시간의 제약이 없이 그때그때 필요한 업무지시를 하였고, 총무는 이에 따른 돌발적인 업무지시를 이행하였다. 비록 고시원 총무들이 특별한 업무가 없어 휴식을 취하거나 공부를 하는 등으로 시간을 보냈다고 하더라도, 그 시간은 고시원 주인의 지휘명령으로부터 완전히 벗어나 자유로운 이용이 보장되는 휴게시간이 아니므로 근로를 위한 대기시간에 해당한다.[229)]

4) 우편운송 차량기사

우편물 운송차량의 운전직에 종사하는 직원들은 격일제 근무형태로 근무하는 도중에 수시로 수면이나 식사 등의 휴식을 취하여 왔다. 그러나 이는 어디까지

---

227) 법무 811-28682, 선고일자: 1980.5.15.

228) 대법원 2017.12.13, 2016다243078.

229) 서울중앙시법 2017.6.23, 2017노922.

leaving work at a specific time. In other words, such periods were not provided freely away from the employer's direction and supervision.[230)]

5) Nursing assistants

The labor contract of nursing assistants who worked a three-shift schedule specified a four-hour rest period during the night shift and the availability of a night-time sleeping room. However, in reality they often could not sleep there due to emergency calls from patients at the nursing hospital where they worked. Such periods should be regarded as waiting hours for work.[231)]

III. Legal Standard Working Hours

> **Labor Standards Act Article 50 (Working Hours)** ① Working hours per week shall not exceed 40 hours excluding recess hours. ② Working hours per day shall not exceed 8 hours excluding recess hours.
>
> **Article 69 (Work Hours [for minors])** Working hours of a person aged between 15 and 18 shall not exceed 7 hours per day and 35 hours per week. However, the working hours may be extended up to an hour per day, or 5 hours per week, by an agreement between the parties concerned.
>
> **Occupational Safety and Health Act Article 139 (Restriction on Extension of Working Hours for Harmful or Dangerous Work)** With respect to a worker who is engaged in harmful or dangerous work prescribed by Presidential Decree, the employer shall not have him work in excess of 6 hours per day or 34 hours per week.

Working hours stipulated in the Labor Standards Act are regulated in units of one day and one week. The purposes of standard working hours are to rehabilitate the employee from mental and physical fatigue, preserve labor service, and guarantee the employee's right to participate in social and cultural activities. Legal standard working hours regulated in the Labor Standards Act are as follows:

230) Supreme Court ruling on May 27, 1993: 92da24509.

231) Supreme Court ruling on Sept. 8, 2016: 2014do8873.

나 일정한 시각에 출근하여 퇴근할 때까지 항상 사업장 내에서 운전업무 등의 노무제공을 위하여 대기하는 상태에서 그 공백시간에 틈틈이 이루어진 것이지 결코 일정한 수면시간이나 휴식시간이 보장되어 있지 않으므로 사업주의 지휘, 감독으로부터 벗어나 자유로운 휴게시간으로 이용한 것이 아니다.[230]

5) 요양보호사

3교대로 근무하는 요양보호사의 근로계약서에는 야간 근무시간 중 4시간의 휴게시간이 명시되어 있다. 요양보호사들이 잠을 잘 수 있는 야간수면실도 운영했지만 실제로는 요양 대상자가 비상벨을 누르는 경우가 많아 잠을 제대로 이루지 못하고 늘 대기상태에 있었다. 이에 대해 법원은 요양보호사의 당해 야간근무 중 휴게시간은 근로시간으로 보았다.[231]

Ⅲ. 법정근로시간

근로기준법 제50조【근로시간】

① 1주간의 근로시간은 휴게시간을 제외하고 40시간을 초과할 수 없다.

② 1일의 근로시간은 휴게시간을 제외하고 8시간을 초과할 수 없다.

제69조【연소자의 근로시간】 15세 이상 18세 미만인 자의 근로시간은 1일에 7시간, 1주에 35시간을 초과하지 못한다. 다만, 당사자 사이의 합의에 따라 1일에 1시간, 1주에 5시간을 한도로 연장할 수 있다.

산업안전보건법 제139조【유해·위험작업에 대한 근로시간 제한 등】

① 사업주는 유해하거나 위험한 작업으로서 높은 기압에서 하는 작업 등 대통령령으로 정하는 작업에 종사하는 근로자에게는 1일 6시간, 1주 34시간을 초과하여 근로하게 해서는 아니 된다.

근로기준법은 1일과 1주를 단위로 하여 근로시간을 규제하고 있다. 이는 긴 시간 동안 근로함에 따라 발생하는 정신적·육체적 피로에서 회복시켜 근로자

230) 대법원 1993.5.27, 92다24509.
231) 대법원 2016.9.8, 2014도8873.

Type of Employee	Standard working hours	Overtime	Night/holiday work
General Employees	8 hours per day; 40 hours per week	Mutual agreement; 12 hours per week	No limit
Female employees within one year after giving birth	8 hours per day; 40 hours per week	Mutual agreement; 2 hours per day; 6 hours per week; 150 hours in one year	Individual agreement; Approval from the Minister of Employment and Labor
Pregnant employees	8 hours per day; 40 hours per week	Not allowed	Specified request; Approval from the Minister of Employment and Labor
Employees under 18 years of age	7 hours per day; 35 hours per week	Mutual agreement; 1 hour per day; 5 hours per week	Individual agreement; Approval from the Minister of Employment and Labor
Employees working under harmful and dangerous conditions	6 hours per day; 34 hours per week	Not allowed	

Ⅳ. Contractual Working Hours

1. Concept

Contractual working hours shall be determined between the worker and employer in the range of working hours pursuant to Article 50(Work Hours) and Article 69(Work Hours for Minors) of the Labor Standards Act, or Article 139(Hazardous and Dangerous Work) of the Occupational Safety and Health Act. This means that the contractual working hours must be set within the statutory working hours. Article 17 of the Labor Standards Act requires wage, contractual working hours and other working conditions to be specified in the process of making an employment contract. Therefore, wage defined in the employment contract are limited to 40 hours a week, and in principle, inclusive wage are a violation of the Labor Standards Act. Article 58 stipulates that if a worker fails to calculate working time by working all or part of the working hours outside the workplace due to business trips or other reasons, he/she shall be deemed to have worked the contractual working hours. Even for part-time workers, "the employer shall obtain the consent of

로 하여금 노동력을 보전하고 사회적·문화적 활동을 통해 인간다운 생활을 할 수 있도록 하기 위함이다.

근로기준법에 규정된 법정근로시간을 요약하면 다음과 같다.

구 분	기준근로시간	연장근로	야간·휴일근로
근로자(원칙)		당사자 합의 1주 12시간	제한 없음
산후 1년 미만 여성 근로자	1일 8시간 1주 40시간	당사자 합의 1일 2시간 1주 6시간 1년 150시간	본인 동의 고용노동부 장관 인가
임신 중인 근로자		불 가	명시적 청구 고용노동부 장관 인가
연소근로자 (15세이상–18세미만)	1일 7시간 1주 35시간	당사자 합의 1일 1시간 1주 5시간	본인 동의 고용노동부 장관 인가
유해·위험 작업 근로자	1일 6시간 1주 34시간	연장근로 불가	

Ⅳ. 소정근로시간

1. 소정근로시간의 개념

소정근로시간은 근로기준법 제50조(법정근로시간), 제69조(연소자의 근로시간) 또는 「산업안전보건법」 제139조(유해 위험한 작업)에 따른 근로시간의 범위에서 근로자와 사용자 사이에 정한 근로시간을 말한다. 이는 법정 근로시간 내에서 소정근로시간을 정해야 하는 것을 말한다. 근로기준법 제17조는 근로계약 체결 시 임금과 소정근로시간, 기타의 근로조건을 명시하도록 하고 있다. 따라서 근로계약에서 정하는 임금은 1주 40시간 내에서 정하도록 하고 있으므로, 원칙상 포괄임금은 근로기준법 위반이 된다. 근로기준법 제58조는 근로자가 출장이나 그 밖의 사유로 근로시간의 전부 또는 일부를 사업장 밖에서 근로하여 근로시간을 산정하기 어려운 경우에는 소정근로시간을 근로한 것으로 본다고 규정하고 있다. 단시간 근로의 경우에도 “사용자는 단시간 근로자에 대하

the employee concerned if they have a part-time worker work beyond the contractual working hours prescribed in Article 2 of the Labor Standards Act. In this case, such employee cannot work more than 12 hours a week. The employer shall pay the part-time worker an additional 50% or more of the ordinary wage for the overtime exceeding the contractual working hours"(Article 6 of the Act on the Protection Etc. of Fixed-term and Part-time Employees). In the past, overtime pay was introduced only for working hours exceeding legal standard working hours. However, for part-time workers, the overtime pay shall be paid if the working hours exceed contractual working hours(introduced on March 18, 2014). This means that if the part-time worker has 20 contractual working hours per week, an additional wage shall be paid for the hours exceeding those 20 contractual working hours.

2. Reasons for limiting work hours

Contractual working hours refer to the time within the legal standard working hours that the worker has to work. Here, legal standard working hours generally refer to 40 hours per week and 8 hours per day. The 12-hour limitation on extended work is for hours in excess of statutory working hours(Article 53 of the LSA). Overtime work for part-time workers is also recognized within a limit of 12 hours beyond the weekly contractual working hours of part-time workers. That is, extended hours for part-time workers are judged based on contractual working hours rather than legal standard working hours(Article 6 of the Act on the Protection Etc. of Fixed-term and Part-time Employees). In Article 17 of the LSA, stipulating the contractual working hours in the employment contract is mandatory, and then based upon this, wage and contractual working hours are determined. The purpose for making it mandatory to list the contractual working hours in the employment contract is to ensure that workers are able to pursue happiness and maintain human dignity while providing work within statutory working hours.

3. Calculating Contractual Working Hours

Contractual working hours are working hours within the legal standard working hours on which the employer and the employees have agreed. It is a concept mainly used to

여 근로기준법 제2조의 소정근로시간을 초과하여 근로하게 하는 경우에는 당해 근로자의 동의를 얻어야 한다. 이 경우, 1주에 12시간을 초과하여 근로하게 할 수 없다. 사용자가 단시간 근로자의 소정근로시간을 초과하는 연장근로에 대하여 통상임금의 100분의 50이상을 가산하여 지급하여야 한다" 고 규정하고 있다(기간제법 제6조). 기존에는 법정근로시간을 초과하는 근로시간만 연장근로에 따른 연장근로가산수당을 지급하도록 하였으나, 단시간 근로자의 경우에는 법정근로시간에 미치지 못하더라도 소정근로시간을 초과하는 경우 연장근로가산수당을 지급하도록 하고 있다(2014년 3월 18일 도입). 예를 들어, 이는 단시간 근로자의 소정근로시간이 주 20시간인 경우 이를 초과했을 때 연장근로에 대한 가산임금을 지급해야 한다는 것이다.

2. 소정근로시간으로 제한하는 이유

소정근로시간은 법정근로시간 내에서 근로자와 사용자가 일하기로 정한 시간을 말한다. 여기서 법정근로시간이라고 하면 일반적으로 1주 40시간, 1일 8시간을 말한다. 연장근로는 법정근로시간을 초과하여 최대 1주 12시간까지로 제한하고 있다(근기법 제53조). 단시간 근로자의 연장근로도 단시간 근로자의 1주 소정근로시간에 가산하여 12시간 한도 내에서 인정된다. 즉, 단시간 근로자의 연장근로는 법정근로시간이 아닌 소정근로시간을 기준으로 판단한다(기간제법 제6조). 근로기준법 제17조에서는 근로계약서의 소정근로시간을 필수 기재사항으로 하여, 임금과 소정근로시간을 정하도록 하고 있다. 근로시간을 근로계약서에 필수사항으로 소정근로시간을 기재하도록 한 취지는, 근로자 가 법정근로시간 내에서 근로를 제공함으로써 인간의 존엄성을 지키면서 행복 추구가 가능한 근로조건을 보장하기 위한 것이다.

3. 소정근로시간의 계산

소정근로시간이라 함은 법정근로시간의 범위 안에서 근로자와 사용자 간에 정한 근로시간을 말한다. 소정근로시간은 주로 일급·월급을 시간급으로 환산

convert daily pay or monthly pay into hourly pay. Accordingly, the hourly ordinary wage is differentiated by the contractual working hours. Contractual working hours determine the hourly ordinary wage, which is calculated by the day, week, or month, then divided by the working hours of the given period. Contractual hours also include the wage paid as an additional allowance for overtime work. They are the standard hours of payment for calculating wage.

(1) In the case of a weekly 5-day work week (8 hours daily) with one day of paid leave and one day of unpaid leave

Week	Month
[8 hrs x 5 days] + 8 hrs = 48 hrs (Duty hours) (Paid leave)	48 hrs × 4.345 weeks ≒ 209 hours

(2) Contractual working hours for employees between the ages of 15 and 18 years (in the case where there is no regulation provided by the company)

Week	Month
[7 hrs x 5 days] + 7 hrs = 42 hrs (Duty hours) (Paid leave)	42 hrs × 4.345 weeks ≒ 182 hours

(3) Contractual working hours for employees working under harmful and dangerous conditions (i.e., engaged in submarine or diving work) (in cases of 6 hours for 6 days and 4 hours for one day a week)

Week	Month
[6 hrs x 5 days] + 6 hrs = 36 hrs (Duty hours) (Paid leave)	36 hrs×4.345 weeks≒ 156 hours

하기 위해 사용하는 개념으로, 소정근로시간을 얼마로 할 것인가에 따라 시간급 통상임금에 차이가 난다. 소정근로시간은 시간 외 근로에 대한 가산임금의 산정에 있어서는 법률상 일·주·월 등에 의한 임금을 그 기간의 소정근로시간으로 나눈 임금을 가지고 계산하도록 하고 있기 때문에 소정근로시간은 임금의 지급대상이 된다.

(1) 주 5일(5일 8시간)을 근로하기로 하고 1일은 유급휴일, 1일은 무급휴일로 처리하는 경우

주	월
[8시간×5일] + 8시간 = 48시간 (근로제공의무시간) (유급처리시간)	48시간 × 4.345주 ≒ 209시간

(2) 15세 이상 18세 미만의 월 소정근로시간(노사 간 별도 정함이 없는 경우)

주	월
[7시간×5일] + 7시간 = 42시간 (근로제공의무시간) (유급처리시간)	42시간 × 4.345주 ≒ 182시간

(3) 유해·위험작업종사자(잠함·잠수작업근로자)의 월 소정근로시간(노사간 별도 정함이 없고 5일 6시간인 경우)

주	월
[6시간×5일] + 6시간 = 36시간 (근로제공의무시간) (유급처리시간)	36시간 × 4.345주 ≒ 156시간

V. Overtime, Nighttime and Holiday Work

The Labor Standards Act: Article 50 (Work Hours)

① Working hours per week shall not exceed forty hours excluding recess hours.
② Working hours per day shall not exceed eight hours excluding recess hours.

Article 53 (Restrictions on Extended Work)

① If the parties concerned reach agreement, the working hours stipulated in Article 50 may be extended up to twelve hours per week.
② If the parties concerned reach agreement, the working hours stipulated in Article 51 may be extended up to twelve hours per week, and the working hours under Article 52 may be extended up to twelve hours per week averaged during an adjustment period pursuant to subparagraph 2 of Article 52.

Article 56 (Extended, Night or Holiday Work)

① Employers shall pay an additional 50 percent or more of the ordinary wage for extended work (work during the hours as extended pursuant to the provisions of Articles 53 and 59, and the proviso of Article 69).
② Notwithstanding paragraph (1), with regards to holiday work employers shall pay additionally according to the following subparagraphs:
1. Holiday work of 8 hours or less: 50 percent of the ordinary wage
2. Holiday work beyond 8 hours: one hundred percent of the ordinary wage
③ Employers shall pay an additional 50 percent of the ordinary wage for night work (work between 10 P.M. and 6 A.M.)

1. Overtime

(1) Overtime limits

Overtime refers to working hours that exceed the standard working hours specified in the Labor Standards Act. Adult employees may extend their working hours up to 12 hours per week through mutual agreement by the parties concerned, with no limit on daily working hours.

There has been confusion as to what constitutes "one week". Things used to be based on 5 or 6 days, with the weekly holiday excluded. Therefore, there were 40 working hours plus up to 12 hours overtime, and then 8 hours of holiday work or 16 hours over 2 holidays could be added, which could total 68 hours a week. However, on March 20, 2018, Article 2 of the Labor Standards Act was amended to include the definition that "one week refers to seven days including holidays." Due to this, the maximum working hours per week is now

Ⅴ. 연장근로, 야간근로와 휴일근로

근로기준법 제50조【근로시간】

① 1주간의 근로시간은 휴게시간을 제외하고 40시간을 초과할 수 없다.

② 1일의 근로시간은 휴게시간을 제외하고 8시간을 초과할 수 없다.

제53조【연장 근로의 제한】

① 당사자 간에 합의하면 1주간에 12시간을 한도로 제50조의 근로시간을 연장할 수 있다.

② 당사자 간에 합의하면 1주간에 12시간을 한도로 제51조의 근로시간을 연장할 수 있고, 제52조 제2호의 정산기간을 평균하여 1주간에 12시간을 초과하지 아니하는 범위에서 제52조의 근로시간을 연장할 수 있다.

제56조【연장·야간 및 휴일 근로】

① 사용자는 연장근로(제53조·제59조 및 제69조 단서에 따라 연장된 시간의 근로를 말한다)에 대하여는 통상임금의 100분의 50 이상을 가산하여 근로자에게 지급하여야 한다.

② 제1항에도 불구하고 사용자는 휴일근로에 대하여는 다음 각 호의 기준에 따른 금액 이상을 가산하여 근로자에게 지급하여야 한다.

1. 8시간 이내의 휴일근로: 통상임금의 100분의 50
2. 8시간을 초과한 휴일근로: 통상임금의 100분의 100

③ 사용자는 야간근로(오후 10시부터 다음 날 오전 6시 사이의 근로를 말한다)에 대하여는 통상임금의 100분의 50 이상을 가산하여 근로자에게 지급하여야 한다.

1. 연장근로

(1) 연장근로의 제한

연장근로(시간 외 근로)란 근로기준법에서 정한 기준근로시간을 초과하는 근로를 말한다. 성인 근로자의 경우, 주 12시간 한도에서 당사자 간의 합의에 의해 연장근로를 할 수 있으나, 1일 연장근로의 한도는 없다.

기존에 1주라는 개념에 혼란이 있어왔다. 보통 1주는 휴일을 제외하고 5일이나 6일을 기준으로 하였기 때문에 근로시간이 주 40시간과 최대 12시간까지의 연장근로에 휴일근로 1일 8시간 또는 2일 16시간을 포함하여 총 60시간에서 68시간까지 근무가 가능하였다. 그러나 2018년 3월 20일 근기법 제2조 정의 규정에서 "7항,"1주"란 휴일을 포함한 7일을 말한다"고 명시하고 있다. 이

52 hours including holidays. Employers shall be punished for violations with imprisonment of not more than 2 years or a fine of not more than KRW 20 million(Article 110 of the LSA, Penal Provisions).

Article 2 (Definitions)
① Terms used in this Act are defined as follows
7. The term “one week” refers to seven consecutive days including holidays.

Before revision	After revision
Max working hours per week: 68 × 68 hrs = 40 hrs + 12 hrs + 16 hrs (if there are 2 holiday days)	Max working hours per week: 52 × 52 hrs = 40 hrs + 12 hrs

An employer shall not permit a pregnant employee to work overtime. However, an employer can allow a returning female worker within one year after childbirth to work overtime up to two hours per day, six hours per week, and 150 hours per year. A minor’s overtime shall not exceed one hour per day and 6 hours per week(Article 74, 75, and 69).

The term “minor” refers to a worker who is between 15 and 17 years of age. Working hours for minors cannot exceed 7 hours per day and 35 hours per week. However, if agreed between the parties, they may be extended 1 hour per day and 5 hours per week. That is, a minor can work up to 8 hours a day and 40 hours a week. Employers shall be punished for violations with imprisonment of not more than 2 years or a fine of not more than KRW 20 million(Article 110 of the LSA, Penal Provisions).

(2) Overtime and additional allowances

Employers shall pay an additional 50% of ordinary wage for overtime, night, and holiday work. The additional pay shall be made for the employee’s overtime after calculating it into his/her ordinary wage. In cases where contractual working hours(e.g., four hours per day) in the collective agreement or rules of employment are fewer than the legal standard working hours, an additional allowance needs to be paid for extended working hours exceeding the contractual working hours regardless of whether they exceed the legal standard working hours. In this case, if the part-time employee worked for 8 hours, the employer shall pay the basic pay for four hours and the overtime allowance for six hours: for four hours extended work and an additional two hours for overtime, which will be 10 hours’ wage in total(Article 6 of the Act on the Protection Etc. of Fixed-term and Part-time Employees).

로 인하여 1주의 최대 근무시간은 휴일을 포함하여 52시간이 된다. 이를 위반하는 경우에는 2년 이하의 징역 또는 2천만원 이하의 벌금에 처한다(근기법 제110조 벌칙).

> **법 제2조【정의】**
> ① 이 법에서 사용하는 용어의 뜻은 다음과 같다. 〈개정 2018.3.20〉
> 7. "1주"란 휴일을 포함한 7일을 말한다

개정 전	개정 후
1주 최대 근로 가능시간: 68시간 × 68시간 = 40시간 + 12시간 + 16시간 (휴일이 2일 경우)	1주 최대 근로 가능시간: 52시간 × 52시간 = 40시간 + 12시간

임신 중인 여성 근로자에 대하여는 연장근로를 시키지 못한다. 다만, 출산 후 1년이 경과되지 아니한 여성 근로자의 경우 1일 2시간, 1주 6시간, 1년 150시간 한도에서 연장근로를 할 수 있다. 연소자의 연장근로는 1일 1시간, 1주 5시간을 초과할 수 없다(근기법 제74조, 제75조, 제69조).

연소자라고 하면 15세 이상 18세 미만인 근로자를 말한다. 연소자의 근로시간도 1일 7시간, 1주 35시간을 초과할 수 없다. 다만, 당사자 간에 합의한 경우 1일 1시간, 1주 5시간 한도로 근로시간을 연장할 수 있다. 즉, 이는 1일 최대 8시간, 1주 40시간이 된다. 이를 위반하는 경우에는 2년 이하의 징역 또는 2천만원 이하의 벌금에 처한다(근기법 제110조 벌칙).

(2) 연장근로와 가산임금

사용자는 연장·야간·휴일근로에 대하여는 통상임금의 50% 이상을 가산하여 지급해야 한다. 가산임금은 근로자가 연장근로에 대하여 통상임금에 가산하여 지급한다. 단체협약·취업규칙 등에서 법정근로시간에 미달하는 근로시간을 정하고 있는 경우에는 그 소정근로시간(예: 1일 4시간 근무)을 초과하고 법정근로시간을 초과하지 않는 경우라도 가산임금을 지급해야 한다. 이 경우 하루에 8시간을 일한 경우, 4시간에 대한 임금과 4시간 연장에 근로에 대한 6시간 포함하여 총 10시간의 임금을 주어야 한다(기간제법 제6조 [단시간 근로자의 초과근로 제한]).

2. Night Work

Night working hours range from 10 p.m. to 6 a.m. the following day.

Regardless of working hours within the contractual working hours, compensation for night work shall be paid separately as an additional allowance. In cases where overtime, off-day work, and night work overlap, an additional allowance shall be paid for each one respectively. For employees falling under Article 63 of the Labor Standards Act(exceptions may apply), an additional allowance will not be paid for overtime or off-day work, but shall be paid for night work.

3. Holiday Work

150% of the ordinary wage shall be paid for up to eight hours of holiday work, and 200% shall be paid for hours of holiday work over eight hours. When overtime work and holiday work overlap, in the past it was very confusing to calculate. However, it is meaningful that this amendment clarifies what to do with such overlap. Employers shall be punished for violations with imprisonment of not more than 3 years or a fine of not more than KRW 30 million(Article 109 of the LSA, Penal Provisions).

4. The compensatory leave system

The compensatory leave system is introduced only upon written agreement with the workers' representative, and involves vacation being granted in lieu of the wages that normally must be paid for overtime work, night work, and holiday work. The specifics of implementation must also be agreed upon in writing with the employee representative, and can be decided freely by labor and management within the scope of the existing Labor Standards Act.[232] The details of the written agreement with the workers' representative should include ① the scope of eligible workers, ② the scope of compensatory working hours, ③ the settlement period, and ④ how compensatory leave is to be used.

(1) Scope of eligible workers: The system can apply uniformly to all workers or only to specific workers.

---

232) Kim, Ki-seon, "Introduction of the Vacation Savings Account System for Working Hours," Monthly Labor Review, June 2018, p. 24.

2. 야간근로

야간근로란 오후 10시부터 익일 아침 6시까지 사이의 근로를 말한다.

소정근로시간 이내의 근로일지라도 야간근로일 경우에는 가산임금을 지급해야 한다. 연장·야간·휴일근로가 중복된 경우 각각 가산하여 지급한다. 제63조의 적용제외 근로자(근로시간·휴게·휴일규정 적용 제외)에 대해서는 연장근로·휴일근로에 대한 가산임금의 지급문제는 발생하지 않으나, 야간근로에 대해서는 가산임금을 지급해야 한다.

3. 휴일근로

1일 8시간 이내의 휴일근로에 대해서는 통상임금의 50%를 가산하여 지급하고, 1일 8시간을 초과하는 휴일근로에 대해서는 통상임금의 100%를 가산하여 지급한다. 이는 연장근로에 해당되어 50% 가산수당을 지급해야 함에도 불구하고 연장근로와 휴일근로가 중복되는 경우 휴일근로 가산수당 할증률 적용하여 연장근로와 휴일근로 가산률(가산율) 중복지급 논란을 법률로 명확히 정리하였다. 이를 위반한 자는 3년 이하의 징역 또는 3천만원 이하의 벌금에 처한다.

4. 보상휴가제

보상휴가제는 근로자대표와의 서면 합의에 따라 가산임금을 지급해야 하는 연장근로, 야간근로, 그리고 휴일근로에 대하여 임금을 지급하는 것을 갈음하여 휴가를 지급하는 제도이다. 보상휴가에 대한 구체적인 시행방법을 근로자대표와의 서면합의로 정하도록 하고 있고, 세부적인 시행방법에 대해 기술한 내용이 없으므로 기존의 근로기준법을 적용하는 범위내에서 노사 간에 자유롭게 정할 수 있도록 하고 있다.[232] 보상휴가제의 실시에 관하여 근로자대표와의 서면합의의 내용은 ① 대상근로자의 범위, ② 대상근로시간의 범위, ③ 정산기간, ④ 보상휴가의 사용방법 등을 포함하여야 할 것이다.

(1) 대상근로자의 범위: 전체 근로자에게 일률적으로 적용할 것인지, 희망하는

232) 김기선, “근로시간저축휴가제의 도입방향”, 월간 노동리뷰, 2018년 6월호, 24면.

(2) Scope of compensatory working hours: Overtime, holiday, and night work shall be subject to the system. What needs to be decided is whether or not any additional wage will be paid for the working hours subject to the compensatory leave system.

(3) Settlement period: This is where the length of time for which compensatory leave can be banked, which shall be no more than three years, in consideration of the extinctive prescription for wages.

(4) How compensatory leave is to be used: Does accumulated compensatory leave have to be used at once or is it divisible? In addition, measures necessary for the company to guarantee long-term leave need to be described, as do details on monetary compensation for the compensatory leave not used during the settlement period.

Ⅵ. Exception: Surveillance · Intermittent Employees

1. Concept

If an employer has received permission from the Minister of Employment and Labor, some rules of the Labor Standards Act concerning working hours, recess, and holidays will not apply to surveillance or intermittent employees, and the employer will not be obligated to pay overtime allowances and holiday work allowances.[233)] This means, when paying fixed monthly wage to surveillance or intermittent employees, the employer does not have to pay additional overtime allowance or holiday work allowance for overtime or holiday work. The employer can even pay lower than minimum wage. Here, "surveillance or intermittent employees" mean those employees whose jobs require a relatively lower intensity of labor and less physical fatigue and mental tension than others. Although some jobs share similar characteristics to surveillance or intermittent work, identical rules to normal employees concerning working hours shall continue to apply to those jobs, if the employer hasn't applied for approval to have them recognized as exceptions by the Minister of Employment and Labor, or if the employer's application for exception was rejected. In relation to this matter, I would like to look into the necessity for exceptions to the Labor Standards Act for certain jobs, requirements for approval, and cases that have been approved or have not been approved.

---

233) Supreme Court ruling on November 22, 1996, 96da30571.

근로자에 한하여 적용할 것인지에 대한 대상근로자의 범위를 설정할 수 있다.

(2) 대상근로시간의 범위: 보상의 대상이 되는 근로시간은 연장근로, 휴일근로, 야간근로이다. 소정근로시간 외에 추가로 지급되는 가산임금 전체를 할 것인지 여부를 결정한다.

(3) 정산기간: 적립 가능한 보상기간에 대해 단기로 할 것인지, 장기로 할 것인지에 대해 결정한다. 이 경우 최대 임금소멸시효를 감안하여 3년 이내로 한다.

(4) 보상휴가의 사용방법: 축적된 보상휴가에 대해 개별적으로 사용할 것인지, 아니면 집단적으로 사용할 것인지에 대해 결정한다. 그리고 장기간의 휴가사용이 가능하도록 회사에서 필요한 조치 등에 대해 기술하여 장기간의 휴가보장이 될 수 있도록 한다. 또한 보상휴가의 정산기간에 대해 사용하지 못한 보상휴가에 대한 금전보상 내용을 포함한다.

Ⅵ. 적용의 제외: 감시 단속적 근로자

1. 개 념

감시 단속적 근로자에 대하여 노동부장관의 승인을 받은 경우에는 근로기준법 상 근로시간, 휴게 및 휴일에 관한 규정이 적용되지 않게 되어, 원칙적으로 사용자는 근로자에게 시간외근로수당 및 휴일근로수당을 지급할 의무가 없다.[233] 즉, 감시 단속적 근로자에 대해서는 월 일정액의 임금을 지급하고 연장, 휴일근로에 대해 별도의 연장근로수당, 휴일근로수당 등을 지급하지 않아도 된다. 여기서 감시 단속적인 근로는 다른 일반근로자와 비교하여 노동강도가 낮고 신체적 피로나 정신적 긴장이 적은 업무를 말한다. 비록 업무의 특징이 감시 단속적 근로라고 추정되더라도 노동부의 승인을 받지 않았거나 적용제외 신청이 거부된 경우에는 일반근로자와 동일한 근로시간에 관한 규정이 적용된다. 이와 관련하여 적용제외 승인의 필요성, 승인요건 및 승인·불승인 사례를 살펴보고자 한다.

233) 대법원 1996.11.22, 96다 30571.

2. Necessity of Exception

While reviewing labor cases that deal with surveillance or intermittent work, I have found it very important, and sometimes essential, for employers to receive approval to make exceptions to the Labor Standards Act for surveillance or intermittent employees.

(1) Exclusive driver (chauffeur) for a company executive

In the morning, a chauffeur employed by Company "A" picks up the executive assigned to him, drives him to the office, and then finishes the day by taking him home in the evening. In cases where the director provides special receptions for corporate clients, the driver has to leave the workplace in the middle of night. In some cases, he may have to drive the executive to golf courses or other places on weekends or holidays. In situations like this, the time involved in picking up the executive before work, time spent waiting in the evening, and time spent waiting during dinners or golf meetings for clients shall be calculated as working hours and paid in overtime allowance for the extra working hours. If the inclusive wage system is applied, the maximum working hours per week(including overtime) are 52 hours, so working hours exceeding 52 hours per week shall be paid an additional overtime allowance. Since inclusive wage only include the legally allowed extended working hours(12 hours per week), the company would have to pay extra overtime wage for hours worked above 52, to cover the extended working hours and holiday work. In order to deal with this situation more appropriately, the employer should submit an application to the Minister of Employment and Labor for exception to be made to the statutory rules regulating working hours, recess and holiday work for surveillance and intermittent employees. Once approval is received, the employer does not have to calculate working hours for surveillance and intermittent employees concerning extended working hours or holiday work.

(2) Employees responsible for maintenance of air-conditioning, heating equipment and electricity

Company "B" is a manufacturer that runs three shifts in its plant. Employees responsible for maintaining air-conditioning, heating equipment and electricity work 12 hour days in two shifts. Their annual wage at entry level were about 30 million won or less, but the actual wage they received amounted to not less than 50 million won after accumulation of overtime and weekly holiday work allowances, etc. Despite having long working hours, the

2. 적용제외 승인의 필요성

감시 단속적 근로와 관련하여 본인이 직접 수임하여 처리하였던 사례를 몇 가지 살펴보면, 감시 단속적 근로자에 대한 '적용제외 승인'을 받는 것이 얼마나 중요한가를 알 수 있다.

(1) 전속 운전기사

A 회사에 고용된 전속 운전기사는 담당 임원을 픽업하여 출근시키고, 또한 저녁에는 퇴근시켜 주면 하루의 일과가 끝난다. 그런데 임원은 사업상 접대를 할 경우에는 심야에 퇴근해야 하고, 또한 주말이나 휴일에도 골프 모임 등에 동행하여 운전을 해야만 했다. 이러한 경우, 출근시간 전에 픽업하는 시간, 저녁 퇴근 시 대기시간, 손님 접대나 골프접대에서의 대기시간 모두 근로시간으로 간주하여 모두 연장근로수당을 지급해야 한다. 포괄임금으로 적용하는 경우에도 일주일에 최대 52시간에 대한 임금까지는 일정액으로 지급할 수 있으나 주 52시간을 초과하는 근로시간에 대해서는 모두 연장근로수당을 지급해야만 한다. 이유는 포괄임금으로 지급하는 것은 법정 연장근로시간 (주 12시간)까지만 포함한 범위이므로 회사는 추가 연장근로, 휴일근로에 대하여 그 초과분의 임금을 지급할 의무가 발생한다. 이와 같은 문제를 해결하기 위해서는 '감시 단속적 근로'에 대한 근로시간, 휴게, 휴일에 대한 근로기준법 적용제외 신청을 하여 노동부로부터 승인을 받아야 한다. 승인된 이후부터는 근로시간, 휴일 근로 등에 대한 시간계산과 가산임금의 적용이 제외된다.

(2) 냉난방, 전기 등의 관리 직원

회사 B는 제조업체로 3교대제로 공장을 가동시키고 있었다. 공장의 냉난방 및 전기를 담당하는 직원들의 경우에는 1일 12시간씩 2교대로 투입되었다. 이들의 입사 시 연봉은 약 3000만원 이었지만, 실제 수령하는 금액은 연장근로수당, 휴일근로수당 등이 가산되어 5000만원 이상에 달하였다. 장시간 근무라 하지만, 실질적으로 업무의 강도나 실제 근무시간은 총 근로시간의 절반에도 미치지 못했다. 이에 대해 직법한 근로시간 관리와 적합한 임금수준을 유지하

intensity of work is lower than for other employees, and the number of hours they actually have to perform some service is less than half of their total shift hours. In order to maintain an acceptable wage level under such long working hours, the company has to receive permission from the MOEL for exception to be made to the statutory rules regulating working hours, recess and holiday work for such employees. If permission is given, the company is free of legal obligations to pay extra allowances for employees on duty beyond the weekly maximum extended working hours, or holiday work.

3. Requirements for "Exclusions from Application" to be Approved

(1) Provision of 'exceptions to application' (Labor Standards Act)

Article 63 (Exclusion from Application) The provisions of this Chapter, and Chapter V, as to working hours, recess, and holidays shall not apply to workers who are engaged in any work described in the following subparagraphs:

1. cultivation of arable land, reclamation work, seeding and planting, gathering or picking-up or other agricultural and forestry work;
2. livestock breeding, catching of marine animals and plants, cultivation of marine products or other cattle-breeding, sericulture and fishery business;
3. surveillance or intermittent work, for which the employer has obtained the approval of the Minister of Employment and Labor;
4. any other work prescribed by Presidential Decree. ("Work provided for by Presidential Decree" in subparagraph 4 of Article 63 of the Act means managerial and supervisory work and work of handling secret affairs irrespective of types of work.)

(2) Approval procedures (Enforcement Decree to the LSA)

Article 10 (Application of exceptions to working hours, etc. under the LSA)

① When an employer wants permission to exclude employees from application of the Labor Standards Act regarding working hours, etc. for those engaged in surveillance or intermittent work in accordance with Article 63 (paragraph 3) of the LSA, he shall submit an application for exemption from the statutory rules for surveillance or intermittent employees with the designated form, Attachment #7, to the head of the Regional Labor Office.

② surveillance employee, stipulated in Paragraph 1, is an employee who provides surveillance as his main function and has relatively less mental and physical fatigue.

③ An intermittent employee, stipulated in Paragraph 1, is an employee who works intermittently and has more recess hours than actual working hours or has long waiting hours.

④ If the head of the Regional Labor Office approves the application according to Paragraph 1, a certificate permitting exemption for surveillance or intermittent employees, Attachment #8, shall be issued.

기 위해서 회사가 당장 취하여야 할 조치는 해당 직원들 업무에 대해 '감시 단속적 근로'에 대한 '적용제외 승인'을 노동부로부터 받는 일이었다. 그렇게 되면, 가산임금이나 연장근로의 법리로부터 자유로워진다.

3. 적용예외 승인

(1) 적용예외에 대한 법 규정 (근로기준법)

제63조【적용의 제외】 이 장과 제5장에서 정한 근로시간, 휴게와 휴일에 관한 규정은 다음 각 호의 어느 하나에 해당하는 근로자에 대하여는 적용하지 아니한다.

1. 토지의 경작·개간, 식물의 재식(재식)·재배·채취 사업, 그 밖의 농림 사업
2. 동물의 사육, 수산 동식물의 채포(채포)·양식 사업, 그 밖의 축산, 양잠, 수산 사업
3. 감시 또는 단속적으로 근로에 종사하는 자로서 사용자가 노동부장관의 승인을 받은 자
4. 대통령령으로 정하는 업무에 종사하는 근로자 (법 제63조 제4호에서 "대통령령으로 정한 업무"란 사업의 종류에 관계없이 관리·감독 업무 또는 기밀을 취급하는 업무를 말한다.)

(2) 승인절차에 대한 규정 (근로기준법 시행규칙)

제10조【근로시간 등의 적용제외 승인 신청 등】

① 사용자는 법 제63조 제3호에 따라 감시 또는 단속적으로 근로에 종사하는 자에 대한 근로시간 등의 적용 제외 승인을 받으려면 별지 제7호 서식의 감시적 또는 단속적 근로종사자에 대한 적용 제외 승인 신청서를 관할 지방노동관서의 장에게 제출하여야 한다.

② 제1항에 따른 승인 대상이 되는 감시적 근로에 종사하는 자는 감시업무를 주 업무로 하며 상태적(상태적)으로 정신적·육체적 피로가 적은 업무에 종사하는 자로 한다.

③ 제1항에 따른 승인 대상이 되는 단속적으로 근로에 종사하는 자는 근로가 간헐적·단속적으로 이루어져 휴게시간이나 대기시간이 많은 업무에 종사하는 자로 한다.

④ 관할 지방노동관서의 장은 제1항에 따른 신청에 대하여 승인을 할 경우에는 별지 제8호 서식의 감시적 또는 단속적 근로종사자에 대한 적용 제외 승인서를 내주어야 한다.

(3) Criteria for approval (Working Regulations of Labor Inspectors)

Article 68 (Approval of exceptions for those working in surveillance and intermittent workers)

① Approval of exceptions for "those working in surveillance", according to Article 63 (paragraph 3) of the Labor Standards Act and Article 10 (paragraph 2) of the Enforcement Decree to the LSA, shall be issued when the following criteria are satisfied:

1. the employee holds a position requiring less mental and physical fatigue, such as a guard, security guard, watchman of products, or keeper of measurement machines, or in exceptional cases, other jobs requiring continuous watch and mental tension;
2. the employee works on a surveillance job as an occupation, but often engages in other temporary jobs; or in exceptional cases, if the employee has to implement other jobs repeatedly or is engaged in other plural duty;
3. the employee works fewer than 12 hours per day under the employer's supervision, or works a 24-hour shift every other day, and either
   a) 8 or more consecutive hours are provided for sleep or recreation, OR
   b) there is an agreement between the employer and apartment building security guards and the employer provides the guards with an off-period of 24 hours the following day.

② Approval of exceptions for "those working in intermittent work", according to Article 63 (paragraph 3) of the Labor Standards Act and Article 10 (paragraph 2) of the Enforcement Decree of the LSA shall be issued when the following criteria are satisfied:

1. the employee is free during ordinary hours, but his/her job entails a lot of waiting to prevent such things as machinery breakdowns or accidents, or for machine maintenance;
2. the employee's actual working hours are fewer than the waiting hours within an 8-hour period, provided that, if the employee works a 24-hour shift every other day, the employee must be granted a 24-hour off-day on the day following the shift;
3. the employee with waiting hours shall be provided with rest facilities free of charge.

③ Working hours for employees who fit under Paragraph 1 and Paragraph 2 shall be calculated as averages per certain period (one week or one month).

4. Cases Approved and Rejected

(1) Approved cases

1) Those working on weekends or at night to maintain a building and its facilities are considered intermittent employees.[234)]

2) Security guards at apartment buildings and those working in an electrical or boiler room are considered to be engaged in surveillance or intermittent work and LSA rules

234) MOEL Guidelines: Sept. 5, 1987, Gungi 01254-14337.

(3) 승인여부 판단기준 (근로감독관 업무지침)

제68조【감시·단속적 근로에 종사하는 자에 대한 적용제외 승인】

① 「근로기준법」제63조 제3호 및 같은 법 시행규칙 제10조 제2항에 따른 "감시적 근로에 종사하는 자"의 적용제외 승인은 다음 각 호의 기준을 모두 갖춘 때에 한한다.

1. 수위·경비원·물품감시원 또는 계수기감시원 등과 같이 심신의 피로가 적은 노무에 종사하는 경우. 다만, 감시적 업무이기는 하나 잠시도 감시를 소홀히 할 수 없는 고도의 정신적 긴장이 요구되는 경우는 제외한다.
2. 감시적인 업무가 본래의 업무이나 불규칙적으로 단시간 동안 타 업무를 수행하는 경우. 다만, 감시적 업무라도 타 업무를 반복하여 수행하거나 겸직하는 경우는 제외한다.
3. 사업주의 지배하에 있는 1일 근로시간이 12시간 이내인 경우 또는 다음 각 목의 어느 하나에 해당하는 격일제(24시간 교대) 근무의 경우
   가. 수면시간 또는 근로자가 자유로이 이용할 수 있는 휴게 시간이 8시간 이상 확보되어 있는 경우
   나. 가목의 요건이 확보되지 아니하더라도 공동주택 경비원에 있어서는 당사자 간의 합의가 있고 다음 날 24시간의 휴무가 보장되어 있는 경우

② 「근로기준법」제61조 제3호 및 같은 법 시행규칙 제10조 제3항에 따른 "단속적 근로에 종사하는 자"의 적용제외 승인은 다음 각 호의 기준을 모두 갖춘 때에 한한다.

1. 평소의 업무는 한가하지만 기계고장 수리 등 돌발적인 사고발생에 대비하여 대기하는 시간이 많은 업무인 경우
2. 실 근로시간이 대기시간의 반 정도 이하인 업무로 8시간 이내인 경우. 다만, 격일제(24시간 교대) 근무인 경우에는 당사자간의 합의가 있고 다음 날 24시간의 휴무가 보장되어야 한다
3. 대기시간에 근로자가 자유로이 이용할 수 있는 수면 또는 휴게시설이 확보되어 있는 경우

③ 제1항 및 제2항의 근로시간은 일정기간(주 또는 월 등)의 평균적 개념으로 산정한다.

4. 승인 및 불승인 사례

(1) 승인사례

1) 건물시설관리를 위해 휴일 및 야간에 대기하는 자는 단속적 근로에 종사하는 자에 해당된다.[234)]

2) 아파트 경비원과 아파트 관리소 내의 전기실, 기관실 직원은 감시·단속적

234) 행정해석: 근기 01254-14337, 1987.9.5.

concerning working hours, recess and holidays shall not be applicable.[235)]

3) A guard supervisor who is in charge of general management of security resources is considered to be engaged in surveillance work.[236)]

4) A private policeman whose job requires a relatively lower intensity of labor than others in his/her field, is considered to be engaged in surveillance work.[237)]

(2) Rejected cases

1) A watchman at a railroad crossing (flagman) is not a surveillance or intermittent employee.

A certain watchman at a railroad crossing controls the trains passing 42 to 50 times per day, and also helps prevent accidents with pedestrians or passing cars. In reviewing the frequency of this watchman's checks and the constant attention needed to prevent accidents, this job cannot easily be classified as surveillance or intermittent work.[238)]

2) Janitors at court are not intermittent employees.

Janitors at court start work early in the morning, and continue according to a certain work schedule, excluding designated recess hours. Some individuals have to work even during recess hours. They are not classified as intermittent employees, because they do not provide work intermittently.[239)]

Ⅶ. Exception: Managerial and Supervisory Positions

1. Concept

Managerial and supervisory positions refer to employees who have managerial or supervisory authority over other employees or deal with classified information and whose start/finish time at work is not strictly regulated because they are given discretion

235) MOEL Guidelines: Feb. 5, 1990, Gungi 01254-1626.

236) MOEL Guidelines: July 27, 1993, Supreme Court 92da46462.

237) Supreme Court ruling on Apr. 25, 1997, 95da4056

238) MOEL Guidelines: Nov. 14, 2001, Gungi 68207-3901.

239) Seoul District Court ruling July 12, 2003, 2002 Guhap 19050.

근로자로 근로시간, 휴게, 휴일에 관한 적용이 제외된다.[235]

3) 경비계장은 경비원들을 관리·감독하여 경비업무 전반을 총괄하는 것이므로 감시적 근로에 종사하는 경비직 직원에 해당된다.[236]

4) 청원경찰은 업무의 성격상 통상의 근로보다 노동의 밀도나 강도가 낮은 감시적 근로에 해당한다.[237]

(2) 불승인 사례

1) 철도 건널목 관리원은 감시·단속적 근로자에 해당되지 않는다.

철도 건널목 관리원의 업무가 1일 42~50회의 열차통행에 대한 업무뿐 아니라 건널목 통행자 및 차량의 건널목 통행 시 발생될 수 있는 각종 사고예방에 관한 업무를 하고 있는 경우라면 업무의 빈도, 안전사고 방지를 위한 주의 정도 등을 감안할 때 감시·단속적 근로로는 보기 어렵다고 사료된다.[238]

2) 법원 청소직 근로자는 단속적 근로자에 해당되지 않는다.

법원 청소직 근로자는 매일 아침 일찍 업무를 시작, 일정한 시간표에 따라 정해진 휴식시간을 제외하고는 계속 업무를 수행하고 있고, 개인에 따라서는 휴식시간에도 업무를 계속해야 하는 경우가 있으므로 반드시 간헐적으로 근로를 제공하고 있다고 볼 수 없어 단속적 근로자에 해당하지 않는다.[239]

Ⅶ. 적용의 제외: 관리 감독자

1. 관리 감독자의 개념

노무관리상 지휘, 감독 권한이 있으며 업무에 있어 재량권이 인정되어 출·퇴근시간이 엄격하게 제한되지 않는 감독이나 관리의 지위에 있는 자 또는 기밀

235) 행정해석 근기 01254-1626, 1990.2.5.

236) 대법원 1993.7.27, 92다46462.

237) 대법원 1997.4.25, 95다4056.

238) 행정해석: 근기 68207-3901, 2001.11.14.

239) 서울행판 2003.6.12, 2002구합19050.

in their work. Article 63(Exclusions from Application) of the LSA regulates that the provisions regarding working hours, recess and holiday shall not apply to managerial and supervisory positions.

2. MOEL Guidelines and Judicial Ruling

"The provisions of Chapter 4 and Chapter 5 of the LSA as to working hours, recess, and holidays shall not apply to persons engaged in management and supervision"(Article 63(4ho) of the LSA and Article 34 of its Enforcement Decree). Here, "persons engaged in management and supervision" refers to those in managerial positions in the decision-making process of working conditions. This position shall be determined collectively in consideration of whether the person participates in deciding labor management or has authority for supervision and control in labor management regardless of his/her formal designation, whether the person's working hours are strictly regulated(such as time to arrive at and leave the workplace), whether the person receives a special allowance due to the position, etc.

Administrative guidelines explain, for those in the position of "section manager" who are authorized to plan and implement general duties and detailed job assignments for their subordinates, and control their business trips, overtime, and vacations, even though the section manager did not receive a special allowance in accordance with that position, if the section manager has not been strictly regulated in time of arrival at and leaving the workplace, the section manager shall be considered as a person who is in line with the employer in determining working conditions and other forms of labor management.[240)]

The Supreme Court has ruled that working hours, recess and holidays stipulated by the Labor Standards Act do not apply to persons in managerial and supervisory positions who decides their subordinates' working conditions, and do not have their times of arrival at and leaving the workplace strictly regulated, and have flexibility in their own working hours. Persons in these positions cannot receive additional allowances for overtime exceeding contractual working hours or holiday work according to the Labor Standards Act.[241)]

---

240) MOEL Guidelines Kunjung-41, on Mar. 3, 2011.

241) Supreme Court ruling on Feb. 28, 1989, 88DaKa2974.

취급자를 말한다. 현행 근로기준법 제63조(적용제외)에는 관리감독자에 대해서는 근로시간, 휴게와 휴일에 관한 규정을 적용하지 않는다고 규정하고 있다.

2. 행정해석과 판례

"관리·감독업무에 종사하는 근로자(제63조 제4호 및 시행령 제34조)"는 근로기준법 제4장 및 제5장에서 정한 근로시간, 휴게와 휴일에 관한 규정을 적용하지 않는다. 여기서 "관리·감독업무에 종사하는 자"라 함은 근로조건의 결정 기타 노무관리에 있어서 경영자와 일체적인 지위에 있는 자를 말하는 것으로 사업장 내 형식적인 직책에도 불구하고 노무관리방침의 결정에 참여하거나 노무 관리상의 지휘·감독 권한을 가지고 있는지의 여부, 출·퇴근 등에 있어서 엄격한 제한을 받는지 여부, 그 지위에 따른 특별수당을 받는 여부 등을 종합적으로 검토하여 판단하여야 할 것이다.

행정해석은 회사의 위임전결규정 등의 자료에 의하여 실장이 일반 업무에 대한 방침 및 소관업무에 관한 세부계획 수립 및 집행 등에 대한 결정권과 소속 직원에 대한 출장, 연장근로 지시, 휴가 승인 등 노무관리상의 지휘·감독 권한을 가지고 있는 것으로 보이는 경우 비록 그 지위에 따른 특별수당을 지급받지 않는다고 하더라도 일반 직원과 달리 출·퇴근 등에 있어서 엄격한 제한을 받지 않는 경우라면 전반적으로 근로조건의 결정 기타 노무관리에 있어 경영자와 일체적인 지위에 있는 자로 볼 수 있다고 해석하고 있다.[240)]

판례는 부하직원의 근로조건 결정 및 기타 노무관리에 있어 경영자의 지위에 있으면서 기업 경영상의 필요에 의하여 출·퇴근에 관하여도 엄격한 제한을 받지 아니하고 자기의 근무시간에 관한 융통성을 가지고 있어 회사의 감독, 관리의 지위에 있던 자는 근로기준법에서 정한 근로시간, 휴게와 휴일에 관한 규정이 적용되지 아니한다. 이러한 위치에 있는 자는 평일의 규정 내 잔업시간은 물론, 일요일 근무에 대해서도 근로기준법 소정의 시간 외 또는 휴일근무라 하여 같은 근로기준법에서 정한 가산금을 지급받을 수는 없다고 판시하고 있다.[241)]

---

240) 행정해석: 근정과-41, 2011.3.3.

241) 대법원 1989.2.28, 88다카2974.

3. Related cases

A labor case has occurred due to escalating disputes between directors in April 2015. The Employee began a lawsuit against the Company and visited the Gangnam Labor Office to claim the Company had violated the Labor Standards Act, and had not paid additional allowance for her overtime work. As the Employee's job title as the managing director placed her in the "directors" group, the question is whether or not this high position is included in 'persons to be excluded from the application of working hours, recess and holidays' stipulated by the Labor Standards Act.

The Employee claimed that she had never received any additional allowance for overtime or holiday work during her service period, and that she was entitled to additional allowances for overtime and holiday work for the past three years. The Employee requested the information of her office PC's "on-and-off" data to check her working time as she had not recorded it in the related documents. The Company responded that the Employee is not entitled to overtime work allowance or holiday work allowance due to her high position as the managing director, putting her in a managerial and supervisory position according to Article 63 of the LSA.

The Employee in this case is not a department head due to the combination of two departments, but has received the high salary of a director, twice the incentives of other employees, and her time of arrival at and leaving the workplace has not been strictly controlled as it has been for other employees. In consideration of these facts, the Gangnam Labor Office in charge of this case concluded that the Employee in this case is in a managerial and supervisory position and can be excluded from the provisions on working hours, recess and holiday provisions in Article 63 of the Labor Standards Act.

Whether the managing director of a foreign company shall be entitled to an additional allowance for overtime work shall be determined collectively in consideration of not only the official designation of the employee as being in a high position but also the manager's authority, observance of commuting time, and any special allowances assigned to the position.[242)]

---

242) Ha, Kaprae,「The Labor Standards Act (27th edition)」Joongan Economy, 2015, page 315.

3. 관련 사례

외국기업에서, 2015년 4월에 임원간의 갈등이 노동사건으로 확대된 사건이 발생하였다. 이 사건의 근로자는 회사가 연장근로에 대한 가산임금을 지급하지 않는 등 근로기준법을 위반하였다고 '강남고용지청'에 회사를 고소하였다. 이 사건의 근로자 직급이 임원에 속하는 '상무'로 근로기준법상 '근로시간, 휴게, 휴일의 적용제외자'로 인정받을 수 있는지의 여부이다.

이 사건의 근로자는 근무기간 중 연장근로와 휴일근로를 많이 하였음에도 한 번도 가산임금을 받아본 적이 없다고 주장하면서, 과거 3년간 연장근로수당과 휴일근로수당을 청구하였다. 근로자는 관련된 자료를 기록하고 있지 않기 때문에 '본인 업무용 컴퓨터 사용기록(on-off 자료)'를 요청하였다. 이에 대해 회사는 이 사건의 근로자는 직급상 상무직급으로 회사의 임원에 해당되므로 근로기준법 제63조의 규정에 따른 '관리감독자'로 연장근로, 휴일근로에 대해 적용대상자가 아니라고 판단하여 지급하지 않았다.

본 사건에서 외국기업의 '상무'와 같이 상당한 직급을 가지고 있음에도 불구하고, 단지 관리자이지 부서장이 아닌 경우에 관리 감독자인지 여부에 대해 판단을 하기 어려운 경우가 많다. 이 사건의 근로자인 경우에는 부서의 통폐합으로 인해 부서장은 아니지만, 고위의 직급에 임원급의 임금, 일반 근로자의 2배 이상의 인센티브를 받고 있으며, 출퇴근시간에 대해서도 일반근로자와 달리 엄격히 통제 받지 않았다. 이러한 사정을 고려하여 이 사건을 담당한 강남노동지청은 이 사건의 근로자를 근로기준법 제63조에 따른 근로시간, 휴일, 휴게에 대해 예외를 인정받을 수 있는 관리·감독자로서 인정하였다.

외국기업의 상무가 연장근로에 대한 가산임금을 지급여부에 대한 판단은 직급의 고하(高下)만을 가지고 판단할 것이 아니라 관리자로서의 권한, 출퇴근 시간준수 의무, 지급에 따른 특별수당 지급여부 등을 복합적으로 고려하여 판단하여야 할 것이다.[242)]

---

242) 하갑래,『근로기준법(제27판)』, 중앙경제, 2015, 315면.

Section 2: Flexible Working Hours

Productivity refers to the amount produced or achieved in a limited time. The term "52-hour week" originated from the introduction of 'one week' in Article 2 of the Labor Standards Act, which states that "one week is seven days, including a holiday."[243)]

For this reason, 40 hours constitute a statutory work week, while the weekly working hours become a maximum 52 hours when maximum overtime(up to 12 hours a week) is allowed. To see greater results while reducing working hours, a flexible working time system that focuses on the characteristics of the work is urgently needed. When I was engaged in wage consultations for a French company responsible for operation of Subway Line 9 in 2006, what the manager told me remains vivid. "Koreans are working 44 hours per week, but are less productive than those who work 32 hours per week." When I thought about it at the time, I figured this was because Koreans are constantly working extended hours and on holidays due to labor market rigidity. Most Korean companies still work from 9 am to 6 pm, Monday through Friday. To be more efficient during these traditional working hours, various flexible working hours urgently need to be introduced into the Labor Standards Act.

The Labor Standards Act includes ① flexible working hours, ② selective working hours, ③ deemed working hours, and ④ discretionary working hours, ⑤ paid time-off leave, etc. Ways to adopt and use these flexible working hours are described in more detail below.[244)]

---

243) The Labor Standards Act for the related article was revised around the concept of one week (Mar. 30, 2018).

244) MOEL (MOEL), "Flexible Working Hour System Guidelines", Sept. 2019; MOEL, "Q&As on a Flexible Working Hour System", Dec. 2017.

제2절 유연적 근로시간제

생산성은 제한된 시간에 더 많은 성과를 내는데 달려 있다. 최근 주 52시간제라는 용어가 생기게 된 것은 근로기준법 제2조에서 "1주라 함은 휴일을 포함한 7일로 한다" 고 명시하면서부터다.[243)]

1주의 법정근로시간인 40시간에 연장근로 한도인 12시간을 더하면 52시간이 된다. 근로시간이 줄어들면서도 더 많은 성과를 내기 위해서는 업무의 특성에 맞추어 집중하는 유연근로시간제가 절실히 필요하다. 필자가 2006년도 지하철 9호선 관리를 맡게 된 프랑스회사를 임금컨설팅 하던 중 관리자가 한 말이 아직도 귀에 생생하다. "한국인들은 주당 44시간 근무하면서 주당 32시간 근무하는 자신들보다 생산성이 떨어진다"고 하였다. 이는 우리나라는 경직된 근무시간으로 인해 연장, 휴일근로 등이 보편화 되었기 때문이라고 생각한다. 아직도 우리나라 대부분 기업은 근무시간이 월요일부터 금요일까지, 오전 9시부터 오후 6시까지 일한다. 이러한 전통적인 근무시간에 업무의 효율을 극대화하기 위해서는 근로기준법에서 허용하고 있는 다양한 유연근로시간제의 도입이 절실히 요구된다.

근로기준법에는 이와 관련하여 ① 탄력적 근로시간제, ② 선택적 근로시간제, ③ 간주근로시간제, ④ 재량근로시간제, ⑤ 보상휴가제 등이 있다. 이러한 유연 근로시간제에 대해 구체적으로 살펴보고자 한다.[244)]

243) 근로기준법 개정(2018.3.20)으로 1주의 개념 도입.

244) 고용노동부, "유연근로시간제 가이드", 2019.9; 고용노동부, "유연근무제 Q&A", 2017.12.

Ⅰ. Selection of Employee Representatives[245)]

1. Purpose

The Labor Standards Act requires written agreement from or consultation with the employee representative for matters such as changes in working hours, etc. "This employee representative refers to the labor union, where there is an organized labor union representing more than half the employees at a business or workplace; or shall refer to a person who represents more than half the employees, where there is no such organized labor union"(Article 24(3) of the LSA). However, this article does not explain the entire scope of "employee" covered by employee representation, the selected unit or method used in selecting the employee representative, manner of representation, effect of the written agreement, etc. Here, I would like to bring attention to clear administrative guidance and judicial rulings concerning these matters to better understand related laws and operations.

<Items Requiring Written Agreement from or Consultation with Employee Representative>

LSA	Written Agreement or Consent Required
Article 51	Three-month flexible working hour system
Article 52	Selective working hour system
Article 57	System of using leave as compensation
Article 58 (2)	Hours deemed working hours for "those ordinarily required to carry out duties"
Article 58 (3)	Discretionary working hours
Article 59	Exceptions in applying working and recess hours for such particulars as transportation
Article 62	Substitution of paid leave

2. Scope of Employee

(1) Scope of employee

The following criterion is used to evaluate whether or not there is an organized labor union representing more than half the employees. The scope of employees participating in voting for the employee representative is calculated as follows:

245) This section is based upon the Administrative Guide: Kungi 68207-735 (June 5, 1997) including related administrative guidance and judicial rulings.

Ⅰ. 도입요건: 근로자대표의 선정[245)]

1. 목 적

근로기준법은 사용자가 근로시간제도의 변경 등에 있어 일정한 사항에 대하여 근로자대표와 서면합의 또는 협의를 하도록 하고 있다. 이 경우 근로자대표는 "당해 사업 또는 사업장에 근로자의 과반수로 조직된 노동조합이 있는 경우에는 그 노동조합, 근로자의 과반수로 조직된 노동조합이 없는 경우에는 근로자의 과반수를 대표하는 자"를 의미한다(근기법 제24조 제3항). 그러나 동 규정만으로 근로자대표를 선출하는 근로자의 범위, 근로자대표의 선정단위 및 선정방법, 근로자대표의 대표권 행사방법, 서면합의서의 효력 등이 명확하지 않다. 따라서 이에 관련한 문제에 대한 명확한 행정해석 기준과 판례 내용을 제시하여 법 해석과 운영을 이해하고자 한다.

〈근로자대표와의 서면합의·동의 및 협의내용〉

근로기준법	서면합의 또는 동의
제51조	3월 단위로 탄력적 근로시간제
제52조	선택적 근로시간제의 도입과 관련된 사항
제57조	선택적 보상휴가제
제58조 제2항	사업장 밖 간주근로시간제에 있어 '업무수행에 통상 필요한 시간 간주
제58조 제3항	재량근로에 있어 근로시간으로 간주하는 시간
제59조	운수업 등 특수업종에 있어 연장근로 및 휴게시간의 특례
제62조	연차휴가 유급휴가의 대체

2. 근로자의 범위와 근로자대표의 선정단위

(1) 근로자의 범위

노동조합이 근로자의 과반수를 조직하고 있는지의 여부를 판단하는 기준이 되거나 근로자대표를 선출함에 있어 투표에 참여하는 근로자의 범위는 다음과 같이 산정한다.

245) 근기 68207-735, 1997.6.5. 행정해석기준으로 유사행정해석 및 판례 추가하여 정리.

The scope of employees covered by employee representation		
= Employees under LSA Guidelines (Article 2 of the LSA (1))	-	Employers under LSA Guidelines (Article 2 of the LSA (2))

The term "employer" under the LSA means ① a business owner, or ② a person responsible for management of a business or ③ a person who works on behalf of a business owner with respect to matters relating to employees. Here, "a person who works on behalf of a business owner with respect to matters relating to employees" is an employee who has the dual position of employee and employer, and so shall be excluded from employees covered by employee representation. Although he/she is considered an employee to whom agreements apply, he/she acts specifically in the interest of the employer in the course of making written agreements.

(2) Unit selected for employee representation

The employee representative shall be selected from a unit of a business or workplace. Accordingly, in cases where one business is composed of several workplaces, if the company wants to introduce new working hour systems to the business unit, the employee representative shall be selected from that business unit, or if the company wants to introduce items to some designated workplace, the employee representative shall be selected from employees at those workplaces.

3. Choosing the Employee Representative

(1) Where there is an organized labor union representing more than half the employees

Whether the labor union represents more than half the employees shall be estimated in the unit of the business where the employer wants to select an employee representative; and shall be estimated in a unit of the workplace for that unit of the workplace. If the labor union represents more than half the employees, it is taken for granted that the labor union becomes the union representative(e.g. the chairman of the union branch) who has been authorized to represent the labor union.

근로자대표를 선출하는 근로자의 범위	=	근로기준법상의 근로자 (법 제2호 제1호)	-	근로기준법상의 사용자 (법 제2호 제2호)

근로기준법상 사용자는 ① 사업주, ② 사업경영담당자, ③ 그밖에 근로자에 관한 사항에 대하여 사업주를 위하여 행위하는 자를 말한다. 여기서 '그밖에 근로자에 관한 사항에 대하여 사업주를 위하여 행위하는 자'는 근로자와 사용자의 이중적 지위를 갖는 자로 근로자 산정에서 제외된다. 이유는 설사 이들이 근로자로 향후 합의 내용의 적용을 받더라도 노사서면 합의과정에서는 사용자를 위하여 대리하는 자로 볼 수 있기 때문이다.

(2) 근로자대표의 선정단위

근로자대표는 당해 사업 또는 사업장 단위로 선정되어야 한다. 따라서 하나의 사업이 수 개의 사업장으로 구성되어 있는 경우, 근로시간제도를 사업단위로 도입하고자 하면 근로자대표는 사업단위로 선정하고, 일부 사업장에만 도입하고자 하면 일부 사업장 단위로 선정해야 한다.

3. 근로자대표 선정방법

(1) 근로자 과반수로 조직된 노동조합이 있는 경우

노동조합이 근로자의 과반수를 조직하고 있는지의 여부는 사업단위로 도입하는 경우는 사업단위에서, 사업장 단위로 도입하는 경우는 사업장 단위에서 판단해야 한다. 노동조합이 근로자 과반수를 조직하고 있으면 근로자대표는 당연히 노동조합의 대표자 또는 노동조합으로부터 대표권을 위임받은 자(예, 노동조합지부장)가 된다.

(2) Where there is no organized labor union representing more than half the employees

Where there is no organized labor union representing more than half the employees, an employee representative shall be selected. In this case, there are no particular restrictions to the method of selection, but in situations where the employees are informed that an employee representative will be authorized to represent them in introduction of a working hour system, it is acceptable to receive employee opinions. Accordingly, direct voting is not always necessary; it is also possible to choose multiple representatives. In cases where a Labor-Management Council has been established by the Act on the Promotion of Workers' Participation and Cooperation(the Labor-Management Council Act) in a business or workplace to introduce a new working hour system, the employee members can be regarded as employee representatives.

The employee representative for the purpose of consulting with the employer shall be selected by independent and voluntary decision-making by the employees after they are informed of the reason for choosing employee representation. It is also acceptable to choose the employee representative through employees' general meeting or individual signatures on circulating representative lists. If an employer asks the employees to choose an employee representative, the employees autonomously determine procedures and methods of selection without intervention by the employer, and select someone(even though some employees could not participate) that represents more than half of the employees, the person shall be regarded as the employee representative.[246)]

(3) Invalid employee representatives

Agreement from or consultation with an employee who does not justifiably represent the employees is not legally valid.

1) In cases where a company does not receive written agreement from the employee representative in introducing a three month or less flexible working hour schedule, but instead receives individual written agreements from more than half the employees, this is a violation of related labor laws.[247)]

---

246) MOEL Guidelines 68207-1472, Nov. 13, 2003.

247) MOEL Guidelines 1167, Apr. 29, 2008.

(2) 노동조합이 근로자 과반수를 조직하지 못하고 있는 경우

노동조합이 근로자의 과반수를 조직하지 못하고 있는 경우에는 근로자의 과반수를 대표하는 자를 선정하여야 한다. 이 경우 선정방법에는 특별한 제한이 없으며, 근로시간제도에 대한 대표권을 행사한다는 것을 근로자에게 주지시킨 상태에서 근로자의 의사를 모으는 적당한 방법이면 된다. 따라서 반드시 직접투표에 의하지 않아도 되며, 1인의 대표는 물론 복수의 근로자대표를 선정하는 것도 가능하다. 근로시간제도를 도입하고자 하는 사업 또는 사업장단위에 '근로자참여 및 협력증진에 관한 법률'(이하 '근참법')에 의한 노사협의회가 설치되어 있으며 그 근로자위원을 근로자대표로 볼 수 있다.

경영상의 이유에 의한 해고 문제에 대하여 "사용자와 협의를 할 근로자의 대표자를 선출한다는 것을 근로자들에게 주지시킨 상태에서 근로자들의 자유로운 의사결정이 보장되는 적당한 방법이면 될 것으로 사료되는 바, 근로자들의 집회를 통한 선출이나 회람을 통한 서명 등의 방법도 무방할 것이다. 사용자가 근로자대표의 선출을 요청하고 그에 따라 근로자들이 사용자의 개입이 배제된 상태에서 자율적으로 근로자대표 선출을 위한 절차나 방법을 결정하고 근로자대표를 선출하였다면 그 과정에서 일부 근로자들이 참여하지 못하였다 하더라도 선출된 자가 근로자의 과반수에 대한 대표성을 가지고 있다면 근로자대표가 아닌 자로 보기는 어렵다."[246]

(3) 근로자대표로서 인정받지 못한 사례

근로자대표로서 대표성이 없는 자와의 승인 또는 협의는 법적인 효력을 가질 수 없다.

1) 3개월 이내 단위 탄력적 근로시간제를 도입하면서 근로자대표와의 서면합의가 아닌 대상 근로자 과반수의 개별적 서면 동의를 받는 경우에는 법적 요건을 갖추지 못한 것이다.[247]

---

246) 행정해석: 근기 68207-1472, 2003.11.13.

247) 행정해석: 근로조건지도과-1167, 2008.4.29.

2) Article 3 of the rules for implementation of the Labor-Management Council Act stipulates that the employee representative shall be selected by direct and secret vote, but this does not cover the method of voting. Vote counting is frequently computerized according to laws related to elections, but electronic voting has not yet been stipulated and related technical matters were not yet officially verified, and so it is difficult to accept its official use in reality.[248)]

4. Method of Representation by the Employee Representative

(1) In cases where a written agreement is made as a supplement to the collective agreement

In cases where the employer makes a supplementary agreement to the collective agreement with the union chairman or the person commissioned to be the employee representative, the agreement can affect the collective agreement.

(2) In cases where a written agreement is made with an employee representative of the Labor-Management Council

Since a written agreement cannot change the existing collective agreement, if such agreement is incompatible with the current collective agreement, separate procedures to revise the collective agreement shall be taken so as to apply to the employees under the collective agreement. Employees to whom the collective agreement does not apply can be included in the written agreement. This written agreement can be applicable without revising the existing rules of employment. However, revising the existing rules of employment is highly recommended in order to maintain consistency in working conditions.

(3) In cases where a written agreement is made with a new employee representative

The effectiveness is considered to be the same as a written agreement with the employee representative of the Labor-Management Council.

---

248) MOEL Guidelines 68107-335, Nov. 12, 1998.

2) 근참법 시행령 제3조 제1항은 근로자위원을 직접·비밀·무기명투표에 의하여 선출하도록 명시하고 있으나 투표방법에 관한 사항은 명시된 바가 없다. 현행 선거관련법상 전산조직을 이용한 개표는 명문화되어 실시 중이나 전자투표에 관하여는 명시된 바가 없으며 기술적인 문제가 검증되지 않아 아직까지는 현실적으로 활용하기에 곤란하다.[248)]

4. 근로자대표의 대표권 행사방법

(1) 노동조합이 대표권을 행사하는 경우

노동조합의 대표자 또는 노동조합으로부터 대표권을 위임받은 자가 대표권을 행사한다. 단체협약의 보충협약으로 체결하거나, 단체협약과는 별개의 서면합의서로 작성할 수 있다.

(2) 노사협의회 근로자위원이 대표권을 행사하는 경우

서면합의의 방식은 노사협의회의 근로자위원들이 정한 대표권 행사방법에 따르면 되고, ① 1인의 대표자를 선출하거나, ② 당해 사업에 한하여 1인의 근로자위원에게 대표권을 위임하거나 ③ 별도의 의사결정 방법을 설정하거나(예를 들어 과반수의 찬성, 2/3 이상의 찬성 등) ④ 근로자위원 전원이 서면합의에 참여하는 등의 모든 방법이 가능하다. 사용자가 일방적으로 일부 근로자위원과만 서면합의 하는 경우에는 법적 효력이 발생하지 않는다.

(3) 새롭게 근로자대표를 선정하는 경우

1인의 근로자대표가 선정된 경우는 선정된 대표가 대표권을 행사하면 된다. 복수의 근로자대표가 선정되는 경우는 노사협의회 근로자 위원이 대표권을 행사하는 방법에 준하여 대표권을 행사한다.

---

248) 행정해석: 노사 68107-335, 1998.11.12.

5. Effect of Written Agreements

When a written agreement is concluded between the employer and the employee representative, the company does not need individual employee agreement. The effects of signing the written agreement differ as follows:

(1) In cases where a written agreement is made as a supplement to the collective agreement

In cases where the employer makes a supplementary agreement to the collective agreement with the union chairman or the person commissioned to be the employee representative, the agreement can affect the collective agreement.

(2) In cases here a written agreement is made with an employee representative of the Labor-Management Council

Since a written agreement cannot change the existing collective agreement, if such agreement is incompatible with the current collective agreement, separate procedures to revise the collective agreement shall be taken so as to apply to the employees under the collective agreement. Employees to whom the collective agreement does not apply can be included in the written agreement. This written agreement can be applicable without revising the existing rules of employment. However, it is very desirable to revise the existing rules of employment in order to maintain consistency in working conditions. When revising the rules of employment in accordance with the written agreement, the employer does not have to again hear the opinion of or obtain agreement from the employee representative or other employees.

Ⅱ. Flexible Working Hour System

1. Purpose

"Flexible working hours" means shortening the working hours of other working days or other weeks while extending working hours on particular working days or particular weeks, so that the average working hours of a certain period shall be within the statutory standard working hours(40 hours per week). For an example, if you work 45 hours(9 hours x 5 days) in the first week and 35 hours(7 hours x 5 days) in the second week, they will equal 40 hours per week on average, meaning an overtime allowance will not have to be paid for the 5 extended working hours in the first week.

5. 서면합의의 효력

사용자와 근로자대표 사이에 서면합의가 유효하게 성립되면 개별근로자의 동의는 필요하지 않다. 서면합의 주체에 따른 효력은 다음과 같다.

(1) 단체협약의 보충협약의 형식으로 체결하는 경우

노동조합의 대표자 또는 노동조합으로부터 위임을 받은 자와 단체협약의 보충협약의 형식으로 체결하는 경우에는 단체협약의 효력을 변경하는 효력이 발생한다.

(2) 노사협의회 근로자 위원과의 서면합의 형식으로 체결하는 경우

단체협약을 변경하는 효력은 발생하지 않으므로, 단체협약에 배치되는 경우 단체협약의 적용을 받는 근로자에게도 적용하려면 별도로 단체협약의 개정절차를 밟아야 한다. 단체협약의 적용을 받지 않는 근로자에게는 서면합의만으로도 적용 가능하다. 취업규칙과 관련해서는 반드시 기존 취업규칙의 변경이 없어도 적용이 가능하다. 다만 근로조건 규정의 통일성을 기하기 위해 기존 취업규칙을 변경하는 것이 바람직하다. 취업규칙을 변경하는 경우 별도의 취업규칙 변경절차(근로자대표 또는 근로 과반수의 의견청취 또는 동의) 거치지 않아도 된다.

Ⅱ. 탄력적 근로시간제

1. 의 의

'탄력적 근로시간제'란 어떤 근로일이나, 어떤 주의 주당 근로시간을 연장시키는 대신 다른 근로일, 다른 주의 근로시간을 단축시킴으로써, 일정 기간의 평균 근로시간을 법정기준근로시간(1주 40시간) 내로 맞추는 제도를 말한다. 예를 들어, 2주 단위 탄력적 근로시간제에서 첫째 주에 45시간(9시간×5일), 둘째 주에 35시간(7시간×5일) 근무 시, 주당 평균 근로시간이 40시간이므로, 첫째 주에 법정근로시간을 초과한 5시간분에 대한 가산수당이 발생하지 않는다.

근로자의 입장에서는 실근로시간 단축, 출퇴근일수의 감소 및 휴일의 증가로 여가활용이 쉬워지는 장점이 있는 반면, 근로시간 변경에 따른 생체리듬 변화, 피로

From the perspective of workers, it is easy to utilize leisure time by reducing working hours, decreasing the number of commuting days, and increasing holidays, while they face changes in biorhythm that cause greater fatigue while their real wage decrease due to reduced overtime allowance. From the perspective of employers, it is possible to reduce labor costs by increasing the efficiency of working hours and reducing the demand for overtime by arranging working hours to proactively respond to market conditions and management, avoiding a fixed statutory time system that is too strict.

The flexible working hour system is designed to increase efficiency in a workforce by adjusting the length of working time according to seasonal, monthly, or daily fluctuations in workload.

Under it, the employee works additional hours beyond the legal standard working hours for a specific period such as two weeks, one month, three months or six months on the condition that the average working hours for a certain period of a day or week shall not exceed the standard working hours. In this case, the employer is not violating the working hour rules of the LSA, nor is he/she obliged to pay an additional allowance for the extended hours. This system is designed to benefit the employer by allowing him/her to adjust working hours according to seasonal changes in production volume.

2. Introducing a Flexible Working Hour System

Article 51 (Flexible Working Hour System)

① An employer may have a worker work in accordance with the rules of employment (or in accordance with rules or regulations equivalent thereto) for a specific week in excess of working hours prescribed in Article 50 (1), or for a specific day in excess of working hours prescribed in Article 50 (2), on condition that average working hours per week in a certain unit period of not more than two weeks do not exceed the working hours under Article 50 (1), and provided that working hours in any particular week shall not exceed forty-eight hours.

② Where an employer reaches an agreement in writing with a workers' representative on the following enumerated items, the employer is allowed to have a worker work for a specific week in excess of the working hours under Article 50 (1), or for a specific day in excess of the working hours under Article 50 (2), on the condition that average working hours per week in a certain unit period of not more than three months do not exceed the working hours under Article 50 (1). However, working hours for a specific week, and for a specific day shall not exceed fifty-two hours and twelve hours respectively:

1. scope of workers subject to this paragraph; 2. unit period (a unit period not exceeding three months); 3. working days in a unit period and working hours for each working day; and 4. other matters prescribed by Presidential Decree.

③ The provisions of paragraphs (1) and (2) shall not apply to workers aged between fifteen and eighteen, and pregnant female workers.

④ If an employer needs to have a worker work in accordance with the provisions of paragraphs (1) and (2), the employer shall prepare measures to ensure that the existing wage level is not lowered.

증대, 연장근로수당의 지급축소에 따른 실질 임금이 감소되는 단점이 있다. 사용자의 입장에서는 고정적 법정 기준시간제도가 가지는 엄격성을 탈피하여 시장 상황, 경영 등에 탄력적으로 대응하도록 근로시간을 배치하여 근로시간의 효율성을 높이고 연장근로 수요를 줄임으로써 인건비 절감이 가능하다는 장점이 있다.

탄력적 근로시간제는 계절별·월별·요일별 업무량의 변화가 있는 경우에 근로시간을 탄력적으로 배치함으로써 효율적인 인력관리를 하려는 데 그 목적이 있다.

탄력적 근로시간제란 2주간, 1개월간, 3개월간, 6개월간 등 일정한 기간을 평균하여 1일간 또는 1주일간 근로시간이 법정기준 근로시간을 초과하지 않으면 특정일 또는 특정 주에 기준근로시간을 초과하더라도 근로시간 위반이 아님은 물론 초과한 시간에 대해 연장근로에 대한 가산수당을 지급하지 않아도 되는 장점이 있는 제도이다. 일이 많을 때는 근로를 길게 하고 일이 적을 때는 근로시간을 짧게 하는 등 근로시간 운용에 탄력성을 부여하기 위한 제도이다.

2. 도입방법

근로기준법 제51조【탄력적 근로시간제】

① 사용자는 취업규칙(취업규칙에 준하는 것을 포함한다)에서 정하는 바에 따라 2주 이내의 일정한 단위기간을 평균하여 1주간의 근로시간이 제50조 제 1항의 근로시간을 초과하지 아니하는 범위에서 특정한 주에 제50조 제 1항의 근로시간을, 특정한 날에 제5조 제 2항의 근로시간을 초과하여 근로하게 할 수 있다. 다만, 특정한 주의 근로시간은 48시간을 초과할 수 없다.

② 사용자는 근로자대표와의 서면 합의에 따라 다음 각 호의 사항을 정하변 3개월 이내의 단위기간을 평균하여 1주 간의 근로시간이 제50조 제1항의 근로시간을 초과하지 아니하는 범위에서 특정한 주에 제50조 제 1항의 근로시간을, 특정한 날에 제50 조 제2항의 근로시간을 초과하여 근로하게 할 수 있다. 다만, 특정한 주의 근로시간은 52시간을, 특정한 날의 근로시간은 12시간을 초과할 수 없다.

1. 대상 근로자의 범위
2. 단위기간(3개월 이내의 일정한 기간으로 정하여야 한다)
3. 단위기간의 근로일과 그 근로일별 근로시간
4. 그밖에 대통령령으로 정하는 사항

③ 제1항과 제2항은 15세 이상 18세 미만의 근로자와 임신 중인 여성 근로자에 대하여는 적용하지 아니한다.

④ 사용자는 제1항 및 제2항에 따라 근로자를 근로시킨 경우에는 기존의 임금 수준이 낮아지지 아니하도록 임금보전방안(賃金補塡方案)을 강구하여야 한다.

Article 51-2 (Flexible working hour system exceeding 3 months)

① Where an employer reaches an agreement in writing with a workers' representative on the following enumerated items, the employer is allowed to have a worker work for a specific week in excess of the working hours under Article 50 (1), or for a specific day in excess of the working hours under Article 50 (2), on the condition that average working hours per week in a certain unit period exceeding 3 months and not exceeding 6 months, do not exceed the working hours under Article 50 (1). However, working hours for a specific week, and for a specific day shall not exceed fifty-two hours and twelve hours respectively:

1. Scope of target workers;
2. Unit period (shall be set as a fixed period exceeding 3 months and not exceeding 6 months);
3. Working hours per week in unit period; and
4. Other matters prescribed by Presidential Decree.

② In the case of working pursuant to Paragraph (1), the employer shall give the worker a continuous break of 11 hours or more before the start of the next working day after the end of the working day. However, if it is inevitable as prescribed by Presidential Decree, such as natural disasters, the written agreement with a workers' representative shall be followed.

③ The employer shall notify the worker of the working hours for each working day of the week two weeks before the start of the working day of each week pursuant to Paragraph (1) ③.

④ When inevitable reasons such as unpredictable natural disasters, machine breakdowns, and sudden increase in workload occur at the time of written agreement with a workers' representative pursuant to Paragraph (1), the employer shall work for one week on average within the unit period under Paragraph (1) ②. As long as the time is maintained, the matters referred to in paragraph (1) ③ may be changed after consultation with a workers' representative. In this case, prior to the commencement of the changed working day, the employee shall be notified of the working hours for each working day.

⑤ In the case of engaging workers to this flexible working hours pursuant to paragraph (1), the employer shall adjust or establish wage items so that the existing wage level does not decrease, or prepare wage preservation measures such as payment of additional wages, and shall report to the Minister of Employment and Labor. However, this is not the case if a wage preservation plan has been prepared through written agreement with a workers' representative.

⑥ The provisions of paragraphs (1) through (5) shall not apply to workers aged between fifteen and eighteen, and pregnant female workers.

An employer may adopt "flexitime" on a 2-week basis by modifying the rules of employment and on a 3-month(6-month) basis by reaching agreement with the employee representative. In a flexitime scheme on a 2-week basis, the hours of work in a particular week may not exceed 48; in a flexitime scheme on a 3-month(6-month) basis, the hours of work in a particular week and on a particular day may not exceed, respectively, 52 and 12 hours, respectively(Article 51, 51-2 of the LSA).

제51조의2【3개월을 초과하는 탄력적 근로시간제】 ① 사용자는 근로자대표와의 서면 합의에 따라 다음 각 호의 사항을 정하면 3개월을 초과하고 6개월 이내의 단위기간을 평균하여 1주 간의 근로시간이 제50조제1항의 근로시간을 초과하지 아니하는 범위에서 특정한 주에 제50조제1항의 근로시간을, 특정한 날에 제50조제2항의 근로시간을 초과하여 근로하게 할 수 있다. 다만, 특정한 주의 근로시간은 52시간을, 특정한 날의 근로시간은 12시간을 초과할 수 없다.

1. 대상 근로자의 범위
2. 단위기간(3개월을 초과하고 6개월 이내의 일정한 기간으로 정하여야 한다)
3. 단위기간의 주별 근로시간
4. 그 밖에 대통령령으로 정하는 사항

② 사용자는 제1항에 따라 근로자를 근로시킬 경우에는 근로일 종료 후 다음 근로일 개시 전까지 근로자에게 연속하여 11시간 이상의 휴식 시간을 주어야 한다. 다만, 천재지변 등 대통령령으로 정하는 불가피한 경우에는 근로자대표와의 서면합의가 있으면 이에 따른다.

③ 사용자는 제1항제3호에 따른 각 주의 근로일이 시작되기 2주 전까지 근로자에게 해당 주의 근로일별 근로시간을 통보하여야 한다.

④ 사용자는 제1항에 따른 근로자대표와의 서면합의 당시에는 예측하지 못한 천재지변, 기계 고장, 업무량 급증 등 불가피한 사유가 발생한 때에는 제1항제2호에 따른 단위기간 내에서 평균하여 1주간의 근로시간이 유지되는 범위에서 근로자대표와의 협의를 거쳐 제1항제3호의 사항을 변경할 수 있다. 이 경우 해당 근로자에게 변경된 근로일이 개시되기 전에 변경된 근로일별 근로시간을 통보하여야 한다.

⑤ 사용자는 제1항에 따라 근로자를 근로시킬 경우에는 기존의 임금 수준이 낮아지지 아니하도록 임금항목을 조정 또는 신설하거나 가산임금 지급 등의 임금보전방안(賃金補塡方案)을 마련하여 고용노동부장관에게 신고하여야 한다. 다만, 근로자대표와의 서면합의로 임금보전방안을 마련한 경우에는 그러하지 아니하다.

⑥ 제1항부터 제5항까지의 규정은 15세 이상 18세 미만의 근로자와 임신 중인 여성 근로자에 대하여는 적용하지 아니한다.

취업규칙 변경을 통하여 2주 이내 단위의 탄력적 근로시간 제도를, 근로자대표와의 합의를 통하여 3개월(6개월) 이내 단위의 탄력적 근로시간 제도를 도입하여 운영할 수 있다. 취업규칙(2주 단위) 또는 근로자대표와의 서면합의(3개월 단위, 6개월 단위)에 의하여 탄력적 근로시간제를 도입하는 경우, 일정한 기간(2주, 3개월, 6개월)을 평균하여 1주간의 근로시간이 40시간을 초과하지 않는 범위 내에서 1일 8시간, 1주 40시간을 초과하여 근로 시킬 수 있다. 다만, 2주 단위의 탄력적 근로시간제의 경우 특정주의 근로시간이 48시간을 초과할 수

(1) Introduction of flexible working hours up to two weeks

Flexible working time up to two weeks can be prepared through the establishment and revision of employment rules. In order to introduce this system through the employment rules, the opinion of the labor union representing the majority of workers or an employee representative representing the majority of workers shall be heard, and consent obtained if introduction of the system will disadvantage the workers.

(2) Introduction of flexible working hours up to 3 months and more than 3 months

This system requires a labor-management agreement. The employer shall receive a written agreement from the labor union which comprises a majority of the workers, or the employee representative representing the majority of workers. The contents of the written agreement shall include ① the scope of the affected workforce, ② the unit period, ③ the working day in the unit period, and the working hours for each working day, and ④ the validity period of the written agreement.

1) The scope of the covered workers does not necessarily have to include all workers, and can apply only to some workers engaged in certain business sectors, industries and occupations. However, it cannot apply to young workers(between 15 and 18 years old) and pregnant women workers.

2) Since the unit period is up to 6 months, it can be implemented in various unit periods such as 6 months, 3 months, 2 months, 1 month, or 3 weeks.

3) The working days and working hours for each working day shall be specified. Workers shall be notified of the work schedule before the start of the unit period by specifying the work day by work type and working hours by work day in the work schedule. However, in the flexible working hour system exceeding 3 months, the employer shall notify the employee of the working hours for each working day of the week by two weeks before starting the working day of each week. Working hours in a particular week may not exceed 52, and working hours on a particular day shall not exceed 12. If more than that, an overtime allowance shall be paid.

4) There is no special limitation on the validity of a written agreement. If an expiration date is set, an automatic renewal clause or an auto-expansion clause may be provided if the expiration date has passed.

없고, 3월(6월) 단위의 탄력적 근로시간제의 경우 특정주의 근로시간은 52시간을, 특정일의 근로시간은 12시간을 초과할 수 없다.

(1) 2주 이내 탄력적 근로시간제 도입

2주 이내 탄력적 근로시간제는 취업규칙의 작성 및 변경을 통하여 도입할 수 있다. 취업규칙을 통해 제도를 도입하고자 할 때는 근로자 과반수를 대표하는 노동조합 또는 근로자 과반수의 의견을 들어야 하며, 동 제도 도입으로 근로자에게 불이익하게 작용하는 경우에도 그 동의를 얻어야 한다.

(2) 3개월 이내와 3개월 초과하는 탄력적 근로시간제 도입

3개월 이내 탄력적 근로시간제의 경우는 노사 서면합의로 도입하여야 하는데, 서면합의 하여야 할 대상은 근로자의 과반수로 조직된 노동조합이 있는 경우에는 그 노동조합, 그렇지 않은 경우에는 근로자 과반수를 대표하는 자가 이에 해당한다. 서면합의 내용에 포함해야 할 사항은 ① 대상근로자의 범위, ② 단위기간, ③ 단위기간에 있어서의 근로일 및 그 근로일별 근로시간, ④ 서면합의의 유효기간이다.

1) 대상근로자의 범위는 반드시 전체 근로자를 대상으로 하여야 하는 것은 아니어서 일정 사업부문, 업종, 직종 등에 따라서 그에 종사하는 일부 근로자에 한하여만 적용할 수 있다. 다만, 연소근로자(15세 이상 18세 미만) 및 임신 중인 여성 근로자에게는 적용할 수 없다.

2) 단위기간은 6개월 이내의 기간이므로 6개월 단위, 2개월 단위, 1개월 단위, 3주 단위 등 다양한 단위기간으로 실시 가능하다.

3) 근로일 및 근로 일별 근로시간을 명시해야 한다. 근무일정표에 근무형태별 근무일과 근무일별 근로시간을 명시한 근무일정을 단위기간 개시 전까지 근로자에게 고지하면 된다. 그러나 3개월을 초과하는 탄력적근로시간제에서 사용자는 각 주의 근로일이 시작되기 2주전까지 근로자에게 해당 주의 근로일별 근로시간을 통보하여야 한다. 특정 주의 근무시간이 52시간을, 특정일의 근로시간이 12시간을 초과할 수 없으며, 초과할 경우 연장근로에 해당한다.

4) 서면합의 유효기간에 대해서는 특별한 제한이 없다. 또한, 유효기간을 설정하는 경우 유효기간이 경과할 경우를 대비하여 자동갱신 조항을 두거나 자동연장조항을 둘 수 있다.

<table>
<tr><th></th><th>Two week flexible working hour system</th><th>Flexible working hour system for less than three months or more than three months</th></tr>
<tr><td>Concept</td><td>Two-week flexible working hours can be efficiently used anytime without employees' additional consent.</td><td>This system is extended to flexible working hours longer than two weeks, which is effective when used in seasonal business, construction, exporting companies, etc.</td></tr>
<tr><td>Eligibility</td><td>① Specified in the rules of employment
② Equal to or less than 48 hours per week
③ Specific weeks and days fixed</td><td>① An employer shall obtain a written agreement from the employee representative on the following items:
- Scope of the employees affected;
- Unit period;
- Working days in the unit period and working hours for each working day; and (Exceeding 3 months: Working hours per week in unit period)
- Effective period of the written agreement
② A maximum of 6 months (less than 3 months and more than 3 months)
③ Working hours shall not exceed 52 per week, 12 per day
④ Exceeding 3 months: Break time of 11 hours or more from the end of the working day before the start of the next working day shall be guaranteed.</td></tr>
<tr><td>Effect</td><td colspan="2">① Exclusion of additional allowances
- No obligation for an additional allowance is given for extended working hours exceeding legal standard hours for a specific week or a specific day.
② Measures to maintain current wage
- An employer shall take measures to ensure that the existing wage level is not lowered (Paragraph ④ of Article 51, LSA).
- In the case of flexible working hours exceeding three months, it is obligatory to prepare a wage preservation plan and report it to the Minister of Employment and Labor (however, when a wage preservation plan is prepared by written agreement between labor and management, the reporting obligation is exempted)</td></tr>
<tr><td>Exceptions</td><td colspan="2">① Minors (those aged 15 to 18)
② Pregnant employees</td></tr>
</table>

3. Cases of Use

(1) At a brick factory[249)]

"We are using sand, special cement, and water to make differentiated bricks in the factory. In January each year, temperatures drop below 20 degrees below zero, and when the water completely freezes at 20 degrees below zero, which makes it almost impossible to produce bricks. So, workers come to work normally and perform chores such as cleaning rather than producing bricks. But in March, the situation is completely different. As construction starts in

249) Kim, Boksoo, "Practical Use of the Flexible Working Hour System," Labor Law, June 2018.

구 분	2주 단위 탄력적 근로시간제	3월이내와 3개월 초과 단위 탄력적 근로시간제
의 의	2주 단위 탄력적 근로시간제는 취업규칙에서 정하는 바에 의해 실시되므로, 근로자들의 별도의 동의 없이 유용하게 활용할 수 있음	이 제도는 2주단위 탄력적 근로시간제 보다 탄력성의 범위를 넓힌 것으로서 주로 계절적 사업, 건설업, 수출산업 등에서 유용하게 활용할 수 있음
실시 요건	① 취업규칙에서 규정해야 함. ② 1주 48시간 이내일 것 ③ 특정주, 특정일을 명확히 지정할 것	① 근로자대표와 아래 사항을 서면 합의 – 대상근로자의 범위 – 단위기간 – 근로일 및 근로일별 근로시간(3개월 초과: 단위기간의 주별 근로시간) – 서면합의 유효기간 ② 6월 이내 (3월 이내와 3월 초과) ③ 1주52시간, 1일 12시간을 초과 하지 못함 ④ 3개월 초과: 근무일 종료 후 다음 근무일 개시 전까지 11시간 이상의 휴식 시간 보장
실시 효과	① 가산임금 적용제외 – 특정주 또는 특정일에 법정기준근로시간을 초과하여 근로하더라도 연장근로가 아니므로 가산임금을 지급할 의무가 없음 ② 임금보전방안 강구 – 사용자는 탄력적 근로시간제를 도입할 경우 기존의 임금수준이 저하되지 않도록 임금보전방안을 강구해야 함(근로기준법 제51조 제4항) – 3월 초과 탄력적 근로시간제에서는 임금보전방안 마련하여 고용노동부장관에 신고 의무 (단, 노사 서면합의로 임금보전방안 마련시 신고의무 면제)	
적용 제외	① 연소자(15세 이상 18세 미만자) ② 임신 중인 여성 근로자	

3. 활용방법

(1) 벽돌공장 도입사례[249)]

“우리 공장은 모래, 시멘트 특수원료, 물을 배합해서 차별화된 벽돌을 만들고 있다. 그런데 매년 1월이 되면 기온이 영하 20도 밑으로 내려가고 영하 20도에서는 물이 완전히 얼어 버리기 때문에 벽돌 생산을 할 수가 없다. 그렇지만, 직원들은 정상적으로 출근해서 청소 등 잡무를 수행한다. 그런데 3월이 되면 상황이 완전히 달라진다. 건설공사가 본격적으로 시작되기 때문에 벽돌 주문이 밀려들어 연장근로를 할 수밖에 없다.” 이러한 회사의 경우 탄력적 근로시간제

249) 김복수, “탄력적 근로시간제도의 실무적 활용”, 〈노동법률〉, 2018.6.

earnest, there is no choice but to work overtime due to the large volume of brick orders." In this company, a flexible working hour system can solve the problem. Workers work 30 hours per week in January, 40 hours per week in February, and 50 hours per week in March. In this case, the average working hours per week are 40, and so the company is not obligated to pay overtime allowance in March, even though their weekly work exceeds 40 hours.

(2) Luxury brand stores

December is peak season, and so customers shop a lot and store workers work overtime. On the other hand, January is offseason and customers don't go to luxury brand stores, leaving workers with not much to do. In these stores, the introduction of flexible working hours can reduce labor costs and increase work efficiency. In December, during the peak season, workers work 52 hours a week, but in January, the off-season, workers can work 28 hours a week.

Ⅲ. Selective Working Hour System

1. Purpose

The selective working hour system is a system that, by setting only the total working hours of the settlement period within one month, allows workers to select their own working time for days and for weeks within the standard working time range, and to freely determine the commute time of each day and each week. In other words, the system sets only the total working hours within one month and leaves the start and end times of working hours up to the workers. A selective working hour system therefore gives workers the choice of specific commute time, which enables them to increase work efficiency and improve their quality of life.

The selective working hour system introduced in Korea allows employees to decide for themselves the time of their arrival and departure from the office, or choose the daily working hours within the range of total working hours described by a specific period unit within one month. This system is useful in helping professionals or business managers improve work efficiency and providing housewives with work opportunities. Under this

도를 통해서 문제를 해결할 수 있다. 1월은 주당 30시간, 2월은 주당 40시간, 3월은 주당 50시간 근로한다. 이 경우 주 평균이 40시간이 되기 때문에 회사는 주당 40시간을 초과하는 3월에도 연장수당을 지급해야 할 의무가 없다.

(2) 명품매장의 도입사례

연말인 12월은 성수기라 고객들이 쇼핑을 많이 하기 때문에 일손이 많아 직원들은 연장근로를 한다. 이에 반해 1월에는 비수기라 고객들이 매장을 많이 찾지 않기 때문에 매장은 한가한 편이다. 이러한 매장의 경우, 탄력적 근로시간제를 도입하여 인건비를 줄이고 업무의 효율을 가져올 수 있다. 성수기인 12월에는 매주 52시간을 근무하고, 비수기인 1월은 매주 28시간을 근무하게 한다면 매장의 생산성을 향상시킬 수 있다.

Ⅲ. 선택적 근로시간제

1. 의 의

선택적 근로시간제란 1개월 이내의 정산기간의 총 근로시간만을 정하고 각 일, 각 주의 출퇴근 시각을 자유롭게 결정하여 기준근로시간 범위에서, 근로자가 근로시간을 임의로 선택할 수 있는 제도로 1개월 이내의 총 근로시간만 정하고 근로시간의 시작 및 종료시각을 근로자의 결정에 맡기는 제도이다. 따라서 선택적 근로시간제는 구체적으로 출퇴근 시각에 대한 근로자의 선택권을 인정함으로써 근로자가 일과 생활의 조화를 이루어 업무의 효율성을 높이고 삶의 질을 향상시킬 수 있다.

우리나라에서 도입하고 있는 선택적 근로시간제는 1개월 이내의 일정기간 단위로 정하여진 총 근로시간 범위 내에서 출·퇴근시간 및 1일의 근로시간을 근로자가 자율적으로 결정할 수 있는 제도로 전문직·사무관리직 등의 업무 능률 향상과 주부의 취업을 용이하게 할 수 있다는 장점이 있다. 이 제도를 도입할 경우 근로자에게는 출·퇴근 편의나 여유 있는 사회생활의 기회가 주어지고, 경

system, employees have convenience in commuting and the right to a more relaxing social life, while the employer benefits from higher productivity and a reduction in inefficient working hours.

The Labor Standards Act: Article 52 (Selective Working Hour System)

① Where an employer has reached a written agreement on each of the following subparagraphs with the workers' representative regarding a worker who is entrusted with the decision as to when to begin and finish work in accordance with the rules of employment (including those equivalent to rules of employment), the employer may have workers work in excess of the working hours per week set by paragraph (1) of Article 50, or the working hours per day set by paragraph (2) of Article 50 on the condition that average working hours per week computed on the basis of adjustment period of not more than one month(three months in case of research and development of new products or technologies) do not exceed the working hours prescribed in paragraph (1) of Article 50:

1. scope of workers subject to this paragraph (excluding workers between the age of 15 and 18)
2. adjustment period
3. total working hours within an adjustment period
4. starting and finishing time of working hours, if a mandatory work period is in force
5. starting and finishing time of working hours which are allowed to be selected by workers; and
6. other matters as determined by Presidential Decree.

Enforcement Decree to the Labor Standards Act: Article 29 (Agreed-upon Matters regarding Selective Work Hours System)

"Other matters as prescribed by Presidential Decree" under subparagraph 6 of Article 52 of the Act mean standard working hours (working hours per day based on which the employer and the workers' representative agree to calculate paid leave, etc.).

2. Types of Selective Working Hour Systems

(1) Fully selective working hour system

Under a fully selective working hour system, the employee decides on the commuting hours during the period of flexible working hours and the employer does not interfere with the allocation of employee working hours. That is, there is no mandatory range of working hours other than the selective working hours.

(2) Partly selective working hour system

Under a partly selective working hour system, the employee is entrusted with the

영자에게는 생산성 증대나 낭비 작업시간의 감소 등의 효과가 있어 사회 전체의 생산성이 증가될 것이다.

근로기준법 제52조【선택적 근로시간제】

① 사용자는 취업규칙(취업규칙에 준하는 것을 포함한다)에 따라 업무의 시작 및 종료 시각을 근로자의 결정에 맡기기로 한 근로자에 대하여 근로자대표와의 서면 합의에 따라 다음 각 호의 사항을 정하면 1개월(신상품 또는 신기술의 연구개발 업무의 경우에는 3개월로 한다) 이내의 정산기간을 평균하여 1주간의 근로시간이 제50 조 제1항의 근로시간을 초과하지 아니하는 범위에서 1주간에 제50조 제1항의 근로시간을, 1일에 제5조 제2항의 근로시간을 초과하여 근로하게 할 수 있다.

1. 대상 근로자의 범위(15세 이상 18세 미만의 근로자는 제외한다)
2. 정산기간
3. 정산기간의 총 근로시간
4. 반드시 근로하여야 할 시간대를 정하는 경우에는 그 시작 및 종료 시각
5. 근로자가 그의 결정에 따라 근로할 수 있는 시간대를 정하는 경우에는 그 시작 및 종료 시각
6. 그밖에 대통령령으로 정하는 사항

근로기준법 시행령 제29조【선택적 근로시간제에 관한 합의사항】

법 제52 조 제6호에서 "그밖에 대통령령으로 정하는 사항"이란 표준근로시간(유급휴가 등의 계산 기준으로 사용자와 근로자대표가 합의하여 정한 1일의 근로시간)을 말한다.

2. 선택적 근로시간제의 종류

(1) 완전 선택적 근로시간제

정산기간 중에 출·퇴근이 근로자의 결정에 맡겨 있고 근로자의 근로시간 배열에 사용자가 관여하지 않는 선택적 근로시간제로 의무 근로시간대는 없고 선택적 근로시간대만 있는 경우를 말한다.

(2) 부분 선택적 근로시간제

정산기간 중의 출·퇴근을 근로자의 결정에 맡긴 상태에서 일정한 시간대를 정하여 그 시간에는 근로자가 사용자로부터 시간적 구속과 구체적 업무지시를

decision to begin and finish tasks, while receiving hourly supervision and concrete job directions from the employer during specified hours. However, during a different range of working hours, the employee decides when to begin and finish work and arranges the amount of working hours.

The mandatory range of working hours is called the "core time," while the selective range is called the "flexible time." Usually, the core time and flexible time are settled automatically through a written agreement between employer and employee. The employer makes the most of the core time, during which he/she can give necessary orders and manage meetings, directions, etc.

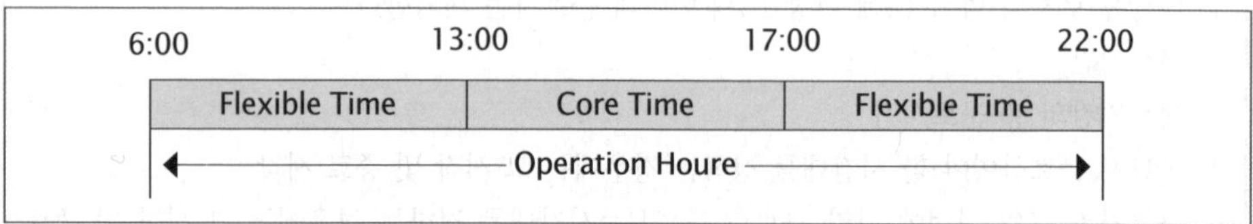

3. Introducing a Selective Working Hour System

(1) Introduction through the rules of employment

Employers shall stipulate that the start and end times of work are left up to the worker's decision for a group of workers subject to selective working hours through the establishment or revision of employment rules.

(2) Written agreement with the employee representative

To introduce the selective working hour system, a written agreement with the labor union or worker representative representing the majority of the workers is required. The written agreement shall include ① scope of workers subject to this system, ② adjustment period(within one month), and the total working hours within an adjustment period, ③ starting and finishing time of working hours, if a mandatory work period is in force(core time), ④ starting and finishing time of working hours which are allowed to be selected by workers(selective time), and ⑤ standard working hours to form the basis for granting paid leave.

받고 나머지 시간에 대해서는 출·퇴근 및 근로시간 배열이 근로자의 결정에 맡겨지는 근로시간제를 말한다.

근로자가 의무적으로 출근해야 하는 시간대를 의무적 근로시간대(Core Time), 재량에 맡겨진 시간대를 선택적 근로시간대(Flexible time)라고 부른다. 선택적 근로시간대와 의무적 근로시간대를 구분하여 설정하는 것은 노·사가 서면합의를 통해 자율적으로 결정할 사항이며, 회의, 지시사항 등 필요한 지휘명령을 위하여 의무 근로시간대를 설정한다.

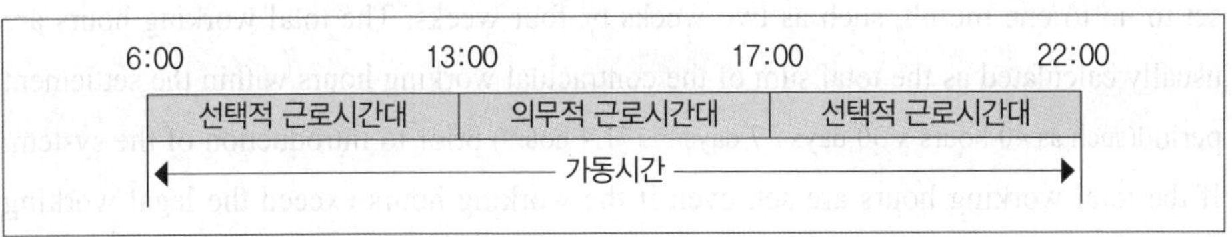

3. 도입방법

(1) 취업규칙을 통해 도입

사용자는 취업규칙의 작성 또는 변경을 통해 선택적 근로시간제의 대상이 되는 근로자 집단에 대해 업무의 시작 및 종료시각을 근로자의 결정에 맡긴다는 내용을 기재하여야 한다.

(2) 근로자대표와의 서면합의

선택적 근로시간제를 도입하려면 근로자의 과반수를 대표하는 노동조합 또는 근로자대표와 서면합의를 해야 한다. 서면합의 내용에 포함되어야 할 사항은 ① 대상근로자의 범위, ② 정산기간(1개월 이내) 및 그 기간에 있어 총 근로시간, ③ 반드시 근로하여야 할 시간대를 정한 경우에는 그 시작 및 종료시각(core time), ④ 근로자가 그의 결정에 따라 근로할 수 있는 시간대를 정하는 경우에는 그 시작 및 종료시각(selective time), ⑤ 유급휴가 부여 등의 기준이 되는 표준근로시간이다.

1) The scope of covered workers

In general, it is easy to apply the system to managers and supervisors who do not have strict restrictions on commuting, etc., and professional, research, and office workers who place more emphasis on quality than the amount of work. However, this system can be introduced at any workplace.

2) Settlement period and total working hours

The period for which the worker chooses to provide the work by themselves can be set to up to one month, such as two weeks or four weeks. The total working hours are usually calculated as the total sum of the contractual working hours within the settlement period(such as 40 hours x 30 days / 7 days = 171.4 hours) prior to introduction of the system. If the total working hours are set, even if the working hours exceed the legal working hours per day or per week within the total working hours of the settlement period, they will not be considered extended working hours subject to overtime allowance.

3) Core working hours and selective working hours

Core working hours is the time when the worker must work, while selective working hours is the time when the worker can decide on their own whether to provide work.

4) Standard working hours

Standard working hours refers to the one day's working hours set by labor and management, which becomes the basis for calculation of paid leave, etc. in the selective working hour system. When using paid leave, it is considered that the standard working hours of 1 day are used.

4. Using a Selective Working Hour System

If the above conditions are satisfied, the employer may extend weekly working hours to more than 40 and daily working hours beyond 8 to the extent that the average working hours per week during the period of flexible working hours within the given month do not exceed 40. In this case, additional allowance for extended work is not provided.

1) 대상근로자의 범위

일반적으로 출퇴근 등에 엄격 제한을 받지 않는 관리, 감독업무 종사자, 근로의 양보다는 질이 중시되는 전문직, 연구직, 사무직 종사자 등에 제도 적용이 용이하나, 사업장 여건이 허락되는 경우 대부분 사업장에서도 도입이 가능하다.

2) 정산기간, 총 근로시간

근로자가 스스로 선택하여 근로를 제공할 정산기간을 1개월 이내에서 2주, 4주 등으로 설정할 수 있다. 총근로시간은 일반적으로 제도 도입 전을 기준으로 정산기간 상당의 소정근로시간 합계로 계산한다(예: 40시간 × 30일 / 7일 = 171.4시간). 총 근로시간을 정하게 되면 정산기간의 총 근로시간 범위 내에서 일, 주 단위 법정근로시간을 초과하여 근무하더라도 연장근로가 되지 않는다.

3) 의무 근로시간대 및 선택적 근로시간대

의무 근로시간대는 근로자가 반드시 근로하여야 할 시간대이며, 선택 근로시간대는 근로자가 스스로의 결정에 의하여 근로제공 여부를 결정할 수 있는 시간대를 말한다.

4) 표준근로시간

표준근로시간은 선택적 근로시간제에서 노사가 유급휴가 등의 계산기준으로 정한 1일의 근로시간을 말한다. 유급휴가 사용 시 1일의 표준근로시간을 사용한 것으로 간주한다.

4. 활용방법

상기 실시요건을 충족하는 경우 1월 이내의 총 근로시간을 평균하여 1주의 평균 근로시간이 40시간을 초과하지 아니하는 범위 안에서 근로기준법 제50조에 규정된 1주 40시간, 1일 8시간의 기준근로시간을 초과하여 연장근로 할 수 있다. 이 경우에 연장근로수당이 발생하지 않는다.

(1) General selective working hour system

Selective working hours are divided into mandatory working hours and selective working hours. The standard working hours, based on the calculation of paid leave, are from 09:00 to 18:00. For example, workers are given discretionary hours at 07:00-11:00 for coming to the office and 15:00-20:00 for leaving the office. The mandatory(core) working hours for all workers are 11:00-15:00.

(2) Jobs where it is difficult to check working hours and with significant waiting time(00 company, which specializes in renewable energy)

Employees were dissatisfied because they did not get paid overtime due to difficulty in verifying their work hours. Also, as for after-sales service, irregular overtime occurred frequently and there were many hours spent waiting. The company introduced a selective working hour system on a monthly basis for sales and after-service teams through written agreements with labor representatives after consultations between labor and management. As a result, it was possible to adjust working hours according to the work volume while reducing unnecessary waiting time and overtime, improving flexibility and efficiency in work.[250)]

(3) Jobs related to types of irregular work

Company 00, which is a refrigeration facility installation and management company, works according to project schedules requested by clients and their companies due to the nature of work. There has been a lot of overtime due to irregular work schedules(including nighttime and holiday work). The company introduced a selective working hour system, which allowed each worker to manage their arrival time to work and their departure time from work according to the circumstances of their client companies. This has minimized unnecessary overtime. As a result, workers were able to adjust their working hours according to their clients' schedules, which made it possible to reduce overtime that had been due to irregular schedules.[251)]

---

250) MOEL, "Flexible Working Hour System Guidelines", Sept. 2019, p. 52.

251) Ibid., pp. 53-54.

(1) 의무 선택적 근로시간제

일반적 근로시간제로 의무적 근로시간대와 선택적 근로시간대로 나누어 운용한다. 유급휴가 등의 계산을 기준으로 삼는 표준근로시간대는 오전 9시에서 저녁 6시이다. 예를 들어, 근로자에게 재량이 주어지는 출근시간대는 오전 7시에서 오전 11시, 퇴근시간대는 오후 3시에서 저녁 8시이다. 그리고 모든 근로자가 의무적으로 근무해야 하는 의무 근로시간대는 오전 11시에서 오후 3시까지이다.

(2) 근무시간 확인이 어렵고 대기시간이 많은 업종의 경우(예: 신재생 에너지 전문업체인 ○○기업)

영업직의 경우 근무시간을 확인하기 어렵다는 이유로 연장근로수당을 지급하지 않아 직원들의 불만이 많았다. 특히, A/S 업무는 업무 특성상 불규칙적인 연장근로가 자주 발생하였고 대기상태가 많았다. 이 회사는 노사 간 협의 과정을 거쳐 근로자대표와의 서면합의로 영업직과 A/S 팀을 대상으로 1개월 단위로 선택적 근로시간제를 도입하였다. 그 결과 업무량에 따른 근로시간 조정이 가능하여, 유연하고 효율적인 업무수행으로 불필요한 대기시간 및 연장근로를 감소시켰다.[250)]

(3) 불규칙적인 근로가 이루어지는 업종

냉동기기 설치와 관리 업체인 ○○기업은 업무 특성상 고객사 및 거래처가 원하는 프로젝트 일정에 따라 근로가 이루어져 불규칙적인 연장, 야간, 휴일 근무가 발생하는 등 장시간 근로가 많이 발생했다. 이 기업은 선택적 근로시간제를 도입하여 각 근로자가 담당하고 있는 고객사의 사정에 맞게 출, 퇴근시간을 운영할 수 있도록 하여 일률적인 출, 퇴근시간에 따른 불필요한 연장근로 발생을 최소화하였다. 그 결과, 고객사의 스케줄에 따라 근로자 스스로 근로시간을 조정할 수 있게 되어 불규칙한 근로시간에 따른 연장근로를 감소시켰다.[251)]

---

250) 고용노동부, "유연근로시간제 가이드", 2019.9, 52면.

251) 고용노동부, "유연근로시간제 가이드", 2019.9, 53~54면.

Ⅳ. Deemed Working Hours System

1. Purpose

The deemed working hours system is a system for recognizing working hours when it is difficult for a worker to calculate all or part of his or her working time outside the workplace due to business or other reasons. In this case, in principle, the prescribed contractual working hours are considered to be worked. However, in cases where work in excess of the predetermined working hours is normally required for the performance of the work, the required time is generally regarded as working time. If labor and management have determined in advance the generally necessary working hours in writing, such working hours are regarded as performed. The deemed working hour system outside the workplace is sometimes referred to as an authorized labor system, and was established to make calculation of working hours more reasonable in consideration of the increasing number of working hours outside the workplace due to development of the service industry and automation. Areas where difficulties exist in calculating working hours include sales, AS service, business trips, taxi driving, reporters' work, and working from home.

2. Introducing a Deemed Working Hours System

Labor Standards Act, Article 58: Special Cases for Calculation of Work Hours

① When it proves difficult to calculate the work hours of an employee because he/she performs his duty in whole or in part outside the workplace owing to business trips or other reasons, the hours shall be calculated as contractual working hours, provided that, in cases where it is ordinarily necessary for an employee to work in excess of contractual working hours to carry out said duty, it shall be deemed that the employee has worked for the hours ordinarily required to carry out that duty.

② Notwithstanding the proviso of paragraph ①, in cases where there exists a written agreement between the employer and the employee representative of the workplace concerned, the hours determined in the agreement shall be regarded as those ordinarily required to carry out the relevant duty

(1) Provision of work outside the workplace

Work outside the workplace shall be judged by comprehensive consideration of the place of work and the type of work performed. Working outside the workplace is a situation in

Ⅳ. 간주근로시간제

1. 의 의

간주 근로시간제란 근로자가 출장 또는 그 밖의 사유로 근로시간의 전부 또는 일부를 사업장 밖에서 근로하여 근로시간을 실제로 측정하기 어려운 경우에 근로시간을 인정하는 제도이다. 이 경우에 원칙적으로 소정근로시간을 근로한 것으로 보나, 당해 업무의 수행을 위해 통상적으로 소정근로시간을 초과한 근로가 필요한 경우에는 통상 필요한 시간을 근로시간으로 인정하며, 통상 필요한 시간을 노사가 따로 서면 합의한 경우에는 그 시간을 근로시간으로 인정한다. 사업장 밖 간주 근로시간제는 인정근로제로 표현하기도 하는데 서비스산업의 발달과 자동화의 진전 등으로 사업장 밖에서 근로하는 사례가 증가하고 있는 현실을 반영하여 근로시간을 보다 합리적으로 정하기 위하여 제정된 것이다. 근로시간의 산정이 어려운 업무로 영업, A/S 업무, 출장업무, 택시운전업무, 기사 취재업무, 재택근무 등을 들 수 있다.

2. 도입방법

> **제58조【근로시간 계산의 특례】**
> ① 근로자가 출장이나 그 밖의 사유로 근로시간의 전부 또는 일부를 사업장 밖에서 근로하여 근로시간을 산정하기 어려운 경우에는 소정근로시간을 근로한 것으로 본다. 다만, 그 업무를 수행하기 위하여 통상적으로 소정근로시간을 초과하여 근로할 필요가 있는 경우에는 그 업무의 수행에 통상 필요한 시간을 근로한 것으로 본다.
> ② 제1항 단서에도 불구하고 그 업무에 관하여 근로자대표와의 서면 합의를 한 경우에는 그 합의에서 정하는 시간을 그 업무의 수행에 통상 필요한 시간으로 본다.

(1) 사업장 밖의 근로제공 일 것

사업장 밖 근로는 근로 장소와 근로수행 형태를 종합적으로 고려하여 판단해야 한다. 근로장소는 소속 사업장에서의 장소 이탈을 전제로 하여 근로자가 자신의 본래 소속 사업장의 근로시간 관리로부터 벗어나 있는 상황을 말한다. 근

which a worker deviates from the management of working hours at his or her own place of work. The form of work performance refers to the conduct of work without specific direction and supervision from the employer's working time management organization.

(2) Difficulty in calculating working hours

It is difficult to calculate working hours, because the work start and finish time outside the workplace are discretionary for the workers concerned, and because the workers concerned work the length of working hours according to their working conditions. Therefore, if it is possible to calculate working hours when the specific direction and supervision of the employer directly affects the workers working outside, the deemed working hour system shall not apply to those workers.

(3) Introducing the system

If(1) and(2) above are met, the agreed-upon working hours shall be considered as working hours, regardless of actual working hours, as one of three: ① predetermined working hours, ② time normally required for the performance of work, or ③ agreed working hours between labor and management.

3. Using a Deemed Working Hours System

(1) Overseas business trips

When traveling overseas for business or returning home, flight time, immigration procedures, and travel time are likely to exceed actual working hours. In such cases, it is desirable to establish a written agreement with the worker representative. Generally, the company guarantees paid or alternative leave for the time required for the work through overseas business regulations. In this regard, the courts and the MOEL consider working time spent abroad as working hours.[252)]

(2) Work outside the workplace

If the working hours are difficult to calculate because the employee performs duty

---

252) Suwon District Court ruling on Nov. 25, 2016: 2015 gadan 505758; MOEL Guidelines on June 14, 2001: 68207-1909.

로수행형태는 사용자의 근로시간 관리조직으로 부터의 구체적인 지휘, 감독을 받지 않고 근로를 수행하는 것을 말한다.

(2) 근로시간을 산정하기 어려울 것

근로시간 산정이 어려운 경우는 사업장 밖 근로의 시업시각과 종업시각이 해당 근로자의 자유에 맡겨져 있고, 근로자의 조건이나 업무상태에 따라 근로시간의 장단이 결정되는 경우를 말한다. 따라서 사업장 밖 근로라 하더라도 사용자의 구체적인 지휘, 감독이 미치는 경우에는 근로시간의 산정이 가능하므로 그 적용대상에서 제외된다.

(3) 도입방법

위의 (1)과 (2)을 충족한 경우, 근로자가 실제 근로한 시간과 관계없이 ① 소정근로시간, ② 업무수행에 통상적으로 필요한 시간, ③ 노사가 서면으로 합의한 시간 중 어느 하나를 근로시간으로 본다.

3. 활용방법

(1) 해외출장

장거리 해외출장을 위해 이동하거나 귀국 시 비행시간, 출입국 수속시간, 이동시간 등은 실제 시간이 소정근로시간을 초과할 가능성이 높다. 이러한 경우 근로자대표와 서면 합의를 통해 정하는 것이 바람직하다. 일반적으로 회사는 해외출장규정을 통해서 그 업무에 필요한 시간만큼 유급이나 대체휴무를 보장한다. 이와 관련하여 법원과 고용노동부는 해외출장 중 소비한 시간은 근로시간으로 판단하고 있다.[252)]

(2) 외근근로

사업장 외에서의 근무로 근로시간 산정이 어려운 경우 근로시간과 임금의 계

---

252) 수원지방법원 2016.11.25, 2015가단505758; 근기 68207-1909, 2001.6.14.

outside the workplace, disputes are likely to arise between employee and employer about calculation of wage. As a solution, the deemed working hour system has been introduced to recognize those outside working hours as fixed working hours.

V. Discretionary Work System

1. Concept

The discretionary work system is a system that requires the delegation of work method to worker discretion in light of the nature of the work.

Workers have a lot of discretion in the way they work according to technological advances, information-orientation of work, increasing economic share of the services industry, increasing share of knowledge labor, etc., and so their remuneration depends on the quality of work rather than the amount of working hours.

Professional work that requires creativity, such as research and development, information processing system analysis, design, news article composition, and editorial work, is not appropriately regulated by the amount of working hours like general workers. But it is desirable for both labor and management to leave their working hours to the discretion of such professional workers rather than to directly control them.

2. Introducing a Discretionary Work System

Labor Standards Act: Article 58 (Special Cases for Calculation of Work Hours)

③ For tasks designated by Presidential Decree as those tasks which need, in light of their characteristics, worker discretion with regard to the ways to perform them, the worker shall be deemed to have worked such working hours as determined by a written agreement between the employer and the workers' representative. Such written agreement shall contain each of the items described in the following subparagraphs:

1. provisions as to work to be provided;
2. provisions in which the employer will not give directions to the worker regarding how to perform the work, and how to allocate working hours; and
3. provisions in which computation of working hours shall be determined by the written agreement concerned.

산 등을 둘러싸고 노·사간 분쟁의 소지가 있으므로, 간주근로시간제를 도입하여 일정시간을 근로한 것으로 인정할 수 있는 근거를 마련한 것이다.

Ⅴ. 재량 근로시간제

1. 의 의

재량근로시간제란 업무의 성질에 비추어 업무수행방법을 근로자의 재량에 위임할 필요가 있는 업무로 사용자가 근로자대표와 서면합의로 정한 근로시간을 소정근로시간으로 인정하는 제도이다.

산업전반에서 기술혁신, 정보화, 서비스업 비중 증가, 지식노동 증가 등에 따라 일하는 방식에 있어서 근로자의 재량 여지가 많고, 그 보수도 근로시간의 양보다 근로의 질(성과)에 따라 결정되는 것이 적합한 전문적 업무가 증가하고 있다.

연구개발 업무, 정보처리시스템 분석, 설계업무, 기사의 취재, 편집업무 등 창의성 발휘가 필요한 전문적 업무에 대해서는 일반근로자와 같이 근로시간의 양으로 동일하게 규제하는 것이 부적절하므로 사용자의 구체적 지시에 따라 업무를 수행케 하는 것보다 근로자의 재량에 맡기는 것이 노사 쌍방을 위하여 바람직하다.

2. 도입방법

근로기준법 제58조【근로시간 계산의 특례】

③ 업무의 성질에 비추어 업무 수행 방법을 근로자의 재량에 위임할 필요가 있는 업무로서 대통령령으로 정하는 업무는 사용자가 근로자대표와 서면 합의로 정한 시간을 근로한 것으로 본다. 이 경우 그 서면 합의에는 다음 각 호의 사항을 명시하여야 한다.

1. 대상 업무
2. 사용자가 업무의 수행 수단 및 시간 배분 등에 관하여 근로자에게 구체적인 지시를 하지 아니한다는 내용
3. 근로시간의 산정은 그 서면 합의로 정하는 바에 따른다는 내용

(1) Work considered discretionary

Work that may be targeted as discretionary is limited to the work prescribed in Article 31 of the Enforcement Decree to the Labor Standards Act. In view of the nature of the work, it must be given to worker discretion. Workers shall not be given specific instructions on how to perform the work, but this shall be left to their full discretion, while the employer can direct the basic content of the work. However, the employer shall not give specific instructions regarding the distribution of working hours to workers.

1) Research and development of new products or technologies, and research in the areas of the humanities or social or natural sciences
2) Design or analysis for data processing systems
3) Gathering, compiling and editing of news for a newspaper, broadcasting or publication business
4) Design or creation of clothing, interior decoration, industrial goods, advertisement, etc.
5) Work as a producer or director in the business of producing broadcasting programs, motion pictures, etc. and
6) Consultation, advice, appraisal or agency with the delegation or commission of others in the affairs of accounting, legal cases, tax payment, legal affairs, labor management, patents, appraisal, etc.

(2) There must be written agreement on statutory matters

To introduce a discretionary work system, the employer must specify the tasks concerned, and other necessary items through a written agreement with the employee representative. The statutory matters that must be included in the written agreement include: ① provisions as to tasks to be provided; ② provisions in which the employer would not give directions to the worker regarding method of performance, and how to allocate working hours; and ③ provisions in which the computation of working hours shall be determined by the written agreement concerned.

3. Using a Discretionary Working Hour System

In order for the company to adopt and use discretionary work hours in certain

(1) 재량근로의 업무에 해당할 것

재량근로의 대상으로 할 수 있는 업무는 근로기준법 시행령 제31조에서 규정한 업무에 한정된다. 업무의 성질에 비추어 업무수행방법은 근로자의 재량에 위임할 필요가 있는 업무여야 한다. 수행 수단에 관한 구체적인 지시를 받지 않아야 하지만 업무수행을 완전히 근로자 재량에 맡겨야 한다는 것은 아니므로 업무의 기본적 내용을 지시할 수 있다. 그러나 사용자는 근로자의 근로시간 배분에 관하여 구체적인 지시를 하지 않아야 한다.

1) 신상품 또는 신기술의 연구개발이나 인문사회과학 또는 자연과학 분야의 연구 업무
2) 정보처리시스템의 설계 또는 분석 업무
3) 신문, 방송 또는 출판 사업에서의 기사의 취재, 편성 또는 편집 업무
4) 의복, 실내장식, 공업제품, 광고 등의 디자인 또는 고안 업무
5) 방송 프로그램, 영화 등의 제작 사업에서의 프로듀서나 감독 업무
6) 회계, 법률사건, 납세, 법무, 노무관리, 특허, 감정평가 등의 사무에 있어 타인의 위임, 위촉을 받아 상담, 조언, 감정 또는 대행을 하는 업무

(2) 법정 사항에 대한 서면합의가 있어야 함.

재량근로제를 도입하기 위해서는 사용자가 근로자대표와 서면합의를 통하여 대상업무를 등을 구체적으로 명시하여야 한다. 서면합의에 반드시 포함시켜야 할 법정사항은 ① 대상업무, ② 사용자가 업무의 수행 수단 및 시간 배분 등에 관하여 근로자에게 구체적인 지시를 하지 아니한다는 내용, ③ 근로시간의 산정은 그 서면 합의로 정하는 바에 따른다는 내용이다.

3. 활용방법

기업이 조직 내 특정 직종이나 부서, 직무 등에 재량 근로시간제를 도입해 활용하기 위해서는 그 적용대상이 ① 위에 언급한 6가지의 재량근로대상업무에

occupations, departments, and duties within the organization, ① it must fall under one or more of the six discretionary work tasks mentioned above, ② discretionary rights in work performance shall be allocated and ③ a written agreement with the worker representative shall pre-exist the discretionary work hours.

Ⅵ. Compensatory Leave System

Labor Standards Act: Article 57 (Compensatory Leave System)
An employer may, in lieu of paying additional wage, grant leave to a worker to compensate for the extended, night and holiday work prescribed in Article 56, pursuant to a written agreement with the workers' representative.

1. Requisites to Utilizing a Compensatory Leave System

There shall be a written agreement between the employer and the employee representative. Without such an agreement, the system shall not be legally in effect. If there is a labor union organized by the majority of employees, the union shall represent all workers. If there is no union, then an employee representative shall represent the workers. The written agreement shall be a document signed by both parties concerned.

2. Criteria for Using Leave as Compensation

wage paid for extended work, night work, and holiday work, and leave rendered as compensation, shall be of equal value. Accordingly, an additional allowance mentioned in Article 56 of the LSA shall be considered. This means that, if two hours were spent in extended work, wage would be valued at 3 hours, including additional allowances. In cases where extended work, holiday work, and night work overlap, wage including each additional allowance shall be compensated with leave.

The parties concerned shall agree upon whether compensatory leave should be rendered as total wage with an additional allowance or only as an additional allowance.

해당되어야 하고, ② 대상업무 수행에 있어 재량이 인정되어야 하고, ③ 근로자대표와의 서면합의가 있어야 한다.

Ⅵ. 보상휴가제

> **근로기준법 제57조【보상 휴가제】**
> 사용자는 근로자대표와의 서면 합의에 따라 제56조에 따른 연장근로·야간근로 및 휴일근로에 대하여 임금을 지급하는 것을 갈음하여 휴가를 줄 수 있다.

1. 보상휴가제 도입 요건

근로자대표와의 서면합의가 있어야 하며, 동 요건을 갖추지 못하면 효력이 없다. 근로자대표는 근로자 과반수로 조직된 노동조합이 있으면 그 노동조합, 근로자 과반수로 조직된 노동조합이 없으면 근로자 과반수를 대표하는 자이며, 서면합의는 노사 당사자가 서명한 문서의 형태로 작성되어야 한다.

2. 보상휴가 부여 기준

연장·야간·휴일근로에 대한 임금과 이에 갈음하여 부여하는 휴가 사이에는 동등한 가치가 있어야 하므로 근로기준법 제56조에 의한 가산임금까지 감안되어야 한다. 따라서 연장근로를 2시간 한 경우 가산임금을 포함하면 총 3시간분의 임금이 지급되어야 하므로 3시간의 휴가가 발생한다. 연장·휴일·야간근로가 중복된 경우에는 가산임금을 포함하여 산정된 임금에 해당하는 휴가가 발생한다.

보상휴가제의 적용대상을 연장근로 등에 대한 가산임금을 포함한 전체 임금으로 할지, 가산임금 부분만 할지는 노사 서면합의로 정한 바에 따른다.

3. Providing Compensatory Leave

1) Leave, according to the regulations, shall be rendered within contractual working hours. Whether the leave shall be used in a unit of hours or days in regards to accumulation depends on the agreement between the parties concerned.

2) In the Act, where the system of using leave as compensation is regulated in a written agreement, details shall be specified in separate written agreements between the parties concerned. They include: ① whether the rendering of leave will be decided by the employee or the employer, and ② whether the leave will be applied to all employees uniformly or selectively. It also considers ③ whether the employer shall allow workers to ask for allowances, and ④ whether the employer will allow workers to ask for leave, if they are not allowed to ask for allowances.

Accordingly, in cases where all employees agree upon using leave uniformly in the written agreement, the employer shall not have to pay an allowance for each employee, since Article 56 of the Labor Standards Act(Extended, Night or Holiday Work) is not being violated.

3) Using leave as compensation is a system in which an employer provides leave instead of allowances, which means the employer shall have to pay allowances if the leave cannot be granted. Unlike annual paid leave, the employer cannot waive wage payment with measures to promote the use of leave.

The right to ask for an allowance is given from the day following the expiry date of the unused leave. If this rule is violated, it is regarded as a violation of Article 56 of the Labor Standards Act. It is not a violation of the Act if the employer pays the allowance sometime between the expiration date of leave and the regular payment date of wage in the first following month.

3. 휴가 부여방법

1) 동 규범에 의한 휴가는 소정근로시간 중에 부여되어야 한다. 휴가를"시간" 단위로 부여할지 이를 "일" 단위로 부여할지는 노사 서면합의로 정하는 바에 따른다.

2) 법 규정에는 노사 서면합의로 보상휴가제를 도입할 수 있는 근거만 있으므로 세부적인 사항은 노사 서면합의에 의해 노사가 자율적으로 정할 수 있다. 즉, 부여 방식은 ① 근로자의 청구에 의할 것인지 사용자가 일방적으로 지정할 것인지, ② 전 근로자에게 일률적으로 적용할 것인지 희망하는 근로자에 한하여 적용할 것인지 등의 사안과 ③ 임금청구권은 휴가 청구권과 임금청구권의 선택을 인정할 것인지 ④ 임금청구권을 배제하고 휴가 청구권만 인정할 것인지 등이다.

노사 서면합의에 의해 전 근로자에게 일률적으로 적용하고 휴가사용권만 인정하기로 한 경우에는 개별 근로자가 이에도 불구하고 임금을 청구하더라도 사용자는 이에 응할 의무가 없으며, 근로기준법 제56조(야간·연장 및 휴일근로) 위반 등의 문제가 발생하지 않는다.

3) 보상휴가제는 임금지급에 갈음하여 휴가를 부여하는 제도이므로 어떠한 이유로든 휴가를 부여하지 않은 경우에는 그에 대한 임금이 지급되어야 한다. 연차유급휴가와는 달리 사용자가 휴가사용촉진조치를 통해 임금지급의무를 면제받을 수 없다.

임금청구권은 휴가를 사용할 수 없게 된 것이 확정된 날의 다음 날부터 행사할 수 있으며, 위반 시에는 근로기준법 제56조 위반이 된다. 다만, 휴가를 사용할 수 없게 된 것이 확정된 날의 다음 날부터 최초로 도래하는 임금 정기지급일에 위 임금을 지급한 경우에는 법 위반으로 보지 않는다.

Ⅶ. Work-from-Home Systems[253)]

1. Jobs Suitable for Working from Home and Required Equipment

(1) The concept of working from home

Working from home provides flexibility when a work space is provided in a home and utilizes information & communication technology and the facilities and equipment necessary for the work. Regular working from home involves most of the work being done from home, while occasional working from home involves only part of the week spent working from home and the other part at the office. This would include, for example, Mondays and Tuesdays at home working and the rest of a 5-day work week in the office.

(2) Jobs suitable for working from home

Jobs that allow workers to work independently and involve the performance of individual tasks, jobs that have little or no face-to-face contact with customers, and jobs that do not need to be performed at a specific location are all suitable for a work-from-home system. Such a system is particularly easy to introduce into fields such as program and game development, web design, book publication, distance education, financial and insurance marketing, civil complaint consulting, planning and administrative processing, and computational work.

1) Suitable tasks

① Work with little or no face-to-face contact with customers

② Work allowing a high degree of independence and little need for approval or reporting, or organizational management that allows a high degree of independence due to little need for cooperation between organizations

③ Work easy to quantify in work performance evaluations and

---

253) Reference: MOEL, "Manual on the Introduction and Operation of a Systematic Flexible Working System", Dec. 2017; MOEL, "How Korean Companies Will Put Flexible Work into Action", Nov. 2016; MOEL Guidelines (kungi 68201-4085, Dec. 29, 2000): "Standards for Application of the Labor Standards Act with Those Working from Home"; MOEL, "Flexible Working Hours Guide", Aug. 2019; Lee, Seunggil, "Status of Those Working from Home in Terms of Labor Law", Labor Law, Aug. 2001, vol. 123.

Ⅶ. 재택근무제[253)]

1. 재택근무제의 적합한 업무와 업무환경 구비요건

(1) 재택근무의 의의

재택근무란 정보통신기술을 활용하여 "자택"에 업무공간을 마련하고, 업무에 필요한 시설과 장비를 구축한 환경에서 근무하는 유연한 근무 형태이다. 재택근무는 대부분의 근무를 재택으로 하는 상시형 재택근무와 일주일 중 일부만을 재택근무를 하는 수시형 재택근무로 구분할 수 있다. 수시형 재택근무는 근무일 중 일부는 재택근무, 일부는 사무실에서 근무하는 형태로 실시할 수 있다. 예를 들면, 주 5일 중 월요일과 화요일에는 재택근무를 하고, 나머지 수요일에서 금요일은 사무실에서 근무하는 방식이다.

(2) 재택근무제에 적합한 업무

재택근무는 독립적이면서도 개별적인 업무수행이 가능하거나, 고객과의 대면접촉이 거의 없는 직무, 특정한 장소에서 이루어지지 않아도 되는 직무 등에 적합하다. 특히, 프로그램 및 게임개발, 웹 디자인, 도서출판, 원격교육, 금융 및 보험마케팅 등의 업종이나, 민원 상담, 기획 및 행정처리 업무, 전산 업무 등의 분야에 도입이 용이하다.

1) 적용 가능 업무

① 고객과의 대면접촉이 거의 없는 업무
② 결재·보고가 적은 독립성이 강한 업무, 기관 간 업무협조가 적어 조직운영의 독립성이 높은 업무
③ 업무실적 평가의 계량화가 쉬운 업무

253) 참고자료: 고용노동부, "체계적인 유연근무제 도입·운영을 위한 매뉴얼, 2017.12; 고용노동부, "유연근로제 우리 기업은 어떻게 운영할까요", 2016.11; 고용노동부 행정해석(근기 68201-4085, 2000.12.29): "재택근로자에 대한 근로기준법 적용기준"; 고용노동부, "유연근로시간제 가이드", 2019.8; 이승길, "재택근로자의 노동법적 지위", 노동법률, 2001.8, vol.123.

④ Jobs determined by managers with approval authority after considering business characteristics and working conditions of the department.

2) Unsuitable tasks

① Jobs where there is significant security risk due to insufficient security measures in the relevant business

② Jobs involving safety inspections, equipment inspections, and accident handling measures, etc., where the person responsible should be there to do such jobs, or the risk will inevitably and significantly increase if the work were to be done from home

③ Jobs where the work must always be carried out in a specific place for the purpose of receiving and processing civil complaints

④ Jobs where other serious obstacles are expected before business(administrative) objectives can be achieved.

(3) Equipment needed when working from home

A certain level of working environment and work facilities(seats, PCs, etc.) are needed at home so that the work can be performed in an identical or very similar environment to the regular office.

1) Preparing work space

As contact with family members can disrupt work performance, employers need to ensure that those working from home have an independent space dedicated to work.

2) Construction of an IT infrastructure

The company will need to provide the basic IT devices and networks needed to do business at home. These would include computers and accessories, printers, communication equipment, and personal web cameras for video conferencing. The company will also need to provide the necessary solutions(electronic payment, messenger, file sharing, project management, etc.) when accessing office systems or performing company work.

④ 승인권자가 업무특성 및 부서 근무여건을 고려하여 정한 업무

2) 근무허가가 불가능한 경우

① 해당업무의 보안대책이 미흡하여 재택근무를 수행하는 경우 심각한 보안 위험이 예상되는 경우

② 안전점검, 장비점검, 사고처리 등 해당업무의 수행을 위하여 반드시 특정의 장소에 항상 위치하여야 하거나 재택근무를 수행하는 경우 현저히 그 위험성이 증가하는 경우

③ 민원사무의 접수 및 처리 등을 위하여 특정의 장소에서 항상 업무를 수행하여야 하는 경우

④ 그밖에 사업(행정) 목적을 달성하는 것에 심각한 지장이 발생할 수 있는 경우

(3) 재택근무 업무환경의 구비요건

재택근무자가 사무실에서 업무를 수행할 때와 동일하게 업무를 수행하기 위해서는 재택근무지에 근무환경 및 업무시설(좌석, PC 등)을 구축하는 것이 필요하다.

1) 업무수행 공간 확보

재택근무는 가족이나 친지 등과의 접촉으로 업무수행에 차질을 야기할 수 있으므로 재택근로자로 하여금 업무수행을 위한 독립된 전용공간을 확보하도록 한다.

2) IT 인프라 구축

회사는 자택에서 업무를 수행하는 데 필요한 기본적인 IT 기기 및 네트워크를 제공한다. 컴퓨터 및 부속장비, 복합기, 통신장비, 화상회의를 위한 개인용 웹 카메라 등 업무 속성에 따라 관련 장비를 지원한다. 사무실 시스템에 접속하거나 업무를 수행할 때 필요한 솔루션(전자결재, 메신저, 파일공유, 프로젝트 관리 솔루션 등)도 제공한다.

3) Cost burden

It is common for the employer to bear the communication expenses related to working from home, the cost of information and communication equipment, and work-related consumable items.

4) Security measures

Working from home requires measures to protect information security. Such measures may include ① providing a solution to security threats that may occur when accessing an office system from home, and to support with related technologies, ② introduction of a computer that leaves all work and records on the cloud rather than individual computers, ③ actions to prevent family members of the employee working from home from accessing any company data, ④ safe disposal of document waste, and ⑤ preparation of measures to ensure security of the home office space and computers(such as shutting them down automatically) when the employee is not at the work-from-home location.

2. Introducing a Work-from-Home System

Introduction of a work-from-home system requires ① a written agreement with the workers' representative, ② changes in the labor contract with individual workers, and ③ changes in the rules of employment. Even when a work-from-home system needs to be revised, the employer must follow the above 3 steps again. However, when the work-from-home system will apply only to a particular worker, only that worker's consent is needed.

(1) Written agreement with the workers' representative

The Labor Standards Act(Article 58(2)) requires a written agreement with the employees' representative when working outside the workplace, such as working from home. The time required for the performance of work is usually determined through a written agreement, but the content of the rest of the written agreement is not otherwise specified. Eventually, if the working hours for a work-from-home system are determined in a written agreement, the details of place of work and those to whom the agreement applies should be included.

3) 비용부담

재택근무와 관련된 통신비, 정보통신기기 비용, 소모성 비품 등은 사용자가 부담하는 것으로 하는 것이 일반적이다.

4) 보안대책

재택근무는 일반 가정에서 업무를 수행하기 때문에 정보보안 등을 위한 대책을 마련해야 한다. 예를 들어, ① 가정에서 사무실 시스템 접속 시 발생할 수 있는 보안 위협에 대해 해결방안을 마련하고 관련 기술을 개발, ② 단말기에 기록을 남기지 않는 클라우드 방식의 컴퓨터 도입, ③ 재택근무자의 다른 가족 구성원이 정보 보호 관련 데이터 등에 접근하지 못하도록 할 것, ④ 폐기문서의 안전한 처리, ⑤ 재택 사무공간 및 컴퓨터 잠그기 등이 있다.

2. 재택근로제 도입 방법

재택근무제의 도입을 하기 위해서는 ① 근로자대표와 서면합의, ② 개별 근로자와 근로계약서 작성 ③ 취업규칙의 변경절차가 필요하다. 일부 조건을 변경할 경우에도 위의 3가지 절차를 거쳐야 한다. 다만, 특정 근로자에 대한 재택근무의 경우, 혹은 간헐적으로 이루어지는 재택근무의 경우에는 해당 근로자의 동의만으로도 제도의 도입이 가능하다.

(1) 근로자대표와 서면합의의 내용

근로기준법(제58조 제2항)에서는 재택근무처럼 사업장 밖에서 근무가 이루어질 경우 근로시간을 근로자대표와의 서면합의로 정할 수 있는 규정을 두고 있다. 다만, 업무수행에 기본적으로 필요한 시간을 서면합의를 통해 정할 수 있도록 하고 있을 뿐, 나머지 서면합의에 꼭 포함되어야 하는 내용에 대해서는 달리 규정하고 있지 않으므로 재택근무제 도입 운영에 따른 근로시간을 서면합의에서 정할 경우, 업무수행에 필요한 평균 근로시간 이외의 근무장소, 적용 대상자 등에 대한 내용을 기본적으로 포함시킬 수 있을 것이다.

(2) Changes to the employment contract

1) Since the details of workplace and working hours are legally required to be specified in the employment contract, the working contract must reflect the changed workplace and working hours under the work-from-home system(regular work from home).

2) For occasional work from home at a certain frequency and time while the company workplace remains the main workplace, it is necessary to state in the employment contract that work at a certain frequency and time outside the workplace is possible. However, as is the case for remote work, it is common for employment contracts to stipulate that uniform working conditions such as working place, working hours, and holidays are subject to employment rules or collective agreements. In this case, even if it is not specified in the employment contract, it is recognized in the employment rules that the company fulfilled its obligation to notify workers of compulsory working conditions.[254)]

(3) Changes to rules of employment

When introducing a work-from-home system, whether there is a need to change the existing rules of employment needs to be confirmed. Any changes shall be reflected in the existing rules of employment.

1) If there is no change to the rules of employment

When comparing the working conditions of working from home with those of ordinary workers at the workplace, if there are no changes in working conditions besides workplace, individual consent of the worker who wants to work from home is all that is needed. There is no need to change the rules of employment.

2) When the rules of employment need to be changed

If the employer requires all workers in the business or workplace to work from home.

---

254) MOEL Guidelines: Labor Standards Team-5809, Aug. 7, 2007.

(2) 근로계약서의 작성 및 변경

1) 근무장소와 근로시간에 대한 내용은 법적으로 근로계약서에 명시해야 할 사항이기 때문에 제도도입에 따라 변경된 근무장소 내지 근로시간의 내용을 반영하여 근로계약서를 작성 또는 변경해야 한다(재택근무 상시형).

2) 사업장을 주된 근무장소로 하면서 일정 빈도 및 시간을 재택근무 방식으로 근무하는 수시형의 경우에는 주 근무장소와 함께 일정 빈도 및 시간을 주된 근무장소 외의 장소에서 근무할 수 있다는 내용을 근로계약서에 함께 명시하여야 한다. 다만, 원격근무와 마찬가지로 근무장소·근로시간·주휴일 등 통상적인 근로조건에 대해서는 취업규칙이나 단체협약 등에 따른다고 규정하는 경우가 일반적이다. 이 경우 근로계약서에 명시되어 있지 않은 사항이라도 취업규칙에 명시되어 있고 이를 해당 근로자에게 주지시키면 명시의무를 이행한 것으로 인정된다.[254)]

(3) 취업규칙 변경

재택근무제 도입 시 기존 취업규칙을 변경할 필요가 있는지 검토하고 변경이 필요한 항목이 있다면 선별하여 기존의 취업규칙에 반영한다.

1) 취업규칙의 변경이 없는 경우

재택근무를 하는 근로자와 통상근로자를 비교하여 근무장소 외의 다른 근로조건에 변경이 없는 경우에는 재택근무를 하고자 하는 근로자의 개별적 동의를 받아 실시하는 것으로 가능하며, 반드시 취업규칙을 변경할 필요는 없다.

2) 취업규칙을 변경해야 하는 경우

사용자가 해당 사업 또는 사업장의 근로자 전체를 대상으로 일괄적으로 재택근무를 시행하는 경우에는 취업규칙을 변경해야 한다.

---

254) 노동부 행정해석: 근로기준팀-5809, 2007.8.7.

3. Application of the Labor Standards Act

(1) Attendance management

The Labor Standards Act regulations on working hours and rest also apply to workers working from home. However, working from home is a form of labor in which working hours and daily home life cannot easily be separated due to the nature of the workplace. It is difficult to manage and supervise such working hours as the employees are at home. In the end, it is left to the worker whether to fulfill the duty to provide work during the specified working hours. However, online attendance records and information and communication devices can provide some assistance with worker management.

(2) Working hours, overtime, night work allowance

When the work-from-home system is introduced, whether or not an overtime allowance, night work allowance, or holiday work allowance occurs depends on the specified working time for the worker or the time normally required to perform the work and the range of working hours established by the labor-management agreement.

In principle, if the teleworkers(which is another term referring to those working from home for an employer) required to perform a specific task in accordance with the employer's instructions work overtime, at night or during a holiday, overtime or nighttime work allowance must be paid. However, it is desirable to prepare a similar procedure for general workers to apply for overtime, night, and holiday work in advance and be approved by the employer before working those hours. For example, a procedure might include reporting in advance plans to work over a holiday to obtain the employer's permission and then report the outcome in detail.

(3) Leave and rest time for teleworkers

If the rules of employment do not provide separate rules for leave and rest for ordinary workers working from home, the employment rules on working hours, leave, and rest for ordinary workers apply. In this regard, it is desirable for the employer to set in advance the matters concerning working hours and non-working hours(for example, non-working hours due to vacation or sick leave).

3. 근로기준법의 적용

(1) 근태관리

재택근무에 종사하는 근로자도 근로기준법상의 근로시간 및 휴식에 관한 규정이 적용된다. 다만, 재택근무는 그 성질상 근로자의 근무시간대와 일상생활 시간대가 혼재되지 않을 수 없는 근로형태이며 "자택"에서 근로가 이루어지기 때문에 사생활의 침해 없이 근로자가 소정근로시간 동안 성실히 업무에 전념하였는가를 관리·감독하는 것은 어렵다. 결국, 소정근로시간 동안의 근로제공 의무나 직무전념 의무의 이행 여부는 근로자에게 맡겨질 수밖에 없고, 정보통신기기를 통한 온라인 출퇴근기록 등으로 재택근무자의 근로시간을 관리하는 것은 가능하다.

(2) 근로시간, 연장근로수당, 야간근로수당

재택근무제 도입 시 반드시 해당 근로자에 대한 소정근로시간 또는 업무 수행에 통상 필요한 시간, 그리고 노사합의로 정한 근로시간의 범위에 따라 연장근로수당이나 야간근로수당, 휴일근로수당에 대한 발생 여부가 달라지게 된다.

사용자의 지시에 따라 특정업무를 수행하는데 필요한 시간이 연장·야간·휴일근로를 발생 시킬 경우 원칙적으로 그에 대한 연장근로, 야간근로수당을 지급해야 한다. 다만, 전술한 바와 같이 재택근무제도 특성상 명확한 근로시간 산정이 어려우므로 근로자가 연장·야간·휴일근로를 사전에 신청하여 사용자의 허가를 받도록 하는 유사한 절차를 마련하는 것이 바람직하다.

(3) 재택근무자의 휴가와 휴식 시간

취업규칙에서 재택근로에 종사하는 통상근로자들에 대한 휴가 및 휴식에 관해서 별도의 규정을 두고 있지 않는 경우에는 통상적 근로에 종사하는 근로자들의 근로조건이 그대로 적용된다. 이와 관련하여 사용자는 근로시간과 비 근로시간(예컨대 휴가나 병가 등으로 인하여 근로하지 못하는 시간)에 관한 사항을 사전에 약정에 두는 것이 바람직하다.

(4) Job training and compulsory training

It is unavoidable that workers who work remotely or from home are susceptible to some concern that they may lag behind their colleagues in development of their abilities, etc., because working from home does make it difficult to have the educational opportunities normally obtained during on-the-job training(OJT). When a separate in-house education or training system or legally-required program is run, this should be reflected in the employment rules. In particular, as education on safety and health(Article 29 of the Industrial Safety and Health Act), preventing sexual harassment(Article 13 of the Equal Employment Act), and protecting personal information(Article 28 of the Personal Information Protection Act) is normally run for workplace workers, the employer will need to provide equal training opportunities to those working from home.

(5) Safety and health standards

Depending on the nature of their work, if it falls under the safety and health standards in the Occupational Safety and Health Act, those working from home will need to follow those rules. Accidents arising during the work at home will be considered occupational accidents and those injured/ill are eligible to insurance benefits under the Industrial Accident Compensation Insurance Act. However, accidents caused by workers' actions unrelated to work are not recognized thus.[255)]

(6) Performance evaluation

When employees are working from home(full time), it is desirable to establish a system so that workers do not worry about performance evaluation and personnel management issues because they are not working at the normal workplace. The most difficult thing for companies who have workers providing work from home is ensuring efficiency from those workers. In the course of evaluating work performance, teleworkers are often less productive and feel less managed. It is a good idea for the company to do the following: ① measure the performance of teleworkers based on visible results; ② manage the quality of work from teleworkers, and ③ implement performance evaluations for teleworkers as necessary, and report summary results and explain to them their ongoing progress.

---

255) MOEL Guidelines: Medical Care 0509-90, Feb. 14, 1996.

(4) 직무교육과 의무교육

원격이나 재택근무를 하는 근로자는 OJT(On the Job Training)에 의한 교육기회를 얻기 어려운 측면이 있으므로 능력개발 등에서 다른 동료근로자들에 비하여 뒤처질 수 있다는 불안감을 갖지 않도록 조치를 취하는 것이 바람직하다. 따라서 통상근로자와는 별도의 사내교육이나 연수제도, 법정교육을 위한 프로그램 등을 운영하는 경우에는 이를 취업규칙에 반영하여야 한다. 특히, 법정교육인 산업안전·보건교육(산업안전보건법 제29조), 성희롱 예방교육(남녀고용평등법 제13조), 개인정보 보호교육(개인정보 보호법 제28조) 등은 사업장 근로자와 차등적 적용되어서는 안 되기 때문에 그에 대한 대처방안을 마련하는 것이 좋다.

(5) 안전보건 기준

업무의 특성에 따라 산업안전보건법상 안전보건기준에 해당하는 경우에는 이를 준수하여야 한다. 재택근무 중에 해당업무가 원인이 되어 발생한 재해는 업무상 재해로 산업재해보상보험법상 보험급여의 대상이 된다. 다만, 근로자의 사적 행위를 원인으로 하여 발생한 재해는 업무상 재해로 인정되지 않는다.[255]

(6) 성과평가

재택근무(상시형)의 경우 근로자가 사무실에 출근하지 않기 때문에 성과평가 등을 걱정하는 일이 없도록 별도의 성과평가 및 인사관리 제도를 구축하는 것이 바람직하다. 재택근무를 제공하는 회사가 가장 어렵게 느끼는 점은 재택근무의 효율성이다. 따라서 ① 회사는 보이는 결과에 의해 재택근무자의 결과물을 측정하고, ② 재택근무자의 업무의 질을 관리하며, ③ 필요시 재택근무자에 대해 수행평가를 시행하고, 요약 결과나 진행과정 등에 대해 보고하도록 하는 것이 좋다.

---

255) 노동부 행정해석: 요양 0509-90, 1996.2.14.

Section 3: Statutory and Contractual Holidays

Ⅰ. Statutory Holidays

Labor Standards Act: Article 55 (Holidays)

① Employers shall allow workers an average of one or more paid holidays per week.
② Employers shall provide paid holidays for holidays declared by Presidential Decree: Provided, that the holidays can be shifted to other working days upon a written agreement with the workers' representative.

LSA Enforcement Decree: Article 30 (Holidays)

① Paid holidays under Article 55 (1) of the Act shall be granted to a person who has shown perfect attendance for the contractual working days during one week. <Amended by Presidential Decree No. 29010, Jun. 29, 2018>
② "Holidays prescribed by Presidential Decree" in the main sentence of Article 55 (2) of the Act means the holidays under any subparagraphs (excluding subparagraph 1) of Article 2 of the Regulations on Holidays of Government Offices and the alternative statutory holidays under Article 3 of the same Regulations.

Regulations on Holidays of Government Offices[256)]

Article 2 (Public Holidays) Statutory holidays of government offices shall be as follows: Provided, that statutory holidays of embassies and legations abroad shall be the statutory holidays among the national holidays of Korea and statutory holidays of residing nations:
1. Sundays;
2. The March 1 Independence Movement Day, Independence Day, National Foundation Day of Korea, and Hangul (Korean alphabet) Day;
3. The first day of January; 4. The day preceding Seollal (Korean New Year's Day), Seollal, and the day following Seollal (the last day of December, and the first and second days of January on the lunar calendar);
5. Deleted; 6. Buddha's Birthday (the eighth day of April on the lunar calendar);
7. The fifth day of May (Children's Day); 8. The sixth day of June (Memorial Day);
9. The day preceding Chuseok (Korean Thanksgiving Day), Chuseok, and the day following Chuseok (14th, 15th, and 16th days of August on the lunar calendar);
10. The 25th day of December (Christmas Day);
10-2. Election days for elections on the termination of terms of office referred to in Article 34 of the Act on Election of Public Officials and the Prevention of Election Malpractices;
11. Other days the Government designates from time to time.

256) [Enforcement Date] The amendment of Article 55 paragraph (2) shall be effective on a date specified in a pertinent subparagraph:
1. With regard to businesses that employ 300 people or more, public institutions: Jan. 1, 2020
2. With regard to businesses that employ 30 to fewer than 300 people: Jan. 1, 2021
3. With regard to businesses that employ 5 to fewer than 30 people: Jul. 1, 2022

제3절 법정휴일과 약정휴일

Ⅰ. 법정휴일

근로기준법 제55조【휴일】

① 사용자는 근로자에게 1주에 평균 1회 이상의 유급휴일을 보장하여야 한다.

② 사용자는 근로자에게 대통령령으로 정하는 휴일을 유급으로 보장하여야 한다. 다만, 근로자대표와 서면으로 합의한 경우 특정한 근로일로 대체할 수 있다.

근로기준법 시행령 제30조【휴일】

① 법 제55조제1항에 따른 유급휴일은 1주 동안의 소정근로일을 개근한 자에게 주어야 한다.

② 법 제55조제2항 본문에서 "대통령령으로 정하는 휴일"이란 「관공서의 공휴일에 관한 규정」 제2조 각 호(제1호는 제외한다)에 따른 공휴일 및 같은 영 제3조에 따른 대체공휴일을 말한다.

관공서의 공휴일에 관한 규정[256)]

제2조【공휴일】 관공서의 공휴일은 다음 각 호와 같다. 다만, 재외공관의 공휴일은 우리나라의 국경일 중 공휴일과 주재국의 공휴일로 한다.

1. 일요일.
2. 국경일 중 3·1절, 광복절, 개천절 및 한글날
3. 1월 1일
4. 설날 전날, 설날, 설날 다음 날(음력 12월 말일, 1월 1일, 2일)
5. 삭제.
6. 부처님오신날 (음력 4월 8일)
7. 5월 5일 (어린이날)
8. 6월 6일 (현충일)
9. 추석 전날, 추석, 추석 다음날 (음력 8월 14일, 15일, 16일)
10. 12월 25일 (기독탄신일)

10의2. 「공직선거법」 제34조에 따른 임기만료에 의한 선거의 선거일

11. 기타 정부에서 수시 지정하는 날

---

256) [시행일] 제55조제2항의 개정규정은 다음 각 호의 구분에 따른 날부터 시행한다.

1. 상시 300명 이상의 근로자를 사용하는 사업 또는 사업장, 공공기관: 2020년 1월 1일
2. 상시 30명 이상 300명 미만의 근로자를 사용하는 사업 또는 사업장: 2021년 1월 1일
3. 상시 5인 이상 30명 미만의 근로자를 사용하는 사업 또는 사업장: 2022년 1월 1일

Article 3 (Alternative Public Holidays)

① Where a public holiday specified in any of subparagraphs 2 through 10 of Article 2 falls under any of the following cases, the first non-public holiday following the public holiday (referring to a day other than the public holidays under the subparagraphs of Article 2; hereinafter the same shall apply) shall be an alternative public holiday: <Amended on May 4, 2023>

1. Where a public holiday under subparagraph 2, 6, 7 or 10 of Article 2 overlaps with a Saturday or Sunday;
2. Where a public holiday under subparagraph 4 or 9 of Article 2 overlaps with a Sunday;
3. Where a public holiday under subparagraph 2, 4, 6, 7, 9 or 10 of Article 2 is not a Saturday or Sunday and overlaps with any of the other public holidays listed in subparagraphs 2 through 10 of Article 2.

② Where the alternative public holiday under paragraph (1) overlaps on the same day, the alternative holidays shall last until the first non-public holiday following such alternative public holiday.

③ Where the alternative public holiday under paragraphs (1) and (2) falls on a Saturday, the first non-public holiday thereafter shall be an alternative public holiday.

1. Weekly Holidays

An employer shall grant a weekly holiday with pay at least once a week on average, provided that the employee concerned has worked all of the contractual working days (as determined in the rules of employment, etc.) for the preceding week. It is advisable that weekly holidays, which are not necessarily Sundays, should be stated in the rules of employment or other forms of company rules. Once a weekly holiday is fixed on a specific day (for example, Sunday), it is possible that an employee who was absent from work on a working day might use the weekly holiday without pay. An employee who has worked on a weekly holiday shall be paid an additional 50% of the normal wage for the hours worked (Article 56 of the LSA).

The interval between a weekly off-day and the following weekly off-day shall be ideally within 7 days. However, Article 55 shall not apply to a short-term employee whose weekly average contractual hours for a 4-week period are less than 15.

1) Inclusion or non-inclusion of paid weekly holiday[257)]

If an employer pays employees according to a monthly wage system, the monthly wage shall be considered to include a paid weekly allowance, barring exceptional situations.[258)] If the employee receives fixed allowances along with basic hourly wages every month

257) MOEL Guidelines: Kunrokijun-2455, on July 8, 2008.

258) Supreme Court ruling on May 24, 1994, 93Da32514.

제3조【대체공휴일】
① 제2조제2호부터 제10호까지의 공휴일이 다음 각 호의 어느 하나에 해당하는 경우에는 그 공휴일 다음의 첫 번째 비공휴일(제2조 각 호의 공휴일이 아닌 날을 말한다. 이하 같다)을 대체공휴일로 한다. 〈개정 2023. 5. 4.〉
1. 제2조제2호·제6호·제7호 또는 제10호의 공휴일이 토요일이나 일요일과 겹치는 경우
2. 제2조제4호 또는 제9호의 공휴일이 일요일과 겹치는 경우
3. 제2조제2호·제4호·제6호·제7호·제9호 또는 제10호의 공휴일이 토요일·일요일이 아닌 날에 같은 조 제2호부터 제10호까지의 규정에 따른 다른 공휴일과 겹치는 경우
② 제1항에 따른 대체공휴일이 같은 날에 겹치는 경우에는 그 대체공휴일 다음의 첫 번째 비공휴일까지 대체공휴일로 한다.
③ 제1항 및 제2항에 따른 대체공휴일이 토요일인 경우에는 그 다음의 첫 번째 비공휴일을 대체공휴일로 한다.

1. 주휴일

1주일간 소정근로일수(취업규칙 등에 일하도록 정해진 날)를 개근하면, 1주일에 평균 1회 이상의 유급휴일을 주어야 한다. 휴일은 취업규칙 등에 특정일을 정하여 주는 것이 바람직하며 반드시 일요일일 필요는 없다. 휴일이 특정되어 있는 경우(예: 일요일) 주중에 결근한 근로자에게는 휴일을 무급으로 줄 수 있다. 주휴일에 근로하면 그날의 근로에 대해 통상임금의 50/100을 가산하여 지급하여야 한다(근로기준법 제56조).

주휴일에서 다음 주휴일까지의 간격은 7일 이내가 바람직하다. 다만, 근로기준법 제18조 규정에 따라 4주간을 평균하여 1주간의 소정근로시간이 15시간 미만인 단시간 근로자에게는 같은 법 제55조의 주휴일규정이 적용되지 않는다.

1) 유급 주휴일 수당 산정 여부[257)]

근로자에 대한 임금을 월급으로 지급할 경우 특별한 사정이 없는 한 월급에는 유급 휴일에 대한 임금도 포함된 것으로 볼 수 있으며,[258)] 시급제 사원이 기본 시급과 함께 매월 고정 수당을 월급의 형태로 지급받는 경우, 그 고정 수당 중에는 유급 휴일에 대한 임금의 성격을 갖는 부분도 포함되어 있는 것으로 보

257) 행정해석: 2008.07.08. 근로조건지도과-2455.
258) 대법 1994.05.24. 선고 93다32514 판결.

in a monthly wage system, such fixed allowances shall be interpreted to have similar characteristics as wages for paid weekly holiday allowance.[259)]

2) The weekly holiday does not normally apply to daily workers, but if a daily worker works for six consecutive days, a paid weekly holiday shall be provided.[260)]

Weekly holiday allowance under the Labor Standards Act shall be given to a worker who fulfills his/her weekly contractual working hours. However, in principle, the weekly holiday shall not be given to daily workers because it is not possible to calculate weekly contractual working hours for daily workers, as they engage in daily employment contracts.

The purpose for providing a weekly holiday is to reduce the accumulated fatigue on workers after one week's work, thereby helping to protect their health and to provide time to participate in social and cultural activities. If a daily worker works for 6 consecutive days per week without absence, actual working days (and not contractual working days) shall be applied and weekly holiday shall be granted. The employer shall pay weekly holiday allowance separately from wages for daily workers, unless the affected worker agrees to receive the weekly holiday allowance in advance, with their daily wages.

(1) Inclusion or non-inclusion of paid weekly holiday

If a worker hired for hourly or daily wage continues to work, an additional weekly holiday allowance shall be paid. If wages are calculated on a monthly basis, the weekly holiday allowance shall be included in the monthly wage. A related precedent states that the hourly or daily wage system does not include weekly holiday pay, which is a statutory allowance under Article 55 of the Labor Standards Act (LSA), paid even if the employees do not actually work on such paid holidays. Therefore, if a worker on the hourly or daily wage system receives a fixed allowance paid for a certain period of time exceeding one month, he or she can claim the difference between the weekly holiday pay calculated based on the newly calculated hourly wage and the previously paid fixed allowance, and this is not a duplicated pay for the weekly holiday pay." [261)]

---

259) Supreme Court ruling on Apr. 24, 1998, 97Da28421.

260) MOEL Guidelines: Kungi 68207-424, on Apr. 2, 1997.

261) Supreme Court ruling on Jan. 28, 2010, 2009da74144; see also Supreme Court ruling on Aug. 20, 2014, 2014da6275

는 것[259)]이 판례의 입장이다.

2) 일용근로자의 경우 주휴일이 적용되지 않지만, 계속해서 1주일에 6일을 근무한 경우 일용근로자에게도 임금과 별도로 주휴일을 유급으로 부여하여야 한다.[260)]

근로기준법상의 주휴일은 1주간의 소정근로일수를 개근한 자에게 주도록 되어 있으므로 근로계약이 1일단위로 체결되어 1주간의 소정근로일수를 산정할 수가 없는 일용근로자에게는 원칙적으로 주휴일을 부여할 수 없다.

그러나 주휴일의 부여 목적이 1주간의 근로로 인하여 축적된 근로자의 피로를 풀어주고 건강을 확보하게 하며, 여가의 이용을 가능케 하여 사회적·문화적 생활을 할 수 있도록 하는데 있다. 따라서 일용근로자가 계속적으로 근로를 한다면 이때에는 소정근로일수 대신 실 근로일수를 기준으로 하여 1주일에 6일을 개근하였으면 주휴일을 부여하여야 한다. 한편, 일용근로자의 경우 주휴수당을 포함하여 임금을 지급받기로 사전에 약정하지 않은 한 주휴수당은 임금과는 별도로 지급되는 것이므로 주휴일이 부여된 일용근로자에게는 임금과는 별도로 주휴수당을 지급하여야 한다.

(1) 유급 주휴일 수당 산정 여부

시급, 일급으로 고용된 근로자가 계속해서 근무하는 경우에는 주휴수당을 별도로 추가하여 지급하여야 하고, 월급으로 계산된 임금의 경우에는 주휴수당이 월 급여에 포함되어 있다. 관련 판례는 "시급제 또는 일급제는 근로기준법 제55조에 따라 부여되는 유급휴일에 실제로 근무를 하지 않더라도 근무를 한 것으로 간주하여 지급되는 법정수당인 주휴수당이 포함되어 있지 않다. 따라서 시급제 또는 일급제 근로자가 1개월을 초과하는 일정기간마다 지급되는 고정수당을 받았다면 새로이 산정한 시간급 통상임금을 기준으로 계산한 주휴수당액과의 차액을 청구할 수 있고, 이를 주휴수당의 중복 청구라고 할 수 없다."고 판시하고 있다.[261)]

259) 대법 1998.04.24. 선고 97다28421 판결.
260) 행정해석: 1997.04.02. 근기 68207-424.
261) 대법원 2010.1.28. 선고 2009다74144 판결, 대법원 2014.8.20. 선고 2014다6275 판결 참조

2. Labor Day

Labor Day is officially May 1st by establishment of the Labor Day Act (Mar. 9,1994). This day is counted as a paid holiday according to the Labor Standards Act. The designation of Labor Day as a paid holiday under the Labor Standards Act is an exception for private autonomy. By defining Labor Day as a legal paid holiday, it ensures an additional annual day off for ordinary workers, beyond the regular holidays, contributing to the improvement of their working conditions. Moreover, historically, Labor Day is a product of labor movements where workers, as a concept opposing employers, fought for the enhancement of working conditions.[262)]

3. Public Holidays

Public holidays, according to Regulations on Holidays of Government Offices[263)] include: Sunday; Independence Movement Day, National Liberation Day, National Foundation Day, Hangul Proclamation Day, New Year's Day (Jan. 1st); Lunar New Year's Day (Dec. 31~Jan. 2 on the lunar calendar), Thanksgiving Day (Aug. 14~16 on the lunar calendar); Buddha's Birthday (Apr. 8 on the lunar calendar), Christmas Day (Dec. 25), Children's Day (May 5), Memorial Day (June 6), and Election Day (designed to elect new officials in accordance with the Act on Election of Public Officials and the Prevention of Election Malpractices), and other particular days specified by the Government.

4. Holiday Work

Article 56 (Extended, Night or Holiday Work)

① An employer shall, in addition to the ordinary wages, pay employees at least 50/100 thereof for extended work (referring to the work during the hours extended pursuant to Articles 53 and 59 and to the proviso to Article 69).

② Notwithstanding paragraph (1), an employer shall, in addition to the ordinary wages, pay employees who perform work on a holiday an amount the same as or more than the following amounts:

1. Holiday work for up to eight hours: 50/100 of ordinary wages;
2. Holiday work exceeding eight hours: 100/100 of ordinary wages

---

262) Constitutional Court decision on May 28, 2015, 2013Hunma343.

263) Presidential Decree 24273, Dec. 28, 2012.

2. 근로자의 날

근로자의 날은 "근로자의 날 제정에 관한 법률(1994.3.9)"에 의해 매년 5월 1일로 지정되어 있다. 이 날은 근로기준법에 의한 유급휴일이다. 근로자의 날을 근로기준법에 의한 유급휴일로 한다고 규정한 것은 사적 자치의 예외로서 근로자의 날을 법정유급휴일로 정함으로써 일반근로자에게 법정유급휴일을 주휴일 외에 연간 1일 더 보장하여 그 근로조건을 향상시킨다는 의미를 갖는 것이다. 더욱이 역사적으로 볼 때 근로자의 날은, 사용자에 대항하는 개념으로서의 근로자가 근로조건의 향상을 위해 투쟁하였던 노동운동의 산물이다.[262]

3. 국가 공휴일

관공서의 공휴일에 관한 규정[263]에 따른 공휴일은 일요일; 국경일 중 3.1절, 광복절, 개천절 및 한글날, 1월1일, 설날(음 12.31 ~ 1.2), 추석날(음8.14 ~ 8.16), 석가탄신일(음4.8), 기독탄신일(양12.25), 어린이날(5.5), 현충일(6.6), 공직선거법에 따른 임기만료에 의한 선거의 선거일, 기타 정부에서 수시 지정하는 날이다.

4. 휴일근로

第56条【연장·야간 및 휴일 근로】

① 사용자는 연장근로(제53조·제59조 및 제69조 단서에 따라 연장된 시간의 근로를 말한다)에 대하여는 통상임금의 100분의 50 이상을 가산하여 근로자에게 지급하여야 한다.

② 제1항에도 불구하고 사용자는 휴일근로에 대하여는 다음 각 호의 기준에 따른 금액 이상을 가산하여 근로자에게 지급하여야 한다.

1. 8시간 이내의 휴일근로: 통상임금의 100분의 50
2. 8시간을 초과한 휴일근로: 통상임금의 100분의 100

---

262) 헌법재판소 2015. 5. 28. 선고 2013헌마343 결정

263) 대통령령 제24273호, 2012.12.28.

1) Additional allowance

An additional allowance is paid for work provided during paid or unpaid holidays. In cases where extended work and holiday work overlap, allowances shall be paid in a combined sum. For the two-shift every-other-day work system, the off-day is differentiated from a holiday without work duty, thus an additional allowance shall not be paid even if the employee works on the off-day.

2) Prior substitution of holiday

Prior substitution of holiday signifies a system in which the employee works on the designated off-days and instead takes another day off from work, through prior arrangement of the parties concerned in the collective agreement or rules of employment. In this case, the original holiday becomes a regular working day. Consequently, neither a holiday allowance nor an additional paid holiday allowance shall be provided.

3) MOEL guidelines and judicial rulings

① For work on paid holidays, the rate of payment shall be 250 percent: 100 percent for paid holiday, 100 percent for actual work, and 50 percent as an additional allowance.[264)]

② Weekly holiday and monthly and annual paid leave shall be calculated according to the attendance rate for the total number of days after omitting the period of a justified labor strike.[265)]

③ Weekly holidays and monthly and annual paid leave are calculated according to the attendance rate of working days excluding the period of justified labor strikes. Those days of no work due to unjustified labor strike shall be treated as absences.[266)]

④ The act of substituting leave with allowances promptly after monthly and annual leave was granted is forfeiting the employee from use of leave.[267)]

⑤ Whether the employee maintains perfect attendance or a 80 percent attendance is determined from the first day he/she began working for the company; but the attendance rate can be calculated from January 1st of each year according to collective agreement or rules of employment.[268)]

---

264) MOEL Guidelines: Kungi 1455-15569, on May 20, 1981.

265) MOEL Guidelines: Kungi 01254-4245, on Mar. 20, 1990.

266) MOEL Guidelines: Kungi 01254-198, on June 16, 1990.

267) MOEL Guidelines: Kungi 1451-9020, on Apr. 6, 1984.

268) MOEL Guidelines: Kungi 68207-646, on Apr. 4, 1998.

1) 가산임금

유급휴일·무급휴일을 구별하지 않고 가산임금을 지급해야 한다. 연장근로와 휴일근로가 겹치는 경우에는 연장근로수당과 휴일근로수당을 함께 지급한다. 격일제 근로형태 하에서의 휴무일은 처음부터 근로의무가 없는 휴일과는 다른 것이므로, 이러한 휴무일에 근로하더라도 가산임금이 적용되지 않는다.

2) 휴일의 사전대체

단체협약이나 취업규칙 등으로 노사가 미리 약정하여 지정된 휴일에 근로를 하고 다른 날에 휴일을 부여하는 제도를 '휴일의 사전대체'라고 한다. 이 경우 원래의 휴일은 평일 근로가 되어 유급휴일 수당과 휴일근로 가산수당을 지급하지 않을 수 있다.

3) 휴일 관련된 판례 및 행정해석

① 유급휴일 근로 시 임금지급률은 유급당연지급분 100% 휴일근로분 100%, 가산임금 50%를 합한 250%이다.[264)]

② 주휴일, 연·월차 유급휴가는 정당한 쟁의행위기간을 제외한 나머지 근로일수에 대한 출근율에 따라 산정 지급되어야 한다.[265)]

③ 주휴일, 연·월차유급휴가 산정 시 정당한 쟁의행위로 인한 파업기간은 동 기간을 제외한 근로일수에 대한 출근율에 따르고, 불법쟁의행위로 근로를 제공하지 않은 날은 결근으로 처리해도 무방하다.[266)]

④ 연·월차휴가 발생 즉시 일방적인 금전 대체지급은 사실상 휴가를 박탈하는 것으로 부당하다.[267)]

⑤ 1년간 개근했는지 또는 8할 이상 출근했는지 여부는 근로자가 입사한 날을 기산점으로 하여 계산하는 것이 원칙이나 단체협약, 취업규칙 등에 의해 매년 1월 1일을 기산점으로 계산할 수도 있다.[268)]

---

264) 행정해석: 1981.5.20. 근기 1455-15569.
265) 행정해석: 1990.3.20. 근기 01254-4245.
266) 행정해석: 1990.6.16. 근기 01254-198.
267) 행정해석: 1984.04.06. 근기 1451-9020.
268) 행성해석: 1998.4.4. 근기 68207-646.

⑥ When extended work and night work overlap, 50 percent or more of ordinary wage shall be paid for each.[269)]

Ⅱ. Contractual Holidays

Unlike statutory holidays, contractual holidays must be stipulated in the rules of employment or collective agreement in order to be legally recognized as paid or unpaid holidays. Statutory holidays shall be granted on particular dates and if work is done on those days, the company shall pay an additional holiday work allowance. Statutory holidays consist of a weekly holiday (Article 55 of the LSA: An employer shall allow a worker on the average one or more paid holidays per week), Labor Day (Act Concerning Establishment of Labor Day: The day of May 1st shall be proclaimed as Labor Day and is a paid holiday as determined by the National Labor Relations Commission) and public holidays as confirmed by the government. However, contractual holidays are determined exclusively by the employer regarding particular dates and whether the holidays are paid or unpaid. If an employee works on a holiday stipulated as paid, the company shall pay an additional overtime allowance.

	Statutory	Contractual
Holiday	1) Weekly Holidays (Article 55) 2) Labor Day (Establishment of Labor Day on May 1st) 3) Public holidays	Company holidays (e.g. Company foundation day)
Remarks	1) Obligated by law 2) Wage is paid	1) Based upon collective agreement, rules of employment, etc. 2) Issue of payment depends on mutual agreement

Corporate holidays refer to paid off-days, such as Company Foundation Day, Labor Union Day, etc., that the company has designated in the collective agreement and the rules of employment.

In cases where contractual holidays are settled as paid off-days, employees are exempted from providing labor. If they have to work on contractual holidays like paid public holidays, they are entitled to paid wages (100%), which are already included in monthly wages, and additional holiday work allowance (150%) (Article 56 (Extended, Night or Holiday Work) of the LSA).

---

269) MOEL Guidelines: Kungi 01254-7592, on May 12, 1987.

⑥ 연장근로와 야간근로 중복 시 통상임금의 50/100 이상을 각각 가산하여 지급하여야 한다.[269)]

Ⅱ. 약정휴일

약정휴일은 법정휴일과 다르게 반드시 취업규칙이나 단체협약으로 정해진 경우에 인정되는 것으로 사용자가 무급휴일 또는 유급휴일로 운용할 수 있다. 법정휴일의 경우에는 해당되는 특정 일자에 반드시 휴일을 부여하거나 근로자가 근무할 경우에는 그에 따른 별도의 휴일근로수당을 지급해야 한다. 법정휴일은 「근로기준법」 제55조에 의한 주휴일(사용자는 근로자에게 1주일에 평균 1회 이상의 유급휴일을 주어야 한다), 「근로자의 날 제정에 관한 법률」에 의한 근로자의날(5월 1일을 근로자의 날로 하고 이 날을 「근로기준법」에 의한 유급휴일로 한다.)과 국가가 인정한 국가 공휴일이 있다. 그러나, 약정휴일은 날짜지정이나 유급 또는 무급을 전적으로 사용자의 판단에 따른다. 약정휴일이 유급으로 정해진 경우에 약정휴일에 근무한 경우에는 휴일근로수당을 지급해야 한다.

구 분	법 정	약 정
휴 일	1) 주휴일(근로기준법 제55조) 2) 근로자의 날 (근로기준법) 3) 국가공휴일	기업의 휴일 (회사창립일등)
특 징	1) 법에 근거하여 의무적으로 부여 2) 임금지급(유급)	1) 부여 여부, 부여 조건 등이 단체 협약, 취업규칙 등을 통해 결정됨 2) 임금지급 여부도 결정하는 바에 따름

회사가 정한 회사의 창립일, 노조설립일 등으로 회사가 단체협약이나 취업규칙으로 유급휴일로서 인정하는 경우에 해당된다.

약정휴일을 유급으로 설정한 경우에는 그 약정휴일에는 근로제공의무가 제외되며, 이 약정휴일에 사용자의 지시에 의해 근로를 제공한 경우에는 근로제공이 없더라도 지급받을 수 있었던 임금(100%)과 휴일근로 가산임금(150%: 근로기준법 제56조: 가산임금)을 추가로 지급해야 한다.

269) 행정해석: 1987.5.12. 근기 01254-7592.

Section 4: Statutory Leave and Contractual Leave

Ⅰ. Annual Paid Leave

1. Concept

Annual paid leave is intended to provide paid leave(separately from paid weekly holidays) to allow workers the opportunity to pursue good health and relaxation.[270)] More specifically, the Constitutional Court stated the purpose for annual leave: “Rest hours or weekly holidays are primarily for the physiological recovery of workers who have accumulated physical or mental fatigue due to daily or weekly work. Annual paid leave is designed to give workers freedom from work for a period of time and to have the opportunity to engage in social and cultural civic life by providing a voluntary leave period without a loss of wage.[271)] The Supreme Court also explains, “It is purposed to provide an opportunity for mental and physical recreation and improve cultural access by exempting workers from the obligation to work for a certain period of time.”[272)] Therefore, the objective of annual leave is to improve the quality of life of workers by providing time for rest and the pursuit of cultural life in terms of relaxation from work.[273)]

Annual paid leave(Article 60) in the Labor Standards Act prescribes the use of leave in principle, but also specifies compensation for unused days. ① As for the number of leave days and the requirements for the occurrence of annual paid leave, An employer shall grant 15 days’ paid leave to a worker who has registered not less than 80 percent of attendance during one year(Article 1). After the first year of service, an employer shall grant one day’s paid leave for each two years of consecutive service in addition to the 15 days’ paid leave to a worker who has worked consecutively for 3 years or more. In this case, the total number of leave days including the additional leave shall not exceed 25(Article 4).

---

270) Lim, Jongryul, Labor Law, Park Young Sa, 2016, p. 454.

271) Supreme Court ruling on May 28, 2015. 2013 hunma 619 (The purpose of annual paid leave).

272) Supreme Court ruling on Dec. 26, 2003. 2011 da 4629 (The purpose of annual paid leave).

273) Kim, Hongyoung, “Improvement of System for Annual Paid Leave to Secure Time for Rest,” Study on Labor Laws, 2016 Vol. 40, Seoul University’s Labor Law Society, p. 165.

제4절 법정휴가와 약정휴가

Ⅰ. 연차유급휴가

1. 연차휴가의 의의

연차휴가는 근로자의 건강하고 문화적인 생활을 실현하기 위하여 유급주휴일과 별도로 유급휴가를 부여하려는 것이다.[270] 좀 더 구체적으로 헌법재판소도 연차휴가의 취지를, "휴게시간이나 주휴일은 하루 또는 일주일의 노동으로 육체적·정신적 피로가 누적된 근로자들의 생리적인 회복을 위한 것이 주목적이라면, 연차유급휴가는 임금 삭감 없이 휴가기간을 스스로 결정할 수 있게 함으로써 근로자들이 노동으로부터 일정기간 해방되고 사회적·문화적 시민생활을 영위할 수 있는 기회를 보장하기 위한 것이다."라고 기술하고 있다.[271] 이에 대해 대법원도 "근로자에게 일정 기간 근로의무를 면제함으로써 정신적·육체적 휴양의 기회를 제공하고 문화적 생활의 향상을 기하려는데 그 취지가 있다."라고 설명한다.[272] 따라서 연차휴가에 대한 설명의 공통점은 근로에 대한 휴식의 측면에 문화적 생활의 측면을 덧붙여 근로자의 생활 질을 향상시키는 것이라 할 수 있다.[273]

우리나라 근로기준법상의 연차유급휴가(제60조)는 휴가사용을 전제로 하지만, 미사용 시 금전보상을 명시하고 있다. ① 휴가일수 및 발생요건을 살펴보면 "1년간 80% 이상 출근한 근로자에게 15일의 연차유급휴가를 주어야 한다(제1조). 3년 이상 계속하여 근로한 근로자에게 최초 1년을 초과하는 계속근로연수 매 2년에 대해 1일을 가산한 유급휴가를 주어야 하고, 최대 25일을 한도로 한다(제4조)." ② 사

270) 임종률, 「노동법」, 박영사, 2020, 454면.
271) 헌법재판소 2015.5.28, 2013헌마619(연차휴가의 취지).
272) 대법원 2003.12.26, 2011다4629(연차휴가의 취지).
273) 김홍영, "휴식 보장을 위한 연차휴가의 제도개선론", 「노동법연구」, 2016 상반기 제40호, 서울대노동법연구회, 165면.

② Regarding the use of annual leave, an employer shall grant paid leave upon request by a worker. However, the leave period concerned may be changed, if granting the leave as requested by the worker might cause serious impediment to the operation of the business(Article 5). Paid leave can be used continuously over a certain day or several days. Here, if a worker requests a leave day by designating a desired date(a claim for leave), the employer can adjust the date of the leave in consideration of the work. ③ In relation to the guarantee of annual paid leave, the annual paid leave shall be granted as paid off-days on the normal working days of the worker(Article 5). Therefore, annual paid leave shall not be granted on weekly holidays, unpaid holidays, or other paid holidays. ④ Regarding compensation for unused annual leave, "the annual paid leave will expire if not exercised for one year"(Article 7). This means that in the event that an employee fails to use the annual paid leave, the employer shall pay the employee for the unused paid leave.[274)]

2. Details

Annual paid leave shall be granted to an employee with perfect attendance for their contractual working hours during one year. This is designed to provide leave to an employee who has served his/her contractual working hours for a long duration, so he/she can recover from fatigue from extended work and refresh his/her mind and body.

LSA Article 60 (Annual Paid Leave):

① An employer shall grant 15 days' paid leave to a worker who has registered not less than 80 percent of attendance during one year.
② An employer shall grant one day's paid leave per month to a worker whose consecutive service period is shorter than one year or whose attendance is less than 80 percent, if the worker has offered work without absence throughout the month.
③ (Deleted)
④ After the first year of service, an employer shall grant one day's paid leave for each two years of consecutive service in addition to the leave prescribed in paragraph (1) to a worker who has worked consecutively for 3 years or more. In this case, the total number of leave days including the additional leave shall not exceed 25.
⑤ An employer shall grant paid leave pursuant to paragraphs (1) through (4) upon request of a worker, and shall pay ordinary wage or average wage prescribed in employment rules or other regulations during the period of leave. However, the leave period concerned may be changed, in case granting the leave as requested by the worker might cause a serious impediment to the operation of the business.

---

274) Supreme Court ruling on Dec. 26, 2013. 2011 da 4629 (Unused annual leave allowance is regarded as wage.)

용방법을 보면 연차휴가는 근로자가 청구한 시기에 휴가를 주어야 하지만, 근로자가 청구한 시기에 휴가를 주는 것이 사업 운영에 막대한 지장이 있는 경우에는 그 시기를 변경할 수 있다(제5조). 유급휴가는 특정일 또는 여러 날에 걸쳐 연속적으로 사용할 수 있다. 여기서 근로자는 원하는 날짜를 지정하여 휴가를 청구하면(휴가청구권) 사용자는 업무의 상황을 고려하여 휴가 청구일을 조정할 수 있다(시기변경권). ③ 연차유급휴가 보장과 관련하여 연차유급휴가는 근로자의 근무일에 유급으로 보장해주어야 한다(제5조). 따라서 연차유급휴가는 주휴일이나 무급휴무일, 약정휴일에 부여해서는 아니 된다. ④ 미사용 연차휴가에 대한 보상과 관련하여 "연차유급휴가는 1년간 행사하지 아니하면 소멸된다. 다만, 사용자의 귀책사유로 사용하지 못한 경우에는 그러하지 아니하다(제7조)." 이는 근로자가 연차유급휴가를 사용하지 못한 경우에 사용자는 이에 따른 미사용 수당을 지급해야 한다는 것이다.[274]

2. 연차휴가의 내용

연차휴가는 1년 이상 근속한 근로자에게 부여하는 유급휴가로서 장기간 소정의 근로를 한 근로자에게 그에 따른 피로를 회복하고 심신의 재충전을 위하여 부여하는 휴가이다.

근로기준법 제60조【연차 유급휴가】

① 사용자는 1년간 80퍼센트 이상 출근한 근로자에게 15일의 유급휴가를 주어야 한다.

② 사용자는 계속하여 근로한 기간이 1년 미만인 근로자 또는 1년간 80퍼센트 미만 출근한 근로자에게 1개월 개근 시 1일의 유급휴가를 주어야 한다.

③ (삭제)

④ 사용자는 3년 이상 계속하여 근로한 근로자에게는 제1항에 따른 휴가에 최초 1년을 초과하는 계속 근로 연수 매 2년에 대하여 1일을 가산한 유급휴가를 주어야 한다. 이 경우 가산휴가를 포함한 총 휴가 일수는 25일을 한도로 한다.

⑤ 사용자는 제1항부터 제4항까지의 규정에 따른 휴가를 근로자가 청구한 시기에 주어야 하고, 그 기간에 대하여는 취업규칙 등에서 정하는 통상임금 또는 평균임금을 지급하여야 한다. 다만, 근로자가 청구한 시기에 휴가를 주는 것이 사업 운영에 막대한 지장이 있는 경우에는 그 시기를 변경할 수 있다.

274) 대법원 2013.12.26, 2011다4629(미사용 연차유급휴가 수당은 임금이다.).

An employer shall grant 15 days of annual leave with pay to an employee who has recorded 80% or higher in workplace attendance. An employer shall grant 1 holiday with pay per month of full attendance to his/her employees who have worked less than 1 year. The days an employee is absent from work due to an occupational accident, pre- and post-natal leave and childcare leave, shall be treated as days worked.

For an employee who has worked 3 years or longer, the employer shall grant an additional 1 day in paid holiday for every 2 years following the first year, with the number of additional holidays limited to 25. An employer shall grant his/her employee annual leave on the day(s) that the employee wants to use his/her annual leave. However, when the employer believes that allowing the use of annual leave on the desired day(s) would do great harm to his/her business, he/she may reschedule the timing of annual leave. An employer may have his/her employee take a day off on a particular working day in lieu of an annual leave day with pay, as long as he/she and the employee representative have reached a written agreement to do so.

Given that annual leave days may be saved for a year and can be split for use on several occasions, it is advisable that a ledger of leave days saved be recorded and maintained for each individual employee.

⑥ In applying paragraphs (1) through (3), a period falling under any of the following subparagraphs shall be considered a period of attendance:
1. A period during which a worker is unable to work due to occupational injuries or diseases;
2. A period during which a pregnant woman does not work on leave taken pursuant to paragraphs (1) through (3) of Article 74;
3. A period during which a worker does not work on parental leave due to article 19 paragraph (1) of the Equal Employment Opportunity and Work-Family Balance Act.

⑦ The leave referred to in paragraphs (1) through (4) shall be forfeited if not used within one year. However, this shall not apply in cases where the worker concerned has been prevented from using the leave due to any cause attributable to the employer.

<Example of Calculating Leave Per Service Year>

~1 yr	1~2	2~3	3~4	4~5	5~6	10~11	15~16	20~21	21~22	25~
11(1 per mo.)	15	15	16	16	17	19	22	24	25	25

The Supreme Court ruling on October 14, 2021 (2021 da 227100) ruled that the annual leave days for one-year fixed-term workers amounted to 11 days, not 26. Even in the case of retirees, the Supreme Court ruling on June 28, 2018 (2016 da 48297) ruled that, in cases where the calculation

사용자는 근로자가 1년간 8할 이상 출근 시 15일의 유급휴가를 주어야 한다. 1년 미만의 근속자에 대해서는 1개월간 개근 시 1일의 유급휴가를 주어야 한다(단, 업무상 재해로 휴업한 기간, 산전·후 휴가기간과 육아휴직기간은 출근한 것으로 보아야 한다).

3년 이상 계속 근로한 근로자에 대하여 최초 1년을 초과하는 매 2년마다 1일을 가산하되 25일을 상한으로 한다. 연차휴가에 대하여 사용자는 근로자의 청구가 있는 시기에 주어야 한다. 다만, 근로자가 청구한 시기에 휴가를 주는 것이 사업운영에 막대한 지장이 있는 경우에는 그 시기를 변경할 수 있다. 근로자대표와 서면합의를 하게 되면 연차 유급휴가일에 갈음하여 특정 근로일에 근로자를 휴무시킬 수 있다.

연차 휴가는 1년간에 걸쳐 분할사용이 가능하므로 휴가 적치대장을 작성하여 개인별로 관리하는 것이 바람직하다.

> ⑥ 제1항부터 제3항까지의 규정을 적용하는 경우 다음 각 호의 어느 하나에 해당하는 기간은 출근한 것으로 본다.
> 1. 근로자가 업무상의 부상 또는 질병으로 휴업한 기간
> 2. 임신 중의 여성이 제74조 제1항부터 제3항에 따른 보호휴가로 휴업한 기간
> 3. 「남녀고용평등과 일·가정 양립 지원에 관한 법률」제19조 제1항에 따른 육아휴직으로 휴업한 기간
>
> ⑦ 제1항부터 제4항까지의 규정에 따른 휴가는 1년간 행사하지 아니하면 소멸된다. 다만, 사용자의 귀책사유로 사용하지 못한 경우에는 그러하지 아니하다.

〈근속연수별 휴가 산정례〉

년 이상~ 년 미만	~1년 미만	1~2	2~3	3~4	4~5	5~6	10~11	15~16	20~21	21~22	25~
휴가 일수	11(매월 1일)	15	15	16	16	17	19	22	24	25	25

2021년 10월 14일 대법원(2021다227100)은 1년 기간제 근로자의 연차 휴가 수당은 26일이 아니라 11일이라는 판결을 하였다. 기업의 정년 퇴직자의 경우에도 2018년 6월 28일 대법원(2016다48297)은 연차휴가 기산점을 매년 1월 1일부터 12월 31일로 하고 있는 경우, 퇴직일이 12월 31일인 경우 그 다음해에

period of annual leave is from January 1 to December 31 of each year, if the retirement date is December 31, there was no annual leave allowance owing in the following year.

(1) Rights related to annual paid leave

1) Right to request annual paid leave

Annual paid leave is designed to help with maintenance of an efficient labor force and provide a balanced life through the spiritual and physical rest of employees who attended work fully during the preceding year. Accordingly, an employer shall grant 15 days of paid leave to an employee who has a workplace attendance rate of 80 percent or higher over the preceding year(Article 60(1) of the Labor Standards Act). An employee is granted the right to annual paid leave according to his/her workplace attendance rate of the preceding year.

2) Right to request unused annual paid leave allowance

The right to request unused annual paid leave allowance is the right to ask for an allowance as compensation for the unused annual paid leave days if the employee provided labor service without using the annual paid leave accrued as remuneration for work for the previous year. This right occurs after the right to request annual paid leave expires. There is also the right to ask for an allowance as compensation for unused annual paid leave for the number of unused annual paid leave days due to the termination of an employment contract, for example, upon retirement. However, when the employer takes measures to promote the use of Annual Paid Leave, the right to request an allowance for unused annual paid leave expires(Article of 61 of the LSA).

(2) Whether to include annual paid leave allowance into average wage when calculating severance pay

1) Unused annual paid leave allowance already occurring before retirement

By the criteria of attendance rate during the year prior to the retirement year, 3/12 of the unused annual paid leave allowance occurring the year prior to the retirement year shall be included in the basic wage items used to calculate average wage for severance pay.

2) Unused annual paid leave allowance occurring only due to retirement

The unused annual paid leave allowance that the employee is granted due to retirement in the retirement year according to the attendance rate of the year before the retirement year shall not

발생하는 연차휴가수당은 없다고 판시하였다.

(1) 연차휴가에 관련된 권리

1) 연차유급휴가청구권

연차유급휴가는 전년도에 계속 근로한 근로자에 대해 정신적·육체적 휴양을 통한 노동의 재생산 유지와 문화생활의 기회를 부여하기 위해 마련된 것이다. 따라서 사용자는 근로자가 전년도에 8할 이상 출근한 경우에는 15일의 유급휴가를 부여하여야 하고(근로기준법 제60조), 근로자는 전년도의 출근율에 따라 유급휴가청구권이 발생한다.

2) 연차유급휴가 미사용수당 청구권

연차유급휴가 미사용수당 청구권은 근로자가 전전년도의 근로한 대가로 발생한 유급휴가를 전년도에 사용하지 아니하고 근로를 제공한 경우 그 미사용 연차유급휴가 일수에 해당하는 연차유급휴가 미사용수당을 사용자에 대하여 청구할 수 있는 권리로 유급휴가 청구권이 소멸된 시점에 발생한다. 또한, 퇴직 등 근로관계가 종료되는 근로자가 이로 인해 사용하지 못하는 미사용 휴가일수에 해당하는 수당을 사용자에 대하여 청구할 수 있는 권리이다. 다만 사용자가 근로기준법에 따른 연차유급휴가 사용촉진을 한 경우 유급휴가 미사용수당 청구권이 소멸된다(근로기준법 제61조).

(2) 연차유급휴가 수당의 퇴직금 산정을 위한 평균임금 포함여부

1) 퇴직하기 전 이미 발생한 연차유급휴가 미사용수당

퇴직 전전년도 출근율에 의하여 퇴직 전년도에 발생한 연차유급휴가 중 사용하지 아니하고 근로한 일수에 대한 연차유급휴가 미사용수당액의 3/12을 "퇴직금 산정을 위한 평균임금 산정 기준임금"에 포함한다.

2) 퇴직으로 인해 비로소 지급사유가 발생한 연차유급휴가 미사용수당

퇴직 전년도 출근율에 의하여 퇴직 연도에 발생한 연차유급휴가를 사용하지

be included in the basic wage items used to calculate average wage for severance pay, because the unused annual paid leave allowance is not wage paid during calculation of average wage.

3. Promoting the Use of Annual Paid Leave

Article 61 (Measures to Urge Employees to Take Annual Paid Leave)

① Where any employee's paid leave is terminated by time limitation pursuant to the main sentence of Article 60 (7) because the employee fails to take his/her paid leave although the relevant employer has taken the measures falling under each of the following subparagraphs to urge employees to take their respective annual leave pursuant to Article 60 (1) and (4) (which excludes the monthly leave given for employees who have worked less than one year, in accordance with Article 60(2)), the relevant employer is not obligated to compensate the employee for his/her failure to take the paid leave, and the employee's failure to take the paid leave shall be deemed not to fall under the reasons attributable to the employer provided for in the proviso to Article 60 (7):

1. Any employer shall notify in writing every employee of the number of days of his/her paid leave that has not been taken, and shall urge every employee to notify the employer of a period he/she is planning for the paid leave after determining on such period within ten days, at the six month point before the period under the main sentence of Article 60 (7) expires;
2. Notwithstanding the encouragement referred to in subparagraph 1, if the employee fails to notify the employer of a period during which he/she is planning to take all of part of his/her remaining paid leave within ten days from the date he/she is urged to take his/her paid leave, the employer shall notify the employee in writing after setting a period for his/her paid leave, by no later than two months before the period under the main sentence of Article 60 (7) expires.

② Where any employee's paid leave is terminated by time limitation pursuant to the main sentence of Article 60 (7) because the employee fails to take his/her paid leave although the relevant employer has taken the measures falling under each of the following subparagraphs to urge employees to take their respective annual leave pursuant to Article 60 (2): the monthly leave given for an employee who has worked less than one year, the relevant employer is not liable to compensate the employee for his/her failure to take the paid leave, and the employee's failure to take the paid leave shall be deemed not to fall under the reasons attributable to the employer provided for in the proviso to Article 60 (7):

1. Any employer shall notify in writing every employee of the number of days of his/her paid leave that has not been taken, and shall urge every employee to notify the employer of a period he/she is planning for the paid leave after determining on such period within ten days, at the three month point prior to one year of his/her service;
2. Notwithstanding the encouragement referred to in subparagraph 1, if the employee fails to notify the employer of a period during which he/she is planning to take all of part of his/her remaining paid leave within ten days from the date he/she is urged to take his/her paid leave, the employer shall notify the employee in writing after setting a period for his/her paid leave, by no later than one month before the end of his/her first year.

아니하고 퇴직함으로써 발생한 연차유급휴가 미사용수당은 평균임금의 정의상 산정사유 발생일 이전에 그 근로자에 대하여 지급된 임금이 아니므로 "퇴직금 산정을 위한 평균임금 산정 기준임금" 에 포함되지 아니한다.

3. 연차유급휴가 사용촉진제도

제61조【연차 유급휴가의 사용 촉진】

① 사용자가 제60조 제1항·제2항 및 제4항에 따른 유급휴가(계속하여 근로한 기간이 1년 미만인 근로자의 제60조 제2항에 따른 유급휴가는 제외한다)의 사용을 촉진하기 위하여 다음 각 호의 조치를 하였음에도 불구하고 근로자가 휴가를 사용하지 아니하여 제60조 제7항 본문에 따라 소멸된 경우에는 사용자는 그 사용하지 아니한 휴가에 대하여 보상할 의무가 없고, 제60조 제7항 단서에 따른 사용자의 귀책사유에 해당하지 아니하는 것으로 본다.

1. 제60조 제7항 본문에 따른 기간이 끝나기 6개월 전을 기준으로 10일 이내에 사용자가 근로자별로 사용하지 아니한 휴가 일수를 알려주고, 근로자가 그 사용 시기를 정하여 사용자에게 통보하도록 서면으로 촉구할 것
2. 제1호에 따른 촉구에도 불구하고 근로자가 촉구를 받은 때부터 10일 이내에 사용하지 아니한 휴가의 전부 또는 일부의 사용 시기를 정하여 사용자에게 통보하지 아니하면 제60조 제7항 본문에 따른 기간이 끝나기 2개월 전까지 사용자가 사용하지 아니한 휴가의 사용 시기를 정하여 근로자에게 서면으로 통보할 것

② 사용자가 계속하여 근로한 기간이 1년 미만인 근로자의 제60조 제2항에 따른 유급휴가의 사용을 촉진하기 위하여 다음 각 호의 조치를 하였음에도 불구하고 근로자가 휴가를 사용하지 아니하여 제60조 제7항 본문에 따라 소멸된 경우에는 사용자는 그 사용하지 아니한 휴가에 대하여 보상할 의무가 없고, 같은 항 단서에 따른 사용자의 귀책 사유에 해당하지 아니하는 것으로 본다.

1. 최초 1년의 근로기간이 끝나기 3개월 전을 기준으로 10일 이내에 사용자가 근로자별로 사용하지 아니한 휴가 일수를 알려주고, 근로자가 그 사용 시기를 정하여 사용자에게 통보하도록 서면으로 촉구할 것. 다만, 사용자가 서면 촉구한 후 발생한 휴가에 대해서는 최초 1년의 근로기간이 끝나기 1개월 전을 기준으로 5일 이내에 촉구하여야 한다.
2. 제1호에 따른 촉구에도 불구하고 근로자가 촉구를 받은 때부터 10일 이내에 사용하지 아니한 휴가의 전부 또는 일부의 사용 시기를 정하여 사용자에게 통보하지 아니하면 최초 1년의 근로기간이 끝나기 1개월 전까지 사용자가 사용하지 아니한 휴가의 사용 시기를 정하여 근로자에게 서면으로 통보할 것. 다만, 제1호 단서에 따라 촉구한 휴가에 대해서는 최초 1년의 근로기간이 끝나기 10일전까지 서면으로 통보하여야 한다.

If an employee has not used the leave days saved within the year, he/she shall be paid for the unused days of leave at average or ordinary wage, as prescribed in the rules of employment. However, if the employees have not used their annual leave despite the employer strongly promoting its use, the employer is exempted from the obligation to provide monetary compensation for the unused annual leave.

1) In the means to promote the use of leave, the employer has the right to change the date selected by the employee for the claiming of his/her leave, as the employee's leave rights are restricted since the employer shall only promote the use of leave shortly before the leave expires.

2) When an employee specifies the period for using leave upon the employer's request, the specified period shall be admitted in principle, and the leave shall be effective during no other period. If the employer decides on the period instead, because the employee fails to do so, it shall also remain unchanged. However, if the employee specifies the leave period, but it is deemed to seriously impede the operation of the business to allow leave for that specified period, the period concerned may be altered.

3) Regarding promotion of the use of annual leave, it is frequent for companies to take formal measures without assigning annual leave for definite working days to employees and in this way avoid paying allowance for the unused annual leave. That is, companies promote the use of annual leave by informing through email only. In cases where the employees come to work on days designated for annual leave, companies do not pay annual leave allowance for unused annual leave owing to their efforts to promote the use of annual leave. However, as this case shows that the company did not provide the use of annual leave on the designated days, the fact that employees could not use annual leave was due to reasons attributable to the employer and the employer shall pay an unused annual leave allowance.

MOEL Guidelines

The 'written document' mentioned in Article 61 of the LSA refers to a paper document. Electronic documents are only possible in exceptional cases where the company has handled every operation by means of electronic documents in the process of its drafting, obtaining approval and

근로자가 1년 이내에 연차 휴가를 사용하지 않고 근로한 경우에는 그 근로일수(휴가일수)만큼 취업규칙에서 정하는 바에 따라 평균임금 또는 통상임금을 지급하여야 한다. 그러나 다음과 같은 사용자의 적극적인 사용촉진 조치에도 불구하고 근로자가 연차유급휴가를 사용하지 않는 경우 금전보상의무가 면제된다(근기법 제61조).

1) 휴가사용촉진조치를 하는 경우에도 근로자의 시기 지정권과 사용자의 시기 변경권은 인정된다. 다만, 휴가사용 촉진조치는 휴가사용 기간이 얼마 남지 않은 상태에서 이루어지는 것이므로 동 권리의 행사도 제한을 받는다.

2) 근로자가 사용자의 휴가시기 지정 촉구에 따라 휴가 시기를 지정한 경우에는 원칙적으로 그 지정한 시기에 휴가를 사용해야 하며, 다른 시기에 시기 지정권을 행사할 수 없다. 근로자가 휴가시기를 지정하지 않아 사용자가 그 휴가시기를 지정한 경우에는 사용자는 원칙적으로 그 지정한 시기를 변경할 수 없다. 다만, 사용자가 근로자로부터 휴가사용 시기를 지정받은 경우에 그 지정받은 대로 휴가를 부여하는 것이 사업운영에 막대한 지장을 초래하는 경우에는 휴가시기를 조정하여 지정할 수 있다.

3) 사용자가 연차휴가 사용촉진조치에 대해 형식적 조치만을 취하고 실질적으로 연차휴가를 부여하지 않으면서도 미사용 연차휴가 수당을 지급하지 않는 경우가 많다. 즉, 연차휴가 사용촉진 조치를 이메일로 통보하면서, 휴가일자에 출근하여 근무를 하는 경우 회사가 휴가사용촉진조치를 다 하였기 때문에 미사용 연차수당을 지급하지 않아도 된다고 생각하는 경우가 많다. 하지만, 이러한 경우에 사용자가 휴가를 보장하지 않은 것이라 볼 수 있기 때문에 사용자의 귀책사유로 휴가를 사용하지 못한 것으로 간주하여 미사용 연차휴가수당을 지급해야 한다.

행정해석

근로기준법 제61조의 서면은 종이로 된 문서를 의미하고 전자문서는 회사가 전자결재체계를 완비해 전자문서로 모든 업무의 기안, 결재, 시행과정을 관리하는 경우에만 예외적으로 가능하

implementing through equipped electronic work-processing systems.[275)] Accordingly, informing by email in the course of promoting the use of annual leave cannot be regarded as notification by written document.[276)]

If the employee has submitted a vacation plan with stipulated dates of leave after the employer has promoted the use of annual leave, the stipulated dates of leave shall be regarded as the employee's declaration of intention to use his/her annual leave. In cases where the employee comes to work on the stipulated date of leave, if the employer received the employee's labor and did not express an objection to his/her coming in to work, it shall be regarded that the employer has approved the labor service on the expected date of leave, and so the employer shall pay an unused leave allowance.[277)]

4. Substitution of Annual Paid Leave

The employer may, through a written agreement with the labor representative, have employees take a paid leave on a particular working day in substitution of annual paid leave(Article 62 of the LSA). The particular working day means a particular day among contractual working days required for labor duty. Accordingly, the employer cannot, pursuant to Article 62 of the LSA, substitute a paid leave day with contractual holiday and leave, nor with statutory holiday and leave.

5. MOEL Guidelines and Judicial Rulings

(1) If an employment contract expires before the employee uses their annual paid leave, how much can he/she receive as annual paid leave allowance?

The right to use annual leave as paid days off is acquired definitely as remuneration for labor when the employee has worked for a one-year period. As soon as the employee acquired the right to annual paid leave, his employment was terminated due to retirement, etc. before using his annual paid leave. In this case, while the right to use annual paid leave requires continuous labor service, this cannot be granted due to retirement. However, the right to request annual paid leave allowance does not require continuous

275) MOEL Guidelines: Kunjung-1128, on Feb. 7, 2012.

276) MOEL Guidelines: Kunjung-6488, on Nov. 1, 2013.

277) MOEL Guidelines: Limjang-285, on Oct. 21, 2005.

다.[275] 이에 연차유급휴가의 사용촉진조치와 관련해 이메일로 통보하는 것이 근로자 개인별로 서면촉구 또는 통보하는 것에 비해 도달 여부의 확인 등이 불명확한 경우, 서면촉구 또는 통보하였다고 인정되기 어렵다.[276)]

휴가사용 촉진조치에 의하여 근로자가 휴가사용 시기를 정하여 사용자에게 휴가 사용계획서를 제출하였다면 그 지정된 시기에 연차유급휴가를 사용하겠다는 의사표시로 볼 수 있을 것이므로 휴가를 청구한 것으로 볼 수 있다. 다만, 근로자가 휴가사용 시기를 지정하고도 출근한 경우 사용자가 노무수령 거부의 의사표시 없이 근로를 제공받았다면 휴가일 근로를 승낙한 것으로 보아야 하므로 연차유급휴가 근로수당을 지급하여야 한다.[277]

4. 연차유급휴가의 대체

사용자는 근로자대표와의 서면합의에 의하여 연차유급휴가일에 갈음하여 특정 근로일에 근로자를 휴무시킬 수 있다(근로기준법 제62조). 여기서 특정근로일이라 함은 근로의무가 있는 '소정근로일' 중의 특정일을 의미한다. 따라서 사용자는 법정 휴일·휴가뿐만 아니라 약정 휴일·휴가로 근로기준법 62조의 규정에 의한 휴가를 대체할 수 없다.

5. 연차휴가와 관련된 주요 판례 및 행정해석

(1) 연차유급휴가를 사용하기 전 근로관계가 종료된 경우 받을 수 있는 연차휴가 수당의 범위

유급(연차휴가수당)으로 연자휴가를 사용할 권리는 근로자가 1년간 소정의 근로를 마친 대가이며 확정적으로 취득하는 것이므로, 근로자가 연차유급휴가권을 취득한 후 연차유급휴가를 사용하기 전에 퇴직 등의 사유로 근로관계가 종료된 경우, 근로관계의 존속을 전제로 하는 연차휴가를 사용할 권리는 소멸한다 할지라도 근로관계의 존속을 전제로 하지 않는 연차휴가수당을 청구할 권리는 그대로 잔존하는 것이어서, 근로자는 근로관계 종료 시까지 사용하지 못한

---

275) 행정해석: 근정과-1128, 2012.2.7.
276) 행정해석: 근정과-6488, 2013.11.1.
277) 행정해석: 임장팀-285, 2005.10.21.

labor service and so shall be compensated as a paid allowance. Accordingly, the employee can request an annual paid leave allowance equivalent to the whole number of annual paid leave days unused up to the employment termination date.[278)]

(2) Generally, absence refers to days that the employee did not, without prior authorization, provide labor on the contractual working day as decided by both labor and management[279)]

There is no regulation concerning "absence" stipulated in the Labor Standards Act, but in general it means that the employee, without authorization, did not provide labor on the contractual working day on which both labor and management decided labor would be provided. However, the day or period to be excluded in calculation of the contractual working days, or deemed as attendance, shall not be deemed an absence pursuant to the following(Labor Standard 68207-709, May 30, 1997, 'Criteria for evaluation of contractual working days and attendance'):

① Statutory or contractual holidays(excluded from the calculation of contractual working days)
- Weekly holidays under the Labor Standards Act
- Contractual holidays under the collective bargaining agreement or the rules of employment
- Holidays or periods regarded as the equivalent of the above.

② Day or period suspended for work duty due to special reasons(excluded from the calculation of contractual working days)
- A period of shutdown due to a cause attributable to the employer
- A period of justifiable strike
- Day or period regarded as the equivalent to the above

③ Day or period deemed as attendance by the laws or its characteristics
- A period of suspension of work due to industrial accident, a period of maternity leave or a period of childcare leave
- A period of training in the reserve forces
- A period of training in civil defense or a period of mobilization
- Days off to exercise civil rights

---

278) Supreme Court ruling on May 27, 2005, 2003Da48549, 2003Da48556.

279) MOEL Guidelines: Labor Standard-4336, on Aug. 18, 2004.

연차휴가일 수 전부에 상응하는 연차휴가수당을 사용자에게 청구할 수 있는 것이다.[278]

(2) 일반적으로 결근일이란 법령의 범위 내에서 노사 당사자가 근로를 제공하기로 정한 날인 '소정근로일'에 근로자가 임의로 근로를 제공하지 아니한 날을 의미한다.[279]

근로기준법상 '결근'의 개념에 관하여 규정한 바는 없으나, 일반적으로 결근일이란 법령의 범위 내에서 노사 당사자가 근로를 제공하기로 정한 날인 '소정근로일'에 근로자가 임의로 근로를 제공하지 아니한 날을 의미한다고 볼 수 있을 것이다. 다만, 소정근로일수 계산에서 제외되거나 출근한 것으로 보아야 하는 다음 각 호의 날 또는 기간에 근로하지 아니한 경우를 결근으로 보아서는 안 된다.

① 법령이나 약정에 의한 휴일(소정근로일수 계산에서 제외)
- 근로기준법에 의한 주휴일
- '근로자의 날 제정에 관한 법률'에 의한 근로자의 날
- 취업규칙이나 단체협약 등에 의한 약정휴일
- 기타 이상의 날에 준하여 해석할 수 있는 날 또는 기간

② 특별한 사유로 근로제공의무가 정지되는 날 또는 기간(소정근로일수 계산에서 제외)
- 사용자의 귀책 사유로 인한 휴업기간
- 적법한 쟁의행위기간
- 기타 이상의 기간에 준하여 해석할 수 있는 날 또는 기간

③ 법령상 또는 그 성질상 출근한 것으로 보아야 하는 날 또는 기간
- 업무상 재해로 인한 휴업기간, 산전후휴가기간, 육아휴직기간
- 예비군 훈련기간
- 민방위 훈련 또는 동원기간
- 공민권 행사를 위한 휴무일

278) 대법원 2005.5.27, 2003다48549; 2003다48556.
279) 행정해석: 근로기준과-4336, 2004.8.18.

- Annual and monthly paid leave and menstruation leave
- Other days or periods regarded as equivalent of the above

(3) Providing annual and monthly paid leave to part-time employees[280)]

According to the related Presidential Decree(Table 1-2) to the LSA, annual and monthly paid leave for part-time employees shall be calculated by hourly units(1 hour deemed for periods shorter than 1 hour) by the following method:

Number of annual leave days for full-time employee(Part-time employee contractual working hours/Full-time employee contractual working hours) × 8 hours

Contractual working hours of short-term employees or full-time employees shall be the contractual working hours per week.(However, if a part-time employee's contractual working hours are not regular, the contractual working hours shall be averaged for contractual working hours of 4 weeks).

Annual paid leave shall be granted as a one day unit, and use shall be granted according to the amount of contractual working hours.

Example) Part-time employee who works 4 hours per day and 6 days per week

- Annual leave (hours): Number of annual leave days for full-time employee (15 days) x [part-time employee's contractual working hours (24 hours) / full-time employee's contractual working hours (40 hours)] x 8 hours = 72 hours

Ⅱ. Contractual Leave

1. Concept

Contractual leave refers to paid vacation, free of the obligation to provide labor in accordance with employer approval, a collective agreement or the rules of employment. Such leave includes congratulatory and condolence leave, sick leave, summer vacation, and other special leave, etc. Contractual leaves are not statutory like annual paid leave, or maternity/paternity leave, but were introduced to maintain traditional Korean values and improve employee wellbeing, and can be stipulated as paid, partially paid, or unpaid leave. A company that does not stipulate these contractual leaves is not in violation of the Labor Standards Act.

---

280) MOEL Guidelines: Labor Standards, Dec. 17, 2002.

– 연월차유급휴가, 생리휴가 기간
– 기타 이상의 날 또는 기간에 준하여 해석할 수 있는 날 또는 기간

(3) 단시간 근로자의 연차휴가 산정방법[280)]

근로기준법시행령 별표1의2에 의거 단시간 근로자의 연차휴가는 다음의 방식에 의하여 시간단위로 산정(1시간 미만은 1시간으로 간주) 통상근로자의 연차유급휴가일수×(단시간 근로자의 소정근로시간/통상근로자의 소정근로시간)×8시간 단시간 근로자 또는 통상근로자의 소정근로시간은 1주간의 소정근로시간으로 함(단시간 근로자의 1주간 소정근로시간이 불규칙한 경우에는 4주간의 소정근로시간을 평균한 시간으로 함). 연차유급휴가는 "1일" 단위로 소정근로일에 부여하되, 동일의 소정근로시간 만큼 연차휴가를 사용한 것으로 한다.

예) 1주간 1일 4시간씩 6일 근무하는 근로자의 경우
– 연차휴가(시간):통상근로자의 연차휴가일 수(15일)×[단시간 근로자의 소정근로시간 (24시간) / 통상근로자의 소정근로시간 (40시간)]×8시간=72시간

Ⅱ. 약정휴가

1 개 념

약정휴가는 사용자의 승인, 단체협약이나 취업규칙으로 유급휴가를 제공함으로써 근로 제공의무를 면제해주는 휴가로 경조휴가, 병가, 하계휴가, 특별휴가 등이 있다. 약정휴가는 연차유급휴가, 산전산후휴가, 배우자 출산휴가와 같이 근로기준법으로 보장된 것이 아니라 한국의 전통적 가치를 존중하고 근로자들의 복지차원에서 도입된 휴가라 할 수 있다. 이러한 약정휴가를 설정해놓지 않았다고 하여 근로기준법을 위반한 것이 아니며, 회사의 재량에 따라 유급, 부분적 유급, 또는 무급으로 설정하여 운용할 수 있다.

280) 행정해석. 근기 68207-3373, 2002.12.17.

2. Types of Contractual Leave

(1) Congratulatory and condolence leave

Many companies provide congratulatory and condolence leave for wedding and funeral services in accordance with traditional Korean rituals. Although the coverage and number of leaves vary from company to company, such leave is granted in addition to annual paid leave. A maximum of five leave days are given for an employee's wedding as congratulatory leave, five days as condolence leave in the event of the death of an employee's direct family member, and one day for a parent's 60th birthday.

(2) Sick leave

Should an employee be unable to carry out his/her duties due to non-occupational injury or illness, the employee shall use annual paid leave to receive medical treatment and shall bear the medical expenses him/herself as there is no statutory sick leave. Government employees can use up to 60 days per year as sick leave according to Article 18 of the Government Employee Service Regulations(Sick Leave). In the private sector, if an employee has used up all his/her annual leave days, he/she may request unpaid leave to take care of illness or injury. If the employee has to continually be absent in order to receive treatment for his/her illness or injury, the company can dismiss the employee for reasons attributable to the employee. Many companies have some restricted types of sick leave, such as follows.

Type 1	No regulation for sick leave days. Annual paid leave shall be used instead.
Type 2	"The company may grant unpaid sick leave of up to 90 days per calendar year."
Type 3	"If an employee requires an extended time of absence due to accident or illness unrelated to his/her duties, he/she may request to use paid leave. The period shall not exceed 14 calendar days, provided that the accrued annual leave has been used up already
Type 4	"In case of a leave of absence due to non work-related injury or illness, 90% of monthly ordinary wage shall be paid for the first month, 70% for the second month and 50% for the third to sixth months."

2. 약정휴가의 유형

(1) 경조휴가

많은 회사들이 한국의 오래된 관혼상제의 전통에 따라 혼례와 상례에 관련하여 경조휴가를 부여하고 있다. 그 대상범위나 부여일 수가 다를 수 있지만, 일반적으로 연차유급휴가와 별개로 추가적으로 유급휴가를 부여한다. 본인 결혼의 경우 5일 이내, 직계가족의 사망 시에 5일 이내, 부모님의 환갑의 경우 1일을 부여한다.

(2) 병 가

근로자가 업무 외에 발생한 개인적 질병이나 부상으로 인하여 직무를 수행할 수 없을 때는 법정 병가가 인정되지 않기 때문에 본인의 연차유급휴가를 사용하여 요양을 해야 하고 또는 치료비 일체도 근로자 개인이 부담해야 한다. 다만, 공무원인 경우에는 국가공무원 복무규정 제18조(병가) 규정에 의해 연 60일까지 유급병가를 사용할 수 있다. 따라서 병가규정이 없는 일반 회사의 경우에 근로자는 병가를 신청할 수 없기 때문에 자신에게 주어진 잔여 연차유급휴가를 사용하여 치료하여야 하고, 연차유급휴가를 모두 사용한 경우에는 무급휴직을 청구하게 된다. 근로자가 질병 또는 부상 치료를 위해 계속해서 결근하는 경우에는 회사는 근로자의 귀책 사유로 인한 통상해고를 할 수 있다. 많은 회사들이 취업규칙에 제한적인 유급 병가규정을 설정하고 있는데 그 유형은 나음과 같다.

유형1	병가규정 없음. 이 경우 연차휴가로 사용하여야 함
유형2	"회사는 역년으로 90일까지의 병가를 지급할 수 있다. 병가는 무급으로 한다."
유형3	"직원이 업무 외의 사고나 질병으로 장기간 결근해야 할 경우, 연차휴가를 모두 사용하고 휴일을 포함하여 14일을 초과하지 않는 범위 안에서 유급 병가를 신청할 수 있다."
유형4	"개인상 병에 의한 휴직일 경우에는 최초 1개월: 월 통상급여의 90%; 2개월 차: 월 통상급여의 70%; 3~6개월 차: 월 통상급여의 50%를 지급한다."

(3) Summer vacation

Summer vacation refers to contractual leave of a maximum one week besides annual paid leave during the heat of the summer in order to promote employee morale. This summer leave is used collectively by production companies, while smaller companies generally use annual paid leave days as summer vacation.

3. Relationship between Labor Law and Contractual Leave

(1) It is impossible to change the date for congratulatory or condolence leave or to apply for it retroactively[281)]

Congratulatory and condolence leave refers to paid leaves granted on particular days or for a particular period to the corresponding employee in accordance with the collective agreement or rules of employment so that the employee can participate in congratulatory or condolence events. It is not possible to change the period of leave nor apply for them retroactively.

(2) Congratulatory and condolence leave not granted during labor strikes[282)]

According to the Labor Standards Act(LSA), holiday refers to a day when the employee is exempted from the obligation to provide labor to the employer, while leave refers to days exempted from the obligation to provide work even though the employer is available to receive the labor service. While contractual holidays or contractual leave stipulated by a collective agreement or rules of employment are not statutory holidays where workers are exempted from the obligation to provide labor according to the Labor Standards Act(LSA), workers are to be so exempted from work on working days due to special agreement between employer and employees. Accordingly, if there is a certain condition where the employer, in reality, can neither receive the employee's labor nor exempt him/her from providing labor, then the contractual holiday or contractual leave cannot occur. However, for those who did not participate in strikes during labor disputes, whether a contractual holiday or contractual leave occurred should be judged according to whether the employer could receive the employee's labor or not.

---

281) MOEL Guidelines: Kungi 68207-1452, on Sept. 14, 1994.

282) MOEL Guidelines: Kungi 68207-883, on Dec. 15, 1999.

(3) 여름휴가

여름휴가는 연차유급휴가와 별도로 직원들의 사기진작을 위해 한여름에 1주일 이내에서 지급하는 약정휴가제도이다. 주로 제조업체에서 집단적으로 사용하고, 소규모 사업장의 경우에는 연차휴가를 대체해서 여름휴가로 사용하기도 한다.

3. 노동법과 약정휴가와의 관계

(1) 경조휴가 시기변경권 불가능 및 소급 불가[281)]

경조휴가는 노사가 단체협약이나 취업규칙 등으로 경조일의 기념이나 경조사 참여를 보장하기 위해 해당 근로자에게 특정일 또는 특정기간에 유급으로 부여하는 휴가로서 사용자의 휴가시기에 따른 변경권 행사가 불가능하고 또한 그 기일이 경과하면 휴가 사용목적이 소멸되어 휴가청구권 또한 소멸한다.

(2) 쟁의행위 기간 중 경조유급휴가는 발생하지 않음[282)]

근로기준법상 휴일이라 함은 근로자가 사용자에 대하여 근로 제공의무가 없는 날을 말하며, 근로기준법상 휴가라 함은 사용자가 근로자의 노무수령을 할 수 있는 상태임에도 사용자가 그날의 근로제공의무를 면제시켜 주는 것을 말한다. 노사 간 단체협약 또는 취업규칙에서 정한 이른바 약정휴일 또는 약정휴가의 경우는 근로제공의무가 없는 근로기준법상 휴일과는 달리 근로 제공의무가 있는 날임에도 노사 간 특약에 의하여 사용자가 근로자의 근로 제공의무를 면제시켜 준 것으로 보아야 할 것이다. 따라서 사용자가 사실상 근로자의 노무제공을 수령할 수 없고 사용자의 면제행위도 행사할 수 없는 상태였다면 약정휴일 또는 약정휴가 자체가 발생하지 아니한다. 다만 파업기간 중 파업 미참석자의 경우에는 사용자가 근로자의 노무제공을 수령할 수 있는 상태인지의 여부에 따라 판단해야 한다.

---

281) 행정해석: 근기68207-1452, 1994.9.14.
282) 행정해석: 근기68207-883, 1999.12.15.

(3) Calculation of average wage during periods of leave[283)]

Average wages where an employee came to resign after a period of leave from work that the employee took with approval from the employer due to non-occupational injury, illness or other reason shall be calculated as follows: average wages to calculate severance pay refer to the amount calculated by dividing the total amount of wages paid to the relevant employee during three calendar months prior to the date of calculation by the total number of calendar days during those three calendar months(Article 2 of the LSA). If the amount calculated by this method is lower than the ordinary wage of the employee concerned, the amount of the ordinary wage shall be deemed as average wage. In cases where the period of average wage calculation includes a period during leave from work with approval from the employer caused by non-occupational injury, illness, or other reason, the period and wages paid for that period shall be deducted respectively from the basis period for the calculation of average wage and the total amount of average wage(Article 2 of the Enforcement Decree to the LSA). Therefore, in cases where an employee took a leave of absence for non-occupational injury, illness or other reason in accordance with Article 2(8) of the Enforcement Decree to the LSA(with approval from the employer), the remaining period and wages excluding the period mentioned above shall be used for the calculation of average wage. If the leave of absence exceeds three months, the first day of the leave of absence shall be the date for calculating average wages based on the previous three months. In any case, if the amount calculated above is lower than the ordinary wage of the employee concerned, the ordinary wage shall be deemed as average wage.

(4) In cases where changes to contractual leave in the rules of employment is considered disadvantageous[284)]

A particular company has provided 5 to 10 days of "health vacation" per year according to rank and length of service, but did not set any restrictions on the time of use. If it were to later decide to allow its use only after annual paid leave is used up, this would be restricting free use of the contractual leave. It would be acceptable and applicable after consent is received according to the appropriate procedures(Article 94 of the LSA).

---

283) MOEL Guidelines: Retirement Pension Dept-518, on Oct. 21, 2008.

284) MOEL Guidelines: Working Conditions Inspection Team-1774, on Mar. 25, 2009.

(3) 휴직기간의 평균임금 산정방법[283)]

업무 외 부상이나 질병, 그 밖의 사유로 사용자의 승인을 받아 휴업한 후 퇴직하게 된 경우에 평균임금을 다음과 같이 계산한다. 퇴직금 산정을 위한 평균임금은 이를 산정하여야 할 사유가 발생한 날 이전 3개월 동안에 그 근로자에게 지급된 임금의 총액을 그 기간의 총일수로 나눈 금액을 말하며(「근로기준법」 제2조), 이러한 방법으로 산출된 평균임금액이 당해 근로자의 통상임금보다 저액일 경우에는 그 통상임금을 평균임금으로 하도록 정하고 있다. 평균임금 산정기간 중에 업무 외 부상 또는 질병으로 사용자의 승인을 받아 휴업한 경우에는 그 기간과 그 기간에 지불된 임금은 평균임금 산정기준이 되는 기간과 임금의 총액에서 각각 공제하도록 규정하고 있다(근로기준법시행령 제2조). 따라서 근로자가 업무 외 부상이나 질병, 그 밖의 사유로 사용자의 승인을 받아 휴업한 기간일 경우에는 동기간을 제외한 나머지 일수 및 임금을 대상으로 평균임금으로 산정하여야 하며, 휴직한 기간이 3개월을 초과하여 평균임금 산정기준기간이 없게 되는 경우에는 휴직한 첫 날을 평균임금산정 사유 발생일로 보아 이전 3월간을 대상으로 평균임금을 산정하여야 한다. 아울러, 위와 같은 방법으로 산출된 평균임금액이 당해 근로자의 통상임금보다 저액일 경우에는 그 통상임금액을 평균임금으로 하여야 한다.

(4) 약정휴가 사용변경은 취업규칙 불이익변경[284)]

회사에서는 직급, 근속연수에 따라 1년에 5~10일의 건강휴가를 부여하고 있고 그 사용 시기에 관하여는 별도의 제한을 두고 있지 않았다. 그러나, 종전에는 건강휴가의 사용시기에 대하여 아무런 조건 없이 허용하다가 이를 연차유급휴가 소진 이후에만 사용할 수 있도록 변경하는 것은 결과적으로 자유로운 사용이 제약되는 것으로, 이는 불이익한 변경에 해당하고 따라서 소정의 동의절차(근로기준법 제94조 제1항)를 거쳐야 유효하게 적용될 수 있다.

---

283) 행정해석: 퇴직연금복지과-518, 2008.10.21.
284) 행정해석: 근로조건지도과-1774, 2009.3.25.

Chapter 5

Working Environment

Section 1: Industrial Safety and Health

I. Concept

On April 16, 2014, a ferry named Sewol, bound for Jeju island from Incheon, sank in the ocean near Jindo Island, and about 300 passengers lost their lives. This is known as the "Sewol ho Accident," one of the worst tragedies in Korea, and one which could have been avoided if the employer had fulfilled his duty to observe safety regulations.

The current Occupational Safety & Health Act(hereinafter referred to as "the Act") requires the employer to establish a management system for occupational safety and health, to prepare preventative measures for harmful and dangerous equipment, facilities, materials, working environment, etc., and at the same time to periodically provide workers the necessary safety and health education to prevent industrial accidents from happening. Also, in cases where an employer is found to have violated the Act, the employer is punished immediately so that activities to protect occupational safety and health and avoid accidents become habitual. Workers can also be punished with a fine for negligence when they violate the Act.

Occupational safety cannot be emphasized enough, as it protects personnel, property, and investment by preventing accidents. This Act, which stipulates the observance of occupational safety and health regulations, is very complicated, and enumerated with many technical articles, and so here I have attempted to define the management structures of the Act clearly and divide the employer's duties according to their characteristics in order to make the Act more easily and clearly understood.

In particular, major changes to the Act, which was enforced from January 16, 2020, included:

Chapter 5

근로환경

제1절 산업안전과 보건

Ⅰ. 의 의

2014년 4월 16일 인천에서 제주로 향하던 여객선 세월호가 진도 인근 해상에서 침몰하면서 승객 300여 명이 사망했다. 이른바 세월호 사건인 이 비극적인 대형 사고는 사업장 내의 안전준수의무를 다했다면 피할 수 있었던 사건이었다.

현행 산업안전보건법(이하 '산안법'이라 한다)은 사업주가 산업재해를 사전에 예방하기 위해 산업안전·보건의 관리체계를 갖추고, 위해·위험한 기구, 시설, 물질, 작업환경 등에 대해 예방조치를 취하고, 동시에 근로자들에게 안전과 보건에 관한 교육을 주기적으로 실시하도록 하고 있다. 또한 사업주가 산안법을 위반한 경우, 즉시 처벌하도록 하여 사업장에서 산업안전보건 예방활동이 생활화되도록 그 준수의무를 엄격히 부과하고 있다. 특히, 근로자도 산안법 위반 시 과태료가 부과된다.

산업안전은 아무리 강조해도 지나치지 않을 정도로 중요하고 이를 사전에 예방함으로써 인적·물적·재정적 보호를 할 수 있다. 이러한 산업안전을 준수해야 하는 내용을 담은 산안법은 열거식으로 표현되어 너무 복잡하고 그 적용범위도 잘 이해가 되지 않는 부분이 많다. 이에 본고는 실무상 산안법의 관리체계 및 사업주의 의무를 그 업무 성격으로 구분해 쉽게 이해해보고자 한다.

특히, 2020년 1월 16일부터 전면개정 시행된 산안법 주요 변경내용은 ① 적용범위를 확대하여 근로자에서 노무제공자로 확대, ② 중대재해에 대해 해당 작

① expanding coverage and expanding from workers to labor providers; ② introducing such shutdowns for serious disasters; and ③ strengthening penalties for accidents.

Ⅱ. The Scope of Application[285)]

1. Extended purpose and scope of application

(1) Purpose

The purpose of this Act is to maintain and promote the safety and health of those who provide work by preventing industrial accidents through establishment of standards on industrial safety and health and clarifying where the responsibility lies, and by creating a comfortable working environment(Article 1). As the Industrial Accident Compensation Insurance Act recognizes the occupational accidents for persons in special types of employment, the Occupational Safety and Health Act extends the scope of industrial accidents from workers to those who provide work, which include not only workers but also special types of workers and delivery workers for safety and health measures(Articles 77 and 78 of the Act).[286)]

(2) Scope of application

This Act shall apply to all businesses: Provided that this Act may not apply wholly or partially to businesses taking into consideration the degree of harm and hazard, the type and scale of business, the location of business, etc. Generally, those excluded from application are ① public administration, education service, foreign agencies; ② businesses that use only office employees; and ③ any business that ordinarily employs fewer than 5 workers(Article 3).

285) Kim, Hyungbae「Labor Law」, 26th, ed., Parkyoung Publishing Co. 2018, page 474-487; Kim, Hyungbae/Park Ji-soon, 「Lectures on Labor Law 」8th ed. Shinjosa, 2019, pp. 341-348.

286) The Industrial Accident Compensation Insurance Act: Article 125 (Special Case concerning Persons in Special Types of Employment)(1) Notwithstanding Article 6, the business which receives labor service, from persons who engage in jobs prescribed by Presidential Decree, among the persons who are not subject to the Labor Standards Act, etc., even though they offer labor service similar to that of employees regardless of the type of contract, and therefore need protection from occupational accidents, and who also meet all the following requirements (hereafter in this Article referred to as "persons in special types of employment"), shall be deemed business subject to this Act: <Amended on January 27, 2010>

1. They mainly provide one line of business with labor service necessary for the operation thereof on a routine basis, and receive payment for such service and live on such pay;
2. They do not use other persons to provide such labor service.

업중지 도입, ③ 재해발생에 대해 처벌규정을 강화하는 내용을 포함하고 있다.

Ⅱ. 산업안전보건법의 적용범위와 관리체계[285)]

1. 목적과 적용범위의 확대

(1) 목 적

산안법은 산업안전 및 보건에 관한 기준을 확립하고 그 책임의 소재를 명확하게 하여 산업재해를 예방하고 쾌적한 작업환경을 조성함으로써 노무를 제공하는 자의 안전 및 보건을 유지하고 증진함을 목적으로 한다(산안법 제1조). 산업재해보상보험법이 특수형태 근로종사자에 대한 산재재해를 가입을 인정해줌에 따라 산업안전보건법도 산업재해의 범위를 근로자에서 근로를 제공하는 자로 확대하여 근로자뿐만 아니라 특수형태의 근로자와 배달종사자에 대한 안전조치 및 보건조치를 추가적으로 도입하였다(산안법 제77조, 제78조).[286)]

(2) 적용범위

산안법은 모든 사업에 적용되는 것이 원칙이나, 유해·위험의 정도, 사업의 종류·규모 및 사업의 소재지 등을 고려하여 법의 전부 또는 일부를 적용하지 아니한다. 일반적으로 ① 순수행정업무, 교육서비스 업무, 외국기관, ② 사무직 근로자만을 사용하는 사업장, ③ 상시 근로자 5명 미만을 사용하는 사업장은 법의 일부를 적용제외하고 있다(산안법 제3조, 영 제2조의2 및 별표1).

---

285) 김형배, 『노동법』, 제26판, 박영사, 2018, 474~487면; 김형배·박지순, 『노동법강의』, 제8판, 신조사, 2019, 341~348면.

286) 산업재해보상법 제125조 【특수형태근로종사자에 대한 특례】 ① 계약의 형식에 관계없이 근로자와 유사하게 노무를 제공함에도 「근로기준법」 등이 적용되지 아니하여 업무상의 재해로부터 보호할 필요가 있는 자로서 다음 각 호의 모두에 해당하는 자 중 대통령령으로 정하는 직종에 종사하는 자(이하 이 조에서 "특수형태근로종사자"라 한다)의 노무(勞務)를 제공받는 사업은 제6조에도 불구하고 이 법의 적용을 받는 사업으로 본다. 〈개정 2010.1.27〉

1. 주로 하나의 사업에 그 운영에 필요한 노무를 상시적으로 제공하고 보수를 받아 생활할 것
2. 노무를 제공함에 있어서 타인을 사용하지 아니할 것.

2. Management structure

(1) Appointment duties

1) The general manager is in charge of safety and health management

The general manager is responsible for general control of occupational safety and health and supervises safety and health managers. Accordingly, the general manager shall be capable of managing the company's business(e.g., plant manager)(Article 15). Companies that ordinarily employ 50 workers or more engaged in manufacturing etc., companies that ordinarily employ 100 workers or more engaged in wholesale and retail sales, etc., and companies that ordinarily employ 300 or more engaged in pure office administration, such as finance, etc., must appoint a general manager to be in charge of safety and health management.

2) Supervisor

An employer shall designate the head of a division within the management structure, who directly manages and supervises production work and employees involved therein or who takes charge of such a position, to carry out safety- and health-related duties such as safety and health inspections(Article 16).

3) Safety manager and health manager

An employer shall assign a safety(health) manager at the workplace to assist the employer or the general manager in technical matters concerning safety among the matters regarding safety and health, and to instruct and advise the supervisor on such matters.

The business owner of a manufacturing company or etc., ordinarily hiring 50 workers or more shall generally appoint a safety(health) manager, but for companies with fewer than 300 employees, the business owner may assign the safety(health) manager an additional safety management job or refer to a professional institution to perform the necessary safety management measures(Articles 17 and 18).

(2) Industrial safety and health committee

The business owner shall establish an industrial safety and health committee comprised of an equal number of worker and employer representatives for workplaces ordinarily

2. 관리체계

(1) 선임의무

1) 안전보건 관리책임자

관리책임자는 안전보건관리를 총괄 관리하며, 안전관리자 및 보건관리자를 지휘·감독한다. 관리책임자는 당해 사업장에서 사업을 실질적으로 총괄 관리하는 자(예를 들면, 공장장) 이어야 한다(산안법 제15조, 영 제9조 및 별표 1의2). 선임의무는 제조업 등의 상시근로자 50인 이상 사업장, 도소매업 등의 상시 근로자가 100인 이상 사업장에 적용되고, 금융 등 순수사무직은 300인 이상 사업장에 적용된다.

2) 관리감독자

경영조직에서 생산과 관련되는 업무와 그 소속 직원을 직접 지휘·감독하는 부서의 장 또는 그 직위를 담당하는 자로 하여금 직무와 관련된 안전·보건에 관한 업무로서 안전·보건점검 등 업무를 수행하도록 하여야 한다(산안법 제16조, 영 제10조).

3) 안전(보건)관리자

사업장에 안전(보건)관리자를 두어 안전(보건)에 관한 기술적인 사항에 관하여 사업주 또는 관리책임자를 보좌하고 관리감독자에게 조언·지도하는 업무를 수행하게 하여야 한다. 제조업 등의 상시 50명 이상의 근로자를 사용하는 사업주는 안전(보건)관리자를 두어야 한다. 다만, 300인 미만의 사업장에서는 안전(보건)관리업무를 겸직하게 하거나 안전(보건)관리 대행기관에 위탁할 수 있다(산안법 제17조/제18조, 영 제12조 제1항 및 별표3).

(2) 산업안전 보건위원회 설치

상시 근로자를 100인 이상 사업장 및 50인 이상 100인 미만으로 사용하고 있는 유해위험사업의 사업주는 노사 동수(同數)로 구성되는 산업안전 보건위원회를 두어야 한다. 회의는 분기별로 실시 하고, 의결사항을 게시해야 하며, 이

hiring more than 100 employees, or which has between 50 to 100 employees engaged in dangerous work. The committee shall meet once per quarter and its decisions shall be posted, and shall be faithfully implemented(Article 24).

(3) Safety and health management regulations

In order to maintain safety and health in the workplace, an employer shall prepare safety and health management regulations, post and/or keep them in the workplace, and notify workers thereof. The employer and workers shall observe the safety and health management regulations(Article 25). These rules shall apply to workplaces ordinarily hiring 100 workers or more; provided that for service businesses like finance, etc. these rules shall apply to workplaces ordinarily hiring 300 workers or more.

Ⅲ. Employer's Duties

1. Report industrial accidents

In cases where a worker dies due to an occupational accident, or is injured or contracts an illness requiring medical treatment for three days or more, the employer shall submit to the Minister of Employment & Labor an accident investigation form regarding the occupational accident within one month from the occurrence date of the occupational accident. Provided, in cases where a "serious accident" occurs, the employer shall report it without delay(Article 57).

2. Measures to prevent harm & hazards

(1) Notice of substance of acts and subordinate statutes

The business owner shall inform workers of the major aspects of orders enacted under this Act by posting them at each workplace(Article 34).

(2) Attachment of safety signs

The business owner shall install or attach safety and health signs to warn employees of dangerous facilities and places in the workplace and provide emergency drills to promote safety awareness(Article 37).

를 성실히 이행해야 한다(산안법 제24조, 영 제25조 및 별표6의2).

(3) 안전보건관리규정

사업장의 안전·보건을 유지하기 위하여 안전보건관리규정을 작성하여 각 사업장에 게시하거나 갖춰 두고, 이를 근로자에게 알려야 한다. 안전보건관리규정을 작성하거나 변경할 때는 산업안전 보건위원회의 심의·의결을 거쳐야 한다. 사업주와 근로자는 안전보건관리규정을 지켜야 한다(산안법 제25조, 영 제26조 및 별표6의2). 이 규정은 상시 근로자 100인 이상 사업장에 적용되고, 금융 등 서비스 업종은 상시 근로자 300인 이상 사업장에 적용된다.

Ⅲ. 사업주의 의무

1. 산업재해 보고

사업주는 산업재해로 사망자가 발생하거나 3일 이상의 휴업이 필요한 부상을 입거나 질병에 걸린 사람이 발생한 경우에는 해당 산업재해가 발생한 날부터 1개월 이내에 산재 내용을 산업재해조사표에 작성하여 관할 지방고용노동관서의 장에게 제출하여야 한다. 다만, 사업주는 '중대재해'가 발생한 경우에는 지체 없이 보고하여야 한다(산안법 제57조).

2. 예방조치 의무

(1) 법령 요지의 게시

사업주는 산안법과 법에 의한 명령의 요지를 상시 각 사업장에 게시·비치하여 근로자로 하여금 알게 하여야 한다(산안법 제34조).

(2) 안전표지의 부착

사업주는 사업장의 유해 또는 위험한 시설 및 장소에 대한 경고·비상시 조치의 안내 기타 안전의식을 고취하기 위하여 안전보건표지를 설치하거나 부착하여야 한다(산안법 제37조).

(3) Safety and health measures

The business owner shall take measures necessary to prevent the following hazards in operating the business: ① hazards caused by machines, tools or other equipment; ② hazards caused by explosive, combustible or inflammable substances; ③ hazards caused by electricity, heat or other forms of energy; ④ Hazards caused by improper work methods in excavating, quarrying, loading and unloading, timbering, transporting, operating, dismantling, handling of heavy objects, etc.; and ⑤ hazards in places where workers might easily trip and fall, sand, structures, etc.,(Article 38).

The business owner shall take measures necessary to prevent the following from causing health problems commonly encountered in the course of business operations: gas, dust, high temperatures, low temperatures, remnants, precision work, poor ventilation or lighting, computer terminals, radiation, simple repetitive actions, etc(Article 39).

(4) Suspension of operation due to a serious accident or possible risk

If there is imminent danger of an industrial accident, or if a serious accident has occurred, the business owner shall take necessary measures for safety and health, such as immediately suspending operations, evacuating workers from the workplace, etc., until work can be resumed after meeting safety requirements(Article 51).

If an industrial accident seems impending, any worker can suspend work and evacuate. In this case, he/she shall report it without delay to the immediate superior officer, who shall take appropriate measures to rectify the situation(Article 52).

(5) Measures in case of a serious accident

1) Employer's measures

The employer shall immediately take necessary measures concerning safety and health, such as stopping work immediately and evacuating workers from the workplace when a serious accident occurs. In addition, the employer shall report to the Minister of Employment and Labor without delay if he finds out that a serious disaster has occurred(Article 54).

2) Measures by the Minister of Employment and Labor

The Minister of Employment and Labor shall, when a serious accident occurs and if it is determined that there is an immediate danger of recurrence, ① if the work during which

(3) 안전상의 조치 및 보건상 조치

사업주는 사업을 행함에 있어 ① 기계·기구 기타 설비에 의한 위험, ② 폭발성·인화성·발화성 물질 등에 의한 위험, ③ 전기·열·기타 에너지에 의한 위험, ④ 굴착·채석·하역·벌목·운송·조작·운반·해체·중량물 취급 기타 불량한 작업방법에 의한 위험 및 ⑤ 추락·붕괴·낙하·천재지변 등으로 인하여 위험발생이 예상되는 장소 등 작업수행상 위험을 방지하기 위해 필요한 조치를 하여야 한다(산안법 제38조).

사업주는 사업을 행함에 있어 가스·분진, 고온·저온, 배출물, 정밀공작, 환기·조명, 컴퓨터 단말기 조작, 방사선, 단순 반복 작업 등에 따라 발생하는 건강장해를 예방하기 위하여 필요한 조치를 취하여야 한다(산안법 제39조).

(4) 중대재해·위험시 작업중지

사업주는 산업재해발생의 급박한 위험이 있을 때 또는 중대재해가 발생하였을 때는 즉시 작업을 중지시키고 근로자를 작업장소로부터 대피시키는 등 필요한 안전·보건상의 조치를 행한 후 작업을 재개하여야 한다(산안법 제51조). 근로자는 산업재해 발생의 급박한 위험이 있는 경우 작업을 중지하고 대피할 수 있으며(작업중지권), 이 경우 지체 없이 이를 직속 상급자에게 보고하고, 상급자는 이에 대한 적절한 조치를 취하여야 한다(산안법 제52조).

(5) 중대재해 발생 시 조치

1) 사업주 조치

사업주는 중대재해가 발생하였을 때는 즉시 해당 작업을 중지시키고 근로자를 작업장소에서 대피시키는 등 안전 및 보건에 관하여 필요한 조치를 하여야 한다. 또한, 사업주는 중대재해가 발생한 사실을 알게 된 경우에는 지체없이 고용노동부 장관에게 보고하여야 한다(산안법 제54조).

2) 고용노동부 장관의 조치

고용노동부 장관은 중대재해가 발생하였을 때 ① 중대재해가 발생한 해당

the serious accident occurred is continuing, or ② if similar work to the work during which the serious accident occurred is continuing, give an order to cease the work. In addition, the Minister of Employment and Labor shall stop the work in case of unavoidable circumstances such as the occurrence of a serious accident due to the collapse of earth and sand, fire, explosion, leakage of harmful or dangerous materials, and the spread of industrial accidents around the place where such serious accident occurred.

The Minister of Employment and Labor shall lift the suspension of work after deliberation by a review committee composed of experts on the work environment, if the employer requests cancellation of the above cases(Article 55).

(6) Other measures to prevent harm and hazards

Article 80 (Protective Measures, etc. for Harmful or Dangerous Machines, Instruments, etc.)	Machines and instruments requiring harmful or hazardous work or operated by power, shall not be transferred, leased, installed or used, or displayed for the purpose of transfer or lease, without taking protective measures for the prevention of harm and hazards.
Article 83 (Safety Certification)	To assess the safety of harmful or dangerous machines, instruments, equipment, protective devices and personal protective equipment, the Minister of Employment & Labor may determine and announce safety certification criteria concerning safety performance, the manufacturer's technological capacity, production systems, etc.
Article 93 (Safety Inspection)	An employer who uses harmful or dangerous machines and equipment shall receive a safety inspection on whether the performance of the harmful or dangerous machines, etc. meet safety standards.
Article 118 (Permission to Manufacture, etc.)	A person who intends to manufacture or use "substances subject to permission"shall obtain, in advance, permission from the Minister of Employment & Labor. This provision shall also apply if the person intends to make a change to anything that has previously been permitted.
Article 119 (Asbestos Investigation) Article 122 (Asbestos Disposal or Removal by Asbestos Disposal or Removal Service Provider)	If structures or facilities are to be demolished or dismantled, the owner or lessee, etc., of the structures or facilities shall conduct a "general asbestos investigation" and record and keep the results thereof. The owner, etc., of structures or facilities subject to an institutional asbestos investigation shall have an "asbestos disposal or removal service provider"dispose of or remove the asbestos.
Article 114 (Preparation, Keeping, etc. of Material Safety Data Sheets)	A person who transfers or supplies a chemical and/or chemical-containing preparations meeting the classification standards pursuant to "target chemicals" shall make and provide a Material Safety Data Sheet (MSDS) to the person to whom they are transferred or supplied.
Article 36 (Risk Assessment)	An employer shall identify hazards and determine the potential for harm caused by structures, machines, instruments, equipment, raw materials, gas, vapor, dust, etc., work behavior or work, determine the level of risk, and take measures under this Act and any order issued under this Act according to the findings, and if necessary to prevent risks or health problems for workers, take additional measures as required.

작업 ② 중대재해가 발생한 작업과 동일한 작업에 해당하는 작업으로 인하여 해당 사업장에 산업재해가 다시 발생할 급박한 위험이 있다고 판단되는 경우에는 그 작업의 중지를 명할 수 있다. 또한 고용노동부 장관은 토사·구축물의 붕괴, 화재·폭발, 유해하거나 위험한 물질의 누출 등으로 인하여 중대재해가 발생하여 그 재해가 발생한 장소 주변으로 산업재해가 확산될 수 있다고 판단되는 등 불가피한 경우에는 해당 사업장의 작업을 중지할 수 있다. 고용노동부 장관은 사업주가 위 사례에 대한 작업중지의 해제를 요청한 경우에는 작업중지 해제에 관한 전문가 등으로 구성된 심의위원회의 심의를 거쳐 작업중지를 해제하여야 한다(산안법 제55조).

(6) 그 밖의 예방조치 의무

제80조 【유해·위험 기계·기구 등의 방호조치 등】	누구든지 유해하거나 위험한 작업을 필요로 하거나 동력(動力)으로 작동하는 기계·기구에 대해 유해·위험 방지를 위한 방호조치를 하지 아니하고는 양도, 대여, 설치 또는 사용에 제공하거나, 양도·대여의 목적으로 진열하여서는 아니 된다
제83조 【안전인증】	고용노동부 장관은 유해하거나 위험한 기계·기구·설비 및 방호장치·보호구의 안전성을 평가하기 위하여 그 안전에 관한 성능과 제조자의 기술 능력 및 생산 체계 등에 관한 안전인증기준을 정하여 고시하여야 한다.
제93조 【안전검사】	유해하거나 위험한 기계·기구·설비를 사용하는 사업주는 유해·위험기계등의 안전에 관한 성능이 고용노동부 장관이 정하여 고시하는 검사기준에 맞는지에 대하여 고용노동부 장관이 실시하는 안전검사를 받아야 한다.
제118조 【제조 등의 허가】	"허가대상물질"을 제조하거나 사용하려는 자는 미리 고용노동부 장관의 허가를 받아야 한다. 허가받은 사항을 변경할 때에도 또한 같다.
제119조 【석면조사】 제122조 【석면해체 제거업자를 통한 석면 해체·제거】	건축물이나 설비를 철거하거나 해체하려는 경우에 해당 건축물이나 설비의 소유주 또는 임차인 등은 "일반석면조사"한 후 그 결과를 기록·보존하여야 한다. 기관석면조사 대상으로서 함유량과 면적 이상의 석면이 함유되어 있는 경우 건축물이나 설비의 소유주등은 "석면해체·제거업자"로 하여금 그 석면을 해체·제거하도록 하여야 한다.
제114조 【물질안전보건자료 작성, 비치 등】	화학물질 및 화학물질을 함유한 제제 중 분류기준에 해당하는 화학물질 및 화학물질을 함유한 제제를 양도하거나 제공하는 자는 이를 양도받거나 제공받는 자에게 모두 기재한 자료, 즉 "물질안전보건자료(MSDS)"를 작성하여 제공하여야 한다.
제36조 【위험성 평가】	사업주는 건설물, 기계·기구, 설비, 원재료, 가스, 증기, 분진 등에 의하거나 작업행동, 그밖에 업무에 기인하는 유해·위험요인을 찾아내어 위험성을 결정하고, 그 결과에 따라 이 법과 이 법에 따른 명령에 의한 조치를 하여야 하며, 근로자의 위험 또는 건강장해를 방지하기 위하여 필요한 경우에는 추가적인 조치를 하여야 한다.

3. Safety and health measures for contractor businesses

(1) Safety measures

The business owner of a contractor business shall institute safety measures to prevent industrial accidents which can occur when those employed by the business owner and the contractor work simultaneously at the same place(Article 63).

(2) Prohibition of contract for harmful and dangerous work

Sectors of work recognized as harmful or dangerous to safety and health shall not apply under a separate contract without the approval of the Minister of Employment & Labor(Article 58).

(3) Setting aside of funds for safety management

Upon entering into a subcontract or independently executing construction, shipbuilding or repair work, or other projects, funds for industrial safety and health management shall be set aside for activities to prevent occupational accidents when planning subcontract or project costs(Article 72).

4. Safety & health education (Chapter 3 of the Act)

In order to prevent possible safety-related accidents while working, the employer shall provide education for new workers, regular education for existing workers, education for workers changing jobs within the company, and special education as necessary.

(1) Regular education

The employer shall periodically conduct employee education on safety and health issues(one hour or longer each month for office/sales workers, two hours or longer per month for production workers, and 16 hours per year for supervisors).

(2) New workers' education

When hiring workers, the employer shall provide safety and health education regarding their respective jobs for 8 hours or longer(one hour for daily workers).

3. 도급사업의 안전·보건조치

(1) 안전조치의무

동일한 장소에서 행하여지는 사업의 일부를 도급에 의하여 행하는 경우에, 사업주는 그가 사용하는 근로자와 그의 수급인이 사용하는 근로자가 동일한 장소에서 작업할 때에 생기는 산업재해를 예방하기 위하여 필요한 조치를 취해야 한다(산안법 제63조).

(2) 유해·위험작업의 도급금지

안전보건상 유해 또는 위험하다고 인정되는 작업은 고용노동부 장관의 인가를 받지 아니하고는 그 작업만을 분리하여 도급을 줄 수 없다(산안법 제58조).

(3) 안전관리비의 계상

건설업, 선박건조·수리업 등을 타인에게 도급하는 자와 이를 자체 사업으로 영위하는 자는 도급계약을 체결하거나 자체 사업계획을 수립할 경우 산업재해 예방을 위한 '표준안전관리비'를 도급금액 또는 사업비에 충당(계상)하여야 한다(산안법 제72조).

4. 안전보건 교육실시(산안법 제3장)

근로자의 작업수행 과정에서 발생 가능한 안전사고를 예방하기 위하여 근로자에게 정기교육, 채용 시 교육, 작업내용 변경 교육, 특별교육을 실시하여야 한다.

(1) 정기교육

사업주는 당해 사업주의 근로자에 대하여 정기적으로 안전·보건에 관한 교육을 실시하여야 한다(사무직·판매직 근로자 매월 1시간 이상, 생산직 근로자 매월 2시간 이상, 관리감독자 연 16시간 이상).

(2) 채용 시 교육

근로자를 채용할 때는 해당업무와 관련되는 안전보건교육을 8시간(일용근로자 1시간) 이상하여야 한다.

(3) Education when changing jobs within the company

When changing the contents of their jobs, the employer shall provide safety and health education regarding their changed jobs for 2 hours or longer(one hour for daily workers).

(4) Special education

The employer shall provide safety and health education for 16 hours or longer to workers working in harmful and/or hazardous workplaces(two hours for daily workers).

5. Management of worker health

(1) Evaluating the working environment

An employer of a business dealing with dangerous or harmful chemical substances or producing a high level of noise shall evaluate the working environment within 20 days from the date when a new workplace or work process is added or when there is any change in the existing workplace or work processes. An additional evaluation shall be made every 3 months for 1 year. The evaluation results shall be reported to the local labor office within 30 days from the completion date of the evaluation(Article 129).

(2) Health examinations

The business owner shall periodically conduct health examinations of the workers. Health examinations must also be given upon the hiring of new workers(Article 125).

1) Employees who are required to take a special medical checkup(as they are engaged in work dealing with harmful substances or materials) shall have a medical checkup before they are assigned to the work. In addition, medical checkups shall be conducted for them whenever necessary.

2) All employers shall ensure that a general medical checkup is conducted at least once every two years for employees engaged in office work and at least once every year for other employees.

3) When an employer receives the results of a special medical checkup from the medical service provider, he/she should take any measures necessary to protect the employee's health and then report to the jurisdictional local labor office.

(3) 작업내용 변경교육

작업내용을 변경할 때는 2시간(일용근로자 1시간) 이상 변경된 작업에 대한 산업안전보건 교육을 하여야 한다.

(4) 특별교육

유해·위험작업에 종사하는 근로자에 16시간 이상, 일용근로자는 2시간 이상의 안전보건교육을 시켜야 한다.

5. 근로자의 보건관리

(1) 작업환경의 측정

유해화학물질 취급, 소음발생 등 유해한 작업은 작업장 또는 작업공정이 신규로 가동되거나 변경되는 경우 그 날로부터 30일 이내에 작업환경 측정을 실시하고, 그 후 측정결과에 따라 6개월에 1회 이상 측정하여 시료채취를 마친 날부터 30일 이내에 지방노동관서에 보고하여야 한다(산안법 제125조).

(2) 건강진단

사업주는 정기적으로 근로자에 대한 건강진단을 실시하여야 한다. 근로자를 채용할 때에도 또한 같다(산안법 제129조).

1) 특수건강진단 대상업무에 종사하는 근로자의 경우 배치 전 건강진단, 특수건강진단, 수시건강진단, 임시건강진단을 실시하여야 한다.

2) 사무직에 종사하는 근로자는 2년에 1회 이상, 그밖에 근로자에 대하여는 1년에 1회 이상 '일반건강진단'을 실시하여야 한다.

3) 건강진단기관으로부터 특수건강진단 결과를 통보 받은 때는 근로자의 건강을 유지하기 위하여 필요한 조치를 한 후 지방노동관서에 보고하여야 한다.

(3) Prohibition or restriction of work for sick persons

For persons diagnosed with infectious disease or mental illness, or any other condition that can be aggravated by work, the business owner shall prohibit or restrict work according to the medical diagnosis. However, upon recovery, the business owner shall, without delay, permit the employee to resume their original work(Article 138).

(4) Extending working hours prohibited

The business owner shall not have an employee who is engaged in harmful or dangerous work working more than six hours per day or thirty-four hours per week(Article 139).

(5) Restriction of employment by qualification

The business owner shall not allow any persons other than those who have the qualifications, license, experience, and/or required skills, to perform harmful or dangerous work(Article 140).

(6) Documenting & keeping records

Documented records concerning appointment of safety and health personnel and the examinations on harmfulness and toxicity of new substances shall be kept for 3 years(internal inspection records shall be kept for 2 years). Records on working environment evaluations and employee medical examinations shall be kept for 5 years(Article 164).

(7) Enhanced penalties for employers for occupational accidents

1) Employers, contractees, and contractors who fail to comply with their safety or health care obligations and cause the death of any worker shall be punished by imprisonment for not more than seven years, or a fine not exceeding 100 million won. The offense is aggravated up to one-half of the sentence if the identical offense is repeated within 5 years(Article 167).

2) In case a worker dies due to a representative's or other worker's violation of safety or health care obligations, not only shall such offender be punished accordingly, but the corporation or contractor shall also be punished by a fine of up to 1 billion won(Joint penalty provision: Article 128).

3) If the court convicts a person for the death of a worker due to a violation of health and safety measures, he or she may have a 200-hour study-attendance order necessary to prevent industrial accidents in addition to the punishment(Article 174).

(3) 질병자의 취업 제한

사업주는 전염병·정신병 또는 근로로 인하여 병세가 현저히 악화될 우려가 있는 질병에 걸린 자에 대하여는 의사의 진단에 따라 근로를 금지하거나 제한하여야 한다. 그러나 근로자가 건강을 회복한 때는 사업주는 해당 근로자를 지체 없이 취업시켜야 한다(산안법 제138조).

(4) 유해·위험작업의 근로시간 연장제한

사업주는 유해·위험한 작업에 종사하는 근로자에 대하여는 1일 6시간, 1주 34시간을 초과해 근로는 금지된다(산안법 제139조).

(5) 자격 등에 의한 취업 제한

사업주는 유해 또는 위험한 작업에 있어서는 그 작업에 필요한 자격·면허·경험 또는 기능을 가진 근로자 외의 자를 취업하게 하여서는 아니 된다(산안법 제140조).

(6) 서류작성 및 보존

안전보건관계자 선임, 신규 화학물질 유해·위험성조사 관련서류는 3년간 보존하고 작업환경 측정결과 기록서류와 근로자 건강진단결과표 등 서류는 5년간 보존하여야 한다(산안법 제164조).

(7) 재해발생에 대한 사업주 강화된 처벌내용

1) 사업주, 수급인, 도급인도 안전조치나 보건조치 의무를 불이행하여 근로자를 사망에 이르게 한 경우 7년 이하의 징역 또는 1억원 이하의 벌금을 부과하되, 형을 선고받고 형이 확정된 후 5년 이내에 동일한 죄를 범한 경우 그 형의 2분의 1까지 가중된다(제167조).

2) 대표자나 그 밖의 종업원이 안전조치나 보건조치 의무를 위반하여 근로자가 사망한 경우 그 행위자를 벌하는 외에 그 법인사업주 또는 도입인에게 10억원 이하 벌금을 부과한다(양벌규정 제173조).

3) 법원이 안전보건조치 위반으로 근로자를 사망에 이르게 사람에게 유죄 판결 선고를 할 경우에는 200시간 범위에서 산업재해 예방에 필요한 수강명령을 부과할 수 있다(제174조).

Section 1-2. The Relationship between and the Occupational Safety and Health Act

Ⅰ. Introduction

The Serious Accidents Punishment Act (hereinafter referred to as the "SAPA") was enacted on January 8, 2021. The Occupational Safety and Health Act (hereinafter referred to as the "OSH Act" or "OSHA") was also completely revised from January 2020 to reduce fatal industrial accidents. However, as fatal accidents have not decreased, a Serious Accidents Punishment Act was introduced that is much stronger than the existing penal provisions of the OSH Act.[287] The Serious Accidents Punishment Act covers both major industrial accidents occurring on company premises as well as major fatal accidents/incidents out in society at large, such as the Sewol ferry accident and the air purifier disinfectant fatalities. The legislative purpose of this law is to punish employers, managers, and corporations for fatal accidents from actions in violation of the obligation to follow the mandatory measures to protect safety and health, so that companies can ① secure the workers' (and the general populations') right to safety, and ② prevent fatalities from negligent practices or a deficient safety management system.[288] This aims to protect workers and the general population from injury or death (Article 1 of the SAPA).

However, the current OSH Act requires that employers establish a management system for occupational safety and health, to take steps to prevent incidents with harmful/dangerous equipment, facilities, materials, working environment, etc., and at the same time to periodically provide workers with the necessary safety and health education to further work to reduce industrial accidents. In cases where an employer is found to have violated the Serious Accidents Punishment Act, the employer will be punished immediately, to further incentivize other employers to make it a habit to protect occupational safety and health and work to avoid accidents. The Serious Accidents Punishment Act is a punitive law that imposes strong penalties on business owners whose workplaces have been the site of a fatal incident, while the OSH Act is a preventative law against industrial accidents.

---

287) Safety Journal, "The obligation to secure safety and health of employers has been further strengthened", Jan. 15, 2021; Daily Labor News, "[The total amended Occupational Safety and Health Act is insufficient] The number of deaths from industrial accidents increased in 2020", Jan. 5, 2021: Industrial accident fatalities did not decrease between 2018 and 2020 (971, 855 and 860, respectively).

288) Proposer: Chairman of the Legal Affairs and Judicial Council of the National Assembly, Reasons for the legislative proposal in "Draft of a Serious Accidents Punishment Act", Jan. 2021.

제1절의 2. 중대재해처벌법과 산업안전보건법과의 관계

Ⅰ. 의 의

중대재해처벌에 관한 법률(이하 "중대재해처벌법") 2021년 1월 8일 제정되었다. 산업안전보건법(이하 "산안법")도 2020년 1월부터 전면개정 되어 중대산업재해를 예방하고 있음에도 불구하고 중대재해가 줄어들지 않자 기존의 처벌조항보다 훨씬 강력한 중대재해처벌법을 도입하게 되었다.[287] 중대재해 처벌법은 기업에서 발생하는 중대 산업재해뿐만 아니라 세월호 참사, 가습기 살균제 참사와 같은 사회적 참사인 중대시민재해까지 포함하고 있다. 이 법의 입법취지는 안전보건 조치의무를 위반하여 인명사고가 발생한 중대재해에 대해 사업주와 경영책임자, 그리고 법인을 처벌함으로써 ①근로자를 포함한 종사자와 일반시민의 안전권을 확보하고, ②기업의 조직문화 또는 안전관리 시스템 미비로 인해 일어나는 중대재해사고를 사전에 방지하는데 있다.[288] 이를 통해 근로자와 시민들의 생명과 신체를 보호하는 것을 목적으로 한다(법제1조).

현행 산안법은 사업주가 산업재해를 사전에 예방하기 위해 산업안전 · 보건의 관리체계를 갖추고 유해·위험한 기구, 시설, 물질, 작업환경 등에 대해 예방조치를 취하고, 동시에 근로자들에게 안전과 보건에 관한 교육을 주기적으로 실시하도록 의무를 부과하고 있다. 즉 사업주가 산안법을 위반한 경우, 즉시 처벌하도록 하여 사업장에서 산업안전보건 예방활동이 생활화되도록 그 준수의무를 엄격히 부과하고 있는 것이다. 따라서 산안법은 산재사고를 예방하기 위한 사전적 예방조치를 위한 법이고, 중대재해처벌법은 중대재해를 야기한 사업주에 대해 강력한 처벌을 하기 위한 사후 처벌법이라 할 수 있다.

이에 중대재해처벌법과 산업안전보건법의 비교를 통해 중대재해처벌법의 목적과 역할을 이해하고 두 법의 상호관계에 대해 구체적으로 살펴보고자 한다.

---

287) 안전저널, "사업주의 안전보건 확보의무 한층 강화됐다", 2021.1.15 보도; 매일노동뉴스, "[전부개정 산업안전보건법 역부족] 2020년 산재사고 사망자 늘었다", 2021.1.5. 보도: 산업재해 사망사고 2018년 971명, 2019년 855명, 2020년 860명으로 줄지 않음.

288) 제안자: 법제사법위원장, "중대재해의 처벌 등에 관한 법률안"에서 입법제안 이유, 2021. 1.

The purpose of the Serious Accidents Punishment Act will be better understood through comparison with the Occupational Safety and Health Act. I will also look at the relationship between the two laws in detail.

II. The Concept of Fatal Accident and Duties of the Employer

1. Concept of fatal accident

Fatal accidents as stipulated in the Serious Accidents Punishment Act, are accidents where ① one or more deaths have occurred, ② two or more persons are injured and require treatment for six months or more due to the same accident, or ③ three persons contract an occupational illness (such as acute poisoning) due to the same hazard within one year (Article 2 of the SAPA).[289] The OSH Act specifies fatal industrial accidents as the following: ① one or more deaths have occurred, ② two or more people are injured at the same time and require at least 3 months of medical care, or ③ 10 or more people are injured or contract an occupational illness at the same time (Article 2 of the OSH Act, Article 3 of the Enforcement Regulations). Therefore, it can be seen that the SAPA and the OSHA have similar definitions of "fatal accident."

2. The scope of application and responsibilities of employers

The Serious Accidents Punishment Act does not apply to workplaces with fewer than five regular workers (Article 3 of the SAPA). However, the OSH Act applies to all workplaces. All or part of the law may not apply in consideration of the degree of harm or risk, business type and size, and business location. In general, some provisions are excluded for ① pure administrative work, educational service work, foreign institutions, ② workplaces using only white-collar workers, and ③ workplaces employing fewer than five regular workers (Article 3 of the OSH Act, Article 2-2 of its Enforcement Decree, Appendix 1). The difference in scope of application is that the OSH Act describes all required occupational safety and health measures for the entire workplace, while the Serious Accidents Punishment Act is limited to fatal and other serious accidents.

---

289) The Serious Accidents Punishment Act is divided into fatal industrial accidents and fatal civil accidents. A fatal civil accident is an accident ① caused by defects in design, manufacture, installation, or management of specific raw materials or products, public facilities or public transportation means, ② in which 10 or more people are injured and require medical care, or ③ 10 or people become sick and need treatment for at least 3 months due to the same cause (Article 2 of the SAPA, section 2).

Ⅱ. 중대재해 개념과 사업주의 의무

1. 중대재해의 개념

중대재해처벌법에서 정한 중대재해라고 하면 사망자가 1명 이상 발생하거나 동일한 사고로 6개월 이상 치료가 필요한 부상자가 2명 이상 발생 또는 동일한 유해요인으로 급성중독 등 직업성 질병자가 1년 이내 3명 이상 발생한 재해를 말한다(법제2조2호).[289] 산안법에서 정한 중대산업재해는 산업재해 중 사망 등 재해 정도가 심하거나 다수의 재해자가 발생한 경우로 사망자가 1명 이상 발생한 재해이거나 3개월 이상 요양이 필요한 부상자가 동시에 2명 이상 발생한 재해 또는 부상자 또는 직업성 질병자가 동시에 10명 이상 발생한 재해로 기술하고 있다(법제2조, 시행규칙제3조). 따라서 중대재해처벌법과 산안법에서 정한 중대재해에 대한 정의는 유사하다고 볼 수 있다.

2. 적용범위와 사업주의 책임범위

중대재해처벌법은 상시 근로자가 5인 미만인 사업장에는 적용되지 않는다(법제3조). 그러나 산안법은 모든 사업장에 적용된다. 다만, 유해·위험의 정도, 사업의 종류·규모 및 사업의 소재지 등을 고려하여 법의 전부 또는 일부를 적용하지 아니한다. 일반적으로 ① 순수행정업무, 교육서비스 업무, 외국기관, ② 사무직 근로자만을 사용하는 사업장, ③ 상시 근로자 5명 미만을 사용하는 사업장은 법의 일부를 적용하지 않고 있다(산안법 제3조, 영 제2조의2 및 별표1). 산안법은 사업장의 산업전반에 관한 산업안전보건조치를 기술한데 비해, 중대재해처벌법은 중대재해에만 국한되어 있다.

중대재해처벌법과 산안법 모두 보호대상자가 근로기준법상의 근로자 뿐만 아니라 근로를 제공하는 자로 폭넓게 보고 있다. 이는 ①「근로기준법」상의 근로

289) 중대재해처벌법은 중대산업재해와 중대시민재해로 구분하고 있다. 중대시민재해는 특정 원료 또는 제조물, 공중이용시설 또는 공중교통수단의 설계, 제조, 설치, 관리상의 결함을 원인으로 하여 발생한 재해로 ①사망자가 1명 이상 발생, ②동일한 사고로 2개월 이상 치료가 필요한 부상자가 10명 이상 발생, ③동일한 원인으로 3개월 이상 치료가 필요한 질병자가 10명 이상 발생하는 재해를 말한다(법제2조3호).

In both the Serious Accidents Punishment Act and the Occupational Safety and Health Act, persons protected goes beyond only workers as defined in the Labor Standards Act, to include all those who provide work. This includes ① workers as defined in the Labor Standards Act, ② those who provide labor for the purpose of income for the execution of business, regardless of type of employment relationship, such as contract, service-based, or consignment, and ③ all contractors at each level in a multi-contract project (Article 2 (7) of the SAPA).

In the Serious Accidents Punishment Act, the person responsible for reducing the risk of fatal accidents is specified as the employer and head of operations (Articles 3 and 4 of the SAPA). "Employer" refers to a person who runs his or her own business or a person who conducts business by receiving the labor of others (Article 2 (8) of the SAPA). The head of operations refers to a person who has the authority and responsibility to represent the business and is in charge of it, or a person who is in charge of safety and health related to work (Article 2 (9) of the SAPA).

However, while the OSH Act places on employers the duty to maintain and promote worker safety and health, the implementation of specific safety and health management responsibilities can be delegated to a person (the safety and health manager) who substantially supervises site offices, factories and etc. (Articles 5, 15, 38, 39 of the OSHA). Accordingly, when an accident occurs at an actual workplace, legal sanctions are imposed mainly on the general manager in charge of safety and health, such as the site manager and the plant manager, rather than the representative director.

3. Employer's obligations

The Serious Accidents Punishment Act stipulates the obligation of the employer to take actions to protect safety and health, and provides for severe penalties for fatal accidents due to the employer violating his or her obligations. In the event that a fatal accident occurs because of a violation of the obligation to protect safety, penalties will be imposed. Conversely, if the employer fulfills his or her duty to put safety and health measures in place, penalties can be avoided.

Employers and heads of operations must establish a safety and health management system to reduce risk and hazards to safety and health in workplaces that are substantially controlled, operated, and managed, and take measures to prevent recurrence in the event a fatal accident occurs (Article 4 of the SAPA). Actions to protect safety and health shall also be taken when subcontracting, servicing, or entrusting a third party to engage in the required work, to prevent fatal industrial accidents from occurring among third party employees. However, this is limited to cases where the employer, corporation, or institution is substantially responsible for controlling, operating, and managing the facility, equipment, and place where the third party employees are working (Article 5

자, ② 도급, 용역, 위탁 등 계약의 형식에 관계없이 그 사업의 수행을 위하여 대가를 목적으로 노무를 제공하는 자, ③사업이 여러 차례의 도급에 따라 행하여지는 경우에는 각 단계의 수급인까지 포함한다(법제2조7호).

중대재해처벌법에서는 중대재해에 대해 책임의 주체를 사업주와 경영책임자로 명시하고 있다(법제3조,제4조). 사업주라 하면 자신의 사업을 영위하는 자, 타인의 노무를 제공받아 사업을 하는 자를 말한다(법제2조8호). 그리고 경영책임자라고 하면 사업을 대표하고 사업을 총괄하는 권한과 책임이 있는 사람 또는 이에 준하여 안전보건에 관한 업무를 담당하는 사람을 말한다(법제2조9호)

그러나 산안법은 사업주에게 근로자의 안전과 건강을 유지 증진시킬 의무를 부여하면서도 구체적인 안전보건관리 책임의 이행에 관하여는 현장사업소, 공장 등 사업장을 실질적으로 총괄하는 사람(안전보건관리책임자)에게 위임할 수 있도록 규정되어 있다(산안법 제5조, 제15조, 제38조, 제39조). 이에 따라 실제 사업장에서 안전사고가 발생할 경우에 대표이사가 아닌 현장소장, 공장장 등 현장의 안전보건 관리책임자 위주로 법적 제재가 이루어지고 있다.

3. 사업주의 의무

중대재해처벌법은 사업주의 안전보건조치 의무를 명시하고 있고 이를 위반하여 발생한 중대재해에 대하여 엄벌에 처하고 있는데 이는 중대재해가 발생하였다고 해서 무조건 사업주를 처벌하는 것이 아니라, 사업주와 경영책임자가 안전 및 보건 확보의무를 위반해 중대재해가 발생한 경우에 처벌을 받게 되는 것이다. 따라서 사업주가 안전보건조치 의무를 다한 경우에는 처벌을 면할 수 있다.

사업주와 경영책임자는 실질적으로 지배·운영·관리하는 사업장에서 종사자의 안전·보건상 유해 또는 위험을 방지하기 위해 안전보건관리체계의 구축하고, 재해 발생 시 재발방지 대책의 수립 등의 조치를 해야 한다(법제4조). 또한 제3자에게 도급, 용역, 위탁 등을 할 때에는 제3자의 종사자에게 중대산업재해가 발생하지 않도록 안전보건 상의 조치를 이행하여야 한다. 다만 이 경우에는 사업주나 법인 또는 기관이 그 시설, 장비, 장소 등에 대하여 실질적으로 지배·운영·관리하는 책임이 있는 경우에 한정한다(법제5조).

산안법에서 사업주는 중대재해가 발생하였을 때는 즉시 해당 작업을 중지시

of the SAPA).

Under the OSH Act, when a fatal accident occurs, the employer must immediately stop the related work and take steps necessary to protect the safety and health of other workers, such as evacuating the workplace. In addition, the employer must immediately report to the Minister of Employment and Labor when he/she becomes aware that a fatal accident has occurred (Article 54 of the OSHA). When a fatal accident occurs, the Minister of Employment and Labor can order all work to stop in relation to ① the job in which the fatal accident occurred, ② the job(s) corresponding to the job in which the fatal accident occurred, if it is determined that there is an imminent risk of recurrence at that workplace. Upon request of the employer whose work has been suspended, the Minister of Employment and Labor shall lift the suspension of work after decision by a deliberation committee composed of experts on cancellations of work suspensions (Article 55 of the OSH Act). In accordance with the revised OSH Act (January 2020), the Minister of Employment and Labor shall issue an order to suspend work to a workplace where a fatal accident has occurred. Work can be resumed at the workplace only after a considerable period of time has elapsed, which places a significant burden on the company.

Ⅲ. Penalties and Employer's Responsibilities

1. Penalties for employer and head of operations

The Serious Accidents Punishment Act applies stronger penalties for fatal accidents than the OSH Act, with fines up to 10 times higher. If at least one person dies due to a violation of the safety and health measures by the employer or head of operations, the employer or head of operations will be sentenced to imprisonment for at least one year or a fine of not more than KRW 1 billion. Penalties are also imposed for injuries or occupational illness. If two or more persons are injured and require treatment for at least six months due to the same accident, or if three or more persons contract an occupational illness within one year due to the same hazards, the employer and/or head of operations shall be sentenced to imprisonment for no more than 7 years or a fine imposed of not more than KRW 100 million won. (Article 6 (2) of the SAPA). If the same type of fatal accident recurs within five years, the penalties are levied again but increase by half (Article 6 (3) of the SAPA). In addition, the person in charge of corporate management at that workplace must attend and complete safety and health education. If the education is not completed without justifiable reason, a fine of not more than KRW 50 million is imposed (Article 8 of the SAPA).

키고 근로자를 작업장소에서 대피시키는 등 안전 및 보건에 관하여 필요한 조치를 하여야 한다. 또한 사업주는 중대재해가 발생한 사실을 알게 된 경우 지체 없이 고용노동부 장관에게 보고하여야 한다(산안법 제54조). 고용노동부 장관은 중대재해가 발생하였을 때 ①중대재해가 발생한 해당 작업, ②중대재해가 발생한 작업과 동일한 작업에 해당하는 작업으로 인하여 해당 사업장에 산업재해가 다시 발생할 급박한 위험이 있다고 판단되는 경우에는 그 작업의 중지를 명할 수 있다. 고용노동부 장관은 사업주가 그 사업장의 작업중지의 해제를 요청한 경우에는 작업중지 해제에 관한 전문가 등으로 구성된 심의위원회의 심의를 거쳐 작업중지를 해제하여야 한다(산안법 제55조). 고용노동부는 개정된 산안법에 따라 2020년 1월 이후로 중대재해가 발생한 사업장의 경우 작업중지 명령을 내리고 상당한 시일이 지난 후 에야 비로소 사업주가 그 해당 작업장에 작업을 재개할 수 있어 기업체에 많은 부담을 주고 있다.

Ⅲ. 처벌내용과 사업주의 책임

1. 사업주와 경영책임자의 처벌

중대재해처벌법은 중대재해에 대한 처벌 수준을 기존의 산안법에 비해 더욱 더 엄격하게 적용하고 있으며, 특히 벌금의 경우 최대 10배나 높다. 안전보건조치 의무 위반으로 사망자가 1명이상 발생한 경우에 사업주 또는 경영책임자는 1년 이상의 징역 또는 10억원 이하의 벌금에 처해진다. 부상이나 직업병 질병자가 발생한 경우에도 처벌된다. 동일한 사고로 6개월 이상 치료가 필요한 부상자가 2명 이상 발생한 경우와 동일한 유해요인으로 직업성 질병자가 1년 이내에 3명 이상 발생한 경우 사업주와 경영책임자는 7년 이하의 징역 또는 1억원 이하의 벌금에 처해진다(법제6조제2항). 또한 동일한 중대재해가 5년 이내에 다시 발생한 경우에는 기존의 처벌의 2분의 1까지 가중한다(법제6조제3항). 그리고 중대재해가 발생한 법인의 경영책임자는 안전보건교육을 이수하여야 한다. 정당한 사유없이 교육을 이수하지 아니한 경우에는 5천만원 이하의 과태료가 부과된다(법제8조).

A person who causes the death of a worker for violating the obligation to take measures for occupational safety and health under the OSH Act shall be punished by imprisonment for not more than 7 years or a fine not exceeding KRW 100 million. If the same type of fatal accident recurs, the punishment is levied again, but also increased by half (Article 167 of the OSH Act).

2. Joint penal provisions

The Serious Accidents Punishment Act imposes a fine of not more than KRW 5 billion won for corporations and up to KRW 1 billion won for injuries or occupational illness. However, if a corporation has taken considerable care and supervision to prevent violation but a fatal accident still occurred, no fine will be imposed (Article 7 of the SAPA). The OSH Act imposes a fine of not more than KRW 1 billion on corporations for the same case where one person or more has died due in a fatal accident (Article 173 of the OSHA). The Serious Accidents Punishment Act has strengthened penalties at least fivefold over the existing OSH Act.

3. Punitive damage compensation

The Serious Accidents Punishment Act introduces a punitive damage compensation system that is not found in the OSH Act. In the event that an employer or head of operations intentionally or by gross negligence violates the obligation to take measures to protect safety and health and this results in a fatal accident, the relevant employer or corporation shall be held liable for compensation not exceeding 5 times the damage suffered by the injured person, or the survivors. However, this does not apply if the accident occurs despite the corporation having given considerable attention and supervision of the relevant risks and hazards (Article 15 of the SAPA). The courts shall decide the amount of punitive damage compensation in consideration of the following seven items: ① the severity of intentional or unintentional negligence, ② the type and details of the violation of the obligation to protect, ③ the scale of the damage caused by violation of the obligation to protect, ④ the economic benefit obtained by the employer or the corporation due to violation of the obligation to protect, ⑤ the duration and number of violations, ⑥ the corporation's property holdings, and ⑦ the extent of the corporation's efforts to mitigate the damage and prevent recurrence.

As there has been no punitive damage compensation system so far, damages have been based only on calculations of the amount of compensation for industrial accidents and civil damages. According to this method, when a worker dies from an industrial accident, the company handles it through industrial accident compensation insurance and is not held liable for compensation. However, if the

산안법에서 산업안전보건 조치의무를 위반하여 근로자를 사망하게 한 자는 7년 이하의 징역 또는 1억원 이하의 벌금에 처한다. 그리고 동일한 중대재해가 발생한 경우 그 형의 2분의 1까지 가중된다(산안법제167조).

2. 양벌 규정

중대재해처벌법은 중대재해로 1명 이상 사망한 재해에 대해서는 법인은 50억원 이하의 벌금, 부상자나 직업병 발생 시에는 10억원 이하의 벌금이 부과된다. 다만, 법인이 그 위반 행위를 방지하기 위해 상당한 주의와 감독을 한 경우에는 벌금이 부과되지 않는다(법제7조). 산안법은 중대재해로 인해 1명이상 사망한 동일한 사안에 대해 법인에 10억원 이하의 벌금을 부과하고 있다(산안법제173조). 중대재해처벌법의 처벌 수위가 기존법에 비해 5배 이상 강화되었다고 할 수 있다.

3. 징벌적 손해배상

중대재해처벌법에는 산업법에 없는 징벌적 손해배상제도를 도입하였다. 사업주 또는 경영책임자가 고의 또는 중대한 과실로 안전보건 조치 의무를 위반하여 중대재해를 발생하게 한 경우, 해당 사업주 또는 법인이 중대재해로 손해를 입은 사람에 대하여 그 손해액의 5배를 넘지 않는 범위에서 배상책임을 진다. 다만, 법인이 해당 업무에 대해 상당한 주의와 감독을 한 경우에는 적용되지 않는다(법제15조). 이 징벌적 손해배상의 경우에 법원은 다음의 7가지를 고려하여 배상액을 결정한다. ① 고의 또는 중대한 과실의 정도, ② 의무 위반행위의 종류 및 내용, ③ 의무 위반행위로 인하여 발생한 피해의 규모, ④ 의무 위반행위로 인하여 사업주나 법인이 취득한 경제적 이익, ⑤ 의무 위반행위의 기간·횟수, ⑥ 법인의 재산상태, ⑦ 법인의 피해구제 및 재발방지 노력의 정도 등이다.

현행까지는 징벌적 손해배상제도가 없었기 때문에 산재보상과 민사상 손해배상액을 기준으로만 손해배상액을 산정하였다. 기존의 방식을 보면, 근로자가 산재 사망한 경우 회사는 산업재해보상보험으로 처리하고, 그 보상책임을 면하

company is liable for negligence in the event of a worker's death, such as due to a lack of safety measures, the company shall be liable for damages under the Civil Act in addition to compensation from the workers' industrial accident compensation insurance to the survivors. The scope of compensation provided under he Civil Act refers to all damages to the injured person/survivors in relation to the company's negligence and considerable causality, with the range of damage recognized by court rulings divided into active, passive, and mental damage. In general, when a worker dies, the scope of passive loss include income (lost income from the time of death to what would have been the time of retirement) and retirement allowance (loss of severance pay due to early termination of employment). Funeral expenses are active damage, while any alimony is included in mental damage.

In the future, it will be possible to request up to 5 times the amount of compensation for existing damages available under he Civil Act when industrial accidents result in death. As a result, the bereaved family and the company will need to engage in a prolonged period of determination of compensation for the bereaved due to disputes over whether an employer was negligent or not, which will act as a considerable burden on the company's ability to quickly handle the aftermath of fatal accidents.[290)]

IV. Implementation Date and Application

The Serious Accidents Punishment Act has a grace period of one year and comes into effect on January 1, 2022. For workplaces with fewer than 50 regularly hired workers (or construction companies engaged in an average project value of less than KRW 5 billion), there is a three-year grace period, meaning the Act comes into effect on January 1, 2024.

Fatal accidents are classified in the SAPA as fatal industrial accidents and fatal civil accidents. Major industrial accidents are handled by Ministry of Employment and Labor inspectors, who investigate the situation for workers and contractors who are directed and supervised by the employer concerned. Since a fatal civil accident involves members of the public who are using a facility or public mode of transportation, the Ministry of Justice, through police officers, has jurisdiction. Therefore, since the two different ministries have jurisdiction over fatal accidents separately, differences in interpretation and disposition of the law are expected in its enforcement, leading to some confusion.[291)]

290) Chung, Daewon. "Major Details and Topics in the Serious Accidents Punishment Act," HR Insight, Jan. 11, 2021.
291) FKI press release, "Concerns about side effects of the Serious Accidents Punishment Act," Jan. 1, 2021.

게 하였다. 그러나 근로자의 사망에 있어 회사의 안전조치 미흡 등 회사의 과실 책임이 있는 경우에는 회사가 유족에게 산재보상 외에 민사상 손해배상 책임을 져야 한다. 민사상 손해배상의 범위는 회사의 과실과 상당인과관계에 있는 재해자의 모든 손해를 말하며, 판례에서 인정하는 손해배상의 범위는 적극적손해, 소극적손해, 정신적손해로 구분하고 있다. 일반적으로 근로자가 사망한 경우, 그 범위는 소극적 손해로 일실수입(사망한 시점에서 퇴직시점까지의 잃게 된 수입금)과 일실퇴직금 (조기퇴직으로 인해 발생하는 퇴직금 손해액), 적극적 손해로서의 장례비, 그리고 정신적 손해비용인 위자료로 구성되어 있다.

앞으로 산업현장에서 발생한 산재사망사건에 있어 기존의 민사상 손해배상액에 추가로 5배까지도 요구할 수 있게 되었다. 이로 인해 유족과 회사는 사업주의 과실에 대한 다툼으로 유족보상금 확정이 장기화 될 것이고 이것은 기업체에 상당한 부담으로 작용할 것이다.[290)]

Ⅳ. 시행시기와 적용

중대재해처벌법은 1년의 유예기간을 두고 있어 2022년 1월부터 적용된다. 또한 상시근로자 50인 미만의 사업장의 경우 (건설업의 경우 50억원 미만의 공사)에 대해서는 3년의 유예기간을 두고 있어 2024년 1월부터 적용된다.

중대재해처벌법에서의 중대재해는 중대산업재해와 중대시민재해로 구분된다. 중대산업재해는 고용노동부의 근로감독관이 맡게 되고, 적용대상은 근로자와 그 사업의 지시와 감독을 받는 종사자가 된다. 중대시민재해의 대상은 시설을 이용하는 일반 시민이 되므로 이를 관할하는 것은 법무부 소속의 일반 사법경찰관이 된다. 따라서 2개의 서로 다른 부처가 중대재해를 나누어서 관할하기 때문에 법의 집행에 있어 법의해석과 처분에 차이가 예상되어 다소 혼란이 예상된다.[291)]

---

290) 정대원, "중대재해처벌법 주요 내용 및 이슈", HR Insight, 2021. 1. 11.

291) 전경련 보도자료, "중대재해기업처벌법 부작용 우려", 2021.1.6.

Section 1-3. The Serious Accidents Punishment Act and Employer Obligations

Ⅰ. Introduction

The Occupational Safety and Health Act (hereinafter referred to as the "OSH Act") was completely revised in January 2020 to prevent fatalities and other serious industrial accidents that regularly occur at industrial sites, but fails to significantly contribute to preventing serious accidents. This is because, in an industrial accident, only the site manager responsible for the safety of the work site is punished. The employer, who is actually responsible for the project escapes responsibility, because it is next to impossible to prove an employer is intentionally negligent under criminal law.[292] Korea's Supreme Court denied the charge of manslaughter against an employer for occupational negligence when the onsite director was supervising construction at the site, and determined that a worker killed in an accident at work was not under the supervision of the employer during construction.[293] In fact, if employers remain unpunished, awareness of the risk of industrial accidents will remain inadequate, and employers will remain less willing to invest in the personnel, funding, and effort necessary to prevent industrial accidents.

On April 29, 2020, 38 workers died and approximately 10 workers were injured during a fire at the Icheon Logistics Warehouse construction site. This was shocking news, and resulted in passage of the Act on the Penalty of Fatal Accidents (hereinafter referred to as the "Serious Accidents Punishment Act" or "SAPA") on January 26, 2021. The SAPA will come into effect January 27, 2022, after a one-year grace period. However, businesses with fewer than 5 employees will remain exempt, while businesses with 6-49 employees will have a three-year grace period (until January 2024).

The purpose of the SAPA is "to stipulate the punishment of employers, business managers, civil servants and corporations, etc. to prevent accidents and protect the lives

---

292) Kwon, Hyuk. "Legal Systemic Status and Legislative Policy Significance of the Serious Accidents Punishment Act," Labor Law Forum (34), Labor Law Theory and Practical Society, November 2021, p. 4.

293) Supreme Court ruling on Nov. 24, 1989: 89do1618.

제1절의 3. 중대재해 처벌법과 사업주의 대응방안

I. 의 의

산업현장에서 끊임없이 발생하는 사망사고 등의 중대 산업재해를 예방하기 위해서 2020년 1월에 산업안전보건법(이하 "산안법")이 전면 개정되었지만, 중대재해를 예방하는데 큰 기여를 하지 못하고 있다. 그 이유는 산재사고가 발생한 경우에 작업현장의 안전을 책임진 담당자만 처벌되었지 죄형법정주의와 사업주의 고의과실을 입증할 수 없다는 이유로 사업주는 형사처벌을 받지 않기 때문이다.[292] 산재 사고에 대해 대법원은 현장소장이 현장에서 공사감독을 하였고, 그 공사에 관하여 대표이사의 관리감독을 받지 않는 근로자가 작업중 사고를 당한 경우 대표이사의 업무상 과실치사죄를 부정하였다.[293] 사실상, 대표이사가 처벌을 받지 않는 이상 산재사고에 대한 경각심이 부족하고, 산재예방에 필요한 인원, 예산, 노력 등이 부족할 수 밖에 없다.

2020년 4월 29일, 이천 물류창고 건설현장 화재 사고로 인하여 38명이 사망하고 10여명이 부상을 당한 사고가 발생하여 사회적으로 중대재해에 대한 경각심을 심어주었다. 이러한 중대산업재해를 예방하기 위해 국회는 2021년 1월 26일 중대재해 처벌 등에 관한 법률(이하 "중대재해처벌법")을 제정하였다. 이 법은 1년 간의 유예를 두고 2022년 1월 27일에 시행된다. 다만, 5인 미만 사업장은 적용이 제외되고, 50인 미만 사입장은 다시 3년의 유예를 두어 2024년 1월부터 전면 시행된다.

이 중대재해처벌법의 목적은 "사업 또는 사업장에서 인체에 해로운 원료나 제조물을 취급하면서 안전·보건 조치의무를 위반하여 인명피해를 발생하게 한 사업주, 경영책임자 공무원 및 법인의 처벌 등을 규정함으로써 중대재해를 예방하고 종사자의 생명과 신체를 보호하는 것이다." 즉, 중대재해처벌법은 사업주의 안전조치 미흡으로 인하여 발생한 중대재해에 대해 사업주나 경영책임자

292) 권혁, "중대재해처벌법의 법체계적 지위와 입법정책적 의의", 노동법포럼(34), 노동법이론 실무학회, 2021. 11. 4면.

293) 대법원 1989.11.24. 선고 89도1618 판결.

and health of workers." In other words, it seeks to prevent industrial accidents through strict punishment for inadequate safety measures at a place of employment. In order for an employer to avoid liability for a serious industrial accident, they must fulfill the safety and health obligations required by this Act and the Enforcement Decree as well as the safety and health measures under the OSH Act. In this regard, I would like to take a detailed look at the specific details and applied practices.

II. Main Details of the Serious Accidents Punishment Act

The SAPA consists of four chapters and 16 articles, covering general rules, serious industrial accidents, serious civil accidents, and supplementary rules.

1. Understanding the key definitions

Some terms used in this law are different from other laws.

1) "Serious industrial accident" refers to an accident resulting in (i) one or more fatalities, (ii) two or more persons injured in the same accident and requiring treatment for at least six months, (iii) three or more people in the accident becoming ill and requiring treatment for three months or longer for the same cause. In the OSH Act, serious accidents were defined in the enforcement regulations of the OSH Act, and so there was some ambiguity, but in the SAPA, the definition of serious accidents is clearly explained in the Act.

2) "Employee" refers to (i) a worker as defined in the Labor Standards Act, (ii) a person who provides labor in return for reward for the purpose of operation of the business, regardless of the type of contract, such as subcontract, service, or consignment. Their protection was more extended than workers under the Labor Standards Act. The term "employer" has also been expanded to include those who run their own business and those who are provided with the labor of others.

3) "Business manager, etc." refers to a person who has a relationship of equal responsibility with the employer, and who has the authority to represent the business and responsibility for its management, or a person in charge of safety and health-related tasks equivalent thereto. In other words, "employer" refers to actual owners of the company and those with the authority to make company-wide decisions.

까지도 엄격하게 처벌함으로써 산업재해를 예방하기 위한 법이다. 중대산업재해가 발생하더라도 사업주가 책임을 면하기 위해서는 산안법상의 안전과 보건 조치뿐만 아니라 사업주로서 이 법과 시행령에서 요구하는 안전보건확보의무를 이행하여야 한다. 이에 대해 구체적인 내용과 실천 사항에 대해 구체적으로 살펴보고자 한다.

Ⅱ. 중대재해처벌법의 주요 내용

이 법은 총칙, 중대산업재해, 중대시민재해, 보칙 등 총 4개의 장, 16개의 조항으로 구성되어 있다.

1. 주요 개념 이해

이 법에서 거론되는, 타 법과는 다른 의미를 지니고 있는 몇 가지의 주요용어를 살펴보자.

1) "중대산업재해"라고 하면 (i) 사망자가 1명 이상 발생, (ii) 동일한 사고로 6개월 이상 치료가 필요한 부상자가 2명 이상 발생, (iii) 동일한 원인으로 3개월 이상 치료가 필요한 질병자가 3명 이상 발생한 경우를 말한다. 산안법의 중대재해의 경우에는 시행규칙으로 정하여 모호한 부분이 있었지만, 중대재해처벌법에서는 법문으로 정해 중대산업재해의 개념을 명확히 하고 있다.

2) "종사자"라고 하면 (i) 근로기준법상의 근로자, (ii) 도급, 용역, 위탁 등 계약의 형식에 관계없이 그 사업의 수행을 위하여 대가를 목적으로 노무를 제공하는 자 등이다. 이는 산안법의 근로기준법상의 근로자보다 그 보호대상이 확대되었다. 따라서 "사업주"의 개념도 자신의 사업을 영위하는 자와 타인의 노무를 제공받아 사업을 하는 자로 확대되었다.

3) "경영책임자등"이란 사업주와 대등한 책임관계를 가지고 있는 자를 말하며, 사업을 대표하고 사업을 총괄하는 권한과 책임이 있는 사람 또는 이에 준하는 안전보건에 관한 업무를 담당하는 사람을 말한다. 즉, 회사의 대표이사나 실질적인 소유주를 말한다.

2. Obligations of employers and business managers to secure safety and health (Article 4)

An employer or business manager shall work to protect the safety and health of workers in the business or workplace they control, operate, or manage, in consideration of the business or workplace scale and characteristics. Specifically, they are responsible for: (i) Ensuring the establishment and implementation of a safety and health management system, including the necessary personnel and funding to prevent serious accidents; (ii) Ensuring orders from the local government for improvement, correction, etc., are followed in accordance with relevant laws and regulations; (iii) Taking the administrative measures necessary to fulfill their obligations under relevant laws and regulations related to safety and health, and (iv) Measures necessary for fulfillment of obligations under safety and health related laws and regulations. Parts (i) and (iv) above are explained in detail in the Enforcement Decree to the Serious Accidents Punishment Act.

3. Details on punishment of employers and business managers when serious industrial accidents occur

(1) Punishment of employers and business managers

If the employer or business manager is found to be responsible for the violation of safety and health requirements in the SAPA, resulting in an accident that kills one or more persons, the employer or business manager shall be subject to a minimum one year of imprisonment or a fine of not more than KRW 1 billion. Penalties are also imposed for injuries or occupational illness. If two or more persons are injured and require treatment for at least six months due to the same accident, or if three or more persons suffer an occupational illness within one year due to the same hazards, the employer or business manager shall be subject to imprisonment of a maximum 7 years imprisonment or a fine of not more than KRW 100 million (Article 6 (2)). If the same type of fatal accident recurs within five years, the penalties shall be increased by 50% (Article 6 (3)). In addition, the person in charge of corporate management at that workplace must attend and complete safety and health education. If the person in charge of corporate management fails to complete the education without justifiable reason, a fine of not more than KRW 50 million shall be imposed (Article 8 of the SAPA, Article 6 of the Enforcement Decree).

2. 사업주와 경영책임자의 안전과 보건 확보의무 (제4조)

사업주 또는 경영책임자는 사업주나 법인이 실질적으로 지배·운영·관리하는 사업 또는 사업장에서 종사자의 안전·보건상 유해 또는 위험을 방지하기 위하여 그 사업 또는 사업장의 특성 및 규모 등을 고려하여 안전과 보건 확보의무 조치를 이행하여야 한다. 세부 조치내용은 다음과 같다.

(i) 재해예방에 필요한 인력 및 예산 등 안전보건관리체계의 구축 및 그 이행에 관한 조치, (ii) 재해 발생 시 재발방지 대책의 수립 및 그 이행에 관한 조치, (iii) 중앙행정기관·지방자치단체가 관계 법령에 따라 개선, 시정 등을 명한 사항의 이행에 관한 조치, (iv) 안전·보건 관계 법령에 따른 의무이행에 필요한 관리상의 조치. 앞에서 밑줄 친 (i)과 (iv)은 시행령에서 구체적으로 설명하고 있다.

3. 중대산업재해 사업주와 경영책임자의 처벌 내용

(1) 사업주와 경영책임자의 처벌

안전보건조치 의무 위반으로 사망자가 1명 이상 발생한 경우에 사업주 또는 경영책임자는 1년 이상의 징역 또는 10억원 이하의 벌금에 처해진다. 부상이나 직업병 질병자가 발생한 경우에도 처벌된다. 동일한 사고로 6개월 이상 치료가 필요한 부상자가 2명 이상 발생한 경우와 동일한 유해원인으로 직업성 질병자가 1년 이내 3명 이상 발생한 경우 사업주와 경영책임자는 7년 이하의 징역 또는 1억원 이하의 벌금에 처해진다(법 제6조 제2항). 또한 동일한 중대재해가 5년 이내에 다시 발생한 경우에는 기존의 처벌의 2분의 1까지 가중한다(법 제6조 제3항). 그리고 중대재해가 발생한 법인의 경영책임자는 안전보건교육을 이수하여야 한다. 중대산업재해가 발생한 법인의 경영책임자 등이 정당한 사유 없이 20시간 이내의 안전보건교육을 이수하지 아니한 경우에는 5천만원 이하의 과태료가 부과된다(법 제8조, 시행령 제6조).

(2) Joint penal provisions

The Serious Accidents Punishment Act imposes a fine of not more than KRW 5 billion for corporations and up to KRW 1 billion for injuries or occupational illness. However, if a corporation has taken considerable care and supervision to prevent violation but a fatal accident still occurs, no fine shall be imposed (Article 7 of the SAPA).

(3) Punitive compensation for damage

The Serious Accidents Punishment Act introduces punitive compensation for damage, which is nonexistent in the OSH Act. In the event that an employer or head of operations intentionally, or by gross negligence, violates his or her obligation to take measures to protect safety and health and this results in a fatal accident, the relevant employer or corporation shall be held liable for compensation not exceeding 5 times the damage suffered by the injured person, or the surviving family. However, this does not apply if the accident occurs despite the corporation having given considerable attention to implementing safety measures and supervision over the relevant risks and hazards (Article 15 of the SAPA).

Ⅲ. Requirements for Employer Immunity in the Event of a Serious Industrial Accident

Even if a serious industrial accident occurs, there will be no punishment if the employer has fulfilled his or her duty to protect safety and health. Specific details are described in the establishment of a safety and health management system (Enforcement Decree Article 4) and administrative measures necessary for fulfillment of obligations in accordance with safety- and health-related laws (Enforcement Decree Article 5).[294)]

1. Establishment of a safety and health management system and implementation measures (Enforcement Decree Article 4)

The details of the safety management and health management system required by Article 4 Paragraph 1 of the Serious Accidents Punishment Act are explained in nine clauses in Article 4

294) Ministry of Employment and Labor, "Fatal Accident Punishment Act – Related to Serious Industrial Accidents," November 2011.

(2) 중대산업재해의 양벌규정

중대재해처벌법은 중대재해로 1명 이상 사망한 재해에 대해서는 법인은 50억원 이하의 벌금, 부상자나 직업병 발생 시에는 10억원 이하의 벌금이 부과된다. 다만, 법인이 그 위반 행위를 방지하기 위해 상당한 주의와 감독을 한 경우에는 벌금이 부과되지 않는다(법 제7조).

(3) 징벌적 손해배상

중대재해처벌법에는 산업법에 없는 징벌적 손해배상제도를 도입하였다. 사업주 또는 경영책임자가 고의 또는 중대한 과실로 안전보건 조치 의무를 위반하여 중대재해를 발생하게 한 경우, 해당 사업주 또는 법인이 중대재해로 손해를 입은 사람에 대하여 그 손해액의 5배를 넘지 않는 범위에서 배상책임을 진다. 다만, 법인이 해당 업무에 대해 상당한 주의와 감독을 한 경우에는 적용되지 않는다(법제15조).

Ⅲ. 중대산업재해 발생 시 사업주의 면책을 위한 요건

중대산업재해가 발생하였더라도 사업주가 안전과 보건확보의 의무를 다한 경우에는 처벌받지 않는다. 그 구체적인 내용은 안전보건관리 체계구축(시행령 제4조)와 안전보건 관계 법령에 따른 의무이행에 필요한 관리상의 조치(시행령 제5조)에서 기술하고 있다.[294)]

1. 안전보건관리체계 구축 및 이행조치(시행령 제4조)

중대재해처벌법 제4조의 제1항에 의해 요구되는 안전관리보건관리 체계에 관한 세부 내용은 시행령 제4조에서 9가지로 설명하고 있다. 이에 대해 사전준비, 전담조직 구성과 배치, 위험성 사전평가, 종사자의 의견청취, 재해 발생 시 대응 매뉴얼 작성, 그리고 용역직원 관리 등의 6개 분야로 나누어 볼 수 있

294) 고용노동부, "중대재해처벌법 - 중대산업재해 관련", 2011. 11.

of the Enforcement Decree. These can then be divided into six areas: i) preventative measures, ii) organization and arrangement of an exclusive organization, iii) prior hazard and risk assessment, iv) listening to workers' opinions, v) creating an emergency response manual of actions to be taken in the event of a serious accident, and vi) managing service agency personnel.[295)] Since companies have different hazards and risks according to the size, characteristics, etc. of their business or workplace, and the manpower and financial situation are different, it is difficult to uniformly determine specific means and methods to control those hazards and risks, and so room must be made to allow for autonomous reasonable judgment.

(1) Establishment of safety and health goals and management policies, and budgeting and execution (Clause 1 and 4).

The goals and management policies related to safety and health may overlap substantially with the employer's plans for safety and health as stipulated in Article 14 of the OSH Act (Reporting to and Approval of the Board of Directors, etc.). However, if the safety and health plan established and reported by the employer considers the situation of the workplace every year, the safety and health goals and management policies required by the Serious Accidents Punishment Act are always considered in each sector while carrying out their business. Such a plan shall contain the basic management philosophy and general guidelines for decision-making regarding safety and health (Clause 1).

The individual employer or business manager shall formulate a budget and ensure the existence of funds necessary for the provision of personnel, facilities, and equipment related to safety and health to prevent serious accidents and decrease risk and the occurrence of hazards, etc. (Clause 4).

(2) Exclusive organization and personnel arrangement (Clause 2, 5, 6)

According to the Occupational Safety and Health Act, individual employers or corporations must have at least three persons in charge of safety and health in all workplaces: a safety manager, a health manager, and an occupational health doctor. In addition, together, they should form an exclusive organization. This exclusive organization is to be in charge of overall management of safety and health for a business or workplace (Clause 2).

An employer or business manager shall assign a safety manager, health manager, and

295) Jeon, Hyeong-bae. "Issues in Interpretation of the Fatal Accident Punishment Act," Labor Law Forum (34), Labor Law Theory and Practice Society, November 2021, pp. 278-282.

다.[295] 모든 기업은 사업 또는 사업장의 규모, 특성, 등에 따른 각기 다른 유해, 위험요인을 가지고 있고 인력과 재정사정이 다르므로 유해, 위험 요인을 통제하는 구체적인 수단, 방법을 일률적으로 정하기 어려우며, 이것은 기업 여건에 맞게 자율적인 판단이 이루어져야 한다.

(1) 안전보건목표와 경영방침 설정, 그리고 예산의 편성과 집행 (제1호, 제4호)

안전과 보건에 관한 목표와 경영방침은 산안법 제14조(이사회 보고 및 승인 등)가 규정하는 대표이사의 안전과 보건에 관한 계획과 상당 부분 중복될 수 있다. 다만, 대표이사가 수립하여 보고하는 안전보건계획은 매년 사업장의 상황을 고려한 안전보건 경영계획이라면, 중대재해처벌법이 요구하는 안전과 보건에 관한 목표와 경영방침은 사업을 수행하면서 각 부문에서 항상 고려하여야 하는 안전보건에 관한 기본적인 경영철학과 의사결정의 일반적인 지침이 담겨 있어야 한다(제1호).

개인사업주 또는 경영책임자는 재해예방을 위해 필요한 안전과 보건에 관한 인력, 시설, 장비의 구비와 유해, 위험 요인의 개선 등에 필요한 예산을 편성하고, 편성된 예산 목적에 맞게 집행하도록 하여야 한다(제4호).

(2) 전담조직과 인력의 배치 (제2호, 제5호, 제6호)

산업안전보건법에 따라 개인사업주나 법인은 모든 사업장에 안전과 보건을 담당하는 안전관리자, 보건관리자, 안전보건관리 담당자, 산업보건의 등 총 3명 이상을 두어야 한다. 또한 이들로 구성된 전담조직을 두어야 한다. 이 전담조직은 사업 또는 사업장의 안전과 보건에 관하여 총괄 관리하는 업무를 담당한다(제2호).

개인사업주나 경영책임자는 산안법에 따른 안전관리자, 보건관리자, 안전보건관리자 및 산업보건의를 배치하여야 한다. 다만, 다른 법령에서 해당 인력의 배치에 대해 달리 정하고 있는 경우에는 그에 따르고, 배치해야 할 인력이 다른

---

295) 전형배, "중대재해처벌법의 해석상 쟁점", 노동법포럼 (34), 노동법이론실무학회, 2021. 11. 278-282면.

occupational health doctor in accordance with the OSH Act. However, if other laws and ordinances stipulate otherwise for the allocation of relevant personnel, those other laws or ordinances shall be followed. In cases where the personnel to be allocated concurrently hold other duties, time for fulfillment of safety and health responsibilities shall be guaranteed in accordance with the standards set and announced by the Minister of Employment and Labor (Clause 6).

The employer or business manager shall grant the necessary authority to the person(s) in charge of safety and health management and shall grant the funding necessary for such person(s) to fulfill the tasks prescribed in the OSH Act, and evaluate and manage whether the relevant tasks are faithfully performed at least once every six months (Clause 5).

(3) Prior hazards and risk assessment (Clause 3)

The employer or business manager shall prepare business procedures to identify and mitigate hazards and risk according to the characteristics of the business or workplace, and confirm, at least once every six months, whether such identification and mitigation has been carried out. However, if the procedure for risk assessment is prepared in accordance with Article 36 of the Occupational Safety and Health Act, the risk assessment is conducted according to said procedure and the implementation reported, confirmation of whether these activities have been carried out shall be considered to have taken place.

(4) Listening to the opinions of workers (Clause 7)

The employer shall prepare procedures to hear the opinions of employees on matters related to safety and health at a business or workplace, and shall confirm, every six months, that improvement measures have been prepared and implemented. If any abnormalities or omissions are identified, the employer shall be responsible for taking necessary countermeasures. However, when an occupational safety and health committee, as defined in the OSH Act, and the safety and health consultative body discuss, deliberate, or decide on the safety- and health-related situation of a related business or workplace, it shall be deemed that the opinions of the relevant workers have been heard.

(5) Creation of a manual on action to be taken in the event of a serious industrial accident (Clause 8)

The employer shall prepare a manual covering actions to occur in the event a serious industrial accident has occurred or imminent risk of occurrence of such an industrial accident exists in the business or workplace. The employer shall check whether measures are taken according to the manual

업무를 겸직하는 경우에는 고용노동부장관이 정하여 고시하는 기준에 따라 안전과 보건에 관한 업무 수행시간을 보장해야 한다(제6호).

개인사업주 또는 경영책임자는 안전보건 관리책임자가 산안법에 정해진 업무를 수행할 수 있도록 필요한 권한과 예산을 부여하고, 해당 업무를 충실히 수행하는지를 반기 1회 이상 평가 관리하여야 한다(제5호).

(3) 유해·위험요인의 평가 (제3호)

개인사업주 또는 경영책임자는 사업 또는 사업장의 특성에 따른 유해·위험요인을 확인하여 개선하는 업무절차를 마련하고, 해당 업무절차에 따라 유해·위험요인의 확인 및 개선이 이루어지는지를 반기 1회 이상 점검한 후 필요한 조치를 하여야 한다. 다만, 산업안전보건법 제36조에 따른 위험성평가를 하는 절차를 마련하고, 그 절차에 따라 위험성 평가를 직접 실시하거나 실시하도록 하여 실시 결과를 보고받은 경우에는 해당 업무절차에 따라 유해·위험요인의 확인 및 개선에 대한 점검을 한 것으로 본다.

(4) 종사자의 의견 청취 (제7호)

사용자는 사업 또는 사업장의 안전·보건에 관한 사항에 대해 종사자의 의견을 듣는 절차를 마련하고, 그 절차에 따라 의견을 들어 재해 예방에 필요하다고 인정하는 경우에는 그에 대한 개선방안을 마련하여 이행하는지를 반기 1회 이상 점검한 후 필요한 조치를 한다. 다만, 산업안전보건법에 따른 산업안전보건위원회와 안전 및 보건에 관한 협의체에서 사업 또는 사업장의 안전·보건에 관하여 논의하거나 심의、의결한 경우에는 해당 종사자의 의견을 들은 것으로 본다.

(5) 중대산업재해 발생 시 조치를 위한 매뉴얼 작성 (제8호)

사용자는 사업 또는 사업장에 중대산업재해가 발생하거나 발생할 급박한 위험이 있을 경우를 대비하여 다음에 관한 내용을 포함한 매뉴얼을 마련하고, 해당 매뉴얼에 따라 조치하는지를 반기 1회 이상 점검한다. 그 포함 내용은 다음과 같다. (i) 작업 중지, 근로자 대피, 위험요인 제거 등 대응조치, (ii) 중대산업재해를 입은 사람에 대한 구호조치, (iii) 추가 피해방지를 위한 조치

at least once every six months. The manual shall include the following: (i) Response measures such as cessation of work, evacuation of workers, and removal of hazards; (ii) Relief measures for persons injured in serious industrial accidents; and (iii) Measures to prevent further damage.

(6) Management of external service agency workers (Clause 9)

When work is subcontracted, outsourced, or entrusted to a third party, standards and procedures are to be prepared to ensure the safety and health of third-party workers, which are to be inspected by the employer at least every six months. The standards and procedures are to include the following: (i) Those receiving the contract, service, entrustment, etc., are to have standards and procedures in place to evaluate the third party's ability and technological level to take the actions necessary to prevent industrial accidents; (ii) Those receiving the contract, service, entrustment, etc., shall have their own standards for funding the management of safety and health; and (iii) Those receiving the contract, service, entrustment etc. in the construction and shipbuilding industries shall have their own standards for construction period or building period for the safety and health.

2. Administrative measures necessary for the fulfillment of obligations under safety and health-related laws and regulations (Enforcement Decree Article 5)

(1) The employer shall inspect, at least every six months, to confirm that the obligations under safety and health-related laws have been fulfilled.

(2) As a result of the inspection or report in (1) above, if it is confirmed that the obligations under safety and health-related laws and regulations have not been fulfilled, the employer shall take action necessary to fulfill those obligations, such as assigning additional manpower or providing additional funding and ensuring its execution.

(3) The employer shall inspect at least every six months whether safety and health education on hazardous and dangerous work, which is mandatory in accordance with safety and health-related laws and regulations, has been provided. If the employer is not the one to directly engage in the inspection, he or she shall receive a report on the findings from those the employer delegates to perform the inspection.

(4) The employer shall take the action necessary to ensure that any unfulfilled education requirements identified in such an inspection or related report in accordance with (3) above, takes place, providing additional manpower and/or funding as necessary and without delay.

(6) 용역직원 관리 (제9호)

사용자는 제3자에게 업무의 도급, 용역, 위탁 등을 하는 경우에는 종사자의 안전·보건을 확보하기 위해 다음에 관한 기준과 절차를 마련하고, 그 기준과 절차에 따라 도급, 용역, 위탁 등이 이루어지는지를 반기 1회 이상 점검한다. 그 기준과 절차는 다음과 같다. (i) 도급, 용역, 위탁 등을 받는 자의 산업재해 예방을 위한 조치 능력과 기술에 관한 평가기준·절차, (ii) 도급, 용역, 위탁 등을 받는 자의 안전·보건을 위한 관리비용에 관한 기준, (iii) 건설업 및 조선업의 경우 도급, 용역, 위탁 등을 받는 자의 안전·보건을 위한 공사기간 또는 건조기간에 관한 기준.

2. 안전·보건 관계 법령에 따른 의무이행에 필요한 관리상의 조치 (시행령 제5조)

(1) 사용자는 안전·보건 관계 법령에 따른 의무를 이행했는지 반기 1회 이상 점검하고, 직접 점검하지 않은 경우에는 점검이 끝난 후 지체 없이 점검 결과를 보고받는다.

(2) 위 (1)에 따른 점검 또는 보고 결과, 안전·보건 관계 법령에 따른 의무가 이행되지 않은 사실이 확인되는 경우에는 인력을 배치하거나 예산을 추가로 편성·집행하도록 하는 등 해당 의무 이행에 필요한 조치를 한다.

(3) 안전·보건 관계 법령에 따라 의무적으로 실시해야 하는 유해·위험한 작업에 관한 안전、보건에 관한 교육이 실시되었는지를 반기 1회 이상 점검하고, 직접 점검하지 않은 경우에는 점검이 끝난 후 지체 없이 점검 결과를 보고받는다.

(4) 위 (3)에 따른 점검 또는 보고 결과, 실시되지 않은 교육에 대해서는 지체 없이 그 이행의 지시, 예산의 확보 등 교육 실시에 필요한 조치를 한다.

Section 2: The Workplace Harassment Prevention Law

The Workplace Anti-Bullying Act was enacted in January 2019 and came into effect in July of the same year. Three incidents contributed to enactment of this law. The first case is known as the "nut rage" incident involving an executive of Korean Air in 2014. Vice President Cho 00, a daughter of Korean Air's owners, exploded in rage that her macadamia nuts were served in a bag, not on a plate, verbally abusing the flight attendant and the chief flight attendant and forcing both to kneel and apologize to her. Ms. Cho then ordered the plane—heading for a runway at New York's John F. Kennedy Airport to fly to Seoul—to return to the boarding gate where she ordered the chief flight attendant to get out. Then, the plane departed.[296)] In 2019, Korean Air was ordered by the court to pay 70 million won to former chief flight attendant Park 00, for the personnel disadvantages received as a result of the incident.[297)] The second case involves a nurse who killed herself, leaving a suicide note that said, "Workplace harassment makes it difficult to work." In March 2019, the Labor Welfare Corporation's Disease Judgment Committee recognized the incident as an industrial accident caused by workplace harassment. In the third case, at the end of 2018, a video surfaced of Yang 00, chairman of WeDisk, a start-up IT company, calling in an ex-employee and brutally assaulting him in the office. Yang is currently in prison for this and other illegal business activities.[298)]

Until recently, investigation and treatment of workplace harassment has been entirely up to companies.[299)] There were only two related rules when the Workplace Anti-Bullying Act was enacted. First, rules of employment had to include procedures for dealing with workplace harassment and for remedy. Second, employers were to be punished if they disadvantage those who report harassment in the workplace. The procedures for handling reports of bullying were entirely up to the employer, which did little to actually resolve the problem. Accordingly, in

296) Moon, Kangboon, "Is this workplace harassment?" 2020. Gadian, p. 34.

297) Seoul High Court ruling on Nov. 5, 2019.

298) Moon, Kangboon, "Is this workplace harassment?" 2020. Gadian, pp. 35-36.

299) Shin, Kwonchul, "Legal Concepts and Criteria for Determining the Occurrence of Bullying in the Workplace," Labor Law (69), Korean Labor Law Association, Mar. 2019, p. 228.

제2절 직장 내 괴롭힘 방지법

직장 내 괴롭힘 방지법이 2019년 1월에 도입되어 동년 7월부터 시행되었다. 직장 내 괴롭힘 방지법 제정에 결정적인 계기가 되었던 3가지의 관련된 사건이 사회적 이슈가 되었다. 첫 번째 사건은 2014년, D항공의 '땅콩 회항' 사건이다. D항공 소유주 일가인 조○○ 부사장이 마카다미아(Macadamia) 땅콩을 봉지 채 서비스한 것을 문제 삼아 승무원에게 폭언을 하고 사무장을 불러 무릎을 꿇리고 빌도록 했는데, 그래도 화가 안 풀려 뉴욕공항에서 서울로 향하던 항공기를 돌려 사무장을 내려놓은 뒤 출발한 사건이다.[296] 2019년 이 사건으로 인사상 불이익을 받은 박○○ 전 사무장에게 D항공이 7000만 원 배상을 해야 한다는 판결이 나왔다.[297] 두 번째 사건은 2018년 2월 서울아산병원의 신입 간호사가 "태움(병원 내 집단 괴롭힘) 때문에 일하기 힘들다"는 유서를 남기고 자살한 사건이다. 이 사건에 대해 2019년 3월 근로복지공단의 질병판정위원회는 직장 내 괴롭힘으로 인해 발생한 산업재해로 인정하였다. 세 번째 사건은 2018년 말 신생 IT 기업 WD의 양○○ 회장이 퇴사한 직원을 불러 사무실에서 무차별 폭행을 하는 동영상이 공개된 사건이다. 그는 현재 이 사건과 더불어 불법 기업 활동으로 법정 구속되어 형을 살고 있다.[298]

직장 내 괴롭힘에 대한 조사와 처리는 선적으로 회사에 맡겨져 있다.[299] 이 직장 내 괴롭힘 법령 도입 시에는 관련 규칙이 두 가지만 있었다. 첫째 직장 내 괴롭힘에 대한 내용과 구제절차를 취업규칙의 필수기재 사항으로 하였고, 둘째 직장 내 괴롭힘을 신고한 자에게 불이익을 주는 경우 해당 사업주를 처벌하도록 하는 내용이었다. 이러한 취업규칙에 근거하여 괴롭힘 사건을 처리하는 방식은 사업주에게 전적으로 맡겨 놓았기 때문에 실질적 문제해결이 되지 못했다. 이에

296) 문강분, "이것도 직장 내 괴롭힘 인가요?" 2020. 가디언, 34면.

297) 서울고등법원 2019.11.5.선고 2019나2004517 판결.

298) 문상분, 위 출판물, 35-36면.

299) 신권철, "직장 내 괴롭힘의 법적 개념과 요건", 노동법학(69), 한국노동법학회, 2019.3. 228면.

April 2021, the following five employer obligations were added in amendments to the relevant laws. Employers are now obligated to: ① Prohibit bullying in the workplace, ② Conduct objective investigations of reported bullying incidents in the workplace, ③ Take appropriate actions to protect alleged victims, ④ Establish and carry out disciplinary action in response to bullying in the workplace, and ⑤ Comply with confidentiality requirements related to harassment investigations in the workplace, with fines levied for negligence.

When determining whether bullying has occurred in the workplace, the criteria are somewhat complex given the blur between the employer's discretionary personnel rights and the employee's personal rights. I will take a look at the related details and criteria for judgement herein.

Ⅰ. Concept & Criteria of Determining Workplace Harassment

The Labor Standards Act (Article 76-2) prohibits harassment in the workplace, which is defined as "an act of inflicting physical or mental pain on other workers or worsening the working environment through an abuse of the superior position of the employer or relationships in the workplace." There are four components to workplace harassment: ① Defined target: employer or employee, ② Abuse of position: Using position or work relationship against the target, ③ Repeated actions towards the target, or assigning of tasks, unnecessary for performance of contracted work: Actions beyond the appropriate scope of work, ④ Infringements of human rights and/or degradation of the working environment: Any action that causes physical or mental pain or worsens the working environment. All four factors above must be met for an incident to qualify as workplace harassment.

1. Explanation of the factors in harassment[300)]

(1) Defined target: Employer or employee

The Labor Standards Act (Article 2 (2)), defines an employer as someone in charge of managing the business, or a person who acts on behalf of the employer with respect to

300) Ministry of Employment and Labor, "Manual for Judgment and Prevention of Harassment in the Workplace," 2019, pp. 24-27.

2021년 4월「근로기준법」개정을 통해, 사용자의 실질적인 직장 내 괴롭힘에 대한 국가적 관여를 강제하면서 다음의 5가지 사항을 추가하였다. ① 사업주의 직장 내 괴롭힘 금지의무, ② 직장 내 괴롭힘 사건에 대해 객관적 조사 실시의무, ③ 피해근로자에 대한 적절한 보호조치의무, ④ 직장 내 괴롭힘 행위자에 대한 필요한 징계조치, ⑤ 직장 내 괴롭힘 조사와 관련된 내용에 대해 비밀준수 의무 등 신설조항과 과태료 조항의 도입이다.

직장 내 괴롭힘을 판단하면서 사용자의 재량적 인사권과 근로자의 인격권 사이에서 직장 내 괴롭힘 판단기준에 대해 다소 애매모호한 점이 많아 이와 관련된 내용과 판단기준에 대해 구체적으로 살펴보고자 한다.

Ⅰ. 직장 내 괴롭힘의 개념과 판단기준

「근로기준법」제76조의2는 직장 내 괴롭힘을 금지하고 있다. 직장 내 괴롭힘을 "사용자 또는 근로자는 직장에서의 지위 또는 관계 등의 우위를 이용하여 업무상 적정범위를 넘어 다른 근로자에게 신체적·정신적 고통을 주거나 근무환경을 악화시키는 행위"로 규정하고 있다. 직장 내 괴롭힘의 구성요소는 다음의 4가지이다. ① 주체 : 사용자 또는 근로자, ② 지위의 활용 : 직장에서의 지위나 관계 등에서의 우위, ③ 업무일탈 : 업무의 적정범위 이상의 행위, ④ 인적, 환경적 침해행위 : 근로자에게 신체적, 정신적 고통을 주거나 근무 환경을 악화시키는 행위. 위의 4가지 요소를 모두 충족해야만 직장 내 괴롭힘에 해당한다.

1. 괴롭힘의 판단요소[300)]

(1) 주체 : 사용자 또는 근로자

직장 내 괴롭힘에서 금지의 주체는 사용자와 근로자이다. 「근로기준법」(제2조 제2항)에서 사용자라고 하면 사업주 또는 사업 경영 담당자, 그 밖에 근로자에 관한 사항에 대하여 사업주를 위하여 행위 하는 자를 말한다. 사업경영담당자

300) 고용노동부, "직장 내 괴롭힘 판단 및 예방 대응 매뉴얼", 2019. 24-27면.

matters related to workers. Someone in charge of managing the business does not have to be the business owner but is in charge of general business management, and refers to someone who represents a business externally after comprehensive delegation from the business owner for all or part of the business management. Anyone who acts on matters related to workers for the business owner is delegated authority from the business owner or the person in charge of business management, and is involved in making personnel decisions, such as hiring and dismissal of those within their own realm of responsibility, directing and supervising the workers on the job, and working conditions. It also refers to someone who can decide and execute matters related to working conditions. Relatives of the employer are included in the scope of "employer" with revision of the Labor Standards Act in 2021 (Article 116). "Employer" includes those with an advantage over other workers, such as via position or work relationship.

In the worker dispatch relationship, according to the Act on the Protection, etc., of Dispatched Workers, a bullying agent in the workplace can also include an employer who directly supervises and directs the work of a dispatched worker.

(2) Abuse of position: Using position or work relationship, etc., against the target

Harassment in the workplace mainly occurs in places where there is a strong organizational culture or authoritarian hierarchy. It occurs mainly in the form of actions by people with superior social or economic status using their power and superior status against those less socially privileged.[301)]

A superior relationship refers to one in which it is likely to be difficult for those in lower positions to resist any bullying behavior. An abuse of position refers to an offender using their superiority against someone in a command-and-control relationship, or even if it is not a direct command-order relationship, it is to use the higher position or rank system. Workplace harassment does not occur unless it involves the abuse of superiority in position or relationship.

---

301) Lee, Soo-Yeon, "The Concept of Workplace Harassment and Judgment Criteria", Ewha Gender Law 10(2), Ewha Womans University Gender Law Research Institute, Aug. 2018, p. 119.

는 사업주가 아니면서 사업경영 일반을 책임지는 자로서, 사업주로부터 사업 경영의 전부 또는 일부에 대해 포괄적인 위임을 받고 대외적으로 사업을 대표하거나 대리하는 자를 말한다. 근로자에 관한 사항에 대해 사업주를 위하여 행위하는 자는 사업주 또는 사업경영 담당자로부터 권한을 위임받아 자신의 책임 아래 근로자 채용, 해고 등 인사처분을 할 수 있고, 직무상 근로자의 업무를 지휘, 감독하며 근로조건에 관한 사항을 결정하고 집행할 수 있는 자를 말한다. 2021년 「근로기준법」 개정으로 직장 내 괴롭힘을 행한 사용자에 대한 벌칙(1천만 원 이하의 과태료)을 부과하는 조항(제116조)이 신설되었다. 이 벌칙은 사용자의 배우자, 4촌의 혈족과 인척이 해당 사업 또는 사업장의 근로자이면서 직장 내 괴롭힘을 행한 경우에도 부과된다(시행령 59조의3). 여기서 금지의 주체인 근로자라고 하면 다른 근로자에 대해 직장에서의 지위나 관계 등의 우위를 가진 자를 말한다.

근로자파견관계에서는 파견법에 따라 파견 중인 근로자의 경우 직접 업무를 감독하고 지시하는 사용사업주도 직장 내 괴롭힘 행위자로 인정된다.

(2) 지위의 활용 : 직장에서의 지위나 관계 등에서의 우위

직장 내 괴롭힘은 조직문화나 권위주의적 위계질서가 강한 곳에서 주로 발생한다. 이는 사회적 경제적으로 우월한 지위에 있는 사람들이 사회적 약자를 대상으로 권력형, 우월적 지위를 이용한 행위의 형태로 주로 발생한다.[301)]

우위성이라고 하면 피해자가 괴롭힘 행위에 대해 저항 또는 거절이 어려울 가능성이 높은 관계를 의미한다. 지위의 우위는 괴롭힘 행위자가 지휘명령 관계에서 상위에 있거나 직접적인 지휘명령 관계가 아니어도 직위, 직급체계상 상위에 있음을 이용하는 것이다. 관계의 우위는 행위자가 피해자와의 관계에서 우위에 있는지는 특정 요소에 대해 사업장 내에서 통상적으로 이루어지는 평가를 바탕으로 판단한다. 따라서 직장에서의 지위나 관계 등의 우위를 이용한 것이 아니라면 직장 내 괴롭힘에 해당되지 않는다.

301) 이수연, "직장 괴롭힘의 개념과 판단기준에 관한 판례법리", 이화젠더법학 10(2), 이화여자대학교 젠더법학연구소, 2018.8. 119면.

(3) Repeated actions towards the target, or assigning of tasks, unnecessary for performance of contracted work: Actions beyond the appropriate scope of work

Actions that are inappropriate and recognized as exceeding the scope of work can be classified into the following seven categories.

① Violence and intimidation: Actions that involve direct physical force or the threat of physical force, such as directly or indirectly inflicting violence on an object.

② Verbal behavior, such as violent, abusive language or gossip: If it is determined that gossip is spread to a third party, such as in an open place, to damage the victim's reputation, it is beyond the appropriate scope for work. In particular, continuous and repetitive verbal abuse or abusive language can seriously harm the victim's personal rights and cause mental pain, so engaging in it constitutes an act beyond the appropriate scope for work.

③ Orders to perform tasks related to assistance with non-work affairs: These are orders that exceed the appropriate scope of work and beyond what is considered normally acceptable in human relations. Examples include continuous and repetitive instructions to run personal errands related to daily life.

④ Bullying and exclusion: Intentional disregard and exclusion in the process of performing work are acts that are beyond the appropriate scope of work and beyond the social norm. Examples include intentionally not providing important information related to work or excluding someone entitled to participation in the decision-making process without justifiable reason, forcing someone to move or leave the department without good reason, discriminating against someone in training, promotion, rewards, or routine benefits without good reason, etc.

⑤ Repetitive instructions for work unrelated to the employment contract: If instructions are given to an employee repeatedly to do work that is unrelated to that specified at the time the labor contract was signed, and if a justifiable reason is not recognized, it amounts to an act beyond the appropriate scope for work. Examples including menial tasks only when an employee was hired for specific other tasks, or giving the employee little work without justifiable reason.

⑥ Assigning an excessive amount of work: If the action is judged to be inappropriate, such as not allowing even the minimum amount of time physically necessary for the task, without unavoidable reasons, it is beyond the appropriate scope of work.

⑦ Interfering with smooth business performance: Actions that interfere with smooth business

(3) 업무일탈 : 업무의 적정범위 이상의 행위

업무의 적정범위를 넘는 것으로 인정되는 행위는 다음의 7가지로 분류할 수 있다.

① 폭행 및 협박 행위 : 신체에 직접 폭력을 가하거나 물건에 폭력을 가하는 등 직, 간접의 물리적 힘을 행사하는 폭행이나 협박행위는 업무상 적정범위를 넘은 행위이다.

② 폭언, 욕설, 험담 등 언어적 행위 : 공개된 장소에서 이루어지는 등 제3자에게 전파되어 피해자의 명예를 훼손할 정도인 것으로 판단되면 업무상 적정범위를 넘은 행위이다. 특히, 지속 반복적인 폭언이나 욕설은 피해자의 인격권을 심각하게 해치고 정신적인 고통을 유발할 수 있으므로 업무상 적정범위를 넘는 행위이다.

③ 사적 용무 지시 : 개인적인 심부름을 반복적으로 시키는 등 인간관계에서 용인될 수 있는 부탁의 수준을 넘어 행해지는 것은 업무상 적정범위를 넘은 행위이다. 예)사적인 심부름 등 개인적인 일상생활과 관련된 일을 하도록 지속적, 반복적으로 지시하는 것

④ 집단 따돌림과 배제시킴 : 업무수행 과정에서의 의도적 무시와 배제는 사회통념을 벗어난 업무상 적정 범위를 넘어선 행위이다. 예) 정당한 사유 없이 업무와 관련된 중요한 정보제공이나 의사결정 과정에서 배제시키는 것. 정당한 이유 없이 부서이동 또는 퇴사를 강요하는 것. 정당한 이유 없이 훈련, 승진, 보상, 일상적인 대우 등에서 차별하는 것 등.

⑤ 업무와 무관한 일을 반복 지시 : 근로계약 체결 시 명시했던 업무와 무관한 일을 근로자의 의사에 반하여 지시하는 행위가 반복되고 그 지시에 정당한 사유가 인정되지 않는다면 업무상 적정범위를 넘어선 행위이다. 예)근로계약서 등에 명시되어 있지 않은 허드렛일만 시키거나 일을 거의 주지 않는 것.

⑥ 과도한 업무 부여 : 업무상 불가피한 사정이 없음에도 불구하고 해당업무 수행에 대해 물리적으로 필요한 최소한의 시간마저도 허락하지 않는 등 그 행위가 타당하지 않은 것으로 판단되면 업무상 적정범위를 넘어선 행위이다.

⑦ 원활한 입무수행을 방해하는 행위 : 업무에 필요한 수요 비품(컴퓨터, 전화

performance, such as not providing essential equipment (computers, telephones, etc.) necessary for business, or blocking access to the Internet or company intranet, are beyond social norms and inappropriate for business.

(4) Infringements of human rights and/or degradation of the working environment

This refers to actions of an employer or a worker that inflict physical or mental pain on another worker through harassment in the workplace or worsening the working environment. It can be said that the working environment has been degraded if an employer intentionally moves certain workers to work in front of the washroom, embarrassing them or creating an environment in which workers cannot perform their duties properly. Intention of the offender is not a prerequisite to determining that actions directly cause physical or mental pain or worsen the working environment.

2. Criteria for Determining Workplace Harassment

(1) Conflict between the employer's right to order work and the employee's personal rights

In determining whether or not bullying has occurred in the workplace, there are cases in which the employer's right to order work and the employee's personal rights are in conflict. In labor disputes, an employer's exercise of personnel rights in a way that violates the employee's personal rights is often viewed as illegal under the Civil Act.

The employer's right to command work is one of the personnel rights, which is an authority unique to the employer and necessary to maintain and establish corporate order. The courts have ruled that employers have considerable discretion in determining the extent of personnel management necessary for business, since they are responsible for personnel.[302] In contrast, the Constitutional Court argues that the right to work includes not only the "right to a place to work" but also "the right to a reasonable environment in which to work," with the latter a basic right to protect against infringement on human dignity. It has ruled that this right includes the right to demand a healthy working environment, fair compensation for work, and guarantee of reasonable working conditions.[303]

---

302) Supreme Court ruling on July 22, 2003: 2002do7225, and many similar rulings.

303) Constitutional Court decision on Nov. 28, 2002: 2001hunba50; Constitution Court decision on Aug. 30, 2007: 2004hunma670.

등)을 제공하지 않거나, 인터넷 사내 인트라넷 접속을 차단하는 등 원활한 업무 수행을 방해하는 행위는 사회 통념을 벗어난 행위로서 업무상 적정 범위를 넘어선 행위이다.

(4) 인적, 환경적 침해행위

사용자나 근로자가 다른 근로자에게 직장 내 괴롭힘을 통해 근로자에게 신체적, 정신적 고통을 주거나 근무환경을 악화시키는 행위이다. 사업주가 의도적으로 특정 근로자를 화장실 앞으로 업무자리를 옮겨 창피를 주거나 근로자가 제대로 된 업무를 수행할 수 없는 환경을 조성하는 경우 근무환경을 악화시켰다고 볼 수 있다. 행위자의 의도가 없었더라도 그 행위로 인해 신체적, 정신적 고통을 느꼈거나 근무환경이 예전보다 나빠졌다면 인정될 수 있다.

2. 직장 내 괴롭힘의 판단기준

(1) 사용자의 업무지시권과 근로자의 인격권과 충돌

직장 내 괴롭힘 여부를 판단함에 있어서 사용자의 업무지시권과 근로자의 인격권이 충돌되는 경우가 있다. 노동분쟁에서 사용자의 인사권 행사가 근로자의 인격권을 침해한 경우에는 민법상의 불법행위로 구성되는 경우가 많다.

사용자의 업무지시권은 인사권으로 기업질서의 유지와 확립을 위해 사용자가 가지는 고유한 권한이다. 사용자의 인사명령에 대해 법원은 인사권자인 사용자의 권한에 속하므로 업무상 필요한 범위에서는 상당한 재량을 가진다고 한다.[302] 이에 반해, 헌법재판소는 근로의 권리가 "일할 자리에 관한 권리" 뿐만 아니라 "일할 환경에 관한 권리"도 함께 내포하고 있고, 후자는 인간의 존엄성에 대한 침해를 방어하기 위한 자유권적 기본권의 성격도 갖고 있어 건강한 작업환경, 일에 대한 정당한 보수, 합리적인 근로조건의 보장 등을 요구할 수 있는 권리 등을 포함한다고 밝히고 있다.[303]

---

302) 대법원 2003.7.22. 선고 2002도7225 판결 등. 다수

303) 헌법재판소 2002. 11. 28. 선고 2001헌바50 결정; 헌법재판소 2007. 8. 30. 선고 2004헌마670 결정.

Here, in determining the appropriate scope of work, it is necessary to determine whether the employer's right to order the work or the worker's personal rights should take precedence. In this case, it is necessary to determine whether or not it is illegal to determine certain work as falling within the appropriate scope for a job through an "evaluation of conflicting fundamental rights."[304] Of the requirements for determining whether an action constitutes workplace harassment, whether or not it departs from the appropriate scope of work needs to be determined so that conflicts over the basic rights of the employer and employee can be harmoniously resolved.[305] This is determined in the light of sound common sense and practices of the social community, and whether there is rationality or substantiality in common social concepts, etc., which shall be judged individually and in relationship to each other.[306] However, since the problem of workplace harassment arises on the premise of an imbalance of power and infringes on the personal rights of workers, an evaluation of conflicting fundamental rights is required from the perspective of the victim, and should focus more on the protection of personal rights.[307]

(2) Criteria for determining whether workplace harassment has occurred

The factors and criteria suggested by the court can be used to determine whether workplace harassment has occurred. This shall be decided by considering and evaluating the following collectively: "

① the relationship between the offender and victim,

② the motive and intention of the act,

③ the timing, place, and situation,

④ the details of the victim's explicit or presumed reaction,

⑤ the content and extent of the act, and

⑥ the repetition or continuity of the act."[308]

---

304) Naver Korean dictionary: An evaluation to compare and judge the legal interests of conflicting fundamental rights.

305) Lee, Sang-Gon, "A Study on Improvement of the Law on Bullying in the Workplace," PhD Thesis, Graduate School of Ajou University, Aug 2020, pp. 163-164.

306) Supreme Court ruling on Feb. 10, 1998: 95da39533: Whether the employer is liable for compensation for harassment in the workplace.

307) Lee, Sang-Gon, "A Study on Improvement of the Law on Bullying in the Workplace," PhD Thesis, Graduate School of Ajou University, Aug. 2020, p. 165.

308) Supreme Court ruling on Feb. 10, 1998: 95da39533.

여기서 업무의 적정범위에 대한 판단에 있어 사용자의 업무 지시권을 우위에 두어야 하는지 아니면 근로자의 인격권 보호를 우위에 두어야 하는지를 판단해야 한다. 이 경우 업무상 적정범위는 '이익형량[304]'을 통해서 위법성 여부가 판단되어야 한다.[305]

직장 내 괴롭힘의 성립요건 중 '업무상 적정범위 일탈' 여부는 사용자와 근로자의 기본권이 상호 조화적으로 해결될 수 있도록 목적에 부합하는 이익형량이 요구된다. 즉, 두 기본권이 충돌할 경우 어느 기본권을 우위에 두어야 하는지의 여부는 사회공동체의 건전한 상식과 관행에 비추어 볼 때 용인될 수 있는 정도의 것인지, 사회통념상 합리성이 없거나 상당성 결여 여부 등을 종합하여 개별적, 상대적으로 판단해야 할 것이다.[306] 다만, 직장 내 괴롭힘의 문제는 힘의 불균형을 전제로 하여 발생되고 근로자의 인격권을 침해한다는 점에서, 인격권 보호에 주안점을 두고 피해근로자의 관점에서 다소 상향된 이익형량이 요구된다.[307]

(2) 직장 내 괴롭힘의 판단기준

법원이 제시한 직장 내 성희롱의 위법성 판단요소와 기준을 살펴보면 직장 내 괴롭힘 여부를 판단하는 기준으로 삼을 수 있을 것이다. 괴롭힘 행위인지의 여부는

① 위법행위와 관련한 행위자와 피해자의 관계
② 행위의 동기와 의도
③ 시기와 장소 및 상황
④ 피해자의 명시적 또는 추정적 반응의 내용
⑤ 행위의 내용과 정도
⑥ 행위의 반복성이나 지속성 등을 종합하여 노동인격의 침해여부를 가려야 할 것이다.[308]

---

304) 법률사전: 서로 충돌하는 기본권의 법익을 비교하고 판단하여 결정하는 일.
305) 이상곤, "직장 내 괴롭힘 법제의 개선방안 연구", 아주대학교 대학원 박사학위 논문, 2020. 8. 163-164면.
306) 대법원 1998.2.10. 선고 95다39533 판결: 직장 내에서 성희롱 관련 사용자의 배상책임 여부.
307) 이상곤, "직장 내 괴롭힘 법제의 개신방안 연구", 위의 논문, 165면.
308) 대법원 1998.2.10. 선고 95다39533 판결

Simply put, it is possible for an employer to infringe on human and personal rights or worsen the employment environment with position (power relations), related work (work relations), or other actions unwanted by the receiving party that are outside the scope of the relevant work (harassment, abusive language, etc.).[309)]

The employer is the exerciser of authority, while the employee has voluntarily consented to perform subordinate duties. Therefore, it is not easy to distinguish if harassment has occurred or if the employee is simply unhappy with work duties.[310)] Nevertheless, if the above criteria are individually reviewed and judged comprehensively, it is believed that clarity will emerge in each individual case as to whether or not workplace harassment has occurred.

The Workplace Anti-Bullying Act, introduced in July 2019, is a major influence on reducing the existing patriarchal authoritarian culture in the workplace and guaranteeing the personal rights of workers. Nevertheless, if resolving workplace harassment is left up to companies, there will be no effective results any time an employer deals with bullying half-heartedly. Amendment to the Workplace Anti-Bullying Act in April 2021 includes provisions to punish employers for engaging in or failing to take the appropriate action for workplace harassment, and obligate employers to conduct an objective investigation if they become aware of workplace harassment. This amendment is particularly helpful to workers. In the future, when harassment occurs in the workplace, the Ministry of Employment and Labor will thoroughly review the incident and actively intervene and punish any employers who fail to take appropriate action, which will work to drastically reduce recurrence. Actions to prevent workplace harassment and provide practical remedies when it does happen can be expected to occur at the same time.

---

309) Kim, Elim, "Gender Equality and Law," Korea National Open University Press and Culture Center, 2013, p. 242.

310) Shin, Kwonchul, "Legal Concepts and Criteria for Determining the Occurrence of Bullying in the Workplace," p. 243.

이를 단순히 정리하면, 사용자가 지위를 이용하여(권력관계), 업무와 관련하여(업무관련성), 상대방이 원하지 않는 행동(괴롭힘, 언동 등)을 함으로써, 인권 및 인격권을 침해하거나 고용환경을 악화시키는지 여부를 판단하는 것이다.[309)]

직장 내 괴롭힘의 판단에 있어 행위자인 사용자는 권한 행사자로서 외관을 갖추고 있고, 피해자인 근로자는 근로의무의 수행원으로서 자발적 동의에 의해 이루어진다. 따라서 이를 구분하기는 쉽지 않다.[310)] 그럼에도 불구하고 위의 기준을 가지고 개별적으로 검토하여 종합적으로 판단한다면 직장 내 괴롭힘 여부 판단에 있어 개별 사안별로 분명한 기준이 나올 것이라고 본다.

2019년 7월 시행된 직장 내 괴롭힘 방지법은 직장 내에서 기존의 가부장적 권위주의적 조직 문화를 개선하고 근로자들의 인격권 보장에 큰 역할을 하였다. 그럼에도 불구하고 회사의 자율에 맡겨져 노사간 스스로 문제해결을 시도하면서, 사용자가 실질적으로 직장 내 괴롭힘 사건에 있어 큰 열의가 없을 경우에는 실효적 효과를 가져올 수가 없었다. 그래서 이번 2021년 4월에 새롭게 도입된 직장 내 괴롭힘 방지법에서는 사용자가 직장 내 괴롭힘 행위자인 경우 처벌을 할 수 있는 조항이 신설되었고, 사용자가 직장 내 괴롭힘을 인지한 경우 객관적 조사를 하여야 할 의무조항이 도입되어 실질적으로 근로자에게 도움이 된다는 것에 그 의미가 있다. 앞으로 직장 내 괴롭힘 사건 발생시 고용노동부에서는 적극적 개입을 통해 사용자가 사건을 철저히 조사하여 관련자를 처벌하게 할 것이고, 이로 인해 차후 사건 재발을 방지할 수 있는 획기적인 변화를 가져올 것이다. 이를 통해 직장 내 괴롭힘 사건에 대한 실질적 구제조치와 예방조치가 동시에 이루어질 수 있을 것이라 기대한다.

309) 김엘림, “남녀평등과 법”, 한국방송통신대학교 출판문화원, 2013, 242면.
310) 신권철, “직장 내 괴롭힘의 법적 개념과 요건”, 위의 논문, 243-244면.

Ⅱ. The Workplace Harassment Prevention Law and the Employer's Duty

Recently workplace harassment within large corporations has become a social problem. Every day it seems that the executives of these companies are reported by the media on issues such as abusive language, assault, and inhumane treatment of their employees, but these acts which are revealed to the public are but the tip of the iceberg. According to a survey by the Korea Labor Institute,[311)] 66.3% of respondents said that they had experienced direct harassment at their workplace in the past five years. Also, according to the Human Rights Commission's survey,[312)] 73.3% of respondents experienced workplace harassment over the past year. The average number of harassment was 10.0 cases, the experience of personal harassment was 39.0%, and the experience of collective harassment was 5.6%. These workplace harassments have resulted in negative reactions such as consideration of resignation (66.9%), less confidence in the company and its senior officials (64.9%), a decline in work performance and concentration (64.9%), and a reluctance to relate with peers (33.3%).

The damage due to workplace harassment continues to grow and so the Workplace Harassment Prevention Law was enacted because of public demand for improvement. The details are described below.

1. Content of the Workplace Harassment Prevention Law

(1) The employer's obligation to prohibit workplace harassment

Article 76-2 (Prohibition of Workplace Harassment) in the Labor Standard Act: the employer or an employee shall not cause physical or mental suffering or deteriorate the working environment, exceeding the appropriate level of bearable limits, by taking advantage of his or her position or relationship in the workplace.

---

311) Keunjoo Kim/Kyunghee Lee, 「A Survey of Workplace Harassment and The Countermeasures」, Korean Labor Institute, December 2017.

312) Sungsoo Hong et al, 「A Survey of Workplace Harassment」, The National Human Rights Commission of Korea, November 2017.

Ⅱ. 직장 내 괴롭힘 방지법과 사용자의 의무

최근 대기업의 직장 내 괴롭힘이 언론에 보도되는 사회 문제가 되고 있다. 이들 회사의 임원들이 직원에 대한 폭언, 폭행, 비인간적인 대우 등의 문제가 사실로 드러난 괴롭힘의 행위이지만 여전히 이것은 빙산의 일각이라 할 수 있다. 한국노동연구원의 조사에 따르면, 과거 5년간 직장 내 괴롭힘에 대해 '직접적 피해 경험'이 있다고 응답한 응답자가 전체 응답자 중 66.3%로 나타났다.[311] 또한 국가인권위원회의 조사에 따르면, 1년간의 직장 내 괴롭힘 피해를 경험하였다고 응답한 응답자는 전체 응답자의 73.3%였고, 피해 경험 행위의 개수는 평균 10.0개로 나타났으며, 괴롭힘 경험 중 개인적 괴롭힘 경험이 39.0%, 집단적 괴롭힘 경험이 5.6%로 나타났다. 이러한 직장 내 괴롭힘으로 인해 이직을 고민(66.9%)하거나, 상급자나 회사에 대한 신뢰가 하락(64.9%) 하고, 그 밖에 업무 능력이나 집중도 하락(64.9%) 동료들과의 관계가 멀어짐 (33.3%) 등의 부정적 영향이 발생하고 있다.[312]

직장 내 괴롭힘의 피해가 커지고 있고, 이에 대한 개선을 위한 사회적 요구로 인하여 직장 내 괴롭힘 금지 관련「근로기준법」,「산업재해보상보험법」,「산업안전보건법」이 개정되었다. 아래에서는 직장 내 괴롭힘법의 주요내용과 실무적 적용에 대해 구체적으로 살펴보고자 한다.

1. 직장 내 괴롭힘 방지법 내용

(1) 사용자의 직장 내 괴롭힘 금지의무 명시

「근로기준법」제76조의2(직장 내 괴롭힘의 금지): 사용자 또는 근로자는 직장에서의 지위 또는 관계 등의 우위를 이용하여 업무상 적정범위를 넘어 다른 근로자에게 신체적·정신적 고통을 주거나 근무환경을 악화시키는 행위를 하여서는 아니 된다.

---

311) 김근주, 이경희,「직장 내 괴롭힘 실태와 제도적 규율 방안」, 한국노동연구원, 2017.12.
312) 홍성수외 7명,「직장 내 괴롭힘 실태조사」, 국가인권위원회, 2017.11.

(2) Obligations of the employer in case of an occurrence of workplace harassment (Article 76-3 of the LSA)

① Anyone who has learned the occurrence of workplace harassment may report such fact to the employer.

② Where an employer receives a report under paragraph (1) or becomes aware of the occurrence of workplace harassment, the employer shall, without delay, conduct an objective investigation of the persons involved to ascertain the fact.

③ Where necessary to protect employees who suffer or claim to suffer workplace harassment (hereinafter referred to as "victimized employees, etc.") while investigation under paragraph (2) is conducted, the employer shall take appropriate measures for the victimized employees, etc., such as transferring their place of work or ordering them a paid leave of absence. In such cases, the employer shall not take measures contrary to the will of the victimized employees, etc.

④ Where the occurrence of workplace harassment is verified as a result of investigation under paragraph (2), the employer shall take appropriate measures for the victimized employees, etc., such as transferring their place of work, giving them a lateral transfer or ordering them a paid leave of absence, if the victimized employees, etc. make a request.

⑤ Where the occurrence of workplace harassment is verified as a result of investigation under paragraph (2), the employer shall, without delay, take necessary measures, such as taking disciplinary measures against the perpetrator of workplace harassment or transferring his or her place of work. In such cases, before taking disciplinary measures, etc., the employer shall hear opinions of the victimized employees, etc. on such measures.

⑥ No employer shall dismiss employees who report the occurrence of workplace harassment, victimized employees, etc., or treat them unfavorably.

⑦ No person who investigates the occurrence of workplace harassment pursuant to paragraph (2), who receives a report on the details of investigation, or who participates in the investigation process of workplace harassment shall divulge confidential information learned in the course of investigation to any other persons against the will of the victimized employees, etc.: Provided, That the same shall not apply where the investigator reports matters relating to the investigation to the employer or provides necessary information at the request of a relevant institution.

(2) 직장 내 괴롭힘 발생 시 사용자의 조치 의무(근기법 제76조의3)

① 누구든지 직장 내 괴롭힘 발생 사실을 알게 된 경우 그 사실을 사용자에게 신고할 수 있다.

② 사용자는 제1항에 따른 신고를 접수하거나 직장 내 괴롭힘 발생 사실을 인지한 경우에는 지체 없이 당사자 등을 대상으로 그 사실 확인을 위하여 객관적으로 조사를 실시하여야 한다.

③ 사용자는 제2항에 따른 조사 기간 동안 직장 내 괴롭힘과 관련하여 피해를 입은 근로자 또는 피해를 입었다고 주장하는 근로자(이하 "피해근로자등"이라 한다)를 보호하기 위하여 필요한 경우 해당 피해근로자등에 대하여 근무장소의 변경, 유급휴가 명령 등 적절한 조치를 하여야 한다. 이 경우 사용자는 피해근로자등의 의사에 반하는 조치를 하여서는 아니 된다.

④ 사용자는 제2항에 따른 조사 결과 직장 내 괴롭힘 발생 사실이 확인된 때에는 피해근로자가 요청하면 근무장소의 변경, 배치전환, 유급휴가 명령 등 적절한 조치를 하여야 한다.

⑤ 사용자는 제2항에 따른 조사 결과 직장 내 괴롭힘 발생 사실이 확인된 때에는 지체 없이 행위자에 대하여 징계, 근무장소의 변경 등 필요한 조치를 하여야 한다. 이 경우 사용자는 징계 등의 조치를 하기 전에 그 조치에 대하여 피해근로자의 의견을 들어야 한다.

⑥ 사용자는 직장 내 괴롭힘 발생 사실을 신고한 근로자 및 피해근로자등에게 해고나 그 밖의 불리한 처우를 하여서는 아니 된다.

⑦ 제2항에 따라 직장 내 괴롭힘 발생 사실을 조사한 사람, 조사 내용을 보고받은 사람 및 그 밖에 조사 과정에 참여한 사람은 해당 조사 과정에서 알게 된 비밀을 피해근로자등의 의사에 반하여 다른 사람에게 누설하여서는 아니 된다. 다만, 조사와 관련된 내용을 사용자에게 보고하거나 관계 기관의 요청에 따라 필요한 정보를 제공하는 경우는 제외한다.

(3) Amendment to the Industrial Accident Compensation Insurance Act

Article 37 (1) of the IACI Act, which lists reasons for acceptance as occupational diseases, has added "illness caused by work-related mental stress, such as workplace harassment and abuse of the worker pursuant to Article 76-2 of the Labor Standards Act".

(4) Amendments to the Industrial Safety and Health Act

Article 4 of the ISH Act (Government obligations) added a new item: "10. Establishment, guidance and support of measures to prevent workplace harassment pursuant to Article 76-2 of the Labor Standards Act".

2. Explanation of Workplace Harassment

(1) Definition of workplace harassment

It is meaningful that the definition of workplace harassment clearly defines the obligations of the related employer and the standard of related harassment incidents. Until this concept was established, the labor law had no legal obligation or liability for workplace harassment. It is very meaningful that the Labor Standards Act has stipulated a definition of workplace harassment in order to strengthen the obligations of employers and to protect the workers with measures to receive remedy for workplace harassment. Therefore, under the existing legal system, the measures that a victim who had been harassed in the workplace could take to the employer included

① a claim for damages based on the liability of the victim for illegal acts (Article 750 of the Civil Act),

② a suit for damages (violation of the obligation of safety considerations by labor contract) (Article 390 of the Civil Act), and

③ a complaint under Article 30 (Human Rights Violation) of the National Human Rights Commission Act.

④ By informing the labor inspector and the Minister of Employment and Labor of the damages incurred, an employee can seek redress directly through filing a legal complaint for violation of Article 116.

(3)「산업재해보상보험법」 개정

업무상 질병으로 인정하는 사유를 열거한「산업재해보상보험법」 제37조 1항에 "「근로기준법」 제76조의2에 따른 직장 내 괴롭힘, 고객의 폭언 등 업무상 정신적 스트레스가 원인이 되어 발생한 질병"을 추가되었다.

(4)「산업안전보건법」 개정

「산업안전보건법」 제4조(정부의 책무)에서 "「근로기준법」 제76조의2에 따른 직장 내괴롭힘 예방을 위한 조치기준 마련, 지도 및 지원"(제10호)을 신설하였다.

2. 직장 내 괴롭힘 방지법 설명

(1) 직장 내 괴롭힘 정의 규정

직장 내 괴롭힘의 정의를 규정함으로써 관련된 사업주의 의무와 업무상 재해의 기준을 명확하였다는 점에서 의미가 있다. 이 개념이 정립되기 전에는 노동법상 직장 내 괴롭힘에 대한 법적인 의무나 책임관계를 갖지 못했다. 일반적으로 근로자들이 직장 내 괴롭힘을 이유로 권리구제를 받는 경우가 거의 없었다는 점에서, 이번「근로기준법」에 직장 내 괴롭힘의 정의를 명문화 함으로써 사업주의 의무를 강화하고 근로자의 보호방안을 마련하였다는데 큰 의미가 있다. 따라서 현재의 법제하에서 직장 내 괴롭힘을 당한 피해 근로자가 사용자를 대상으로 취할 수 있는 조치로는

① 가해근로자의 불법행위에 대한 사용자 책임을 이유로 한 손해배상 청구소송 (「민법」 제750조),

② 채무불이행(근로계약상 안전배려의무 위반)을 이유로 한 손해배상 소송(「민법」 제390조),

③「국가인권위원회법」 제30조(인권침해)에 기한 진정제기

④ 근로감독관, 고용노동부장관에 피해를 통보, 진정할 수 있고 제116조 위반으로 검사에게 직접 고소할 수 있는 방법이 생겼다.

(2) Establishment of the employer's duty for action in case of workplace harassment

In case of workplace harassment, the victim or a third party can notify the employer. An employer who has been informed of the occurrence of workplace harassment must conduct an investigation to confirm the fact. In the course of this investigation, measures should be taken to protect the victim and, if the investigation confirms the workplace harassment, disciplinary action should be taken without delay.

(3) The addition of 'workplace harassment' in the required items of the Rules of Employment

An employer who routinely employs 10 or more workers must fill out the 12 required items in the Rules of Employment and report them to the Minister of Employment and Labor (Article 93 of the LSA). Here is the required item added in relation to workplace harassment: "11. Matters concerning prevention and measures in case of occurrence of workplace harassment." In other words, it is stipulated in the Rules of Employment that the company has implemented measures related to workplace harassment.[313)]

(4) Penalties applicable for unfavorable treatment by an employer

It is regulated as the employer's duty, in the self-governing rules, that the employer should explore preventive measures against workplace harassment and take appropriate measures. However, if disadvantageous treatment of victims is taken, the employer should and can be severely punished, similar to the Equal Employment Act. In other words, Article 110 of the Labor Standards Act stipulates "imprisonment for up to three years or a fine of not more than KRW 30 million in violation of Article 76-3 (Paragraph 6) of this Act".

(5) Amendment to the Industrial Accident Compensation Insurance Act

The current Article 37 (1) of the IACI Act did not recognize occupational accidents caused by workplace harassment, but the revised law does recognize an occupational accident due to "illness caused by work-related mental stress such as workplace

---

313) Labor Ministry Guideline: "Operational Guides for the Rules of Employment", LSA Dept-1119, April 24, 2009.

(2) 직장 내 괴롭힘 발생 시 사용자의 조치 의무 신설

직장 내 괴롭힘 발생시에 피해근로자나 제3자가 사용자에 신고할 수 있다. 신고를 받았거나 직장 내 괴롭힘 발생을 인지한 사용자는 그 사실관계 확인을 위한 조사를 실시하여야 한다. 이 조사과정에서 피해근로자를 보호를 위한 조치를 하여야 하고, 조사결과 직장 내 괴롭힘이 사실로 확인되는 경우에는 지체 없이 징계조치를 하여야 한다.

(3) 취업규칙의 필요적 기재사항 중 직장 내 괴롭힘 추가

취업규칙은 상시 10명이상의 근로자를 사용하는 사용자는 필요적 기재사항 12가지를 기재한 취업규칙을 작성하고 고용노동부장관에게 신고하도록 하고 있다(「근로기준법」 제93조). 여기에 필요적 기재사항으로 "11. 직장 내 괴롭힘의 예방 및 발생 시 조치 등에 관한 사항"이 추가되었다. 즉, 직장 내 괴롭힘과 관련한 자체적인 회사의 조치 사항을 취업규칙에 명문화하여 이를 준수하도록 하고 있는 것이다.[313)]

(4) 직장 내 괴롭힘을 신고한 근로자와 피해자에 대한 해고 등 불이익 처우 시 벌칙

직장 내 괴롭힘에 대한 예방과 발생시 조사하여 합당한 조치를 하여야 하는 사업주의 의무는 법적인 의무가 자치규정으로 사업주 스스로 지켜야 하도록 규정화 되어 있다. 그러나 이러한 과정에서 피해근로자에 대한 불이익 처우에 대해서는 사용자가 강력한 처벌을 받을 수 있도록 「남녀고용평등법」과 동일하게 사용자의 법적 의무를 부과하고 있다. 즉, 「근로기준법」 제110조에 "이 법 제76조의3인 6항 위반 시, 3년 이하의 징역 또는 3천만 원 이하의 벌금"을 규정하고 있다.

(5) 「산업재해보상보험법」 개정

현행 산업재해보상보험법」제37조 1항에는 직장 내 괴롭힘에 의한 업무상 재해를 인정하지 않았으나, 개정법은 "직장 내 괴롭힘, 고객의 폭언 등 업무상 정

313) "취업규칙 해석 및 운영지침", 근로기준과-1119, 2009.4.24.

harassment", and so this article will provide a legal basis to occupational accidents. Diseases caused by workplace harassment were difficult to have recognized as a work-related injury by the Korea Workers' Welfare Corporation, and were accepted exceptionally only after complicated legal disputes. However, with the revised law, the Welfare Corporation has opened the way for victims to be recognized more quickly in the first work-related accident assessment stage.

(6) Amendments to the Industrial Safety and Health Act

Workplace harassment has an adverse effect on the mental and physical health of the workers, undermining their opportunity to work in a healthy environment. Therefore, the amendment to Article 4 of the ISH Act, to prevent illness caused by workplace harassment, imposes upon the government an obligation to act. In this regard, the Ministry of Employment and Labor has prepared'A Practical Manual for the Prevention of Workplace Harassment and Countermeasures Against It', which will be distributed to all companies. Unfortunately, this obligation to prevent workplace harassment is defined as an obligation of the state rather than a direct obligation of the employer, so that the employer is not responsible for violations of the ISH Act.

3. The Effect of the Workplace Harassment Prevention Law

It is not easy for ordinary workers to take legal action for harassment against a workplace because such matters take a considerable amount of time and money. However, the amendment to the Labor Standards Act clarifies the concept of workplace harassment, and in particular the obligation of prohibition of workplace harassment by an employer, along with the obligation to implement relief procedures that will enable victims to receive protection and relief from workplace harassment more quickly.

신적 스트레스가 원인이 돼 발생한 질병"도 업무상 재해로 인정받을 수 있는 법적 근거를 마련했다. 기존의 직장 내 괴롭힘으로 발생한 질병은 근로복지공단에서 업무상 재해로 인정받기 어려웠고, 공단의 불승인 결정에 불복하여 법원에서 힘겹게 다투고 나서야 권리를 구제받을 수 있었다. 그러나, 이번 개정법으로 인해 앞으로는 근로복지공단의 최초 업무상 재해 심사 단계에서 더욱 신속하게 피해를 구제 받을 수 있는 길이 열리게 되었다.

(6)「산업안전보건법」개정

직장 내 괴롭힘은 근로자의 정신적, 신체적 건강에 악영향을 끼쳐 해당 근로자의 건강한 근로의 기회를 훼손하게 되므로 직장 내 괴롭힘으로 발생하는 질병을 예방하는 차원에서 산업안전보건법 개정안 제4조는 직장 내 괴롭힘 예방에 관한 정부의 조치의무를 부과하고 있다. 이와 관련하여 고용노동부는 직장 내 괴롭힘에 대한 '직장 내 괴롭힘 판단 및 예방·대응 실무 매뉴얼'을 제작하여 기업에서 배포할 예정이다. 아쉬운 것은 이러한 직장 내 괴롭힘 예방의 의무를 사업주의 직접 의무가 아닌 국가의 의무로 규정함으로써 사업주가 산업안전보건법 위반으로부터는 책임을 면하고 있다는 점이다.

3. 직장 내 괴롭힘 방지법의 효과

기존에도 직장 내 괴롭힘이 발생한 경우에는 경우에 따라 그에 대한 민사상 손해배상이나 형사상 고소가 가능하였으나 그러한 법적 조치를 취한다는 것은 상당한 시간과 비용이 들기 때문에 일반 근로자가 현실적으로 직장 내 괴롭힘으로부터 구제받는 것은 쉽지 않았다. 그러나 이번「근로기준법」개정안은 직장 내 괴롭힘의 개념을 분명히 하였고, 특히 사업주의 직장 내 괴롭힘 금지와 구제절차 이행 의무를 규정함으로써 피해근로자가 직장 내 괴롭힘으로부터의 보호와 구제를 더욱 신속하게 받을 수 있게 되었다.

Section 3: The Employer Obligations in the Recruitment Process

I. Concept

Recruitment of workers is in principle the employer's prerogative, and for years there were no laws to regulate it. While the employment documents and recruitment review costs required by employers when hiring employees are a great burden to job seekers, there have been rare instances where the employer has returned the employment documents voluntarily or has returned them when requested by the job seeker. In addition, there have been irregularities in the recruitment process, such as retaining business suggestions of job seekers, and posting false recruitment advertisements for the purpose of promoting companies.[314)] As a result, the Act on the Fairness of the Recruitment Procedures(hereinafter referred to as the "Recruitment Procedure Act" or "the RPA") was enacted in 2014, and employers who ordinarily employ more than 30 workers fall under this Act, which limits their rights in the recruitment process(Article 3).

Numerous recruiting scandals have occurred recently in both public and private companies, and so a need was perceived for systematic supplementation in order to guarantee the fairness of the recruitment process.[315)] On July 17, 2019, the Recruitment Procedure Act was partially amended and implemented. The RPA prohibits certain hiring practices(Article 4-2, Paragraph 1), and also prohibits the act of giving or receiving goods, entertainment, or property during recruitment(Article 402, Paragraph 2). In addition, a penal clause(Article 17) has been established to handle violations, which implements effective sanctions.

In this article, I will look closely at how strictly unfair employment practices can be

---

314) Lee, Seunggil/Lee, Jooho, "Employment Freedom and Restrictions on Labor Laws: Focused on the Recruitment Procedure Act" 「Social Law Research」, Volume 26, Aug. 2015, Korean Social Law Association, p. 112.

315) Shin, Kwonchul, "Fairness in Recruiting – Focused on Employment Irregularities" 「Labor Law Studies」(67), August 2018, Korea Labor Law Society, pp. 95-96.

제3절 채용절차에 있어 사업주의 의무

Ⅰ. 개 념

기업에서 근로자 채용은 원칙상 사용자의 고유권한 사항으로, 기존에는 이를 규율하는 법이 없었다. 사용자가 근로자를 채용하고자 할 때 요구하는 채용서류와 채용심사 비용은 구직자들에게 큰 부담이 되고 있으나, 우리나라의 채용 시장의 관행상 사용자가 이를 적극적으로 반환하거나 구직자의 요구에 따라 돌려주는 경우는 거의 희박하다. 또한, 사용자가 근로자를 채용할 의사가 없으면서 구직자의 사업 아이디어를 수집하거나, 사업장을 홍보하기 위한 목적으로 거짓으로 채용하거나 구인 공고를 내는 등 채용과정에서 부조리가 발생하고 있다.[314] 이에 2014년 채용절차의 공정화에 관한 법률(이하 "채용절차법")이 제정되면서 상시 30명 이상 근로자를 사용하는 사업장의 경우, 채용과정에서 발생하는 사용자의 권한을 일부 제한하고 있다(제3조).

그리고 최근 공·사기업체에서 채용비리 사건들이 연이어 발생되면서 채용절차의 공정성을 담보할 수 있도록 제도적 보완의 필요성이 대두되었다.[315] 이에 2019년 7월 17일자로 채용절차법이 일부 개정되었다. 이번 채용절차법 일부 개정 사항은 "누구든지 법령을 위반하여 채용에 관한 부당한 청탁, 압력, 강요 등의 행위를 할 수 없도록 금지하고(제4조의2 제1호), 누구든지 채용과 관련하여 금전, 물품, 향응 또는 재산상의 이익을 제공하거나 수수하는 행위를 할 수 없도록 금지(제4조의2 제 2호)하는 내용을 담고 있습니다. 또한, 이를 위반 시 벌칙 조항(제17조)을 신설해 실효성 있는 제재방안을 포함하고 있다.

---

314) 이승길, 이주호, "노동법상 사용자의 채용자유와 제한 – 채용절차법을 중심으로–, 「사회법 연구」, 제26조, 2015.8, 한국사회법학회, 112면.

315) 신권철, "채용의 공정 – 채용비리를 중심으로, 「노동법학」(제67), 2018.9. 한국노동법학회, 95~96번.

sanctioned and also at employers' obligations in the process of hiring.

Ⅱ. Sanctions against Unfair Hiring Practices

1. Prohibition against false advertising (Article 4 of the RPA)

Employers shall not put out false recruitment advertisements for purposes such as collecting ideas or publicizing the workplace under the pretense of recruitment. Any employer who puts out a false recruitment advertisement in violation of this Act shall be punished by imprisonment of up to five years or a fine not exceeding KRW 20 million(Article 16 of the Act). This Article was designed to protect the interests of job applicants and to prevent social and other damages.[316)]

In addition, the employer shall not make changes to the recruitment advertisement that are adverse to any specific job seeker without justifiable reason, or adversely change the working conditions presented in the recruitment advertisement without justifiable reason after employing the job seeker. The employer shall not force the applicant to assign his ownership of intellectual property rights such as employment documents and related papers. In violation of this, the employer a fine of up to KRW 5 million will be levied(Article 17).

This implies that a change in the type of job, type of employment and/or working conditions proposed in the recruitment advertisement by the employer violates the principle of good faith, and shall not be allowed in consideration of the need to protect the trust of jobseekers in the job announcement. The prohibition against changing the working conditions as presented in the recruitment advertisement is intended to protect the interests of the job seeker by prohibiting an unfavorable change of working conditions, considering the fact that the job seeker is in an inferior position to the employer. In addition, the copyright and intellectual property rights of the jobseekers are protected by related laws such as the Copyright Act and the Framework Act on Intellectual Property, but because of the lack of substantive protection, the introduction of such restrictions in the RPA will enlarge the scope of direct protection.[317)]

---

316) Ministry of Employment and Labor, "Practical Manual for Fair Recruitment Procedures", 2015, pp. 23-25.

317) Ibid., p. 37.

본고에서는 채용상 불공정 제재와 채용상 지켜야 할 의무에 대해 자세히 살펴본다. 이를 통해 채용절차에 있어 사업주의 의무를 이해하는 데 도움이 되었으면 한다.

Ⅱ. 채용상 불공정 제재

1. 거짓 채용광고 금지 (법 제4조)

사용자는 근로자를 채용할 의사가 없으면서 채용을 가장하여 아이디어를 수집하거나 사업장을 홍보하기 위한 목적 등으로 거짓의 채용광고를 내면 안 된다. 이를 위반하면 5년 이하 징역 또는 2,000만원 이하 벌금의 형사 처벌을 받게 된다(법 제16조). 이는 취업하기 위해 채용광고를 보고 응모한 구직자의 권익을 보호하고, 사회적 비용과 피해의 발생을 방지하기 위한 것이다.[316)]

또한, 사용자는 정당한 사유 없이 채용광고 내용을 구직자에게 불리하게 변경하거나 구직자를 채용한 후 정당한 사유 없이 채용광고에서 제시한 근로조건을 불리하게 변경해서는 안 된다. 그리고 사용자는 구직자에게 채용서류 및 이와 관련한 저작권 등의 지식 재산권을 자신에게 귀속하도록 강요해서도 안 된다. 이를 위반하면 500만원 이하 과태료를 부과 받게 된다(법 제17조).

이는 사용자가 채용공고에서 제시한 직종, 고용형태 및 근로조건을 임의로의 변경은 신의성실의 원칙에 맞지 않고 구직자의 구인공고에 대한 신뢰는 보호할 필요성이 있음을 고려한 것이다. 채용광고에 제시된 근로조건의 변경금지는 구직자가 사용자에 비하여 열위에 있는 현실을 감안하여 근로조건을 구직자에게 불리하게 변경하는 것을 금지하여 구직자의 권익을 보호하려는 취지이다. 그리고 구직자가 제출한 저작권이나 지적재산권에 관하여서는 「저작권법」과 「지식재산기본법」등 관련 법령에서 그 권리를 보호하고 있지만, 실질적 보호가 미흡하기 때문에 채용절차법에서 금지규정을 도입하면서 직접적인 보호의 범위가 확대되었다.[317)]

---

316) 고용노동부, "채용절차 공정화에 관한 법률 업무 매뉴얼", 2015, 23~25면.
317) 고용노동부, "채용절차 공정화에 관한 법률 업무 매뉴얼", 2015, 37면.

2. Prohibition against unfair recruiting (Article 4-2 of the RPA)

Whether or not an employer hires a particular individual is the employer's own prerogative, and needs to be respected. However, if employees are being hired through open competition rather than individual recruitment, they should be given fair competition opportunities based on the job announcement. The revised Law on Recruitment Procedures enacted in July 2019 is intended to prevent unfair employment practices and to prevent actions such as unfair requests, pressure and force that hinder sound employment and social order; this Act also prohibits the offering or receiving of money or goods. It imposes a fine of up to KRW 30 million for violations.

Although the existing penalties for unfair employment apply to business obstruction under the Criminal Act, there are limits to the application for criminal offenses. Therefore, the Recruitment Procedure Act introduced this new content and can now punish unfair recruitment practices under labor law. In order to establish a business obstruction in Article 314[318)] of the Criminal Act in the case of unfair recruitment, it is necessary to have an illegal act in the form of hierarchy or power information-processing, and the action must interfere with human affairs; that is, the work of others. However, there is a legal limit to applying the Criminal Act because the person who engages in illegal recruitment is usually the decision-maker of the company, and the recruitment work corresponds to his original work and does not correspond to an 'other person's work'.[319)] Therefore, it is meaningful that we can now partially supplement the vacancy in punishment of unfair recruitment practices in the Criminal Act by introducing the prohibition against unfair recruitment practices in the Recruitment Procedure Act.[320)]

---

318) Article 314 (Interference with Business)
(1) A person who interferes with the business of another by the method of Article 313 or by the threat of force, shall be punished by imprisonment for not more than five years or by a fine not exceeding fifteen million won.
(2) Any person who interferes with another person's business by damaging or destroying any data processor, such as a computer, or special media records, such as electromagnetic records, or inputting false information or improper order into a data processor, or making any impediment in processing any data by other way, shall also be subject to the same punishment as referred to in paragraph (1).

319) Jung, Jongchul, "Illegal Recruitment and Related Legal Responsibility" 「Labor Law」, June 2018, Jungangkyungjae.

320) Shin, Kwonchul, "Fairness of Recruitment – Focused on Falsified Recruitment, 「Labor Law Study」(67th), Sept. 2018. Korean Labor Law Society, pp. 95-96.

2. 채용비리 금지 (법 제4조의2)

사용자가 누구를 채용할지 여부는 사용자의 고유권한 이므로 존중되어야 한다. 그러나 사용자가 개별채용이 아닌 공개경쟁을 통해 채용하는 경우에는 채용공고에 따른 공정한 경쟁의 기회를 부여하여야 한다. 이번 2019년 7월에 개정 시행된 채용절차법은 공정한 취업기회를 박탈하고 건전한 고용질서와 사회통합을 저해하는 채용비리 등을 방지하기 위하여 채용에 관한 부당한 청탁, 압력, 강요 등의 행위 및 채용과 관련하여 금전, 물품 등을 제공하거나 수수하는 행위를 금지하고 있다. 이를 위반하는 경우 3천만원 이하의 과태료를 부과하고 있다.

기존의 채용비리에 대한 처벌은 형법의 업무방해죄를 적용하였으나, 법리상 업무방해죄의 적용에는 한계가 있기 때문에 이번 채용절차법에서는 위의 내용을 새롭게 명시하여 노동법으로써 불공정 행위를 처벌하도록 하고 있다. 채용비리에 있어 형법 제314조[318]의 업무방해죄가 성립되기 위해서는 위계나 위력 정보처리 등을 통한 수단상의 위법이 있어야 하고, 사람의 업무 즉 타인의 업무에 대한 방해가 있어야 한다. 그런데 부정채용의 관여자는 통상 해당 회사의 의사결정권자로서 채용업무는 본연의 업무에 해당하고 업무방해죄 성립을 위한 '타인의 업무'에는 해당되지 않는다는 법률상의 한계가 존재하였다.[319] 따라서 이번 채용비리를 채용절차법에서 금지함으로써 기존에 채용비리행위 제재에 대한 공백을 일부 보완하였다는데 그 의미가 있다.[320]

318) 제314조【업무방해】① 제313조의 방법 또는 위력으로써 사람의 업무를 방해한 자는 5년 이하의 징역 또는 1천500만원 이하의 벌금에 처한다. ② 컴퓨터등 정보처리장치 또는 전자기록등 특수매체기록을 손괴하거나 정보처리장치에 허위의 정보 또는 부정한 명령을 입력하거나 기타 방법으로 정보처리에 장애를 발생하게 하여 사람의 업무를 방해한 자도 제1항의 형과 같다.

319) 정종철, "부정채용과 그에 따른 법적 책임", 「노동법률」, 2018.6, 중앙경제사.

320) 신권철, "채용의 공정 - 채용비리를 중심으로", 앞의 논문, 95~96면.

3. Prohibition against requesting personal information that is not relevant to the job (Article 4-3 of the Act)

The employer is not allowed to require that the applicant include personal information in the basic recruitment form that is not required for the performance of his/her job, or to collect it as evidence material. Such restricted personal information shall be collected and processed only in accordance with the following: ① the physical condition of the applicant's appearance, height, weight, etc., ② the area of origin of the applicant, marital status and property; ③ education, occupation, and property. A fine of up to KRW 5 million will be imposed for violations. However, in the legislative process, the attachment of an identification photo to the employment documents was excluded from the collection restrictions. The reason for this is that ID photos are considered a necessary part of the applicant's identity verification in both the recruitment review and the interview.[321)]

4. Prohibition against jobseekers paying for recruitment review (Article 9 of the Act)

The employer shall not incur any monetary cost(recruitment review fee) for the job seeker other than the cost of submitting the job application document. However, if there is an unavoidable circumstance due to the specific nature of the workplace or occupation, it may be approved by the Minister of Employment and Labor to have a job seeker pay a portion of the recruitment review fee. A fine of up to KRW 3 million is imposed for violations.

Here, recruitment review costs are directly related to the recruitment, such as the cost of planning and preparing the recruitment, the recruitment ad, etc., and recruiting applicants, which refers to any indirect costs. The employer shall be fully liable for this cost in accordance with the principle of beneficiary burden.[322)]

---

321) Kwak, Younghee, "Although the Recruitment Procedure Act has passed, it is still possible to request an 'ID photo'",「Labor Law」, May 2019, Jongankyungjae.

322) MOEL, above manual, pages 64-65.

3. 직무와 관련 없는 개인정보 요구 금지 (법 제4조의3)

사용자는 구직자에 대하여 그 직무의 수행에 필요하지 아니한 개인정보를 기초심사자료에 기재하도록 요구하거나 입증자료로 수집하여서는 아니된다. 그러한 수집이 제한된 개인정보는 ① 구직자의 본인의 용모, 키, 체중 등의 신체적 조건, ② 구직자 본인의 출신지역, 혼인여부 및 재산, ③ 구직자 본인의 직계 존비속 및 형제자매의 학력, 직업, 재산 등이다. 이를 위반한 경우, 500만원 이하의 과태료를 부과한다. 다만, 입법과정에서 채용서류에 증명사진 부착은 수집제한에서 제외되었다. 그 이유는 증명사진의 경우는 채용 시험이나 면접에서 수험생 동일성 확인을 위해 반드시 필요한 자료라고 판단하였기 때문이다.[321)]

4. 구직자에게 채용심사 비용 부담 금지 (법 제9조)

사용자는 채용심사를 목적으로 구직자에게 채용서류 제출에 드는 비용 외 일체의 금전적 비용(채용심사비용)을 부담시킬 수 없다. 다만, 사업장 및 직종의 특수성으로 인해 불가피한 사정이 있는 경우, 고용노동부 장관의 승인을 받아 구직자에게 채용 심사 비용 일부를 부담하게 할 수 있다. 이를 위반시 300만원 이하의 과태료를 부과한다.

여기서 채용심사 비용은 사용자가 채용을 계획하고 준비하는데 드는 비용부터, 채용광고 등의 비용, 채용서류를 접수 받은 후 해당 구직자에 대한 채용적격 여부를 심사하는데 드는 비용 등 채용과 관련하여 사용자에게 직접 또는 간접적으로 발생하는 일체의 비용을 말한다. 이 부분에 대해 수익자부담원칙에 따라 사용자가 전적으로 부담하여야 한다.[322)]

321) "채용절차법 통과됐지만, '증명사진'은 요구 가능하다", 「노동법률」, 2019. 5, 중앙경제사.

322) 고용노동부, "채용절차 공정화에 관한 법률 업무 매뉴얼", 2015, 64~65면.

Ⅲ. Employer Obligations in the Recruitment Process

1. Obligation to notify

The employer has obligations to inform job seekers of four things. Job seekers should be notified that the recruitment documents have been properly received, that the recruitment schedule and procedures are ongoing, the status of their recruitment, and of the right for rejected applicants to have their documents returned. Notification methods include posting on a homepage, text transmission by mobile phone, e-mail, fax, and telephone. Notifications must be made without delay for the relevant matters in the recruitment procedure.

1) Notice upon receiving application documents: Acceptance of application documents(Article 7, Clause 2 of the RPA)
2) Notice during the recruitment process: recruitment schedule and recruitment process(Article 8)
3) Notice of status of application for recruitment: whether the job seeker has been hired or not(Article 10)
4) Notice if employment has been denied: return of employment documents, etc(Article 11, Paragraph 6).[323)]

2. Obligation to return documents (Articles 11 and 17, Paragraph 3)

Since the employer requires various evidence of qualifications when hiring, job seekers are required to pay an average of KRW 155,000 per application to verify their qualifications, meaning the average cost for a job seeker to get a job amounts to KRW 4,495,000(when applying 29 times).[324)] If a job seeker receives their employment documents back, this can reduce the cost of finding a job.

If a job seeker who is not hired requests the return of his recruitment documents, the employer shall send or deliver the documents to the jobseeker within 14 days from the date on which the jobseeker requested them, after confirming the job seeker's identification. However, the company shall not be obliged to return any documents submitted through the homepage or e-mail or

---

323) Specific items employers need to tell job seekers (I) the fact that the job seeker may claim the return of the hiring document; (ii) the type and scope of the hiring document to be returned; Implementation period, (v) return method and cost burden, (vi) retention period and destruction of employment documents.

324) A number given by the recruitment company 'Human' to the Korean lawmaker, Kyeryun Shin on Feb. 3, 2013.

Ⅲ. 채용상 지켜야 할 의무

1. 고지의무

사용자는 구직자에 대하여 총 4번의 고지 의무가 있다. 채용서류가 잘 접수되었는지, 채용일정 및 과정은 어떻게 진행되고 있는지, 채용여부 및 불합격자 서류반환 청구권한이 있음을 고지하여야 한다. 고지방법은 채용절차에 있어 해당사항에 대해 지체없이 홈페이지 게시, 휴대전화에 의한 문자전송, 전자우편, 팩스, 전화 등을 이용한다.

1) 응시 접수 단계에서의 고지: 채용서류의 접수사실(법 제7조 제2항)
2) 채용 과정 단계에서의 고지: 채용일정 및 채용과정(법 제8조)
3) 채용 확정 단계에서의 고지: 채용여부(법 제10조)
4) 채용 확정 후의 고지: 채용서류 등의 반환 등(법 제11조 제6항).[323]

2. 서류반환 의무(법 제11조, 제17조 제3항)

사용자가 근로자를 채용과정에 있어 구직자의 능력을 파악하기 위해 다양한 종류의 자격증명서, 입증자료 등을 요구하기 때문에 구직자가 기업 1개소를 지원하는데 부담비용이 평균 15만5천원(경제적 비용 6만3천원+시간적 비용 9만2천원)이고, 취업 성공시 까지 1인당 449만 5천원(29회 지원)에 달한다고 조사되었다.[324] 구직자가 채용서류를 돌려받게 되면 그만큼 구직에 필요한 비용을 절감할 수 있다.

사용자는 최종 채용이 거절된 구직자가 채용서류 반환을 청구하는 경우에는 본인임을 확인한 후 구직자가 반환을 청구한 날로부터 14일 안에 구직자에게 채용서류를 발송하거나 전달해야 한다. 다만, 홈페이지 또는 전자우편으로 제

---

323) 사용자가 구직자에게 알려야 할 구체적인 사항 (i) 채용서류의 반환을 청구할 수 있다는 사실, (ii) 반환청구 대상 채용서류의 종류 및 범위, (iii) 반환청구 제출 방법, (iv) 반환 청구기간 및 이행기간, (v) 반환 방법 및 비용부담, (vi) 채용서류의 보관기간 및 파기이다.

324) 신계륜 민수통합당 의원이 취업전문사이트 '사람인'에 의뢰해 설문조사 결과(2013.2.3).

documents which were voluntarily submitted by the applicant without the employer's request. To be prepared for such requests, the employer shall keep the employment documents for a period no less than 180 days, which shall begin 14 days from the date the job seeker was officially not hired, and notify the job seeker of the period of retention. In principle, the cost of returning the employment documents is borne by the employer. However, the job seeker may be liable to pay expenses to receive the documents according to the individual application. If the company does not fulfill its obligation to retain the employment documents, or if the company does not notify the job seeker, the employer will be subject to a penalty of up to KRW 3 million.

3. Storing and deleting documents

The employer shall keep the employment documents for the period prescribed by Presidential Decree. However, the employer shall be deemed to have fulfilled the obligation to return the employment documents if the employment documents are lost due to natural disaster or other reasons not caused by the employer(Article 11(3)). The retention period is from the date of recruitment application to the date of request for the return of documents. If the company is requested to return the documents, the employer must send them by special delivery from the post office(Article 3 of the Enforcement Decree to the Act).

The employment documents contain the job seeker's personal information, and as the need for privacy is paramount, the documents should be destroyed after a certain period of time. If the period for requesting return expires or if the employment documents are not returned, the employment documents must be destroyed in accordance with the Personal Information Protection Act(Article 11, Paragraph 4).[325] The destruction of employment documents shall take place within 5 days after this period expires, as stated in the Personal Information Protection Act.[326] The methods acceptable for destroying personal information are: ① For electronic files: permanent deletion in a way that cannot be restored; ② For recorded, printed, written or other recording media: shredded or incinerated(Article 16 of the Enforcement Decree to the Personal Information Protection Act).

---

325) Article 21 (Destruction of Personal Information) (1) A personal information controller shall destroy personal information without delay when the personal information becomes unnecessary owing to expiry of the retention period, attainment of the purpose for processing the personal information, etc.: Provided, that this shall not apply where the retention of such personal information is mandatory under other statutes.

326) Ministry of Public Administration and Security, Ministry of Employment and Labor, "Guidelines for Personal Information Protection - Personnel and Labor Fields", 2012, p. 23.

출했거나 사용자의 요구 없이 자발적으로 구직자가 채용서류를 제출한 경우는 반환 의무를 지지 않는다. 사용자는 구직자의 반환 청구에 대비해 구직자의 채용여부가 확정된 후 14일부터 180일 안에서 회사가 정한 기간만큼 채용서류를 보관해야 하며, 보관 기간은 구직자에게 고지해야 한다. 채용서류 반환에 드는 비용은 원칙적으로 사용자가 부담하나, 구직자의 신청에 따라 수취인 부담으로 발송하는 경우에는 구직자가 부담할 수도 있다. 만약, 채용서류의 보관 의무를 다하지 않거나 이러한 사실을 구직자에게 알리지 않으면 과태료 300만원 이하에 처해지게 된다.

3. 서류의 보관 및 삭제

사용자는 대통령령으로 정하는 기간 동안 채용서류를 보관해야 한다. 다만, 천재지변이나 그밖에 사용자에게 책임 없는 사유로 채용서류가 멸실된 경우, 사용자는 채용서류의 반환 의무를 이행한 것으로 본다(제11조 제3항). 보관 기간은 반환 미청구 시 채용서류의 반환을 청구일까지, 반환 요청 시에는 채용서류를 첨부한 특수취급 우편물의 발송일까지 또는 구직자에게 전달한 시점까지이다(시행령 제3조).

채용서류에는 구직자의 개인정보가 담겨있어 사생활 보호의 필요성이 높으므로 일정 기간이 지나면 그 서류를 파기해야 한다. 반환 청구기간이 지나거나 채용서류를 반환하지 않은 경우「개인정보 보호법」[325]에 따라 채용서류를 파기해야 한다(법 제11조 제4항). 이 경우 채용서류의 파기할 시점은 개인정보 보호법에서 명시하고 있듯이 '지체 없이'(5일 이내) 파기해야 한다.[326] 개인정보의 파기방법은 ① 전자적 파일 형태인 경우: 복원이 불가능한 방법으로 영구 삭제, ② 기록물, 인쇄물, 서면, 그 밖의 기록매체인 경우: 파쇄 또는 소각한다(개인정보 보호법시행령 제16조).

---

325) 개인정보 보호법 제21조【개인정보의 파기】①개인정보처리자는 보유 기간의 경과, 개인정보의 처리 목적 달성 등 그 개인정보가 불필요하게 되었을 때는 지체 없이 그 개인정보를 파기하여야 한다. 다만, 다른 법령에 따라 보존하여야 하는 경우에는 그러하지 아니한다.

326) 행정안정부, 고용노동부, "개인정보보호 가이드라인-인사,노무분야", 2012, 23면.

Section 4: The Anti-corruption Act (the Kim Young-Ran Act)

I. Concept

Even though Korea has reached the status of a developed country, many indices still show that the morality of public officials is perceived as being relatively low. According to a survey by the Anti-Corruption and Civil Rights Commission(ACRC), on the corruption perception index, 53.4% of the people who participated in the survey responded that civil servants are corrupt. Even in an international evaluation in 2018, Korea's Corruption Perceptions Index ranked 57; in 30th place out of 37 OECD countries.[327] Accordingly, it became necessary to legislate a comprehensive anti-corruption act in order to overcome the limitations of the existing anti-corruption laws(the Criminal Act, the Public Service Ethics Act, etc.) in preventing corruption, get rid of the corruption within the public services, and reach a transparent society. Thus, the "Improper Solicitation and Graft Act(hereinafter referred to as the "Kim Young-Ran Act" or the "Anti-corruption Act") was enacted on March 27, 2015 at the suggestion of Kim Young-Ran, chief of the ACRC, and was implemented on September 28, 2016. This Kim Young-Ran Act includes in its scope of application employees engaged in media companies, private schools, and even the spouses of employees, and so affects the lives of ordinary people.[328] In particular, this Act contains joint penal provisions that can be used to punish a company when an employee violates this law regarding improper solicitation or provision of financial or other advantages, and so all companies should implement thorough precautions for the purpose of ensuring the avoidance of any joint punishment.

Hereunder, I will review the Kim Young-Ran Act in terms of its principles and the exceptions to what is considered improper solicitation and prohibited financial or other advantages, after which I will also carefully examine its joint penal provisions, their application, and the necessary efforts required of a company.

---

327) Document issued by the Anti-Corruption and Civil Rights Commission in 2019.

328) The scope of application is much wider, and so several petitions to the Constitution Court were submitted, but all were rejected. Constitutional Court ruling on July 28, 2016 (2015 Hunma 236, 412, 662, 273 combined cases).

제4절 부패방지법 (김영란법)

Ⅰ. 의 의

우리나라는 선진국에 이르렀음에도 불구하고 여러 지표에서 나타나는 공직사회의 도덕성은 낮은 편이다. 2018년 국민권익위원회의 부패인식도 조사결과 국민의 53.4%가 공직사회가 부패하였다고 응답하였으며, 2018년 국제적 기준에서도 우리나라 부패인식지수(CIP)는 57점(100점 만점)으로 OECD 회원국 기준 37개국 중 30위를 차지하였다.[327] 따라서 부패방지를 위한 기존의 법체계의 한계와 공직사회의 부패를 추방하고 투명한 사회로의 진입을 위해 부패방지법 제정이 절실히 요구되었다. 이에 '부정청탁 및 금품 등 수수의 금지에 관한 법률'(이하 '김영란법' 또는 '청탁금지법')이 국가권익위원회 김영란 위원장의 제안으로 2015년 3월 27일 제정 되어 2016년 9월 28일 시행되었다. 이 김영란법은 공직자의 범위에 언론인, 사립학교 관계자, 심지어 그 배우자까지 포함시킴으로써 일반국민들의 생활과도 밀접하게 관련되어 있다.[328] 특히 양벌규정이 김영란법에 포함되어 직원의 부정청탁과 금품제공이 회사의 사용자 책임으로까지 확대 적용됨에 따라 회사의 면책을 위한 철저한 조치가 필요하게 되었다.

아래에서는 김영란법의 주요 내용인 불법청탁과 금품수수의 원칙과 예외에 대해 살펴보고, 기업체에서 관심이 있는 양벌규정에 대해 구체적으로 언급하고자 한다.

327) 국민권익위원회 자료, "부정청탁 및 금품 등 수수의 금지에 관한 법률 해설" 2019.
328) 적용대상의 너무 광범위하다 하여 위헌심사까지 청구하였으나, 모두 기각되었다. 헌법재판소 2016.7.28, 2015헌마236, 412, 662, 673(병합) 결정.

Ⅱ. The Anti-corruption Act

1. Concept and scope of application

(1) Concept

The purpose of this Act is to ensure that civil servants and relevant persons fulfill their duties in an upright manner and to secure the public's confidence in public institutions by forbidding improper solicitation of civil servants or other relevant persons and by prohibiting them from accepting financial or other advantages. This Act is composed of two major parts: anti-solicitation measures and prohibited financial and other advantages.

(2) Scope against application

1) "Civil servants and relevant persons" refers to

① civil servants and employees working in

② public service-related organizations,[329)]

③ public institutions,

④ schools of various levels and educational corporations, and

⑤ media companies.

2) Spouses of civil servants and relevant persons

3) Private persons performing public duties:

① members of various committees,

② persons who have authority delegated by a public institution,

③ persons on assignment from the private sector to a public institution,

④ professionals who engage in deliberation or assessment in relation to public duties.

4) General people

persons who improperly solicit civil servants or who offer them financial or other advantages

---

329) Public service-related organizations: The Bank of Korea, public companies (Korea Electric Power Corporation, etc.); local corporations (Seoul Metro, etc.); government-invested corporations/subsidiary organizations (Korean Red Cross, etc.); work assignment organizations (National Agricultural Cooperative Federation, etc.); institutes appointing directors (Korea Workers' Compensation and Welfare Service, etc.).

Ⅱ. 청탁금지법의 내용

1. 목적 및 적용 범위

(1) 목 적

김영란법은 공직자에 대한 부정청탁과 금품수수를 금지함으로써 공직자의 공정한 직무수행을 보장하고 공공기관에 대한 국민의 신뢰를 확보하는 것을 목적으로 한다. 이 청탁금지법은 부정청탁 그리고 금품수수의 금지라는 두 개의 축으로 이루어져 있다.

(2) 적용 범위

청탁금지법이 적용되는 자는 아래와 같다.

1) 공직자 등은

① 공무원,

② 공직 유관단체의 직원,[329)]

③ 공공기관의 직원,

④ 사립학교의 교직원,

⑤ 언론사의 직원을 말한다.

2) 공직자 등의 배우자

3) 공무수행인

① 각종 위원회에 참여하는 민간위원,

② 공공기관의 업무를 위임받는 자, 위탁하는 자,

③ 공공기관에 파견근무 하는 민간인,

④ 심의·평가 업무를 담당하는 외부 전문가

4) 일반국민

공직자 등에게 부정청탁을 하거나 금품을 제공한 민간인.

---

329) 공직유관단체: 한국은행, 공기업(한국전력공사 등), 지방공사(서울메트로 등), 정부출자/ 출연/ 보조기관(대한적십자사 등), 입무위탁기관(농협중앙회 등), 임원선임기관(근로복지공단 등).

2. Prohibition of improper solicitation[330)]

(1) Details (14 types)

① Authorization, permission, and any other actions,

② mitigating or remitting various administrative dispositions or punishments,

③ intervening or exerting influence in the appointment, promotion, or any other personnel management of civil servants,

④ using influence so that a person is appointed to or rejected from a position which is involved in the decision-making of a public institution,

⑤ using influence so that a specific individual is chosen or rejected by a public institution,

⑥ using influence so that duty-related confidential information on tenders, auctions, etc., is disclosed,

⑦ using influence so that a specific person is selected or rejected as a party to a contract,

⑧ intervening or exerting influence so that subsidies, etc., are assigned to, provided to, invested in, or deposited with a specific person,

⑨ using influence so that a specific person buys, exchanges and/or uses goods and services that are produced, provided or managed by public institutions beyond the normal monetary value,

⑩ using influence so that admissions, grades, performance tests or other matters related to schools of various levels are handled and/or manipulated,

⑪ using influence so that physical examination for conscripts, assignment to a military unit, appointments or any other matters related to military service are handled in a specific way,

⑫ using influence so that, in various assessments and judgments performed by public institutions, specific assessments or judgments are made,

⑬ using influence so that a certain person is selected or rejected as the subject of administrative guidance, control, inspection or examination, or where the outcome thereof is manipulated or discovered violations are ignored, and

⑭ using influence so that the investigation, judgment, adjudication, decision, conciliation, arbitration, or settlement of a case or any other equivalent function is handled in a specific manner.

---

330) Punishment for improper solicitation (Articles 22, 23 of the Act)

Violation	Punishment
A stakeholder improperly solicits a civil servant directly	None
A stakeholder improperly solicits a civil servant through a third party	Fine for negligence not exceeding KRW 10 million
A person improperly solicits a civil servant on behalf of a third party (private person)	Fine for negligence not exceeding KRW 20 million
A civil servant improperly solicits another civil servant on behalf of a third party	Fine for negligence not exceeding KRW 30 million
A civil servant or relevant person who performs functions as directed by an improper solicitation	Imprisonment for not more than two years or a fine not exceeding KRW 20 million

2. 부정청탁금지[330)]

(1) 내용(14가지)

청탁금지법은 직접 또는 제3자를 통하여 직무를 수행하는 공직자 등에게 부정청탁을 하는 것을 금지하였다.

① 인가·허가 등 직무처리,
② 행정처분·형벌부과 감경·면제,
③ 채용·승진 등 인사 개입,
④ 공공기관 의사결정 관여 직위 선정·탈락 등에 개입,
⑤ 공공기관 주관 수상·포상 등 선정·탈락에 개입,
⑥ 입찰·경매 등에 관한 직무상 비밀 누설,
⑦ 특정인 계약 당사자 선정·탈락에 개입,
⑧ 보조금 등의 배정·지원, 투자 등에 개입,
⑨ 공공기관이 생산·공급하는 재화 및 용역의 비정상적 거래,
⑩ 학교 입학·성적 등 업무처리·조작,
⑪ 징병검사 등 병역 관련 업무처리,
⑫ 공공기관이 실시하는 각종 평가·판정 업무 개입,
⑬ 행정지도·단속 등 대상 선정·배제, 위법사항 묵인,
⑭ 사건의 수사·재판 등 업무처리이다.

330) 부정청탁에 대한 제재(청탁금지법 제22조, 제23조)

위반 행위자	제재수준
직접 부정청탁을 한 이해당사자	제재 없음.
제3자를 위하여 부정청탁을 한 이해당사자	1천만원 이하 과태료
제3자를 위하여 부정청탁을 한 일반인	2천만원 이하 과태료
제3자를 위하여 부정청탁을 한 공직자 등	3천만원 이하 과태료
부정청탁에 따라 직무를 수행한 공직자 등	2년 이하 징역 또는 2천만원 이하 벌금

(2) Exceptions

In order not to discourage claiming legitimate rights, claiming, or demanding, the following 7 items are permitted under the Anti-corruption Act:

① Requesting certain actions, such as asking for remedy against or resolution of infringement of a right; ② Publicly soliciting a civil servant or relevant person to take a certain action; ③ Where an elected public official, political party, civil society organization, etc., conveys a third party's complaints and grievances the public interest; ④ Requesting or demanding that a public institution complete a certain duty within a statutory deadline, or inquiring or asking verification about progress; ⑤ Applying or making a request for verification or certification of a certain duty or juristic obligation; ⑥ Requesting an explanation or interpretation of systems, procedures or Acts and/or subordinate statutes related to a certain duty in the form of an inquiry or consultation; and ⑦ Any other conduct not deemed as contravening social norms.

3. Acceptance of financial or other advantages[331)]

(1) Details

The previous Anti-Corruption Act required both a "work-related connection" and clear "benefits given in return for favors" in order for an action to be subject to punishment, but this new Act does not require directly-related "bribery in return for favors", and any civil servant who receives KRW 1 million or more will be punished without the need for any work-related connection. In cases where a civil servant or relevant person accepts, requests, or promises to receive any financial or other advantage with a value in excess of KRW 1 million at one time or a total of KRW 3 million within the same fiscal year from the same person, regardless of the relationship between such offer and his or her duties, he/she is

331) Punishment for Graft (Articles 22, 23 of the Act)

Violation	Punishment
· A civil servant receives a financial or other advantage in excess of KRW 1 million at one time or a total of KRW 3 million within the same fiscal year from the same person, regardless of a connection to his or her duties · A civil servant does not report the fact that his or her spouse received a financial or other advantage · A person provides a financial or other advantage	Imprisonment for not more than three years or a fine not exceeding KRW 30 million
· A civil servant receives a financial or other advantage not exceeding KRW 1 million in connection with his or her duties, regardless of whether such offer is given in exchange for favors · A civil servant does not report such financial or other advantage received by his or her spouse · A person provides a financial or other advantage to a civil servant or his or her spouse.	Fine for negligence of two to five times the received amount
· A civil servant receives an honorarium exceeding the allowable limit for an outside lecture	Fine for negligence not exceeding KRW 5 million

(2) 예 외

정당한 권리, 주장 또는 요구가 위축되는 것을 방지하기 위하여 아래의 7가지에는 청탁금지법이 적용되지 않는다.

① 법령·기준에서 정한 절차, 방법에 따른 요구, 건의 등, ② 공개적으로 특정 행위를 요구, ③ 선출직 공직자, 시민 단체 등이 공익 목적으로 제3자 고충민원 전달, ④ 법정기한 내 업무처리 요구 진행상황 확인·문의, ⑤ 직무 또는 법률관계에 관한 확인, 증명 등 신청·요구, ⑥ 질의·상담을 통한 법령·제도 등 설명·해석 요구, ⑦ 기타 사회상규에 위배되지 않는 행위.

3. 금품수수금지[331)]

(1) 내 용

기존의 뇌물죄는 처벌을 위해 '직무관련성'과 '대가성'을 모두 필요로 하지만, 청탁금지법은 '대가성'을 요구하지 않고, 100만원을 초과하는 금품의 수수에는 직무관련성도 없어도 처벌된다. 공직자가 받은 물품이 1회 100만원 또는 회계연도 기간 300만원을 초과하는 경우에는 직무 관련 여부와 관계없이 공직자와 제공(제공의 약속)한 자 모두 처벌된다. 다만, 수수한 금품이 1회 100만원 이하, 회계연도 300만원 이하인 경우에는 직무관련이 있어야 처벌된다.

여기서 금품 등이라 함은 금전, 물품 기타의 재산적 이익뿐만 아니라 편의 제공과 사람의 수요·욕망을 충족시키기에 족한 일체의 유형·무형의 이익을 포함

331) 금품수수에 대한 제재 (청탁금지법 제22조, 제23조)

위반행위자	제재수준
·1회 100만원 또는 매 회계연도 300만원 초과 금품 등 수수 공직자들 ·배우자의 위 금품 등 수수 사실을 알고도 신고하지 않은 공직자등 ·위 금품 등을 공직자등 또는 그 배우자에게 제공한 자	3년 이하 징역 또는 3천만원 이하 벌금
·직무와 관련하여 1회 100만원 이하의 금품 등을 수수한 공직자 등 ·배우자의 위 금품 등 수수 사실을 알고도 신고하지 않은 공직자 등 ·위 금품 등을 공직자 등 또는 그 배우자에게 제공한 자	수수금액의 2배 이상 5배 이하 과태료
·외부강의 등 초과 사례금을 수수한 후 신고·반환을 하지 아니한 공직자등	500만원 이하 과태료

subject to criminal punishment. However, in instances where less than KRW 1 million is accepted at one time, or less than a total of KRW 3 million within the same fiscal year, the civil servant is subject to criminal punishment only if there is a connection with his/her duty.

Financial and other advantage refers to money, goods, and other financial gain, as well as tangible or intangible gains which provide convenience or satisfy the person's needs or desires. Examples are ① money, property, hotel vouchers, memberships, admission tickets, etc., ② meals, alcohol or golf, provision of transportation, etc., ③ providing economic benefits such as relief of debt, provision of employment, offering of favors, etc.

"Work-related connection" refers to the "duties handled by one's position." Examples are: ① duties authorized generally and abstractly under the law, ② duties performed actually or habitually, ③ duties to support or influence decision makers, and ④ duties closely related to the job.

(2) Exceptions

There are 8 valid situations for accepting financial or other advantages:

① Financial or other advantages which a senior civil servant or relevant person offers to his or her subordinates to either raise their morale or console, encourage, or reward them; ② Food and drink, congratulatory or condolence money, gifts, or other items that are offered to facilitate performance of duties or for social relationships, rituals, or assistance to festivities and funerals, the value of which is within the limit provided by Presidential Decree: - Meals are allowed to a value of not exceeding KRW 50,000; - Gifts are allowed to a value of not exceeding KRW 150,000 for agricultural and fishing gifts, and up to KRW 300,000 during traditional holidays); - Congratulatory and condolence payments are allowed to a value of not exceeding KRW 50,000(However, up to KRW 100,000 for congratulatory and condolence); ③ Financial or other advantages that are offered from a legitimate source due to a private transaction; ④ Financial or other advantages that relatives(under Article 777 of the Civil Act) of a civil servant or relevant person offer; ⑤ Financial or other advantages that employees' mutual aid societies, clubs, alumni associations, ethnic societies, friendship clubs, religious groups, social organizations, etc. related to a civil servant or relevant person offer to their members in accordance with the rules prescribed by the respective organizations, and financial or other advantages from those who have long-term and continuous relationships with a civil servant or relevant person; ⑥ Financial or other advantages that are uniformly provided by an organizer of an official event related to the duties of a civil servant or relevant person to all participants thereof, including transportation,

한다. 구체적으로 ① 금전, 부동산, 숙박권, 회원권, 입장권 등, ② 음식물, 주류, 골프 등의 접대, 교통·숙박 등의 편의 제공, ③ 채무 면제, 취업 제공, 이권 부여 등 경제적 이익제공이 있다.

직무관련성은 '그 지위에 수반하여 취급하는 사무'를 의미한다. 구체적으로 ① 법령상 일반적·추상적 권한에 속하는 직무, ② 사실상·관례상 처리하는 직무, ③ 결정권자를 보좌하거나 영향을 줄 수 있는 직무행위, ④ 직무와 밀접한 관련이 있는 직무행위를 포함한다.

(2) 예 외

다만, 법을 위반하지 않고 금품수수가 가능한 8가지 사항이 있다.

① 공공기간이 지급하거나 상급공직자가 위로 격려, 포상 등의 목적으로 하급 공직자에게 제공하는 금품, ② 원활한 직무수행 사교·의례, 경조금 목적으로 제공되는 5만원 이내 음식물, 5만원 이내 선물(다만, 농수산물 선물은 15만원 한도, 명절 선물 기간중에는 30만원), 5만원 이내 경조사비(다만, 화환, 조화는 10만원한도), ③ 사적 거래로 인한 채무의 이행, 정당한 권원에 의하여 제공되는 금품, ④ 공직자등의 친족이 제공하는 금품 등(친족: 배우자, 8촌 이내의 혈족, 4촌 이내의 인척), ⑤ 공직자등 관련 단체가 내부 기준에 따라 구성원에게 제공하는 금품이나 장기적이고 지속적 친분관계를 맺고 있는 자가 질병 등으로 어려운 처지에 있는 공직자등에게 제공하는 금품 등, ⑥ 공직자등의 직무와 관련한 공식적 행사에서 주최자가 참석자에게 통상적인 범위에서 일률적으로 제공하는 교통, 숙박, 음식물 등, ⑦ 불특정 다수인에게 배포하기 위한 기념품, 홍보용품 등이나 경연, 추첨 등을 통하여 제공하는 경품, 상품 등, ⑧ 그밖에 다른 법령, 기준 또는 사회상규에 따라 허용되는 금품 등이 이에 해당된다.

accommodation, and food and drink; ⑦ Souvenirs or promotional goods distributed to many and unspecified persons, or awards or prizes that are given by a contest or lottery; and ⑧ Financial or other advantages that are permitted by any other Acts and/or subordinate statutes, standards or social norms.

III. Joint Penal Provisions and Employer's Obligations

1. Concept

The joint penal provisions refer to a system of punishing the employee and the employer together for violations of the law by the employee in the course of his/her work. Article 24 of the Anti-corruption Act(Joint Penal Provisions) stipulates that "Where an employee commits a violation: improper solicitation and/or provision of financial or other advantage, the violator and his/her employer are punished together. Provided, that this shall not apply where the employer has not been negligent in giving due attention and supervision concerning the relevant duties so as to prevent such violation."

The Supreme Court ruled, concerning the reasons for the employer to be exempted from liability, that whether the employer has been negligent in giving due attention and supervision shall be determined by considering the following items collectively: ① the violation and its relevant situation, such as the purpose for enacting that law, the severity of damages coming from infringing rights due to violation of the relevant law, and the purpose for introducing the joint penal provisions in that law; ② the concrete details of the violation and actual damage caused by the violation of this law; and ③ the size of the business, along with the degree of command and supervision by the employer; and ④ the company's efforts to prevent violations.[332)]

2. Related cases[333)]

(1) Improper solicitation

Case 1: In a case where employee X of a construction company solicited civil servant

332) Supreme Court ruling on February 25, 2010 (2009do5824), on Sep. 9, 2010 (2008do7834), etc.

333) Document issued by the Anti-Corruption and Civil Rights Commission in 2016.

Ⅲ. 양벌규정과 사용자 의무

1. 개 념

양벌규정이란 근로자의 업무관련 위반행위에 관하여 그 행위자만을 처벌하는 것이 아니고 행위자를 고용한 사용자도 행위자와 같이 처벌하는 제도를 말한다. 청탁금지법 제24조(양벌규정)에서는 근로자가 이 법을 위반하는 금품수수와 부정청탁의 위반행위를 한 경우에는 그 행위자를 벌하는 외에 그 사용자도 처벌한다고 규정하고 있다. 다만, 사용자가 그 위반행위를 방지하기 위하여 해당 업무에 관하여 상당한 주의와 감독을 게을리하지 아니한 경우에는 면책된다는 규정을 함께 마련하고 있다.

판례는 양벌규정의 면책사유인 "법인이 상당한 주의 또는 관리감독 의무를 게을리하였는지 여부는 ① 당해 위반행위와 관련된 모든 사정, 즉 당해 법률의 입법 취지, 처벌조항 위반으로 예상되는 법익 침해의 정도, 그 위반행위에 관하여 양벌규정을 마련한 취지 등은 물론 ② 위반행위의 구체적인 모습과 그로 인하여 실제 야기된 피해 또는 결과의 정도, ③ 법인의 영업 규모 및 행위자에 대한 감독가능성 또는 구체적인 지휘감독 관계, ④ 법인이 위반행위 방지를 위하여 실제 행한 조치 등을 전체적으로 종합하여 판단하여야 한다"고 판시하고 있다.[332)]

2. 구체적 사례[333)]

(1) 부정청탁

사례1: 건설회사 소속 직원X가 건축법령을 위반하여 건축허가를 내어 줄 것을 00구청 건축허가 담당공무원A에게 청구한 경우: 건설회사는 양벌규정 적용 시 2천만원 이하의 과태료를 부담한다.

332) 대법원 2010.2.25, 2009도5824; 대법원 2010.9.9, 2008도7834 등.
333) 권익위원회 자료, 2016.

A of 00 District Administration Office for permission for a building project in violation of construction laws: In applying the joint penal provisions, the construction company will receive a fine not exceeding KRW 20 million.

Case 2: In a case where employee X of a construction company solicited civil servant A of 00 District Administration Office for permission for a building project, providing whiskey worth KRW 700,000: If "bribery" as defined in the Criminal Act, is applied, the construction company will not be punished by the joint penal provisions, but if the case is not admitted as "bribery" under the Criminal Act, the joint penal provision is applied and a fine will be given, not exceeding KRW 20 million.

(2) Accepting financial or other advantages

Case 1: While a construction company was waiting to receive a construction permit from the District Administration Office, in a case where employee X provided whiskey worth KRW 700,000 to the civil servant in charge of construction permits, employee Y provided gift tickets worth KRW 500,000 to the same person, and employee Z provided a meal equivalent to KRW 200,000 to the same person, all in different work-related meetings: In applying the joint penal provisions, the construction company shall bear a fine of between KRW 2.8 million and KRW 7 million won.

Case 2: In a situation where employees X and Y of a construction company invited newspaper reporters A, B, C, D to a work-related dinner and spent KRW 120,000 for the dinner, and paid KRW 240,000 at the bar in a second location: As entertainment of the civil servants by employees X and Y is evaluated as one behavior, in applying the joint penal provision, one fine will be levied, which will be between KRW 120,000 and KRW 300,000 won: A fine for negligence of two to five times the received amount →(120,000/6 persons) +(240,000/6 persons) = KRW 60,000.

사례2: 건설회사 소속 직원X가 건축허가를 내어 줄 것을 00구청 건축허가 담당공무원A에게 청탁하면서 70만원 상당의 양주를 전달한 경우: 건설회사는 형법상 '뇌물'로 인정 시 건설회사 측에는 양벌규정은 적용되지 않는다. 그러나 형법상 '뇌물'로 인정되지 않을 시에는 양벌규정을 적용하여 2천만원 이하의 과태료를 부담한다.

(2) 금품수수

사례1: 건설회사는 00구청에 건축허가를 신청하여 심사 대기 중인 상황에서, 구청 건축허가 담당공무원A에게 건설회사 소속의 임원 X가 70만원 상당의 양주를, 직원 Y는 50만원 상당의 상품권을, 직원 Z는 20만원 상당의 식사를 각각 업무로 만난 자리에서 제공한 경우: 건설회사는 양벌규정 적용 시 280만원~700만원 과태료를 부담한다.

사례2: 건설회사의 소속직원X, Y가 직무와 관련한 회식에서 언론사 직원 A,B,C,D를 초청하여 1차에서 식사비용 12만원, 2차에서 술값 24만원을 결제한 경우: 근로자X, Y, 의 일련의 행위는 1개의 행위로 평가되므로, 양벌규정 적용 시 1개의 과태료 부과하여 12만원~30만원 과태료를 부담한다. 과태료의 근거는 수수금액의 2배 이상 5배 이하: (12만원/6명)+(24만원/6명)=6만원

Section 5: The Personal Information Protection Act and Personnel Management

Ⅰ. Concept

Personal information is easily obtained in our internet-driven information society, and there have been many cases of abuse. Recently, financial companies, search engines, game companies, and others have been the victims of information hacking, resulting in a plethora of spam mail, illegal use of other people's names, voice phishing, and identity theft. Accordingly, in the endeavor to provide a consistent code to protect personal information, the Personal Information Protection Act was signed into law on March 29, 2011, and enforced from September 20, 2011. This act is a general law that combines all laws related to protection of personal information and contains strong penal provisions. It also covers all processes of gathering personal information, both on- and offline. The Ministry of Public Administration & Security has enforced the law after the six month period between September 20, 2011 and March 29, 2012 for intensive guidance.

Ⅱ. The Personal information Protection Act

The Personal information Protection Act regulates matters concerning the use of personal information in order to protect and promote people's rights and interests by protecting them from unwanted collection, leakage, illegal use and abuse of their personal information. The law includes the following six major subjects.

제5절 개인정보 보호법

Ⅰ. 의 의

인터넷 활용이 빈번한 정보화 사회로 인하여 개인정보를 쉽게 획득할 수 있고, 이를 남용하는 사례가 많이 발생하고 있다. 최근에 금융회사, 검색엔진 사이트, 게임사에서의 해킹 등으로 인하여 많은 개인정보가 대량으로 유출된 바 있고, 이것이 스팸메일, 명의도용, 보이스 피싱, 신분증 위조 등의 형태로 변화되어 추가 피해를 발생 시키고 있다. 이에 따라 개인정보에 보호에 일관성 있는 조치를 위하여 「개인정보 보호법」이 2011.3.29 제정되었고 2011.9.30 부로 시행되고 있다. 이 법은 개인정보 보호에 대한 법을 통합하는 일반법이며 강력한 처벌조항을 가지고 있다. 따라서 이 법은 일반 온라인 정보뿐만 아니라 오프라인의 개인정보를 다루는 모든 업무에 적용된다. 주관부서인 행정안전부는 법 시행 후 6개월간(2011.9.30~ 2012.3.29)은 계도기간을 거친 후 시행에 들어갔다.

이러한 개인정보를 보호하기 위한 이 법에 대한 주요 내용을 먼저 알아보고, 회사의 노무관리 차원에서 어떤 대응이 필요한지에 대해 살펴보고자 한다.

Ⅱ. 주요 내용

「개인정보 보호법」은 개인정보의 수집, 유출, 오용, 남용으로부터 사생활의 비밀을 보호함으로써 국민의 권리와 이익을 증진하고자 개인정보 처리에 관한 사항을 규정하고 있다. 이 법의 다음의 6가지 주요 내용을 포함하고 있다.

1. Expansion of scope

The Personal information Protection Act is a general law applying to the relationship between individuals and those collecting their personal information. Previously, personal information was protected in specifically designated ways through separate laws such as the Information & Communication Act and the Credit Information Act, but the protections offered there have been expanded and applied to all handlers of personal information working in either the public or private sector. Accordingly, this law also applies to companies that do not conduct any online business.

2. Expansion of protection

The scope of protection of personal information covers not only information processed electronically, but also paper records such as those used in civil service Offices, etc. Personal information means data that distinguishes or reveals individual identity(including name, resident registration number, date of birth, address, etc.) and data that reveals an individual's past and current conditions and situations(including educational background, financial status, medical history and health, etc.).

3. Restrictions on use of unique identifying information

Unique identifying information provided to the individual by law, such as resident registration numbers, shall be prohibited, in principle, from processing. In cases where a specific law requires such information, or where it is deemed obviously necessary for the urgent benefit of life, body or property of a subject of information or a third party, gathering such information is permitted. Individual resident registration numbers shall not be required on websites. Any person violating this shall be punished with imprisonment of up to five years or with a fine not exceeding 50 million won.

4. Restrictions against use of video recording devices

Installation and operation of video recording devices in open places is now restricted. A video recording device is any instrument, such as CCTV(closed-circuit television) or network cameras, which is installed and remains in a designated place and is meant to videotape objects and/or people, or transmit the video recordings through a wired

1. 보호의무 적용대상의 확대

「개인정보 보호법」은 일반법으로 개인정보처리자와 정보주체(대상 개인)와 관계에 적용된다. 기존에는 「정보통신법」이나 「신용정보법」등과 같이 개별법에 따라 시행되던 개인정보 보호 의무대상을 공공 및 민간 부문의 모든 개인정보처리자로 확대 적용하고 있다. 따라서 인터넷을 기반으로 영업을 하지 않는 일반회사의 경우에도 동일하게 개인정보 보호에 관하여 동일한 법 적용이 된다.

2. 개인정보 보호범위의 확대

컴퓨터 등에 의해 처리되는 정보 외 동사무소 민원신청서류 등 종이문서에 기록된 개인정보도 보호대상에 포함하고 있다. 개인정보란 개인의 정체성(identity)을 구별하거나 밝혀낼 수 있는 정보(성명, 주민등록번호, 생일, 주소, 등) 및 특정 개인의 과거 및 현재의 상황이나 상태를 나타낼 수 있는 정보(교육상황, 재정상황, 진료 및 건강 상태 등)를 말한다.

3. 고유 식별정보 처리 제한

주민번호 등 법령에 따라 개인을 고유하게 구별하기 위해 부여된 고유 식별정보는 원칙적으로 처리가 금지되어 있다. 법령에서 규정하였거나 정보주체 또는 제3자의 급박한 생명, 신체, 재산의 이익을 위하여 명백히 필요하다고 인정되는 경우 처리가 가능하다. 인터넷에서 회원가입 조건으로 본인의 주민번호를 사용하지 못하도록 되어 있다. 이를 위반 시 5년 이하의 징역 또는 5천만 원 이하의 벌금에 처한다.

4. 영상정보 처리기기 규제

공개된 장소에 영상정보 처리기기 설치 및 운영을 제한하고 있다. “영상정보 처리기기”란 일정한 공간에 지속적으로 설치되어 사람 또는 사물의 영상 등을 촬영하거나 이를 유, 무선망을 통하여 전송하는 일체의 장치로서 폐쇄회로텔레

or wireless network. The arbitrary use of such operations in a way that differs from its intended purpose, recording video in places other than the originally intended area, and recording of voices, are all prohibited. Any person violating this shall be punished with imprisonment of up to three years or with a fine not exceeding 30 million won.

5. Collection and use of personal information

The collection of personal information must satisfy certain criteria, and any information gathered shall only be used in the specified way. These criteria are: ① the target person must have agreed to give such information; ② an article of law exists which requires the collection of such information in order to observe the law; ③ it is needed by a public agency to carry out duties assigned by related law; ④ it is necessary for one party to enter into or implement a legal contract with the individuals concerned; ⑤ such information is urgently necessary to protect life, body, and interest of individuals and/or third parties; ⑥ it is necessary for the justifiable interests of the handler of such information, and is more important than the rights of individuals. In this last case, it shall be closely related to the justifiable interest of the handler of such information, and shall not exceed a reasonable scope. A person who violates this shall be punished with a fine for negligence up to 50 million won.

6. Duty to report leaks of personal information

When recognizing that personal information has been leaked, the handler of such information shall notify the individuals concerned of this fact without delay, and shall include: ① the details of the leaked personal information; ② the time the leak occurred, and any related details; ③ information about how the individual can minimize any damage caused by the leak; ④ any countermeasures the handler of such information has taken, and procedures for remedy for any damage; and ⑤ the contact information of the department individuals can contact to report any resulting damage.

Any person violating this duty to report leaks of personal information shall be punished with a fine for negligence of up to 30 million won. Any person responsible for failing to report to the appropriate government authority on the way the organization handled the leak shall be punished with a fine for negligence of up to 30 million won.

비전(CCTV) 및 네트워크 카메라를 말한다. 설치 목적을 벗어난 카메라 임의조작, 다른 곳을 비추는 행위, 녹음 기능을 금지하고 있다. 이를 위반하는 경우에는 3년 이하의 징역 또는 3천만 원 이하의 벌금에 처한다.

5. 개인정보 수집 및 이용

개인정보 수집에 대해 일정한 사유가 있는 경우로 제한하고 있으며, 그 목적에 맞게 이용하도록 하고 있다. 그 일정한 사유란, ① 정보주체의 동의가 있는 경우, ② 법률에 특별한 규정이 있거나 법령상 의무를 준수하기 위하여 불가피한 경우, ③ 공공기관이 법령 등에서 정하는 소관 업무의 수행을 위하여 불가피한 경우, ④ 정보주체와의 계약의 체결 및 이행을 위하여 불가피하게 필요한 경우, ⑤ 명백히 정보주체 또는 제3자의 급박한 생명, 신체, 재산의 이익을 위하여 필요하다고 인정되는 경우, ⑥ 개인정보처리자의 정당한 이익을 달성하기 위하여 필요한 경우로서 명백하게 정보주체의 권리보다 우선하는 경우, 이 경우 개인정보처리자의 정당한 이익과 상당한 관련이 있고 합리적인 범위를 초과하지 아니하는 경우로 한다. 이를 위반한 경우 5천만 원 이하의 과태료를 부과한다.

6. 개인정보 유출통지 및 신고제 도입

개인정보 처리자는 개인정보가 유출되었음을 알게 되었을 때는 지체 없이 정보주체에게 다음의 사실을 알려야 한다. ① 유출된 개인정보의 항목, ② 유출된 시점과 그 경위, ③ 유출로 인하여 발생할 수 있는 피해를 최소화하기 위하여 정보주체가 할 수 있는 방법 등에 관한 정보, ④ 개인정보 처리자의 대응조치 및 피해 구제절차, ⑤ 정보주체에게 피해가 발생한 경우 신고 등을 접수할 수 있는 담당부서 및 연락처.

개인정보 유출에 대한 통지의무를 위반한 경우에는 3천만 원 이하의 과태료를 부과한다. 또한, 조치결과의 신고를 하지 아니한 경우에는 3천만 원 이하의 과대료를 부과한다.

III. Management of Personnel and Personal Information

Laws related to the protection of personal information are applied equally to most companies. Regarding the management of personnel, the main issues are the management of employees' personal information and the company use and management of video recording devices.

1. Details on management of employees' personal information

Collecting and using personal information is tightly restricted, but in cases where an employee enters into an employment contract to offer work in return for wage from the employer, the employer shall know the employee's name, resident registration number, address, wage information, and other necessary data, as this is an example of what is necessary for one party to enter into or implement a legal contract with the individuals concerned. These items of personal information are essential to management of personnel regarding the four social insurances, year-end income tax adjustment, and issuance of various certificates. Accordingly, no individual agreement is necessary regarding the use of personal information in this way. However, it is still necessary for the employer to inform the employee of the collection and use of his/her personal information related to the making of an employment contract. This notification shall include the purpose for collecting the personal information, where to read and/or correct such information, the period it will be retained, and management after he/she leaves the company, etc.

Can personal information obtained through resumes, etc. at the time of hiring be exempt from the requirement for consent from employees to collect or use their information, as it can be considered necessary for one party to enter into or implement a legal contract with the individuals concerned?[344)]

According to the Enforcement Decree (Article 27) to the Labor Standards Act, the employer shall record the employees' name, resident registration number, matters on the basis of wage calculation, and other working conditions in the wage ledger. In other cases such as the collection and use of job seekers' personal information, consent does not have to be given, according to Article 1 (subparagraph 4) of the Enforcement Decree to the Labor Standards Act (Making and implementing a contract). The information about individual employees shall generally be used not only for employment contracts, but also other purposes such as welfare, labor union management, training, etc. Furthermore, as companies are likely to gather such sensitive information, it is greatly desirable to inform the employees concerned of the use of personal information from employment-related documents, and the period of use, etc.

In cases where the employer collects unique and sensitive identifying information such as resident registration number at the time of employment, excluding where there are concrete reasons to gather such information due to related law, it shall be necessary for the employer to receive separate agreement from the employees concerned.

334) Explanation of Laws and Decrees Concerning Protection of Personal information (the Ministry of Public Administration & Security, on Dec. 2011, p. 90)

Ⅲ. 개인정보와 인사관리

개인정보 보호와 관련하여 일반 회사에도 동일하게 적용된다. 인사관리와 관련 하여서는 주로 직원 개인정보 관리에 대한 내용과 영상정보처리기기의 사용, 관리와 관련이 있다.

1. 회사 내 직원 개인정보 관리

개인정보를 수집하여 이용하는 것을 엄격하게 제한하고 있지만, 근로자가 사용자에게 근로를 제공하고 사용자는 이에 대해 임금을 지급하는 근로계약을 체결할 경우에는 사용자는 근로자의 성명, 주민등록번호, 주소, 임금, 기타의 일체의 자료를 반드시 알아야 한다. 이는 "계약의 체결, 이행을 위해 불가피하게 필요한 경우"에 해당된다. 이러한 근로계약에 따른 4대보험 관리, 연말정산, 각종 증명서 발급, 그리고 퇴직 후의 사용증명서 발급을 위해 개인정보 관리가 필수적이라 할 수 있다. 따라서 개인정보 사용에 대한 개인동의서는 필요 없다고 할 수 있다. 그러나 근로자의 동의서를 받지 않는다 하더라도 근로계약 체결 시 근로계약서 내용에 개인정보 수집, 이용에 관한 사항을 알리는 것이 필요할 것이다. 그 내용은 개인정보 수집 목적, 열람 및 정정 방법, 보유기간, 퇴직 후 직원 정보 처리에 대한 절차 등이다.

직원 채용 시 이력서 등을 통하여 얻게 되는 직원 개인정보는 "정보주체와의 계약의 체결 및 이행을 위하여 불가피하게 필요한 경우"에 해당하는 것으로 보아 그 수집·이용에 대하여 동의가 면제되는 것으로 볼 수 있는지[344)]

「근로기준법 시행령」 제27조에 의하면 사용자는 직원의 성명, 주민등록번호, 임금 계산기초가 되는 사항과 기타 근로조건에 관한 사항을 임금 대장에 기록하여야 하는 바, 이는 법령이 정한 경우에 해당한다. 기타 정보의 경우에도 구직예정자의 개인정보 또한, 그 수집, 이용과 관련하여 법 제15조 제1항 제4호 (계약의 체결 및 이행에 필요한 경우)에 의하여 구직예정자의 동의가 면제될 수 있을 것이다. 다만 기본적으로 직원에 관한 정보는 계약체결 목적뿐만 아니라 복지, 노조관리, 교육 등의 목적으로 활용될 여지가 높고 민감정보를 수집할 여지가 있기 때문에, 채용 시에는 입사서류에 채용을 포함한 회사의 개인정보 이용 목적, 기간 등을 명확히 기재하여 대상자에게 알리는 것이 바람직하다.

채용 시에 주민등록번호 등 고유 식별정보와 민감정보를 수집하는 경우에는 법령에 구체적인 근거가 있는 경우를 제외하고 정보주체에게 별도의 동의를 얻어야 한다.

334) 개인정보 보호법령 해설집 (행정안전부, 2011.12, 90페이지)

2. Company use and management of video recording devices

Video recording devices shall not be installed or operated in public places. Exceptions are as follows: ① In cases where its use is concretely permitted by law and/or decree; ② In cases where its use is necessary to prevent or investigate crime; ③ In cases where its use is necessary for facility security and prevention of fire; ④ In cases where its use is necessary to enforce traffic laws; and ⑤ In cases where its use is necessary to collect, analyze and distribute traffic information. While use of video recording devices is permitted in these cases, the company shall set up a board notifying employees of the presence of such recording devices.

"Public places" refers to places like roads, parks, plazas, and other places the public is free to use. The lobby of a company building can be used by many unspecified people, so it is included in the restrictions on installing a video recording device. However, the inner rooms and hallways of the company building, where access is strictly controlled and only to internal employees and those receiving permission, would be considered closed to the public, and so are excluded from restrictions on installation of video recording devices. Provided, in cases where the video recording device was installed and is in operation to collect individual imagery information, other protections of privacy still apply. That is, when a company obtains the employee's permission, and when the recording is necessary to accomplish the justifiable interests of the handler of such information, installing and operating a video recording device is allowed.

Case: Monitoring the Workplace[335)]

Some companies install and operate video recording devices to monitor work activities. Such video recording devices installed in the workplace have been the cause of conflict between the employer's authority to supervise work and workers' right to privacy. Workplaces off-limits to outsiders are in principle "closed places", and Article 25 (Restrictions on use of video recording devices) does not apply, while the principle of general protection of privacy does. In relation to this, the Act concerning the Promotion of Worker Participation and Cooperation stipulates that management shall consult employees before installing video recording devices such as CCTVs, which can be done through labor-management discussions, where a balance between monitoring work and protecting privacy may be struck.

---

335) Explanation of Laws and Decrees Concerning Protection of Personal Information (Ministry of Public Administration and Security, Dec. 2011, p. 166)

2. 회사 내 영상정보처리기기의 사용과 관리

누구든지 공개된 장소에 영상정보처리기기를 설치, 운영하여서는 아니된다. 다만, 허용되는 경우는 다음과 같다. ① 법령에서 구체적으로 허용하는 경우, ② 범죄를 예방 및 수사를 위하여 필요한 경우, ③ 시설안전 및 화재 예방을 위하여 필요한 경우, ④ 교통단속을 위하여 필요한 경우, ⑤ 교통정보의 수집, 분석 및 제공을 위하여 필요한 경우이다. 이렇게 허용되는 경우에도 정보주체가 쉽게 인식할 수 있도록 안내판 등을 설치하여야 한다.

「공개된 장소」란 도로, 공원, 광장 등의 공공장소와 불특정 다수가 출입하거나 이용할 수 있도록 허용된 장소를 의미한다. 기업 건물의 로비 등은 불특정 다수가 출입하고 있으므로 여기에 설치된 영상정보처리기기는 설치제한규정에 적용된다. 그러나 출입이 엄격히 통제되고 있고 내부 직원이나 허가를 받은 사람만 출입이 허용되는 기업 사옥의 내부 공간은「비공개된 장소」에 해당하므로 설치제한규정을 적용을 받지 않는다. 다만, 이 경우에 기업이 업무를 목적으로 개인 영상정보를 수집하기 위하여 내부 공간에 영상정보처리기기를 설치, 운영하는 경우에는 이 법의 다른 개인정보 보호원칙이 적용된다. 즉, 그 구성원의 동의를 받거나 개인정보 처리자의 정당한 이익을 달성하기 위하여 필요한 경우 등에 한하여 영사정보처리기기 설치, 운영이 허용된다.

사례: 근로 모니터링[335)]

민간기업 등에서 근로 모니터링 등을 목적으로 영상정보처리기기를 설치·운영하는 경우가 있다. 근로 공간에 설치된 영상정보처리기기는 사용자 측의 근로 관리권한과 근로자 측의 사생활 보호권이 서로 상충될 우려가 있다.

외부인의 출입이 통제되는 근로공간은 원칙적으로 '비공개된 장소'에 해당하므로 이 법 제25조는 적용되지 않으며, 그 외의 일반적 개인정보보호 원칙의 적용을 받는다.

이와 관련하여,「근로자참여 및 협력증진에 관한 법률」에서는 CCTV와 같은 근로자 감시 장비는 노사 양자의 협의사항으로 규정하고 있으므로, 근로 모니터링 목적의 CCTV 설치 범위 및 사생활 침해 방지조치 등을 노사 협의에 따라 정하여 설치·운영할 수 있다.

335) "개인정보 보호법령 해설집" (행정안전부, 2011.12, 166페이지)

Chapter 6

Dismissals

Section 1: Understanding Dismissal

Ⅰ. Duties of Employer and Employees

The employment contract is a legal agreement entered into where a worker offers work, in return for which an employer pays wages. Here, the main obligations of workers is to provide work, and employers to pay wages in return. Workers must faithfully provide the work specified in the employment contract at a fixed time and place. If the worker fails to do so for reasons attributable to the worker, the employer may claim compensation for damages or terminate the employment contract (Article 390 of the Civil Act). Even if the employer fails to receive the worker's work, the entire wage must be paid for work already performed (Article 538 of the Civil Act). The Civil Act governs relations between equal parties and places clear responsibilities in the event of a breach of obligations. However, the Labor Standards Act imposes separate restrictions against violation of the main obligations between parties to ensure workers' right to life and that employers pay wages promptly.

In addition to the main obligations in these employment contracts, workers are obligated to be faithful and employers are obligated to protect, both on the "good faith" principle between contracting parties.[336)] Workers are obligated to protect the interests of the employer without engaging in acts that violate that employer's interests. Employers also have a duty

336) Lim, Jongryul, 「Labor Law」 18th ed., Parkyoungsa, 2020, p. 360; Supreme Court ruling on Nov. 28, 2013: 2011da60247.

해고제도

제1절 해고의 이해

Ⅰ. 근로자와 사용자의 의무

근로계약은 근로자가 사용자에게 근로를 제공하고 사용자는 이에 대하여 임금을 지급하는 것을 목적으로 체결된 계약이다. 여기서 근로자와 사용자의 주된 의무는 근로제공과 임금의 지급이다. 근로자는 근로계약서에 기재된 업무를 정해진 시간과 장소에서 성실하게 제공해야 하는데 근로자의 귀책사유로 근로제공 의무를 이행하지 못하게 되면, 사용자는 근로자에게 손해배상을 청구하거나 근로계약을 해지할 수 있다(민법 제390조). 또한 사용자가 근로자의 근로를 수령하지 못한 경우에도 임금 전액을 지급해야 한다(민법 제538조). 민법은 대등한 당사자간의 관계이므로 의무위반에 명확한 책임을 가하고 있다. 그러나 근로기준법은 당사자의 주된 의무위반에 대해 근로자의 생존권 보장과 사용자의 신속한 급여지급을 위해 별도의 제한 규정을 두고 있다.

이러한 근로계약의 주된 의무와 함께 계약당사자의 신의성실 원칙에 따른 의무로 근로자는 성실의무, 사용자는 보호의무를 부담한다.[336] 근로자는 근로관계에 있어 사용자의 이익을 침해하는 행위를 하지 않고 그 이익을 보호해야 하는 성실의무를 진다. 사용자도 근로관계에 있어 근로자의 이익을 보호해야 하는 보

---

336) 임종률, 「노동법」 18판, 박영사, 2020, 360면; 대법원 2013.11.28. 선고 2011나60247.

to protect the workers with whom working relations have been established.[337)]

In this regard, I would like to examine how the employee's duty of integrity and the employer’s duty to protect are applied in actual cases.

A. Employees’ Duty of Integrity and Impact of Violations

Even if there are no such provisions in the employment contract, workers are obligated to be faithful in accordance with the principle of good faith in the Civil Act. Such integrity obligations include the duty to maintain trade secrets, to be faithful, to avoid engaging in concurrent business with the employer’s competitors, and to comply with regulations.

1. Duty to maintain trade secrets

Regarding trade secrets, the Supreme Court stated in a ruling, “Not only in a contract obligating the maintenance of confidentiality during the existence of a contractual relationship or after its termination, but also in the absence of such provisions, it is believed that [employees] have agreed to such obligations by the good faith principle.[338)] The Unfair Competition Prevention and Trade Secret Protection Act (hereinafter the “Unfair Competition Prevention Act”) also regulates the maintenance of trade secrets and imposes liability for damages and criminal liability for violations thereof. However, the period for keeping such trade secrets after resignation is limited due to the great concern about limiting the freedom of occupation.[339)]

Related Case (1): As head of the research department of a writing instrument manufacturer, an employee who had acquired technical information corresponding to a trade secret quit and began working for a competitor company after that company offered a higher salary and a better position. He disclosed the entire body of technical information to that competitor and used it to produce ink. Such an act is a violation of the obligation to maintain trade secrets, as it is for the purpose of obtaining an unjust profit contrary to good manners or social order.[340)]

---

337) Ha, Kaprae,「The Labor Standards Act」33rd ed., Joongang Economy, 2020, pp. 149-165.

338) Supreme Court ruling on Dec. 23, 1996: 96 da 16605.

339) Seoul High Court ruling on Nov. 12, 2002: 2002 ra 313.

340) Supreme Court ruling on Dec. 23, 1996: 96 da 16605, This is a violation of the regulation on trade secrets, in accordance with Article 2 (3) of the Unfair Competition Prevention Act.

호의무를 진다.[337]

이와 관련하여, 근로자의 성실의무와 사용자의 보호의무가 현장에서 어떻게 적용되고 있는지 살펴보고자 한다.

A. 근로자의 성실의무와 위반의 효력

근로자는 근로계약에 규정이 없어도 민법상 신의성실원칙에 따른 성실의무를 진다. 그러한 성실의무에는 영업비밀유지업무, 충실의무, 경쟁업체에 대한 겸업금지 규정, 청렴의무 등을 진다.

1. 영업비밀 유지의무

대법원은 영업비밀에 대해서 "계약관계 존속 중은 물론 종료 후라도 반드시 명시적으로 계약에 의하여 비밀유지의무를 부담하기로 약정한 경우뿐만 아니라 그러한 규정이 없었다고 하더라도 신의성실의 원칙 또는 묵시적으로 그러한 의무를 부담하기로 약정하였다고 보고 있다.[338] 「부정경쟁방지 및 영업비밀보호에 관한 법률」(이하 "부정경쟁방지법")도 영업비밀유지를 규정하고 이를 위반한데에 대한 손해배상책임과 형사책임을 부과하고 있다. 그러나 근로자 퇴직 후의 영업비밀 유지기간은 직업선택의 자유를 제한할 우려가 크기 때문에 제한적으로 해석한다.[339]

관련사례(1) : 필기구 제조업체의 연구실장으로 영업비밀에 해당하는 기술정보를 습득한 자가 경쟁회사로부터 고액의 급여와 상급 직위를 보장받기로 하고 전직하였다. 그는 경쟁 회사에 그 전 회사의 기술정보를 공개하고 이를 사용하여 잉크를 생산하였다. 그러한 행위는 선량한 풍속 및 기타 사회질서에 반하는 부정한 이익을 얻을 목적에서 행하여진 것으로 영업비밀 유지의무 위반행위에 해당한다.[340]

---

337) 하갑례, 「근로기준법」 제33판, 중앙경제, 2020, 149-165면.

338) 대법원 1996.12.23. 선고 96다16605.

339) 서울고등법원 2002.11.12 선고 2002라313 판결.

340) 대법원 1996.12.23. 선고 96다16605: 부정경쟁방지와 영업비밀에 관한 법 제2조 제3호 (라)목 영업비밀보호 규정 위반

Related Case (2): A company's membership information used to produce educational materials and sell educational services, has independent economic value, and is considered useful management information for business activities that are kept confidential only with considerable effort. Such information is considered a trade secret specified in the Unfair Competition Prevention Act. A particular defendant used such member information to personally conduct class business activities for some inactive members. Although the defendant was obligated to keep such member information a trade secret, the defendant violated this, gained profit from it, inflicted damage on the plaintiff as the holder of the trade secret, and is therefore obligated to compensate the plaintiff for resulting damages.[341)]

2. Violation of the duty to be faithful

A worker using his/her employer's trade secrets for personal gain is a violation of the obligation to protect trade secrets. Violations of this duty justify the company taking actions for disciplinary dismissal.

Related Case: Although real estate speculation is activity that falls within the realm of private life, a certain company was established for the purpose of stabilizing public residential life and improving welfare through the development and supply of housing sites and construction of housing. When considering the purpose for an urban development corporation to be established and the duties of workers responsible for real estate compensation, an employee of an urban development corporation engaging in real estate speculation resulted in a profoundly negative impact on social evaluation of the corporation.[342)]

3. Violation of the prohibition against concurrent, interfering employment

Related Case: As the concurrent employment of a worker at another workplace is a private matter, it is unfair to prohibit entirely and comprehensively any second job that does not hinder corporate order or that employee's provision of labor. However,

341) Seoul High Court ruling on Sept. 19, 2012: 2012 na 1391.

342) Supreme Court ruling on Dec. 13, 1994: 93 nu 23275.

관련사례(2) : 교육서비스업과 교육자료 제작 판매업 등을 목적으로 하는 회사의 회원정보는 공공연히 알려져 있지 아니하고 독립된 경제적 가치를 가지는 것으로 상당한 노력에 의하여 비밀로 유지된 영업활동에 유용한 경영상의 정보로써 부정경쟁방지법에서 정한 영업비밀에 해당한다. 피고가 회원정보를 이용하여 휴회 회원들 중 일부 회원들을 대상으로 개인과외 영업행위를 하였다. 피고는 회원정보를 영업비밀로 유지하여야 할 의무가 있음에도 이를 위반하여 그 영업비밀을 사용하여 이익을 얻고 그 영업비밀의 보유자인 원고에게 손해를 입힌 것이므로 이로 말미암은 손해를 배상할 의무가 있다.[341)]

2. 충실의무 위반

회사의 영업비밀을 이용하여 개인의 이득을 취하는 경우에도 영업비밀유지의무위반에 해당한다. 이를 위반하여 해고한 조치는 정당하다.

관련사례 : 근로자의 징계사유인 부동산투기행위가 근로자의 사생활에서의 비행에 불과하다고 할지라도, 택지의 개발과 공급, 주택의 건설 등을 통하여 시민의 주거생활의 안정과 복지향상을 목적으로 설립한 도시개발공사의 설립목적, 부동산보상 관련업무를 담당하는 근로자의 업무내용 등의 여러 사정을 종합적으로 고려하면, 도시개발공사 소속 근로자의 부동산투기행위는 객관적으로 그 공사의 사회적 평가에 심히 중대한 악영향을 미치는 것으로 평가될 수 있는 경우라고 할 것이다.[342)]

3. 겸직 금지의 위반

관련사례 : 근로자가 다른 사업장에 겸직하는 것은 근로자 개인능력에 따른 사생활의 범주에 속하는 것이므로 기업질서나 노무제공에 지장이 없는 겸직까지 전면적, 포괄적으로 금지하는 것은 부당하다. 그러나 노무제공에 지장을 줄 정도의 장시간의 겸직, 또는 경쟁회사의 이사에 취임하는 경우 등이 금지대상이 될

---

341) 서울고등법원 2012.09.19. 선고 2012나1391 판결.

342) 대법원 1994. 12. 13. 선고 93누23275 (경향사업 관련 판결)

it is reasonable to prohibit full-time employment with another company that serves to hinder such provision of labor, or serving as a director of a competitor company, with disciplinary dismissal a justifiable consequence of violating this prohibition.[343)]

B. Employer's Obligation to Protect and Impact of Violations

Employers are obligated to protect workers in accordance with the principle of good faith inherent in the employment contract. Typical examples are the duty to consider safety, the using employer's duty to dispatched workers, and the duty to prevent sexual harassment in the workplace.

1. Obligation to consider safety

Employers are obligated to take the necessary measures to prevent harm to life, body, and health while workers are providing labor in good faith in accordance with the employment contract. If the employer fails in these obligations, resulting in a worker being injured in some way, the employer shall be liable for neglect resulting in injury.[344)]

1) Case: A worker fell from a ladder while working and was injured. While the worker was working on the ladder, the employer had a safety obligation to take measures whereby other workers would secure the ladder to the ground so that the worker would not slip off. The employer neglected to do so. Therefore, the employer must compensate the worker for injury. Since the worker neglected to take action him or herself to prevent an accident, the company's responsibility is limited to 70%.[345)]

2) Case: An accident occurred in which a worker was hit in the left eye by some bent rebar (resulting in blindness in that eye) during rebar removal work. The employer was obligated to conduct safety training and provide and require the wearing of safety equipment, but neglected to do so. Therefore, the company's liability is limited to 80% in

343) Supreme Court ruling on Dec. 13, 1994: 93 nu 23275.

344) Supreme Court ruling on Feb. 23, 1999: 97 da 12082.

345) Chuncheon District Court ruling on Aug. 10, 2016: 2014 gadan 11050.

수 있고 이를 원인으로 한 징계 및 해고사유는 정당성을 인정받을 수 있다.[343)]

B. 사용자의 보호의무와 위반의 효력

사용자는 근로계약에 내재된 신의성실원칙에 따른 근로자를 보호해야 하는 의무를 진다. 대표적인 것이 안전을 배려할 의무, 파견근로자에 대한 사용사업주의 의무, 직장 내 성희롱예방 의무 등이다.

1. 안전을 배려할 의무

사용자는 근로계약에 수반되는 신의성실 원칙에 따라 근로자가 노무를 제공하는 과정에서 생명, 신체, 건강을 해치는 일이 없도록 필요한 조치를 마련하여야 할 보호의무를 부담한다. 이러한 의무를 위반하여 근로자가 손해를 입은 경우 사용자는 채무불이행으로 인한 손해배상책임을 진다.[344)]

1) 사례 : 이 사건 근로자가 사다리에 올라가 작업하다가 떨어져 부상을 입었다. 당시 근로자가 사다리 위에 올라가서 작업을 하고 있었을 때 사용자는 근로자에게 사다리에서 미끄러지지 않도록 지상에서 고정하여 줄 다른 근로자와 공동작업을 할 수 있도록 조치할 안전배려의 의무가 있었다. 사용자는 근로자가 안전하게 작업할 수 있도록 필요한 조치를 취하여야 할 이 의무가 있음에도 불구하고 이를 게을리한 과실이 있다. 따라서 사용자는 근로자가 입은 손해를 배상할 책임이 있다. 그리고 근로자도 스스로 사고를 방지하려는 노력을 소홀히 한 과실이 있으므로 회사의 과실 책임은 70%로 제한한다.[345)]

2) 사례 : 근로자가 철근제거작업 중 휘어진 철근에 눈을 가격당하여 왼쪽 눈이 실명된 사고가 발생하였다. 이 산재사건에 대해 사용자는 안전교육을 실시하고 안전장비를 지급하고 보호장비를 착용하도록 해야 하는 의무가 있었다. 그러나 사용자는 이에 필요한 안전교육을 하지 않았고, 안전장비를 갖추지 않았고, 장비를 미

343) 대법원 94.12.13. 선고 93누23275 판결.
344) 대법원 1999.2.23. 선고 97다12082 판결.
345) 춘천지방법원 2016.8.10. 선고 2014가단11050 판결.

calculating the amount of compensation that the company should pay.[346)]

2. Using employer obligations to dispatched workers

In terms of preventing and managing accidents, a using employer is responsible for the dispatch employees it uses as if the using employer was the original employer.

Related Case: An industrial accident occurred involving a worker who had signed an employment contract with a dispatching company but was working at the using employer's workplace. On November 15, 2005 at 3:35 am, while removing debris from a plastic injection machine, the worker's right arm and hand were crushed and lacerated. The worker demanded additional civil injury compensation from the using employer in 2010 after having received lump sum compensation for treatment and disability through the dispatch company's industrial accident insurance. The using employer claimed there was no relationship between it and the dispatched worker, and the extinctive prescription for illegal activities had expired since 3 years had passed since the incident. In response, the Supreme Court stated in its ruling, "Although the using employer did not have any direct employment contract with the plaintiff, the using employer was able to control and manage the plaintiff's labor through a worker dispatch contract. This is regarded as an employer-worker relationship. Therefore, it is fair to say that the using employer is obligated to consider safety as if it were a using employer." The employer's duty to protect was recognized as grounds for injury compensation (Article 390 of the Civil Act), with the extinctive prescription determined to be 5 years instead of 3 years.[347)]

3. Obligation to prevent sexual harassment in the Workplace

Employers must ensure a work life free from sexual harassment in the workplace. In the event sexual harassment occurs in the workplace, the employer shall take action to prevent recurrence, as well as suitable disciplinary action towards the instigator of the sexual harassment. The employer shall endeavor to make relief efforts and prevent

346) Daegu District Court ruling on Apr. 19, 2019: 2018 gadan 115280.

347) Supreme Court ruling on Nov. 28, 2013: 2011 da 60247.

착용하게 하여 사고를 미연에 방지해야 함에도 이를 의무를 게을리하였다. (중략) 이에 회사가 배상해야 할 손해액 산정에 있어 회사의 책임을 80%로 제한한다.[346]

2. 파견근로자에 대한 사용사업주의 의무

근로자파견관계에 있어 근로계약이 없는 파견근로자가 사용사업주 업무를 수행하다가 업무상 사고를 당한 경우, 사용사업주는 그 재해를 당한 파견근로자에 대해서도 사용자 책임을 진다.

관련사례 : 근로자가 파견회사와 근로계약을 체결하고 사용사업주에게 파견되어 업무를 시작한지 6일째 되는 날, 산재사고가 발생하였다. 근로자는 2005년 11월 15일 03시 35분경 플라스틱 사출기의 이물질을 제거하던 중 오른쪽 손과 팔 부분이 압착되어 절단되는 사고가 발생하였다. 재해자는 파견회사의 산재보험으로 치료 및 장해보상 일시금을 모두 받은 후, 2010년경 사용사업주에게도 민사상 손해배상을 청구한 사건이다. 이에 대해 사용사업주는 파견근로자와 근로계약 관계가 없고, 불법행위에 따른 소멸시효도 3년이므로 시효가 지났다고 주장하였다. 이에 대해 대법원은 “사용사업주와 원고 사이에 직접적인 고용계약은 존재하지 않지만 근로자파견계약에 의해 원고의 노무를 지배 · 관리할 수 있었고, 이러한 양자의 관계는 고용계약 및 근로자파견계약을 매개로 한 실질적인 사용자와 근로자의 관계라고 본다. 따라서 사용사업주는 원고에 대해 사용자로서 안전배려의무가 있다고 할 것이다.”라고 판단하였다. 사용자의 보호의무는 채무불이행에 따른 손해배상(민법 제390조) 규정으로 인정하고 그 소멸시효도 3년이 아닌 5년으로 판단하였다.[347]

3. 직장 내 성희롱예방 의무

사용자는 직장 내 성희롱이 없는 직장 생활을 보장해야 한다. 직장 내 성희롱이 발생한 경우, 필요한 조치를 통해 성희롱 가해자에게 적합한 징계와 함께 사건 재발방지를 위해 노력해야 하고, 피해자를 위한 구제노력과 제2의 피해가

346) 대구지방법원 2019.4.19. 선고 2018가단115280 판결.
347) 대법원 2013.11.28. 선고 2011다60247 판결.

secondary damage to the victim. If the employer fails in this obligation, the employer shall be liable for damages due to illegal acts as well as criminal punishment for violating the Equal Treatment Act.

Related Case: A worker (the plaintiff) complained about sexual harassment in the workplace and asked for prompt and appropriate remedy. However, not only did the defendant (company) ignore the complaint, it also took disciplinary and other unfavorable action, such as a suspension from work, against the plaintiff. The company also took discriminatory and unfair disciplinary action against fellow workers who helped the plaintiff, thereby preventing the plaintiff from receiving any help from friendly colleagues in the workplace and isolating her from other colleagues. As a result of the company's actions, the plaintiff received "secondary damage" in which she was exposed to negative reactions, negative public opinion, disadvantageous treatment, and mental anguish for complaining about sexual harassment in the workplace and "causing a problem." The mental stress suffered by the plaintiff is believed to be considerable. Accordingly, as the employer, in accordance with Article 756 of the Civil Act, the company shall compensate the plaintiff for mental injury incurred by its violation of Article 14 (2)[348)] of the Equal Employment Act and as an employer in violation of its duty to protect.[349)]

Ⅱ. Relationship between the Labor Standards Act and the Civil Act regarding Termination of Employment

The Civil Act and Labor Standards Act are often regarded as equivalent when it comes to employment. However, strictly speaking, there are many areas where the Labor Standards Act does not apply and/or has limited application. The Labor Standards Act applies to a limited number of legal provisions for a workplace with fewer than five persons, but does not apply to workplaces with only relatives and housekeepers living together. Issues that are not stipulated

348) Article 14 (Measures to Be Taken in Case of Sexual Harassment at Work) (2) Upon receiving a report as prescribed in paragraph (1) or discovering an occurrence of sexual harassment in the workplace, the employer shall immediately conduct an investigation to confirm the facts. In such cases, the employer must ensure that the worker who has reportedly suffered from sexual harassment on the job or who has claimed that sexual harassment occurred (hereinafter referred to as the "employee victim etc.") does not feel sexually humiliated during the investigation process.

349) Seoul High Court ruling on Apr. 20, 2018: 2017 na 2076631.

가지 않도록 노력해야 한다. 이를 위반한 경우에는 사용자는 남녀고용평등법을 위반한 형사처벌 뿐만 아니라 불법행위에 따른 손해배상 책임을 진다.

관련사례 : 피고(회사)는 근로자인 원고가 이 사건 직장 내 성희롱으로 인한 피해를 호소하며 신속하고 적절한 구제조치를 취해 줄 것을 요청하는데도 이를 무시하고 오히려 성희롱 피해를 입은 원고에게 근거 없는 혐의를 씌워 부당한 징계처분을 하거나 대기발령 등의 불리한 조치를 하였다. 더구나 피고는 원고를 도와준 동료 근로자에게 까지 차별적이고 부당한 징계처분을 함으로써 원고로 하여금 직장 내에서 우호적인 동료들의 도움을 받을 수 없도록 하였고, 다른 동료들로부터 고립되는 처지에 놓이게 하였다. 피고의 이러한 행위로 인해 원고는 이 사건 직장 내 성희롱 피해 사실을 알리고 문제를 삼는 과정에서 오히려 부정적 반응이나 여론, 불이익한 처우 또는 그로 인한 정신적 피해에 노출되는 이른바 '2차 피해'를 입었고, 그로 인해 원고가 입은 정신적 고통은 상당할 것으로 판단된다. 따라서 피고는 원고에 대하여 남녀고용평등법 제14조 제2항[348]을 위반하였고, 또한 사용자로서 보호의무를 위반하였기에 원고가 입은 정신적 손해를 배상할 책임이 있다.[349]

Ⅱ. 고용종료와 관련 근로기준법과 민법과의 관계

고용과 관련된 법률관계는 민법과 근로기준법에서 규정하고 있다. 다만, 근로기준법은 5인 미만의 상시 근로자를 사용하는 사업 또는 사업장에 제한적으로 적용되고, 동거하는 친족만을 사용하는 경우와 가사사용인에 대해서는 법이 적용되지 않는다. 근로기준법에 규정되지 않은 부분은 민법 제2조의 신의성실 원칙과 권리남용금지의 원칙, 그 밖의 조항이 적용된다. 민법상 고용에

348) 제14조(직장 내 성희롱 발생 시 조치) ② 사업주는 제1항에 따른 신고를 받거나 직장 내 성희롱 발생 사실을 알게 된 경우에는 지체 없이 그 사실 확인을 위한 조사를 하여야 한다. 이 경우 사업주는 직장 내 성희롱과 관련하여 피해를 입은 근로자 또는 피해를 입었다고 주장하는 근로자가 조사 과정에서 성적 수치심 등을 느끼지 아니하도록 하여야 한다.

349) 서울고등법원 2018.4.20. 선고 2017나2076631 판결.

in the Labor Standards Act are subject to the principle of good faith and the prohibition against abuse of rights in Article 2 of the Civil Act, as well as some other provisions of thatAct. The employment section of the Civil Act has only 9 provisions in total but is considered the general law in labor law. As there are some differences in details and application when it comes to termination of employment, it is necessary to distinguish between the Civil Act and the Labor Standards Act. Five of the nine provisions in the Civil Act on employment are related to the termination of employment contracts.[350] In our capitalist economic system, as the Civil Act is based on the principle of freedom of contract, one party to the contract can freely terminate it on the premise of certain requirements or damages. However, if employment contracts allow employers, who are in a socially and economically superior position to employees in the labor contract relationship, to unilaterally dismiss employees, employee ability to maintain their livelihoods, based as it is upon earnings from employment, is threatened by unemployment at any time, which places them in an unequal and oppressive relationship.[351]

For this reason, the Labor Standards Act was enacted under the Constitution towards improving the equity of such relationsand to guarantee human dignity and the right to pursue happiness as a basic right of workers.[352]

A. The Need to Distinguish between the Different Types of Termination of Employment

1. Divisions in law

There are three types of termination of employment under the Civil Act. First, if employment is terminated when the contract period expires, it is recognized that renewal of the contract is

350) The five provisions of the Civil Act on the termination of employment contracts: ① Article 658 (Content of Service and Right of Rescission for the Future); ② Article 659 (Lapse of Three Years or More and Right to Give Notice of Rescission of Contract for the Future); ③Article 660 (Notice of Rescission for Future of Contract of Employment in which No Period has been Fixed); ④ Article 661 (Unavoidable Cause and Right to Rescind Contract for the Future); and ⑤ Article 663 (Employer's Bankruptcy and Notice of Rescission of Contract for the Future).

351) Lim, Jongyul, 「Labor Law」, 14th ed., Parkyoungsa, 2016, p.528; Kim, Allim, 「The Labor Protection Law」, KNOU Press, 2013, p. 213.

352) Article 32 of the Constitution of Korea: (3) Standards of working conditions shall be determined by Act in such a way as to guarantee human dignity.

관한 총 9개 조항은 노동법의 일반법적 효력을 가진다. 고용관련 민법 9가지 조항 중 5개가 고용계약 해지와 관련이 있다.[350] 자본주의 경제체제에서 민법은 계약자유의 원칙을 기본원리로 하고 있기 때문에 계약당사자 일방은 일정한 요건이나 손해배상을 전제로 자유롭게 계약을 해지할 수 있다. 그러나 근로자와 사용자 사이의 근로계약 관계에서 사회적, 경제적으로 우월한 위치에 있는 사용자가 자유롭게 근로계약을 해지할 수 있도록 하면 취업을 해야 생계를 유지할 수 있는 근로자는 언제든지 실직될지 모르는 위협부담을 항상 안고 있으므로 불평등하고 억압적인 관계에 놓이게 된다.[351]

이러한 불평등 관계를 개선하고, 근로자의 기본적인 권리인 인간의 존엄성과 행복추구권을 보장해주기 위해 헌법에 준하여 근로기준법이 만들어졌다.[352]

A. 고용의 종료에 대한 구분의 필요성

1. 법령상 구분

민법상 고용의 종료는 3가지로 규정하고 있다. 첫째, 고용기간이 만료한 때에 고용이 종료하며, 일정한 요건하에 묵시적 갱신을 인정한다(민법 제662조). 둘째, 약정기간이 3년을 넘거나 또는 기간의 약정이 없는 경우 당사자에게 해지통고권을 부여하며, 해지 통고 후 일정기간이 경과하면 해지 효력이 발생한다(민법 제659조, 제660조). 셋째, 특정한 사유가 있는 경우에 해지권의 발생을 인정하는 것이다(민법 제657조, 제658조, 제661조, 제663조). 이와 같이 민법에 의한 계약종료는 당사자간의 대등한 계약이므로, 필요한 경우에 자유롭게 해지할 수 있다는 것을 전제로 하고 있다.

---

350) 민법상 고용해지 관련 5개 조항은 ①노무의 내용과 해지권(민법 제658조), ②3년이상의 경과와 해지통고권(제659조), ③기간의 약정이 없는 고용의 해지통고(제660조), ④부득이한 사유와 해지권(제661조), ⑤사용자파산과 해지통고(민법 제663조)이다.

351) 임종률, 「노동법」, 제14판, 박영사, 2016, 528면; 김엘림, 「근로보호법」, 방송대 출판부, 2013, 213면.

352) 헌법 제32조 ③ 근로조건의 기준은 인간의 존엄성이 보장되도록 법률로서 정한다.

granted under certain circumstances (Article 662 of the Civil Act). Second, if the contract term is for more than three years or there has been no contract for a period of time, the right of notice of termination shall be granted to each party, and at this time, termination will take effect after a specific period of time (Articles 659 and 660). Third, there is recognition of the right of termination under certain circumstances (ArWticles 657, 658, 661, and 663). A contract under the Civil Act is a contract between parties, so it is presumed that it can be cancelled if necessary.

However, in the Labor Standards Act, unilateral termination of a labor contract by an employer amounts to an unfair dismissal and becomes subject to remedy applications for unfair dismissal. Provided, however, that this shall not be the case if the contract period is fixed, the period required for the completion of the work is specified and attained, or if the employee reaches retirement age. For an employment contract with a definite period of time, if the contract is longer than two years, the contract type becomes to a non-fixed term (Article 4 of the Fixed-term Employment Act).

2. Just cause for termination

The Civil Act allows either party to freely and unilaterally terminate the employment contract as it is freely concluded between the parties in accordance with the principle of freedom of contract.

However, the Labor Standards Act stipulates that employers cannot dismiss, suspend, or discipline a worker without justifiable reason (Labor Standards Act (LSA), Article 23). According to the LSA, it is impossible to notify an employee of unilateral termination of an employment contract in a manner that would be acceptable under that Act. This is because the LSA's aim is to protect employees. However, it is possible to terminate an employment contract for justifiable reason. Justifiable grounds are situations where an employee is liable to such an extent that the employment relationship cannot be continued under social norms, or there is inevitable management necessity.[353)]

Whether or not the employment relationship cannot in fact be continued depends on a variety of factors such as the purpose and nature of the business, the conditions of the workplace, the status of the worker, the motivation behind the employee's violations and/or actions affecting the company, and previous behavior. The situation must be reviewed and judged with comprehensive consideration of these factors.[354)]

353) Supreme Court ruling on July 8, 2003, 2001doo8018.

354) Supreme Court ruling on May 28, 2009, 2007doo579.

그러나 근로기준법에서는 사용자가 근로계약을 일방적으로 해지하는 것은 부당해고가 되어 법적으로 부당해고 구제신청의 대상이 된다. 다만, 근로계약 기간을 정한 경우 기간의 만료, 업무완성에 필요한 기간을 정하였거나 정년제 근로자가 정년에 도달한 경우 등은 근로관계의 자동 소멸 사유로 해고에 해당되지 않는다. 한편, 기간의 정함이 있는 근로계약의 경우에도 원칙적으로 2년을 초과하는 경우에는 기간의 정함이 없는 무기계약직으로 계약의 형태가 변경되어 정년이 될 때까지 고용이 계속 된다고 볼 수 있다 (기간제법 제4조).

2. 정당한 사유 유무

민법은 계약자유의 원칙에 따라 고용계약을 당사자간에 자유롭게 체결한 것과 마찬가지로 계약해지도 어느 일방이 자유롭게 해지할 수 있다.

그러나 근로기준법은 사용자는 "정당한 이유없이 근로자에게 해고, 휴직, 정직, 감봉, 기타의 징계를 하지 못한다"라고 명시하고 있다(근기법 제23조). 근로기준법상 근로계약 관계에서는 민법의 일방적 계약해지 통보가 불가능하다고 할 수 있다. 이는 근로기준법이 근로자 보호를 목적으로 하고 있기 때문이다. 그래도 정당한 사유가 있는 경우에는 근로계약의 해지가 가능하다. 판례에 의하면 정당한 사유는 사회통념상 고용관계를 계속할 수 없을 정도로 근로자에게 책임이 있는 사유가 있거나 부득이한 경영상의 필요가 있는 경우를 말한다.[353] 고용관계를 계속할 수 없을 정도인지 여부는 사업의 목적과 성격, 사업장의 여건, 근로자의 지위 및 직무의 내용, 비위행위의 동기, 그 행위의 기업질서에 대한 영향, 과거의 근무 태도 등 여러 사정을 종합적으로 검토하여 판단해야 한다.[354]

---

353) 대법원 2003.7.8. 선고 2001두8018 판결.

354) 대법원 2009.5.28. 선고 2007두979 판결.

B. Termination of Employment Contracts under the Labor Standards Act

Under the Labor Standards Act, unilateral termination of labor relations by an employer is allowable only under very specific circumstances. It is not easy to break employment relations with employees unless the contract is fixed-term. There must be legitimate reasons, limited by the time of termination, and termination must be carried in adherence withstrict dismissal procedures. Unilateral notice of termination of an employment contract by the employer becomes unfair dismissal and is subject to applications for remedy against unfair dismissal through a local or national labor relations committee.

1. Expiration of and exceptions to employment terms

According to Article 4 of the Fixed-term Employment Act, "the employer may utilize the services of a fixed-term employee to the extent that employment does not exceed two years, or to the extent that repeated renewal of the fixed-term employment contract does not exceed two years. However, in exceptional cases, where the period required for completion of the project is set, the age of the employee is 55 or more, the person is engaged in a professional position like 25 national qualifications, if his/her earned income per year is in the top 25% of Korean nationals, even if it exceeds 2 years, the contract can be terminated upon expiration of the applicable term.

2. Limitations to termination for just cause

Article 23 of the Labor Standards Act stipulates that employers cannot dismiss employees without justifiable grounds. According to the Labor Standards Act, it is impossible in employment contracts to provide a Civil Act-related unilateral notice of contract cancellation. This is because the LSA aims to protect workers. However, if there is justifiable cause, it is possible to terminate a labor contract. The Labor Standards Act provides justifiable grounds for dismissal as specified below.[355)]

① The employee took a bribe for allowing an inflow of flawed products from a supplier that has upset the production process of the company;

② The employee caused another person to drive a business vehicle without authorization, which

355) The MOEL Ordinance, related to Article 26 of the LSA.

B. 근로기준법에서 근로계약의 종료

근로기준법상 사용자의 일방적인 근로관계의 종료는 엄격하게 제한하고 있다. 근로계약은 기간의 정함이 있는 계약이 있지 않은 이상 근로자와의 고용관계를 단절하기가 쉽지 않다. 정당한 사유를 필요로 하고, 해고시기에 제한을 받으며, 해고절차에 있어서도 엄격한 절차를 거쳐야만 정당한 계약종료를 할 수 있다. 사용자의 일방적 계약종료 통지는 부당해고가 되어 노동위원회를 통한 구제신청의 대상이 된다.

1. 고용기간의 만료와 예외

기간제법 제4조에 따르면, "사용자는 2년을 초과하지 아니하는 범위 안에서 또는 기간제 근로계약의 반복 갱신이 2년을 초과하지 아니하는 범위 안에서 기간제 근로자를 사용할 수 있다. 다만, 사업완료에 필요한 기간을 정한 경우, 연령이 만 55세이상인 경우, 전문직종에 종사하는 자로서 25개의 국가자격을 갖춘 자, 박사학위를 취득한 후 해당분야에서 근로를 제공하는 경우, 등은 예외사유로 2년을 초과하여 기간제 근로자로 사용할 수 있다.

2. 정당한 사유에 의한 제한

근로기준법 제23조는 사용자는 정당한 이유없이 근로자를 해고하지 못한다고 명시하고 있다. 근로기준법상 근로계약 관계에서는 민법의 일방적 계약해지 통보가 불가능하다고 할 수 있다. 이는 근로자 보호를 목적으로 하고 있기 때문이다. 그래도 정당한 사유가 있는 경우에는 근로계약의 종결이 가능하다.[355]

① 납품업체로부터 금품 또는 향응을 제공받고 불량품을 납품받아 생산에 차질을 가져온 경우

② 영업용 차량을 임의로 타인에게 대리운전하게 하여 교통사고를 일으킨

355) 근로기준법 제26조와 관련 근로기준법 시행규칙 별표

resulted in an accident;

③ The employee provided confidential information on the business to a competitor, which adversely affected the business;

④ The employee made up or disseminated ungrounded facts or masterminded unlawful collective actions that caused a considerable disturbance to the business;

⑤ The employee took advantage of his/her job position or committed breach of trust to misappropriate, embezzle, or use company money for private purpose for a long time (e.g., embezzling the proceeds from operation of a company vehicle);

⑥ The employee stole or carried products or material out of the company without authorization;

⑦ The employee, being engaged in personnel management, treasury or accounting, manipulated the records or produced fraudulent statements that caused damage to the business;

⑧ The employee deliberately destroyed company equipment or property, causing considerable disturbance to the business; or

⑨ The employee deliberately committed acts which seriously disturbed the business or caused considerable financial damage to the company.

3. Restrictions on layoffs

According to Article 24 of the Labor Standards Act, if an employer dismisses an employee for managerial reasons, the employer must: ① have a need for urgent management changes; ② make efforts to avoid dismissal; ③ select employees to be dismissed by establishing reasonable, fair criteria for dismissal, and ④ notify the employee representative 50 days in advance to discuss these efforts to avoid dismissal and selection of the employees subject to dismissal. If the above four criteria are met, it will be a legitimate dismissal under Article 23 of the Labor Standards Act. Therefore, there are strict restraints on terminating an employment contract for reasons attributable to an employer but not the employee.

경우

③ 사업의 기밀, 기타 정보를 경쟁관계에 있는 다른 사업자 등에게 제공하여 사업에 지장을 가져온 경우

④ 허위사실을 날조·유포하거나 불법 집단행동을 주도하여 사업에 막대한 지장을 가져온 경우

⑤ 영업용차량 운송수입금을 부당하게 착복하는 등 직책을 이용하여 공금을 착복·장기유용·횡령하거나 배임한 경우

⑥ 제품 또는 원료 등을 절취 또는 불법 반출한 경우

⑦ 인사·경리·회계담당 직원이 근로자의 근무상황 실적을 조작하거나 허위 서류 등을 작성하여 사업에 손해를 끼친 경우

⑧ 사업장의 기물을 고의로 파손하여 생산에 막대한 지장을 가져온 경우

⑨ 기타 사회통념상 고의로 사업에 막대한 지장을 가져오거나 재산상 손해를 끼쳤다고 인정되는 경우

3. 정리해고의 제한

근로기준법 제24조의 정리해고의 제한 규정에 의거, 사용자는 경영상의 이유에 의하여 근로자를 해고할 경우 ① 긴박한 경영상 필요가 있어야 하고, ② 해고회피노력을 다하여야 하며, ③ 해고대상자를 합리적이고 공정한 기준으로 선정하여야 하고, ④ 해당근로자에게는 해고 50일 전에 통보하고, 사용자는 해고회피노력과 해고 대상자 선정에 관하여 협의하여야 한다고 명시하고 있다. 위의 네 가지 기준을 충족한 경우에 근로기준법 제23조에 있는 정당한 해고사유가 된다. 즉, 근로자의 귀책사유가 없이 사용자의 귀책사유로 근로자와의 근로계약을 해지하고자 할 경우에는 엄격한 제한을 받는다.

4. Restrictions on timing of dismissal

The employer shall not dismiss any employee during a period of temporary interruption of work for medical treatment of an occupational injury or disease or within 30 days thereafter, or any female employee during a period of temporary interruption of work before or after childbirth as provided herein or within 30 days thereafter (Article 23 of the LSA). This provision is designed to protect employees from the risk of unemployment during periods when employees lose their ability to work or when they cannot perform effective job searches.[356)] If an employee is dismissed in violation of this, the penalty clause is applied and the action invalidated by law. However, if the employer cannot continue the business or pays an adequate lump sum compensation for the injury or illness on the job, the period of dismissal is not exceptionally limited (Article 23 of the LSA).

5. Restrictions on procedures for dismissal

(1) Notice of dismissal

According to Article 26 of the Labor Standards Act, the employer shall give at least 30 days' notice before dismissing an employee. If this is not done, ordinary wages of at least thirty days shall be paid to the worker. This provision applies even in cases where there is legitimate reason for dismissal. Of course, if there are no justifiable reasons for dismissal, notice of dismissal does not amount to just cause for dismissal.

(2) Written notice of dismissal

Under Article 27 of the Labor Standards Act, if an employer intends to dismiss an employee, the employer shall notify the employee of the reason(s) for dismissal and the date of such dismissal, in writing. In the absence of this written notice, the dismissal shall have no effect. This regulation mandates that the employer be careful when dismissing employees. Such notice is designed to clarify the reason(s) for dismissal and date of dismissal so that any related dispute can be easily resolved and the employee can take appropriate action against the dismissal.[357)]

---

356) Lim, Jongyul, 「Labor Law」, 14th ed., Parkyoungsa, 2016, p. 543; Supreme Court ruling on Aug. 27, 1991, 91nu3321.

357) Supreme Court ruling on Oct. 27, 2011, 2001da42324.

4. 해고시기의 제한

사용자는 근로자가 업무상 부상 또는 질병의 요양을 위하여 휴업한 기간과 그 후 30일 동안, 산전 산후의 여성이 근로기준법에 따라 휴업한 기간과 그 후 30일간은 해고하지 못한다(근로기준법 제23조). 근로자가 노동력을 상실한 기간이나 효과적인 구직활동을 할 수 없는 기간동안 근로자를 실직의 위험으로부터 보호하려는 취지에서 설정한 규정이다.[356] 이를 위반하여 근로자를 해고한 경우 벌칙조항이 적용되고, 사법상 무효가 된다. 다만, 사용자가 업무상 부상 또는 질병에 대하여 일시보상을 하였거나 사업을 계속할 수 없는 경우에는 예외적으로 해고 시기의 제한을 받지 않는다(근기법 제23조).

5. 해고절차의 제한

(1) 해고의 예고

근로기준법 제26조에 의하면, 사용자는 근로자를 해고하려면 적어도 30일전에 예고해야 하고, 30일전에 예고를 하지 않은 때에는 30일분 이상의 통상임금을 지급해야 한다. 해고 예고 규정은 해고의 정당한 여부와는 별개의 사안으로, 정당한 사유가 없는 경우 해고예고 자체를 하였다고 해고의 정당한 해고사유가 되는 것은 아니다.

(2) 해고의 서면통지

근로기준법 제27조에 의하면, 사용자는 근로자를 해고하려면 해고의 사유와 시기를 서면으로 통지해야 한다. 이 서면의 통지가 없는 경우에는 해고의 효력이 없다. 이 규정은 사용자가 근로자를 해고하는데 신중을 기하게 하는 한편, 해고의 존부 및 시기와 그 사유를 명확하게 하여 사후에 이를 둘러싼 분쟁이 적정하게 해결되고, 근로자에게는 해고에 적절히 대응할 수 있도록 하려는 것이다.[357]

---

356) 임종률, 「노동법」, 제14판, 박영사, 2016, 543면; 대법원 1991.8.27. 선고 91누3321 판결.
357) 대법원 2011.10.27. 선고 2011다42324 판결.

C. Termination of an Employment Contract according to the Civil Act

1. Expiration of employment terms & exceptions

If the parties set a term for employment, the employment shall terminate upon expiration of that period, unless renewed by mutual agreement of the parties before or after the expiration. If, however, after the expiration, the employee continues to provide labor without an agreement for renewal and the employer does not take action within areasonable period of time, the Civil Act interprets that the employee has been rehired under the same conditions (Article 662). However, termination of the contract may then be given at any time by the parties, which shall take effect one month after the receipt of notice (Articles 662 and 660). The Civil Act considers shorter-term contracts are more favorable between two parties in terms of the principle of freedom of contract.[358)]

2. Notice of dismissal

(1) Long-term employment

The period of employment can be determined by agreement between the parties, but when employment has continued for a very long period of time, there is potential to restrict the freedom of the parties regarding the employment relationship. Therefore, the Civil Act stipulates that when a contract term of employment exceeds 3 years or until the end-of-life of one party or a third party to the parties, either party may give notice of termination at any time after three years (Article 659). In such cases, termination will take effect three months from the date on which the other party receives such notice (Article 659). The maximum term for fixed-term employment contracts is limited to three years. This is to avoid disadvantage to the employee by lengthening the period of employment. In other words, the employment contract between comparably equal parties, according to the Civil Act, must be for a short enough period to protect employees.

---

358) Yang, Jaehyun, "A Study on the Employment Contract in the Civil Act," PhD thesis for Soongshil University, 2010, p. 66.

C. 민법에서 고용계약의 종료

1. 고용기간의 만료와 예외

당사자가 고용기간을 정한 경우 그 기간의 만료로 고용은 종료한다. 다만, 고용기간이 만료되기 전 또는 만료된 후에도 당사자의 합의로 이를 갱신할 수 있다. 그런데 고용기간이 만료한 후에 갱신기간의 합의 없이 근로자가 계속해서 노무를 제공하고 이에 대해 사용자가 상당한 기간 내에 이의를 제기하지 않는 경우, 민법은 당사자의 의사로 간주하여 전 고용과 동일한 조건으로 다시 고용한 것으로 본다(민법 제662조 제1항). 다만 기간의 정함이 없는 고용의 경우 당사자는 언제든지 계약해지의 통고를 할 수 있고, 그 통고를 받은 때부터 1개월이 지나면 해지의 효력이 생긴다(민법 제662조, 제660조). 이는 민법의 계약자유의 원칙으로 대등한 양 당사자는 계약기간이 짧을수록 더 유리한 계약으로 간주하고 있다.[358]

2. 해고통고

(1) 고용기간이 장기인 경우

고용기간은 당사자의 합의로 정할 수 있지만, 그것이 지나치게 장기인 때에는 고용관계의 특성상 당사자의 자유를 구속하는 문제가 있다. 그래서 민법은 고용의 약정기간이 3년을 넘거나 또는 당사자의 일방 혹은 제 3자의 종신까지로 된 때에는, 각 당사자는 3년을 경과한 후 언제든지 계약해지의 통고를 할 수 있는 것으로 정한다(민법 제659조). 이 경우 상대방이 해지의 통고를 받은 날로부터 3개월이 지나면 해지의 효력이 생긴다(민법 제659조). 기간의 정함이 있는 고용계약의 최장기간을 3년으로 제한하고 있다. 이는 고용기간을 길게 함으로써 노무자에게 불이익을 주지 않기 위한 것이다. 다시 말해, 고용기간이 짧아야 근로자를 보호할 수 있다는 민법상 대등한 당사자 계약의 특징이다.

358) 양재현, "민법상 고용계약에 관한 연구", 숭실대학교 법학박사 학위논문, 2010, 66면.

(2) In cases where there is no agreement on contract period

In the absence of an agreement on the term of employment, each party may at any time notify the other of termination of the contract (Article 660 of the Civil Act). In this case, termination shall take effect one month from the date on which the other party receives notice of termination (Article 660). However, when remuneration is determined by a period of time, the termination will become effective upon passing of the first pay period after the notice has been received (Article 660).[359)]

3. Termination of employment

Notice of termination of an employment contract can be given at any time in the following instances. The termination becomes effective upon the time notification reaches the other party:

1) By the employee: should the employer assign the employer's right to a third party without the employee's consent (Article 657 of the Civil Act: Exclusivity of Rights and Duties);
2) By the employee: should the employer request that the employee provideslabor not agreed to in the employment contract (Article 658 of the Civil Act: Content of Service and Right of Rescission for the Future);
3) By either employee or employer: in unavoidable circumstances (Article 661 of the Civil Act: Unavoidable Cause and Right to Rescind Contract for the Future); and
4) By the employee (or bankruptcy trustee): If the employer receives a bankruptcy determination; even if there is agreement on the term of employment, the employee or bankruptcy trustee may terminate the contract (Article 663 of the Civil Act: Employer's Bankruptcy and Notice of Termination of Contract for the Future).

D. Comments

There are few benefits to be gained by making comparisons between the Civil Act and the Labor Standards Act. The Civil Act establishes rights and obligations based on the

---

359) For example, if you give a notice of cancellation in April, your contract will be cancelled the first period after 1 June.

(2) 기간의 약정이 없는 경우

고용기간의 약정이 없는 때에는 각 당사자는 언제든지 계약해지의 통고를 할 수 있다(민법 제660조). 그 경우 상대방이 해지의 통고를 받은 날로부터 1개월이 경과하면 해지의 효력이 생긴다(제660조). 다만 기간으로 보수를 정한 때에는, 통고를 받은 당기 후의 1기를 경과함으로써 해지의 효력이 생긴다(민법 제660조).[359)]

3. 고용해지

고용계약해지 통고는 다음의 경우에 언제든지 할 수 있다. 상대방에게 그 통지가 도달한 때부터 통고기간이 필요 없이 해지의 효력이 생긴다.

1) 사용자가 근로자의 동의 없이 그 권리를 제삼자에게 양도한 경우(민법 제657조 : 권리의무의 전속성)
2) 사용자가 약정하지 아니한 노무의 제공을 요구한 때나 근로자가 약정한 기한이 없는 경우(민법 제658조: 노무의 내용과 해지권).
3) 고용기간의 약정이 있는 경우에도 부득이한 경우 있는 때에는 당사자는 계약을 해지할 수 있다(민법 제661조: 부득이한 사유와 해지권).
4) 고용기간의 약정이 있는 때에도 사용자가 파산선고를 받은 경우에는 노무자 또는 파산관재인은 계약을 해지할 수 있다(제663조: 사용자파산과 해지통고).

D. 의견

민법이 일반법의 차원에서 대등한 당사자 간의 계약관계를 기준으로 권리와 의무 관계를 정립하였다고 본다면, 근로기준법은 특별법으로서 강행규정으로 사용자가 지켜야 하는 의무들을 명시하고 있기 때문이다. 따라서 특별법인 근

359) 예를 들어, 매우러 초일부터 말일까지를 기간으로 임금을 선정하여 월급을 주기로 하였는데 4월에 해지통고를 한 경우에는 당기 후의 1기를 경과한 때, 즉 6월 1일부터 해지의 효력이 생긴다.

contractual relationship between equal parties at the level of general law, while the Labor Standards Act stipulates enforcement regulations in a special law that the employer must comply with. Therefore, as the Civil Act is more comprehensive and there are limitations on application of the Labor Standards Act, the Civil Act can be interpreted additionally or applied in a supplementary fashion for cases not covered under the Labor Standards Act.

Ⅲ. Criteria for Determining Whether Forced Resignation is Agreed Resignation or Dismissal

There are two ways to terminate employment: one is voluntary resignation and the other is dismissal, which is a unilateral decision by the employer. Resignations do not cause labor disputes as the employee chooses to resign, whereas dismissals require a justifiable reason in accordance with Article 23 of the LSA since they terminate the employment relationship without mutual consent.

Forced resignations are in the grey area between resignation and dismissal, and refer to cases where the employee does not wish to quit but must submit a letter of resignation at the employer's insistence, whereupon the employer terminates the employment relationship. In this case, it would seem that there would be no labor dispute about whether this was a dismissal or not because the employer simply terminated the employment by accepting the letter of resignation submitted. In relation to this, the Civil Act (Article 107: Declaration of Untrue Intention) stipulates, "A declaration of intent shall be valid, even if the declarant has made it with the knowledge that such declaration is different from his intent: Such declaration of intent shall be void if the other party was aware, or should have been aware, of the real intent of the declarant." Judicial rulings have shown that if an employer receives letters of resignation from all employees but dismisses them selectively, such terminations are considered dismissals, whereas if employers pay certain employees a voluntary early retirement bonus and, in return for that, receive a letter of resignation before engaging in managerial dismissals due to urgent business reasons, these are considered mutually agreed resignations.

There are no substantial or stipulated criteria for determining if forced resignations are agreed resignations or de facto dismissals, resulting in frequent labor disputes. I would like to look at related cases and review the legal criteria for such determinations.

로기준법이 일반법인 민법에 우선 적용되며, 민법은 근로기준법에 규정이 없는 경우에만 보충적으로 적용된다.

Ⅲ. 권고사직과 해고

근로관계를 종결하는 데에는 근로자가 스스로 그만두는 사직과 사용자의 일방적 의사표시인 해고로 구분된다. 사직은 근로자가 스스로 사직 의사표시를 하고 그만 두는 경우로 노동법적 다툼의 문제가 될 여지가 없다. 반면 해고의 경우에는 사용자가 일방적 의사표시로 근로관계를 단절하기 때문에 실질적 유효 요건으로 근로기준법 제23조 1항의 규정에 따른 정당한 사유가 있어야 한다.

그런데 사직과 해고의 경계에 해당하는 권고사직은 근로자가 사직하고 싶지 않은 내면의 의도가 있지만, 사용자의 권고에 의해 어쩔 수 없이 사직서를 제출하고 사용자가 이를 수용함으로써 고용관계를 단절하는 것이다. 이 경우 외형상 제출된 사직서를 수리하는 것으로 사직에 의한 근로관계 종결이기 때문에 해고의 다툼이 있을 수 없을 것 같이 보인다. 이와 관련하여 민법 제107조(진의 아닌 의사표시)는 규정에 의하면, “의사표시는 표의자가 진의 아님을 알고 한 것이라도 그 효력이 있다. 그러나 상대방이 표의자의 진의 아님을 알았거나 이를 알 수 있었을 경우에는 무효로 한다.”라고 규정하고 있을 뿐이다. 판례는 사용자가 일괄 사직서를 받은 후 선별적 사직을 수용하는 경우에는 해고에 해당되는 반면에 사용자가 긴박한 경영상 이유로 경영상 해고를 단행하기에 앞서 특정 근로자들에게 희망퇴직금을 지급하고 그 대가로 사직서를 제출 받고 퇴직처리 한 경우에는 합의퇴직으로 보았다.

이러한 사직서 제출에 따른 퇴직처리, 즉 권고사직이 합의퇴직인지 해고인지를 구분하는 문제에 관하여 법 규정상 구체적이고 명확한 기준이 없기 때문에 법적 다툼으로 이어지는 경우가 많다. 따라서 이와 관련된 사례들을 중심으로 그 법적 판단기준을 살펴보고자 한다.

A. Cases Determined to be Dismissals

In cases where an employee was unilaterally forced by the employer to submit a resignation letter to the company, the resignation can be invalidated because it was not the employee's actual intent to resign. Judicial rulings have shown that when an employer forced an employee to submit a letter of resignation and terminated the employment based upon the received letter, this was considered de facto dismissal as the decision to terminate employment was a unilateral employer decision. In addition to this, dismissal without justifiable reason is equal to unfair dismissal.[360] Following are some cases where resignation was considered de facto dismissal.

1. Employee unable to enter the country if a resignation letter was not submitted

An employee who was working overseas had to enter the country to undergo medical treatment for an illness, but the company insisted that he submit a letter of resignation if he wished to enter the country, and so he did so, although that was not his original intent. In this case, the employee's letter of resignation was not considered a valid reason for termination of employment.[361]

2. All employees submitted letters of resignation, after which the company terminated employment with all of them

A company's quality team was strongly criticized by the quality management director for quality problems. The quality team held a meeting where they decided that the entire team would submit letters of resignation to the board members to show their desperate determination to improve their work. The letters of resignation were not meant to express an actual intention to resign, but to apologize for the quality problems collectively, and express their intention to not repeat them. However, the company accepted their letters of resignation and terminated employment with everyone on the quality team. Included were low-ranking employees who had to submit their letters of resignation in solidarity with the other members of the quality team (including the quality management director and the team leader). This termination was judged as unfair dismissal.[362]

---

360) Supreme Court ruling on July 12, 1991, 90da11554

361) Supreme Court ruling on Sep. 1, 1992, 92da26260

362) Seoul Administrative Court ruling on Nov 25, 2008, 2008guhap27674

A. 해고에 해당하는 사례

사직의 의사가 없는 근로자로 하여금 사용자의 일방적 강요에 의하여 어쩔 수 없이 사직서를 작성하여 제출한 경우에는 근로자의 진의 아닌 의사표시가 존재하므로 무효라 할 수 있다. 판례도 사용자가 근로자로부터 사직서를 제출 받고 이를 수리하는 형식을 취하여 근로계약관계를 종료시킨다고 할지라도 사직의 의사 없는 근로자로 하여금 어쩔 수 없이 사직서를 작성 제출하게 한 경우에는 실질적으로는 사용자의 일방적 의사에 의하여 근로계약관계를 종료시키는 것이어서 해고에 해당하고 정당한 이유 없는 해고조치는 부당해고와 다름없는 것으로 판단하고 있다.[360] 근로자의 진의 아닌 의사표시와 관련된 사례들은 다음과 같다.

1. 사직하지 않는 이상 입국이 금지된 경우

해외근로자가 업무상 재해의 치료를 위하여 중도 귀국함에 있어 "미리 사직의 뜻이 담긴 사직서를 제출하지 아니하면 귀국시켜 줄 수 없다"는 회사의 강요에 어쩔 수 없이 본의에 반하여 사직서를 제출한 것이라면 그 사직서 제출에 의한 사직은 무효이다.[361]

2. 일괄 사직서 제출 및 전원 퇴직처리

품질관리 팀원들은 품질 관리를 맡고 있는 상무로부터 품질 불량과 관련하여 강하게 질책을 받았고, 이에 대하여 품질관리팀은 자체 회의를 거쳐 팀원 전체의 사직서를 작성하여 임원회의에 제출하였다. 그 팀원 전체의 사직서는 그 내용대로 사직하겠다는 의사가 아니라 종래의 행위에 대한 잘못을 통감하여 책임지는 자세로 새로이 일하겠다는 각오의 의사표시였다. 이에 대해 회사는 품질관리팀 전원을 해고하였다. 해고자들은 품질관리팀의 하위 직원에 불과하며, 팀 전체의 업무 처리가 문제되어 상무나 팀장이 사직서를 작성하는 상황에서 팀원 전체가 동참하는 차원에서 어쩔 수 없이 사직서를 제출한 것이므로 이는 부당한 해고에 해당된다.[362]

---

360) 대법 1991.7.12, 90다11554

361) 대법 1992.9.1, 92다26260

362) 서울행법 2008.11.25, 2008구합27674

3. All employees submitted letters of resignation, but the company only terminated selected employees

A company received orders from the supervisory office to terminate a certain number of employees, and in implementing this order, the company forced all employees to submit letters of resignation. The applicant for remedy against unfair dismissal had to submit a letter of resignation along with his other coworkers, against his will. The company then terminated employment for six employees. This case was considered a dismissal because employment was, in reality, terminated by unilateral decision of the employer.[363)]

4. Personnel at the managerial level or higher were forced to submit letters of resignation, which the company accepted

A company president ordered all senior managers to submit letters of resignation so that they could get recognition from the chairman of the board. All managers had to submit their resignations against their will, which the company accepted, and terminated employment with all of them. These terminations were ruled to be unilateral dismissals by the company president.[364)]

5. A company terminated employment with all employees after receiving their letters of resignation, and hired them again

All employees had to submit letters of resignation according to company business policy. The company accepted these resignations and terminated employment relations. They were then rehired. Since there was no gap in time between their resignations and rehiring, it was determined that the employees had not truly intended to resign when they submitted their letters of resignation, and that the employer was aware that the employees resigned only on the condition of reemployment. Therefore, the company's terminations based upon the letters of resignation were not valid.[365)]

---

363) Supreme Court ruling on Feb 9, 1993, 91da44452

364) Supreme Court ruling on Apr 29, 1994, 93nu16185

365) Supreme Court ruling on May 10, 1988, 87daka2578

3. 일괄사직서 제출 및 선별적 퇴직 처리

감독관청으로부터 일정 수의 임직원을 선발하여 해직시킬 것을 지시받고 이를 시행함에 있어 모든 직원들로 하여금 일괄적으로 사직서를 제출하도록 하므로 원고는 사직할 의사가 없으면서도 부득이 다른 직원들과 함께 사직서를 제출하였는데 회사가 6명의 사직서만을 수리하여 면직시켰다면 이는 실질적으로는 회사의 일방적 의사에 의하여 근로관계를 종료시키는 것이어서 해고에 해당한다.[363)]

4. 특정 간부이상 사직서 일괄제출 및 전원 사직 처리

회사의 대표이사가 부장급 이상 간부들에 대해 이사장에게 재신임을 묻겠다고 하면서 일괄하여 사직서를 제출하도록 지시를 하여 간부들은 모두 사직할 의사 없이 일괄하여 사직서를 제출하였으며, 회사는 제출된 사직서에 따라 해당 근로자 전부를 퇴직처리 하였다. 이는 실질적으로 대표이사의 일방적 의사에 의하여 근로계약관계를 종료시킨 것으로서 해고에 해당한다.[364)]

5. 일괄 사직서 처리 및 재입사 처리

근로자가 회사의 경영방침에 따라 사직원을 제출하고 회사가 이를 받아들여 퇴직처리를 하였다가 즉시 재입사하는 형식을 취함으로써 근로자의 그 퇴직전 후에 걸쳐 실실석인 근로관계의 단절이 없이 계속 근무하였다면 그 사직원 제출은 근로자가 퇴직을 할 의사 없이 퇴직의사를 표시한 것으로 비진의 표시에 해당하고 재입사를 전제로 사직원을 제출하게 한 회사 또한 그와 같은 진의 아님을 알고 있었다고 할 것이므로 위 사직원 제출과 퇴직처리에 따른 퇴직의 효과는 생기지 아니한다.[365)]

---

363) 대법 1993.02.09, 91다44452
364) 대법 1994.04.29, 93누16185
365) 대법 1988.5.10, 87다카2578

6. An employee was transferred only after submitting a letter of resignation, in accordance with company policy

In cases where an employee transfers from the parent company to its subsidiary, or from the subsidiary to the parent company, whether continuous employment exists or not depends on whether the employee actually intended to resign or is simply following company requirements that he/she resign before such a transfer. If the employee submitted a letter of resignation to the parent company or the subsidiary with the real intention of terminating the employment relationship, received severance pay and later was hired by the parent company or its subsidiary again, it can be regarded that his/her employment with the previous entity has been terminated. However, if the employee had to resign and be rehired by the company in accordance with the parent company's unilateral policy, and so submitted a letter of resignation (without really intending to terminate the employment relationship), even if the employee received severance pay, the employment shall not be considered terminated as the employee had no intention to do so in actuality.[366)]

7. Employees with poor performance results forced to quit by the employer

Korea Rural Community Corporation was required to downsize its workforce in accordance with a government management innovation plan. The Corporation selected some employees to terminate without reasonable or fair criteria and forced them to submit letters of resignation. These forced resignations were considered dismissals since they were unilateral decisions by the employer.[367)]

B. Cases Determined to be Agreed Resignations

The criteria for determining agreed resignation refer to conditions where the employee submits a letter of resignation without really desiring to resign, but resignation is admitted in his or her best interest. This may be considered agreed resignation. The following legal

366) Supreme Court ruling on Mar. 28, 1997 95da51397.

367) Supreme Court ruling on June 14, 2002, 2001du11076

6. 그룹사 방침에 따라 사직서 제출 후 다시 자회사로 전출된 경우

근로자가 모회사로부터 자회사로, 다시 자회사로부터 모회사로 전출되는 경우에 근로자가 자의에 의하여 계속 근로관계를 단절할 의사로써 모회사 또는 자회사에 사직서를 제출하고 퇴직금을 지급받은 다음 자회사 또는 모회사에 다시 입사하였다면 전자와의 근로관계는 일단 단절될 것이지만, 그것이 근로자의 자의에 의한 것이 아니라 모회사의 경영방침에 의한 일방적인 결정에 따라 퇴직과 재입사의 형식을 거친 것에 불과하다면 이러한 형식을 거쳐서 퇴직금을 지급받았더라도 근로자에게 근로관계를 단절할 의사가 있었다고 할 수 없고 따라서 계속적 근로관계도 단절되지 않는다.[366)]

7. 저평가자에게 일방적 권고사직 한 경우

정부의 공기업 경영혁신 계획에 따라 인력감축의 일환으로 농어촌진흥공사가 구조조정대상자를 선정함에 있어 합리적이고 공정한 기준 없이 일부 근로자를 문제직원으로 확정하여 그에 대하여 사직을 종용함으로써 권고사직 형식으로 근로계약관계를 종료시킨 경우 이는 실질적으로 해고에 해당한다.[367)]

B. 합의퇴직에 해당되는 사례

합의퇴직에 대한 판단기준은 진의 아닌 의사표시였지만, 이를 진의의 의사표시로 인정할 수 있는 것이라면, 합의퇴직의 성격으로 판단할 수 있다는 점이다. 다음과 같은 법적 논리를 가지고 이를 판단한다.

비록 사용자가 사직의사 없는 근로자로 하여금 어쩔 수 없이 사직서를 작성·제출하게 한 후 이를 수리하여 근로계약관계를 종료시키는 경우라도, 사용자가 사직서 제출에 따른 사직의 의사표시를 수락함으로써 사용자와 근로자 사이의 근로계약관계가 합의퇴직에 의하여 종료된 것으로 볼 수 있으므로 사용자의 해

366) 대법 1997.03.28, 95다51397
367) 대법 2002.6.14, 2001두11076

principle can be used as criteria for judgment.

Even though an employer forces an employee to submit a letter of resignation against his will, then accepts the resignation and terminates employment, this may not be dismissal, but an agreed resignation. A certain employee outwardly expressed his intention to resign as fitting the situation, even though that was not his real intention. Therefore, even though he did not want to resign, if he judged that expressing his intention to do so was the best thing he could do under the circumstances, it can be understood that his real intention was to express regret, not actually resign.[368)]

1. Voluntary resignation in relation to dismissal for managerial reasons

Even though the employees of a certain company did not wish to resign, they submitted letters of resignation as they seemed the best plan of action when collectively considering the economic situation, the company's redundancy plans, and the company's early retirement bonus, and the interests of both sides. The employment relationship between the employees and the company was terminated as the resignation was deemed to be mutually agreed after the employees submitted letters of resignation as recommended by the company.[369)]

2. An employee was pressured to submit a letter of resignation rather than resigning for disciplinary reasons

Even though an employee did not wish to resign at the time he submitted a letter of resignation, he chose his best option, which was to avoid disciplinary dismissal and resign, as a way of gaining severance pay and future employment rather than seek judgment on the validity of disciplinary dismissal under those circumstances. The letter of resignation was considered valid as his resignation corresponded to his expression of true intention.[370)]

---

368) Supreme Court ruling on Apr. 25, 2003, 2002da11458

369) Supreme Court ruling on Apr. 22, 2002, 2002da65066

370) Supreme Court ruling on Apr. 25, 2000, 99da34475

고라고 볼 수 없다. 특히 진의 아닌 의사표시에 있어서의 '진의'란 특정한 내용의 의사표시를 하고자 하는 표의자의 생각을 말하는 것이지 표의자가 진정으로 마음속에서 바라는 사항을 뜻하는 것은 아니므로 표의자가 의사표시의 내용을 진정으로 마음속에서 바라지는 아니하였다고 하더라도 당시의 상황에서는 그것이 최선이라고 판단하여 의사표시를 하였을 경우에는 이를 내심의 효과의사가 결여된 진의 아닌 의사표시라고 할 수 없다.[368)]

1. 경영상 해고와 관련된 희망퇴직

근로자들은 사직을 선뜻 받아들일 수는 없었다 할지라도 그 당시의 경제상황, 피고회사의 구조조정 계획, 피고회사가 제시하는 희망퇴직의 조건, 퇴직할 경우와 계속 근무할 경우에 있어서의 이해관계 등을 종합적으로 고려하여 당시의 상황으로 그것이 최선이라고 판단한 결과 사직원을 제출 하였다. 따라서 근로자들과 회사 사이의 근로관계는 근로자들이 회사의 권유에 따라 사직의 의사표시를 하고 회사가 이를 받아들임으로써 유효하게 합의퇴직 되었다고 본다.[369)]

2. 징계해고 보다 권고사직 처분을 위해 사직서 제출한 경우

근로자가 사직원 제출 당시 자기의 의사표시를 진정으로 바라지 아니하였다 하더라도 당시 상황에서는 징계면직처분의 효력을 다투는 것보다는 퇴직금 수령 및 장래를 위하여 재심을 통한 징계해고의 취소를 받는 것이 최선이라고 판단하여 그 의사표시를 한 것으로써 근로자에게 그 의사표시에 상응하는 사직의 효과의사가 있었다고 본다.[370)]

368) 대법 2003.4.25, 2002다11458
369) 대법 2003.4.22, 2002다65066
370) 대법 2000.4.25, 99다34475

Section 2: Justification of Disciplinary Dismissal

An employer can exercise the right to disciplinary action for an employee's violation of service regulations to maintain order within the company, provided, however, that it is justified when the organization implements the action fairly as authorized by the collective agreement or rules of employment.

The employer shall observe the following basic principles for disciplinary action. First, a different application of disciplinary punishment shall not be given for the same violation of the same regulation. The previous disciplinary action precludes any following disciplinary actions. Second, disciplinary action cannot be taken retroactively. Once a considerable time has passed after an employer has become aware that an employee acted in a way that justifies disciplinary action, the employer can no longer take such action, as it would, in effect, be retroactive discipline. Third, the employee shall not be punished twice for the same violation. Fourth, an employer shall observe the disciplinary process described in the collective agreement and rules of employment to guarantee fair implementation of disciplinary action and to promote reasonable operation of the disciplinary system.

The employer exercises his right to take disciplinary action by punishing an employee who violates company regulations in order to maintain managerial order and promote productivity. The purpose of this disciplinary action is to prevent recurrence of identical violations and to restore company order. The employer's authority to take disciplinary action is discretionary but shall be exercised within boundaries set by the Labor Standards Act. That is, "No employer shall dismiss, lay off, suspend, or transfer an employee, or reduce wages, or take other punitive measures against an employee without justifiable reasons" (Article 23 (1) of the LSA). Therefore, disciplinary action without justifiable reason is null and void, as it is an abuse of the employer's right.

In cases where an application for remedy against unfair dismissal is submitted to the Labor Commission, judgment criteria for justifiable disciplinary action may be classified under the following three principles: 1) Whether there was a justifiable reason for disciplinary action,

제2절 징계해고의 정당성 판단기준

사용자는 기업질서 유지를 위하여 종업원의 복무규율 위반에 대해 징계권을 행사할 수 있다. 다만, 그 절차에 있어 단체협약이나 취업규칙에 정하는 바에 따라 권한 있는 기관에 의해 공정하게 행사한 경우에 한하여 정당성을 갖는다.

사용자는 징계권 행사시 다음의 기본 원칙을 준수하여야 한다. 첫째, 동일한 규칙에 동일한 정도의 행위에 대한 징계처분의 종류와 정도는 상이해서는 안 되며 전례의 처분은 후례의 징계처분을 구속한다. 둘째, 징계는 소급해서 징계할 수 없다. 따라서 상당한 기간이 경과한 경우 소급하여 징계하면 위법한 징계가 된다. 셋째, 근로자는 동일한 범죄에 대하여 거듭 처벌받지 아니한다. 넷째, 징계권의 공정한 행사를 확보하고 징계제도의 합리적인 운영을 도모하기 위해서는 단체협약이나 취업규칙에 정한 징계절차를 준수해야 한다.

징계권 행사는 경영질서를 유지하고 생산성 향상을 도모하기 위해 근로자의 사규 위반사항에 대해 사용자가 제재를 가하는 것이다. 이러한 징계의 목적은 근로자에게 적절한 제재를 가하여 동일한 사건이 재발됨을 막고자 함이며, 이를 통해 사내질서를 회복·유지하기 위함이라 할 수 있다. 징계에 대한 사용자의 권한은 재량 사항이나 근로기준법에 의해 제한을 받는다. 즉, “사용자는 근로자에게 정당한 이유 없이 해고, 휴직, 정직, 전직, 감봉, 그 밖의 징벌을 하지 못한다(근기법 제23조 제1항).” 따라서 정당한 사유가 없는 징계는 사용자의 권리를 남용한 것으로 그 징계는 무효가 된다.

노동위원회가 부당해고 구제신청사건을 판단함에 있어 적용하는 기준은 크게 다음 세가지로 나누어 볼 수 있다. 이 세가지 원칙은 1) 징계의 사유가 존재하는지 여부, 2) 징계의 양정이 적당한지 여부, 3) 징계의 절차를 준수하였는지의 여부가 그것이다. 징계의 정당성 판단기준에 있어, 주요쟁점은 ‘징계의 사유’보다는 ‘징계 양정’이나 ‘징계 절차’에 있는 경우가 많다. 아래에서는 징계의 세

2) Whether the severity of punishment was appropriate, and 3) Whether disciplinary process was observed. In judging the criteria for disciplinary action, there has been no dispute over the "reasons for disciplinary action,"but there has been a lot of dispute over "severity of punishment" and "disciplinary process." I would like to look at some concrete guidelines and labor cases related to the three judgment criteria for disciplinary action.

I. Reasons for Disciplinary Action

The employer shall clearly stipulate reasons for disciplinary action related to company service regulations in the rules of employment or other appropriate document, in order to implement disciplinary action. This regulation of disciplinary action shall satisfy the need for justifiable reason under the precondition that "the employer cannot discipline the employee without justifiable reason" from Article 23 (1) of the LSA.

1. Individual behaviors

(1) Insincere work attitude such as absence without notice, etc.

Negligence in the rules of employment refers to poor work performance, insincere attendance, arriving late, leaving early, avoiding duties, etc. However, such cases of job negligence are behavior commonly displayed by many employees in providing labor service. Therefore, they may be subject to a wage reduction or personnel evaluation, but not to disciplinary punishment.

Nevertheless, negligence of duty can induce disciplinary punishment in such cases where the employee is negligent without permission, or the employee's behavior disrupts company order regardless of reporting the cause in advance, or where the employee repeats the same mistakes after repeated warnings from the company.

Poor work attitude indicates behavior that degrades work efficiency or reduces productivity due to lack of concentration on duty. Absences without permission, neglecting work, or frequently arriving late to work can account for a poor evaluation of work attitude. Poor work attitude cannot naturally be subject to disciplinary action, but when the employee neglects or does not abide by warnings given by the company, he/she may be subject to disciplinary action.

① In the event the company regulates, for example in its rules of employment, insincere

가지 판단 기준에 관한 유사사례를 통해 구체적인 내용을 들여다보고자 한다.

Ⅰ. 징계의 사유

사용자가 근로자를 징계처분 하기 위해서는 취업규칙 등 복무규정으로 징계 사유를 명확하게 해야 한다. 이러한 징계에 관한 규정은 근로기준법 제23조 제1항인 "정당한 이유 없이 징벌을 할 수 없다"라는 대 전제 내에서 정당한 징계의 사유를 찾아야 한다.

1. 개별적 행위

(1) 무단결근

직무태만은 취업규칙의 징계처분 사유로 구체적으로 근무성적 불량, 무단결근, 출근 불량, 잦은 지각, 조퇴, 직장이탈 등이 여기에 속한다. 그러나 직무태만의 유형들은 근로계약상 노무를 일부 또는 전부 제공하지 않는 행위이므로, 일반적으로 채무 불이행으로 임금삭감의 대상이 되거나 인사고과의 평가 대상이 될 수 있을 뿐이며 징계처분의 대상이라고 할 수 없다.

이들 행위가 징계처분의 대상이 될 수 있기 위해서는 무단으로 행한 경우 또는 그 이유를 제출하였다고 할지라도 기업질서를 문란케 하는 데 큰 영향을 미치는 경우 또는 주의를 받고도 개선하지 않고 그 빈도가 많은 경우 등이라고 할 수 있다.

근무태도 불량은 주로 업무에 전념하지 않아 업무의 효율성을 저하시키거나 생산량을 저하시키는 행위를 말한다. 무단결근이나 직무태만·잦은 지각 등이 근무태도의 평가대상에 해당된다. 성적불량 자체만으로 징계처분의 대상이 당연히 되는 것은 아니나 수차례의 시정지시·교육 참가의 명령에도 이를 태만히 하거나 개선하지 않는 경우에는 징계의 대상이 될 수 있다.

① 취업규칙 등에 "며칠 이상" (또는 월 몇 회 이상) "무단결근한 때" 형식으로

work attitude such as 'absence without notice' by stipulating its right to take disciplinary dismissal action "when 'absent without notice' exceeds a certain number of days (in a month)," such stipulations shall not be null and void, even if they violate the Labor Standards Act. Accordingly, if an employee is repeatedly absent from work without notice, the company has justifiable reason to take disciplinary dismissal actions against him.[371)]

② In the rules of employment, if the company stipulates that exceeding a certain number of 'absences without notice' as a justifiable reason for taking disciplinary dismissal action, it does not indicate an accumulation of the total number of 'absent days without notice' without limit to a certain period of time. But it should be interpreted that there is a limit to an employee's total number of 'absent days without notice' within a given recognized fixed period.[372)]

(2) Poor performance (low sales performance)

In every company there are employees who perform very well, and those who perform poorly. Companies pay incentives to good workers, while they take action with poor employees to ensure better performance in the future. In some instances, companies may dismiss poorly-performing employees, and in such cases, the labor laws have strict standards designed to protect employees. Generally, for disciplinary dismissal to be deemed justifiable, there needs to be justification in 1) reason for dismissal, 2) the severity of disciplinary action, and 3) disciplinary procedures. Justification for dismissing under-performing employees should be determined by considering not only the criteria required for normal disciplinary dismissal, but also occupational characteristics related to poor performance by the particular employee. In order to dismiss employees with poor records, a company needs to maintain a detailed checklist to verify that it has provided sufficient opportunities to these employees for improvement and that the poor performance has been ongoing for a long period of time(refer to Table 1).[373)]

---

371) Supreme Court ruling on Sep. 26, 1986, 89DaKa5475.

372) Supreme Court ruling on May 9, 1989, 88DaKa4277.

373) Koo Keunseo,「Justification for Dismissal of Poor Performers」Labor Law Theory and Practice Association, Nov. 2011; Bang, Sangin,「Legal Issues Surrounding Poor Performers」, Monthly Labor Law Feb. 2010; Cho, Sanguk,「Management of Poor Performers」, Monthly Labor Law, Dec. 2012; Kim, Sunghee,「Dismissal of Poor Performers」, Gangwon Law Studies, Feb. 2012.

무단결근 등 불성실 근무를 징계해고사유로 규정한 경우, 이러한 취업규칙 등의 규정은 특별한 사정이 없는 한 근로기준법에 위반되어 무효라고 할 수 없으므로 근로자에게 위 규정에 해당되는 무단결근 등의 사유가 있을 때 이를 징계해고의 사유로 삼아 해고하는 것은 정당한 이유가 된다.[371)]

② 취업규칙 등에 일정기간 이상의 결근일수를 기준으로 하여 징계해고사유로 규정하고 있는 경우, 그 의미는 일정한 기간적 제한 없이 합계 며칠 이상의 무단결근을 한 모든 경우를 가리키는 것이 아니라, 상당하다고 인정되는 일정한 기간 내에 합계 며칠 이상의 무단결근을 한 경우를 뜻한다고 제한적으로 해석하여야 한다.[372)]

(2) 저성과자

어느 회사나 영업을 잘하는 근로자와 못하는 근로자가 있다. 영업을 잘하는 근로자에게는 인센티브를 주고, 그렇지 못한 근로자에게는 영업을 다시 잘할 수 있도록 인사 상 적합한 조치를 취해야 한다. 그런데 회사에 영업실적이 저조한 '저성과자'에 대하여 인사 상 극단적인 조치인 '해고'를 하는 경우가 있는데, 이와 관련하여 노동법은 엄격한 기준을 가지고 근로자를 보호하고 있다. 일반적으로 정당한 징계해고가 되려면 해고의 사유, 징계의 양정과 절차가 정당해야 한다. 특히, 저성과자에 대한 해고는 일반적인 징계해고의 기준과 함께 '영업실적 저조'라는 업무적 특성을 고려해 판단해야 한다. 저성과자를 해고하려면 영업성과 향상을 위한 충분한 기회의 부여 여부, 계속 영업실적의 저조 등을 확인하기 위한 자세한 체크리스트(점검표)가 필요하다.[373)]

---

371) 대법원 1989.09.26 선고 89다카5475 판결

372) 대법원 1989.05.09 선고 88다카4277 판결

373) 구건서,「저성과자 해고에 대한 정당성 판단」, 노동법이론 실무학회, 2011년 11월; 방상진,「성과부진자 관리제도의 법률문제」,『노동법률』, 중앙경제, 2010년 2월; 조상욱,「저성과자 관리방안」,『노동법률』, 중앙경제 2012년 12월; 김승희,「저성과자에 대한 해고의 정당성 판단을 중심으로」,『강원법학』, 강원대학교, 2012. 2.

<Checklist: Meeting Requirements for Justifiable Dismissal of Poor Performers>

1. Are the criteria for determining poor performers objective and reasonable?	1) Objective criteria should be applied. 2) Poor performance should be sustained for a reasonably long time. 3) Sales are not expected to show much improvement.
2. Is the evaluation of poor performers objective and impartial?	1) Objective and impartial evaluation must be used. 2) Multiple evaluators should be used to assess the sales performance. 3) Absolute evaluation is preferable to relative evaluation.
3. Does the company endeavor to motivate poor performers to improve?	1) Sufficient advance warning must be given to the low performer. 2) A Performance Improvement Program (PIP) should be in operation. 3) Continuous improvement coaching and mentoring shall be provided. 4) Occupational support for poor performers shall be available.
4. Are there any guidelines regarding the dismissal of poor performers in the collective agreement or rules of employment?	1) Rules for handling poor performers should exist. 2) Sufficient explanation regarding the dismissal of poor performers should be provided. 3) Systematic procedures such as evaluation of sales performance, notification of evaluation results, and work expectations should be implemented.
5. Is the poor performance serious enough to deserve termination of employment according to social norms?	1) The poor performance must be serious enough to be accepted as such according to social norms. 2) The company must consider many factors, such as the company's business situation, the employee's working conditions, and past practices of disciplinary action.

(3) Disregard of rules

Failure to yield to company discipline signifies that the employee is disturbing the company's order, violating working rules with unacceptable behavior, violating dress codes, etc., which are matters concerning the freedom to private life. Disruption of company order disrupts team work in the company, thereby disturbing peace and order through behavior that negatively influences the company.

In general, company order is regulated in the rules of employment. Even if there is no specific regulation on it in the rules of employment, the employee shall have an additional duty bound by the labor contract, which is not to disturb the company's group activities.[374)]

---

374) Supreme Court ruling on July 29, 1994, 94da4295.

〈저성과자 해고의 정당성을 갖추기 위한 체크리스트〉

1. 저성과자 선발기준은 객관적이고 합리적이었는가?	1) 객관적 선발기준이 있어야 한다. 2) 저성과는 상당기간 지속되어야 한다. 3) 성과 개선 가능성이 낮아야 한다.
2. 저성과자 평가가 객관적이고 공정하였는가?	1) 객관적이고 공정한 평가가 이루어져야 한다. 2) 다수 평가자가 근무성적을 평가하는 것이 바람직하다. 3) 상대평가 보다는 절대평가가 필요하다.
3. 회사는 저성과자의 성과 향상을 위해 노력 하였는가?	1) 저성과자에 대해 사전에 충분한 경고를 주어야 한다. 2) 성과향상 프로그램(PIP)을 운영해야 한다. 3) 지속적인 코칭과 멘토링을 해야 한다. 4) 저성과자에 대한 업무지원을 하여야 한다.
4. 저성과자 해고에 대한 단체협약이나 취업규칙에 근거 규정이 있었는가?	1) 저성과자 해고에 대한 근거규정이 있어야 한다. 2) 저성과자 해고에 대해 사전에 충분한 설명이 있어야 한다. 3) 체계적 실적·성과평가, 평가결과통보와 개선지시가 규정에 따라 체계적으로 이루어져야 한다.
5. 저성과는 사회통념상 고용관계를 유지할 수 없을 정도로 현저하였는가?	1) 저성과가 현저히 저조하여 사회통념상 수용할 수 없을 정도여야 한다. 2) 기업이 처한 상황, 근로자의 근무여건, 징계관행 등을 고려해 판단해야 한다.

(3) 직장 질서문란

직장규율을 문란케 하는 행위란 직장 내에서의 풍기문란이나 복장위반 등과 관련된 근무수칙을 위반하는 등 근무기강을 문란하게 하는 행위로 사생활의 자유와 관련된 문제가 대두되고 있다. 직장질서의 문란행위는 사업장 내의 공동작업을 곤란하게 하거나 기업에 불리한 영향을 미치는 특정근로자의 행동으로 인해 직장의 평화와 질서가 교란되는 것을 말한다. 일반적으로 직장질서는 취업규칙에 의하여 규율되고 있으나, 취업규칙에 직장질서에 관한 규정이 없다고 해도 근로자는 근로계약상 부수적 의무로 기업 공동생활의 진행에 침해가 되는 행위를 중지할 의무가 있다.[374)]

374) 대법원 1994.7.29 선고 94다4295 판결

(4) Misrepresentation of educational background and career, concealment and falsification of information in the resume, etc.

Misrepresentation of one's past career is deemed a justifiable reason for disciplinary punishment, not when it may distort the company's assessment of the employee's work abilities, character, trust, etc., but when it disturbs the structure of working conditions such as wage level and position due to past critical misrepresentation of career, or when the falsified information infringes upon the company's actual order and proves damaging to the employer.

Common examples include misrepresentation of educational achievement and jobs done, concealment of ideology or faith, concealment of imprisonment or disciplinary action data, etc.

① Where an employee is found to have falsified or concealed his education or experience, the company may have chosen not to hire him/her or may have chosen not to provide the same working conditions. This assumption justifies taking appropriate disciplinary dismissal actions.[375)]

② Even if an employee who conceals his/her low education background has no problem handling his/her work and even if he works diligently over a long period, the right for the company to take justifiable disciplinary dismissal action remains unchanged.[376)]

③ In the event where false education and career details in the resume is the result of a mistake or where such fallacy is trivial, under special circumstances such as inappropriateness based on social norms, to warrant a dismissal, the company may not have justifiable reason to take dismissal action.[377)]

(5) Use of violence against colleagues or superiors

In the rules of employment and the collective agreement, any violent behavior by an employee towards his colleagues or superiors is usually a reason for disciplinary dismissal. This is generally necessary to reflect tight disciplinary principles for the purpose of maintaining management order and shall not be deemed as a violation of the principles of the Labor Standards Act. However, where disciplinary dismissal is based on such reason of violence, the company shall consolidate various aspects of pre- and post-events including the motive and the rightness or wrongness, etc., of such misconduct so that its adoption of such disciplinary dismissal measures can be deemed

375) Supreme Court ruling on June 23, 2000, 98da54940.

376) Supreme Court ruling on Mar. 14, 1989, 87daKa3196.

377) Supreme Court ruling on Mar. 26, 1993, 98do4672.

(4) 학력, 경력의 사칭, 은폐, 이력서의 허위기재

경력사칭이 정당한 징계사유가 되기 위해서는 허위 기재로 말미암아 근로자의 노동력, 인격, 신뢰성 등에 대한 사용자의 평가를 그르치게 하거나, 하였을 위험성이 있다는 것만으로는 부족하고 근로자의 과거의 중요한 경력사칭으로 인하여 임금수준, 직급결정 등 근로조건의 체계를 문란케 하거나 적정한 노무배치를 저해하는 등 현실적으로 직장질서가 침해되어 사용자가 구체적 피해를 입었어야 한다.

경력사칭의 대표적인 형태는 학력의 사칭, 경력의 사칭, 사상·신조의 은폐, 전과·징계사실의 은폐, 노조 임원임의 은폐 등이 있다.

① 근로자가 입사 시 이력서상의 학력, 경력을 사칭 또는 은폐하여 채용된 후 근무하다가 이 사실이 발각되었을 경우, 채용 당시 회사가 그와 같은 허위기재 사실을 알았더라면 근로자를 고용하지 않았을 것이거나 적어도 동일 조건으로는 고용하지 아니하였을 것으로 보이는 한, 정당한 징계해고사유가 된다.[375)]

② 근로자가 낮은 학력을 숨기고 취업하였으나 모자라는 학력 때문에 하는 일에 지장을 받은 일도 없고 오랜 기간 동안 성실히 근무하여 왔다고 하더라도 정당한 징계해고사유가 됨에는 변함이 없다.[376)]

③ 입사 시 이력서상의 학력, 경력의 허위사항 기재가 작성자의 착오로 인한 것이거나 그 내용이 극히 사소하여 그것을 징계해고사유로 삼는 것이 사회통념상 타당하지 않다는 등의 특별한 사정이 있는 경우에는 정당한 해고사유가 되지 아니한다.[377)]

(5) 동료·상사에 대한 폭력행사

취업규칙이나 단체협약에서 근로자가 직장동료 또는 상사 등에 대한 폭력행위를 한 것을 징계해고사유로 규정하는 것은 통상적으로 회사의 경영질서 유지를 위하여 사원들의 엄격한 근무기강의 확립이 요구된다는 점에서 근로기준법

375) 대법원 2000.6.23 선고 98다54940 판결.
376) 대법원 2000.6.23 선고 98다54940 판결.
377) 대법원 1989.3.14 선고 87다카3196 판결.

as based on justifiable reason and not the result of an abuse of disciplinary rights.[378)]

2. Disobeying company directions

(1) Disobeying orders regarding personnel movement, such as workplace, job, or company transfers

As an employer has power over personnel management, he/she may be quite free to redeploy his/her employees so long as it is necessary for business purposes. Nevertheless, he/she shall give a justifiable reason for any act of transferring an employee to another position. In order to determine whether an act of redeployment is justifiable or not, consideration shall be made about its necessity for business purposes, its implications on the employee's quality of life, comparability of the previous position and the new one, and compliance with the good-faith principle in the personnel transfer process.

① Since transferring employees is included in the employer's original authority to manage the workforce, such a personnel management order shall be respected as one of the employer's discretionary rights. This cannot be regarded as illegal except in cases where this violates the Labor Standards Act or amounts to an abuse of this right. Whether such a personnel transfer amounts to an abuse of this right or not shall be estimated after comparing and considering the necessity of the transfer for operation of the business and financial disadvantage to the employee. If an employee's financial disadvantage due to the personnel transfer is not unreasonable but is an "ordinary difficulty," this personnel order shall be deemed a justifiable right in managing personnel, and not an abuse of that right.[379)]

Regarding justification for personnel transfer, whether the company has sincerely consulted with the employee concerned in advance or not can be one important factor in determining justifiable implementation of the personnel right. However, it is not an abuse of the employer's personnel management rights if the only supporting reason is that the employer did not go through this procedure.[380)]

---

378) Supreme Court ruling on Mar. 13, 1992, 91da39559.

379) Supreme Court ruling on Oct. 11, 2007, 2007do11566.

380) Supreme Court ruling on Oct. 13, 1995, 94da52928

에 위배되는 무효의 규정이라고 할 수 없다. 다만, 근로자의 폭력행사를 징계해고사유로 한 해고처분의 경우에는 특히 그 비행의 동기와 경위 등 전후의 여러 가지 사정을 종합하여 판단한다.[378)]

2. 업무명령위반

(1) 전근, 전보, 전적 등 인사이동에 관한 명령불응

근로자에 대한 인사권은 사용자의 권한에 속하므로 업무상 필요한 범위 내에서 상당한 재량을 가지고 배치전환 할 수 있으나, 정당한 이유없이 전보, 전직 등을 할 수 없다. 정당한 이유는 업무상 필요성, 업무상 필요와 근로자 생활상의 이익에 미치는 영향과 비교형량, 인사이동 절차에서 신의성실의 원칙 등으로 판단한다.

① 근로자에 대한 전보나 전직은 원칙적으로 인사권자인 사용자의 권한에 속하므로 업무상 필요한 범위 내에서는 사용자는 상당한 재량을 가지며, 그것이 근로기준법에 위반되거나 권리남용에 해당되는 등 특별한 사정이 없는 한 유효하고, 전보 처분 등이 권리남용에 해당하는지의 여부는 전보의 업무상 필요성과 전보에 따른 근로자의 생활상의 불이익을 비교 교량하여 결정되어야 하고, 업무상의 필요에 의한 전보 등에 따른 생활상의 불이익이 근로자가 통상 감수하여야 할 정도를 현저하게 벗어난 것이 아니라면, 이는 정당한 인사권의 범위 내에 속하는 것으로 권리남용에 해당하지 않는다.[379)]

전보처분 등을 함에 있어서 근로자 본인과 성실한 협의절차를 거쳤는지 여부는 정당한 인사권의 행사인지 여부를 판단하는 하나의 요소라고는 할 수 있다. 그러나 그러한 절차를 거치지 아니하였다는 사정만으로 전보처분 등이 권리남용에 해당하여 당연히 무효가 된다고는 할 수 없다.[380)]

---

378) 대법원 1992.03.13 선고 91다39559 판결
379) 대법원 2007.10.11.선고 2007두11566
380) 대법원 1995. 10. 13. 선고 94다52928 판결

② If an employee is absent from work out of defiance of a personnel movement order, such as workplace transfer, job transfer or company transfer, the company may be justified in taking disciplinary dismissal action as such absence may be deemed absence without notice based on its employment policy or as disobedience to a reasonable order for which the company has discretionary right. Whether the reason for disciplinary dismissal is justifiable or not depends on whether the employer's order for workplace transfer, job transfer, or company transfer is reasonable or not.[381)]

③ In the event a dismissed employee is reinstated to his job based on the court's judgment of the dismissal as unfair or based on a relief order, advice, etc., from the Labor Commission, the company shall carry out the reinstatement of such dismissed employee to his previous job. While reinstating the employee, the employer shall consider any personnel arrangement already made during the time of dismissal until reinstatement, business necessity, and change of working environment, etc., so as to assign appropriate work to the reinstated employee. Even if the newly assigned job is somewhat different from the previous job, it shall be deemed to have reinstated him/her justifiably because this belongs to the realm of the employerv's fundamental authority and right of management. However, if the employee resorts to actions such as resisting such reinstatement and rejecting the work for a long time, it becomes a reason for dismissal.[382)]

(2) Violation of directions

Refusing to follow directions at work means the employee is neglecting company principles and risking industrial accidents by resisting necessary directions, disobeying them without legitimate reasons, or independently performing a duty that actually requires a superior's permission.

① In the event the employer instructs the employee to perform extra work or work overtime in excess of contractual working hours agreed on between labor and management, and the standard working hours stipulated in the Labor Standards Act, but where such instructions are legitimate and justifiable, it can be a reason for justifiable disciplinary dismissal if the employee refuses. Without such justification, it cannot be reason for disciplinary dismissal.[383)]

② In the event an employee who received disciplinary action is to submit a written explanation,

381) Supreme Court ruling on May 10, 1994, 93da47667.

382) Supreme Court ruling on July 29, 1994, 94da4295.

383) Supreme Court ruling on Aug. 23, 1994, 93nu21514.

② 근로자가 사용자의 전근, 전보, 전적 등 인사이동에 관한 명령에 반발하여 회사에 출근하지 않아 이것이 취업규칙상 무단결근 또는 회사의 업무상 정당한 명령에의 위반이라는 징계해고사유에 해당되는 경우가 있다. 이것이 징계해고사유로 정당한 이유가 있는 것인지의 여부는 결국 사용자의 전근, 전보, 전적 명령 등의 정당성 여부에 달려 있다.[381)]

③ 일단 해고한 근로자를 다시 원직에 복직시키는 것과 관련하여, 사용자가 해고하였던 근로자를 해고무효 확인판결이나 노동위원회의 구제명령, 권고 등에 따라 복직시키면서 해고 이후 복직 시까지 해고가 유효함을 전제로 이미 이루어진 인사질서, 사용자의 경영상의 필요, 작업환경의 변화 등을 고려하여 복직 근로자에게 그에 합당한 일을 시킨 경우, 그 일이 비록 종전의 일과 다소 다르더라도 이는 사용자의 고유권한인 경영권의 범위에 속하는 것이므로 정당하게 복직시킨 것으로 보아야 하므로, 이러한 복직조치에 응하지 않으면서 장기간 그 작업을 거부하는 등의 행위는 징계사유에 해당한다고 한다.[382)]

(2) 지시명령 위반

업무상의 지시명령 위반이란 업무상 필요한 지시·명령에 반항하거나 정당한 이유 없이 복종하지 않는 행위 또는 상사의 허락을 얻지 않으면 안 되는 사항에 대하여 허가 없이 자의적인 행위를 함으로써 직장의 규율을 현저하게 문란케 하고 업무상 재해를 발생케 한 경우의 행위라고 할 수 있다.

① 사용자가 노사 간의 합의로 정한 "소정근로시간" 또는 근로기준법에 정한 "기준근로시간"을 넘어 근로자에게 초과근무 또는 시간외근로를 명한 경우나 휴일근로를 명한 경우 이것이 적법, 정당한 근무명령이라면 근로자가 이를 거부한 것은 정당한 징계해고사유로 될 수 있지만, 그렇지 않은 경우라면 근로자가 이를 거부하였다고 하여 징계해고사유로 삼을 수 없다.[383)]

② 취업규칙 등에서 징계처분을 당한 근로자는 시말서를 제출하도록 규정되

381) 대법원 1994.5.10 선고 93다47667 판결
382) 대법원 1994.7.29 선고 94다4295 판결
383) 대법원 1994.8.23 선고 93누21514 판결

if the employee rejects submitting such a written explanation as required by the disciplinary procedure, this can be deemed as disobedience to a justifiable instruction and may become a new reason for disciplinary action. However, such non-submission of a written explanation is a light violation, and if the employer chooses the most severe dismissal action from the other available types of disciplinary punishment for it, the employer may generally be deemed to have abused his/her right to take disciplinary action, unless there is special reason for doing so.[384)]

3. Delinquency in private life

(1) Prohibition against concurrent employment

Most rules of employment prohibit concurrent employment. The employee shall obtain the company's permission prior to becoming a director or employee at a different company or organization, and shall not be employed at an identical or similar type of company for a certain period of time after leaving the company.

An employee's holding of another job with another company is a private matter and based on his individual ability. It is therefore unjustifiable to completely and comprehensively prohibit the holding of another job which does not interfere with corporate order or the provision of his labor service. Pursuant to this, where the holding of such other job poses a hindrance to the said employee's provision of labor service to the company due to the length of time in the other job or the holding of a directorship position in a competitor company, such concurrent jobs may be prohibited, in which case disciplinary dismissal is possible.[385)]

(2) Delinquency outside of business and criminal offenses (Delinquency in private life)

When an employee's delinquency outside of business affects reliability or human relations with other co-workers inside the company and disrupts labor relations, it can induce disciplinary action. However, such behavior and conduct are in the realm of the employee's private life and, while it may account for social criticism, cannot be the sole cause of disciplinary action in principle. It can only be considered as necessitating disciplinary action when the offense infringes on company order.

---

384) Supreme Court ruling on Dec. 24, 1991, 90da12991.

385) Supreme Court ruling on Dec. 13, 1994, 93nu23275.

어 있는 경우 징계처분에 따른 시말서 부제출은 그 자체가 사용자의 업무상 정당한 명령을 거부한 것으로서 새로운 징계사유가 될 수 있다고 한다. 그러나 그 징계사유가 종전 징계처분에 뒤따르는 시말서 부제출이라는 가벼운 비위로 특단의 사정이 없는 한 이것만으로 징계종류 중 가장 무거운 해고를 선택한 것은 징계권의 범위를 일탈한 것으로 보는 것이 일반적이다.[384)]

3. 업무외 사생활 범주

(1) 이중취업 금지

대부분의 취업규칙에는 다른 회사나 단체의 임원 또는 종업원이 되거나 영리를 목적으로 하는 업무에 종사하려고 할 때에는 회사의 승인을 받도록 하거나 퇴직 후 일정 기간은 동종 또는 유사회사에 취직하거나 겸업하지 못하도록 규정하여 이중취업금지 의무를 부과하고 있다.

근로자가 다른 사업장에 겸직하는 것은 근로자 개인능력에 따른 사생활의 범주에 속하는 것이므로 기업질서나 노무제공에 지장이 없는 겸직까지 전면적, 포괄적으로 금지하는 것은 부당하다. 따라서 노무제공에 지장을 줄 정도의 장시간의 겸직, 경쟁회사의 이사에 취임하는 경우 등이 금지의 대상이 될 수 있고 이를 징계해고사유로 하는 것만이 정당성을 인정받을 수 있다.[385)]

(2) 업무 이외의 비행과 형사범죄 (사생활에서의 비행)

근로자의 업무 이외의 비행이 인격적 신뢰영역 또는 사업체 내에서의 동료근로자와의 관계 등에 영향을 미쳐 근로관계가 침해되는 경우에는 징계처분의 사유가 된다. 그러나 방종하거나 부도덕한 품행은 사적생활의 영역에 속하는 것이므로 사회적으로 비난받거나 위법한 경우라 하더라도 원칙적으로 징계처분의 사유에 해당되지 않으나, 그로 인해 기업질서가 침해되는 경우에는 징계처분으로 고려될 수 있다.

---

384) 대법원 1991.12.24 선고 90다12991 판결

385) 대법원 1994.12.13 선고 93누23275 판결.

The reason for an employer to have disciplinary rights is to maintain regulations and order within the legal framework necessary for smooth implementation of the company's business activities. Therefore, an employee's delinquency in private life can only be a reason for justifiable disciplinary dismissal if it is directly related to business activities or if it is likely to damage social evaluation of the company.[386)]

(3) In the event an employee is convicted of a criminal offense

In the collective bargaining agreement or rules of employment, where reason for disciplinary dismissal includes "in the event the employee is convicted of a criminal offense," the purpose for such inclusion is to recognize that such judgment of guilt may affect the company in the following ways: (1) the employee's basic responsibility in providing labor service is not possible for a long time so the employer cannot accomplish the purpose of the labor contract; (2) the employer and the employee cannot expect to maintain normal labor relations due to loss of a trust, and this causes harm to the ability to maintain corporate order due to a loss of reliable relations or human relations with other employees inside the company; and (3) depending on the employee's position and characteristics of the criminal act, the company may suffer significant damage to its reputation or trust, or there may be negative influence on its business transactions.[387)]

4. Labor union activities

(1) Protection of the company's right to maintain corporate order

① A labor union officer wore a vest decorated with union propaganda. Although the company warned him several times that he would be punished according to company regulations if he continued to wear the vest during working hours, he ignored the warnings. The company decided to discipline him by suspending him from office for two months. This was deemed as a fair labor practice.[388)]

---

386) Supreme Court ruling on Dec. 13, 1994, 93nu23275.

387) Supreme Court ruling on May 23, 1997, 97da9239.

388) National Labor Commission decision on July 15, 2001: 2001buno32.

사용자가 근로자에 대하여 징계권을 행사할 수 있는 것은 사업 활동을 원활하게 수행함에 필요한 범위 내에서 규율과 질서를 유지하기 위한 데에 그 근거를 두고 있다 할 것이다. 그러므로 근로자의 사생활에서의 비행사실 등은 사업활동에 직접 관련이 있거나 기업의 사회적 평판(신뢰도)를 훼손할 염려가 있는 것에 한하여 정당한 징계해고사유가 될 수 있다.[386)]

(3) 형사상 범죄로 유죄판결

단체협약이나 취업규칙 등에 징계해고사유로서 "형사상의 범죄로 유죄판결을 받았을 경우"를 규정하고 있다. 그 규정의 취지는 통상 그러한 유죄판결로 인하여 1) 근로자의 기본적 의무인 근로제공의무를 이행할 수 없는 상태가 장기화되어 근로계약의 목적이 달성될 수 없게 되었기 때문이다. 2) 사용자와 근로자의 신뢰관계가 상실됨으로써 근로관계의 유지가 기대될 수 없게 되었거나 기업 내의 다른 종업원과의 신뢰관계나 인간관계가 손상되어 직장질서의 유지를 저해하게 되었기 때문이다. 3) 당해 근로자의 지위나 범죄행위의 내용에 따라서는 사용자인 회사의 명예나 신용을 심히 훼손하거나 거래관계까지 악영향을 미치게 되기 때문이다.[387)]

4. 집단행동과 노동조합 활동

집단적 노사관계법에 위반된 불법집단행동은 징계의 정당한 사유가 될 수 있다.

(1) 기업질서 유지권 보호

① 노동조합간부가 노조간부로서의 역할을 충실히 하겠다는 이유로 노조활동 문구가 새겨진 조끼를 착용하고 근무한 행위에 대해 사용자의 수차례에 걸친 경고와 사규에 의해 처벌하겠다는 통보에도 불구하고 계속 조끼를 착용하고 근무한 노조간부의 행위에 대해 회사가 사규에 의해 출근정지 2월의 징계를 내린 것은 부당노동행위가 아니다.[388)]

---

386) 대법원 1994.12.13 선고 93누23275 판결.
387) 대법원 1997.05.23 선고 97다9239 판결
388) 중앙노동위원회 2001.6.15 선고 2001부노32 결정

② Although a behavior is partly related to union activities, if the disciplinary dismissal was for a reason stipulated clearly in the rules of employment, then the dismissal is not unfair.[389)]

③ Where the company dismissed an employee due to his anti-government agitation, promotion of distrust, lying on a resume, etc., if the company's dismissal was not to retaliate for his union activities, but to take disciplinary measures against the harm to company order, then this is not unfair labor practice.[390)]

④ Despite an employee's status as a labor union officer, so long as there was no evidence that the company took disciplinary action on account of its dislike for the union, then the action cannot be said to be unfair labor practice.[391)]

⑤ If the disciplinary dismissal for an illegal industrial action and the employee's contempt for the representative director was justifiable and not nominal, then it is not regarded as unfair labor practice.[392)]

⑥ Distribution of pamphlets during break time inside company facilities cannot be punished by disciplinary action unless it disturbs the employees or violates the company's order.[393)]

(2) Labor union activities

① In order for an employee's behavior to be categorized as justifiable union activity the Supreme Court has held that the following requirements must be met: First, the behavior must be seen as an activity on behalf of the labor union or to obtain implied authority or approval for the labor union (Characteristic). Second, the behavior must be necessary to maintain and improve the employees' working conditions and to enhance their economic and social status, and must assist in enforcing employee unity (Purpose). Third, the activity must be outside working hours, except for special provisions granting permission to the contrary in the rules of employment or collective agreement, or except for repeated labor practice or the employer's consent (Time). Fourth, union activities inside the workplace shall follow the reasonable conditions based on the employer's right to manage the

389) Supreme Court ruling on Aug. 10, 1990: 89nu8217.

390) National Labor Commission decision on Feb. 18, 1991: 90buno251.

391) National Labor Commission decision on June 12, 2000: 2000buno35.

392) Administrative Court ruling on Oct. 5, 2000: 99gu35764

393) Supreme Court ruling on Nov. 12, 1991, 91nu4146.

② 징계해고가 명백히 취업규칙에 정해진 해고사유에 해당한다면 노조활동을 한 부분이 인정되더라도 그 해고는 부당해고가 아니다.[389)]

③ 정당성이 없는 반정부선동, 노사불신조장, 이력서 허위기재 등을 이유로 한 해고가 조합활동에 보복이라기보다는 업무질서문란에 대한 조치라면 부당노동행위가 아니다.[390)]

④ 노동조합간부라도 징계사유에 대한 징계양정이 정당하고 달리 노동조합을 혐오하여 징계하였다는 명백한 증거가 없는 한 부당노동행위로 인정할 수 없다.[391)]

⑤ 불법쟁위행위와 대표이사에 대한 모욕을 이유로 해고한 것이 표면상의 이유에 불과한 것이 아니고 정당한 경우는 부당노동행위라고 볼 수 없다.[392)]

⑥ 휴게시간 중의 기업 내에서 유인물 배포는 다른 근로자의 휴식을 방해하거나 구체적으로 직장질서를 문란하게 하는 것이 아닌 한 휴게시간의 자유이용에 비추어 사용자의 허가를 받지 않았다는 이유로 징계처분을 할 수 없다.[393)]

(2) 노동조합 활동

① 대법원은 근로자의 행위가 노동조합의 활동으로 정당하다고 인정받기 위해서는 다음과 같은 요건을 갖출 것을 요구한다. 첫째, 행위의 성질상 노동조합의 업무를 위한 활동으로 볼 수 있거나 노동조합의 묵시적 수권 혹은 승인을 받았다고 볼 수 있는 것이어야 한다(성질). 둘째, 근로조건의 유지, 개선과 근로자의 경제적 지위의 향상을 도모하기 위하여 필요하고 근로자들의 단결 강화에 도움이 되는 행위이어야 한다(목적). 셋째, 취업규칙이나 단체협약에 별도의 허용규정이 있거나 노동관행, 사용자의 승낙이 있는 경우 외에는 취업시간 외에 행해져야 한다(시기). 넷째, 사업장 내의 조합활동에 있어서는 사용자의 시설관리권에 바탕을 둔 합리적인 규율이나 제약에 따라야 하고, 폭력과 파괴행위 등

389) 대법원 1990.8.10. 선고 89누8217 판결
390) 중앙노동위원회 1991.2.18 선고 90부노251 결정
391) 중앙노동위원회 2000.6.12 선고 2000부노35 결정
392) 서울행정법원 2000.10.5 선고 99구35764 판결
393) 대법원 1991.11.12 선고 91누4164 판결

facility and the activities must not involve violence to persons or property (Method).[394)]

② If a union member does not follow the union's opinion determined by the decision-making process of the labor union, or if the union member opposes or criticizes a labor union decision or policy, the behavior is considered voluntary and a purely personal activity, and is not considered union activity.[395)]

③ Running for a position as a union delegate is clearly engaging in union activity. Furthermore, applying to the Ministry of Employment and Labor for unpaid allowances such as bathing allowance and reserve army training allowance pursuant to the rules of employment shall be considered union behavior if the purpose is to improve the employees' working conditions and enhance their economic and social status, which can be interpreted as behavior to obtain the implied authority or approval of the labor union. This is justifiable and permissible union activity.[396)]

④ Even though it is company policy to require the company's prior approval or permission before distributing handouts, this requirement cannot prohibit every union activity including justifiable activity to maintain and improve working conditions. Whether such activity is justifiable shall not only be judged by the company's position but also various other factors, such as the handout's contents, number of pages, time and method of distribution, effect on the company or the work, etc.[397)]

⑤ Distribution of handouts during non-working recess hours is permissible even if the union member did not obtain prior permission, unless the distribution negatively affected other employees' work, obstructed free use of their recess hours, or corrupted the company's order concretely. Although the handout distributed by the union member is designed to promote working conditions, if its content creates extreme distrust or hatred toward management and endangers public morals by distorting or exaggerating conditions, the employer's disciplinary dismissal is justifiable and such action is not unfair labor practice.[398)]

---

394) Supreme Court ruling on May 15, 1990, 90do357; Apr. 10, 1992, 91do3044

395) Supreme Court ruling on Sep. 25, 1992, 92da18542

396) Supreme Court ruling on Aug. 10, 1990, 89nu8217

397) Supreme Court ruling on Dec. 23, 1997, 96nu11778

398) Supreme Court ruling on Feb. 9, 1993, 92da20880

의 방법에 의하지 않는 것이어야 한다(방법).[394)]

② 노동조합의 결의를 거쳤다거나 구체적인 지시에 의한 조합의사에 따르지 않고 노동조합의 결정이나 방침에 반대하거나 이를 비판하는 행위는 조합원으로서의 자발적이고 순전히 개인적인 활동에 불과하므로 노동조합의 활동에 해당하지 않는다.[395)]

③ 노동조합원이 조합대의원으로 출마한 행위는 노동조합의 행위에 해당함이 분명하고, 취업규칙에 의하여 지급하도록 정하여진 목욕권과 예비군훈련기간의 수당을 지급하지 않는다고 노동부에 진정한 행위는 노동조합의 목적인 근로조건의 유지개선, 기타 근로자의 경제적 지위향상을 도모하기 위한 행위이다. 따라서 조합의 묵시적 승인 내지 수권을 얻은 행위라고 보아야 할 것이므로 노동조합의 업무를 위한 정당한 행위로 본다.[396)]

④ 유인물 배포행위의 경우에는, 그에 대하여 회사의 사전승인이나 허가를 받도록 하고 있다 할지라도 근로자들의 근로조건의 유지, 향상이나 복지증진을 위한 정당한 행위까지 금지할 수는 없다. 그 행위가 정당한가 아닌가는 회사의 승인이나 허가 여부만을 가지고 판단할 것은 아니고, 그 유인물의 내용 매수, 배포의 시간 대상 방법, 이로 인한 기업이나 업무의 영향 등 여러 가지 사정을 고려하여야 한다.[397)]

⑤ 취업시간 아닌 주간의 휴게시간 중의 유인물의 배포는 다른 근로자의 취업에 나쁜 영향을 미치거나 휴게시간의 자유로운 이용을 방해하거나 구체적으로 직장질서를 문란하게 하는 것이 아닌 한 허가를 얻지 아니하였다는 이유만으로 정당성을 잃는다 할 수 없다. 그러나 조합원이 배포한 유인물이 비록 근로조건개선을 목적으로 한 것이라도 그 내용이 사실을 왜곡 또는 과장한 것으로써 경영진에 대한 극도의 불신 내지 증오심을 유발하게 하여 직장질서를 문란하게 할 위험성이 있다면 이를 이유로 한 사용자 측의 징계해고는 정당하며 부당노동행위가 아니다.[398)]

394) 대법원 1990.5.15 선고 90도357 판결; 대법원 1992.4.10 선고 91도3044 판결
395) 대법원 1992.9.25 선고 92다18542 판결
396) 대법원 1990.8.10 선고 89누8217 판결
397) 대법원 1997.12.23 선고 96누11778 판결
398) 대법원 1993.2.9 선고 92다20880 판결

⑥ If some contents in the handout damages the character, honor, reputation, etc. of other employees or some parts of the contents stipulated in the document are falsified, exaggerated or distorted, then if the purpose of distributing the handout was not to infringe on other employees' rights or interests, but to maintain and improve working conditions, to promote employee welfare and enhance their economic and social status, and if the content of the handout was true as a whole, the employee distributing a handout is a justifiable union activity.[399)]

⑦ A distributed handout contained contents slandering the company. The handout might cause hostile feelings against the company and was not handed out directly to the employees, but was spread over the employer's plant in secret. Even though the time for distributing handouts is during the labor union's delegate election campaign, this handout may bring concrete danger by infringing on the employer's right to facility management and violate corporate order and so it is not justified.[400)]

⑧ The company stipulated in its rules of employment that handouts distributed inside the workplace shall obtain the employer's prior approval, with the company able to take disciplinary action against employees who violate this stipulation. The stipulation cannot be invalidated just because it might violate the provision in the Constitution guaranteeing freedom of speech.[401)]

⑨ Although the labor dispute was resolved, the company's operations returned to normal, and the union repeatedly urged the union member to come back to work, he did not return to his driving job for an extended period because he was still participating in labor union activities and seeking to disrupt company operations. If the company dismisses him for the above reason, this decision is hard to categorize as an unfair labor practice taken in retaliation for his union activities, such as participating in strikes occurring previously.[402)]

⑩ In cases where the labor union in a company with a day and night shift had to hold

---

399) Supreme Court ruling on May 22, 1998, 98da2365

400) Supreme Court ruling on June 23, 1992, 92nu4253

401) Supreme Court ruling on September 30, 1994, 94da4042

402) Supreme Court ruling on October 23, 1990, 89nu4666

⑥ 유인물로 배포된 문서에 기재되어 있는 문언에 의하여 타인의 인격, 신용, 명예 등이 훼손 또는 실추되거나 그렇게 될 염려가 있다. 또한 문서에 기재되어 있는 사실관계의 일부가 허위이거나 표현이 다소 과장되거나 왜곡된 점이 있다 하더라도, 그 문서를 배포한 목적이 타인의 권리나 이익을 침해하려는 것이 아니라 근로조건의 유지 개선과 근로자의 복지증진 기타 경제적 사회적 지위의 향상을 도모하기 위한 것으로 문서의 내용이 전체적으로 보아 진실한 것이라면 이는 근로자의 정당한 활동범위에 속한다.[399]

⑦ 배포한 유인물이 사용자의 허가를 받지 아니하였을 뿐만 아니라 허위사실을 적시하여 회사를 비방하는 내용을 담고 있는 것이어서 근로자들로 하여금 사용자에 대하여 적개감을 유발시킬 염려가 있는 것이고, 위 유인물을 근로자들에게 직접 건네주지 않고 사용자의 공장에 은밀히 뿌렸다는 것이다. 이는 사용자의 시설관리권을 침해하고 직장질서를 문란시 킬 구체적인 위험성이 있는 것으로 비록 위 유인물의 배포시기가 노동조합의 대의원선거운동기간이었다고 할지라도 위 배포행위는 정당화 될 수 없다.[400]

⑧ 사업장 내에서의 기업질서를 유지하기 위하여 사업장 내에서의 유인물 배포에 관하여 취업규칙에서 사용자의 허가를 얻도록 한 허가규정이나 이를 위반한 근로자에 대하여 징계할 수 있도록 한 징계규정이 언론의 자유를 보장한 헌법 조항을 위반했다고 하여 무효라고 할 수 없다.[401]

⑨ 노사분규가 수습되어 회사의 업무가 정상적으로 돌아왔음에도 불구하고 회사의 근무촉구에 따르지 않고 노동조합활동을 위한 것임을 내세워 장기간 승무에 임하지 아니하여 회사의 업무에 지장을 주었다면, 회사가 이를 이유로 하여 해고한 것은 사내질서 유지를 위한 사용자 고유의 징계권의 행사라고 보여진다. 이를 가지고 그 이전에 있었던 농성참여 등 조합활동에 대한 보복으로 이루어진 부당노동행위라고 보기 어렵다.[402]

⑩ 주야교대근무 기업에서 근무시간 중에 쟁의행위 찬반투표를 위한 조합총

399) 대법원 1998.5.22 선고 98다2365 판결
400) 대법원 1992.6.23 선고 92누4253 판결
401) 대법원 1994.9.30 선고 94다4042 판결
402) 대법원 1990.10.23 선고 89누4666 판결

a general meeting to discuss the pros and cons of an industrial action, and informed the employer of the general meeting, although the general meeting was held during working hours, it is permissible union activity.[403)]

⑪ In case where, in the interest of pursuing better working conditions by instigating employees to go on illegal strikes, lashing out at company managers, and violating the employer's instructions to return to work, disciplinary dismissal according to the prescribed process is legal and justifiable.[404)]

⑫ It is not justifiable for employees to use annual leave or monthly leave collectively and they can face disciplinary action if found to be involved in collective bargaining.[405)]

⑬ After an employer and a labor union end collective bargaining on wages, some employees with complaints might continue to strike in spite of the employer's directions to get back to work. In this case, it is justifiable for the company to open a disciplinary committee and dismiss the employees because of their long-term absence.[406)]

(3) Labor union officer position and activity

① When an employee received a personnel order to change jobs or transfer to another department under the employer's rightful authority, the employee was absent from work for over 20 days and disobeyed the personnel order, concluding that the company was retaliating against him for his demands for improved working conditions. Since the behavior was a severe violation, the termination of his labor contract was justifiable.[407)]

② A full-time labor union officer basically maintains labor relations with the employer, keeping his status as an employee, but is considered suspended from duty and exempt from his work obligation. On the other hand, as the employer implements training programs during working hours which the employees are obliged to attend, such occasion is like providing work for the company. If there is a special provision according to the

---

403) Supreme Court ruling on February 22, 1994, 93do613

404) Supreme Court ruling on Apr. 13, 1993, 92Na50580.

405) Supreme Court ruling on Dec. 22, 1992, 92Da43272.

406) Supreme Court ruling on Nov. 9, 1990, 90nu3621.

407) National Labor Commission ruling on Nov. 16, 2016: 2016buhae956

회를 개최하는 것이 불가피하고 그 총회 소집을 사전에 사용자에게 통보하여 충분히 대비할 수 있는 여유를 준 사정 등이 있는 경우에는 취업시간 중에 조합 총회를 소집하였더라도 정당성이 상실되지는 않는다.[403)]

⑪ 노동조합원들이 냉각기간을 거치지 아니한 불법파업을 선동하고 회사관계자들에게 폭언을 하고 승차지시를 어기는 등 허용된 범위를 넘어서 요구를 관철하려 한 경우 회사 측이 소정의 절차를 거쳐 징계해고 한 것은 절차적으로 적법할 뿐만 아니라 실체적으로도 정당하다.[404)]

⑫ 연·월차휴가를 집단적으로 청구하는 것은 올바른 권리행사가 아니며 단체교섭과 관련된 경우에는 준법투쟁으로서 쟁의행위가 된다.[405)]

⑬ 사용자와 노동조합이 임금에 관한 협약을 마무리 지었으나 이에 불만을 품고 동조하는 일부 근로자들과 함께 농성을 계속하던 중 여러 차례에 걸쳐 사용자로부터 근무지시를 받고도 정상근무를 거부한 경우 징계위원회의 심의를 거쳐 장기결근 등의 사유를 들어 이들을 해고한 것은 정당하다.[406)]

(3) 노동조합 간부의 신분 및 활동

① 근로자가 원칙적으로 사용자의 권한에 속하는 전직이나 전보명령을 받고서도, 스스로 이를 자신의 사용자에 대한 근로조건개선 요구 등에 대한 보복이라고 단정하고 위 명령에 불응한 채 20여일이 넘도록 무단결근을 계속하였다면 이와 같은 행위는 근로자와 사용자 사이의 근로계약관계를 지속하게 하는 것이 현저히 불공정 또는 부당하다고 인정될 정도의 무거운 비위행위에 해당한다. 따라서 이를 이유로 근로자를 징계해고한 사용자의 조치는 정당하다.[407)]

② 노동조합전임자는 사용자와 사이에 기본적으로 노사관계는 유지되고 근로자로서의 신분도 그대로 가지지만 휴직상태에 있는 근로자와 유사하여 근로제공의무가 면제된다. 한편 사용자가 근로시간을 대체하여 근로자에 대하여 실시하는 교육, 연수, 훈련 등 거기에 참가하는 것이 근로자의 의무로서 강제되는 한 근로제공과 다를

403) 대법원 1994.2.22 선고 93도613 판결
404) 대법원 1993.04.13 선고 92다50980 판결
405) 대법원 1992.12.22 선고 92다43272 판결
406) 대법원 1990.11.09 선고 90누3621 판결
407) 중앙노동위원회 2016.11.16 선고, 중앙2016부해956 결정

collective agreement, it is difficult to treat participating in the training as wrong.[408)]

③ When a union member is absent because he was campaigning for election as a labor union delegate, this is not justifiable reason for absence from work and therefore is cause for dismissal by the company.[409)]

Ⅱ. Severity of Disciplinary Punishment

1. Principles

(1) In regulating reasons for disciplinary action in the rules of employment, the company can stipulate various levels of disciplinary punishment for identical cases. The company can regulate standard types of disciplinary punishment for violations, but it can also stipulate heavier punishment according to the severity of the violations. For the most part, it is up to the company what disciplinary punishment they wish to give. However, this discretion requires a socially acceptable balance between the reasons for disciplinary action and the disciplinary punishment. In cases where the employer gives a very heavy punishment for a light violation, the disciplinary action becomes an abuse of the employer's right and becomes null and void.[410)]

(2) In cases where there are several violations of company regulations that the employee should be punished for, whether disciplinary dismissal is justifiable shall not only be determined by each individual violation. Instead, the employer shall include all violations when considering dismissal, and reach a decision based on whether the violations are serious enough to discontinue employment relations in terms of socially acceptable common sense.[411)]

(3) In choosing a type of disciplinary punishment, the employer shall first review the

408) Supreme Court ruling on Nov. 23, 1999, 99da45246

409) Supreme Court ruling on Feb. 11, 1992, 91da5976

410) Supreme Court ruling on Jan 11, 1991: 90daka21176

411) Supreme Court ruling on Dec 9, 1997: 97nu9161

바 없으므로 단체협약 등에 따른 정함이 없다면 근로제공의무가 면제된 노동조합전임자가 그러한 교육 등에 참가하지 않았다 하여 바로 잘못이라고 보기는 어렵다.[408]

③ 운수회사의 노동조합 대의원선거에 입후보하여 그 선거운동을 한다는 이유로 회사의 배차지시를 거부하고 결근한 것은 정당한 사유에 의한 결근이라고 볼 수 없어 징계해고사유에 해당된다.[409]

Ⅱ. 징계의 양정

1. 원칙

(1) 취업규칙에서 징계사유를 규정함에 있어 동일한 징계사유에 대하여 여러 등급의 징계가 가능한 것으로 규정하였다든가, 어떤 징계사유에 대하여 원칙적인 징계의 종류를 규정하면서 예외적으로 정상에 따라 보다 무거운 징계를 할 수 있는 것으로 규정하였다든가 하는 경우에 그 중 어떤 징계처분을 선택할 것인지는 징계권자의 재량에 속한다. 그러나 이러한 재량은 징계권자의 자의적이고 편의적인 재량에 맡겨져 있는 것이 아니며, 징계사유와 징계처분과의 사이에 사회통념상 상당하다고 보여지는 균형의 존재가 요구된다. 따라서 경미한 징계사유에 대하여 가혹한 제재를 가하다든가 하는 것은 권리의 남용으로서 무효라고 하지 않으면 안 된다.[410]

(2) 근로자에게 여러 가지 징계혐의 사실이 있는 경우, 이에 대한 징계해고처분이 적정한지의 여부는 그 사유 하나씩 또는 그 중 일부의 사유만 가지고 판단할 것이 아니고, 전체의 사유에 비추어 사회통념상 근로관계를 계속할 수 없을 정도로 근로자에게 책임이 있는지 여부에 의하여 판단하여야 한다.[411]

(3) 징계해고처분이 적정한지의 여부는 전체의 사유에 비추어 사회통념상 근로관계를 계속할 수 없을 정도로 근로자에게 책임 있는지의 여부에 의하여 판단하여야 한다. 징계종류 선택의 자료로서 피징계자의 평소 소행과 근무성적, 당해 징계처분 사유 전

408) 대법원 1999.11.23 선고 99다45246 판결
409) 대법원 1992.2.11 선고 91다5976 판결
410) 대법원 1991.1.11. 선고 90다카21176 판결
411) 대법원 1997. 12. 9. 선고 97누9161 판결

employee's previous attitude, performance results, and severity of the violations.[412)]

(4) If there is an admitted reason for disciplinary punishment, the kind of disciplinary punishment the employer shall apply is at the employer's discretion. If the employer determines disciplinary action according to appropriate criteria for the severity of disciplinary punishment, unless such criteria are unreasonable, and if such application was not inappropriately used to dismiss particular employees, such disciplinary action is legal, and does not violate the principle of balanced application.[413)]

(5) Dismissal is justifiable only when the employee commits so serious a violation that the company cannot reasonably continue the employment relationship any longer. Whether the violation is a terminable offence shall be decided after considering all factors, such as the business target and characteristics, workplace conditions, the employee's status and job responsibilities, the incident's motivation and context, possible danger of obstructing corporate order, and his/her previous work attitude.[414)]

2. Types of disciplinary action

(1) Verbal warning

A warning is given to point out the employee's violation, to ask for self-correction, and to prevent any further violations. It is called a verbal warning, because it does not require a written explanation.

(2) Written reprimand

A reprimand is a disciplinary action that involves scolding someone for a mistake. This method demands that the employee submit a written explanation and asks for self-correction. In some cases, additional consequences may follow the reprimand. Accordingly, a detailed explanation of the reprimand shall not necessarily be prescribed.

---

412) Supreme Court ruling on Feb 12, 2004: 2003du127578

413) Supreme Court ruling on Oct. 12, 2007, 2007Du7093

414) Supreme Court ruling on Dec. 28, 2007, 2006da33999.

후에 저지른 비위행위 사실 등은 징계양정에 있어서 참작자료로 삼을 수 있다.[412)]

(4) 징계사유가 인정되는 경우에 징계권자가 피징계권자에 대하여 어떤 징계를 선택할 것인지는 원칙적으로 징계권자의 재량에 속한다. 징계권자가 징계양정기준에 따라 징계처분을 하였을 경우 정해진 징계 양정기준이 전혀 합리성이 없다거나 특정의 근로자만을 해고하기 위한 방편이라는 등의 특별한 사정이 없는 한 징계처분은 정당하다.[413)]

(5) 해고처분은 사회통념상 고용관계를 계속할 수 없을 정도로 근로자에게 책임 있는 사유가 있는 경우에 행하여져야 그 정당성이 인정된다. 사회통념상 당해 근로자와의 고용관계를 계속할 수 없을 정도인지의 여부는 당해 사용자의 사업의 목적과 성격, 사업장의 여건, 당해 근로자의 지위 및 담당직무의 내용, 비위행위의 동기와 경위, 이로 인하여 기업의 위계질서가 문란하게 될 위험성 등 기업질서에 미칠 영향, 과거의 근무태도 등 여러 가지 사정을 종합적으로 검토하여 판단하여야 한다.[414)]

2. 징계의 종류

(1) 구두경고

비위행위를 행한 근로자에 대하여 징벌의 의미로 비위행위를 지적하고 반성을 촉구하며, 동일한 비위행위를 다시 저지르지 않도록 사용자가 촉구하는 것을 말한다. 시말서를 받지는 않으므로 일종의 훈계라고 할 수 있다.

(2) 서면경고

견책이란 원래 잘못을 꾸짖는다는 의미인데 징계의 한 종류로 사용되고 있다. 보통 근로자에게 시말서를 제출하는 방법으로 비위행위의 반성을 촉구하는 것이 보통이다. 또 사정에 따라서는 견책을 받는 것을 요건으로 하여 부가적인 불이익이 따르는 경우도 있다. 따라서 견책의 내용은 반드시 확정되어 있는 것이라 보기 어렵다.

---

412) 대법원 2004.2.12. 선고 2003두127578 판결
413) 대법원 2007.10.12. 선고 2007두7093 판결
414) 대법원 2007.12.28. 선고 2006다33999 판결.

(3) Wage reduction

If a wage reduction is allowed without limit, the employee may easily be taken advantage of. Thus, Article 95 of the Labor Standards Act regulates that the amount of reduced wage for each infraction shall not exceed 50% of one day's average wage of the relevant worker, with the total amount of reduction to not exceed one-tenth of the total amount of wages in one pay period.

However, if the employee arrives late or leaves early for personal reasons, wage reduction in this case is not a disciplinary measure but a matter of wage calculation.

(4) Demotion

Demotion is a disciplinary action that lowers an employee's position, rank, or salary grade, significantly impacting their working conditions.

(5) Suspension from office

This disciplinary action concerns suspending those employees who violate company regulations while retaining their status. Wages are also unpaid during the suspension period.

However, under extended suspensions, the employee cannot receive wages or to seek another job, and so the period shall be limited to 6 months.

(6) Disciplinary dismissal

This is a disciplinary action to sever all labor relations with the employee whose violation is so severe that the company cannot expect managerial order without excluding him/her.

3. Related cases

(1) An employer dismissed an employee for a minor violation, even though the employee had received awards several times. As this disciplinary action was the heaviest form of punishment, it

(3) 감급

감급을 무제한으로 인정하면 근로자의 생활을 궁핍하게 하므로 근로기준법 제95조는 이에 대하여 '1회의 액이 평균임금의 1일분의 반액을 초과하거나 총액이 임금지급기간에 있어서의 임금 총액의 10분의 1을 초과하지 못한다.'고 규정하고 있다. 그러나 원래 근로자가 자기의 귀책사유로 인하여 지각·조퇴를 한 경우에 사용자가 임금감액을 하는 것은 하나의 임금계산방법에 의한 것이므로 본 조에서 말하는 '감급의 제재'에는 해당되지 아니함에 유의하여야 한다.

(4) 강등

강등은 직위, 직급, 호봉이 낮아지는 인사발령조치로 근로조건에 큰 영향을 미치는 중징계이다.

(5) 정직

기업질서에 위반한 근로자에 대하여 종업원으로서의 신분은 유지시킨 채 일정 기간 출근을 정지시키고 노무의 수령을 거부하여 직무에 해당하는 근로를 시키지 않음으로써, 그 기간 중에 임금을 지급하지 않는 징계처분이다.

다만, 출근정지가 너무 장기간에 걸쳐 있으면 당해 근로자는 임금을 얻을 수 없고, 그렇다고 하여 타사에 취업하는 것이 허용되는 것도 아니므로 감급의 제한보다 오히려 가혹한 결과를 가져오게 된다. 따라서 그 기간은 최장 6개월 이내로 제한하여야 한다.

(6) 징계해고

경영질서에 대한 침해행위가 매우 중대하여 근로자를 경영 외로 배제하지 않으면 경영질서를 유지할 것을 기대할 수 없다고 판단되는 근로자와의 근로관계를 단절하는 제재이다.

3. 사례

(1) 여러 차례 표창을 받은 경력이 있는 근로자의 사소한 잘못에 대하여 징계처분 중 가장 무거운 파면처분을 택한 것은 징계재량권의 범위를 일탈한 것이라 할

went beyond the employer's right to take disciplinary action.[415)]

(2) An employer dismissed an employee for one incident of misbehavior. From all the options available, the employer chose what appeared to be the heaviest form of punishment. Furthermore, as this employee's one incident of misbehavior was not judged to be a common sense reason to discontinue employment relations, the disciplinary dismissal was determined to be an abuse of the employer's right to take disciplinary action, and was null and void.[416)]

(3) After a transfer to another department, an employee did not show any improvement in attitude over a long period, despite receiving repeated warnings for negligence at work, so dismissal was justifiable. Since having been transferred to the business department, an employee's intentionally negligent behavior at work became reason for disciplinary punishment under the company's service regulations. Providing labor is the most fundamental obligation that an employee has, and his high position as a general manager would make him more likely to become a target for criticism. Although the company had warned him several times directly and indirectly, through transfer, reprimand, and employment without a specific job, etc. for his repeated negligence, he did not show any regret or improvement. His behavior infringed seriously enough on the need for reliability with the company that it decided to break the employment contract. In considering motives, causes, and process of the employee's negligence, it was judged that dismissal of this employee was within the realm of the employer's right to take disciplinary action. Accordingly, the Seoul District Court agreed with the National Labor Commission's ruling that this dismissal was justifiable.[417)]

Ⅲ. Required Disciplinary Procedures

1. Importance of Disciplinary Procedures

Justifiable disciplinary action is estimated by whether the following three aspects are justifiable: reasons for discipline, severity of punishment, and disciplinary procedures. Of

---

415) Supreme Court ruling on Sep. 13, 1978: 76nu228

416) Supreme Court ruling on Mar. 22, 1996: 95nu3763

417) Seoul District Court ruling on Oct 20, 2006: 2005guhap35810

것이다.[415)]

(2) 오로지 1회에 그친 비위행위에 대하여 징계의 종류 중 가장 무거운 해고를 선택한 것은 그 징계의 양정이 너무 무겁다. 또한 위 행위 하나만을 가지고 사회통념상 근로계약을 계속시킬 수 없을 정도로 책임 있는 사유라고도 볼 수 없으므로 본 해고는 회사가 부당하게 징계권을 남용한 것으로써 무효로 본다.[416)]

(3) 전보조치 이후 장기적인 직무태만행위에 대해 수차례 경고를 했음에도 불구하고 개선의 태도를 보이지 않았다면 해고는 정당하다. 원고가 지식경영팀 전보 조치 이후 의도적으로 그 직무를 태만히 하여온 이상 이는 회사의 상벌관리 규정상의 징계사유에 해당한다. 원고의 비위행위는 근로계약에 있어서 근로자의 가장 기본적 의무인 성실한 근로제공의무를 위반하였다. 특히 원고가 부장의 직위에 있는 간부직원이라는 점에서 그 비난가능성이 크고, 원고의 직무태만에 대하여 회사가 여러 차례 전보, 견책, 무보직 조치 등을 통해 수차례 직·간접적인 경고를 하였음에도 불구하고 전혀 개선되지 아니하는 등 원고가 전혀 반성의 태도를 보이지 아니한 점 등에 비추어 원고의 이러한 행위는 참가인 회사와의 정상적인 근로계약관계를 유지할 수 없을 정도로 참가인 회사와의 신뢰관계를 전면적으로 침해한 것이라 할 것이다. 원고의 직무태만의 동기와 원인, 그 과정을 살펴볼 때 참가인 회사가 원고에 대하여 한 이 사건 해고는 정당한 징계재량권 범위 내에서 이루어진 것이라 할 것이다. 따라서 이 사건 해고가 정당하다고 판정한 이 사건 재심판정은 적법하다.[417)]

Ⅲ. 징계절차

1. 징계절차의 중요성

징계의 정당성을 따질 때, 징계의 사유, 양정 및 절차가 모두 정당해야 정당한 징계를 한 것으로 판단한다. 특히 징계의 절차와 관련하여 징계의 사유가 충

415) 대법원 1978.9.13. 선고 76누228 판결
416) 대법원 1996.3.22. 선고 95누3763 판결
417) 서울행정법원 2006.10.20. 선고 2005구합35810 판결

special note is that if the employer does not follow appropriate disciplinary procedures, the disciplinary action is null and void even though there is sufficient reason for disciplinary action and the severity of punishment is reasonable. Disciplinary procedures fall into two categories. The first is a written notice (of dismissal etc.): if the employer fails to issue a written notice of dismissal, any dismissal will be considered unfair even though there is justifiable reason for dismissal. Secondly, if a provision exists in the rules of employment or collective agreement stipulating disciplinary procedures, the employer shall observe these procedures to ensure disciplinary action is justifiable. If these procedures are not observed, disciplinary action cannot be considered in effect despite the justifiability of the reasons. However, if no regulations are stipulated in the rules of employment or collective agreement concerning disciplinary procedures such as opportunity for the employee to attend the disciplinary action hearing and represent his/her own views, disciplinary action is considered to be in effect without disciplinary procedures. In this article, required disciplinary procedures will be clarified, using as reference related labor cases that Kangnam Labor Law Firm has represented.

2. Disciplinary process

(1) Written notification of reasons for dismissal

An employer who wants to dismiss an employee shall give written notice as to the cause for dismissal and the date of dismissal. If the employer dismisses the employee without giving such written notification, the dismissal shall be rendered null and void (LSA Article 27).

(2) Observation of disciplinary process

An employer shall observe the disciplinary process guidelines described in the collective agreement and rules of employment to guarantee fair implementation of the disciplinary action and to promote reasonable operation of the disciplinary system.

1) In cases where the disciplinary process has been regulated in the collective agreement, rules of employment, etc., the disciplinary process must be observed. If there is no procedural provision stipulated, disciplinary punishment may still be valid.[418)]

---

418) Supreme Court ruling on Jan. 24, 1989: 88daka7313

분히 있고 징계의 양정이 타당하더라도 그 절차를 준수하지 않으면 징계자체가 무효로 된다는 점이다. 이 징계의 절차는 2가지 유형으로 분류할 수 있다. 첫째는 해고 등의 서면통지이다. 해고의 서면통지를 하지 않은 경우, 정당한 해고사유가 있었더라도 부당한 해고로 판정한다. 둘째, 회사의 취업규칙 및 단체협약에서 징계의 절차를 정한 경우에는 반드시 이 절차규정을 준수해야만 정당한 징계가 된다. 즉 이러한 절차를 지키지 않는 경우에는 징계사유가 정당하더라도 그 징계의 효력은 인정되지 않는다. 그러나, 취업규칙이나 단체협약에 징계대상자의 출석 및 진술기회부여 등에 관한 절차가 규정되어 있지 않다면 그와 같은 절차를 밟지 아니하고 징계절차를 진행해도 징계의 효력이 인정된다. 이 징계의 절차와 관련하여 필자가 경험한 사례를 중심으로 그 정당성에 대해 살펴보고자 한다.

2. 징계의 절차

(1) 해고사유 등의 서면통지

사용자는 근로자를 해고하려면 해고사유와 해고시기를 서면으로 통지하여야 한다. 사용자가 해고사유와 시기를 서면으로 통지하지 않고 근로자를 해고하면 무효가 된다.(근기법 제27조)

(2) 징계절차의 준수

징계권의 공정한 행사를 확보하고 징계제도의 합리적인 운영을 도모하기 위해서는 단체협약이나 취업규칙에서 정한 징계절차를 준수해야 한다.

1) 징계절차가 단체협약이나 취업규칙 등에 규정되어 있는 경우 징계절차의 준수는 유효여건이지만, 이와 같은 절차규정을 두지 않은 경우에는 그러한 절차를 밟지 않았다고 하여 징계처분이 무효가 되는 것은 아니라 할 것이다.[418]

418) 대법원 1989.1.24. 선고 88다카7313 판결

2) According to disciplinary regulations based on collective bargaining and the rules of employment, the company shall include the union chairman in the disciplinary action committee and shall give the employee in question opportunity to attend, state his/her opinion, and submit verification documents. However, if the company dismisses an employee without observing the disciplinary process guidelines, even if disciplinary punishment is justifiable, this dismissal is invalid because the company did not follow the disciplinary process.[419)]

3) The rules of employment stipulate that the employee in question shall be given an opportunity to express his/her opinions in the disciplinary process, which means that the company shall give the employee opportunity to attend and state his/her opinion at the disciplinary action committee. Therefore, the company shall inform the employee of the time and place of the disciplinary meeting so as to provide the employee ample time to prepare his/her statement and verification documents. When a specific disciplinary action committee met at 2pm on January 26, 2001 and concluded with disciplinary dismissal, the employee in question received notification of the disciplinary hearing by mail, just that day. This did not give the employee enough time to prepare his statements or verification documents, so such delayed notification is illegal.[420)]

4) The collective agreement includes guidelines for disciplinary dismissal if an employee is absent without permission or leaves early without permission. If a company dismisses an employee for these behaviors, without engaging in the decision-making process through a disciplinary action committee (thereby following the entire disciplinary process), disciplinary dismissal cannot be recognized as a valid course of action.[421)]

3. Case one: written notice[422)]

Located in Mokdong, Seoul, "G" Institute employed about 20 teachers, both native English and Korean, to teach elementary and middle school students. Intending to balance

419) Supreme Court ruling on July 9, 1991: 90da8077

420) Supreme Court ruling on Jun 25, 2004: 2003du15317

421) Seoul High Court ruling on Jul 8, 2008: 2007nu34776

422) Seoul Labor Commission 2010buhai2283: Unfair dismissal involving GKI Language Institute.

2) 단체협약이나 취업규칙 또는 이에 근거를 둔 징계규정에서 징계위원회의 구성에 노동조합의 대표자를 참여시키도록 되어 있고 또 징계대상자에게 징계위원회에 출석하여 변명과 소명 자료를 제출할 기회를 부여하도록 되어 있음에도 불구하고 이러한 징계절차를 위배하여 징계해고를 하였다면 이러한 징계권의 행사는 징계사유가 인정되는 여부에 관계없이 절차에 있어서의 정의에 반하는 처사로 무효다.[419)]

3) 취업규칙의 징계결정에서 징계대상자에게 소명의 기회를 부여하여야 한다고 규정하고 있는 것은 징계대상자에게 징계위원회에 출석하여 변명과 소명자료를 제출할 수 있는 기회를 부여한 것이므로 피고학원은 원고에게 변명과 소명자료를 준비할 만한 상당한 기간을 두고 개최일시와 장소를 통보하여야 한다. 징계해고가 의결된 징계위원회의 개최통보서가 원고의 집으로 통보된 것은 징계위원회 개최 당일(2001. 1. 26)로 징계위원회에 참석할 시간적 여유 또는 변명과 소명자료를 준비할 만한 시간적 여유를 주지 않고 촉박하게 이루어진 통보이므로 이는 부적법하다.[420)]

4) 근로자의 무단결근 및 무단 조퇴는 원고의 단체협약상의 해고 등의 징계사유에 해당된다 할 것이나 원고는 근로자를 해고하면서 단체협약 등에서 근로자를 징계하고자 할 경우에는 징계위원회의 의결을 거치도록 하는 절차를 전혀 지키지 아니하고 한 징계 처분은 원칙적으로 효력을 인정할 수 없으므로, 이 사건 해고는 절차적 정당성이 없어 무효다.[421)]

3. 사례 1 : 서면통보와 관련된 노동사건[422)]

서울 목동에 있는 G학원은 원어민 강사 및 한국인 강사 20여명을 채용하여 초중등 학생들에게 영어교습을 하는 학원을 운영하고 있다. 이 학원 원장은 원어민 강사와 한국인 강사의 비율을 맞추기 위해 원어민 강사 (이하, “이 사건 근

419) 대법원 1991.7.9. 선고 90다8077 판결

420) 대법원 2004.6.25. 선고 2003두15317 판결

421) 서울행정법원 2008.07.08. 선고 2007누34776 판결

422) 서울2010부해2283 지케이아이 어학원

the number of native teachers with Korean teachers, the principal of the institute verbally notified two foreign teachers in the middle of August of their coming dismissal, due to being estimated as the teachers with the lowest skills. On August 27, these two teachers were dismissed. The employer then sent written notification of dismissal to the two teachers (hereinafter referred to as "the Employees") by text message and regular mail. The Employees applied to the Seoul Labor Commission for remedy on November 24, 2010.

The Labor Commission held a judgment hearing and stated the following:

"Both parties have stated their claims in this dismissal case, and the main point is placed on justification for dismissal: whether or not the reasons, procedures, and severity of punishment are appropriate. In estimating the justification for dismissal in this case, Article 27 of the Labor Standards Act states this basic requirement: 'If an employer intends to dismiss an employee, the employer shall notify the employee of the reasons for dismissal and the date of such dismissal in writing. Dismissal shall take effect only after written notification is given to the employee.' The employer claimed that he sent the employees written notification of dismissal by regular mail, but since the employer could not verify this fact with evidence, it is hard to believe that the employer properly implemented the procedures of giving written notice for dismissal stipulated in Article 27 of the Labor Standards Act. Accordingly, these dismissals are unfair without having to review whether the reasons for dismissal are justifiable. This Labor Commission has concluded that the employer should pay each employee 9.5 million won, which is the amount that the employees were supposed to receive each month in lieu of reinstatement."

The employer claims that it would not be fair to give 20 million won as compensation, instead of a few hundred thousand won, on account of one missed document: written notification of dismissal. However, Article 27 of the Labor Standards Act clearly regulates that employers shall give written notification of dismissal, along with reasons for dismissal and effective date, before the dismissal takes effect. This means that written notification is an essential requirement for dismissal to be legally effective. This act is designed to make the employer seriously consider the effects dismissal has on employee security, and to clearly resolve labor issues such as unfair dismissal and unpaid severance pay.

로자"라 함) 중 자질이 떨어진다고 판단한 2명의 외국인 강사에 대해 8월 중순경에 해고를 통보하고 8월 27일에 해고를 하였다. 이 사건 사용자는 근로자들에게 사전에 해고통보를 구두로 하였으며, 퇴직 후인 2010년 9월 2일 핸드폰 문자와 일반우편으로 이 사건 근로자들에게 서면으로 해고통보를 하였다고 주장하였다. 그래서 이 사건의 근로자들은 서울지방노동위원회에 2010년 11월 24일 부당해고 구제신청을 하였다.

이에 노동위원회는 다음과 같이 판단하였다.

"이 사건에 관한 당사자의 주장요지가 위와 같으므로 이 사건의 주요 쟁점은, 이 사건 해고의 정당성 여부, 즉 그 사유, 절차 및 양정이 적정한 지 여부에 있다 하겠다. 이 사건 해고의 정당성에 대하여 살펴보면 근로기준법 제27조 제1항에서는 '사용자는 근로자를 해고하려면 해고사유와 해고시기를 서면으로 통지하여야 한다.'고 규정하고 있고, 제2항에서는 '근로자에 대한 해고는 제1항에 따라 서면으로 통지하여야 효력이 있다.' 고 규정하고 있다. 이 사건 근로자들에게 해고통보서를 우편으로 보냈다고 주장하고 있으나, 해고통보서를 우편으로 보낸 사실을 입증하지 못하고 있으므로 이 사건 사용자가 근로기준법 제27조에서 정하고 있는 해고의 서면통지절차를 이행하였다고 인정하기는 어렵다. 따라서 이 사건 해고는 사유의 정당성 여부를 살펴볼 필요도 없이 부당하다 할 것이다. 한편, 우리 위원회는 이 사건 근로자들이 원직복직을 원치 않으므로 판정일까지 이 사건 근로자들이 매월 지급받은 임금상당액을 기준으로 이 사건 근로자 1, 2에 대하여 각각 9백5십 만원을 지급하는 것이 적정하다〉고 판단된다."

이 사건 사용자는 서면해고통보서 하나 때문에 몇 만원도 아닌 2천 만원을 보상해야 한다는 것에 대해 반발하고 노동위원회의 판단에 대해 공정한 판정이라 할 수 없다고 주장하고 있다. 이에 반해 근로기준법 제27조는 사용자가 근로자를 해고하려면 해고사유와 해고시기를 서면으로 통지하여야 그 효력이 발생하도록 규정하여, 이러한 서면통보가 해고의 효력요건임을 명시하고 있다. 이는 근로자의 생활에 막대한 지장을 초래하는 해고 문제가 신중하게 다루어지도록 하고 부당해고 및 퇴직금과 관련하여 분쟁이 발생하였을 때 이를 명확히 해결하기 위함이다.

4. Case two : labor case on disciplinary procedures[423)]

MiHang Transportation operated a taxi business in Yeosu, South Jeolla Province, with 40 employees. On September 6, 2006, two employees led a group of about 10 union members to the president's office to protest, swore at the employer and threatened to disclose company corruption to the police.

The company called a disciplinary action committee hearing with four committee members appointed by the company according to the rules of employmentand determined disciplinary action for violation of employee responsibility: suspension for three months without pay. The National Labor Commission's judgment was as follows:

"The reason for disciplinary action against the Employees was for cursing the employer in the process of protesting company decisions, which has been proven as actual fact after looking into voice recordings, related employee statements, and related video materials. However, even though reason exists for disciplinary action against the Employees, justification for disciplinary action requires legality in disciplinary procedures as well as reasons for disciplinary action. The employer claimed 'disciplinary action was justifiable since the company formed a disciplinary action committee according to the rules of employment. The collective agreement was invalid as of May 1, 2005 due to cancellation by the employer on October 29, 2004. This means that rules related to composition of the disciplinary action committee are considered contractual parts of the collective agreement, not normative. Therefore, normal disciplinary procedures do not have to be followed in this case.' However, according to Article 31(1) of the Labor Union Act, standards concerning working conditions and other matters concerning the treatment of employees as prescribed in the collective agreement are given normative effect. This normative portion would be transformed to working conditions of individual employees and remain effective in their labor contracts, even in cases where the current collective agreement has expired and a new collective agreement has not yet been concluded. These normative portions consist of matters concerning wages, various allowances, working hours, holidays, leave, kinds and benefits of industrial accident compensation, severance pay, service regulations, promotion, reward and punishment, and dismissal. Accordingly, regulations concerning the composition of a disciplinary committee

---

423) National Labor Commission 2007buhae92: Case of unfair suspension involving Mihang Taxi Company.

4. 사례 2 : 징계절차와 관련된 노동사건[423)]

전라남도 여수의 택시회사인 미항교통은 근로자 40여 명을 고용하여 택시운수업을 영위하고 있다. 2006년 9월 6일 조합원 10여 명이 사장실에 몰려와 항의하던 중, 이 사건 근로자1, 2가 주동이 되어 대표이사에게 욕설을 하고 회사의 비리를 고발하여 회사 문을 닫게 하겠다고 협박을 하였다.

이에 회사에서는 취업규칙에 따라 회사가 지명한 4명의 징계위원으로 징계위원회를 소집하여 이 사건 근로자들에게 "종업원의 책무위반"을 이유로 무급정직 3개월의 징계처분을 하였다. 이 사건에 대해 중앙노동위원회는 다음과 같이 판단하였다.

"이 사건 근로자들에 대한 징계사유는 2006년 9월 6일에 있었던 대표이사와 이 사건 근로자들 사이의 언쟁 과정에서 이 사건 근로자들이 한 욕설은 이 사건 녹취록, 관련자들의 자술서 및 관련 영상자료 등을 보건대 사실이 인정되어 징계사유는 인정된다. 그러나 이 사건 근로자들에 대한 징계사유가 인정된다고 하더라도 사용자의 징계처분이 정당성을 인정받으려면 징계사유뿐만 아니라 징계절차 또한 적법하여야 한다. 이 사건 사용자는 동 단체협약에 대하여 2004년 10월 29일 해지통보 하여 2005년 5월 1일자로 실효되었고, 더욱이 징계위원회 구성 등의 문제는 단체협약의 채무적 부분에 해당하므로 규범적 부분과는 달리 이 사건에 그 효력이 미치지 못하므로 취업규칙에 의거 징계위원회를 구성하였으므로 징계절차는 정당하다고 주장한다. 그러나 노동조합법 제33조 제1항에 따라 단체협약의 내용 중 근로조건 그 밖의 근로자의 대우에 관하여 정한 부분에 대하여는 규범적 효력이 부여되고 있다. 이와 같은 규범적 부분은 단체협약의 유효기간이 만료되고 새로운 협약이 체결되지 아니한 경우라도 개별근로자의 근로계약 내용이 그 효력을 유지한다. 규범적 부분에는 임금, 각종 수당, 근로시간, 휴일, 휴가, 재해보상의 종류와 산정방법, 퇴직금, 복무규율, 승진, 상벌 및 해고 등에 관한 사항 등이 포함된다고 할 것이어서 이 사건 단체협약상 상벌위원회 구성 등에 관한 규정은 규범적

---

423) 중노위 2007부해92 유한회사 미항교통 부당정직 재심신청

shall be considered normative."[424)]

"If so, although disciplinary action against the Employees followedjustifiable procedures according to the collective agreement, the employer did not compose a disciplinary action committee of three persons representing labor and three representing management, as regulated by the collective agreement, at the time of punishing the employees concerned. Instead, the employer punished the Employees through a disciplinary action committee consisting of members selected onlyby the employer in accordance with the rules of employment. This disciplinary action therefore had procedural mistakes, is unfair, and lacking justification."

In conclusion, despite having a justifiable reason for suspending the Employees without pay, this disciplinary action was judged as unfair because the employer did not observe disciplinary procedures. Upon judgment by the first Labor Commission, the company should have taken new disciplinary action according to legitimate disciplinary procedures, as this is possible. "In cases where a conclusion of unfair dismissal is reached due to a violation of disciplinary procedure, the employee is considered to have never been dismissed. The employer can then take new disciplinary action by following corrected disciplinary procedures, as this does not violate the principle of good-faith or of prohibition against double punishment."[425)]

5. Details of disciplinary procedures

(1) General disciplinary procedures

In general, disciplinary procedures are implemented in the following order. However, if the company does not have any procedures in its regulations, these steps are not necessary.

1) Occurrence of reason for disciplinary action
2) Investigation of actual facts and obtaining of evidence
3) Approval from employer for disciplinary action
4) Directions from the employer to the chairman of the disciplinary action committee to take disciplinary action
5) Employee is informed of time and place of the disciplinary action hearing

---

424) Supreme Court ruling on Feb. 23, 1996, 94nu9177

425) Supreme Court ruling on Dec. 5, 1995, 95da36138

부분에 해당한다.[424)]

그렇다면 이 사건 근로자들에 대한 징계처분은 단체협약에 따른 정당한 절차를 거쳐야하는데도 이 사건 사용자는 이 사건 근로자들 징계 시 단체협약에 따른 노사 3인 동수로 구성된 상벌위원회를 구성하지 아니하고 취업규칙에 따라 사용자 측이 선임한 징계위원으로만 구성된 징계위원회에서 징계하였는바, 이는 절차상 하자가 있어 그 정당성을 인정할 수 없는 부당한 징계에 해당한다."

결론적으로 이 사건에 있어 사용자의 정직 처분은 징계의 사유가 정당함에도 불구하고, 징계의 절차를 준수하지 않아 부당 정직으로 판정을 받았다. 이 경우회사에서는 해당 초심지노위의 판정이 있었을 때, 다시 적법한 징계절차를 밟아서 재(再)징계를 했어야 했다. 징계절차를 위반하여 무효로 된 징계에 대하여 다시 정당하게 징계절차를 거쳐 다시 징계를 하는 것은 가능하다. "징계해고에 관한 절차 위반을 이유로 해고무효 판결이 확정된 경우 소급하여 해고되지 아니한 것으로 보게 될 것이지만, 그 후 같은 징계사유를 들어 새로이 필요한 제반 징계절차를 밟아 다시 징계처분을 한다고 해도 일사부재리의 원칙이나 신의칙에 위배되지 않는다."[425)]

5. 징계의 절차와 관련된 내용

(1) 징계의 일반적 절차

징계는 일반적으로 다음의 순서로 진행된다. 다만, 회사 규정에 징계의 절차 규정이 없는 경우에는 절차를 생략할 수 있다.

1) 징계사유의 발생
2) 사실관계 조사 및 증거확보
3) 징계의결 요구에 대한 인사권자의 결재
4) 인사권자가 징계위원장에게 징계의결 요구서 발송
5) 징계위원회의 개최일시, 장소를 지정하고 출석통지

424) 대법원 1996. 2. 23. 선고 94누9177 판결
425) 대법원 1995. 12. 5. 선고 95다36138 판결.

6) Disciplinary action hearing held
7) Determination of disciplinary action
8) Employer notified of actions taken
9) Final decision on disciplinary action by the employer
10) Employee is informed of the final decision on disciplinary action.

(2) Composition of disciplinary action committees

If the company has in its rules of employment or collective agreement that disciplinary action shall be taken through its disciplinary action committee, then this regulation shall be observed. In principle, this disciplinary action committee is composed of those appointed by the employer. However, in cases where the disciplinary action committee in the collective agreement is regulated to be composed of an equal number of representatives from the labor union and the company, or shall include the labor union chairman, this disciplinary procedure must be observed in order for disciplinary action to be justifiable.

(3) Employee opportunity to represent own views

If, according to the collective agreement, the employee concerned is to be given an opportunity to state his/her own views or submit related evidence, this procedure shall be observed. In this case, the employer shall inform the employee of the hearing date, time, and place with considerable advance warning in the course of providing this opportunity to the employee concerned to represent his/her own views.

(4) Articles requiring labor union consultation or consent

In cases where the collective agreement requires, the employer shall consult with or receive agreement from the labor union in advance concerning disciplinary decisions.

6) 징계심의

7) 징계의결

8) 징계위원장이 인사권자에게 징계의결 결과통보

9) 인사권자의 징계처분 확정

10) 인사권자가 피징계자에게 징계처분 결과 통보

(2) 징계위원회의 구성

취업규칙이나 단체협약에 징계를 하고자 할 경우 징계위원회를 거쳐야 한다는 규정이 있을때는 이를 반드시 지켜야 한다. 징계위원회는 원칙적으로 사용자가 위촉하는 자로 구성된다. 그러나 단체협약에 징계위원회를 구성할때 노사동수 참석 또는 노동조합의 대표자가 참석하도록 되어 있는 경우에는 반드시 이를 준수해야지만 정당한 징계절차가 된다.

(3) 소명기회 부여

규정에 징계대상자에게 출석하여 변명과 소명자료를 제출할 기회를 부여하여야 한다고 명시되어 있는 경우에는 징계절차에서 반드시 지켜야 한다. 소명기회를 부여함에 있어서는 상당한 시간을 두고 개최일시와 장소를 통보하여야 한다.

(4) 노동조합과의 협의, 합의 조항

단체협약에 징계처분에 관하여 노동조합과 사전에 협의 또는 합의를 거치도록 되어 있다면 그와 같은 절차 또한 지켜야 한다.

Section 3: Ordinary Dismissal

I. Concept and Types of Ordinary Dismissal

1. Concept

Ordinary dismissal refers to termination of the employment contract due to the failure of the employee to fulfill hisher obligation to provide labor service in accordance with the employment contract. Therefore, ordinary dismissal requires a reason, attributable to the employee, that the employee cannot provide work.[426] A reason attributable to the employee means that the employee falls into the remarkable condition where the employee becomes mentally or physically unable to provide the work, which is the employee's main obligation according to the employment contract, and as a result, cannot carry out his assigned work sufficiently in the workplace.[427] That is, the term employment contract in the Labor Standards Act means a contract which is entered into for a worker to offer work and for an employer to pay wages for that work(Article 2 of the Labor Standards Act). As the reason the employee cannot provide work according to the employment contract is attributable to the employee, the employer can terminate the employment contract on the grounds of the employee's severe violation of the employment contract. This is referred to as ordinary dismissal.

2. Types of ordinary dismissal

In most cases, ordinary dismissal is for reasons attributable to the employee, but court rulings also place termination of an employment contract due to company bankruptcy or voluntary closure in the category of ordinary dismissal.

---

426) Jun, Hyungbae, A Study on the Justification for Ordinary Dismissal by Type, Seoul Labor Relations Commission, 2011, p. 1.

427) Lim, Jongryul, 「Labor Law」, 13th ed., 2015, Parkyoungsa, p. 353.

제3절 통상해고

Ⅰ. 통상해고의 의의와 유형

1. 통상해고의 의의

통상해고란 근로자가 근로계약상의 근로제공 의무를 이행하지 못하여 사용자가 채무불이행을 이유로 근로계약을 해지하는 해고이다. 따라서 통상해고가 정당한 해고가 되기 위해서는 근로자가 근로를 제공하지 못한다는 사실이 있어야 하는 근로자의 귀책사유가 있어야 한다.[426] 여기서 '근로자의 귀책사유'란 근로계약상 근로자의 의무인 근로제공에 필요한 정신적, 육체적 또는 기타 적격성을 현저하게 저해하는 사정이 근로자에게 발생하여 그 결과 근로자가 사업장 내에서 자신의 지위에 해당하는 업무를 충분히 감당할 수 없게 된 경우를 말한다.[427] 즉, 근로계약은 근로자는 사용자에게 근로를 제공하고 사용자에는 이에 대해 임금을 지급하는 관계이기 때문에, 근로계약에 의한 근로제공을 제대로 할 수 없는 귀책사유가 근로자에게 있을 때 사용자는 근로자가 근로계약의 중대한 위반을 한 것을 이유로 근로계약을 해지할 수 있는 경우가 통상해고라 할 수 있다.

2. 통상해고의 유형

통상해고는 대부분이 근로자측의 원인에 의하여 해고가 발생한다. 다만, 판례는 폐업 시 회사정리절차에서 회사측의 원인에 의해 근로계약을 해지하는 것도 통상해고로 보고 있다.

---

426) 전형배, 통상해고 유형별 정당성 판단 사례연구, 서울지방노동위원회, 2011, 1면.
427) 임종률, 「노동법」, 제18판, 2020, 박영사, 523면.

(1) Dismissal due to reasons attributable to the employee

1) In cases where the employee is not qualified for the work, or lacks the necessary vocational skills

① In cases where the employee is unable to obtain a qualification certificate essential for work, or fails an examination required for appropriate work performance, or he/she lacks the necessary professional knowledge or skills, this may be grounds for ordinary dismissal.[428)] ② If the employee's work performance has been evaluated as very poor, the employer cannot dismiss the employee for that reason only. However, in cases where the employee's work ability has been evaluated remarkably deficient in objective reviews, a dismissal may be determined as attributable to the employee.[429)] ③ In cases where the employee has a severe handicap after completing medical treatment for an occupational injury, if the employee cannot carry out or completes his previous assignments very poorly, the employer may be justified in dismissing the employee.[430)]

2) In cases where the employee is sick with an illness that makes it unreasonably difficult to provide work.

① In cases where a driver has become blind, or in cases where a cook has contracted an incurable infectious disease, dismissal is regarded as attributable to the employee.[431)] ② In cases where the employee is injured due to actions unrelated to work, and cannot work as normal for a considerable time even after taking a leave of absence twice, dismissal may be justifiable.[432)]

3) In cases where potential exists for a company's secrets to be leaked

In cases where an employee is in a position to know a company's business secrets and has a close relationship, through marriage, with a competitor's management, or the employee has a close relative or friendly relationship with a competitor company's directors, dismissal may be acceptable to prevent the leakage of business secrets.[433)]

---

428) Supreme Court ruling on July 25, 1989, 88DaKa25595.

429) Seoul Civil Court ruling on Apr. 12, 1990, 89Gahap33263.

430) Supreme Court ruling on Nov. 12, 1996, 95Nu15728.

431) Supreme Court ruling on Dec. 6, 1996, 95Da45934.

432) Administrative Court ruling on Mar. 3, 2006, 2005Guhap14158.

433) Constitution Court decision on Mar. 31, 2005, 2003Hunba12

(1) 근로자의 귀책사유에 의한 통상해고

1) 업무에 대한 자격을 갖추고 못하고 있거나 직무능력이 부족한 경우

사례로는, ① 직업상 요구되는 자격증을 받지 못한 것, 직무상 요구되는 시험이나 검사의 불합격, 전문적 지식이나 기능의 부족 등이 이에 해당된다.[428] ② 인사고과에 의한 근무성적평정의 결과가 나쁜 경우 그 사실만으로 근로자를 해고할 수는 없으며, 근무자의 직무능력이 현저히 부족하다는 것이 객관적으로 판단되는 경우에만 일신상의 사유가 인정된다고 본다.[429] ③ 근로자의 업무상 부상에 관한 요양종결에 따라 상당한 신체장해가 남아 있어 종전의 담당 업무를 수행할 수 없거나 부적합하게 되었음을 이유로 한 회사의 근로자에 대한 해고는 정당하다.[430]

2) 계약상의 노무제공을 곤란하게 하는 질병의 경우

사례로는, ① 운전사가 눈이 멀게 된 경우 또는 요리사가 불치의 전염병에 감염된 경우에는 일신상의 해고 사유가 인정된다.[431] ② 업무와 무관한 폭력사건으로 상해를 입어서 2차례의 휴직에도 불구하고 업무를 수행함에 있어 상당한 지장을 초래할 수밖에 없어 보인다면 해고는 정당하다.[432]

3) 기밀누설 위험의 경우

기업 경영상 비밀유지가 요구되는 지위에 있는 근로자가 경쟁기업주와 인척관계에 있거나 해당 근로사와 가까운 친척 또는 친교관계에 있는 자가 경쟁기업체에 있어서 사업상의 기밀이 누설될 위험이 있는 경우이다.[433]

---

428) 대법원 1989.7.25, 88다카25595.
429) 서울민사법원 1990.4.12, 89가합33263.
430) 대법원 1996.11.12, 95누15728.
431) 대법원 1996.12.6, 95다45934.
432) 행정법원 2006.3.3, 2005구합14158.
433) 헌법재판소 2005.3.31, 2003헌바12 결정; 김형배·박지순, 「노동법 강의」, 제8판, 2019, 신조사, 317면.

(2) Dismissal due to reasons attributable to the employer

1) In cases where a bankruptcy administrator dismisses all employees after the declaration of bankruptcy, this dismissal is not managerial dismissal, but ordinary dismissal, and so the company does not need to follow the requirements in the Labor Standards Act as to the process for dismissal for managerial reasons.[434)]

2) In cases where the employer has made every effort to resolve financial problems, and has concluded that closing the business is the most reasonable method, and closed the business and dismissed the employees, these dismissals are justifiable.[435)]

3) In cases where the employer has dismissed an employee because the work that was supposed to be carried out is no longer needed, this dismissal is not for managerial reasons, but is ordinary dismissal. [436)]

4) In cases where an employee was hired to work at a specific workplace, and the company's license to use the specific workplace has expired, dismissal of that employee may be justifiable. [437)]

II. Advantages to Ordinary Dismissal

1. Ease of dismissal

In cases where the employee neglects his primary duty in the employment contract to provide work, or carries out his assigned duties insufficiently, the employer can notify the employee of termination of his employment contract. This ordinary dismissal serves to increase the number of reasons for terminating the employment contract and make flexibility in manpower management possible.

There are three types of dismissal: ordinary dismissal, disciplinary dismissal, and managerial dismissal. Here, disciplinary dismissal and managerial dismissal have strict requirements and procedures that must be followed for the dismissal to be determined justifiable.

434) Supreme Court ruling on Feb. 27, 2004, 2003Du902.

435) Administrative Court ruling on Apr. 18, 2006, 2005Guhap34015.

436) Supreme Court ruling on Oct. 29, 1996, 96Da22198.

437) Administrative Court ruling on July 19, 2005, 2004Guhap39723.

(2) 사용자의 귀책사유에 의한 통상해고

1) 파산관재인이 파산선고로 인하여 파산회사가 해산한 후 사업의 폐지를 위하여 행하는 해고는 정리해고가 아니라 통상해고에 해당하는 것이어서, 정리해고에 관한 근로기준법 규정이 적용될 여지가 없다.[434)]

2) 자금난 해소를 위한 노력을 하다가 폐업하는 것이 가장 합리적인 방법이라는 판단하에 법인 해산결의를 하고 근로자들을 해고하였다면 정당한 이유에 의한 해고이다.[435)]

3) 근로계약상 근로자가 사용자를 위하여 한국에서 수행하기로 하였던 업무가 종료되었음을 이유로 해고하였다면 정리해고가 아니라 통상해고로서 정당한 사유가 있다.[436)]

4) 근로계약 체결 시 특정장소에서 근무할 조건으로 근로계약을 체결하였다면 그 장소에 대한 국유재산 사용허가가 취소되어 국유재산을 반환하는 시점에서 이루어진 근로계약 해지는 정당하다.[437)]

Ⅱ. 통상해고가 필요한 이유

1. 해고의 용이성

근로자가 근로계약의 주 의무인 근로제공 의무를 게을리 한다든지 약속된 근로제공을 불완전하게 한 경우에는 사용자는 그 근로계약을 해지를 통보할 수 있다. 이러한 통상해고는 근로관계의 해지의 내용을 확대하며 사용자의 유연한 인력운용을 가능하게 해준다.

해고의 종류에는 통상해고, 징계해고, 경영상 해고(정리해고)로 구분된다. 그런데, 징계해고나 경영상 해고는 엄격한 요건과 절차를 준수하여야 정당한 해고로 인정받을 수 있다.

---

434) 대법원 2004.2.27, 2003두902.
435) 행정법원 2006.4.18, 2005구합34015.
436) 대법원 1996.10.29, 96나22198.
437) 행정법원 2005.7.19, 2004구합39723.

Disciplinary dismissal requires the employer to follow the disciplinary procedures stipulated in the collective agreement or the rules of employment. If the employer does not do so, the dismissal becomes unfair even though the reason was serious enough to justify dismissal. In one case, the courts ruled, the collective agreement, the rules of employment, and its related rules regulated that the employer should form a disciplinary action committee that includes a labor union representative, and provide the employee concerned the opportunity to attend the disciplinary action committee meeting where he/she may explain his side and submit any defending documents. However, if the employer dismisses the employee concerned in violation of the disciplinary procedures, this dismissal is unfair and invalid regardless of any justifiable reason for dismissal.[438)]

Managerial dismissal requires very strict criteria and the employer to comply with procedures according to dismissals for managerial reasons in Article 24 of the Labor Standards Act to be determined justifiable in accordance with Article 23(1) of the same Act. These conditions and procedures for managerial dismissal are: ① there must be an urgent necessity in relation to the business; ② the employer shall make every effort to avoid dismissal; ③ the employer shall follow reasonable and fair criteria for the selection of those persons subject to dismissal; and ④ the employer shall inform and consult in good faith with the labor union(where there is no such organized labor union, the employee representative) regarding the methods for avoiding dismissals and the criteria for dismissal at least 50 days before the intended date of dismissal. The above four conditions and procedures should be observed in order for managerial dismissals to be determined justifiable.

2. No need for procedures of dismissal

Ordinary dismissal does not become unfair if procedures required for disciplinary and managerial dismissals are not followed. In this review, ordinary dismissal plays a role in reducing the restrictions on dismissal, and is used when there are reasons attributable to the employee, unlike disciplinary and managerial dismissals. Related examples include:

① Ordinary dismissal does not require that disciplinary procedures be followed, such as holding a disciplinary action committee meeting and providing opportunity for the employee to explain his opinions.[439)]

---

438) Supreme Court ruling on July 9, 1991, 90Da8087.

439) Supreme Court ruling on Sept. 24, 1991, 91Da13533.

먼저, 징계해고의 경우, 단체협약이나 취업규칙에 징계규정을 둔 경우 반드시 이를 준수하여야 하며, 이를 준수하지 않은 경우에는 정당한 징계해고 사유가 존재하더라도 부당한 해고이다. 판례에는 단체협약이나 취업규칙 또는 이에 근거를 둔 징계규정에서 징계위원회의 구성에 노동조합의 대표자를 참여시키도록 되어 있고, 또 징계대상에게 징계위원회에 출석하여 변명과 소명자료를 제출할 기회를 부여하도록 되어 있음에도 불구하고 이러한 징계절차를 위배하여 징계해고를 하였다면 이러한 징계권의 행사는 징계사유가 인정되는 여부에 관계없이 절차를 위반하는 경우에는 무효이다.[438] 라고 판단하고 있다.

또한, 경영상 해고(정리해고)의 경우에도 근로기준법 제24조의 규정은 정리해고의 요건과 절차를 갖춘 경우에 동법 제23조의 1항의 규정에 의한 정당한 이유가 있는 해고로 명문화하고 있다. 그러한 정리해고의 정당한 요건과 절차는 첫째, 경영상 해고에 의하여 근로자를 해고하려면 긴박한 경영상의 필요가 있어야 하다. 둘째, 해고를 피하기 위한 노력을 다하여야 한다. 셋째, 합리적이고 공정한 해고의 기준을 정하고 해고대상자를 선정하여야 한다. 넷째, 해고를 피하기 위한 방법과 해고의 기준 등에 관하여 근로자의 과반수를 대표하는 노동조합(그러한 노동조합이 없는 경우 근로자대표)에게 50일 전에 통보하고 성실하게 교섭하여야 한다. 이와 같은 4 요건과 절차를 준수해야만 정당한 경영상 해고이다.

2. 해고의 절차규정의 완화

통상해고는 징계해고나 정리해고의 절차규정을 지키지 않는다고 하여도 부당한 해고에 해당되지 않는다. 통상해고는 이러한 면에서 해고의 제한규정을 완화해주는 역할을 한다고 할 수 있다. 이는 징계해고나 정리해고가 아니고 해고의 사유가 근로자 일신상의 이유에 있기 때문이다.

사례로 ① 통상해고는 징계위원회를 개최하고 근로자에게 소명의 기회를 주는 등 징계해고와 같은 절차를 거칠 필요가 없다.[439]

---

438) 대법원 1991.7.9, 90다8087.

439) 대법원 1991.9.24, 91다13533.

② A certain employee claimed that dismissal was unfair because the company did not follow the procedures of holding a personnel committee meeting and did not request submission of a doctor's medical certificate, as stipulated in the collective agreement. However, there were no rules stipulated in the company's collective agreement or the rules of employment that the company had to hold a personnel committee meeting for dismissals besides disciplinary dismissal. The company did not need to hold a personnel committee meeting to confirm there was a reason to dismiss the employee, so this dismissal is not simply illegal because the company did not follow the procedures for dismissal.[440)]

III. Considerations in Determining Justification for Ordinary Dismissal

1. Good faith principle

Where a reason for ordinary dismissal has not become serious enough to terminate employment, dismissing the employee without sufficient consideration of the employee's situation according to the principle of good faith and sincerity will be determined unjustifiable and an abuse of managerial rights by the employer. For example, in cases where the employer intends to dismiss an employee due to a physical disability, if the employee can be rehabilitated or otherwise recover from that disability in a relatively short time, it would be necessary to keep the employee for a certain period of time by way of assigning him to lighter work.

2. Observance of legal procedures

Ordinary dismissal should be prepared for with legal procedures. As ordinary dismissal is a unilateral action by the employer to terminate the employment contract, the employer must follow the procedural requirements in the Labor Standards Act if an employer intends to dismiss an employee. The employer shall notify the employee of the reason(s) for dismissal and the date of such dismissal in writing(Article 27 of the LSA). The employer shall give notice to the employee at least thirty days before the planned dismissal. If notice is not given thirty days before the planned dismissal, ordinary wages of at least thirty days shall be paid to the employee in lieu of notice(Article 26 of the LSA). A written notification of dismissal is related to the justification for dismissal, but such advance notice of dismissal can be substituted with money.

440) Supreme Court ruling on Dec. 6, 1996, 95Da45934.

② 퇴직처분이 인사위원회의 개최와 단체협약상 정해진 의사의 진단서 발급 절차 없이 된 것이어서 해고절차가 위법하거나 신의칙에 반한다는 주장에 대하여, 피고 회사의 단체협약이나 취업규칙상 조합원 또는 종업원을 징계해고가 아닌 다른 사유로 해고 시 인사위원회를 개최 규정이 없고, 퇴직사유의 존부 판단에 해당 근로자의 권익을 위하여 반드시 인사위원회의 심사 기타 절차를 거쳐야만 할 필요성이 있는 것도 아니므로 이와 같은 절차를 거치지 않았다 하여 퇴직처분이 위법하게 되는 것은 아니다.[440)]

Ⅲ. 통상해고의 정당성 요건

1. 신의칙의 원칙

통상해고의 사유의 정당성에 있어서도 그 사유가 근로관계를 더 이상 지속시킬 수 없는 정도에 이르지 아니함에도 신의성실에 따르는 기본적인 배려 없이 근로계약을 해지한다면 권리남용에 해당해 정당성이 없다. 예컨대, 근로자의 신체장애(physical disability)로 해고 시 그 장해가 해소 또는 완화될 가능성이 있는 경우라면 일정기간 유예기간을 두고 배치전환 등을 하여 근무하도록 하면서 관찰하는 것이 필요하다.

2. 법정절차 요건의 준수

통상해고의 절차규정의 정당성 요건을 갖추어야 한다. 통상해고도 근로계약관계를 종료시키는 사용자의 일방적 의사표시이므로 근로기준법의 해고의 일반적인 절차규정을 지켜야 한다. 해고 시 해고 사유와 해고 효력일자가 기재된 '서면통보'를 해야 하며(근기법 제27조), 또한 30일 전에 통보하여야 하고 30일 전 해고예고통보가 없는 경우에는 해고예고 수당을 지급해야 한다(근기법 제26조). 해고서면 통보는 해고의 정당성과 효력을 가지는 조항이지만, 해고 예고의무는 금전으로 대체할 수 있기 때문에 정당성과는 아무런 관련이 없다.

440) 대법원 1996.12.6, 95다45934.

According to judicial rulings, ordinary dismissal does not require the observation of procedural regulations for other forms of dismissal. If there are no regulations in the collective agreement or rules of employment requiring a personnel committee meeting to be held for dismissals outside of disciplinary dismissal, a failure to follow such disciplinary dismissal procedures is not illegal.[441)] As the dismissal is an ordinary dismissal, the employer does not have to consider the procedures that involve holding a disciplinary committee meeting or provide opportunity for the employee to explain his opinion.[442)]

Ⅳ. Ordinary Dismissal Due to Poor Performance[443)]

Possession of insufficient skills for the job and poor work performance is considered reasons for ordinary dismissal. In order for such dismissals to be justifiable, certain conditions must be met.

Remarkably insufficient skills for a job and poor work performance can be reasons for ordinary dismissal despite the lack of reason for disciplinary action, since the purpose for a labor contract is for an employee to offer work for wages and for the employer to pay wages for that work. A remarkable failure to fulfill the obligation to provide work can become a reason for terminating the employment contract. However, as Article 23 of the Labor Standards Act restricts such dismissals, there should be a justifiable reason why poor performance or a failure to provide the contractual work is serious enough to dismiss the employee. The court stipulates that justifiable reasons for a dismissal due to poor work performance or a failure to provide the contractual work mean that the employee's work performance is too poor to maintain employment relations according to socially accepted understanding. Such situations shall be judged on a case-by-case basis.[444)] Additionally, the Labor Relations Commission has also decided that an employer's dismissal of an employee for failure to provide contractual work serious enough to make it impossible to maintain employment relations shall be deemed ordinary, not disciplinary, dismissal.

---

441) Supreme Court ruling on Dec. 6, 1996, 95Da43934.

442) Supreme Court ruling on Sept. 24, 1991, 91Da13533.

443) On Dec. 30, 2015, the Minister of Employment and Labor, Ki-kwon Lee announced MOEL Guidelines for Ordinary Dismissal Due to Poor Performance. These guidelines will be the main guide to judging criteria for ordinary dismissal. For further details, please see the book, Jung, Bongsoo, 「Manual for Lawful Dismissal」, KangNam Labor Law Firm, 2019, pp. 156-169.

444) zSupreme Court ruling on Feb. 9, 2007 (2007Du18287).

통상해고 시 해고절차규정의 준수 여부에 대하여 판례는 준수하지 않아도 된다고 판시하고 있다. 회사의 단체협약이나 취업규칙상 조합원 또는 근로자를 징계해고가 아닌 다른 사유로 해고 시 인사위원회를 개최하여야 한다는 규정이 없다면, 그 절차를 거치지 않은 퇴직처분이 위법하지 않다.[441] 해고가 통상해고인 이상 회사가 징계위원회를 개최하고 소명의 기회를 주었는지 여부에 대하여는 심리를 하지 않아도 무방하다.[442]

Ⅳ. 저성과자에 대한 통상해고 지침[443]

업무능력 결여, 근무성적 부진은 통상해고 사유에 해당하며, 그 해고가 정당하기 위해서는 일정한 요건을 갖추어야 한다.

근로제공에 대한 임금의 지급이라는 근로계약의 본질을 고려할 때 업무능력의 현저한 결여, 근무성적이 부진한 경우에는 별도의 징계사유가 없더라도 통상해고의 사유가 된다. 근로계약은 근로자의 근로 제공과 사용자의 임금 지급을 목적으로 하는 계약으로 업무수행 능력의 현저한 결여는 근로제공 의무를 불완전하게 이행하는 것으로 이는 근로계약 해지 사유에 해당하기 때문이다. 그러나 법 제23조에서 해고를 제한하고 있으므로 업무능력 결여 또는 근무성적의 부진이 해고까지 이르기 위해서는 정당한 이유가 있어야 한다. 판례는 업무능력 결여, 근무성적 부진을 이유로 한 해고의 정당한 이유를 근로자의 근무성적이 사회통념상 고용관계를 유지할 수 없을 정도로 객관적으로 불량한 정도에 이른 경우를 의미한다고 판시 하면서 사안별로 정당성을 판단한다.[444] 아울러 노동위원회도 근무성적 불량으로 인하여 근로관계를 더 이상 유지하기 곤란할 정도에 이른 경우 징계해고가 아닌 통상해고의 정당성을 인정한다.

---

441) 대법원 1996.12.6, 95다43934.

442) 대법원 1991.9.24, 91다13533.

443) 2015.12.30. 고용노동부 이기권장관이 발표한 “저성과자에 대한 통상해고 지침” 이 지침은 노동위원회의 심판에서 있어 저상과자 해고에 대한 판단기준이 될 것이라 예상된다. 자세한 내용은 다음을 참고 바람. 정봉수, 「해고 매뉴얼」, 강남노무법인, 2019, 156-169면.

444) 대법원 2007.2.9, 2006두18287.

Section 4: Justification of Dismissal during a Probationary Period

Ⅰ. Principle

Even though an employee is hired with the requirement to undergo a probationary period, his dismissal shall be for a 'justifiable reason' in accordance with Article 23 of the Labor Standards Act.[445)]

Even though an employee is hired with the requirement to undergo a probationary period, his dismissal shall be for a 'justifiable reason' in accordance with Article 23 of the Labor Standards Act, because his labor contract was established just like that of a non-probationary employee. Provided, that the probationary system is designed to set a probationary period in order to judge whether or not the probationary employee shows competence for the job before confirming regular employment. The employer does not have to apply the same requirements for a regular employee's dismissal when deciding whether he will continue or cancel the regular contract at the time the probationary period is over, or during the probationary period. Accordingly, it is possible to refuse to hire him because of negative evaluations relating to ability to do the job. It is also possible to dismiss him or to refuse regular employment when there is a justifiable reason for dismissal. Under this view, the probationary period plays a role in easing restrictions for dismissal.[446)]

1. Justification for dismissal of a probationary employee during a probationary period[447)]

The employer shall not dismiss an employee without a justifiable reason in accordance with Article 23 of the Labor Standards Act. Whether or not there is a justifiable reason

---

445) Seoul District Court ruling on Feb. 12, 1999, 98 gu 15558

446) Supreme Court ruling on Jan. 11, 1994, 92 da 44695; Sept. 8, 1987, 87 daka 555

447) MOEL Guideline: Aug. 4, 2006, Labor Standards Team-4040

제4절 수습기간 중의 해고의 정당성

Ⅰ. 원 칙

일정한 수습기간을 두고 고용된 시용근로자라고 할지라도 그에 대한 해고에 있어서는 근로기준법 제23조 소정의 '정당한 이유'가 있어야 한다.[445)]

일정한 수습기간을 두고 고용된 시용근로자라고 할지라도 정식으로 채용된 경우와 마찬가지로 근로계약 관계는 성립한 것은 틀림이 없으므로 그에 대한 해고에 있어서도 근로기준법 제23조 소정의 '정당한 이유'가 있어야 한다. 다만, 시용근로제도는 확정적인 근로관계를 맺기에 앞서서 정식채용을 전제로 하여 당해 근로자의 업무적격성 및 일반적격성 등 당해 직업과 관련된 능력 등을 판단하기 위하여 시용기간을 두는 것으로서, 그 수습기간 종료 후의 정식채용 여부 또는 수습기간 중의 해고에 관하여는 통상의 근로자에 대한 해고와 동일한 기준에 따라야 한다고 볼 수는 없고, 업무적격성이나 일반적격성에 대한 부정적 평가로 인하여 정식채용을 거부하거나 해고할 만한 합리적 이유가 있을 때는 그 해고 또는 정식채용의 거절이 가능하다고 할 것이고, 이러한 측면에서 시용근로제도는 해고의 규제를 어느 정도 완화하는 기능이 있다고 보지 않을 수 없다.[446)]

1. 수습기간 중인 근로자의 해고의 정당성[447)]

근로기준법 제23조에 의해 사용자는 정당한 이유 없이 근로자를 해고할 수 없으며, 해고의 정당한 이유가 있는지는 사회통념상 당해 근로자와의 계속적인

445) 서울행정법원 1999.2.12, 98구15558.
446) 대법원 1994.1.11, 92다44695; 대법원 1987.9.8, 87다카555.
447) 행정해석: 근로기준팀-4040, 2006.8.4

for dismissal shall be estimated on a case by case basis according to whether there is a special reason why the employer cannot continue to maintain employment of the employee. However, the probationary period shall be a period for deciding whether or not to offer formal employment for the new employee after evaluating his/her abilities to be able to fulfill the required duties. Accordingly, the scope of justifiable reasons for the new employee's dismissal is wider than that for a regular employee.

2. The employer shall not take disciplinary action, such as dismissal, toward a probationary employee without justifiable reason. However, the range of justifiable reasons is wider than for a regular employee.[448)]

The employer shall not take disciplinary action, such as dismissal, toward a probationary employee without justifiable reason. However, the range of justifiable reasons is wider than for a regular employee. Provided, that the probationary period shall be a reasonable period in consideration of the job characteristics. If the period is extended unfairly, the extension is not effective in view of social acceptability: in cases where the probationary period exceeds 3 months, the requirement to give advance notice of dismissal stipulated in Article 26 of the LSA shall apply.

II. Justifiable Dismissal

1. It is justifiable to refuse formal employment to an employee in a probationary period on account of poor performance, negligence of duty, non-cooperative relationships with other coworkers, etc.[449)]

A certain employee was hired on a six-month probationary basis by a certain company. Since the probationary employee displayed remarkably poor performance compared to other probationary employees, was insincere at work, and could not get along with his coworkers, superiors or workers from related companies, the team leader gave him a low evaluation rating. The employer decided against hiring the probationary employee

448) MOEL Guideline: Nov. 12, 1990, Kungi 01254-15636

449) Seoul District Court ruling on May 22, 2005, 2004 guhap 30122

근로관계 유지를 기대할 수 없을 정도의 사정이 있는지에 따라 개별적·구체적 사안별로 판단하여야 한다. 다만, 수습사용 기간은 당해 근로자가 앞으로 담당하게 될 업무를 수행할 수 있는가에 관하여 그 능력 등을 평가하여 본채용 여부를 결정하기 위한 기간으로서 해고를 정당시할 수 있는 이유의 범위가 정상근로자의 경우보다 넓다.

2. 수습근로자라 하더라도 정당한 이유없이 해고 등의 징벌을 하지 못하나 그 정당성의 범위는 일반 근로자에 비해 넓다고 할 것이다.[448)]

수습근로자라 하더라도 근로기준법 제23조에 따라 정당한 이유없이 해고 등의 징벌을 하지 못하나 그 정당성의 범위는 일반근로자에 비해 넓다. 다만, 수습기간은 업무의 성격 등을 고려하여 합리적인 기간이어야 하고 이를 부당하게 장기화할 경우 그러한 계약은 사회통념 등을 고려할 때 그 효력이 없으며, 수습기간이 3개월을 초과할 경우 동법 제26조에 규정된 해고예고의 적용을 받게 된다.

Ⅱ. 정당한 해고

1. 수습기간 중인 근로자를 업무실적 저조, 근무태도 불성실, 직원들과의 융화 결여 등을 이유로 채용 거절한 것은 정당하다.[449)]

참가인 근로자는 원고회사에 6개월의 시용기간을 정한 수습직원으로 입사했다. 그러나 참가인은 수습으로 근무하는 동안 다른 수습직원에 비해 업무실적이 현저히 저조하고, 근무태도가 불성실했으며 동료직원이나 상급자 및 관련업체 직원들과도 제대로 융화하지 못한 점, 이러한 구체적 자료를 기초로 팀장이 참가인에 대해 낮은 근무평가를 하였고 그에 대한 검증과 인사위원회의 심의를

---

448) 행정해석 근기 01254-15636, 1990.11.12.
449) 서울행정법원 2005.3.22, 2004구합30122.

because of the low evaluation rating. Based on these circumstances, the refusal of regular employment cannot be seen as unfair dismissal.

2. It is justifiable to refuse to hire a probationary employee.[450)]

A certain company estimated that continuous employment was unsuitable and refused to hire a probationary employee during the probationary period stipulated in the rules of employment. The reason was that, while on duty, the probationary employee(a hotel manager) spoke violently to and threatened the managing director who was checking attendance. In view of the purpose of a probationary period, his dismissal is objective, reasonable and justifiable according to socially accepted ideas.

3. It is justifiable to refuse to hire a probationary employee who did not describe his key role in a district labor union in his resume.[451)]

A certain probationary employee did not describe in his resume his experience as a vice-training/PR chief of the Metal Workers Union in Seoul - East Area when he submitted a job application, and so the company could not evaluate his character comprehensively. It was considered justifiable for the company to refuse to hire him because of the omission of his previous union experience from his resume and negligence of duty.

4. It is justifiable to dismiss a probationary employee on account of negligence of duty.[452)]

A certain probationary employee received complaints from customers because there were too much or too little food available due to his miscalculation of the necessary amount. Furthermore, he resisted his supervisor's warnings and disturbed company order. Therefore, the company's dismissal of him for his negligence of duty was seen as justifiable exercise of the employer's personnel rights.

---

450) NLRC decision on July 2, 2001 2001 Buhae 199

451) NLRC decision on July 2, 2001, NLRC 2001 Buhae 144

452) NLRC decision on Aug. 11, 2000, NLRC 2000 Buhae 282

거쳐 참가인에 대한 채용거절이 이루어진 점 등을 고려할 때 이 사건 채용거절이 사회통념상 합리성을 일탈한 부당해고라고 볼 수 없다.

2. 수습근로자에 대한 본 채용 거부는 정당하다.[450)]

관광호텔의 당직 지배인이 출근점검을 하는 관리이사에게 폭언, 협박한 사실에 대해 근로자로서 계속근로가 부적당하다고 판단, 취업규칙에서 정한 수습기간을 적용하여 본 채용을 거부한 것은 근로계약상 유보된 해약권을 행사한 것이라 할 것이고, 이는 본래 수습기간을 둔 목적에 비추어 사회통념상 객관적이고 합리적이어서 정당하다고 할 것이다.

3. 이력서에 지역노조 재임 사실을 기재하지 않은 수습사원의 채용거부는 정당하다.[451)]

수습근로자인 피신청인이 입사 시 제출한 이력서에 서울동부지역 금속노동조합 교육선전부 차장으로 재임하고 있는 사실을 기재하지 아니하여 신청인 회사가 고용하려고 하는 피신청인에 대한 전인격적인 판단을 그르치게 한 것과 불성실한 근무태도를 사유로 피신청인을 근무부적격자로 보아 신청인이 피신청인에 대하여 한 본 채용 거부는 합리적인 이유가 있고 사회통념상 상당한 것으로 보여진다.

4. 수습사용 중에 있는 근로자에게 근무태도 불량을 이유로 한 해고조치는 정당하다는 사례[452)]

신청인(사용자)은 피신청인(근로자)이 수습사용중에 있으면서도 반찬의 소요량을 제대로 파악하지 못하여 반찬이 남거나 부족하게 됨으로써 고객으로부터 항의를 받았으며, 이러한 일로 상급자인 주방장이 주의를 주면 이에 반항하고

---

450) 중앙노동위원회 2001.7.2, 2001부해199 결정.
451) 중앙노동위운회 2001.6.8, 2001부해144 결정.
452) 중앙노동위원회 2000.8.11, 2000부해282 결정.

5. It is justifiable exercise of personnel rights if an employer dismisses a probationary employee on account of negligence of duty.[453)]

It is justifiable exercise of personnel rights for an employer to dismiss a taxi driver during his probationary period for neglecting his duties(late for work) and quarreling with his superior's instructions.

6. Even though the employer made a comprehensive personnel evaluation with some subjective aspects during a probationary period, which became a reason for dismissal, it is not unfair enough to deny the entire results of the evaluation.[454)]

Even though the employer made a comprehensive personnel evaluation with some subjective aspects during a probationary period, which became a reason for dismissal, it is not unfair enough to deny the entire results of the evaluation. Because the employee cannot verify that the company manipulated the results afterwards, his dismissal is justifiable.

7. It is justifiable to dismiss a probationary employee without disciplinary process on account of negligence of duty in accordance with the rules of employment.[455)]

It is justifiable to dismiss an employee in the middle of a three-month probation period without disciplinary process for neglecting his duties during that period.

---

453) NLRC decision on Jan. 21, 2000, NLRC 99 Buhae 626

454) NLRC decision on Apr. 8, 1999, NLRC 99 Buhae 64

455) NLRC decision on Mar. 16, 1998, NLRC 97 Buhae 329

직장질서를 문란시키는 등 근무태도 불량을 사유로 해고조치하였음은 정당한 인사권행사로 볼 수 있다

5. 성실의무를 다 하지 아니한 수습 근로자에 대한 징계해고는 사용자의 정당한 인사권 행사이다.[453)]

택시회사에 수습기간 중에 있는 운전기사가 회사 상사의 지시에 대하여 언쟁을 하고 지각을 하는 등 근로자로서의 성실의무를 다하지 아니하여 징계해고한 것은 사용자의 정당한 인사권의 행사이다.

6. 해고처분의 근거로 삼은 수습기간 중의 종합평가가 주관적인 평가부분이 다소 없지 아니하나 평가결과 자체의 인정을 좌우할 수 있는 정도에 이르지 아니하므로 정당한 해고라고 본다.[454)]

신청인에 대한 해고처분의 근거로 삼은 수습기간중의 종합평가는 주관적인 평가부분이 다소 없지 아니하나 평가결과자체의 인정을 좌우할 수 있는 정도에 이르지 아니하고, 신청인은 피신청인회사가 평가내용을 사후에 조작하였다고 주장하나 이를 입증하기 어려워 정당한 해고라고 판정한 사건이다.

7. 취업규칙에 따라 근무태도가 불량한 수습근로자를 징계절차 없이 해고한 것은 정당하다.[455)]

입사일로부터 3개월간을 수습기간으로 정하고 근무 중이던 신청인이 그간에 근무태도가 불량하여 피신청인이 수습 중인 신청인을 징계절차 없이 본채용을 거부한 것은 정당하다

453) 중앙노동위원회 2000.1.21, 중앙노동위원회 99부해626 결정.
454) 중앙노동위원회 1999.4.8, 99부해64 결정.
455) 중앙노동위원회 1998.3.16, 97부해329 결정.

Ⅲ. Unfair Dismissal

1. Despite the employee being under a probationary period, it is unfair to dismiss him on account of a lack of job skills when he did not receive any customer orders within a short period of time (i.e., only two months).[456)]

According to a certain company's personnel regulations, new employees have a two-month probationary period, during which a company can cancel employment for a lack of skill with the job, insufficient qualifications, and other job eligibility issues during a probationary period. A certain employee was hired with the expectations of receiving orders from 000 company and its subsidiary, but this did not happen, nor was any effort made on his part to attract orders. Therefore, the company cancelled his employment due to poor job performance and in accordance with its regulations. Despite the employee having a probationary period, it is hard to conclude he lacked the job skills needed simply by the fact that he did not receive any sales orders within a short period of time(i.e., about two months). Verifiable evidence that would support this is hard to come by sufficiently to justify his dismissal. Accordingly, this dismissal was deemed null and void because it was implemented without justifiable reason.

2. As long as a probationary evaluation was not objective or reasonable enough to refuse regular employment, such a refusal amounts to unfair dismissal that abuses the right of the employer's reserved cancellation.[457)]

A certain company had not cancelled the employment of any probationary employees since its foundation. Certain probationary employees had not been informed regarding the criteria and methods for evaluating their work, and the probationary evaluation system(which used an evaluation table) was not introduced until the last month of the probationary period(i.e., June 7, 2001). This made it difficult to judge whether the probationary employees had been evaluated continuously during their probationary period.

---

456) Seoul District Court ruling on Jan. 16, 2004, 2003 Kahap 54613

457) Administrative Court ruling on Aug. 27, 2002, 2002 guhap 7210

Ⅲ. 부당한 해고

1. 수습기간중에 있는 근로자라 하더라도 2개월 여의 단기간 내에 수주실적이 없다고 하여 업무적격성 결여를 이유로 해고한 것은 부당하다.[456)]

피고 회사는, 피고 회사 인사관리규정에 의하면 신입 또는 경력으로 입사한 자는 인사 후 2개월간의 수습기간을 가지되 수습기간 중 업무수행능력, 자질, 기타 업무적격성이 결여된 것으로 인정되는 자에 대하여는 채용을 취소할 수 있도록 정하고 있다. 원고의 경우 주식회사 ○○ 및 그 계열사로부터 SI 사 업을 수주해 줄 것을 기대하고 그를 영입하였으나, 수주 실적이 없는 것은 물론 수주를 위한 노력 마저도 기울이지 않아 업무적격성이 결여되어 있다는 판단 아래 위 인사관리규정에 따라 수습채용을 취소하면서 원고에 대한 퇴임발령을 한 것이라는 취지의 주장이다. 설령 원고가 수습기간 중에 있는 근로자였다고 하더라도, 2개월여의 단기간 내에 수주실적이 없다고 하여 원고의 업무 적격성이 결여되어 있었다고 인정하기는 어렵다고 할 것이고, 그밖에 원고에 대한 퇴임발령을 정당화할 만한 합리적인 사유가 있었다는 점을 인정할 증거도 없으므로, 피고 회사의 이 부분 주장 또한 받아들이지 아니한다. 결국, 이 사건 해고처분은 정당한 이유 없이 이루어진 것이어서 무효라고 할 것이다.

2. 수습평가 결과가 정식채용을 거부할 정도로 객관적·합리적 이유가 없는 이상, 정식채용 거절은 유보해약권을 남용한 부당해고이다.[457)]

원고회사는 창사 이후 공개채용에 의해 선발한 수습사원을 채용취소 한 적이 한번도 없었고, 참가인들 등 수습사원들에 대하여 수습평가의 기준과 방법 등이 제대로 공고되거나 교육되지도 않은 것으로 보이며, 수습사원평가표에 의한 계량화된 수습평가제도 자체가 수습기간 만료 월인 2001.6.7 수립되어 수습기

456) 서울지방법원 2004.1.16, 2003가합45613.
457) 서울행정법원 2002.8.27, 2002구합7210.

In considering all those aforementioned conditions, even though they received a 'C', low enough to cancel employment, this was not judged objective or reasonable enough to refuse regular employment on account of the negative evaluation of their occupational and job skills according to socially accepted ideas. Therefore, the employer's refusal of regular employment amounted to unfair dismissal that abused the right of reserved cancellation.

3. If their labor contracts do not contain a clear article that applies a probationary period, employees shall be regarded as regularly employed. Cancellation of this employee's labor contract is not simply contract termination, but dismissal.[458)]

Unless there is a clear article that applies a probationary period in a labor contract between employer and employee, employees shall be regarded as regularly employed and not probationary. Dismissal of an employee shall be evaluated by whether or not there is a justifiable reason for dismissal of a regular employee.

4. It is unjustifiable to cancel employment immediately because of errors in the employment application document without giving an opportunity to rectify those errors and without evaluating job skills and attitude during a probationary period.[459)]

The probationary work system is to set a probationary period for the purpose of estimating an employee's vocational skills in the process of regular employment before finalizing the labor contract. Therefore, because this is a system designed to set aside a certain period of time to decide whether or continue employment, it serves to ease dismissal restrictions. However, despite being a probationary employee whose contract period is fixed for a certain period of time, if the employee is hired just like regular employees, his or her dismissal shall require justifiable reason in accordance with Article 23 of the Labor Standards Act.

---

458) Supreme Court ruling on Nov. 12, 1999, 99 da 30473

459) LRC on Aug. 22, 2002, 2002 Buhae 104

간 동안 위 평가표에 의한 지속적인 평가가 이루어져 온 것으로 보기에는 부족한 측면이 있는 점 등의 제반 사정을 종합하여 보면, 비록 참가인들이 수습평가 결과 채용취소가 가능한 미 등급을 받았다 할지라도, 사회통념상 참가인들의 직업적 능력이나 업무적격성에 대한 부정적 평가로 인하여 정식채용을 거부할 정도로 객관적이고 합리적인 이유가 있다고는 판단되지 않는다. 그러므로 원고가 참가인들의 정식채용을 거절한 것은 유보해약권을 남용한 것으로서 부당해고에 해당한다.

3. 근로계약에서 사용기간이 적용된다고 명시하지 않는 이상 정식사원으로 채용된 것으로 보아 사용계약의 해지가 아닌 해고이다.[458)]

피고가 원고와의 근로계약에서 시용기간을 적용할 것인가 여부를 명시하지 아니한 이상 원고는 시용근로자가 아닌 정식 사원으로 채용된 근로자라고 인정된다고 할 것이므로 원고에 대한 해고가 정식근로자에 대한 해고로서 정당한 사유가 있는지 여부를 판단하였어야 할 것이다.

4. 시용기간중의 근무능력 및 태도 등에 대한 어떠한 평가도 없이 단지 입사서류의 하자를 들어 보완할 수 있는 기회를 주지 않은 채 곧바로 채용 취소는 정당하지 않다.[459)]

시용 근로제도는 확정적인 근로관계를 맺기에 앞서서 정식채용을 전제로 하여 당해 근로자의 직업적 능력을 판단하기 위하여 시용기간을 두는 것으로서 확정적인 근로계약의 체결 여부를 일정 정도 보유하는 제도이기 때문에 해고규제를 완화하는 기능이 있기는 하나, 일정한 수습 기간을 두고 고용된 시용 근로자라고 할지라도 정식으로 채용된 경우와 마찬가지로 근로계약 관계는 성립한 것임에는 틀림이 없으므로 그에 대한 해고에 있어서도 근로기준법 제23조 소정의 '정당한 이유'가 있어야 한다.

---

458) 대법원 1999.11.12, 99다30473.

459) 경북지방노동위원회 2002.8.22, 2002부해104 결정.

5. Where there is no probationary period stipulated, dismissing an employee for abstract reasons is an abuse of the right to manage personnel.[460)]

A certain employer hired an experienced employee through an online advertisement. Although the employer informed the employee of the three-month probationary period verbally in the job interview, there was no evidence to verify this. The employer said that the employee had been dismissed due to a lack of foreign language ability and interpreting skills and poor ability to form working relationships. As these judgements were based subjectively on the employer's views, it is an abuse of the right to manage personnel to dismiss the employee where the existence of a probationary period is in doubt.

6. Despite a justifiable reason for dismissal, it is unfair to cancel employment unilaterally without a disciplinary process for the employee who finishes his or her probationary period.[461)]

Under the company's collective bargaining agreement(CBA), employee probationary periods were to expire in six months despite the absence of a company regulation regarding this, unless there is special agreement between the two related parties. As a probationary temporary driver, the company argued that the CBA did not apply to a certain employee, who was dismissed due to a car accident occurring after the probationary period had ended and the occurrence of unexcused absences from work. Within the company, the CBA applied to a majority of employees holding the same kind of job, so an employee who has already passed a probationary period shall be entitled to the disciplinary process stipulated in the CBA.

7. Justification for refusing regular employment of a contracted employee subject to a probationary period.[462)]

The educational foundation, Chun Hae School, refused regular employment to some

460) NLRC on July 25, 2002, 2002 Buhae 288

461) LRC on Aug. 14, 2001, 2001 Buhae 73

462) NLRC on May 14, 2001, 2001 Buhae 32, 33

5. 수습기간이 정해지지 않은 상태에서 추상적인 사유를 이유로 해고한 것은 인사권 남용이다.[460)]

신청인은 인터넷 채용광고를 통해 경력사원으로 피신청인을 채용했고 면접당시 구두로 3개월의 수습기간을 통보했다고 하나 입증할 만한 증거가 없다. 또 신청인은 해고사유에 대해 피신청인이 외국어 실력부족 및 통역기술 부족과 업무 및 조직 내 인간관계에 제대로 적응하지 못하였다는 것을 제시하나 대부분이 신청인의 주관적인 판단으로 보여진다. 징계절차에 대해서도 수습기간 여부가 불명한 상태에서 사유 또한 추상적이어서 이를 이유로 피신청인을 해고한 것은 인사권 남용한 경우에 해당된다.

6. 귀책사유가 인정되더라도 수습기간을 도과한 근로자에 대해 징계절차에 의하지 않고 일방적으로 채용 취소한 것은 부당하다.[461)]

피신청인회사 단체협약 의해 신청인의 수습기간은 근로계약 당사자간의 약정 등 특별한 사정이 없는 한 사용자에 의한 별도의 조치가 없다해도 6개월 기간의 만료로 수습기간이 종료된 것이다. 또 회사는 신청인이 임시직 수습기사로서 단협의 적용을 받지 않아 수습기간 후에 발생한 교통사고 및 무단결근에 대해 채용취소한 것이라 주장하나 회사는 동종 근로자 반수 이상이 하나의 단협적용을 받는 사업장으로 이미 수습기간이 도과한 신청인에 대해 단협에서 정한 징계절차를 배제한 채 일방적으로 채용취소한 것이므로 부당하다.

7. 수습기간제 계약 근로자에 대한 본 채용 거부의 정당성 여부[462)]

학교법인 춘해학원에서 수습기간제 근로계약을 체결하고 근로한 근로자들이 근무태만, 상급자의 지시위반, 근무평정결과 업무부적격자로 평가되어 본 채

---

460) 중앙노동위원회 2002.7.25, 2002부해288 결정.

461) 지방노동위원회 2001.8.14, 2001부해73 결정.

462) 중앙노동위원회 2001.5.14, 2001부해32,부해33 결정.

probationary employees due to negligence of duty, violation of directions, and poor personnel evaluations that disqualified them. However, the employer did not provide concrete data showing that these probationary employees had not followed their superiors' instructions. Despite whether or not the personnel ratings were reasonable, the employer did not have relevant regulations in place nor was there evidence that personnel ratings had been given objectively and fairly. At a similar university, probationary employees continued to work after expiry of their probationary periods, which gave them the expectation that their employment would continue. It is unfair dismissal to terminate a labor contract simply due to expiry of a contract period for probationary employees without objective and justifiable reasons.

8. Justification for refusing regular employment of a probationary employee.[463)]

A certain employer dismissed(refused to grant regular employment) to probationary employees(tour bus drivers) for physically fighting with their colleagues after drinking. However, the violent incident occurred outside the workplace and after work. After the incident, the parties involved reconciled amicably. Accordingly, the employer's refusal to grant regular employment to the probationary employees was an abuse of the right to manage personnel and was considered unfair dismissal.

9. The company confirmed a position, salary table and announced the personnel orders for a newly hired employee. However, if the company does not describe a probationary period in the labor contract, he/she shall be considered a regular employee.[464)]

When hiring a new employee a certain employer confirmed position and salary table(4th level 2 ho), and then assigned him to the general affairs team in a personnel order, which means he was hired as a regular employee. Then, the employer dismissed him for lacking job skills, but considering this was his first job after graduation, this amounted to unfair dismissal and an abuse of the employer's personnel management right.

---

463) NLRC on Mar. 21, 2001, 2000 Buhae 574

464) NLRC on Nov. 2, 1998, 98 Buhae 427

용을 거부한 이 사건의 경우, 상급자의 지시에 따르지 않았다는 구체적인 입증자료를 신청인이 제시하지 못하여 이를 인정하기 어렵고, 근무평가와 관련하여 근무평정의 합리성 여부에 불구하고 근무평정에 대한 관련규정이 없을 뿐만 아니라 객관적이고 공정하게 이루어졌다고 볼 만한 근거가 없고, 동대학에는 수습기간제 계약기간 만료 이후에도 계속 근로하는 관행과 계속 근로할 수 있다는 기대가 예정되어 있다고 보여지므로 신청인이 객관적으로 인정받을 수 있는 정당한 사유없이 피신청인과의 근로계약 기간 만료를 이유로 일방적으로 종료시킨 것은 부당해고에 해당된다.

8. 수습근로자에 대한 본채용 거부의 정당성 여부[463)]

관광버스 회사의 운전기사인 수습근로자들이 동료들과 음주 후 서로 다투고 폭행사고를 발생 시킨 사실에 대하여 사용자가 이를 이유로 해고(본채용거부)한 이 사건의 경우, 위 폭행사고가 근무시간 이후 회 사 밖에서 우발적으로 일어났고 이 사고 후 폭행 관련 당사자 사이에 원만한 합의가 이루어 점에 비추어 사용자가 단순히 수습근로자라는 이유만으로 본채용을 거부한 것은 인사권을 남용한 부당해고에 해당 한다

9. 신규채용 시 직급·호봉과 근무부서를 확정, 인사발령했으며 근로계약서에 수습근로에 관한 사항이 명기되지 않았다면 정식직원으로 인정되어야 한다.[464)]

신청인이 신규채용 시 직급과 호봉(4급2호)을 부여받았고 근무부서(총무과)를 확정하여 인사발령된 점 등으로 보아 수습이 아닌 정식직원으로 채용된 것을 인정할 수 있고, 피신청인이 신청인에 대한 해고사유로 삼은 업무능력 부족 등의 이유는 신청인이 사회 초년생인 것을 고려할 때 해고까지 한 것은 인사권을 남용한 부당한 해고이다.

---

463) 중앙노동위원회 2001.3.21. 2000부해574.

464) 중앙노동위원회 1998.11.2. 98부해427 결정.

Section 5: Remedy for Unfair Dismissal, etc.

I. Procedures to Request Remedy for Unfair Dismissal, etc.

If an employer dismisses, lays off, suspends, or transfers a worker, or reduces wage, or takes other punitive actions against a worker without justifiable reason, the worker may apply to the Labor Relations Commission for remedy. In addition, any labor union whose rights have been infringed by unfair labor practices may also do so(Article 28 of the Labor Standards Act, Article 28 of the Union Act). As these labor disputes are dynamic, continuous, and collective, administrative agencies or courts cannot always be expected to handle them fairly, promptly, and reasonably, due to the inflexibility of bureaucracy and lack of experience of some agencies. The Labor Relations Commission is an independent administrative agency that has the authority and the ability to resolve labor disputes fairly, promptly, and in a way that is appropriate to the professional situation at hand.[465)]

When a worker, without justifiable cause, is dismissed, laid off, suspended, transferred, has his/her wages reduced or receive any other punitive action, he/she may request remedial action from the Labor Relations Commission(LRC). Such applications for remedy shall be made within 3 months from the date of the allegedly unfair act in question. If the LRC determines the dismissal is unfair, it may order the employer concerned to restore the dismissed worker to the previous job or pay monetary compensation to the worker(Article 30(3) of the LSA).

In cases where the worker doesn't want to return to the previous workplace, the employer shall provide the worker with money or other valuables that are at least equal to the wages which the worker would have been paid during the period of his/her absence if he/she had not been dismissed. Money or other valuables at least equivalent to the wage includes monetary compensation for the unfair dismissal, and is paid in lieu of reinstatement.

An employer who fails to comply with a remedial order from the LRC for unfair dismissal or disciplinary measures(suspension from office, position change, pay cut, etc.)

465) Lee, Byungtae, 「Labor Law」(7th ed.), Jongang Kyungjae, 2008, p. 487.

제5절 부당해고 등에 대한 구제

Ⅰ. 부당해고 등의 구제신청·심사절차

노동관계의 분쟁은 유동적이고 계속적이고 집단적인 성격을 가지고 있어 그 해결을 일반 행정기관이나 사법기관에서 처리할 경우, 관료주의성, 경직성, 비전문성 등으로 인해 공정하고 신속하며 합리적인 해결을 기대하기 어려운 측면이 있다. 이러한 이유로 인해 독립된 행정기구로 설치된 노동위원회를 통하여 노동분쟁을 신속·공정하고 합리적으로 처리하고 있다. 따라서 노동위원회의 준사법적 권한에 의해 결정되는 내용은 법원에 의한 해결에 비해 합목적성, 신속성 및 전문성을 보장할 수 있는 장점을 가지고 있다.[465)]

사용자가 근로자에 대하여 정당한 이유 없이 해고, 휴직, 정직, 전직, 감봉 기타 징벌을 한 때는 당해 근로자는 노동위원회에 구제를 신청할 수 있다. 근로자는 노동위원회에 해고가 있는 날로부터 3월 이내에 구제신청을 하여야 한다. 부당해고로 판정되면 노동위원회는 근로자의 원직복직 또는 금전보상제를 명할 수 있다(근기법 제30조 제3항).

금전보상제는 근로자가 원직복직을 원하지 않는 경우 근로자가 해고기간동안 근로를 제공하였다면 지급받을 수 있었던 임금 상당액 이상의 금품을 근로자에게 지급토록 하는 것이다. 임금상당액 이상의 금품은 해고기간 동안의 임금상당액과 위로금을 포함하여 원직복직을 대신한 것이다.

부당해고 등(해고, 정직, 전직, 감봉 포함)에 대한 구제명령을 정당한 이유 없이 이행하지 않는 경우 이행강제금이 부과된다(근기법 제33조). 이행강제금의 대상은 지방노동위원회 및 중앙노동위원회의 구제명령이 되며 당사자가 이의를 제기하여 행정소송을 제기한 경우라도 이행강제금이 부과된다. 부과금액은 3천

465) 이병태, 노동법, 세7판, 중앙경제, 2008, 487면.

shall pay a fine(Article 33 of the LSA). This fine shall be imposed on any employer who has received, and ignored, a remedial order from the National or Regional Labor Relations Commission. Even should the employer refuse to accept the order and file an administrative suit, the fine shall still be imposed. The fine may not exceed 30 million won, but may be imposed up to twice a year for a maximum of 2 years. An employer who fails to comply with the finalized remedial order shall be imprisoned for a term not exceeding 1 year or a fine not exceeding 10 million won(Article 111 of the LSA).

1. The Procedure for Handling Tasks in Adjudication Meetings

The Labor Relations Commission reviews applications and admits, rejects or cancels labor cases, determines eligibility of the parties involved, investigates, conducts interviews and holds judgment hearings within 60 days after the initial application date.

(1) Applications for remedy

If an employer dismisses or treats a worker unfairly, the worker may apply to the Labor Relations Commission for remedy. This application for remedy shall be made within three months from the date on which the unfair dismissal and/or related actions took place(or from the date of termination in cases where such activities continue). The worker must apply for remedy with the Labor Relations Commission nearest his/her workplace regarding unfair dismissal or unfair labor practice.

(2) Investigation

The Labor Relations Commission shall, without delay, conduct necessary investigations and inquiry of the parties concerned, upon receipt of an application for remedy. The Labor Relations Commission shall ① designate an investigator responsible for the process of investigation, ② demand the applicant submit evidence of the reason(s) for the application, ③ deliver a copy of the application for remedy or statement of reasons to the employer, and give opportunity for rebuttal and associated evidence to explain the employer's actions, and, ④ if necessary, order the parties, witnesses or other related persons to attend a hearing and give their testimonies. Further investigation will then be carried out as deemed necessary.[466)]

466) Article 45 and 46 of the Enforcement Decree of the LRC Act.

만원을 한도로 1년에 2회, 2년까지 부과할 수 있다. 확정된 구제명령을 이행하지 않는 자에 대해서는 벌칙(1년 이하의 징역 또는 1천만원 미만의 벌금)이 부과된다(근기법 제111조).

1. 노동위원회 심판회의의 업무 처리 절차

노동위원회는 구제신청서가 접수된 날로부터 60일 이내에 신청요건(당사자 적합 여부 등), 사실조사를 거친 후 당사자 및 증인에 대한 심문을 다루는 심문회의와 판정회의를 거쳐 사건의 인정과 기각, 각하 여부를 결정한다.

(1) 신 청

부당해고 판정 내지 부당노동행위 판정과 관련한 심판은 근로자가 관할 지방노동위원회에 구제를 신청함으로써 개시된다. 근로자의 신청은 사용자의 부당해고 또는 부당노동행위가 행해진 날(그러한 행위가 계속될 경우 그 종료일)부터 3개월 이내에 행해져야 한다. 관할 지방노동위원회는 부당해고 또는 부당노동행위가 발생한 사업장의 소재지를 관할하는 지방노동위원회를 말한다.

(2) 조 사

노동위원회는 구제가 신청된 사건에 대해 지체 없이 필요한 조사와 관계 당사자에 대한 심문을 한다. 조사의 과정으로 ① 노동위원회가 담당 조사관을 지정하고, ② 신청인에게 신청 이유를 소명하기 위한 증거 제출을 요구하고, ③ 피신청인에게 구제신청서 및 이유서의 부본을 송부하여 그에 대한 답변서 및 그 이유의 소명을 위한 증거의 제출을 요구하고, ④ 필요한 경우 당사자, 증인 또는 참고인의 출석을 요구하여 진술을 듣고 사실조사를 하는 과정이 진행된다.[466)]

466) 노동위원회규칙 제45조 및 제46조.

(3) Hearing

The Labor Relations Commission shall hold a hearing within 60 days from the date the application was received. This hearing is to review documented evidence both parties have submitted, and information gathered during investigation, and then decide whether unfair dismissal or unfair labor practice actually took place. The committee members(public-interest, worker and employer representative members) assigned to the case shall attend the hearing, have both parties verify their claims, and interview witnesses and other related persons. At the judgment hearing right after the hearing, the public interest committee members shall decide whether unfair dismissal or unfair labor practice took place. The worker and employer committee members may also interview the parties to the case and witnesses, and give their opinions before the public interest committee members give their decision during the judgment hearing.

〈Burden of Proof〉

1) Regarding decisions disadvantageous to certain personnel such as dismissal, the first burden of proof is on the employer to verify whether the worker committed a particular action, whether such action violated the rules of employment, and whether the disciplinary action, severity and suitability of punishment is justified. Regarding unfair labor practice, the first burden of proof is on the worker and the labor union to verify the employer's intention to commit the unfair labor practice, unfair treatment, and/or the existence of domination and interference.[467)]
2) However, regarding an employer's statements of reasons for decisions disadvantageous to certain personnel such as dismissal, the burden of proof then falls on the worker to verify that he/she did not commit a particular action, that he/she did not violate the rules of employment, and/or that the punishment was too severe or unsuitable to the violation. Regarding unfair labor practices, the employer also has a burden of proof to verify that he/she did not intend to commit an unfair labor practice, or give disadvantageous treatment to the company personnel due to their union activities, or obstruct those union activities, or cause deterioration to the union organization.[468)]

(4) Settlement

Labor cases filed for remedy at the Labor Relations Commission are often resolved between the two parties peacefully before going to the judgment stage of the Commission's activities. Such settlement not only helps to restore labor-management

467) Supreme Court ruling on Aug 14, 1992, 91da29811

468) Supreme Court ruling on Sep 10, 1996, 95nu16738

(3) 심 문

노동위원회는 구제신청이 이루어진 사건 접수일로부터 60일 이내에 심문회의를 열어 부당해고 또는 부당노동행위의 성립 여부를 판단하기 위해 사건에 대한 심문을 진행하게 된다. 심문회의는 당사자가 제출하는 증거서류와 조사 절차 중에 수집된 증거 자료에 대해 심사를 하여 부당해고 또는 부당노동행위의 성립여부를 판단하기 위한 사전 절차이다. 사건을 배정받은 공익위원 및 노사위원이 출석하여, 당사자의 쌍방에게 자신의 주장을 입증하게 하고, 증인과 참고인을 심문하기도 한다. 공익위원은 심문회의에서 심문을 한 후 판정회의에서 부당해고 또는 부당노동행위의 성립 여부를 판단하여 의결한다. 심문회의에 참석한 근로자위원과 사용자위원은 당사자나 증인을 심문할 수 있고, 판정회의에서 공익위원이 판정을 의결하기 전에 자신의 의견을 개진할 수 있다.

〈입증책임〉

1) 해고 등 불이익한 인사조치의 정당성에 관하여 근로자의 특정한 행위의 존재, 그 행위가 취업규칙 등 징계사유에 해당하는 사실, 징계절차의 정당성, 징계양정 및 형평의 적정성 등에 관한 1차적인 입증책임은 사용자에게 있고, 부당노동행위 성립에 관하여 부당노동행위의 의사, 불이익 처분, 지배개입행위의 존재 등에 대한 1차적인 입증책임은 근로자·노동조합에 있음.[467)]
2) 그러나 해고 등 불이익한 인사조치에 있어서 사용자의 정당성 주장에 대하여 근로자가 특정행위의 부존재, 취업규칙 등의 징계사유에 해당하지 않는 점, 징계절차 및 양정상의 하자 등을 주장하는 경우에 그 입증책임은 근로자에게 있고, 부당노동행위에 있어서 사용자가 부당노동행위 의사의 부존재, 인사조치가 조합활동에 대한 불이익처분이 아니며 인사조치로 인하여 조합활동의 장애, 조직력의 약화가 없었던 점 등을 주장하는 경우에 그 입증책임은 사용자에게 있는 것임.[468)]

(4) 화 해

노동위원회에 구제가 신청된 사건 중에는 노동위원회로부터 판정이 내려지지 않고 당사자 간 화해로 당해 사건을 해결하는 경우가 많다. 화해는 노사 당사자 간 대립된 입장을 해소시켜 이후의 원활한 노사관계를 회복시켜 줄 수 있으며, 또한, 사용자가 임의로 합의한 바는 자발적으로 이행되므로 노동위원회가 구제

467) 대법원 1992.8.14, 91다29811.
468) 대법원 1996.9.10, 95누16738.

stability, but also aids implementation of the employer's agreement more effectively than a remedy order from the Labor Relations Commission. The Labor Relations Commission can always recommend or arrange a draft of settlement for both parties in the process of investigation and interview. Once settlement is established, the statement of settlement is composed, which has the same effect as settlement decided by a court.[469)]

(5) Judgment

The judgment hearing is for the purpose of determining whether unfair dismissal or unfair labor practice has occurred, and takes place after the hearing. The judgment hearing is held with all three public interest committee members, and resolutions pass with approval from at least two of the three committee members. The Labor Relations Commission issues an order for remedy to the employer when it is deemed that unfair dismissal or unfair labor practice has occurred, or cancels the application for remedy if it is deemed that they have not. The Labor Relations Commission shall deliver a letter of the verdict to the employer and workers concerned within 30 days of the date of judgment.

(6) Details in orders for remedy

The Labor Commission, upon arrival of the application for remedy, shall carry out an investigation into factual aspects of the case and conduct an inquiry of the parties concerned and, based on the outcome of the investigation and the inquiry, may issue an order for a remedial action by the employer or decide to dismiss or return the application for remedy when the case is found not to be subject to unfair labor practice.[470)]

※ The application may be dismissed or returned in any of following cases:
- When the applicant union is not a union organization recognized under the Trade Union Act;
- When the filing is made after 3 months from occurrence of the alleged unfair labor practice;
- When it is clear that the action in question is not an act of unfair labor practice; or
- When the remedy is neither beneficial to the employee nor possible to achieve.

---

469) Article 16-3 of the Labor Relations Commission Act

470) Article 84 of the Trade Union Act.

명령으로 강제하는 것보다 그 이행이 담보되는 면도 있다. 노동위원회는 조사 및 심문 과정에서 언제든지 당사자에게 화해안을 제시하고 화해를 권고하거나 주선할 수 있다. 화해가 성립하면 화해조서(和解調書)를 작성하는데, 이 화해조서는 재판상 화해와 동일한 효력을 가진다.[469)]

(5) 판 정

노동위원회의 심판회의는 심문을 종료하면 판정회의를 개최하여 부당해고 또는 부당노동행위의 성립 여부를 판정한다. 판정회의는 공익위원 3인의 전원 출석으로 개의하고 위원 3인 중 과반수인 2인이 찬성하여야 성립한다. 부당해고 또는 부당노동행위가 성립한다고 판정한 때는 사용자에게 구제명령을 내리며, 성립되지 않는다고 판정한 때는 그 구제신청을 기각하는 결정을 한다. 노동위원회는 판정회의가 있은 후 30일 이내에 판정서를 당해 사용자와 신청인에게 각각 교부한다.

(6) 구제명령의 내용

노동위원회는 부당노동행위 신청에 대한 사실조사를 통하여 부당노동행위가 성립한다고 판정한 때는 사용자에게 구제명령을 하며, 부당노동행위가 성립되지 아니한다고 판정한 때는 구제신청을 기각 또는 각하의 판정을 하게 된다.[470)]

※ 각하 사유

- 신청한 노동조합이 노조법상의 노동조합이 아닌 경우
- 제척기간인 발생일 이후 3개월이 지난 경우
- 부당노동행위가 아닌 것이 명백한 경우
- 구제의 실익이 없거나 불가능한 경우 등

469) 노동위원회법 제16조의3.
470) 노조법 제84조.

1) Dismissal cases
① Rehabilitation
If a new labor contract is drawn in the form of re-employment, it is violating the purpose of rehabilitation, so the employer shall reinstate the dismissed employee to his/her pre-dismissal position or equivalent position.
② Back pay(Retroactive pay)
The employer shall pay the amount of wage the employee could not receive during the dismissal period. However, if the employee has earned any income from post-employment, the amount of back pay shall be adjusted according to the income earned.
2) Conditional contract (Yellow-dog contract)
The contract shall be nullified.
3) Refusal of collective bargaining
Order for Initiation of collective bargaining or collective agreement shall be given.
4) Domination or interference
Remedy is almost impossible, but such behaviors shall be at least stopped or prevented from reoccurrence.

2. Failure to comply with an order for remedy (Enforcement levy)

Employers are required to obey orders for remedy, and penalties are applied if they fail to do so(Article 111 of the LSA, Article 89 of the Trade Union Act). However, this criminal punishment is valid after the remedy order is confirmed finally. If an employer, after receiving a remedy order from the LRC and a decision on reexamination concerning a remedy order from the National Labor Relations Commission, fails to comply by the compliance deadline, an enforcement levy not exceeding 20 million won shall be imposed on the employer. The LRC may impose this enforcement levy twice a year for up to two years from the date the initial order for remedy was issued, or until the order is complied with. If an order for remedy issued by the LRC is canceled in accordance with a decision rendered by the National Labor Relations Commission after reexamination or a confirmed court ruling, the LRC shall immediately stop imposing the enforcement levy and return any monies already paid, by virtue of its authority or upon request of the employer.

Controversy may arise when deciding “fulfillment” of the remedy order if there are no criteria to determine “fulfillment” of the orders from the Labor Relations Commission. There will be disputes among parties and the LRC in understanding these conditions. So, the purpose of pursuing complete fulfillment is to prevent these disputes, ensure the effectiveness of an order for remedy, and resolve labor disputes in the early stages(Article 79 of the Rules on the LRC).

1) 해고의 경우

① 원직복귀

재고용이라는 형식으로 근로계약을 체결하는 것은 원상회복 취지에 어긋나며 해고 전의 직무 또는 그에 상당한 직에 복직시켜야 한다.

② 임금의 소급지불(back pay)

해고기간 중 받지 못한 임금 상당액을 지급하여야 한다. 그러나 해고된 후 다른 곳에 취업하여 얻은 수입이 있을 경우 원상회복에 의해 그 수입부분은 공제할 수 있다.

2) 조건부계약(황견계약)의 경우

계약서를 파기한다.

3) 단체교섭 거부의 경우

단체교섭 개시명령이나 단체협약 체결명령을 내린다.

4) 지배·개입의 경우

이에 대한 구제는 대단히 곤란한 것으로 원상회복이 불가능한 경우가 많으나 그 행위의 중지 또는 재발방지를 명한다.

2. 구제 명령의 불이행 (이행강제금)

사용자는 구제명령이 있을 때는 이에 따라야 한다. 사용자가 명령을 따르지 않는 경우에는 형벌이 부과된다(근기법 제111조, 노조법 제89조). 그러나 이것은 명령이 확정된 이후에야 해당된다. 사용자가 노동위원회의 판정에 불복하여 재심을 신청하거나 행정소송을 제기하는 경우 명령은 확정되지 않는다. 이 경우, 부당해고 구제에서는 확정되지 않은 구제명령에 대해서도 이행을 강제하는 이행강제금 제도가 인정된다. 노동위원회는 구제명령 또는 중앙노동위원회의 재심판정을 받은 후 이행기한까지 구제명령을 이행하지 아니한 사용자에게 2천만 원 이하의 이행강제금을 부과한다. 노동위원회는 최초의 구제명령을 한 날을 기준으로 매년 2회의 범위에서 구제명령이 이행될 때까지 반복하여 이행강제금을 부과·징수할 수 있다(2년 한도). 노동위원회는 중앙노동위원회의 재심판정이나 법원의 확정판결에 따라 노동위원회의 구제명령이 취소되면 직권 또는 사용자의 신청에 따라 이행강제금의 부과·징수를 즉시 중지하고 이미 징수한 이행강제금을 반환하여야 한다.

여기서 사용자의 구제명령 이행과 관련하여 논란이 되는 부분은 사용자의 부당해고 등에 대한 이행 기준(履行基準)이 없는 경우, 그 이행 여부에 대한 해석을 둘러싸고 근로자·사용자와 노동위원회 사이에 마찰이 야기될 우려가 있다는 점이다.

1. Fulfillment of an order to reinstate the worker to his/her previous job is when the employee has been assigned the same position the employee had when he/she was dismissed, with the same kind of work duties, or when the employee has been assigned other work duties with his/her prior consent. However, if the same position or work is no longer available for unavoidable reasons, assigning a similar position or work duties to the employee can be regarded as fulfillment of the order for remedy.
2. Fulfillment of the duty to pay the amount equivalent to wages is when the total amount of wages that the worker would have received, up to the time of complete payment, is paid to the worker.
3. Fulfillment of an order for monetary compensation is when the amount stipulated in the written judgment is paid.
4. Fulfillment of other orders for remedy occurs when the items stated in the written judgment are implemented.
5. In cases where the parties agree to a settlement other than an order for remedy for unfair dismissal, fulfillment occurs when that settlement is implemented.

3. Procedures for appeal

If an employer or worker is aggrieved by an order for remedy or decision to dismiss rendered by a Regional Labor Relations Commission, he/she may apply to the National Labor Relations Commission for reexamination within ten days of the date on which he/she received the notice of the order for remedy or decision to dismiss the application. The procedures for application to the National Labor Relations Commission are the same as the procedures for application to the LRC. An employer or worker may file a lawsuit in accordance with the Administrative Litigation Act against the decision made by the National Labor Relations Commission after reexamination within fifteen days from the date on which he/she received the notice of decision on reexamination. If an employer or worker is aggrieved by the decision of the National Labor Relations Commission and appeals to the Administrative Court, the National Labor Relations Commission becomes a defendant and the worker(the employer) becomes a defendant assistant participant. If no application for reexamination is made and no administrative lawsuit is filed within the periods listed above, the order for remedy, decision to dismiss or decision on reexamination shall be considered confirmed.

4. Monetary compensation system

The monetary compensation system was introduced so that workers not wishing to be reinstated can still receive remedy. Under the monetary compensation system, the Labor Relations Commission may order the employer to pay the worker an amount not less than the wages he/she would have received if he/she had worked during the period after he/she was

따라서 이행 기준에 대한 판단은 완전이행(完全履行)을 전제로 하고 있으며, 그 목적은 이러한 마찰을 사전에 예방하고, 구제명령의 실효성을 확보하며, 노사분쟁의 조기 해결을 도모하고자 함이다(노동위원회 규칙 제79조). 그 기준은 다음과 같다.

1. 원직복직의 이행은 당해 근로자에게 해고 등을 할 당시와 같은 직급과 같은 종류의 직무를 부여하였거나 당해 근로자의 동의를 얻어 다른 직무를 부여하였는지 여부. 다만, 같은 직급이나 직무가 없는 등 불가피한 사유가 발생한 때는 유사한 직급이나 직무를 부여한 경우를 말함
2. 임금상당액 지급의무 이행은 구제명령의 이행기일까지 그 금액을 전액 지급한 경우를 말함
3. 금전보상을 내용으로 하는 구제명령은 주문에 기재된 금액을 전액 지급한 경우를 말함
4. 그 밖의 구제명령의 이행은 그 주문에 기재된 대로 이행한 경우를 말함
5. 당사자가 부당해고 구제명령과 다른 내용으로 합의하고 그 내용대로 이행한 경우 완전 이행으로 간주

3. 불복절차

지방노동위원회의 구제명령 또는 기각결정에 불복이 있는 관계 당사자는 중앙노동위원회에 재심을 신청할 수 있다. 재심신청 기간은 판정서를 송달받은 날부터 10일 이내이다. 중앙노동위원회의 재심절차는 지방노동위원회에서 초심절차와 동일하게 진행된다. 중앙노동위원회의 재심판정에 대하여 관계 당사자는 행정소송법에 정하는 바에 따라 취소소송을 제기할 수 있다. 제소 기간은 재심판정서를 송달받은 날로부터 15일 이내이다. 회사(근로자)가 중앙노동위원회의 결정에 불복하여 행정소송을 제기한 경우, 피고가 중앙노동위원회가 되고, 당해 근로자(사용자)는 피고보조참가인이 된다. 재심신청 기간 내에 재심을 신청하지 않거나 제소 기간 내에 행정소송을 제기하지 않는 경우, 그 구제명령, 기각결정, 재심판정은 확정된다.

4. 금전보상제도

근로자가 부당해고에 대한 구제방법으로 결정된 원직복직을 희망하지 않는 경우, 노동위원회의 구제명령에 따라 사용자가 임금상당액 이상의 금품을 지급하고 근로관계를 종료할 수 있는 금전보상제도가 도입되었다. 임금상당액 이상의 금품은 해고기간 동안의 임금상당액과 위로금을 포함하여 원직복직을 대신한 것으로서, 노동위원회가 근로자의 귀책사유, 해고의 부당성 정도 등을 고려하여 결정한다. 금전보상제도가 도입됨으로써 정당한 이유 없는 해고의 구제방식을 다양화하

dismissed, in lieu of ordering that the worker be reinstated. An amount equivalent to wages(or more) includes some additional compensation as well, which shall be determined by the LRC after considering such things as any worker fault, and degree of unfairness of the dismissal, etc. This monetary compensation system has contributed to worker rights by providing alternatives in remedy for unfair dismissals. However, in actual practice this monetary compensation system has been used on a limited basis because it permits the minimum compensation equal only to the wages the worker would have received during the period after dismissal. Accordingly, in order to promote the monetary compensation system, it would be reasonable to require compensation equal to the total salary during the period after dismissal, a certain amount of compensation for the trouble and inconvenience of taking action, and the costs related to the application for remedy.

(1) Applicants

Only an employee or his/her legal agent can apply for financial compensation.

(2) Application Period

An employee who intends to apply for financial compensation must apply between the date of application for remedy and the date on which notification for judgment hearing is received.

(3) Application Requirements

An employee wishing financial compensation instead of reinstatement shall submit an application for financial compensation to the Labor Relations Commission. In this application, the employee shall stipulate the amount of desired compensation, and method and details of calculation. Reference data, such as the employment contract, pay slip(s), etc., shall also be attached.

(4) Calculation of Compensation

The compensation period shall be from the date of dismissal to the date of judgment on the case, and the amount shall include equivalent salary. Equivalent salary means the amount that the employee would have likely received if he/she had been able to work normally during the time between dismissal and judgment on the case, including expenses etc., caused by the dismissal. The judgment committee shall determine the amount by considering collectively the degree of unfair dismissal, the degree of employee fault, the employee's intermediate income accrued from the date of dismissal to the date of judgment, and the type of employment contract.

여 권리구제의 실효성을 증대시켰다고 할 수 있다. 그러나 실무에 있어서 금전보상제도는 금전보상이 해고기간 중에 받을 수 있었던 임금에 한정되어 최소한의 보상만 인정하고 있기 때문에 제한적으로만 사용되고 있다. 따라서 금전보상제도를 활성화하기 위해서는 해고기간 동안의 임금, 일정액의 위자료, 구제신청에 소요된 비용 등도 인정하는 것이 타당하다고 본다.

(1) 신청권자

금전보상명령 신청은 부당해고 구제신청을 한 근로자(또는 그 대리인)만 할 수 있다.

(2) 신청기간

금전보상명령을 신청하고자 하는 근로자는 구제신청서를 제출한 후 심문일정통지를 받기 전까지 신청하여야 한다.

(3) 신청방법

복직명령 대신 금전보상명령을 원하는 근로자는 "금전보상명령 신청서"를 노동위원회에 제출하여야 한다. 이 때 근로자는 신청서에 근로자가 원하는 보상금액과 그 산출내역을 기재하여야 하며 근로계약서·임금명세서 등 소명자료를 첨부해야 한다.

(4) 보상금 산정

보상금액의 산정기간은 해고일로부터 당해 사건의 판정일까지로 하며, 보상금액은 임금상당액을 포함한 총금액으로 한다. "임금상당액"은 근로자가 해고일로부터 판정일까지 정상적으로 근로를 제공하였더라면 받을 수 있었던 금액을 말한다. 보상금은 임금상당액과 부당해고로 인한 위로금·비용 등을 포함하는 것이다. 심판위원회는 해고의 부당성 정도, 근로자의 귀책 정도, 근로자가 해고일로부터 판정일까지 근로자가 얻은 중간수입, 근로계약의 형태 등을 종합적으로 고려하여 결정한다.

5. Unfair dismissal and monetary compensation

Matters related to monetary compensation for unfair dismissal are not dealt with by the Labor Relations Commission. However, the courts may require an employer to make monetary compensation to the employee for purposely dismissing him/her even though that dismissal is evidently unfair.

[Related ruling][471] In cases where an employer dismisses an employee to push him/her out of the workplace without a justifiable reason for disciplinary dismissal, or in cases where the reason for dismissal was clearly unfair considering the content of the rules of employment, or in cases where the employer could recognize that the dismissal would be unfair if he/she had paid a little attention, that disciplinary dismissal would be an abuse of the employer's right to discipline the employee. If this dismissal is unfair enough to be accepted as against social norms or socially accepted rules, this not only becomes an unjustifiable dismissal according to Paragraph 1 of Article 23 of the Labor Standards Act, but also an illegal act that inflicts emotional distress on the employee concerned.

II. Compromise as a Means of Settling Labor Disputes

1. Concept

Of the total labor cases brought to the Labor Relations Commission, the percentage of cases resolved through compromise has gradually increased: 25% in 2010, 32% in 2011, 34% in 2012 and 34 % in 2013.[472] This reflects the LRC's view that compromise is one of the most important methods to resolving labor disputes, a view it has held since the provision Compromise was introduced into the Labor Commission Act in April 2007.[473] LRC judgments result in one party winning all the benefits, while the other loses all, which may result in an appeal that extends the labor dispute beyond what was expected.

Compromise plays a role in preventing resolution of labor cases from such delays, and

471) Supreme Court ruling on Feb. 23, 1999, 98da12157 [Confirmation of Unfair Dismissal].

472) MOEL, White Paper on Labor and Employment, 2014.

473) Lee, Sungil & Cho, Sungkwan, A Study on Improving Operation of the Labor Relations Commission, 「Thesis Papers on Labor Laws」 No. 27, Comparative Labor Law Society, 2013.

5. 부당해고와 위자료

부당해고에 대한 위자료 문제는 노동위원회에서는 다루지 않는다. 그러나 법원에서는 부당해고가 명백함에도 불구하고 사용자가 근로자를 해고하는 경우에는 불법행위가 되어 위자료 지급명령을 내린 경우도 있다.

[관련판례[471)]] 사용자가 근로자를 징계해고할 만한 사유가 전혀 없는데도 오로지 근로자를 사업장에서 몰아내려는 의도하에 고의로 어떤 명목상의 해고사유를 만들거나 내세워 징계라는 수단을 동원하여 해고한 경우나, 해고의 이유로 된 어느 사실이 취업규칙 등 소정의 해고사유에 해당되지 아니하거나 해고사유로 삼을 수 없는 것임이 객관적으로 명백하고 또 조금만 주의를 기울이면 이와 같은 사정을 쉽게 알아볼 수 있는데도 그것을 이유로 징계해고에 나아간 경우 등 징계권의 남용이 된다. 이것이 우리의 건전한 사회통념이나 사회상규상 용인될 수 없음이 분명한 경우에 있어서는 그 해고가 근로기준법 제23조 제1항에서 말하는 정당성을 갖지 못하여 효력이 부정되는 데 그치는 것이 아니라, 위법하게 상대방에게 정신적 고통을 가하는 것이 되어 근로자에 대한 관계에서 불법행위를 구성한다.

Ⅲ. 화해를 통한 노동분쟁 해결

1. 의의

노동위원회에 접수된 전체사건 중 화해로 종결된 사건의 비율이 2010년 기준 25%, 2011년 32%, 2012년 34%, 2013년 34 %로 점차 확대되고 있다.[472)] 이는 2007년 4월 '노동위원회법'에 '화해조항'이 명문으로 도입된 이후 노동위원회가 화해제도를 노동분쟁을 해결하는 중요한 수단으로 간주하고 있기 때문이다.[473)] 노동위원회의 판정은 어느 한 당사자의 일방적 이익을 가져오고, 다른 상대방에게는 모든 것을 잃는 결과를 가져오기 때문에 이에 대한 불복으로 인하여 노동분쟁

---

471) 대법원 1999.2.23, 98다12157【해고무효확인및임금청구】.

472) 고용노동부, 「고용노동백서」, 2014.

473) 이승길·조성관, 노동위원회의 운영상 개선방안에 관한 소고, 「노동법논집」, 제27호, 비교노동법학회, 2013.4, 260면.

aims for amicable conclusion between the company and employee concerned. Despite this important role, the compromise system is regarded as a method of anything goes to solve disputes in actual practice. Accordingly, it is necessary to understand the use of compromise through actual labor cases resolved reasonably in such a way, and seek how to make more frequent use of it.

2. The Legal Status of Compromise and its Use

(1) The legal status of compromise

The Civil Act stipulates(in Articles 731 and 732) that a compromise shall become effective when the parties have agreed to terminate a dispute between themselves by mutual concession. A contract of compromise shall have the effect that the rights conceded by one of the parties are thereby extinguished and the other party will, in turn, acquire the pertinent rights by virtue of the compromise. Judicial rulings have agreed that when reaching a compromise, the previous agreement is extinguished by virtue of the newly established effects of the compromise, and the compromise becomes legally binding regardless of any contradicting content in the previous agreement.[474)]

According to Article 16-3 of the Labor Commission Act, the LRC may recommend conciliation or present a proposal for such at the request of the parties concerned or by virtue of its authority before a judgment, order or decision is rendered pursuant to Article 84 of the Trade Union & Labor Relations Adjustment Act or Article 28 of the Labor Standards Act. The conciliation statement shall have the same effect as a compromise imposed by the courts in accordance with the Civil Procedure Act.

(2) Use of compromise

1) Designing the compromise

The compromise process in an unfair dismissal case brought to the LRC begins with the necessary time to consider the compromise, when a judge in the judgment hearing has suggested a compromise and one of the parties has accepted it. In general, the party requesting a compromise in the course of an unfair dismissal case is regarded as having a weaker claim, and so a compromise is seldom requested before the judgment hearing starts.

---

474) Supreme Court ruling on Sept. 22, 1992: 92Da25335.

이 장기화 되는 경향이 있다. 화해는 회사와 근로자가 해고 사건을 원만하게 해결하도록 하여 노동분쟁이 장기화 되는 것을 사전에 방지하는 역할을 수행한다. 화해제도의 이러한 중요한 역할에도 불구하고, 실무에서 우연하게 이루어지는 분쟁해결 방식으로 간주되고 있다. 따라서 화해를 통해 노사분쟁을 합리적으로 해결한 실사례에서 화해제도를 이해하고, 이를 적극적인 활용방법을 모색할 필요가 있다.

2. 화해의 법적지위 및 활용

(1) 화해의 법적 지위

민법에서 '화해'는 당사자가 상호 양보하여 당사자 간의 분쟁을 중지할 것을 약정함으로써 그 효력이 생긴다. 화해계약은 당사자 일방이 양보한 권리가 소멸되고 상대방이 화해로 그 권리를 취득하는 효력이 있다(제731조, 제732조). 판례의 입장도 화해의 효력에 대해 화해계약이 성립되면 특별한 사정이 없는 한 그 창설적 효력에 의하여 종전의 법률관계를 바탕으로 한 권리의무관계는 소멸되는 것이므로 계약당사자 간에는 종전의 법률관계가 어떠하였느냐를 묻지 않고 화해계약에 의하여 새로운 법률관계가 생기는 것으로 봤다.[474)]

노동위원회법(제16조의3호)에 따르면, 노동위원회는 「노동조합 및 노동관계조정법」 제84조 또는 「근로기준법」 제28조의 규정에 따른 판정·명령 또는 결정이 있기 전까지 관계 당사자의 신청 또는 직권에 의하여 화해를 권고하거나 화해 안을 제시할 수 있다. 당사자가 합의해 작성된 화해조서는 「민시소송법」에 따른 '재판상 화해'의 효력을 갖는다.

(2) 화해의 활용

1) 화해의 선택

노동위원회의 부당해고 사건에 있어 화해는 주로 심문회의에서 공익위원이 화해를 권고하고 어느 일방이 이를 수용할 때, 화해의 시간이 부여되는 방식으로 진행된다. 보통 부당해고 사건을 진행함에 있어 어느 일방이 화해를 요구할 경우에

474) 대법원 1992.9.22, 92다25335.

If the employer feels likely to lose the case, a compromise is quite acceptable. This is the case also if the employer feels he has the potential to win the case, if the cost of settlement is much lower, as the compromise will prevent the employee from appealing. From the employee's viewpoint, a compromise is desirable if he/she does not wish to continue working for the employer, has gotten a new job, or feels he/she cannot win the case.

2) Settlement money

Settlement money is normally calculated by the employee's wage. In cases where the employee has a favorable position in a dismissal case, he/she requests monetary compensation up to one year's wages, considering the wages that should have been received during the dismissed period and the ability to earn more upon reinstatement at the workplace. However, if the employee has an unfavorable position in the dismissal case, he/she usually accepts a compromise with the settlement money covering only the period of dismissal. Accordingly, after the LRC has investigated the facts related to the justification for dismissal in the judgment hearing, it will suggest a compromise including a cash settlement.

Should a considerable gap exist between what each party feels is acceptable, the LRC will endeavor to narrow the gap through mediation to encourage settlement. Nevertheless, if there is no compromise reached, the LRC tends to avoid a quick judgment and instead opts to give both parties time to consider ways to reach a compromise.

(3) Difference between compromise and monetary compensation

Monetary compensation is a system where the company provides the employee monetary compensation if the employee does not desire reinstatement upon such a verdict in an unfair dismissal case(Article 30 of the Labor Standards Act). Any requirement for monetary compensation shall begin when an employee receives notification of the judgment hearing date, with the calculation period for compensation calculated from dismissal date to judgment date(Articles 64 and 65 of the Labor Relations Regulation). Accordingly, monetary compensation can be claimed for wages missed during the period after dismissal, and as this amount cannot include compensation for emotional damage, the compensation is relatively low and limited.[475)] On the other hand, since a compromise is not related to the level of monetary compensation, the greater the possibility for unfair

475) Cho, Sunghye, Critical Review of the Monetary Compensation System for Unfair Dismissal, 「Labor Strategy Studies」, 2009, vol. 9, p. 154.

는 이를 요구하는 일방이 자신들의 주장이 약하다는 것을 인정하는 모습으로 비춰질 것을 우려하여 심문회의까지는 화해를 먼저 제안하지 않는 경우가 많다.

사용자의 입장에서는 부당해고로 판정이 날 가능성이 높을 경우 화해를 수용한다. 또한, 정당한 해고로 인정받을 것이 확실시되더라도 합의금이 아주 적다면 근로자가 재심신청을 사전에 방지하기 위해 화해를 수용하기도 한다. 반면에, 근로자는 복직이 되더라도 ① 계속 근무가 불가능한 경우, ② 새로운 직장에 취업한 경우, ③ 부당해고로 인정받기가 어려운 경우 합의를 수용한다.

2) 화해의 금액

화해 금액은 보통 '근로자의 급여'를 기준으로 계산된다. 해고 사건에 있어 근로자가 유리한 입장에 놓여 있으면, 해고기간의 임금과 추가로 근무하면 받을 수 있는 기간에 대한 임금을 요청하기 때문에 1년 치의 급여를 합의금으로 청구하기도 한다. 이에 반해 근로자가 해고사건에 대해 불리한 경우에는 해고기간의 임금 정도만 받고 화해하는 경우가 많다. 따라서 노동위원회는 부당해고 여부를 판정하기에 앞서 심문회의에서 사실관계를 통해 해고가 정당한지 부당한지를 어느 정도 심문이 있은 이후에 화해를 권유하며 합의금도 제시하게 된다. 양 당사자의 합의금액이 차이가 난 경우에는 노동위원회의 조정을 통해 합의금이 어느 정도 좁혀져서 합의가 되도록 유도한다. 그럼에도 불구하고 최종적으로 합의되지 않은 경우 심문회의에서 곧바로 부당해고 여부를 판정하지 않고, 며칠의 기회를 주어 회사와 근로자가 합의하기도 한다.

(3) 화해와 금전보상과의 차이

'금전보상제도'는 부당해고로 판정받았으나 근로자가 원직복직을 원치 않아 대신 금전으로 보상하는 제도이다(근기법 제30조). 금전보상 청구는 심문회의 개최일을 통보받기 전까지 하여야 하며, 보상금액의 산정기간은 해고일로부터 당해 사건의 판정 일까지로 한다(노동위원회 규칙 제64조, 제65조). 따라서 금전보상은 해고기간 동안의 임금만 청구할 수 있으며, 해고에 대한 정신적 보상(위자료)에 대해서는 인정되지 않기 때문에 보상금이 낮아 제한적으로 사용될 수밖에 없다.[475)]

---

475) 조성혜, 부당해고 시 금전보상제도에 대한 비판적 검토, 「노동정책연구」, 2009, 제9권, 154면

dismissal to be determined, the higher the compensation request will be, while the lower the possibility for unfair dismissal to be determined, the lower the compensation request will be: for example, one month's wage, equivalent to the one month compensation requirement for a failure to give advance notice of dismissal.

3. Labor cases resolved through compromise

(1) A case brought against Company A

Company A, a Taiwanese semiconductor company with five Korean employees at its Korean branch is selling semiconductor components to Korean electronics companies. For the past few years, this company has been in deficit, and determined that the branch manager's poor sales skills were to blame. The company dismissed the branch manager without notice, and paid him the required one month compensation in August 2014. The branch manager then applied to the LRC for remedy for unfair dismissal.

The LRC held a judgment hearing on November 19, 2014 where the branch manager claimed that the poor sales performance that the company claimed was partly due to the high prices of the company's semiconductors, his legal status was not as an employer since he only worked as a sales manager, and the Korean branch was a sales office and not an autonomous organization. These claims greatly weakened the company's chances of winning the case.

The LRC estimated that as the branch manager had lost the company's confidence, he would be unable to work effectively upon reinstatement, and suggested a compromise be reached, which both parties accepted. In the judgment hearing, the employee demanded 12 months' wages as a condition for settlement, while the company responded with an offer for 3 months' wages in consideration of the already-paid compensation for no advance notice of dismissal, and the labor attorney's service fees. The LRC judge then proposed compensation equal to 8 months' wages to both parties, but the company rejected it. The LRC then explained that the parties would have one week to consider methods for settlement, and that a judgment would be made if the two parties were unable to reach agreement by that time.

When the company's labor attorney explained to the company that the LRC was more

이에 반해 화해는 금전보상 수준에 대한 어떠한 구속 없기 때문에 부당해고로 판정될 가능성이 높으면 더 많은 합의금을 청구할 수 있고, 반면에 정당한 해고로 판정될 가능성이 높으면 1개월 치 해고예고수당 정도의 임금으로 합의되는 경우도 있다.

3. 화해를 통한 노동분쟁 해결사례

(1) A 회사의 해고 사건

A회사는 대만계 반도체 회사로 한국에 5명의 직원을 사용하고 반도체 부품을 전자회사에 판매하고 있다. 최근에 회사는 적자가 계속되고 있어 이에 대한 원인이 한국 지사장의 영업능력 부족이라 판단하였다. 이에 회사는 2014년 8월에 해고예고수당 만을 지급하고 지사장을 즉시 해고하였다. 곧바로 지사장은 부당해고 구제신청을 노동위원회에 신청하였다.

노동위원회는 2014.11.19. 심문회의를 개최한 바, 회사가 주장하는 지사장의 영업실적 부족의 원인 중 하나로 회사의 반도체 가격경쟁력이 높지 않았고, 지사장의 지위가 사용자인지에 대해 실제로 영업부서장 정도의 역할만 하였고, 독립된 사업체의 대표자 역할을 하지 못하였다는 사실관계가 확인됨으로써 회사에 불리한 분위기였다.

노동위원회는 지사장이 복직한다면 회사의 신임을 잃은 이상 계속 근로가 불가능하다고 판단하게 되었다. 이러한 상황에서 노동위원회는 화해를 제시한바, 회사와 지사장은 화해하겠다고 의사표시를 하였다. 이 심문회의의 화해 조건으로 근로자는 12개월의 임금보상을 요구한바, 회사는 해고예고수당과 공인노무사의 수임료 등을 고려해 3개월의 임금보상 한다고 입장을 표명하였다. 이에 공익위원은 당사자 쌍방에게 8개월의 임금보상(안)을 제시하였으나, 회사는 이를 거부하였다. 이에 노동위원회는 1주의 화해기간을 추가로 주면서 동 기간 내 합의하지 않으면 부당해고의 여부를 판정한다고 하였다.

이에 회사를 대리한 공인노무사는 현재 회사가 지방노동위원회에서 불리한 입장이고, 부당해고로 판정 시 재심절차 등 추가적 법률비용이 발생한다는 점을 설

in favor of the employee's claims and additional costs would result if they appealed a verdict of unfair dismissal, the company agreed to increase the settlement to 5 months' wages. The company's labor attorney then persuaded the employee's labor attorney(whose client had already accepted the judge's proposal for 8 months' wages) that the employee's severance pay would be reduced by two months considering that there had been fewer than 5 employees for some years previously. The employee then reduced his claim by an additional two months and accepted 6 months' wages as a settlement. In the end, the company's labor attorney successfully persuaded the company to accept this small difference, which also accepted the employee's compromise. Ultimately, 5 1/2 months' wages in compensation was accepted by both parties.

(2) A case brought against Company B

Company B is a Korean branch office of a multinational company with head offices in Switzerland. An employee was assigned to the Korean branch office as a senior director on December 1, 2012, signing a two year contract. He had adjusted to Company B very well and worked faithfully, but suddenly received a letter of dismissal from Company B on August 30, 2013. The reason given for dismissal was suspicion that the employee had been involved in unfair price transactions with a customer while working at the head office in 2012. However, Company B did not investigate the incident thoroughly, and simply dismissed the employee immediately pursuant to a request from the head office. The judgment hearing at the LRC was held for this case on December 17, 2013.

As the company had dismissed the employee pursuant to a request from the head office without observing the disciplinary process stipulated in the rules of employment, it was very clear that unfair dismissal would be the verdict. The LRC Chairman suggested the parties settle the case, to which both parties agreed.

However, settlement was difficult due to significant difference of opinion on adequate compensation. The employee was unwilling to return to work, while the company could not win the case. When he considered that there were only 11 months left in his contract and he was unsure about continuing to work at the head office after completing it, the employee decided to accept 9 months' average wage as compensation. The company agreed, and the settlement was finalized as 9 months' average wage.

명해 회사가 추가 5개월 치의 임금보상을 합의안으로 받아 냈다. 한편, 근로자 측도 공익위원의 제시 안을 수용한 상태로 8개월 치 임금보상 합의안은 수용하겠다는 입장이었다. 이에 사측 공인노무사는 근로자 측 공인노무사에게 연락해 실제로 퇴직금 계산에 있어 상시 근로자 수 5인 이내의 기간을 고려할 경우 약 2개월 치 임금이 축소된다는 사실을 설명하면서 기존의 8개월 치 임금보상에서 6개월 치로 조정하였다. 최종 1개월 치 임금보상 차이에 대해 회사를 추가적으로 설득하였고, 노측에게도 추후 근로자가 부담해야 할 위험을 설명해 5.5개월 치로 양보해 최종 합의에 이르렀다.

(2) B회사의 해고사건

B회사는 스위스에 본사를 둔 다국적 기업의 한국지사이다. 근로자는 2012.12.1에 한국지사에 상무로 발령을 받아 새로이 2년간의 근로계약을 체결하고 근무를 시작하였다. 근로자는 성실히 근무하던 중 갑작스럽게 2013.8.30 에 해고통지를 받았다. 해고 이유는 근로자가 2012년 본사에서 근무 시 거래업체와 부당거래에 관여한 것이었다. B회사는 본 사안을 자체 조사하지 않은 채 B회사 본사의 해고요청 통지에 따라 그 근로자를 해고하였다. 이에 근로자는 노동위원회에서 부당해고 구제신청을 하였고, 이 사건과 관련해 노동위원회의 심문회의가 2013.12.17 오후에 열렸다.

심문회의에서 B회사가 본사의 요청에 의해 취업규칙에 의한 징계절차도 거치지 않은 채 근로자를 일방적으로 해고한 것이 인정되어 부당해고로 판정될 것이 명백하였다. 심문회의 의장은 양 당사자에게 합의를 제안한 바, 이를 수용하였다.

하지만 합의금액에 대해서는 다툼이 있어 쉽게 해결되지 않았다. 근로자도 업무복귀가 사실상 어려운 상황이었고, 회사도 부당해고 판정을 피해갈 수 없는 입장이었다. 근로자는 계약기간이 11개월가량밖에 남아 있지 않았기 때문에 11개월 치의 임금보상을 요구하였다.

이에 대해 회사는 부당해고로 판정이 날 경우의 위험 등을 고려해 6개월 치 임금보상을 제시하였다. 최종 양 당사자가 상호 양보해 9개월 치에 조정된 임금보상으로 합의되었다.

Chapter 7

Employment Adjustment

Section 1: Dismissal for Managerial Reasons[476)]

Ⅰ. Concept

Dismissal for managerial reasons is to reduce the number of employees due to organizational restructuring in order to adjust to economic, industrial, and technical changes, or to renew a group of employees. Dismissal for managerial reasons discharges employees not because of any fault, as in ordinary or disciplinary dismissal, but on account of managerial business conditions.

A dismissal with proper cause shall satisfy the following conditions. If these items are satisfied, the employer can be exempt from legal responsibility as proper cause under the four conditions of Article 23(1).

① Urgent necessity in relation to the business; ② efforts were made to avoid dismissal; ③ fair criteria for the selection of those persons subject to dismissal; ④ the employee representative is informed 50 days in advance and after consulting in good faith.

Each of the above qualifications is not defined or fixed, but shall be determined flexibly in relation to meeting other requirements in actual cases. Whether the dismissal for managerial reasons in a substantial case meets each of the above requirements shall be judged synthetically in consideration of each individual situation related to each requirement.[477)]

---

476) Jung Bongsoo, 「Workplace Restructuring Manual」, KangNam Labor Law Firm, 2018.

477) Supreme Court ruling on Nov. 13, 2003, 2003Du4119.

Chapter 7

구조조정

제1절 경영상 해고[476)]

Ⅰ. 의 의

경영상 이유에 의한 해고란 경제적·산업구조적·기술적 성격에 기인한 기업 합리화 계획에 따라 근로자의 인원수를 줄이거나 인원구성을 바꾸기 위하여 행하는 해고로서 일반적으로 정리해고라고 한다. 정리해고는 통상해고, 징계해고와는 달리 근로자에게 직접적인 귀책사유가 없음에도 사용자 측의 경영사정으로 행하여진다는 특성이 있다.

정리해고가 정당한 해고가 되기 위해서는 다음의 4가지 필수요건을 모두 갖추어야 한다. 사용자가 이러한 조건을 모두 충족하여야만 근로기준법 제23조 제1항에 의한 정당한 이유가 있는 해고로서 사용자는 그 책임을 면할 수 있다.

① 긴박한 경영상의 필요가 발생, ② 해고회피노력, ③ 합리적이고 공정한 해고대상자의 선정, ④ 근로자대표에 대한 50일 전 통보 및 성실한 협의

각 요건의 구체적 내용은 확정적·고정적인 것이 아니라 구체적 사건에서 다른 요건의 충족 정도와 관련하여 유동적으로 정해지는 것이므로, 구체적 사건에서 경영상 이유에 의한 당해 해고가 위 각 요건들을 모두 갖추어 정당한지 여부는 위 각 요건을 구성하는 개별 사정들을 종합적으로 고려하여 판단하여야 한다.[477)]

476) 정봉수, 「인력 구조조정 매뉴얼」, 강남노무법인, 2018.
477) 대법원 2003.11.13, 2003두4119.

Ⅱ. Requirements

> Article24 of the LSA. Restrictions on Dismissal for Business Reasons
> ① Where an employer wishes to dismiss a worker for business reasons, there must be an urgent necessity in relation to the business. It shall be deemed that there is such an urgent business necessity in the case of a business transfer, merger, or acquisition of the business to prevent business deterioration.
> ② In a case following under paragraph(1) , the employer shall make every effort to avoid dismissal and shall establish and follow reasonable and fair criteria for the selection of those persons subject to dismissal. In any case, there shall be no discrimination on the basis of gender.
> ③ Where there is an organized labor union representing more than half of the workers at a business or business location, the employer shall inform and consult in good faith with the labor union (where there is no such organized labor union, this shall refer to a person who represents more than half of the workers - hereinafter referred to as "employee representative") regarding the methods for avoiding dismissals and the criteria for dismissal under the provisions of paragraph(2) at least 50 days before the intended date of dismissal.

1. Urgent necessity in relation to business

Here, urgent necessity in relation to business is not only limited to conditions in which the company needs to prevent bankruptcy, but also includes conditions in which the company must reduce its employees in order to prevent imminent danger.[478)]

▶ Concrete examples

① When facing financial crisis due to continuous business deterioration;
② Termination of certain production lines due to business deterioration;
③ In cases of business transfer, merger, or acquisition of the business to prevent business deterioration;
④ In cases where personnel reduction is admitted as objectively reasonable(this not only includes dismissal due to business deterioration but also dismissal for technological reasons to promote productivity or to change the working structure to recover or to promote competitiveness and introduce new technology, and dismissals due to company restructuring after technological innovation); and
⑤ In cases where there is a surplus of employees due to business restructuring, such as streamlining the organization, etc.

---

478) Supreme court ruling on Sept. 26, 2003, 2001Du10776.

Ⅱ. 경영상 해고의 요건

근로기준법 제24조【경영상 이유에 의한 해고의 제한】

① 사용자가 경영상 이유에 의하여 근로자를 해고하려면 긴박한 경영상의 필요가 있어야 한다. 이 경우 경영 악화를 방지하기 위한 사업의 양도·인수·합병은 긴박한 경영상의 필요가 있는 것으로 본다.

② 제1항의 경우에 사용자는 해고를 피하기 위한 노력을 다하여야 하며, 합리적이고 공정한 해고의 기준을 정하고 이에 따라 그 대상자를 선정하여야 한다. 이 경우 남녀의 성을 이유로 차별하여서는 아니 된다.

③ 사용자는 제2항에 따른 해고를 피하기 위한 방법과 해고의 기준 등에 관하여 그 사업 또는 사업장에 근로자의 과반수로 조직된 노동조합이 있는 경우에는 그 노동조합(근로자의 과반수로 조직된 노동조합이 없는 경우에는 근로자의 과반수를 대표하는 자를 말한다. 이하 "근로자대표"라 한다)에 해고를 하려는 날의 50일전까지 통보하고 성실하게 협의하여야 한다.

1. 긴박한 경영상의 필요성의 존재

여기서 긴박한 경영상의 필요라 함은 반드시 기업의 도산을 회피하기 위한 경우에 한정되지 아니하고, 장래에 올 수도 있는 위기에 미리 대처하기 위하여 인원삭감이 객관적으로 보아 합리성이 있다고 인정되는 경우도 포함된다.[478)]

▶ 구체적 사례

① 계속되는 경영악화로 경영위기 직면

② 경영악화로 일부 사업 폐지

③ 경영악화를 방지하기 위한 사업의 양도·인수·합병의 경우

④ 인원 삭감이 객관적으로 보아 합리성이 인정되는 경우(경영악화라는 경제적 이유뿐만 아니라 생산성 향상, 경쟁력 회복·증강에 대처하기 위한 작업형태의 변경, 신기술 도입이라는 기술적 이유와 기술혁신에 따라 생기는 구조조정을 이유로 한 해고 등)

⑤ 기타 직제개편 등 경영합리화 조치를 단행함으로써 잉여 노동력이 발생하는 경우 등

---

478) 대법원 2003.9.26, 2001두10776.

(1) Degree of urgent necessity

1) In practice, a workforce cut for urgent managerial reasons must be carried out not merely to overcome the poor performance of a business but also to change work organization or introduce new technologies with a view to improving productivity or restoring or strengthening competitiveness, or to keep up with the innovations and structural changes in the industry. Namely, dismissal for managerial reasons has been conducted on the grounds of technological needs as well as managerial needs. Accordingly, the requirement of urgent managerial reasons should not be interpreted to mean that only the need to keep the business afloat is justifiable. Rather, it seems that when a workforce reduction is reasonable in objective terms, an urgent managerial reason for dismissal exists.[479)]

2) According to a Supreme Court ruling, The requirement of 'urgent managerial reasons' should not be interpreted to mean that only the need to keep the business afloat makes dismissal justifiable. Rather, it seems that when workforce reduction is reasonable in objective terms, 'urgent managerial reasons for dismissal exist. That is, a workforce cut for urgent managerial reasons has been carried out not merely to overcome the poor performance of a business but also to change the work organization or introduce new technologies with a view to improving productivity or restoring or strengthening competitiveness, or to keep up with the innovations and structural changes in the industry.[480)]

(2) Continuity of necessity in relation to business

Urgent necessity in relation to business for the purpose of dismissal for managerial reasons requires deterioration of the business by which the company is obliged to reduce a number of employees, and the financial difficulties that have been repeated and cannot be expected to be overcome in the near future. Accordingly, the fact that a strike by the union made it impossible to maintain normal business operations does not give the employer the right to close the business for urgent necessity in relation to business.[481)]

---

479) Supreme Court ruling on Dec. 10, 1991, 91Da8647.

480) Supreme Court ruling on May 11, 1999, 99Du1809.

481) Supreme Court ruling on May 12, 1992, 91Nu13076.

(1) 긴박성의 정도

1) 정리해고의 요건으로 첫째 요건인 기업 경영상의 필요성이라는 것은 기업의 인원삭감조치가 영업 성적의 악화라는 기업의 경제적 이유뿐만 아니라, 생산성의 향상, 경쟁력의 회복 내지 증강에 대처하기 위한 작업형태의 변경, 신기술의 도입이라는 기술적인 이유와 그러한 기술혁신에 따라 생기는 산업의 구조적 변화도 이유로 하여 실제 이루어지고 있고 또한 그럴 필요성이 충분히 있다는 점에 비추어 보면 반드시 기업의 도산을 회피하기 위한 것에 한정할 필요는 없고, 인원삭감이 객관적으로 보아 합리성이 있다고 인정될 때는 긴박한 경영상의 필요성이 있는 것으로 넓게 보아주어야 함이 타당하다.[479)]

2) "긴박한 경영상의 필요성이라 함은 반드시 기업의 도산을 회피하기 위한 경우에 한정되지 아니하고 인원삭감이 객관적으로 보아 합리성이 있다고 인정될 경우에 포함되는 것으로 보아야 한다." 즉, 기업의 인원삭감조치가 영업 성적의 악화라는 기업의 경제적인 이유뿐만 아니라 생산성의 향상, 경쟁력의 회복 내지 증강에 대처하기 위한 작업형태의 변경, 신기술의 도입이라는 기술적인 이유와 그러한 기술혁신에 따라 생기는 산업의 구조적 변화를 이유로 하는 경우에도 인정된다.[480)]

(2) 경영상 필요성의 계속성

경영상 해고를 위한 "긴박한 경영상의 필요성"을 인정하기 위하여서는 적어도 기업이 일정 수 이상의 근로자를 감원하지 않으면 안 될 경영악화 또는 기업 재정상의 어려움이 계속적으로 누적되어 왔고 장래에도 쉽사리 해소되지 않을 개연성이 있어야 한다. 따라서 노동조합의 파업 등의 사유로 단순히 일시적으로 정상적인 경영이 어려웠다는 사정만으로는 "긴박한 경영상의 필요"가 있다고 할 수 없다.[481)]

---

479) 대법원 1991.12.10, 91다8647.
480) 대법원 1999.5.11, 99두1809.
481) 대법원 1992.5.12, 90누9421.

(3) Examination of necessity in relation to business

It is the basic inclination in judicial rulings that the matter of urgent necessity in relation to business shall not be estimated on the basis of business portions or a certain branch's business condition, but shall be estimated synthetically by evaluating the entire business.

1) Abolition of a related department due to cessation of production or reduced production[482)]

A company whose business is to produce aggregates and ready-mix has been in operation beside the Han river, but has to stop producing aggregates and reduce its business volume. Therefore, the company had to abolish certain workplaces and reduce business volume. This case was considered an urgent necessity in relation to business.

2) Abolition of one section due to managerial reasons and merger of all employees to other business[483)]

A school corporation, which was operating a hospital, abolished an Industrial Health Section and assigned the related jobs to its subsidiary Industrial Health Research Center. Then, the school dismissed all employees concerned in order to transfer them with similar working conditions to the Research Center. These actions were held as justifiable dismissals.

3) Reorganization designed for business improvement[484)]

In the course of being transferred to the private sector, a public company had to prepare for free market competition in the fertilizer industry, cope with decreasing competitiveness due to careless business practices, and streamline or revise the organization to resolve deficit issues. Therefore, the dismissals were justifiable.

4) Abolition of a few business parts which are chronically losing money while the total business is profitable[485)]

In view of the total business, the company recorded surpluses in business performance. However, some business parts were chronically losing money due to work inefficiency.

---

482) Supreme Court ruling on Jan. 12, 1990, 88DaKa34094.

483) Supreme Court ruling on Dec. 22, 1987, 87DaKa2011.

484) Supreme Court ruling on June 14, 1994, 93Da48823.

485) Administrative Court ruling on Nov. 7, 2000, 2000Gu11672.

(3) 경영상 필요성의 심사 대상

"긴박한 경영상의 필요성"이 있는지 여부는 일부 사업부분 또는 지점만의 경영사정을 기준으로 판단해서는 안 되며 사업 전체를 대상으로 종합적으로 판단해야 한다는 것이 판례의 기본적인 태도이다.

1) 생산의 중단, 축소로 인한 작업부서의 폐지[482)]

골재 생산, 레미콘 제조를 업으로 하는 기업이 한강 구역 내에서 골재 생산을 중단, 축소할 수밖에 없고 이에 따라 일정 공구 사업소를 폐지하여 사업규모가 대폭 축소된 경우에 경영상 해고를 위한 긴박한 경영상의 필요성 인정

2) 경영상 이유로 과를 폐지하고 법인 산하 타 사업장으로 흡수한 경우[483)]

병원을 경영하는 학교법인이 병원의 산업 보건과를 경영상의 이유로 폐지하고 그 업무를 산하의 산업보건연구소로 이관하면서 그 직원들을 근로조건이 비슷한 위 연구소로 이동시키기 위하여 해고 처분한 것이라면 정당한 이유가 있는 것으로 유효하다.

3) 경영 개선을 위한 기구 개편[484)]

경영상 해고가 기업이 민영화되는 과정에서 비료 가격 자유경쟁체제로 전환 및 비료산업구조의 변화에 대비하고, 종래의 방만한 경영에 따른 경쟁력 하락을 타개하기 위하여 적자요인을 해소하기 위해 기구를 효율적으로 축소, 개편해야 할 필요성에 의하여 이루어신 것이라면 정당

4) 전체가 흑자인 경영하에 만성적인 적자인 일부 사업 부문의 폐지[485)]

사업 전체의 경영사정을 종합하여 볼 때 전체 경영실적에서 흑자를 기록하고 있다 하더라도 일부 사업 부문의 비효율로 인하여 만성적인 적자를 기록하고 있고 그러한 만성적인 적자가 해당 사업 부문의 구조적인 문제에 기인한 것일 때는 해당 사업 부문을 폐지하는 것은 정당하다.

482) 대법원 1990.1.12, 88다카34094.
483) 대법원 1987.12.22, 87다카2011.
484) 대법원 1994.6.14, 93다48823.
485) 행정법원 2000.11.7, 2000구11672.

As such chronic deficit is due to an organizational problem, the dismissal of employees by the abolition of the corresponding business parts can be accepted as justifiable.

5) In cases where the company has abolished one business part since it has operated two business parts separately[486)]

An employer can abolish his business corporation and dismiss all employees, which, in principle, is the owner's managerial right. If the company owner closed his corporation in an attempt to disturb the labor union's activities, this can be considered an unfair labor practice. The employer operated his own business, but, due to a business reason, he separated his business into two business units, and divided their personnel, facilities, and accounting. However, although the two businesses have very different internal business operations, they cannot be deemed as different entities because the businesses are owned by the same person. In this case, if one business part is abolished, it can be interpreted as streamlining the business rather than abolishing one business. Therefore, the employer cannot dismiss all employees working in the abolished business unit.

6) Workforce reduction is allowed as a result of the decision to contract out a part of the business in order to resolve economic difficulty in that area of the business.

A company, after suffering a 4-year long deficit in a particular business department, decided to contract out the department in an effort to resolve the deficit issues and, as a consequence, dismissed the employees working in the department. In this case, it is acknowledged that such employee dismissal was done for an urgent managerial reason.[487)]

2. Efforts to avoid dismissal

An employer has made efforts to avoid dismissal by taking all kinds of managerial measures to cope with business difficulties facing the company. However, if he/she cannot overcome his business difficulties through these efforts, and if he/she cannot expect any other measures except for dismissal, dismissal for managerial reasons can be accepted as a last resort.

---

486) Supreme Court ruling on May 12, 1992, 90Nu9421.

487) Supreme Court ruling on Dec. 22, 1995, 94Da52119.

5) 경영진의 사정으로 분할하여 운영하던 사업 중 하나를 폐지한 경우[486)]

사용자가 그 경영의 사업체 전부를 폐업하고 이에 따라 그 소속 근로자 전원을 해고하는 것은 원칙적으로 기업 경영의 자유에 속하는 것으로서 노동조합의 단결권 등을 방해하기 위한 위장 폐업이라는 등의 특별한 사정이 없는 한 부당노동행위가 된다고 할 수는 없겠지만 어떤 기업이 하나의 영업 허가를 가지고 동 종의 사업을 경영하면서 그 경영진의 사정 때문에 그 사업을 2개 이상의 단위로 분할하여 그 인적, 물적 설비를 서로 독립시키고 회계를 서로 분리하여 경영하여 왔다 하더라도 그 경영주체가 동일한 인격체라면 그 회사 내부의 분리경영이라는 사정이 있다 하여 이를 별개의 사업체로 볼 수는 없는 것이며, 이러한 경우 여러 개의 사업 단위 중 하나의 사업단위를 폐지하기로 하였다 하더라도 이는 사업 축소에 해당 될 뿐 사업 전체의 폐지라고 할 수는 없는 것이어서 그 사업체가 폐업되었음을 전제로 하여 그 단위 사업에 속한 전체 근로자를 해고할 수는 없다고 본다.

6) 경영난을 해소하기 위하여 해당 사업부문을 외부 하도급제로 운영하기로 함에 따라 잉여인력을 감축하는 것은 가능하다.

4년 가까이 계속된 적자 등으로 인한 경영난을 해소하기 위하여 해당 사업부문을 외부 하도급제로 운영하기로 함에 따라 잉여인력을 감축한 경우, 긴박한 경영상의 필요성을 인정한다.[487)]

2. 해고의 회피를 위한 노력

기업이 당면한 경영상의 어려움을 타개하기 위하여 실현 가능한 경영상의 모든 조치를 강구하는 등 "해고 회피노력"을 기울였으나 그러한 노력만으로는 경영상의 곤란을 극복할 수 없었거나, 해고 이외의 다른 경영상의 조치를 취하는 것이 기대하기 곤란한 사정이 있어 부득이 최후의 수단으로써 경영상 해고를 할 수밖에 없음이 인정되어야 한다.

---

486) 대법원 1992.5.12, 90누9421호.
487) 대법원 1995.12.22, 94다52119.

(1) Concrete methods to avoid dismissal

① Improvement of business policies or a change of managers, or business rationalization through scientific and rational management of production methods
② Reduction of office size and integration of the organization
③ Transfer of personnel
④ Reduction of outsourced personnel(subcontract, temporary, or dispatched employees)
⑤ Cessation of new hiring and discontinuance of renewal of short term contracts
⑥ Reduction of production, cessation of holiday/overtime work, use of unused leave(annual and monthly leave) and applying selective working hours
⑦ Reduction of directors' wages, abolition of bonuses or special allowances exceeding the collective agreement's standards, and other cost-saving measures
⑧ Temporary suspension(closing, employees stay at home)
⑨ Promotion of early retirement or voluntary application for retirement

(2) Judicial rulings about efforts to avoid dismissal

1) In case where there are no other methods except dismissal[488)]

A company abolished its Business Unit 1 due to urgent necessity in relation to business and is about to dismiss all employees. Business Unit 1 and Business Unit 2 have not had any business relations in the sharing of history, operating management, and/or exchanging employees, and each business unit has maintained its own independence. In this case, the company has no obligation to avoid dismissal by transferring or dispatching the employees belonging to Business Unit 1.

2) In cases where there is no effort to avoid dismissal, such as transferring employees to another plant or temporarily closing, etc.[489)]

A company closed a plant in a certain area due to chronic deficit and did not transfer employees to other plants. The company did not take efforts to avoid dismissal, such as temporary suspension, etc. Therefore, it can be admitted that the company did not complete efforts to avoid dismissal.

---

488) Supreme Court ruling on May 12, 1992, 90Nu9421.

489) National Labor Relations Commission 92Buhae341.

(1) 해고 회피노력의 구체적인 방안

① 경영방침의 개선이나 경영진의 교체 및 작업 방식의 과학화, 합리화 등을 통한 경영 합리화 방안
② 사무실 규모의 축소 및 기구 통폐합
③ 전직(배치전환) 등의 노력 이동 방법
④ 외부인력(하도급, 임시직, 파견 근로자) 사용 축소
⑤ 신규 채용(중도 채용 포함)의 중단, 유기계약자(계약직 근로자) 계약 갱신 중단
⑥ 단축 조업, 휴일·시간 외 근로의 중단, 휴가(연월차휴가 등) 소진 등 근로의 분산에 의한 시간적 조치
⑦ 임원수당의 삭감, 상여금이나 단체협약 수준 이상의 특별 수당의 지급 폐지와 같은 제 경비의 발령
⑧ 퇴직 장려 및 희망(명예) 퇴직자의 모집

(2) 해고 회피 노력에 관한 판례

1) 사실상 해고조치 이외에 마땅한 방법이 없는 경우[488)]

긴박한 경영상의 필요에 따라 제1 사업부를 폐지하면서 근로자를 정리해고 함에 있어서 만약 제1사업부와 제2 사업부가 연혁적인 면에서나 실제 운영상 경영진은 물론 그 근로자들에 대하여도 완전히 인적, 물적 설비가 분리되어 있고 서로 교류가 없어서 그 소속 근로자도 다른 사업부와는 전혀 관계가 없는 독립 단위라고 인식하는 상태에서 근무하여 왔다면, 전근이나 전보 등의 방법에 의하여 제1사업부 소속 근로자에 대한 해고를 회피할 조치를 취하여야 한다고 할 수 없다.

2) 타 공장 전보나 일시 휴직 등의 해고회피 노력을 하지 않은 경우[489)]

사업의 만성적인 적자로 ㅇㅇ지역의 공장을 폐쇄하면서 재심 신청인을 본사나 다른 지역의 공장으로 전보시키지 아니한 점이나, 달리 일시 휴직 등 해고회피노력을 찾아볼 수 없으므로 해고 회피를 위한 노력을 다하지 않은 점을 인정한다.

488) 대법원 1992.5.12, 90누9421.
489) 중노위 92부해341호.

3) In cases where there are no efforts to promote voluntary retirement, streamline the working process, etc.[490)]

When a company was expected to reduce personnel in the winter season, it did not promote voluntary retirement, but rather hired new employees. The company also did not make efforts to establish concrete plans to promote the efficiency of production and to prepare for the time to reduce personnel. Therefore, it cannot be held that the company did its best to avoid dismissal.

4) Exceptions for efforts to avoid dismissal[491)]

A company whose business is to produce, sell, and export clothing has three plants: Plant A, Plant B, and Plant C. Plant A produces high-quality female clothing, Plant B produces clothing for export, and Plant C produces low-quality products like socks for their major products. Plant A requires very high quality machinery and skilled workers and pays higher wages than Plant B, which produces a great amount of clothing for export in a mass-production line. Plant C requires simple skills from its workers and pays less than Plant B. Therefore, each plant operation is too different to exchange employees. When the company decided to close Plant B due to urgent necessity in relation to business and dismissed all employees without transferring its employees to Plant A and Plant C, it can be accepted that the company made efforts to avoid dismissal.

3. Fair and unfair criteria for the selection of those persons subject to dismissal

Criteria for the selection of those persons subject to dismissal are normally described in the collective agreement or rules of employment and can be admitted as long as they are unbiased and generally accepted in society. However, if not specified, an employer can set reasonable and fair principles and select those persons subject to dismissal.

If an employer selects one of the three criteria - age, service period, and service record - without considering other conditions such as employees' dependents, property, health, etc., that criteria cannot be validated as rational or fair.[492)]

---

490) National Labor Relations Commission 94Buhae317.

491) Supreme Court ruling on Dec. 22, 1992, 92Da14779.

492) Seoul District Court ruling on Feb. 11, 2000, 99Gahap55101.

3) 희망퇴직자의 모집, 작업 방식의 합리화 등의 노력이 없었던 경우[490)]

동절기 인원감축이 예상된 상황에서 희망퇴직자를 모집한 사실이 없고 오히려 신규 채용한 바 있으며, 작업 방식의 합리화를 위한 구체적인 계획을 수립하여 인원감축에 대비한 노력이 보이지 않는 등으로 보아 해고회피를 위한 최선의 노력을 다하였다고 볼 수 없다.

4) 해고 회피 노력에 대한 예외 사례[491)]

섬유류 제조, 판매 및 수출 사업을 하는 회사가 그 산하에 (갑), (을), (병)의 3개 공장을 두고, (갑)공장에서는 국내 여성용 고급 의류를, (을)공장에서는 수출용 의류를, (병)공장에서는 양말류를 주로 제조하고 있는데, 이 중 (갑)공장은 고급 여성 의류를 생산하므로 기술과 숙련이 필요하며 라인 작업에 따라 수출용 의류를 다량 제조하는 (을)공장에 비하여 고임금이 지급되었고, (병)공장은 단순 노동에 속하는 작업이어서 (을)공장보다 저임금이 지급되는 등 근로자들의 교류가 행하여지기 어려운 사정이 있다면, 긴박한 경영상의 필요에 따라 (을)공장을 폐업, 그 소속 근로자들을 전부 해고하면서 (갑)이나 (병)공장에 전근시키지 않은 것만으로는 해고 회피 조치를 다하지 않았다고 볼 수 없다.

3. 해고대상자 선정의 공정성

해고대상자 선정기준이 단체협약·취업규칙 등에 정해져 있으면 사회통념상 합리성이 인정되는 한 그 기준에 따르면 되고, 정해져 있지 않다면 해고시점에서 사용자가 합리적이고 공정한 원칙을 정하여 이에 따라 해고대상자를 선정하면 될 것이다.

근로자의 부양의무 유무, 재산, 건강상태 등 각자의 주관적인 사정을 고려함이 없이 연령, 재직기간, 근무성적 등 3가지 기준 중 어느 하나에만 해당하면 다른 기준을 고려함이 없이 감축대상자로 선정한 것은 합리적이고 공정하다 할 수 없다.[492)]

---

490) 중노위 94부해317호.

491) 대법원 1992.12.22, 92다14779.

492) 서울지방법원 2000.2.11, 99가합55101.

▶ **Concrete examples of considerations**

① Protection of employee and employee's family: Employee's age, length of service, number of dependents, income of the spouse, property, etc.
② Benefit to the company: employee's work performance, job skills, experience, craftsmanship, prizes or penalties, etc.
③ Status within, or degree of loyalty to, the company: Daily worker, part-timer, temporary worker, etc.

(1) Fair criteria for selecting those subject to dismissal

1) When an employer selects those subject to dismissal based on age, service years, number of dependents, faithfulness in attendance, rewards and punishments, certificates of qualification, etc., this selection is reasonable and fair criteria for dismissal because objectively measurable methods and distinguishable criteria were applied after considering subjective situations for each employee and the company synthetically.[493)]

2) Concerning the criteria and method used to select those subject to dismissal for managerial reasons, the employer shall not consider only one factor, like employee job skills, but also consider employee living conditions, equity between employees, etc. The criteria and methods to be used are mostly at the employer's discretion, but the criteria and methods of selection decided upon by mutual agreement between the employer and the employee representative are considered reasonable, unless they are extremely subjective or unjustifiable.[494)]

3) In cases where dismissal of employees for managerial reasons must be done, it is desirable that the employer shall not only select those employees working in a division that will be abolished, but also select those subject to dismissal from throughout the company, as employees are transferable in personnel management.[495)]

4) If an employer excludes some employees in production from those subject to dismissal for managerial reasons, it shall be accepted as reasonable if they are skilled craftsmen and possess essential certificates of qualification to operate production lines.[496)]

5) Even though the only employees dismissed for managerial reasons were labor union

---

493) Administrative Court ruling on Nov. 22, 2005, 2005Guhap15694.

494) Administrative Court ruling on Apr. 28, 2006, 2005Guhap5086.

495) MOEL Guidelines: Kungi 68207-1905.

496) Supreme Court ruling on June 14, 2002, 2000Du8486.

▶ 구체적 사례

① 근로자의 생활보호 측면(근로자의 연령, 근속기간, 부양가족 수, 배우자의 소득, 재산상태 등)

② 기업의 이익 측면(평소근무성적, 근로능력, 경험, 숙련도, 상벌 등)

③ 기타 기업에의 귀속성의 정도(일용, 아르바이트, 임시직 등)

(1) 정당한 대상자 선정 기준

1) 회사가 근로자의 연령, 근속연수, 부양 가족 수, 근로자의 근태, 상벌, 자격증 소지 여부 등을 기준으로 정리해고 대상자를 선정한 것은 근로자의 주관적인 사정과 회사 측 사정을 종합적으로 고려하여 객관적으로 계량화와 판별이 가능한 기준에 따라 합리적이고 공정한 기준에 따른 것이라 할 것이다.[493)]

2) 정리해고 대상자의 선정기준 및 방법에 대하여는 근로자의 업무능력만을 기준으로 하여야 하는 것은 아니고 근로자의 생활사정, 근로자 사이의 공평성 등을 기준으로 하는 것도 가능하며, 사용자에게 상당한 재량이 있고 특히 근로자대표의 동의를 얻어 결정된 선정기준 및 방법은 지나치게 자의적이거나 불합리한 것이 아닌 한 합리성을 부인할 수 없다 할 것이다.[494)]

3) 경영상 해고 시 폐지되는 사업에 근무하던 근로자만을 해고의 대상으로 할 것이 아니라 인사교류가 가능한 전 근로자를 대상으로 하는 것이 바람직하다.[495)]

4) 생산직 근로자들 중 일부를 정리해고 대상에서 제외시켰다고 하더라도 참가인 회사의 생산 작업을 위하여 반드시 필요한 자격증을 소지한 자이거나 숙련 기능공이었다면, 해고대상자 선정에서도 합리적인 것으로 보아야 한다.[496)]

5) 정리해고가 조합원들만을 대상으로 삼았다 하더라도 사전에 노조와의 협

493) 행정법원 2005.11.22, 2005구합15694.

494) 행정법원 2006.4.28, 2005구합5086.

495) 행정해석: 근기 68207-1905, 1998.8.10.

496) 내법원 2002.6.14, 2000누8486.

members, this is justifiable if the employer consulted with the labor union in advance and dismissed them according to objective and fair criteria.[497)]

(2) Unfair criteria for selecting those subject to dismissal

1) Criteria that only considers company circumstances

1) In the selection of those subject to dismissal, if the employer considers educational background as the sole criteria for dismissal, proposes voluntary resignation only to those with lower educational levels, and dismisses the employees concerned without making any effort to avoid dismissal, these dismissals would be unfair because they were not done according to the required procedures.[498)]

2) When dismissing temporary employees for managerial reasons, a local government made no effort to avoid dismissal and dismissed temporary employees according to age, from the oldest, without determining reasonable and fair criteria for dismissal. The local government also implemented the dismissals unilaterally, without consulting with the employee representative, so these dismissals were unfair, and an abuse of the right to manage personnel.[499)]

3) An employer selected employees subject to dismissal for managerial reasons on the basis of age as unilateral and subjective criteria. If the employer did not consider the degree of disadvantage for the employees concerned, the necessity of social protection, contribution made, or employee attitudes during their service period, etc., this dismissal cannot be seen as having reasonable and fair criteria.[500)]

4) It is difficult to accept as fair dismissal for managerial reasons an employer's selection of those subject to dismissal only on the basis of disciplinary punishment received by certain employees. Even though such criteria are accepted as reasonable, most disciplinary punishment of the employees concerned cannot be accepted as justifiable reason for dismissal in view of their procedures, timing, and purpose.[501)]

5) In one case, a company unilaterally decided that length of employment would be the main criteria in choosing employees to dismiss for managerial reasons. In other words, those who

---

497) Seoul Appellate Court ruling on Nov. 20, 2000Nu6963.

498) National Labor Relations Commission 2004Buhae78 on July 28.

499) National Labor Relations Commission 2001Buhae192 on June 12.

500) Administrative Court ruling on Dec. 11, 2001, 2001Gu26794.

501) Seoul Appellate Court ruling on July 3, 2003, 2002Nu11860.

의를 거쳐 객관적이고 합리적인 기준에 의해 행해졌다면 정당하다.[497)]

(2) 정당하지 못한 대상자 선정 기준

1) 회사 측 사정만을 고려한 기준

1) 해고대상자 선정에 있어서도 학력을 기준으로만 선정하여 이 기준에 미달되는 재심신청인 등을 오직 희망퇴직만을 권유하였을 뿐 다른 해고 회피노력은 다하지 아니하고 정리해고 한 것은 절차상 하자로 인한 부당해고에 해당한다.[498)]

2) 지방자치단체가 일용직 근로자를 정리해고 함에 있어서 해고회피 노력을 하지 아니하고, 합리적이고 공정한 해고의 기준을 정함이 없이 '고령자순'으로 해고대상자를 선정하여 근로자대표와의 사전 협의 등이 없이 일방적으로 해고처분한 것은 인사권의 남용으로서 부당해고에 해당한다.[499)]

3) 이 사건에서 원고가 연령이라는 일방적이고 획일적인 기준에 의하여 참가인들을 정리해고 대상자로 선정한 것은 참가인들에게 미치는 불이익의 정도나 사회적 보호의 필요성, 근무기간 동안의 기여도나 근무태도 등을 전혀 감안하지 아니한 것으로서 공정하고 합리적인 해고기준을 적용하였다고 볼 수 없다.[500)]

4) 참가인 회사가 징계전력만을 기준으로 하여 정리해고 대상자를 선정한 조치의 합리성은 이를 선뜻 인정하기 어렵고, 설사 그러한 기준의 합리성을 어렵사리 인정한다 하더라도 원고들에 대한 징계처분들 중 상당수는 그 절차 내지 시기 및 목적 등의 면에서 그 공정성이 의심스럽다.[501)]

5) 장기간 조직을 위하여 성실하게 근무한 직원이 단지 장기 근속자라는 이유만으로 연령을 불문하고 우선적으로 정리해고 대상자로 선정될 수 있도록 하

---

497) 서울고등법원 2001.11.29, 2000누6963.
498) 중앙노동위원회 2004.7.8, 2004부해78.
499) 중앙노동위원회 2001.6.12, 2001부해192.
500) 행정법원 2001.12.11, 2001구26794.
501) 서울고등법원 2003.7.3, 2002누11860.

had served the company longer, although they had contributed more than other workers to the company, were still more likely to be dismissed for managerial reasons. Other things, like work attitude, were also considered, but they were not weighted as heavily against an employee in determining dismissal as length of employment. Therefore, this selection cannot be accepted as reasonable and fair.[502)]

6) If the employer did not engage in prior consultations with the employee representative regarding criteria for dismissal for managerial reasons and the possible methods for avoiding dismissal, dismissal for managerial reasons is illegal since correct procedures were not followed in choosing objective and socially justifiable rationale.[503)]

2) Criteria deficient in reasonableness and fairness

1) In cases where the employer selected as subject to dismissal for managerial reasons those employees who did not agree to transfer and also did not agree to voluntarily resign, this selection cannot be justifiable based upon reasonable criteria.[504)]

An employer notified one of his employees several times of the intention to dismiss him for managerial reasons because of his constant refusal to transfer to another department. After consulting with the labor union, the employer dismissed the employee for managerial reasons, particularly because he did not agree on a transfer and also did not respond to suggestions to voluntarily resign. This selection for dismissal cannot be accepted as being done according to objective and reasonable criteria. Even though the employer consulted with the labor union, this selection for dismissal violated the principles of the Labor Standards Act and cannot be accepted.

2) Even though requirements for dismissal for managerial reasons were satisfied, choosing those to be dismissed for managerial reasons by vote cannot be admitted as justifiable.[505)]

An employer selected those employees subject to dismissal only by means of a vote by committee members, without any objective evaluation materials or evaluation criteria. This dismissal for managerial reasons could be affected by individual relationships more than by company criteria, so there is a great possibility for unfair results.

3) An employer dismissed an employee who refused to accept an honorary resignation

502) Administrative Court ruling on July 7, 2000, 99Gu34600.

503) Seoul Appellate Court ruling on Dec. 2, 1999, 99Nu4930.

504) Administrative Court ruling on Nov. 27, 2007, 2007Guhap16103.

505) Administrative Court ruling on June 16, 2000, 99Gu30967.

고, 그 반영비율 역시 근무태도의 비중보다 높게 책정한 것은 합리성과 공정성을 갖추고 있다고 보기 어렵다.[502)]

6) 근로자대표와 사이에 정리해고 대상자 선정기준 및 해고회피와 관련하여 아무런 사전협의절차를 거치지도 아니한 이상 정리해고는 객관적 합리성과 사회적 정당성을 갖추지 못한 위법한 것이다.[503)]

2) 합리성과 공정성을 상실한 기준

1) 전출에 동의하지 아니하고, 희망퇴직에도 응하지 않았다 하여 정리해고 대상자로 선정한 것은 합리적인 기준에 의한 해고대상자 선정이라 할 수 없다.[504)]

참가인은 원고에 대하여 종전부터 전출에 동의하지 아니한다는 이유로 수차례 정리 해고할 것임을 통지하다가 노동조합과의 협의로 원고가 전출에 동의하지 아니하고, 희망퇴직에도 응하지 아니하였다는 사정을 들어 원고를 특정하여 정리해고 대상자로 선정한 것은 도저히 객관적이고 합리적인 기준에 의하여 해고대상자를 선정한 것이라고 할 수 없고, 비록 이것이 노동조합과의 협의를 거친 것이라고 하더라도 이와 같은 해고대상자 선정은 위 근로기준법의 취지를 도외시하는 것으로서 용납될 수 없다.

2) 정리해고의 요건이 충족되었다 하더라도 해고 대상자를 투표로 선정하는 것은 정리해고의 정당성을 인정받을 수 없다.[505)]

이무런 객관적인 평가자료나 평가기준 없이 단순히 위원들의 투표만으로 그들을 정리해고 대상으로 선정한 것은 정리해고가 그 대상자에게 미치는 불이익 정도와 정리해고 실시 목적에서 기업의 입장보다 개인적인 친소관계가 영향을 미치므로 그 결과가 왜곡될 가능성이 크다.

3) 인건비 절감의 효과가 거의 없는 명예퇴직 권유를 받아들이지 않자 해고

---

502) 행정법원 2000.7.7, 99구34600.
503) 서울고등법원 1999.12.2, 99누4930.
504) 행정법원 2007.11.27, 2007구합16103.
505) 행정법원 2000.6.16, 99구30967.

recommended by the employer, even though his dismissal wouldn't have any effect in reducing labor costs. This cannot be accepted as a socially fair and objective dismissal for managerial reasons.[506)]

As one method to avoid dismissal, the employer proposed honorary resignation and a position transfer to short-term contract employment to an employee who was going to retire from the company in 9 months. As the employer would not be able to reduce his labor costs by dismissing this employee, this dismissal, because the employee would not voluntarily resign, cannot be accepted as fair or objective.

4) Even though collective bargaining has stipulated the order of and method by which employees are subject to dismissal, if the employer selects the employees subject to dismissal simply at his own discretion, this selection is not made in a justifiable way but is a violation of reasonable and fair criteria.[507)]

5) In cases where some workplaces of a business are closed but others in the same business are still in operation, it is not possible to dismiss all the employees of the closed workplaces by citing an urgent managerial reason as the reason for dismissal.

When there are some workplaces in operation, although others are closed, this constitutes a business curtailment, not a complete closure. Therefore, the employer may not dismiss all employees only at the closed workplaces just because the workplaces are closed.[508)]

4. Sincere consultations with the employee representative

When an employer tries to consult with the employee representative in good faith but cannot reach an agreement, the dismissal of the employee according to the employer's own criteria is not invalid; provided, however, that the criteria shall be reasonable and fair as a precondition.

In some cases, the collective agreement provides that the employer should reach agreement with the union on any dismissal for managerial reasons. If this is the case and if the union keeps resisting the proposed layoff without giving a justifiable reason for such resistance, any layoff that the employer carries out without agreement by the union is legally effective. There was a case where an urgent managerial reason required a massive layoff and the employer had

506) Seoul Appellate Court ruling on July 16, 1998, 97Gu47660.

507) Seoul Appellate Court ruling on Dec. 12, 2003Nu4838.

508) Supreme Court ruling on Jan. 26, 1993, 92Nu3076.

한 것은 정리해고로서 객관적 합리성과 사회적 상당성을 지닌 것으로 볼 수 없다.[506)]

정년을 불과 9개월 정도 앞두고 있던 참가인에 대하여는 해고회피노력의 일환으로 명예퇴직과 계약직 사원으로의 근무를 권유하였는데, 그 경우 원고 회사가 얻을 수 있는 인건비 절감의 효과는 거의 없는 점 등에 비추어 볼 때, 참가인이 원고 회사의 명예퇴직 권유를 받아들이지 않자 참가인을 해고한 것은 정리해고로서 객관적 합리성과 사회적 상당성을 지닌 것으로 볼 수 없다.

4) 단체협약상 정리해고 대상 근로자의 순위가 규정되어 있음에도 근로자 전체를 정리해고 대상자로 선정한 것은 합리적이고 공정한 기준에 따른 것이라고 할 수 없다.[507)]

5) 일부 사업장을 폐쇄하였을지라도 다른 사업장에서 사업을 계속하고 있는 경우에는 폐쇄된 사업장의 "모든 근로자"를 정리해고 할 수 없다.

일부 사업장을 폐쇄하였다고 하더라도 다른 사업장에서 사업을 계속하고 있는 이상 사업을 축소한 것에 지나지 아니할 뿐 사업 전체를 폐지한 것이라고 할 수는 없으므로, 그 사업장의 폐쇄만을 이유로 그 사업장에 종사하는 모든 근로자를 다 해고할 수 있는 것은 아니다.[508)]

4. 근로자대표와의 성실한 사전 협의

성실하게 협의하였으나 합의에 이르지 못한 경우에는 사용자가 일방적으로 정한 정리해고 기준에 따라 해고하여도 이를 무효라 할 수 없다. 다만 이 때 사용자가 일방적으로 정한 정리해고 기준이 합리적이고 공정하다는 것이 전제가 되어야 할 것이다.

정리해고를 할 경우에 노동조합의 합의가 있어야 한다는 단체협약이 체결되어 있는 회사에서 노동조합 측이 합리적 근거나 이유 없이 무작정 정리해고를

506) 서울고등법원 1998.7.16, 97구47660.
507) 서울고등법원 2003.12.12, 2003누4838.
508) 대법원 1993.1.26, 92누3076.

good-faith consultations with the union in advance and did his best to minimize dismissals. Given this, it seems that the union, which refused to agree to the planned layoffs without giving a justifiable reason for such refusal, abused its right to refuse, which states that the collective agreement requires a bilateral accord on dismissal for managerial reasons. As the employer failed to reach agreement with the union because of a reason attributable to the union, the layoffs were effective.[509)]

▶ **Concrete examples**

① An employer shall inform the employee representative on the methods for avoiding dismissals and the criteria for dismissal 50 days prior to the date of dismissal. ② An employer shall consult in good faith.

※ Employee representative: Where there is an organized labor union representing more than half of the workers at a business or business location, the labor union becomes the employee representative; however, where there is no such organized labor union, the employee representative shall refer to a person who represents more than half of the workers.

(1) Unit selected for employee representation

The employee representative shall be selected from a unit of a business or workplace. However, in cases where target employees are defined by particular occupations or positions, the employee representative shall be one who represents these targeted employees. Accordingly, if these particular targeted employees are not entitled to union membership, it would be pointless to consult with the labor union concerning the managerial reduction of these targeted employees. In a hospital where the employer intends to reduce employees of 4th rank or higher, consulting with the labor union as an employee representative of 5th rank and lower would be unacceptable as the employer has not consulted in good faith with an appropriate employee representative.[510)]

(2) Method of employee representative selection

1) Where there is an organized labor union representing more than half the employees

Whether the labor union represents more than half the employees shall be estimated in the unit of the business where the employer wants to select an employee representative

509) Administrative Court ruling on Mar. 7, 2000, 99Gu20694.

510) Seoul Appellate Court ruling on Mar. 25, 2005, 2004Nu4613.

반대하는 경우, 합의가 없이 행한 정리해고는 유효하다. 즉, 단체협약에 합의 조항을 두고 있는 경우라 하더라도 정리해고를 해야 할 긴박한 상황이 존재하여 노동조합과 사전협의를 하고 진지한 노력을 다했음에도 불구하고 노동조합 측이 수십 차례 집회를 여는 등 합리적 근거나 이유를 제시함이 없이 무작정 정리해고를 반대함으로써 사전합의를 하지 못한 경우라면, 이는 노동조합 측이 합의거부권을 남용한 것이라 할 것이므로 노동조합 측과 합의가 없었다고 하더라도 정리해고는 유효하다.[509)]

▶ 구체적 사례

① 근로자대표에게 해고회피 방안 및 해고기준 등에 관하여 해고일 50일전까지 통보하고, ② 이에 관하여 성실하게 협의

※ 근로자대표: 근로자의 과반수로 조직된 노동조합이 있으면 그 노동조합을 말하며, 그러한 노동조합이 없으면 근로자의 과반수를 대표하는 자를 말함.

(1) 근로자대표의 선정단위

근로자대표는 당해 사업 또는 사업장 단위로 선정되어야 한다. 그러나 대상이 특정한 직종 또는 직급으로 한정되는 경우 그 대상자를 대표하는 자와의 협의가 필요하다. 따라서 그 특정 부문이 당초 노동조합에 가입할 수 없는 경우라면 감원에 관한 노동조합과의 협의는 무의미하다. 병원에서 4급 이상 직원을 감원함에 있어 5급 이하 직원들로 구성된 노동조합(근로자대표)을 상대로 협의한 것은 성실한 협의의무를 다했다고 보기 어렵다.[510)]

(2) 근로자대표 선정방법

1) 근로자 과반수로 조직된 노동조합이 있는 경우

노동조합이 근로자의 과반수를 조직하고 있는지 여부는 사업단위로 도입하는 경우는 사업단위에서, 사업장단위로 도입하는 경우는 사업장단위에서 판단

509) 행정법원 2000.3.17, 99구20694.

510) 서울고등법원 2005.3.25, 2004누4613.

and shall be estimated in a unit of the workplace for the unit of the workplace. If the labor union represents more than half the employees, it is taken for granted that the labor union becomes the representative of the employees or the person(e.g. chairman of the union branch) who has been authorized to represent the labor union.

2) Where there is no organized labor union representing more than half the employees

For dismissals for managerial reasons, the employee representative for the purpose of consulting with the employer shall be selected by independent and voluntary decision-making by the employees, after they are informed of the reason for choosing employee representation. It is also acceptable to choose the employee representative through employee congregation or individual signatures on circulating representative lists. If an employer asks the employees to choose an employee representative, the employees autonomously determine procedures and methods of selection without intervention by the employer, and select someone(even though some employees could not participate) that represents more than half of the employees, the person shall be regarded as the employee representative.[511)]

(3) Invalid employee representatives

Agreement from or consultation with an employee who does not justifiably represent the employees is not legally valid.

1) Even though an employer had explained the deterioration of business to team leaders in manager-level plenary meetings and asked them for their opinions in selection of target employees for managerial dismissal, this is not company consultations with an acceptable employee representative.[512)]

2) Because the company did not comply with substantial conditions in the course of managerial dismissal and, furthermore, consulted with an arbitrary organization and not an employee representative, this dismissal for managerial reasons is unfair.[513)]

---

511) MOEL Guidelines 68207-1472, on Nov. 13, 2003.

512) Administrative Court ruling on Sept. 7, 2007, 2006Guhap25285.

513) Seoul Appellate Court ruling on June 20, 2003, 2002Nu14739.

해야 한다. 노동조합이 근로자 과반수를 조직하고 있으면 근로자대표는 당연히 노동조합의 대표자 또는 노동조합으로부터 대표권을 위임 받은 자(예, 노동조합 지부장)가 된다.

2) 노동조합이 근로자 과반수를 조직하지 못하고 있는 경우

경영상의 이유에 의한 해고 문제에 대하여 "사용자와 협의를 할 근로자의 대표자를 선출한다는 것을 근로자들에게 주지시킨 상태에서 근로자들의 자유로운 의사결정이 보장되는 적당한 방법이면 될 것으로 사료되는 바, 근로자들의 집회를 통한 선출이나 회람을 통한 서명 등의 방법도 무방할 것이다. 사용자가 근로자대표의 선출을 요청하고 그에 따라 근로자들이 사용자의 개입이 배제된 상태에서 자율적으로 근로자대표 선출을 위한 절차나 방법을 결정하고 근로자대표를 선출하였다면 그 과정에서 일부 근로자들이 참여하지 못하였다 하더라도 선출된 자가 근로자의 과반수에 대한 대표성을 가지고 있다면 근로자대표가 된다."[511]

(3) 근로자대표로서 인정받지 못한 사례

근로자대표로서 대표성이 없는 자와의 승인 또는 협의는 법적인 효력을 가질 수 없다.

1) 팀장 및 간부급 전체회의에서 회사의 경영난을 알리고 감축대상자의 선정 등에 관한 간부직원들의 의견을 구하였다하여 근로자대표와 성실하게 협의하였다고 보기 어렵다.[512]

2) 정리해고 시 실질적 요건도 갖추지 못하고 근로자대표가 아닌 임의조직과 협의를 거쳐 이루어진 정리해고는 부당하다.[513]

511) 행정해석: 근기 68207-1472, 2003.11.13.
512) 행정법원 2007.9.7, 2006구합25285.
513) 행정법원 1999.12.24, 99구12679.

Ⅲ. Implementation of Dismissal for Managerial Reasons

Article 24 of the LSA. Restrictions on Dismissal for Business Reasons

④ When an employer intends to dismiss workers under the provisions of paragraph ① exceeding the fixed limit prescribed by Presidential Decree, he/she shall report to the Minister of Employment and Labor pursuant to the relevant provision of the Presidential Decree.

Enforcement Decree Article10-2. Report of Dismissal Plan for Managerial Reasons

① An employer shall report to the Minister of Employment and Labor 30 days before he/she desires to dismiss for the first time, if he/she intends to dismiss the number of workers as prescribed in paragraph 4 of Article 24, which is referred to in the following subparagraphs:

1. A business or workplace which ordinarily employs fewer than 99 workers: 10 or more;
2. A business or workplace which ordinarily employs more than 100, but not exceeding 999: 10 percent or more of workers ordinarily employed; and
3. A business or a workplace which ordinarily employs more than 1,000 workers: 100 or more.

② The report as prescribed in paragraph (1) shall include the following matters:

1. Reason for dismissal;
2. Number of workers to be dismissed;
3. Items consulted on with the labor representative; and
4. Dismissal schedule.

An employer shall inform individual employees 30 days prior to dismissal or pay allowance for non-advance notice(ordinary wages for 30 days) even in the event of dismissal for managerial reasons. As a procedural condition, the employer shall report to the Minister of Employment and Labor if dismissing more than a certain number of employees. Whether the Minister of Employment and Labor is notified or not does not undermine the effect. That is, reporting to the Minister is not a requisite to justify a dismissal for managerial reasons, but a requisite for processing.

The Labor Standards Act regulates that during times of managerial dismissal, An employer intending to dismiss more than 10% or more of the total number of workers in any given month shall report to the Minister of Employment and Labor, 30 days prior to first dismissal, the dismissal plan stipulating ① reasons for dismissal; ② number of workers to be dismissed; ③ details of consultations with a representative of workers; and ④ dismissal schedule(Article 24(paragraph 4) of the LSA). However, this clause does not include any necessary conditions or procedures to satisfy the need for justification of managerial dismissal, nor does it include penal provisions. It therefore leaves in question whether the company has to observe this clause or not.

Provided, Article 33(Report of Large Changes in Employment) of the Basic Employment Policy Act regulates that if changes in the volume of employment due to the automation,

Ⅲ. 경영상 이유에 의한 해고 실시

근로기준법 제24조

④ 사용자는 제1항의 규정에 의하여 대통령령이 정하는 일정 규모 이상의 인원을 해고하고자 할 때는 대통령령이 정하는 바에 따라 고용노동부 장관에게 신고를 하여야 한다.

시행령 제10조의2【경영상의 이유에 의한 해고계획의 신고】

① 법 제24조 제4항의 규정에 의하여 사용자는 1월 동안에 다음 각호의 1에 해당하는 인원을 해고하고자 하는 경우에는 최초로 해고하고자 하는 날의 30일전까지 고용노동부 장관에게 신고하여야 한다.(1998.2.24 신설)

1. 상시근로자 수가 99인 이하인 사업 또는 사업장: 10인 이상
2. 상시근로자 수가 100인 이상 999인 이하인 사업 또는 사업장:상시근로자 수의 10% 이상
3. 상시근로자 수가 1000인 이상 사업 또는 사업장: 100인 이상

② 제1항의 규정에 의한 신고에는 다음 각 호의 사항이 포함되어야 한다.

1. 해고의 사유,
2. 해고예정인원,
3. 근로자대표와의 협의내용,
4. 해고의 일정

경영상 이유에 의한 해고를 실시할 경우에도 사용자는 근로자 개인에게 30일 전 해고예고 또는 해고수당(통상임금의 30일분)을 지급하고 해고한다. 절차적 요건으로서 일정 규모 이상의 인원을 해고하고자 할 때는 고용노동부 장관에게 신고하여야 한다. 고용노동부 장관에게 신고하지 않았다고 하여 해고의 효력이 부인되는 것은 아니다. 즉, 고용노동부 장관에의 신고는 정리해고의 성립요건은 아니고 절차적 요건이다.

근로기준법은 정리해고를 할 경우에 '사용자가 1개월 동안에 해고하려는 인원수가 총 근로자 수의 10%를 초과할 경우에는 최초 해고하려는 날의 30일전까지 해고사유, 해고예정인원, 근로자대표와의 협의한 내용, 해고일정 등을 포함한 해고계획을 노동부장관에게 신고하여야 한다'라고 규정하고 있다(제24조 제4항). 그러나 정리해고의 정당성을 갖추기 위한 요건과 절차에 이 조항은 포함되지 않고 벌칙조항도 없다. 이에 대해 이를 준수하여야 하는지가 문제된다.

이 조항은 미준수시 벌칙조항이 없을 뿐만 아니라 정리해고의 정당성을 결정하는 사유나 절차에도 해당되지 않는다. 다만, 고용정책기본법 제33조(대량 고

installation or expansion of production facilities or the reduction, adjustment, etc. of business scale reach the level prescribed by Presidential Decree, the employer shall report to the head of the competent employment security office on matters related to the changes. If the employer neglects this clause, a fine up to 3 million won can be levied. The level prescribed by Presidential Decree is 30 persons or more per workplace or a company ordinarily hiring fewer than 300 employees; and 10% or more of the total employees for workplaces or companies ordinarily hiring 300 employees or more. Accordingly, even though there is no influence on justification for managerial dismissal, it is desired that employers report to the Minister of Employment and Labor 30 days prior to managerial dismissal in order to avoid the fine for negligence and promote acceptance of eligibility for unemployment benefits later.

Ⅳ. Obligation to Reemploy Preferentially

Article 25 of the LSA. Preferential Reemployment

① When an employer who has dismissed workers under the provisions of Article 24 wishes to reemploy workers within 3 years of the date of dismissal, he/she shall consider the duties of the workers prior to their dismissal and make every effort to preferentially reemploy them if they so desire.

② The Government shall take the necessary measures for dismissed workers under the provisions of Article 24 such as stabilization of livelihood, reemployment, and vocational training on a priority basis.

When an employer who has dismissed workers under the provisions of Article 24 of the Labor Standards Act wishes to reemploy workers within 3 years of the date of dismissal, he/she shall consider the duties of the workers prior to their dismissal and make every effort to preferentially reemploy them, if they so desire. Recently, the Supreme Court ruled, "If an employer who dismissed a worker for managerial reasons hires a new worker for the same position without confirming with the dismissed worker as to whether he or she wishes to return to work or not, this new employment can be seen as violating the obligation to re-employ. In this case, the dismissed worker can claim compensation for damages due to the employer failing to fulfill the obligation to re-employ. This compensation shall be equivalent to wages from the time when the obligation to re-employ occurred to the time the employer hires the dismissed worker."[514)]

514) Supreme Court ruling on November 26, 2020, 2016 da 13437.

용변동신고 등) 제1항은 사업주는 생산설비의 자동화, 신설 또는 증설이나 사업규모의 축소, 조정 등으로 인한 고용량(雇傭量)의 변동이 대통령령으로 정하는 기준에 해당하는 경우에는 그 고용량의 변동에 관한 사항을 직업안정기관의 장에게 신고하여야 한다. 고 규정하고 이를 이행하지 않으면 300만원 이하의 과태료를 부과할 수 있도록 하고 있다. 대통령이 정하는 기준은 '상시 근로자 300명 미만 사업(장)에는 30인 이상; 상시 근로자 300명 이상인 사업(장)은 상시 근로자 총수의 100분의 10이상이다.' 따라서 비록 정리해고의 정당성에 영향을 미치지 않지만, 과태료 문제와 차후 실업급여의 원활한 수급 등을 위해서 정리해고 30일 전에 노동부장관에게 신고하는 것이 바람직하다.

Ⅳ. 우선 재고용 의무

근로기준법 제25조【우선 재고용 등】

① 제24조에 따라 근로자를 해고한 사용자는 근로자를 해고한 날부터 3년 이내에 해고된 근로자가 해고 당시 담당하였던 업무와 같은 업무를 할 근로자를 채용하려고 할 경우 제24조에 따라 해고된 근로자가 원하면 그 근로자를 우선적으로 고용하여야 한다.

② 정부는 제24조에 따라 해고된 근로자에 대하여 생계안정, 재취업, 직업훈련 등 필요한 조치를 우선적으로 취하여야 한다.

근로기준법 제24조에 의해 정리해고를 행한 사용자는 근로자를 해고한 날로부터 3년 이내에 해고된 근로자가 해고 당시 담당하였던 업무와 같은 업무를 할 근로자를 채용하려고 할 경우 제24조에 따라 해고된 근로자가 원하면 그 근로자를 우선적으로 고용하여야 한다. 최근 대법원은 "경영상 이유에 의하여 근로자를 해고한 사용자가 해고 근로자에게 고용계약 체결의사를 확인하지 않은 채 제3자를 채용하였다면 우선 재고용의무를 위반한 것으로 볼 수 있다. 해고 근로자는 사용자가 위 규정을 위반하여 우선 재고용의무를 이행하지 않은 데 대하여, 우선 재고용의무가 발생한 때부터 고용관계가 성립할 때까지의 임금 상당 손해배상금을 청구할 수 있다"고 판시하고 있다.[514)]

514) 대법원 2020.11.26, 2016다13437.

Section 2: Matters for Consideration when Planning Managerial Dismissals

I. Legal Issues

1. Concept

Dismissal for managerial reasons(hereby referred to as managerial dismissal) refers to when an employer dismisses an employee for urgent business reasons. As managerial dismissal is implemented without reasons attributable to the employee, there are strict requirements an employer must follow. Such dismissal may be accepted as justifiable according to Article 23 of the Labor Standards Act(LSA) if the employer satisfies four requirements: ① There exists urgent necessity in relation to the business; ② Efforts were made to avoid dismissal; ③ Fair criteria was used in the selection of those persons subject to dismissal; and ④ The employee representative was notified 50 days in advance and sincere consultations were done with him/her.

There are some items that need to be considered in reality in the process of satisfying the above four requirements. Firstly, in cases where the collective agreement includes an employment stabilization agreement on managerial dismissal or a clause requiring the labor union's agreement in the process of managerial dismissal, how the company might deal with them is a matter of concern. Secondly, in a company with only one labor union that represents only production workers, whether an employee representative for white collar employees is needed or not when white collar employees are included in those being dismissed for managerial reasons, must also be considered.

2. Restrictions on managerial dismissal in the collective agreement

(1) Agreements on procedures for managerial dismissal in the collective agreement

In cases where the collective agreement contains clauses requiring agreement from the

제2절 정리해고 시 고려사항

Ⅰ. 법적 쟁점

1. 의 의

경영상 이유에 의한 해고(이하 정리해고라 함)는 회사가 긴박한 경영상 이유가 있을 때 사용자가 일방적으로 근로자를 해고하는 것이다. 이러한 정리해고는 근로자의 귀책사유 없이 행해지는 해고이기 때문에 그 요건을 엄격하게 갖추어야 한다. 정리해고는 ① 긴박한 경영상의 필요성, ② 해고회피의 노력, ③ 합리적이고 공정한 해고기준, ④ 50일 전에 근로자대표에게 통보 및 협의라는 4가지 조건을 갖추어야 근로기준법 제23조에 의한 정당한 해고로 인정받을 수 있다.

그런데, 이 4가지 요건을 갖추는 과정에서 실무상 부딪치게 되는 몇 가지 고려해야 할 사항들이 있다. 첫째, 단체협약으로 고용안정협약이나 절차상 합의조항을 두었을 때 어떻게 합리적으로 대처해야 하는지가 문제 된다. 둘째, 생산직 근로자만으로 구성된 노동조합이 있는 사업장에서 사무직 근로자까지 정리해고를 하고자 할 경우, 사무직 근로자들을 대표하는 근로자대표를 선출해야 하는지가 문제 될 수 있다.

2. 단체협약에 따른 정리해고 제한규정

(1) 단체협약상 정리해고 절차에 대한 합의 조항

아래의 사례와 같이 단체협약에 해고대상자 선정이나 위로금 책정에 대한 합의조항이 있는 경우, 노동조합과의 합의가 없이는 정리해고를 할 수 없는지가 문제가 될 수 있다. 또한, 노동조합과의 합의가 되지 않은 경우에 어떤 조

labor union on those subject to managerial dismissal and the early retirement package(ERP) bonus(as seen in the box below), the company may not be able to reach an agreement with the labor union. If the company cannot reach agreement with the labor union, how can the company select those subject to dismissal and how can it determine an ERP bonus?

Collective Bargaining: Article 27 (Reduction of Personnel) 1. When the Company intends to reduce personnel due to urgent business reasons, it shall inform the Labor Union of the reason(s) 60 days prior to dismissal and agree with the Labor Union on the criteria and procedure for choosing those subject to dismissal, and ERP bonus. (The order of priority follows voluntary applicants and late joiners).

The phrases in the collective agreement, the company shall agree with the labor union and The order of priority follows late joiners can be the biggest barriers in the process of managerial dismissal. This is because these phrases form the essential procedures to follow, which are The Company can conduct managerial dismissal, but must do the following: ① Notify the labor union 60 days in advance; ② Reach agreement with the labor union on the criteria and procedures for choosing those subject to managerial dismissal, and ③ Reach agreement with the labor union on details of the ERP bonus. It is important that the company follows such procedures.

As for the ERP bonus, reaching an agreement is likely to be difficult as the company expects a lower amount while the labor union may insist on the maximum amount. Therefore, since the company has sufficiently consulted with the labor union regarding the level of the ERP bonus, it is not necessary for the two parties to reach agreement. The next condition is that the company shall reach agreement with the labor union regarding the criteria for choosing those subject to dismissal. If the two parties cannot reach such agreement, the company shall adhere to procedures that choose voluntary applicants and late-joiners first. This means that the company has to respect seniority and select late-joiners as those subject to managerial dismissal in cases where there is no agreement on the matter. If the company has to unilaterally dismiss some employees for managerial reasons, it does not have to pay an ERP bonus to those Union members. The most beneficial course for both parties is to make every effort to reach an agreement on reasonable criteria for dismissal. Accordingly, in order to handle the restrictions on managerial dismissal, both parties are required to set up an appropriate ERP bonus through sufficient consultation, and work hard to reach an agreement on fair criteria for dismissal. Otherwise the company will have to dismiss simply based on seniority.

건으로 해고대상자를 선정할 것인지가 문제될 수 있다. 이 문제에 대해 아래 단체협약의 내용과 관련하여 판단 및 이에 대한 행정해석과 판례의 내용을 살펴본다.

> **단체협약 제27조【인원 정리】** 1. 회사는 경영상 부득이한 사유로 인원을 정리하고자 할 때는 최소한 60일 이전에 정리사유를 통보하고 정리대상자의 선정과 절차, 위로금은 조합과 합의한다. (우선순위는 희망자, 입사역순으로 한다.)

위의 단체협약 내용 중 조합과 합의한다와 우선순위는 입사역순으로 한다는 규정이 정리해고 시 가장 큰 장애요인으로 작용할 수 있다. 왜냐하면 이러한 조항은 회사는 정리해고를 할 수 있다. 다만, 회사가 정리해고를 할 경우에는 ① 60일전 통보, ② 정리대상자 선정과 절차, ③ 위로금은 조합과 합의한다는 정리해고의 절차규정에 해당되기 때문이다. 회사 측으로는 이 절차규정을 지키기 위해 어떤 과정을 거쳐야 하는지가 핵심문제가 된다.

희망퇴직금에 대해서는 회사는 적정하게, 노동조합은 최대로 많이 요구하기 때문에 합의되기 어렵다. 따라서 희망퇴직금은 적정한 수준에서 성실하게 협의가 이루어졌다면 문제가 없다. 여기서 다음 조건인 '정리대상자에 대해 조합과 합의한다'는 규정이 있다. 합의가 되지 않을 경우에는 우순순위를 '희망자, 입사역순'으로 한다고 규정하고 있다. 합의가 되지 않을 때는 반드시 입사역순으로 정리해고 대상자를 선정해야 한다. 이 경우, 회사 측이 일방적으로 정리해고를 하는 경우에 해당하므로, 조합원들에게 위로금을 지급할 필요가 없고, 퇴직위로금을 받지 못하기 때문에 조합원에게도 손해가 된다. 최대한 합리적인 해고 기준을 선정하는 것이 노동조합과 회사 모두에게 유리하다는 얘기다. 따라서 위 정리해고 제한규정을 해결하기 위해서는 충분한 노사협의의 과정을 통해 희망퇴직금을 적정하게 설정하고 또한 입사 역순으로 우선순위를 선정하지 않기 위해 노동조합과 반드시 합의에 이르는 것이 바람직하다.

○ Judicial ruling 1) In cases where there is an article requiring prior agreement with the labor union regarding personnel dismissal in the collective agreement, such personnel dismissal outside of this process is invalid.[515)]

In cases where there are articles in the collective agreement articles requiring prior agreement and consent with the labor union regarding personnel dismissal, or requiring an agreement on personnel dismissal through consultations with the labor union, the dismissals of personnel outside of this process shall be regarded as invalid in principle. However, even though the collective agreement contains a requirement of such prior agreement with the labor union, the employer's personnel management rights are not always only what can be implemented according to the agreement or consent of the labor union. If it is regarded that the labor union has abused the right of prior agreement or given up a right of prior agreement intentionally, it is valid for the employer to carry out personnel dismissal without receiving the labor union's agreement.

○ Judicial ruling 2): While a prior agreement with the labor union has been made necessary for times of managerial dismissal, consultation alone would be sufficient.[516)]

As managerial dismissal is a significantly sensitive managerial decision to be made by the management body, it cannot be an item for collective bargaining in principle. Although this is the case, the collective agreement can include an article requiring the company to decide or implement managerial dismissal based on agreement with the labor union. In this case, it shall not be determined that the company has given up or severely restricted its own managerial rights. In reviewing the article in the collective agreement requiring prior agreement with the labor union, its does not mean that the company shall have the labor union's prior agreement before making managerial decisions, but the clause of the agreement shall be translated as sufficient consultation to ensure reasonableness and fairness in the company efforts to give the labor union the opportunities necessary to deliver in advance its opinions on the criteria for managerial dismissal etc., and shall in good faith refer to the union's opinions.

(2) Employment stabilization agreement

Details on employment adjustment cannot be topics for collective bargaining. However, if the company accepted the union's demand and stipulated it in the collective agreement,

515) Supreme Court ruling on July 15, 2010, 2007Du15797.

516) Seoul Appellate Court on July 10, 2003, 200Na58138.

○ 판례1) 노동조합과 인사처분에 관한 사전합의 조항이 단체협약에 규정된 경우 그 절차를 거치지 아니한 인사처분은 원칙적으로 무효이다[515)]

사용자가 인사처분을 할 때 노동조합의 사전 동의나 승낙을 얻어야 한다거나 노동조합과 인사처분에 관하여 논의하여 의견의 합치를 보아 인사처분을 하도록 단체협약 등에 규정된 경우에는 그 절차를 거치지 아니한 인사처분은 원칙적으로 무효로 보아야 한다. 다만 이처럼 사전합의조항을 두고 있다고 하더라도 사용자의 인사권이 어떠한 경우를 불문하고 노동조합의 동의나 합의가 있어야만 행사할 수 있는 것은 아니고, 「노동조합이 사전합의권을 남용하거나 스스로 사전합의권의 행사를 포기하였다고 인정되는 경우」에는 사용자가 이러한 합의 없이 한 인사처분도 유효하다고 보아야 한다.

○ 판례2) 정리해고 시 합의키로 한 경우에도 노조와 협의만으로 충분하다고 본 사례[516)]

정리해고 등의 실시 여부는 경영주체에 의한 고도의 경영상 결단에 속하는 사항으로서 이는 원칙적으로 단체교섭의 대상이 될 수 없다. 사용자인 피고가 정리해고의 실시 등 경영권의 본질에 속하여 단체교섭의 대상이 될 수 없는 사항에 관하여 노동조합과 합의하여 결정 혹은 시행하기로 하는 내용의 단체협약 조항이 있다고 하더라도 쉽게 사용자의 경영권의 일부 포기나 중대한 제한을 인정하여서는 아니 된다. 위 단체협약의 합의조항의 문구내용 등에 비추어, 이 사건에 있어 위 단체협약의 합의조항은 정리해고의 실시 등 경영상 결단을 하기 위해서는 반드시 노동조합의 사전 동의를 요건으로 한다는 취지가 아니라 사전에 노동조합에게 해고의 기준 등에 관하여 필요한 의견을 제시할 기회를 주고 노동조합의 의견을 성실히 참고하게 함으로써 구조조정의 합리성과 공정성을 담보하고자 하는「협의」의 취지로 해석한다.

(2) 고용안정협약

구조조정에 대한 내용은 단체협약의 대상이 될 수 없지만, 사용자가 노동조합의 요구를 수용하여 단체협약으로 명시한 경우에는 사용자에게 이를 준수해

515) 대법원 2010.7.15, 2007두15797.

516) 서울고등법원 2003.7.10, 2002나58138.

the employer has an obligation to observe this. A decision by the Seoul Appellate Court states While merging with Company B, Company A will continue the employment of all personnel, and shall not, after the merger, dismiss personnel unilaterally.[517)] And a Supreme Court ruling: The company shall not engage in managerial dismissal for the next five years.[518)] In cases where such an employment stabilization agreement is introduced to the collective agreement, it is doubtful whether the company can implement managerial dismissal in light of urgent business necessity. In general, judicial rulings explain that in cases where a company's very survival is at risk due to financial crisis, or where a company is experiencing very negative business changes it had not anticipated at the time the employment stabilization section was agreed to in the collective agreement, this agreement does not have to be honored. However, in all other cases, this agreement remains valid.

- ○ Judicial ruling: Managerial dismissal in conflict with the employment stabilization agreement is unfair dismissal.[519)]

Employment adjustments like managerial dismissal are sensitive managerial decisions of the management body and shall not be items for collective bargaining in principle. However, the collective agreement, which is a written document of agreements made through collective bargaining between the company and the labor union, has no limitations in details, as long as they do not violate law or good public order and customs. In cases where the employer decides to limit unilateral managerial dismissal and concludes an employment stabilization agreement with the labor union, this agreement shall be considered a normative portion of the collective agreement as the standards concerning working conditions and the treatment of workers. Accordingly, unless there is a special situation like the unfairness of continuing the effectiveness of the collective agreement in light of changes that could not be expected at the time the Agreement was concluded, the company's decision to oppose the Agreement is invalid in principle.

3. Employee representative for white collar employees

In cases where there is a labor union consisting of only production workers, and which represents the majority of all employees, when the company intends to include white collar employees in its plans for managerial dismissal for business reasons, is it acceptable to only

517) Supreme Court ruling on May 26, 2011, 2011Do7526.

518) Supreme Court ruling on Oct. 24, 2003, 2003Da43278 (Daewoo Motors).

519) Administrative Court ruling on July 1, 2011, 2010Guhap35272.

야 할 의무가 발생한다. 이러한 조항의 예는 다음과 같다. A회사가 B회사를 인수하면서 전 종업원에 대하여 전원 고용을 승계하도록 하며, 인수 후 인위적인 구조조정을 실시하지 않도록 한다.[517] 노사가 향후 5년간 정리해고를 하지 않기로 한다.[518] 이러한 고용안정조항을 단체협약으로 체결한 경우, 회사의 긴박한 경영상의 이유로 정리해고를 할 수 있는가에 대한 의문이 생길 수 있다.

판례는 '회사가 존폐위기에 처할 심각한 재정적 위기에 도래하였다거나 예상하지 못하였던 급격한 경영상 변화가 있는 경우 등 협약 체결 당시 예상하지 못하였던 사정 변경이 있어 협약의 효력을 유지하는 것이 객관적으로 기대불가능한 경우'를 제외하고는 이 협약의 효력은 유효하다고 본다.

○ 판례: 고용안정협약 및 합의에 반하는 정리해고는 부당해고에 해당한다[519]

정리해고 등 기업의 구조조정 여부는 사용자에 의한 고도의 경영상 결단에 속하는 사항으로서 이는 원칙적으로 단체교섭 대상이 되지 아니한다. 그러나 단체협약은 사용자와 노동조합 사이에 이루어진 단체교섭 결과 성립된 합의사항을 문서화한 것으로 강행법규나 공서양속에 위반되지 않는 한 그 내용에 제한이 없고, 사용자가 스스로 경영상 결단에 의하여 근로자들에 대한 정리해고를 제한하기로 하여 노동조합과 이른바 고용안정협약을 체결한 경우 이는 근로조건 기타 근로자의 대우에 관한 것으로서 단체협약의 규범적 부분에 해당한다. 따라서 협약체결 당시 예상하지 못하였던 사정변경이 있어 협약의 효력을 유지하는 것이 객관적으로 보아 부당한 경우와 같은 특별한 사정이 없는 한 이에 반하는 행위는 원칙적으로 무효이다.

3. 사무직 근로자에 대한 근로자대표

생산직으로만 구성된 노동조합이 근로자의 과반수로 조직되어 있는 경우, 사무직에 대하여 경영상의 이유에 의한 해고를 하려 할 때, 생산직으로만 구성된 노동조합하고만 협의하여도 문제가 없는지가 논쟁이 될 수 있다.

---

517) 대법원 2011.5.26, 2011두7526.

518) 대법원 2003.10.24, 2003다43278(대우자동차 사건).

519) 행정법원 2011.7.1, 2010구합35272.

engage in consultations with the labor union representing only production workers?

In cases where the company intends to conduct managerial dismissal covering all employees, even though white collar employees are not members of this labor union, the labor union, if it is the majority union, can represent white collar employees. There should therefore be no legal issues from the absence of a white collar employee representative. However, if those subject to managerial dismissal are not production workers, but only white collar employees, the labor union cannot be the employee representative, and an employee body representing the white collar employees shall be established.

- Judicial ruling: Consultation with an employee representative shall not be considered as sincere if the employee representative and the labor union have no interest in matters related to personnel reduction of a particular group of employees subject to managerial dismissal.[520)]

Article 24(paragraph 3) of the Labor Standards Act is designed to provide opportunities for those potentially subject to managerial dismissal to have their own representing body put forward their interests to the company. In cases where downsizing predominantly affects employees of 4th rank or higher, it is necessary to consult with employee representatives who represent the interests of employees at 4th rank or higher. The employee representatives with which the hospital consulted regarding managerial dismissal represented employees of 5th rank or lower and the labor union was a minority labor union also representing employees of 5th rank or lower, the employee representatives and labor union members were not those potentially affected by managerial dismissal. Therefore, consultation with these employee representatives and the labor union cannot be regarded as sincere consultation with the employee representative required for managerial dismissal.

- Administrative Guidelines[521)]: Who is the main employee representative for consultations on dismissal for managerial reasons?

When planning managerial dismissals involving all employees, the company shall consult with the labor union representing the majority of employees. However, in cases where dismissal for managerial reasons targets employees of a particular rank, it is desirable to consult with the labor union composed of those employees of that particular rank so as to prevent labor disputes.

---

520) Administrative Court ruling on Jan. 30, 2004, 2003Guhap18866.

521) MOEL Guidelines: Labor Directions-3856, on Sept. 18, 2008.

회사 전체를 대상으로 구조조정을 하고 있는 경우에 사무직 근로자가 노동조합에 가입되어 있지 않더라도 노동조합은 과반수 노동조합으로 사무직 근로자들을 대표 한다고 할 수 있다. 따라서 사무직 근로자대표를 특별히 구성하지 않아도 법적인 문제는 없다. 그러나 정리해고 대상이 생산직이 아닌 사무직만 해당 될 경우에는 노동조합이 근로자대표가 될 수 없고, 사무직근로자 중에 근로자대표를 선정해야 한다.

○ 판례: 정리해고와 거의 이해관계를 갖고 있지 아니한 근로자대표 및 노동조합과의 감원에 대한 협의는 근로자대표와 성실한 협의를 하였다고 볼 수 없다[520)]

정리해고 시 근로자들의 이해관계를 대변할 수 있는 조직과의 협의를 통하여 이해관계를 조절함을 목적으로 하고 있는 근로기준법 제24조 제3항의 취지에 비추어 보면, 근로자 중 주로 4급 이상의 직원을 감원하기로 하는 경우 4급 이상 직원들의 이해관계를 대변할 수 있는 근로자대표와의 협의도 필요하다. ○ 병원이 정리해고와 관련하여 협의하였다고 하는 근로자대표는 모두 5급 이하의 직원들로 구성된 근로자대표와 근로자의 반수를 넘지 않고 주로 5급 이하의 근로자로 구성된 노동조합이라는 것이고, 위 근로자대표와 노동조합 조합원은 대부분 정리해고 대상자가 아니어서 이 사건 정리해고와 거의 이해관계를 갖고 있지 아니하므로, 위와 같은 근로자대표 및 노동조합과의 감원에 대한 협의는 근로자대표와 성실한 협의를 하였다고 볼 수 없다.

○ 경영상 이유에 의한 해고시 협의주체인 근로자대표 관련[521)]

회사의 전체직원을 대상으로 정리해고를 하는 경우에는 근로자의 과반수로 조직된 노동조합과 협의하여야 할 것이다. 다만, 경영상 이유에 의한 해고가 전체 근로자의 과반수가 되지 않는 특정 직급만을 대상으로 할 경우에는 해당 특정 직종으로 조직된 노동조합의 참여를 허용하는 것이 노사분쟁의 예방을 위해서 바람직할 것이다.

520) 행정법원 2004.1.30, 2003구합18866.

521) 행정해석: 근로조건 지도과-3856, 2008.9.18.

II. Voluntary Early Retirement Programs

1. Necessity for voluntary early retirement programs

It is difficult to dismiss employees when following all the requirements for Dismissal for Managerial Reasons under the Labor Standards Act. As this dismissal requires the employer to follow specific procedures to verify managerial reasons, many companies replace dismissals for managerial reasons by adopting a voluntary Early Retirement Program("ERP") instead. Voluntary early retirement means that the employee chooses to resign(rather than being pressured to), which can be a positive situation by giving employees more options than if they were dismissed for managerial reasons. If the company pays employees an additional ERP bonus and employees accept it, personnel reduction will take place even without dismissal for managerial reasons. This situation frees the company from any risk of violating the related laws, as well as the need to enter into legal proceedings or report to the Ministry of Employment and Labor.

Recently, a number of companies that have dismissed employees for managerial reasons, or were in the process of dismissing for managerial reasons, have lost lawsuits for unfair dismissal because of a lack of effort to avoid those dismissals, so ERPs can be an alternative to dismissal for managerial reasons. Thus, I would like to concretely review some implementation methods for ERP, as well as considerations to be made when using an ERP instead of dismissing for managerial reasons.

2. Implementation of voluntary early retirement programs

(1) Concept

Voluntary early retirement refers to terminating employment when the employee submits a letter of resignation voluntarily upon accepting an employer's recommendation that he/she do so. Here, as the employer intends to dismiss the employee for unilateral business reasons(without reasons attributable to the employee), it is necessary for the employer to offer sufficient rewards to the employee so that the employee willingly submits a letter of resignation. During the time before imminent dismissal for managerial reasons, voluntary early retirement with bonuses might be the best option for the employee, rather than being fired without compensation.

Ⅱ. 희망퇴직제도

1. 의 의

근로기준법에 의한 경영상 해고(정리해고)는 법적인 요건이 까다로울 뿐만 아니라 회사는 이 해고의 요건을 입증하여야 하는 의무가 발생하기 때문에, 많은 기업들은 희망퇴직제를 정리해고 대신으로 시행하고 있다. 희망퇴직은 직원 스스로가 사직서를 제출한다는 의미에서 정리해고보다는 직원에게 선택권을 부여한다. 회사가 퇴직위로금을 지급하고, 직원은 이를 수용하는 방식이므로 근로기준법 제24조에 의한 정리해고와는 상관없이 인원 감축을 하는 것이므로, 법적인 절차 및 노동부 신고의무 등이 없으며, 법 위반의 문제가 발생하지 않는다.

최근에 정리해고를 실시했거나 실시 중인 기업들 중 상당수가 근로기준법에 의한 "정리해고의 요건과 절차"가 미흡했다는 이유로 "부당해고" 판정을 받고 있어 희망퇴직제 또는 퇴직위로금을 지급하고, 고용관계를 정리하는 것이 대안이 될 수 있다. 이에 정리해고의 대안인 희망퇴직제도에 대해 실시방법 및 고려사항에 대해 구체적으로 검토하고자 한다.

2. 희망퇴직 실시

(1) 희망퇴직의 개념

희망퇴직은 사용자가 근로자에게 퇴직을 권유하고 근로자는 이를 받아들여 사직서를 제출하는 형식을 통해 근로관계를 종결하는 것을 의미한다. 그러나 근로자의 귀책사유 없이 회사의 일방적인 경영상 사유 등으로 근로자를 해고시키기 때문에 근로자가 사용자의 사직 제의를 수용하고 자발적으로 사직서를 제출하기 위해서는 그 근로자에게 충분한 반대급부를 제공해야 한다. 이런 경우 정리해고를 앞둔 근로자의 입장에서는 보상 없이 정리해고 당하는 것보다는 수용 가능한 퇴직위로금을 수령하는 희망퇴직을 하는 것이 최선의 선택으로 볼 수 있다.

(2) Matters to be considered when planning ERPs

In companies adopting ERPs, competent employees may find employment with other companies after receiving their ERP bonus. Although the main purpose of ERPs is to terminate incompetent or unproductive employees, they may also impact the company negatively should they lose competent employees as well. Therefore, it is necessary to establish a clear purpose and clear methods ahead of the implementation of an ERP. That is, if plans for an ERP mostly attract employees not specifically targeted for early retirement by the company, the company needs to have the authority to reject applications.

(3) Establishment of an ERP bonus

The employer's major concern may usually be focused on the level of financial compensation rather than legal disputes with the employees concerned. In cases where voluntary early retirement is used as a means of dismissing employees, whether that ERP becomes successful or not is greatly dependent upon the level of ERP bonus. Generally speaking, in determining ERP bonuses, the employer needs to consider both length of service of the employees(reflecting their contribution to the company) and the company's ability to pay those bonuses. The employer needs to pay special attention when determining the level of compensation, recognizing that the first ERP bonus paid out will become the standard for any following ERP cases.

(4) Informing employees subject to voluntary early retirement

The ideal method is for the company to specify which employees will be subject to voluntary early retirement from those who fall behind their peers in terms of skills and performance. In this case, the company creates a list of employees under consideration in advance, explains the ERP to them, and asks them to accept. If the company cannot persuade some employees to accept the ERP, then the company can begin dismissing for managerial reasons, following the guidelines under the Labor Standards Act. The employer needs to make clear to the employees that there will be no benefits should they refuse the ERP and wait to be dismissed for managerial reasons. In cases where employees are dismissed for managerial reasons, the company is not obligated to pay any financial compensation like the ERP bonus.

(2) 희망퇴직 계획 시 유의사항

희망퇴직제도를 시행하는 경우에 회사에서 능력이 있는 직원들이 퇴직위로금을 지급받고 타 회사로 전직하는 경우를 예상할 수 있다. 그러나 희망퇴직을 실시하는 궁극적인 목적은 능력이나 성과가 떨어지는 직원을 대상으로 인원 감축을 하고자 하는 것인데 반해 실제로는 유능한 인재를 잃어버리는 결과가 발생할 수도 있다. 따라서 희망퇴직제도를 시행할 경우에는 목적과 방법을 사전에 명확히 설정하여 발표하여야 한다. 즉, 불특정 다수의 직원들이 퇴직을 희망하는 경우에 회사는 반드시, 사직서를 반려할 수 있는 권한을 가지고 있어야 한다.

(3) 퇴직위로금 설정

협상 대상자와 법적인 부분에 대한 언급보다는 퇴직위로금의 금전적인 보상 수준이 해결 방안이 될 것이다. 대부분의 회사에서 정리해고의 일환으로 희망퇴직을 실시하는 경우, 희망퇴직의 성공여부는 퇴직위로금의 수준에 따라서 결정된다. 따라서 회사는 직원들에게 제시할 퇴직위로금의 수준을 사전에 정해두는 것이 가장 중요하다. 일반적으로 퇴직위로금을 결정할 경우에는 해당 근로자의 기여도를 반영할 수 있는 근속연수에 따라 결정되고, 또한, 회사의 지급능력에 따라 결정된다. 회사의 퇴직위로금은 한 번 정하여 지급하게 되면, 이것이 기준이 되어 차후 다른 대상 근로자들의 기준이 되기 때문에 신중히 결정하여야 한다.

(4) 희망퇴직 대상자에 대한 통보

업무능력이나 성과가 떨어지는 직원을 대상으로 희망퇴직 대상자를 지명하여 희망퇴직제도를 시행하는 것이 가장 바람직한 방법이다. 이 경우에는 사전에 회사에서 퇴직자를 선별하여, 희망퇴직제도의 프로그램을 설명하고, 명예퇴직을 시키는 것이며, 회사의 설득 노력에도 불구하고 이를 거부하는 경우에는 회사는 근로기준법에 의한 정리해고를 실시해야 할 것이며, 정리해고는 퇴직위로금 등의 반대급부가 없다는 것을 인식시켜야 한다. 즉, 정리해고를 할 경우에는 퇴직위로금 등 금전적인 보상의무가 없다.

(5) Implementing the ERP together with dismissals for managerial reasons

In cases where employees do not accept the ERP that the company offers, the employer needs to dismiss those employees for managerial reasons, following the guidelines in the Labor Standards Act. In these cases, timing is important. If the desired number of personnel accept the ERP, it is not necessary to announce any dismissals. If dismissals are announced at the same time as the ERP, some serious problems may occur in the company's organizational atmosphere or in the ERP bonus. Accordingly, it is recommended that the company announce the ERP before basic requirements and legal procedures needed to dismiss employees for managerial reasons. If the number of ERP applications exceeds the target, it is not necessary to dismiss any employees for managerial reasons. If the number of ERP applications falls short of the target, it is necessary to implement the basic requirements and legal procedures to begin dismissing employees for managerial reasons. That is, the company should begin dismissing the selected employees for managerial reasons if the number of applications for the ERP is insufficient. At the same time, the employees should be informed that there will be no ERP bonuses upon dismissal for managerial reasons. In this case, the managers-in-charge who directly consult with the employees subject to voluntary early retirement need to be properly trained.

In cases where it is desired that only specific employees accept early retirement, it is recommended not to announce the ERP to all employees, but to only inform the employees subject to early voluntary resignation. Those employees who accept the ERP will finish their employment when they receive the ERP bonus and submit their letters of resignation. However, the rest of the company's contract employees will finish employment when their contract period has expired. In this case, cancellation notices for contract employees also need to be considered.

3. Other programs outside of ERP bonuses

It is necessary to develop other programs to reduce the psychological impact on an employee from sudden resignation. That is, personnel reduction should be implemented with legal severance pay + ERP bonus + outplacement + unemployment allowance.

(5) 정리해고와 병행하여 실시

직원들이 회사에서 시행하는 희망퇴직을 수용하지 않을 경우에는 근로기준법에 의한 정리해고를 실시하여야 하며, 이 경우 정리해고의 발표 시점이 중요하다. 희망퇴직으로 인하여 인원정리가 원만히 해결되었다면, 굳이 정리해고를 발표할 필요성은 없다. 희망퇴직과 동시에 정리해고를 발표한다면, 직원들의 조직 분위기 및 보상금 등에 관하여 문제가 발생할 수 있다. 따라서 정리해고의 기준과 법적인 절차의 발표 전에 희망퇴직제도를 먼저 발표하고, 퇴직자 모집(지명)이 100%가 되었을 경우에는 정리해고를 발표할 필요가 없으나, 100%가 되지 않았을 경우에는 정리해고의 수단을 퇴직자 모집과 병행하여 실시한다. 즉, 희망퇴직을 하지 않을 경우에는 정리해고를 할 수밖에 없고, 정리해고를 실시하여 해고를 하는 경우에는 퇴직위로금이 지급되지 않는다는 것을 명확히 전달하여야 한다. 이 경우 퇴직 대상자와 협상을 진행하는 관리자에 대한 교육이 필요하다.

모든 직원들에게 적용하지 않고, 일부 직원에게만 적용하는 경우에는 전체 직원들에게 희망퇴직제도를 발표하지 말고, 희망퇴직 해당 직원들에게만 개별적으로 접촉을 하여 희망퇴직제도를 적용하는 것이 효율적이다. 해당 직원들이 희망퇴직위로금을 받고 사직서를 제출하는 경우에는 그것으로 회사와 고용관계가 종료되는 것이기 때문이다. 그 이외의 계약직 사원에 대해서는 고용계약기간의 만료와 동시에 계약해지를 하면 될 것이다. 이 경우 계약직의 고용계약해지는 별도로 검토를 하어야 할 것이다.

3. 퇴직위로금 이외의 프로그램

갑작스런 퇴직으로 인하여 직원들의 심리적인 불안감이 발생할 수 있으므로 이를 최소화할 수 있는 다양한 프로그램을 개발할 필요성이 있다. 즉, “법정 퇴직금 + 퇴직위로금 + 전직지원서비스 + 실업급여”를 통하여, 고용조정을 실시할 수 있도록 한다.

Section 3: Business Mergers and Business Transfers

Ⅰ. Concept

Due to the deteriorating economy, corporate business adjustments, mergers and acquisitions have recently become frequent. As corporations are restructured, employees often continue to maintain employment while their employer changes. This is known as a business transfer: the employees and their duties remain the same, but the employer does not. As there is no clear explanation stipulated in the Commercial Act, the Civil Act or Korean labor law of how business transfers are to affect employment relations or working conditions for employees, we have to depend on judicial precedent for issues that arise. Herein I will review the legal principles of business transfers, the details and limitations of transferred employment, and relation with the rules of employment or collective agreements.

Ⅱ. Mergers and Employment Relationships

A merger refers to two or more companies integrating into a single entity. There are two types of mergers: consolidation, in which two or more different companies are disassembled to build a single new company; and merger, in which one company takes over the business of another company(or companies) to become a larger one.

In the event of a merger, the effective contracts of employment and the existing rules of employment at the merged company(or companies) shall be taken over comprehensively by the new merging company. Wages and other working conditions shall remain unchanged, and the years of consecutive work, for the purpose of computing retirement pay and annual paid leave, shall be carried over. To the extent that the employment relationship remains the same, the existing collective agreement shall also be retained. Accordingly, both the normative and contractual parts of the collective agreement shall be taken over by the new company as its rights or obligations to the labor union(s) and employees of

제3절 합병, 영업양도 시 근로관계

Ⅰ. 의 의

최근 경기악화로 인하여 기업의 구조조정과 M&A(인수 및 합병)가 활발히 진행되고 있다. 이 경우 사업조직의 변동이 발생되는데, 근로자는 고용을 계속 유지하면서 사업주가 교체된다. 이렇게 사업주는 변경되었지만 동일한 영업이나 업무를 하면서 근로자가 고용을 유지하는 것을 영업양도라고 한다. 이 영업양도에 있어서 상법, 민법, 그리고 노동법에는 근로자의 고용관계나 근로조건의 변동에 대한 명확한 규정이 없기 때문에 관련 내용에 대해 판례의 법리에 의존할 수밖에 없다. 아래에서는 판례에 있는 영업양도의 기본 법리, 근로관계의 승계의 내용과 한계, 그리고 취업규칙이나 단체협약과의 관계에 대해 자세히 알아보고자 한다.

Ⅱ. 합병 시 근로관계

합병이란 2이상의 기업이 하나의 기업으로 합쳐지는 것으로, 기존의 모든 회사가 해산하면서 새로운 회사로 합쳐지는 '신설합병'과 나머지 다른 회사를 한 회사가 흡수하는 '흡수합병'으로 나뉜다.

합병이 이루어지면 피합병회사의 근로계약이나 취업규칙은 합병회사에 포괄적으로 승계된다. 임금이나 근로시간 등 모든 근로조건이 종전과 동일하고 연차유급휴가나 퇴직금 산정에서 계속 근무연수도 합병과 무관하게 합산하여 계산하여야 한다. 근로관계가 동일한 이상 단체협약의 효력도 당연히 승계된다. 이에 따라 단체협약의 규범적 부분이나 채무적 부분 모두 노동조합과 근로자에 대한 합병회사의 권리의무로 승계된다.

근로관계가 포괄적으로 승계되는 경우에는 근로자의 종전의 근로계약상의 지위

the merged company(companies). In cases where the existing working conditions were succeeded inclusively, existing status under the previous employment contract succeeded and the employee's working conditions according to previous employment relations are maintained identically in the succeeded company. In order for the employer to one-sidedly revise the existing working conditions, or apply new working conditions that are unfavorable to the employees, the employer shall obtain agreement by a collective decision-making method from the majority of employees who are still under the previous employment contract. Accordingly, without such consent, there is no legal effect of any employer-revised working conditions or the rules of employment of the new company on employees of the previous company, if such rules were to be disadvantageous to said employees. In this case, employees who work at the new company are subject to the previous rules of employment.[522)]

Ⅲ. Legal Principles of Business Transfer

1. Basic principles

1) Business transfers involve the transferring of a business from one entity to another, while retaining the people, property, and business identity. Partial business transfers are also possible. When a business transfer occurs, responsibility for employment of the employees concerned shall be handed over inclusively to the transferee in principle. Whether an employee previously transferred from another company is accepted as part of a business transfer shall be decided not by how much property was transferred, but by whether the transferred business organization was totally or partially retained. For example, if all property is transferred after an organization is liquidated, it is not a business transfer. On the other hand, if a business facility partially retains its organization when it is handed over, and if the transferred portion retains its previous role, this is a business transfer.[523)]

2) Business transfers can involve the entire business or a particularly important portion being transferred. In order for the transfer of a particularly important portion to be

522) Supreme Court ruling on Dec. 23, 1996, 95da32631.

523) Supreme Court ruling on Mar. 29, 2002, 2000doo8455 (Unfair dismissal); July 27, 2001, 99doo2680.

도 승계되는 것이어서 종전의 근로관계에 따라 근로한 근로자는 승계한 법인에서도 종전의 근로관계와 동일한 근로관계를 유지하게 되고, 사용자가 일방적으로 취업규칙을 변경하거나 종전의 근로관계보다 불이익하게 승계한 법인의 취업규칙을 적용하기 위하여서는 종전의 근로계약상 지위를 유지하던 근로자 집단의 집단적 의사결정 방법에 의한 동의 등의 사정이 있어야 하며 이러한 동의 등이 없는 한 사용자가 일방적으로 종전의 근로조건을 근로자에게 불리하게 변경하거나 종전의 근로조건보다 불이익하게 승계한 법인의 취업규칙을 적용하는 것은 효력이 없다 할 것이므로 이 경우 종전의 근로조건을 그대로 유지한 채 승계한 법인에서 근무하게 되는 근로자에 대하여는 종전의 취업규칙이 그대로 적용된다.[522)]

Ⅲ. 영업양도의 기본법리

1. 영업양도의 기본 원칙

1) 영업양도라 함은 일정한 영업목적에 의하여 조직화된 업체 즉, 인적·물적 조직을 그 동일성은 유지하면서 일체로서 이전하는 것으로서 영업 일부만의 양도도 가능하다. 이러한 영업양도가 이루어진 경우에는 원칙적으로 해당 근로자들의 근로관계가 양수하는 기업에 포괄적으로 승계된다. 여기서 영업의 동일성 여부는 양도계약 관계가 영업의 양도로 인정되느냐 안 되느냐는 단지 어떠한 영업재산이 어느 정도로 이전되어 있는가에 의하여 결정 되는 것이 아니고 거기에 종래의 영업조직이 유지되어 그 조직이 전부 또는 중요한 일부로서 기능할 수 있는가에 의하여 결정된다. 예를 들어, 영업재산의 전부를 양도했어도 그 조직을 해체하여 양도했다면 영업의 양도는 되지 않는 반면, 그 일부를 유보한 채 영업시설을 양도했어도 그 양도한 부분만으로도 종래의 조직이 유지되어 있다고 사회관념상 인정되면 그것을 영업의 양도라 본다.[523)]

2) 사업양도는 전부 또는 중요한 일부에 대해서도 가능하며, 근로관계 승계의 효과가 발생하는 사업의 일부 양도가 있다고 하기 위해서는 적어도 양도되는 사

522) 대법원 1996.12.23, 95다32631.
523) 대법원 2002.3.29, 2000두8455(부당해고); 대법원 2001.7.27, 99두2680.

accepted as a business transfer, the transferred business must be able to at least operate its systematic function and perform the particular business involving the business facilities and the employees therein in the same way before and after the business transfer.[524)]

3) Whether a business transfer has occurred or not shall be determined by whether the transferred business can perform the same profitable business as before through the transferred property as a systematic organization while also managing the previous level of business without starting anew.[525)]

2. Exceptions

(1) Conditional business transfers

If a business is transferred, labor relations between the transferor(original employer) and the employees are transferred inclusively to the transferee(new employer) in principle, unless there are special conditions imposed in the transfer agreement. If one of the conditions between the parties involved in the transfer is to exclude some employees, those excluded employees will not be transferred. Such a condition shall be justifiable under Article 23(1) of the Labor Standards Act, because it is equivalent to actual dismissal. However, it is not justifiable to dismiss an employee on account of a business transfer.[526)]

(2) Contract for sale and purchase of property

When POSCO(the transferee) purchased a particular business section operated by Sami Special Steel Company(the transferor), the transferee took over only the assets of the plant but not its claims and liabilities. The transferee took on most of the employees from the transferor, but employed them individually after dismantling the previous personnel organizations upon transfer and hiring them again under a probationary period, after which it placed them in new positions according to the transferee's new business schedule. This was not a business transfer, but rather transfer of an asset.[527)]

---

524) Supreme Court ruling on June 9, 2005, 2002da70822.

525) Supreme Court ruling on Nov. 25, 1997, 97da35085.

526) Supreme Court ruling on June 28, 1994, 93da33173.

527) Supreme Court ruling on July 27, 2001, 99doo2680: Sami Special Steel; Lim, Jongyul, 「Labor Law」, 18th ed., Park Young Sa, 2020, p. 522.

업의 물적 시설과 인적 구성이 일정한 사업목적을 일관성 있게 사업양도 전이나 그 후에 있어서 수행할 수 있는 기능적 일체성을 유지할 수 있어야 한다.[524)]

3) 영업양도가 있다고 볼 수 있는지의 여부는 양수인이 당해 분야의 영업을 경영함에 있어서 무(無)로부터 출발하지 않고 유기적으로 조직화된 수익의 원천으로서의 기능적 재산을 이전받아 양도인이 하던 것과 같은 영업적 활동을 계속하고 있다고 볼 수 있는지의 여부에 따라 판단되어야 한다.[525)]

2. 영업양도의 예외

(1) 특약이 있는 영업양도

영업이 양도되면 반대의 특약이 없는 한 양도인과 근로자 사이의 근로관계는 원칙적으로 양수인에게 포괄적으로 승계되고, 영업양도 당사자 사이에 근로관계의 일부를 승계의 대상에서 제외하기로 하는 특약이 있는 경우에는 그에 따라 근로관계의 승계가 이루어지지 않을 수 있으나, 그러한 특약은 실질적으로 해고나 다름이 없으므로 근로기준법 제23조 제1항 소정의 정당한 이유가 있어야 유효하다. 영업양도 그 자체만을 사유로 삼아 근로자를 해고하는 것은 정당한 이유가 있는 경우에 해당한다고 볼 수 없다.[526)]

(2) 인력 제외한 자산매매계약

포스코(양수인)가 삼미특수강(양도인)이 경영하던 특정의 사업부문을 인수할 때에 공장의 자산은 인수하고 채권, 채무는 전혀 인수하지 않으면서 양도인 소속 근로자 대다수를 채용했지만 수습기간을 거쳐 재배치하는 등 그 인적 조직을 해체하고 양수인의 방침에 따라 재구성을 하였다. 이 경우에는 사업의 양도가 아니라 자산양도로 인정된다.[527)]

524) 대법원 2005.6.9, 2002다70822.
525) 대법원 1997.11.25, 97다35085.
526) 대법원 1994.6.28, 93다33173.
527) 대법원 2001.7.27, 99두2680, 삼미특수강 사건, 임종률, 노동법, 박영사, 제14판, 522면.

Ⅳ. Business Transfers and Employment Relations

1. Principles

1) When making a contract to purchase some parts of another company, in cases where the buying company agrees to take over the rights and duties of the employees working at that business section inclusively, their employment is transferred to the buying company in principle. However, the employment relations transferred at this time refer to the employment conditions the buying company agreed to as of the signing date of the contract, but does not include an employee who was dismissed from that business section prior to the contract-signing date or who was in the middle of a legal dispute regarding claims of unfair dismissal.[528)]

2) In the event of a business transfer, an employee's employment relations are transferred to the transferee company and considered to be continuous. Just because the transferred employee received severance pay at the time of business transfer, does not mean that the employee was terminated by the previous company(the transferor) and beginning new employment with the company that purchased the business. Provided, that if the employee submitted a resignation letter voluntarily and then received severance pay, it can be regarded that the employee agreed to the termination of employment. In contrast, in cases where an employee had to resign and be re-hired by the company according to its unilateral decision and in accordance with its business policy, even though the employee receives severance pay, the employment has not been terminated.[529)]

2. Exceptions

1) Employment relations transferred in a business transfer refer to those with the employees working at the particular section being transferred as of the signing date of the contract, but do not refer to employees who were dismissed from that business section prior to the contract signing date, even if they were in the middle of a legal dispute over claims of unfair dismissal. However, if it is clear that the transferee company knew that

---

528) Supreme Court ruling on May 25, 1993, 91da41750; July 14, 1997, 91da40276.

529) Supreme Court ruling on Nov. 13, 2001, 2000da18608: Severance pay.

Ⅳ. 영업양도와 근로관계의 승계

1. 원 칙

1) 다른 기업의 사업부문의 일부를 양수하는 계약을 체결하면서 그 물적 시설과 함께 그 사업부문에 근무하는 근로자들에 대한 권리의무도 함께 포괄승계받기로 약정하는 경우에도 원칙적으로 해당 근로자와의 근로관계는 영업양수인에게 승계된다. 다만, 이때 승계되는 근로관계는 그 계약체결일 현재 실제로 그 영업부문에서 근무하고 있는 근로자와의 근로관계만을 의미한다고 할 것이고, 계약체결일 이전에 해당 영업부문에서 근무하다가 해고 또는 면직된 근로자로서 그 해고 및 면직처분의 효력을 다투는 근로자와의 근로관계까지 승계하는 것은 아니다.[528)]

2) 영업양도의 경우에는 특별한 사정이 없는 한 근로자들의 근로관계 역시 양수인에 의하여 계속적으로 승계되는 것으로, 영업 양도 시 퇴직금을 수령하였다는 사실만으로 전 회사와의 근로관계가 종료되고 인수한 회사와 새로운 근로관계가 시작되었다고 볼 수 없다. 다만, 근로자가 자의에 의하여 사직서를 제출하고 퇴직금을 지급받았다면 계속 근로의 단절에 동의한 것으로 볼 여지가 있지만, 이와 달리 회사의 경영방침에 따른 일방적 결정으로 퇴직 및 재입사의 형식을 거친 것이라면 퇴직금을 지급받았더라도 계속 근로관계는 단절되지 않는다.[529)]

2. 예 외

1) 영업양도에 의하여 승계되는 근로관계는 계약체결일 현재 실제로 그 영업부문에서 근무하고 있는 근로자와의 근로관계만을 의미하고, 계약체결일 이전에 해당 영업부문에서 근무하다가 해고된 근로자로서 해고의 효력을 다투는 근로자와의 근로관계까지 승계되는 것은 아니다. 그러나 근로자들이 회사의 전적명령에 동의하지 아니함으로써 전적명령 자체가 아무런 효력이 없음이 객관

528) 대법원 1993.5.25, 91다41750; 대법원 1997.7.14, 91다40276.

529) 대법원 2001.11.13, 2000다18608【퇴직금】.

the orders of the transferor company to the transferring employees were not valid(as the employees rejected them), and accepted the business transfer clearly knowing this fact, the employment relations of those employees would be transferred to the transferee company as they are.[530)]

2) In the event of a business transfer, employment relations with the employees concerned are transferred inclusively in principle, but if opposing the transfer to the transferee company, the employees can choose to stay with the transferor company or resign from both the transferee and transferor companies. The employee may also choose, upon his/her own volition, to resign from the transferor company and thereby terminate continuous employment, and then seek a new job with the transferor company. At this time, the employee's intention to oppose the business transfer should be expressed to the transferor company or the transferee company within a reasonable time from the date that the employee came to be aware of the business transfer.[531)]

Ⅴ. Applicability of Rules of Employment and Collective Agreement

1. The rules of employment

1) If employment relations were transferred inclusively, the employee can expect to have the same working conditions with the transferee company as he/she had with the previous company(transferor). In cases where the employer intends to change the rules of employment unilaterally or require the transferred employees to agree to comparatively disadvantageous rules of employment with the transferee company(the new employer), the employer shall obtain the consent of the majority of employees to whom the transferor company's rules of employment apply, by means of a collective decision-making process. Without this type of agreement, the employees concerned shall not be subject to the transferee company's rules of employment, but shall remain subject to the previous rules of employment as they are.[532)]

530) Supreme Court ruling on May 31, 1996, 95da33238.

531) Supreme Court ruling on May 10, 2012, 2011da45217: Severance pay.

532) Supreme Court ruling on Jan. 28, 2010, 2009da32362.

적으로 명확하게 되었을 뿐만 아니라, 양수회사가 영업양수를 할 당시 근로자들에 대한 전적명령이 아무런 효력이 없게 된 사실을 알고 있었음이 명백하다면, 특별한 사정이 없는 한 근로자들의 근로관계가 양수회사에게 그대로 승계된다.[530)]

2) 영업양도가 이루어진 경우에는 원칙적으로 해당 근로자들의 근로관계가 양수하는 기업에 포괄적으로 승계되는 것이지만 근로자가 반대의 의사를 표시함으로써 양수기업에 승계되는 대신 양도기업에 잔류하거나 양도기업과 양수기업 모두에서 퇴직할 수 있다. 또한, 이와 같은 경우 근로자가 자의에 의하여 계속근로관계를 단절할 의사로 양도기업에서 퇴직하고 양수기업에서 새로이 입사할 수도 있다. 이때 근로관계 승계에 반대하는 의사는 근로자가 영업양도가 이루어진 사실을 안 날로부터 상당한 기간 내에 양도기업 또는 양수기업에게 표시하여야 한다.[531)]

Ⅴ. 취업규칙과 단체협약의 변동

1. 취업규칙과의 관계

1) 근로관계가 포괄적으로 승계되는 경우에는 근로자는 승계한 법인에서도 종전의 근로관계와 동일한 근로관계를 유지하게 되고, 사용자가 일방적으로 취업규칙을 변경하거나 종전의 근로관계보다 불이익하게 승계한 법인의 취업규칙을 적용하기 위해서는 종전의 근로계약상 지위를 유지하던 근로자 집단의 집단적 의사결정 방법에 의한 동의가 있어야 하며, 이러한 동의가 없는 한 승계한 법인의 취업규칙을 적용할 수 없다. 이 경우 종전의 근로조건을 그대로 유지한 채 승계한 법인에서 근무하게 되는 근로자에 대하여는 종전의 취업규칙이 그대로 적용된다.[532)]

---

530) 대법원 1996.5.31, 95다33238.
531) 대법원 2012.5.10, 2011다45217(퇴직금).
532) 대법원 2010.1.28, 2009다32362.

2) In cases where employment relations are transferred inclusively due to business transfer or company merger, the transferor employer's contract working conditions shall be transferred. If the severance pay regulations from the transferor company are superior to the severance pay regulations of the transferee company, the inferior transferee severance pay regulations shall not apply after the transfer unless the transferee company obtains the transferred employees' consent through the collective decision-making process stipulated in Article 94(1) of the Labor Standards Act. After the employment relations are transferred inclusively, if the transferee company's severance pay system is inferior to that of the transferor company, the transferor company's severance pay system shall be continuously applied to the employees from the transferor company. As a result, two different severance pay systems would be operated in one company. In this exceptional case, two different severance pay systems can be legitimately established and applied.[533)]

2. Relation to the collective agreement

1) Even though employment relations were transferred inclusively in the business transfer, if the company newly agrees with the labor union through a collective agreement that the previous working conditions would change, or be adjusted or unified with the transferee company's working conditions, this new collective agreement shall be applicable.[534)]

2) Even though multiple companies are merged, the collective employment relations and working conditions between the merged companies and their employees are transferred and continue to apply as they were in the pre-merger companies until the labor union representing those employees can make a new collective agreement that unifies the different working conditions. Even though the labor union of the new company has a union shop membership system, the merged company's employees will not automatically become members of the new company's labor union, until the labor union representing all employees(including the merged company's employees) agree on union shop membership or conclude a collective agreement on the issue with the employees from the merged company.[535)]

533) Supreme Court ruling on Dec. 26, 1995, 95da41659: Severance pay.

534) Supreme Court ruling on Oct. 10, 2001, 2001da24051: Wage.

535) Supreme Court ruling on May 14, 2004, 2002da23185.

2) 영업양도나 기업합병 등에 의하여 근로계약 관계가 포괄적으로 승계된 경우에 근로자의 종전 근로계약상의 지위도 그대로 승계되는 것이므로, 승계 후의 퇴직금 규정이 승계 전의 퇴직금 규정보다 근로자에게 불리하다면 근로기준법 제94조 제1항 소정의 당해 근로자집단의 집단적인 의사결정 방법에 의한 동의 없이는 승계후의 퇴직금 규정을 적용할 수 없는 것이다. 근로관계가 포괄적으로 승계된 후의 새로운 퇴직금제도가 기존 근로자의 기득이익을 침해하는 것이어서 그들에게는 그 효력이 미치지 않고 부득이 종전의 퇴직금 규정을 적용해야 해서 결과적으로 하나의 사업 내에 별개의 퇴직금제도를 운용하는 것으로 되었다고 하더라도, 이러한 경우에까지 차등 있는 퇴직금제도를 설정한 경우에 해당한다고는 볼 수 없다.[533)]

2. 단체협약과의 관계

1) 회사의 합병에 의하여 근로관계가 승계되어 종전 취업규칙이 그대로 적용되더라도 합병 후 노동조합과의 사이에 단체협약의 체결을 통하여 합병 후 근로자들의 근로관계 내용을 단일화하기로 변경, 조정하는 새로운 합의가 있으면 그 새로운 단체협약이 유효하게 적용된다.[534)]

2) 복수의 회사가 합병되더라도 피합병회사와 그 근로자 사이의 집단적인 근로관계나 근로조건은 합병회사와 합병 후 전체 근로자들을 대표하는 노동조합과의 사이에 단체협약의 체결을 통해 근로자들의 근로관계 내용을 단일화하기로 변경, 조정하는 새로운 합의가 있을 때까지는 피합병회사의 근로자들과 합병회사 사이에 그대로 승계된다. 합병회사의 노동조합이 유니언 숍의 조직형태를 취하고 있었다고 하더라도 위에서 본 바와 같은 피합병회사의 근로자들까지 아우른 노동조합과 합병회사 사이의 새로운 합의나 단체협약이 있었을 때까지는 피합병회사의 근로자들이 자동적으로 합병회사의 노동조합의 조합원으로 되는 것은 아니다.[535)]

533) 대법원 1995.12.26, 95다41659 [퇴직금].
534) 대법원 2001.10.30, 2001다24051 [임금].
535) 대법원 2004.5.14, 2002다23185.

Chapter 8

Retirement Management

Section 1: Retirement Age System

Ⅰ. Concept

The retirement age system is a system whereby the employer-employee relationship is terminated when an employee reaches the appropriate retirement age as stipulated by the rules of employment or an employment contract, regardless of any intention on the part of the employee to renew the employment contract or his/her ability to work. Previously, Korean labor law regarding retirement age gave only a recommendation, not a compulsory stipulation, but a statutory retirement age system became effective in May of 2013. Accordingly, any retirement age system that had considered retirement age to be lower than 60 years of age became null and void, and retirement age was automatically set to 60. In addition to this, a rank-based retirement age system is now considered justifiable if it was the result of a labor-management agreement, but with introduction of the statutory retirement age system, any retirement age set lower than 60 years of age is now invalid. In situations where a company that did not previously have a retirement age regulation introduces one due to the compulsory retirement age law, it is recognized that this can be a disadvantageous revision of working conditions, and such unilateral revision is invalid as well.

<Act on Prohibition of Age Discrimination in Employment & Elderly Employment Promotion, May 22, 2013>

Article 19 (Retirement Age) ① When an employer sets a retirement age, he/she shall set it at 60 years of age or older.

② Regardless of Subparagraph ①, in cases where the employer has previously set a retirement age at lower than 60 years of age, his/her retirement age policy shall be regarded as having been set at 60 years of age.

퇴직 관리

제1절 정년제

Ⅰ. 정년제의 의의

'정년제'란 당해 사업장의 취업규칙 또는 근로계약에서 정한 연령이 되면 근로자의 재계약 의사 및 근로능력 여하에도 불구하고 근로계약 관계를 종료시키는 제도를 의미한다. 정년제에 대한 노동법 규정은 강행규정이 아닌 노력 조항이었으나, 2013년 5월 법률개정에 따라 법정 정년제가 도입되었다. 이에 따라 기존의 기업체가 사용하고 있던 만 60세가 되지 못한 정년제는 무효가 되고, 무효가 된 정년제는 만 60세의 정년제도로 자동변경 된다. 또한, 기존의 노사합의로 수용한 직급 정년제가 인정되었으나, 법정 정년제가 도입됨에 따라 만 60세 이내에서는 무효가 된다. 정년을 정하지 않은 회사가 법정 정년제 도입을 이유로 정년제를 도입하는 경우에는 근로조건의 불이익 변경이 되고 이러한 일방적인 변경은 규범적 효력이 없다.

〈「고용상 연령차별금지 및 고령자고용촉진에 관한 법률」(2013.5.22)〉

제19조【정년】 ① 사업주는 근로자의 정년을 60세 이상으로 정하여야 한다. ② 사업주가 제1항에도 불구하고 근로자의 정년을 60세 미만으로 정한 경우에는 정년을 60세로 정한 것으로 본다.

Ⅱ. Application of the Statutory Retirement Age System[536)]

1. In cases where a company has a previously-established retirement age lower than the statutory retirement age

Any retirement age that was previously established at lower than the statutory age of 60 years is null and void due to enforcement of the statutory retirement age, and such invalid retirement age system will be revised so it is in accordance with the compulsory retirement age of 60 years. Accordingly, any such previous retirement age system that a company has stipulated in their regulations is null and void due to introduction of the statutory retirement age, and that statutory retirement age shall become the company's retirement age.

2. In cases where a company which did not previously have a retirement age establishes one due to introduction of the statutory retirement age

1) **Judicial ruling:**[537)] In a situation where a transportation company that did not have a regulation for retirement age established a retirement age, the company's employees could have worked without any age restriction until such time as the company established a retirement age regulation. Once the company established the retirement age regulation, only those employees who passed a review committee could work past the retirement age. This introduction of a retirement age regulation is considered to be an unfavorable change in the working conditions, because it deprives employees of their existing rights and interests.

2) **Judicial ruling:**[538)] Certain employees had worked continuously without any age limitation until their employer established a new retirement age regulation. Because of this new regulation, employees who reached 60 years of age could continue to work as daily workers afterwards. Therefore, this new regulation of the retirement age deprives the employees of their rights and interests, and is considered a disadvantageous revision of working conditions.

---

536) MOEL Guidelines related to handling the retirement age system《Kungi68201-690, on Mar. 3, 2010》

537) Supreme Court ruling on May 16, 1997, 96Da2507.

538) Busan District Court ruling on Sept. 7, 2007, 2007Gahap2704.

Ⅱ. 법정 정년제의 적용[536)]

1. 법정정년에 미치지 못한 정년제 사업장의 경우

법정정년인 60세 미만으로 설정된 정년은 법정정년제 실시로 인하여 무효가 되고, 그 무효가 된 정년제는 60세 정년이 강제적으로 적용된다. 따라서 기존 회사에서 설정된 정년제는 법정 정년제 도입으로 인해 무효가 되고 법정정년이 회사의 정년이 된다.

2. 정년규정이 없던 회사가 법정정년제 도입으로 정년제를 설정한 경우

1) **판례:**[537)] 취업규칙에 정년규정이 없던 운수회사에서 정년규정을 신설한 경우, 그 운수회사의 근로자들은 정년제 규정이 신설되기 이전에는 아무런 제한 없이 계속 근무할 수 있었으나, 그 정년규정의 신설로 인하여 정년에 이르고, 회사의 심사에 의하여 일정한 경우에만 정년을 넘어서 근무할 수 있도록 되었다면 이와 같은 정년제 규정의 신설은 근로자가 가지고 있는 기득의 권리나 이익을 박탈하는 불이익한 근로조건을 부과하는 것에 해당한다.

2) **판례:**[538)] 근로자들은 정년규정이 신설되기 전에는 만 60세를 넘더라도 아무런 제한 없이 계속 근무할 수 있었던 사실이 인정되고, 정년규정의 신설로 인하여 비로소 만60세로 정년에 이르게 되고 피고와의 협의에 의하여 일용직의 신분으로만 만60세를 넘어서 계속 근무할 수 있게 되었으므로, 위와 같은 정년제 규정의 신설은 근로자가 가지는 기득의 권리나 이익을 박탈하는 불이익한 근로조건을 부과하는 것에 해당한다고 할 것이다.

536) 정년제 관련 업무처리 지침《행정해석: 근기 68201-690, 2000.3.10》.
537) 대법원 96다2507, 1997.5.16.
538) 부산지방법원 2007.9.7, 2007가합2704.

3. In cases where a company continues to employ employees after reaching retirement age

If an employee has continued to work with the employer's implied consent after reaching retirement age, the employer cannot terminate employment just because the employee has exceeded the retirement age unless there are special circumstances. When re-employing retirees after their retirement age: if the contract period is fixed, expiration of such contract period is reason to terminate employment; if the contract period is not fixed, it is possible to dismiss the employee only when there is a justifiable reason for dismissal.

4. In cases where the company has a rank-based retirement age system under the statutory retirement age system

If the retirement age can be regulated differently in accordance with title or rank within the workplace, and if the company has established reasonable criteria regarding work characteristics, content, and type of work that the employees provide, the company can then regulate the retirement age by rank(rank-based retirement age system) or as tenure-based employment that cannot be renewed(the tenure-based retirement age system).[539)] The company can also implement two retirement age systems at the same time: a general retirement age system and a rank-based tenure system.[540)] However, this regulation becomes null and void once the statutory retirement age is introduced, but is possible and valid for the period exceeding the statutory retirement age.

5. In cases where an employee is undergoing medical treatment

In cases where an employee is receiving medical treatment due to an occupational accident, the employment relationship shall be continued up to the retirement age.[541)]

---

539) Supreme Court ruling on Apr. 9, 1991, 90Da16245.

540) Labor Standard Team-856, on Oct. 31, 2005.

541) MOEL Guidelines: Kungi 01254-9824, on July 6, 1991.

3. 정년제 경과 후 계속 사용한 경우

정년이 경과한 후에도 사용자의 묵시적 동의하에 계속해서 근로하였다면 특별한 사정이 없는 한 정년초과 만을 이유로 해고할 수 없다. 정년퇴직자 재고용시의 근로계약 기간의 만료시점은 정년 이후 재고용계약 시 근로계약 기간을 정할 경우는 동 계약기간의 만료로, 기간을 정하지 않은 경우에는 해고의 정당한 사유가 있는 때에 해고가 가능하다.

4. 법정 정년제에서 직급정년제가 존재하는 경우

정년규정은 당해 사업장에 있어서 근로자가 제공하는 근로의 성질, 내용, 근무형태 등 제반 여건에 따라 합리적인 기준을 둔다면 같은 사업장 내에서도 직책 또는 직급에 따라 달리 정할 수 있다.[539] 따라서 직급별로 임기를 정하고 임기만료 이후 연임하지 못하면 퇴직토록 하는 방식의 직급별 임기제(또는 직급정년제)를 시행하거나, 일반정년제와 직급별 임기제를 함께 시행한다 하더라도 이를 반드시 법위반으로 보기는 어렵다.[540] 그러나 이 규정은 법정정년제 도입한 이후에는 법정 정년이내에서는 무효이고, 법정 정년 이후에는 가능하다고 할 수 있다.

5. 요양 중인 자의 정년이 된 경우

업무상 재해를 당하여 요양 중인 근로자가 정년에 달한 경우 사용종속관계는 정년일 전일까지 유지된다.[541]

539) 대법원 1991.4.9, 90다16245.

540) 행정해석: 근로기준팀-856, 2005.10.31.

541) 행정해석: 근기 01254-9824, 1991.7.6.

6. In cases where the company has hired an employee older than the retirement age at the age of hiring

In cases where the company was aware that the employee was older than the retirement age stipulated by the rules of employment, and hired the employee anyway, it is unfair to dismiss the employee due to the retirement age in the rules of employment.[542)]

7. Retirement age and retirement date

The retirement date shall be clearly stipulated in order to prevent dispute between employer and employees. If the retirement date has not previously been stipulated, but has habitually continued on a certain day in practical repetition, such habitual practice is the date of termination. In the following samples, I clarify the appropriate retirement dates in various situations for an employee born on April 1, 1965

1) If the retirement age was stipulated as 60 years of age, the retirement date becomes the first day exceeding 60 years of age, which means April 1, 2025.
2) If the retirement date is the first day of retirement age, the effective date would be April 1, 2025.
3) If the retirement date is stipulated as the last day of the month after reaching retirement age, the retirement date would be April 30, 2025.
4) If the retirement date is stipulated as the last day of the quarter after reaching retirement age, the retirement date would be July 30, 2025.
5) If the retirement date is the last day of the first half-year after reaching retirement age, the effective date would be June 30, 2025.
6) If the retirement date is the last day of the year when retirement age is reached, retirement becomes effective on December 31, 2025.
7) If the retirement date is the last day of retirement age, the effective date would be March 31, 2026.

---

542) MOEL Guidelines: Kungi 68207-658, on Apr. 18, 1994.

6. 정년연령이 넘은 근로자를 채용한 경우

채용 당시 근로자의 연령이 취업규칙에서 정한 정년 이상인 사실을 알고서 근로자를 채용하였다면 취업규칙상의 정년을 이유로 해고하는 것은 부당하다.[542)]

7. 정년과 퇴직시점

퇴직시점을 명확히 하여야 한다. 정년퇴직 시점에 대한 노사 간 다툼을 방지하기 위해서는 정년해당 연령을 시기(始期)나 종기(終期)을 정하는 것이 바람직하다. 퇴직시점을 명확히 정하지 않고 관행적으로 운용해 온 경우에는 그 관행에 따라 퇴직시점이 결정된다. 정년을 법정정년으로 하고 있는 A사업장에서 일하는 근로자 甲(생년월일이 1965년 4월 1일)의 정년으로 인한 퇴직 시점은 다음과 같다.

1) 정년이 60세라는 경우: 만60세에 도달(시작)하는 날을 말한다(대법 71다2669, 1973.6.12). 2025년 4월 1일.
2) 정년퇴직 시점을 정년이 시작된 첫날로 규정한 경우: 갑의 정년퇴직 시점은 2025년 4월 1일
3) 정년에 도달한 달의 말일로 규정한 경우: 갑의 정년퇴직 시점은 2025년 4월 30일
4) 정년에 도달한 해의 분기 말일로 규정한 경우: 정년에 도달한 해의 2/4분기 말일로 규정하고 있다면 갑의 정년퇴직 시점은 2025년 6월 30일
5) 정년에 도달한 해의 반기 말일로 규정한 경우: 정년에 도달한 해의 상반기 말일로 규정하고 있다면 갑의 정년퇴직 시점은 2025년 6월 30일
6) 정년에 도달한 해의 말일로 규정한 경우: 갑의 정년퇴직 시점은 2025년 12월 31일
7) 정년이 종료되는 날로 규정한 경우: 갑의 정년퇴직 시점은 2026년 3월 31일

542) 행정해석: 근기 68207-658, 1994.4.18.

Section 2: Retirement Benefit Plans

Ⅰ. Concept

The Employees' Retirement Benefit Guarantee Act Chapter 2. Severance Pay System Article 8 (Establishment of a Severance Pay System)

① An employer who intends to set up a severance pay system shall set it up in a way that it can pay workers who retire 30 days or more of average wages for each year of their consecutive service as severance pay.

② Notwithstanding the provisions of paragraph (1), an employer may, in cases where a worker demands, pay the worker the amount of severance pay corresponding to his/her consecutive service period earlier than his/her retirement. In this case, the consecutive service period to be used for the calculation of the amount of severance pay accumulated thereafter shall be reckoned anew from the time when balances were settled.

Chapter 3. Establishment of a Retirement Pension Plan Article 2 (Definition)

7. Defined benefit retirement pension plan refers to a retirement pension plan under which the level of benefits a worker will receive is determined in advance.
8. Defined contribution retirement pension plan refers to a retirement pension plan under which the level of contributions an employer shall make to pay benefits is determined in advance.

Retirement benefit plans consist of the Severance Pay Plan, Defined Benefit Retirement Pension Plan, and Defined Contribution Retirement Pension Plan. The three plans are equivalent in value. Companies established since December 2005 are required to carry one or more of the three plans.

As there is no provision on qualifying causes of retirement for entitlement to severance pay, an employer shall give severance pay in all cases of termination of the employment relationship due to the employee's resignation or death, the company's disorganization, completion of the work, the employee reaches the retirement age, or the employee is dismissed for disciplinary reasons.

제2절 퇴직급여제도

Ⅰ. 퇴직금제도의 의의

근로자퇴직급여보장법 제2장 퇴직연금제도 제8조【퇴직금제도의 설정】

① 퇴직금제도를 설정하고자 하는 사용자는 계속 근로기간 1년에 대하여 30일분 이상의 평균임금을 퇴직금으로 퇴직하는 근로자에게 지급할 수 있는 제도를 설정하여야 한다.

② 제1항의 규정에 불구하고 사용자는 근로자의 요구가 있는 경우에는 근로자가 퇴직하기 전에 당해근로자가 계속 근로한 기간에 대한 퇴직금을 미리 정산하여 지급할 수 있다. 이 경우 미리 정산하여 지급한 후의 퇴직금 산정을 위한 계속 근로기간은 정산시점부터 새로이 기산한다.

제3장 퇴직연금제도의 설정 제2조【정의】

7. "확정급여형 퇴직연금"이라 함은 근로자가 지급받을 급여의 수준이 사전에 결정되어 있는 퇴직연금을 말한다.
8. "확정기여형 퇴직연금"이라함은 급여의 지급을 위하여 사용자가 부담하여야 할 부담금의 수준이 사전에 결정되어 있는 퇴직연금을 말한다.

퇴직급여제도라 함은 퇴직금제도, 확정급여형 퇴직연금, 확정기여형 퇴직연금을 말한다. 세 가지 제도는 모두 동등한 가치를 갖는 것으로 간주되며, 2005년 12월 이후 신설되는 사업장은 세 제도 중 한 가지 이상의 제도를 설정하여야 한다.

퇴직의 사유는 제한이 없기 때문에 근로자의 사직, 사망 또는 기업의 소멸, 일의 완료, 정년의 도래 및 징계 해고 등 근로계약이 종료되는 모든 경우에 지급된다.

Ⅱ. Severance Pay System

1. Requirements of severance pay

(1) Those eligible for severance pay shall be employees under the Labor Standards Act.

1) Whether to pay severance pay to an employee who was appointed as a company director

In cases where an employee was appointed as company director without terminating employment, the matters related to severance pay shall be evaluated as follows: ① In cases where the director fulfills his duties with the authority of a representative director or executive director commissioned by the company by means of the Commercial Act and the Civil Act and receives a service fee, the director cannot be deemed an employee under the Labor Standards Act. Therefore, his severance pay occurs from the time when he was appointed as director(on the terminated date of employment according to the LSA). The negative prescription is also calculated from the same date. ② In cases where, despite the director's title, he maintains subordinate relations to the employer and is actually in an employee position, the severance pay occurs from the time when the director resigns from the company. The negative prescription is also calculated from the same date.[543)]

2) Calculating severance pay for a person assigned to a regular position from that of a daily worker

The consecutive years of employment to calculate severance pay for an employee who worked for the company as a daily worker but was reemployed as a regular employee shall be considered collectively based on the concrete facts as follows: If a temporary employee quit his temporary position, the employer accepted it, and he followed employment procedures by applying for a regular position, his previous labor contract was terminated effectively regardless of the new employment. However, if the temporary employee was rehired to a regular position while maintaining temporary employment, this is only a transfer to a regular position from an irregular position and his employment cannot be deemed effectively terminated.[544)]

---

543) MOEL Guidelines: Wage 68200-814 2001.11.27.

544) MOEL Guidelines: Wage 68207-581 2000.11.14.

Ⅱ. 퇴직금 제도

1. 퇴직금 지급요건

(1) 퇴직금 지급 대상자: 근로기준법상의 근로자여야 한다.

1) 직원이 임원으로 선임된 경우 퇴직금 지급 여부

재직 중인 직원이 근무기간의 단절 없이 이사로 선임된 경우에 있어 퇴직금을 둘러싼 법률관계는 아래와 같이 판단하여야 한다. ① 이사가 상법 및 민법에 의하여 회사의 업무대표권 또는 집행권을 위임받아 업무를 수행하고, 보수를 받는 등 근로기준법상 근로자로 볼 수 없는 경우에는 임원으로 선임된 날(근로기준법상의 근로관계가 종료된 날)을 기준으로 퇴직금 지급청구권이 발생하고, 소멸시효 또한 이날부터 기산된다. ② 명칭만 이사일 뿐 사용자와 여전히 고용종속 관계를 유지하고 있는 등 사실상 근로기준법상의 근로자에 해당되는 경우에는 이사로서 퇴직한 날을 기준으로 퇴직금 지급 청구권이 발생하고, 이날부터 소멸시효가 기산된다.[543)]

2) 일용직으로 근무하다가 정규직으로 전환된 경우의 퇴직금 산정방법

동일한 사업장에서 일용직으로 입사하여 근무하다가 정규직으로 임용되어 계속 근로한 근로자의 퇴직금 계산을 위한 계속근로연수 판단은 아래와 같이 구체적인 사실관계를 종합적으로 고려하여야 한다. 근로자의 자발적인 의사에 따라 일용직 사직의사 표시와 사용자의 사직수리가 이루어진 이후에 정규직으로의 전환을 위한 시험응시 등 임용절차를 거친 경우라면 이는 정규직 임용 여부와는 관계없이 기왕의 일용직에 대한 근로관계는 유효하게 단절된 것으로 볼 수 있을 것이나, 일용직 근로관계를 계속 유지하고 있는 상태에서 정규직으로의 채용이 이루어진 경우라면 이는 일용직에서 정규직으로 전환된 것에 불과한 것이므로 근로관계가 유효하게 단절되었다고는 볼 수 없다.[544)]

---

543) 행정해석: 임금 68200-814, 2001.11.27.
544) 행정해석: 임금 68207-581, 2000.11.14.

3) If a retired employee is rehired by the same company, the employer cannot make a special contract that excuses the employer from severance pay obligations, as this violates law. The agreement is null and void.

When rehiring a retired employee, the company shall pay severance pay to the employee whose service period has become at least one year after the re-employment. Even if both parties agreed there would be no severance pay, this agreement violates law and becomes null and void.[545)]

4) Whether a full-time lecturer at an entrance exam institute is entitled to severance pay

If a full-time lecturer registered as an individual service provider provided labor service to the employer under substantial employment relations, he/she can receive severance pay. Whether or not a person is an employee under the Labor Standards Act shall be determined by whether the employee provides labor service to the employer under subordinate relations for the purpose of wages in a business or workplace regardless of the contract type. Full-time lecturers at the institute worked every day(6 days per week), which was distinct from other part-time lecturers, received a fixed amount of wages, and observed service regulations and personnel regulations such as starting time and finishing time. They are therefore employees who provide labor service under subordinate relations.[546)]

5) If a person has continuously maintained daily employment formally as a daily employee, the Labor Standards Act shall apply to them and the employer shall pay severance pay to the daily employee who has served at least one year.

If a person has been a daily worker formally but maintained daily employment without cessation, he/she shall be considered a regular employee. It is not true that the continuity of employment shall be estimated by the employee providing an average of 25 days or more of work per month, but also if the employee provided 4 to 15 days on average every month. As daily employees have provided labor service for 4 or 5 days every month without exception, they shall be considered continuously employed and the Labor

545) MOEL Guidelines: Kungi 68207-584 1999.03.12.

546) Seoul District Court ruling on Nov. 10, 2006, 2004Gadan69638.

3) 정년퇴직자가 동일 사업장에 재고용 시 퇴직금 부지급은 강행법규 위반으로 무효이다.

정년퇴직한 근로자를 재고용하는 경우에도 재고용 시점부터 계속 근무한 기간이 1년 이상이면 퇴직금을 지급하여야 한다. 당사자 간에 이를 지급하지 않기로 합의하였다 하더라도 동 합의는 강행법규 위반으로 무효이다.[545]

4) 입시학원 종합반 전임강사가 퇴직 시 퇴직금을 받을 수 있는지 여부

개인사업자로 등재된 입시학원 종합반 전임강사가 실질적인 종속관계로 사용자에게 근로를 제공했다면 퇴직 시 퇴직금을 받을 수 있다. 근로기준법상 근로자에 해당 되는지 여부는 그 계약형식에 상관없이 실질에 있어 근로자가 사업 또는 사업장에 임금을 목적으로 종속적인 관계에서 사용자에게 근로를 제공했는지 여부에 따라 판단해야 한다. 원고들은 학원에서 재학생반 전임강사로 다른 시간강사 내지 단과반 강사들과 달리 매일(주 6일) 출근하며 고정적인 월급을 받았던 점, 출퇴근 시간 등 학원 강사들에 대한 복무규정과 인사규정이 시행됐던 점 등에 비추어 종속적인 관계에서 근로를 제공한 근로자로 봄이 상당하다.[546]

5) 형식상 일용근로자로 되어 있다 하더라도 일용관계가 계속되어온 경우, 상용근로자로 보아 근로기준법을 적용해야 하고 1년 이상 근로한 자에 대하여는 퇴직금을 지급해야 한다.

형식상으로는 비록 일용근로자로 되어 있다고 하더라도 일용관계가 중단되지 않고 계속되어 온 경우에는 상용근로자로 보아야 한다. 또한 근로자가 월평균 25일 이상 근무하여야만 근로관계의 계속성을 인정할 수 있는 것은 아니며, 매월 빠뜨리지 않고 4, 5일 내지 15일 정도씩 계속하여 일해 온 경우에는 근로관계의 계속성이 인정된다. 원고들이 피고회사에서 일용근로자로 근무하는 동안 매월 빠뜨리지 않고 최소한 4, 5일 이상 계속하여 근무해 온 사실을 인정할 수 있으므로 원고들에 대하여도 계속적 근로관계가 인정되어 근로기준법이 적용

545) 행정해석: 근기 68207-584, 1999.3.12.

546) 서울서부지방법원 2006.11.10, 2004가단69638.

Standards Act shall be applied to them.[547)]

6) The Labor Standards Act applies to illegal migrant employees, and they are entitled to severance pay.

The term employee used in Article 2 of the Labor Standards Act means a person, regardless of occupation, who offers work to a business or workplace for the purpose of earning wages. In Article 6 of the Act, an employer shall not take discriminatory action in relation to the working conditions on the grounds of nationality. The Labor Standards Act is applicable to foreign migrant employees, unless there are special reasons otherwise. Accordingly, the rules of severance pay stipulated in the Labor Standards Act apply to illegal migrant employees.[548)]

(2) Consecutive years of employment: The employee shall serve continuously for at least one year.

Years of continuous employment refer to the period from the time when the employee began working for the company to the time when the employee resigned from the company.

The period of disciplinary suspension from work due to an employee's own reasons shall be included in the period of continuous employment, which is the basic data for calculating severance pay, if a person maintains subsidiary employment relations with his employer.[549)]

According to Article 8(1) of the Employee Retirement Benefit Security Act, an employer shall pay severance pay equivalent to the average wage for thirty days or more for each one year of continuous employment. The period of continuous employment in this Act means the period from establishment of the labor contract to its termination. The period in which the employee did not provide labor service, but was in subordinate employment relations with an employer, shall be included into the period of continuous employment for calculating severance pay. Accordingly, the period of disciplinary suspension from work due to the employee's own reasons shall be included in the period of continuous employment as the basic data for calculating severance pay, so long as an employee has maintained subsidiary employment relations with his employer.

---

547) Seoul District Court ruling on Apr. 19, 95Gahap11509.

548) Supreme Court ruling on Aug. 26, 1997, 97Da18875.

549) MOEL Guidelines: Retirement Benefit Security Team-1596.

되어야 할 것이다.[547)]

6) 불법체류 외국인 근로자에게도 근로기준법상의 퇴직금 규정이 적용된다.

근로기준법 제2조에 근로자라 함은 직업의 종류를 불문하고 사업 또는 사업장에 임금을 목적으로 근로를 제공하는 자를 말한다고 규정하고 있고, 또 같은 법 제6조에 의하면 사용자는 근로자에 대하여 국적을 이유로 근로조건에 대한 차별적 대우를 하지 못한다고 규정하고 있으므로 특별한 사정이 없는 한 외국인 근로자에 대하여도 근로기준법이 적용된다 할 것이다. 따라서 불법체류 외국인 근로자에게도 근로기준법상의 퇴직금 규정이 적용된다.[548)]

(2) 계속근로연수: 1년 이상 계속 근로한 자라야 함.

계속근로연수는 원칙적으로 근로자가 입사한 날부터 퇴직일까지의 기간을 말한다.

근로자의 귀책사유로 인한 징계정직기간의 경우 사용종속관계가 유지되고 있다면 퇴직금 산정의 기초가 되는 계속 근로기간에 포함하는 것이 타당하다.[549)]

근로자퇴직급여 보장법 제8조 제1항에 의하면 퇴직금은 계속 근로기간 1년에 대하여 30일분 이상의 평균임금을 지급하여야 한다. 동법에서 계속 근로기간이라 함은「근로계약을 체결하여 해지될 때까지의 기간」을 의미하므로, 실제로 근로를 제공하지 않은 기간이라 하더라도 사용종속관계가 유지되고 있는 기간은 퇴직금 산정을 위한 계속근로연수 산정 시 포함하여야 한다. 따라서 근로자의 귀책사유로 인한 징계정직기간의 경우에도 사용종속관계가 유지되고 있다면 특별한 사정이 없는 한 그 기간은 퇴직금 산정의 기초가 되는 계속 근로기간에 포함하는 것이 타당할 것이다.

547) 서울지방법원 1996.4.19, 95가합 11509.

548) 대법원 1997.8.26, 97다18875.

549) 행정해석: 퇴직급여보장팀-1596, 2006.5.11.

2. Calculation of severance pay

The ERBG Act stipulates that severance pay is calculated as average wage equivalent to 30 days for each year of the relevant worker's continuous service. In the defined benefit (DB) pension system, an amount calculated as the average wage of 30 days for each year of continuous service is deposited into the retirement pension account. In the defined contribution (DC) retirement pension system, 1/12 of the total annual wage is deposited into the retirement pension account. This is equivalent to 8.3% of the annual salary. Because a defined contribution (DC) retirement pension system pays a fixed amount each year, it cannot be recalculated later because the ordinary wage is higher than the average wage. As such, it can be said that severance pay is clarified by calculating the average wage, which is the total wage, in the ERBG Act.

In this way, severance pay and retirement pension are calculated with the average wage, which is the total wage. The reason for calculating and paying the average wage is to protect the living wage of workers and to match a certain wage level in terms of severance pay or accident compensation. The Labor Standards Act provides three ways to protect the level of average wage.[550] First, if the average wage is lower than the ordinary wage, it is stipulated that the ordinary wage shall be the average wage (Article 2, Paragraph 2). Second, the calculations of average wage exclude the probationary period of workers, periods of absence due to reasons attributable to the employer, periods of maternity leave, periods of recovery from work-related illnesses or accidents, periods of childcare leave, periods of legal industrial action, etc. This is an exception to the calculation of average wage, and is a limited enumeration provision to prevent the average wage from being unreasonably low in special cases for workers.[551] Third, despite the exceptions to the above Enforcement Regulation to the Labor Standards Act, if the average wage fluctuates significantly due to the worker's accidental circumstances, the notice on special cases for calculating the average wage determined by the MOEL (Article 4 of the Enforcement Decree to the LSA) is applied.[552]

550) Supreme Court ruling on Jan. 14, 2021: 2020da207444.

551) Supreme Court ruling on July 25, 2003: 2001da12669.

552) Supreme Court ruling on June 25, 2020: 2018da292418.

2. 퇴직금의 산정

근퇴법에서 퇴직금은 근로자의 계속근로연수 1년에 대해 30일분의 평균임금으로 지급한다고 규정하고 있다. 확정급여(DB) 연금제도도 근로자의 계속근로연수 1년에 대해 30일분의 평균임금으로 계산한 금액을 퇴직연금 통장에 적립한다. 확정기여(DC) 퇴직연금은 연간임금총액의 12분의 1만큼 퇴직연금계좌에 적립한다. 이는 연봉 대비 8.3%에 해당하는 금액이다. 확정기여(DC) 퇴직연금제도는 매년 확정된 금액을 지급하는 것이므로 나중에 평균임금 보다 통상임금이 더 높다는 이유로 다시 산정할 수 없다.[550] 이와 같이 근퇴법에서 퇴직금 계산은 임금총액인 평균임금으로 계산한다는 것을 명확히 한 것이라 할 수 있다.

이렇게 퇴직금과 퇴직연금은 임금총액인 평균임금으로 계산한다. 평균임금으로 계산하여 지급하는 이유는 근로자의 생활임금 수준을 보호하여 퇴직금이나 재해보상에 있어 일정한 급여수준을 보장해 주기 위한 취지이다. 따라서 근로기준법은 평균임금의 수준을 보호하기 위해서 다음 3가지 방법을 제시하고 있다. 첫째, 평균임금이 통상임금 보다 저액일 경우에는 그 통상임금액을 평균임금으로 한다고 규정하고 있다(제2조 제2항). 둘째, 근로자의 수습기간, 사용자의 귀책 사유로 인한 휴업기간, 출산휴가기간, 업무상 질병이나 사고로 요양한 기간, 육아휴직기간, 정당한 쟁의행위기간 등의 경우에는 그 기간을 제외하고 평균임금을 계산하게 된다. 이는 평균임금 산정의 예외로 근로자의 특별한 경우에 평균임금이 부당히 낮게 산정되는 것을 막기 위한 제한적 열거규정이다.[551] 셋째, 위의 근로기준법 시행령의 예외에도 불구하고 근로자의 우연한 사정으로 평균임금의 변동이 심한 경우에는 고용노동부가 정하는 평균임금산정특례 고시에 따른다 (근기법 시행령 제4조)[552].

550) 대법원 2021. 1. 14 선고 2020다207444 판결.
551) 대법원 2003. 7. 25. 선고 2001다12669 판결.
552) 대법원 2020. 6. 25 선고 2018다292418 판결

1) Suspension period from work due to the employee's personal reasons shall be included in the period for calculating average wages.

Average wage to calculate severance pay in Article 2 of the Labor Standards Act means the amount calculated by dividing the total wages paid to a relevant employee during the three calendar months immediately before the day on which a cause for calculating his average wages occurred by the total number of calendar days during those three months. If the amount calculated in this way is lower than the ordinary wage of the employee concerned, the ordinary wage shall be deemed his average wage. In cases where the average wage calculating period includes a period of time falling under any points in Subparagraphs 1 to 8 of Article 2(1) of the Enforcement Decree to the LSA, the period and wages paid for that period shall be deducted respectively from a basis period for the calculation of average wages and the total amount of average wage. However, the period in which the employee did not provide labor service due to his own reasons, such as absence, shall not be excluded from the basis period for the calculation of average wages. Accordingly, in cases where the employee did not provide labor service during the basis period to calculate severance pay due to his personal reason like absence, the identical period shall be included into a basis period of average wage and calculated for severance pay.[553)]

2) Including bonuses paid through one year into the amount subject to calculation of average wage.

There are no regulations stipulated in labor law about matters concerning payment of bonuses, but bonuses shall be deemed wages as remuneration for work when they are stipulated in the rules of employment for payment conditions, amount, and payment period, or when they have been paid so habitually to all employees that the employee may have natural expectations to receive a bonus as a matter of course. On the other hand, in cases where the payment rate of bonuses was established per year-unit and paid for the period exceeding one month, the total amount of bonus paid for a certain month shall not be included into calculation of average wage. The bonuses shall be calculated by dividing the total amount of bonuses paid to a relevant employee during the twelve calendar months before the day on which a cause for calculating his average wage occurred by the total number of calendar months, which is 3/12 times the total amount of bonuses paid per year.[554)]

---

553) MOEL Guidelines: Wages 68207-132,2003.02.27.

554) MOEL Guidelines: Wages 68207-120.

1) 휴직기간이 근로자 귀책사유에 해당되는 경우 평균임금산정 기준기간에 포함하여 평균임금을 산정하여야 한다.

퇴직금 산정을 위한 평균임금은 근로기준법 제2조의 규정에 의거 이를 산정하여야 할 사유가 발생한 날 이전 3월간에 지급된 임금총액을 그 기간의 총일수로 나눈 금액을 말하며, 이러한 방법으로 산출된 평균임금액이 당해 근로자의 통상임금보다 저액일 경우에는 그 통상임금액을 평균임금으로 하도록 정하고 있다. 평균임금 산정기간 중에 같은 법 시행령 제2조 제1항 제1호 내지 제8호에 해당하는 기간이 있는 경우에는 그 기간과 그 기간 중에 지불된 임금은 평균임금 산정기준이 되는 기간과 임금의 총액에서 각각 공제하도록 규정되어 있다. 그러나 결근 등 근로자 귀책사유에 의하여 근로를 제공하지 못한 기간은 평균임금 산정기준이 되는 기간에서 공제하도록 규정되어 있지 아니하다. 만일 평균임금 산정기준이 되는 기간에 근로를 제공하지 못한 사유가 결근 등 근로자 귀책사유에 해당되는 경우에는 동기간도 평균임금산정 기준기간에 포함하여 평균임금을 산정하여야 한다.[553)]

2) 1년간 지급받은 상여금을 평균임금 대상금품에 산입하는 방법

상여금의 지급 등에 대하여는 노동관계법에 별도 규정되어 있지 아니하나, 취업규칙 등에 지급조건, 금액, 지급시기가 정해져 있거나 전 근로자에게 관례적으로 지급하여 사회통념상 근로자가 당연히 지급받을 수 있다는 기대를 갖게 되는 경우에는 근로의 대상성을 갖는 임금으로 보고 있다. 한편 상여금의 지급률을 연간단위로 설정하여 1개월을 넘는 단위로 지급하고 있는 경우에는 이를 지급받은 그 월의 임금으로 취급하여 일시에 전액을 평균임금에 산입하는 것이 아니며, 평균임금을 산정하여야 할 사유가 발생한 날 이전 12개월의 기간 동안에 지급 받은 상여금 전액을 그 기간 동안의 근로월수로 분할 계산하여 즉, 3/12을 평균임금산정 기준 임금총액에 산입한다.[554)]

---

553) 행정해석: 임금 68207-132, 2003.2.27.

554) 행정해석: 임금 68207-120.

3) In cases where the severance pay regulation has been revised justifiably in the middle of the consecutive work period, the calculation of severance pay shall apply to the severance pay regulation effective at the time of retirement. The calculation shall not be applied differently for the period before and after revision of the severance pay regulation.[555)]

3. Prohibition against discriminating system for severance pay

1) Discriminating in severance pay between full-time and part-time employees violates the prohibition against different application.[556)]

Article 34(2) of the Labor Standards Act prohibits establishment of different severance pay systems according to job classification, title, business classification, etc. in one workplace and requires one severance pay system. If a company differentiates its application of severance pay for full-time employees than it does for part-time employees, it violates the prohibition against discrimination. Even though the company hires full-time employees and part-time employees differently and applies different hiring procedures, job characteristics, promotion/transfer, etc., discrimination of severance pay shall not be justified without reasonable cause.

2) That the company included the amount equivalent to severance pay into the monthly wage for foreign pilots amounted to different application between foreign employees and native employees.[557)]

If a company agrees to include an amount equivalent to severance pay into the monthly wage for foreign pilots, this means that the company will not pay severance pay at the time of retirement for foreign pilots. This is a different system of severance pay, prohibited by Article 28(2) of the previous Labor Standards Act, than for the native pilots who receive severance pay when quitting their jobs. Therefore, foreign pilots can apply for severance pay by the rules of employment applying to the majority of employees.

555) Supreme Court ruling on Sept. 10, 1996, 95Da15414.

556) Seoul District Court ruling on Oct. 20, 2000, 2000Kahap8606.

557) Supreme Court ruling on Mar. 27, 1998, 97Da19725.

3) 계속근무기간의 중간에 퇴직금규정이 유효하게 변경된 경우 퇴직금을 산출함에 있어서는 전체 근무기간에 대하여 퇴직 당시에 유효한 퇴직금 규정을 적용해야 하는 것이지 퇴직금규정 변경 전후의 기간을 나누어 변경 전 근무기간에 대해 변경 전의 규정을 적용할 것은 아니다.[555)]

3. 퇴직금 차등제도 금지

1) 정규직직원과 시간제 직원에 대해 차등의 퇴직금 제도를 두어 차별하는 것은 차등금지원칙에 위반된다.[556)]

근로기준법 제34조 제2항은 하나의 사업 내에서 직종, 직위, 업종 등에 따라 차등의 퇴직금 제도를 두는 것을 금지하고 하나의 퇴직금 제도를 적용하도록 하는 것인 바, 피고회사가 정규직직원과 시간제 직원에 대해 차등의 퇴직금 제도를 두어 차별하는 것은 위 차등금지원칙에 위반하는 것이라고 보아야 할 것이고, 정규직직원과 시간제 직원 사이에 피고회사 주장과 같은 채용절차, 근로의 성격, 승급 전보조치의 유무 등에서 차이가 있다고 하더라도 이것이 위와 같은 차별을 정당화할 합리적인 이유가 된다고 할 수 없다.

2) 외국인 조종사에 대하여는 월급여 속에 퇴직금 상당액을 포함시켜 지급하기로 한 것은 내국인 근로자와의 사이에 차등제도를 설정한 것이다.[557)]

외국인 조종사에 대하여는 월급여 속에 퇴직금 상당액을 포함시켜 지급하기로 합의하였다고 하더라도, 이는 결국 외국인 조종사에 대하여는 퇴직 시에 퇴직금을 지급하지 않는다는 것이므로, 퇴직 시에 퇴직금을 지급받는 내국인 근로자와의 사이에 구 근로기준법 제28조 제2항이 금지하는 차등제도를 설정한 것이라 할 것이고, 따라서 원고는 피고에 대하여 최다수 근로자에 대한 퇴직금 제도임이 기록상 분명한 피고의 취업규칙에 따른 퇴직금을 청구할 수 있다.

---

555) 대법원 1996.9.10, 95다15414.
556) 서울지방법원 2000.10.20, 2000가합8606.
557) 대법원 1998.3.27, 97다19725.

3) If there are two different applications of severance pay, such as the rules of employment regulating a cumulative severance pay system for native employees and individual employment contracts regulating a singular severance pay system for foreign workers, this violates the regulation that prohibits different application of severance pay.[558)]

4. Paying severance pay

Interim severance pay is implemented only in cases where an employee requests it, but the employer is not obligated to agree to the employee's request. Even if there are relevant regulations regarding the interim severance pay system in the rules of employment or the collective agreement, individual employees must request it concretely and then it can be handled as interim severance pay.

1) In cases where reason to reduce severance pay occurs after payment of interim severance pay, such as abolition of a cumulative severance pay system, the reduced severance pay system applies to that company. The reduced severance pay system calculates both the previously paid interim severance pay and final severance pay, and the company may pay severance pay after deducting the amount already paid.[559)]

According to Article 34(1) of the Labor Standards Act, the liability of an employer to pay severance pay occurs when employment is terminated. However, according to Article 34(3) of the LSA, an employer may, upon the request of an employee, even before his/her retirement, pay severance pay calculated on the basis of consecutive years of employment. Interim severance pay does not differ in characteristics from normal severance pay. In cases where reason to reduce severance pay occurs after payment of interim severance pay, the reduced severance pay system shall apply to that company. The company will calculate the previously paid interim severance pay and the final severance pay, and then the company shall pay severance pay(or expect a refund if overpaid) after deducting the amount it already paid as interim severance pay.[560)]

---

558) Supreme Court ruling on Nov. 28, 1997, 97Da24511.

559) MOEL Guidelines: Wage Policy Team-1173, 2004.4.8.

560) Supreme Court ruling on May 6, 2003, 2001Da54977.

3) 퇴직금 지급에 관하여 누진제를 적용하도록 규정한 국내 직원에 대한 취업규칙과 달리 해외 기능공에 대해서는 개별 근로계약에 의해 단수제를 적용한 경우, 퇴직금 차등제도 금지 규정에 위반된다.[558)]

4. 퇴직금 지급방법

근로자의 퇴직금 중간정산 요구가 있는 경우에 시행이 가능하나, 근로자의 요구에 사용자가 반드시 응해야 할 의무가 있는 것은 아니며, 취업규칙이나 단체협약에 퇴직금 중간정산제 실시를 위한 근거를 마련하고 있다 해도 개별근로자의 별도의 구체적인 요구가 있어야만 유효한 퇴직금 중간정산으로 인정된다.

1) 중간정산 후 퇴직금 감액사유가 발생한 경우(퇴직금 누진제 폐지) 퇴직금 감액규정을 적용하여 중간정산 퇴직금액과 최종 퇴직금액을 산정하고 이미 지급된 금액을 공제하여 퇴직금을 지급할 수 있다.[559)]

근로기준법 제34조 제1항의 규정에 의하여 사용자의 퇴직금 지급의무는 근로계약이 종료된 때에 발생하는 것이다. 다만, 동조 제3항에 의하여 근로자의 요구가 있는 때는 근로자가 퇴직하기 전에 당해 근로자가 계속 근로한 기간에 대한 퇴직금을 미리 정산하여 지급할 수 있으나, 중간정산 퇴직금이라고 하여 퇴직금과 별도의 성격을 갖는 것은 아니므로, 달리 볼 특별한 사정이 없는 한 퇴직금 중간정산이 있은 후에 퇴직급여규정에 정하고 있는 퇴직금 감액사유가 발생한 경우에는 이미 중간정산 된 부분에 대하여도 퇴직급여 규정상의 감액규정이 적용되는 것이고, 사용자로서는 중간정산 된 근로기간과 그 후의 근로시간에 대하여 각각 위 감액규정을 적용하여 중간정산 퇴직금액과 최종 퇴직금액을 산정하고 여기에서 이미 지급된 금액을 공제하고 퇴직금을 지급(초과지급의 경우에는 환수)할 수 있다고 사료된다.[560)]

558) 대법원 1997.11.28, 97다24511.
559) 행정해석: 임금정책과-1173, 2004.4.8.
560) 대법원 2003.5.16, 2001다54977.

2) Is it possible to pay interim severance pay to all employees with the consent of the majority of employees?[561)]

According to Article 34(3) of the Labor Standards Act, an employer may, upon request of an employee, even before his retirement, pay severance pay calculated on the basis of consecutive years of employment. In this case, the number of consecutive years of employment for the calculation of severance pay after such advance payment shall be reckoned anew from the moment of the latest adjustment of balances. Although this interim severance pay was established previously for the relevant regulation or criteria of the interim severance pay in the collective agreement or rules of employment, it shall require concrete requests from an individual employee before implementation. Accordingly, even the consent of more than 50% of all employees does not satisfy the requirements for interim severance pay to all the employees.

3) Even though the company pays some amount as severance pay in the wages paid every month, this does not amount to payment of severance pay.[562)]

The severance pay stipulated in Article 34(1) of the Labor Standards Act occurs on the condition of termination of employment relations, and, in principle, will not occur during the middle of the labor contract. Even if the employer agrees with an employee to pay a certain amount of money as severance pay inside wages paid every month, this cannot be valid as payment of severance pay stipulated in Article 34(1) of the Labor Standards Act.

4) A contract giving up the right to request severance pay or to launch a civil suit is a violation of the Labor Standards Act, and shall be null and void even if an employee signs it.[563)]

Severance pay is remuneration characteristic of deferred wages to be paid in return for continuous employment to an employee who retires after serving a certain period of time. The concrete right to request severance pay occurs on condition of the fact of termination of continuous employment. A contract giving up the right to request severance pay or to launch a civil suit is a violation of the Labor Standards Act, and shall be null and void due to violation of the Labor Standards Act even if an employee signs it.

---

561) MOEL Guidelines: Wages 68200-111, 2002.02.20.

562) Supreme Court ruling on Mar. 11, 2005, 2005Do467.

563) Supreme Court ruling on Aug. 23, 2002, 2001Da41568.

2) 퇴직금 중간정산을 집단적 동의를 받아 시행할 수 있는지[561)]

근로기준법 제34조 제3항의 규정에 의거 사용자는 근로자의 요구가 있는 경우에는 근로자가 퇴직하기 전에 당해 근로자가 계속 근로한 기간에 대한 퇴직금을 미리 정산하여 지급할 수 있으며, 이 경우 미리 정산하여 지급한 후의 퇴직금 산정을 위한 계속근로연수는 정산 시점부터 새로이 기산하도록 정하고 있다. 이러한 퇴직금 중간정산은 단체협약이나 취업규칙 등에 퇴직금 중간정산을 실시할 수 있는 근거나 기준을 정하고 있는 경우에도 개별근로자의 구체적 요구가 있어야만 시행할 수 있는 것이다. 따라서 전체 근로자의 50%이상의 동의만으로는 퇴직금 중간정산의 요건을 적법하게 갖추었다고 볼 수는 없다.

3) 근로관계가 계속되는 동안 매월 지급되는 임금 속에 퇴직금이라는 명목의 금원을 지급하였다고 하여도 퇴직금 지급으로서의 효력은 없다.[562)]

근로기준법 제34조 제1항에서 규정한 퇴직금이란 퇴직이라는 근로관계의 종료를 요건으로 하여 비로소 발생하는 것으로 근로계약이 존속하는 동안에는 원칙으로 퇴직금 지급의무는 발생할 여지가 없는 것이므로 사용자와 근로자들 사이에 매월 지급받는 임금 속에 퇴직금이란 명목으로 일정한 금원을 지급하기로 약정하고 사용자가 이를 지급하였다고 하여도 그것은 근로기준법 제34조 제1항에서 정하는 퇴직금 지급으로서의 효력은 없다.

4) 퇴직금청구권을 포기하거나 민사소송을 제기하지 않겠다는 부제소특약은 근로기준법에 위반되어 무효이다.[563)]

퇴직금은 사용자가 일정기간을 계속하여 근로하고 퇴직하는 근로자에게 그 계속근로에 대한 대가로서 지급하는 후불적 임금의 성질을 띤 금원으로서 구체적인 퇴직금청구권은 계속근로가 끝나는 퇴직이라는 사실을 요건으로 하여 발생되는 것인바, 최종 퇴직 시 발생하는 퇴직금청구권을 사전에 포기하거나 사전에 그에 관한 민사상 소송을 제기하지 않겠다는 부제소특약을 하는 것은 강행법규인 근로기준법에 위반되어 무효이다.

---

561) 행정해석: 임금 68200-111, 2002.2.20.

562) 대법원 2005.3.11, 2005도467.

563) 대법원 2002.8.23, 2001다41568.

Ⅲ. The Retirement Pension Plan

1. Concept

Before December 2005, there were only two types of retirement payments stipulated in the Labor Standards Act: the Statutory Severance Pay Plan, to be paid upon resignation, and the Interim Severance Pay Plan, which could be paid while the employee was still employed. However, in December 2005, the Employee Retirement Benefit Security Act(hereinafter referred to as the ERBS Act) was enacted and introduced something new: the Retirement Pension Plan, which can take the form of either a Severance Pay System or a Retirement Pension Plan. The Retirement Pension Plan is also further broken down into three types: the Defined Benefit Plan, the Defined Contribution Plan and the Individual Retirement Plan. Under these plans and upon retirement, employees can receive gains made from investment of their pension funds, either as a lump sum or monthly pension from an outside financial agency.

The ERBS Act, revised July 26, 2012, strengthened the Retirement Benefit Plan to ensure the retirement benefit is used as income during old age, rather than extra income before retirement. Interim severance payments are now restricted, and at least one of only seven reasons must exist.[564)] The Individual Retirement Plan has also been introduced.

---

564) Enforcement Decree (Article 3) to the Employee Retirement Pension Security Act (Reasons for Interim Severance Pay) ①

1. Where an employee who has not owned a house has purchased a house in his/her own name;
2. Where an employee who has not owned a house makes a key money deposit (according to Article 303 of the Civil Act) or a security deposit (according to Article 3-2 of the Housing Lease Protection Act) for the purpose of moving into a residence. In this case the employee can only apply for the retirement pension one time during employment in a company or business;
3. Where an employee, employee's spouse according to Article 50 (Paragraph 1) of the Income Tax Act, or his/her dependent family member has received medical care for six months or more;
4. Where an employee has been declared bankrupt under the Debtor Rehabilitation and Bankruptcy Act within five years from the time of providing the retirement reserve as collateral;
5. Where an employee has received a decision for commencement of a rehabilitation proceeding under the Debtor Rehabilitation and Bankruptcy Act within five years from the time of providing the retirement reserve as collateral;
6. Where wages are decreasing due to the Wage Peak System according to rules from Paragraph 1 ~ 3 of Article 28 (1) of the Enforcement Decree to the Employment Insurance Act; and
7. Where other reasons and conditions prescribed by Ordinance of the Ministry of Employment and Labor, such as natural disasters, etc., are met.

Ⅲ. 퇴직연금제도

1. 의 의

2005년 12월 이전에는 근로기준법 퇴직금제도(근로자가 퇴사할 할 때 일시금으로 받는 법정 퇴직금제도와 근로자가 재직 중에 받을 수 있는 퇴직금중간정산제도)만 존재하였으나, 2005년 12월 근로자퇴직급여보장법(근퇴법)이 제정되면서 퇴직연금제도가 도입되었다. 현행 퇴직급여제도는 퇴직금제도와 퇴직연금제도로 구성된다. 여기서 퇴직연금제도는 확정급여형(DB) 퇴직연금제도, 확정기여형(DC) 퇴직연금제도, 개인형퇴직연금제도(IRP)로 3가지 형태로 구성된다. 퇴직연금제도는 회사가 근로자의 재직기간 동안 퇴직급여의 지급에 필요한 재원을 외부 금융기관에 적립하면, 근로자가 퇴직할 때 적립된 재원으로부터 연금 또는 일시금의 퇴직급여를 받아 노후생활에 사용할 수 있도록 하는 제도이다.

2012년 7월 26일 개정된 근퇴법은 근로자의 퇴직급여가 생활자금으로 소모되지 않고 노후에 소득재원으로 사용될 수 있도록 퇴직금 제도를 정비하였으며, 크게 2가지의 특징을 갖는다. 첫째 특징은 퇴직금 중간정산의 엄격한 제한이다. 즉, 퇴직금을 재직 중에 중간정산할 수 있는 사유가 7가지로 한정된다.[564] 둘째

564) 근로자퇴직급여보장 시행령 제3조【퇴직금의 중간정산 사유】①

1. 무주택자인 근로자가 본인 명의로 주택을 구입하는 경우
2. 무주택자인 근로자가 주거를 목적으로 「민법」 제303조에 따른 전세금 또는 「주택임대차보호법」 제3조의2에 따른 보증금을 부담하는 경우. 이 경우 근로자가 하나의 사업 또는 사업장에 근로하는 동안 1회로 한정한다.
3. 근로자, 근로자의 배우자 또는 「소득세법」 제50조 제1항에 따른 근로자 또는 근로자의 배우자와 생계를 같이하는 부양가족이 질병 또는 부상으로 6개월 이상 요양을 하는 경우
4. 퇴직금 중간정산을 신청하는 날부터 역산하여 5년 이내에 근로자가「채무자 회생 및 파산에 관한 법률」에 따라 파산선고를 받은 경우
5. 퇴직금 중간정산을 신청하는 날부터 역산하여 5년 이내에 근로자가「채무자 회생 및 파산에 관한 법률」에 따라 개인회생절차개시 결정을 받은 경우
6. 「고용보험법 시행령」 제28조 제1항제1호부터 제3호까지의 규정에 따른 임금피크제를 실시하여 임금이 줄어드는 경우
7. 그밖에 천재지변 등으로 피해를 입는 등 고용고용노동부 장관이 정하여 고시하는 사유와 요건에 해당하는 경우

In cases where retirement pension holders resign before retirement, opening of an IRP is mandatory, and funds are transferred as a lump sum from the previous employer to either the new employer's pension plan, or an IRP account. The accumulated retirement benefit in this IRP account will, by law, be kept and managed until the employee is 55.

2. Differences between the Severance Pay System and the Retirement Pension Plan

The differences between the Retirement Pension Plan and the Severance Pay System are as follows.

1) Under the Retirement Pension Plan, the company deposits the retirement contributions with an outside financial agency, and the employee receives a retirement benefit from the financial agency upon resignation. Under the Severance Pay System, the employer pays a pre-determined amount in severance pay upon employee resignation.

2) The Defined Benefit Plan is the same as the severance pay system, with the amount calculated in the same way: multiplying the average wage for each of the most recent three months by the years of service. The Defined Contribution Plan requires a deposit of 1/12 of the employee's annual salary every year, with the individual retirement benefit varying according to performance of fund investments.

3) In cases where an employee receives a lump sum from the Retirement Pension Plan, he/she shall receive it into an IRP. However, under the Severance Pay System, the employee can still receive a lump sum as before, as there is no obligation to transfer to an IRP in the Severance Pay System. However, the employee can open an IRP account and receive payment there if He/she wishes.

4) The Retirement Pension Plan guarantees the principal funds contributed, as they are managed by an outside agency. Under the Defined Benefit Plan also, the principal deposited outside is guaranteed. However, the Severance Pay System has a weakness in that should the company go bankrupt, the funds may not be available, since they were deposited within the company.

5) The Retirement Pension Plan requires regular retirement contributions to an outside agency, which can reduce the company's financial burden as it does not have to pay out large amounts upon resignation, contrary to the severance pay system. As the severance pay should be paid in full as a lump sum upon retirement, the company will have a heavier financial burden.

특징은 개인형퇴직연금제도(IRP)를 도입이다. 이 IRP 제도는 퇴직연금제도에 가입한 근로자가 중도 퇴직하는 경우 의무적으로 가입하여야 하며, 이직 또는 조기 퇴직으로 인해 수령한 퇴직 일시금은 반드시 IRP계좌로 이전되며, 이 적립된 퇴직급여는 55세까지 의무적으로 보관, 운용할 수 있도록 한 제도이다.

2. 퇴직금제도와 퇴직연금제도 비교

퇴직금제도와 퇴직연금제도의 차이점을 비교하면 다음과 같다.

1) 먼저 퇴직연금제도는 근무기간 중 일정금액의 퇴직급여를 금융기관에 사외 적립하고, 근로자 퇴직시점에 금융기관이 퇴직급여를 지급하는 방식으로 운영한다. 퇴직금제도에서는 근로자가 퇴직할 때 회사가 산정된 금액의 퇴직급여를 직접 지급한다.

2) DB제도는 퇴직급여 산정방식이나 지급되는 금액 등이 퇴직금제도와 동일하다. 따라서 퇴직금 제도와 DB제도의 경우 퇴직 전 최근 3개월의 평균임금에 근속연수를 곱한 금액이 지급금액이 된다. 반면, DC제도에서는 연간 임금총액의 12분의 1 이상을 매년 적립하고, 가입자 개개인의 운용성과에 따라 퇴직급여 수령액이 달라진다.

3) 지급방법은 퇴직연금제도에서는 퇴직 일시금을 지급받을 경우에 반드시 IRP로 수령해야 한다. 그러나 퇴직금제도에서는 퇴직급여의 IRP 강제이전 의무가 없기 때문에 기존방식처럼 일시금으로 퇴직급여를 지급하면 되고, 원하는 근로자는 별도로 IRP를 개설하여 퇴직급여를 수령할 수도 있다.

4) 퇴직연금제도는 사외적립방식이므로 사외 적립된 비율만큼 수급권이 보호되며, DB제도 전액 적립 시 지급액 전액에 대하여 수급권이 보호된다. 반면 퇴직금제도의 경우 퇴직급여를 사내에 유보하므로 회사가 도산하면 근로자가 퇴직급여를 못 받을 가능성이 높다.

5) 퇴직연금제도에서는 퇴직급여를 주기적으로 사외에 적립함으로써 비용 부담을 분산하고 있어 사용자의 재정부담이 경감되나 퇴직금제도에서는 근로자 퇴직 시 일시에 퇴직금을 지급해야 하므로 회사의 재정부담이 가중된다.

3. Necessity for and concept of the Retirement Pension Plan

(1) Necessity for the Retirement Pension Plan

From the employee's perspective, the reasons necessitating the Retirement Pension Plan are as follows: Firstly, it is necessary to supplement the social welfare system. Currently, most people depend on the National Pension only. However, this is not enough for necessities. With three levels of social security(National Pension, Retirement Pension, and Individual Pension), the employee will be far better prepared. Secondly, it is necessary to protect the right for employees to secure their retirement benefits. If the company goes bankrupt, the employee will most likely not receive wages of any kind. To ensure benefits do not remain unpaid, companies shall deposit their contributions at an outside financial agency through the Retirement Pension Plan. From the employer's perspective, the reasons necessitating the Retirement Pension Plan are as follows: Firstly, companies can reduce corporate tax through the Retirement Pension Plan. Only 20% of the retirement benefit reserve each year can be considered business expenses, and each year this percentage will be reduced 5% until 2016, when there will be no tax benefit at all. However, 100% of retirement reserve for the Retirement Pension Plan can be claimed as a tax deduction each year. Secondly, the Defined Benefit Plan aids in reducing company debt, as the retirement pension deposit is deducted from the retirement reserve. The Defined Contribution plan allows the total amount the company has paid into the retirement benefit each fiscal year to be regarded as actual retirement payout, thereby reducing company debt. Thirdly, companies introducing the Retirement Pension Plan can also save from a reduction in wage claim premiums: 50% of the premiums multiplied by the guaranteed rate covered by the Defined Contribution retirement benefit.

(2) Introduction of the Retirement Pension Plan

The employer shall establish pension regulations and obtain consent from the employee representative and permission from the Ministry of Employment and Labor before introducing the Retirement Pension Plan. Upon employee retirement, the financial agency shall pay out a lump sum or a regular pension from the retirement fund the employer deposited. The retirement pension company(trustee) will be a financial agency such as a bank, insurance company, or securities firm, and perform operational management and asset management. Operational management includes design of the retirement pension, operational method of the assets, and

3. 퇴직연금제도의 필요성 및 도입

(1) 퇴직연금제도의 필요성

근로자의 입장에서 퇴직연금이 필요한 이유는 첫째, 사회보장제도의 보충효과를 위해서 필요하다. 현재 노후자금은 국민연금에만 의존하고 있는 경우가 대부분인데, 노후 대비를 국민연금만으로 하기에는 많이 부족하다. 따라서 국민연금, 퇴직연금, 개인연금의 3층 노후보장수단이 필요하다. 둘째, 퇴직금 수급권 보장 차원에서 필요하다. 기업이 도산할 경우에 근로자는 퇴직금을 받을 수 없다. 이를 해결하기 위해서는 퇴직연금제도를 통해 퇴직급여를 사외 금융기관에 안전하게 예치할 필요가 있다.

사용자 입장에서 퇴직연금이 필요한 이유는 첫째, 법인세 절감 효과를 들 수 있다. 퇴직금제도로 사내적립을 한 경우 2012년 기준으로 적립금 추계액의 20%만 손비로 인정되며, 매5%씩 감소하여 2016년에는 사내적립금에 대한 손비인정이 없어진다. 그러나 퇴직연금제도는 추계액 범위 내에서 기업 납입금의 100%가 비용으로 인정을 받는다. 둘째, 회사의 부채비율 개선효과가 있다. DB형 제도에 가입하게 되면 퇴직연금예치금을 퇴직급여충당금에서 차감형식으로 표시하여 기업의 부채비율 개선효과가 있고, DC형 제도로 가입했을 경우 당해 회계기간에 회사가 납부한 퇴직연금 부담금 전액을 퇴직급여(비용)으로 인식하므로 기업의 퇴직부채가 소멸되는 효과가 있다. 셋째, 퇴직연금제도를 도입한 기업에 대해서는 임금채권부담금이 일정부분 경감되어 이를 통한 추가적인 비용절감을 할 수 있다. 경감 금액은 부담금의 50%에 퇴직연금제도로 지급 보장되는 비율을 곱한 금액이다.

(2) 퇴직연금제도의 도입

퇴직연금을 도입하기 위해서는 사용자는 근로자대표의 동의를 얻어 연금규약을 작성하고 고용노동부의 승인을 받아야 한다. 퇴직연금사업자(금융기관)은 근로자 퇴직 시 기업이 적립한 퇴직급여를 퇴직 근로자에게 일시금 또는 연금으로 지급한다. 퇴직연금사업자는 은행, 보험, 증권사 등의 금융기관이 있으며

administration. Asset management includes such tasks as depositing contributions and paying out retirement benefits, maintaining and managing assets, establishing and managing/operating the account.

4. Types of Retirement Pension Plan

(1) The Defined Benefit Retirement Plan (DB)

1) Concept

Under the Defined Benefit plan the company deposits 60% or more of the retirement contributions expected for the year to an outside agency, and the financial agency pays 100% of the retirement benefit within its obligation to pay.[565)] The Defined Benefit plan is characterized by a prior confirmation of the severance payment. This is calculated in the same way as in the existing Severance Pay System, and is equal to the final month's total wage. Severance pay is calculated by multiplying the average monthly wage(over the final 3 months) before resignation/ retirement by the years of service.

2) Characteristics

As the amount of retirement benefit is determined beforehand, plans for the retirement years are possible. As the company contributes to and manages the retirement reserve directly, the employee is free of those responsibilities. One disadvantage is that transferring the retirement deposits to another company is difficult. Depositing additional money or withdrawing money early is not allowed by law, but it is possible to borrow the money as a secured loan, for the following purposes: 1. First-time purchase of a house; 2. Medical treatment for 6 months or longer for the employee or his/her dependents; 3. Decision for commencement of a rehabilitation proceeding; 4. Bankruptcy; or 5. Other reasons and conditions such as natural disasters, etc., prescribed by Ordinance of the Ministry of Employment and Labor. The DB Plan is suitable for companies with job security, low turnover, and who provide high salary increases.

---

565) The Minimum Reserve is the amount equivalent to 60% of the Standard Mandatory Reserve from July 26, 2012 to the end of 2013. After this period, the Minimum Reserve is to increase 10% every two years, becoming 70% of the Standard Mandatory Reserve from 2014 to the end of 2015, then 80% of the Standard Mandatory Reserve from 2016 to the end of 2017, and the rate stipulated by decree of the Minister of Employment and Labor from 2018 on.

운용관리와 자산관리의 업무를 수행한다. 운용관리 업무는 퇴직연금 제도설계, 자산의 운용방법 제시, 행정적 측면의 제도운영이 있고, 자산관리 업무는 부담금 수령 및 퇴직급여지급, 자산의 보관 및 관리, 계좌의 설정 및 관리, 운용지시를 이행하는 일이다.

4. 퇴직연금제도의 종류

(1) 확정급여(DB) 퇴직연금제도

1) 개 념

DB제도는 회사가 기준책임준비금의 60%이상을 사외 금융기관에 예치하고,[565] 금융기관이 지급의무가 있는 범위의 100%를 지급하는 방식이다. 확정급여형은 근로자가 받을 퇴직금이 기존 퇴직금 제도와 동일하게 최종임금 수준에 따라 퇴직금이 결정된다. 퇴직금은 퇴직 시의 평균임금에 근속연수를 곱하여 산정하며 이 때 퇴직 시의 평균임금은 최종 3개월간의 평균임금입니다.

2) 특 징

DB제도는 퇴직할 때 받을 급여수준이 확정되었기 때문에 안정적인 노후설계가 가능하며, 부담금 납입과 적립금 운영을 기업이 대신하므로 근로자의 부담이 없는 반면 직장 이동에 따른 연금의 이동성이 원활하지 못하다. 또한, 추가납입이나 중도인출은 불가하고 법정 사유에 한해 담보내출만 가능하다. 그 법정사유는 무주택자의 주택구입, 본인 또는 부양가족의 6개월 이상 요양, 파산선고, 개인회생절차 개시, 기타 천재사변 등으로 고용노동부 장관이 인정하는 경우이다. 따라서 DB제도는 기업이 ① 안정적이고 이직률이 낮으며, ② 임금상승률이 높은 경우에 적합한 제도이다.

---

565) 사용자의 최소적립금은 2012년 7월 26일부터 2013년 말까지는 기준책임 준비금의 60%에 해당하는 금액이며, 그 후 매 2년마다 10%씩 상승한다. 2014년부터 2015년 말까지는 최소적립금은 70%, 2016년부터 2017년 말까지는 기준책임준비금의 80%, 2018년 이후 부터는 고용노동부령에서 성하는 비율을 적용한다.

3) Eligibility

The employee receives retirement pension or lump sum allowance upon retirement. The retirement pension is available for those who are 55 years old or older and have subscribed to it for 10 years or more. In this case, the beneficiary period shall be 5 years or longer. The lump sum payment is paid to those who were not eligible for pension and who want to receive it as a lump sum payment. This lump sum payment means that the retirement benefit is transferred to the IRP account.

(2) The Defined Contribution Retirement Plan (DC)

1) Concept

The level of contribution the employer and employee make is predetermined by pension law, with the employee's final retirement benefit determined by the company's contributions and the employee's investment gains. Investment outcomes are up to the employee and the final payment depends on the performance of his or her investments. The employer deposits 1/12 of the employee's annual salary every year. A retirement payment is deposited every month, like an interim severance payment. Final payout is determined by performance of the employee's investments. The employee's retirement benefit is equal to company contributions and investment returns.

2) Characteristics

Employees can put additional money into this fund. As the fund is separately managed, it is easy to move it to another company, plus, payout can be higher than the Defined Benefit plan if the investment returns are good. However, management of the retirement funds is at the risk of each employee, who is responsible for choosing appropriate investments. The companies that are more suited to the Defined Contribution plan are ① Companies with lower salary increases and ② Companies implementing an annual salary system.

3) Eligibility

The employer deposits 1/12 of the employee's annual salary every year. The employee manages the retirement fund, and will receive it as a monthly pension or lump sum payment upon retirement. The retirement pension is available for those who are 55 years old or older and have subscribed to for 10 years or more. In this case, the beneficiary period shall be 5 years or longer. The lump sum payment is paid to those who were not

3) 수급요건

퇴직 시에 연금 또는 일시금으로 수령한다. 연금수령은 연금가입자가 55세 이상으로서 가입기간이 10년 이상, 이 경우 연금의 지급기간은 5년 이상이어야 한다. 일시금은 연금수급자격을 갖추지 못했거나 일시금 수령을 원하는 자에 지급하며, 일시금은 IRP계좌로의 전환을 의미한다.

(2) 확정기여(DC) 퇴직연금제도

1) 개 념

DC제도는 기업의 퇴직급여 부담금 수준을 노사가 사전에 연금규약으로 확정하고 부담금을 납부하는 제도로 근로자의 최종 퇴직급여 수령액은 기업이 부담한 금액과 근로자 개인의 운용수익에 따라 결정된다. 사용자는 가입자의 연간 임금총액의 12분의 1에 해당하는 금액을 퇴직급여의 부담금으로 납부하여야 한다. 매년 발생하는 퇴직급여를 개인별로 적립하는 점에서 매년 중간정산을 하는 것과 유사하다. 근로자 개인의 운용 성과에 따라 향후 받을 퇴직급여 수령액이 달라질 수 있으며, 운용결과에 대한 책임은 근로자가 진다. 근로자가 받을 퇴직급여는 기업부담금과 운용수익을 합한 금액입니다.

2) 특 징

DC 제도는 근로자 추가부담금 납입이 가능하며, 적립금이 개인별로 관리되므로 직장이동시 적립금의 이동성이 편리하며, 운용수익률 예상치가 급여상승률 보다 높을 경우 확정급여형보다 유리하다. 그러나, 적립금 운용을 위한 근로자 각자의 노력이 요구되고, 금융상품 선택과 운용에 따른 위험부담이 있다. DC제도가 적합한 기업은 ① 임금인상률이 낮은 기업, ② 연봉제를 실시하는 기업 등이다.

3) 수급요건

사용자가 매년 근로자 연간 임금총액의 1/12 이상을 근로자 계좌에 적립하면, 근로자가 직접 적립금을 운용하다가 퇴직 시 연금 또는 일시금의 형태로 받을 수 있다. 연금수령은 연금가입자가 55세 이상으로서 가입기간이 10년 이

eligible for pension or who want to receive it as a lump sum payment. This lump sum payment means that the retirement benefit is transferred to the IRP account.

The Defined Contribution Plan holder can legally withdraw the deposit or borrow the money as a secured loan during employment for the following reasons: ① First-time purchase of a house; ② Medical treatment for 6 months or longer for the employee or his/her dependents; ③ Decision for commencement of a rehabilitation proceeding; ④ Bankruptcy; or ⑤ Other reasons and conditions such as natural disasters, etc., prescribed by Ordinance of the Ministry of Employment & Labor.

(3) The Individual Retirement Plan (IRP)

1) Concept

The Individual Retirement Plan can take the form of a Company IRP or an individual IRP. The Company IRP is a retirement pension plan as described in the Employee Retirement Benefit Security Act and is acceptable as a retirement benefit scheme for companies that employ 9 or fewer employees. It operates in basically the same way as the Defined Contribution plan, but companies do not have to create the pension rules. In cases where the company later employs 10 or more employees, the Defined Contribution plan shall be adopted. The Individual IRP was designed for the employee to be able to manage his or her own retirement benefit until retirement or until receiving it if resignation occurs earlier.

2) Characteristics/Eligibility

Under the Retirement Pension Plan, when the employee resigns or retires, the retirement benefit shall be transferred to an IRP. Upon reaching the age of 55, the employee can receive a regular retirement pension or lump sum payment. The IRP reserve cannot be withdrawn earlier than the required age except for the legal reasons described in Article 2 of the Enforcement Decree to the ERBS Act: Reasons for Offering Right to Receive Benefits as Collateral. However, The Retirement Pension Plan(DB, DC, Company IRP) shall be transferred to the IRP except in the following situations: ① The subscriber receives payment after age 55 upon retirement; ② The subscriber returns the borrowed money with wage collateral; ③ The retirement fund is equal to 1.5 million won or less, as stipulated by the Minister of Employment and Labor.

상, 이 경우 연금의 지급기간은 5년 이상이어야 한다. 일시금은 연금수급자격을 갖추지 못했거나 일시금 수령을 원하는 자에 지급하며, 일시금은 IRP계좌로의 전환을 의미한다.

DC 제도에 있어 법정 사유에 한하여 적립금 담보대출 또는 중도인출이 가능하다. 그 법정사유는 무주택자의 주택구입, 본인 또는 부양가족의 6개월 이상 요양, 파산 선고, 개인회생절차 개시, 기타 천재사변 등으로 고용노동부 장관이 인정하는 경우이다.

(3) 개인형퇴직연금제도 (IRP)

1) 개 념

개인형 퇴직연금제도는 기업형 IRP제도와 퇴직 후의 개인형 IRP제도로 구분할 수 있다. 기업 IRP는 상시 근로자 10인 미만의 사업장인 경우 퇴직급여 제도로 인정된다. 기본적 운용구조는 DC제도와 동일하나, 퇴직연금규약 작성의무가 없다. 향후 근로자가 10인 이상이 될 경우 DC로 전환해야 한다. 개인형 IRP는 근로자가 이직 또는 조기 퇴직 시 수령한 퇴직급여를 은퇴할 때까지 보관, 운용할 수 있도록 한 제도이다.

2) 특징 · 수급요건

퇴직연금제도에서 퇴직 또는 이직하는 경우에는 퇴직급여를 반드시 개인형 IRP로 이전해야 한다. 이 경우, IRP 적립금은 55세 이후에 연금으로 수령하거나 일시금으로 수령할 수 있다. IRP의 적립금은 자유로이 인출할 수 없으며, 인출을 원하는 경우에는 법정사유(시행령 2조: 담보대출사유)에 해당되어야 한다. 다만, 퇴직연금제도(DB, DC, 기업IRP)에서 퇴직시 개인 IRP로 강제이전이 제외되는 경우는 다음과 같다(시행령9조). ① 가입자가 55세 이후에 퇴직하여 급여를 받는 경우, ② 가입자가 퇴직급여를 담보로 대출받은 금액 등을 상환하기 위한 경우, ③ 퇴직급여액이 고용노동부 장관이 정하는 금액(150만원) 이하인 경우이다.

Section 3: Extension of Working Age for Manual Workers

I. Introduction

On February 21, 2019, the Supreme Court ruled that extends the working age of ordinary manual workers from the current 60 to 65.[566] The retirement age for manual workers went from 55 to 60 through another Supreme Court decision in 1989 and has remained there for the past 30 years. This most recent Supreme Court ruling in February 2019 will bring many changes to society.

In the immediate term, this change will use 65 years of age for calculating civil damage compensation for people who are not salaried workers such as the unemployed, minors, students, full-time housewives and general manual workers. However, considering that the working age of manual workers goes together with the statutory retirement age prescribed by the Act on Prohibition of Age Discrimination in Employment & Elderly Employment Promotion(hereafter, the Elderly Employment Act),[567] which was set at 60 years in 2013, extension of the working age for manual workers to 65 years will influence society in a great number of ways, in terms not only of changing compensation for damages, but also lending momentum to further extending the statutory retirement age. It is especially related to the low birth rate and societal aging in Korea. The proportion of the population aged 65 or older in Korea reached 14.3% in 2018, which makes the nation an aged society, and will reach 20% in 2025, when it will be considered a super-aged society. [568]

---

566) Working age means the maximum age someone is available for employment. The court determines the working age not only after considering social and economic conditions such as the average age of the nation, the economy, and employment conditions, etc., but also after examining a variety of other conditions such as the number of workers in each age group, the employment rate and the labor participation rate (Supreme Court Decision on April 13, 2012, 2009 da 77198, 77204).

567) To accelerate employment of retirement-aged people, the Act on the Employment Promotion of the Elderly was enacted on December 31, 1991. This Act became the Act on the Prohibition of Age Discrimination in Employment and Elderly Employment Promotion on March 21, 2008 (hereinafter referred to as the Elderly Employment Act).

568) According to the United Nations, if the number of those aged 65 or older reaches 7% of a nation's total population, that nation is considered an aging society; if 14%, it is an aged society; and if 20%, it is a super-aged society; Ha, Kaprae, 「Labor Standards Act」, 33rd ed., Joongang Economy, 2020, p. 603; National

제3절 육체노동자 가동연한

Ⅰ. 의 의

대법원은 2019년 2월 21일 일반 육체노동자 가동연한(취업가능한 연령)[566]을 기존 60세에서 65세로 연장하는 전원합의체 판결을 내렸다. 육체노동자 가동연한은 1989년 대법원 전원합의체 판결을 통하여 55세에서 60세로 변경되어 지난 30 년간 60세로 유지되어 왔으나 최근 2019년 2월에 육체노동자들의 취업가능 연령을 65세로 연장한 것은 사회적으로 큰 변화를 예고하지 않을 수 없다.

당장 이러한 변화로 일반 육체노동자뿐 아니라 무직자, 미성년자, 학생, 전업주부 등 소득활동을 하고 있지 않은 국민들의 민사상 손해배상액 산정 기준 나이를 기존 60세에서 65세로 적용할 것이다. 다만, 육체노동자 가동연한과 그 궤를 같이 하는 고령자고용법[567]에서 규정하는 법정정년이 현재 2013년부터 60세로 정하고 있는 점을 고려해보았을 때, 이번 육체노동자의 취업가능 가동연한을 65세로 연장한 것은 단순히 손해배상의 추가보상뿐 아니라 법정정년의 연장요구 등 우리 사회 전반에 다양한 영향을 미치게 될 것으로 예상된다. 특히 우리나라가 당면한 저출산 고령화 문제와도 상당한 관련이 있다. 우리나라의 65세 이상의 인구비율은 2018년에 14.3%로 이미 고령화 사회에 진입했고, 2025년 20%로 초고령 사회로 진입할 것이다.[568]

---

566) 가동연한은 취업가능연령으로 법원은 국민의 평균여명, 경제수준, 고용조건 등의 사회적, 경제적 여건 외에 연령별 근로자 인구수, 취업률 또는 근로참가율 및 직종별 근로조건과 정년 제한 등 제반 사정을 조사하여 도출된다(대법원 2012.4.13, 2009다77198; 77204).

567) 고령화사회를 맞아 고령자들의 고용을 촉진하기 위해 1991.12.31.「고령자고용촉진법」이 제정되었고, 2008.3.21에 이 법이「고용상연령차별금지 및 고령자고용촉진에 관한 법률」(이하, '고령자고용법')로 명칭이 변경되었다.

568) UN에서는 65세 이상의 인구비율이 7% 이상이면 고령화 사회, 14% 이상이면 고령사회, 20% 이상이면 초고령 사회로 본다; 하갑래,「근로기준법」제28판, 중앙경제, 603면; 통계청,「장래인구특별추계 2017-2067」, 2019.3, 12면.

Ⅱ. Changes to Legal Environment

Damage caused by illegal acts includes direct damages, indirect damages and consolation money.[569] Direct damage refers to illegal activities that result in medical expenses, nursing care costs, funeral expenses, repair of damaged vehicles, and other expenses for the victim and/or the victim's family. Indirect damages refer to gains that could have been realized if the illegal act had not been committed. These include lost earnings during the working period and lost severance pay.[570] In this regard, compensation for higher automobile insurance premiums and compensation for civil damages due to work accidents are directly affected.

1. Automobile insurance damages

On May 1, 2019, the age limit for calculating compensation for damages was raised from 60 to 65 years. The contents of this report are as follows: ① extended working age for death and disability, ② consolation money calculation for death and disability, and ③ suspension allowance due to injuries.

For example, if a 35-year-old daily worker is killed in a traffic accident, he would theoretically have had 25 more years of work until his 60th birthday, losses of 277 million won would have to be compensated. However, in the future it will be 30 years, and 320 million won would have to be compensated. The loss of work due to an injury for a 62-year-old worker has been estimated at 0 won, but according to the revised law, it will be 14.5 million won.

<Example of increased lost earnings due to extended working ages in auto insurance compensation[571]>

Division	Victim	Present 60 years	Changed 65 years	Difference
Death	35 years	277 million won	320 million wo	250 million won
Injuries	62 years	0 won	145 million won	145 million won

Statistical Office, 「Future Population Special Estimation 2017-2067」, Mar. 2019, p. 12.

569) The Seoul Central District Court has set a benchmark of 100 million won as consolation money for mental anguish suffered by the family of victims of traffic accidents and occupational accidents that occur after March 1, 2015, without any fault attributed to the deceased person.

570) "Damage Claims Law", Judicial Research and Training Institute, 2008, p. 108.

571) Supreme Court ruling on Nov. 28, 2018: 2018da248909; Data at a public hearing from the Compensation Insurance Association.

Ⅱ. 육체노동자 가동연한 연장에 따른 법적 환경의 변화

불법행위로 인한 손해는 적극적 손해, 소극적 손해 및 위자료[569]로 구성된다. 적극적인 손해는 불법행위로 인한 피해자의 금전 지출을 의미하며, 치료비, 간병비, 장례비, 피해 차량 수리비 등이 이에 해당한다. 소극적 손해는 불법행위가 없었더라면 얻을 수 있었으나 불법행위가 발생하였기 때문에 얻을 수 없게 된 이익을 의미하며, 가동연한 동안의 일실수입과 일실퇴직금이 이에 해당된다.[570] 이와 관련하여 자동차 보험의 보상과 업무상 재해의 민사상 손해배상이 직접적 영향을 받고 있다.

1. 자동차 보험 손해배상금

손해배상금 산정에 있어 취업가능연한과 관련된 연령기준을 2019년 5월 1일부터 현행 60세에서 65세로 상향됨에 따라, 각 보험사는 자동차보험 표준 약관을 변경하였다. 그 내용은 ① 사망, 후유장애 상실수익액 취업가능연한, ② 사망, 후유장애 위자료 감액 연령, ③ 부상으로 인한 휴업손해액 취업가능연한 등이 현 60세에서 모두 65세로 상향조정 되었다.

예를 들어, 35세 일용직 근로자가 교통사고로 사망했을 경우 지금까지는 60세까지 25년 동안 일한 것으로 가정하고 상실수익액 2억 7,700만원을 지급했다. 그러나 앞으로는 30년 일한다고 보고 3억 200만원을 주게 된다. 62세 일용근로자의 부상으로 인한 휴업손해는 지금까지 0원이었으나, 변경된 법에 따르면 1,450만원을 받는다.

〈자동차보험 대인배상에서 가동연한 상향에 따른 일실이익 증가 예시[571]〉

구 분	피해자	현행(60세)	변경(65세)	증 감
사망 상실수익액	35세 일용근로자	2억7,700만원	3억200만	2,500만원
부상 휴업손해	62세 일용근로자	0원	1,450만원	1,450만원

569) 서울중앙지방법원은 2015년 3월 1일 이후 교통과 산재사고의 정신적 위자료에 있어 피해자 측의 과실이 없이 사망한 경우 1억원을 기준으로 삼고 있다.

570) 「손해배상소송」, 사법연수원, 2008, 108면 참조

571) 대법원 2018다248909 판결 관련 2018.11.28. 공개변론 손해보험협회 발표자료.

2. Estimated civil damages for industrial workers

In the event that an employee dies from an industrial accident, the company refers compensation to industrial accident compensation insurance. However, if the company is deemed partly liable, such as for failing to have sufficient safety measures in place, which resulted in the death of the worker, the company shall be liable for civil damages in addition to industrial accident compensation for the surviving family. The extent of the civil damages shall be the loss of the victim whose death has a significant causal relationship to the company's negligence, while the scope of damages recognized are categorized as direct damage, indirect damage and mental damage. In general, if a worker dies, compensation shall cover the sum of medical expenses, hospital expenses, negative expenses, lost work income(loss incurred from the time of death to the point of retirement) and a one-time retirement allowance(severance pay due to early retirement), and mental damage. Lost labor earnings used to be calculated up to the age of 60, but now will be calculated up to the age of 65, which increases the amount of civil damage compensation.

2. 산재 근로자의 민사상 손해배상 산정

근로자가 산업재해로 사망한 경우에 회사는 산업재해보상보험으로 처리하고, 그 보상책임을 면하게 된다. 그러나 근로자의 사망에 있어 회사의 안전조치 미흡 등 회사의 과실 책임이 있는 경우에는 회사는 재해자의 유족에 대해 산재보상 외에 민사상 손해배상 책임을 져야 한다. 민사상 손해배상의 범위는 회사의 과실과 상당 인과관계에 있는 재해자의 모든 손해를 말하며, 판례에서 인정하는 손해배상의 범위는 적극적손해, 소극적손해 및 정신적손해로 구분하고 있다. 일반적으로 근로자가 사망한 경우, 그 배상 범위는 적극적 손해인 병원비와 장의비, 소극적 손해인 일실수입(사망한 시점에서 퇴직시점까지의 잃게 된 수입금)과 일실퇴직금(조기퇴직으로 인해 발생하는 퇴직금 손해액), 그리고 정신적 손해인 위자료로 구성되고 있다. 여기서 일실수입은 지금까지는 60세까지를 기준으로 계산하였지만, 앞으로는 65세까지 계산하므로 민사상 손해배상액이 증가한다.

Chapter 9

Female Workers

Section 1: Prohibiting Discrimination in Employment

I. Concept

The Equal Employment Opportunity and Work-Home Balance Assistance Act has been established to prohibit any discrimination on the basis of gender in determining working conditions for recruitment, employment, wages, promotion, training, etc.

Equal Employment Act). Article 37 (Penal Provisions)

① If an employer discriminates against men or women in worker age limit, retirement and dismissal in violation of Article 11, he/she shall be punished by imprisonment of 5 years or less or a penalty of 30 million won or less.

② If an employer commits an act in violation of any of the following subparagraphs, he/she shall be punished by imprisonment of three years or less or a penalty of 30 million won or less:

1. If an employer does not pay the equal wage for the work of equal value in the same business in violation of Article 8(1);

④ If an employer commits a violation falling under any of the following subparagraphs, he/she shall be punished by a penalty of 5 million won or less:

1. In violation of Article 7, an employer discriminates against men or women based on gender in recruitment and hiring, or when recruiting and hiring female workers, if an employer presents or demands certain physical conditions, including appearance, height, weight, etc., unmarried status, etc., which are not required to perform a certain job;
2. In violation of Article 9, if an employer discriminates against men or women in managing welfare programs such as payment of money and goods or loans other than wages in a bid to support workers lives; and
3. In violation of Article 10, if an employer discriminates against men or women in training, posting and promotion.

Chapter 9

여성 근로자

제1절 여성차별 금지

Ⅰ. 의 의

여성차별 철폐를 위하여 '남녀고용평등 및 일·가정 양립에 관한 법률'이 제정되었으며, 모집, 채용, 임금, 승진, 교육 등 제반 근로조건의 결정과 관련하여 남녀 성차별을 금지하고 있다.

남녀고용평등 및 일·가정 양립에 관한 법 제37조【벌칙】

① 사업주가 제11조를 위반하여 근로자의 정년·퇴직 및 해고에서 남녀를 차별(중략) 경우에는 5년 이하의 징역 또는 3천만원 이하의 벌금에 처한다.

② 사업주가 다음 각 호의 어느 하나에 해당하는 위반행위를 한 경우에는 3년 이하의 징역 또는 3천만원 이하의 벌금에 처한다.

1. 제8조 제1항을 위반하여 동일한 사업 내의 동일 가치의 노동에 대하여 동일한 임금을 지급하지 아니한 경우

④ 사업주가 다음 각 호의 어느 하나에 해당하는 위반행위를 한 경우에는 500만원 이하의 벌금에 처한다.

1. 제7조를 위반하여 근로자의 모집 및 채용에서 남녀를 차별하거나, 여성 근로자를 모집·채용할 때 그 직무의 수행에 필요하지 아니한 용모·키·체중 등의 신체적 조건, 미혼 조건 등을 제시하거나 요구한 경우
2. 제9조를 위반하여 임금 외에 근로자의 생활을 보조하기 위한 금품의 지급 또는 자금의 융자 등 복리후생에서 남녀를 차별한 경우
3. 제10조를 위반하여 근로자의 교육·배치 및 승진에서 남녀를 차별한 경우

Ⅱ. Criteria for Evaluating Gender Discrimination

The term discrimination refers to applying different conditions of employment or work to workers or disadvantaging certain workers without reasonable cause on the basis of gender, marital status, status in the family, pregnancy, childbirth, etc. Even should an employer apply the same terms and conditions of employment to male and female employees, if the number of male or female employees who meet the conditions is significantly lower than that of the employees of the opposite gender, bringing unfavorable consequences to the employees of a particular gender, and the employer cannot justify those terms and conditions of employment, this case shall be regarded as discrimination in employment(Article 2(1)).

However, the employer concerned shall not be deemed discriminative, when, because of the nature of the work concerned, it is inevitable to employ workers of a particular gender for the work; the employer takes actions to protect maternity, such as pregnancy, delivery, and baby nursing, of female employees; or the employer takes the affirmative action to increase equality in employment in accordance with the relevant law and regulations.

In solving disputes related to gender discrimination, the employer shall take responsibility in verifying whether or not appropriate measures are reasonable.

Ⅲ. Types of Gender Discrimination

1. Prohibition against Discrimination during Recruitment and Hiring

When recruiting and hiring female workers, an employer shall not present or demand certain physical conditions such as appearance, height, etc., which are not required to perform a certain job for which the employee seeks employment(Article 7).

The following cases in recruiting and hiring may be classified as gender discrimination:

- Females are not allowed equal opportunity as males during recruitment.
- Limited conditions apply only to females such as: Recruitment of male employees; Men between ages 25~30, women who are unmarried.
- Men and women are recruited separately or a desired number per gender is assigned as(n) men for managerial positions:(n) women for sales positions, or in cases where a certain job is limited to female employees.

Ⅱ. 성차별의 판단 기준

성차별이라 함은 사업주가 여성 근로자에게 혼인 또는 가족상의 지위, 임신 등의 사유로 합리적인 이유 없이 근로조건을 달리하거나 불이익한 조치를 취하는 것을 말한다. 사업주가 채용 또는 근로의 조건을 동일하게 적용하더라도 그 조건을 충족시킬 수 있는 남성 또는 여성이 다른 한 성에 비하여 현저히 적고 그로 인하여 특정 성에게 불리한 결과를 초래하며 그 기준이 정당한 것임을 입증할 수 없는 경우에도 차별에 해당한다(법 제2조 1호).

단, 직무의 성질상 특정 성이 불가피하게 요구되는 경우, 근로여성의 임신·출산·수유 등 모성보호를 위한 조치를 취하는 경우, 법률에 의한 적극적 고용개선조치를 취하는 경우는 차별로 보지 않는다.

성차별과 관련한 분쟁을 해결할 때 분쟁 대상이 되는 조치가 합리적인지 여부를 입증할 책임은 사업주에게 있다.

Ⅲ. 성차별의 유형

1. 모집 · 채용 시 차별 금지

사용자는 근로자의 모집과 채용에 있어서 여성에게 남성과 평등한 기회를 주어야 하고, 직무수행에 필요 없는 용모·키 등 신체적 조건을 제시해서는 안 된다(법 제7조).

모집과 채용에 있어서 다음과 같은 경우에는 성차별이다.

- "남자 모집" 같이 여성에게 응모기회를 주지 않는 경우
- "남녀사원 모집. 단, 남자는 25~30세, 여자는 미혼에 한함" 등과 같이 여성에게만 제한적인 조건을 부여한 경우
- "관리직 남자0명, 판매직 여자0명"과 같이 남녀를 분리 모집하거나 성별 채용인원을 배정하는 경우 또는 특정 직종에 여성의 채용기회를 제한하는 경우

- Regardless of the same education and job experience, a lower position is given to women: e.g. Managerial position, 5th grade: female high school graduates; managerial position, 4th grade: male high school graduates.
- After hiring the employees under the same conditions, men are hired as regular employees, but women as irregular employees.
- In an interview, female applicants are asked more difficult questions than were asked of male applicants.

However, there are exceptions for certain businesses such as entertainment businesses when hiring actors and models, etc. that must consider gender or appearance; security businesses, etc. that hire only males; and those businesses which are prohibited by law from hiring women or allowed to hire only females.

2. Prohibition against Discrimination in Wage and Welfare Programs

An employer shall pay equal wages for equal work in the same business. The criteria for equal work shall include skills, effort, responsibilities, working conditions, etc., required to perform work(Article 8).

Concerning wages and welfare programs, the following cases are examples of gender discrimination:

- For work of equal value, the employer pays a lower wage to females than to males solely on account of gender.
- Existence of a different wage table based upon gender
- The employer keeps a separate criteria(based on gender) for adjustment of wage level or promotion for workers having similar backgrounds, job experience, schooling, etc.
- Family allowance is rendered differently according to a classification of gender such as male employee with spouse.
- The employer places a higher than expected wage level on male workers based upon their military service.

– "관리직 5급: 고졸자 여자, 관리직 4급:고졸 남자"와 같이 동일한 학력, 경력 등에도 불구하고 여성을 낮은 직급으로 모집하는 경우
– 똑같은 조건으로 사원을 모집한 후 남자는 정규직, 여자는 임시직 등으로 발령하는 경우
– 구술시험에서 남성보다 여성에게 더 어려운 질문을 하는 등 불리한 대우를 하는 경우

그러나 배우·모델 등 예술 분야와 같이 직무 성질상 불가피하여 성별이나 용모를 제한하는 경우, 수위 등 직무수행 상 불가피하게 남성으로 해야 하는 경우, 법령에 의거 여성채용이 제한되는 직종에 여성을 채용하지 않거나 여성만을 모집하는 경우는 차별이 아니다.

2. 임금 · 복리후생에서 차별 금지

사용자는 임금 등 근로조건을 결정할 때 '동일 노동가치 동일 임금' 원칙을 준수해야 한다. 동일 노동가치 동일 임금 원칙이란 업무수행에 요구되는 기술, 노력, 책임, 작업조건 등에서 볼 때 서로 비교되는 남·녀간의 노동이 동일하거나 유사한 경우에는 동일한 임금을 지급해야 한다는 원칙을 말한다(법 제8조).

임금·복리후생에 있어서 다음과 같은 경우에는 성차별이다.

– 동일노동 동일가치임에도 불구하고 여성이란 이유로 남성에 비해 임금을 적게 지급하는 경우
– 성별 호봉표를 적용하는 경우
– 경력·학력 등 객관적인 조건이 같음에도 불구하고 호봉 산정이나 승급상 다른 기준을 적용하는 경우
– 가족수당을 '배우자가 있는 남성 근로자'와 같이 성별 기준에 의해 차등 지급하는 경우
– 군복무자에 대해 복무 기간을 상회하여 호봉을 가산하거나 미필자인 남성 근로자에게 호봉을 가산하는 경우

3. Prohibition of Discrimination during Training, Deployment, and Promotion

An employer shall not discriminate against men or women during training, deployment, or promotion on account of marital status, pregnancy, childbirth or gender. The employer also shall not exclude women from certain positions, nor discriminate against men by depriving them of any chance for promotion(Article 10).

Concerning general personnel issues such as transfer, promotion, retirement, etc., the following is gender discrimination:

- Unfavorable personnel transfer on account of marital status, pregnancy, childbirth, etc.
- Separate assignments given to a specific gender to subsidiary work, a special job or field.
- No opportunity given to women; promotion is harder for women than men.
- Assignment by gender when applying employment management system per course.

4. Prohibition against Discrimination on Retirement Age Limit, Retirement and Dismissal

An employer shall not discriminate against men or women in respect to their retirement age limit, retirement, or dismissal. The employer also shall not draw a labor contract stipulating marriage, pregnancy or childbirth of working women as cause for retirement(Article 11).

Retirement age limit is the age in which the labor contract automatically expires. Provided that it is not regulated by law, the retirement age shall be determined in the collective agreement, rules of employment, etc.

The following cases for retirement age limit, retirement and dismissal are examples of gender discrimination:

- Different retirement age for men and women in the same workplace
- When marriage compels retirement
- Dismissal for managerial reasons of which the criteria is based upon gender
- Dismissal due to marriage, pregnancy or childbirth of working women
- Disadvantageous reasons for disciplinary action

Ⅳ. Gender Discrimination Remedy System

Please refer to Chapter 10, “Management of Non-Regular Workers,” Section 2, for the system on correcting discrimination.

3. 교육, 배치, 승진 시 차별 금지

사용자는 근로자의 교육, 배치, 승진에 있어서 혼인, 임신, 출산 또는 여성인 것을 이유로 고과내용을 구분하여 편성하면 안 되며, 일정한 직무에 여성을 배치하는 것을 제외하거나 승진 시 승진 기회를 박탈하는 등 남성과 차별 대우를 해서는 안 된다(법 제10조).

이동, 승진, 퇴직 등 제반 인사사항에 있어서 다음과 같은 경우에는 성차별이다.

- 혼인, 임신, 출산 등의 이유로 불이익하게 인사이동을 하는 경우
- 보조 업무, 특정 직무나 분야에 구분하여 배치하는 경우
- 승진기회를 박탈하거나 승진을 남성에 비해 어렵게 하는 경우
- 코스별 고용관리 제도를 적용할 때 성별 기준에 의한 배치를 하는 경우

4. 정년, 퇴직, 해고 시 차별 금지

사용자는 여성인 것을 이유로 정년, 퇴직, 해고에 관하여 차별을 하지 못하며, 채용 시 혼인, 임신, 출산을 퇴직 사유로 예정하는 내용의 근로계약을 체결해서는 아니 된다(법 제11조).

정년은 근로관계가 자동적으로 종료되는 연령을 정한 것이며, 법령에 별도로 정해지지 않았으므로 노사가 단체협약, 취업규칙 등에 의해 자유롭게 정할 수 있다.

정년, 퇴직, 해고에 있어서 다음과 같은 경우에는 성차별이다.

- 동일 직종에서의 남녀 정년 차별
- 결혼퇴직제
- 성차별적인 해고 대상의 선정 기준
- 혼인, 임신, 출산 등을 이유로 해고
- 불리한 징계 사유

Ⅳ. 성차별 구제제도

'제10장 비정규직 관리' 제2장의 차별시정제도 참고 바람.

Section 2: Sexual Harassment at Work

"Sexual harassment at work" refers to a situation where an employer, a senior, or an employee sexually humiliates or offends another employee with sexually charged behavior or language using status at work or in relation to work, or gives disadvantages in employment on account of a failure respond positively to sexual advances or other sexual requests.

Sexual harassment can occur anywhere within or outside the company premises. If a superior takes advantage of his/her position, it counts as sexual harassment. Sexual harassment can also occur inside a vehicle during a business trip, or during a collective dinner, etc.

Ⅰ. Concept

Act on Equal Employment and Work-Family Reconciliation Article 2 (Definition)

(2) "Sexual harassment at work" in this Act refers to a situation where an employer, a senior, or an employee makes another employee feel sexually humiliated or offended by using sexually charged behavior or language using their high status at work or in relation to work, or provides a disadvantage in employment on account of a rejection of a sexual gesture or other requests.

1. Using their high status at work or in relation to work

1) This applies to an employer or employee using their status at work or in connection to work, whether the situation takes place inside the workplace or in a public area.

2) Although it occurs outside working hours and outside the workplace, it is sexual harassment if it is connected to work performance.

3) The concept of workplace includes a customer's office, dinner with a business partner, business partner's or customer's house, etc., if there is a connection to work.

제2절 직장 내 성희롱

직장 내 성희롱이란 사업주, 상급자, 근로자가 직장 내의 지위를 이용하거나 업무와 관련하여 다른 근로자에게 성적인 언어나 행동 또는 이를 조건으로 고용상의 불이익을 주거나 성적 굴욕감을 유발하게 하여 고용환경을 악화시키는 것을 말한다.

직장 내 성희롱은 사업장 안이나 밖 어디서나 발생할 가능성이 있으며, 상급자가 그 지위를 이용하거나 업무와 관련이 있다면 성립된다. 예를 들어 출장 중인 차 안이나 업무와 관련이 있는 전체회식 장소 등에서 발생하는 성희롱도 직장 내 성희롱이다.

Ⅰ. 성희롱의 개념

> **남녀고용평등 및 일·가정 양립에 관한 법 제2조【정의】**
> “직장 내 성희롱”이라 함은 사업주·상급자 또는 근로자가 직장 내의 지위를 이용하거나 업무와 관련하여 다른 근로자에게 성적 언동 등으로 성적 굴욕감 또는 혐오감을 느끼게 하거나 성적 언동 그 밖의 요구 등에 대한 불응을 이유로 고용에 있어서 불이익을 주는 것을 말한다.

1. 지위를 이용하거나 업무 등과 관련하여

1) 행위 장소가 직장 내인지 여부를 불문하고 공공기관의 종사자, 사용자 또는 근로자의 지위를 이용하거나 기타 업무 관련성이 존재하는 경우를 말한다.

2) 근무시간 외에 직장을 벗어난 곳이라 하더라도 업무수행과 관련성이 존재하는 경우에 성희롱이 성립한다.

3) 거래처의 사무실, 거래 관계자와의 회식장소, 거래 관계자 및 고객의 자택 등도 업무관련성이 있으면 직장의 개념에 포함한다.

4) Although there is no connection in regards to rank in the workplace, there is a connection with the counterpart of a customer company that the employee has to contact in connection with work.

2. Environmental and conditional sexual harassment

(1) Environmental sexual harassment

Environmental sexual harassment is where an employer, a senior, or an employee sexually humiliates or offends another employee with sexually charged behavior or language using a higher status at work or in connection to work, or creates a disadvantage in their employment.

(2) Conditional sexual harassment

Conditional sexual harassment is where an employer, a senior, or an employee disadvantages another employee by using their higher status at work or in connection to work on account of rejection to sexual advances or demands.

Ⅱ. Types of Sexual Harassment and Criteria for Determining its Occurrence

1. Types of sexual harassment

(1) Physical behaviors

① Physical contact like kissing, hugging from in front or behind

② Touching the body, like the breast, backside, etc.

③ Behaviors such as forcing a massage or caressing

(2) Verbal behaviors

① Sying a filthy joke or speaking lustful and indecent words, including in telephone conversations

② Likening appearance to sexual things

4) 반드시 직장 내의 상하관계가 성립하지 아니하여도 업무와 관련하여 필연적으로 접촉하게 되는 거래처의 업무 담당자와의 관계 등도 포함된다.

2. 환경형 성희롱과 조건형 성희롱

(1) 환경형 성희롱

사업주, 상급자, 근로자가 직장 내의 지위를 이용하거나 업무와 관련하여 다른 근로자에게 성적 언어나 행동 등으로 성적 굴욕감을 유발하여 고용환경을 악화시키는 것이 '환경형 성희롱'이다.

(2) 조건형 성희롱

사업주, 상급자, 근로자가 직장 내의 지위나 업무와 관련하여 다른 근로자에게 성적 언어나 행동 요구 불응을 이유로 고용상의 불이익을 주는 것이 '조건형 성희롱'이다.

Ⅱ. 성희롱의 유형과 판단기준

1. 성희롱의 유형

(1) 육체적 행위

① 입맞춤이나 포옹, 뒤에서 껴안는 등의 신체적 접촉행위
② 가슴·엉덩이 등 특정 신체부위를 만지는 행위
③ 안마나 애무를 강요하는 행위

(2) 언어적 행위

① 음란한 농담을 하거나 음탕하고 상스러운 이야기를 하는 행위(전화통화를 포함한다)
② 외모에 대한 성적인 비유나 평가를 한 행위

③ Asking about sexual relationships or facts, or intentionally distributing information of a sexual nature

④ Forcing or requesting sexual relations

⑤ Forcing a woman to sit close and fill glasses at a dinner meeting, etc.

(3) Visual behaviors

① Putting up or displaying lustful photos, pictures, drawings, etc., including distribution by email or fax

② Intentionally exposing or touching one's own physical parts in a sexual manner

(4) Other language or behavior which makes other workers feel sexually humiliated or offended as a socially accepted notion.

2. Criteria for determining whether an action amounts to sexual harassment

(1) Concept

In evaluating sexual harassment, the victim's subjective conditions must be considered. As a socially accepted idea, how a reasonable person evaluates or copes with a situation against the particular controversial behaviors involved must also be considered in the victim's case. Accordingly, you should review whether the situation created a threatening and hostile employment environment as a result and hindered work efficiency.

(2) Concrete details in evaluating what amounts to sexual harassment

1) Undesired behaviors

Whether a certain behavior is considered sexual harassment shall be determined for each case after totally considering all situations and a record of the characteristics of the sexual language or behavior involved and the incident-occurring background. Of course, it is not sexual harassment when two parties want or agree to have a sexual relationship.

However, it is sexual harassment when one party does not want such behavior. An undesired act shall not require repeating or recurring. A one-time sexual act can be regarded as sexual harassment.

③ 성적인 사실관계를 묻거나 성적인 내용의 정보를 의도적으로 유포하는 행위
④ 성적인 관계를 강요하거나 회유하는 행위
⑤ 회식자리 등에서 무리하게 옆에 앉혀 술을 따르도록 강요하는 행위

(3) 시각적 행위

① 음란한 사진·그림·낙서·출판물 등을 게시하거나 보여주는 행위(컴퓨터 통신이나 팩시밀리 등을 이용하는 경우를 포함한다)
② 성과 관련된 자신의 특정 신체부위를 고의적으로 노출하거나 만지는 행위

(4) 그밖에 사회통념상 성적 굴욕감 또는 혐오감을 느끼게 하는 것으로 인정되는 언어나 행동

2. 성희롱의 판단기준

(1) 성희롱 여부의 판단 개념

성희롱 여부의 판단 시에는 피해자의 주관적 사정을 고려하되, 사회 통념상 합리적인 사람이 피해자의 입장이라면 문제가 되는 행동에 대하여 어떻게 판단하고 대응하였을 것인가를 함께 고려하여야 하며, 결과적으로 위협적·적대적인 고용환경을 형성하여 업무능률을 저해하게 되는지를 검토하여야 한다.

(2) 성희롱 판단의 구체적 내용

1) 원하지 않는 행위

어떤 행위가 성희롱을 구성하는지의 여부에 관한 결정은 성적 언동의 성격과 사건이 일어나게 된 배경 등 모든 상황과 기록을 전체적으로 고려하여 사안별로 결정한다. 물론 양 당사자가 원하고 상호합의가 된 성적관계나 교제는 성희롱이 아니다.

그러나 상대가 원치 않은 행위일 경우에는 성희롱이 해당된다. 원하지 않는 행위는 반드시 반복적이거나 계속 일어날 필요는 없다. 단 한 번의 성적 행동이라도 성희롱으로 간주될 수 있다.

2) Victim's perspective

Evaluating whether sexual harassment has occurred at work is to determine if the situation made the victim feel sexually humiliated or offended. In this case, whether or not the offender intended to sexually harass does not matter. That is, the criteria for determining whether sexual harassment has occurred at work is important, and how the victim was affected by the sexual language or behavior.

3) No clear expression of intention required

Recognition of sexual harassment does not require that the alleged victim prove that the alleged offender intended to sexually harass. The undesired behavior in practice shall be estimated objectively in consideration of the victim's language and behavior or surrounding circumstances.

4) Whole circumstances considered during the incident

Whether sexual harassment was or was not committed shall be reviewed by considering totally the recorded events and all surrounding circumstances. All facts and circumstances related to the work environment where the sexual harassment occurred shall be organized and recorded totally and synthetically. Also, a review of the records shall be implemented from all points of view and considering all circumstances.

(3) Judicial ruling[572)]

Sexual language and behaviors equating to 'workplace sexual harassment' in accordance with Article 2(2) of the Equal Employment Act refer to physical relations between a man and a woman or physical, linguistic and visual behaviors in relation to the male or female physical appearance. These behaviors mean that a normal and average person would feel sexually humiliated or offended if that person were in the victim employee's situation in view of the social community's healthy common sense and socially accepted notions. The condition in which these behaviors are considered sexual harassment does not require intention from the offender, but shall consider the relation with the victim employee, place and situation where such behaviors happened, the counterpart's explicit and presumptive reactions and details of such behaviors,

572) Judgment of sexual harassment: Supreme Court ruling on June 14, 2007, 2005Du6461

2) 피해자의 관점

직장 내 성희롱 여부를 판단하는 결정적인 기준은 그 행위로 인해 피해자가 성적인 굴욕감이나 혐오감을 느꼈는지의 문제이다. 피해자가 성적인 굴욕감이나 혐오감을 느꼈다면 성희롱이 성립될 수 있다. 이때 행위자가 성희롱을 할 의도가 있었는지 없었는지의 여부는 판단기준에 영향을 줄 수 없다. 즉 직장 내 성희롱의 여부는 성적인 언동으로 인해 피해자가 어떤 영향을 받았는지가 가장 중요한 기준이 된다.

3) 명시적인 의사 표현이 없어도 성립

성희롱 피해자가 반드시 행위자에게 직접 그 행위를 원치 않는다는 명시적인 의사표시를 하여야만 성희롱이 성립되는 것은 아니다. 그 행위가 실제로 원하지 않는 행위였음은 피해자의 언행이나 주변 정황을 고려하여 객관적으로 판단한다.

4) 피해 발생 당시의 총체적인 상황고려

성희롱을 구성하느냐 구성하지 않느냐는 전체기록과 상황의 총체성으로 검토되어야 한다. 즉 성희롱을 유발한 작업환경에 관련된 모든 사실과 상황들이 총체적이고 종합적으로 구성되고 기록되어야 한다. 또한, 그 기록에 대한 검토는 그 사건이 발생한 모든 상황을 고려한 전체 맥락의 관점에서 실시되어야 한다.

(3) 판 례[572)]

남녀고용평등법 제2조 제2호에서 규정한 '직장 내 성희롱'의 전제 요건인 '성적 언동 등'이란 남녀 간의 육체적 관계나 남성 또는 여성의 신체적 특징과 관련된 육체적, 언어적, 시각적 행위로서 사회 공동체의 건전한 상식과 관행에 비추어 볼 때 객관적으로 상대방과 같은 처지에 있는 일반적이고도 평균적인 사람으로 하여금 성적 굴욕감이나 혐오감을 느끼게 할 수 있는 행위를 의미하고, 위 규정상의 성희롱이 성립하기 위해서는 행위자에게 반드시 성적 동기나 의도가 있어야 하는 것은 아니지만, 당사자의 관계, 행위가 행해진 장소 및 상황, 행위에 대한 상대방의 명시적 또는 추정적인 반응의 내용, 행위의 내용 및

572) 성희롱 판단: 대법원 2007.6.14, 2005두6461.

characteristics and degree of the behavior, whether such behavior was one time only or repeated, and other concrete situations. So, such behaviors should be ones during which a normal and average person in the same situation would also feel sexually humiliated or offended in an objective sense. In such cases, these behaviors should be admitted as sexual harassment that resulted in the counterparty feeling sexually humiliated and offended.

Ⅲ. Employer's Duty to Prevent Sexual Harassment

1. Prohibition against sexual harassment at work

Employers, senior workers, or workers shall not engage in sexual harassment at work(Article 12).

※ Article 39 (Fine for Negligence) ① An employer who commits an action in violation of Article 12 shall be punished by a fine for negligence of ten million won or less.

2. Education to prevent sexual harassment at work

An employer shall implement an educational program one or more times per year to prevent sexual harassment at work and create a safe work environment for workers. Employers and employees shall be required to take education to prevent sexual harassment(Article 13 ①, ②).

The preventive program shall include the following items: ① Laws concerning sexual harassment; ② Procedures or criteria for remedy in the event of sexual harassment at work; ③ Consultation for grievances and procedures for remedy for victims of sexual harassment at work; ④ Other items necessary to prevent sexual harassment at work.

A preventive program can be implemented through employee seminars, morning meetings, conferences in consideration of the size of the business and the situation. Simply distributing or putting up educational materials cannot be deemed as implementation of preventive training.

※ Article 39 (Fine for Negligence) ③ Any employer who failed to implement the measures prescribed in Article 13(1) shall be punished by a fine for negligence of 3 million won or less.

정도, 행위가 일회적 또는 단기간의 것인지 아니면 계속적인 것인지 여부 등의 구체적 사정을 참작하여 볼 때, 객관적으로 상대방과 같은 처지에 있는 일반적이고도 평균적인 사람으로 하여금 성적 굴욕감이나 혐오감을 느낄 수 있게 하는 행위가 있고, 그로 인하여 행위의 상대방이 성적 굴욕감이나 혐오감을 느꼈음이 인정되어야 할 것이다.

Ⅲ. 성희롱 예방을 위한 사업주 의무

1. 성희롱의 금지

사업주, 상급자 또는 근로자는 직장 내 성희롱을 하여서는 아니된다(법 제12조).

※ 제39조【과태료】① 사업주가 위반한 행위를 한 경우에는 1천만원 이하의 과태료에 처한다.

2. 성희롱의 예방 교육

사업주는 직장 내 성희롱을 예방하고 근로자가 안전한 근로환경에서 일할 수 있는 여건 조성을 위하여 직장 내 성희롱의 예방을 위한 교육을 연 1회 이상 실시하여야 한다. 사업주와 근로자는 성희롱 예방 교육을 받아야 한다(법 제13조 제1항, 제2항).

성희롱 예방 교육에는 다음 각 호의 내용이 포함되어야 한다.

① 직장 내 성희롱에 관한 법령, ② 해당 사업장의 직장 내 성희롱 발생 시의 처리절차와 조치 기준, ③ 해당 사업장의 직장 내 성희롱 피해근로자의 고충상담 및 구제 절차, ④ 그밖에 직장 내 성희롱 예방에 필요한 사항

성희롱 예방 교육은 사업의 규모나 특성 등을 고려하여 직원연수·조회·회의, 인터넷 등 정보통신망을 이용한 사이버 교육 등을 통하여 실시할 수 있다. 다만, 단순히 교육자료 등을 배포·게시하거나 전자우편을 보내거나 게시판에 공지하는 데 그치는 등 근로자에게 교육 내용이 제대로 전달되었는지 확인하기 곤란한 경우에는 예방 교육을 한 것으로 보지 아니한다.

※ 법 제39조【과태료】③ 제13조 제1항의 규정에 의한 조치를 하지 아니한 자는 300만원 이하의 과태료에 처한다.

3. Measures to be taken when sexual harassment is reported at work

The employer shall take disciplinary action and other equivalent measures without delay upon the confirmation of sexual harassment at work(Article 14).

1) Upon receiving a report or discovering an occurrence of sexual harassment in the workplace, the employer shall immediately conduct an investigation to confirm the facts. In such cases, the employer must ensure that the worker who has reportedly suffered from sexual harassment on the job or who has claimed that sexual harassment occurred(hereinafter referred to as the "alleged employee victim etc.") does not feel sexually humiliated during the investigation process.

2) In protecting an alleged employee victim etc. during the investigation, the employer shall take appropriate measures such as changing that person's place of work or providing paid leave if necessary. In any case, the employer shall not take action that goes against the will of the alleged employee victim, etc.

3) If the investigation confirms that sexual harassment has occurred on the job against the alleged employee victim(upon confirmation, hereafter referred to as the "employee victim"), the employer shall take measures as necessary and as requested by the employee victim, such as changing the place of work, transferring, or providing the employee victim with paid leave.

4) If the investigation identifies the perpetrator of sexual harassment on the job, the employer shall immediately change the perpetrator's place of work or take other disciplinary actions. In such cases, the employer shall listen to the view of the employee victim on the disciplinary action before carrying it out.

5) Persons who investigate the report of sexual harassment on the job as prescribed in paragraph 2), who receive such a report, or who participate in the investigation process shall not divulge the confidential information they learn during the investigation against the will of the employee victim etc.: Provided, that this shall not apply to cases where they are reporting information relevant to the investigation to the employer or providing necessary information upon request from relevant institutions.

※ In violation of 1) to 5) above: Article 39 (Fine for Negligence) (2) An employer who commits an action in violation of Article 14(1) shall be punished by a fine for negligence of five million won or less.

6) Employers shall not take any of the disadvantageous actions listed in the following subparagraphs against an employee who reports sexual harassment or against an(alleged) employee victim etc.:

3. 성희롱 발생 시 조치

성희롱이 발생 시 다음과 같은 조치를 하여야 하다(법 제14조).

1) 사업주는 직장 내 성희롱 신고를 받거나 직장 내 성희롱 발생 사실을 알게 된 경우에는 지체 없이 그 사실 확인을 위한 조사를 하여야 한다. 이 경우 사업주는 직장 내 성희롱과 관련하여 피해를 입은 근로자 또는 피해를 입었다고 주장하는 근로자가 조사과정에서 성적 수치심 등을 느끼지 아니하도록 하여야 한다.

2) 사업주는 직장 내 성희롱 조사 기간 동안 피해근로자등을 보호하기 위하여 필요한 경우 해당 피해근로자등에 대하여 근무장소의 변경, 유급휴가 명령 등 적절한 조치를 하여야 한다. 이 경우 사업주는 피해근로자등의 의사에 반하는 조치를 하여서는 아니 된다.

3) 사업주는 직장 내 성희롱 조사 결과 직장 내 성희롱 발생 사실이 확인된 때는 피해근로자가 요청하면 근무장소의 변경, 배치전환, 유급휴가 명령 등 적절한 조치를 하여야 한다.

4) 사업주는 직장 내 성희롱 조사결과 직장 내 성희롱 발생 사실이 확인된 때는 지체 없이 직장 내 성희롱 행위를 한 사람에 대하여 징계, 근무장소의 변경 등 필요한 조치를 하여야 한다. 이 경우 사업주는 징계 등의 조치를 하기 전에 그 조치에 대하여 직장 내 성희롱 피해를 입은 근로자의 의견을 들어야 한다.

5) 직장 내 성희롱 발생 사실을 조사한 사람, 조사 내용을 보고 받은 사람 또는 그밖에 조사 과정에 참여한 사람은 해당 조사 과정에서 알게 된 비밀을 피해근로자등의 의사에 반하여 다른 사람에게 누설하여서는 아니 된다. 다만, 조사와 관련된 내용을 사업주에게 보고하거나 관계 기관의 요청에 따라 필요한 정보를 제공하는 경우는 제외한다.

※ 제39조【과태료】사업주가 법 제14조 제6항을 위반한 행위를 한 경우에는 500만원 이하의 과태료에 처한다.

6) 사업주는 성희롱 발생 사실을 신고한 근로자 및 피해근로자등에게 다음 각 호의 어느 하나에 해당하는 불리한 처우를 하여서는 아니 된다.

① Expulsion, dismissal or any disadvantageous measures corresponding to rejection of the worker's status;
② Unfair personnel actions such as levying penalties, suspending, reducing wages, demoting, or limiting promotion;
③ Unfair personnel actions such as relieving of all duties or reassigning duties against the worker's will;
④ Discriminative evaluations of achievement, peer evaluations or unfair payment of wages or bonuses based on such unfair evaluations;
⑤ Limiting educational or training opportunities to develop and/or improve vocational abilities;
⑥ Perpetrating actions such as bullying, physical or verbal abuse which inflict emotional or physical damage, or neglecting to stop the occurrence of such actions;
⑦ Any other disadvantageous measures against the will of the worker who reported the sexual harassment or against the employee victim etc.
※ Article 37 (Penal Provisions) (2) An employer who commits an act in violation of Article 14(6) shall be punished by imprisonment of three years or less or a penalty of 30 million won or less.

4. Application to dispatch employees

When the provision of Article 13(1) is applied to a workplace where dispatch employees are used pursuant to the Act relating to Protection, etc. of Dispatch Employees, the using employer prescribed in Article 2(4) of the Act relating to Protection, etc. of Dispatch Employees shall be regarded as the employer prescribed in this Act.

Ⅳ. Employer's Procedures in Dealing with Sexual Harassment Cases

Upon receiving a complaint of sexual harassment, the employer shall conduct interviews, investigate the facts, implement appropriate measures, such as disciplinary punishment, etc. and then inform the alleged victim-employee.

- 1st stage: Receipt of sexual harassment report

The person-in-charge of a help organization in the company, personnel or labor department receives the case.

① 파면, 해임, 해고, 그밖에 신분 상실에 해당하는 불이익 조치
② 징계, 정직, 감봉, 강등, 승진 제한 등 부당한 인사조치
③ 직무 미부여, 직무 재배치, 그밖에 본인의 의사에 반하는 인사조치
④ 성과평가 또는 동료평가 등에서 차별이나 그에 따른 임금 또는 상여금 등의 차별 지급
⑤ 직업능력 개발 및 향상을 위한 교육훈련 기회의 제한
⑥ 집단 따돌림, 폭행 또는 폭언 등 정신적·신체적 손상을 가져오는 행위를 하거나 그 행위의 발생을 방치하는 행위
⑦ 그밖에 신고를 한 근로자 및 피해근로자등의 의사에 반하는 불리한 처우

※ 제37조【벌 칙】사업주가 위반한 행위를 한 경우에는 3년 이하의 징역 또는 3천만 원 이하의 벌금에 처한다.

4. 파견근로에 대한 적용

「파견 근로자보호 등에 관한 법률」에 의하여 파견근로가 행해지는 사업장에 대하여 제13조 제1항의 규정을 적용함에 있어서는 「파견 근로자보호 등에 관한 법률」 제2조 제4호의 규정에 의한 사용사업주를 이 법에 의한 사업주로 본다(법 제34조).

Ⅳ. 성희롱의 처리절차

직장 내 성희롱 관련 내용이 접수되면 사업주는 당사자 상담과 조사를 통하여 사실관계를 확인하고, 징계 등 적절한 조치와 함께 처리 결과를 피해근로자에게 통보하는 순서로 처리한다.

– 1단계: 성희롱 접수

회사 내의 고충처리 절차에 따라 고충처리기구의 담당자나 인사부서, 노무부서에서 접수한다.

- 2nd stage: Interviews and investigation

Upon receiving the report, the person-in-charge shall quickly interview and thoroughly investigate. If necessary, the investigator can hear the suspect's testimony instead by organizing a face-to-face meeting between the alleged victim and the suspect.

The person-in-charge shall weigh the collected information obtained during investigations. As soon as the person-in-charge draws an official opinion, it shall be reported to the employer.

- 3rd stage: Confirmation and disciplinary action

Upon confirming that sexual harassment has occurred, the employer shall take appropriate measures such as transferring the offender to a different department or position, issuing a warning or reprimand, suspending from work, or dismissing the offender. If light disciplinary punishment such as a warning fails to deter the offender from repeating the sexual harassment, the employer shall take harsher disciplinary measures. Also, the victim may request a transfer to another department.

- 4th stage: Report of the results

Upon closing the investigation, the company shall notify the(alleged) victim and the(alleged) offender of the results.

- 5th stage: Preventative actions

The employer shall pay special concern to the victim employee after the closure of a confirmed case of sexual harassment to prevent further harassment of that employee.

〈Reference : Burden of Proof〉

In cases of workplace harassment or sexual harassment, the burden of proof is crucial. Generally, it lies with the person making the claim, and if they fail to prove it, they lose the case. However, according to Article 30 (Burden of Proof) of the Equal Employment Act, "the burden of proof in disputes related to this Act shall be borne by the employer." Therefore, in matters related to this law, if an employee claims they have a grievance or have suffered damage, they only need to provide evidence that could lead judges or members of the labor commission to reasonably infer that the problems are related to the law.[573] In this particular case, even though the employer and the victim provided different explanations for the occurrence of harassment and sexual misconduct, the Supreme Court recognized P's claims of workplace harassment and sexual harassment as true, as it was reasonable to assume that such events had occurred.

---

573) Kim, El-lim, "Employer's Responsibility for Sexual Harassment in the Workplace - Supreme Court Decision 95da39533, February 10, 1998," in Labor Case Law: 100 Cases, First Edition, Korean Labor Law Association, Parkyoungsa, 2014.

– 2단계: 상담과 조사

사건 접수를 하면 피해자와 성희롱 용의자에게 신속하게 성희롱 사건 전모를 듣고 공정하고 세심하게 조사한다. 필요한 경우에는 피해자의 입장을 성희롱 용의자와의 대면 대신 증인의 증언을 통해 들을 수 있다.

고충처리 담당자는 조사과정에서 취득한 개인정보를 양자의 사생활 보호 측면에서 비밀로 지켜야 한다. 공식 조사된 결과가 직장 내 성희롱이라고 판단되면 담당자는 사업주에게 보고한다.

– 3단계: 확인과 징계절차

사업주는 성희롱 사실이 확인되면 성희롱 행위자에 대해 부서 이동, 경고, 견책, 전직, 대기발령, 정직, 해고 등의 적절한 조치를 취해야 한다. 경고 등 가벼운 징계로 행위자가 성희롱 행위를 멈추지 않을 경우 더욱 강한 징계 조치를 해야 한다. 또한, 성희롱 피해자가 원하는 경우 본인의 근무 부서를 이동시킬 수 있다.

– 4단계: 결과 통지

조사를 종결할 때는 피해자와 성희롱 행위자 모두에게 조사 결과를 통지한다.

– 5단계: 사후 재발 방지

사업주는 성희롱 사건에 대한 조치 후에도 향후 피해근로자에 대한 성희롱 문제가 재발하지 않도록 관심을 가져야 한다.

〈참고 : 입증책임〉

직장내 괴롭힘이나 성희롱 사건은 입증책임이 중요하다. 일반적으로 입증 책임은 이를 주장하는 사람이 이를 입증해야 하고 입증하지 않으면 패소한다. 그러나 남녀고용평등법 제30조(입증책임)에서는 "이 법과 관련한 분쟁해결에서 입증책임은 사업주가 부담한다." 이에 따라 이 법과 관련된 문제에 관하여 근로자는 고충과 피해를 받았음을 법관, 노동위원회 위원 등 판단자들이 추측할 수 있을 정도의 실증을 주거나 증거를 제출하면 된다.[573)]

---

573) 김엘림, "직장 내 성희롱 사용자 책임 – 대법원 1998. 2. 10. 선고 95다39533 판결," 「노동판례백선 초판」, 한국노동법학회 편, 박영사, 2014.

Section 3: Protection of Motherhood

Ⅰ. Understanding Motherhood Protection

The Korean government is taking steps to protect motherhood through specific provisions stipulated by the Constitution of the Republic of Korea[574)] as well as other practical provisions stipulated by various labor laws. Despite these protection laws, the birthrate has decreased to an average of just 0.68 persons per couple as of 2024, and the government has strengthened its efforts in response towards revising labor laws designed to promote workforce participation by women and also increase the birthrate.

Ⅱ. Protection of Maternal Employees

A maternal employee refers to a woman who is pregnant or is within her first year after childbirth, and is therefore provided special protection under the various laws so designed.

1. Employment in hazardous/dangerous work prohibited

Employers shall not assign maternal employees to mentally and physically hazardous work. In addition, they shall not assign women aged 18 or older who are not pregnant to work that is hazardous to their possible future pregnancy and/or childbirth. Occupations that are prohibited are described in the attached Table 4 of the Presidential Decree(Article 65 of the LSA(Labor Standards Act)).

2. Restrictions on extended work, night work and holiday work

(1) Extended work

Employers shall not place pregnant female employees on overtime duty or flexible work,

574) Constitution of the Republic of Korea (Article 36, Subparagraph 2): The State shall endeavor to protect mothers.

제3절 여성보호

Ⅰ. 여성보호의 의의

우리나라는 모성과 관련하여 헌법에 의한 명시적 보호규정[574]과 노동법에 의한 실천적 보호규정을 두고 엄격하게 모성을 보호하고 있다. 이러한 법률적 보호규정에도 불구하고 출산율이 계속 떨어져 2024년에는 0.68명에 까지 하락함에 따라 여성근로를 장려하고 출산율을 높이기 위한 노력이 노동법에 반영되고 있다.

Ⅱ. 임산부 보호

임산부는 임신 중이거나 산후 1년이 지나지 아니한 여성을 말하며, 이 기간 동안 모성보호를 위한 각종 보호 규정을 통해 특별한 보호를 받는다.

1. 유해·위험한 사업에 사용금지

사용자는 임산부를 도덕상 또는 보건 상 유해·위험한 사업에 사용하지 못한다. 특히, 임산부가 아닌 18세 이상의 여성을 보건 상 유해·위험한 사업 중 임신 또는 출산에 관한 기능에 유해·위험한 사업에 사용하지 못한다. 이와 관련 임산부의 금지직종은 근로기준법시행령 별표 4호에 명시하고 있다(근기법 제65조).

2. 연장근로, 야간근로, 휴일근로의 제한

(1) 연장근로(근로기준법 제51조, 제71조, 제74조)

사용자는 임신 중의 여성 근로자에게 연장근로 및 탄력적 근로를 하게 하여

574) 헌법 제36조 제2항: 국가는 모성의 보호를 위하여 노력하여야 한다.

and, in the event of such a request from the employee, she shall be assigned light duties. Employers shall not permit women for whom less than one year has passed since childbirth to work more than 2 hours in overtime per 8-hour work day, and 6 hours per work week of 40 hours, even if so agreed in a collective agreement(Article 51, 71, 74 of the LSA).

(2) Night work and holiday work (Article 70 of the LSA)

Employers shall not assign maternal employees to work at night(from 10 P.M to 6 A.M.) or on holidays. However, exception to such restrictions on night work and holiday work are possible in cases where the employer obtains permission in advance from the Minister of Employment and Labor and ① there is consent from the employee for whom less than one year has passed since childbirth; or ② a pregnant woman makes such a request.

3. Protection leave for maternal employees

(1) Maternity leave

Employers shall grant pregnant female employees 90 days of maternity leave(①120 days if a woman is pregnant with two or more babies; ②100 days if a woman gives birth to a premature baby who is admitted to the neonatal intensive care unit.), to be used before and after childbirth. In such cases, a minimum of 45 days(60 days for multiple babies) shall be allocated after childbirth. At the end of the maternity leave, the employer shall allow the female employee to return to the same work, or other work at the same rate of pay as before the leave. The first 60 days(75 days for multiple babies) of leave shall be paid. The remaining 30 days(or 45 days for multiple babies) qualify for reimbursement of up to 2.1 million won through employment insurance, provided, that for companies[575)] eligible for preferential support, the employee concerned will receive the first 60 days' maternity leave allowance(up to 2.1 million won per month) from employment insurance. In this case, the employer will pay the amount of the ordinary wage exceeding the government subsidy(Article 74 of the LSA).

Employers shall not dismiss any female employee during a period of temporary interruption of work before or after childbirth as provided herein and within 30 days thereafter. For the purpose of calculating annual paid leave, the maternity leave shall be regarded as attended days. Also, in calculating the average wage for purposes of severance payment, the period

575) Preferentially Supported Companies (Article 12 of the Presidential Decree to the LSA)

서는 아니 되며, 그 근로자의 요구가 있는 경우에는 쉬운 종류의 근로로 전환하여야 한다. 사용자는 산후 1년이 지나지 아니한 여성에 대하여는 단체협약이 있는 경우라도 1일의 8시간 근무에 2시간, 1주일 40시간 근무에 6시간을 초과하는 연장근로를 시키지 못한다.

(2) 야간근로 및 휴일근로(근기법 제70조)

사용자는 임산부를 야간근로(오후 10시부터 오전 6시까지)와 휴일 근로를 근로시키지 못한다. 다만, 예외적으로 사용자가 노동부장관의 인가를 받고, ① 산후 1년이 지나지 아니한 여성의 동의가 있는 경우와 ② 임신 중의 여성이 명시적으로 청구하는 경우에는 야간근로와 휴일근로가 가능하다.

3. 임산부의 보호휴가

(1) 출산휴가

사용자는 임신 중의 여성에게 출산 전과 출산 후를 통하여 90일(①한 번에 둘이 상 자녀를 임신한 경우에는 120일; ②미숙아를 출산하여 신생아 집중치료실에 입원하는 경우에는 100일)의 출산전후휴가를 주어야 한다. 이 경우 휴가 기간의 배정은 출산 후에 45일(한 번에 둘 이상 자녀를 임신한 경우에는 60일) 이상이 되어야 한다. 사용자는 출산전후휴가 종료 후에는 휴가 전과 동일한 업무 또는 동등한 수준의 임금을 지급하는 직무에 복귀시켜야 한다. 사용자는 출산휴가 중 최초 60일(한 번에 둘 이상 자녀를 임신한 경우에는 75일)은 통상임금을 지급해야 한다. 나머지 30일은 고용보험에서 최대 210만원까지 통상임금을 보전해 준다. 다만, 우선지원 대상기업[575]은 국가로부터 최초 60일에 대해서도 매월 210만원까지 지원을 받을 수 있는데, 이 경우에는 정부지원금을 초과하는 통상임금에 대해서만 유급으로 지급하면 된다(근기법 제74조).

출산휴가는 해고 제한에 해당되어 사용자는 근로자가 산전·산후의 여성이 이 법에 따라 휴업한 기간과 그 후 30일 동안은 해고하지 못한다. 연차유급휴

575) 우선지원 대상기업의 상시 사용하는 근로자 기준(고용보험법시행령 제12조 관련)

of maternity leave and the wage paid during the maternity period shall be deducted from the calculation of average wage required to be included in the period and wage.

<Maternity Leave Benefits>

* Amount of maternity leave benefits for companies eligible for priority support

<table>
<tr><th></th><th></th><th>1st month</th><th>2nd month</th><th>3rd month</th></tr>
<tr><td rowspan="2">Preferentially-Supported Companies</td><td rowspan="2">Ordinary wage</td><td colspan="2">Employer's burden (amount exceeding 2.1 million won)</td><td>Unpaid leave</td></tr>
<tr><td colspan="3">Subsidized by the Employment Insurance Fund (up to 2.1 million won per month; up to 6.3 million won for three months)</td></tr>
<tr><td>Large Companies</td><td>Ordinary wage</td><td colspan="2">Employer's burden
(100% of ordinary wage)</td><td>Unpaid leave:
Subsidy of up to 2.1 million won</td></tr>
</table>

1) Maximum amount: 6.3 million won (2.1 million won per month) in cases where the amount of ordinary wage corresponding to 90 days of maternity leave or miscarriage/stillbirth leave exceeds 6.3 million won, provided that in cases where the period of payment of maternity leave benefits, etc., is less than 90 days, the amount shall be calculated based on the number of actual leave days; and
2) Minimum amount: an amount equivalent to ordinary wage for the period of payment of the maternity leave benefits, etc., calculated using the hourly minimum wage as the hourly ordinary wage of the employee in cases where the hourly ordinary wage of the employee is lower than the hourly minimum wage applied on the beginning date of maternity leave or miscarriage/stillbirth leave in accordance with the Minimum Wage Act

(2) Advance maternity leave

In cases where an employee who is or was recently pregnant requests leave due to a miscarriage or other pregnancy-related reason, the employer shall allow her to take leave at any time prior to the expected due date. In any case, 45 or more continuous days(60 days for multiple babies) shall be provided after childbirth or miscarriage. Reasons for advance maternity leave are as follows(Article 74 of the LSA).

Type of Industry (Classification Code)	Number of Employees
1. Manufacturing (C);	Up to 500 persons
2. Mining (B); 3. Construction (F); 4. Transportation (H); 5. Publishing, filming, broadcasting, and IT services (J); 6. Facility management and company support services (N); 7. Professional, science and technology services (M); 8. Health and social security insurance services (Q).	Up to 300 persons
9. Wholesale and retail services (G); 10. Hotel and restaurant services (I); 11. Finance and insurance (K); 12. Art, sports, and other leisure-related services (R);	Up to 200 persons
13. Other businesses	Up to 100 persons

가 계산에 있어 출산휴가는 출근한 것으로 본다. 퇴직금 계산을 위한 평균임금 산정에 있어서도 출산휴가 기간과 그 기간 중에 지급된 임금은 평균임금 산정 기준이 되는 기간과 임금의 총액에서 뺀다.

〈출산휴가 급여지원〉

* 출산휴가 급여지원

<table>
<tr><th></th><th></th><th>1개월</th><th>2개월</th><th>3개월</th></tr>
<tr><td rowspan="2">우선지원기업 근로자</td><td rowspan="2">통상
임금</td><td colspan="2">사업주 부담 (210만원 초과 통상임금)</td><td>무급</td></tr>
<tr><td colspan="3">고용보험기금 지원 (상한 월 210만원, 3개월 630만원)</td></tr>
<tr><td>대규모기업 근로자</td><td>통상
임금</td><td colspan="2">사업주 부담 (통상임금 100%)</td><td>무급: 고보지원
상한 210만원</td></tr>
</table>

1) 상한액: 출산전후휴가기간 또는 유산 · 사산휴가기간 90일에 대한 통상임금에 상당하는 금액이 630만원(월 210만원)을 초과하는 경우에는 630만원. 다만, 출산전후휴가 급여등의 지급기간이 90일 미만인 경우에는 일수로 계산한 금액으로 한다.

2) 하한액: 출산전후휴가 또는 유산 · 사산휴가기간 시작일 당시 적용되던 「최저임금법」에 따른 시간 단위에 해당하는 최저임금액 보다 그 근로자의 시간급 통상임금이 낮은 경우에는 시간급 최저임금액을 시간급 통상임금으로 하여 산정된 출산전후휴가 급여등의 지원기간 중 통상임금에 상당하는 금액

(2) 조기출산휴가

사용자는 임신 중인 여성 근로자가 유산의 경험 등 사유로 출산휴가를 청구하는 경우 출산 전 어느 때라도 휴가를 나누어 사용할 수 있도록 하여야 한다. 이 경우 출산 후의 휴가 기간은 연속하여 45일(한 번에 둘 이상 자녀를 임신한 경우에는 60일) 이상이 되어야 한다(근기법 제74조, 시행령 제43조).

여기서 조기 출산휴가의 사유는 다음과 같다.

산업분류(분류기호)	상시 근로자 수
1. 제조업(C);	500명 이하
2. 광업(B), 3.건설업(F), 4.운수업(H), 5.출판, 영상, 방송통신 및 정보서비스업(J), 6. 사업시설관리 및 사업지원 서비스업(N), 7.전문, 과학 및 기술 서비스업(M), 8.보건업 및 사회보험 서비스업(Q)	300명 이하
9. 도매 및 소매업(G), 10.숙박 및 음식점업(I), 11.금융 및 보험업(K), 12.예술, 스포츠 및 여가관련 서비스업(R)	200명 이하
13. 그 밖의 업종	100명 이하

① In cases where a pregnant employee went through a miscarriage or stillbirth in the past;
② In cases where a pregnant employee is over 40 years of age at the time of the request for maternity leave; and
③ In cases where a pregnant employee submits a medical document issued by a hospital that describes the danger of miscarriage or stillbirth.

(3) Maternity leave for miscarriage or stillbirth

At the request of a female employee who has suffered a miscarriage or stillbirth, the employer shall grant her leave for miscarriage or stillbirth, except where the miscarriage is the result of an artificially-induced abortion. If a female employee who has had a miscarriage or stillbirth asks for maternity leave, she must submit to the employer an application for miscarriage or stillbirth leave, providing the reason for the request for leave, the date of the miscarriage or stillbirth and the pregnancy period, along with a medical certificate issued by a medical organization. In cases of miscarriage or stillbirth, the employer shall pay the ordinary wage for the period given for maternity leave, just as with a normal maternity leave, as follows:
① A pregnancy period of less than 15 weeks: ten days from the date of miscarriage or stillbirth;
② A pregnancy period of 16 weeks or more but less than 21 weeks: thirty days from the date of miscarriage or stillbirth;
③ A pregnancy period of 22 weeks or more but less than 27 weeks: sixty days from the date of miscarriage or stillbirth; and
④ A pregnancy period of 28 weeks or more: ninety days from the date of miscarriage or stillbirth.

(4) Reduced working hours during the pregnancy period

In cases where a female employee who is pregnant for 12 weeks or less or 32 weeks or more applies for reduced working hours, the employer shall allow it. High-risk pregnant women, particularly those experiencing preterm labor or carrying multiple pregnancies, can obtain a doctor's diagnosis and use reduced working hours throughout their entire pregnancy. Provided that the pregnant employee's current working hours are fewer than 8 per day, the employer may reduce her working hours to 6 hours per day. The employer cannot reduce the wage of the employee due to the reduced working hours(Article 74 of the LSA).

① 임신한 근로자에게 유산·사산의 경험이 있는 경우
② 임신한 근로자가 출산전후휴가를 청구할 당시 연령이 만 40세 이상인 경우
③ 임신한 근로자가 유산·사산의 위험이 있다는 의료기관의 진단서를 제출한 경우

(3) 유산·사산휴가

사용자는 임신 중인 여성이 유산 또는 사산한 경우로서 그 근로자가 청구하면 유산·사산 휴가를 주어야 한다. 다만, 인공 임신중절 수술에 따른 유산의 경우는 그러하지 아니하다. 이 경우, 유산 또는 사산한 근로자가 유산·사산휴가를 청구하는 경우에는 휴가 청구 사유, 유산·사산 발생일 및 임신기간 등을 적은 유산·사산휴가 신청서에 의료기관의 진단서를 첨부하여 사용자에게 제출하여야 한다. 사용자는 유산·사산휴가도 출산휴가와 같이 주어진 휴가범위 내에서 통상임금을 지급해야 한다(근기법 제74조, 시행령 제43조).

① 임신기간이 15주 이내인 경우: 유산 또는 사산한 날부터 10일 까지
② 임신기간이 16주 이상 21주 이내인 경우: 유산 또는 사산한 날부터 30일 까지
③ 임신기간이 22주 이상 27주 이내인 경우: 유산 또는 사산한 날부터 60일 까지
④ 임신기간이 28주 이상인 경우: 유산 또는 사산한 날부터 90일까지

(4) 임신기간 중 단축근로

사용자는 임신 후 12주 이내 또는 32주 이후에 있는 여성 근로자가 1일 2시간의 근로시간 단축을 신청하는 경우 이를 허용하여야 한다. 특히 조기 진통, 다태아 임신 등 고위험 임산부는 의사의 진단을 받아 임신 전 기간에 대해 근로시간 단축을 사용할 수 있다. 다만, 1일 근로시간이 8시간 미만인 근로자에 대하여는 1일 근로시간이 6시간이 되도록 근로시간 단축을 허용할 수 있다. 사용자는 근로시간 단축을 이유로 해당 근로자의 임금을 삭감하여서는 아니 된다(근기법 제74조 제7항, 제8항).

(5) Allowing paid time off for prenatal examinations

If a pregnant female employee requests time off from work to receive a regular prenatal health checkup, the employer shall allow her to do so. An employer shall not reduce an employee's wage on the grounds that she took time off for the relevant health checkup. The paid time off allowance for prenatal examinations is as follows: ① one time every two months up to the 7th month of pregnancy; ② one time per month during the 8th and 9th months; ③ one time every two weeks during the 10th month or later(Article 74-2 of the LSA, Article 10 of the Protection of Motherhood Act).

4. Paternity Leave

If an employee requests leave on the grounds of his spouse giving birth, the employer shall grant him paid leave of up to 20 days. The leave may not be used after a lapse of 120 days from the date when the employee's spouse gave birth(Article 18-2 of the Equal Employment Opportunity and Work-Family Balance Act). Paternity leave will also be usable on three separate periods if desired.

To reduce the burden on SMEs of this extended period of paid leave, the government will pay for 20 days of those paternity leave benefits(100% of normal wage) for SME workers.

5. Infertility Treatment Leave

An employer must provide up to 6 days of leave per year to employees who request time off for infertility treatment, such as artificial insemination or in vitro fertilization. The first 2 days of this leave must be paid. However, if granting leave at the requested time would cause significant disruption to the normal operation of the business, the employer may reschedule the leave in consultation with the employee.

Employers are prohibited from taking adverse actions, such as dismissal or disciplinary measures, against employees for using infertility treatment leave. Additionally, employers must not disclose any information learned during the leave request process to others without the consent of the employee who applied for the leave(Article 18-3 of the Equal Employment Opportunity and Work-Family Balance Assistance Act).

(5) 태아건강 검진시간 보장

사용자는 임신한 여성 근로자가 정기건강진단을 받는데 필요한 시간을 청구하는 경우 이를 허용하여 주어야 한다. 사용자는 건강진단 시간을 이유로 그 근로자의 임금을 삭감하여서는 아니 된다. 정기건강검진 실시기준은 ① 임신 7월까지는 매 2월에 1회 ② 임신 8월에서 9월까지는 매 1월에 1회 ③ 임신 10월 이후에는 매 2주에 1회이다(근기법 제74조의 2, 모자보건법 제10조).

4. 배우자 출산휴가

사용자는 근로자가 배우자의 출산을 이유로 휴가를 청구하는 경우에 20일의 유급휴가를 주어야 한다. 배우자 출산휴가는 근로자의 배우자가 출산한 날부터 120일이 지나면 사용할 수 없다.(고평법 제18조의 2) 배우자 출산휴가는 3회에 한해서 분할하여 사용할 수 있다.

휴가기간 확대에 따른 중소기업의 부담을 덜어주기 위해 정부는 중소기업(우선지원 대상기업) 근로자의 유급 20일분에 대해서는 배우자 출산휴가급여(통상임금의 100%)를 지급한다.

5. 난임치료휴가

사업주는 근로자가 인공수정 또는 체외수정 등 난임치료를 받기 위하여 휴가를 청구하는 경우에 연간 6일 이내의 휴가를 주어야 하며, 이 경우 최초 2일은 유급으로 한다. 다만, 근로자가 청구한 시기에 휴가를 주는 것이 정상적인 사업 운영에 중대한 지장을 초래하는 경우에는 근로자와 협의하여 그 시기를 변경할 수 있다.

사업주는 난임치료휴가를 이유로 해고, 징계 등 불리한 처우를 하여서는 아니 된다. 사업주는 난임치료휴가의 청구 업무를 처리하는 과정에서 알게 된 사실을 난임치료휴가를 신청한 근로자의 의사에 반하여 다른 사람에게 누설하여서는 아니된다(남녀고용평등법 제18조의3).

6. Nursing hours

A female employee who has an infant under twelve months of age shall be allowed to take paid nursing recesses, twice per day for at least 30 minutes each(Article 75 of the LSA).

Ⅲ. Childcare Leave and Reduced Working Hours for the Childcare Period

1. Childcare Leave[576)]

Employers shall grant childcare leave if an employee asks for it to take care of his/her child(including an adopted child) aged 8 or under who is attending up to the 2nd grade of elementary school. This shall not apply in such cases where ① an employee has offered continuous services in the business concerned for less than 6 months prior to the scheduled date of childcare leave, or ② an employee's spouse is on childcare leave for the same infant. An employee who intends to apply for childcare leave shall submit to his/her employer an application with documentation verifying the birth date of the infant to be cared for, not less than 30 days prior to the scheduled start date of leave.

The period of childcare leave shall be one year or less. The childcare leave can be used all at once or at four different times, up to a total period of one year. However, to promote shared parental care, if each parent takes at least three months of parental leave, or in cases involving single parents or parents of children with severe disabilities, the leave may be extended up to 18 months. The period of childcare leave shall be included in the employee's continuous service period. Employers shall not dismiss or give any other unfavorable treatment to a employee on account of taking childcare leave, nor dismiss the employee concerned during the childcare-leave period; provided that this shall not apply if the employer is not able to continue operating his/her business. After the end of the childcare leave, the employer shall restore the employee to the same work as before the leave, or any other work paying the same level of wage. In calculating the attendance rate for the annual paid leave, the period of childcare leave shall be included for the contractual working hours,

576) Article 19 of the Equal Employment Act: Article 10 and 11 of its Presidential Decree, Article 70 of the Employment Insurance Act

6. 육아시간

생후 1년 미만의 유아를 가진 여성 근로자가 청구하면 1일 2회 각각 30분 이상의 유급 수유 시간을 주어야 한다(근기법 제75조).

Ⅲ. 육아휴직과 육아기 근로시간 단축

1. 육아휴직[576)]

사용자는 근로자가 만 8세 이하 또는 초등학교 2학년 이하의 자녀(입양한 자녀를 포함한다)를 양육하기 위하여 육아휴직을 신청하는 경우에 이를 허용하여야 한다. 다만, 육아휴직을 시작하려는 날의 전날까지 해당 사업에서 계속 근로한 기간이 6월 미만인 근로자 그리고 같은 영유아에 대하여 배우자가 육아휴직을 하고 있는 근로자는 제외된다. 육아휴직을 신청하려는 근로자는 휴직개시 예정일의 30일전까지 해당 자녀의 출생 등을 증명할 수 있는 서류를 첨부하여 육아휴직신청서를 사용자에게 제출하여야 한다.

육아휴직의 기간은 1년 이내로 하며, 1회에 1년간 사용하든지 총 사용기간1년 이내에서 4회에 한하여 분할 사용할 수 있다. 다만, 부모 맞돌봄 확산을 위해 부모가 각각 육아휴직을 3개월 이상 사용하는 경우와 한부모 또는 중증 장애아동의 부모는 육아휴직을 1년 6개월 까지 사용할 수 있다. 육아휴직 기간은 근속기간에 포함한다. 사용자는 육아휴직을 이유로 해고나 그 밖의 불리한 처우를 하여서는 아니 되며, 육아휴직 기간에는 그 근로자를 해고하지 못한다. 다만, 사업을 계속할 수 없는 경우에는 그러하지 아니하다. 사용자는 육아휴직을 마친 후에는 휴직 전과 같은 업무 또는 같은 수준의 임금을 지급하는 직무에 복귀시켜야 한다. 연차유급휴가의 개근여부 계산에 있어 육아휴직기간은 소정근로일수계산에서 포함되기 때문에 육아휴직기간에 대해서 연차유급휴가가 발생한다. 기간제 근로자 또는 파견 근로자의 육아휴직 기간은 사용기간 또는 근

576) 고평법 제19조, 시행령 제10조, 제11조, 고용보험법 제70조

which means that the annual paid leave is granted for the period of actual work. The period of childcare leave for a fixed-term employee or a dispatched employee shall not be included in the employment period or the dispatched period.

2. Reduction of working hours for the childcare period(Article 19 of the Equal Employment Act, Article 73-2 of the Employment Insurance Act):

If an employee eligible to ask for childcare leave requests a reduction of working hours instead of childcare leave, the employer shall grant it. However, the employer is not required to grant it in cases where it is not possible to hire replacement personnel, and where it causes a considerable difficulty for the normal operation of business If the employer does not grant the reduction of working hours for the childcare period, the employer shall notify the employee in writing of the reason for such decision, and have the employee take normal childcare leave or else consult with the employee as to whether to support him/her through other measures. Employers shall not apply unfavorable working conditions to an employee who works reduced working hours for the childcare period on grounds of the working hour reduction, except when applying them in proportion to the usual working hours.

The eligible age for children under the reduced working hours for childcare is up to 12 years old (6th grade). Any unused period of childcare leave may be doubled and applied toward the reduced working hours for childcare. If childcare leave is not utilized, reduced working hours for childcare may be extended up to a maximum of three years. The minimum usage period is set at one month, allowing for flexibility to meet short-term caregiving needs, such as during school vacations. If the employer grants a reduction of working hours for the childcare period to the relevant employee, the working hours after reduction shall be a minimum of 15 hours per week but shall not exceed 35 hours per week. Employers shall not dismiss or give any other disadvantageous treatment to the employee on account of the working hour reduction. After the period of working hour reduction is over, the employer shall restore the employee to the original work or to other work paying the same level of wage as before the reduction of working hours.

로자파견기간에 산입하지 아니한다.

2. 육아기 근로시간 단축

사용자는 육아휴직을 신청할 수 있는 근로자가 육아휴직 대신 육아기 근로시간 단축을 신청하는 경우에 이를 허용하여야 한다. 다만, 대체인력 채용이 불가능한 경우, 정상적인 사업 운영에 중대한 지장을 초래하는 경우 등의 경우에는 그러하지 아니하다. 사업주가 육아기 근로시간 단축을 허용하지 아니하는 경우에는 해당 근로자에게 그 사유를 서면으로 통보하고 육아휴직을 사용하게 하거나 그 밖의 조치를 통하여 지원할 수 있는지를 해당 근로자와 협의하여야 한다. 고용보험으로부터 근로자가 수령하는 육아기 근로시간 단축급여는 정상적인 육아휴직 급여를 기준으로 단축된 근로시간에 비례한 금액으로 한다. 사업주는 육아기 근로시간 단축을 하고 있는 근로자에 대하여 근로시간에 비례하여 적용하는 경우 외에는 육아기 근로시간 단축을 이유로 그 근로조건을 불리하게 하여서는 아니 된다(고평법 제19조의 2, 고용보험법제73조의 2).

육아기 근로시간 단축 대상 자녀 연령은 12세(초6) 까지 이고, 육아휴직 미사용기간은 두 배 가산하여 육아기 근로시간 단축에 사용할 수 있다. 육아휴직을 사용하지 않은 경우 육아기 근로시간 단축을 최대 3년 까지 사용할 수 있다. 최소 사용단위기간도 1개월로하여 방학 등 단기적 돌봄 수요에 사용할 수 있다. 사용자가 해당 근로자에게 육아기 근로시간 단축을 허용하는 경우 단축 후 근로시간은 주당 15시간 이상이어야 하고 35시간을 넘어서는 아니 된다. 사용자는 육아기 근로시간 단축을 이유로 해당 근로자에게 해고나 그 밖의 불리한 처우를 하여서는 아니 된다. 사용자는 근로자의 육아기 근로시간 단축기간이 끝난 후에 그 근로자를 육아기 근로시간 단축 전과 같은 업무 또는 같은 수준의 임금을 지급하는 직무에 복귀시켜야 한다.

IV. Menstruation Leave

An employer shall, if requested by a female worker, grant her one day's menstruation leave per month (Article 73).

Menstruation leave is given to female employees who suffer from physical and/or mental difficulties at work due to her menstruation. The leave shall be granted to an employee who requests it, regardless of whether or not she has come to work for all the contractual working days of the given month. On the basis of the revised law that now recognizes menstruation leave as unpaid leave, the employer does not have to pay an allowance for the use of the leave, if requested. However, allowance shall be paid if both parties agree differently in the collective agreement, rules of employment or labor contract. Though menstruation leave is now considered unpaid, it is permitted by law to consider it paid so as to have no effect on attendance in calculating the number of contractual working days and rate of attendance for weekly holiday, annual paid leave, etc.

Ⅳ. 생리휴가

사용자는 여성인 근로자가 청구하는 때는 월 1일의 생리휴가를 주어야 한다(근기법 제73조, 생리휴가).

생리휴가는 여성 근로자가 생리로 인하여 신체적·정신적으로 근로에 어려움을 겪지 않도록 생리 사실에 기하여 본인이 청구할 경우에 부여하여야 한다. 또한, 생리휴가는 1월간 소정근로일수 만근 여부와 관계없이 근로자가 청구하면 부여하여야 한다. 생리휴가가 유급에서 무급으로 개정됨에 따라 생리휴가를 청구 시 휴가사용에 대하여 임금지급의무가 없다. 다만, 단체협약, 취업규칙, 근로계약 등에 의거 당사자간에 달리 약정한 바가 있으면 그에 따라야 할 것이다. 생리휴가가 무급으로 개정되었더라도 법에 의하여 부여되는 휴가이므로 주휴일, 연차휴가 등을 부여하기 위한 소정근로일수 및 출근율 산정 시 소정근로일수에 포함하고 그날은 출근한 것으로 보아야 한다.

Chapter 10

Management of Irregular Employees

Section 1: Types of Irregular Employees

Ⅰ. Concept

The labor structure is variably extending to include part-time employees, short-term employees, dispatched employees, etc., and labor management is more flexible with the contract period, as the labor market is becoming more intricate and labor restrictions strictly enforced. According to the Labor Standards Act, Article 16(Term of Contract), "the term of a labor contract shall not exceed one year, except in cases where there is no fixed term or where there is otherwise a fixed term as necessary for the completion of a certain project." This article does not define the employee as regular or irregular, contract or term in accordance with term of contract. However, we can define a short-term employee as one whose term of contract is less than one year. We can also define a part-time employee as one whose contractual work hours per week are shorter than those of a full-time employee engaged in the same kind of work at the workplace concerned. We generally call short-term and part-time employees as irregular employees.[577)]

577) MOEL Guidelines: Dec. 24, 2004, Kungi-1650.

비정규직 관리

제1절 비정규직의 의의와 유형

Ⅰ. 의 의

노동시장이 복잡해지고 노동규제가 강화됨에 따라 단시간 근로자, 단기간 근로자, 파견 근로자 등 근로형태의 다양화와 고용계약 기간의 관리를 통해 노무관리의 유연성을 높이는 것이 추세이다. 구근로기준법 제16조는 근로계약 기간에 대하여 '근로계약은 기간의 정함이 없는 것과 일정한 사업완료에 필요한 기간을 정한 것을 제외하고는 그 기간은 2년을 초과하지 못한다.'고 규정하고 있다. 그와 같은 근로계약 기간에 따라 근로자를 정규직이나 비정규직, 계약직 또는 기간제 근로자 등으로 구분하여 정의하고 있지는 않으나, 근로계약 기간이 2년 미만인 근로자를 '단기계약 근로자', 1주간의 소정근로시간이 당해 사업장의 동종업무에 종사하는 통상근로자의 근로시간보다 짧은 근로자를 '단시간 근로자'라 한다. 일반적으로 이와 같은 단기계약근로자 또는 단시간 근로자를 비정규직 근로자라 한다.[577)]

577) 행정해석: 근로기준과-1650, 2004.12.24.

Ⅱ. Part-Time Employees

1. Concept

The term part-time worker in Article 2 of the Labor Standards Act(LSA) means an employee whose contractual working hours per week are shorter than those of a full-time worker engaged in the same kind of job at the same workplace. For example, since a full-time worker works 40 hours per week, a worker who has worked 8 hours for 4 days a week(32 hours per week) is considered a part-time worker.

The concept of part-time worker includes employment is in ① one-week units, ② contractual working hours, and ③ shall be compared to the working hours of regular workers.

1) The one-week basis shall be the working hours of the week if the working hours are constant every week, but the average of 4 weeks shall be calculated for the weekly contractual working hours when weekly working hours are not constant(Article 18 of the LSA).

2) The number of contractual working hours per day for part-time workers is the number of hours divided by the number of days for a full-time worker for that period.[578)] In other words, the calculation may vary depending on the total number of days worked by a full-time worker over a four-week period. Contractual working hours is defined as the working hours determined between the worker and the employer within the range of legal working hours, so the contractual working hours should be equal to or less than the legal working hours(Article 2 of the LSA).[579)]

The calculation method for the contractual working hours per day is as follows: ① 6 hours per day from Monday to Friday and a 5-day working per week: [(30 hours × 4 weeks)/(5 days × 4 weeks) = 6 hours]. Or ②, if a regular worker works 6 days a week: [(30 hours × 4 weeks)/(6 days × 4 weeks) = 5 hours].

3) The full-time workers for comparison are defined as "full-time workers engaged in the same kind of job in the same workplace" in Article 2 of the "Act on the Protection etc.

---

578) Enforcement Decree to the LSA, Article 9 [Attachment No. 2].

579) The LSA, Article 50 (Work hours) 40 hours per week and 8 hours per day; Article 69 (Working hours for minors) 7 hours per day and 40 hours per week; Article 139 of the Occupational Safety and Health Act (Harmful and dangerous work) 6 hours per day and 34 hours per week.

Ⅱ. 단시간근로자

1. 단시간 근로자의 의의

단시간 근로자"란 1주 동안의 소정근로시간이 그 사업장에서 같은 종류의 업무에 종사하는 통상 근로자의 1주 동안의 소정근로시간에 비하여 짧은 근로자를 말한다(근로기준법 이하 '근기법' 제2조). 즉, 통상근로자의 1주 소정근로시간이 40시간이라면, 1일 8시간씩 1주 4일 근무한 경우에도 1주 근로시간이 32시간이 되기 때문에 단시간 근로자에 속한다.

단시간 근로자의 개념은 ① 1주 기준, ② 소정근로시간, ③ 통상근로자의근로시간이 포함된 내용이다.

1) 1주의 기준은 매주 근로시간이 일정한 경우에는 그 주의 근무시간이 되지만, 각 주마다 근무시간이 일정하지 않은 경우에는 4주를 평균하여 1주의 근로시간을 산정한다(근기법 제18조).

2) 단시간 근로자의 1일 소정근로시간 수는 4주 동안의 소정근로시간을 그 기간의 통상 근로자의 총 소정근로일 수로 나눈 시간 수로 한다.[578] 즉, 통상근로자의 4주 기간 동안의 총 소정근로일수에 따라 산정이 달라질 수 있다. 소정근로시간은 법정근로시간[579]에 따른 근로시간의 범위에서 근로자와 사용자 사이에 정한 근로시간을 말하므로 소정근로시간은 법정근로시간과 같거나 작아야 한다(근기법 제2조).

구체적인 예를 가지고 1일 소정근로시간을 계산해보자면, ① 월요일부터 금요일까지 매일 6시간을 근무하고 통상근로자가 주5일을 근무하는 경우: (30시간×4주) / (5일×4주) = 6시간이 된다. ② 그러나 동일한 근로시간을 근무하더라도 통상근로자가 주6일을 근무하는 경우: (30시간×4주) / (6일×4주) = 5시간이 된다.

3) 통상근로자의 기준은『기간제 및 단시간 근로자 보호 등에 관한 법률』(이하

578) 근로기준법 시행령 제9조, [별표 2]
579) 근기법 제50조는 1주 40시간, 1일 8시간; 제69조(연소자의 근로시간)는 1일 7시간, 1주 40시간; 산업안전보건법 제139조(유해위험한 근로자의 근로시간) 1일 6시간, 1주 34시간.

of Fixed-Term and Part-Time Workers"(FPA). The court has explained that whether or not the work of the employee selected as a comparable worker corresponds to the work of the same or similar type as the work of a part-time worker is not based on the work content as specified in the rules of employment or the employment contract, but on the basis of the work actually performed by full-time workers. However, even if the tasks they perform are not completely in agreement with one another and there are some variances in the scope, responsibilities and authority of the tasks, they are considered to engage in similar tasks unless there is a substantive difference in the content of the main task.[580)]

2. Legal working conditions of part-time workers

Working conditions for part-time workers shall be determined on the basis of the relative ratio of their working hours in comparison to those of full-time workers engaged in the same kind of job in the same workplace(Article 18 of the LSA).

That is, even part-time workers are subject to all the provisions of the Labor Standards Act, but for statutory holidays and leaves, the principle of proportional working hours of ordinary workers is applied.[581)]

(1) Employment contracts and rules of employment

1) Employment contract

The employment contract of part-time workers must be issued in writing. For violations, a penalty of KRW 5 million is imposed(Articles 17 and 24 of the FPA). The items that must be included in the labor contract include: ① Matters concerning the contract period; ② Matters concerning working hours and rest hours; ③ Matters concerning components, calculation and payment methods of wages; ④ Matters concerning holidays and leave; ⑤ Matters concerning the place of work and required work; ⑥ Work days and working hours of each work day. The reason for requiring the employer to make labor contracts in writing is to prevent disputes for violation of the Labor Standards Act.

---

580) Supreme Court ruling on Oct. 25, 2012: 2011do7045.

581) For details, related information is in the Labor Standards Act and Article 9 of the Enforcement Decree to the LSA attachment, Table 2, the FPA, the Minimum Wage Act, etc.

기단법) 제2항은 당해 사업 또는 사업장의 동종 또는 유사한 업무에 종사하는 통상근로자로 하고 있고, 법원은 이에 대해 비교대상 근로자로 선정된 근로자의 업무가 단시간 근로자의 업무와 동종 또는 유사한 업무에 해당하는지 여부는 취업규칙이나 근로계약 등에 명시된 업무 내용이 아니라 근로자가 실제 수행하여 온 업무를 기준으로 하여 판단하되, 이들이 수행하는 업무가 서로 완전히 일치하지 아니하고 업무의 범위 또는 책임과 권한 등에서 다소 차이가 있다고 하더라도 주된 업무의 내용에 본질적인 차이가 없다면, 특별한 사정이 없는 이상 이들을 동종 또는 유사한 업무에 종사한다고 보고 있다.[580)]

2. 단시간 근로자의 법정 근로조건

단시간 근로자의 근로조건은 그 사업장의 같은 종류의 업무에 종사하는 통상근로자의 근로시간을 기준으로 산정한 비율에 따라 결정되어야 한다(근기법 제18조). 즉, 단시간 근로자도 근로기준법상 제 규정을 모두 적용 받지만, 법정휴일이나 휴가에 있어서는 통상근로자의 근로시간 비례원칙이 적용된다.[581)]

(1) 근로계약과 취업규칙

1) 근로계약

단시간 근로자의 근로계약은 서면으로 작성하고 교부해야 한다. 이를 위반하는 경우에는 과태료 500만원이 부과된다(기단법 제17조, 제24조). 근로계약에 필수적으로 포함되어야 하는 사항은 ① 근로계약 기간에 관한 사항, ② 근로시간·휴게에 관한 사항, ③ 임금의 구성항목·계산방법 및 지불방법에 관한 사항, ④ 휴일·휴가에 관한 사항, ⑤ 취업의 장소와 종사하여야 할 업무에 관한 사항, ⑥ 근로일 및 근로일별 근로시간이다. 근로계약 작성의무를 엄격하게 구속하는 이유는 장차 근로기준법의 위반 분쟁을 사전에 예방하기 위함이다.

580) 대법원 2012.10.25, 2011두7045.

581) 그 자세한 내용은 근기법 및 근기법 시행령 제9조, [별표 2]), 기단법, 최저임금법 등에 따라 정리함.

2) Rules of employment (ROE)

The employer may create rules of employment that apply to part-time workers separately from those that apply to full-time workers. If an employer wants to make or change the rules of employment, the employer shall consult with the majority of part-time workers to whom the ROE will apply. However, if the ROE are to be modified in a manner that is unfavorable to the part-time workers, the employer must obtain the consent of the majority of the part-time workers(Article 94 of the LSA). The purpose for this is to prevent the employer from unilaterally lowering the working conditions of part-time workers.[582)]

(2) Wages

① The wage calculation unit for a part-time worker is based on the hourly wage. If hourly wage is calculated as daily ordinary wage, the number of hours worked per day is multiplied by the hourly wage. ② The wage shall be paid in full to the worker directly in Korean currency, and shall be paid at least once per month on a fixed date(Article 43 of the LSA). ③ For part-time workers, the average wage of 30 days or more for one year of continuous work shall be paid as severance pay. In this case, if the average wage is less than the ordinary wage, the ordinary wage must be paid as severance pay(Article 2 of the LSA). Also, in establishing a severance pay system for part-time workers, there should be no difference from that of the severance pay system for full-time workers. ④ Even if there is no comparable full-time worker, the minimum wage under the Minimum Wage Act must be paid.

(3) Working hours

1) The contractual working hours of part-time workers are strictly protected. The employer must obtain the consent of the part-time worker to have the part-time worker work beyond the contractual working hours, and in instances such as this the Act(FPA) also stipulates that the part-time worker shall not work more than 12 additional hours from the contractual working time of one week. The employer shall pay part-time workers at least 50/100 of the ordinary wage for overtime work exceeding the contractual working hours within the legal working hours(8 hours per day, 40 hours per week). Under the

---

582) Supreme Court ruling on May 28, 1990: 90da19647.

2) 취업규칙

사용자는 단시간 근로자에게 적용되는 취업규칙을 통상근로자에게 적용되는 취업규칙과 별도로 작성할 수 있다. 취업규칙을 작성하거나 변경하고자 할 경우에는 적용대상이 되는 단시간 근로자 과반수의 의견을 들어야 하며, 이를 단시간 근로자에게 불이익하게 변경하는 경우에는 단시간 근로자 과반수의 동의를 받아야 한다(근기법 제94조). 이는 사용자가 일방적으로 단시간 근로자의 근로조건을 저하시키는 것을 예방하기 위한 법적 취지이다.[582)]

(2) 임 금

① 단시간 근로자의 임금산정 단위는 시간급을 원칙으로 하며, 시간급 임금을 일급 통상임금으로 산정할 경우에는 1일 소정근로시간 수에 시간급 임금을 곱하여 산정한다. ② 임금은 통화로 직접 근로자에게 그 전액을 지급하여야 하고, 매월 1회 이상 일정한 날짜를 정하여 지급하여야 한다(근기법 제43조). ③ 단시간 근로자의 계속근로연수 1년에 대해 30일분의 이상의 평균임금을 퇴직금으로 지급해야 한다. 이 경우 평균임금이 통상임금보다 적으면 그 통상임금액을 퇴직금으로 지급해야 한다(근기법 제2조). 또한, 단시간 근로자의 퇴직금제도를 설정함에 있어서 통상근로자의 퇴직금제도에 차등을 두어서는 아니 된다. ④ 단시간 근로자의 비교대상 근로자가 없는 경우에도 최저임금법에 따른 최저임금 이상을 지급해야 한다.

(3) 근로시간

1) 단시간 근로자의 소정근로시간은 엄격하게 보호되고 있다. 사용자는 단시간 근로자에 대하여 소정근로시간을 초과하여 근로하게 하는 경우에는 당해 근로자의 동의를 얻어야 하며, 이 경우에도 1주 소정근로시간에 12시간을 초과하여 근로하게 할 수 없다고 명시하고 있고 소정근로시간을 초과하여 연장근로를 하는 경우에는 법정근로시간(1일 8시간, 1주 40시간) 이내에도 불구하고 그

582) 대법원 1990.5.28, 90다19647.

Labor Standards Act, an additional wage of 50% or more of ordinary wage is paid only for overtime work exceeding legal working hours, but for part-time workers, payment of additional wages is prescribed even if the contractual working hours are exceeded within the legal working hours(Article 6 of the FPA).

2) Part-time workers are also paid an additional 50% for holiday work as specified in the rules of employment, and 100% for holiday work exceeding 8 hours(Article 56 of the LSA).

3) If a part-time worker performs night work between 10 pm and 6 am on the following day, the employer shall pay wages with an additional allowance equivalent to 50/100(Article 56 of the LSA).

(4) Holidays and annual paid leave

Holidays and annual paid leave for part-time workers are applied equally in accordance with the principle of proportional working hours for full-time workers.

1) Holidays

An average of one paid holiday per week worked shall be guaranteed, for which the contractual working hours of one day must be paid. When calculating wages according to hourly wage, the employer shall pay an additional weekly holiday allowance. However, in the case of a part-time worker who has been employed for weekend or holiday work, the weekly holiday should be given as a paid holiday on a non-weekend day.

① Calculating 6 hours per day from Monday to Friday, 5 days' work per week for full-time workers and payment of KRW 10,000 per hour: [(30 hours × 4 weeks)/(5 days × 4 weeks) = 6 hours], results in [6 hours × KRW 10,000 = KRW 60,000]. ② However, if full-time workers are working for 6 days a week: [(30 hours × 4 weeks)/(6 days × 4 weeks) = 5 hours], the result is [5 hours × KRW 10,000 = KRW 50,000].

2) Annual paid leave

The employer shall grant part-time workers a number of days of annual paid leave equal to that of full-time workers. Annual paid leave is calculated in hours, with less than one hour counting as one hour. Also, in case of monthly paid leave for those working less than one year, the contractual working hours of one day per each month should be given as monthly paid leave. The criteria for granting annual paid leave for part-time workers

초과근로에 대한 통상임금의 100분의 50 이상을 가산하여 지급하여야 한다. 근로기준법의 경우 법정근로시간을 초과하는 연장근로에 대해서만 통상임금의 100분의 50 이상의 가산임금을 지급하지만, 단시간 근로자의 경우에는 소정근로시간을 초과할 경우에도 가산임금의 지급을 규정하고 있다(기단법 제6조).

2) 단시간 근로자도 취업규칙에 명시된 휴일근로에 대해 100분의 50을 가산해서 지급하고, 8시간을 초과하는 휴일근로에 대해서는 100분의 100을 가산한다(근기법 제56조).

3) 단시간 근로자가 오후 10시부터 다음 날 오전 6시 사이 야간근로를 하는 경우에는 100분의 50을 가산한 임금을 지급해야 한다(동법 제56조).

(4) 휴일과 연차유급휴가

단시간 근로자의 휴일과 연차유급휴가는 통상근로자의 근로시간 비례원칙에 따라 동일하게 적용된다.

1) 휴 일

1주에 평균 1회 이상의 유급휴일을 보장하여야 한다. 이 경우 1일의 소정근로시간을 유급으로 주어야 하며, 시간급으로 임금을 계산할 경우에는 유급 주휴수당을 추가적으로 계산하여 지급해야 한다. 다만, 주말 근무나 휴일을 대체하기 위해 채용된 단시간 근로자의 경우에는 주말이 아닌 날에 주휴일을 유급으로 주어야 한다.

① 월요일부터 금요일까지 매일 6시간, 통상근로자는 주5일 근무하고, 시간급 1만원인 경우: [(30시간×4주) / (5일×4주) = 6시간]이 되므로 [6시간×1만원 = 6만원]이 된다. ② 그러나 통상근로자가 주6일을 근무하는 경우: [(30시간×4주) / (6일×4주) = 5시간]이 된다. [5시간×1만원 = 5만원]이 된다.

2) 연차유급휴가

사용자는 단시간 근로자에게 연차유급휴가 횟수를 통상근로자와 같이 동등하게 부여하여야 한다. 이 경우 연차유급휴가는 시간단위로 계산하고, 1시간 미만은 1시간으로 본다. 또한, 근속연수 1년 미만자의 월차유급휴가의 경우에도 매월 1일의 소정근로시간을 월차유급휴가로 주어야 한다. 단시간 근로자의 언

are as follows:

$$\text{Number of annual leave days for full-time workers} \times \frac{\text{Number of hours worked for part-time workers}}{\text{Number of annual leave days for full-time workers}} \times 8 \text{ hours}$$

If a part-time worker works 20 hours a week, this works out to [15 days ×(20 hours/40 hours) × 8 hours = 60 hours]. In other words, each four hours is guaranteed as an annual paid leave day.

3) Maternity leave

The employer shall give 90 days of pre- and post-natal maternity leave for pregnant part-time female workers, with the first 60 days of maternity leave being paid. ① The maternity leave allowance is the amount calculated as the hourly wage of a part-time worker multiplied by the contractual working hours of one day and multiplied by 60 days. ② The remaining 30 days can be paid as maternity leave benefits as stipulated by the Employment Insurance Act(Article 74 of the LSA). Assuming that a part-time worker is paid KRW 10,000 per hour, and the contractual working hours is 5 hours per day. ① The maternity leave allowance is KRW 10,000 × 5 hours × 60 days = KRW 3,000,000. ② The maternity leave benefit is KRW 10,000 × 5 hours × 30 days = KRW 1,500,000.

3. Prohibition against discriminatory treatment and exceptions to application

(1) Prohibition against discriminatory treatment

An employer shall not give discriminatory treatment to any part-time employee on the grounds of his/her employment status compared to full-time workers engaged in the same or similar kinds of work in the business or workplace concerned. It is necessary to pay various allowances etc. in accordance with the rules of employment and employment contracts, and not discriminate against ordinary workers. The subjects of discriminatory treatment are ① Wages;[583] ② Regular bonuses, holiday bonuses, etc. and bonuses paid

583) Article 2 of the LSA: The term wages in this Act means wages, salaries and any other money or valuable goods an employer pays to a worker for his/her work, regardless of how such payments are termed.

차휴가부여의 기준은 다음과 같다.

$$\text{통상근로자의 연차휴가일수} \times \frac{\text{단시간 근로자의 소정근로시간}}{\text{통상 근로자의 소정근로시간}} \times 8\text{시간}$$

단시간 근로자가 주20시간 근무하는 경우, 15일×(20시간/40시간)×8시간 = 60시간이다. 즉, 1일 연차유급휴가로 4시간이 보장되어야 한다.

3) 산전후휴가

사용자는 임신 중인 단시간 여성 근로자에 대하여 출산 전과 출산 후를 통합하여 90일의 출산전후휴가를 부여하여야 한다. 이 경우 출산전후휴가 중 최초 60일은 유급으로 한다. 단시간 근로자의 시간급에 1일의 소정근로시간을 곱하고 이에 60일을 곱한 금액을 ① 산전후 유급수당으로 사업주로부터 지급받고, 나머지 30일분은 고용보험법에서 정한 바에 따라 ② 산전후휴가급여를 지급받을 수 있다(근기법 제74조). A의 시간급이 10,000원이고, 1일 소정근로시간이 5시간인 경우 ① 산전후휴가 유급수당은 10,000원×5시간×60일 = 3,000,000원이고, ② 산전후휴가급여는 10,000원×5시간×30일 = 1,500,000원으로 계산된다.

3. 차별적 처우의 금지와 적용의 제외

(1) 차별적 처우의 금지

사용자는 단시간 근로자임을 이유로 당해 사업 또는 사업장에서 동종 또는 유사한 업무에 종사하는 기간의 정함이 없는 근로계약을 체결한 근로자에 비하여 차별적 처우를 하여서는 아니 된다. 취업규칙과 근로계약에 따라 각종 수당 등을 지급하여야 하고, 통상근로자와 차별을 하여서는 아니된다는 것이다. 차별적 처우의 대상은 ① 임금,[583] ② 정기상여금, 명절상여금 등 정기적으로 지

583) 근기법 제2조: "임금"이란 사용자가 근로의 대가로 근로자에게 임금, 봉급, 그밖에 어떠한 명칭으로든지 지급하는 일체의 금품을 말한다.

regularly; ③ Incentives according to business performance; ④ Other matters concerning working conditions and benefits, etc.(Article 2 of the FPA) If a part-time employee has received discriminatory treatment, he/she may file a request for correction with the Labor Relations Commission; this shall not apply if six months have passed since such discriminatory treatment occurred(or since such treatment ended in cases of continuous discriminatory treatment). The procedures for this are the same as those for remedy application of an unfair dismissal case(Articles 8, 10 to 15 of the FPA). The employer shall not discriminate against the part-time worker for the reason that he has applied for correction of discrimination(Article 16 of the FPA). If the employer fails to carry out the correction order from the Labor Relations Commission without just cause, he shall be fined up to KRW 100 million(Article 24 of the FPA).

(2) Exceptions to application

With respect to workers whose contractual working hours is an average of less than 15 hours per week over a four-week period(or the employment period, if they have been employed for less than four weeks), the following shall not apply: ① weekly holiday allowance(Article 55), ② annual paid leave(Article 60), ③ monthly paid leave(Article 60), and ④ severance pay(Article 34). In addition, employment insurance, national pension and national health insurance are excluded, while industrial accident compensation insurance is not.

If the employer sets the contractual working hours of one week to 14 hours, and concludes an employment contract by adding an additional 2 hours of fixed overtime work every day(for 5 days), the Ministry of Employment and Labor has decided that the total working hours, including fixed extended working hours, are defined as working hours actually taken, as long as there is no reason to believe otherwise. In such case, part-time workers are subject to severance pay. However, it is possible to exclude from fixed working hours if it is not fixed overtime work but extension work due to an agreement with the company at that time.[584)]

584) MOEL Guidelines: Working Standards-5085, Dec. 1, 2009.

급되는 상여금, ③ 경영성과에 따른 성과급, ④ 그 밖의 근로조건 및 복리후생 등에 관한 사항이다(기단법 제2조). 차별에 대한 구제신청은 노동위원회를 통해 할 수 있으며, 차별적 처우가 있은 날(계속되는 차별적 처우는 그 종료일)로부터 6개월 이내에 제기하여야 하며 절차는 부당해고 구제신청사건에 준한 절차와 같다(기단법 제8조, 제10조 내지 제15조). 사용자는 단시간 근로자가 차별시정을 신청한 것을 이유로 그에게 불리한 처우를 하지 못한다(동법 제16조). 사용자가 노동위원회의 시정명령을 정당한 이유없이 이행하지 아니한 경우에는 1억원 이하의 과태료에 처한다(동법 제24조)

(2) 단시간 근로자의 적용제외

4주 동안(4주 미만으로 근로하는 경우에는 그 기간)을 평균하여 1주 동안의 소정근로시간이 15시간 미만인 근로자에 대하여는 ① 주휴일(제55조), ② 연차유급휴가(제60조), ③ 월차유급휴가(제60조), ④ 퇴직금(제34조), ⑤ 4대보험 중 산재보험을 제외한 고용보험, 국민연금, 국민건강보험이 적용되지 않는다.

사용자가 1주 소정근로시간을 14시간으로 정하고 추가로 매일 2시간씩(5일) 고정연장근로를 하는 것으로 근로계약을 체결한 경우, 노동부는 '필요에 따라 연장근로를 실시하기로 정했다고 보기는 어려운 점 등으로 보아 달리 볼 사정이 없는 한(고정연장근로를 포함한 시간이) 당사자간 근로하기로 미리 정한 근로시간'이라며 해당 근로자는 퇴직금 지급 대상이라고 판단했다. 다만, 고정된 연장근로가 아니라 그때그때 일시적 필요에 따라 당사 합의로 연장근로가 이루어졌다면 소정근로시간에서 제외할 수는 있을 것이다.[584)]

584) 근로기준과-5085, 2009.12.1.

Ⅲ. Short-Term Contract Employees

1. Concept

Those whose contract period is less than two years are referred to as short-term contract employees(hereinafter called short-term employees). Regardless of what they are called, or whether their contracts are like that of daily workers, contracted workers, temporary employees, commissioned employees, etc., short-term employee simply refers to an employee employed for less than two years. Though they may be termed short-term employees, the term excludes those who have repeated or renewed their contracts several times.

2. Labor contract

Most articles in the Labor Standards Act apply to short-term employees in principle. With respect to a business or workplace with 4 employees or fewer, only selected provisions of the Labor Standards Act such as wage, weekly holidays, recess hours, etc. are applied.

When hiring a short-term employee, a labor contract must be drafted and submitted that specifies the following items:

① Matters concerning each constituent item of wage, and the methods of calculation and payment;

② Matters concerning work start and finish times for the employee, recess hours, and holidays;

③ Matters concerning place of employment and work to be performed; and

④ Matters concerning other working conditions.

An employer shall also keep a register of workers with information including name, date of birth, personal history, etc., wage ledger concerning the payrolls paid, and other important documents concerning the labor contract for three years. With respect to a daily worker who has been employed for a period of less than thirty days, a register may not be needed.

3. Wage payment and calculation

For contracts exceeding one month, wages shall be paid at least once a month on a fixed day. For daily workers who are hired on a daily basis, wages shall be paid each day

Ⅲ. 기간제 근로자

1. 기간제의 의의

기한을 정한 근로계약에 의해 고용한 근로자 중 근로계약 기간이 2년 미만인 근로자를 2년 미만 단기계약 근로자(이하 "단기간 근로자"라 함)라 한다. 일용직·계약직·임시직·촉탁직 등 계약형태와 명칭을 불문하고 계속 근로기간이 2년 미만인 단기계약직 근로자를 의미하며, 비록 단기간 근로자라 할지라도 수차례에 걸쳐 근로계약이 반복 갱신되어 계속근로연수가 사실상 2년 이상인 경우는 제외된다. 단기간 근로자에 대해서도 원칙적으로 근로기준법의 관련 조항이 적용된다. 단, 상시 5인 미만의 근로자를 사용하는 사업 또는 사업장은 임금, 주휴, 휴게시간 등 근로기준법의 일부 조항만 적용된다.

2. 근로계약

단기간 근로자를 고용할 경우 다음의 사항을 명시한 근로계약서를 작성·교부해야 한다.

① 임금의 구성항목, 계산방법, 지불방법에 관한 사항
② 근로시간의 시업시각과 종업시각, 휴게시간, 휴일에 관한 사항
③ 취업의 장소, 종사해야 할 업무에 관한 사항
④ 기타 근로조건에 관한 사항

또한, 성명, 생년월일, 이력 사항 등을 기재한 근로자 명부, 임금을 지급한 임금대장 등 근로계약에 관한 중요한 서류를 작성하여 3년간 보관해야 한다. 다만, 30일 미만의 일용 근로자에 대해서는 근로자 명부를 별도로 작성할 필요가 없다.

3. 임금의 지급과 계산

근로계약 기간이 1개월 이상인 경우에는 매월 1회 이상 일정한 기간을 지정하여 임금을 지급한다. 다만, 일 단위로 근로계약을 체결하는 일용직 근로자의 경

upon fulfilling the contractual working hours.

The wage of a daily worker is calculated by the hourly or daily wage rate in principle. The hourly wage is calculated into a daily wage by multiplying the number of contractual working hours of one day by the hourly wage rate.

Contractual working hours of one day for a construction worker or guard usually include extended or night work, so an additional allowance may be rendered in the inclusive wage of one day. In this case, the ordinary wage of one day can be gained through an inclusive inverse calculation.

For example, if the labor contract is drawn for 10 working hours a day and 120,000 won as a daily wage, then the ordinary wage of one day is 87,273 won:

- Hourly wage = 120,000 won [8 hours×(2 hours1.5)] = 10,909 won
- Ordinary wage of one day = 10,909 won(hourly wage) 8 hours(number of contractual working hours of one day) = 87,273 won

4. Working hours, holidays and leave

1) Working hours shall not exceed 40 per week and 8 per day excluding recess hours, but if the parties concerned agree, working hours may be extended up to 12 hours per week. Accordingly, construction workers can sign a contract for 10 working hours per day.

If a daily worker renews his/her daily contract for 5 consecutive days, one paid holiday shall be provided. However, if he/she is eligible to receive one paid holiday after 5 consecutive working days, but the contract terminates the day before expecting a paid holiday, the holiday shall not be paid. Thus, for daily workers in construction or manufacturing, holiday allowance is often omitted in a calculation of payment which multiplies the number of days to a daily wage rate. Accordingly, if a daily worker maintains full attendance for the corresponding week, the weekly holiday allowance shall be additionally paid for each weekly holiday.

2) A monthly paid leave shall be given to an employee with perfect attendance for the contractual working hours of the month, but the accumulated use of monthly paid leave is only available before the contract terminates. If the contract terminates on the day the monthly paid leave can be used, the leave shall not be granted.

우는 근로계약서에 명기된 근로시간 종료 직후에 매일 임금을 지급해야 한다.

일용직 근로자의 임금산정은 원칙적으로 시간급 또는 일급 단위를 원칙으로 하며, 시간급 임금을 일급 통상임금으로 산정할 경우에는 1일의 소정근로시간 수에 시간급 임금을 곱하여 산정한다.

건설현장 노무직, 경비직 등과 같이 1일의 소정근로시간이 연장근로나 야간근로를 예정하고 있어 근로계약상 연장근로 또는 야간근로에 대한 가산임금을 포함한 금액을 1일의 포괄 임금으로 하고 있는 경우에는 일급 통상임금을 포괄 역산방식에 의해 산출할 수 있다.

예를 들어 1일 10시간을 근로시간으로 하고 일당 120,000원으로 근로계약을 한 경우 1일 통상임금은 다음과 같이 87,273원이 된다.

· 시간급 임금 = 120,000원 ÷ [8시간+(2시간 × 1.5)] = 10,909원
· 일 통상임금 = 10,909원 × 8시간(1일 소정근로시간) = 87,273원

4. 근로시간, 휴일, 휴가

1) 휴게시간을 제외한 실근로시간이 1일 8시간, 1주간 40시간을 초과할 수 없지만, 당사자 합의하에 1주 12시간 범위 내에서 연장근로를 할 수도 있다. 따라서 건설현장 같은 경우 1일 10시간 근로조건으로 근로계약을 체결해도 무방하다.

일용직 근로자가 근로계약을 반복적으로 체결하여 5일간 계속 근로한 경우에는 1일의 유급휴일을 주어야 한다. 다만, 5일간 계속 근로함으로써 유급 주휴일 부여 요건을 충족한 경우라도 주휴일을 부여해야 할 날 직전 일에 근로관계가 종료된 때는 주휴일을 부여하지 않을 수 있다. 그러므로 건설현장이나 제조업에서 일용 근로자의 경우 단순히 출근일수에 일당을 곱하여 임금을 산정하는 방법은 주휴수당을 누락시킨 결과가 되어 해당 주간을 만근할 경우에는 추가로 주휴일 수를 파악하여 주휴수당을 지급해야 한다.

2) 1월간 소정근로일을 개근한 경우에는 월차유급휴가를 부여하되 월차유급휴가의 적치 사용은 근로관계가 종료되는 때까지 가능하다.

If the short-term employee renews his/her contract for more than one year, annual paid leave shall be provided.

5. Accident compensation and dismissal

If a short-term employee suffers an occupational injury or disease, he/she is eligible for industrial accident compensation insurance in principle. Industrial accident compensation insurance does not cover workers who can be treated within 4 days for injury sustained during an industrial accident, but the rules concerning accident compensation in the Labor Standards Act are applicable instead. Even if the contract of a short-term employee expires during a period of temporary interruption of work for medical treatment of an occupational injury or disease, he/she can continue to receive medical attention and wages during business suspension until he/she recovers, or, alternatively, receive a lump sum compensation payment.

If there is a justifiable reason for dismissal, an employer can immediately dismiss the following employees without advance notice as stipulated in the Labor Standards Act(Article 26 of the LSA): ① Where the employee worked consecutively less than 3 months; ② Where it is impossible to continue business because of natural disaster, armed conflict, or other unavoidable causes; and ③ Where a worker has caused considerable difficulties to business, or damage to property on purpose. In the case of a short-term contract of less than one year, the labor contract terminates automatically when the contract period expires and does not require advance notice of dismissal.

6. Employment insurance

A short-term employee qualifies for employment insurance. However, employment insurance is not available to workers whose contractual working hours are fewer than 60 per month(15 per week) and to workers over 65 years of age.

7. Severance pay

If a daily-work contract is repeatedly extended for more than one year, severance pay shall be provided. If a short-term employee has a one-year labor contract, severance pay shall be provided upon termination of the contract period.

단기간 근로자가 계약이 갱신되어 재고용이 되면 최초 입사일로부터 1년이 경과하는 경우에는 연차유급휴가를 부여해야 한다.

5. 재해보상과 해고

단기간 근로자가 업무수행 중 재해를 당하면 원칙적으로 산재보험에 적용된다.

산재보험이 적용되지 않는 4일 미만의 재해인 경우 근로기준법상의 재해보상 규정이 적용되며, 2년 미만 단기계약 근로자가 업무상 부상 또는 질병으로 인해 요양하고 있는 기간 중에는 근로계약 기간의 만료와 관계없이 부상·질병이 완쾌되거나 일시 보상을 행할 때까지 요양보상, 휴업보상 등을 해줘야 한다.

① 근로자가 계속 근로한 기간이 3개월 미만인 경우, ② 천재·사변, 그 밖의 부득이한 사유로 사업을 계속하는 것이 불가능한 경우, ③ 근로자가 고의로 사업에 막대한 지장을 초래하거나 재산상 손해를 끼친 경우에는 근로기준법이 정한 해고예고의 절차를 거치지 않고 즉시 해고할 수 있다(근기법 제26조). 2년 미만 단기 근로계약의 경우에는 원칙적으로 근로계약 기간의 만료로 자동적으로 근로관계가 해지되기 때문에 해고예고 절차가 필요 없다.

6. 고용보험

단기간 근로자에 대해서도 고용보험이 적용된다. 다만, 1개월의 소정근로시간이 60시간(1주간 15시간) 미만인 자, 65세 이상인 단기간 근로자에 대해서는 고용보험이 적용되지 않는다.

7. 퇴직금

일용직 근로자일지라도 일용계약이 반복하여 갱신되면 1년을 초과하여 근무할 경우 퇴직금을 지급해야 한다. 단기계약직이 1년을 계약기간으로 한 경우에도 퇴직금을 지급해야 한다.

Ⅳ. Dispatched Employees

1. Concept of worker dispatch

The term employee dispatch refers to a system in which the sending employer, while maintaining employment relations after hiring a worker, engages the worker to work for a using employer with directions and orders under a worker dispatch contract.(Article 2-1 of Act Relating to Protection, etc. for Dispatched Workers; hereinafter called Worker Dispatch Act).

1) In an outsourcing contract, one party promises to complete the work assigned and the opposite party pays remuneration for the work provided(Article 664 of the Civil Act).

2) In a commission, one party entrusts the opposite party with partial work and the opposite party accepts it(Article 680).

3) An outsourcing contract is distinguished from worker dispatch, based upon whether the contractor party or the contracted party conducts business independently or not, without comparing outsourcing contracts and commission(Notification 98-32 from the Ministry of Employment and Labor).

2. Length of dispatch period

The service period for dispatched workers shall not exceed one year. However, if an agreement is obtained by the sending employer, the using employer, and the dispatched worker, then the period may be extended only once.

The purpose of Article 6 in the Worker Dispatch Act is to treat the dispatched employee as a regularly hired employee when the using employer continues to use the dispatched employee for more than two years. It is also designed to prevent the increased use of illegally dispatched employees. Accordingly, using a dispatched employee for more than two years under the above referenced Article means that the using employer uses the same dispatched employee for more than two years. Based upon understanding of the above, if the using employer has replaced the dispatched employee with an interval period of less than two years, the using employer does not have a legal obligation to hire the dispatched employee.

In cases where the employer has utilized the same dispatched employee for more than two years, he shall be responsible for the employee not as the using employer of a

Ⅳ. 파견 근로자

1. 파견근로의 의의

파견사업주가 근로자를 고용한 후 그 고용관계를 유지하면서 근로자 파견계약의 내용에 따라 사용사업주의 지휘·명령을 받아 사용사업주를 위하여 근로에 종사하게 하는 것을 근로자파견이라 한다(근로자파견법 제2호 제1호).

1) 도급이란 당사자 일방이 어떤 일을 완성할 것을 약정하고 상대방이 그 일의 결과에 보수를 지급할 것을 약정하는 계약을 말한다(민법 제664조).

2) 위임이란 당사자 일방이 상대방에 대하여 사무 처리를 위탁하고 상대방이 이를 승낙하는 계약을 말한다(민법 제680조).

3) 근로자파견사업과 구별하기 위한 위장도급 여부를 판단할 때는 도급·위임을 구분하지 않고, 수급인 또는 수임인이 사업주로서의 독립성을 가지고 사업을 행하느냐에 따라 판단하고 있다(노동부고시 제98-32호).

2. 파견기간

1년 이내를 원칙으로 하되, 파견사업주·사용사업주·파견 근로자 간의 합의가 있는 경우 1회에 한하여 1년 더 연장 가능하다(최장 2년).

'근로자파견법' 제6조(파견기간)의 입법취지는 사용사업주가 파견 근로자를 2년 이상 사용하는 경우에는 파견 근로자를 고용한 것으로 간주함으로써 파견 근로자의 정규직화를 촉진하고, 무분별한 파견 근로의 확산을 방지하는데 있으며, 동조에서 파견 근로자를 2년 이상 사용하는 경우라 함은 동일 파견 근로자를 2년 이상 사용하는 경우를 의미한다. 따라서 A라는 직무에 서로 다른 파견 근로자를 2년 미만을 주기로 교체하여 사용하는 경우에는 사용사업주가 파견 근로자를 고용할 법률상 의무는 없다.

사용사업주가 동일한 파견 근로자를 2년을 초과하여 사용할 필요가 있는 경우에는 동 사업주로 하여금 「파견 근로자의 사용사업주」로서의 책임이 아니라

dispatched employee, but as an employer under the Labor Standards Act.[585)]

Even if the worker was illegally dispatched, when he/she has worked for more than two years at the using employer's company, the using employer shall employ the worker as a regular employee, in accordance with Article 6, Paragraph 3 of the Worker Dispatch Act.

3. Jobs to which the worker dispatch system applies

(1) Jobs available at all times

Jobs permitted for worker dispatch shall be those 32 jobs judged suitable for that purpose given their nature and the expertise, skills, or experiences they require and prescribed by Presidential Decree, but excluding direct production jobs in the manufacturing fields(Article 5(1) of the Worker Dispatch Act).

(2) Jobs available for a limited time

In companies where labor shortages(due to workers on leave for child birth, illness, injury) or an urgent need to temporarily/occasionally secure manpower, the worker dispatch system shall be permitted(Article 5(2) of the Worker Dispatch Act).

(3) Jobs where worker dispatch is not allowed (Article 5 (3) of the Act):

① Jobs performed at the construction site;

② Unloading activities in the harbor transport business;

③ Activities of seamen;

④ Hazardous and dangerous activities(Article 58 of the Occupational Safety and Health Act);

⑤ Work subject to issuance of health management pocketbooks;

⑥ Work of medical persons and medical technicians;

⑦ Driving work in the passenger vehicle transport business(city, local, and chartered buses, taxis); and

⑧ Driving work in the freight vehicle transport business.

---

585) Seoul Appellate Court ruling on Mar. 14, 2003, 2002Nu2521.

「근로기준법상 사용자」로서의 책임을 진다.[585)]

불법적인 파견 근로자의 경우에도 2년 이상 실질적으로 기업체에서 일하였다면 근로자파견법 제6조 제3항에 근거해 사용사업체가 정식 근로자로 직접 고용해야 한다.

3. 파견대상 업무

(1) 상시 허용 업무

근로자 파견사업은 제조업의 직접 생산 공정 업무를 제외하고 전문지식·기술·경험 또는 업무의 성질 등을 고려하여 적합하다고 판단되는 업무로서 대통령령이 정하는 32개 업무를 대상으로 한다(파견법 제5조 제1항).

(2) 일시 허용 업무(파견법 제5조 제2항).

출산·질병·부상 등으로 결원이 생긴 경우 또는 일시적·간헐적으로 인력을 확보하여야 할 필요가 있는 경우에는 근로자 파견사업을 행할 수 있다.

(3) 절대 금지 업무(파견법 제5조 제3항).

① 건설현장업무
② 항만운송사업
③ 선원
④ 유해·위험업무(산업안전보건법 제58조)
⑤ 건강관리수첩의 교부 대상 업무(석면, 염화 비닐 등을 취급하는 11개 업무)
⑥ 의료인 및 의료기사
⑦ 여객자동차 운송사업(시내버스, 시외버스, 전세버스, 일반택시)
⑧ 화물 운송사업(화물자동차, 특수자동차)

585) 서울고등법원 2003.3.14, 2002누2521.

Korean Standard Classification of Occupations	Types of jobs
120	Computing professionals
16	Administration, business, and finance professionals (excludes administration professionals(161))
17131	Patent professionals
181	Archivists, librarians and related professionals(excludes the job of librarians (18120))
1822	Translators and interpreters
183	Creative writers and actors
184	Movie, drama, and broadcasting professionals
220	Computing associate professionals
23219	Other electric engineers and technicians
23221	Telecommunication technicians
234	Drawing (including CAD) technicians
235	Optical and electronic instrument handling jobs (limited to subsidiary work. Excludes clinical pathologists(23531), radiology technicians(23532), other medical instrument technicians(23539)
252	Education associate professionals excluding regular education
253	Other education associate professionals
28	Artistic, entertainment and sports associate professionals
291	Management associate professionals
317	Administration support clerks
318	Library, mail and related clerks
3213	Debt collectors and related workers
3222	Telephone switchboard operators (excludes where it is considered the core service in the concerned business)
323	Clients handling clerks
411	Bodyguards and related workers
421	Cooks (excludes those cooks in tourism and hotels as stipulated in Article 3 of the Tourism Promotion Act)
432	Travel Guidelines
51206	Petrol pump attendants
51209	Other shop salespersons
521	Telephone salespersons
842	Motor vehicle drivers
9112	Building cleaners
91221	Guards and security guards (excludes guard duties in Article 2 (1) of the Guard Act)
91225	Parking attendants
913	Delivery, transportation, and meter men

한국표준 직업분류 (통계청고시 제2000-2호)	대 상 업 무
120	컴퓨터관련 전문가의 업무
16	행정, 경영 및 재정 전문가의 업무
17131	특허 전문가의 업무
181	기록 보관원, 사서 및 관련 전문가의 업무
1822	번역가 및 통역가의 업무
183	창작 및 공연예술가의 업무
184	영화, 연극 및 방송관련 전문가의 업무
220	컴퓨터관련 준전문가의 업무
23219	기타 전기공학 기술공의 업무
23221	통신 기술공의 업무
234	제도 기술 종사자, 캐드 포함의 업무
235	광학 및 전자장비 기술 종사자의 업무
252	정규교육이외 교육 준전문가의 업무
253	기타 교육 준전문가의 업무
28	예술, 연예 및 경기 준전문가의 업무
291	관리 준전문가의 업무
317	사무 지원 종사자의 업무
318	도서, 우편 및 관련 사무 종사자의 업무
3213	수금 및 관련 사무 종사자의 업무
3222	전화교환 및 번호안내 사무 종사자의 업무
323	고객 관련 사무 종사자의 업무
411	개인보호 및 관련 종사자의 업무
421	음식 조리 종사자의 업무
432	여행안내 종사자의 업무
51206	주유원의 업무
51209	기타 소매업체 판매원의 업무
521	전화통신 판매 종사자의 업무
842	자동차 운전 종사자의 업무
9112	건물 청소 종사자의 업무
91221	수위 및 경비원의 업무(「경비업법」 제2조 제1호에 따른 경비업무를 제외한다.)
91225	주차장 관리원의 업무
913	배달, 운반 및 검침 관련 종사자의 업무

(4) Restrictions on worker dispatch

Companies who are experiencing the following situations cannot dispatch workers:

① companies in which industrial disputes are taking place(Article 43 of the Trade Union Act)

② Companies in which employees are being or have just been dismissed for managerial reasons(Article 24 of the LSA).

4. Duties of the sending employer and using employer

Employee dispatch is fundamentally based on a three-way relationship between the agency employer, the using employer, and the employee. As the employee dispatch mechanism involves distinction in the hiring and using process, the responsibilities of an employer as prescribed in Labor Standards Act are divided between the sending employer and the using employer.

(1) Sending employer

Provided that the sending employer is the one who has hired the dispatched employee, he/she holds the employer's responsibility for most articles in the Labor Standards Act. That is, Chapter 2(Labor Contract), Chapter 3(Wages), wage-related articles in Chapter 4(Working Hours and Recess), labor contract and wage articles in Chapter 5(Females and Minors), and Chapter 8(Accident Compensation), where the sending employer is the employer.

(2) Using employer

A using employer is in charge of the dispatched employee and holds employer responsibility concerning the employee's start and finish times, recesses, extended work, holiday, etc.

[Worker Dispatch Relations]

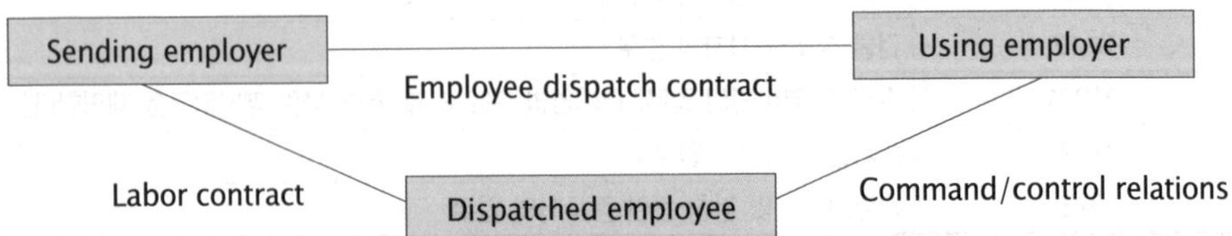

(4) 근로자파견의 제한(파견법 제16조)

① 쟁의행위 중인 사업장에 파견 금지(노조법 제43조 관련)
② 정리해고 후 파견 근로자의 사용 제한(근기법 제24조 관련)

4. 파견사업주 및 사용사업주의 의무

근로자파견은 파견사업주, 사용사업주와 근로자의 3자간의 관계를 기초로 성립하여, 근로자에 대한 고용과 사용이 분리됨으로써 근로기준법상의 사용자 책임이 나누어진다.

(1) 파견사업주

파견사업주는 파견 근로자를 고용하는 자이니만큼 근로기준법 대부분의 조항에 대하여 사용자책임을 진다. 즉, 근로기준법 제2장 근로계약, 제3장 임금, 제4장 근로시간 및 휴식 중 임금과 관련한 부분, 제5장 여성과 소년 중 근로계약 및 임금에 관한 부분, 제8장 재해보상에 대하여는 파견사업주만을 사용자로 본다.

(2) 사용사업주

사용사업주는 파견 근로자를 지휘·명령하여 업무를 수행한다. 따라서 출퇴근시간, 휴게, 연장근로, 휴일근로 등 관하여 사용사업주가 사용자책임을 진다.

〈근로자파견계약〉

파견사업주
사용사업주
(근로자파견계약서)
고용계약관계
(근로계약서)
파견근로자
지휘·명령관계

(3) Joint responsibility of sending employers and using employers

Sending and using employers shall assume joint responsibility for the following articles: Equal Treatment, Prohibition of Forced Labor, Elimination of Intermediary Exploitation, Guarantee of Exercise of Civil Rights, and Duty to Report and Attend in Chapter 1(General Provisions); Chapter 7(Apprenticeship); Chapter 11(Rules of Employment); and Chapter 12(Penal Provisions)(Article 34 of the Worker Dispatch Act).

5. Occupational Safety and Health Act

By regulating special cases related to application of the Occupational Safety and Health Act, the using employer shall be deemed an employer dispatching work to the dispatched worker for the dispatch period(Article 35).

<Employer's Responsibilities in Employees' Health Checkup>

Items	Employer's responsibility	Remarks
• Health checkup upon hiring • General health checkup	Sending employer	① Explain health results to the employees ② Send the result of health checkup to the using employer
• Special health checkup • Temporary health checkup	Using employer	① Explain health results to the employees ② Send the result of health checkup to the sending employer

Ⅴ. Specially Hired Service Providers

1. Concept

Specially hired service providers refer to those who provide labor service on a regular basis in a specific workplace, but who are not yet recognized as employees. Typical jobs include golf-club caddies, home-study teachers, cement truck drivers, and telemarketers. They are not generally recognized as employees because they are not in a subordinate relationship with the employer due to their job characteristics, and also do not provide exclusive services to the employer. However, in recent judicial rulings, if a person is exclusively attached to one workplace, and if there is a considerable subordinate

(3) 파견사업주·사용사업주의 공동책임

근로기준법 제1장 총칙 중의 균등처우, 강제근로의 금지, 중간착취의 배제, 공민권 행사의 보장, 보고·출석의무 등의 규정, 제7장 기능습득, 제9장 취업규칙, 제10장 기숙사, 제11장 근로감독관 등 및 제12장 벌칙규정은 파견사업주와 사용사업주가 공동책임을 진다(파견법 제34조).

5. 산업안전보건법

산업안전보건법 적용에 관한 특례를 마련하여 파견중인 근로자의 파견근로에 관하여는 사용사업주를 산업안전보건법상 사업주로 보아 사업주 책임을 부과시키고 있다(파견법 제35조).

〈근로자건강진단에 관한 사용자 책임〉

항 목	사용자 책임	비 고
·채용 시건강진단 ·일반건강진단	파견사업주	① 건강진단 결과를 근로자에게 설명 ② 건강진단 결과를 사용사업주에게 송부
·특수건강진단 ·임시건강진단	사용사업주	① 건강진단결과를 근로자에게 설명 ② 건강진단결과를 파견사업주에게 송부

Ⅴ. 특수고용종사자

1. 의 의

특수고용 종사자는 특정 사업장에서 노무를 실질적으로 제공하고 있지만, 노동법이 인정하는 근로자로 인정받지 못하는 자들을 말하며, 대표적인 사례로는 골프장 캐디, 학습지 교사, 레미콘 운송차주, 텔레마케터 등 있다. 이들이 노동법의 근로자로 인정받지 못하는 이유는 이들의 업무속성이 사용자와의 사용종속관계가 없을 뿐만 아니라 하나의 사업주에 대해 전속성이 없기 때문이다. 그러나 최근에는 하나의 사업장에 종속되어 있고, 사용자로부터 사용종속 관계가 어느 정도 인정되는 특수고용 종사자를 노동법의 근로자로 인정하는 판례가 발

relationship with the employer, such a person can be considered an employee. Previous judgment criteria depended on whether the base pay was given, whether the four social security insurances were subscribed to, and whether income tax was paid. But as these things can be determined arbitrarily by the employer, given his or her economically superior position, determining whether someone is an employee must now be through determining whether an actual subordinate relationship to the employer has existed or not.

2. Characteristics of the Work

Whether a telemarketer who is a specially hired service provider is an employee or not is decided by how much of a subordinate relationship exists between the employer and the at-home telemarketer at the place of work. Telemarketers are usually engaged in business such as selling insurance, selling targeted real estate, distance sales, etc. Unlike a person working at a call-center, his/her main earnings are determined by their individual sales performance, so it is not entirely accurate to call such a person an employee.

In the beginning, telemarketers were handled as outsourced or commissioned labor, and no real problems existed. However, companies have gradually been using telemarketers to directly increase operational profits. In this process the company comes to supervise the telemarketer directly, which affects the telemarketer's status as a commissioned service provider under the Civil Act to that more like an employee to which the labor laws apply. As the telemarketer's status changes this way, employers need to handle dismissals carefully, deal with severance pay, annual leave, social security insurances, and other protections granted by Korean labor law. Accordingly, employers need to recognize that telemarketers' status can change from commissioned service provider(under the Civil Act) to an employee(under labor law) according to the degree of employer involvement in the telemarketer's work. When using telemarketers, it is necessary to consider in advance whether the telemarketer shall be considered self-employed or an employee exclusively supervised and directed.

생하고 있다. 이런 판례는 노동법이 인정하는 근로자인지 여부는 실질적으로 사용종속 관계에 있었는지 여부를 가지고 판단하여야 하며, 기존의 중요한 판단기준이 되었던 기본급 지급여부, 4대보험 가입여부, 근로소득세의 원천징수 여부는 사용자가 경제적으로 우월한 지위를 이용하여 임의로 결정할 여지가 크기 때문에 이러한 부분만을 가지고 결정할 것이라 아니라고 본다.

2. 업무의 특징

특수고용 종사자 중, 특히 텔레마케터의 근로자성 인정여부는 사업주가 텔레마케터의 업무수행에 있어 어느 정도의 사용종속성을 가지느냐에 따라 유동적으로 결정된다. 텔레마케터는 보험모집, 기획부동산 중계, 원거리 판매 등에 종사하고 있으며, 주 수입원이 그 개인의 판매 실적에 따라 보수가 결정되기 때문에 근로자성에 대한 다툼이 많다.

기업들이 처음에는 텔레마케터를 도급 또는 사무위임의 형태로 사용하였기 때문에 별 문제가 발생하지 않았다. 하지만, 점차적으로 기업들이 영업이익의 확대를 위하여 텔레마케터의 업무수행에 직접적으로 관여하게 된다. 이러한 과정에서 기업은 텔레마케터를 직접적으로 관리감독을 할 수밖에 없게 되는데, 이렇게 되면 텔레마케터의 신분이 민법의 수임인에서 노동법의 근로자로 변하게 된다. 이렇게 신분이 변경된 텔레마케터의 경우, 사용자는 노동법상의 해고의 제한, 퇴직금, 연차휴가, 사회보장보험 등의 책임을 져야 한다. 따라서 사용자는 텔레마케터의 업무에 대한 사용자의 구속 강도에 따라 텔레마케터의 신분이 민법의 수임인에서 노동법의 근로자로 변경될 수 있다는 사실을 인지하고, 텔레마케터를 운영할 때는 텔레마케터를 자유소득자로 사용할 것인지 아니면 전속적으로 관리·감독하는 근로자로 사용할 것인지에 대해 고민을 해야 할 것이다.

Section 2: Protection of Irregular Employees

Ⅰ. The Discrimination Correction System for Irregular Employees

1. Concept

The discrimination correction system is based on guidelines newly introduced in the Short-term Employee Act and the Employee Dispatch Act. It is designed to prohibit disadvantageous treatment(without justification) regarding wages and other working conditions of non-regular employees(short-term, part-time, or dispatched employees) in comparison with target employees(term-less contract employees, ordinary employees, or directly hired employees). Discriminative treatment can be rectified through the remedy process of the Labor Relations Commission.

The discrimination correction system for non-regular employees does not mean that the employer shall keep all working conditions of non-regular employees the same as working conditions for regular employees. However, the employer is prohibited from disadvantageous treatment without justification. That is, the employer is allowed to discriminate if there is a justifiable reason based on productivity, job skills, etc.

2. The discrimination correction system for short-term and part-time employees

(1) Those eligible for correction of discrimination

Those who can be protected from an employer's discriminative treatment shall be employees according to the Labor Standards Act and also be a short-term or part-time employee.

(2) Requests for correction of discrimination

If a fixed-term or part-time employee has received discriminatory treatment, he/she

제2절 비정규직의 보호

Ⅰ. 비정규직의 차별시정제도

1. 차별시정제도 의의

차별시정제도는 '기간제법'과 '파견법'에서 새로이 도입된 제도이다. 차별시정제도는 사용자가 비정규직 근로자(기간제, 단시간, 파견 근로자)를 비교대상 근로자(무기계약근로자, 통상근로자, 직접고용근로자)에 비하여 임금 그 밖의 근로조건 등에 있어서 합리적인 이유 없이 불리하게 처우하는 것을 금지하는 제도이며, 차별적 처우에 대해서는 노동위원회를 통해 시정 절차를 마련하고 있다.

비정규직 근로자에 대한 차별금지제도는 비정규직 근로자의 모든 근로조건을 정규직 근로자의 근로조건과 동일하게 대우하라는 것은 아니며, 합리적 이유 없이 불리하게 처우하는 것을 금지하는 것이다. 즉, 생산성, 숙련도 차이 등 합리적 이유가 있는 경우에는 비정규직 근로자에 대하여 차등 대우하는 것이 허용된다.

2. 기간제, 단시간 근로자의 차별시정제도

(1) 차별시정신청권자

사용자의 차별처우로부터 보호를 받을 수 있는 차별시정신청권자는 근로기준법상의 근로자이어야 하며, 근로자 중에서도 기간제 근로자 및 단시간 근로자이어야 한다.

(2) 차별적 처우의 시정신청

기간제 근로자 또는 단시간 근로자는 차별적 처우를 받은 경우 노동위원회에

may file a request for correction with the Labor Relations Commission, within six months after such discriminatory treatment occurred or since such treatment ended in cases of continuous discriminatory treatment(Article 9 of the Short-term Employee Act). The period of time which shall be examined to determine if the employee is considered short-term or part-time is not when the application for correction of discrimination is made but the time the employer allegedly engaged in the discriminative behavior.

(3) The scope of wages and other working conditions in prohibiting discrimination (Article 2 of the Short-term Employee Act)

① Wages pursuant to subparagraph 5 of Article 2(1) of the Labor Standards Act

② Regular bonus, etc. and bonuses paid regularly

③ Incentives according to business performance and

④ Other matters concerning working conditions and benefits, etc.

The scope of wages and other working conditions deals with working conditions regulated in the Labor Standards Act and working conditions stipulated in the collective agreement, rules of employment and/or labor contract. Therefore, the scope includes not only wages but also working hours, holidays, leave, safety, health, and industrial accident compensation.

(4) Target employees for comparison

The judgment of discrimination for short-term and part-time employees shall require the existence of target employees for comparison. Target employees not only play a role as providing comparison criteria to estimate disadvantageous treatment, but also as the basis and criteria for the Discrimination Correction Committee to determine parameters of the correction order. In comparison to short-term employees, target employees shall be term-less contract employees engaged in the same or similar jobs in the business or workplace(Article 8(1) of the Short-term Employee Act). In comparison to part-time employees, the target employees shall be ordinary employees who were engaged in the same or similar jobs in the business or workplace(Article 8(2) of the Short-term Employee Act).

same or similar job means jobs that are similar in classification, duties, and specification. That is, they will be considered synthetically based on the possibility of substitution within each group of employees.

그 시정을 신청할 수 있다. 다만, 차별적 처우가 있은 날(계속되는 차별적 처우는 그 종료일)부터 6개월 이내에 신청하여야 한다(기간제법 제9조). 기간제, 단시간 근로자 인정여부에 대한 판단은 차별시정 신청 당시가 아니라 사용자에 의한 차별처우가 있었던 때를 기준으로 한다.

(3) 차별처우 금지영역 (기간제법 제2조)

① 근로기준법 제2조 제1항 제5호에 따른 임금
② 정기상여금, 명절상여금 등 정기적으로 지급되는 상여금
③ 경영성과에 따른 성과금
④ 그밖에 근로조건 및 복리후생 등에 관한 사항.

즉, '임금 그 밖의 근로조건 등'의 범위는 ㉠ 근로기준법이 규율하는 근로조건과 ㉡ 단체협약, 취업규칙 또는 근로계약 등에 의한 근로조건으로서, 근로관계에서 발생하는 임금을 비롯하여 근로시간, 휴일, 휴가, 안전, 보건 및 재해보상 등이 포함될 것이다.

(4) 비교대상 근로자

기간제, 단시간 근로자에 대한 차별판단을 위해서는 이들 주체와 비교할 수 있는 다른 대상이 존재하여야 한다. 비교대상 근로자는 불리한 처우가 있었는지 여부를 판단하는 비교기준으로서의 역할뿐만 아니라 시정명령의 내용을 결정하는 근거 및 기준으로서의 역할도 수행하게 된다. 기간제 근로자의 비교대상 근로자는 ① 당해 사업 또는 사업장에서 ② 동종 또는 유사한 업무에 종사하는 ③ 기간의 정함이 없는 근로계약을 체결한 근로자(기간제법 제8조 제1항)가 된다. 단시간 근로자의 비교대상 근로자는 ① 당해 사업 또는 사업장의 ② 동종 또는 유사한 업무에 종사하는 ③ 통상근로자(기간제법 제8조 제2항)가 된다.

'동종 또는 유사한 업무'란 직종, 직무 및 작업내용이 동일성, 유사성을 가진 업무를 말한다. 즉, 업무성격의 유사성, 업무에 있어서 각 근로자의 집단의 상호대체 가능성 등을 종합 고려하여 판단하여야 할 것이다.

[Related ruling[586)]]

A target comparison employee to evaluate whether there has been discriminatory treatment regarding a fixed-term employee refers to other workers engaged in the same or similar kinds of work under a non-fixed-term labor contract in the business or workplace concerned. Whether the work of the target employee selected for comparison is the same or similar kinds of work is not determined by the work stipulated in the rules of employment or the employment contract, but shall be determined by the work that the fixed-term employee actually performs. Even though the work of the target comparison employee and of the fixed-term employee in question does not match and is different in scope, responsibility and authority, if the primary duties are not essentially different, it is deemed that they are engaged in the same or similar work.

(5) Disadvantageous treatment

Disadvantageous treatment means that short-term and part-time employees receive poorer treatment in wages or other working conditions in comparison to target employees. In judging whether or not there is disadvantageous treatment, it is a principle that detailed items relating to wages and working conditions paid to short-term and part-time employees shall be compared with detailed items paid to target employees.

As disputes occur, comparable wages and working hours shall be categorized and compared as follows: ① In cases where some aspect of wages and working conditions are better for target employees but other aspects are lower; and ② in cases where short-term and part-time employees are treated disadvantageously in comparison with target employees on particular wages and working conditions; and ③ in cases where the employer provides other purpose-based wages and working conditions. In this case, payment in accordance with actual provision of labor service(overtime, nighttime, holiday work allowances, etc.) shall be exempted from the scope of comparison.

In cases where it is hard or impossible to compare detailed items or categories because of the inclusive wage system or annual salary system, the wages and working conditions of target employees shall be compared and estimated overall.

586) Supreme Court ruling on Oct. 25, 2012, 2011doo7045, [Correction of Discrimination].

[관련판례[586)]]

기간제 근로자에 대하여 차별적 처우가 있었는지를 판단하기 위한 비교 대상 근로자로 「당해 사업 또는 사업장에서 동종 또는 유사한 업무에 종사하는 기간의 정함이 없는 근로계약을 체결한 근로자」를 들고 있다. 비교 대상 근로자로 선정된 근로자의 업무가 기간제 근로자의 업무와 동종 또는 유사한 업무에 해당하는지는 취업규칙이나 근로계약 등에 명시된 업무 내용이 아니라 근로자가 실제 수행하여 온 업무를 기준으로 판단하되, 이들이 수행하는 업무가 서로 완전히 일치하지 않고 업무의 범위 또는 책임과 권한 등에서 다소 차이가 있다고 하더라도 주된 업무의 내용에 본질적인 차이가 없다면, 특별한 사정이 없는 이상 이들은 동종 또는 유사한 업무에 종사한다고 보아야 한다.

(5) 불리한 처우

불리한 처우란 기간제, 단시간 근로자가 비교대상 근로자에 비하여 임금 그 밖의 근로조건 등에 있어서 낮은 대우를 받는 것을 의미한다. 불리한 처우의 여부를 판단함에 있어서 기간제, 단시간 근로자에게 지급되는 임금 및 근로조건의 세부지급항목이 존재하는 경우 이에 상응하는 비교대상 근로자의 세부지급항목과 비교하여 판단하는 것이 원칙이다.

세부지급 항목별 비교가 현실적으로 ① 임금 및 근로조건에 있어서 특정 부분은 비교대상 근로자보다 높은 반면 다른 특정 부분은 낮은 경우, ② 기간제, 단시간 근로자가 특정 임금 및 근로조건에 대해 비교대상 근로자에 비하여 불리한 처우를 받았다고 주장하는 반면, 사용자는 그 특정 임금 및 근로조건에 대신하여 다른 명목의 임금 및 근로조건을 제공하였음을 주장하여 다투는 경우에는, 비교 가능한 임금 및 근로조건을 하나의 범주로 묶어 비교, 판단할 수 있을 것이다. 이 경우 실제로 제공된 근로에 따라 지급되는 급부(연장, 야간, 휴일 근로수당 등)는 비교범주에서 제외된다.

포괄산정임금제 또는 연봉제로 산정하여 세부지급항목별 또는 범주화에 의한

---

586) 대법원 2012.10.25, 2011두7045【차별시정재심판정취소】.

As part-time employee wages are based on hourly wages, calculating ordinary employee wages into hourly wages is necessary to confirm whether or not there is disadvantageous treatment. In this case, the comparison basis shall be hourly wages calculated from ordinary wages per contractual working hour.

(6) Justifiable reasons

1) Concept of justifiable reason

If there is a justifiable reason that the employer treats short-term and part-time employees disadvantageously in comparison to target employees, disadvantageous treatment will not be considered discriminatory. Here, without justifiable reason means that there is no reason to treat fixed-term employees differently, or that even though such a reason exists, the method or degree is not accepted as appropriate. Whether there is justifiable reason for discrimination shall be determined upon considering collectively the type and scope of the work, responsibility and other working conditions of the fixed-term employees.[587)]

2) Short-term employees and employment period

When the employer applies wages and other working conditions in proportion to the employment period for short-term employees and this resulted in disadvantageous treatment, it can be accepted as justifiable.

3) Part-time employees and principle of protection by time proportion

Working conditions of part-time employees shall be determined on the basis of a relative ratio computed by comparing the work hours of part-time employees with those of full-time employees engaged in the same kind of work at the pertinent workplace, which is an application of the proportional time principle(Article 18(1) of the Labor Standards Act). Accordingly, it is justifiable to apply wages and divisible working conditions in proportion to time.

---

587) Supreme Court ruling on Oct. 25, 2012, 2011doo7045 [Correction of Discrimination].

비교가 곤란하거나 불가능한 경우에는 비교대상 근로자의 임금 및 근로조건을 전체적으로 비교, 판단할 수 있을 것이다.

단시간 근로자는 시간급 임금으로 정해지기 때문에 불리한 처우가 있는지를 확인하기 위해서는 통상근로자의 임금을 시간급 임금으로 환산하여야 한다. 이 경우 소정근로시간에 대하여 통상적으로 지급하는 임금을 기준으로 산정된 시간급을 원칙으로 한다.

(6) 합리적 이유

1) 합리적 이유의 의의

사용자가 기간제, 단시간 근로자를 비교대상 근로자에 비하여 불리하게 처우함에 합리적 이유가 있다면 당해 불리한 처우는 정당화되고 차별처우에 해당하지 않게 된다. 여기서 「합리적인 이유가 없는 경우」란 기간제 근로자를 달리 처우할 필요성이 인정되지 않거나, 달리 처우할 필요성이 인정되는 경우에도 그 방법·정도 등이 적정하지 않은 경우를 의미한다. 그리고 합리적인 이유가 있는지는 개별 사안에서 문제가 된 불리한 처우의 내용 및 사용자가 불리한 처우의 사유로 삼은 사정을 기준으로 기간제 근로자의 고용형태, 업무 내용과 범위·권한·책임, 임금 그 밖의 근로조건 등의 결정요소 등을 종합적으로 고려하여 판단해야 한다.[587)]

2) 기간제 근로자와 취업기간

사용자가 기간제 근로자에 대하여 취업기간에 따라 임금 그 밖의 근로조건을 비례적으로 적용한 결과, 비교대상 근로자에 비해 불리한 처우가 발생하는 경우 합리적 이유가 인정될 수 있을 것이다.

3) 단시간 근로자와 시간비례보호의 원칙

단시간 근로자의 근로조건은 그 사업(장)의 동종 또는 유사한 업무에 종사하는 통상근로자의 근로시간을 기준으로 산정한 비율에 따라 결정되는, 이른바 시간비례의 원칙이 적용된다(근기법 제18조 제1항). 따라서 임금 및 분할 가능한 근로조건을 시간비례에 따라 적용하는 경우 합리적인 이유가 인정될 것이다.

587) 대법원 2012.10.25, 2011두7045【차별시정재심판정취소】.

4) Disadvantageous treatment in accordance with short-term employment

The difference in wage and working conditions in accordance with characteristics of short-term employment, such as employment type(e.g., short-term employee), can be regarded as justifiable. It will also be considered as justifiable when the employer excludes short-term employees from wages and working conditions paid based on long-term employment and/or continuous service, such as long-term service allowance and compensational special bonuses for those retiring after long-term employment.

5) Disadvantageous treatment due to employment conditions and criteria

If an employer discriminates against an employee justifiably on account of different employment factors(such as career, qualifications, etc.), the disadvantageous treatment can be justifiable when such factors determine wages, etc.

6) Disadvantageous treatment based on employment methods and procedures

Even though employment methods and procedures(open employment/closed employment, written tests/interviews, etc.) are different, if short-term and part-time employees provide labor service under the same conditions as target employees, then disadvantageous treatment is not justifiable solely because of different employment methods and procedures. However, if the employer applies employment methods and procedures differently in order to reflect different work performance ability, it can be utilized as indirect evidence to confirm differences in work performance ability.

7) Difference in job scope

As job scope is directly related to quality and quantity of work and becomes an important factor in determining wages, target employees shall be selected carefully in consideration of differences in job scope. Disadvantageous treatment in wages and working conditions due to differences in job scope can be regarded as justifiable.

8) Difference in authority and responsibilities related to job

It can be justifiable to discriminate based on wages in accordance with the level of authority and responsibility. If the employer pays allowances(position allowance, title allowance, etc.) corresponding to the level of authority and responsibility, even though the

4) 기간제 근로자라는 단기고용의 특성에 따른 불리한 처우

기간제근로라는 고용형태, 즉 단기고용이라는 특성에 따른 임금 및 근로조건 등에서 차이는 합리적 이유가 있는 것으로 본다. 또한, 장기고용 및 계속근로를 전제로 지급하는 임금 및 근로조건, 예컨대 장기근속수당, 장기근속 퇴직자에 대한 공로 보상적 특별지급금품 등에서 기간제 근로자를 배제하는 것은 합리적 이유가 있는 것으로 볼 수 있을 것이다.

5) 채용 조건, 기준에 불리한 처우의 근거를 두는 경우

사용자가 불리한 처우를 정당화하는 합리적 이유로서 채용 조건, 기준(경력 및 자격증 등의 요건)이 다름을 주장하는 경우, 채용 조건, 기준이 당해 사업장의 임금결정요소라면 이 범위 내에서 불리한 처우는 정당화될 수 있을 것이다.

6) 채용 방법, 절차에 불리한 처우의 근거를 두는 경우

채용방법, 절차는 다르나(공개채용·비공개채용, 필기시험·면접 등), 기간제, 단시간 근로자가 비교대상 근로자와 동일한 조건 및 내용의 근로를 제공하는 경우 채용 방법, 절차가 다르다는 사정만으로는 불리한 처우를 정당화하는 합리적 이유가 될 수 없다. 다만, 사용자가 상이한 업무수행능력을 반영하기 위해 채용 방법, 절차를 달리 한 것이라면 이는 업무수행능력 차이를 뒷받침하는 간접적인 증거로 활용될 수 있을 것이다.

7) 업무의 범위가 다른 경우

업무범위는 근로의 양, 질과 직결되고 임금결정의 중요한 요소가 되므로 업무범위의 차이를 엄격하게 고려하여 비교대상 근로자를 선정하여야 하며, 업무범위의 차이로 인한 임금 및 근로조건 등에서 불리한 처우는 합리적인 이유가 있는 것으로 볼 수 있다.

8) 업무의 권한, 책임 등이 다른 경우

권한, 책임의 정도에 따라 임금에 차이를 두는 것도 합리적 이유로 인정될 수 있다. 권한, 책임의 정도를 임금결정에는 반영하지 않더라도 그에 상응하는 대

level of authority and responsibility were not reflected in determining wages, it can be justifiable to exclude such allowances for short-term and part-time employees who do not have such authority and responsibilities.

9) Low labor productivity

If the reason short-term and part-time employees' labor productivity is low is because of a lack of previous experience and/or prejudice and not the result of their service, then discriminatory practices are not justifiable. However, it is justifiable if the employer discriminates on wages according to a wage system based on low labor productivity in comparison with target employees.

10) Disadvantageous treatment in accordance with decision factors for wages and working conditions

It can be regarded as justifiable when the employer considers relevant factors(duties, abilities, skills, technology, qualifications, career, educational background, service years, responsibilities, achievements, performance, etc.) of labor service in determining wages and pays different wages in accordance with such differences.

11) Legal allowances

Legal allowances, which are allowances to be paid by law, are additional allowances(Article 56 of the LSA) for overtime, nighttime and holiday work, annual paid leave allowance, etc.(Article 60(5) of the LSA).

3. The discrimination correction system for a dispatched employee

(1) Characteristics

Both using and sending employers are prohibited from discriminative behavior under the Employee Dispatch Act. Even though the discrimination correction system for dispatched employees is regulated identically to the discrimination prohibition for short-term and part-time employees, the system is different in content and interpretation because of the characteristics of dispatch employment.

In terms of both legislative consideration of the discrimination prohibition system in

가를 별도의 수당명목(직책수당, 직급수당 등)으로 지급하는 경우, 만약 기간제, 단시간 근로자가 이러한 권한과 책임을 갖고 있지 않다면 당해 기간제, 단시간 근로자를 수당 지급대상에서 제외하여도 합리적 이유가 인정될 수 있을 것이다.

9) 노동생산성이 낮은 경우

기간제, 단시간 근로자의 노동생산성이 낮다는 것이 직접적인 근로의 결과에서 확인된 것이 아니라 선험적 평가 및 편견에 의한 것이라면 이는 합리적인 이유로 인정될 수 없다. 그렇지만 실제 업무수행 결과인 근로의 질이 비교대상 근로자에 비해 낮음을 이유로 임금체계에 따라 차등을 두었다면 이는 합리적 이유로서 인정될 수 있을 것이다.

10) 임금 및 근로조건의 결정요소에 따른 불리한 처우

임금을 결정함에 있어 근로제공에 관련된 요소들(직무, 능력, 기능, 기술, 자격, 경력, 학력, 근속연수, 책임, 업적, 실적 등) 중 어떠한 요소에 따라 결정되는지를 확인하고 그 요소의 차이로 인하여 불리한 임금을 받는 경우는 합리적 이유가 있다고 볼 수 있다.

11) 법정수당의 경우

법정수당은 법에 의해 지급할 의무가 있는 수당으로 연장, 야간, 휴일근로 가산수당(근기법 제56조), 연차유급휴가수당(근기법 제60조 제5항) 등이 있다.

3. 파견 근로자의 차별시정제도

(1) 특 징

파견법에서 차별행위 금지주체로 근로계약 체결당사자인 파견사업주뿐만 아니라 사용사업주까지 규정한 것은 입법 정책적 고려에서 도입된 것이다. 따라서 파견 근로자에 대한 차별시정제도는 기간제, 단시간 근로자에 대한 차별금지와 동일한 형식으로 규정되어 있다 하더라도 고용관계와 사용관계가 분리된 파견근로의 특성에 비추어 실질적으로는 내용상 및 해석상 차이가 있을 수 있다.

the Employee Dispatch Act and the special characteristics of dispatch employment, the scope of prohibition shall be limited to wages and other working conditions established in accordance with the dispatched employees' labor provisions and entry to the workplace.

The using and sending employer are both considered parties responsible for avoiding discriminative behaviors and, therefore, will share the responsibility of implementing any correction orders, including fines levied for failure to implement correction orders.

(2) Applying for correction of discrimination

1) The dispatched employee as an applicant for discrimination correction

The term dispatched employee means a person who is subject to employee dispatch as a person employed by a sending employer(Article 2(5) of the Employee Dispatch Act). Regardless of the form of contract, if the employee is a dispatched employee in reality, then he/she can be apply for correction of discrimination.

2) Illegally dispatched employee and applying for correction of discrimination

Under the Employee Dispatch Act, an illegal dispatch occurs when the employer: ① violates the permitted jobs of a dispatched employee; ② violates the length of dispatch period, or ③ operates a non-licensed dispatch business.

(3) Subjects prohibiting discriminative treatment: sending employer and using employer

The Employee Dispatch Act(Article 21(1)) states that Neither sending nor using employers shall treat a dispatched employee in a discriminatory manner on account of them being a dispatched employee. Accordingly, the persons responsible for prohibiting discriminative behavior are the sending employer and the using employer. In addition, they will become the employers concerned for correcting discrimination. According to Article 34 of the Employee Dispatch Act, the sending employer is responsible for wages, annual paid leave, etc. as per the Labor Standards Act, while the using employer is responsible for working hours and recess, use of leave, etc.

(4) The scope of prohibited discriminative treatment

In regards to discriminative treatment, the dispatched employees' wages and other

파견법상 차별금지제도의 입법 정책적 측면과 고용관계 및 사용관계로 분리되는 파견근로의 특수성을 감안할 때 차별처우 금지영역은 파견 근로자의 근로제공 및 사업장 편입에 따라 형성되는 '임금 그 밖의 근로조건 등'이 될 것이다.

사용사업주와 파견사업주 양자는 각각 사용자 책임영역에 따라 차별행위 금지주체일 뿐만 아니라 시정명령을 받는 주체 및 확정된 시정명령 불이행시 과태료 납부책임의 주체가 된다.

(2) 차별시정신청권자

1) 차별시정신청권자로서의 파견 근로자

"파견 근로자"라 함은 파견사업주가 고용한 근로자로서 근로자파견의 대상이 되는 자이다(파견법 제2조 제5호). 계약의 형식과 상관없이 실질이 파견 근로자이면 차별시정의 신청권자가 될 수 있다.

2) 불법 파견 시 파견 근로자도 차별시정신청권자임

파견법상 불법파견은 ① 파견대상 업무를 위반하거나, ② 파견기간을 위반하거나, ③ 무허가 파견을 행하는 경우에 발생한다.

(3) 차별처우 금지주체:파견사업주와 사용사업주

파견법에서는 "파견사업주와 사용사업주는 파견 근로자임을 이유로 차별적 처우를 하여서는 아니된다"(제21조 제1항)고 규정하고 있다. 따라서 차별행위의 금지의무자는 파견사업주와 사용사업주이며, 각각 사용자 책임영역에 따라 차별시정의 피신청인이 될 수 있다. 파견법 제34조의 규정에 따라 근로기준법상의 임금, 연차유급휴가 등에 관한 사항은 파견사업주가, 근로시간과 휴게, 휴일의 부여 등은 사용사업주가 사용자로서 책임을 지게 된다.

(4) 차별처우 금지영역

차별처우 금지영역으로서 '임금 그 밖의 근로조건 등'의 범위는 파견 근로자의 경우 고용관계와 사용관계(지휘명령관계)가 분리되는 고용형태의 특수성으로

working conditions are analyzed differently from that of short-term and part-time employees because the dispatched employee has particular characteristics of employment. Working conditions established in relation to the dispatched employee's labor provision and entry to the using employer's workplace shall not be discriminatory, and the sending employer and a using employer shall not discriminate against the dispatched employee by treating them less favorably than employees the using employer hired directly. However, such things like family allowance paid to directly-hired employees are not related to working conditions established by labor provisions and entry to workplace. Accordingly, differences in such things are not prohibited.

(5) Target employees for comparison

The dispatched employee's target employees for estimating discrimination shall be employees engaged in the same or similar jobs in a using employer's workplace(Article 21(1) of the Dispatch Employee Act).

(6) Disadvantageous treatment and justifiable reasons

1) Basic principle

Whether there is disadvantageous treatment or not and whether such treatment is justifiable or not shall be estimated by considering the dispatch employment characteristics. Even though there is disadvantageous treatment, it can be justifiable if the reason(such as exclusion of promotion opportunities) is attributable to the type of dispatch employment.

2) Wages of a dispatched employee

If a dispatched employee is subject to disadvantageous treatment in regard to wages, as the responsible person for the payment of wages is the sending employer, the dispatched employee can apply for a correction against the sending employer. In this case, when the amount that a dispatched employee received from the sending employer is less than the amount paid to the target employee in comparison engaged in the same or similar job, it is discrimination.

3) Other working conditions of a dispatched employee

Other working conditions of a dispatched employee shall include items related to

인하여 차별처우 금지영역의 범위가 기간제, 단시간 근로자와는 다르다. 파견 근로자로서의 근로제공 및 사용사업주의 사업장에의 편입에 따라 형성되는 근로조건은 차별처우 금지영역에 해당되며, 파견사업주 및 사용사업주는 사용사업주가 직접 고용한 근로자와 차별해서는 아니된다. 근로제공 및 사업장 편입에 따른 근로조건이 아닌 나머지 부분(예: 직접 고용한 근로자 신분에 기하여 지급되는 가족수당 등)은 임금 그 밖의 근로조건 등(제2조 제7호)에 포함된다고 볼 수 없을 것이므로 차별처우가 금지되는 영역에 해당되지 않을 것이다.

(5) 비교대상 근로자

차별판단을 위한 파견 근로자의 비교대상 근로자는 "사용사업주의 사업내의 동종 또는 유사한 업무를 수행하는 근로자"이다(파견법 제21조 제1항).

(6) 불리한 처우와 합리적 이유

1) 기본원칙

파견 근로자에 대한 불리한 처우의 유무와 합리적인 이유의 유무는 파견근로의 특성을 고려하여 판단하게 된다. 설사 불리한 처우가 있는 경우에도 그 원인이 파견근로라는 고용형태의 속성으로 인한 경우에는 합리적 이유가 있는 것으로 볼 수 있다(예: 승진기회의 배제 등).

2) 파견 근로자의 임금

파견 근로자가 임금에 있어서 불리한 처우를 받고 있는 경우 임금지급에 대한 사용자 책임은 파견사업주가 지므로 파견사업주를 피신청인으로 하여 차별적 임금의 시정을 신청할 수 있다. 이 경우 파견 근로자가 파견사업주로부터 지급받은 임금이 '사용사업주가 직접 고용한 사용사업주 사업내의 동종 또는 유사 업무 수행 근로자(비교대상 근로자)'에게 지급한 임금에 비해 적다면 차별의 문제가 제기될 수 있다.

3) 파견 근로자의 그 밖의 근로조건 등

파견 근로자의 "그 밖의 근로조건 등"에서 "① 파견 근로지로서의 근로제공"

working conditions in accordance with labor provision of a dispatched employee and entry to a using employer's workplace.

4. Discrimination correcting procedures

In cases where a short-term employee, part-time employee, or dispatched employee is subject to discriminative treatment, the employee can apply for correction with the Labor Relations Commission within six months from the date the discriminative treatment occurred(or the last day for continuing discriminative treatment)(Article 9(1) of the Short-term Employee Act, Article 21(2) of the Employee Dispatch Act).

In regards to the penal provision, it shall not apply to the discriminative behavior itself. If the employer does not implement a correction order after the Labor Relations Commission has found discriminative treatment, the Minister of Employment and Labor can level a fine of up to 100 million won against the employer. The Minister can also order the employer to submit the status of implementation of the correction order. If the employer has not obeyed the order without justifiable reason, he/she can be fined up to 5 million won.

Ⅱ. Limits on Employment Period for Fixed-term Employees and Exceptions[588)]

1. Concept

We can distinguish employment contracts into three categories based upon employment period. They are ① contracts without fixed-term, ② contracts necessary for completion of a project, and ③ short-term employment contracts within two years. Since the protection laws for irregular employees came into effect July 1st, 2007, the employment period is determined to be within two years, excluding the contract without fixed period, and in cases where the labor contract has been renewed for more than two years, the contract becomes one without a fixed term. Accordingly, as the employment contract reaches the end of the two

588) Reference: Article 4 (Employment of Fixed-term Employees) of the Fixed-Term Employee Act; Article 3 (Exceptions to Limit on Employment Period of Fixed-term Employees).

및 "② 사용사업주의 사업장에의 편입"에 따른 근로조건과 관련된 사항이 포함될 것이다.

4. 차별시정절차

기간제 근로자, 단시간 근로자 및 파견 근로자가 차별적 처우를 받은 경우에는 동차별적 처우가 있은 날(계속되는 차별적 처우는 그 종료일)부터 6월 이내에 노동위원회에 그 시정을 신청할 수 있다(기간제법 제9조 제1항, 파견법 제21조 제2항).

차별적 처우를 한 경우 차별행위 그 자체에 대해서는 벌칙이 부과되지 않는다. 차별적 처우로 판정한 노동위원회의 시정명령이 확정된 후에도 사용자가 정당한 이유 없이 이행하지 않을 경우 고용노동부 장관이 사용자에게 1억원 이하의 과태료를 부과하게 된다. 또한, 고용노동부 장관은 확정된 시정명령에 대하여 사용자에게 이행상황을 제출할 것을 요구할 수 있으며, 정당한 이유 없이 이행상황 제출요구에 불응하는 경우 500만원 이하의 과태료를 부과한다.

Ⅱ. 기간제 근로자의 사용기간 제한과 예외[588)]

1. 의 의

근로계약에 있어 사용기간을 가지고 분류할 때 3가지로 분류할 수 있다. 즉 ① 기간의 정함이 없는 계약, ② 사업완료에 필요한 기간을 정한 계약, ③ 2년 이내의 단기간 근로계약이다. 비정규직 보호법이 시행된 2007년 7월 1일 이후부터는 기간의 정함이 없는 근로계약을 제외하고는, 그 계약기간을 2년 이내로 하고 근로계약이 갱신 반복하여 2년을 초과할 경우에는 기간의 정함이 없는 근로계약으로 전환된다. 따라서 사용자는 2년을 초과하는 시점에서 정규직으로 전환하든지 아니면 근로관계를 해지해야 한다.

---

588) 참조: 기간제법 제4조(기간제 근로자의 사용)와 시행령 제3조(기간제 근로자 사용기간 제한의 예외)

year period, the employer shall decide whether to give the employee a permanent position or terminate employment relations. Even though the employment contract has been renewed repeatedly several times, employment is estimated to be terminated due to expiration of the valid period as the employer did not renew his/her last employment contract. In reality, employers have to receive a judgment through the labor commission or the court to confirm whether the employment that had been renewed repeatedly several times was deemed an employment contract without a fixed period. Generally in court rulings, in cases where a fixed term employee had worked for at least five years and renewed his/her employment contract four times or more, the contract was regarded as expired when it was no longer renewed; but in cases where the fixed term employee had worked for about six years and renewed his/her employment contract at least five times, the contract was regarded as transferred to employment without fixed term when renewal did not happen.[589] The protection laws for irregular employees limit the period of the fixed-term employment to two years to clarify any disputes regarding employment period. However, even though the employment period for fixed-term employees is regulated, some exceptions were introduced due to business characteristics, work characteristics, relations with other laws, and legislative policies.

2. Limit on employment period for fixed-term employees

Article 4 of the Fixed-Term Employee Act regulates that an employer may hire a fixed-term employee for a period not exceeding two years(for repeated fixed-term labor contracts, the sum of the periods of such contracts shall not exceed two years.) Accordingly, the employer cannot use fixed-term employees more than two years, and if he/she does, the employee is regarded as a regular employee. That means, if the employment contract was terminated after exceeding two years, the employee's status changes to regular or non-fixed-term employment. Accordingly, the Fixed-Term Employee Act was designed to avoid disputes over repeated and renewed employment by stipulating the two year limit on the employment period, and to promote temporary employees into regular positions. The reasons to limit the employment period of fixed-term employees include preventing

589) National Human Rights Commission, Survey on labor conditions and the human rights of fixed-term employees Nov. 2008.

그 동안 수차례에 걸쳐 근로계약이 갱신 반복 되었어도 그 계약기간이 정해져 있는 이상 그 기간 만료로 근로계약이 종결되는 것으로 판단하였다. 현실에서 근로계약이 수차례 걸쳐 갱신반복 되어 기간의 정함이 없는 근로계약이 되기 위해서는 노동위원회나 법원을 통해 판단을 받아야 했다. 보통 판례에서는 5년 정도 근무하고 계약이 4번 갱신된 경우에 새로운 계약 갱신이 없는 경우에는 그 계약이 단절된 것으로 간주하고 있으며, 이와 다르게 6년 정도 근무하고 계약이 5번 정도 갱신된 경우에 새로운 계약 갱신이 없는 경우에는 그 계약이 무기계약직으로 전환된 것으로 보고 있다.[589] 비정규직 보호법은 바로 이러한 계약기간에 대한 논쟁을 명확하기 하기 위해 사용기간을 2년으로 도입하였다. 그러나 기간제 근로자의 사용기간이 강행규정임에도 불구하고 사업의 특성, 업무의 특성, 다른 법과의 관계, 입법 정책적 고려에 의하여 사용기간에 대한 예외도 설정하였다.

2. 사용기간의 제한

기간제법 제4조는 "사용자는 2년을 초과하지 아니하는 범위 안에서 (기간제 근로계약의 반복갱신 등의 경우에는 그 계속근로 한 총기간이 2년을 초과하지 아니하는 범위 안에서) 기간제 근로를 사용할 수 있다."고 규정하고 있다. 따라서 사용자는 2년을 초과하여 기간제 근로자를 사용할 수 없고, 2년을 초과할 시에는 정규직으로 고용된 것으로 간주된다. 즉 사용자는 근로자와의 근로계약 기간이 2년을 초과하는 만료 시에 그 근로자를 정규직이나 무기계약직으로 간주하여 해고할 수 없다. 따라서 기간제법은 기존의 계약기간의 반복 갱신 등으로 인한 다툼에 대해 명확히 2년을 명시하여 더 이상의 혼란을 막고, 해당 근로자를 정규직으로 유도하고 있다. 기간제 근로자의 사용기간에 대한 제한을 둔 이유는 첫째, 기존의 근로계약의 갱신 반복으로 인한 법적 다툼을 명확히 법으로 정하는 것이고, 둘째로 명시한 2년의 기간이 정규직화를 유도하는 적절한 시기라고 판단하였기 때문이다.

---

589) 국가인권위원회의 무기계약직 근로자 노동인권상황 실태조사 2008.11.

legal disputes from renewed or repeated employment contracts, and induce fixed-term employees to gain regular positions. Many other countries restrict fixed-term employment. Korea does not, but seeks to protect them by limiting the employment period.

3. Exceptions to the fixed-term employment period and purposes

(1) Cases where the period is needed to complete a project or particular task

If a construction project is proved objectively to be a fixed-term business requiring a certain amount of time to complete, an employment contract can be made for the period required to complete the project in excess of two years. This project-based exception is limited to temporary or one-time business. This includes: ① construction projects; ② temporary surveyors during statistical survey periods; ③ temporary commissioned projects; and ④ secretaries of a part-time director with a three-year contract period.

(2) Cases where a fixed-term employment contract is made with the aged

The Elderly Employment Promotion Act was established to promote the employment of older people, with elderly referring to those aged 55 and over. Employment of such persons has no employment period limits for fixed-term employment contracts.

(3) Cases where a job requires professional knowledge and skills

These cases refer to any of the following: ① The employed person holds a doctoral degree and is engaged in the relevant field; ② The employed person holds a national technical qualification of technician level and is engaged in the relevant field; and ③ The employed person holds a professional qualification(in one of 25 approved fields) and is engaged in the relevant field. Those with doctoral degrees, national technical qualifications of technician level, or professional qualifications issued by the government for 25 fields are generally recognized as specialist with professional knowledge and skills in a particular field. This exception was adopted in reflection of the characteristics of jobs involving these professional specialists. Technician refers to a person who holds a national technical qualification at technician level pursuant to the National Technical Qualifications Act. Professional certificate holder refers to a

기간제 근로자를 사용하는 경우, 외국의 경우에는 사용사유제한을 두는 경우가 있으나, 한국에서는 사용사유 제한에 대해서는 아무런 규정이 없으며 대체로 기간제한을 두고 정규직화를 유도하고 있다.

3. 사용기간의 예외

(1) 사업의 완료 또는 특정한 업무의 완성에 필요한 기간을 정한 경우

건설공사 등의 일정한 시간이 걸리는 유기사업이라는 것이 객관적으로 명백하면, 비록 근로계약 기간이 2년을 넘더라도 그 사업이 끝나는 때까지의 기간을 정하여 근로계약을 체결하는 것이 인정된다. 이 경우, 원칙적으로 한시적이거나 1회성 사업의 특성을 갖는 경우로 한정된다고 보아야 한다. 이러한 사업완료나 특정한 업무의 완성이 필요한 사업이나 업무는 다음과 같다. ① 건설공사현장 근로, ② 통계조사기간 동안의 임시조사원, ③ 한시적으로 수행되는 위, 수탁계약업무, ④ 3년 임기 비상근회장 비서업무 등이 있다.

(2) 고령자와 근로계약을 체결하는 경우

「고령자고용촉진법」은 고령자 고용을 촉진하기 위해 제정된 것으로 고령자라고 함은 만 55세부터 말한다. 고령자를 사용하는 경우에는 그 근로계약의 사용기간 적용을 제외하고 있다.

(3) 전문적 지식·기술의 활용이 필요한 경우

① 박사 학위를 소지하고 해당 분야에 종사하는 경우, ② 기술사 등급의 국가기술 자격을 소지하고 해당 분야에 종사하는 경우, ③ 국가에서 발행하는 25개 전문국가자격 소지자가 해당 분야에 종사하는 경우

박사학위 소지자, 기술사 소지자, 국가에서 발행하는 25개의 전문직 자격사의 경우에는 일반적으로 해당 분야의 전문적 지식과 기술을 갖춘 전문가로서 인식되고 있고, 그 전문가 집단 소속의 특성을 고려한 것이라 볼 수 있다. 기술사는 국가기술자격법에 따른 기술사 자격을 소지한 경우를 말하고, 전문자격사

specialist who is qualified in at least one of the 25 fields recognized by the government in relevant law.[590)]

(4) In cases where a separate law defines the employment period of fixed-term workers differently

1) The Regulations for Contractual Position of Public Servants regulate that the employment period for such public servants shall be a necessary period within five years.

2) The Enforcement Decree on Staffing Educational Personnel and The Private School Act regulates that the employment period of fixed-term teachers shall be up to one year, and if necessary, can be extended up to 3 years.

3) The Act on Foreign Workers' Employment regulates that foreign workers can be employed for up to three years after entering Korea.

---

590) 1. A certified architect according to Article 7 of the Certified Architect Act
2. A certified public labor attorney according to Article 3 of the Certified Public Labor Attorney Act
3. A certified public accountant according to Article 3 of the Certified Public Accountant Act
4. A customs house broker according to Article 4 of the Customs Act
5. A patent attorney according to Article 3 of the Patent Attorney Act
6. A lawyer according to Article 4 of the Lawyer Act
7. An Actuary according to Article 182 of the Insurance Business Act
8. A loss adjuster according to Article 182 of the Insurance Business Act
9. A real estate appraiser according to Article 23 of the Act concerning the Notification of Real Estate Price and Appraisal and Assessment on Real Estate
10. A veterinarian according to Article 2 of the Veterinary License Act
11. A certified tax attorney according to Article 3 of the Certified Tax Attorney Act
12. A pharmacist according to Article 3 of the Pharmaceutical Affairs Act
13. An oriental medicine pharmacist according to Article 4 of the Pharmaceutical Affairs Act
14. An oriental medicine salesman according to Article 45 of the Pharmaceutical Affairs Act
15. An oriental medicine dispensing chemist in the attachment to Article 2 of the Enforcement decree to the Pharmaceutical Affairs Act
16. A doctor according to Article 5 of the Medical Act
17. A dentist according to Article 5 of the Medical Act
18. An oriental medicine doctor according to Article 5 of the Medical Act
19. A certified management consultant according to Article 46 of the Act concerning the Promotion of Small and Medium Companies and their Products
20. A certified technology consultant according to Article 46 of the Act concerning the Promotion of Small and Medium Companies and their Products
21. A business pilot according to Article 26 of the Civil Aeronautics Act
22. A transportation pilot according to Article 26 of the Civil Aeronautics Act
23. An air traffic controller according to Article 26 of the Civil Aeronautics Act
24. A flight engineer according to Article 26 of the Civil Aeronautics Act
25. An aviation specialist according to Article 26 of the Civil Aeronautics Act

는 관련법에 의거하여 국가에서 인정하는 25개의 분야에서 자격을 갖춘 자를 말한다.[590)]

(4) 다른 법령에서 별도의 기간을 정해져 있는 경우

1) 계약직 공무원 규정은 "계약직공무원의 채용기간은 5년의 범위 안에서 당해 사업의 수행에 필요한 기간으로 한다."라고 규정하고 있다.

2) 교육공무원임용령과 사립학교법는 "기간제교원의 임용기간은 1년이내로 하되, 필요한 경우 3년의 범위 내에서 그 기간을 연장할 수 있다."라고 규정하고 있다.

3) 외국인근로자의 고용 등에 관한 법률은 "외국인근로자는 입국한 날부터 3년의 범위에서 취업활동을 할 수 있다."라고 규정하고 있다.

---

590) 1. 「건축사법」 제7조에 따른 건축사
2. 「공인노무사법」 제3조에 따른 공인노무사
3. 「공인회계사법」 제3조에 따른 공인회계사
4. 「관세사법」 제4조에 따른 관세사
5. 「변리사법」 제3조에 따른 변리사
6. 「변호사법」 제4조에 따른 변호사
7. 「보험업법」 제182조에 따른 보험계리사
8. 「보험업법」 제186조에 따른 손해사정사
9. 「부동산가격공시 및 감정평가에 관한 법률」 제23조에 따른 감정평가사
10. 「수의사법」 제2조 제1호에 따른 수의사
11. 「세무사법」 제3조에 따른 세무사
12. 「약사법」 제3조에 따른 약사
13. 「약사법」 제4조에 따른 한약사
14. 「약사법」 제45조에 따른 한약업사
15. 대통령령 제14319호 약사법 시행령 일부개정령 부칙 제2조에 따른 한약조제사
16. 「의료법」 제5조에 따른 의사
17. 「의료법」 제5조에 따른 치과의사
18. 「의료법」 제5조에 따른 한의사
19. 「중소기업진흥 및 제품구매촉진에 관한 법률」 제46조에 따른 경영지도사
20. 「중소기업진흥 및 제품구매촉진에 관한 법률」 제46조에 따른 기술지도사
21. 「항공법」 제26조에 따른 사업용 조종사
22. 「항공법」 제26조에 따른 운송용 조종사
23. 「항공법」 제26조에 따른 항공교통관제사
24. 「항공법」 제26조에 따른 항공기관사
25. 「항공법」 제26조에 따른 항공사

(5) In cases where there is a justifiable reason

1) If a fixed-term employee is needed to fill a vacancy arising from a worker's temporary suspension from duty or dispatch until the worker returns to work: In cases where an employee has taken a leave of absence after giving birth, contracting an illness, doing military service, etc., and took a long-term dispatch, a fixed-term employee can be used to fill it.

2) The period needed for a worker to complete schoolwork or vocational training is defined: When an employee has taken the chance to develop his/her job skills, his/her employment period shall be exceptional for its limit.

(6) Consideration of legislative policies (this exception is gradually extended)

1) In cases where the earned income falls within the highest 25% : Where the earned income of fixed-term employees engaged in occupations like managers, professionals, and other similar jobs according to the Korean Standard Classification of Occupations falls within the highest 25%, there is no limit to employment period(earned income is based on the average annual earned income of the past two years);

2) Where jobs are provided to develop the public's vocational competency, promote employment and offer necessary social services in accordance with other laws such as the Basic Employment Policy Act and the Employment Insurance Act;

3) Where jobs are provided to promote the employment of discharged soldiers and grant them livelihood stability pursuant to Article 3 of the Support for Discharged Soldiers Act;

4) Where a person who has professional military knowledge or skills recognized by the Minister of Defense is engaged in the relevant field or where a person teaches national security and military science in a university pursuant to subparagraph 1 of Article 2 of the Higher Education Act;

5) Where a person with exceptional experience is engaged in a field related to national security, national defense, diplomacy or unification;

6) Where a person is engaged in work specified in any of the following items in a school under Article 2 of the Higher Education Act(including graduate schools under Article 30 of the same Act): ① Work of a teaching assistant under Article 14 of the Higher Education Act; or ② Work of an adjunct teacher, professor emeritus, part-time instructor, visiting teacher, etc., under Article 7 of the Enforcement Decree to the Higher Education Act;

(5) 합리적인 사유가 있는 경우

1) 휴직, 파견 등으로 결원이 발생하여 당해 근로자가 복귀할 때까지 그 업무를 대신할 필요가 있는 경우: 출산, 질병, 군 입대 등으로 인한 기존 근로자가 휴직하거나 장기 파견된 경우 당해 근로자를 대체하는 등이 해당된다.

2) 근로자가 학업, 직업훈련 등을 이수함에 따라 그 이수에 필요한 기간을 정한 경우: 근로자가 자주적으로 직업능력을 개발하고자 하는 경우에는 근로계약기간을 예외로 하고 있다.

(6) 입법 정책적 배려(비정규직보호법 도입 이후 기간사용제한 지속적 확대)

1) 근로소득 상위 100분의 25에 해당하는 경우: 근로소득은 최근 조사한 고용형태별 근로실태조사의 대분류표에 의한 관리자, 전문가 및 관련 종사자 직업에 종사하는 자의 근로소득이 근로자 상위 100분의 25에 해당하는 경우에는 기간제로 근무 시에 사용기간 제한에 해당되지 않는다. 근로소득은 최근 2년간의 연평균 근로소득으로 한다.

2) 고용정책기본법, 고용보험법 등 다른 법령에 따라 국민의 직업능력 개발, 취업 촉진 및 사회적으로 필요한 서비스 제공 등을 위하여 일자리를 제공하는 경우

3) 제대군인 지원에 관한 법률 제3조에 따라 제대군인의 고용증진 및 생활안정을 위하여 일자리를 제공하는 경우

4) 국방부장관이 인정하는 군사적 전문적 지식, 기술을 가지고 관련 직업에 종사하거나 고등교육법 제2조 제1호에 따른 대학에서 안보 및 군사학과목을 강의하는 경우

5) 특수한 경력을 갖추고 국가안전보장, 국방 외교 또는 통일과 관련된 업무에 종사하는 경우

6) 고등교육법 제2조에 따른 학교에서 다음 각 목의 업무에 종사하는 경우(2010.2.4. 도입) ① 고등교육법 제14조에 따른 조교의 업무, ② 고등교육법 시행령 제7조에 따른 겸임교원, 명예교수, 시간강사, 초빙교원 등의 업무

7) Where a part-time worker's weekly working hours, under Article 18 of the Labor Standards Act, is evidently short;

8) Sports athletes under subparagraph 4 of Article 2 of the National Sports Promotion Act and where a person is engaged in teaching sports pursuant to subparagraph 6 of the same Article;

9) Where a person is directly engaged in research work or directly involved in research work as an assistant, such as by carrying out experiments, surveys, etc., in any of the following research institutions:

① National or public research institutions; ② Government-invested research institutions established under the Act on the Establishment, Operation and Fosterage of Government-Invested Research Institutions and the Act on the Establishment, Operation and Fosterage of Government-Invested Science and Technology Research Institutions; ③ Specific research institutions under the Support of Specific Research Institution Act; ④ Research institutions established under the Act on the Establishment and Operation of Local Government-Invested Research Institutes; ⑤ Public institution-affiliated research institutions under the Act on the Management of Public Institutions; ⑥ Company- or university-affiliated research institutions; and ⑦ Research institutions which are a corporation established under the Civil Act or any other Act.

Ⅲ. Right of Fixed-term Workers to Expect Renewal of their Employment Contract

1. Concept

The frequency of the use of non-regular workers in Korea has occurred due to their overuse through managerial dismissal and worker dispatch laws, in efforts to cope with the IMF financial crisis in 1997. In order to limit the use of non-regular workers and encourage their use as full-time workers whenever possible, the Act on the Protection, etc. of Fixed-term and Part-time Workers(hereinafter referred to as the "Fixed-term Workers Act") was enacted. For the protection of irregular workers, the Fixed-term Workers Act, enacted in 2007, stipulates that fixed-term workers can be used for a maximum of two years, and after two years, the fixed-term worker is regarded as a non-fixed term worker(Article 4 of the Act). This regulation was introduced to limit the use of fixed-term workers and to eliminate employment insecurity by promoting the renewal of their fixed-term employment in cases where fixed-term workers had worked for more than two years.

7) 근로기준법 제18조 제3항에 따른 1주 동안의 소정근로시간이 뚜렷하게 짧은 단시간 근로자를 사용하는 경우

8) 국민체육진흥법 제2조 제4호에 따른 선수와 같은 조 제6호에 따른 체육지도자 업무에 종사하는 경우

9) 아래의 연구기관에서 연구업무에 직접 종사하는 경우 또는 실험, 조사 등을 수행하는 등 연구업무에 직접 관여하여 지원하는 업무에 종사하는 경우

① 국공립연구기관, ② 정부출연연구기관 또는 과학기술분야에 설립된 정부출연 연구기관, ③ 특정연구기관, ④ 지방자치단체가 설립한 연구기관, ⑤ 공공기관의 부설 연구기관, ⑥ 기업 또는 대학의 부설 연구기관, ⑦ 다른 법률에 따라 설립된 법인의 연구기관

Ⅲ. 기간제 근로자의 갱신기대권

1. 의 의

우리나라의 비정규직 문제는 1997년도 IMF의 금융위기를 극복하고자 정리해고법과 파견근로법의 도입으로 무분별하게 비정규직 근로자를 사용하면서 발생하게 되였다. 기간제 비정규직 근로자 사용을 제한하고 가급적 정규직 사용을 유도하기 위해 비정규직 보호법인『기간제 및 단시간 근로자 보호 등에 관한 법률』(이하 "기간제법")이 제정되었다. 비정규직 보호를 위하여 2007년부터 시행된 기간제법은 기간제 근로자를 최대 2년동안 사용할 수 있고, 이 기간을 초과할 경우 무기계약직으로 간주하도록 하고 있다(법 제4조). 이 규정은 기간제 근로자의 사용을 제한하고, 기간제 계약직원이 반복 갱신되어 2년 이상 근무할 경우 정규직화로 유도하여 고용불안을 해소하기 위해 도입되었다.

기간제법 제4조에는 분명히 2년 이내에서 기간제 근로자를 사용할 수 있다고 규정화되어 있고, 2년 제한규정의 예외대상을 별도로 정하고 있다. 갱신기대권은 기간제 근로계약에 갱신 조건을 가진 근로계약 등이 있거나, 기간제 근로자에게 갱신될 수 있다는 확신을 갖게 한 경우에는 기간제 2년 사용제한의 예외

Article 4 of the Fixed-term Workers Act stipulates that fixed-term workers can be used for two years, with some exceptions. Nevertheless, the right to expect renewal is assured in cases where the fixed-term contract can be renewed, with a condition; the worker expects to have his/her fixed-term contract renewed. In addition, the exemption clauses of fixed-term employment are exceptional for repeated employment contracts for professional workers and aging workers, which add to confusion at the workplace, making it necessary to establish the details and specific criteria for this. In this regard, I would like to specifically examine the laws, precedents, and reasons for the right to expect renewal.

2. Restriction on term of fixed-term workers in Article 4 of the Fixed-term Workers Act and the right to expect renewal

(1) Details of Article 4 of the Fixed-term Workers Act

Article 4 of the Fixed-term Workers Act limits the period of use for fixed-term workers to two years.[591] The reason this limitation is as follows: ① In Article 16 of the previous version of the Labor Standards Act, the upper limit is set as one year, but there is no restriction on the total period of use through repeated renewal of the labor contract. This enabled employers to take advantage of repeating an employment contract for less than one year as a means of avoiding the restriction against dismissal according to Article 23 of the LSA. This has increased the number of workers in fixed-term contracts; and ② it is a principle that employment is terminated automatically upon termination of the contract. However, if an employment contract is renewed

591) The Fixed-term Workers Act: Article 4 (Employment of Fixed-term Employees) ① An employer may employ a fixed-term employee for a period not exceeding two years (in cases where a fixed-term labor contract is repeatedly renewed, the total consecutive employment period shall not exceed two years.): Provided that an employer may employ a fixed-term employee for more than two years in any of the following cases:

1. Where the period required for completion of a project or particular task is defined;
2. Where a fixed-term employee is needed to fill a vacancy arising from a worker's temporary suspension from duty or dispatch;
3. Where the period required for a worker to complete his/her education or vocational training is defined;
4. Where a fixed-term labor contract is made with an elderly person as defined in Article 2 Subparagraph 1 of the Elderly Employment Promotion Act;
5. Cases prescribed by Presidential Decree, where the job requires professional knowledge and skills or is offered as part of the government's welfare or unemployment measures;
6. Other cases prescribed by Presidential Decree, where there are reasonable grounds equivalent to those described in subparagraphs 1 through 5.

② If an employer employs a fixed-term employee for more than two years, even though grounds under the proviso to paragraph (1) do not exist or cease to exist, the fixed-term employee shall be considered a worker who has made a non-fixed term labor contract.

대상인 전문직종 근로자나 고령자의 경우에도 모두 인정되고 있어, 사업 현장에서 혼란을 주고 있다. 따라서 이에 대한 구체적인 판단기준의 정립이 필요하다고 하겠다. 이에 대해 갱신기대권과 관련된 법령, 판례내용, 갱신거절의 합리적 사유에 대해 구체적으로 살펴보고자 한다.

2. 기간제법의 기간제한(법 제4조)과 갱신기대권

(1) 기간제법 제4조의 내용

기간제법 제4조는 기간제 근로자의 사용기간을 2년으로 제한하고 있다.[591] 그 이유는, ① 구 근로기준법 제16조에 근로계약 기간을 정하는 경우는 1년을 상한으로 하고 있으나 기간을 정한 근로계약의 반복갱신을 통한 총 사용기간에 대하여는 아무런 제한이 없어서 사용자들이 1년 이내의 근로계약을 반복 갱신함으로써 근로기준법 제23조의 해고 제한규정을 회피하는 수단으로 활용하여 왔고 이에 따라 기간제 근로자의 규모가 증가하게 되었으며, ② 법원이 계약기간 만료 시 고용관계가 자동 종료되는 것을 원칙으로 하되 근로계약이 수차례 반복 갱신된 경우에는 기간의 정함이 없는 근로계약으로 해석하는 경우도 있으나, 그 경우 계약 관행, 당사자의 의사, 갱신에 대한 기대가능성, 직무특성 등

591) 기간제법 제4조【기간제 근로자의 사용】① 사용자는 2년을 초과하지 아니하는 범위 안에서(기간제 근로계약의 반복갱신 등의 경우에는 그 계속근로한 총기간이 2년을 초과하지 아니하는 범위 안에서) 기간제 근로자를 사용할 수 있다. 다만, 다음 각 호의 어느 하나에 해당하는 경우에는 2년을 초과하여 기간제 근로자로 사용할 수 있다.
1. 사업의 완료 또는 특정한 업무의 완성에 필요한 기간을 정한 경우
2. 휴직·파견 등으로 결원이 발생하여 당해 근로자가 복귀할 때까지 그 업무를 대신할 필요가 있는 경우
3. 근로자가 학업, 직업훈련 등을 이수함에 따라 그 이수에 필요한 기간을 정한 경우
4. 「고령자고용촉진법」 제2조 제1호의 고령자와 근로계약을 체결하는 경우
5. 전문적 지식·기술의 활용이 필요한 경우와 정부의 복지정책·실업대책 등에 따라 일자리를 제공하는 경우로서 대통령령이 정하는 경우
6. 그밖에 제1호 내지 제5호에 준하는 합리적인 사유가 있는 경우로서 대통령령이 정하는 경우
② 사용자가 제1항 단서의 사유가 없거나 소멸되었음에도 불구하고 2년을 초과하여 기간제 근로자로 사용하는 경우에는 그 기간제 근로자는 기간의 정함이 없는 근로계약을 체결한 근로자로 본다.

several times, it may be interpreted as being an employment contract without a fixed term. In that case, as the habitual practice of the contract, the intention of the parties, the expectation of renewal, the nature of the work, and other various factors need to be considered, it has been pointed out that the workers are not likely to win a dismissal case, and that such dismissal cases are inconsistent, which led to enactment of the Fixed-term Workers Act.[592] Since the adoption of the Fixed-term Workers Act, even if an employment contract is repeated a number of times, there is no such dispute because the term can only be a limit of two years. However, in instances of a fixed-term labor contract where there are conditions for renewal even if there is no provision for renewal, if trust exists in the relationship for renewal of the fixed-term contract, the right to expect renewal is still valid even after introduction of the Act.

(2) The right to expect contract renewal

The right to expect renewal is not specified in the Fixed-term Workers Act, but has been consistently recognized in court rulings, and has the same role as the subsidiary clause of Article 4 of the Fixed-term Workers Act. The right to expect renewal means that if a contract is signed for fixed-term employment, but a contract renewal is reasonably expected, if the employer refuses to renew the contract with no reasonable justification, the effect is similar to unfair dismissal. In this case, any employment after the contract expires shall be regarded as a renewal of the old labor contract.[593]

The Supreme Court concluded, "In the case of a term of employment contract, the employment contract between the parties shall be terminated without waiting for a separate action such as dismissal of the employee when the period expires. However, ① except in a case where the original period is renewed over a long period of time and the fixed period is only a form;[594] ② in cases where there is a provision stipulated in the employment contract and the rules of employment that the fixed-term contract will be renewed if certain requirements are met despite the expiration of the period; or ③ if there is a trust relationship between the parties that the employment contract will be renewed if certain requirements are met, even if there is no such specific provision; the refusal to renew the employment contract can be considered dismissal rather than termination of the contract due to expiration of contract period.[595] Since enactment

592) Labor Law Practice Study,「Labor Standards Act Translation II」Parkyoungsa, 2010, pp. 17-18.

593) Noh, Kiljoon,「A study of the fixed-term employment contract」, Graduate School of Ajou University (Doctoral thesis), 2018, p. 37.

594) Supreme Court ruling on Feb. 24, 2006, 2005doo 5673.

595) Supreme Court ruling on Apr. 14, 2011, 2007doo1729; Supreme Court ruling on Nov. 10, 2016, 2014doo 45765.

다양한 사정들을 고려함에 따라 실무상 근로자가 승소하기가 쉽지 않고 사례별로 일관성이 없다는 지적을 받아 왔기 때문에 이를 입법적으로 해결하는데 있다.[592] 기간제법 도입 이후에는 근로계약이 수차례 반복되더라도 2년을 한도로 정하여 기간제를 사용할 수 있기 때문에 더 이상의 다툼이 없어지게 되었다. 다만, 기간제 근로계약 등에 있어 갱신에 대한 조건을 설정하였거나 그러한 규정이 없더라도 계약의 갱신에 대해 신뢰관계가 성립된 경우 인정되는 갱신기대권은 기간제법 도입 이후에도 계속 효력을 가지고 있다.

(2) 갱신기대권

갱신기대권은 기간제법에는 명시되어 있지 않으나, 판례에서 일관적으로 인정되어온 권리로 기간제법 제4조의 부속조항과 같은 역할을 하고 있다. '갱신기대권'이란 기간제 근로계약을 체결하였으나 근로자에게 계약갱신에 대한 정당한 기대권이 인정되는 경우 사용자가 '합리적 이유' 없이 계약갱신을 거절한다면 부당해고와 같이 아무런 효력이 없고, 이 경우 기간만료 후의 근로관계는 종전의 근로계약이 갱신된 것과 동일하다는 판례법리이다.[593]

대법원은 "근로계약 기간을 정한 경우 근로계약 당사자 사이의 근로계약은 그 기간이 만료함에 따라 사용자의 해고 등의 별도의 조치를 기다릴 것이 없이 당연히 종료된다. 그러나 ① 예외적으로 당초 정해진 기간이 장기간에 걸쳐 갱신이 반복되어 그 정한 기간이 단지 형식에 불과하게 된 경우,[594] ② 근로계약이나 취업규칙으로 기간만료에도 불구하고 일정한 요건을 충족하면 갱신된다는 취지의 규정을 두고 있는 경우나 ③ 그러한 규정이 없더라도 당사자 사이에 일정한 요건이 충족되면 근로계약이 갱신된다는 신뢰관계가 형성된 경우에는 근로계약 갱신거절은 계약기간만료에 의한 계약의 종결이 아니라 해고에 해당된다."고 판시하고 있다.[595] 기간제법 제정을 통해 원칙적으로 총 계약기간이 2년 한도로 법제화 되어 위의 ①의 문제는 어느 정도 해결되었다. 그러나 ②와

---

592) 노동법실무연구회, 「근로기준법 주해Ⅱ」, 박영사, 2010, 17~18면.

593) 노길준, 「기간제 근로계약에 관한 연구」, 아주대학교 대학원(박사학위 논문), 2018, 37면.

594) 대법원 2006.2.24, 2005두5673.

595) 대법원 2011.4.14, 2007두1729; 대법원 2016.11.10, 2014두45765.

of the Fixed-term Workers Act, the total contract period is limited to two years in principle, and the above issue ① was solved to some degree. However, since issues ② and ③ arise from the expectation of conditional renewal and the right to expect renewal, disputes have often arisen between workers and employers.

3. Reasonable justification for refusing to renew after recognition of the right to expect renewal

(1) Reasons to refuse renewal

A Supreme Court ruling[596)] provides the criteria: "If a reasonable expectation that an employment contract will be renewed is granted to a worker, it is ineffective for the employer to unfairly refuse to renew the employment contract without reason. If there is reasonable justification to not renew the contract, even if the employee has a reasonable expectation of renewal, such reasons can be evaluated by considering the following: ① The employer's purpose and characteristics of the business, workplace conditions, the employee's position and job responsibilities; ② The process of signing an employment contract; ③ Whether or not the requirements and procedures for renewal of the employment contract are set up and its operational status; and ④ Whether the employee bears responsibility or not. The reason for refusal and the procedure should be judged based on socially-accepted standards, on the basis of being objective, reasonable and fair, and the burden of proof for such matters shall be borne by the employer."

Even if legitimate expectation of renewal of a fixed-term worker's employment contract is recognized, it is sufficient for the employer to refuse to renew the contract if there is reasonable justification which is deemed equivalent to socially-accepted standards, which is a relaxed standard rather than a legitimate reason.[597)] This is because it would suggest that reasonable justification trumps the renewal expectation, or that the expectation of renewal has changed.

596) Supreme Court ruling on Oct. 12, 2017.10.12, 2015doo44493.

597) Seoul Appeal Court ruling Sep. 30, 2010, 2009noo36233.

③은 조건부 갱신, 갱신에 대한 기대권으로부터 발생하기 때문에 근로자와 사용자 간에 분쟁이 발생하는 경우가 많다.

3. 갱신기대권이 인정된 이후 갱신거절의 합리적 사유

(1) 갱신거절의 합리적 사유

판례[596]는 "근로자에게 근로계약이 갱신될 수 있으리라는 정당한 기대권이 인정되는 경우 사용자가 이에 위반하여 합리적인 사유 없이 부당하게 근로계약의 갱신을 거절하는 것은 부당해고와 마찬가지로 아무런 효력이 없다. 근로자에게 이미 형성된 갱신에 대한 정당한 기대권이 있음에도 불구하고 사용자가 이를 배제하고 근로계약의 갱신을 거절한 데에 합리적 이유가 있는지가 문제될 때는 다음을 고려하여 판단. ① 사용자의 사업 목적과 성격, 사업장 여건, 근로자의 지위 및 담당 직무의 내용, ② 근로계약 체결 경위, ③ 근로계약의 갱신에 관한 요건이나 절차의 설정 여부와 그 운용 실태, ④ 근로자에게 책임 있는 사유가 있는지 여부 등 당해 근로관계를 둘러싼 여러 사정을 종합하여 갱신 거부의 사유와 그 절차가 사회통념에 비추어 볼 때 객관적이고 합리적이며 공정한지를 기준으로 판단하여야 한다. 그러한 사정에 대한 증명책임은 사용자가 부담한다."라는 기준을 제시한다.

기간제 근로자의 근로계약 갱신에 대한 정당한 기대권이 인정된다고 하더라도 사용자가 그 계약을 갱신 거절하는 데에는 해고 제한의 기준인 정당한 이유보다는 완화된 기준인 사회통념상 상당하다고 인정되는 합리적 사유가 있으면 충분하다.[597] 왜냐하면 갱신기대권을 대체할 수 있는 합리적 사유를 제시하거나 갱신기대권이 소멸했다는 사실을 제시하면 될 것이기 때문이다.

---

596) 대법원 2017.10.12, 2015두44493.

597) 서울고등법원 2010.9.30, 2009누36233.

(2) Related labor cases

1) Cases where there is no reason to refuse to renew the contract

1) Worker A entered into an employment contract for two years from October 26, 2010 to October 25, 2012. According to the contract, it could be renewed one month before the expiry date. One month before expiration of the contract, the company informed worker A that the labor relationship would be terminated on October 25, the expiry date of the employment contract. The company informed worker A that the personnel evaluation results were not good, which was the reason for termination of the contract. However, at that time, the company's personnel evaluation criteria were vague, and objectivity was low.[598)]

2) The company is a foundation that operates social work support projects for unemployed people. It hired worker A on October 26, 2010, who then worked as a team leader supporting establishment of the social enterprise. The enterprise informed worker A on September 24, 2012 that the employment contract would expire on October 25, 2012. One month before expiration of the contract, the company considered whether or not it would switch to full-time employment through personnel evaluation.[599)]

3) Seoul Metropolitan Government Facility Management Corporation had concluded contracts for the transportation of persons with disabilities by setting a contract period of one year with the driver, and then did not renew the contract. It is stated that the Call Taxi for the Handicapped by the City of Seoul is to renew the contract period on a yearly basis and that the purpose for this is to be able to replace unsatisfactory people. This service for the disabled cannot be regarded as a temporary business and has term extension regulations for the contract with drivers. Considering the aforementioned, it is considered that the drivers who belong to this facility management corporation are granted the right to expect that their fixed-term contract will be renewed.[600)]

---

598) Supreme Court ruling on Nov. 10, 2016, 2014doo45765: As there was no objectivity in the personnel evaluation, the case was determined as unfair dismissal.

599) Seoul Appeal Court ruling on Nov. 6, 2014, 2013noo53679: At the end of the term contract period, the company evaluated whether to convert to full-time employment through personnel evaluation. The worker expected renewal, and the company was not fair in its personnel evaluation.

600) Supreme Court ruling on Apr. 14, 2011, 2007doo1729: It is a regular business which re-contracts on a yearly

(2) 갱신기대권 관련 사건 사례

1) 계약갱신 거절에 합리적 사유가 없는 경우

1) 근로자 A는 2010년 10월26일 부터 2012년 10월25일까지 2년을 기간으로 한 근로계약을 체결했다. A가 회사와 합의한 근로계약에 따르면, 근로계약 만료 1개월 전에 재계약할 수 있다는 내용이 포함되어 있다. 근로계약 만료 1개월 전인 2012.9.24 회사는 A에게 근로계약 만료일인 10월25일자로 근로관계를 종료한다고 통보했다. 회사는 근로계약 해지사유로 '인사평가 결과가 좋지 않다'고 A에게 통보했다. 그러나 당시 회사의 인사평가 기준은 모호했고 객관성도 떨어졌다.[598)]

2) 회사는 실업자의 사회적 일자리 지원사업 등을 운영하는 재단법인이고, 근로자는 2010년 10월 26일 입사하여 사회적 기업 설립지원팀장 등으로 근무하였다. 재단법인은 2012년 9월 24일 근로자에게 2012년 10월 25일에 근로계약 기간이 종료된다는 내용을 통보하였다. 회사는 계약만료 1개월 전, 인사평가를 통해 정규직 전환 여부를 판단하였고, 대상자 4명 중, 본 근로자만 정규직 전환에서 탈락하였다.[599)]

3) 서울시 시설관리공단이 계약기간을 1년으로 정하여 장애인 콜택시 운행에 관한 위·수탁계약을 체결하고 장애인콜택시의 운행업무를 수행하던 운전자 갑 등에게 계약에서 정한 위탁기간이 만료되었음을 이유로 갱신계약 체결 대상자 선정을 위한 심사에서 탈락시켰다. 서울시의 장애인콜택시 운영계획에 계약기간을 1년 단위로 갱신하도록 하면서 그 취지가 부적격자의 교체에 있음을 명시하고 있고, 장애인콜택시 사업을 한시적·일시적 사업이라고 볼 수 없는 점, 위·수탁 계약에서 위탁기간 연장 규정을 두고 있는 점 등을 종합하면, 시설관리공단 소속 운전자들 에게는 기간제 근로계약이 갱신되리라는 정당한 기대권이 인정된다고 본다.[600)]

---

598) 대법원 2016.11.10, 2014두45765. 인사평가의 객관성이 없기 때문에 부당해고로 인정

599) 서울고등법원 2014.11.6, 2013누53679. 기간제 계약기간이 만료되는 시점에서 인사평가를 통해 정규직 전환여부를 평가함. 근로자는 갱신기대권을 가졌고, 회사는 평가에 공정성이 없었다.

600) 대법원 2011.4.14, 2007두1729. 1년 단위로 재 계약하는 상시 업무인데, 회사는 인사평가를

2) For some occupations, the right to expect renewal is recognized

1) In a specific plaintiff's case(who was an in-house lawyer), his/her labor contract cannot be regarded as having no fixed term, as the plaintiff worked four times over five years while renewing the labor contract. The plaintiff had reason to expect renewal as he/she had been responsible for necessary tasks as the lawyer for the company and had had the contract renewed several times, cultivating the expectation this would continue as long as he/she wished to continue to work.[601)]

2) The defendant, Gimcheon City, had commissioned the plaintiffs(members of the symphony orchestra) as non-permanent members since December 1, 2004, and entered into two-year contracts with them. However, the City suddenly did not renew after contract expiration in January 2011. Gimcheon City had decided to select new members through a new screening process before the final contract expired, and in November 2011, it announced hiring for a Gimcheon City arts group. The City asked the plaintiffs to join the new screening test. The candidates' current address of Daegu or Gyeongbuk as of the announcement date was added as a qualification requirement for common examination. Because of this, plaintiffs who lived in Seoul, Milyang, and Busan failed to meet the qualification requirements and so Gimcheon City refused to renew their contracts.[602)]

3) Company S entered into an employment contract with the plaintiffs for one year in October 2011, after which they worked as a golf course management team with no updated contracts until February 2014. Company S's retirement age was 55, and the plaintiffs had already reached this age before or during the term of the contract. Company S signed an employment contract with the plaintiffs in March 2014 which set the work period for one additional year, and notified the plaintiffs in January 2015 that their contract period would expire in February. In the case of the plaintiffs, it can be said that the retirement age did not convert them into unqualified workers. It could be expected that

---

basis. The company refused to renew the contract through personnel evaluation. There was no fairness or objectivity in the personnel evaluation.

601) Seoul District Court ruling on Apr. 19, 2012: 2011gahap 21933. Professional jobs for which there is no limit of 2 years for employment term in Article 4 of the Fixed-term Workers Act, yet the job holders have the right to expect renewal.

602) Supreme Court ruling on Oct. 12, 2017: 2015doo44493. When a job is excluded from Article 4 of the Fixed-term Workers Act, the right to expect renewal is applicable.

2) 기간제 2년 한도의 예외직종의 경우에도 갱신기대권이 인정된 경우

1) 이 사건 원고(사내변호사)의 경우 근로계약을 기간의 정함이 없는 것으로 볼 수는 없으나, 원고가 5년간 4회에 걸쳐 근로계약을 갱신하면서 근무하였고, 방송국 운영을 위하여 상시적, 지속적으로 필요한 업무를 담당하였으며, 그동안 사내변호사들이 스스로 계속 근무를 희망하는 한 근로계약이 갱신되었다는 등의 사정이 있었다면 원고는 근로계약 갱신에 대한 합리적 기대권을 가진다.[601)]

2) 피고인 김천시는 2004년 12월 1일부터 원고들을 교향악단에 비상임 단원으로 위촉해 2년 단위로 위촉계약을 체결하고, 기간만료까지 정기평정을 통해 수차례 재 위촉해 왔다. 그런데 김천시는 갑자기 2011년 1월 위촉기간 만료 후 원고를 재 위촉하지 않았다. 김천시는 최종 위촉계약 만료 전 신규전형을 통해 단원 선발을 결정하고 2011년 11월 김천시 시립예술단 모집공고를 냈다. 그리고 원고들에게 해당 신규전형에 응시하도록 했다. 공통응시자격요건에 '공고일 현재 주소가 대구, 경북으로 되어 있는 자'가 추가 됐다. 이로 인해 당시 주소가 서울, 밀양, 부산이던 원고들이 응시자격을 갖추지 못하였기 때문에 불합격했고, 김천시는 갱신을 거부하였다.[602)]

3) 골프장 S사는 원고들과 2011년 10월 근무기간을 1년으로 하는 근로계약을 체결하였고, 이후 2014년 2월까지 새로운 근로계약을 체결하지 않은 채 골프장 코스관리팀 사원으로 일하였다. S사의 정년은 만 55세였는데, 원고들은 기간제 근로계약을 체결하기 전이나 계약기간 중에 이미 정년에 도달한 상태였다. S회사는 2014년 3월 원고들과 다시 근무기간을 1년으로 정하는 근로계약을 체결했는데, 이듬해인 2015년 1월 원고들에게 계약기간이 2월에 만료된다고 통보하였다. 원고들에게는 정년이 도과하여 기간의 정함이 없는 근로자로 전환될 수는 없다고 하더라도 근로계약이 갱신되리라는 기대권이 인정된다고 봄이 타당하고, 그 갱신거절의 정당한 이유를 찾아볼 수도 없으므로 이 사건 근

통해 계약 갱신을 거부하였다. 이에 대해 인사평가의 공정성과 객관성이 없었다.

601) 서울중앙지법원 2012.4.19, 2011가합21933. 기간제법 제4조의 기간제 2년의 한도에 예외적인 전문직도 갱신기대권에 적용된다는 판례임.

602) 대법원 2017.10.12, 2015두44493. 기간제법 제4조의 적용제외대상의 경우에도 갱신기대권을 인정한 판결이다.

the labor contract would be renewed, and that there was no reason to refuse the renewal, and so it was deemed as unfair dismissal.[603)]

3) Cases where the right to expect renewal cannot be established

1) A certain employee had been working as a full-time professional commissioner in the Civil Rights Commission with a contract period ending December 31, 2008, and worked as a professional adviser from January 1, 2009 to December 31, 2009. He had to resign because of contract expiration. There was no right to expect renewal because the Commission announced that this job was not a position which would be converted into non-fixed employment, in accordance with its regulations on irregular workers in public institutions.[604)]

2) Hyundai Motor Company employed a fixed-term worker and renewed the employment contract 14 times over short periods of 2 weeks to a maximum of 6 months. After 2 years, it notified the worker of expiry of the contract, which was not renewed on January 31, 2015. There were no precedent cases in which other irregular workers in the company became full-time workers, and so there was no right to expect renewal because, while the position was constantly needed, it was regarded as a temporary task to fill the vacancies of regular workers.[605)]

Ⅳ. Guidelines for Determining if Subcontracting is Actually Illegal Dispatch and Related Cases

1. Introduction

Dispatched workers are used for the flexibility and reductions to labor costs they entail for companies. However, as dispatched workers can only be used for 2 years and only for a limited range of jobs, companies have been looking for a way to make use of workers in a similar way. In-house subcontract workers are one way to gain the continuous benefit that dispatch employment cannot provide. In-house subcontracting requires independence and expertise. However, many companies in Korea do not outsource these specialized

603) Supreme Court ruling on Feb. 3, 2017: 2016doo50563.

604) Seoul Appeal Court ruling on Aug. 18, 2011: 2011noo9821.

605) Seoul Administrative Court ruling on Oct. 20, 2016: 2015goohap71068.

로계약 종료는 부당해고에 해당한다고 판시하였다.[603)]

3) 갱신기대권이 성립되지 않는 경우

1) 원고들은 2008년 6월19일 국민권익위원회에 계약기간을 2008년 12월31일까지로 하여 상근전문위원으로 채용되어 근무하다가 2008년 12월 경 다시 계약기간을 2009년 1월1일부터 2009년 12월31일까지로 하여 전문자문위원으로 근무하였고, 동년 12월31일 계약기간 만료로 퇴직하였다. 국민권익위원회가 해당직군 채용공고를 내면서 '공공기관 비정규직 근로자 등에 관한 규정에 따라 무기계약 전환대상자는 아님' 이라고 공고한 사실이 있기 때문에 갱신기대권이 없다.[604)]

2) 현대자동차는 기간제 근로자를 채용하면서 짧게는 2주일에서 많게는 6개월 단위로 14회에 걸쳐 근로계약을 반복하여 사용하다가 2년이 되는 시점에서 계약만료를 통보하고 2015년 1월31일에 계약갱신을 하지 않았다. 이에 대해 법원은 기존의 다른 기간제 근로자가 정규직으로 변경된 전례가 없었고, 업무가 상시적 계속적으로 필요하지만 정규직 근로자의 업무공백을 메우기 위한 한시적 업무로 판단하여 갱신기대권을 인정하지 않았다.[605)]

Ⅳ. 불법파견 판단지침과 판단 사례

1. 개 요

파견근로자를 사용하는 것은 기업체에서 고용의 유연화와 인건비 절감차원에서 큰 도움이 되기 때문이다. 그러나 이러한 파견근로자는 제한된 업종에 한해, 2년 밖에 사용할 수 없어 기업체에서는 파견근로 형태로 계속 유지할 수 있는 방법을 모색하게 되었다. 이러한 파견과 같은 효과를 가지면서 지속적으로 사용할 수 있는 것이 사내하도급이다. 사내하도급은 업무의 독립성과 전문성을 요구하고 있다. 그러나 우리나라의 많은 회사들이 이러한 전문적인 업무에 대

603) 대법원 2017.2.3, 2016두50563.
604) 서울고등법원 2011.8.18, 2011누9821.
605) 서울행정법원 2016.10.20, 2015구합71068.

tasks, but often make use of in-house subcontracting for simple work or to increase their manpower for lower costs. If a company directs and orders subcontract workers in their work, this will be judged illegal dispatch and the employer will be subject to criminal punishment and an obligation to directly employ the in-house subcontract worker(Article 6-2 of the Dispatch Act).

To prevent illegal dispatch, on April 19, 2007, the Ministry of Employment and Labor has provided Guidelines on Determining 'Dispatch Workers' to Distinguish between Dispatch and Subcontracting. Nevertheless, the use of illegal dispatch and disguised subcontracting have expanded across all industries. Accordingly, on December 30, 2019, the Ministry of Employment and Labor began emphasizing the criteria through its Guidelines on Criteria for Determining Dispatch Workers.

2. Determining Illegal Dispatch

(1) Understanding Illegal Dispatch

The term worker dispatch means a system in which a sending employer, while maintaining employment relations with a worker after hiring, has the worker work for a using employer under the direction and order of the using employer in accordance with a worker dispatch contract(Article 2 of the Dispatch Act). Whether or not it is a worker dispatch is judged based on the facts rather than the name or form of the contract between the using and sending employers.

A contract for work becomes effective when one of the parties has agreed to perform a certain job and the other has agreed to pay remuneration for such work(Article 664 of the Civil Act). This means that the subcontractor, at his own discretion and responsibility, uses his own employed workers to complete the work. In-house subcontracting refers to having a subcontractor perform some of the work in the contractor's workplace. When a subcontractor worker receives commands and control from the contractor at the contractor's workplace and provides work to the contractor, a dispatch relationship is established. In this case, it is illegal because the contractor does not meet the legal requirements for dispatch workers.[606)]

---

606) Lim, Jongyul, Labor Law (18th Ed.), Parkyoungsa, 2020, p. 647; Ka, Kapryel, The Labor Standards Act (33rd Ed.), Joongang Kyungjei, 2020, p. 793.

하여 외주를 주는 것이 아니라 인건비를 아낄 수 있는 단순업무나 부족한 인력을 하도급이라는 형태로 활용하는 경우가 많다. 기업체가 하도급 근로자의 업무를 지휘·명령하게 되면 이는 불법파견으로 인정되어 직접고용의무와 함께 형사처벌을 받게 된다(파견법 제6-2조).

고용노동부는 불법파견을 방지하기 위하여 "파견과 도급의 구분을 위한 '근로자 파견'의 판단지침 지침" (2007.4.19)을 제시하였다. 그럼에도 불구하고 불법파견과 위장도급이 전산업으로 확대되어 왔다. 이에 고용노동부는 기존의 지침에 추가하여 "근로자파견 판단기준에 관한 지침"(2019.12.30)을 통해 판단기준을 구체화하고 있다.

2. 불법파견 여부 판단

(1) 불법파견의 이해

근로자파견이란 파견사업주가 근로자를 고용한 후 그 고용관계를 유지하면서 근로자파견계약의 내용에 따라 사용사업주의 지휘·명령을 받아 사용사업주를 위한 근로에 종사하게 하는 것이다(파견법 제2조). 근로자파견에 해당하는지 여부는 사용사업주(원청)와 파견사업주(하청)간 체결한 계약의 명칭이나 형식보다는 그 사실관계를 기준으로 판단한다.

도급이란 수급인이 어떤 일을 완성할 것을 약정하고, 도급인은 그 일의 결과에 대해 보수를 시급할 것을 약정함으로써 성립하는 계약이다(민법 제664조). 수급인이 스스로의 재량과 책임 하에 자기가 고용한 근로자를 사용하여 일을 완성하는 것을 의미한다. 사내하도급은 자신의 사업장 내에서 이루어지는 업무의 일부를 도급업체로 하여금 수행하도록 하는 것을 말한다. 수급인의 근로자가 도급인의 사업장에서 도급인의 지휘·명령을 받고 도급인에게 근로를 제공하는 경우에는 파견관계가 성립하는데, 이 경우 근로자파견요건을 갖추지 못하였기 때문에 불법파견이 된다.[606)]

606) 임종률, 노동법(제18판), 박영사, 2020, 647면; 하갑래, 근로기준법(제33판), 중앙경제, 2020, 793면.

(2) Procedures for Determining Disguised Subcontracting and Illegal Dispatch

First, whether the subcontractor is a substantive company needs to be verified. If there is no substantive employer entity, the subcontractor workers are given direct employment instructions. When a subcontract employer entity is recognized, the next step is to judge whether disguised subcontracting is occurring or not.

1) Determining the substantive employer entity

When engaged in subcontracting using external personnel within the company, first review whether the subcontractor is recognized as an employer entity. If the subcontractor entity is not recognized as the employer, the subcontract workers are deemed to have a direct labor contract relationship with the contractor company.

2) Determining whether a subcontract worker is dispatched

When a subcontractor is recognized as the substantive employer entity, next to be determined is whether the contractor actually exercises command and control over the subcontract workers, and whether a subcontract worker is in fact a dispatch worker.

3. Criteria for Determining Disguised Subcontracting and Related Cases

(1) Whether a Subcontractor is the Substantive Employer Entity

The Supreme Court provides the following criteria in relation to a subcontract to hide the employment relationship in a contract. As a person hired by the original employer provides labor service for a third party at the third party's location, to be regarded as an employee of the third party, his employment shall satisfy the following: ① The original employer does not have independence in management and works as an agent of the third party in managing employees; ② The original employer's business entity is nothing more than formal and nominal, and the employee shall be subordinate to the third party in reality; ③ The party that actually pays wages to the employee is the third party; ④ The party to which the person provides labor service is the third party. Based on these criteria, it should be concluded that there was already an implicit employment contract made between the employees and the third party.[607)]

607) Hyundae Mipo Shipbuilding Company: Supreme Court ruling on Sept. 23, 2003 2003du3420.

(2) 위장도급과 불법파견 판단절차

우선, 하도급 업체가 실체가 있는 회사인지 확인한다. 실체가 없으면 해당 하도급 근로자를 직접고용 하라는 지시를 내린다. 하도급의 실체가 인정되는 경우에는 그 다음으로 하도급 회사의 위장도급 여부를 판단한다.

1) 수급인의 사업주로서의 실체 판단

기업체 내에서 외부인력을 활용하여 업무를 수행하는 경우, 우선 수급인이 사업주로서 실체가 인정되는지 여부를 검토한다. 수급인이 사업주로서 실체가 인정되지 않는 경우에는 수급인 소속 근로자는 도급인 회사에 직접적인 근로계약관계가 있음을 인정한다.

2) 근로자파견 해당 여부 판단

수급인이 사업주로서 실체가 인정되는 경우에는 도급인 회사가 수급인 소속 근로자를 실제로 지휘·명령하여 사용하는지를 검토하여 근로자파견에 해당하는지 여부를 판단한다.

3. 위장도급 판단기준과 사례

(1) 수급인이 사업주로서의 실체 판단

대법원은 근로계약 관계를 숨기기 위한 도급계약과 관련하여 다음과 같은 기준을 제시하고 있다. "원고용주에게 고용되어 제3자의 사업장에서 제3자의 업무에 종사하는 자를 제3자의 근로자라고 할 수 있으려면, 원고용주는 사업주로서의 독자성이 없거나 독립성을 결하여 제3자의 노무대행기관과 동일시 할 수 있는 등 그 존재가 형식적, 명목적인 것에 지나지 아니하고, 사실상 당해 근로자는 제3자와 종속적인 관계에 있으며, 실질적으로 임금을 지급하는 자도 제3자이고, 또 근로제공의 상대방도 제3자이어서 당해 근로자와 제3자 간에 묵시적 근로계약관계가 성립되어 있다고 평가될 수 있어야 한다"[607]

---

607) 현대미포조선 사건: 대법원 2003.9.23, 2003두3420.

Whether the subcontractor is recognized as a substantive employer entity is determined by considering whether the subcontractor has an entity and independence as employer regardless of the type and name of the contract between the subcontractor and contractor. However, if the subcontractor has some degree of entity and independence as a business owner, it is judged that there is a substantive entity as employer.[608)]

1) Rights to hire, dismiss, etc.

Review whether the subcontractor decides on the working conditions and personnel affairs of the worker.

2) Responsibility to raise funds and make the necessary expenditures

Review whether the subcontractor raises its own money for establishing a business, renting an office, and other tasks.

3) An employer's legal responsibilities

Review whether the subcontractor has withheld earned income tax, whether or not its workers have been subscribed to the four social insurance plans, and whether rules of employment have been established and enforced.

4) Responsibility for providing machinery, facilities, tools and instruments

Review whether the subcontractor possesses the machinery, facilities, and legal documentation necessary to do business independently.

5) Professional skills and experience

Review whether the subcontractor plans the business independently, exercises management decision-making power and has the professional skills or experience necessary for the business.

---

608) Supreme Court ruling on Feb. 26, 2015, 2010da106436.

수급인이 사업주로서 실체가 인정되는지 여부는 수급인과 도급인 사이에 체결된 계약의 형식, 명칭 등과 관계없이 수급인이 사업주로서의 독자성이나 독립성을 갖추고 있는지를 종합적으로 고려하여 판단한다. 그러나 수급인이 어느 정도의 사업주로서 독자성이나 독립성이 있는 경우에는 사업주로서의 실체가 있다고 판단한다.[608)]

1) 채용, 해고 등의 결정권

수급인이 소속 근로자의 근로조건과 인사노무 관련 사항을 결정하는지 여부를 검토한다.

2) 소요자금 조달에 대한 책임

수급인이 사업체 설립비용, 사무실 임대비용, 기타 사업을 하기 위해 필요한 자금을 스스로 마련하는지 여부를 검토한다.

3) 법령상 사업주로서의 책임

수급인이 근로소득세 원천징수와 4대보험 가입여부, 취업규칙을 마련하여 시행하였는지를 검토한다.

4) 기계, 설비, 기자재의 소유

수급인이 독자적으로 사업을 하기 위해 필요한 기계, 설비, 기자재 등을 소유여부를 검토한다.

5) 전문적 기술·경험

수급인이 사업에 필요한 전문적 기술이나 경험을 가지고 독자적으로 사업을 기획하고 경영상 의사결정권을 행사하는지 여부를 검토한다.

608) 대법원 2015.2.26, 2010다106436.

(2) Related Cases

1) Cases of substantive employer entity recognized

〈Kumho Tire: Supreme Court ruling on Dec. 22, 2017, 2015 da 32905〉

① A subcontractor established a separate company away from the contractor, acting as an independent business entity, and registering the business; ② joined the 4 social security insurances; and ③ prepared separate employment rules and controlled working status.

〈Incheon Airport Corporation: Supreme Court ruling on July 25, 2013. 2012 da 79439〉

① Subcontractors have separate employment rules, control working status, and exercise disciplinary rights; ② They signed service contracts with other companies besides this contractor, and hired 2,730 workers assigned to several companies.

2) Cases of a substantive employer entity denied

〈SK Insight: Supreme Court ruling on Sept. 23, 2003. 2003du 3420〉

① The contractor instructs the subcontractor's employees to work without distinction from its own employees, and performs all personnel management directly; ② The subsidiary of the contractor holds 100% of the stock of the subcontractor, and this subcontractor carries out the contractor's work.

➡ The contractor only used the subcontractor's business registration in order to take advantage of workers in the form of disguised subcontract. However, in reality, there is an employment contract relationship as if they'd been hired directly.

〈Hyundai Mipo Shipbuilding: Supreme Court ruling on July 10, 2008. 2005da75088〉

① The subcontractor has been contracted for about 25 years handling assigned tasks from the contractor, who notified the subcontractor of hiring, disciplinary requests, and a list of eligible persons for promotion; ② The contractor decides working hours and overtime work for the subcontractor workers, and assigns them to work other than the contracted work; ③ The contractor pays the bonus, severance pay, etc. directly to the subcontractor workers.

➡ Actually, without having independence in business performance or in business management, the subcontractor functions as a business unit of the contractor or as a worker provision agency.

4. Criteria for Determining Illegal Dispatch and Related Cases

The Supreme Court set the standard precedent for illegal dispatch as follows. Whether employment is employee dispatch or not shall, regardless of the formal and nominal contract made between the two parties, be determined by collectively considering the purpose of the

(2) 판단 사례

1) 사업주로서 실체를 인정한 사례

〈금호타이어 사건: 대법원 2017.12.22, 2015다32905〉
① 하청이 원청과는 별도의 회사를 설립하여 독립적 사업주체로 활동하고 사업자 등록, ② 4대보험 가입, ③ 독자적인 취업규칙 마련 및 이를 근거로 근태관리권 행사

〈인천공항공사 사건: 대법원 2013.7.25, 2012다79439〉
① 하청이 별도의 취업규칙, 근태관리 및 징계권 행사, ② 해당 원청 외에 타 업체와도 용역 계약 체결, 소속 근로자 2,730여명이 여러 업체에서 용역업무 수행

2) 사업주로서 실체를 부인한 사례

〈SK인사이트 사건: 대법원 2003.9.23, 2003두3420〉
① 원청이 하청근로자들에 대해 원청 직원들과 구분 없이 업무를 지시하고 제반 인사관리 직접 수행, ② 하청은 원청의 자회사가 주식 100%를 보유, 원청의 업무만 도급 받아 수행
➡ 원청은 위장도급의 형식으로 근로자를 사용하기 위해 하청의 법인격을 이용한 것에 불과, 실질적으로는 직접 채용한 것과 마찬가지로 근로계약관계가 존재한다.

〈현대미포조선 사건: 대법원 2008.7.10, 2005다75088〉
① 하청은 약25년간 오직 원청으로부터 업무를 도급받아 수행하면서 원청이 채용여부 결정, 징계요구, 승진대상자 명단 통보, ② 원청이 근로시간과 연장근로를 결정하여 작업지시, 도급업무 외의 원청 업무도 수행하도록 함, ③ 원청이 상여금, 퇴직금 등 직접 지급
➡ 실질적으로는 업무수행의 독자성이나 사업경영의 독립성을 갖추지 못한 채 원청의 일개 사업부서로 기능하거나 노무대행기관의 역할을 수행

4. 불법파견 판단기준과 사례

대법원은 불법파견에 대해 다음과 같이 기준판례를 제시하였다. "근로자파견에 해당하는지 여부는 당사자의 형식적이고 명목상 정한 계약형식과 상관없이, 계약 목적 또는 대상의 특정성, 전문성 및 기술성, 계약당사자의 기업으로

contract or job characteristics, specialty and technology, business registrations of the contracting parties and managerial independence, and the using employer's actual command and control.[609)]

(1) Substantial Contractor Command and Control

Whether the contractor directly or indirectly instructs the subcontractor workers on the specifics of the work to be performed is reviewed, and whether the subcontractor workers are significantly controlled by these instructions and commands from the contractor. Even if the subcontractor's field manager gives specific instructions and orders to the subcontractor workers, it can be a sign of dispatch employment if the subcontractor's field manager only conveys decisions not made by the subcontractor. However, if ① the contractor only determines such things to an appropriate extent for a contractor, such as specifying the scope of the subcontractor's work, while specific work details are determined and instructions on such are conveyed by the subcontractor's field manager and ② the contractor does not order subcontractor workers on a regular basis, but instead it instructs only in emergencies or only in temporary situations, then requiring subcontractor workers to follow the contractor's safety and health instructions as required in accordance with Article 63 of the Occupational Safety and Health Act does not, in itself, mean the subcontract workers are actually dispatch workers.

<Related Cases>

<Examples of command and control that determines dispatch employment>

- In cases where the contractor has decision-making authority to assign work to the subcontractor's workers, and decides the place and time.[610)]
- In cases where the contractor prepares a work manual or work instructions with work methods and details, etc., and issues it to the subcontractor's workers, and they have to perform the work accordingly.[611)]

< Examples of when command and control do not determine dispatch employment>

- When the subcontractor establishes its own work plans to execute the contract, and accordingly and independently determines the number of workers to be put to the work, the work arrangement and changes, and work time.
- Even if the contractor is involved in the work of subcontractors, such as by placing a work manual, etc., in cases where the subcontractor workers carry out their work in accordance with their own field manager's work instructions.[612)]

---

609) Hyundai Motor Case: Supreme Court ruling on Feb. 23, 2012, 2011doo7076.

610) Hyundai Motor Case: Supreme Court ruling on Feb. 26, 2015, 2010da106436.

611) Kumho Tire Case: Supreme Court ruling on Dec. 22, 2017, 2015da32905.

612) KT&G Case: Supreme Court ruling on Jan. 25, 2017, 2014da211619.

실체 존부와 사업경영상 독립성, 계약 이행에서 사용사업주의 지휘명령권 보유 등을 종합적으로 고려하여 그 근로관계의 실질을 따져서 판단하여야 한다."[609)]

(1) 원청의 상당한 지휘·명령

도급인이 수급인 소속 근로자에 대해 직·간접적으로 업무수행의 구체적 사항에 관한 지시를 하고, 수급인 소속 근로자가 이에 구속되는지 등 상당한 지휘·명령 인정여부를 검토한다. 수급인의 현장대리인이 수급인 소속 근로자에게 구체적인 지휘·명령을 하였다고 하여도 도급인이 결정한 사항을 전달하는 것에 불과한 경우에는 근로자파견의 징표에 해당할 수 있다. 다만, ① 도급인은 도급 작업의 범위를 특정하는 등 도급인의 권한에 속하는 정도의 지시만 하고, 구체적인 작업내용은 수급인의 현장 대리인이 결정하여 지시하는 경우, ② 도급인이 수급인 소속 근로자에게 상시적으로 지시하는 것이 아니라 긴급상황이나 일시적으로 지시하는 경우, ③ 산업안전보건법 제63조에 따라 도급인의 안전조치 및 보건조치를 해야 하는 경우에는 근로자파견의 징표에 해당한다고 보기 어렵다.

〈판단 사례〉

〈지휘·명령에 해당될 수 있는 경우〉 ○ 원청이 하청근로자에 대해 일반적인 작업배치와 변경결정권을 가지고, 작업장소, 작업시간 등을 결정한 경우[610)] ○ 원청이 작업방법과 내용 등이 기재된 업무매뉴얼이나 작업지침 등을 작성하여 하청근로자에게 교부하고, 하청근로자는 그에 따라 업무를 수행한 경우[611)] 〈지휘·명령에 해당되기 어려운 경우〉 ○ 하청이 계약이행을 위한 작업계획을 자체적으로 수립하고, 이에 따라 작업에 투입할 근로자 수, 작업배치와 변경, 작업시간 등을 독자적으로 결정하는 경우 ○ 원청이 업무매뉴얼을 두는 등의 방법으로 하청근로자들의 업무에 관여했더라도, 하청소속 현장관리인이 작업지시를 하면서 근태관리 한 경우[612)]

609) 현대차 사건: 대법원 2012.2.23, 2011두7076.
610) 현대차 사건: 대법원 2015.2.26, 2010다106436.
611) 금호타이어 사건: 대법원 2017.12.22, 2015다32905.
612) KT&G 사건: 대법원 2017.1.25, 2014다211619.

(2) Subcontractor's Actual Engagement in the Contractor's Business

① Subcontractor workers can consist of groups working with the contractor's workers, ② groups performing work besides the contractual work, and ③ those who substitute for contractor workers in the event of the latter's absence. In these cases, it will be reviewed whether the subcontractor workers have actually been transferred to engagement in the contractor's own business.

If a subcontractor worker performs the same work in the same space as a contractor worker, there is a high chance it will be deemed dispatch employment. Even if the workplaces are the same, it is difficult to assume that the individual workers are included in the contractor's business when they perform the work independently according to the contract purpose of the subcontractor.

<Related Cases>

<Examples of when actual engagement in contractor's business determines dispatch employment>

- o (Same workplace) When subcontractor and contractor workers are placed in the same group and perform the same tasks together.[613)]
- o (Different workplace) When subcontractor and contractor workers are spatially separated, but subcontractor workers participate in one of a series of processes or subdivided work steps in one process and are closely linked.[614)]

<Examples of when actual engagement in contractor's business do not determine dispatch employment>

- o (Same workplace) Even if subcontractor workers work together in the same space as contractor workers, when the details of the work are different and the work is done independently and has no relation to the work of the contractor workers.[615)]
- o (Different workplace) When subcontractor workers do not perform the same tasks when mixed with contractor workers.[616)]

---

613) Hyundai Motor Case: Supreme Court ruling on Feb 26, 2015, 2010da106436.

614) Kumho Tire Case: Supreme Court ruling on Dec 22, 2017, 2015da32905.

615) KT&G Case: Supreme Court ruling on Jan. 25, 2017, 2014da211619.

616) Korea Tire Case: Supreme Court ruling on Dec. 13, 2018: 2015na2023411.

(2) 도급인 사업으로의 실질적 편입

① 수급인 소속 근로자가 도급인 소속 근로자와 하나의 작업 집단으로 구성되어 공동 작업을 하거나, ② 도급인이 수급인 소속 근로자에게 계약상 업무 외의 업무도 수행하도록 하거나, ③ 도급인의 근로자 결원 발생 시 수급인 소속 근로자로 하여금 대체하도록 하는 등 도급인이 수급인 소속 근로자를 자신의 근로자와 마찬가지로 자신의 사업에 편입하였는지의 여부다.

수급인 소속 근로자가 도급인 소속 근로자와 같은 공간에서 같은 업무를 공동작업을 통해 수행하는 경우 근로자파견에 해당할 개연성이 높다. 근무 장소가 같더라도 개별 근로자들이 소속된 수급인의 계약 목적에 따른 업무를 각자 독립적으로 수행하는 경우에는 도급인의 사업에 편입되었다고 보기 어렵다.

〈판단 사례〉

〈원청 사업 편입에 해당될 수 있는 경우〉

- (같은 장소) 하청근로자와 원청근로자가 같은 조에 배치되어 동일한 업무를 함께 수행하는 경우[613)]
- (다른 장소) 하청근로자와 원청근로자의 작업장소가 공간적으로 떨어져 있더라도, 하청근로자들이 일련의 공정 중 하나, 또는 하나의 공정 중 세분화된 작업단계에 참여하고 밀접하게 연동되어 진행되는 경우[614)]

〈원청 사업에의 편입에 해당된다고 보기 어려운 경우〉

- (같은 장소) 근로자가 도급인소속 근로자와 같은 공간에서 함께 근무하더라도, 업무내용이 서로 다르고, 도급인소속 근로자의 업무와 무관하게 독립적으로 이루어지는 경우[615)]
- (다른 장소) 하청근로자가 원청근로자와 혼재하여 동일한 업무를 수행하는 것이 아니고, 공정 간 유기성도 크지 않은 경우[616)]

---

613) 현대차 사건: 대법원 2015.2.26, 2010다106436.
614) 금호타이어 사건: 대법원 2017.12.22, 2015다32905.
615) KT&G 사건: 대법원 2017.1.25, 2014다211619.
616) 한국타이어 사건: 대법원 2018.12.13, 2015나2023411.

(3) Personnel and Labor-related Decisions

Reviewing who makes decisions related to personnel and labor determines whether the subcontractor exercises management authority independently.

<Related Cases>

<Examples of the subcontractor being unable to exercise personnel rights> o New placements of subcontractor workers must be approved by the contractor, and subcontractor workers must be replaced if the contractor requests it.[617)] o The contractor decides the subcontractor's working hours and whether overtime is to be performed, etc.[618)] <Examples of the subcontractor being able to exercise personnel rights> o When subcontractors provide training necessary to perform their jobs at their workplace, and have basic authority on recruiting and disciplinary action to directly manage the work time and worker attendance.[619)]

(4) Subcontractor Expertise and Technology

Whether the work to be performed by the subcontractor worker(s) is specifically determined shall be reviewed, as well as whether it is distinct from the work of contractor workers and whether the subcontractor has the necessary expertise and technology.

<Related Cases>

<Examples of the subcontractor lacking the needed expertise and technology> o When the subcontractor's scope of work is undefined and it simply carries out the work assigned by the contractor. o When the subcontractor's work is the same as that of the contractor and is not clearly classified.[620)] <Examples of the subcontractor possessing the needed expertise and technology> o In cases where the subcontractor's work is performed independently from the contractor's work. o When subcontractor workers perform only the work specified in the contract, but do not perform additional work under direction of the contractor.[621)]

617) Gunpo-si Case: Supreme Court ruling on July 22, 2016, 2014da222794.

618) Hyundai Motor Case: Supreme Court ruling on Feb. 26, 2015, 2010da106436.

619) KT&G Case: Supreme Court ruling on Jan. 25, 2017, 2014da211619.

620) Hyundai Motor Case: Supreme Court ruling on Feb. 26, 2015, 2010da106436.

621) KT&G Case: Supreme Court ruling on Jan. 25, 2017, 2014da211619.

(3) 인사노무 관련 결정

수급인이 업무에 투입될 하도급 근로자의 인사노무와 관련된 사항을 결정하고 관리 권한을 독자적으로 행사하는지 검토한다.

〈판단 사례〉

〈인사권을 행사하지 않은 경우〉

- ○ 하청이 근로자를 신규 배치하는 경우 원청의 승인을 받아야 하고, 원청이 근로자의 교체를 요구하면 하청은 이를 반드시 따르도록 되어 있는 경우[617)]
- ○ 하청근로자의 업무시간, 연장근로 여부 등을 원청이 결정하는 경우[618)]

〈인사권을 행사한 경우〉

- ○ 하청이 업무수행에 필요한 교육을 자체적으로 실시하고, 채용 · 징계 등에 관한 기본적 권한을 가지고 근로자들의 근태관리를 직접 한 경우[619)]

(4) 업무의 전문성과 기술성

수급인 소속 근로자가 수행할 업무가 구체적으로 확정되어 있는지, 도급인 소속 근로자의 업무와 구별되고 전문성과 기술성이 있는지를 검토한다.

〈판단 사례〉

〈전문성·기술성 등이 없는 경우〉

- ○ 하청의 고유하고 특유한 업무가 별도로 있는 것이 아니라 원청의 필요에 따라 하청의 업무가 결정되는 경우
- ○ 하청근로자의 업무가 원청근로자의 업무와 동일하여 명확히 구분되지 않는 경우[620)]

〈전문성·기술성 등이 인정되는 경우〉

- ○ 하청근로자의 업무가 원청근로자의 업무와 달라 독립적으로 이루어지는 경우
- ○ 하청근로자가 도급계약에서 정한 업무만 수행하고, 원청의 지시에 따른 추가적인 업무는 수행하지 않는 경우[621)]

---

617) 군포시 사건: 대법원 2016.7.22, 2014다222794.
618) 현대차 사건: 대법원 2015.2.26, 2010다106436.
619) KT&G 사건: 대법원 2017.1.25, 2014다211619.
620) 현대차 사건: 대법원 2015.2.26, 2010다106436.
621) KT&G 사건: 대법원 2017.1.25, 2014다211619.

(5) Company Organization and Facilities

It is reviewed whether the subcontractor has an independent business organization, equipment, or equipment necessary to achieve the purpose of the contract as a party to the contract.

<Related Cases>

<Examples of the subcontractor lacking an independent corporate organization and facilities>
- o If the subcontractor has not invested its own technology or capital.[622]
- o If the subcontractor does not have separate human and material facilities, does not have specific expertise and consists simply of a large number of workers.[623]

<Examples of the subcontractor possessing independent corporate organization and facilities>
- o The subcontractor has an organization to achieve the purpose of the contract, and is actually working for a number of companies besides the relevant contractor.[624]

Ⅴ. Disguised Outsourcing Cases and Criteria for Judgment

1. Introduction

The greater utilization of dispatched employees has benefited companies in maintaining labor flexibility and in reducing labor costs. However, the ban of hiring dispatched employees for more than two consecutive years has consequently forced companies to seek internal outsourcing. Although the company may offer an outsourcing contract, it treats the employee like a dispatched employee in practice. Addressing this issue, the Supreme Court clearly distinguished the difference between a dispatched employee and outsourcing employee with its judicial ruling. The following will review the main contents from the rulings that outlined dispatch and outsourcing and the criteria for 'worker dispatch'. There have been two recent cases heard by the Supreme Court which provide good examples of this. In this article, I would like to look at the details of these rulings and review the criteria used in making their decisions.

---

622) Hyundai Motor Case: Supreme Court ruling on Feb. 26, 2015, 2010da106436.

623) Kumho Tire Case: Supreme Court ruling on Dec. 22, 2017, 2015da32905.

624) KT&G Case: Supreme Court ruling on Jan. 25, 2017, 2014da211619.

(5) 기업조직과 설비 등 보유

수급인이 도급계약 등의 당사자로 계약의 목적을 달성하기 위하여 필요한 독립적 기업조직이나 설비, 장비 등을 갖추고 있는지를 검토한다.

〈판단 사례〉

〈독립적 기업조직·설비를 갖추지 못한 경우〉
- ㅇ 하청의 고유기술이나 자본이 투입되지 않는 경우[622]
- ㅇ 하청이 별도의 인적·물적 시설을 갖추지 않고 다수의 근로자들로만 구성되어 있고, 특유의 전문성도 갖추지 않은 경우[623]

〈독립적 기업조직·설비를 갖춘 경우〉
- ㅇ 하청이 도급계약 목적 달성을 위한 조직을 갖추고 있고, 실제로 해당 원청 외의 다수 업체를 상대로 업무를 수행하고 있는 경우[624]

V. 사내 하도급의 위장도급 사례

1. 의 의

파견근로자를 사용하는 것은 기업체에서 고용의 유연화와 인건비 절감 차원에서 큰 도움이 되었다. 그러나 이러한 파견근로자는 2년 밖에 사용할 수 없기 때문에 기업체에서는 파견근로 형태로 계속 유지할 수 있는 방법을 모색하면서, 사내 도급이 확산되어 왔다. 기업체에서는 사내도급 형태를 갖추었지만, 실질적으로는 근로자 파견관계와 같이 직접 도급근로자를 지휘, 명령하는 하는 경우가 많이 있었다. 이러한 문제에 대해, 대법원은 사내도급과 파견근로를 명확히 구분하는 판결을 내놓으면서 이 판단기준을 명확히 구분하였다. 이와 관련하여 최근 대표적인 대법원 판례 2개가 나왔는데 이 판례들을 통해 그 판단기준을 살펴보고자 한다.

---

622) 현대차 사건: 대법원 2015.2.26, 2010다106436.
623) 금호타이어 사건: 대법원 2017.12.22, 2015다32905.
624) KT&G 사건: 대법원 2017.1.25, 2014나211619.

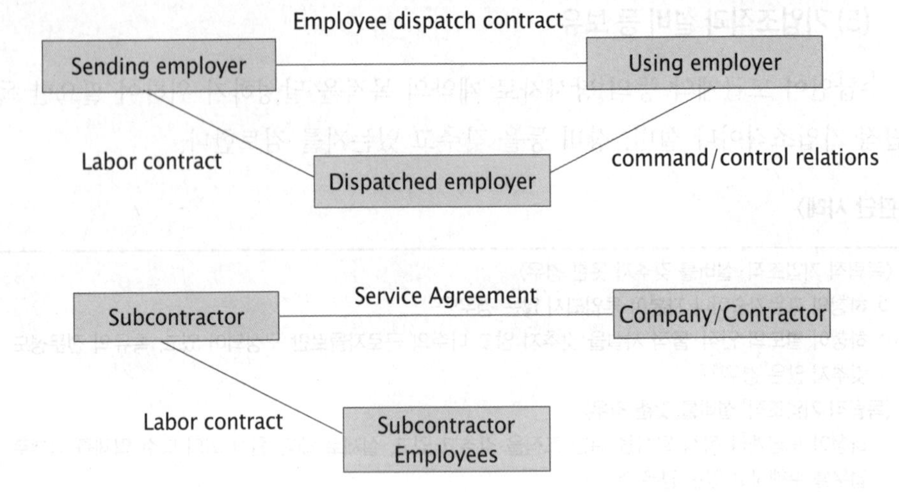

2. Case of Disguised Outsourcing by Hyundai Mipo Shipbuilding Company (1/2)

(1) Summary

Hyundai Mipo Shipbuilding Company(hereinafter "the Shipbuilder") terminated a service contract with Yongin Company(hereinafter "the Subcontractor") when a labor union was established inside the Subcontractor. Right after termination of this contract, all 30 employees(hereinafter "the applicants") of the Subcontractor were dismissed, and the company closed down on January 31, 2003. The applicants filed a claim for confirmation of employee status against the Shipbuilder. Busan Appellate Court rejected this claim on the grounds that the service agreement between the Shipbuilder and the Subcontractor could be recognized as an outsourcing contract. However, the Supreme Court overturned the Appellate Court's decision, stating that it was possible to recognize the Shipbuilder and the Subcontractor's employees as having an implied employment contract.

(2) Supreme Court Ruling[625)]

1) Legal principles for implied employment

As a person hired by the original employer provides labor service for a third party at the

625) Supreme Court ruling on July 10, 2008, 2005da75088.

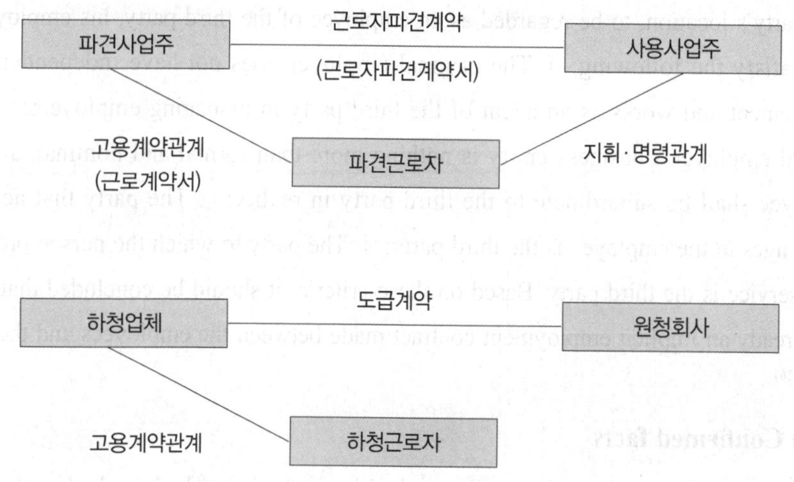

2. 현대미포조선 위장도급 사례 (1/2)

(1) 사건개요

현대미포조선(이하 “원청회사”)은 사내하청인 용인기업(이하 “하청업체”)에 노동조합이 설립되자 하청업체와의 도급계약을 해지하였고, 이에 따라 하청업체는 2003년 1월 31일에 폐업되었다. 이로 인하여 하청업체에 소속된 근로자 30명은 모두 해고되었고, 이들은 원청회사를 상대로 ‘근로자지위 확인청구소송’을 제기했다. 하급심인 부산고등법원은 원청회사와 하청업체 간에 도급관계가 인정된다고 보아 근로자들의 청구를 기각하였으나 대법원은 원청회사와 하청업체의 근로자들 간에 묵시적인 근로계약 관계가 인정된다는 판결을 하였다.

(2) 대법원 판결[625)]

1) 묵시적 계약관계 법리

‘원고용주에게 고용되어 제3자의 사업장에서 제3자의 업무에 종사하는 자를 제3자의 근로자라고 할 수 있으려면, 원고용주는 사업주로서의 독자성이 없거나 독립성을 결하여 제3자의 노무대행기관과 동일시 할 수 있는 등 그 존재가

625) 대법원 2008.7.10, 2005다75088.

third party's location, to be regarded as an employee of the third party, his employment shall satisfy the following: ① The original employer does not have independence in management and works as an agent of the third party in managing employees; ② The original employer's business entity is nothing more than formal and nominal, and the employee shall be subordinate to the third party in reality; ③ The party that actually pays wages to the employee is the third party; ④ The party to which the person provides labor service is the third party. Based on these criteria, it should be concluded that there was already an implicit employment contract made between the employees and the third party.[626)]

2) Confirmed facts

The Subcontractor where the applicants had been employed had worked exclusively for the Shipbuilder as an outsourcing partner to inspect and repair marine engine heat exchangers, safety valves, etc. for the previous 25 years. The Shipbuilder required that employees who wished to work for the Subcontractor pass a skills test before being hired by the Subcontractor. They were then qualified to receive an additional allowance directly paid by the Shipbuilder. Furthermore, the Shipbuilder had substantive authority for employment and promotion of the Subcontractor's employees, including the ability to demand disciplinary action or choosing candidates for promotion.

In addition, the Shipbuilder directly monitored the applicants' attendance(including if they left work early), leaves, overtime, hours worked, and their work attitude. The Shipbuilder also determined the volume of work, working methods, work orders, and when and how the applicants would cooperate, and directly assigned work duties or placed applicants for substantive work duties through the Subcontractor's responsible manager. The Shipbuilder required the applicants to complete its own work assignments in addition to work given by the Subcontractor, paying a certain wage even when there was no work from the Subcontractor by assigning other duties such as receiving education, cleaning of the workplace, and assisting other departments in their work. The Shipbuilder directly supervised and managed the applicants.

626) Supreme Court, Sep 23, 2003 2003du3420

형식적, 명목적인 것에 지나지 아니하고, 사실상 당해 근로자는 제3자와 종속적인 관계에 있으며, 실질적으로 임금을 지급하는 자도 제3자이고, 또 근로제공의 상대방도 제3자이어서 당해 근로자와 제3자 간에 묵시적 근로계약관계가 성립되어 있다고 평가될 수 있어야 한다'.[626)]

2) 사실관계

원고들이 소속된 하청업체는 약 25년간 오직 피고 회사로부터 선박엔진 열교환기, 세이프티 밸브의 검사·수리 등의 업무를 수급인 자격으로 수행하여 왔는데, 원청회사는 하청업체가 모집해 온 근로자에 대하여 원청회사가 요구하는 기능시험을 실시한 다음, 그 채용 여부를 결정하였고, 그 시험합격자에게만 원청회사가 직접 지급하는 수당을 수령할 자격을 부여하였으며, 하청업체 소속의 근로자들에 대하여 징계를 요구하거나, 승진대상자 명단을 통보하는 등, 하청업체 소속 근로자들의 채용, 승진, 징계에 관하여 실질적인 권한을 행사하였다.

뿐만 아니라, 원청회사는 원고들의 출근, 조퇴, 휴가, 연장근무, 근로시간, 근무태도 등을 점검하고, 원고들이 수행할 작업량과 작업 방법, 작업 순서, 업무 협력 방안을 결정하여 원고들을 직접 지휘하거나 또는 하청업체 소속 책임자를 통하여 원고들에게 구체적인 작업 지시를 하였으며, 하청업체가 당초 수급한 업무 외에도 원고들로 하여금 원청회사 소속 부서의 업무를 수행하게 하거나, 하청업체의 작업물량이 없을 때에는 교육, 사업장 정리, 타 부서 업무지원 등의 명목으로 원고들에게 매월 일정 수준 이상의 소득을 보장하는 등, 직접적으로 원고들에 대한 지휘감독권을 행사하였다.

더 나아가, 하청업체는 원칙적으로 수급한 물량에 대하여 시간단위의 작업량 단가로 산정된 금액을 원청회사로부터 수령하였지만, 원청회사는 하청업체 소속 근로자들이 선박 수리와 직접적인 관련이 없는 원청회사의 다른 부서 업무지원, 안전교육 및 직무교육 등에 종사하는 경우 이에 대한 보수도 산정하여 그 지급액을 결정하였을 뿐만 아니라, 원고들에게 상여금, 퇴직금 등의 수당을 직접 지급하였다.

---

626) 내법원 2003.9.23, 2003두3420

Furthermore, the Subcontractor was, in principle, supposed to receive a service fee calculated by multiplying each time unit by the volume received, to which the Shipbuilder added the wages paid when Subcontractor employees were engaged in other Shipbuilder-assigned work not directly related to the Subcontractor duties(such as fixing the marine engines). The Shipbuilder also paid bonuses and severance pay directly to the applicants.

While the Subcontractor handled income tax deductions, income reports, and bookkeeping for its employees under its own business name and registration, it used offices provided by the Shipbuilder, as well as all required facilities such as rooms for its own employee education.

3) Judgment

Upon review of the confirmed facts in B above, and based on the legal principle mentioned in A, it can be determined that even though the Subcontractor had entered into a formal outsourcing contract with the Shipbuilder and had a formal structure in which its own employees(the applicants) performed the necessary labor service, the Subcontractor did not substantially manage itself in terms of work performance or management of its business. The Subcontractor worked just like a department of the Shipbuilder would, or as a labor management agency for the Shipbuilder. Rather, as it is assumed that the Shipbuilder received subordinate labor service from the applicants and decided their working conditions(including wages), an implied employment should be estimated to exist between employees of the Subcontractor and the Shipbuilder, just as if the Shipbuilder had hired the applicants directly.

3. Case of Disguised Outsourcing by Hyundai Motor Company (2/2)

(1) Summary

While Yesung Company(hereinafter "the Subcontractor"), an in-house outsourcing company of the Hyundai Motor Factory – Ulsan(hereinafter "HMC"), was engaged in assembling automobile parts, it dismissed its 15 employees(hereafter "the applicants") on February 2, 2005, due to union activities. The applicants then filed for remedy for unfair dismissal and unfair labor practices against HMC and the Subcontractor, immediately

마지막으로, 하청업체는 사업자등록 명의를 가지고 소속 근로자들에 대한 근로소득세 원천징수, 소득신고, 회계장부 기장 등의 사무를 처리하였으나, 이러한 사무는 피고 회사가 제공하는 사무실에서 이루어졌을 뿐만 아니라, 하청업체는 독자적인 장비를 보유하지 않았으며, 소속 근로자의 교육 및 훈련 등에 필요한 사업경영상 독립적인 물적 시설을 갖추지 못하였다.

3) 판 단

이러한 사실관계를 본 법리에 비추어 살펴보면, 하청업체는 형식적으로는 원청회사와 도급계약을 체결하고 소속 근로자들인 원고들로부터 노무를 제공받아 자신의 사업을 수행한 것과 같은 외관을 갖추었다고 하더라도, 실질적으로는 업무수행의 독자성이나, 사업경영의 독립성을 갖추지 못한 채, 원청회사의 일개 사업부서로서 기능하거나, 노무대행기관의 역할을 수행하였을 뿐이고, 오히려 원청회사가 원고들로부터 종속적인 관계에서 근로를 제공받고, 임금을 포함한 제반 근로조건을 정하였다고 봄이 상당하므로, 근로자들과 원청회사 사이에는 직접 원청회사가 원고들을 채용한 것과 같은 묵시적인 근로계약관계가 성립되어 있었다고 볼 수 있다.

3. 현대자동차의 위장도급 사례 (2/2)

(1) 사건개요

현대자동차 울산공장(이하 "원청회사")의 사내하도급 업체인 예성기업(이하 "하청업체")은 의장공정을 맡아 업무를 수행하던 중, 노동조활 활동을 이유로 2005년 2월 2일 근로자 15명을 해고하였다. 이에 근로자들은 '부당해고 및 부당노동행위 구제신청'을 원청회사와 하청업체를 상대로 제기하자 하청업체는 곧 바로 폐업하였다. 이 사건은 하급심에서는 원청회사가 사용자가 아니고 실제 사용자인 하청업체는 폐업하였다는 이유로 모두 기각되었으나, 대법원은 원청회사와 하청업체와의 묵시적 고용관계는 부정 하였으나, 원청회사와 하청업체간에 파견관계가 성립된다고 인정하였다. 개정전의 파견법에 따라 근로자의

after the Subcontractor closed down. The applicants' claims were not accepted in the lower courts, who determined that the Subcontractor, who had already closed down, was their real employer, and not HMC. While the Supreme Court did not determine an implied employment relationship existed between HMC and the Subcontractor, it determined that a dispatch relationship did. According to the Employee Dispatch Act before its revision, in cases where a dispatched employee has served more than two years, the applicant is determined to be a direct employee of the using employer.

(2) Supreme Court Ruling[627)]

1) Legal principles for employee dispatch

Whether employment is employee dispatch or not shall, regardless of the formal and nominal contract made between the two parties, be determined by collectively considering the purpose of the contract or job characteristics, specialty and technology, business registrations of the contracting parties and managerial independence, and the using employer's actual command and control.

2) Confirmed facts

Of the work processes directly and indirectly necessary to produce cars, assembly on the conveyer belt system does not require the Subcontractor to possess much in the way of technological or specialized skills, and the Subcontractor can give few instructions to its employees in this process.

The applicants were placed on either side of the conveyor belt assembly line together with regular employees of HMC, carrying out simple and repetitive tasks according to the various instructions prepared and distributed by HMC, and using HMC's own facilities, parts, and supplies. In this manufacturing process, the Subcontractor did not supply its own unique technology or invest its own capital.

HMC possessed the general rights to give the applicants their work duties and change their work area, and determined the volume of work to be finished, working methods and working procedures. HMC directly managed the applicants or indirectly gave them substantial work orders through an on-site manager of the Subcontractor. In considering

627) Supreme Court ruling on February 23, 2012, 200du7076.

근속년수가 2년을 넘는 경우 “고용의제” 조항에 따라 근로자가 사용사업주에 고용된 것으로 본다고 인정을 받았다.

(2) 대법원 판결[627)]

1) 근로자파견 법리

근로자파견에 해당하는지 여부는 당사자의 형식적이고 명목상 정한 계약형식과 상관없이, 계약 목적 또는 대상의 특정성, 전문성 및 기술성, 계약당사자의 기업으로서 실체 존부와 사업경영상 독립성, 계약 이행에서 사용사업주의 지휘명령권 보유 등을 종합적으로 고려하여 그 근로관계의 실질을 따져서 판단하여야 한다.

2) 사실관계

자동차 생산에 직간접적으로 필요한 작업 중에서 컨베이어 시스템에 의한 자동차 조립 업무인 의장 공정은 하청업체의 기술성과 전문성에 대한 요구 정도가 낮고 노무 제공 과정상 하청업체는 그 근로자에 대한 지시권이 미약하다.

하청업체 근로자들은 컨베이어벨트 좌우에 원청회사의 정규직 근로자들과 혼합 배치되어 원청회사 소유의 생산 관련 시설과 부품, 소모품 등을 사용하여 원청회사가 미리 작성하여 교부한 각종 작업지시서 등에 의하여 단순, 반복적인 업무를 수행하였고, 이 과정에서 하청업체의 고유 기술이나 자본 등이 업무에 투입된 바는 없었다.

원청회사는 하청업체 근로자들에 대한 일반적인 작업배치권과 변경결정권을 가지고 있었고, 원청회사의 정규직 근로자와 마찬가지로 하청업체 근로자들이 수행할 작업량과 작업 방법, 작업 순서 등을 결정하였다. 원청회사는 하청업체 근로자들을 직접 지휘하거나 또는 하청업체 소속 현장관리인 등을 통하여 하청업체 근로자들에게 구체적인 작업지시를 하였다. 하청업체 근로자들이 수행하는 업무의 특성 등을 고려하면, 하청업체 현장관리인 등이 그 근로자들에게 구체적인 지휘명령권을 행사하였다 하더라도, 이는 원청회사가 결정한 사항을 전달한

---

627) 대법원 2012.2.23, 2011두7076.

the characteristics of the applicants' work, the responsibility of the on-site manager was simply as the messenger of HMC orders to the applicants.

HMC decided the starting and finishing times of each work shift, recess hours, overtime and night work, shift duties, the pace of manufacturing, etc., for the applicants, and in cases where HMC's regular employees were absent due to occupational accidents or leaves, the applicants would fill in.

3) Judgment

The Appellate Court ruled that, based upon legal principles for employee dispatch and the confirmed facts, the employees were, inactuality, working under HMC's direct supervision after hiring by the Subcontractor and dispatch to HMC.

것에 불과하였다.

원청회사는 하청업체 근로자들에 대하여 시업과 종업 시간의 결정, 휴게시간의 부여, 연장 및 야간근로 결정, 교대제 운영 여부, 작업속도 등을 결정하였고, 원청회사의 정규직 근로자에게 산재, 휴직 등 사유로 결원이 발생하는 경우 하청업체 소속 근로자로 하여금 그 결원을 대체하여 작업하게 하는 경우도 있었다.

3) 판 단

환송심인 고등법원은 '근로자파견 법리'와 사실관계를 바탕으로 근로자가 하청업체에 고용된 후 원청회사에 파견되어 원청회사로부터 직접 노무지휘를 받는 근로관계 있다고 판단하였다.

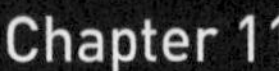

Vulnerable Workers

Section 1: Working Conditions for Minors

Ⅰ. Introduction

Minors are in the process of growing up as adults, so they are less developed physically and mentally, and receive special protection because they are legally required to go to school.[628] Korea's Constitution(Article 32, Paragraph 5) stipulates that special protection shall be accorded to working minors, and Chapter 5 of the Labor Standards Act specifically describes the working conditions of minors. Minors work as short-term workers, fixed-term workers, and workplace trainees in 24-hour convenience stores, fast food restaurants, and production plants. Therefore, when considering their working conditions, it is necessary to consider the conditions at workplaces with fewer than 5 workers in mind. For field trainees in particular, working conditions vary by whether they are working as students or workers.

All the protections in the Labor Standards Act(LSA) apply to working minors as well as adult workers. This includes the prohibitions against discrimination, forced labor, and violence, restrictions on unfair dismissal and managerial layoffs, and the requirement to issue written employment contracts. However, in workplaces with fewer than 5 employees, dismissal restrictions, shut-down allowances, additional wages for overtime work, and annual paid allowances do not apply.[629]

---

628) Lim, Jongyul, Labor Law (18th Ed.), Parkyoungsa, 2020, p. 611; Ha, Kapryel, The Labor Standards Act (33rd Ed.), Joongang Economy, 2020, p. 693.

629) Laws applicable to workplaces ordinarily employing fewer than five people

Chapter 11

취약근로자의 보호

제1절 연소자

Ⅰ. 개 념

연소자는 성인으로 성장하는 과정에 있기 때문에 신체적 정신적으로 미숙하고, 의무교육을 받아야 하기 때문에 특별한 보호의 대상이 된다.[628] 헌법(제32조 제5항)에 연소자의 근로는 특별한 보호를 받아야 한다고 규정하고 있으며, 근로기준법 제5장에서 연소자의 근로조건에 대해 구체적으로 기술하고 있다. 연소근로자는 24시간 편의점, 패스트푸드점, 생산 공장 등에서 단시간 근로자, 기간제 근로자, 현장실습생 등으로 일하고 있다. 따라서 연소근로자의 근로조건을 고려할 때, 연소자, 단시간 근로자, 기간제 근로자, 5인 미만 사업장의 근로조건을 모두 염두에 두고 판단하여야 한다. 특히, 현장실습생의 경우 학생 신분인지 근로자 신분인지에 따라 근로조건이 달라지게 된다.

연소자도 일반근로자와 마찬가지로 근로기준법의 모든 규정이 적용된다. 일반적으로 차별금지, 강제근로의 금지, 폭행의 금지, 근로계약의 서면작성, 부당해고 제한, 정리해고 제한 등에 적용된다. 다만, 5인 미만 사업장의 경우에는 해고제한, 휴업수당, 가산임금, 연차유급수당 등이 적용되지 않는다.[629]

---

628) 임종률, 노동법(제18판), 박영사, 2020, 611면; 하갑례, 근로기준법(제33판), 중앙경제, 2020, 693면.

629) 상시 5인 미만의 근로자를 사용하는 사업 또는 사업장에 적용하는 법규성.

I would like to list the working conditions for minors in detail by sections and special protection regulations together. In addition, I will examine whether trainees are students or workers in legal disputes.

Ⅱ. Scope of Working Minors and Occupations from which They Are Prohibited

1. Scope of Working Minors

In principle, no person under the age of 15 shall be employed as a worker. However, those 13 to 15 years of age with an employment permit issued by the Minister of Employment and Labor may be so employed, as long as the employment does not interfere with their compulsory education(Article 64 of the LSA and Article 35 of its Enforcement Decree). The employer shall keep in the workplace a certificate proving the family relationships and written consent from their parent or guardian for each working minor under 18(Article 66).

2. Prohibited Occupations

Under the Labor Standards Act, employers cannot assign pregnant women or those under 18 years of age to work that involves moral or health hazards or danger(Article 65). Prohibited occupations include high-pressure work and diving work, jobs or businesses that prohibit the employment or entry of children under the age of 18, work in prisons and mental hospitals, work in incineration and slaughter, and work dealing with oil.[630)] However, they can be employed for gas station refueling service for passenger vehicles.

Employers shall not assign women or minors under the age of 18 to work in mines except where the work is temporarily needed to perform the certain duties such as health,

630) Prohibited occupations include: ① In the「Rules on Occupational Safety and Health Standards」, high-pressure work and diving work, ② In the「Construction Equipment Management Act」 and「Road Traffic Act」, etc., driving, and its related works which are prohibited for those younger than 18 years, ③ Jobs or business employment or entry of minors under the age of 18 is prohibited by other laws such as the「Youth Protection Act」, ④ Jobs in prisons and mental hospitals, ⑤ incineration and slaughter, ⑥ handling fuel tasks (excluding refueling passenger vehicles with gasoline), ⑦ Work related to 2-bromopropane handling or exposure, ⑧ Other tasks designated and publicly announced by the Minister of Employment and Labor after deliberation.

연소근로자의 근로조건을 각 부분별 구체적으로 열거하고 특별한 보호규정을 기술하고, 법적인 쟁점이 되는 현장실습생에 대한 판단기준에 대해 살펴보고자 한다.

Ⅱ. 연소자의 범위와 사용금지 직종

1. 연소근로자의 범위

사용자는 15세 미만인 사람은 근로자로 사용하지 못한다. 다만, 예외적으로 고용노동부장관이 의무교육에 지장이 없다고 판단하여 취직인허증을 발급하는 경우에 한해 13세이상 15세미만자도 근로자로 사용할 수 있다(근기법 제64조, 시행령 제35조). 사용자는 18세 미만인 사람에 대하여는 그 연령을 증명하는 가족관계기록사항에 관한 증명서와 친권자(부모) 또는 후견인(친권자 부재)의 동의서를 사업장에 갖추어 두어야 한다(제66조).

2. 사용금지 직종

근로기준법에서 사용자는 임산부와 18세 미만자를 도덕상 또는 보건상 유해·위험한 사업에 사용하지 못한다(제65조). 금지직종은 고압작업 및 잠수작업, 18세 미만 청소년의 고용이나 출입을 금지하고 있는 직종이나 업종, 교도소와 정신병원에서의 업무, 소각과 도살의 업무, 유류를 취급하는 업무 등이다.[630] 다만, 유류를 취급하는 업무 중 주유업무는 제외한다.

사용자는 여성과 18세 미만인 사람을 갱내(坑內)에서 근로시키지 못한다. 다만, 보건의료, 보도취재 등 업무를 수행하기 위하여 일시적으로 필요한 경우에

630) 금지직종은 ① 「산업안전보건기준에 관한 규칙」고압작업 및 잠수작업, ② 「건설기계관리법」, 「도로교통법」 등에서 18세 미만인 자에 대하여 운전, 조종면서 취득을 제한하고 있는 직종과 업종의 운전, 조정업무, ③ 「청소년보호법」 등 다른 법률에서 18세 미만 청소년의 고용이나 출입을 금지하고 있는 직종이나 업종, ④ 교도소와 정신병원에서의 업무, ⑤ 소각과 도살의 업무, ⑥ 유류를 취급하는 업무(주유업무는 제외한다), ⑦ 2-브로모프로판을 취급하거나 노출될 수 있는 업무, ⑧ 그 밖에 고용노동부장관이 심의를 거쳐 지정하여 고시하는 업무.

medicine, news reporting, news coverage, etc(Article 72).[631)]

Employers shall not abuse workers in training, workers on probation or any other apprentice whose purpose is to acquire a technical skill, or assign them to domestic work or other work not related to the acquirement of technical skill(Article 77).

Businesses where entry and employment of minors(under the age of 19) is prohibited under the Youth Protection Act(Article 2, Item 5) are:

(1) Businesses where minors are prohibited from entering or working

entertainment and other bars, video rooms, karaoke rooms(businesses with facilities that make it legal for minors to enter are excluded from the entry ban), telephone rooms, dancing academies, dancing rooms, businesses involving speculative behavior, and those involving the handling of sexual devices.

(2) Businesses prohibited from hiring minors

Accommodation, barber shops, bathing businesses in which a massage room is set up or which is divided into private rooms, tobacco retail, toxic product manufacturing, sales and handling, ticket coffee shop, places selling alcohol like soju bars, beer bars, cafes, etc., music record sales, video sales and rental shops, general game rooms, and comic book rental shops.

Ⅲ. Special Protection of Labor Contracts

Employers seeking to hire minors shall draw up employment contracts for the minors to sign if they so desire in the same position in determining the working conditions(Article 4). In this case, the parents[632)] or guardians[633)] cannot act on behalf of the minor, but

---

631) Article 42 (Jobs Permitted for Working Inside Pits) The jobs for which women and those under the age of eighteen may be placed temporarily inside a pit under Article 72 of the Act shall be as follows:1. Jobs for health, medical treatment and welfare;2. Jobs for the gathering and reporting of news for newspapers, or to publish and produce broadcasting programs;3. Surveying for the purpose of academic research;4. Jobs for management and supervision;5. Practical training work performed in the fields relating to subparagraphs 1 through 4.

632) Civil Act - Article 909 (Custodian)(1) Parents shall have parental authority over their minor child.

633) Civil Act - Article 928 (Commencement of Guardianship for Minors)
Where there is no person with parental authority over a minor or where a person with parental authority is unable to exercise all or part of his/her parental authority, a guardian shall be appointed for the minor.

는 그러하지 아니하다(제72조).[631]

사용자는 양성공, 수습, 그 밖의 명칭을 불문하고 기능의 습득을 목적으로 하는 근로자를 혹사하거나 가사, 그 밖의 기능 습득과 관계없는 업무에 종사시키지 못한다(제77조).

청소년보호법에서 미성년자(19세 미만)에 대해 출입과 고용을 금지하는 업소(청소년 보호법 제2조 5목)는 다음과 같다.

(1) 청소년 출입·고용금지 업소

유흥주점, 단란주점, 비디오방, 노래방(청소년의 출입이 허용되는 시설을 갖춘 업소에는 출입만 가능), 전화방, 무도학원업, 무도장업, 사행행위영업, 성기구 취급업소

(2) 청소년 고용금지 업소

숙박업, 이용업, 목욕장업 중 안마실을 설치하거나 개실로 구획하여 하는 영업, 담배소매업, 유독물 제조·판매·취급업, 티켓다방, 주류판매 목적의 소주방, 호프, 카페 등 형태의 영업, 음반판매업, 비디오물 판매·대여업, 일반게임장, 만화대여업

Ⅲ. 근로계약의 특별보호

연소근로자와 사용자는 근로조건의 결정 시 동등한 지위에서 사유로운 의사에 의하여 근로계약을 작성하여야 한다(제4조). 이 경우 친권자[632]나 후견인[633]

631) 제42조【갱내근로 허용업무】법제72조에 따라 여성과 18세 미만인 자를 일시적으로 갱내에서 근로시킬 수 있는 업무는 다음 각 호와 같다.
1. 보건, 의료 또는 복지 업무
2. 신문·출판·방송프로그램 제작 등을 위한 보도·취재업무
3. 학술연구를 위한 조사 업무
4. 관리·감독 업무
5. 제1호부터 제4호까지의 규정의 업무와 관련된 분야에서 하는 실습업무.

632) 민법 제909조【친권자】① 부모는 미성년자인 자의 친권자가 된다.

633) 민법 제928조【후견인】미성년자에게 친권자가 없거나 친권자가 친권의 전부 또는 일부를 행사할 수 없는 경우에는 미성년후견인을 두어야 한다.

if the employment contract is deemed unfavorable to the minor, they can terminate it later(Article 67). Under the Civil Act, those under the age of 19 cannot engage in legal actions such as signing contracts independently, and so may engage in legal actions only with the consent of a parent or guardian. So, in the Labor Standards Act, those under the age of 18 must submit consent from their parents at the time of employment. However, working minors may independently engage in legal actions such as claiming wages and joining a labor union.

The employer must write and deliver the necessary items in the working minor's employment contract, and if working conditions are changed, a revised employment contract must be issued(Article 17). The written contents shall include: ①(Wages) Wage composition, calculation method, and payment method; ②(Contractual working hours) shall be determined within the legal working hours for minors(7 hours per day, 35 hours per week); ③(Weekly holidays) If workers work more than 15 hours a week, they are entitled to an average of 1 or more paid weekly holidays per week; ④(Paid Leave) Workplaces with five or more employees must guarantee monthly paid leave and annual paid leave; ⑤(Place of employment and work to be engaged in).

Ⅳ. Wages

Employers must pay wages directly, in currency, and in full to working minors, at least once a month on a fixed date(Article 43). When working minors quit or the working relationship is terminated due to dismissal, any owed wages, severance pay, and other money shall be paid within 14 days of the termination(Article 36). Employers must not pay wages to the parents of their minor workers(Article 68). If working children are unable to provide work due to reasons attributable to the employer, they shall be paid 70% of their average wage(Article 46). If an emergency situation such as illness or accident occurs and working minors require immediate payment of wages for work performed before the request date in order to cover the related expenses, employers shall pay wages ahead of payday(Article 45).

Wages must be set at minimum wage at least, and cannot be lowered on account of the worker being a minor. However, for unskilled minors who have signed an employment

이 미성년자의 근로계약을 대리할 수는 없으나, 근로계약이 미성년자에게 불리하다고 인정하는 경우에는 이를 해지할 수 있다(제67조). 민법상 19세 미만인 미성년자는 독자적으로 계약체결 등 법률행위를 할 수 없고, 친권자나 후견인의 동의를 받아 법률행위를 할 수 있다. 노동법에서도 연소근로자는 근로계약시 친권자의 동의서를 제출해야 한다. 그러나 연소근로자는 임금청구, 노동조합 가입 등의 법률행위를 독자적으로 할 수 있다.

사용자는 연소자와 근로계약 체결시 필수 기재사항에 대해 서면으로 작성하여 교부하여야 하고, 근로조건이 변경된 경우 변경된 근로계약서를 교부하여야 한다(제17조). 서면 명시내용은 다음과 같다. ① 임금: 임금의 구성항목, 계산방법, 지급방법. ② 소정근로시간: 연소자의 법정근로시간 내에서 정해져야 한다(1일 7시간, 1주 35시간 이내). ③ 주휴일: 1주 15시간 이상 근무한 경우에는 1주일에 평균 1일 이상의 유급 주휴일을 주어야 한다. ④ 유급휴가: 5인 이상의 사업장은 월차 유급휴가와 연차 유급휴가를 보장하여야 한다. ⑤ 취업의 장소와 종사하여야 할 업무.

Ⅳ. 임금

사용자는 연소근로자에게 임금을 직접, 통화로, 그 전액을 지급하여야 하고, 매월 1회 이상 일정한 기일을 정하여 지급하여야 한다(제43조). 연소근로자가 퇴직하거나 해고로 인하여 근로관계가 종료된 경우에는 14일 이내에 임금, 퇴직금, 기타의 금품을 지급하여야 한다(제36조). 사용자가 임금을 친권자에게 지급하면 안된다(제68조). 사용자의 귀책사유로 연소근로자가 근로를 제공하지 못한 경우에는 평균임금의 70%의 휴업수당을 지급하여야 한다(제46조). 연소근로자가 질병이나 재해 등의 비상한 상황이 발생해 그 비용을 충당하기 위해 임금지급일 전에 기왕의 근로에 대한 임금을 지급해 줄 것을 요구하면 사용자는 지급해야 한다(제45조).

임금은 최저임금 이상으로 책정되어야 하고, 연소자라는 이유로 최저임금을 저하시킬 수 없다. 다만, 1년 이상의 근로계약을 체결하고 수습 중인 근로자의

contract for at least one year, the minimum wage may be reduced up to 10% for the probationary first 3 months. However, this is not applicable to simple labor work(Article 5 of the Minimum Wage Act, or MWA).

If working children quit after continuing to work for one year or more, severance pay equal to the 30 days' average wage per year of continual work shall be paid(MWA, Article 34). However, there is no obligation to pay severance pay if the average working hours are fewer than 15 per week for each 4 week period. If some months the minor works an average of fewer than 15 hours per week and some months the minor works an average of 15 hours or more per week, only the months in which the minor worked an average of 15 hours or more per week are calculated, and severance pay is incurred only when such period is one year or longer(Article 18).

Ⅴ. Special Protection of Working Hours and Rest

The working hours of persons aged 15 to 18 shall not exceed 7 hours per day and 35 hours per week. However, this may be extended by up to 1 hour per day and 5 hours per week if there is agreement between the parties. Since 1 week refers to 7 days including holidays, the longest working hours for working minors shall be 40 hours a week. Therefore, flexible working hours and selective working hours are not applicable to working minors(MWA, Articles 51 and 52).

An employer shall allow a recess period of 30 minutes or more for every 4 working hours and at least 1 hour for every 8 working hours during the work day. During these rest hours, rest should be freely available to working minors(Article 54).

If working minors continue to work for 15 hours or more per week, they are given paid weekly holidays(Article 55). If they have completed their contractual working hours for one week, they are entitled to a weekly leave allowance of one or more days(Article 55). The weekly leave allowance for working minors is determined according to the ratio calculated by the working hours of ordinary workers engaged in the same type of work at the workplace, just as the working conditions for part-time workers(Article 18).[634)]

---

634) For 4 hours a day, 5 days a week, and an hourly wage of 10,000 won, the weekly vacation allowance is calculated according to the proportional principle of short-time workers. (20 hours / 40 hours per week) x 8 hours = 4 hours; 4 hours x 10,000 won = 40,000 won.

경우에는 최저임금의 10%를 감한 범위내에서 정할 수 있다. 그러나 그 업무가 단순 노무업무의 경우에는 해당되지 않는다(최저임금법 제5조).

연소근로자가 1년 이상 계속근무한 후 퇴직하는 경우에는 계속근로년수 1년에 30일분의 평균임금으로 하는 퇴직금을 지급하여야 한다(제34조). 다만, 근로시간이 4주간 평균 1주 근로시간이 15시간 미만인 경우에는 퇴직금 지급의무가 없다. 1주 평균 15시간 미만인 달과 그 이상인 달이 섞여 있는 경우에는 1주 평균 15시간 이상인 달만 계산하여 그 기간이 1년 이상인 경우에 한해 퇴직금이 발생한다(제18조).

Ⅴ. 근로시간과 휴식의 특별보호

15세 이상 18세 미만인 사람의 근로시간은 1일에 7시간, 1주에 35시간을 초과하지 못한다. 다만, 당사자 사이의 합의에 따라 1일에 1시간, 1주에 5시간을 한도로 연장할 수 있다. 1주란 휴일을 포함한 7일을 말하기 때문에 연소근로자가 근로할 수 있는 최장시간은 주40시간이 된다. 따라서 연소근로자에 대해서는 탄력적 근로시간제와 선택적 근로시간제가 적용되지 않는다(제51조, 제52조).

사용자는 연소근로자의 근로시간이 4시간인 경우에는 30분 이상, 8시간인 경우에는 1시간 이상의 휴게시간을 근로시간 중에 주어야 한다. 이 경우 휴게시간은 연소근로자가 자유롭게 이용할 수 있어야 한다(제54조).

연소근로자가 1주 15시간 이상 계속 근무한 경우에는 유급 주휴일을 부여 받는다(제55조). 연소근로자가 1주간 소정근로일수를 개근한 경우에는 1일 이상의 주휴수당을 주어야 한다(제55조). 연소자의 주휴수당은 단시간 근로자의 근로조건과 같이 그 사업장의 같은 종류의 업무에 종사하는 통상 근로자의 근로시간을 기준으로 산정한 비율에 따라 결정된다(제18조).[634)]

---

634) 1일 4시간, 1주일에 5일, 시간급 10,000원 인 경우, 주휴수당은 단시간근로자의 비례원칙에 따라 계산된다(주 20시간 / 40시간)×8시간 = 4시간, 4시간×10,000원=40,000원이 된다.

When working minors have worked for more than the contractual working hours, employers must pay overtime allowance amounting to 50% or more of the normal wage, in addition to the normal wage(Article 6 of the Fixed-Term Employment Act).

Employers are not allowed to have those under the age of 18 work from 10 pm to 6 am or on holidays, unless the employer obtains the consent of those under the age of 18 and approval from the Minister of Employment and Labor(Article 70). According to the approval standards of the Ministry of Employment and Labor,[635)] if nighttime operations are inevitable for fast food restaurants where many minors work part-time, in consideration of the safety of working children, their health, and protecting their ability to learn during the day, the limit is 12 midnight, unless approval from the Minister of Employment and Labor is gained for special reasons. Here, the term special reasons refers to cases where the necessity for night work is accepted and will have no detrimental effect on the health of working minors.

Employers shall give 15 days of annual leave when working minors have attended the workplace for at least 80% of the contracted work hours during one year. Employers shall also provide one day of paid leave for each month to working minors who have continued to work for less than one year or those who have attended the workplace for less than 80 percent of the contracted work hours during one year(Article 60).

Ⅵ. Coverage by the Four Major Social Insurances

In principle, coverage by the four major social insurances are required for working minors. However, if the on-site trainees are students who are not workers, they are not eligible. For working minors, the four insurances are applied slightly differently.

1. Industrial Accident Compensation Insurance

Applies the same as for all workplaces using workers. However, on-site trainees who are not workers are exceptionally eligible for compensation from workers' compensation(Article 123 of the Industrial Accident Compensation Insurance Act).

---

635) Ministry of Employment and Labor Guidelines on approval for minors to engage in night work (Equality Policy Division-July 26, 2004).

연소근로자가 소정근로시간을 초과하여 근무한 경우에는 통상임금의 100분의 50 이상을 가산한 연장근로수당을 지급하여야 한다(기간제법 제6조).

사용자는 18세 미만자를 오후 10시부터 오전 6시 까지의 시간과 휴일에 근로시키지 못한다. 다만, 사용자가 18세 미만자의 동의와 고용노동부장관의 인가를 받으면 야간시간과 휴일에 근로를 할 수 있다(제70조). 고용노동부의 인가기준에 따르면,[635] 연소자가 다수 아르바이트를 하고 있는 패스트푸드점에 대하여 업종의 특성상 야간 가동(영업)이 불가피 하다고 볼 수 있지만, 연소근로자의 건강보호 및 학습보장, 귀가 등 안전을 고려하여 특별한 사유가 없는 한 오후 12시까지 제한적으로 인가한다. 여기서 특별한 사유라 함은 사업주의 야간근로 필요성과 연소근로자의 건강 등에 무리가 없는 경우를 말한다.

사용자는 연소근로자가 1년간 80%퍼센트 이상 출근한 경우에 15일을 연차휴가를 주어야 한다. 사용자는 계속하여 근로한 기간이 1년 미만인 연소근로자 또는 1년간 80퍼센트 미만 출근한 연소근로자에게는 1개월 개근 시 1일의 유급휴가를 주어야 한다(제60조).

Ⅵ. 4대보험 적용

연소근로자에 대해서 4대보험을 원칙적으로 가입해야 한다. 다만, 현장 실습생이 근로자가 아닌 학생 신분이면 4대보험 가입대상이 아니다. 연소근로자에 있어 4대 보험별로 조금씩 다르게 적용된다.

1. 산업재해보상보험

근로자를 사용하는 모든 사업장에 적용되므로 연소근로자에게도 당연히 적용된다. 다만, 근로자가 아닌 현장실습생은 예외적으로 산재보상의 대상이 된다(산재법 제123조).

635) 고용노동부의 연소근로자 야간근로 인가업무 처리지침(평등정책과-2004.7.26).

2. Employment Insurance

Working minors who are employed for 1 day or longer are covered by employment insurance, but short-time workers with fewer than 60 working hours per month are excluded.

3. National Pension and National Health Insurance

The national pension is mandatory for those aged 18 or over and under 60 who work at a workplace. However, the National Health Insurance applies to all workers working in the workplace, regardless of age. The same applies to daily workers whose employment period is shorter than one month, and short-time workers whose contractual working hours per month are fewer than 60.

Ⅶ. Legal Issues related to Working Children

Whether or not the trainees in third grade of vocational high school are workers depends on whether or not they are students. If the main purpose for field training is to develop practical learning abilities to earn high school credits, they cannot be considered workers. However, if on-site trainees are recognized as having a subordinate relationship with the employer, they are considered workers under the Labor Standards Act.

1. Student Status[636)]

In accordance with the Industrial Education Promotion Act, 2 + 1 year public high school students take the 3rd year(1 year) course as students during the 3rd year of high school and engaged in industrial field training. A standard agreement is signed between the business, the school, and the students, and the students engage in on-site practice according to the on-site practice plan prepared in consultation with the business and the school. The business is supposed to evaluate trainee performance during on-the-job

---

636) MOEL Guidelines: Employment support unemployment benefits-262, Jan. 19, 2011; Kungi 68207-1833, May 4, 2002.

2. 고용보험

1일 이상 고용된 연소근로자는 고용보험에 가입되지만, 1개월의 소정근로시간이 60시간 미만인 단시간 근로자는 제외된다.

3. 국민연금과 국민건강보험

국민연금은 사업장에서 근무하는 18세 이상 60세 미만 자이다. 그러나 국민건강보험은 연령과 상관없이 사업장에서 근로를 하는 모든 근로자에게 적용된다. 가입제외 대상은 동일하게 고용기간이 1개월 미만인 일용근로자, 1개월의 소정근로시간이 60시간 미만인 단시간 근로자이다.

Ⅶ. 연소자 관련 법적 쟁점

직업계고등학교 3학년의 실습생이 근로자인지의 여부는 학생 신분인지 아닌지에 따라 달리 적용되고 있다. 현장실습생의 주 목적이 학점이수 등 실질적 학습능력을 위한 것이면 근로자로 볼 수 없다. 그러나 현장실습생이 사업주와의 사용종속관계가 인정되면 근로기준법상 근로자에 해당된다.

1. 학생 신분인 경우[636)]

2+1 체제의 공고실습생은 산업교육진흥법에 의거하여 고교 3년 과정중에 3학년(1년) 과정을 학생의 신분으로 산업체현장에서 현장실습을 실시한다. 산업체, 학교, 학생간에 표준협약서를 체결하고, 산업체와 학교측이 협의하여 작성한 현장실습계획에 따라 학생이 현장실습을 실시한다. 산업체에서는 학교측이 정한 기준에 따라 실습생의 현장실습 내용을 평가하여 그 결과를 학교측에 통보하는 것으로 되어 있다. 현장 실습은 산업교육진흥법에 따라 교육과정의 일부로써 공고생이 향후 산업에 종사하는 데 필요한 지식기술태도 습득을 목적으

636) 행정해석: 고용지원 실업급여과-262, 2011.1.19; 근기 68207-1833, 2002.5.4.

training according to the standards set by the school and notify the school of the results. Field training is a part of the curriculum in accordance with the Industrial Education Promotion Act and aims to help students acquire the knowledge, skills, and attitudes necessary for them to engage in industry in the future. In this case, it is difficult to see the trainee as a worker who provides work for the purpose of wages.

2. Worker status[637)]

Applicants who are expected to graduate are considered workers, if a subordinate relationship is recognized, and the Labor Standards Act is applied. In other words, even if they are trainees who are expected to graduate from high school and their working period is temporary, it cannot be concluded that they are not covered by the Labor Standards Act only for these reasons. In cases where it is recognized that there is a subordinate relationship pursuant to Article 2 of the Labor Standards Act based on the actual relationship between the employer and the trainee regarding the employment contract, the nature and content of work, and whether or not compensation is paid, the Labor Standards Act shall apply to the trainee.

---

637) Supreme Court ruling on June 9, 1987: 86 daka 2920.

로 한다. 이 경우에는 실습생은 임금을 목적으로 근로를 제공하는 근로자로 보기 어렵다.

2. 근로자 신분인 경우[637)]

졸업예정 실습생도 사용종속관계가 인정되면 근로자에 해당되고 근로기준법이 적용된다. 즉 고등학교 졸업예정자인 실습생이고 또 그 작업기간이 잠정적인 것이라 할지라도 바로 이러한 사유만으로 근로기준법을 적용받지 않는 근로자라고 단정할 수는 없다. 사업주와 실습생 사이의 채용에 관한 계약내용, 작업의 성질과 내용, 보수의 여부 등 실질적인 관계에 의하여 근로기준법 제2조의 규정에 의한 사용종속관계가 있음이 인정되는 경우에는 그 실습생은 근로기준법의 적용을 받는 근로자에 해당된다.

637) 대법원 1987.6.9, 86다카2920.

Section 2: Employment of Persons with Disabilities & Their Protection in the Workplace

I. Concept

Persons with disabilities also have the right to pursue happiness with dignity and value as human beings, and are entitled to state protection of these rights(Articles 10 and 34 of the Constitution). In accordance with this principle, employers of at least a certain size are obliged to hire persons with disabilities, and laws prohibiting discrimination against them in employment are being, and have been, implemented. Accordingly, employers shall provide employment opportunities to such persons and shall not discriminate against any workers in personnel management, such as in hiring, promotion, transfer, education and training, etc., merely on the grounds that the workers have disabilities. When discrimination does exist, separate legal remedies are provided to ensure the effectiveness of their protection.

In spite of these strict legal systems, many employers choose to pay the employment levy instead of hiring persons with disabilities. In accordance with the urgent demand for greater awareness of the social acceptability of persons with disabilities, Education on Improving Workplace Awareness of Persons with Disabilities is a new statutory form of education established in 2018, with associated penalties for failures by employers to implement such education. If employers are unable to fulfill their obligation to hire persons with disabilities, companies know they only need to pay the employment levy instead. However, since related and legally-required education has been introduced, what follows is a detailed definition of persons with disabilities, the required employment promotion measures, prohibition against discrimination and remedy for infringed rights, and education on improving workplace awareness of persons with disabilities. We then comprehensively review the working standards for persons with disabilities.[638)]

---

638) Ha, Kap-Rae, 「Labor Standards Act」, 28th edition, Joongang Economy, October 2016, pp. 616-624; Kim, El-Lim, Yun, Ae-Rim, 「Labor Standards Act」, KNOU PRESS, Nov. 2017, pp. 304-309.

제2절 장애인 고용보호

Ⅰ. 의 의

장애인도 인간으로서의 존엄과 가치를 가지고 행복을 추구할 권리를 가지고 있고, 국가는 장애인이 인간다운 생활을 할 수 있도록 보호하여야 한다(헌법 제10조, 제34조). 이러한 취지에 따라 일정규모 이상의 사업주에게 장애인을 의무적으로 고용하도록 하고 불이행에 대해서는 소정의 부담금을 부과하며, 장애인에 대한 고용차별을 금지하는 법이 제정되어 시행되고 있다. 이에 따라 사업주는 장애인에게 고용의 기회를 제공하고, 근로자가 장애인이라는 이유로 채용·승진·전보 및 교육훈련 등 인사 관리상 차별대우를 하여서는 아니 된다. 또한, 장애인이 차별을 받은 경우에는 차별구제의 실효성을 보장하기 위한 별도의 구제조치가 법적으로 마련되어 있다.

엄격한 법적 제도를 마련하였음에도 불구하고 많은 사업주들이 장애인을 고용하지 않아 장애인고용부담금을 납부하는 경우가 많다. 장애인에 대한 사회적 수용의 의식전환이 절실히 필요하다는 요구에 따라 2018년부터 “직장 내 장애인 인식개선 교육”이 법정교육으로 신설되었고, 이를 따르지 않을 시 과태료를 부과하고 있다. 그간 기업에서 장애인 고용의무를 다하지 못하는 경우 장애인 고용부담금 정도만 내는 정도로 인식하고 있었지만, 이제는 장애인과 관련된 내용이 필수교육으로 도입됨에 따라 관련 법의 세부 내용을 알아야 한다. 이하에서는 장애인의 고용보호를 종합적으로 소개하기 위해 장애인에 대한 정의와 고용촉진조치 내용, 차별금지와 권리구제, 그리고 장애인 인식개선 교육의 내용에 대해 구체적으로 설명하고자 한다.[638)]

638) 하갑례, 「근로기준법」, 제33판, 중앙경제, 2020, 616~624면, 김엘림·정봉수, 「근로보호법」, 방송대 출판문화원, 2020, 304~309면.

Ⅱ. Definition of and Obligation to Employ Persons with Disabilities

1. Definitions and related laws

Korea labor law related to persons with disabilities includes the Act on the Employment Promotion and Vocational Rehabilitation of Persons with Disabilities(hereinafter referred to as the "Employment Act for Persons with Disabilities")[639] and the Act on the Prohibition of Discrimination against the Disabled(hereinafter referred to as the "Act Against Discrimination of Persons with Disabilities").[640] The purpose of the Employment Act for Persons with Disabilities is to contribute to the employability of such persons so that they may live as regular members of society through work suited to their abilities(Article 1). Here, the term "person with disabilities" refers to someone who has had his/her long-term working life substantially restricted due to a physical or mental disability that corresponds to the standards prescribed by Presidential Decree.[641] There are 15 types of disability specified in Article 2 of the Enforcement Ordinance of the Act on Welfare for Persons with Disabilities: ① physical disabilities, ② brain lesions, ③ blindness, ④ deafness, ⑤ language disability, ⑥ mental retardation, ⑦ developmental disability, ⑧ mental disorder, ⑨ kidney disorder, ⑩ cardiac disorder, ⑪ respiratory disorder, ⑫ liver disorder, ⑬ facial disorder, ⑭ intestinal fistula and ⑮ epilepsy with other disabilities.

The purpose of this Act Against Discrimination of Persons with Disabilities is to prohibit discrimination on the basis of disability in all aspects of life, and to effectively safeguard the rights and interests of individuals discriminated against on the grounds of the disability, thus enabling them to fully participate in society and establishing their right to equality which will ensure their human dignity and sense of value(Article 1). This law stipulates the concept and criteria for discrimination against persons with disabilities, and also provides a framework for judging discrimination based not only on employment but also access to and use of education, goods and services, judicial and administrative procedures, services and political rights, motherhood

639) The Employment Act for Persons with Disabilities was enacted on Jan 13, 1990, and revised on Nov. 28, 2017. The Ministry of Employment and Labor is in charge.

640) The Act Against Discrimination of Persons with Disabilities was enacted on Apr. 11, 2007, and revised on Dec. 19, 2017. The Ministry of Health and Welfare is in charge.

641) The Enforcement Decree to the Act contains the following : A person determined to have a disability as specified in Article 2 of the Enforcement Decree to the Act on Welfare for Persons with Disabilities; The Enforcement Decree to the Act contains the following: A person determined to have a disability as specified in Article 2 of the Enforcement Decree to the Act on Welfare for Persons with Disabilities.

Ⅱ. 장애인의 정의와 장애인 고용의무

1. 장애인의 정의와 관련 법률

노동법과 관련된 장애인 관련 법으로는 「장애인고용촉진 및 직업재활법(이하 "장애인고용법")」[639]과 「장애인차별금지 및 구제 등에 관한 법률(이하 "장애인차별금지법")」[640] 이 있다. 장애인고용법은 "장애인이 그 능력에 맞는 직업생활을 통하여 인간다운 생활을 할 수 있도록 장애인 고용촉진 및 직업재활을 꾀하는 것"을 목적으로 한다(제1조). 여기서 '장애인'이란 신체 또는 정신상의 장애로 장기간에 걸쳐 직업생활에 상당한 제약을 받는 자로서 대통령령으로 정하는 기준에 해당하는 자[641]를 말한다(제2조 제1항). 「장애인복지법 시행령」 제2조에서 정한 장애인의 종류를 ① 지체장애인, ② 뇌병변장애인, ③ 시각장애인, ④ 청각장애인, ⑤ 언어장애인, ⑥ 정신지체인, ⑦ 발달장애인, ⑧ 정신장애인, ⑨ 신장장애인, ⑩ 심장장애인, ⑪ 호흡기장애인, ⑫ 간장애인, ⑬ 안면장애인, ⑭ 장루·유루장애인, ⑮ 간질장애인의 15종으로 규정하고 있다.

장애인차별금지법은 "모든 생활영역에서 장애를 이유로 한 차별을 금지하고 장애를 이유로 차별을 받은 사람의 권익을 효과적으로 구제함으로써 장애인의 완전한 사회참여와 평등권 실현을 통하여 인간으로서의 존엄과 가치를 구현함"을 목적으로 한다(제1조). 이 법률은 장애인의 차별 개념과 판단기준을 규정하고 고용뿐만 아니라 교육, 재화 및 용역의 접근과 이용, 사법·행정절차 및 서비스와 참정권, 모·부성권, 가족·가정·복지시설, 건강 등에서 차별을 금지하고 차별피해자에 대해 국가인권위원회를 통한 권리구제에 관하여 규정하고 있다. 장애인차별금지법은 다른 법률과의 관계에 대해 "장애를 사유로 한 차별의 금지 및 권리구제에 관하여 이 법에서 규정한 것 외에는 「국가인권위원회법」으

639) 장애인고용법 제정 1990.1.13, 최근 개정 2017.11.28, 고용노동부 관할.
640) 장애인차별금지법 제정 2007.4.11, 최근 개정 2017.12.19, 보건복지부 관할.
641) 장애인고용법 시행령은 「장애인복지법 시행령」제2조의 규정에 의한 장애인의 기준에 해당하는 자와 「국가유공자 등 예우 및 지원에 관한 법률 시행령」 제14조 제3항의 규정에 의한 상이등급에 해당하는 자를 장애인으로 정하고 있다(제3조).

and fatherhood, family, home, welfare facilities, and right to health. It prohibits discrimination and stipulates the right to relief for victims of discrimination through the National Human Rights Commission Act(NHRCA). In Article 9, the Act Against Discrimination of Persons with Disabilities provides that "the prohibition of discrimination on grounds of disability and the right to relief under the Act shall be in accordance with the provisions of the NHRCA, except as provided in this Act."

2. Obligation to employ those with disabilities

An employer who employs 50 or more persons at any time shall be deemed to be obligated to employ persons with disabilities to the rate prescribed by the President(hereinafter referred to as "the mandatory employment rate") up to 5 percent of the total number of employees(Article 28 of the Employment Act for Persons with Disabilities). The mandatory employment rate from 2019 is 31/1000(Article 25 of the Enforcement Decree). Here, "ordinary employment" refers to an employee who has 16 or more working days per month regardless of the type of labor contract. Specifically, the number of employees hired for 16 days or more per month is calculated by dividing the number of months of operation(minus month(s) with fewer than 16 days of operation) for one year(Article 24 of the Enforcement Decree).

The Minister of Employment and Labor may pay an employment incentive calculated in proportion to the number of persons with disabilities who have been hired exceeding the standard employment rate, including employers who are not subject to employment obligations. The payment unit price shall be within the range of the minimum wage converted on a monthly basis, and shall be preferentially set for those with severe disabilities and women with disabilities(Article 30 of the Employment Act for Persons with Disabilities).

3. Employment levy on companies failing to employ persons with disabilities

Employers who do not hire persons with disabilities, or do not meet the mandatory employment rate, must pay an annual employment levy to the Minister of Employment and Labor. However, employers with fewer than 100 permanent employees are exempted from this obligation. Employers subject to the obligation to employ persons with disabilities shall declare in writing their number of permanent employees per month, their number of employees with disabilities and the amount of levy(if any) paid each year by January 31 of the following year, and shall pay the levy for that year. The Employment Levy for Persons with Disabilities is the annual

로 정하는 바에 따른다"(제9조)라고 정하고 있다.

2. 장애인 고용의무

상시 50인 이상의 근로자를 고용하는 사업주는 그 근로자의 총수의 100분의 5의 범위내에서 대통령으로 정하는 비율(이하 "의무고용률"이라 한다) 이상에 해당(그 수의 소수점 이하는 버림)하는 장애인을 고용하여야 한다(장애인고용법 제28조). 2019년 이후의 의무고용률은 1000분의 31로 한다(시행령 제25조). 상시라 함은 근로계약형태와 관계없이 매월 근로일수가 산정일 현재 16일 이상인 근로자를 말한다. 구체적으로 1년 동안 '매월 16일 이상 고용한 근로자 수'를 조업 개월수 (조업일이 16일 미만인 달은 뺀다)로 나누어 산정한다(시행령 제24조).

고용노동부 장관은 고용의무 적용대상이 아닌 사업주를 포함하여 기준고용률을 초과하여 장애인을 고용한 사업주에게 초과 고용한 장애인의 수에 비례하여 산정한 고용장려금을 지급할 수 있다. 지급단가는 월 단위로 환산한 최저임금액의 범위 내여야 하며, 중증·여성장애인에 대하여는 우대하여 정해야 한다(장애인고용법 제30조).

3. 장애인 고용부담금

의무고용률에 미달하는 장애인을 고용한 사업주는 매년 고용노동부 장관에게 장애인고용부담금을 납부하여야 한다. 다만, 상시근로자 수 100인미만의 사업주는 장애인고용부담금 부과를 면제하고 있다. 장애인고용의무대상 사업주는 매년 다음연도 1월31일까지 매월 상시근로자 수와, 고용한 장애인 근로자 수, 부담금의 액수 등이 기재된 서면을 신고하고 해당연도의 부담금을 납부하여야 한다. 장애인 고용부담금은 의무고용률에 따라 고용해야 할 장애인총수에서 매월 상시 고용하고 있는 장애인 수를 뺀 수에 부담기초액을 곱한 금액의 연간 합계액이다(장애인고용법 제33조).

sum of the total number of persons with disabilities to be hired under the mandatory employment rate minus the number of persons with disabilities regularly employed each month multiplied by the burden base amount(Article 33 of the Employment Act for Persons with Disabilities).

Total Levy = {(Total number of persons with disabilities to be hired) - (Total number of persons with disabilities hired annually)} × Base burden

Ⅲ. Discrimination Against Those with Disabilities

1. Contents of discriminations

(1) Criteria for determining discrimination

Direct discrimination is where ① those with disabilities are treated unfavorably, due to their disability, through restriction, exclusion, separation, or denial without justifiable reason(Article 4(1) of the Act Against Discrimination of Persons with Disabilities).

Indirect discrimination refers to ② when persons with disabilities who are not adversely affected by restrictions, exclusion, separation, or rejection in a formal way but still undergo adverse consequences for their disability by applying criteria to them, without justifiable cause, that do not consider their specific situation; ③ where reasonable accommodation is not provided to persons with disabilities without just cause. Here, "reasonable accommodation" refers to that which would enable the person with disability to participate in the same activities as those without disabilities, including facilities, tools, services, etc., taking into consideration the gender of the person with the disability; ④ behavior by a person in a way that directly advertises or promotes adverse treatment such as through restriction, exclusion, separation, rejection, etc. without justifiable reason. In this case, the advertisement usually includes actions deemed to have an advertising effect that promotes adverse treatment. ⑤ In points 1) to 4), discrimination against a person who is dealing or accompanying a person with a disability for the purpose of helping a person with a disability. In this case, acts by persons with disabilities against other persons with disabilities shall also be subject to determination as discrimination on the basis of that which is prohibited by this Act; ⑥ interfering with the legitimate use of assistance animals or devices for those with disabilities, or other acts prohibited by Article 4 against assistance animals and devices for those with disabilities(Article 4 of the Act Against Discrimination of Persons with Disabilities).

부담금 총액 = {(월별장애인 고용의무 인원의 연간합계) − (월별장애인 고용 인원의 연간합계)} × 부담기초액

Ⅲ. 장애인 차별금지

1. 차별의 내용

(1) 차별행위 기준

직접차별은 ① 장애를 사유로 정당한 사유 없이 제한·배제·분리·거부 등에 의하여 불리하게 대하는 경우이다(장애인차별금지법 제4조 제1항).

간접차별은 장애인에 대하여 ② 형식상으로는 제한·배제·분리·거부 등에 의하여 불리하게 대하지 아니하지만 정당한 사유 없이 장애를 고려하지 아니하는 기준을 적용함으로써 장애인에게 불리한 결과를 초래하는 경우, ③ 정당한 사유 없이 장애인에 대하여 정당한 편의제공을 거부하는 경우("정당한 편의"라 함은 장애인이 장애가 없는 사람과 동등하게 같은 활동에 참여할 수 있도록 장애인의 성별, 장애의 유형 및 정도, 특성 등을 고려한 편의시설·설비·도구·서비스 등 인적·물적 제반 수단과 조치를 말한다), ④ 정당한 사유 없이 장애인에 대한 제한·배제·분리·거부 등 불리한 대우를 표시·조장하는 광고를 직접 행하거나 그러한 광고를 허용·조장하는 경우(광고는 통상적으로 불리한 대우를 조장하는 광고효과가 있는 것으로 인정되는 행위를 포함한다), ⑤ 장애인을 돕기 위한 목적에서 장애인을 대리·동행하는 자(이하 "장애인 관련자")에 대하여 제1호부터 제4호까지의 행위를 하는 경우(장애인 관련자의 장애인에 대한 행위 또한, 이 법에서 금지하는 차별행위 여부의 판단대상이 된다), ⑥ 보조견 또는 장애인 보조기구 등의 정당한 사용을 방해하거나 보조견 및 장애인 보조기구 등을 대상으로 제4호에 따라 금지된 행위를 하는 경우를 말한다(장애인차별금지법 제4조).

(2) Exception for discrimination

Actions that are taken in accordance with the following situations are not considered unjustifiable discrimination: ① Excessive burden or considerable difficulty is incurred by avoiding prohibited discrimination, making it inevitable due to the nature of specific work or business performance; ② Active measures taken by this Act or other laws and ordinances to realize the real equality of persons with disabilities and to correct discrimination against persons with disabilities shall not be regarded as discrimination under this Act(Article 4 of the Act Against Discrimination of Persons with Disabilities).

(3) Judgment of discrimination

If there are two or more causes for discriminatory action but the main cause is recognized as due to a disability, the action shall be regarded as discrimination under this Act. When judging discrimination, the gender of the person with the disability, the type and degree of the disability, and other characteristics of the person with disability shall be fully considered(Article 5 of the Act Against Discrimination of Persons with Disabilities).

2. Discrimination correcting organization and remedies for infringed rights

In the event a person is discriminated against in a way prohibited by the Act Against Discrimination of Persons with Disabilities, that person or any person or organization who knows this fact may appeal to the National Human Rights Commission(NHRC). Even if there is no complaint, the NHRC may investigate in its own power when there is reasonable cause to believe discrimination has occurred that is prohibited by the Act Against Discrimination of Persons with Disabilities(Article 38 and 39).

The NHRC shall notify the Minister of Justice of the details of any recommendation for the forbidden discrimination behaviors. The Minister of Justice gets involved in cases where a person who receives a recommendation from the NHRC does not carry out the recommendation without justifiable cause. This can include: ① a failure to implement recommendations for discriminatory acts against multiple persons; ② a failure to implement recommendations for repeated discriminatory acts; and ③ intentionally disregarding a recommendation to disadvantage the person being discriminated against. The Minister of Justice may also get involved if he/she deems a correction order is necessary and the degree of real or potential damage is severe and the effect on the public interest is recognized as serious(Article 43 of the Act

(2) 차별의 예외

위의 차별행위에 해당되지 않는 경우는 다음과 같다. ① 금지된 차별행위를 하지 않음에 있어 과도한 부담이나 현저히 곤란한 사정 등이 있는 경우와 금지된 차별행위가 특정 직무나 사업 수행의 성질상 불가피한 경우이다. ② 장애인의 실질적 평등권을 실현하고 장애인에 대한 차별을 시정하기 위하여 이 법 또는 다른 법령 등에서 취하는 적극적 조치는 이 법에 따른 차별로 보지 아니한다(장애인차별 금지법 제4조).

(3) 차별의 판단

차별의 원인이 2가지 이상이고, 그 주된 원인이 장애라고 인정되는 경우 그 행위는 이 법에 따른 차별로 본다. 차별여부를 판단할 때는 장애인 당사자의 성별, 장애의 유형 및 정도, 특성 등을 충분히 고려하여야 한다(장애인차별금지법 제5조).

2. 차별시정기구와 권리구제

장애인차별금지법에서 금지하는 차별행위로 인하여 피해자 또는 그 사실을 알고 있는 사람이나 단체는 국가인권위원회에 그 내용을 진정할 수 있다. 인권위원회는 진정이 없는 경우에도 장애인차별금지법에서 금지하는 차별행위가 있다고 믿을 만한 타당한 근거가 있고 그 내용이 중대하다고 인정할 때는 이를 직권으로 조사할 수 있다(장애인차별금지법 제38, 39조).

인권위원회가 금지하는 차별행위로 권고를 할 경우에는 그 내용을 법무부 장관에게 통보하여야 한다. 법무부 장관은 인권위원회의 권고를 받은 자가 정당한 사유 없이 권고를 이행하지 아니하는 행위 중 일부 행위에 해당하는 경우로 ① 피해자가 다수인 차별행위에 대한 권고 불이행, ② 반복적 차별행위에 대한 권고 불이행, ③ 피해자에게 불이익을 주기 위한 고의적 불이행, ④ 그밖에 시정명령이 필요한 경우에 대해 그 피해의 정도가 심각하고 공익에 미치는 영향이 중대하다고 인정되는 경우, 피해자의 신청에 의하여 또는 직원으로 시정명령을 할 수 있다(장애인차별금지법 제43조). 그 시정명령은 ① 차별행위의 중지, ② 피해의 원상회복, ③ 차별행위의 재발방지를 위한 조치, ④ 그밖에 차별시

Against Discrimination of Persons with Disabilities). Corrective orders can include ① suspension of the discriminatory acts, ② compensation for damage, ③ implementation of measures to prevent recurrence, and ④ other measures deemed necessary to correct the discrimination.

Any party contesting the order of correction by the Minister of Justice may file an administrative suit within thirty(30) days from the date of receipt of the order. The order of correction shall be finalized if no action has been filed within this period of time(Article 44 of the Act Against Discrimination of Persons with Disabilities). The Minister of Justice may impose a fine of up to KRW 30 million against persons failing to follow a correction order without just cause(Article 50 of the Act Against Discrimination of Persons with Disabilities).

IV. Compulsory Education on Protecting the Rights of Persons with Disabilities

1. Compulsory education & related penalties

Employers shall work to eliminate bias in the workplace against those with disabilities, create stable working conditions for them, and educate their workforce to improve their awareness of persons with disabilities. Mandatory education covers all businesses or workplaces employing morethan 50 workers and shall consist of one hour per year. Employers shall keep records related to the education for 3 years(Articles 5-2, 5-3, 86 of the Employment Act for Persons with Disabilities, and(3) Article 5-2 of the Enforcement Decree).

2. Content of mandatory education

Education to improve workplace awareness of persons with disabilities shall include: ① the definition of disability and types of disability; ② human rights, prohibition of discrimination against, and provision of fair accommodations for persons in the workplace with disabilities; ③ laws and systems related to employment promotion and vocational rehabilitation of persons with disabilities; and ④ other contents deemed necessary to improve workplace awareness of persons with disabilities. This education can be done collectively, as an inquiry or a meeting, or through remote education using the Internet or other communication network, or experiential education in consideration of the size and characteristics of the business(Article 5-2 of the Employment Act for Persons with Disabilities).

정을 위하여 필요한 조치이다.

법무부 장관의 시정명령에 대하여 불복하는 관계 당사자는 그 명령서를 송달 받은 날부터 30일 이내에 행정소송을 제기할 수 있으며, 기간 이내에 행정소송을 제기하지 않은 때는 그 시정명령은 확정된다(장애인차별금지법 제44조). 법무부 장관은 확정된 이행명령을 정당한 사유없이 이행하지 않은 자에 대해 3천만 원 이하의 과태료를 부과할 수 있다(장애인차별금지법 제50조).

Ⅳ. 장애인 고용보호에 대한 의무교육

1. 의무교육 대상 및 벌칙

사업주는 장애인에 대한 직장 내 편견을 제거함으로써 장애인 근로자의 안정적인 근무여건을 조성하고 채용이 확대될 수 있도록 장애인 인식개선 교육을 실시하여야 한다. 필수교육 대상은 50인 이상의 근로자를 고용한 모든 사업 또는 사업장이다. 직장 내 장애인 인식개선 교육을 연간 1회, 1시간 이상 실시하여야 한다. 사업주는 교육 실시 관련 자료를 3년간 보관하여야 하며 이를 위반하여 장애인 인식개선 교육을 실시하지 않거나 관련 교육실시 자료를 3년간 보관하지 않는 경우에는 각각 300만원 이하의 과태료를 부과한다(장애인고용법 제5조의2, 제5조의3, 제86조, 시행령 제5조의2).

2. 의무교육 내용

직장 내 장애인 인식개선 교육에는 다음의 내용을 포함하여야 한다. ① 장애의 정의 및 장애유형에 대한 이해, ② 직장 내 장애인의 인권, 장애인에 대한 차별금지 및 정당한 편의 제공, ③ 장애인 고용촉진 및 직업재활과 관련된 법과 제도, ④ 그밖에 직장 내 장애인 인식개선에 필요한 내용이다. 사업주는 사업의 규모나 특성을 고려하여 직원연수·조회·회의 등의 집합교육, 인터넷 등 정보통신망을 이용한 원격교육 또는 체험교육을 통한 교육을 실시할 수 있다(장애인고용법 제5조의2).

Section 3: Prohibition against Age Discrimination[642]

Ⅰ. Concept

Age discrimination means that a certain person(or a group to which an employee belongs) under similar circumstances creates disadvantages for a person(or a group) of a different age. Employers shall not discriminate against an employee based on age, without a justifiable reason, in each of the following: ① recruitment and employment; ② provision of wages and valuables aside from wages, and benefits packages; ③ education and training; ④ disposition, change of position and promotion; and ⑤ retirement and dismissal. If application of a standard aside from age, without justifiable reason, leads to a result particularly unfavorable to a certain age group, this shall be considered age discrimination. This Act shall apply to any workplace where an employer intends to hire, or has hired, one employee or more, and so this Act covers all legally employable age levels.

Act on Prohibition of Age Discrimination in Employment and Elderly Employment Promotion: Article 23-4 (Penal Provision), Article 24 (Fines for Negligence)

- Employers who discriminate because of age, without a justifiable reason, shall be fined an amount not exceeding 5 million won.
- Any person who fails to carry out a correction order of the labor office shall be imposed a negligence fine not exceeding 30 million won.
- An employer shall not give disadvantageous treatment to an employee, such as dismissal, transfer, disciplinary action, etc., on the grounds that the employee has filed a petition, submitted materials, given answers and testimony, filed a lawsuit, made a report, etc. In violation of this article, the employer shall be punished by imprisonment for not more than two years or by a fine not exceeding 10 million won.

Ⅱ. Justifiable Reasons

The Act is violated when said person or group is discriminated against without justifiable reason. The concept of justifiable reason as general criteria for determining

642) Reference: MOEL Guidelines on Mar. 2009.

제3절 고령자 연령차별 금지[642)]

Ⅰ. 연령차별의 의의

연령차별은 유사한 상황에서 특정인(또는 그가 속한 연령집단)을 다른 연령의 사람(또는 집단)보다도 불이익하게 취급하는 것을 말한다. 사업주는 근로자의 모집·채용, 임금·임금 외의 금품 지급 및 복리후생, 교육·훈련 및 배치·전보·승진, 퇴직·해고에 있어서 합리적인 이유 없이 연령을 이유로 차별하여서는 아니된다. 합리적인 이유 없이 연령 외의 기준을 적용하여 특정 연령집단에게 특히 불리한 결과를 초래하는 경우 이를 차별로 본다. 연령차별금지 관련 법 적용은 근로자를 1명 이상 사용하려 하거나 사용하는 사업 또는 사업장이며, 취업 가능한 모든 연령층을 차별보호의 대상으로 한다.

고용상 연령차별금지 및 고령자고용촉진에 관한 법률제23조의 3【벌칙】, 제24조【과태료】

- 모집·채용에서 합리적인 이유 없이 연령을 이유로 차별한 사업주는 500만원 이하의 벌금에 처한다. (1차 서면경고 조치 후 시정하지 않으면 과태료 부과) (동법 제23조의3)
- 관할 노동청의 시정명령을 정당한 사유 없이 이행하지 아니하는 자에게는 3천만원 이하의 과태료를 부과한다(동법 제24조).
- 사업주는 연령차별행위에 대한 진정, 자료제출, 답변·증언, 소송, 신고 등을 하였다는 이유로 근로자에게 해고, 전보, 징계 그 밖의 불리한 처우를 하여서는 아니된다. 위반 시 2년 이하의 징역 또는 1천만원 이하의 벌금에 처한다(동법 제23조의3).

Ⅱ. 합리적인 이유

연령을 이유로 하는 차별은 "합리적인 이유 없이" 이루어진 경우에 한하여 성립하며, 차별을 허용하는 일반적 판단기준으로서의 '합리적' 개념은 엄격하게

642) 참조: 고용노동부시침, "고용상 연령차별금지 및 고령자고용촉진에 관한 법률", 2009.3.

whether unfair discrimination is occurring shall be interpreted strictly. Namely, the difference(discrimination) of treatment due to age ① shall be implemented to accomplish a justifiable purpose(justification of purpose). Being important under the corresponding circumstances can be interpreted as a justifiable purpose. The discrimination ② shall be unavoidable(necessity of method). If it is possible to accomplish its purpose by using a reasonable method aside from age(if there is a reasonable alternative), using necessity of method as a defense is hard to justify. And ③ the principle of comparison between purpose and method shall be applied. In this case, it shall be appropriate to choose a certain age group to be disadvantaged if it is chosen according to the principle of comparison between purpose and method.

Ⅲ. Types of Discrimination

1. Direct discrimination

Actions where employers discriminate based on age without justifiable reason are direct discrimination. Discriminating based on age means that the reason for the discrimination is the biological age of a certain person(or a certain group), and disadvantageous treatment applies to an employee(or group of employees) according to whether or not he/she has reached a particular age, whether an employee belongs to a group of a particular age or not, and relative difference in age.

2. Indirect discrimination

Indirect discrimination is when a standard is used, aside from age(namely, neutral standard), to disadvantage a certain group or employee. Even though it seems non-discriminative externally, in practical terms, it leads to a result particularly unfavorable to a certain age group(namely, a disadvantage of some sort). So, indirect discrimination occurs when application of a neutral standard is not justifiable. Indirect discrimination also occurs when a certain age group is treated unfavorably compared to another age group, and this judgment of 'disadvantage in result' shall require a comparison between definable age groups.

해석해야 한다. 즉, 연령에 근거한 대우의 차이(차별)는 ① 정당한 목적을 달성하기 위한 것이어야 하고(목적의 정당성), 해당 상황에서 중요한 것이어야 '정당한' 목적으로 해석할 수 있다. 연령을 이유로 한 차등취급은 ② 불가피한 것이어야 하며(수단의 불가피성), 연령 이외의 합리적 수단을 사용하여 목적을 달성할 수 있는 경우(즉, 합리적 대안이 존재하는 경우)에는 수단의 불가피성을 인정하기 어렵고 또한, ③ 목적과 수단 간에는 비례원칙이 적용되는데, 비례원칙에 의하면 수단으로 채택된 연령기준의 정도 및 그에 따른 불이익의 정도가 적정하여야 한다.

Ⅲ. 차별의 종류

1. 직접차별

사업주가 합리적인 이유 없이 연령을 이유로 차별하는 행위는 직접차별에 해당하는 행위이기 때문에 금지되어야 하며, "연령을 이유로" 한다는 것은 차별의 원인이 특정인(또는 특정집단)의 '생물학적' 나이인 경우이며, 특정 연령의 도달 여부, 특정 연령그룹 해당 여부 및 연령의 상대적 차이 등을 불리한 대우의 기준으로 삼는 것이다.

2. 간접차별

간접차별은 연령 외의 기준(즉, 중립적 기준)을 사용함으로써 표면상으로는 아무런 차별이 없어 보이나 실제로는 특정 연령집단의 구성원이 다른 연령집단의 구성원에 비해 불리한 상황에 처하게 되고(즉, 결과적 불이익), 중립적 기준의 적용이 정당하지 않는 경우에 성립한다. 간접차별은 "특정 연령집단의 사람들이 다른 연령집단의 사람들에 비해 불리한 상황에 처하게" 될 것(결과적 불이익)을 요건으로 하며, 결과적 불이익이 있는지의 판단은 서로 다른 연령집단 사이의 비교를 요한다.

Ⅳ. Examples of Age Discrimination at Each Level of Employment

1. Recruitment and employment

A typical type of age discrimination occurring in recruitment and employment is to limit applicant ages(particularly maximum age) or to prefer a particular age group.

- Age limit in open applications for recruitment of 9th grade civil servants
- Age limit in applications for recruitment of female crew of domestic airline companies(Age limit of 25 or younger)
- Age limit in applications for recruitment of university employees(Age limit of 40 or younger)
- Age limit in open applications for recruitment of teachers(Age limit of 40 or younger)

2. Wages, valuables aside from wages, and benefits packages

Actions where employers discriminate between ages for determining wages, other valuables and benefits packages for people in similar positions, are direct discrimination. However, in cases where difference in number of service years reflects different job skills, degrees of responsibility, or difference in performance, and in cases where it is necessary to promote longer service, wage discrimination determined by the number of service years is not regarded as age discrimination and is accepted as reasonable discrimination.

3. Education and training

Employees shall be given equal opportunity for education and training, without discrimination based on age, as they are important methods to develop job skills and are closely related to human resource management and compensation. In selecting eligible employees for various education and training opportunities, like overseas training, if the employer excludes a certain age group based on age without objective and reasonable criteria, this action would fall under age discrimination.

4. Disposition, changes of position and promotion

The employer usually chooses eligible employees for disposition, changes of position, and

Ⅳ. 고용단계별 연령차별 사례

1. 모집·채용

모집·채용단계에서 발생하는 연령차별의 대표적 유형은 지원자의 나이(특히 최고 연령)를 제한하거나 특정 연령층을 선호하는 경우이다.

· 9급 지방공무원 제한경쟁 특별임용시험 응시연령 제한
· 국내 항공사 여자승무원 응시연령 제한(만 25세 이하)
· 대학교원 지원연령 제한(만 40세 이하)
· 교사 신규채용 공개전형 응시연령 제한(40세 이하)

2. 임금, 임금 외의 금품지급 및 복리후생

유사한 상황에서 연령을 기준으로 하여 임금이나 기타 금품, 복리후생에서 불이익을 주는 행위는 연령차별에 해당한다. 근속기간의 차이가 직무능력이나 직무책임도 또는 성과의 차이를 반영하는 것으로 볼 수 있는 경우나, 근로자의 장기근속을 촉진하여야 할 필요가 있는 경우에는 연령차별에 해당하지 않으며, 이런 경우에도 근속기간을 기준으로 하는 임금의 차이는 합리적인 차등에 해당한다.

3. 교육·훈련

교육훈련은 직무능력개발의 중요 수단이자 인사 및 보상에서의 이익과 밀접히 연관되어 있기 때문에 연령에 따른 차별이 없이 평등한 기회가 보장되어야 한다. 해외연수 등 각종 교육훈련의 대상자를 선발함에 있어서 객관적이고 합리적 기준에 의하지 않고 연령을 기준으로 특정 연령집단을 제외하는 것은 원칙적으로 차별에 해당한다.

4. 배치·전보·승진

근로자의 배치·전보 및 승진에서 사용자는 다양한 요소들(예: 직무능력, 조직

promotion by considering various factors, such as job skills, organizational efficiency, teamwork, sense of responsibility, etc. Therefore, the employer's discretion to evaluate and select eligible employees shall be respected, but if the employer, in evaluating and selecting these employees, disadvantages a certain employee or group based on age, this age discrimination is prohibited as an abuse of the employer's discretion. In cases where the employer does not provide opportunity or applies disadvantageous conditions to a certain age group, without justifiable reason, in management of personnel disposition, promotion, etc., and in cases where a certain age group was collectively disposed to or transferred to disadvantageous jobs, or in cases where younger employees were treated preferentially, when compared to more eligible older employees, such acts are considered age discrimination. If there is a remarkable statistic difference between different age groups, discrimination can be suspected.

5. Retirement and dismissal

When an employer establishes criteria to dismiss a certain group of employees due to their advanced age, without considering other factors like job skills, performance, etc. in the process of employment adjustment, this action falls under age discrimination because the employer dismissed employees due to age. Where there is a close relation between service period and wages in the seniority-based salary system, dismissing employees simply because they have been employed a long time, and therefore receive high wages, will be considered indirect discrimination.

V. Exceptions to the Prohibition against Age Discrimination

① A certain age group is inevitably required in consideration of the characteristics of related duties

※ Example: set age limit for an applicant who shall carry out a young man's role in a drama or movie

② There is a difference in the continuous service period, a reasonable difference in wages, or money and valuables, and benefits packages aside from wages

③ Retirement age is set in the labor contract, work rules, or collective agreements, etc.

④ Support measures are implemented to maintain and promote the employment of a certain age group as defined by law

효율성, 인화력, 책임감 등)을 고려하여 적격자를 선택하는 것이 통상적이고, 사용자의 평가·선택에 대한 일정한 재량권을 존중하여야 하지만 연령을 이유로 불이익을 주는 연령차별은 재량권의 일탈로서 금지된다. 배치·승진 등의 인사에서 합리적 이유 없이 특정 연령집단의 구성원들에게는 기회를 부여하지 않거나 상대적으로 불리한 조건을 적용하는 경우, 특정 연령집단을 근로조건이 불리한 직무로 일괄 배치하거나 전보시키는 경우, 보다 나은 자격조건을 갖추었음에도 나이가 적은 자를 우대하는 경우는 원칙적으로 차별에 해당하며, 업적평가나 승진에서 서로 다른 연령집단 사이에 현저한 통계적 차이가 존재하는 경우에는 차별을 의심할 수 있다.

5. 퇴직·해고

기업구조조정 과정에서 직무능력이나 성과 등 다른 요소들에 대한 고려 없이 고령자라는 이유만으로 우선적으로 해고하도록 하는 기준은 연령을 이유로 고용상실이라는 불이익을 주는 것으로 원칙적으로 연령차별에 해당한다. 연공서열형 임금체계 하에서는 연령과 근속기간·임금 사이에는 매우 밀접한 관계가 있으므로 장기근속이나 고임금을 해고기준으로 삼는 경우에는 간접차별 해당된다.

Ⅴ. 차별예외사유

① 직무의 성격에 비추어 특정 연령기준이 불가피하게 요구되는 경우

※ 예시: 연극, 영화 등에서 청년역할의 수행을 위한 연령제한

② 근속기간의 차이를 고려하여 임금이나 임금 외의 금품과 복리후생에서 합리적인 차등을 두는 경우

③ 근로계약, 취업규칙, 단체협약 등에서 정년을 설정하는 경우

④ 법률에 따라 특정 연령집단의 고용유지·촉진을 위한 지원조치를 하는 경우

Section 4: Foreign Workers

Ⅰ. Concept

Most of the human rights violations involving migrant workers occur with non-professional foreign workers. Visiting overseas Korean workers have the freedom to choose their workplace, so there is not much difference in labor law protections from their Korean counterparts. For professional foreign workers, there are some limitations on labor protections in certain areas, but those differences can be resolved by transferring to another workplace. However, there are many limitations for non-professional foreign workers in the protections they receive under Korean labor law. Some examples follow.

① Non-professional foreign workers are not free to change workplaces. They must remain at the same workplace for three years unless there are justifiable reasons for the change of workplace. ② Wages remain at the minimum wage regardless of their skills or how many years of experience they have. ③ Despite the fact that the right to annual paid leave occurs when they work for at least one year(Article 60 of the Labor Standards Act or LSA), most non-professional foreign workers do not receive it. ④ Foreign workers can only receive their severance pay when they return to their home country, not when their employment terminates.

Korea's three labor rights(the right to organize a union, the right to collective bargaining, and the right to collective action) are guaranteed in collective labor relations, and a labor union of illegal workers has even been officially recognized as a legitimate union.[643)] Nevertheless, it is impossible in reality for a company-unit foreign labor union to have continuity in its activities, as all non-professional foreign workers are fixed-term workers, and employers can control the collective behavior of foreign workers. Therefore, it is impossible to actually exercise their three labor rights.

---

643) Supreme Court ruling on June 25, 2015: 2007doo4995. Decided with all judges sitting (Withdrawal of union establishment certificate).

제4절 외국인

Ⅰ. 개 요

외국인근로자의 인권침해는 대부분이 단순기능 외국인근로자에 해당되는 문제로 귀결한다. 동포근로자는 직장선택의 자유가 있어 내국인과의 노동법적 보호의 차이가 많지 않고, 전문외국인력의 경우에는 일정한 부분에 노동법적 보호의 제약이 있지만, 그래도 취업비자나 다른 사업장 이동을 통해 해결이 가능하다. 그러나 단순기능 외국인근로자는 노동법 보호의 한계를 많이 가지고 있다. 단순기능 외국인근로자가 직면한 노동법적 보호가 취약한 사례는 다음과 같다.

① 개별적 근로관계에 있어 사업장 변경이 자유롭지 못하다. 근로계약 기간 3년 동안 사용자가 동의하지 않는 이상 사업장 이동이 불가능하다. ② 임금이 근속연수나 업무숙달과 상관없이 최저임금에 맞추어져 있다. ③ 1년 이상 근무한 경우 연차유급휴가가 발생함(근기법 제60조)에도 불구하고 대부분의 단순기능 외국인근로자는 연차유급휴가를 부여받지 못하고 있다. ④ 퇴직금의 경우에도 퇴직으로 인하여 수령하는 것이 아닌 외국인근로자가 본국으로 귀국할 경우만이 수령 요건이 된다.

집단적 노사관계에 있어서 노동3권이 보장되고 있고, 심지어 불법체류자의 노동조합이 공식적으로 노동조합으로 인정받아 활동 중에 있다.[643] 그럼에도 불구하고 기업단위의 외국인노동조합의 설립과 활동은 현실상 불가능하다. 이는 단순기능 외국인근로자는 모두 기간제 근로자이기 때문에 사용자가 얼마든지 외국인근로자의 단체행동을 통제할 수 있다. 따라서 실질적 노동3권의 행사가 불가능하다.

---

643) 대법원 2015.6.25, 2007두4995 전원합의체 (노동조합설립신고서 반려처분취소).

Regarding social insurances, ① Foreign workers are protected by means of mandatory subscription to Industrial Accident Compensation Insurance, but occupational accidents are not properly handled unless the work-related accident is a serious one.[644] ② Most workplaces do not subscribe their foreign workers to employment insurance as it is not mandatory. ③ For this reason, non-professional foreign workers cannot receive benefits during any unemployment period after termination of employment.[645]

I would like to examine these problems in detail and propose desirable solutions.

Ⅱ. Individual Employment Relations

1. Prohibition against Discrimination

In terms of criteria for determining discrimination, the court proposes two principles: treating the same things differently and different things in the same way. The first requirement in determining whether discriminatory treatment exists is that there must be an identical working group to compare with the situation facing the person claiming to have been discriminated against.[646] Second, discrimination can be deemed justifiable even in the same workplace with workers who are engaged in the same occupation when the discrimination is according to reasonable standards in consideration of various conditions such as the details of the work and the working conditions.[647]

(1) Application to foreign workers

As foreign workers have the right to a decent work environment, the same labor standards apply to them as to Korean workers.[648]

---

644) National Human Rights Commission of Korea, Investigation on the Human Rights Situation of Foreign Workers in the Construction Industry, Research Report on the Human Rights Situation in 2015, p. 9.

645) Supreme Court, Feb. 26, 2002. Verdict 2000da39063 (Reasonable discrimination is not discrimination).

646) Supreme Court ruling on Oct. 29, 2015: 2013 Da1051 (Different wages according to different hiring methods).

647) Supreme Court ruling on Feb. 26, 2002: 2000 da 39063 (Reasonable discrimination is not discrimination).

648) Constitutional Court of Korea ruling on Sept. 29, 2011: 2009 hunma 230352, (Merged); Lee, Sang-yoon, The Status of Foreign Workers under Labor Law, Justice, Korea Law Institute, Dec. 2002, p. 59.

사회보험 관련하여 ① 산재보험의 경우에 당연가입으로 보호가 되고 있지만, 산재사고가 중대재해가 아니고서는 산재처리가 제대로 되고 있지 않다.[644] 고용보험의 경우에도 외국인근로자의 고용보험 가입이 강제가입이 아니라 ② 임의가입으로 되어 있기 때문에 대부분의 사업장이 미가입 되어 있다. ③ 이로 인하여 사업장 변경을 위해 퇴직한 후 구직기간 동안 실업급여 혜택을 받을 수 없는 실정이다.[645]

위에서 언급한 내용들은 대표적인 권리구제의 취약한 사례로 문제를 구체적으로 살펴보고 바람직한 해결방안을 모색하고자 한다.

Ⅱ. 개별적 근로관계 분야

1. 차별금지

차별금지에 대한 '판단기준을 어떻게 보아야 하는가'에 있어 법원은 차별적 처우란 '같은 것을 다르게, 다른 것을 같게 취급하는 것'이라 정의하면서 다음의 두 가지 원칙을 제시하고 있다. 첫째, 차별적 처우에 해당하기 위해서는 우선 그 전제로써 차별을 받았다고 주장하는 사람과 그가 비교대상자로 지목하는 사람이 본질적으로 동일한 업무집단에 속해 있어야 한다.[646] 둘째, 같은 사업장에서 같은 직종에 근무하는 근로자집단이라고 하더라도 근로의 내용, 근무형태 등 제반여건을 고려하여 합리적인 기준을 정하여 차별하는 경우에는 정당한 차별로 인정하고 있다.[647]

(1) 외국인근로자에 대한 적용

외국인근로자는 "일할 근로환경에 관한 권리"로 가지므로, 내국인과 마찬가지로 근로기준법에 정한 근로기준을 적용받는다.[648]

---

644) 국가인권위원회, "건설업 종사 외국인근로자 인권상황 실태조사", 2015년도 인권상황 실태조사 연구용역보고서, 9면.

645) 전광석, 「한국사회보장법론」, 집현재, 2016, 197면.

646) 대법원 2015.10.29, 2013다1051(채용방식에 따른 급여차액 정당).

647) 대법원 2002.2.26, 2000다39063(합리적 기준 차별은 차별이 아님).

648) 헌법재판소 2011.9.29, 2009헌마230·352(병합); 이상윤, "외국인근로자의 노동법상 지위", 「저스티스」, 한국법학원, 2002.12, 59면.

Discrimination against foreign workers, visiting overseas Korean workers, and illegal workers without Korean nationality may occur. The Foreign Employment Act(FEA) stipulates that Workers shall not be treated unfairly because they are foreign workers(Article 22). However, there is a limit to enforcement of anti-discrimination regulations, as this article does not have a related penalty provision, and only covers non-professional workers in the employment-permit system. Therefore, discrimination based on nationality shall fall under the provision in Article 6 of the Labor Standards Act, "No discriminatory treatment of working conditions on the grounds of nationality shall be made" and related penalties.[649)] The Ministry of Employment and Labor(MOEL) also provides guidelines for the remedy of rights(identical to those that apply to Korean workers), even if there are violations of immigration law, such as the worker working illegally at workplaces covered by the Labor Standards Act.[650)] However, if there is a justifiable reason for discrimination, exceptions shall be granted. In principle, discrimination is prohibited, but the following is regarded as justified: ① Discrimination based on skill level, Korean language proficiency, and years of service in working conditions; ② Discrimination based on the contract period of fixed-term workers; and ③ Discrimination related to the Immigration Control Act in terms of visa details.

(2) Related issues

Here are some examples of discrimination over nationality. ① The Constitutional Court of Korea judged that in cases where industrial trainees have actual working relations under the name of training, under the direction and supervision of the employer, providing labor and receiving money in the form of allowances, it is difficult to justify excluding them from the main points of labor standards.[651)] ② A foreigner(Worker A) of Thai nationality entered the country as an industrial trainee but was injured while working illegally. Worker A filed for medical treatment, but the Labor Welfare Corporation did

649) Article 114 of the Labor Standards Act is the penalty provision, which stipulates that a fine of no more than 5 million won shall be imposed.

650) Administrative Interpretation by MOEL on Mar. 10, 2000.

651) Constitutional Court ruling Aug. 30, 2007: 2004 hunma 670 (Industrial Trainee System).

대한민국의 국적을 소유하지 않은 외국인근로자, 해외동포, 불법체류자 등을 대상으로 한 차별이 발생할 수 있다. 외국인고용법은 "사용자는 외국인근로자라는 이유로 부당하게 차별하여 처우하여서는 아니 된다(외고법 제22조)"라고 규정하고 있지만, 이에 대해 처벌규정이 없고 적용범위도 고용허가제와 관련된 단순기능 외국인 근로자에게만 적용되어 차별금지 규정을 집행하는 데에 한계가 있다. 따라서 국적에 의한 차별은 근로기준법 제6조는 "...국적을 이유로 근로조건에 대한 차별적 처우를 하지 못한다" 는 규정과 위반 시 관련 벌칙규정[649]에 따른다고 할 수 있다. 고용노동부에서도 근로기준법이 적용되는 사업장에서 일하는 불법체류자 등과 같이 출입국위반 사항이 있다고 하더라도 내국인과 동일하게 권리구제를 할 수 있도록 지침을 하달하고 있다.[650] 다만, 차별에 합리적인 이유가 있는 경우에는 그 예외가 인정된다. 원칙적으로 차별을 금지하고 있지만, ① 근로조건에 있어 숙련정도나 한국어활용정도, 근속연수 등에 따른 차별은 국적에 의한 차별이 아닌 정당한 차별로 인정하고 있다. ② 기간제 근로자의 계약기간에 따른 차별이 있을 수 있다. ③ 출입국관리법 체류비자관리에 의한 차별 등은 정당한 차별로 인정된다.

(2) 외국인근로자의 적용 사례

국적에 의한 차별의 사례로 ① 헌법재판소는 산업연수생이 연수라는 미명 하에 사업주의 지시·감독을 받으면서 사실상 노무를 제공하고 수당 명목의 금품을 수령하는 등 실질적인 근로관계에 있는 경우, 근로기준법이 보장한 근로기준 중 주요사항을 외국인 산업연수생에 대하여만 적용되지 않도록 하는 것은 합리적인 근거를 찾기 어렵다고 하여 근로기준법을 일부 적용하지 않는 것은 위헌이라고 판단하였다.[651] ② A는 태국 국적 외국인으로 산업연수 체류자격으로 입국하였으나, 체류기간을 초과하여 불법체류자로 근무하던 중에 부상을 입었다. A는 요양신청을 하였으나 공단은 A가 불법 취업한 외국인이라는 이유로

649) 벌칙규정은 근로기준법 제114조로 '500만원 이하의 벌금에 처한다'라고 규정.
650) 노동부 행정해석, 근기 68201-691, 2000.3.10.
651) 헌법재판소 2007.8.30, 2004헌마670 결정 (산업연수생세도).

not permit the accident to be deemed an industrial accident because Worker A was an illegally-employed foreigner. However, the Supreme Court made it clear that while illegal workers are subject to crackdowns, they are still protected by labor law for work already provided.[652] ③ On May 3, 2005, foreign workers in Seoul and Gyeonggi-do filed for establishment of a labor union with the Seoul Regional Labor Administration, but their application for establishment was rejected because some members were illegal workers. A protracted court dispute over recognition of the union took place, but on June 25, 2015, the Supreme Court judges collectively recognized establishment of a union consisting of illegal workers.[653] These three cases apply labor law to foreign workers in the same way as for Koreans, but the origin of discrimination came from their status as foreign workers.

There are many cases of discrimination against workers offering general labor because they are foreigners, on the basis of nationality, differences in skill, and their fixed-term employment. In practice, foreign workers are paid the minimum wage regardless of their work experience or length of service. In contrast, Koreans are paid at least twice the minimum wage and in accordance with how long they have been providing work. This can be regarded as discrimination by nationality.[654] Although discrimination is prohibited on the basis of nationality, it is difficult to prove that discrimination against foreign workers is on the basis of nationality.[655]

2. Annual Paid Leave

The provisions of annual leave for non-professional foreign workers are not specified in the standard labor contract[656] and such leave is rarely granted in reality. Annual leave, however, is an essential part of a labor contract to be included under Article 17 of the

---

652) Supreme Court ruling Sept. 15, 1995: 94 nu 12067 (Rejection of accident as work-related).

653) Supreme Court ruling June 25, 2015: 2007 doo 4995 (Cancellation of rejection of union establishment application).

654) Lee, Jun-il, 「Human Rights Act - Social Issues and Human Rights」, 7th ed., Hongmunsa, August 2017, p. 4.

655) Lee, Soo-yeon, Work from Female Foreign Workers and their Universal Rights, *Korean Social Law Review*, No. 33, Korean Social Law Association, Dec. 12, 2017, p. 128.

656) FEA Enforcement Regulations, Form No. 6 (Standard Labor Contract).

산재 불승인을 하였다. 그러나 대법원은 불법체류는 단속의 대상임을 명백히 하고 있으나, 이미 제공된 사실적 행위의 노동에 대해서는 노동법의 보호가 있어야 한다는 취지에서 불법체류자도 산재보험이 적용된다고 판결하였다.[652] ③ 서울과 경기도의 불법체류자로 구성된 외국인근로자들이 2005년 5월 3일 서울지방노동청에 노동조합 설립신고를 제출하였으나 불법체류자라는 이유로 거부당하였다. 이 노동조합 인정여부에 대해 장기간 법원에서 다툼이 있었으나 2015년 6월 25일 결국 대법원 합의체 판결에서 불법체류자들로 구성된 노동조합의 설립을 인정하였다.[653] 위의 3가지 사례는 내국인과 동일하게 노동법을 적용한 사례이지만, 그 발단은 외국인이라는 이유로 차별을 받은 사례이다.

외국인이라는 이유로 차별받는 사례가 일반노동의 저변에 많이 존재하고 있다. 외국인근로자는 국적이 다르다는 이유, 기능 숙달정도의 차이, 기간제 근로자라는 이유 등으로 차별을 받고 있고, 실무에서는 외국인근로자들의 경우 업무숙달 정도나 장기 근속여부와 상관없이 최저임금을 지급하고 있다. 이에 반해 내국인들의 경우 최저임금의 최소 2배 이상의 임금을 받고 근로를 제공한다. 이는 국적에 의한 차별이라 볼 수 있다.[654] 특히, 국적을 이유로 차별을 금지하고 있지만 외국인근로자에 대한 차별에 대해 국적을 이유로 차별하였다고 입증하기가 어렵기 때문에 차별금지의 적용하는데 어려움이 있다.[655]

2. 연차유급휴가

단순기능 외국인근로자에게 연차휴가 규정은 표준근로계약서에도 명시되어 있지 않고,[656] 실제로 지급하는 경우도 거의 없다. 그러나 연차휴가는 근로기준법 제17조의 근로계약의 작성 중 필수기재사항이고, 당연히 근로의 대가로 지

652) 대법원 1995.9.15, 94누12067(요양불승인처분취소).
653) 대법원 2015.6.25, 2007두4995 전원합의체 판결 (노조설립신고 반려처분취소).
654) 이준일, 「인권법 -사회적 이슈와 인권-」, 제7판, 홍문사, 2017.8, 4면.
655) 이수연, "외국인여성 근로자의 노동과 보편적 권리 보장", 「사회법연구」 제33호, 한국사회법학회, 2017.12, 128면.
656) 외고법 시행규칙 별지 제6호 서식(표준근로계약서).

Labor Standards Act, and of course this legal leave must be granted in return for work.

Annual leave is intended to be in addition to paid weekly leave in order to ensure worker health and cultural experience.[657] The Constitutional Court stipulates that If a break or weekday is primarily intended for the physiological recovery of workers who have accumulated physical and mental fatigue due to daily or weekly work, annual paid leave will be taken without a reduction in wages. By allowing them to make their own decisions, they ensure that workers are free from work for a certain period of time and have the opportunity to enjoy social and cultural life.[658] In response, the Supreme Court explained, "It is intended to provide time for mental and physical recreational opportunities and improve quality of life by exempting workers from working for a certain period of time."[659] Therefore, annual leave can be said to improve the quality of life for workers by granting time to engage in cultural aspects of life and a rest from work.[660]

(1) Application to foreign workers

The international standards for annual paid leave and the standards in Korea's Labor Standards Act can be divided and compared by ① vacation days and occurrence requirements, ② method of use, ③ provision of annual paid leave, and ④ compensation for unused annual leave.

On an international basis, the ILO(International Labour Organization) has adopted Convention No. 52 Annual Paid Leave(1936) and Convention No. 132 Annual Paid Leave(1970)(C132) for annual leave. ① In any case, in relation to the number of leave days and occurrence requirements, a minimum of three weeks must be granted for one year(Article 3 of C132). Workers who have not worked for a year have the right to paid leave in proportion to the period worked(Article 4). ② In relation to the use of annual

657) Lim, Jong-Ryul, Labor Law, 17th Ed., Parkyoungsa, 2019, p. 454.

658) Constitutional Court ruling on May 28, 2015: 2013 hunma 619 (Purpose for annual leave).

659) Supreme Court Dec. 26, 2003. Sentence 2011Da4629 Decision (Purpose for annual leave).

660) Kim, Hong-Young, Improvement of Annual Leave for Securing Rest, Labor Law Research, First Half of 2016, No. 40, Seoul National University Labor Law Association, p. 165.

급해야 하는 법정휴가이다.

연차휴가는 근로자의 건강하고 문화적인 생활을 실현하기 위하여 유급 주휴일과 별도로 유급휴가를 부여하려는 것이다.[657] 헌법재판소도 연차휴가의 취지를, "휴게시간이나 주휴일은 하루 또는 일주일의 노동으로 육체적·정신적 피로가 누적된 근로자들의 생리적인 회복을 위한 것이 주목적이라면, 연차유급휴가는 임금 삭감 없이 휴가기간을 스스로 결정할 수 있게 함으로써 근로자들이 노동으로부터 일정기간 해방되고 사회적·문화적 시민생활을 영위할 수 있는 기회를 보장하기 위한 것이다."라고 기술하고 있다.[658] 이에 대해 대법원도 "근로자에게 일정 기간 근로의무를 면제함으로써 정신적·육체적 휴양의 기회를 제공하고 문화적 생활의 향상을 기하려는데 그 취지가 있다."라고 설명한다.[659] 따라서 연차휴가에 대한 정의는 근로에 대한 휴식의 측면에 문화적 생활의 측면을 덧붙여 근로자의 생활의 질을 향상시키는 것이라 할 수 있다.[660]

(1) 외국인근로자에 대한 적용

연차유급휴가 제도에 대한 국제기준과 우리나라의 근로기준법상 기준에 대해 ① 휴가일수 및 발생요건, ② 사용방법, ③ 연차유급휴가 보장, ④ 미사용 연차휴가에 대한 보상으로 나누어 비교해 볼 수 있다.

국제기준으로 ILO(국제노동기구)는 연차휴가에 대해 제52호 연차유급휴가 협약(1936년)과 제132호 연차유급휴가 개정협약(1970년)을 채택하였다. ① 휴가일수 및 발생요건과 관련하여 어떠한 경우라도 1년에 대해 최소 3주 이상을 주어야 하고(제132호 연차유급휴가협약 제3조), 1년에 미달되는 근로자는 당해 연도에는 당해 연도의 근무기간에 비례하는 유급휴가를 받을 권리를 가진다(동협약 제4조). ② 연차휴가의 사용과 관련하여 연차휴가는 분할 사용이 가능하지만 '적어도 중단되지 아니하는 2주'로 구성되어야 하며(동협약 제8조), 휴가를 받을

---

657) 임종률, 「노동법」, 제18판, 박영사, 2020, 454면.
658) 헌법재판소 2015.5.28, 2013헌마619(연차휴가의 취지).
659) 대법원 2003.12.26, 2011다4629(연차휴가의 취지).
660) 김홍영, 휴식 보장을 위한 연차휴가의 제도개선론, 「노동법연구」, 2016 상반기 제40호, 서울대 노동법연구회, 165면.

leave, it may be divided, but should consist of at least two uninterrupted weeks(Article 8) and must be given within one year from the date of eligibility for leave(Article 9). ③ Annual paid leave during working days must be paid(Article 7). ④ For unused annual leave, workers who have worked for the minimum working period(six months) shall be entitled to paid leave, or in lieu of paid leave, shall be compensated(Article 11).[661)]

According to the Korean Labor Standards Act, annual paid leave(Article 60) presupposes the use of leave, but specifies compensation when not used. ① Looking at the number of vacation days and the occurrence requirements, 15 days of annual paid leave should be given to workers who work at least 80% of one year. Workers who have worked for at least three years must be given paid leave, plus one day for every two years of continuous work in excess of the first year, with a maximum of 25 days(paragraph 4). ② In the method of use, annual leave should be granted at the time when the worker requests it, but if the leave at the time requested by the worker is seriously disruptive to operation of the business, the period may be changed(paragraph 5). Paid leave can be used continuously over a specific day or several days. Here, if the worker requests specific dates(right to claim leave), the employer can adjust it in consideration of the work situation(right to change timing). ③ The guarantee of annual paid leave refers to the leave being granted on working days for the worker(paragraph 5). Therefore, weekly holidays or contracted holidays shall not be included when calculating how much annual leave is used. ④ With respect to compensation for unused annual leave, the leave shall be forfeited if it is not used within one year. However, this shall not apply in cases where the worker concerned has been prevented from using the leave due to any cause attributable to the employer(paragraph 7). This means that if a worker fails to use annual paid leave, the employer must pay an allowance for unused annual paid leave.[662)]

---

661) Park, Il-hoon, 「A Study on the Legal Aspects of the Annual Paid Leave System」, Master's Thesis, Korea University Graduate School, Dec. 2014, pp. 125-140.

662) Supreme Court ruling Dec. 26, 2013: 2011 Da 4629 (Unused annual paid leave allowance is wage); Lee, Su-yeon, Ensuring Labor and Universal Rights of Foreign Women Workers, p. 112; Ministry of Employment and Labor, "Employment Permit System," p. 25.

자격이 발생한 시점부터 1년 이내에 주어야 한다(동협약 제9조). ③ 연차유급휴가는 근무일 중에 유급으로 주어야 한다(동협약 제7조). ④ 미사용 연차휴가에 대해서는 최저 근무기간(6개월)을 근로한 근로자는 고용종료 시에 유급휴가를 받지 않은 근무기간에 비례하는 유급휴가나 이에 갈음하는 보상을 받는다(동협약 제11조).라고 규정하고 있다.[661)]

우리나라 근로기준법상 연차유급휴가(근기법 제60조)는 휴가사용을 전제로 하지만, 미 사용시 금전보상을 명시하고 있다. ① 휴가일수 및 발생요건을 살펴보면 1년간 80% 이상 출근한 근로자에게 15일의 연차유급휴가를 주어야 한다(근기법 제60조 제1항). 3년 이상 계속하여 근로한 근로자에게 최초 1년을 초과하는 계속근로연수 매 2년에 대해 1일을 가산한 유급휴가를 주어야 하고, 최대 25일을 한도로 한다(제4항). ② 사용방법을 보면 연차휴가는 근로자가 청구한 시기에 유급휴가를 주어야 하지만, 근로자가 청구한 시기에 휴가를 주는 것이 사업 운영에 막대한 지장이 있는 경우에는 그 시기를 변경할 수 있다(제5항). 유급휴가는 특정일 또는 여러 날에 걸쳐 연속적으로 사용할 수 있다. 여기서 근로자는 원하는 날짜를 지정하여 휴가를 청구하면(휴가청구권) 사용자는 업무의 상황을 고려하여 휴가 청구일을 조정할 수 있다(시기변경권). ③ 연차유급휴가 보장과 관련하여 연차유급휴가는 근로자의 근무일에 유급으로 보장해주어야 한다(제5항). 따라서 연차유급휴가는 주휴일이나 무급휴무일, 약정휴일에 부담하여서는 아니 된다. ④ 미사용 연차휴가에 대한 보상과 관련하여 연차유급휴가는 1년간 행사하지 아니하면 소멸된다. 다만, 사용자의 귀책사유로 사용하지 못한 경우에는 그러하지 아니하다(제7항). 이는 근로자가 연차유급휴가를 사용하지 못한 경우에 사용자는 연차유급휴가 미사용 수당을 지급해야 한다는 것이다.[662)]

---

661) 박일훈, 「연차유급휴가제도의 법적 쟁점에 관한 연구」, 고려대학교 대학원 석사논문, 2014.12, 125~140면.

662) 대법원 2013.12.26, 2011다4629(미사용 연차유급휴가 수당은 임금이다.); 이수연, "외국인 여성 근로자의 노동과 보편적 권리 보장", 112면; 고용노동부, 「알기 쉬운 고용허가제」, 25면.

(2) Related issues

Annual paid leave must also apply to foreign workers.[663] In the Foreign Employment Act(FEA) Enforcement Rules(Annex 6), the Standard Labor Contract does not specify annual paid leave, which is mandatory under the Labor Standards Act. It prescribes that items not stipulated in the contract will follow the items stipulated in the Labor Standards Act. In reality, most business owners do not grant annual paid leave to non-professional foreign workers. A report by Amnesty International in October 2014 states, "No migrant worker interviewed by Amnesty International received any annual leave or annual leave allowance."[664]

Non-professional foreign workers are also never compensated for annual paid leave. On the other hand, the annual paid leave regulations are applied to professional foreign workers in the same way as they are for Koreans. In 2011, the Supreme Court acknowledged the employment status of native English instructors in a lawsuit over their status filed by 24 native English instructors, and decided that the employer had to pay weekly allowance, annual leave work allowance and severance pay for the working period.[665] Unused annual leave allowances are also to be reflected in the average wage for calculating severance pay. The right of non-professional foreign workers to annual paid leave must be enforced, and if they do not use annual paid leave, they must be paid an allowance equivalent to the number of annual paid leave days. When employment is terminated, any unpaid annual leave allowance and severance pay reflected in average wage calculation can be recalculated and the payment made for the difference, with the employer paying their final wages and allowances within 14 days after the date the employment is terminated. Any delay in payment shall be subject to 20% interest per year as defined by the Labor Standards Act(Article 37).

---

663) Choi, Hong-Yeop, Long-term Employment of Foreign Workers, Labor Law No. 48, Korean Labor Law Association, Dec. 2013, p. 444.

664) Amnesty International, Exploitation and Forced Labor of Foreign Migrant Workers in the Agricultural Industry, Document No. ASA 25/004/2014, Oct. 2014, p. 30.

665) Supreme Court ruling Jun. 11, 2015: 2014 Da 88161 (Employment status of native English instructors).

(2) 외국인근로자의 적용 사례

연차유급휴가는 외국인근로자에게도 당연히 적용되어야 한다.[663] 외국인고용법 시행규칙(별지서식 제6호)의 「표준근로계약서」에는 근로기준법상 필수기재사항인 연차유급휴가 규정이 명시되어 있지 않고, 제11호 "이 계약에서 정하지 않은 사항은 「근로기준법」에서 정하는 바에 따른다." 라고만 규정되어 있다. 또한, 현실에서는 대다수 사업주가 단순기능 외국인근로자에게 연차유급휴가를 지급하고 있지 않고 있다. 2014년 10월 국제앰네스티(Amnesty International)의 보고서에 따르면, "국제앰네스티가 면담한 이주노동자 중 어느 누구도 연차휴가나 연차휴가근로수당을 받은 사람이 없었다."라고 기록하고 있다.[664]

단순기능 외국인근로자들은 연차유급휴가에 대해 전혀 보상받지 못하고 있다. 반면, 전문외국 인력의 경우에는 내국인과 동일하게 연차유급휴가 규정을 적용 받고 있다. 2011년 대법원은 원어민 강사 24명이 제기한 근로자지위 확인소송에서 원어민 강사들의 근로자성을 인정하였고, 근무기간에 대해 주휴수당, 연차휴가근로수당과 퇴직금을 지급하라고 판결하였다.[665] 퇴직금 계산에서 있어서는 미사용 연차휴가수당을 퇴직금계산을 위한 평균임금에 반영하였다. 다시 말해서 전문외국인력에게도 내국인과 동일하게 근로기준법을 적용하였다는 점이다. 따라서 단순기능 외국인근로자도 연차유급휴가를 보장해주어야 하고, 연차유급휴가 미사용 시에는 연차유급휴가 일수에 상당하는 수당을 지급해야 한다. 또한, 퇴직한 경우에는 미사용 연차휴가 수당과 퇴직금 계산을 위한 평균임금 계산에 반영한 퇴직금을 재계산하여 그 차액에 대해 지급을 청구할 수 있고, 퇴사일로부터 14일이 경과한 다음 날부터 지급하는 날까지 근로기준법에서 정한 연 20%의 비율로 계산한 지연손해금을 지급해야 한다(근기법 제37조).

---

663) 최홍엽, "외국인근로자의 장기간 고용과 법적쟁점", 「노동법학」 제48호, 한국노동법학회, 2013.12, 444면.

664) 국제앰네스티, 「한국 농축산업 이주노동자 착취와 강제노동」, 문서번호: ASA 25/004/2014, 2014.10, 30면.

665) 대법원 2015.6.11, 2014다88161(원어민 강사의 근로자 지위 확인).

3. Minimum Wage

(1) Application to foreign workers

The purpose of the Minimum Wage Act(MWA) is to provide financial stability to workers and improve workforce quality by guaranteeing a minimum level of wages. It applies to all businesses or workplaces(Article 1 and 3). The Labor Standards Act applies some regulations to businesses or workplaces that employ five or more permanent workers, while the Minimum Wage Act applies to all workplaces with at least one worker. The MWA also applies to foreign workers, including overseas Korean workers. The MWA does not apply to additional allowances for overtime, holiday work or night work, or meal or housing allowances, but fixed and regularly-paid meal allowances are considered part of ordinary wage(Articles 5 and 6).

(2) Related issues

Disputes in standard work contracts for non-professional foreign workers are often around an employer deducting the cost of lodging from ordinary wage. According to recent MOEL administrative guidelines,[666)] meal allowances can be deducted from wages, but the limit is 20% of the monthly ordinary wage. As a result, wages can be withheld for accommodations and meals. In fact, this can be seen as a violation of the principle of full payment of wages.[667)] In addition, foreign workers in rural areas are often excluded from standards on maximum working hours, rest and holidays under Article 63 of the Labor Standards Act.[668)]

---

666) MOEL, Working Guidelines on Accommodation and Housing for Foreign Workers and Collecting Related Costs, Office in charge of Foreign Workers, Feb. 6, 2017.

667) Article 43 of the LSA and Supreme Court ruling Oct. 23, 2001: 2001 da 25184; Lee, Soo-yeon, Work from Female Foreign Workers and their Universal Rights, p. 113.

668) Amnesty International, Exploitation and Forced Labor of Foreign Migrant Workers in the Agricultural Industry, p. 30.

3. 최저임금

(1) 외국인근로자에 대한 적용

최저임금법은 근로자에 대하여 임금의 최저수준을 보장하여 근로자의 생활안정과 노동력의 질적 향상을 위하는 목적으로 근로자를 사용하는 모든 사업 또는 사업장에 적용된다(최임법 제1조, 제3조). 근로기준법은 일부 규정을 5인 이상 상시근로자를 사용하는 사업 또는 사업장에 적용하고 있는데에 반하여, 최저임금법은 1인 이상 모든 사업장에 적용된다. 특히 외국인근로자도 이 최저임금법에 적용을 받으므로, 단순기능 외국인근로자나 방문취업 근로자의 경우에 최저임금을 기준으로 임금이 책정되고 있다. 연장근로, 휴일근로나 야간근로에 따른 가산수당, 급식비나 주택수당 등은 최저임금에 적용되지 않으나, 여기서 고정적이고 정기적으로 지급되는 급식비는 통상임금에 적용된다(최임법 제5조, 제6조).

(2) 외국인근로자의 적용 사례

최저임금과 관련하여 단순기능 외국인근로자의 표준근로계약서는 숙식비 비용을 삭감함으로써 최저임금법 위반과 관련하여 다툼이 많이 발생한다. 최근 고용노동부의 행정해석을 보면,[666] 숙식비를 임금에서 공제할 수 있도록 하고 있으며 다만, 월 통상임금의 20% 한도로 하고 있다. 따라서 최저임금 기준으로 임금이 책정 되고, 이 최지임금에시 숙소와 식사에 해당하는 비용을 원천징수 할 수 있다고 업무지도를 하고 있다. 사실상 이는 임금전액불 지급원칙에 대해 위반의 소지가 있다고 볼 수 있다.[667] 또한, 농어촌지역의 외국인근로자들은 근로기준법 제63조에 해당되는 근로시간, 휴게, 휴일의 적용제외 대상자이므로 장기간 근로임에도 불구하고 최저임금에도 못 미치는 임금을 받는 경우가 많다.[668]

---

666) 고용노동부 행정해석, "외국인근로자 숙식정보 제공 및 비용징수 관련 업무지침" 외국인력담당관실, 2017.2.6.

667) 관련 근거는 근기법 제43조와 대법원 2001.10.23, 2001다25184(임금 전액지급의 원칙에 대한 예외); 이수연, "외국인여성 근로자의 노동과 보편적 권리 보장", 113면.

668) 국세앰네스티, 「한국 농축산업 이주노동자 착취와 강제노동」, 30면

Ⅲ. Collective Labor Relations

1. Guarantee of the Three Labor Rights

The purpose of establishing a union is to improve working conditions through exercise of the three labor rights. Working conditions refers to the details of labor contracts such as wages and working hours, while other economic and social status of workers refers to the overall living profits of workers including working conditions such as welfare and social security within the company.[669)]

Foreign workers cannot afford to improve working conditions at the current minimum wage unless they ask for a wage increase through collective activities of the union. Therefore, to improve their working conditions, it is necessary to establish labor unions and engage in collective activities. Foreign workers are also entitled to the right to independent association, the right to collective bargaining, and the right to collective action(the three labor rights) guaranteed under Article 33(1) of the Constitution. Foreign workers can join a labor union or create a union consisting only of foreigners.

Until a recent ruling, the Ministry of Employment and Labor stated that it was impossible for illegal workers to establish or join a labor union.[670)] On April 24, 2005, 91 foreign workers living in Seoul, Gyeonggi, and Incheon sat up the Seoul Gyeonggi Incheon Migrant Workers' Union and submitted a report of establishment to the Seoul Regional Labor Office, but their report was rejected. Then, the Migrant Workers' Union filed a lawsuit against the Labor Office in 2005 for its rejection, but the regional court dismissed their lawsuit. However, the Appeal Court and the Supreme Court canceled that dismissal.[671)]

The lawsuit against the rejection of union establishment was finally decided by the Supreme Court on 25 June 2015 along with the decision of the High Court that a union

---

669) Kim, Hyung-bae, Labor Law, 24th Ed., Parkyoungsa, 2015, p. 131.

670) The position of the MOEL and the First Deliberation was that the illegal workers could not have the three labor rights recognized (Seoul Administrative Court ruling on Feb. 7, 2006: 2005 goohap 18266: Union rejected).

671) Supreme Court ruling on June 25, 2015: 2007 doo 4955 (Labor union of illegal foreign workers recognized).

Ⅲ. 집단적 노사관계법

1. 외국인근로자에 노동 3권 보장

노동조합의 설립목적은 노동3권의 행사를 통해 근로조건의 향상을 위한 것이다. '근로조건'이라 함은 임금, 근로시간 등 근로계약 내용을 말하고, '그밖에 근로자의 경제적, 사회적 지위'란 기업 내 복지, 사회보장 등 근로조건 이외 근로자의 생활이익 전반을 말한다.[669)]

외국인근로자는 노동조합의 집단 활동을 통하여 임금인상을 요구하지 않으면 현재의 최저임금에 맞추어진 근로조건을 개선할 여지가 없다. 따라서 외국인근로자의 근로조건 향상을 위해서는 노동조합의 설립과 활동이 필요하다. 외국인근로자도 헌법 제33조 제1항에 보장된 자주적인 단결권, 단체교섭권, 단체행동권을 보장받는다. 노동조합에 가입하거나 외국인들만으로 구성된 노동조합도 만들 수 있다.

외국인 불법체류자의 경우에도 노동조합의 설립 또는 가입이 허용되고 있다. 최근 판결이 있기 전까지는 불법체류자의 노동조합 가입 및 활동에 대해 고용노동부는 노동조합의 설립이 불가하다는 입장이었다.[670)] 이와 관련된 사건으로 2005년 4월 24일 서울, 경기, 인천 지역에 거주하는 외국인근로자 91명이 '서울경기인천 이주근로자 노동조합'을 설립하고 서울지방노동청에 설립신고서를 제출하였으나 거부되었다. 이에 이주노동조합은 2005년 노동청을 상대로 노동조합설립신고 반려처분 취소소송을 제기하였고 패소판결을 받았지만, 항소심과 최종심은 초심판결을 취소하였다.[671)]

본 노동조합설립 거부처분에 대한 소송은 마침내 2015년 6월 25일 대법원 전원합의체 판결을 통해 고등법원의 판결 취지를 유지하는 결정을 받으면서, 불법체류 외국인근로자로 구성된 노동조합도 노동3권을 보장받을 수 있는 길

669) 김형배, 「노동법」 24판, 박영사, 2015, 131면.

670) 고용노동부와 제1심의 입장은 불법체류자는 노동3권을 인정할 수 없다는 입장이었다(서울행정법원 2006.2.7, 2005구합18266, 원고패소).

671) 대법원 2015.6.25, 2007두4955(불법체류 외국인 노동조합 설립 인정).

of foreign workers which included illegal workers was acceptable as a legitimate labor union so as to guarantee the three labor rights. The Supreme Court stated, According to the former The Trade Union Act, workers are those who provide work under subordinate relations with others and live on wages in return. This should include not only those employed by a particular employer, but also those who need the three labor rights protected, including those who are temporarily unemployed or looking for work. It recognizes the broader concept of workers in the Trade Union Act than that found in the Labor Standards Act, and recognizes those living on wages, temporary unemployed, and even job seekers that do not belong to a specific workplace.[672)]

Regarding violation of the Immigration Act, the Supreme Court stated, The Immigration Act is to prohibit the actual act of hiring foreigners without employment qualifications. It is hard to prohibit legal effects such as rights under labor laws accorded to workers in a working relationship already established.[673)] Even though a foreign worker is an illegal worker, the court has confirmed that they have the right to enjoy workers' rights under The Trade Union Act.

2. Related issues

Foreign workers can also seek to improve their working conditions by forming labor unions and signing collective agreements through collective bargaining.[674)] Indeed, it is not easy for individual foreign workers to receive remedy for disputes with an employer. Language is only part of the problem. The real issue is often the vulnerability to disadvantageous retaliation by that employer. One The Trade Union Activity is to allow foreign workers to protect themselves. For this reason, it is a justifiable solution for foreign workers to establish a labor union to secure and improve working conditions. In fact, some other foreign workers(native English speakers) established a labor union in

672) Lim, Jong-Ryul, Labor Law, pp. 53-55; Korean Labor Law Research Group, A Commentary on the Trade Union and Labor Relations Adjustment Act (I), Parkyoung-Sa, 2015, p. 75.

673) Supreme Court ruling on June 25, 2015: 2007 doo 4955 (Labor union of illegal foreign workers recognized).

674) Lim, Jong-Ryul, Labor Law, p. 51.

이 열렸다. 대법원은 "구 노조법상 근로자란 타인과의 사용종속관계 하에서 근로를 제공하고 그 대가로 임금 등을 받아 생활하는 사람을 의미한다. 특정한 사용자에게 고용되어 현실적으로 취업하고 있는 사람뿐만 아니라 일시적으로 실업 상태에 있는 사람이나 구직 중인 사람을 포함하여 노동3권을 보장할 필요성이 있는 사람도 여기에 포함되는 것으로 보아야 한다"고 하였다. 이는 노조법상의 근로자 개념을 근로기준법상의 근로자보다 폭넓게 보아야 하고 특정사업장에 소속되어 있지 않더라도 임금으로 생활하는 자, 일시적인 실업자, 구직자까지도 노조법상 근로자에 포함하는 광의의 근로자 개념을 인정하고 있다.[672)]

특히 출입국관리법의 위반에 대해서 대법원은 "출입국관리 법령에서 외국인고용제한규정을 두고 있는 것은 취업자격 없는 외국인의 고용이라는 사실적 행위 자체를 금지하고자 하는 것뿐이지, 나아가 취업자격 없는 외국인이 사실상 제공한 근로에 따른 권리나 이미 형성된 근로관계에 있어서 근로자로서의 신분에 따른 노동관계법상 제반 권리 등의 법률효과까지 금지하려는 것으로 보기는 어렵다"[673)]고 판시하면서 외국인근로자가 불법체류자임에도 불구하고, 근로를 제공하여 발생한 권리나 노조법상 근로자의 권리를 향유할 권한이 있다는 점을 확인하고 있다.

2. 외국인근로자의 적용 사례

외국인근로자들도 스스로 노동조합을 만들고 단체교섭을 통해 단체협약을 체결하여 근로조건의 향상을 꾀할 수 있다.[674)] 실제로 외국인근로자 개인이 개별 노동문제로 인하여 회사를 상대로 권리구제를 받는 것이 쉽지가 않다. 언어 문제도 있지만, 사용자의 불이익처분으로 인해 계속근로가 불가능한 경우가 많기 때문이다. 외국인근로자들을 스스로 지켜 줄 수 있는 것이 노동조합 활동이다. 이러한 이유로 외국인근로자들이 노동조합을 설립하여 근로조건 개선 및 확보를 하는 것이 권리구제를 받는 합리적인 해결책이다.

---

672) 임종률, 「노동법」 제18판, 박영사, 2020, 53~55면; 노동법실무연구회, 「노동조합 및 노동관계조정법 주해」(I), 박영사, 2015, 75면.

673) 대법원 2015.6.25, 2007두4995 전원합의체 판결(노동조합설립 반려처분취소)

674) 임종률, 「노동법」, 51면.

Avalon Institute in Yeonsu-gu, Incheon in September 2009, and secured better working conditions through collective bargaining.[675)] In November that year, when six native English instructors received late overtime pay from their employer upon orders from the Ministry of Employment and Labor, the employer of the school fired the lead instructor. As a result, concerned about their own job security, the remaining five English instructors set up a labor union to guarantee fair treatment.[676)] The labor union of these English instructors was established under the protection of the Trade Union Act in Korea, and collective agreements were also signed through collective bargaining. However, the institute recruited new native English instructors on the premise that they would not join the labor union, and the original instructors' contract periods expired eventually, so the number of union members gradually decreased to none. Looking at the process of establishment, activity, and extinction of the native instructor's union, it is confirmed that the right to exercise the three labor rights is difficult in reality for foreign workers.

There has been much debate about the recognition of unions established for illegal foreign workers. The logic behind such recognition is that, first, foreign workers without qualifications for employment can also exercise the three labor rights to improve working conditions because they are still workers under the Trade Union & Labor Relations Adjustment Act(The Trade Union Act).[677)] Second, under the Immigration Act, the determination of an illegal stay is only for enforcement purposes, and the basic rights of foreign workers must not be restricted.[678)] Third, restricting the three labor rights for

---

675) ① Report on the establishment of a labor union (Director of Yeonsu-gu, Incheon Metropolitan City): Document number - Regional Economic Division-40378, Nov. 23, 2009; ② Jung, Bong-soo, Establishment of Foreign Instructor Labor Union, Labor Law Magazine, Jan. 2010; Collective Agreement with Foreign Instructor Union, Labor Law Magazine, Aug. 2010, ③ Incheon Regional Labor Relations Commission, Application for Mediation of Labor Disputes in Avalon Education Union (2010 Mediation 6), May 13, 2010.

676) Jung, Bongsoo,「A Study on the Worker Status of Native Korean Instructors」, Master's Thesis, Graduate School of Labor, Korea University, Dec. 2013, p. 87.

677) Jun, Hyung-Bae, Labor Rights of Foreign Workers, Korean Labor Law Review, No. 18, Korean Society of Comparative Labor Law, Apr. 4, 2010, p. 150.

678) Supreme Court ruling Sept. 15, 1995: 94 noo 12067 (Application of Industrial Accident Compensation Insurance to illegal foreign workers), which defined the nature of the Immigration Act as an enforcement regulation; Choi, Hong-Yeop, The Current Status and Issues of Foreign Employment, Labor Law Research, Seoul National University Labor Law Research Association, Dec. 2008, p. 207.

실제 합법적인 체류자격을 가진 외국인근로자(원어민 강사)가 2009년 9월 인천광역시 연수구의 아발론학원에 노동조합을 설립하였고, 단체교섭을 통한 단체협약까지 체결하여 근로조건을 확보한 사례가 있다.[675] 2009년 11월, 원어민 강사 6명이 미지급된 연장근로수당을 고용노동부에 진정하여 수령하게 되자, 학원 원장이 해당 주동자 원어민 강사를 해고하였다. 이에 고용불안을 느낀 원어민 강사 5명이 고용보장을 위해 노동조합을 설립하게 되었다.[676] 이 원어민 강사들의 노동조합은 우리나라의 노동조합법 보호 아래 설립되었고, 또한, 단체교섭을 통해 단체협약까지 체결하였다. 그러나 학원 원장이 새로운 원어민 강사를 노동조합 가입하지 않을 것을 전제로 채용하였고, 기존의 조합원인 원어민 강사들이 계약기간이 만료 되었을 때, 근로계약을 갱신해주지 않아 학원을 그만두게 됨에 따라 조합원이 점차 줄어들어 노동조합이 소멸하게 되었다. 이 원어민 외국인강사의 노동조합 설립, 활동, 소멸 과정을 보면서 외국인 근로자의 노동3권의 행사가 현실에서 어렵다는 사실을 확인할 수 있었다.

불법체류 외국인근로자의 노동조합에 대한 설립의 인정여부에 대해 많은 논쟁이 있었다. 인정해야 한다는 논리는 첫째, 취업자격이 없는 외국인근로자도 노조법상 근로자이므로 근로조건의 개선을 위한 노동3권을 행사할 수 있다.[677] 둘째, 출입국관리법상 불법체류의 신분은 행정 목적상 단속기준에 불과하므로 외국인근로자의 기본권을 제한할 수 없다는 것이다.[678] 셋째, 불법체류자의 노동3권을 제한하는 것은 불법적인 고용을 유인하여 외국인근로자에 대한 인권침해와 인권유린을 방관한다고 할 수 있다.[679] 이에 반해 불법체류자의 노동조

675) ① 노동조합 설립신고(인천광역시 연수구청장) 지역경제과-40378, 2009.11.23; ② 정봉수, "외국인 강사 노동조합 설립", 2010.1, "외국인 강사노동조합의 단체협약 체결" 2010.8, 중앙경제; ③ 인천지방노동위원회, "아발론교육노동조합 노동쟁의 조정신청사건(2010조정6)", 2010.5.13.

676) 정봉수, 「원어민강사의 노동법적 지위에 관한 연구」, 고려대학교 노동대학원 석사학위논문, 2013.12, 87면.

677) 전형배, "외국인근로자의 노동인권",「노동법논총」제18호, 한국비교노동법학회, 2010.4, 150면.

678) 대법원 1995.9.15, 94누12067 판결(불법체류자 산재적용)에서 출입국관리법의 성격을 단속규정이라 정의하고 있다; 최홍엽, "외국인 고용의 현황과 쟁점", 「노동법연구」, 서울대학교 노동법연구회, 2008.12, 207면.

679) 김선일, "취업자격 없는 외국인근로자의 노동조합 설립", 「사법」 제35호, 사법발전재단, 2016.3, 373면.

illegal workers can be said to induce illegal employment of foreigners and human rights violations and abuses.[679] The logic of not recognizing a labor union of illegal workers or restricting the three labor rights is as follows. First, a labor union is to improve working conditions through collective bargaining. Illegal workers cannot improve their working conditions because they are not guaranteed by law.[680] Second, since the activities of labor union officers(if they are also illegal workers) are restricted to exercise of the three labor rights, it can be said that the activities of unions can be related to political movements requiring revision of the Immigration Act. Third, it is doubtful whether a union of illegal workers can be protected by the Trade Union Act, while it is possible for illegal workers to join existing Korean workers' unions. So even if unions of illegal workers are not recognized, such workers can still join and be active in an existing union.[681]

The Supreme Court recognizes the right of a union of illegal foreign workers to exist because illegal workers are still workers as defined by the Trade Union Act, regardless of whether they are foreigners, or whether they are eligible for employment.[682]

Ⅳ. Social Insurances

There are four major insurances: Industrial Accident Compensation Insurance, Employment Insurance, National Health Insurance, and the National Pension Plan.

---

679) Kim, Sun-il, Establishing a Labor Union for Unemployed Foreign Workers, 35, Judicial Development Foundation, Mar. 3, 2016.

680) Park, Jong-Hee / Kang, Sun-Hee, Operation and Improvement of the Legal System on Protecting the Human Rights of Migrant Workers, Korea Law, Vol. 50, Korea University Law Institute, 2008, p. 436; Jeon, Yun-gu, Legal Status of Foreign Workers in the Prohibition of Discrimination, Korean Labor Law Review, No. 28, Korean Society of Comparative Labor Law, Aug. 8, 2013.

681) Kim, Sun-il, Establishing a Trade Union for Unemployed Foreign Workers, 35, pp. 374-375.

682) Supreme Court ruling June 25, 2015: 2007 doo 4955 (Trade union of illegal foreign workers recognized).

합을 인정하지 않거나 노동3권을 제한해야 한다는 논리는 다음과 같다. 첫째, 노동조합의 활동이 단체교섭과 단체협약을 통해 근로조건을 개선하는 활동을 하는 것인데, 불법체류 외국인근로자들은 장래의 근로관계를 법으로 보장받지 못하므로 근로조건의 개선을 이룰 수 없다는 것이다.[680] 둘째, 불법체류의 신분인 노동조합의 임원들의 활동은 노동3권 행사가 제한되므로 노동조합의 활동이 출입국관리법 개정을 요구하는 정치운동이 주된 목적이 될 수 있다고 볼 수 있다. 셋째, 불법체류자의 노동조합이 노조법으로 보호를 받을 수 있는지 의심이 되고, 불법체류자들도 기존의 내국인 노동조합에 가입할 수 있기 때문에 불법체류자의 노동조합을 인정해주지 않아도 내국인의 합법적인 노동조합에 가입하여 활동할 수 있다는 점이다.[681]

이에 대해 대법원은 전원합의체 판결은 불법체류자도 노조법상의 근로자성이 인정되는 한, 그러한 근로자가 외국인인지 여부나 취업자격의 유무에 상관없이 노조법상 근로자의 범위에 포함되므로 불법체류자의 노동조합을 인정하고 있다.[682]

Ⅳ. 사회보험

사회보험은 산업재해보상보험, 고용보험, 국민건강보험, 국민연금이라는 4대보험으로 구성되며, 보험의 내용에 따라 적용을 달리하는 특징이 있다.

680) 박종희·강선희, "이주근로자 인권보호에 관한 법 제도 운영과 개선방안", 「고려법학」 제50권, 고려대학교 법학연구원, 2008, 436면; 전윤구, "차별금지에서 외국인근로자의 법적 지위", 「노동법논총」 제28호, 한국비교노동법학회, 2013.8, 412면.

681) 김선일, "취업자격 없는 외국인근로자의 노동조합 설립", 374~375면.

682) 대법원 2015.6.25, 2007두4995 전원합의체 판결(노동조합설립 반려처분취소)

<Social Insurances and their Application to Foreign Workers>

		Non-professional foreign workers (E-9)	Oversea Koreans H-2, F-4	Professional foreign workers E-1~E-7	Illegal workers
Industrial Accident Compensation Insurance		Applied	Applied	Applied	Applied
Employment Insurance	Unemployment allowance	Optional	Optional	Optional	Not applied
	Vocational development, Job security	Applied	Applied	Applied	Not applied
National Health Insurance		Applied	Applied	Applied (exceptions allowed)	Not applied
Long-term Care Insurance		Excluded	Visiting &Working: excluded; Overseas Korea: Applied	Applied (exceptions allowed)	Not applied
National Pension		Applied	Applied	Applied (Reciprocal)	Not applied

Source: Choi, Hong-yeop, "Social Security of Foreign Workers," p. 175; Roh, Jae-cheol and Ko, Jun-ki, "Problems in and Improvements to Social Insurance Law for Foreign Workers," p. 126.

① Industrial Accident Compensation Insurance applies to foreigners as well, but the remaining social insurances vary in application. ② Regarding Employment Insurance, most foreign workers stay in Korea temporarily, so it is often optional. ③ National Health Insurance is naturally applicable if a foreign worker is employed at a workplace. ④ National Pension is naturally applied in principle, but the principle of reciprocity means it varies in accordance with relations with each foreign country.

The following describes in detail the application of social insurances with foreign workers.

1. Industrial Accident Compensation Insurance (IACI) Act

IACI premiums are fully paid by the employer, and are calculated by multiplying the total income of all workers in the workplace by the insurance rate announced by the government according to the business' risk level. In applying the industrial accident insurance premium rate for the same business, if the premium benefits to workers exceed

〈외국인근로자의 체류자격에 따른 사회보험 적용현황〉

구 분		외국인근로자 E-9(비전문)	동포근로자 H-2(방문취업 F-4(재외동포)	전문외국인력 E-1(교수)~ E-7(특정활동)	불법체류 근로자
산재보험		적용	적용	적용	적용
고용보험	실업급여	임의가입	임의가입	임의가입	미적용
	직업능력 고용안정	적용	적용	적용	미적용
국민건강보험		적용	적용	적용 (예외인정)	미적용
노인장기요양보험		제외	방문취업: 제외 재외동포: 적용	적용 (예외인정)	미적용
국민연금		적용	적용	적용 (상호주의)	미적용

출처: 최홍엽, “외국인근로자의 사회보장”, 175면; 노재철·고준기, “외국인근로자에 대한 사회보험법상의 문제점과 개선방안”, 126면.

① 산업재해보상보험은 외국인도 당연히 적용되지만, 나머지 사회보험은 적용상 차이가 있다. ② 고용보험의 경우 외국인근로자는 한국에서 일시 체류하는 경우가 대부분이므로 본인의 선택에 의해 가입여부를 임의 적용으로 하는 경우가 많다. ③ 국민건강보험은 외국인근로자가 고용을 전제로 사업장에 채용된 경우에는 당연 가입대상이 된다. ④ 국민연금도 당연가입이 원칙이지만 외국 국가와의 관계에 따른 상호주의 원칙이 적용되고 있다.

다음에서는 외국인근로자의 사회보험 적용에 대해 구체적으로 살펴본다.

1. 산재보험법

산재보험료는 사업주가 전액부담하며, 산재보험요율은 사업업종의 위험여부에 따라 정부에서 고시하는 보험요율을 사업장의 보수총액을 곱하여 계산된 보험금을 납부한다. 동일사업의 산재보험료율을 적용함에 있어서 과거 3년간의 보험급여 금액의 85%를 넘거나 75% 이하인 경우 그 사업에 적용되는 보험료율을 50% 범위 안에서 결정해서 인상 또는 인하하여 그 사업에 대한 다음 사업

85% or less than 75% of the previous three years of premium payments, the premium rate applied to the business is determined up to 50% higher or lower for the next business year.[683)] As a result, industrial accident insurance premiums may increase the following year if a lot has been paid out in IACI benefits, which will affect the company's intention to apply to IACI as it can expect higher premiums.[684)]

Insurance benefits shall be paid at the worker's(or survivor's) request if a worker at a workplace covered by IACI has an injury, illness or accident requiring at least four days of medical care. Types of insurance benefits include nursing care, leave of absence, sick compensation pensions, disability, survivor, nursing care, funeral expenses, and vocational rehabilitation.

(1) Application to foreign workers

Since the IACI Act stipulates in Article 1(Purpose) that its purpose is to compensate workers for work-related accidents promptly,[685)] foreign workers must be protected. Regardless of their eligibility for working visas, all are covered by the IACI Act. If a foreigner is injured while providing work, whether he or she is an industrial trainee or an illegal foreign worker, the accident will be compensated for as an occupational accident.[686)] This has been confirmed by a Supreme Court case.[687)] Workers are eligible for workers' compensation in the event of a work injury, regardless of whether they are Korean workers or illegal workers. The Supreme Court has made it clear that illegal stays are subject to crackdowns, but that illegal residents shall also be covered by industrial accident insurance in the sense that workers must be protected by labor law for labor already provided.

The IACI Act is a social insurance system in which the State carries out compensation

683) Lee, Sang-Kook, The Industrial Accident Compensation Insurance Act (I), 3rd Ed., Daemyung Publisher, Jan. 2014, p. 554.

684) Jeon, Kwang-seok, Park, Ji-soon and Kim, Bok-ki, The Social Security Act, 4th Ed., Shinjosa, 2017, p. 188.

685) For the purpose of Article 1 of the relevant laws of the Four Major Social Insurance Acts, the IACI and employment insurance protect workers, and national pension and national health insurance protect citizens. Therefore, the IACI is naturally applied to foreigners as workers.

686) Jeon, Kwang-seok et al, The Social Security Act, p. 163; Choi, Hong-yeop, Social Security of Foreign Workers, pp. 158-159.

687) Supreme Court ruling Sept. 15, 1995: 94 noo 12067 (Withdrawal of decision on disapproval of medical treatment): This is the first case confirmed as a work-related accident involving illegal industrial trainees. The immigration control statute restricts employment of foreigners only to prohibit the actual act of hiring those without employment qualifications. It is hard to think that even the effects of legal rights, such as the rights of labor laws, will be prohibited.

연도의 산재보험료율로 적용한다.[683] 따라서 산재보험 수급으로 인해 다음연도의 산재보험료가 높아지게 될 수 있기 때문에 기업체에서는 가급적 산재보험처리를 기피하게 된다.[684]

보험급여는 산재보험 적용대상 사업장의 근로자가 업무상 사유로 4일 이상의 요양을 요하는 부상, 질병을 얻거나 사망한 경우 당해 근로자(또는 유족)의 신청에 따라 지급한다. 보험급여의 종류에는 요양급여, 휴업급여, 상병보상연금, 장해급여, 유족급여, 간병급여, 장의비, 직업 재활급여가 있다.

(1) 외국인근로자에 대한 적용

「산업재해보상보험법」(이하 "산재보험법"이라 한다)은 제1조(목적)에서 "근로자의 업무상 재해를 신속히 보상하고"라고 규정하여 보호대상을 근로자로 설정하여 두고 있으므로,[685] 외국인근로자는 체류자격과 무관하게 모두 산재보험법을 적용받는다. 외국인 신분이 산업연수생이든지 불법체류 신분이든지 근로를 제공하다가 다친 경우에는 산업재해로 인정하게 되었다.[686] 이는 대법원의 판례에서도 이를 확인하고 있다.[687] 산재보험은 국민여부 또는 불법체류 여부와 상관없이 업무상 재해를 당한 경우에 산재보상의 대상이 된다. 대법원은 불법체류는 단속의 대상임을 명백히 하고 있지만, 이미 제공된 사실적 행위의 노동에 대해서는 노동법의 보호가 있어야 한다는 취지에서 불법체류자도 산재보험이 적용된다고 판결하였다.

산재보험법은 근로자가 업무상 사유로 부상을 당하거나 질병에 걸리는 경우

683) 이상국, 「산재보험법(I)」, 제3판, 대명출판사, 2014.1, 554면.

684) 전광석·박지순·김복기 「사회보장법」 제4판, 신조사, 2017, 188면.

685) 4대사회보험의 관련 법률 제1조 목적에서 산재보험과 고용보험은 보호대상이 근로자이고, 국민연금과 국민건강보험은 보호대상이 국민이다. 따라서 산재보험은 외국인도 근로자로서 당연 적용된다.

686) 전광석/외 2인, 「사회보장법」, 163면; 최홍엽, "외국인근로자의 사회보장", 앞의 논문, 158~159면.

687) 대법원 1995.9.15, 94누12067(요양불승인처분취소). 불법체류자 산업연수생의 최초 산재인정 건이다. "출입국관리 법령에서 외국인고용제한규정을 두고 있는 것은 취업자격 없는 외국인의 고용이라는 사실적 행위 자체를 금지하고자 하는 것뿐이지, 나아가 취업자격 없는 외국인이 사실상 제공한 근로에 따른 권리나 이미 형성된 근로관계에 있어서 근로자로서의 신분에 따른 노동관계법상의 제반권리 등의 법률효과까지 금지하려는 것으로 보기는 어렵다"고 판시하였다.

on behalf of the employer under the Labor Standards Act if a worker is injured or ill from work. Accident compensation is applied to all businesses or workplaces using workers, taking into account the risk, size and place of business. The following types of work are not covered by the IACI Act(Article 6): ① household service ② work for businesses with fewer than five workers in agriculture, forestry, fishing and hunting, etc.[688] Therefore, in the event a business or workplace is not covered by the IACI Act and has an industrial accident requiring medical treatment for three days or less, the Labor Standards Act requires the employer to compensate for the work injury/illness.[689]

(2) Related issues

There are legal and environmental limitations in relation to industrial accident insurance and foreign workers. Legal restrictions are related to application of the Industrial Accident Compensation Act, as workplaces hiring fewer than 5 workers and engaged in agricultural, livestock, and fishery work receive limited coverage for accidents and are excluded from work-related accident compensation.[690] Most agriculture and livestock farming workplaces employ fewer than 5 workers, so there is no industrial accident insurance coverage, and the employer must deal with work accidents him or herself. As an individual employer has a limited amount of property, an injured or ill worker may not be able to receive sufficient compensation.[691]

The environmental limitations of the IACI Act are as follows. First, the industrial accident rate among foreign workers is higher than among workers who are Korean nationals. The reason is that foreign workers do not communicate well in Korean, so safety instructions are not delivered correctly, and they often work in poor workplaces that do not have industrial safety facilities.[692] Second, illegal foreign workers are at risk of forced deportation, so they do not want to get medical treatment unless they are seriously injured. Companies do not want to apply for work-related compensation, but

---

688) Enforcement Decree to the IACI Act, Article 2 (Exclusion of Application of Law), Paragraph 6.

689) Korea Labor Welfare Corporation, Handbook of Workers' Compensation and Employment Insurance in 2019 and Employment, pp. 7-8.

690) Noh, Ho-Chang, Migrant Women and Social Security Law, Journal of Migration and Gender Law, Aug. 2017, pp. 26-27.

691) Amnesty International, Exploitation and Forced Labor of Migrant Workers in the Korean Agricultural Industry, pp. 36-37.

692) National Human Rights Commission of Korea, Survey of the Human Rights Situation for Foreign Workers in the Construction Industry, Human Rights Situation Survey 2015 Research Report, p. 9.

근로기준법상 사업주가 부담해야 할 보상책임을 국가가 대신하여 수행하는 사회보험제도이다. 산재보험은 근로자를 사용하는 모든 사업 또는 사업장에서 적용되는 것을 원칙으로 하면서, 사업의 위험률, 규모 및 사업장소 등을 참작하며 다음 사업은 예외로 산재보험법의 적용을 받지 않는다(산재법 제6조). 제외되는 사업장은 "① 가사서비스업, ② 농업, 임업, 어업, 수렵업 중 상시 5인 미만의 근로자를 사용하는 사업" 등이다.[688] 따라서 산재보험법에서 적용되지 않는 사업이나 사업장의 경우와 3일 이하의 요양을 필요로 하는 산업재해의 경우에는 근로기준법에 따라 사용자가 업무상 재해에 대한 보상을 하여야 한다.[689]

(2) 외국인근로자와 관련된 쟁점

산재보험과 외국인근로자의 관계에 있어 법적용상 제한과 환경적인 한계가 있다. 우선 법적용상 제한은 산재보험법의 적용제외 사업장으로 농업, 축산업, 어업 등은 상시 5인미만 사업장은 산재보험이 적용되지 않는 경우 재해보상에 한계가 있다.[690] 농업과 축산업의 경우에는 대부분 5인 미만 사업장이므로 산재보험이 적용되지 않아 사용자 책임으로 업무상 재해를 처리해야 하는데, 개인사용자의 재산적 한계가 있기 때문에 제대로 보상이 되지 않고 있다.[691]

산재보상법의 환경적인 한계는 다음과 같다. 첫째, 외국인근로자의 산업재해율은 내국인 근로자들에 비해 높다. 그 이유는 외국인근로자의 경우 의사소통이 제대로 되지 않아 안전지시가 정확히 전달되지 않고, 산업안전시설을 갖추지 못한 열악한 사업장에서 일하는 경우가 많고 외국인들 스스로가 숙달된 기능인이기보다는 단순기능 초보자들이 많기 때문이다.[692] 둘째, 불법체류 외국인근로자들은 강제출국의 위험이 있으므로 중대재해가 아닌 한 본인 스스로 산재보험으로 치료를 받지 않으려 한다. 회사들도 산재보험을 신청하지 않고 치

688) 산재법 시행령 제2조(법의 적용 제외 사업) 제6호.

689) 근로복지공단, "2019년 산재·고용보험 가입 및 부과업무 실무편람", 7~8면.

690) 노호창, "이주여성과 사회보장법제", 「이주젠더법학」제9권 제2호, 이화여자대학교 젠더법학연구소, 2017.8, 26~27면.

691) 국제앰네스티, 「한국 농축산업 이주노동자 착취와 강제노동」, 36~37면

692) 국가인권위원회, "건설업 종사 외국인근로자 인권상황 실태조사", 2015년도 인권상황 실태조사 연구용역보고서, 9면

only pay for medical treatment, leaving foreign workers without Industrial Accident Compensation Insurance coverage and vulnerable to permanent effects of injuries.[693] Third, when an industrial accident involves a foreign worker, the employer is afraid that his/her IACI premiums will increase or he/she may be audited by the Labor Office due to work-related accidents frequently occurring at the workplace. There is also the risk of disadvantageous consequences from the Labor Office, and so they pay the medical fees directly for foreign workers. This is often accepted by foreign workers because they do not know the industrial accident compensation system.[694]

2. Employment Insurance Act (EIA)

Employment insurance premiums are classified into unemployment benefits and premiums for employment stability and vocational skills development projects. Unemployment benefit premiums are borne by both workers and employers, while employers are responsible for employment security and vocational skills development projects(Article 6 of the EIA).[695] Unemployment benefits are payable only when a worker is involuntarily unemployed and seeking work.[696]

(1) Application to foreign workers

Employment insurance grants benefits to eligible people to prevent undue hardship from unemployment, promote job-seeking activities and employment, and develop the vocational skills of workers. It thereby contributes to the economic and social development of the nation(Article 1 of the EIA). Employment insurance applies to all businesses or workplaces in principle, with exceptions in consideration of business size. It applies to all workers

---

693) Choi, Hong-yeop, Social Security for Foreign Workers, Democratic Law No. 22, The Korean Society for Democratic Law, 2002, p. 160.

694) Ibid. pp. 160-161.

695) Korea Labor Welfare Corporation, Working Guide for Industrial Accident Compensation Insurance and Employment Insurance in 2019, pp. 7-46.

696) Employment Insurance Act. Article 40 (Eligibility Requirements for Job-Seeking Benefits)

1. The unit period of insurance under Article 41 during the 18-month period (hereinafter referred to as base period) prior to the date of separation shall be not less than 180 days in total;
2. Despite his/her willingness and ability to work, he/she shall be out of employment (including cases where he/she operates a business for the purpose of making profit; hereinafter the same shall apply in this Chapter and Chapter 5);
3. The reasons for separation shall not be any of the reasons for restricting eligibility for benefits under Article 58;
4. He/she shall be actively seeking reemployment;

료비만 부담하여 외국인근로자에게 영구장해가 남는다든지 산재보험법상 보호를 받지 못하는 경우가 많다.[693] 셋째, 사용자가 외국인근로자 산재사고가 발생했을 때 산재보험료 인상이나 산재다발 사업장으로 지정되어 추후 노동관청의 감사나 기타 불이익을 당하기 때문에 가급적 공상으로 처리하는 경우가 많다. 이에 대해 외국인근로자들도 산재보험제도를 잘 모르기 때문에 이를 묵인하는 경우가 많다.[694]

2. 고용보험법

고용보험 보험료는 실업급여와 고용안정·직업능력개발사업의 보험료로 구분하여 부과되는데, 실업급여 보험료는 근로자와 사용자가 각 1/2씩 부담하고, 고용안정·직업능력개발사업 비용은 사용자가 부담한다(고보법 제6조).[695] 실업급여의 수급자격을 갖춘 상태에서 비자발적으로 실업이 되고 구직노력을 하여야 지급된다.[696]

(1) 외국인근로자에 대한 적용

고용보험은 실업의 예방, 고용의 촉진 및 근로자의 직업능력의 개발과 향상을 꾀하고, 근로자가 실업한 경우에 생활에 필요한 급여를 실시하여 근로자의 생활안정과 구직 활동을 촉진함으로써 경제·사회 발전에 이바지하는 것을 목적으로 마련된 사회보험이다(법 제1조). 고용보험은 모든 사업 또는 사업장에 적용되는 것을 원칙으로 하되 사업의 규모를 고려하여 예외규정을 두고 있다. 고용보험은 근로자 입장에서 실업급여를 받는 것이 주 목적이므로 모든 근로자

693) 최홍엽, “외국인근로자의 사회보장”, 「민주법학」 제22호, 민주주의법학연구회, 2002, 160면.
694) 최홍엽, “외국인근로자의 사회보장”, 160~161면.
695) 근로복지공단, “2019년 산재·고용보험 가입 및 부과업무 실무편람”, 7~46면.
696) 고용보험법 제40조【구직급여의 수급 요건】

① 이직일 이전 18개월간(기준기간) 피보험단위기간이 통산하여 180일 이상일 것

② 근로의 의사와 능력이 있음에도 불구하고 취업(영리를 목적으로 사업을 영위하는 경우 포함)하지 못한 상태에 있을 것

③ 재취업을 위한 노력을 적극적으로 할 것

④ 이직사유가 비자발적인 사유일 것 (이직 사유가 법 제 58조에 따른 수급자격의 제한사유에 해당하지 아니할 것)

because its main purpose is to provide stability for unemployed persons, so does not apply if those persons do not need help or are protected by other insurance. Those excluded from employment insurance are: ① 65 years of age or older, ② working fewer than 60 hours a month(15 hours a week), ③ civil servants under the National Civil Service and Local Public Service Act, ④ those to whom the Private School Teachers Pension Act applies, ⑤ sailors under the Seafarers Act, ⑥ foreign workers who are not eligible for residency. However, foreigners with status of residence may subscribe and benefit.

< Foreign Worker Eligibility for Employment Insurance>

Status of Sojourn	Application	Status of Sojourn	Application
A-1(Diplomat)	×	E-1(Professor)	o(Optional)
A-2(Government official)	×	E-2(Foreign language instructor)	o(Optional)
A-3(Agreement)	×	E-3(Research)	o(Optional)
B-1(Visa exemption)	×	E-4(Technology transfer)	o(Optional)
B-2(Tourist/transit)	×	E-5(Professional employment)	o(Optional)
C-1(Temporary news coverage)	×	E-6(Artistic performer)	o(Optional)
C-3(Short-term visit)	×	E-7(Designated activities)	o(Optional)
C-4(Short-term worker)	o(Optional)	E-9(Non-professional employment)	o(Optional)
D-1(Artist)	×	E-10(Crew worker)	o(Optional)
D-2(Student)	×	F-1(Visiting or joining family)	×
D-3(Industrial trainee)	×	F-2(Resident)	o(Compulsory)
D-4(General trainee)	×	F-3(Accompanying spouse/child)	×
D-5(Journalism)	×	F-4(Overseas Korean)	o(Optional)
D-6(Religion)	×	F-5(Permanent resident)	o(Compulsory)
D-7(Supervisor)	o(Reciprocal)	F-6(Marriage to Korean Citizen)	o(Compulsory)
D-8(Corporate investor)	o(Reciprocal)	G-1(Miscellaneous)	×
D-9(International trade)	o(Reciprocal)	H-1(Working holiday)	×
D-10(Job Seeking)	×	H-2(Working visit)	o(Optional)

Source: Korea Labor Welfare Corporation, "Working Guide for Workers and Workers' Compensation and Employment Insurance 2017," p. 18.

※ '×' denotes those foreigners ineligible for employment insurance.

As previously stated, employment insurance is divided into unemployment benefits and employment stability and vocational skills development projects. Unemployment benefits of course include unemployment payments, but also maternity leave allowances

에게 적용되는 것이 원칙이지만, 실업급여의 도움이 필요하지 않거나 다른 보험에서 보호되는 경우에는 적용되지 않는다. 고용보험이 적용제외 되는 근로자는 ① 65세 이상인 자, ② 1월간 소정근로시간이 60시간(1주간 15시간)미만인 자, ③ 국가공무원법 및 지방공무원법에 의한 공무원, ④ 사립학교교원연금법의 적용을 받는 자, ⑤ 선원법에 의한 선원, ⑥ 거주 자격이 없는 외국인근로자 등이다. 다만, 체류자격을 가진 외국인은 임의가입이 가능하다.

〈외국인의 체류자격별 고용보험 적용 여부〉

체류자격	고용보험 적용	체류자격	고용보험 적용
1. 외 교(A-1)	×	19. 교 수(E-1)	○(임의)
2. 공 무(A-2)	×	20. 회화지도(E-2)	○(임의)
3. 협 정(A-3)	×	21. 연 구(E-3)	○(임의)
4. 사증면제(B-1)	×	22. 기술지도(E-4)	○(임의)
5. 관광통과(B-2)	×	23. 전문직업(E-5)	○(임의)
6. 일시취재(C-1)	×	24. 예술흥행(E-6)	○(임의)
7. 단기종합(C-3)	×	25. 특정활동(E-7)	○(임의)
8. 단기취업(C-4)	○(임의)	26. 비전문취업(E-9)	○(임의)
9. 문화예술(D-1)	×	27. 선원취업(E-10)	○(임의)
10. 유 학(D-2)	×	28. 방문동거(F-1)	×
11. 산업연수(D-3)	×	29. 거 주(F-2)	○(강제)
12. 일반연수(D-4)	×	30. 동 반(F-3)	×
13. 취 재(D-5)	×	31. 재외동포(F-4)	○(임의)
14. 종 교(D-6)	×	32. 영주(F-5)	○(강제)
15. 주 재(D-7)	○(상호주의)	33. 영주(F-6)	○(강제)
16. 기업투자(D-8)	○(상호주의)	34. 기 타(G-1)	×
17. 무역경영(D-9)	○(상호주의)	35. 관광취업(H-1)	×
18. 구직(D-10)	×	36. 방문취업(H-2)	○(임의)

출처 : 근로복지공단, “2017년 산재·고용보험 가입 및 부과업무 실무편람”, 18면.

※ ×로 표시된 경우에는 임의가입도 불가함에 유의

고용보험은 실업급여 부분과 고용안정·직업능력개발사업 부분으로 나누어져 있다. 실업급여 보험료는 노사가 절반씩 납부하고, 고용안정사업과 직업능력개발사업 보험료는 사업주가 전액 부담한다. 실업급여 부분은 실업수당과 산전산

and childcare leave benefits. Therefore, foreigners cannot receive maternity leave benefits and childcare leave benefits or unemployment benefits if they do not have employment insurance. If a foreign worker who is staying for employment in Korea does not intend to receive unemployment benefits, he or she may choose not to subscribe.[697)]

Professional foreign workers(E-1 to E-7) can continue to stay on their job search visa(D-10) for six months after termination of an employment contract. However, unemployment benefits are limited for non-professional foreign workers(E-9) even if they subscribe, as they are subject to compulsory deportation if they cannot find another job within 3 months after termination of their previous employment contract(Article 25, paragraph 3 of the Foreign Employment Act). Unemployment benefits are the basic item of social insurance in view of the last hold that workers can depend on when there is no economic return due to unemployment. Therefore, foreign workers should also be able to protect their right to live during a period of unemployment by having to subscribe to the unemployment benefit portion of employment insurance rather than being permitted to opt out.

Premiums for employment security and vocational skills development projects under Employment Insurance are all paid for by the employer. Therefore, workers can participate in a variety of education related to the development of their vocational skills, and can pursue their own education programs with the support of employment insurance. The amount a company can receive for employment security and vocational skills development projects shall be less than the amount paid in employment insurance premiums(240/100 for workplaces receiving preferential support).[698)]

---

697) Korea Labor Welfare Corporation, Working Guide for Industrial Accident Compensation Insurance and Employment Insurance in 2019. Unemployment allowance is excluded for foreign workers in principle. However, foreigners are also eligible in the following cases. (Enforcement Decree to the Employment Insurance Act, Article 3: Excluded Workers).

① Foreigners pursuant to Article 12 of the Enforcement Decree to the Immigration Control Act who have status of residence (D-8), corporate investment (D-8), and trade management (D-9) in accordance with the principle of reciprocity.

② However, the applicant whether he/she can join or not, shall be subject to the discretion of the applicant with the status of residence under Article 23 (1) of the Enforcement Decree to the Immigration Control Act.

③ Residents (F-2), permanent residents (F-5), and resident spouses (F-6) who are allowed to stay for long periods of time under Article 12 of the Enforcement Decree to the Immigration Control Act) are eligible for employment insurance.

698) Jeon, Kwang-seok, Korean Social Security Law, Jiphyunjae, 2016, pp. 416-420.

후 휴가수당 및 육아휴직 급여의 재원이 된다. 따라서 외국인이 고용보험을 가입하지 않으면 실업수당뿐만 아니라 산전산후 휴가수당과 육아휴직 급여를 받을 수 없다. 한국에서 취업을 목적으로 체류하는 외국인근로자중 실업급여를 받을 의도가 없는 경우에는 가입을 하지 않을 수도 있다.[697)]

전문외국인력(E-1~E-7)은 근로계약 종결 후 6개월 이상 구직비자(D-10)를 통해 계속 체류가 가능하기 때문에 실업급여 수령이 가능하다. 그러나 단순기능 외국인근로자(E-9)의 경우에는 비록 실업급여에 가입하더라도 근로계약 종결 후 구직신청을 한 다음 3개월 이내에 다른 사업장에서 취업하지 못할 경우 강제출국 대상이 되므로 실업급여의 혜택이 제한된다(외고법 제25조 제3항). 실업급여는 실업으로 인해 경제적 수익이 없을 때 근로자들이 기댈 수 있는 최후의 보루인 점을 볼 때, 사회보험의 기초항목이라 할 수 있다. 따라서 외국인근로자도 고용보험의 실업급여 부분에 대해 임의가입이 아닌 의무가입으로 전환하여야 실업기간 중 근로자의 생존권을 보호할 수 있을 것이다.

고용보험의 고용안정사업과 직업능력개발 사업은 사업주의 보험료 전액부담으로 진행되는 것이기 때문에 외국인근로자도 모두 적용된다. 따라서 근로자의 직업능력개발에 관련된 제반 교육을 참가할 수 있고, 고용보험의 지원을 받아 자체적으로 교육프로그램을 개발할 수 있다. 회사가 지원받을 수 있는 고용안정사업 및 직업능력개발사업에 관한 금액은 고용보험료 납부액의 100분의 100 이내(우선지원 사업장의 경우에는 100분의 240)이다(고보법 시행령 제42조 제1항).[698)]

---

697) 근로복지공단, "2019년 산재·고용보험 가입 및 부과업무 실무편람": 원칙적으로 고용보험의 실업급여 적용에서 제외하고 있다. 다만, 외국인도 다음의 몇 가지 사항에 해당 될 때 적용의 대상이 된다. (고용보험법 시행령 제3조: 적용제외 근로자)

① 「출입국관리법 시행령」 제12조의 규정에 따른 외국인 중 주재(D-8), 기업투자(D-8), 무역경영 (D-9)의 체류자격을 가진 자는 국가 간의 상호주의 원칙에 따라 법이 적용된다.

③ 그러나 「출입국관리법 시행령」 제23조 제1항에 따른 체류자격을 가진 보험가입 여부는 신청자의 재량에 따른다(임의가입 대상자).

③ 「출입국관리법 시행령」 제12조의 규정에 따른 장기적으로 체류 가능한 영구체류자 [거주(F-2), 영주(F-5), 결혼이민(F-6)]는 고용보험의 당연가입 대상이다.

698) 전광석, 「한국사회보장법론」, 집현재, 2016, 416~420면.

(2) Related issues

Systematic support for vocational skill development of foreign workers is necessary.[699] This will encourage the retention of skilled and professional workers rather than just non-skilled ones. In addition, many labor-management conflicts and industrial accidents occur due to insufficient communication abilities and a lack of understanding of Korean culture. Therefore, policy consideration is required for the development of vocational skills for foreign workers by utilizing the vocational skills development project under Employment Insurance.[700] Article 43 of the UN Convention on the Rights of Foreign Workers states that foreign workers shall enjoy equal treatment with their host country workers in relation to ① the use of vocational guidance and job placement services, ② the use of vocational training and retraining facilities and institutions.[701] In Germany, foreign workers are required to attend at least 600 hours of inclusive education.[702]

Even if a worker chooses to subscribe to Employment Insurance, he/she cannot get the basic benefits provided by the social insurances. Professor Kwang-seok Jeon has stated, It is not reasonable to limit beneficiaries simply because they are foreign subscribers to social insurance. The Social Insurance Act regulates the legal relationship between paying premiums and providing benefits should be equivalent in the event of social risk. Therefore, in the Social Insurance Act, the legal relations related to paying premiums should be integrated with the legal relations related to payment of salaries.[703]

For non-professional foreign workers, it is difficult to receive stable unemployment benefits because Article 25(3) of the Foreign Employment Act stipulates that they must leave the country if they cannot find employment within three months after termination

---

699) Insurance premiums for employment insurance are divided into unemployment benefits and premiums for employment security and vocational skills development projects. Fifty percent of the unemployment benefit portion is paid by workers and 50% by employers, but foreign workers are also beneficiaries of the employment security and vocational skills development projects paid by the employer. Reference: Article 16-10 (Report on Total Amount of Remuneration, etc.) of the Act on Collection of Premiums for Employment Insurance and Industrial Accident Compensation Insurance.

700) Jeon, Gwang Seok et al, Social Security Act, p. 197.

701) Choi, Hong-yeop, UN Convention on the Rights of Migrant Workers and the Reality of Labor Law in Korea, Youngnam Law No. 31, Yeungnam University Institute of Law, Oct. 2010, pp. 525-528.

702) Yoo, Gil-sang et al, Research on Reorganization of Management System for Foreign Workers, Ministry of Employment and Labor, Dec. 2012, p. 157.

703) Jeon, Kwang-seok, Korean Social Security Law, Jiphyunjae, 2016, p. 197.

(2) 외국인근로자와 관련된 쟁점

사업주의 의무부담에 의해 납부되는 직업능력개발 사업에 따라 외국인의 직업능력개발 사업에 대한 체계적인 지원이 필요하다고 할 수 있다.[699] 우선 직업능력을 개발하여 단순기능인이 아닌 숙련공이나 전문기능인으로 발전해 나갈 수 있도록 직업능력에 기회를 주어야 할 것이다. 또한, 의사소통능력 부족과 한국문화의 이해 부족으로 인한 노사갈등이나 산재사고가 다수 발생하고 있어 고용보험의 직업능력 개발사업을 적절히 활용하여 외국인근로자들의 직업능력 개발에도 정책적 배려가 필요하다.[700] UN의 외국인근로자 권리협약 제43조에서도 외국인근로자가 "① 직업지도 및 직업소개 서비스의 이용, ② 직업훈련, 재훈련 시설과 기관의 이용"과 관련하여 고용국 근로자와 평등한 대우를 향유한다고 규정하고 있다.[701] 독일의 경우 외국인근로자는 의무적으로 최소 600시간 통합교육에 참석하여야 한다.[702]

실업급여 가입을 임의로 하면 사회보험이 제공하는 기본적인 보험혜택을 받을 수 없다. 전광석 교수는 "사회보험에서 외국인 가입자라는 이유로 급여를 제한하는 것은 타당하지 않다. 사회보험법은 보험료를 납부하고 사회적 위험이 발생한 경우 보험료에 상응하는 급여를 제공하는 법률관계를 규율하고 있다. 따라서 사회보험법에서 보험료 납부와 관련된 법률관계는 급여지급과 관련된 법률관계와 통일체를 이루어야 한다"고 하면서 외국인근로자의 고용보험 임의가입을 의무가입으로 해야 한다는 입장이다.[703]

단순기능 외국인근로자의 경우에도 외국인고용법 제25조 제3항에 근로계약 종결 후 구식신청 3개월 이내 타 사업장에 취업하지 못하면 출국해야 한다는 규정이 있기 때문에 안정된 실업급여를 받기 어렵다. 그러나 점차 외국인근로

699) 고용보험의 보험료는 실업급여부분과 고용안정사업 및 직업능력개발사업의 보험료로 구분한다. 실업급여부분은 근로자와 사용자가 5:5로 나누어 납부하지만, 고용안정과 직업능력개발 사업은 사업주가 보수총액을 기준으로 납부하기 때문에 그 외국인근로자도 당연적용 근로자가 된다. 참조: 「고용보험 및 산업재해보상보험의 보험료 징수 등에 관한 법률」제16조의10(보수총액 등의 신고) ① 사업주는 전년도에 근로자에게 지급한 보수총액 등을 매년 3월 15일까지 공단에 신고하여야 한다.

700) 전광석외 2인, 「사회보장법」 197면.

701) 최홍엽, "UN의 이주근로자권리협약과 한국의 노동법 현실", 「영남법학」 제31호, 영남대학교 법학연구소, 2010.10, 525~528면.

702) 유길상외 3인, 「외국인력 노입 관리시스템 개편방안 연구」, 고용노동부의 연구용역, 2012.12, 157면.

703) 전광석, 「한국사회보장법론」, 197면.

of their employment contract. Increasingly, however, the importance of unemployment benefits is on the rise due to introduction of the extension of the long-term stay in Korea. Foreign workers must also be enrolled in unemployment benefits before they can receive maternity leave benefits or childcare leave benefits. Therefore, it is necessary to review the optionality for foreign workers in subscribing to employment insurance.[704)]

3. National Health Insurance Act (NHIA)

National Health Insurance aims to improve public health and social security by providing insurance benefits for the prevention, diagnosis, treatment, and rehabilitation of injured and ill people, as well as assist with costs of childbirth and death, and promote health(Article 1 of the NHIA). National Health Insurance is a compulsory insurance that is divided into workplace and regional insurers. Currently, it covers about 97% of all citizens, with other medical services covered under the Medical Benefits Act, which is a form of public assistance for beneficiaries of the Basic Livelihood Subsidy.[705)] The self-employed who do not employ workers, daily workers employed for less than one month, and part-time workers who work less than 60 hours a month are not required to subscribe.[706)]

The insurance premiums for subscribing workers are an amount calculated by multiplying the standard monthly salary by the premium rate, with 50% of the premiums borne by workers and 50% by employers(Article 69). Therefore, the premiums are paid according to the individual's standard monthly salary.[707)]

Long-term care insurance is a social insurance system separate from National Health Insurance. It was introduced in July 2008 due to aging of the population and the necessity to care for the elderly. It provides essential care services such as face washing, bathing, meals, assistance with using the toilet, and nursing care for elderly persons unable to

---

704) Choi, Hong-yeop, Social Security of Foreign Workers, p. 168.

705) Roh, Ho-chang et al, Social Security of Foreigners, Immigration Law, p. 468.

706) National Health Insurance, National Health Insurance Operational Guide in 2019, pp. 33-36.

707) National health insurance premiums are 6.46% of monthly income, with 3.23% each from the employer and the worker. Long-term care insurance premium adds an additional 8.51% from the employer and the worker based upon monthly national health insurance premiums.

자가 장기체류하고 있고, 단기체류 기간은 2012년 도입된 성실근로자 체류기간 연장제도 등의 도입으로 인하여 실업급여의 중요성이 대두되고 있다. 또한, 실업급여에 가입되어 있어야지 출산전후 휴가급여나 육아휴직 급여를 받을 수 있다. 따라서 외국인근로자에 대해 고용보험의 가입을 의무화하는 것에 대해 검토가 필요하다고 본다.[704)]

3. 국민건강보험법

국민건강보험은 국민의 질병이나 부상에 대한 예방, 진단, 치료, 재활과 출산, 사망 그리고 건강증진에 대하여 보험급여를 실시함으로써 국민보건을 향상시키고 사회보장을 증진하기 위함을 목적으로 한다(건보법 제1조). 국민건강보험은 직장가입자와 지역가입자로 구분되는 의무보험으로, 현재 전체국민의 약 97%가 국민건강보험에 적용되고, 그 외에는 기초생활보장수급자 등에 속하는 공공부조에 해당하는 의료급여법에 의하여 의료서비스를 제공받고 있다.[705)] 직장가입자에서 제외되는 자는 근로자를 채용하지 않은 자영업자, 1월 미만 기간동안 고용되는 일용근로자, 비상근 근로자 또는 1개월간의 소정근로시간이 60시간 미만인 시간제 근로자 등이다.[706)]

직장가입자의 보험료는 표준보수월액에 보험료율을 곱한 금액이 되며, 여기서 산출된 금액에 근로자와 사용자가 각각 50%씩 부담한다(건보법 제69조). 따라서 개인의 표준보수월액에 따라 차등 납부가 된다.[707)]

노인장기요양보험은 인구의 고령화와 노인요양의 필요성으로 인해 2008년 7월부터 국민건강보험에서 별도로 도입된 사회보험제도이다. 고령이나 치매·중풍 등의 노인성 질병으로 혼자서는 거동이 불편한 노인에게 세수, 목욕, 식사 배변처

704) 최홍엽, “외국인근로자의 사회보장”, 168면.
705) 노호창외, “외국인의 사회보장”, 「이민법」, 468면.
706) 국민건강보험, “2019 사업장 업무편람”, 33~36면.
707) 국민건강보험료는 2019년 기준 6.46%로 사용자 3.23%와 근로자 3.23%를 납부한다. 여기에 추가되는 노인장기요양보험료는 사용자와 근로자가 각자의 보험건강보험료율에 각각 8.51%를 곱한 금액을 납부한다.

move alone due to age-related diseases such as dementia and stroke.[708] Long-term care insurance premiums are equivalent to 8.51% of National Health Insurance premiums.

(1) Application to foreign workers

All business and local subscribers covered by National Health Insurance are required to pay premiums. However, foreign workers(E-9) and visiting Korean workers(H-2) under the employment permit system in the Foreign Employment Act and in Article 7(4) of the Long-Term Care Insurance Act can be exempted through a separate application process through a nursing care insurance subscriber. All other foreign workers who do not have a basis for exemption are automatically subscribed to long-term care insurance and pay the premium along with the health insurance premium.

(2) Related issues

Foreigners and overseas Koreans are eligible for health insurance if their status of residence is recognized by relevant laws. Employers of native English instructors are required to subscribe for the 4 social insurances, but they often fail to do so for National Pension and National Health Insurance.[709] This is because there is no real penalty for failing to subscribe to National Health Insurance. If non-Koreans are not workplace subscribers, they must be classified as local subscribers and join the compulsory system. However, if they sign contracts with new employers every year, they will not be protected as a local subscriber because their place of residence is unclear.

Article 109 of the NHIA, paragraph 4, states that foreign workers who are staying illegally are not covered by health insurance. Although Korea has about 366,500 illegal workers as of June 2019, this exclusion means they(and their families) find it difficult to receive adequate care for chronic conditions, childbirth and other health events due to

---

708) Article 2 (Definition) of the Long-Term Care Insurance Act. 1. “Elderly people,” etc. are those aged 65 years or older or those under 65 who have age-related diseases such as dementia or cerebrovascular disease. 2. Long-term care benefits means services such as physical activities, household support or care, or cash to pay for such assistance for those who are deemed to have been unable to carry out daily necessary activities on their own for the previous six months.

709) Lee, Byung-Woon and Go, Jun-ki, The Current Status and Problems of Health Care for Foreign Workers, Hanyang Law, 31, Hanyang Law Society, Aug. 2010, p. 333.

리, 간호 등 필요한 요양서비스를 제공하는 제도이다.[708] 장기요양보험료는 건강보험료에 장기요양 보험료율(8.51)을 곱한 금액을 건강보험료와 함께 납부한다.

(1) 외국인근로자에 대한 적용

국민건강보험이 적용되는 모든 사업장가입자나 지역가입자 모두 당연 적용되어 보험료를 납부한다. 다만 「노인장기요양보험법」 제7조 제4항에 따라 외국인고용법의 고용허가제에 속하는 외국인근로자(E-9)와 방문취업 동포근로자(H-2)는 별도의 적용제외 신청절차를 통해 장기요양보험 가입자에서 제외를 받을 수 있다. 제외신청의 근거가 없는 다른 외국인근로자들은 모두 장기요양보험에 자동 가입되어 보험료를 건강보험료와 함께 납부한다.

(2) 외국인근로자와 관련된 쟁점

외국인과 재외국민은 관련법에 의해 체류자격이 인정되는 경우 건강보험 의무가입 대상이다. 원어민 강사의 경우에도 사용자가 4대보험의 의무가입 사업주이지만 국민연금과 국민건강보험을 의도적으로 누락시켜, 원어민 강사가 건강보험 혜택을 받지 못하는 경우가 많다.[709] 이는 국민건강보험에 사업장가입을 하지 않았다고 하여 마땅한 처벌조항이 없기 때문이다. 사업장가입자가 아닌 경우 지역가입자로 분류되어 강제제도 가입해야 하지만, 매년 새로운 사용자와 근로계약을 하는 경우 거주지가 명확하지 않기 때문에 지역가입자로서도 보호되지 않는다.

특히, 불법체류 외국인근로자는 건강보험이 적용되지 않는다고 명시하고 있다(동법 제109조 제4항). 2019년 6월 현재 37만 명의 불법체류 외국인근로자가 상시 체류하고 있는 상태에서 만성질환과 출산 및 육아관련 질환 등 의료수요가 증가하고 있음에도 불구하고 건강보험 적용제외에 따른 과다한 의료비로 인

---

708) 노인장기요양보험법 제2조(정의). 1. "노인등"이란 65세 이상의 노인 또는 65세 미만의 자로서 치매, 뇌혈관성질환 등 노인성 질병을 가진 자를 말한다. 2. "장기요양급여"란 6개월 이상 동안 혼자서 일상생활을 수행하기 어렵다고 인정되는 자에게 신체활동, 가사활동의 지원 또는 간병 등의 서비스나 이에 갈음하여 지급하는 현금 등을 말한다.

709) 이병운·고준기, "외국인근로자의 보건의료 현황과 문제점", 「한양법학」 31, 한양법학회, 2010.8, 333면.

the cost of medical care.[710] Medical insurance should also cover illegal workers so as to guarantee the basic rights of human beings.[711]

4. National Pension Act (NPA)

The National Pension Scheme is a system that pays old-age pensions to citizens who reach a certain age, or pays the pension to the citizen's family if the pensioner is disabled or dies(Article 1 of the NPA). The National Pension Scheme was enacted on January 1, 1988, when the NPA came into effect. Initially, it applied only to workplaces hiring 10 or more workers, but then gradually expanded to every company.(Article 6). However, civil servants, soldiers, and private school workers subject to the Civil Service Pension Act, the Military Pension Act, and the Private School Pension Act, respectively, are excluded from membership. The National Pension Plan is divided into workplace subscribers and regional subscribers, and subscription is mandatory for workplaces that use one or more workers at all times. Excluded from workplace subscribers are the self-employed who do not employ workers, daily workers employed for less than one month, non-employed workers, or part-time workers who work less than 60 hours a month. Premiums are in proportion to income, with 50% borne by the worker and 50% by the employer.[712] The types of benefits under the NPA include old-age pension, survivor's pension, disability pension, and lump-sum refund.[713]

(1) Application to foreign workers

Foreigners working in workplaces are subject to the National Pension Act(Article 126) and foreign nationals residing in Korea shall, of course, become business or regional subscribers. However, if the law equivalent to Korea's NPA in the foreigner's country of citizenship does not apply to Republic of Korea nationals living there, the principle of

710) Lee, Byung-Woon / Go, Jun-ki, p. 335.

711) Choi, Hong-yeop, Social Security for Foreign Workers, pp. 162-164.

712) As of 2021, the National Pension premium is charged 9% of standard monthly income, which is each distributed to 4.5% respectively to the employer and the worker.

713) National Pension Service, A Practical Guide to National Pension Workplaces 2020, pp. 32-36.

하여 제대로 된 보장은 받기가 어렵다.[710] 불법체류근로자에 대해서는 국가정책상 사회보험의 적용을 제외하고 있지만, 헌법상 보장된 인간으로서 기본권 보장을 위해 의료보험 적용이 반드시 필요하다.[711]

4. 국민연금법

국민연금제도는 국민이 납부한 연금재원을 가지고, 해당 국민이 일정한 연령에 이르렀을 때 노령연금을 지급하거나, 연금가입자가 장애나 사망한 경우 그 가족의 생계를 위해 연금을 지급하는 제도이다(국연법 제1조). 국민연금은 1988년 1월 1일 국민연금법 시행으로 시행되어 초기에는 10인 이상 사업장만 적용하다가 그 후 점차적으로 확대하여 국내에 거주하는 18세 이상 60세 미만의 국민은 국민연금의 가입대상이 된다(동법 제6조). 다만, 공무원연금법, 군인연금법 및 사립학교연금법의 적용을 받는 공무원·군인 및 사립학교 직원은 가입대상에서 제외된다. 국민연금 가입대상자는 사업장가입자와 지역가입자로 구분되는데, 상시 1인 이상의 근로자를 사용하는 사업장은 당연적용사업장이 된다. 사업장 가입자에서 적용제외 되는 자는 근로자를 채용하지 않은 자영업자, 1월 미만의 기간 동안 고용되는 일용근로자, 비상근근로자 또는 1개월간의 소정근로시간이 60시간 미만인 시간제 근로자 등이다. 연금보험료는 소득에 비례하여 근로자와 사용자가 각각 50%씩 부담한다.[712] 국민연금법에 따른 급여의 종류는 노령연금, 유족연금, 장애연금, 반환일시금이 있다.[713]

(1) 외국인근로자에 대한 적용

국민연금법 제126조에 따라 국민연금법을 적용 받는 사업장에 사용되는 외국인과 국내에 거주하는 외국인은 당연히 사업장가입자 또는 지역가입자가 된다. 다만, 그 국민연금에 상응하는 연금제도를 그 외국인의 본국법이 대한민국

710) 이병운·고준기, "외국인근로자의 보건의료 현황과 문제점", 335면.
711) 최홍엽, "외국인근로자의 사회보장", 162~164면.
712) 2021년 기준보험료는 기준소득 월액의 9%로 사용자가 4.5%와 근로자가 4.5% 각각 부담한다.
713) 국민연금, "2020년 알기 쉬운 국민연금 사업장 실무안내", 2020, 32~36면.

reciprocity applies. Those not covered by the National Pension Scheme are those here on temporary stay visas or without income.[714)]

National Pension applies to foreign nationals when they are employed at a workplace that must subscribe to it. To receive the pension benefit, the foreign national must have paid into the national pension for at least 10 years and reach the age of 60. This is not easy for most foreign workers to do. In this case, a lump-sum refund will be given, which will be handled in accordance with the social security agreement Korea has with that national's country of citizenship. Lump-sum refunds are only given to those nationals from countries with such social security agreements with Korea(see Table next page).

However, since most of the sending countries in the employment permit system do not have social security agreements with Korea, most foreign workers are ineligible for the national pension, so they cannot receive a lump sum refund.[715)] In this regard, the failure to receive lump sum refunds despite the inability to receive old-age pension benefits raises the issue of a serious limitation on property rights. It also pays foreign workers in countries that do not. In addition, the National Pension Act was amended in January 2015 in accordance with the decision of the Constitutional Court in recognition of the property

---

714) Excluded foreigners: (1) Those who have stayed without permission to extend their stay in accordance with Article 25 of the Immigration Control Act; (2) A person who has not registered as an alien under Article 31 of the Immigration Control Act or who has been issued an order of forced eviction under Article 59 (2) of the same Act; (3) Status of residence (D-1), Study abroad (D-2), Technical training (D-3), General training (D-4), Religion (D-6), Visiting living (F- 1) Person with companion (F-3) and others (G-1).

715) Concerning pension entitlements, the Constitutional Court recognizes property rights by the following logic. In order for rights under public law to be protected by the constitution's protection of property rights, it must meet the following requirements. First, public rights must be attributed to the rights of individuals and made available to the benefit of the individual (private usefulness). Second, they are acquired not by unilateral benefits of the state but by labor, investment or special sacrifice of the rights of the individual. It should be equivalent to the benefits paid (the substantial self-contribution of the beneficiaries), and third, it should contribute to the survival of the beneficiaries. Through these requirements, the right of unilateral benefits of the state, such as social assistance, is excluded from the protection of property rights, and is protected to a degree similar to that of judicial property only if the status of social law is an equivalent to its benefits. Public rights to be received are recognized. In other words, public property rights of that nature are included in the protection of property rights only if the legal status of the public law is so strong that it is comparable to business property rights and deprivation is against the principle of the rule of law. Constitutional Court of Korea decision June 29, 2000: 99 Hunba 289; Constitutional Court of Korea decision on May 28, 2009: 2005 Hunba 20.

국민에게 적용되지 아니하면 해당 외국인에게도 국민연금을 적용하지 않는다는 상호주의의 입장을 취하고 있다. 그리고 국민연금의 가입 적용대상에서 제외되는 외국인은 일시적으로 체류하거나 소득이 없는 외국인이다.[714)]

국민연금은 외국인근로자가 국민연금 사업장에 취업한 경우 당연가입 조건으로 적용되는데 노령연금을 수급하기 위해서는 10년 이상 국민연금에 가입하고 60세의 연령에 도달하여야 한다. 외국인근로자가 이를 충족하기는 쉽지 않다. 이 경우 반환일시금을 수령하는데, 이는 출신국과의 사회보장 협장에 따라 기납부한 국민연금 보험료를 일시반환 받을 수 있다. 여기에 사회보장 협정이 체결된 국가에 대해서만 일시 반환금이 적용된다(다음 페이지 표 참조).

그러나 고용허가제의 송출국가는 대부분이 사회보장협정이 이루어지지 않는 국가이므로 해당 국가의 외국인근로자는 국민연금의 수급권이 없기 때문에 국민연금 가입대상에 일시반환금을 수령할 수 없었다.[715)] 이에 대해 노령연금 혜택을 받을 수 없음에도 불구하고 일시반환금을 수령하지 못하는 것은 재산권의 중대한 제한이라는 문제가 제기되어 상호주의 태도 등을 고려하여 2007년 5월 국민연금법 개정으로 국민연금 반환일시금을 지급하지 않는 국가의 외국인근로자에도 지급하고 있다. 또한, 관련하여 국민연금에 대한 재산권적 가치를 인정한 헌법재판소 결정에 따라 2015년 1월 국민연금법이 개정되어, 국민연금에 상응하는 연금제도가 없는

714) 제외되는 외국인: ① 출입국관리법 제25조에 따라 체류기간연장허가를 받지 아니하고 체류하는 자, ② 출입국관리법 제31조에 따른 외국인등록을 하지 아니하거나 같은 법 제59조 제2항에 따라 강제퇴거명령시가 발급된 자, ③ 체류자격이 문화예술(D-1), 유학(D-2), 기술연수(D-3), 일반연수(D-4), 종교(D-6), 방문동거(F-1), 동반(F-3), 기타(G-1)인 자이다.

715) 연금수급권과 관련하여 헌법재판소는 다음가 같은 논리로 그 재산권성을 인정하고 있다. "공법상의 권리가 헌법사의 재산권 보장의 보호를 받기 위해서는 다음과 같은 요건을 갖추어야 한다. 첫째, 공법상의 권리가 권리주체에게 귀속되어 개인의 이익을 위하여 이용 가능해야 하며(사적 유용성), 둘째, 국가의 일방적인 급부에 의한 것이 아니라 권리주체의 노동이나 투자, 특별한 희생에 의해 획득되어 자신이 행한 급부의 등가물에 해당하는 것이어야 하며(수급자의 상당한 자기기여), 셋째, 수급자의 생존의 확보에 기여해야 한다. 이러한 요건을 통하여 사회부조와 같이 국가의 일방적인 급부에 대한 권리는 재산권의 보호대상에서 제외되고, 단지 사회법상의 지위가 자신의 급부에 대한 등가물에 해당하는 경우에 한하여 사법상의 재산권과 유사한 정도로 보호받아야 할 공법상의 권리가 인정된다. 즉 공법상의 법적 지위가 사업상의 재산권과 비교될 정도로 강력하여 그에 대한 박탈이 법치국가원리에 반하는 경우에 한해, 그러한 성격의 공법싱의 권리가 재산권의 보호대상에 포함되는 것이다." 헌법재판소 2000.6.29, 99헌바289 결정; 헌법재판소 2009.5.28, 2005헌바20 결정.

value of national pensions(Article 126 of the NPA).[716)]

<Countries with Reciprocal Agreements Regarding National Pensions>

Applicable countries	The USA, Canada, Russia, Japan, China and other countries (73)
Workplace-based-only applicable countries (36)	Ghana, Gabon, Grenada, Taiwan, Laos, Lebanon, Mexico, Mongolia, Vanuatu, Venezuela, Belize, Bolivia, Bhutan, Sri Lanka, Sierra Leone, Haiti, Algeria, Ecuador, El Salvador, Yemen, Jordan, Uganda, India, Indonesia, Zimbabwe, Cameroon, Kazakhstan, Kenya, Costa Rica, Ivory Coast, Congo, Columbia, Kyrgyzstan, Thailand, Paraguay, Peru
Non-applicable countries (22)	Nigeria, South Africa, Nepal, East Timor, Malaysia, Myanmar, Bangladesh, Vietnam, Saudi Arabia, Singapore, Iran, Egypt, Cambodia, Pakistan, Georgia, Maldives, Belarus, Swaziland, Armenia, Ethiopia, Tonga, Fiji

Source: National Pension Plan, "A Practical Guide to National Pension Workplaces 2019," 2019, p. 36.

(2) Related issues

It is difficult for foreign workers to receive the Korean old-age pension because they must contribute for a minimum ten years and then reach the age of 60(Article 77 of the NPA).[717)] Therefore, foreign workers who do not meet these requirements can receive the national pension benefit as a lump sum refund when they leave the country.

Non-professional foreigners stay for a short time and most return to their home countries within three to five years. In this case, the national pension paid in the meantime will be received as a lump-sum refund. The national pension premium is 9% of a worker's total income, with workers and employers each paying 4.5%. Therefore, application of the National Pension on non-professional foreign workers who are unlikely to receive the benefits is an additional tax on the employer. The old-age pension for non-professional foreigners with short-term stays cannot help them as they are leaving Korea before their eligible date.[718)]

---

716) Jeon, Kwang-seok, Korean Social Security Law, p. 274. Noh, Ho-Chang, Immigrant Women and Social Security Law, Journal of Migration and Gender Law, Vol. 9, 2ho, Ehwa Women's University Gender Law Research Center, Aug. 2017, pp. 34-35; Lee, Dahae, Citizenship and Labor Citizenship to Protect Migrant Workers, p. 175.

717) In accordance with the National Pension Act of 2007 (No. 8541ho), the pension age began to be adjusted from 2015, with 1 year's delayed benefit every 5 years. From 2033, the right to benefits will change to 65 years old.

718) Lee, Soo-yeon, Ensuring Labor and Universal Rights of Foreign Women Workers, p. 128.

국가의 외국인 경우에는 국민연금의 가입자에서 제외되었다(동법 제126조).[716)]

〈국민연금 상호주의에 의한 적용대상 국가〉

사업장·지역 당연 적용국 (73개국)	미국, 캐나다, 러시아, 일본, 중국과 기타 나라 73개국
사업장 당연 적용·지역 적용제외국 (36개국)	가나, 가봉, 그레나다, 대만, 라오스, 레바논, 멕시코, 몽골, 비누아투, 베네수엘라, 벨리즈, 볼리비아, 부탄, 스리랑카, 시에라리온, 아니티, 알제리, 에콰도르, 엘살바도르, 예맨, 요르단, 우간다, 인도, 인도네시아, 짐바브웨, 카메룬, 카자흐스탄, 케냐, 코스타리카, 코트디부아르, 콩고, 골롬비아, 키르기스스탄, 태국, 파라과이, 페루
사업장·지역 적용 제외국(22개국)	나이지리아, 남아프리카공화국, 네팔, 동티모르, 말레이시아, 미얀마, 방글라데시, 베트남, 사우디아라비아, 싱가포르, 이란, 이집트, 캄보디아, 파키스탄. 그루지야, 몰디브, 벨로루시, 스와질란드, 아르메니아, 이디오피아, 통가, 피지

출처: 국민연금, "2019년 알기 쉬운 국민연금 사업장 실무안내", 2019, 36면.

(2) 외국인근로자와 관련된 쟁점

노령연금 수령자가 되기 위해서는 국민연금의 최소 가입기간 10년과 수급연령 60세[717)]를 충족하여야 하기 때문에 사실상 외국인근로자가 노령연금을 수령하기가 힘들다(국연법 제77조). 따라서 이 요건을 충족하지 못한 외국인근로자는 출국할 때에 국민연금 납입금을 일시 반환금으로 수령할 수 있다.

단순기능 외국인의 경우에는 단기순환방식으로 체류하고 대부분이 3년 내지 5년 이내에 본국으로 돌아간다. 이 경우 그 동안 납부한 국민연금을 반환일시금으로 수령하게 되는데, 국민연금은 근로자와 사용자가 각각 소득의 4.5% 씩 총 9%의 보험료가 적립된다. 따라서 국민연금의 노령연금을 수령할 가능성이 거의 없는 단순기능 외국인근로자에 국민연금을 적용하는 것은 사업주의 입장에서는 추가적 과세라고 할 수 있다. 단기체류가 예정된 단순기능 외국인에 대한 노령연금의 실효성이 감소할 수 밖에 없다고 할 수 있다.[718)]

---

716) 전광석, 「한국사회보장법론」, 274면. 노호창, "이주여성과 사회보장법제", 「이주젠더법학」제9권 제2호, 이화여자대학교 젠더법학연구소, 2017.8, 34~35면; 이다혜, 「시민권과 이주노동–이주노동자 보호를 위한 '노동시민권'의 모색–」, 175면.

717) 2007년 국민연금법(제8541호)에 따라 2015년부터 수급연령이 조정에 들어가 각 5년마다 1세씩 조정이 들어가 각 5년마다 1세씩 영장되어 2033년부터는 65세부터 수급권을 가지는 것으로 변경되었다.

718) 이수연, "외국인여성 근로자의 노동과 보편적 권리 보장", 128면.

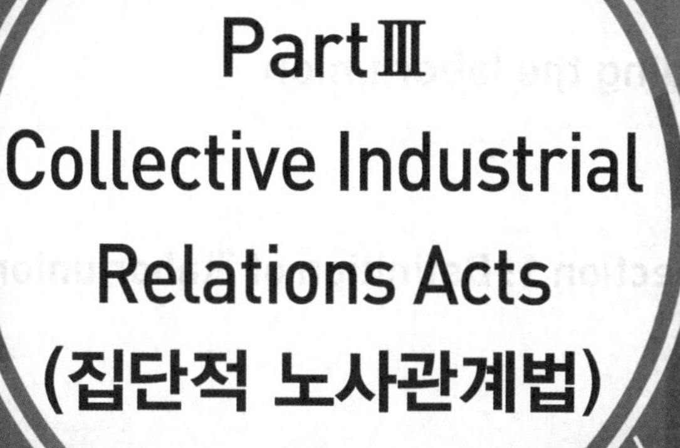

Part Ⅲ Collective Industrial Relations Acts (집단적 노사관계법)

Chapter 12

Understanding the labor union

Section 1: Definition of "labor union"

Ⅰ. Purpose of the Trade Union and Labor Relations Adjustment Act

Article 33 of the Constitution stipulates the three basic rights of labor as the following: to enhance working conditions, workers shall have the right to independent association, collective bargaining and collective action. Actions exercising the right to independent association are accomplished through a labor union. Labor unions can make a collective agreement through collective negotiation as an equal counterpart to the employer for the purpose of maintaining and improving the working conditions of the employees and enhancing their economic and social status. The labor union can also stage a strike where the employees collectively refuse to work as a means to meet their ends.

The purpose of the Trade Union and Labor Relations Adjustment Act(hereinafter, the Trade Union Act) is to maintain and improve working conditions and improve the economic and social status of workers by securing their rights of association, collective bargaining and collective action pursuant to the Constitution, and to contribute to the maintenance of industrial peace and development of the national economy by preventing and resolving labor disputes through fair adjustment of labor relations.[1)]

The Trade Union Act not only considers civil and criminal misbehavior as non-justifiable labor union activities but also prohibits unfavorable treatment of employees(such as dismissal) for justifiable union activities.[2)]

1) Article 1 of the Trade Union Act.

2) Article 3 and Article 4 of the Trade Union Act.

노동조합의 이해

제1절 노동조합법의 이해

Ⅰ. 노조법의 목적

헌법 제33조에 의하면 "근로자는 근로조건의 향상을 위하여 자주적인 단결권, 단체교섭권 및 단체행동권을 가진다"고 노동3권을 규정하고 있다. 근로자의 자주적인 단결권 행사는 노동조합을 통해 이루어지는데, 노동조합은 근로자가 자주적으로 단결하여 근로조건의 유지 개선과 기타 근로자의 경제적 사회적 지위 향상을 도모하기 위하여 사용자와 대등한 당사자로서 단체교섭을 하여 단체협약 체결을 할 수 있다. 또한, 사용자를 압박하기 위해 근로제공을 집단적으로 거부하는 쟁의행위를 할 수 있다.

노동조합 및 노동관계조정법(이하 "노조법" 이라 함)의 목적은 의한 근로자의 단결권·단체교섭권 및 단체행동권을 보장하여 근로조건의 유지·개선과 근로자의 경제적·사회적 지위 향상을 도모하고, 노동관계를 공정하게 조정하여 노동쟁의를 예방·해결함으로써 산업평화의 유지와 국민경제의 발전에 도모하기 위하는 것이다.[1]

노동조합의 정당한 노조활동에 대하여는 민·형사상의 책임이 면제될 뿐만 아니라, 사용자가 정당한 조합활동을 이유로 근로자에게 해고나 기타 불이익을 주는 행위를 금지하고 있다.[2]

---

1) 노조법 제1조.

2) 노조법 제3조, 제4조.

Ⅱ. "Worker" according to the Trade Union Act

Worker according to Article 2(1) of the Labor Standards Act is stipulated as a person who offers work to a business or workplace to earn wages, regardless of the kind of job he/she is engaged in. The concept of employee includes the following factors: ① It is not determined by the kind of job he/she is engaged in; ② the person works at a specific business or workplace; ③ the person offers work to earn wages. In understanding this concept, wage is placed at the center, while the key point to be considered is whether a subordinate relationship exists between the one who performs the work and the one who provides the work. That is, employee means a person who offers work to earn money through a subordinate relationship.[3)] A subordinate relationship is one where a person hired by an employer provides work to that employer, under the employer's direction and orders, and carries out the tasks the employer requires to be done. This means that an employee who offers work to earn wages can be considered a person offering work under a subordinate relationship to an employer.[4)]

Worker according to Article 2(1) of the Trade Union Act is stipulated as a person who lives on wages, salary, or other equivalent form of income earned in pursuit of any type of job. Those who receive a wage are workers under the Labor Standards Act, and those who earn income equivalent to wages are workers under the Trade Union Act. Equivalent income means any reward earned in exchange for providing labor service to another person independently, without a subordinate relationship. Therefore, worker in the Trade Union Act includes workers earning a wage, unemployed persons without income, and those who have no dependent relationship but continue to provide labor for income.[5)] In other words, under the Labor Standards Act, workers have both human and economic dependency, but workers under the Trade Union Act are those with economic dependency only. However, this does not apply to those who provide independent work, such as self-

3) Lim, Jongryul, 「Labor Law」, 14th ed., Parkyoungsa, 2016, p. 32.

4) Labor Standards Act」, 33rd ed., Joongang Economy, 2020, pp. 32-36, Supreme Court ruling on Dec. 7, 2006, 2004da29736.

5) Lim, Jongryul, 「Labor Law」, 14th ed., Parkyoungsa, 2016, p. 35; Supreme Court ruling on Jan. 29, 2015, 2012doo28247.

Ⅱ. 노조법상의 근로자

근로기준법의 근로자는 제2조 제1호에서 "근로자"란 직업의 종류와 관계없이 임금을 목적으로 사업이나 사업장에 근로를 제공하는 자를 말한다고 정의하고 있고, 근로자의 개념 요소를 '직업의 종류를 불문하고', '사업 또는 사업장에', '임금을 목적으로 근로를 제공하는 자'라고 설명하고 있다. 근로자의 개념 설정에서 임금을 그 중심개념으로 두고 있으며, 또한, 노무제공자와 노무이용자 사이에 사용종속관계를 근로자의 핵심적인 요소로 파악하고 있다. 즉, 근로자란 사용종속관계에서 임금을 목적으로 근로를 제공하는 자라고 할 수 있다.[3)] 사용종속관계란 근로자가 사용자에게 고용되어 근로를 제공한다는 것으로, 사용자의 지휘·명령을 받는 근로자는 그 사용자가 원하는 내용의 일을 하는 것을 말한다. 근로자는 근로의 대가로 임금을 받고 노동력을 제공하는 것이므로 '사용종속관계 아래서 근로를 제공하는 자'로 이해할 수 있다.[4)]

노조법상의 근로자는 제2조 제1호에서 "근로자"란 함은 직업의 종류를 불문하고 임금, 급료 기타 이에 준하는 수입으로 생활하는 자로 정의하고 있다. 여기서 임금을 받는 자는 근로기준법상 근로자이고 기타 이에 준하는 수입으로 생활하는 자는 근로자가 아닌 노조법상의 근로자이다. 이러한 수입은 타인에게 종속적 근로는 아니지만 이와 비슷한 노무를 공급하는 등의 대가로 얻는 수입을 말한다. 따라서 노조법의 근로자는 임금수입으로 생활하는 근로자, 수입이 없는 실업자, 종속적인 관계는 없지만, 지속적으로 수입을 위해 노동을 제공하는 자를 포함한다.[5)] 즉, 근로기준법상 근로자는 인적 종속성과 경제적 종속성을 모두 갖고 있지만, 노조법상의 근로자는 경제적 종속성만 있으면 근로자로 포함하고 있다. 그러나 영세 자영업자처럼 독립적인 노무를 제공하는 자나 근로의 의사가 없는 학생이나 구직을 포기한 자는 여기에 해당되지 않는다.

---

3) 임종률, 「노동법」 제18판, 박영사, 2020, 32면.

4) 하갑래, 「근로기준법」 제33판, 중앙경제사, 2020, 32~36면; 대법원 2006.12.7, 2004다29736, 종합반 입시강사의 근로자성.

5) 임종률, 「노동법」, 제18판, 박영사, 2020, 35면; 대법원 2015.1.29, 2012두28247.

employed persons, students who are not ready to work, or those who have given up looking for a job.

A parcel delivery worker is not a worker earning wages per hour from an employer, but an individual contractor who receives a service fee according to the number of parcels delivered. Since such individual contractors are not workers under the Labor Standards Act, they are protected as workers under the Trade Union Act only. Therefore, it is necessary to distinguish the characteristics of these two different types of worker.

If a worker is recognized as a worker under the Trade Union Act, he/she may exercise the three labor rights(independent association, collective bargaining, and collective action) as a worker. Individual parcel delivery people who are registered as individual business owners and whose income depends on the quantity they deliver can only organize labor unions and demand collective bargaining in order to improve their working conditions. In this case, the employer must comply with the collective bargaining requests of labor unions, with the labor unions able to increase their bargaining power through strikes favoring collective bargaining. If an employer's property is damaged through collective bargaining or labor strikes, the employer cannot terminate the contract with the delivery agent or claim damages.[6)]

6) Articles 3, 4, 81 of the Trade Union Act.

택배배달원은 사업장에 소속되어 업무시간당 임금을 받는 근로자가 아니라 배달하는 소포우편물 개수에 따라 용역수수료를 받는 개인사업자에 해당된다. 이러한 개인사업자는 근로기준법상의 근로자가 아니기 때문에 노조법상의 근로자로서만 보호를 받고 있다. 따라서, 근로기준법상 근로자와 구분되는 노조법상 근로자의 의의를 살펴볼 볼 필요가 있다

노조법상의 근로자로 인정되는 경우 노동3권(단결권, 단체교섭권, 단체 행동권)을 행사할 수 있다. 택배 배달원들이 개별 사업자등록을 하고, 배달 수량에 따라 수입을 가져가는 개인 사업자이지만, 근로조건의 향상을 위하여 노동조합을 조직하고 단체교섭을 요구할 수 있다. 이 경우 사용자는 노동조합의 단체협약 요구에 반드시 응해야 하고, 노동조합은 단체교섭을 유리하게 이끌기 위해 파업을 통해 교섭력을 높일 수 있고, 사업주는 단체교섭 과정이나 쟁의행위로 인해 손해를 입은 경우, 택배 배달원과의 용역계약을 해지하거나 손해배상을 청구할 수 없다.[6)]

6) 노조법 제3조, 제4조, 제81조.

Section 2: Requirements to Protect Labor Unions

Employees may organize, at their own discretion, a labor union to maintain or improve their working conditions or promote their social and economic status. There are no statutory restrictions on the organizational structure of a union. Accordingly, employees are free to organize one, whether it is company, industry-level, or occupation-based.

The labor union shall be established under the substantial requirements of Article 2, subparagraph 4, of the Trade Union Act and the formal requirements of Article 10 of the same Act, so it can be recognized and protected under the general rights of the Act. The labor union shall substantially meet the requirements, which include subject, independence, purpose and association. Although the labor union meets the requirements, any person who intends to establish a labor union under the Trade Union Act shall submit a report of establishment, together with the union's bylaws, to administrative agencies such as the Minister of Employment and Labor, the mayors and provincial governors with jurisdiction over the area, and then obtain certificates of report of establishment from the administrative agencies. When a labor union has received these certificates of report, it is considered established as of the time when the Minister of Employment and Labor received the report.

Ⅰ. Substantial Requirements

Article 2 of the Trade Union Act (Definitions)

4. The term labor union means an organization, or associated organizations of workers, formed in a voluntary and collective manner upon the workers' initiative for the purpose of maintaining and improving their working conditions and enhancing their economic and social status. However, an organization shall not be regarded as a labor union in the following cases:

A. An employer, or other persons who always act in the interest of the employer, are allowed to join;

B. Most of its expenditures are paid for by the employer;

C. Its activities are only aimed at mutual support, self-improvement, and other welfare undertakings;

D. Those who are not workers are allowed to join; and

E. Its aims are mainly directed at political issues.

제2절 노동조합이 법적 보호를 받기 위한 조건

근로자들은 자주적으로 단결하여 근로조건의 유지·개선, 기타 근로자의 사회적·경제적 지위의 향상을 도모하기 위하여 노동조합을 결성할 수 있다. 노동조합의 조직형태는 법적 제한이 없으며, 근로자는 자주적인 의사에 따라 기업별, 산업별, 직종별 노조 등을 결성할 수 있다.

노동조합이 노조법상 노동조합으로 인정받아 노동법이 보호하는 제반 권리를 향유하기 위해서는 노조법 제2조 제4호에서 규정하는 실질적 요건과 제10조에서 규정하는 형식적 요건을 모두 구비하여야 한다. 노동조합은 주체성·자주성·목적성 및 단체성이라는 실질적 요건을 갖추어야 하며, 노동조합으로서의 실질적 요건을 갖추고 있다 하더라도 노조법상의 노동조합으로 설립되기 위해서는 설립신고서에 규약을 첨부하여 고용노동부 장관 또는 특별시장·광역시장·도지사 등 행정관청에 이를 제출한 후, 행정관청으로부터 신고증을 교부받아야만 하고, 노동조합이 위와 같이 신고증을 교부받은 경우에는 설립신고서가 접수된 때에 설립된 것으로 보게 된다.

Ⅰ. 실질적 요건

노조법 제2조【정 의】

4. "노동조합"이라 함은 근로자가 주체가 되어 자주적으로 단결하여 근로조건의 유지·개선 기타 근로자의 경제적·사회적 지위의 향상을 도모함을 목적으로 조직하는 단체 또는 그 연합단체를 말한다. 다만, 다음 각목의 1에 해당하는 경우에는 노동조합으로 보지 아니한다.

가. 사용자 또는 항상 그의 이익을 대표하여 행동하는 자의 참가를 허용하는 경우

나. 경비의 주된 부분을 사용자로부터 원조 받는 경우

다. 공제·수양 기타 복리사업만을 목적으로 하는 경우

라. 근로자가 아닌 자의 가입을 허용하는 경우.

마. 주로 정치운동을 목적으로 하는 경우

1. Positive requirements

The labor union shall be an organization or associated organizations of workers, formed in a voluntary and collective manner upon the workers' initiative for the purpose of maintaining and improving their working conditions and enhancing their economic and social status. These positive requirements must be established by the labor union.

(1) Subject of rights: Employees' organization

The labor union shall be formed under a united organization of workers to protect rights. The Trade Union Act defines the term worker as a person who, being subordinate to an employer, works for the employer and receives wages in return, whatever the subordinate relationship with the employer is called(such as employment, subcontracting, commissioning or an untitled contract). In order to determine whether the person is subordinate to the employer or not, it is necessary to examine what is really happening between the two: if wages are given for work under the employer's control and instruction; if wages are given in return for the work; and what kind of work is being provided.

The employees belonging to a union at the employer's company should have a subordinate relationship with the employer. Accordingly, persons who are not subordinate to the employer may not form a legitimate labor union, as defined in the Trade Union Act, at the employer's company.

(2) Independence

The labor union shall be formed as a collective group by the basic principle of establishment. The labor union represents a group separate from the employer and shall behave voluntarily and collectively upon the workers' free will without the intervention of the labor office or the employer. Otherwise it loses its independence.

(3) Purpose

The labor union shall be an organization established for the purpose of maintaining and improving the working conditions and enhancing the economic and social status of workers.

1. 적극적 요건

노동조합은 근로자가 주체가 되어야 하고, 자주적으로 단결하여야 하며, 궁극적으로 근로자의 근로조건 유지·개선 및 경제적·사회적 지위 향상을 목적으로 하여야 한다는 것이 노동조합이 갖추어야 할 적극적인 요건이다.

(1) 주체: 근로자의 조직

노동조합은 근로자가 주체가 되어 단결된 조직이어야 한다. 노조법상의 근로자란 사용자와 사용종속관계 하에서 노무에 종사하고 대가로 임금 등을 받아 생활하는 자를 말하고, 사용자와 사용종속관계가 있는 한 당해 노무공급계약의 형태가 고용, 도급, 위임, 무명계약 등 어느 형태이든 상관없으며 사용종속관계는 사용자와 노무제공자 사이에 지휘 감독관계의 여부, 보수의 노무대가성 여부, 노무의 성질과 내용 등 노무의 실질관계에 의하여 결정된다.

노동조합의 구성원인 근로자와 사용주 사이에는 고용에 따른 종속관계가 있어야 하고 이러한 관계가 없는 자는 노조법이 정한 적법한 노동조합을 조직할 수 없다.

(2) 자주성

노동조합은 '자주적'으로 조직되는 단체이어야 하며, 이는 노동조합의 설립운영의 기본 원칙이다. 노동조합은 사용자와 대항하는 단체이므로 근로자를 대상으로 하여 근로자가 주체가 되어 행정관청, 사용자의 개입에 의하지 않고 근로자가 스스로의 주도권을 가지고 활동하지 않으면 설사 근로자에 의하여 설립되고 운영되더라도 그 자주성은 상실되고 마는 것이다.

(3) 목 적

노동조합은 근로자의 근로조건 유지·개선 및 경제적·사회적 지위 향상을 도모함을 목적으로 조직되는 단체이어야 한다.

2. Negative requirements

The labor union shall be free of the following negative requirements:

(1) An employer, or other persons, who always act in the interest of the employer, are allowed to join.

This is designed to prevent the labor union from becoming a company union and to promote equality and independence by excluding the employer and other persons who act in the interest of the employer. A person who, in relation to the employees of the business, acts in the interest of the employer or represents the employer's interest, is a person who is given a certain mandate and responsibility to determine working conditions and personnel matters or make orders or instructions on work. In order to determine whether a particular person has such a mandate and responsibility, his/her actual and specific duties, rather than his official position or title, should be examined. Although some union members were allowed in by the union despite their ineligibility for membership because they are acting in the interest of the employer, the union does not immediately forfeit its status as a labor union under the Trade Union Act. It will be forfeited only in cases where the autonomy of the labor is infringed in reality or is likely to be infringed.[7)]

(2) Most of its expenditures are paid for by the employer.

The labor union shall not receive regular subsidies or assistance from the employer, other than the least possible support such as an office, office fixtures, etc.

(3) Its activities are only aimed at mutual support, self-improvement, and other welfare undertakings.

The labor union shall be designed to maintain or improve working conditions. If the labor union exists only for the betterment of welfare, it shall not be recognized as a labor union.

(4) Those who are not workers are allowed to join

An employee who was dismissed from the relevant workplace may also maintain

7) Supreme Court ruling on Jan. 19, 2004: 2001da5142.

2. 소극적 요건

노동조합이 배제하여야 할 요건, 즉 결격 요건을 의미한다.

(1) 사용자 또는 항상 그의 이익을 대표하여 행동하는 자의 참가를 허용하는 경우

이는 사용자와 그 이익대표자의 노조참여를 배제시킴으로써 노동조합의 어용화를 방지하고 노사 교섭력의 균형과 자주성을 확보하기 위한 것이다. 사업의 근로자에 관한 사항에 대하여 사업주를 위하여 행동하는 자 또는 사용자의 이익을 대표하여 행동하는 자라 함은 근로자의 인사·급여·노무관리 등 근로조건의 결정 또는 업무상의 명령이나 지휘감독을 하는 등의 사항에 대하여 일정한 권한과 책임을 부여받는 자를 말하는데, 그 권한과 책임의 유무는 직제상의 명칭에 의하여 형식적·획일적으로 판단할 것이 아니라 실질적·구체적으로 판단하여야 한다. 노동조합이 사용자의 이익대표자 참가를 허용함으로써 조합원 중에 일부가 조합원으로서의 자격이 없는 경우, 바로 노조법상의 노동조합의 지위를 상실하는 것이 아니라 이로 인하여 이 법이 규정하는 노동조합의 자주성이 현실적으로 침해되었거나 침해될 우려가 있는 경우에만 노동조합의 지위를 상실한다.[7)]

(2) 경비의 주된 부분을 사용자로부터 원조 받는 경우

노동조합은 사무실이나 집기 등 최소한의 지원 이외의 정기적인 보조금 또는 원조를 사용자로부터 받아서는 아니 된다.

(3) 공제·수양 기타 복리사업만을 목적으로 하는 경우

노동조합은 근로조건의 유지·개선이 본래의 목적이므로 이 목적을 떠나 복리사업만을 목적으로 하는 경우 노동조합이라 할 수 없다.

(4) 근로자가 아닌 자의 가입을 허용하는 경우

그 해당 사업장에서 해고된 자도 조합원의 자격을 유지할 수 있다. 그러나 해

7) 대법원 2004.1.29, 2001다5142.

their union membership. However, a dismissed person cannot serve as a union officer. However, if a dismissed person applies for remedy for unfair labor practices to the Labor Commission, he or she may maintain the status of a union officer until a re-examination by the National Labor Commission is made.

★ **Unemployed person**: This stipulation in Paragraph 4(d) of Article 2 of the Trade Union Act was established to prevent denial of the employee characteristic when a union member is dismissed by an employer, and is used on a very limited basis for cases like this. This stipulation is not applicable to those employees belonging to industrial, occupational and regional unions, which do not need subordinate relationships with particular employers. The 'employee' stipulated by Paragraph 1 and 4(d) of Article 2 of the Trade Union Act does not only refer to employees hired by the particular employer directly, but also to those who are unemployed temporarily and looking for a job, as long as they are entitled to the employee's three rights.

(5) Its aims are mainly directed at political issues.

Before its revision, Article 12 of the Trade Union Act prohibiting unions from engaging in political activities has been deleted and this new article has been replaced to protect the labor union from losing its purpose.

Ⅱ. Formal Requirements

Any person who intends to establish a labor union shall submit a report specifying the related matters, together with the bylaws, to the Minister of Employment and Labor. Upon receiving the certificate of report, the union shall be recognized as established from the time it notifies the Minister of Employment and Labor of its establishment.[8)]

The fundamental reason that the Trade Union Act requires a report on union establishment lies in the need of the competent authorities to protect and guide labor unions to ensure that they are organized into an effective and orderly system and are operated as independent and democratic organizations.

---

8) Article 12 of the Trade Union Act.

고된 자는 조합임원을 맡을 수 없다. 다만, 해고된 자가 노동위원회에 부당노동행위의 구제신청을 한 경우에는 중앙노동위원회 재심판정이 있을 때까지는 조합임원의 지위를 유지할 수 있다.

★ **실업자**: 노조법 제2조 제4호 ④목 단서는 '기업별 노동조합'의 조합원이 사용자로부터 해고됨으로써 근로자성이 부인될 경우에 대비하여 마련된 규정으로, 이와 같은 경우에만 한정적으로 적용된다. 원래부터 일정한 사용자에의 종속관계를 필요로 하지 않는 산업별·직종별·지역별 노동조합 등의 경우까지 적용되는 것은 아니다. 노조법 제2조 제1호 및 제4호 ④목 본문에서 말하는 '근로자'는 특정한 사용자에게 고용되어 현실적으로 취업하고 있는 자뿐만 아니라, 일시적으로 실업 상태에 있는 자나 구직중인 자도 노동3권을 보장할 필요성이 있는 한 그 범위에 포함된다.

(5) 주로 정치운동을 목적으로 하는 경우

이는 종전 노조법 제12조의 정치활동 금지규정을 삭제하는 대신 노동조합의 기능이 노동조합 본래의 목적에서 벗어나지 못하도록 하기 위한 것이다.

Ⅱ. 형식적 요건

노동조합은 일정한 사항을 기재한 신고서에 규약을 첨부하여 고용노동부 장관에게 신고하여야 하며, 설립 신고증을 교부받은 경우에는 설립신고서가 접수된 때에 설립된 것으로 본다.[8)]

노조법이 노동조합의 설립에 관하여 신고주의를 택하고 있는 취지는 소관 행정당국으로 하여금 노동조합에 대한 효율적인 조직체계의 정비·관리를 통하여 노동조합이 자주성과 민주성을 갖춘 조직으로 존속할 수 있도록 노동조합을 보호·육성하고 그 지도·감독에 철저를 기하게 하기 위한 노동정책적인 고려에서 마련된 것이다.

8) 노조법 제12조.

Section 3: Reasons for Disqualification of a Labor Union

Workers are free to establish and join a labor union according to their basic rights guaranteed by the Constitution. However, Trade Union Act stipulates that a union that allows the employer or persons acting on behalf of the employer to become members, that association shall be disqualified from being declared a labor union. The restriction that a labor union shall not allow membership for the employer also extends to representatives of the employer's interests. The Trade Union Act restricts the scope of union membership in this way to ① protect the independence of the union by preventing someone directly representing the employer from joining it and controlling or intervening in its operations and ② maintain the balance of bargaining power between labor and management by preventing the leakage of employer-related confidential information to the union.[9] For this reason, if a worker who is prohibited from joining a labor union joins such a union, that union becomes disqualified as it can no longer serve to protect labor rights under the Trade Union Act.

Recently, more than 100 office workers in a public corporation formed a labor union and received a Certificate of Union Establishment from the Ministry of Employment and Labor(MOEL). However, the employer claimed that some of the union members included workers who are prohibited from joining a labor union under the Trade Union Act, and filed a complaint with the MOEL so as to disqualify the Office Workers' Labor Union. Herein, I would like to examine whether these workers are prohibited from joining a labor union according to the Trade Union Act.

9) MOEL Guidelines: Nojo 01254-665, June 28, 1996.

제3절 노동조합 결격사유

근로자는 헌법으로 보장하고 있는 기본권에 따라 자유롭게 노동조합을 설립하고 가입할 수 있다. 다만, 노조법에서는 노동조합의 결격사유로 '사용자 또는 항상 그의 이익을 대표하여 행동하는 자의 참가를 허용하는 경우'를 규정함으로써 가입 제한 범위를 '사용자' 뿐 아니라 '사용자의 이익대표자'로 넓게 해석하고 있다. 노조법에서 이와 같이 노동조합 가입범위를 제한하는 이유는 ① 사용자에 속하는 자가 노동조합에 가입하여 노동조합의 조직운영에 지배·개입하는 행위를 방지함으로써 노조의 자주성을 보호하고자 하는 것이며 ② 한편으로는 사용자의 노무관련 기밀에 관한 사항이 노조에 누설됨을 예방하여 노사 교섭력의 균형을 기하고자 하는 데 있다.[9] 이러한 이유로 가입이 제한되는 근로자가 노동조합에 가입하는 경우 노조법상 결격사유가 있다고 판단하여 노조법상 노동조합의 권리를 인정받지 못하게 된다.

최근 한 공기업의 사무직 근로자 100여명이 노동조합을 결성하고 고용노동부로부터 '노동조합 설립신고증'을 교부받았다. 그러나 사용자는 노동조합의 조합원 중 노조법상 가입제한범위에 해당하는 직원들이 일부 포함되어 있다고 주장하며 고용노동부에 사무직 노조설립 신고증을 반려해달라는 진정을 제기한 사건이 있었다. 이하에서는 이 사건 사용자의 주장대로 조합원들이 실제 노조법상 가입제한범위에 해당하는지 관련 법리에 따라 검토하고자 한다.

9) 고용노동부 행정해석: 노조 01254-665, 1996.6.28.

Ⅰ. Criteria for Determining Disqualification

1. Requirements for establishing a labor union

Article 2, Paragraph 4 of the Trade Union Act regulates, The term 'labor union' means an organization or associated organization of workers which is formed in a voluntary and collective manner upon the workers' initiative for the purpose of maintaining and improving working conditions, or improving the economic and social status of workers, which is the substantive requirement. Article 10, paragraph 1 of the same Act stipulates that a Report on Establishment shall be submitted to the MOEL, which is the formal requirement. The Trade Union Act explains that in order for such a labor union to be legitimate, it must meet both substantive and formal requirements.

The substantive requirement is designed to assess whether a union has identity, independence, purpose and collective nature,[10)] in which case it is not regarded as a labor union under the Trade Union Act if an employer or other persons who always act in their employer's interests are allowed to join the organization; in cases where most of the expenditures are provided for by the employer; where those who are not workers are allowed to join the organization, etc., the union's identity, independence, purpose and collective nature must be protected.

The formal requirement is for the labor union to report its establishment to and receive a Confirmation of Registration letter from the MOEL. A person who intends to establish a labor union shall prepare a report with the union constitution attached, which describe the union's democratic and independent operations(Article 10(1) of the Act). The MOEL shall return any report filed by a labor union to which any item in Article 12(3) apply(related to disqualification). The purpose of requiring such a report regarding the establishment of a labor union is to ensure it can survive as an independent, democratic organization through effective maintenance and management of the administrative organization.[11)]

10) Lim, Jongyul, 「Labor Law」, 18th ed., Park Young Sa, 2020, p. 60.

11) Supreme Court ruling on Oct. 14, 1997, 96 nu 9829.

Ⅰ. 노동조합의 결격사유 판단기준

1. 노동조합 설립요건

노조법 제 2조 제 4호는 "노동조합이란 근로자가 주체가 되어 자주적으로 단결하여 근로조건의 유지·개선 기타 근로자의 경제적·사회적 지위의 향상을 도모함을 목적으로 조직하는 단체 또는 그 연합단체를 말한다" 고 규정하면서('실체적 요건'), 동법 제 10조 제1항에서 설립신고라는 '형식적 요건'을 규정하고 있다. 노조법은 이와 같이 적법한 노동조합이 설립되기 위해서는 실체적 요건과 형식적 요건을 모두 충족해야 한다는 입장이며 실질적 심사주체는 행정관청이 담당하고 있다.

실체적 요건은 노동조합이 주체성, 자주성, 목적성, 단체성을 갖추었는지 심사하는 것으로, [10] 사용자 또는 항상 그의 이익을 대표하여 행동하는 자의 참가를 허용하는 경우, 경비의 주된 부분을 사용자로부터 원조 받는 경우, 근로자가 아닌 자의 가입을 허용하는 경우 등의 사유에 해당하는 때는 노조법상 노동조합으로 보지 않는다. 이는 노동조합의 실체적 요건인 노동조합의 주체성, 자주성, 목적성과 단체성을 갖추어야 한다는 것이다.

형식적 요건은 노동조합이 설립신고를 하여 신고증을 교부받아야 한다. 노동조합을 설립하고자 자는 노동조합의 민주적 자주적 운영을 명시한 규약을 첨부하여 설립 신고하여야 하고(제10조 제1항), 행정관청은 설립하고자 하는 노동조합이 결격사유에 해당하는 경우에는 설립신고서를 반려하여야 한다(제12조 제3항). 노동조합의 설립에 관하여 신고주의를 택한 취지는 노동조합의 조직체계에 대한 행정관청의 효율적인 정비·관리를 통하여 노동조합이 자주성과 민주성을 갖춘 조직으로 존속할 수 있도록 보호·육성하려는 데에 있다. [11]

---

10) 임종률, 「노동법」, 제18판, 박영사, 2020, 60면.
11) 대법원 1997.10.14, 96누9829.

2. Labor unions that remain unregistered due to their disqualification from establishment

Once the MOEL has received a Report on Establishment, it shall issue a Confirmation of Registration letter within three days,[12] except when ① supplementation is required or ② when it is necessary to reject the report on establishment. Since unions are established under a registration system rather than a permit system, once a Confirmation of Registration letter is issued, the union shall be considered to have been established as of the date of receipt of the Report on Establishment by the MOEL.

1) Supplementation is required if some problem is detected in the Report on Establishment. If a report does not have the union constitution attached or if the union constitution was not enacted by direct, secret and anonymous ballot, an order for supplementation shall be issued, to be fulfilled within 20 days.

2) On the other hand, if the reasons for disqualification are related to the establishment of the union, the MOEL may reject the Report on Establishment. If it sends an order for correction, then correction shall be made by the applying union within 30 days. If it fails to do so within that period, it shall be regarded as an unregistered union.[13]

Notwithstanding the principles of free registration for labor unions, the MOEL shall issue a Confirmation of Registration only to unions that meet certain requirements. Labor unions that are not established in accordance with the Trade Union Act cannot be protected by that Act because they are unregistered. There are three types of unregistered unions: ① No attempt at registration was made, ② The union's Report on Establishment was rejected, or ③ A previously-registered union was disqualified.

If a labor union becomes unregistered, it does not have the following benefits:(1) Immunity from civil and criminal liability(Articles 3 and 4), ② Legal status(Article 6), ③ The right to apply for adjustment in labor disputes, or to apply to the Labor Relations Commission for remedy against unfair labor practices(Articles 7(1) and 82), ④ The right to use a labor union name(Article 7), ⑤ Tax-exempt status(Article 8), ⑥ Authority to engage in collective bargaining and conclude collective agreements(Article 29), ⑦ The right to participate in the procedure for determining a bargaining representative union(Article 29-2), ⑧ The right to engage in collective action during disputes, which

12) Article 19, Paragraph 1 of the Act on the Handling of Civil Complaints: If the period for processing a complaint is set to 5 days or less, it shall be calculated in hours from the time of receipt of the complaint, but holidays and Saturdays shall not be counted. In this case, one day shall consist of eight working hours.

13) Trade Union Act: Article 12(2), (3)-1 ho; Enforcement Decree to the Trade Union Act: Article 9(2).

2. 설립요건 결격사유와 법외 노동조합

설립신고서를 접수한 행정관청은 ① 보완이 필요한 경우 또는 ② 반려해야 할 경우를 제외하고 3일 이내[12]에 신고증을 교부해야 한다. 노동조합의 설립은 허가제가 아니라 신고제라는 점에서 신고증을 교부받은 경우, 설립신고서를 행정관청에 접수한 날부터 노동조합의 법적 효력이 발생된다.

1) '보완이 필요한 경우'는, 일부 미비사항을 개선하면 설립 신고필증이 발행되는 경우인데 설립신고증에 규약이 첨부되어 있지 않거나, 규약을 직접, 비밀, 무기명 투표로 제정하지 않은 경우 보완명령을 하며, 보완기간은 20일이다.

2) 한편 노동조합 설립에 '결격사유'가 포함된 경우 행정관청은 노조설립신고를 반려할 수 있으며, 30일의 기간을 정하여 시정을 요구하고 그 기간 내에 이를 이행하지 아니하는 경우 당해 노동조합에 대하여 법외 노조 판단을 한다.[13]

노동조합은 자유설립 원칙임에도 불구하고, 일정한 요건을 갖춘 노동조합에 대해서만 행정관청은 노동조합 신고증을 교부해주고 있다. 이렇게 노조법에 따라 설립되지 않은 노동조합은 법외 노조라고 하여 노조법의 보호를 받지 못한다. 그 유형으로는 ① 설립신고를 하지 않거나, ② 신고수리가 거부되거나, ③ 신고 수리된 후 사후적으로 법외노조 통보를 받은 단결체가 있다.

법외노조가 되면 박탈되는 노조법상 권리로는 ① 조합활동 및 쟁의행위에서 민·형사상 면책권(제3조 및 제4조), ② 법인격 취득(제6조), ③ 노동쟁의조정신청권 및 부동노동행위 구제신청권(제7조 제1항 및 제82조), ④ 노동조합 명칭사용(제7조), ⑤ 조세면제권(제8조), ⑥ 단체교섭 및 협약체결 권한(제29조), ⑦ 교섭창구 단일화절차 참여권(제29조의2), ⑧ 노동조합의 주도에 의한 쟁위행위(제37조), ⑨ 필수유지업무 근무 근로자의 지정권(제42조의6), ⑩ 특별조정위원에 대한 배제권(제72조), ⑪ 부당노동행위 구제신청권(제81조) 이다.

---

12) 민원처리에 관한 법률 제 19조 제 1항 " 민원의 처리기간을 5일 이하로 정한 경우, 민원의 접수 시각부터 '시간'단위로 계산하되, 공휴일과 토요일은 산입(算入)하지 아니한다. 이 경우 1일은 8시간의 근무시간을 기준으로 한다.

13) 노조법 제12조 제2항, 제3항 제1호, 노조법 시행령 제9조 제2항.

is normally afforded to labor unions(Article 37), ⑨ The right to designate workers for essential maintenance services(Article 42-6), ⑩ The right to be excluded from participating in a special mediation committee(Article 72), and ⑪ The right to apply for redress of unfair labor practices(Article 81).

Ⅱ. Review of Related Cases

The MOEL office will order corrective action if there is a reason to disqualify from registration an existing union or a union that has submitted a Report on Establishment. If the corrective action is not taken, then a Certificate of Registration will not be issued to the reporting union, or registration will be canceled for an already existing union. There are two main reasons for disqualification. First, the union allowed membership for an employer or those working directly for the employer's interests. Second, the labor union's constitution contains content that is undemocratic or violates its independence or the Trade Union Act.

1. In cases where a member is the employer or someone working directly for the employer's interest

Relevant MOEL guidelines explain that those who act on behalf of the employer in matters relating to workers under Article 2(2) of the Trade Union Act are ① those who are engaged in determination of working conditions such as personnel, salary, welfare, labor management, etc.; ② those who have been given a certain authority and responsibility by the employer over matters such as ordering, supervision, etc.; ③ and those in charge of management of personnel and labor such as recruitment, dismissal, and job transfer; ④ those in charge of determining wages, working hours, breaks and other working conditions and confidentiality of labor relations; and ⑤ those with authority or direct involvement in internal and external regulations and other policy decisions. This includes employees and directors in charge of human resources and labor, and employees and managers in charge of management planning. In addition, those who act in the employer's interest in Article 2(4) of the Trade Union Act refer to those acting on behalf of the employer with respect to the workers of the business, such as the employer's assistants, employees in supervisory positions, and employees and directors in charge of accounting in the company, directors' drivers, and security personnel engaged in surveillance, patrols and other policing duties.[14)]

---

14) MOEL Guidelines: nojo 01254-665, June 28, 1996.

Ⅱ. 관련사례 검토

노동조합이 설립을 위해 설립신고서를 행정관청에 제출한 경우, 행정관청은 설립하고자 하는 노동조합에 결격사유가 있는 경우 시정을 명하고 시정되지 않는 경우 신고증을 교부 하지 않거나, 기존의 노동조합에 대해서는 설립신고를 취소시킬 수 있다. 그 결격사유는 주로 2가지로 구분할 수 있다. 첫째, 사용자의 지위에 있는 자와 사용자의 이익대변자의 참가를 허용한 것이며, 둘째, 노조규약이 민주성과 자주성을 잃었거나 노조법을 위반하는 내용을 담고 있는 경우이다.

1. 사용자의 지위에 있는 자나 사용자의 이익대변자가 조합원인 경우

관련 행정해석은 노조법 제2조 제2호에서 그 사업의 근로자에 관한 사항에 대하여 사업주를 위하여 행동하는 자라 함은 ① 근로자의 인사, 급여, 후생, 노무관리 등 근로조건의 결정 또는 업무상의 명령이나 지휘감독을 하는 등의 사항에 대하여 사업주로부터 일정한 권한과 책임을 부여받은 자를 말하는 것으로 채용, 해고, 전보 등 인사·노무관리를 담당하는 자, ② 임금, 근로시간, 휴게시간 기타 근로조건의 결정과 노동관계에 관한 기밀사무를 담당하는 자, ③ 대내외 관계규정 기타의 방침결정에 대하여 권한을 갖거나 이에 직접 관여하는 자로서 일반적으로 인사·노무담당 직원 및 책임자, 경영기획담당 직원 및 책임자 등이 이에 해당한다. 또한, 동법 제2조 제4호 가목 후단의 항상 사용자의 이익을 대표하여 행동하는 자는 그 사업의 근로자에 관한 사항에 대하여 사업주를 위하여 행동하는 자와 유사한 의미를 가지나, 통상 사용자에 전속되어 사용자의 업무를 보조하는 비서, 전용 운전수와 사용자의 지시를 받아 근로자에 관한 감시·감독적 지위에 있는 감사담당 부서의 직원, 그리고 회사 내의 경리·회계를 전담하는 부서의 직원 및 책임자, 회사 내의 재산보호·출입자의 감시·순찰 등의 경찰적 업무를 담당하는 경비직 등이 이에 해당된다.[14)]

14) 고용노동부 행정해석: 노소 01254-665, 1996.6.28.

However, authority and responsibility for determining working conditions such as personnel, salary, welfare, and labor, or for ordering or supervising work should be considered in terms of specific facts such as the degree of involvement in the job and in workers' affairs, rather than only the formal title or status. This should be also judged in consideration of whether this authority has been granted by the employer or the manager in charge of the business and the degree of involvement in matters related to workers. Other details to be reviewed comprehensively are whether the persons in question have access to the employer's confidential information related to plans and policies.[15)]

2. Cancellation of a labor union's registration due to its constitution violating the Act on the Establishment, Operation, Etc. of Trade Unions for Teachers (hereinafter, the Teacher's Union Act)

Korea Teachers' Labor Union(KTU). The KTU is a representative case of disqualification because its constitution violated the Trade Union Act.

(1) Background to the KTU's disqualification[16)]

The KTU was founded in May 1989, and is a nationwide unit labor union that covers elementary and secondary school teachers, consisting of about 50,000 members in 2015. The KTU has been contributing to true education by working against bribery, prohibiting corporal punishment, eradicating private school corruptions, but has also been criticized for opposing the teacher evaluation system and for teaching political ideology.

On June 27, 1999, when the KTU was legalized, it established an additional clause(Article 5) in its Constitution to be able to allow 9 laid-off teachers to join, but this registration report did not include this article when reporting to the MOEL. In other words, in 1999, when the KTU reported its registration form, the provision that allowed it to retain dismissed teachers as members was hidden.

In 2010, the MOEL received a complaint from a conservative NGO that the KTU was keeping the 9 dismissed teachers as members. As a result, it was discovered that the union's

15) MOEL Guidelines: nojo 01254-383, May 24, 1999; nojo 01254-665, June 28, 1966.

16) Internet Encyclopedia: Wikipedia / Wooden Wiki, Search: National Teachers' Union of Korea, accessed on August 18, 2019.

다만, 형식적인 직급 명칭이나 지위보다는 직무내용 및 근로자에 관한 사항에 관여정도 등 구체적인 사실관계를 토대로 인사·급여·후생·노무관리 등 근로조건의 결정 또는 업무상의 명령이나 지휘감독 등에 관한 권한과 책임을 사업주 또는 사업의 경영담당자로부터 부여받고 있는지 여부, 근로자에 관한 사항에 관여정도 등을 감안하여 판단하여야 한다. 또한, 근로관계에 대한 계획과 방침 등 사용자의 기밀에 속하는 사항을 접하고 있는 경우 등 구체적인 사실관계를 종합적으로 검토하여 판단하여야 한다.[15)]

2. 규약위반에 따른 노동조합 설립 취소: 전국교직원노동조합

노조법에 정해진 결격사유 중 규약 기재사항 위반으로 설립이 취소되어 법외노조가 된 대표적 사례가 전국교직원노동조합(전교조)이다.

(1) 전교조의 법외 노조 배경[16)]

전교조는 1989년 5월에 창립되었으며, 초등, 중등 교원을 가입범위로 하는 전국규모의 단위노동조합으로 2015년 기준 5만여명의 조합원으로 구성되어 있다. 전교조는 그 동안 촌지추방, 체벌금지, 사학비리근절 등에 나서 참교육에 기여했다는 평가와 함께 교원평가제 반대, 정치적 이념수업 등으로 부정적 평가도 공존하고 있다.

전교조가 합법화된 1999년 6월 27일 전교조는 해직 교원(9명)도 가입할 수 있도록 내부 규약의 부칙 조항(5조)을 신설하였으나, 행정관청에 설립신고를 할 때는 본 조항이 포함되지 않은 규약을 제출하였다 즉, 1999년 전교조 설립신고 시에 해직자도 조합원 가입범위에 포함된다는 규정을 숨겼다.

고용노동부는 2010년 전교조가 해직자를 조합원으로 두고 있다는 보수성향 시민단체의 진정이 접수되어 전교조의 규약을 점검하였고, 그 결과 전교조의 규

15) 해정해석: 노조 01254-383, 1999.5.24; 노조 01254-665, 1996.6.28.
16) 인터넷 백과사전: 위키피디아·나무위키, "검색어: 전국교직원노동조합", 2019.8.18. 검색.

constitution violated the Trade Union Act[17] and the Teachers' Union Act.[18] So, in May 2010, the MOEL issued an order to the KTU to correct its constitution. The reason given was that dismissed teachers cannot become union members in accordance with Article 2 of the Teachers' Union Act and Article 2(4) of the Trade Union Act, and any union with non-employee members is subject to disqualification. In accordance with Article 9(2) of the Enforcement Decree to the Trade Union Act, the union was disqualified for failing to follow the correction order from the MOEL.

(2) The KTU challenges the judgement as unconstitutional[19]

The KTU challenged the constitutionality of the judgment with the following arguments:(1) The Trade Union Act and Teachers Union Act violate the constitutional right to organize, as they do not allow dismissed workers to join a labor union;(2) Rules not entrusted under legislation enacted by the National Assembly are a violation of legal principle: Article 9(2) of the Enforcement Decree to the Trade Union Act(which the MOEL used to disqualify the KTU), was enacted by the MOEL, and cannot be implemented without the actual Article stipulated in the Trade Union Act, passed in the National Assembly by lawmakers.

(3) Decision of the Constitutional Court[20]

The Constitutional Court dismissed the KTU's constitutional challenge on May 28, 2015. Even if some of the non-teachers are members of the teacher union, it is up to the discretion of the MOEL to decide whether to qualify or disqualify the labor union. In addition, the discretionary judgment of the MOEL on disqualification of the KTU as it includes some persons who are no longer teachers is based on the number of

---

17) Trade Union Act Article 2 (4ho) Disqualification item (4) D. Where those who are not workers are allowed to join the organization, Provided that a dismissed person shall not be regarded as a person who is not a worker, until a review decision is made by the National Labor Relations Commission when he/she has made an application to the Labor Relations Commission for remedy against unfair labor practices. (The underlined provision was deleted due to the revision of the union law in December 2020)

18) Teachers Union Act: Article 2. The term teacher in this Act refers to a person prescribed in Article 19 (1) of the Elementary and Secondary Education Act: Provided that any dismissed persons who have requested remedy for unfair labor practices to the Labor Relations Commission under Article 82 (1) of the Trade Union and Labor Relations Adjustment Act shall be regarded as teachers until a review decision is made by the National Labor Relations Commission under Article 2 of the Labor Relations Commission Act. (The underlined provision was deleted due to the revision of the union law in December 2020)

19) Seoul High Court ruling on Sep. 19, 2014: 2014ah413.

20) Constitutional Court decision on May 28, 2015, 2014 hunma 671, 2014 hunma 21.

약 부칙 5조가 노조법[17]과 교원노조법[18]에 위배된다고 판단하여 2010년 3월 첫 번째 시정명령을 내렸다. 고용노동부의 법외노조 통보 배경은 첫 번째는 교원노조법의 제2조와 노조법 제2조 제4호에 따라서 교원이 아닌 자가 조합원이 될 수 없고, 교원이 아닌 자가 가입된 전교조는 노동조합의 결격사유가 된다는 것이다. 둘째로 노조법 시행령 9조 제2항 따라 설립신고서 반려사유가 발생한 경우 시정을 요구하고 시정명령이 이행되지 않으면 노조설립을 취소한다는 것이다.

(2) 전교조의 위헌심판 제기[19]

전교조는 해직자 가입을 허용하지 않는 노조법과 이를 준용한 교원노조법은 헌법상 단결권을 침해하고 있다는 점. 노조법 시행령 제9조 제2항(행정관청의 노조법 결격사유에 대한 시정명령)에 관하여 국회에서 제정한 법률에서 구체적인 사항을 위임하지 않은 사항은 행정부처가 제정하는 시행령이나 시행규칙에서 정할 수 없다는 점 등을 들면서 위헌심판 청구를 하였다.

(3) 헌법재판소의 판결[20]

헌법재판소는 2015년 5월 28일 전교조의 위헌심판 청구를 기각하는 결정을 내렸고, 그 내용은 다음과 같다. "교원이 아닌 사람이 교원노조에 일부 포함돼 있다 하더라도 이를 이유로 법외노조로 할 것인지 여부는 행정당국의 재량적 판단에 달려 있다. 그리고 조합원 자격을 상실한 사람이 일부 포함돼 있는 노조를 상대로 법외노조통보를 한 재량적 판단에 대해서는 전교조에서 활동하는 자격 없는 조합원의 수, 그러한 조합원들이 교원노조 활동에 미치는 영향, 자격

17) 노조법 제2조 제4호 노동조합 결격사유: 라. 근로자가 아닌 자의 가입을 허용하는 경우. 다만, 해고된 자가 노동위원회에 부당노동행위의 구제신청을 한 경우에는 중앙노동위원회의 재심판정이 있을 때까지는 근로자가 아닌 자로 해석하여서는 아니된다. (단서 조항은 2020년 12월 노조법 개정으로 삭제됨)

18) 제2조【정의】이 법에서 "교원"이란 「초·중등교육법」 제19조 제1항에서 규정하고 있는 교원을 말한다. 다만, 해고된 사람으로서 「노동조합 및 노동관계조정법」 제82조 제1항에 따라 노동위원회에 부당노동행위의 구제신청을 한 사람은 「노동위원회법」 제2조에 따른 중앙노동위원회의 재심판정이 있을 때까지 교원으로 본다. (단서 조항은 2020년 12월 노조법 개정으로 삭제됨)

19) 서울고등법원 2014. 9. 19. 2014아413.

20) 헌재 2015.5.28, 2013헌마671; 2014헌가21.

unqualified members who are active in the union activities, the effect of such members on KTU activities, and the union activities of such unqualified members. This decision to disqualify the KTU is within the legal discretion of the MOEL.

In addition, the Constitutional Court stated, Adoption of the principle of reporting in relation to the establishment of a labor union allows the relevant union to survive as an independent, democratic organization through efficient maintenance and management of the organizational structure of a labor union. It is the purpose of labor policy considerations to protect, foster, and thoroughly guide and supervise.[21)] In particular, since the teachers' union is made up of unit labor unions under one nationwide organization, allowing non-teachers into membership is a reason for disqualification of its establishment under Article 2(4) of the Trade Union Act.

Ⅲ. Comments

If an employer places control over a union by becoming a member himself or having someone directly representing his interests become a member, this amounts to a violation of the union's identity and independence. On the other hand, when a large number of workers directly representing the employer's interest join the union, the company essentially falls under the control of the labor union, as confidentiality of the company's business will be impossible to maintain. This upsets the balance of power between labor and management. Therefore, to maintain this balance, the administrative office needs to be involved in the reasons for disqualification of a labor union from establishment.

In the same way, it should be judged as a disqualified labor union as the White Color Office Workers Union in this case includes the employer's managers and the representatives representing the employer's interests. Accordingly, the administrative office shall check the actual status of the union in accordance with Article 9(2) of the Enforcement Decree to the Trade Union Act, and order corrections within 30 days if reason exists to disqualify the union.

---

21) Constitutional Court decision on July 31, 2008, 2004 hunba 9.

없는 조합원의 노조활동을 금지 또는 제한하기 위한 행정당국의 적절한 조치 여부, 해당 노동조합이 이를 시정할 가능성이 있는지 여부 등을 종합해 볼 때 적법한 재량의 범위 안에 있다"고 판단하였다.

또한, 헌법재판소는 "노동조합법이 노동조합의 설립에 관하여 신고주의를 택하고 있는 것은 소관 행정당국으로 하여금 노동조합의 조직체계에 대한 효율적인 정비, 관리를 통하여 자주성과 민주성을 갖춘 조직으로 존속할 수 있도록 보호, 육성하고 그 지도와 감독에 철저를 기하기 위한 노동 정책적인 고려에 그 취지가 있다"[21]고 판시하고 있다. 특히 전교조가 전국을 대상으로 단위노동조합으로 되어 있기 때문에 노조법 제2조 제4호에 해당되어 교원이 아닌 자의 가입을 허용하는 경우에는 노조 설립의 결격사유가 된다는 것이다.

Ⅲ. 코멘트

사용자가 노동조합을 지배하기 위해 노조법상 사용자의 지위에 있는 자나 사용자의 이익대변자를 조합원으로 가입시킴으로써 노동조합을 사용자의 지배하에 두는 경우에는 노조의 주체성과 자주성을 침해하는 것이다. 이와 반대로 사용자의 이익을 대변하는 자가 노동조합에 다수 가입되어 사용자가 기밀사항을 준수할 수 없을 때 이는 오히려 노동조합이 사용자를 관리하는 상태가 되어 노사간의 힘의 우위가 유지될 수 없다. 따라서 노사간의 대등한 관계 유지를 위해 행정관청은 노동조합 설립의 결격사유에 대해 관여가 필요하다고 할 수 있다.

이와 같은 논리로 이 사건의 공공기관 사무직 노조가 사용자의 지위에 있는 자와 사용자의 이익대변자를 조합원으로 두는 것은 노조설립의 결격사유가 된다고 판단된다. 따라서 행정관청은 노조법 시행령 제9조 제2항에 따라 본 노동조합의 실태를 점검하고 노조의 결격사유가 있는 경우 30일 이내에 시정을 명하고, 기한 내에 시정되지 않는 경우 노조법 위반을 이유로 사무노조에 대해 노조설립을 취소하여야 할 것이다.

---

21) 헌재 2008.7.31, 2004헌바9.

Chapter 13

Labor Unions

Section 1: Establishment and Operation of a labor union

Ⅰ. Establishment of a labor union

Article 10 (Report on Establishment of Trade Union)

(1) Any person who intends to establish a trade union shall submit a report stating the following matters, accompanied by its bylaws provided for in Article 11 to the Minister of Employment and Labor in cases of the trade union in the form of the associated organization and the unit trade union extending over not less than two Special Metropolitan City, Metropolitan Cities, Special Self-Governing City, Dos, and Special Self-Governing Province, to the Special Metropolitan City Mayor, Metropolitan City Mayors and Do Governors in cases of the unit trade union extending over not less than two Sis/Guns/Gus, and to a Special Self-Governing City Mayor, a Special Self-Governing Province Governor, and the head of a Si/Gun/Gu in cases of any other trade unions:
1. Name; 2. The location of the principal office; 3. The number of union members; 4. Names and domiciles of executive officers; 5. Title of an associated organization to which it belongs, if any; 6. In cases of a trade union in the form of an associated organization, the titles of its constituent organizations, the number of union members, location of the main office, and the names and addresses of executive officers.

Article 11 (Regulations)

Any trade union shall enter the matters falling under each of the following subparagraphs in its bylaws in order to guarantee an autonomous and democratic operation of its organization:
1. Name; 2. Purposes and activities; 3. The location of the principal office; 4. Matters concerning union members; 5. Title of an associated organization to which it belongs, if any; 6. Matters concerning a council of delegates, if any; 7. Matters concerning meetings;
8. Matters concerning the representatives and executive officers; 9. Matters concerning union dues and other accounting; 10. Matters concerning modification of the union bylaws;
11. Matters regarding dissolution; 12. Matters concerning the publication of the result of the vote for and against the industrial actions and the keeping and perusal of the roll of voters and ballot papers, etc.; 13. Matters concerning impeachment on representatives or executive officers for

노동조합

제1절 노동조합의 설립과 운영

Ⅰ. 노동조합의 설립

제10조【설립의 신고】

① 노동조합을 설립하고자 하는 자는 다음 각호의 사항을 기재한 신고서에 제11조의 규정에 의한 규약을 첨부하여 연합단체인 노동조합과 2 이상의 특별시·광역시·특별자치시·도·특별자치도에 걸치는 단위노동조합은 고용노동부장관에게, 2 이상의 시·군·구에 걸치는 단위노동조합은 특별시장·광역시장·도지사에게, 그 외의 노동조합은 특별자치시장·특별자치도지사·시장·군수·구청장에게 제출하여야 한다.

1. 명칭;
2. 주된 사무소의 소재지
3. 조합원수
4. 임원의 성명과 주소
5. 소속된 연합단체가 있는 경우에는 그 명칭
6. 연합단체인 노동조합에 있어서는 그 구성노동단체의 명칭, 조합원수, 주된 사무소의 소재지 및 임원의 성명·주소

제11조【규약】

노동조합은 그 조직의 자주적·민주적 운영을 보장하기 위하여 당해 노동조합의 규약에 다음 각 호의 사항을 기재하여야 한다.

1. 명칭; 2. 목적과 사업; 3. 주된 사무소의 소재지; 4. 조합원에 관한 사항; 5. 소속된 연합단체가 있는 경우에는 그 명칭; 6. 대의원회를 두는 경우에는 대의원회에 관한 사항; 7. 회의에 관한 사항; 8. 대표자와 임원에 관한 사항; 9. 조합비 기타 회계에 관한 사항; 10. 규약변경에 관한 사항; 11. 해산에 관한 사항; 12. 쟁의행위와 관련된 찬반투표 결과의 공개, 투표자 명부

violation of the bylaws; 14. Matters concerning the procedures for election of executive officers and delegates; 15. Matters concerning discipline and control.

Article 12 (Issuance of Certificate of Report)

(1) Upon receiving a report on establishment as referred to in Article 10 (1), the Minister of Employment and Labor, the Special Metropolitan City Mayor, Metropolitan City Mayors, a Special Self-Governing City Mayor, Do Governors, a Special Self-Governing Province Governor, or the head of a Si/Gun/Gu shall issue a certificate of report within three days, except for cases provided for in the former part of paragraph(2) and paragraph(3).

(2) When the administrative agencies deems it necessary that a report on establishment or bylaws of a trade union needs to be supplemented because of any omission or other reasons, they shall order a supplement thereof within a specified period of up to 20 days, as prescribed by Presidential Decree. In such cases, a certificate of report shall be issued within three days after receiving the supplemented report on establishment or bylaws.

(3) When a trade union which made a report of establishment falls under any of the following subparagraphs, the administrative agencies shall return the report of establishment they received: 1. When it falls under any item of subparagraph 4 of Article 2; 2. When it fails to supplement a report or bylaws within the specified period, notwithstanding an order of supplement issued pursuant to paragraph (2).

(4) When a trade union receives the certificate of report, it shall be deemed to have been established at the time the Minister of Employment and Labor received the report of establishment.

Labor unions as defined in the Trade Union Act shall meet substantial and formal requirements in order to be established effectively.

Labor unions shall meet the substantial requirements, regarding subject, independence, purpose and association. Although a labor union meets these substantial requirements, any person who intends to establish a labor union in accordance with the Trade Union Act shall submit a report of establishment, together with the bylaws, to administrative agencies such as the Minister of Employment and Labor or a Special Metropolitan City mayor, a Metropolitan City mayor, and provincial governors, and then obtain certificates of report of establishment from the administrative agencies. When a labor union has received these certificates of report, it is construed as having been established at the time when the Minister of Employment and Labor received the report. Generally, although the Trade Union Act guarantees the freedom to set up labor unions, the fundamental reason that the Trade Union Act requires a report on union establishment lies in the need for the relevant authorities to protect and guide labor unions to ensure that they are organized into an effective and orderly system and operate as independent and democratic organizations.[22)]

---

22) Seoul Administrative Court ruling on Apr. 21, 2005: 2004 guhap 35536.

> 및 투표용지 등의 보존 · 열람에 관한 사항; 13. 대표자와 임원의 규약위반에 대한 탄핵에 관한 사항; 14. 임원 및 대의원의 선거절차에 관한 사항; 15. 규율과 통제에 관한 사항
>
> **제12조 【신고증의 교부】**
>
> ① 고용노동부장관, 특별시장·광역시장·특별자치시장·도지사·특별자치도지사 또는 시장·군수·구청장(이하 "행정관청"이라 한다)은 제10조제1항의 규정에 의한 설립신고서를 접수한 때에는 제2항 전단 및 제3항의 경우를 제외하고는 3일 이내에 신고증을 교부하여야 한다.
>
> ② 행정관청은 설립신고서 또는 규약이 기재사항의 누락등으로 보완이 필요한 경우에는 대통령령이 정하는 바에 따라 20일 이내의 기간을 정하여 보완을 요구하여야 한다. 이 경우 보완된 설립신고서 또는 규약을 접수한 때에는 3일 이내에 신고증을 교부하여야 한다.
>
> ③ 행정관청은 설립하고자 하는 노동조합이 다음 각호의 1에 해당하는 경우에는 설립신고서를 반려하여야 한다.
>
> 1. 제2조제4호 각목의 1에 해당하는 경우;2. 제2항의 규정에 의하여 보완을 요구하였음에도 불구하고 그 기간내에 보완을 하지 아니하는 경우
>
> ④ 노동조합이 신고증을 교부받은 경우에는 설립신고서가 접수된 때에 설립된 것으로 본다.

노조법상의 노동조합은 실질적 요건과 설립신고라는 형식적 요건을 갖추어야만 유효하게 설립될 수 있다.

노동조합은 주체성·자주성·목적성 및 단체성이라는 실질적 요건을 갖추어야 하며, 노동조합으로서의 실질적 요건을 갖추고 있다고 하더라도 노조법상의 노동조합으로 설립되기 위해서는 설립신고서에 규약을 첨부하여 노동부장관 또는 특별시장·광역시장·도지사 등 행정관청에 이를 제출한 후, 행정관청으로부터 신고증을 교부받아야만 하고, 노동조합이 위와 같이 신고증을 교부받은 경우에는 설립신고서가 접수된 때에 설립된 것으로 보게 된다. 이처럼 노조법이 노동조합의 설립에 관하여 기본적으로 노동조합의 설립 자유를 보장하면서 신고주의를 채택하고 있는 취지는 소관 행정관청으로 하여금 노동조합에 대한 효율적인 조직체계의 정비·관리를 통하여 노동조합이 자주성과 민주성을 갖춘 조직으로 존속할 수 있도록 노동조합을 보호·육성하고 그 지도·감독에 철저를 기하기 위한 노동정책적인 고려에서 마련된 것으로 풀이된다.[22]

---

22) 서울행정법원 2005.4.21, 2004구합35356.

Those who lose their eligibility for labor union membership due to a change in position can organize a labor union.

If employees lose their eligibility for existing labor union membership due to a change in position, they can establish a new labor union in cases where the part of Article 2 of the Trade Union Act, which states the status of an employer or a person representing the interest of the employer applies.[23)]

Employees that do not come under the scope of the existing union membership can establish a new labor union.

As a labor union organized in a specific business(workplace) allows union membership for 3rd grade position or lower according to its bylaws, employees with 2nd grade position or higher are clearly out of the scope of its membership. If employees with 2nd grade position or higher have not joined an industrial, regional, and/or occupational union and item(a) as described in subparagraph 4 of Article 2, and they are not 'an employer or other persons who always act in the interest of the employer,' they can establish a new labor union within their own scope.[24)]

Ⅱ. Admission of a labor union

Article 5 (Organization and Membership in the labor union)
Workers are free to organize a labor union or to join one, except for public servants or teachers who are subject to other enactments.

It is not justifiable to prohibit a former union member from rejoining the union.[25)]

1) To qualify for union membership, union members shall be employees stipulated under Article 2, Item 1 of the Trade Union Act, shall not fall under Article 2, Item 4(a) of the Act, which prohibits membership in the union for employees with the 'status of an employer or a person representing the interest of the employer', and that membership shall be determined autonomously by the labor union's bylaws.

2) According to Article 5 of the Trade Union Act, employees shall be free to join and leave a labor union. The joining procedures shall be stipulated in the bylaws of the labor union concerned. In cases where the labor union organized with a particular company's employees

23) MOEL Guidelines: Sept. 1, 2003, Nojo 68107-452.

24) MOEL Guidelines: Oct. 1, 2002, Nojo 68107-767.

25) MOEL Guidelines: May 22, 2002, nojo 68107-452.

직급변동으로 조합원 자격을 상실한 자의 노조 설립은 가능하다.

직급변동으로 기존 노동조합의 조합원 자격이 상실된 자의 경우 노조법 제2조 제4호 가목의 「사용자 또는 그의 이익대표자」에 해당되지 않는 경우에는 새로운 노동조합을 설립할 수 있다.[23)]

기존 노조의 조직범위에 포함되지 않은 직급의 근로자들로 새로운 노조를 설립할 수 있다.

특정 사업(장)에 조직된 노동조합이 규약상 조직범위로 3급 이하 근로자들만을 조직범위로 하고 있어 당해 사업(장)의 2급 이상의 근로자들과 조직대상이 명확히 구분되고 동 2급 이상의 근로자들이 산업별·지역별·직종별 노조 등에 가입하고 있지 않다면 동 2급 이상의 근로자들은 동법 제2조 제4호 가목 소정의 '사용자 또는 항상 그의 이익을 대표하여 행동하는 자'에 해당하지 않는 범위 내에서 새로운 노동조합을 설립할 수 있다.[24)]

Ⅱ. 노동조합의 가입

> **제5조【노동조합의 조직·가입】**
>
> 근로자는 자유로이 노동조합을 조직하거나 이에 가입할 수 있다. 다만, 공무원과 교원에 대하여는 따로 법률로 정한다.

노조 탈퇴자의 재가입을 제한하는 것은 정당하지 않다.[25)]

1) 노동조합에 가입할 수 있는 자의 자격 및 범위는 노조법 제2조 제1호의 규정에 의한 근로자로서 동법 제2조 제2호 및 제4호 가목 소정의 사용자 또는 항상 그의 이익을 대표하여 행동하는 자에 해당되지 않는 범위 내에서 당해 노조의 규약으로 자율적으로 정할 사항이다.

2) 동법 제5조의 규정에 의거 근로자들은 자유로이 노동조합에 가입·탈퇴할 수 있는 것이며, 그 가입절차 등은 당해 노동조합의 규약으로 정하도록 하고 있으나 특정 기업의 근로자를 구성원으로 하여 조직한 노동조합의 경우에 근로자의 노조

---

23) 행정해석: 노조 68107-767, 2002.10.1.

24) 행정해석: 노조 68107-767, 2002.10.1.

25) 행정해석: 노조 68107-452, 2002.5.22.

rejects membership applications or obstructs union membership by delaying procedures(e.g., requiring approval of the labor union chairman), the principle is to see them as having been recognized as fully qualified members of the union.

It is not null and void to exclude application of the collective agreement for a certain scope of employees by particularly regulating in the collective agreement those who cannot become members of the labor union.[26)]

According to Article 5 and Article 11 of the Trade Union Act, employees shall be free to establish a labor union or join one. Concretely, the scope of the labor union membership shall be specified in the labor union's bylaws, meaning employees are free to join the labor union and obtain membership in accordance with the bylaws. However, if the labor union and the company mutually agree in the collective agreement to stipulate those who cannot become union members because they are outside the scope of the labor union's membership, the labor union can exclude application of the collective agreement for a certain scope of employees. In this case, it is not null and void even though the provision for the scope of its membership in the collective agreement is different from that of the labor union's bylaws.[27)]

If some union members are not eligible for union membership because the labor union allowed those who are acting in the interest of the employer to join it, the status of the labor union is forfeited only in cases where the autonomy of the labor union has been infringed or is likely to be infringed.[28)]

1) Although some union members are not eligible for membership because the labor union allowed those who are acting in the interest of the employer to join it, the status as a labor union under the Trade Union Act is not forfeited immediately, but only in cases where the autonomy of the labor has been infringed in reality or is likely to be infringed.

2) The employees cannot be treated as employers or those who are acting in the interest of the employer just because they have subordinates or have a supervisory role in relation to their work; their jobs are directly related to determining working conditions such as employment personnel, payroll, welfare, labor management, etc., but they have no authority to determine those items; and their role is only to collect and provide necessary data or submit their opinions for their superiors to make decisions.

---

26) Supreme Court ruling on Jan. 19, 2004: 2001da5142.

27) Supreme Court ruling on Jan. 29, 2004: 2001 da 5142.

28) Seoul Appellate Court ruling on Oct. 28, 1997: 97 ra 94.

가입을 거부 또는 가입절차(위원장의 승인 등)의 해태 등으로 노조 가입을 방해하는 경우에는 원칙적으로 그 근로자의 노동조합 가입원서를 노동조합에 제출한 시기에 조합원 자격을 갖는다.

단체협약에서 노동조합의 조합원이 될 수 없는 자를 특별히 규정하여 일정 범위의 근로자들에 대하여 단체협약의 적용을 배제하는 경우 무효라고 볼 수 없다.[26)]

노조법 제5조, 제11조의 각 규정에 의하면, 근로자는 자유로이 노동조합을 조직하거나 이에 가입할 수 있고, 구체적으로 노동조합의 조합원의 범위는 당해 노동조합의 규약이 정하는 바에 의하여 정하여지며, 근로자는 노동조합의 규약이 정하는 바에 따라 당해 노동조합에 자유로이 가입함으로써 조합원의 자격을 취득하는 것이다. 다만 단체협약에서 노사간의 상호 협의에 의하여 규약상 노동조합의 조직대상이 되는 근로자의 범위와는 별도로 조합원이 될 수 없는 자를 특별히 규정함으로써 일정 범위의 근로자들에 대하여 위 단체협약의 적용을 배제하고자 하는 취지의 규정을 둔 경우에는, 비록 이러한 규정이 노동조합 규약에 정해진 조합원의 범위에 관한 규정과 배치된다 하더라도 무효라고 볼 수 없다.[27)]

노동조합이 사용자의 이익대표자의 참가를 허용함으로써 조합원 중에 일부가 조합원으로서의 자격이 없는 경우 노동조합의 자주성이 현실적으로 침해되었거나 침해될 우려가 있는 경우에만 노동조합의 지위를 상실한다.[28)]

1) 노동조합이 사용자의 이익대표자의 참가를 허용함으로써 조합원 중에 일부가 조합원으로서의 자격이 없는 경우, 바로 노조법상의 노동조합의 지위를 상실하는 것이 아니라 이로 인하여 위 법이 규정하는 노동조합의 자주성이 현실적으로 침해되었거나 침해될 우려가 있는 경우에만 노동조합의 지위를 상실한다고 보아야 할 것이다.

2) 업무상의 명령이나 지휘감독을 할 하급자도 없고 담당 업무가 근로자의 인사·급여·후생·노무관리 등 근로조건의 결정과 직접 관련은 있으나 위 피신청인들이 위 사항들을 결정하는 권한을 가지고 있는 것이 아니라 상급자들이 결정하는데 필요한 자료를 수집·제공하거나 의견을 제출하는 역할에 그칠 뿐이므로 사용자 또는 사용자의 이익대표자라 할 수 없다.

---

26) 대법원 2004.1.29, 2001다 5142.
27) 대법원 2004.1.29, 2001다5142.
28) 서울고법 1997.10.28, 97라 94.

Section 2: Method for Establishing a Labor Union

Ⅰ. Effects of the Establishment of a Labor Union

A labor union, upon receiving a Certificate of Labor Union Establishment, is entitled to the following legal protections[29]:

① Immunity for justifiable industrial actions from civil and criminal liabilities;
② Registering with the competent registration office to make the union an incorporated body;
③ Mediation for labor disputes from the Labor Relations Commission upon request;
④ Remedy for unfair labor practices from the Labor Relations Commission upon request;
⑤ Receiving the status of a labor union;
⑥ Exemption from taxation for its union activities, in accordance with the tax code(except for profit-making activities).

Ⅱ. Procedures for Establishing a Labor Union

To establish a labor union, the employees shall complete an application form for labor union establishment and submit it, along with their union's bylaws, to the related administrative office. The administrative office shall issue a Certificate of Labor Union Establishment as long as there is no reason to reject the application. Before this, the employees who wish to establish a labor union shall hold a general meeting where they shall establish the union bylaws and elect union officials. The administrative office very often requests meeting minutes of the general meeting as verification that the bylaws were legitimately established and union officials properly elected. Therefore the meeting minutes are used to objectively verify that the labor union was established according to legally appropriate procedures.

29) Article 3, 4, 6, and 7 of the Trade Union Act.

제2절 노동조합의 설립방법

Ⅰ. 노동조합의 설립 효과

설립신고증을 교부받은 노동조합은 정당한 노동조합 활동에 대한 민·형사 면책, 노동쟁의조정신청 및 부당노동행위 구제신청을 할 수 있는 등 다음의 법적보호를 받을 수 있다.[29)]

① 정당한 쟁의행위인 경우 민사·형사상 면책된다.
② 관할 등기소에 등기를 하여 법인으로 할 수 있다.
③ 노동위원회에 노동쟁의 조정을 신청할 수 있다.
④ 노동위원회에 부당노동행위 구제신청을 할 수 있다.
⑤ 노동조합이라는 명칭을 사용할 수 있다.
⑥ 노동조합의 본래 목적을 위한 활동을 할 경우 세법이 정하는 바에 따라 조세가 부과되지 않는다(단, 영리가 목적인 사업은 제외).

Ⅱ. 노동조합의 설립절차

노동조합설립은 노동조합 설립신고서를 작성한 후, 규약을 첨부하여, 관할 행정관청에 제출하고, 행정관청은 결격사유가 없는 한 설립신고증을 교부하는 방식으로 진행된다. 우선, 노동조합을 설립하고자 하는 자는 총회를 개최하여 규약제정과 임원을 선출하여야 한다. 행정관청은 규약제정과 임원선출의 적법성에 대한 입증자료로 총회의 회의록을 요구하는 경우가 많다. 이 회의록은 노동조합이 적법한 절차에 따라 결성되었다는 사실을 객관적으로 입증하기 위하여 활용된다.

29) 노조법 3조, 제4조, 제6조 및 제7조.

Section 3: labor union activities

Ⅰ. Internal Activities of a Labor Union

The current Trade Union Act not only considers civil and criminal misbehavior as unjustifiable labor union activities but also prohibits unfavorable treatment of employees (such as dismissal) for justifiable union activities.

However, if union activities take place during working hours or within the company premises, then disputes may arise concerning the employer's right to supervise or manage labor and facilities.

The scope of labor union activities, which are under protection of the Trade Union Act, is not specified by law, but suggested by judicial rulings as follows:

- First, the behavior must be seen as an activity on behalf of the labor union or to obtain implied authority or approval for the labor union (Characteristic).
- Second, the behavior must be necessary to maintain and improve the employees' working conditions and to enhance their economic and social status, and must assist in enforcing employee unity (Purpose).
- Third, the activity must be outside working hours, except for special provisions granting permission to the contrary in the rules of employment or collective agreement, or except for repeated labor practice or the employer's consent (Time).
- Fourth, union activities inside the workplace shall follow reasonable conditions based upon the employer's right to manage the facility and the activities must not involve violence to persons or property (Method).

These criteria shall be the standards for labor union activities if there are no specified rules in the collective agreement or if there are disputes on interpretation of the agreement. In order to prevent such conflicts, it is advisable to stipulate concretely, in the collective agreement, the admitted scope of labor union activities and procedures during working hours or within company premises.

제3절 노동조합의 활동

Ⅰ. 노동조합의 내부 활동

현행 노조법은 정당한 노조활동에 대하여는 민·형사상의 책임이 면제될 뿐만 아니라, 사용자가 정당한 조합활동을 이유로 근로자에게 해고 기타 불이익을 주는 행위를 금지하는 등 이를 보호하고 있다.

그러나 노조활동이 근무시간 중 또는 기업시설 내에서 행하여지는 경우에는 사용자의 경영권, 특히 근로에 관한 지휘·감독권이나 시설관리권과의 마찰이 불가피하게 된다.

노조법상 보호대상이 되는 노조활동의 범위에 대하여서는 법령상 명시적인 규정이 없으나 판례에서는 다음과 같은 기준을 제시하고 있다.

- 첫째, 행위의 성질상 노동조합의 업무를 위한 활동으로 볼 수 있거나 노동조합의 묵시적 수권 혹은 승인을 받았다고 볼 수 있다(성질).
- 둘째, 근로조건의 유지, 개선과 근로자의 경제적 지위의 향상을 도모하기 위하여 필요하고 근로자들의 단결 강화에 도움이 되는 행위여야 한다(목적).
- 셋째, 취업규칙이나 단체협약에 별도의 허용규정이 있거나 노동관행, 사용자의 승낙이 있는 경우 외에는 취업시간 외에 행해져야 한다(시기).
- 넷째, 사업장 내의 조합활동에 있어서는 사용자의 시설관리권에 바탕을 둔 합리적인 규율이나 제약에 따라야 하고, 폭력과 파괴행위 등의 방법에 의하지 않는 것이어야 한다(방법).

이러한 기준은 단체협약에 관한 규정이 없거나 협약 해석상 다툼이 있는 경우 조합활동의 정당성 판단기준이 될 수 있다. 따라서 논란의 소지를 없애기 위하여 근무시간 중 또는 회사 시설물을 이용한 조합활동의 인정 범위와 절차에 대하여 단체협약으로 그 내용을 명백히 규정하는 것이 바람직하다.

조합활동은 회사업무에 지장을 주지 않는 범위 내에서 수행해야 하므로 근무

In principle, union activities shall be arranged outside working hours so as to cause no disturbance in the company's regular work. Otherwise, union activities shall be approved by the employer, unless there is special approval through collective agreement, etc. Specific regulations in the collective agreement are highly recommended.

1. It is not justifiable to prohibit a former union member from rejoining the union.[30)]

1) To qualify for union membership, union members shall be the employees stipulated under Item 1 of Article 2 of the Trade Union Act, shall not fall under Item 4(a) of Article 2 of the Act, which renders ineligible for union membership those who have the status of an employer or a person representing the interests of the employer, and shall be determined autonomously by the labor union's bylaws.

2) According to Article 5 of the Trade Union Act, employees shall be free to join a labor union or leave it. The joining procedures shall be stipulated in the bylaws of the labor union concerned. In cases where a labor union organizing a particular company's employees rejects membership applications or obstructs union membership by delaying procedures(e.g., requiring the approval of the labor union chairman), the principle is to interpret their having been recognized as fully qualified member of the union.

2. A labor union is free to join or withdraw from an associated organization of labor unions.[31)]

Just as a qualified employee can organize, join or depart from a labor union on his/her own volition, a union is also free to join or withdraw from an associated organization as long as such decision is made in an independent and democratic way.

30) MOEL Guidelines: Nojo 68107-452, on May22, 2002.

31) Supreme Court ruling on Dec. 22,1992, 91Nu6726.

시간 외에 행함이 원칙이다. 근무시간 중의 조합활동은 단체협약 등에 별도의 허용규정이 있는 경우 외에는 사용자의 승낙이 있어야 하므로 단체협약에 구체적으로 규정하는 것이 바람직하다.

1. 노조 탈퇴자의 재가입을 제한하는 것은 정당하지 않다[30)]

1) 노동조합에 가입할 수 있는 자의 자격 및 범위는 '노조법' 제2조 제1호의 규정에 의한 근로자로서 동법 제2조 제2호 및 제4호 가목 소정의 사용자 또는 항상 그의 이익을 대표하여 행동하는 자에 해당되지 않는 범위 내에서 당해 노조의 규약으로 자율적으로 정한다.

2) 동법 제5조의 규정에 의거 근로자들은 자유로이 노동조합에 가입·탈퇴할 수 있는 것이며, 그 가입절차 등은 당해 노동조합의 규약으로 정하도록 하고 있으나 특정 기업의 근로자를 구성원으로 하여 조직한 노동조합의 경우에 근로자의 노조 가입을 거부 또는 가입절차(위원장의 승인 등)의 해태 등으로 노조 가입을 방해하는 경우에는 원칙적으로 그 근로자의 노동조합 가입원서를 노동조합에 제출한 시기에 조합원 자격을 갖는다.

2. 노동조합도 자유로운 의사에 따라 연합단체에 가입하거나 탈퇴할 수 있다[31)]

근로자가 자유로이 노동조합을 조직하거나 이에 가입할 수 있는 것과 마찬가지로 노동조합도 대외적으로 자주적이고 대내적으로 민주적인 의사결정에 따라 연합단체에 가입하거나 소속된 연합단체로부터 탈퇴할 수 있다.

---

30) 행정해석: 노조 68107-452, 2002.5.22.

31) 대법원 1992.12.22, 91누6726.

3. It is null and void if a bylaw or election management rule stipulates indirect selection methods in order to prohibit labor union members from selecting delegates directly.[32)]

Article 17 of the Trade Union Act regulates that delegates in the council of delegates, on behalf of the general assembly, the highest decision-making body, shall be elected by direct, secret, and unsigned ballot. The purpose of this guide is to let the union members be engaged in decision-making about the organization and operations of the labor union and to promote democracy inside the labor union. Accordingly, it is null and void if a bylaw or election management rule stipulates an indirect selection method and prohibits labor union members from selecting delegates directly, except in special situations.

4. Criteria to determine whether a union activity is justifiable or not.[33)]

A union activity is justifiable when it is reasonably regarded as an activity of the union or is authorized or approved, explicitly or implicitly, by the union; it is aimed at maintaining or improving working conditions, promoting the economic and social status of employees and bringing the employees closer to one another; it is done outside of working hours, except when the collective agreement otherwise prescribes or the employer has approved union activities during working hours; and, if it is conducted within the premises of the company, it complies with the rules and restrictions based on the employer's right to control the facilities at the workplace and is not an act of violence or destruction.

5. If some of a union's members are against a certain decision or policy of the union, the activity performed to express such opposition is not a union activity.[34)]

If certain union members did not accept the decision or policy of the union and, to express

---

32) Supreme Court ruling on Jan. 14,2000, 97Da41349.

33) Supreme Court ruling on Apr. 11, 1992, 91Do3044.

34) Supreme Court ruling on Sept. 25, 1992, 92Da18542.

3. 조합원이 대의원 선출에 직접 관여하지 못하도록 간접적인 선출방법을 정한 규약이나 선거관리규정 등은 무효이다[32)]

노조법 제16조 제2항이 노동조합의 최고의결기관인 총회에 갈음할 대의원회의 대의원을 조합원의 직접·비밀·무기명투표에 의하여 선출하도록 규정하고 있는 취지는, 노동조합의 구성원인 조합원이 그 조합의 조직과 운영에 관한 의사결정에 관여할 수 있도록 함으로써 조합 내 민주주의 즉 조합의 민주성을 실현하기 위함에 있고 이는 강행규정이라고 할 것이므로, 다른 특별한 사정이 없는 한 위 법 조항에 위반하여 조합원이 대의원의 선출에 직접 관여하지 못하도록 간접적인 선출방법을 정한 규약이나 선거관리 규정 등은 무효라 할 것이다.

4. 노동조합 활동에 대한 정당성 판단[33)]

노동조합의 활동이 정당하다고 하기 위하여서는 행위의 성질상 노동조합의 활동으로 볼 수 있거나 노동조합의 묵시적인 수권 혹은 승인을 받았다고 볼 수 있는 것으로서 근로조건의 유지 개선과 근로자의 경제적 지위의 향상을 도모하기 위하여 필요하고 근로자들의 단결 강화에 도움이 되는 행위이어야 하며, 취업규칙이나 단체협약에 별도의 허용규정이 있거나 관행, 사용자의 승낙이 있는 경우 외에는 취업시간 외에 행하여져야 하고, 사업장 내의 조합 활동에 있어서는 사용자의 시설관리권에 바탕을 둔 합리적인 규율이나 제약에 따라야 하며 폭력과 파괴행위 등의 방법에 의하지 않는 것이어야 할 것이다.

5. 조합원의 일부가 노동조합의 결정이나 방침에 반대하거나 이를 비판하는 행위는 노동조합의 활동이라고 할 수 없다[34)]

조합원의 일부가 노동조합 집행부와 조합원 전체의 의사에 따르지 않고 노동

32) 대법원 2000.1.14, 97다41349.
33) 대법원 1992.4.10, 91도3044.
34) 대법원 1992.9.25, 92다18542.

such opposition, took an action, for example, by handing out printed matter criticizing the decision or policy, such action is arbitrarily initiated by those union members, and not taken under the agreement of the union members. Accordingly, such action is not seen as a union activity, except when there is a particular reason to regard it as either being essential to the union activities or having been approved by the union itself.

Ⅱ. External Activities of a Labor Union

1. Protection of the Employer's Right for Order within the Company

1) A labor union officer had been wearing a vest decorated with union propaganda. Although the company had warned him several times that he would be punished according to company regulations if he continued to wear the vest during working hours, he disregarded the warnings. Therefore, the company decided to discipline him by suspending him from office for two months. That is not unfair labor practice.[35)]

2) Although a behavior is partly related to union activities, if the disciplinary dismissal was for a reason stipulated clearly in the rules of employment, then the dismissal is not an unfair dismissal.[36)]

3) Where the company dismissed an employee due to his anti-government agitation, promotion of distrust, lying on a resume, etc., if the company's dismissal was not in retaliation for his union activities, but to take disciplinary measures against the harm to company order, then this is not an unfair labor practice.[37)]

4) Despite an employee's status as a labor union officer, so long as there is no evidence that the company took disciplinary action on account of its dislike for the union, then the action cannot be said to be an unfair labor practice.[38)]

5) If disciplinary dismissal for an illegal industrial action and an employee's contempt for the representative director was justifiable and not nominal, then it is not regarded as an unfair labor practice.[39)]

---

35) National Labor Relations Commission 2001Buno32, on July 15, 2001.

36) Supreme Court ruling on Aug. 10,1990, 89Nu8217.

37) National Labor Relations Commission 90Buno251, on Feb. 18, 1991.

38) National Labor Relations Commission 2000Buno35, on June 12, 2000.

39) Administrative court ruling on Oct. 5, 2000, 99Gu35764.

조합의 결정 방침에 반대하거나 이를 비판하는 행위는 행위의 성질상 노동조합의 활동으로 볼 수 있다거나 노동조합의 묵시적인 수권 혹은 승인을 받았다고 인정할 만한 사정이 없는 한 조합원으로서 자의적인 활동에 불과하여 노동조합의 활동이라고 할 수 없다.

Ⅱ. 노동조합의 대외적 활동

1. 기업 질서유지권 보호에 의한 제한

1) 노동조합 간부가 노조간부로서의 역할을 충실히 하겠다는 이유로 노조활동 문구가 새겨진 조끼를 착용하고 근무한 행위에 대해 사용자의 수차례에 걸친 경고와 사규에 의해 처벌하겠다는 통보에도 불구하고 계속 조끼를 착용하고 근무한 노조간부의 행위에 대해 회사가 사규에 의해 출근정지 2월의 징계를 내린 것은 부당노동행위가 아니다.[35)]

2) 징계해고가 명백히 취업규칙에 정해진 해고사유에 해당한다면 노조활동을 한 부분이 인정되더라도 그 해고는 부당해고가 아니다.[36)]

3) 정당성이 없는 반정부선동, 노사불신조장, 이력서 허위기재 등을 이유로 한 해고가 조합활동에 보복이라기보다는 업무질서문란에 대한 조치라면 부당노동행위가 아니다.[37)]

4) 노동조합 간부라도 징계사유에 대한 징계양정이 정당하고 달리 노동조합을 혐오하여 징계하였다는 명백한 증거가 없는 한 부당노동행위로 인정할 수 없다.[38)]

5) 불법쟁의행위와 대표이사에 대한 모욕을 이유로 해고한 것이 표면상의 이유에 불과한 것이 아니고 정당한 경우에는 이를 부당노동행위라고 볼 수 없다.[39)]

---

35) 중노위 2001부노32, 2001.6.15.
36) 대법원 1990.8.10, 89누8217.
37) 중노위 90부노251, 1991.2.18.
38) 중노위 2000부노35, 2000.6.12.
39) 행정법원 2000.10.5, 99구35764.

2. labor union activities

1) If a union member does not follow the union's decisions, as determined by the decision-making process of the labor union, or if the union member opposes or criticizes a labor union decision or policy, the behavior is considered voluntary and a purely personal activity, and is not considered union activity.[40)]

2) Running for a position as a union delegate is clearly engaging in union activity. Furthermore, applying to the Ministry of Employment and Labor for unpaid allowances such as bathing allowance and reserve army training allowance pursuant to the rules of employment shall be considered union behavior if the purpose is to improve the employees' working conditions and enhance their economic and social status, which can be interpreted as behavior to obtain the implied authority or approval of the labor union. This is justifiable and permissible union activity.[41)]

3) Even though it is company policy to require the company's prior approval or permission to distribute a handout, this requirement cannot prohibit every union activity including justifiable activities to maintain and improve working conditions. Whether such activity is justifiable shall not only be judged by the company's position but also other factors, such as the handout's contents, number of pages, time and method of distribution, effect on the company or the work, etc.[42)]

4) Distribution of handouts during non-working recess hours is permissible even if the union member did not obtain prior permission, unless the distribution negatively affects other employees' work, obstructs free use of their recess hours, or concretely corrupts order within the corporation. Although the handout distributed by a union member is designed to promote working conditions, if its content creates extreme distrust or hatred toward management and endangers public morals by distorting or exaggerating conditions, the employer's decision to dismiss the employee for disciplinary reasons is justifiable and not an unfair labor practice.[43)]

---

40) Supreme Court ruling on Sept. 25, 1992, 92Da18542.

41) Supreme Court ruling on Aug. 10,1990, 89Nu8217.

42) Supreme Court ruling on Dec. 23, 1997, 96Nu11778.

43) Supreme Court ruling on Feb. 9, 1993, 92Da20880.

2. 노동조합 활동

1) 노동조합의 결의를 거쳤다거나 구체적인 지시에 의한 조합의사에 따르지 않고 노동조합의 결정이나 방침에 반대하거나 이를 비판하는 행위는 조합원으로서의 자발적이고 순전히 개인적인 활동에 불과하므로 노동조합의 활동에 해당하지 않는다.[40)]

2) 노동조합원이 조합대의원으로 출마한 행위는 노동조합의 행위에 해당함이 분명하고, 취업규칙에 의하여 지급하도록 정하여진 목욕권과 예비군훈련 기간의 수당을 지급하지 않는다고 노동부에 진정한 행위는 노동조합의 목적인 근로조건의 유지개선, 기타 근로자의 경제적 지위향상을 도모하기 위한 행위로서 조합의 묵시적 승인 내지 수권을 얻은 행위라고 보아야 할 것이므로 노동조합의 업무를 위한 정당한 행위이다.[41)]

3) 유인물 배포행위의 경우에는, 그에 대하여 회사의 사전승인이나 허가를 받도록 하고 있다 할지라도 근로자들의 근로조건의 유지, 향상이나 복지증진을 위한 정당한 행위까지 금지할 수는 없는 것이므로 그 행위가 정당한가, 아닌가는 회사의 승인이나 허가 여부만을 가지고 판단할 것은 아니고, 그 유인물의 내용 매수, 배포의 시간 대상 방법, 이로 인한 기업이나 업무의 영향 등 여러 가지 사정을 고려한다.[42)]

4) 취업시간 아닌 주간의 휴게시간 중의 유인물의 배포는 다른 근로자의 취업에 나쁜 영향을 미치거나 휴게시간의 자유로운 이용을 방해하거나 구체적으로 직장질서를 문란하게 하는 것이 아닌 한 허가를 얻지 아니하였다는 이유만으로 정당성을 잃는다 할 수 없으나, 조합원이 배포한 유인물이 비록 근로조건 개선을 목적으로 한 것이라도 그 내용이 사실을 왜곡 또는 과장한 것으로서 경영진에 대한 극도의 불신 내지 증오심을 유발하게 하여 직장질서를 문란하게 할 위험성이 있다면 이를 이유로 한 사용자 측의 징계해고는 정당하며 부당노동행위가 아니다.[43)]

---

40) 대법원 1992.9.25, 92다18542.
41) 대법원 1990.8.10, 89누8217.
42) 대법원 1997.12.23, 96누11778.
43) 대법원 1993.2.9, 92다20880.

5) If some contents stipulated in the handout damage the character, honor, reputation, etc. of other employees or some parts of the document are falsified, exaggerated or distorted, then if the purpose of distributing the handout was not to infringe on other employee's rights or interests, but to maintain and improve working conditions, to promote employee welfare, and to enhance their economic and social status, and if the content of the handout was true as a whole, the distribution of the employee's handout is a justifiable union activity.[44)]

6) A distributed handout contained content slandering the company, and may have caused hostile feelings against the company. It was not handed out directly to the employees but was spread over the employer's plant in secret. Even though it was distributed during the labor union's election campaign of delegates, this handout may have brought concrete danger by infringing on the employer's right to manage his facility and violated corporate order, so it is not justifiable.[45)]

7) The company stipulated in its rules of employment that handouts distributed inside the workplace shall obtain the employer's prior approval and the company may take disciplinary action against an employee who violates this rule. The rule is be invalid simply because it might violate the provision of the Constitution guaranteeing freedom of speech.[46)]

8) Although a labor dispute was resolved, the company's operations returned to normal, and the union repeatedly urged a union member to come back to his job, he did not return to his driving job for an extended period because he was still participating in labor union activities and trying to disrupt the operations of the company. If the company dismissed him for the above reason, this decision is hard to categorize as an unfair labor practice taken to retaliate against his union activities(such as participating in previous strikes).[47)]

---

44) Supreme Court ruling on May 22, 1998, 98Da2365.

45) Supreme Court ruling on June 23, 1992, 92Nu4253.

46) Supreme Court ruling on Sept. 30, 1994, 94Da4042.

47) Supreme Court ruling on Oct. 23, 1990, 89Nu4666.

5) 유인물로 배포된 문서에 기재되어 있는 문언에 의하여 타인의 인격, 신용, 명예 등이 훼손 또는 실추되거나 그렇게 될 염려가 있고, 또 문서에 기재되어 있는 사실관계의 일부가 허위이거나 표현이 다소 과장되거나 왜곡된 점이 있다고 하더라도, 그 문서를 배포한 목적이 타인의 권리나 이익을 침해하려는 것이 아니라 근로조건의 유지 개선과 근로자의 복지증진 기타 경제적 사회적 지위의 향상을 도모하기 위한 것으로서 문서의 내용이 전체적으로 보아 진실한 것이라면 이는 근로자의 정당한 활동범위에 속한다.[44]

6) 배포한 유인물이 사용자의 허가를 받지 아니하였을 뿐만 아니라 허위사실을 적시하여 회사를 비방하는 내용을 담고 있는 것이어서 근로자들로 하여금 사용자에 대하여 적개감을 유발시킬 염려가 있는 것이고, 위 유인물을 근로자들에게 직접 건네주지 않고 사용자의 공장에 은밀히 뿌렸다는 것이므로 이는 사용자의 시설관리권을 침해하고 직장질서를 문란 시킬 구체적인 위험성이 있는 것으로서 비록 위 유인물의 배포시기가 노동조합의 대의원선거 운동기간 이었다고 할지라도 위 배포행위는 정당화 될 수 없다.[45]

7) 사업장 내에서의 기업질서를 유지하기 위하여 사업장 내에서의 유인물 배포에 관하여 취업규칙에서 사용자의 허가를 얻도록 한 허가규정이나 이를 위반한 근로자에 대하여 징계할 수 있도록 한 징계규정이 언론의 자유를 보장한 헌법 조항에 위반하여 무효라고 할 수 없다.[46]

8) 노사분규가 수습되어 회사의 업무가 정상적으로 돌아왔음에도 불구하고 회사의 근무촉구에 따르지 않고 노동조합활동을 위한 것임을 내세워 장기간 승무에 임하지 아니하여 회사의 업무에 지장을 주었다면, 회사가 이를 이유로 하여 해고한 것은 사내질서 유지를 위한 사용자 고유의 징계권의 행사라고 보일 뿐 이를 가지고 그 이전에 있었던 농성참여 등 조합활동에 대한 보복으로 이루어진 부당노동행위라고 보기 어렵다.[47]

---

44) 대법원 1998.5.22, 98다2365.
45) 대법원 1992.6.23, 92누4253.
46) 대법원 1994.9.30, 94다4042.
47) 대법원 1990.10.23, 89누4666.

9) In cases where the labor union in a company with a day and night shift has to hold a general meeting to discuss the pros and cons of an industrial action, and informs the employer of the general meeting, although the general meeting is held during working hours, it is permissible union activity.[48)]

3. Position and activities of a labor union officer

1) When an employee received a personnel order to change jobs or transfer to another department under the employer's rightful authority, the employee was absent from work for over 20 days and disobeyed the personnel order, concluding that the company was retaliating against him for his demands for improved working conditions. Since the behavior was a severe violation, the termination of his labor contract was justifiable.

2) A labor union's full-time officer basically maintains labor relations with the employer, keeping his status as an employee, but he is considered suspended from duty and exempt from his work obligations. On the other hand, as the employer implements a training program during working hours, and the employees are obligated to attend, such occasion is like providing work to the company. Unless there is a special provision in the collective agreement stating otherwise, it is difficult to treat participation in the training as wrong.[49)]

3) When a union member was absent because he was campaigning for election as a labor union delegate, this is not a justifiable reason for absence from work and therefore is cause for dismissal by the company.[50)]

---

48) Supreme Court ruling on Feb. 22, 1994, 93Do613.

49) Supreme Court ruling on Nov. 23, 1999, 99Da45246.

50) Supreme Court ruling on Feb. 11, 1992, 91Da5976.

9) 주야교대근무 기업에서 근무시간 중에 쟁의행위 찬반투표를 위한 조합총회를 개최하는 것이 불가피하고 그 총회 소집을 사전에 사용자에게 통보하여 충분히 대비할 수 있는 여유를 준 사정 등이 있는 경우에는 취업시간 중에 조합총회를 소집하였더라도 정당성이 상실되지는 않는다.[48)]

3. 노동조합 간부의 신분 및 활동

1) 근로자가 원칙적으로 사용자의 권한에 속하는 전직이나 전보명령을 받고서도, 스스로 이를 자신의 사용자에 대한 근로조건 개선 요구 등에 대한 보복이라고 단정하고 위 명령에 불응한 채 20여일이 넘도록 무단결근을 계속하였다면 이와 같은 행위는 근로자와 사용자 사이의 근로계약 관계를 지속하게 하는 것이 현저히 불공정 또는 부당하다고 인정될 정도의 무거운 비위행위에 해당한다 할 것이므로 이를 이유로 근로자를 징계해고 한 사용자의 조치는 정당하다.

2) 노동조합전임자는 사용자와 사이에 기본적으로 노사관계는 유지되고 근로자로서의 신분도 그대로 가지지만 휴직상태에 있는 근로자와 유사하여 근로제공의무가 면제되고, 한편 사용자가 근로시간을 대체하여 근로자에 대하여 실시하는 교육, 연수, 훈련 등 거기에 참가하는 것이 근로자의 의무로서 강제되는 한 근로제공과 다를 바 없으므로 단체협약 등에 따른 정함이 없다면 근로제공의무가 면제된 노동조합전임자가 그러한 교육 등에 참가하지 않았다 하여 바로 잘못이라고 보기는 어렵다.[49)]

3) 운수회사의 노동조합 대의원선거에 입후보하여 그 선거운동을 한다는 이유로 회사의 배차지시를 거부하고 결근한 것은 정당한 사유에 의한 결근이라고 볼 수 없어 징계해고 사유에 해당된다.[50)]

---

48) 대법원 1994.2.22, 93도613.
49) 대법원 1999.11.23, 99다45246.
50) 대법원 1992.2.11, 91다5976.

Ⅲ. Full-Time Union Officers

1. Paid Time-Off

According to the Trade Union Act, when an employer subsidizes wages to full-time union officers engaged in duties only for the labor union, this is considered to be unfair labor practice by the employer, and the employer shall be subject to a punishment of up to two years in prison or a fine of 20 million won. Since the time this provision was added to the Trade Union Act in 1997, implementation has been delayed several times, but starting July 1, 2010, it finally went into effect upon revision of the Trade Union Act on December 31, 2009. This revision, however, allows a minimal number of paid full-time union officers by introducing paid time-off for some union activities. The paid time-off can allow for full-time union officers within a maximum number of hours when the labor union and the employer agree on paid time-off. The employer shall not subsidize wages for full-time union officers in cases where there is no agreement between both parties.

This newly revised Act introduced a paid time-off system by tripartite agreement of union, management, and the government. This stipulates that the company can provide a minimal number of paid time-off hours for union activities, even though a wage subsidy for full-time union officers is prohibited. It is regarded as work-provision when labor union officers are engaged in collaborative activities with the company such as collective bargaining or consultation, grievance-handling, industrial safety issues, etc. and labor union maintenance/management tasks designed to promote good relations between labor and management. To determine the maximum number of paid time-off hours and the items considered as paid time-off, a Union Activity Review Commission(UARC) was composed under jurisdiction of the Ministry of Employment and Labor. The UARC consisted of 15 representatives: 5 recommended by labor, 5 by management, and 5 public committee representatives recommended by the government.

The Union Activity Review Commission(UARC) determined the maximum number of paid time-off hours at a conference attended by labor, management and public committee representatives in June 2013, which was announced by the Ministry of Employment and Labor and implemented on July 1, 2013. Wage subsidies for full-time union officers are prohibited, but if the collective agreement stipulates such subsidy, activities for which full-time union officers receive a subsidy from the employer are allowed within the

Ⅲ. 노조 전임자

1. 근로시간면제도

노조법에 의하면 노동조합의 업무에만 종사하는 노동조합의 전임자에게 급여를 제공하게 되면 사용자의 부당노동행위가 되고, 사용자가 부당노동행위를 한 때는 2년 이하의 징역 또는 2000만원 이하의 처벌을 받도록 규정되어 있다. 그러나 이 규정은 1997년 노조법으로 편입된 이후 여러 차례 시행이 계속 유예되다가 2009년 12월 31일 법 개정에 의하여 2010년 7월 1일 부터는 법 취지에 따라 전면적으로 시행되게 되었다. 다만, 노동조합 활동에 일정 부분의 유급 근로시간면제를 인정하여 최소한의 유급전임을 인정하게 되었다. 이 근로시간 면제는 노사가 합의한 경우에만 근로시간면제의 한도 내에서 유급으로 전임을 인정하는 것이기 때문에 노사의 합의가 없는 경우에는 노조 전임자에게 급여를 지급할 수 없다.

이 법 개정에서는 근로시간면제(타임오프)를 신설하여 노조 전임자의 급여금지 규정에도 불구하고 노사정 합의로 노동조합 활동에 대해 최소한의 유급전임을 인정하기로 하였다. 노조 전임자의 교섭·협의, 고충처리, 산업안전 등 노사공동활동과 건전한 노사관계 발전을 위한 노조의 유지 관리업무는 근로한 것으로 간주한다는 내용이다. 이 근로시간면제시간의 한도와 면제시간 항목의 결정을 위해 노동부 산하 근로시간면제심의 위원회를 두며, 노사가 추천하는 위원 각 5인과 정부가 추천하는 공익위원 5인 등 15명으로 구성하기로 하였다.

근로시간면제위원회는 2013년 6월, 노동, 경영계 및 공익위원 등이 참석한 가운데 회의를 열어 근로시간면제 한도를 결정함에 따라 고용노동부는 이를 고시하였으며, 2013.7.1부터 적용된다. 노조 전임자에게 급여지급이 금지 되지만, 노사가 새로운 단체협약으로 합의한 경우에는 노동부가 제시한 근로시간면제의 범위 내에서만 노조 전임자의 유급전임이 인정된다. 노사가 근로시간면제에 대해 단체협약으로 합의하지 못한 경우에는 노조 전임자는 무급이 원칙이 된다.

maximum number of paid time-off hours regulated by the Ministry of Employment and Labor. If there is no such stipulation in the collective agreement, full-time union officers' activities shall not be subsidized financially in principle.

<table>
<tr><th>Number of Union Members</th><th>Maximum Paid Time-Off Hours (Full-Time Union Officers)</th><th>Maximum Number of Part-Time Union Officers</th></tr>
<tr><td>Fewer than 100</td><td>Up to 2,000 hours (1)</td><td rowspan="10">o Companies with fewer than 300 union members: in cases where paid time-off is split between part-time officers, the number of part-time union officers shall not exceed three times the number in parentheses.
o Companies with 300 union members or more: in cases where paid time-off is split between part-time officers, the number of part-time union officers shall not exceed two times the number in parentheses.</td></tr>
<tr><td>100 ~ 199</td><td>Up to 3,000 hours (1.5)</td></tr>
<tr><td>200 ~ 299</td><td>Up to 4,000 hours (2)</td></tr>
<tr><td>300 ~ 499</td><td>Up to 5,000 hours (2.5)</td></tr>
<tr><td>500 ~ 999</td><td>Up to 6,000 hours (3)</td></tr>
<tr><td>1,000 ~ 2,999</td><td>Up to 10,000 hours (5)</td></tr>
<tr><td>3,000 ~ 4,999</td><td>Up to 14,000 hours (7)</td></tr>
<tr><td>5,000 ~ 9,999</td><td>Up to 22,000 hours (11)</td></tr>
<tr><td>10,000 ~ 14,999</td><td>Up to 28,000 hours (14)</td></tr>
<tr><td>15,000 or more</td><td>Up to 36,000 hours (18)</td></tr>
</table>

1) "Number of Union Members" refers to the total number of union members at an identical business or workplace.
2) 2,000 time-off hours required to maintain one full-time union officer (considering ⓐ 2,088 hours = 40 hours per week x 52 weeks + 8 hours; ⓑ annual leave)

2. Activities of full-time union officers

The employer shall admit new employees as full-time union officers when the labor union replaces current full-time union officers who are stipulated in the collective agreement, unless there is a special reason not to do so.[51)]

1) According to Article 24(1) of the Trade Union Act, if provided for in a collective agreement or allowed by employers, employees may be engaged exclusively in affairs of the labor union without providing employers with work specified in their employment contracts.

2) In cases where the collective bargaining agreement does not specify full-time union officers, but regulated the number of full-time union officers, in this case if current full-time union members including the union chairman cannot be engaged exclusively in the affairs of the labor union, the company shall admit new full-time union officers assigned in accordance with the decision or determination of the labor union's organization with justifiable authority in consideration of the purpose of the collective agreement, customary

51) MOEL Guidelines: Oct. 25, 2004, Labor Union Division-3042.

조합원 규모	시간 한도 (전임자 인정인원)	사용가능인원(파트타임)
100명 미만	최대 2,000시간 이내 (1명)	– 조합원수 300명 미만의 구간: 파트타임 으로 사용할 경우 그 인원은 풀타임으로 사용할 수 있는 인원의 3배를 초과할 수 없다 – 조합원수 300명 이상의 구간: 파트타임 으로 사용할 경우 그 인원은 풀타임으로 사용할 수 있는 인원의 2배를 초과할 수 없다
100~199명	최대 3,000시간 이내 (1.5명)	
200~299명	최대 4,000시간 이내 (2명)	
300~499명	최대 5,000시간 이내 (2.5명)	
500~999명	최대 6,000시간 이내 (3명)	
1,000~2,999명	최대 10,000시간 이내 (5명)	
3,000~4,999명	최대 14,000시간 이내 (7명)	
5,000~9,999명	최대 22,000시간 이내 (11명)	
10,000~14,999명	최대 28,000시간 이내 (14명)	
15,000명 이상	최대 36,000시간 이내 (18명)	

1) 규모는 사업 또는 사업장의 전체 조합원수를 의미함

2) 노조 전임자 1인당 연간 2,000시간(ⓐ 2,088 = 주40시간×52주+8시간, ⓑ 연휴 고려) 의 근로시간을 기준으로 책정함.

2. 전임자의 활동

단체협약에 규정된 전임자를 노조에서 변경하는 경우 특별한 사유가 없는 한 인정하는 것이 타당하다.[51]

1) 노조법 제24조 제1항에 의거 근로자는 단체협약으로 정하거나 사용자의 동의가 있는 경우에는 근로계약 소정의 근로를 제공하지 아니하고 노동조합의 업무에만 종사할 수 있다.

2) 단체협약에 전임자를 특정하지 아니한 채 전임자 수만 규정되어 있고 위원장 등 기존 전임자들이 노동조합 업무에 전임할 수 없게 된 경우라면, 단체협약의 체결취지, 그간의 관행 등을 존중하되 달리 볼 특별한 사유가 없는 한 당해 노동조합 내에서 정당한 권한을 가진 기관의 결의·결정에 따라 지정된 자에 대하여 사용자는 노조 전임을 인정하는 것이 타당하다.

51) 행정해석: 노동조합과-3042, 2004.10.25.

acceptance, etc., unless there is a special reason not to do so.

Although full-time union officers were suspended from office as punishment, the employer shall continue to pay them if they were engaged exclusively in affairs of the labor union.[52]

1) Despite being full-time union officers according to Article 24(1) of the Trade Union Act, the employees can only be exempted from providing employers with work specified in their employment contract according to a provision in the collective agreement or consent of the employer, but still maintain their status as employees. Accordingly, the employers can discipline full-time union officers in accordance with reasons for discipline and procedures stipulated in the collective agreement.

2) Although full-time union officers are exclusively engaged in the affairs of the labor union without providing employers with work specified in their employment contract, the officers can receive pay from the employer according to Article 24(2) of the Trade Union Act and Article 6 of its Additional Provision. Therefore, the employer shall pay full-time union officers in agreement with the labor union if full-time union officers have been engaged in affairs of the labor union even though they were suspended office as punishment.

The employer shall pay full-time union officers according to the collective agreement even during illegal strikes.[53]

The pay that the employer provides to full-time union officers who are exempt from the obligation of providing work specified in their employment contract is different from wages paid in return for work. Therefore, the principle, no wage for no work according to Article 44(1) of the Trade Union Act, will not apply directly to full-time union officers, and their pay shall follow the agreement or decision of the labor union and the employer.

It is not legitimate that the union chairman appoints union officers, or that union officers are selected by rounds of applause.[54]

1) Article 11 of the Trade Union Act regulates that all labor unions shall provide for matters concerning the procedures for election of officers in their bylaws in order to guarantee the autonomous and democratic operation of their organizations. Therefore, the election of officers shall be selected by the procedures and methods stipulated in the Trade Union Act and bylaws.

2) On the other hand, Article 16(4) of the Trade Union Act regulates that matters concerning the

---

52) MOEL Guidelines: Nov. 5, 2003, NoJo 68107-573.

53) MOEL Guidelines: Sept. 25, 2001, Nojo 68107-1089.

54) MOEL Guidelines: Aug. 7, 2001, Nojo 68107-884.

노조 전임자가 정직처분을 받았다 하더라도 노동조합의 업무에 종사하고 있다면 전임자 급여를 지급하여야 한다.[52)]

1) 노조법 제24조 제1항 소정의 노동조합의 전임자라 할지라도 단체협약이나 사용자의 동의에 의해 근로계약 소정의 근로를 제공하지 않을 뿐 근로자의 신분은 그대로 유지하고 있으므로 사용자는 단체협약 등에 정한 징계사유와 절차에 따라 해당 노조 전임자에 대한 징계권을 행사할 수 있다.

2) 이와 같이 노조 전임자는 동법 제24조 제2항, 부칙 제6조에 의거 근로계약 소정의 근로를 제공하지 아니하고 노동조합의 업무에만 종사하더라도 2009년 12월 31일까지는 사용자로부터 급여를 지급받을 수 있는 것이므로 사용자는 노조 전임자가 정직처분을 받았다 하더라도 노동조합의 업무에 종사하고 있다면 달리 볼 사정이 없는 한, 노동조합과 합의한 전임자의 급여를 지급하여야 한다.

불법 파업기간이라 하더라도 단체협약상 사용자의 전임자 급여지급 의무가 면제되는 것은 아니다.[53)]

사용자가 근로계약상의 근로제공의무가 면제된 노동조합 전임자에게 지급하는 급여는 근로의 대가로 지급되는 임금과는 상이한 것이므로 노조법 제44조 제1항의 '무노동 무임금'의 원칙이 직접 적용되는 것은 아니며, 노동조합 전임자의 처우에 대하여는 동 법상 별도의 규정을 두고 있지 아니하므로 노사가 합의·결정한 바에 따른다.

노조임원을 위원장이 지명하거나 박수로 선출하는 것은 부적합하다.[54)]

1) 노조법 제11조는 노동조합의 자주적·민주적 운영을 위하여 임원의 선거절차에 관한 사항을 노동조합의 자체규약으로 정하도록 하고 있는바, 임원의 선거는 동법 및 규약 등에 정한 절차와 방법에 따라 선출하여야 한다.

2) 한편, 동법 제16조 제4항의 규정에 의하여 노동조합의 임원은 조합원(또

52) 행정해석: 노조 68107-573, 2003.11.5.
53) 행정해석: 노조 68107-1089, 2001.9.25.
54) 행정해석: 노조 68107-884, 2001.8.7.

election of union officers shall be decided by members through direct, secret, and unsigned ballot. It violates the Trade Union Act when the union chairman appoints union officers or when they were selected by rounds of applause by labor union members. Union officers do not have the right to vote in this election unless they are delegates from the Council of Delegates according to Article 17(2) of the Trade Union Act.

It is null and void for the union bylaws or election management rules to stipulate indirect selection methods as a way of prohibiting labor union members from selecting delegates directly.

Article 17 of the Trade Union Act regulates that delegates in the council of delegates, on behalf of the general assembly, the highest decision-making body, shall be elected by direct, secret, and unsigned ballot. The purpose of this guide is to let the union members be engaged in decision-making about the organization and operations of the labor union and to promote democracy inside the labor union - namely, its democratic characteristics. Accordingly, it is null and void for a bylaw or election management rule to stipulate an indirect selection method and prohibits labor union members from selecting delegates directly, except in special situations.[55]

Ⅳ. Dissolution of a Labor Union

A labor union shall be dissolved in any of the following cases:

1) Occurrence of any of the causes for dissolution prescribed in its bylaws;

2) merger or division of the business concerned;

3) resolution made to do so at a general meeting or by the council of delegates; or

4) decision by the competent authority to do so with the resolution of the Labor Relations Commission, when the union has no executive officials and has not carried out any union activity for 1 year or longer. It is deemed that a labor union has not carried out any union activity for 1 year or longer when it has not collected any membership dues from its member employees or has not called any general meeting or a meeting of delegates for 1 year or longer.

55) Supreme Court ruling on Jan. 14, 2000: 97 da 41349.

는 대의원)의 직접·비밀·무기명투표에 의하여 선출하여야 하는 바, 노동조합의 임원을 노동조합의 위원장이 지명하거나 조합원들의 박수로 선출하는 것은 동법 동조항에 위배되는 것이며, 노동조합의 임원이 동법 제17조 제2항에 의한 대의원회의 대의원이 아닌 한 표결권을 행사할 수 없다.

조합원이 대의원 선출에 직접 관여하지 못하도록 간접적인 선출방법을 정한 규약이나 선거관리규정 등은 무효이다.

노조법 제16조 제2항이 노동조합의 최고의결기관인 총회에 갈음할 대의원회의 대의원을 조합원의 직접·비밀·무기명투표에 의하여 선출하도록 규정하고 있는 취지는, 노동조합의 구성원인 조합원이 그 조합의 조직과 운영에 관한 의사결정에 관여할 수 있도록 함으로써 조합 내 민주주의 즉 조합의 민주성을 실현하기 위함에 있고 이는 강행규정이라고 할 것이므로, 다른 특별한 사정이 없는 한 위 법 조항을 위반하여 조합원이 대의원의 선출에 직접 관여하지 못하도록 간접적인 선출방법을 정한 규약이나 선거관리 규정 등은 무효이다.[55)]

Ⅳ. 노동조합의 해산

노동조합은 법에 정한 일정한 사유가 발생하면 해산된다(노조법 제28조).

1) 규약에서 정한 해산 사유가 발생한 경우

2) 해당 사업의 합병 또는 분할로 소멸한 경우

3) 총회 또는 대의원회의 해산결의가 있는 경우

4) 노동조합의 임원이 없고 노동조합으로서의 활동을 1년 이상하지 아니한 것으로 인정되는 경우로서 행정관청이 노동위원회의 의결을 얻은 경우이다. 여기서 '노동조합으로서의 활동을 1년 이상하지 아니한 것으로 인정되는 경우'란 계속하여 1년 이상 조합원으로부터 조합비를 징수한 사실이 없거나, 총회 또는 대의원회를 개최한 사실이 없는 경우를 의미한다.

---

55) 대법원 2000.1.14, 97다41349.

Chapter 14

Collective Bargaining and collective agreement

Section 1: Understanding Collective Bargaining

Ⅰ. Concept and Forms of Collective Bargaining

1. Concept of collective bargaining

Collective bargaining refers to the negotiation of working conditions by the labor-management council. The labor union and the employer(or employers' association) come to agree collectively on working conditions or other fair rules of labor relations and conclude a collective agreement.

2. Good faith principle

The parties to collective bargaining shall negotiate a collective agreement in good faith and may not abuse their right to collectively bargain in the process. Neither the union nor the employer may refuse or neglect to bargain or conclude a collective agreement without giving a justifiable reason for doing so.[56)]

3. Forms of collective bargaining

(1) Company level collective bargaining(labor union: employer)

Most Korean companies use this form, which is negotiation between the company and

56) Article 30 and Article 81 (3) of the Trade Union Act.

Chapter 14

단체교섭 및 단체협약

제1절 단체교섭의 이해

Ⅰ. 단체교섭의 의의와 방식

1. 단체교섭의 의의

단체교섭이란 노사 간의 협의회를 통한 근로조건의 교섭을 의미하는 개념으로 정의할 수 있으며, 노동조합과 사용자(또는 사용자 단체) 간의 근로조건에 관한 사항 및 기타 노사관계의 공정한 룰(Rule) 설정에 관하여 집단적으로 교섭하여 단체협약이라는 규범을 탄생시키기 위한 사실행위를 말한다.

2. 성실교섭의무

단체교섭의 당사자는 신의에 따라 성실히 교섭하고 단체협약을 체결하여야 하며 그 권한을 남용할 수 없다. 정당한 이유 없이 교섭 또는 단체협약 체결을 거부하거나 해태할 수 없다(노조법 제30조). 사용자가 정당한 사유 없이 교섭을 거부하거나 성실교섭의무에 위반하는 경우에는 부당노동행위가 된다.[56)]

3. 단체교섭의 방식(유형)

(1) 기업별 교섭(노동조합: 사용자)

56) 노조법 제81조 제3호.

the union organized by employees of the company.

(2) Multi-union/employer bargaining(union association: employers' association)

Multi-union/employer bargaining refers to negotiation between an association of local or country-wide unions and the industrial or local employers' association.

Regarding multi-union and employer bargaining, there are three typical industrial labor unions: Metal Workers' Union, Financial Industry Union, and Health & Medical Workers' Union

(3) Diagonal bargaining(associated union: individual company's employer)

The associated union of the company-level union independently engages in collective bargaining with the individual company's employer corresponding to the individual union.

(4) Coordinated bargaining(associated union and individual union: employer)

The associated union participates in joint collective bargaining between an individual union or a branch of an associated union(branch of industrial or occupational union) and the employer.

(5) Multi-group bargaining(several company-level labor unions: employers' association)

Several company-level labor unions unite to negotiate with the employers' association, which is often referred to as combined bargaining or congregation bargaining.

<Forms of Collective Bargaining>

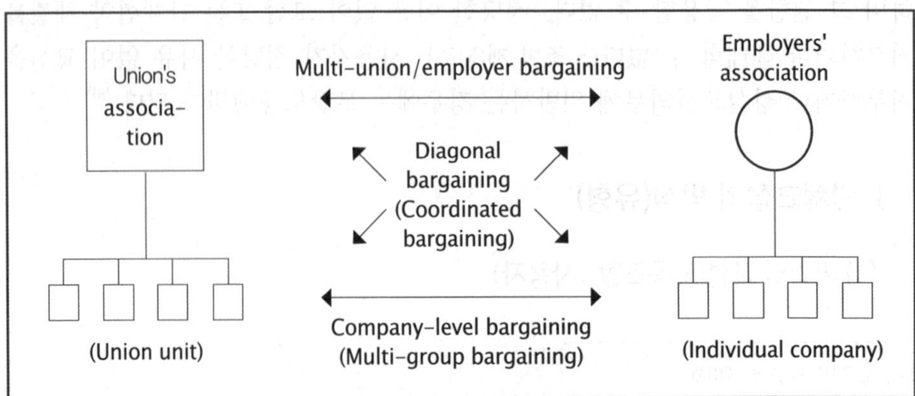

우리나라에서 가장 많이 취하여지는 구조로서 특정기업과 그 기업 내 근로자로 구성된 노동조합이 당사자가 되어 교섭하는 것을 말한다.

(2) 통일교섭(전국적 노동조합 : 전국적 사용자단체)

전국적 또는 지역적인 노동조합과 산업별 또는 지역적인 사용자단체가 교섭하는 것을 통일교섭이라 한다. 통일교섭을 하는 산업별 노동조합은 구성된 금속노조, 금융노조, 보건의료노조가 있다.

(3) 대각선교섭(상부노동조합 : 개별기업의 사용자)

기업별 노동조합이 소속하는 상부단체가 각 기업별 조합에 대응하는 개별기업과 개별적으로 교섭하는 방식이다.

(4) 공동교섭(상부노동조합과 개별노동조합 : 사용자)

기업별 조합 또는 기업단위의 지부(산업별 또는 직종별 조합의 기업단위의 지부)가 행하는 기업별 단체교섭에 있어서 상부단체인 조합이 공동으로 참가하여 교섭하는 방식이다.

(5) 집단교섭(수개의 기업별 노동조합 : 사용자단체)

몇 개의 기업별 조합이 집단화하여 공동으로 사용자 측의 집단과 교섭하는 방식을 말하며 이를 연합교섭 또는 집합교섭이라고 한다.

〈교섭방식〉

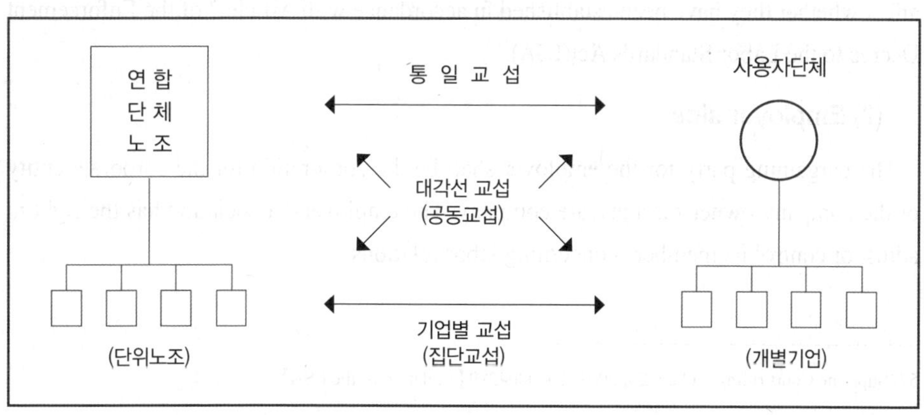

Ⅱ. Parties to Collective Bargaining

1. Collective bargaining party

The collective bargaining parties have a right and duty to engage in collective bargaining and implements it independently.

(1) Employee side

The bargaining party for the employee shall be a legitimate labor union established under requirements demanded by the Trade Union Act. Thus, temporary strike groups, dismissed employees' groups, company organizations, individual employees, or key anti-union members do not have legal authority to demand collective bargaining. Hence, if the employer rejects collective bargaining demands from such groups or persons, it is not recognized as an unfair labor practice.

If a labor union is formed as an industrial or occupational union but its union branch or union unit for the individual company is established under proper requirements such as through formation of union bylaws, union officers, etc. in order to act independently, such a union can be a party to collective bargaining for specific outcomes according to the demands of the union described by the union bylaws or union resolutions as the party to have the right and duty to negotiate.

In cases where the labor union's subordinate organizations like a unit labor union or a branch labor union that have independent bylaws and executive organizations, and conduct activities like an independent entity, such an entity can bargain and conclude a collective agreement regarding organization and labor union members. This does not affect whether they have been established in accordance with Article 7 of the Enforcement Decree to the Labor Standards Act(LSA).[57)]

(2) Employer side

The bargaining party for the employer shall be the corporation for the corporate entity or the company owner for a private company. The employers' association has the right to adjust or control its members concerning labor relations.

---

57) Supreme Court ruling on Feb. 23, 2001, 2000do4299【Violation of the LSA】.

Ⅱ. 단체교섭의 주체(당사자와 담당자)

1. 단체교섭의 당사자

단체교섭의 당사자는 단체교섭에 대한 권리와 의무를 가진 자로서, 단체교섭을 스스로의 이름으로 수행하고 그 성과인 단체협약의 당사자로서 권리와 의무를 부담하는 자를 의미하는 것이다.

(1) 근로자 측

근로자 측 교섭당사자는 법 소정의 노동조합 설립요건을 갖춘 적법한 노동조합이라야 하므로 일시적인 쟁의단, 해고자단체, 직장조직, 개별근로자나 반집행부 간부 등은 단체교섭을 요구할 법적 권한이 없고 사용자가 이를 거부하더라도 부당노동행위가 되지 아니한다.

또한, 노동조합이 산업별 또는 직종별 조합인 경우 기업 단위의 지부 또는 분회는 독자적인 활동을 할 수 있는 하나의 노동조합으로서의 규약, 임원 등의 요건을 갖추고 설립신고를 한 경우에는 협상의 권리·의무의 주체로서 규약이나 결의 등으로 정한 노동조합의 의사에 따라서 한정된 내용에 관하여 교섭의 당사자가 될 수 있다.

노동조합의 하부단체인 분회나 지부가 독자적인 규약 및 집행기관을 가지고 독립된 조직체로서 활동을 하는 경우 당해 조직이나 그 조합원에 고유한 사항에 대하여는 독자적으로 단체교섭하고 단체협약을 체결할 수 있고, 이는 그 분회나 지부가 노조법 시행령 제7조의 규정에 따라 그 설립신고를 하였는지 여부에 영향받지 아니한다.[57)]

(2) 사용자 측

사용자 측의 교섭당사자는 법인기업인 경우에는 그 법인, 개인기업인 경우에는 그 사업주가 된다. 사용자단체는 노사관계에 관하여 그 구성원인 사용자에 대하여 조정 또는 통제를 할 수 있는 단체교섭, 협약체결 권한을 가진 사용자단체라야 단체교섭의 당사자가 될 수 있다.

---

57) 대법원 2001.2.23, 2000도4299【근로기준법위반】.

2. Person-in-charge of collective bargaining

(1) Employee side

The representative of a labor union or delegates of a labor union shall have the authority to negotiate as persons-in-charge of the collective bargaining. The term, "authority to negotiate " includes not only the authority to bargain collectively, but also the authority to conclude a collective agreement reflecting those collective negotiations.[58)]

(2) Employer side

The employer or representative of the employers' association shall be the person-in-charge of the collective bargaining. Here, the employer refers to the company owner in the case of a private company or the representative director in the case of a corporation. The general manager of the branch office or the chief of the labor affairs department can also be the person-in-charge of the collective bargaining through proxy authority of limited scope or special delegation.

Ⅲ. Matters Subject to Collective Bargaining

There are no statutory regulations as to the matters subject to collective bargaining. However, in light of the fact that collective bargaining is fundamentally aimed at maintaining or improving working conditions, the matters subject to collective bargaining shall be those concerning working conditions, those of a collective nature, or those at the disposal of the employer.

1. Effect of collective bargaining on personnel and management

If the employer rejects the demand for collective bargaining on matters violating personnel and management rights, it is not recognized as an unfair labor practice. If the employer accepts the bargaining demands at his/her own discretion and negotiates an agreement on matters of personnel and management, the employer shall implement them accordingly.

---

58) Supreme Court ruling on Apr. 27, 1993, 91noo12257【Collective Agreement】.

2. 단체교섭의 담당자

(1) 근로자 측

노동조합의 대표자 또는 노동조합으로부터 위임을 받은 자는 단체교섭 담당자로서 단체교섭의 권한이 있다. "교섭할 권한"이라 함은 사실행위로서의 단체교섭의 권한 외에 교섭한 결과에 따라 단체협약을 체결할 권한을 포함한다.[58]

(2) 사용자측

사용자 또는 사용자단체의 대표가 단체교섭의 담당자가 된다. 여기서 사용자란 개인기업의 경우에는 기업주 개인을, 법인인 경우에는 대표이사를 의미하는바, 이들이 각각 교섭의 담당자로 된다. 그리고 지점의 지배인 또는 노무부서의 책임자 등은 일정한 범위의 대리권 또는 특별위임에 의하여 단체교섭의 담당자가 될 수 있다.

Ⅲ. 단체교섭의 대상

단체교섭의 대상에 대하여는 법률상 규정이 없으나, 근로조건의 유지·개선을 위한 단체교섭의 본질에 비추어 볼 때, 단체교섭의 대상사항이 되기 위해서는 첫째, 근로조건에 관한 사항, 둘째, 집단적 성격을 띠는 사항, 셋째, 사용자의 처분가능성이 있는 사항이어야 한다.

1. 인사·경영사항에 관한 단체협약의 효력

인사·경영권을 침해하는 사항에 대하여 사용자가 교섭을 거부하더라도 부당노동행위가 성립되지 아니한다. 다만, 사용자가 스스로의 의사에 따라 교섭에 임하여 인사·경영사항에 관한 단체협약을 체결한 경우에는 그 협약의 취지에 따라 성실히 이행하여야 한다.

---

58) 대법원 1993.4.27, 91누12257【단체협약변경명령취소】.

2. Cases where personnel and management rights are violated

1) The union demands agreement on personnel issues(e.g., employment, dismissal, transfer of employees to another division, etc.).

2) The union demands a disciplinary action committee consisting of an equal number of employer and employee representatives and equal treatment after rejection of its disciplinary proposal.

3) The union demands a pre-agreement concerning any merger or acquisition involving the company, plant removal, subcontracting, or outsourcing.

4) The right to bring changes to work organization or the business structure in step with removal or integration of some departments is included in the employer's prerogatives concerning business management. Accordingly, the right cannot be negotiated at a collective bargaining table, and no action that is aimed at negotiating the un-negotiable can be justifiable.[59)]

5) Dismissal for managerial reasons is based on the employer's right to take measures for business purposes. If the union claims that the employer should not dismiss employees for managerial reasons, this is an attempt to restrict the employer's right to manage his own business. Therefore, dismissals for economic reasons cannot be negotiated in the setting of collective bargaining.[60)]

<Compulsory & Optional Items for Collective Bargaining>

	Compulsory items	Optional items	Forbidden items
Definition	An employer should conduct collective bargaining over these matters, upon employee request	An employer may choose to conduct bargaining over these matters, upon employee request	These matters are not negotiable
Collective bargaining	Unfair labor Practice to refuse over compulsory items	Permitted for optional items	
Failure to reach agreement	Industrial action may be taken over compulsory items	No industrial action is Allowed for optional items	
In case of agreement	Collective agreement signed	A collective agreement signed	
Subject to mediation for industrial disputes	Yes	No	
Examples	Working conditions, including wages, hours of work, employee benefits, etc.	- Full-time union officials - Reinstatement of dismissed workers - Union activities during working hours - Business controlling stake - Payment of wages during industrial disputes	- Release of detained workers - Support for a particular political party - Closed shop - Support for a particular religious creed

59) Supreme Court ruling on Jan. 11, 2002, 2001Do1687.

60) Supreme Court ruling on Apr. 24, 2001, 99Do4893.

2. 인사·경영권의 침해 사례

1) 조합원의 인사(채용·해고·부서이동 등)에 노사합의를 요구하는 경우

2) 징계위원회의 노사 동수 구성 및 가부동수 시 부결처리를 요구하는 경우

3) 기업양도, 공장이전, 하도급 및 용역전환 시에 노사간의 사전합의를 요구하는 경우

4) 사용자의 재량적 판단이 존중되어야 할 기구 통·폐합에 따른 조직변경 및 업무분장 등에 관한 결정권은 사용자의 경영권에 속하는 사항으로서 단체교섭 사항이 될 수 없고, 단체교섭 사항이 될 수 없는 사항을 달성하려는 쟁의행위는 그 목적의 정당성을 인정할 수 없다.[59)]

5) 경영상 이유에 의한 해고 역시 경영상의 필요에 의하여 실시되는 사용자의 경영상 조치라고 할 것이므로, 정리해고에 관한 노동조합의 요구내용이 사용자는 정리해고를 하여서는 아니 된다는 취지라면 이는 사용자의 경영권을 근본적으로 제약하는 것이 되어 원칙적으로 단체교섭의 대상이 될 수 없다.[60)]

〈단체교섭 대상 구분〉

	의무 교섭사항	임의 교섭사항	금지 교섭사항
개 념	근로자의 단체교섭 요구 시 사용자는 의무적으로 교섭에 응해야 함	근로자의 교섭요구 시 사용자가 원하는 경우에 임의로 교섭 가능	교섭대상이 될 수 없음
단체교섭 거부여부	교섭 거부 시 부당노동행 위에 해당	거부 가능	거부 가능
단체교섭 결렬 시	쟁의행위 가능	쟁의행위 불가능	
단체교섭 타결 시	단체협약 체결	단체협약 체결	
노동쟁의 조정	조정대상	조정대상이 아님	
구체적인 사례	임금, 근로시간, 후생 등 근로조건에 관한 사항	- 노조 전임자 - 해고자 복직 - 근로시간중의 노조활동 - 경영권 - 쟁의 중의 임금 여부	- 구속자 석방 - 특정정당지지 - Closed Shop - 특정종교지지

59) 대법원 2002.1.11, 2001도1687.

60) 대법원 2001.4.24, 99도4893.

3. Items related to personnel & management rights where bargaining is compulsory

1) The union demands payment of moving costs, settlement expenses, etc. although employee-transfer decision-making is the sole right of the employer.

2) The union demands establishment of personnel criteria related to working conditions for the entire body of employees, such as personnel guidelines, criteria for job assignment and rotation, etc.

3) The union demands pre-judgment or negotiation, although the employer has final decision-making authority for disciplinary punishment or dismissal.

4) In a specific case, the collective agreement provided that the employer should obtain prior consent from the union when setting the services of regular bus drivers, the bus service schedule, and the schedules for on-call drivers and daily-hired drivers. These matters are closely associated with employee working conditions(bus drivers), although they are part of the employer's right to manage his own business. In addition, it does not seem to fundamentally undermine the employer's rights to include them in collective bargaining. Accordingly, they may be negotiated at the bargaining table.[61)]

Ⅳ. Authority to Make Agreements and Delegation Procedures

1. Admission of a union representative's authority to make agreements

Although the negotiating authority of a union representative includes the authority to make agreements, it is a very common practice for the unions of industrial companies to hold a general meeting to review the agreements on account of the union bylaws and demand re-bargaining in case the agreements are not accepted, which usually delays the negotiation process. Thus, the new Article 29, subparagraph 1, of the Trade Union Act endows authority to the union representative to bargain and make collective agreements.

If the union representative or another authorized person is required to put before a

61) Supreme Court ruling on Aug. 26, 1994, 93Nu8993.

3. 인사·경영사항 중 단체협약으로 체결할 수 있는 경우

1) 회사 이전시 이전 에 관한 판단은 경영권의 고유한 사항이나 이전으로 인한 근로자의 이사비용, 정착비용 등의 지불을 요구하는 경우

2) 인사원칙, 배치전환의 기준 등과 같이 전체 근로자의 근로조건과 관련된 '인사기준'의 설정을 요구하는 경우

3) 징계·해고 시에 그 최종 결정권은 회사가 보유한 채 노동조합의 의견을 듣거나 사전협의를 거치도록 요구하는 경우

4) 단체협약 중 조합원의 차량별 고정승무발령, 배차시간, 대기기사 배차순서 및 일당기사 배차순서에 관하여 노조와 사전합의를 하도록 한 조항은 그 내용이 한편으로는 사용자의 경영권에 속하는 사항이지만 다른 한편으로는 근로자들의 근로조건과도 밀접한 관련이 있는 부분으로서 사용자의 경영권을 근본적으로 제약하는 것은 아니라고 보이므로 단체협약의 대상이 될 수 있다.[61]

Ⅳ. 단체협약체결권 및 단체교섭권의 위임

1. 단체협약체결권 인정

노조대표자의 교섭권한에는 체결권한이 포함되는 것임에도 불구하고 산업현장에서는 노조규약을 이유로 합의안을 조합원총회에 부치고 총회에서 부결되면 재교섭을 요구함으로써 교섭이 지연되는 사례가 있어 왔다. 이에 따라 노조법 제29조 제1항에서는 노조대표자가 교섭권한과 함께 체결권한까지 가지고 있음을 명시하고 있다.

노동조합의 대표자 또는 수임자가 단체교섭의 결과에 따라 사용자와 단체협약의 내용을 합의한 후 다시 협약안의 가부에 관하여 조합원총회의 의결을 거쳐야만 한다는 것은 대표자 또는 수임자의 단체협약 체결권한을 전면적, 포괄적으로 제한함으로써 사실상 단체협약 체결권한을 명목에 불과한 것으로 만드

---

61) 내법원 1994.8.26, 93누8993.

general meeting of union members a collective agreement that is negotiated with the employer, this would render ineffective the right of the union representative or the authorized person to conclude a collective agreement. Namely, the right to conclude a collective agreement would be reduced to a mere nominal right. In this light, such provision is against the purpose of the Trade Union Act in force.[62)]

2. Delegation procedures

The delegate to collective bargaining shall receive approval from the general meeting of the union or council of delegates.

Mandating the authority to collective bargaining means that a union authorizes a person or organization other than the union representative to negotiate with the employer on behalf of the union and for the good of the union and its members. Even without a separate procedure of declaring an end to the mandated authority, the union's right to collective bargaining always exists in concurrence with the authorized party's right. In other words, even when a unit union has mandated its right to collective bargaining to an associated organization, the union's right to collective bargaining is retained.[63)]

As long as the branch or chapter of the union is an independent organization with an independent set of rules and a governing body, it may carry out independent collective negotiations and sign collective agreements over the matters peculiar to the organization and its member employees. This is not affected by whether or not the branch or chapter has reported its establishment in accordance with Article 7 of the Trade Union Act.[64)]

Ⅴ. Procedures for Collective Bargaining

(1) Initiating collective bargaining

Collective bargaining is initiated upon the labor union's request. If there already exists

62) Supreme Court ruling on May 12, 2000, 98Do3299.

63) Supreme Court ruling on Nov. 13, 1998, 98Da20790.

64) Supreme Court ruling on Feb. 23, 2001, 2000Do4299.

는 것이어서 현행법의 취지에 위반된다.[62)]

2. 단체교섭권의 위임

단체교섭권 위임은 법 제16조 규정에 따라 반드시 조합원총회 또는 대위원회의 의결을 거쳐야 한다.

단체교섭 권한의 '위임' 이라고 함은 노동조합 조직상의 대표자 이외의 자에게 조합 또는 조합원을 위하여, 조합의 입장에서 사용자 측과 사이에 단체교섭을 하는 사무처리를 맡기는 것을 뜻하고, 그 위임 후 이를 해지하는 등의 별개의 의사표시가 없더라도 노동조합의 단체교섭 권한은 여전히 수임자의 단체교섭 권한과 중복하여 경합적으로 남아 있다고 할 것이므로 단위노동조합이 당해 노동조합이 가입한 상부단체인 연합단체에 그러한 권한을 위임한 경우에 있어서도 단체교섭 권한은 여전히 유지되는 것이다.[63)]

노동조합의 하부단체인 분회나 지부가 독자적인 규약 및 집행기관을 가지고 독립된 조직체로서 활동을 하는 경우 당해조직이나 그 조합원에 고유한 사항에 대하여는 독자적으로 단체교섭하고 단체협약을 체결할 수 있고, 이는 그 분회나 지부가 노조법 시행령 제7조의 규정에 따라 그 설립신고를 하였는지 여부에 영향을 받지 아니한다.[64)]

Ⅴ. 단체교섭의 절차

(1) 단체교섭의 개시

단체교섭은 통상 노동조합의 요청에 따라 개시된다. 다만, 단체협약(임금협약 포함)이 체결되어 있는 경우에는 그 협약의 유효기간 만료시를 전후하여 새로운 단체협약을 체결하기 위한 교섭을 요구하고 교섭이 개시되어야 한다. 그러

---

62) 대법원 2000.5.12, 98도3299.
63) 대법원 1998.11.13, 98다20790.
64) 대법원 2001.2.23, 2000도4299.

an applicable collective agreement(including wage agreement) in the company, collective bargaining for a new collective agreement shall be withheld until termination of the existing agreement.

However, if there is no existing collective agreement, or if the union demands new content, collective bargaining can be initiated at any given time, but it is desirable to develop a method of preliminary bargaining to ensure things run smoothly.

(2) Time and place for collective bargaining

In principle, collective bargaining shall not be held during working hours, unless it has been habitually held during working hours and the employer has allowed this. The place of bargaining is unrestricted, but it is recommended to consider a place where discourse can continue without interruptions.

(3) Procedures for collective bargaining

1) Demands for collective bargaining shall be sent in a written document specifying time, place, major agenda items, representatives, etc. The two parties shall consult and decide on the day and time of bargaining.

2) If the union has demanded collective bargaining several times but the employer continues to postpone it or fails to respond, it is considered to be a refusal to engage in collective bargaining. If the employer responds but does not negotiate in good faith, or proposes demands that are disadvantageous and forces it upon the union, or leaves the office, this is also refusal to engage in collective bargaining.

3) During the effective period of the collective agreement, the union cannot make requests for a new collective agreement(including a collective wage agreement) due to enlargement of the union, replacement of the union representative, etc.

나 단체협약이 없거나 기존의 단체협약에 그러한 내용이 전혀 없는 것은 언제나 교섭을 요구하고 개시할 수 있으나 원만한 단체교섭을 위해서는 예비교섭을 통하여 단체교섭의 방법을 정하는 것이 바람직하다.

(2) 단체교섭의 시간과 장소

단체교섭은 원칙적으로 일과시간에 할 수 없으나 기업별 노조의 특성상 근로의무시간 중 교섭하는 것이 관행화되고 사용자도 이를 인정한다면 이는 무관할 것이며, 단체교섭의 장소는 법상 제한이 없으나 단체교섭의 성격, 즉 평화적인 대화가 될 수 있어야 하므로 이를 저해할 우려가 있는 장소만 아니면 된다.

(3) 단체교섭의 방법

1) 단체교섭의 요구는 서면으로 단체교섭 희망일시·장소·주된 의제·대표자명단 등을 사전에 통보하여야 하고 교섭일시는 쌍방이 협의하여 결정하여야 한다.

2) 일방이 수차 단체교섭을 요구하였음에도 불구하고 상대방이 고의로 교섭을 지연시키거나 불응할 경우 단체교섭의 거부로 간주할 수 있으며 또한, 교섭에 응하였으나 상당한 성의를 가지고 긍정적으로 교섭하지 아니하고 오히려 종전 제안보다 상대방에게 불리한 제안을 계속하거나 강압적으로 제안수락을 강요하며 퇴장하는 행위 등은 단체교섭의 거부로 볼 수 있을 것이다.

3) 단체협약 유효기간 내에 노동조합 조직 확장, 조합대표의 경질 등의 이유로 새로운 단체협약(임금협약 포함) 체결을 요구할 수 없다.

Section 2: Multiple Labor Unions

Ⅰ. Understanding the Multiple Union System[65)]

1. Concept

Effective July 1, 2011, employees are free to organize two or more labor unions in the unit of a business(or workplace) or to join such labor union(s), according to revision of the Trade Union and Labor Relations Adjustment Act(hereinafter referred to as 'the Trade Union Act'). However, this revised law stipulates the application of one unified collective agreement in a business(or workplace) by introducing a single bargaining channel. This is designed to prevent disturbances from duplicate bargaining, different applications of working conditions, and serious disputes between unions.

Generally in the Multiple Union System, only the largest labor union representing more than half of a company's union members will engage in collective bargaining and collective contracting as the bargaining representative union, and has the duty to represent the minority labor unions fairly. Since this Multiple Union System was implemented on July 1, 2011, many changes have occurred in labor relations between employers and the labor unions, both positive and negative. The positive changes include guaranteeing the right to multiple labor unions in one company where employees are free to join the one they like, and even establish their own. The negative changes include weakening of industrial unions as they are now splintered and must choose a bargaining representative union to represent all of them in each workplace or business unit. Some companies have taken advantage of this change by subsidizing or otherwise supporting company-friendly labor unions to the point where they obtain the majority of union membership. In such situations, the existing combative and unfriendly labor unions find themselves generally powerless as they become minority labor unions that have lost their right to bargain and take action collectively.

---

65) This article is based on the Ministry of Employment and Labor Guide, "Manual on multiple labor unions in a business (workplace)" (Dec. 2010).

제2절 복수노조와 교섭창구 단일화

Ⅰ. 복수노조 제도의 개요[65)]

1. 의 의

2010.1.1. "노조법(이하 '노조법'이라 함)"이 개정됨에 따라 2011.7.1부터 근로자들은 사업(장) 단위에서 2개 이상의 노동조합을 자유롭게 설립하거나 가입할 수 있다. 그러나 교섭창구 단일화제도를 도입하여 하나의 사업(장)에 하나의 단체협약이 적용되도록 함으로써 복수노조 허용에 따른 중복 교섭 등 교섭질서의 혼란, 근로조건의 통일성 훼손과 노동조합간 과도한 세력 다툼 및 분열과 같은 산업현장의 혼란을 방지하고 있다.

복수노조는 조합원의 과반수를 대표하는 다수 노조가 교섭대표로서 권한을 가지는 것과 함께 공정대표의무를 부과하여 소수 노조에게도 일정 부분 권한을 가질 수 있도록 하고 있다. 그 뿐 아니라, 복수노조 제도에서는 노사관계에 크고 작은 긍정적 및 부정적 변화가 생겼는데, 긍정적 변화는 근로자의 단결선택권을 보장하여 근로자들의 성향에 맞는 노동조합을 설립할 수 있는 복수노조 시대가 되었다는 것이고, 부정적 변화는 교섭창구가 하나의 사업 또는 사업장 단위로 이루어지면서 산별노조가 약화되었고, 이러한 변화로 인하여 개별 사업 또는 사업장 단위의 친기업 노동조합이 설립되면서 기존의 사측과 대립적인 관계를 유지하였던 강성노조가 소수노조로 되면서 단체교섭권과 단체행동권을 상실하여 노조가 와해되는 경우가 많이 발생하였다는 것이다.

---

65) 참조: "노동부사업(사업장) 단위 복수노조 업무매뉴얼" (2010.12)

2. Determining the representative bargaining union and bargaining methods

(1) Principle

In cases where a company-level labor union was determined and confirmed as the representative bargaining union through the procedures mentioned above, it can conclude a collective agreement by negotiating with the employer. A branch or unit of an umbrella labor union(such as an industrial union) at the business or workplace shall also participate in determining and confirming the representative bargaining union through the procedures mentioned above. Accordingly, if the branch or unit of the umbrella union or the company-level labor union did not participate in determining and confirming the representative bargaining union, it cannot negotiate with the employer. In such a case, if the employer rejects a request for negotiation with the umbrella union, it will not be considered unfair labor practice.

(2) Determining the representative bargaining union case-by-case

1) In cases where there are two company-level labor unions

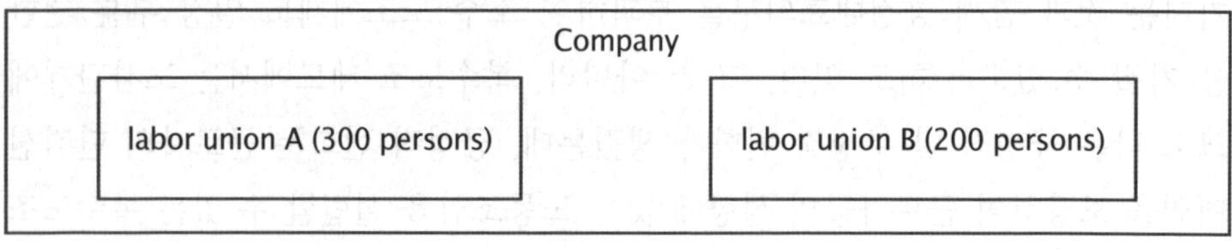

Above all, labor union A and labor union B shall autonomously determine the representative bargaining union. If they fail to do so, labor union A becomes the representative bargaining union as it has the majority of union members.

2) In cases where there are labor unions at the company, local, and industry level

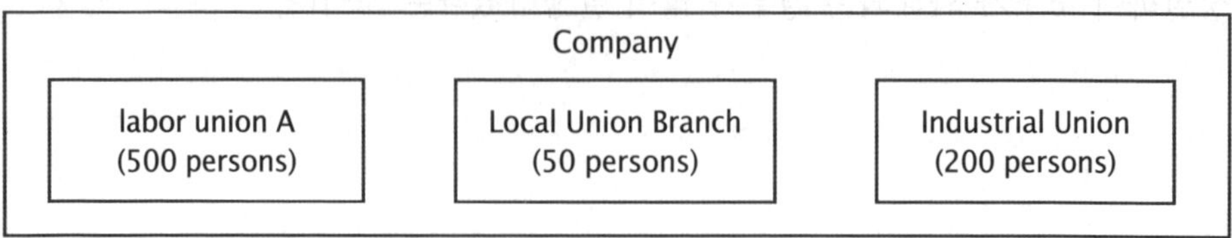

2. 복수노조 유형별 교섭대표노동조합 결정 및 교섭방식

(1) 원 칙

기업별 노동조합은 교섭창구 단일화 절차를 거쳐 교섭대표노동조합으로 결정 또는 확정된 경우에는 사용자와 단체협약 체결을 위한 교섭을 할 수 있다. 산업별 노동조합 등 초기업단위 노동조합의 지부, 분회도 사용자와 교섭하기 위해서는 노동조합과 동일하게 교섭창구 단일화 절차를 거쳐 교섭대표노동조합으로 결정 또는 확정되어야 한다. 따라서 교섭대표노동조합 으로 결정 또는 확정되지 못한 초기업단위 노동조합의 지부, 지회나 기업별 노동조합은 사용자와 교섭할 수 없으며, 초기업단위 노동조합의 집단교섭 등의 요구에 대해 사용자가 이를 거부하더라도 부당노동행위에 해당하지 않는다.

(2) 사례별 교섭대표노동조합 결정방식

1) 기업별 노동조합이 2개가 있는 경우

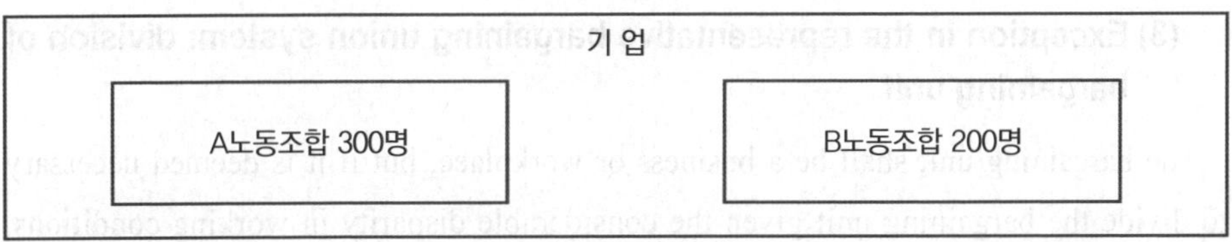

우선, A노동조합과 B노동조합이 자율적으로 교섭대표 노동조합을 합의하여 결정한다. 자율적 단일화가 이루어지지 않을 경우 전체 조합원 500명 중 A노동조합이 과반수를 차지하므로 A노동조합이 교섭대표노동조합으로 결정된다.

2) 기업별, 산업별, 지역별 노동조합 3개가 공존하는 경우

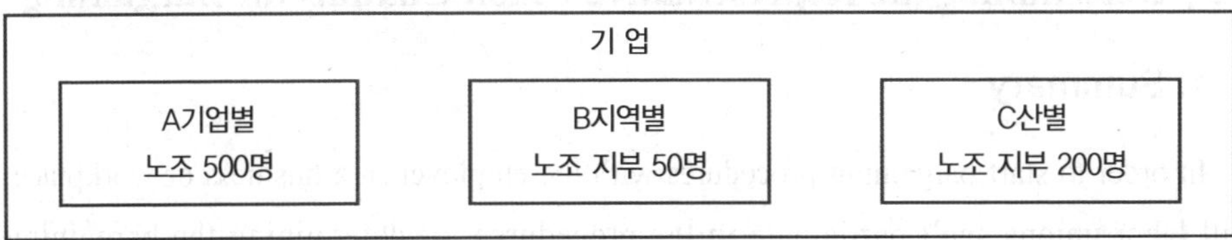

Above all, company-level labor union A, local-level labor union B and Industrial Union C shall autonomously determine the representative bargaining union. If the labor unions fail to do so, labor union A becomes the representative bargaining union as it has the majority of the total 750 union members.

3) In cases where there are two industrial unions and one company labor union

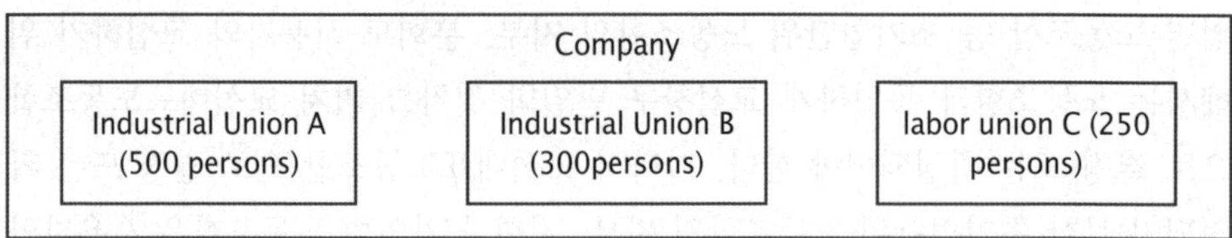

Above all, the three labor unions shall autonomously determine the representative bargaining union. If they fail to do so, none of the labor unions represent a majority of the 1,050 members, but if a particular labor union comes to represent a majority of the members by coalition or commission, that joint union becomes the representative bargaining union as it will now represent a majority of the membership.

(3) Exception in the representative bargaining union system: division of bargaining unit

The bargaining unit shall be a business or workplace, but if it is deemed necessary to divide the bargaining unit given the considerable disparity in working conditions, employment status, bargaining practices, etc., in a business or workplace, the Labor Commission may decide to divide the bargaining unit at the request of either or both of the parties to the labor relationship.

Ⅱ. Determining the Representative Union Channel for Bargaining

1. Summary

In order to start bargaining procedures with the employer in a business or workplace, all labor unions shall participate in the procedures for determining the bargaining channel and determine the representative bargaining union. The regulation to establish a

우선, A기업별 노동조합, B지역별 노동조합 지부, C산업별 노동조합 지부 간 자율적으로 교섭대표노동조합을 결정한다. 자율적 단일화가 이루어지지 않을 경우 전체 조합원 750명중 A기업별 노동조합이 과반수를 차지하므로 A기업별 노동조합이 교섭대표노동조합으로 결정된다.

3) 1개의 산별노동조합과 2개의 기업별 노동조합이 공존하는 경우

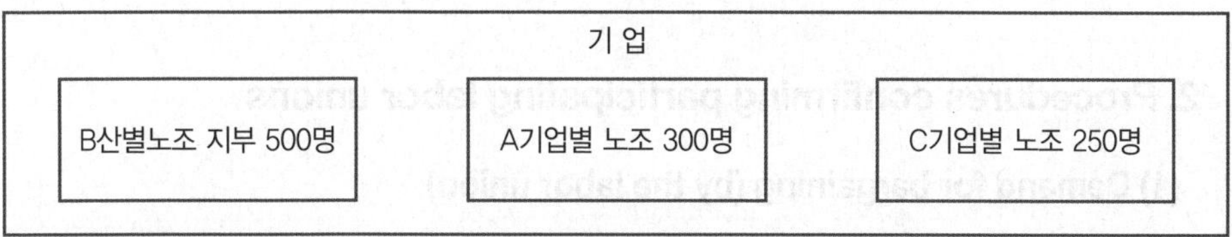

우선, 3개의 노동조합 간 합의에 자율적으로 교섭대표노동조합을 결정한다. 자율적 단일화가 이루어지지 않을 경우 전체 조합원수 1,050명 중 과반수를 차지하는 노동조합이 없으므로 연합이나 위임에 의해 과반수를 차지하는 경우 그 연합체가 과반수 노동조합으로서 교섭대표노동조합의 지위를 획득한다.

(3) 교섭창구 단일화의 예외: 교섭단위 분리

교섭단위는 하나의 사업 또는 사업장이 원칙이나, 당사자의 신청에 의해 현격한 근로조건의 차이, 고용형태, 교섭 관행 등을 고려하여 노동위원회 결정으로 교섭단위를 분리할 수 있다.

Ⅱ. 교섭창구 단일화

1. 의 의

하나의 사업 또는 사업장에서 사용자와 교섭하기 위해서는 해당 사업 또는 사업장의 모든 노동조합은 교섭창구 단일화를 거쳐 교섭대표 노동조합을 정하여야 한다(제29조의2). 교섭창구 단일화에 관한 규정은 강행규정으로 노동조합과 사용자는 반드시 이에 따라야 하므로 사업 또는 사업장의 근로자들이 가입하거나 조직한 모든 노동조합은 노동조합의 '조직형태'와 '조직대상의 중복' 여

bargaining channel is mandatory for both the labor union and the company. Regardless of type of organization or if they duplicate each other, all labor unions which employees of a business or workplace have joined or organized shall participate in the procedures to determine the representative union to be the bargaining channel. Determining the bargaining channel is ① to confirm which labor unions are participating in the bargaining channel and ② to determine a single representative bargaining union.

2. Procedures confirming participating labor unions

(1) Demand for bargaining (by the labor union)

A labor union may begin to request bargaining with the employer three months before the expiration date of the collective agreement. In this case, the request shall be made in writing, including the name of the labor union and the number of union members as of the date of the request for bargaining.

(2) Public notice of the labor union's request for bargaining (by the employer)

Upon receiving a request to bargain from a labor union, an employer shall put a notice on a bulletin board in the business or workplace concerned for seven days from the date of receiving said request. Even should there be only one labor union in that business or workplace, the employer shall post notice of the labor union's request for bargaining as there may be employees who have joined other industrial or local labor unions.

(3) Application by another labor union for bargaining (by the labor union)

If another labor union wants to participate in the collective bargaining, it shall request to do so within the seven-day notice period. Unions that fail to do this will be unable to participate in the procedures to determine a bargaining channel.

(4) Confirmation of labor union request for bargaining (by the employer)

The employer shall give public notice of the submitted request for five days beyond the seven-day notice period. Only labor unions that were confirmed as labor unions requesting bargaining can participate in the procedures to determine the representative bargaining union and apply for redress of any violation of the right for fair representation.

부에 관계없이 교섭창구 단일화 절차에 참여하여야 한다. 교섭창구 단일화는 ① 교섭창구 단일화 절차에 참여하는 노동조합을 확정하고, ② 그 노동조합들 중에서 교섭대표노동조합을 정하는 절차를 거치게 된다.

2. 교섭요구 노동조합의 확정절차

(1) 교섭요구(勞)

사용자와의 교섭을 원하는 노동조합은 어느 노동조합이든지 단체협약 만료일 이전 3개월이 되는 날부터 사용자에게 명칭, 조합원 수 등을 기재한 서면으로 교섭을 요구할 수 있다.

(2) 교섭요구 사실 공고(使)

교섭 요구를 받은 사용자는 교섭 요구를 받은 날로부터 7일간 교섭요구 사실을 해당 사업(장)의 게시판 등에 공고하여야 한다. 사용자가 해당 사업(장)에 노동조합이 1개만 있는 것으로 알고 있더라도 산업별 지역별 노동조합에 가입된 근로자가 있을 수 있으므로 반드시 교섭요구 사실을 공고하여야 한다.

(3) 다른 노조 교섭 참여 신청(勞)

교섭요구 사실에 대한 공고기간(공고일로부터 7일간)내에 하여야 하며, 그 기간에 교섭을 요구하지 않을 경우에는 교섭창구 단일화 절차에 참여할 수 없다.

(4) 참여노조 확정공고(使)

교섭요구 사실에 대한 공고기간이 끝난 다음 날부터 5일간 공고하여야 한다. 교섭요구 노동조합으로 확정된 노동조합만이 교섭대표노동조합 결정 절차에 참여할 수 있고, 공정대표의무 위반 시정신청을 할 수 있다.

3. Procedures for determining the representative bargaining union

(1) Summary

If there is only one labor union confirmed and determined as a labor union requesting bargaining, that labor union shall be the representative bargaining union. If two or more labor unions are confirmed and determined as labor unions requesting bargaining, the labor unions shall determine one representative bargaining union regardless of the type of organization or duplication in organizational coverage and negotiate with the employer. An exception is possible if separate bargaining with the other labor union(s) is accepted by the employer.

(2) Autonomous determination (by the labor union)

The labor unions, after confirmed or determined as labor unions requesting bargaining, can autonomously determine the representative bargaining union within 14 days after such confirmation. As there are no special procedures on or limits to the method used to determine the representative union, the only requirement is that the labor unions collectively agree.

(3) Confirmation of a majority labor union (by the labor union)

A majority labor union is a labor union organized with a majority of the members of all labor unions participating in the procedures for determining the representative bargaining union. If there is no majority labor union, in cases where two or more labor unions share the majority of the members of all labor unions participating in the procedures to establish a single bargaining channel by delegating authority or being united, they will be regarded as the majority labor union. Once the representative bargaining union is determined, the employer shall be notified within five days after expiration of the period for autonomous determination.

(4) Notification of information (by the employer)

Upon receiving notification that a labor union is the majority labor union, the employer shall give public notice of this for five days from the date of receiving that notification to ensure that other labor unions and employees see it.

3. 교섭대표노동조합 결정절차

(1) 개 요

확정된 교섭요구 노동조합이 1개인 경우에는 그 노동조합이 교섭대표노동조합 이며, 사용자와 교섭하여 단체협약을 체결할 수 있다. 확정된 교섭요구 노동조합이 2개 이상인 경우에는 원칙적으로 조직대상의 중복, 조직형태와 관계없이 교섭대표노동조합을 결정하여 사용자와 교섭해야 한다. 다만, 예외적으로 일정한 기간 내에 사용자가 동의하는 경우에는 노동조합과 개별교섭이 가능하다.

(2) 자율적 단일화(勞)

교섭요구 노동조합이 확정된 후 노동조합은 교섭요구 노동조합이 확정 또는 결정된 날로부터 14일 이내에 자율적으로 교섭대표노동조합을 정할 수 있다. 노동조합 간 자율적 단일화 방식에 대해서는 특별한 절차나 제한이 없으므로 참여 노동조합들의 합치된 의사가 반영되는 형태라면 자유롭게 정할 수 있다.

(3) 과반수 노조 통지(勞)

과반수 노동조합은 교섭창구 단일화 절차에 참여한 노동조합 전체 조합원의 과반수를 차지하는 노동조합을 의미한다. 과반수 노동조합이 없더라도 2개 이상의 노동조합이 위임 또는 연합 등의 방법으로 전체 조합원의 과반수가 되는 경우에도 과반수 노동조합으로 인정한다. 과반수 노동조합이라고 주장하는 노동조합은 사용자에게 자신이 전체 조합원의 과반수를 차지하는 과반수 노동조합으로서 교섭대표 노동조합이라는 사실을 자율적 단일화 결정 기한이 만료되는 날부터 5일 이내에 통지하여야 한다.

(4) 공고 통지(使)

사용자는 과반수 노동조합임을 통지 받은 때는 그 통지를 받은 날부터 5일간 그 내용을 공고하여 다른 노동조합과 근로자가 알 수 있도록 하여야 한다.

(5) Joint bargaining representative team (by autonomous or Labor Commission decision)

If there is no majority labor union, the labor unions eligible to jointly participate as the representative bargaining union shall organize a joint bargaining representative team and begin negotiations with the employer. The joint bargaining representative team shall be organized autonomously by the labor unions but if there is no agreement, it will be composed by the Labor Commission. The labor unions eligible to participate in the joint bargaining representative team shall be those whose members make up not less than 10% of the members of all labor unions participating in the procedures to determine the representative bargaining union. The collective agreement that the joint bargaining representative team concludes with the employer shall still apply to members of labor unions who make up less than 10% of the membership of all unions at the business or workplace, and these members shall still be eligible to vote for or against collective action.

Ⅲ. Status of the Representative Bargaining Union

1. Authority and obligations of the representative bargaining union

As collective bargaining and collective action shall be implemented by the representative bargaining union according to the single bargaining channel system, the representative bargaining union has authority as the labor union's party. Accordingly, the representative bargaining union has authority under and obligations to the Trade Union Act to independently conduct collective bargaining, conclude a collective agreement, and lead collective action, etc. The other labor unions cannot refuse the collective agreement concluded by the representative bargaining union, nor take steps that lead to independent collective action.

2. Duration of status of the representative bargaining union

(1) General principle

The representative bargaining union shall retain its status for two years, regardless of the effective period of the collective agreement.

(5) 공동교섭대표단(자율 또는 노동위원회)

과반수 노동조합이 없는 경우에는 확정된 교섭요구 노동조합은 공동교섭대표단을 구성하여 사용자에게 교섭을 요구하여야 한다. 공동교섭대표단은 먼저 노동조합 간 자율적으로 구성하고, 합의가 되지 않을 경우 노동위원회 결정에 따라 구성한다. 공동교섭대표단에 참여할 수 있는 노동조합은 조합원 수가 교섭창구 단일화 절차에 참여한 노동조합 전체 조합원의 10% 이상인 노동조합으로 제한된다. 조합원 수가 전체 조합원의 10% 미만 노동조합 및 그 조합원이라 하더라도 공동교섭대표단이 사용자와 체결한 단체협약은 적용되며, 쟁의행위 찬반투표 대상인원에도 포함된다.

Ⅲ. 교섭대표노동조합의 지위

1. 교섭대표노동조합의 권한 및 의무

교섭창구 단일화 제도의 취지상 단체교섭, 쟁의행위 등은 개별 노동조합이 아닌 교섭대표노동조합을 중심으로 이루어져야 하므로 교섭대표노동조합에게 당사자의 지위를 부여하고 있다. 따라서 교섭대표노동조합은 독립적으로 단체교섭, 단체협약 체결, 쟁의행위 주도 등의 노조법상 권한과 의무를 가진다. 교섭대표노동조합이 아닌 노동조합은 교섭대표노동조합이 체결한 단체협약의 적용을 거부하거나 독자적으로 쟁의행위에 돌입하는 등의 행위를 할 수 없다.

2. 교섭대표노동조합의 지위 유지기간

(1) 일반 원칙

교섭대표노동조합은 단체협약 유효기간에 관계없이 2년을 기준으로 그 지위를 유지한다.

(2) In cases where a new representative bargaining union has been determined

Since the effective period of the previous representative bargaining union has expired, the same representative bargaining union shall retain its status until such time as a new representative bargaining union is determined to renew an expiring collective agreement.

(3) In cases where a new representative bargaining union has not been determined

If the status of a representative bargaining union has expired, and a new one yet to be determined, the existing representative bargaining union shall retain its status as representative bargaining union in relation to implementation of the existing collective agreement until a new representative bargaining union is determined.

(4) In cases where a collective agreement is not concluded within one year

If a representative bargaining union has not concluded a collective agreement within one year since such determination was made, other labor unions may demand bargaining with the employer. Then, a procedure to determine the representative bargaining union agreement is initiated. The reason for this is because the representative bargaining union has not been able to conclude a collective agreement even though it has negotiated with the employer for one year. This may indicate that it has neglected to, or does not intend to properly exercise its bargaining representative authority, or has abused its authority.

Ⅳ. Duty of Fair Representation

The bargaining representative union and the employer shall have the duty of fair representation, which is to treat fairly and avoid discriminating against members of minority labor unions, participating in the procedure for determining the bargaining channel, or the labor unions themselves, without reasonable grounds. If the bargaining representative union and employer engage in discrimination, the affected labor union(s) may request the Labor Relations Commission to remedy such discrimination within three months from the date on which the act is committed. If the Labor Relations Commission recognizes that there has been discrimination without reasonable grounds, it shall issue an order to remedy such

(2) 새로운 교섭대표노동조합이 결정된 경우

교섭대표노동조합 유지기간 만료일 이후 유효기간이 만료되는 단체협약 갱신을 위한 새로운 교섭대표노동조합이 결정된 경우에는 기존 교섭대표 노동조합은 그 결정된 때까지만 그 지위를 유지한다.

(3) 새로운 교섭대표노동조합이 결정되지 못한 경우

교섭대표노동조합의 지위유지기간이 만료되었으나, 새로운 교섭대표노동조합이 결정되지 못한 경우 기존 교섭대표노동조합은 새로운 교섭대표노동조합이 결정될 때까지 기존 단체협약의 '이행'과 관련하여 계속 그 지위를 유지한다.

(4) 1년간 단체협약을 체결하지 못한 경우

교섭대표노동조합으로 결정된 후 1년간 사용자와 단체협약을 체결하지 못한 경우에는 어느 노동조합이든지 사용자에게 교섭을 요구함으로써 새로운 교섭대표노동조합을 정하기 위한 교섭창구 단일화 절차가 개시된다. 이는 교섭대표노동조합이 사용자와 1년간 교섭하였음에도 단체협약을 체결하지 못한 것은 교섭대표권한을 행사할 의사가 없거나 해태 또는 그 권한을 남용한 것으로 보아야 하기 때문이다.

Ⅳ. 공정대표의무

교섭대표노조와 사용자는 교섭창구 단일화 절차에 참여한 소수 노동조합과 그 조합원에 대한 불합리한 차별을 방지하기 위해 공정대표의무를 진다. 공정대표의무란 교섭대표노동조합과 사용자가 소수 노동조합과 그 조합원의 이익을 합리적인 이유 없이 차별하지 않고 공정하게 대표권을 행사할 의무를 말한다. 소수 노조는 교섭대표 노조와 사용자가 차별한 경우에 그 행위가 있은 날부터 3개월 이내에 노동위원회에 시정을 요청할 수 있고, 합리적인 이유 없는

discrimination(Article 29-4 of the Act). One example of the failure to uphold the duty of fair representation is when a bargaining representative union paid union officers from a minor union a much lower rate for paid time-off hours than officers from its own union.[66)]

The Constitutional Court ruled that the system of determining the bargaining representative union is constitutional and declared the following: "Article 29-2 of the Trade Union Act regulates that the system for determining the bargaining representative union was designed to solve potential issues in the following areas: In cases where there are two or more labor unions coexisting in a business or workplace, as these labor unions exercise their bargaining rights respectively, problems that can realistically be anticipated include: hostility between those labor unions or disputes between the labor unions and the company; an increase in the costs associated with collective bargaining due to having to repeat negotiations in the same bargaining areas; management difficulties in preparing multiple collective agreements; and unreasonable differences arising out of the application of different working conditions for members of different unions who are all providing the same or similar work. The system of determining a bargaining representative union as mentioned above has resulted in restrictions of the collective bargaining rights of minority labor unions not selected as the representative union, requiring certain safeguards to minimize these restrictions. One of the safeguards introduced was the duty of fair representation stipulated in Article 29-4 of the Trade Union Act. This was designed to prevent discrimination against: a) minority labor unions not selected as the representative union(and who had participated in determining the bargaining representative unions) or b) their members by assigning the bargaining representative union and employer the duty of fair representation."[67)]

1. Subject

The bargaining representative union and the employer shall not discriminate between the unions participating in the procedure of determining the representative union channel for bargaining, or its members, without reasonable grounds(Article 29-4 of the LUA). It is the bargaining representative union and the employer who bear the duty of fair representation.

---

66) Administrative Court ruling on Apr. 25, 2013, 2012Guhap35498.

67) Constitutional Court decision on Apr. 24, 2012, 2011Hunma338.

차별이라고 인정되는 경우 노동위원회는 그 시정에 필요한 명령을 해야 한다(노조법 제29조의4). 판례에서도 "교섭대표노동조합 전임자에 비해 교섭대표노동조합이 아닌 노동조합 전임자의 근로시간면제 시간을 현저히 적게 배분한 근로시간면제 합의는 공정대표의무를 위반한 것이다"라고 판단하였다.[66)]

헌법재판소는 복수노조의 교섭창구단일화 절차에 대해 합헌결정을 하면서 다음과 같이 명시하였다. "노조법제29조의2는 교섭창구 단일화제도를 규정하고 있는데, 이는 하나의 사업 또는 사업장에 2개 이상의 노동조합이 병존하는 경우 야기될 수 있는 현실적인 문제, 즉 복수의 노동조합이 각각 독자적인 교섭권을 행사할 수 있도록 할 경우 발생할 수 있는 노동조합과 노동조합 상호 간의 반목 및 노동조합과 사용자 사이의 갈등, 동일한 사항에 대해 같은 내용의 교섭을 반복하는 데서 비롯되는 교섭효율성의 저하와 교섭비용의 증가, 복수의 단체협약이 체결되는 경우 발생할 수 있는 노무관리상의 어려움, 동일하거나 유사한 내용의 근로를 제공함에도 불구하고 노동조합 소속에 따라 상이한 근로조건의 적용을 받는 데서 발생하는 불합리성 등의 문제를 효과적으로 해결하는 데 그 취지가 있다. 위와 같은 교섭창구단일화제도는 교섭대표가 되지 못한 노동조합의 단체교섭권을 제한하는 것이므로 그 침해를 최소화하기 위한 장치가 필요한데, 그중 하나로 도입된 것이 노조법 제29조의4에 규정된 공정대표의무로서 이는 교섭대표 노동조합이 되지 못한 소수 노동조합을 보호하기 위해 사용자와 교섭대표 노동조합에게 공정대표의무를 부과하여 교섭창구단일화 절차에 참여한 노동조합 또는 그 조합원에 대한 차별을 금지하는 것이다"[67)]

1. 주체

교섭대표노조와 사용자는 교섭창구 단일화 절차에 참여한 노조 또는 그 조합원 간에 합리적 이유 없이 차별을 하여서는 아니 된다(노조법 제29조의4). 공정

66) 행정법원 2013.4.25, 2012구합 35498.
67) 헌법재판소 2012.4.24, 2011헌마338.

Here, in principle, the bargaining representative union bears the duty of fair representation, but depending on the case, the employer may also bear such duty(duty of non-discrimination) together with the bargaining representative union.[68] However, the employer alone does not assume the duty of fair representation. A minority union removed from the procedure of determining the representative union channel for bargaining has the right to ask the duty of fair representation to the bargaining representative union. Applicants who can claim the duty of fair representation are minority unions that have participated in the representative union channel for bargaining, while unions that did not participate are excluded.

2. Scope

The purpose of the fair representation duty is to prohibit discrimination between labor unions participating in the process of determining the representative union channel for bargaining. The duty of fair representation must be observed not only in the articles of the collective agreement, which is the result of collective bargaining, but also in the process of collective bargaining.[69] In order for the bargaining representative union to treat the minority union equally in the process of collective bargaining and to fulfill the duty of fair representation procedurally and appropriately, it is necessary to provide information about the collective bargaining and the conclusion of a collective agreement to the minority union. However, since the discretion of the majority union is allowed in the collective bargaining process, if a minority union is discriminated against without reasonable cause by deviating or abusing the discretion of the bargaining representative union, the duty of fair representation is violated.[70]

The issues related to the duty of fair representation are ① the scope of union members, the subject of membership, and qualifications, ② the limit of paid time-off and treatment of paid full-time employees, and ③ the union shop issue in the content of the collective agreement. In the course of union activities, ① union fee deduction, ② requirements for recognition of paid union activities, ③ selection of labor-management council members, ④ union office,

68) Park, Jisoon, "The Concepts and Contents of the Duty of Fair Representation", Labor Review, Korea Labor Institute, June 2011, p. 14.

69) Supreme Court ruling on August 30, 2018: 2017 Da 218642.

70) Supreme Court ruling on September 13, 2018: 2017 Doo 40655.

대표의무를 부담하는 자는 교섭대표노조와 사용자이다. 여기서 교섭대표노조가 공정대표의무를 지는 것이 원칙이지만, 사안에 따라서는 사용자도 교섭대표노조와 함께 공정대표의무(차별금지의무)를 부담한다.[68] 그러나 사용자 단독으로 공정대표의무를 지지는 않는다. 그 이유는 교섭창구 단일화 절차에서 파생된 소수노조가 교섭대표 노조에 대한 권리자이기 때문이다. 공정대표의무를 요구할 수 있는 신청인은 창구단일화 절차에 참가한 소수 노조이고, 교섭창구 단일화 절차에 참가하지 않은 노조는 제외된다.

2. 범위

공정대표의무의 내용은 교섭창구단일화 절차에 참여한 노동조합 간 차별을 금지하는 것이다. 공정대표의무는 단체교섭의 결과물인 단체협약의 내용 뿐만 아니라 단체교섭의 과정에서도 준수되어야 한다.[69] 교섭대표노동조합이 단체교섭 과정에서 소수노동조합을 동등하게 취급하고 공정대표의무를 절차적으로 적정하게 이행하기 위해서는 기본적으로 단체교섭 및 단체협약 체결에 관한 정보를 소수노동조합에 적절히 제공하고 그 의견을 수렴하여야 한다. 단체교섭 과정에서 다수노조에게는 재량권이 인정되지만, 교섭대표 노조가 이러한 재량권을 일탈하거나 남용함으로써 소수노조를 합리적 이유 없이 차별하는 경우에는 공정대표의무를 위반한 것이 된다.[70]

단체협약의 내용에서 공정대표의무와 관련해 문제되는 것들은, ①조합원 범위, 가입 대상, 자격, ②근로시간 면제한도 및 면제자 전임자 대우, ③유니온숍 문제 등이며 조합 활동과정에서 문제시 되는 것들은, ①조합비 공제, ②유급 조합활동 인정요건, ③노사협의회 위원 선정, ④노조 사무실, ⑤노조 게시판 등 편의 제공이다. 단체교섭 과정에서 문제되는 것들은, ①교섭 요구안에 대한 의견수렴, ②교섭경과 및 교섭결과의 통지 설명, ③교섭의제 선정 문제

68) 박지순, "공정대표의무의 의의와 내용", 노동리뷰, 2011.6, 14면.
69) 대법원 2018.8.30. 선고 2017다218642
70) 대법원 2018.9.13. 선고 2017두40655 판결

⑤ union bulletin board, etc. are provided for. In the process of collective bargaining, ① gathering opinions on the proposal for negotiations, ② explaining the progress and results of negotiations, and ③ selecting the bargaining agenda are stipulated.[71)]

3. Burden of proof

Responsibility in lawsuits is apportioned according to who has the duty to verify the burden of proof. In general, the burden of proof rests with the party making the claim. However, regarding the burden of proving the duty of fair representation, the Supreme Court has ruled, "If it is recognized that the bargaining representative labor union or the employer discriminated against another union or its members participating in the procedure for determining the representative union channel for bargaining, the fact that such discrimination has reasonable grounds should be verified by the bargaining representative union or the employer with the burden of proof for the claim."[72)] It was determined that the burden of proof rests with the bargaining representative union and the employer, because the legal provisions specify the duty of fair representation which the bargaining representative union and the employer have to a minority union in accordance with Article 29-4 of the Labor Union Act.[73)]

Ⅴ. Legal Issues related to Permission for Multiple labor unions

1. Estimation of a business or workplace

The unit to be considered a single bargaining channel is a business or workplace. It is necessary to estimate whether the business is organically operated as a managing body itself, regardless of the workplace. The corporate entity as a business agent is a single unit, and so all workplaces or business departments in the entity's corporation are regarded as a single bargaining unit. However, despite being a single corporation, if each workplace

71) Lee, Kyungwoo, "Objects of Fair Representation and Judgment Criteria", Labor Law, December 2018, Joong-Ang Kyungjae.

72) Supreme Court ruling on August 30, 2018: 2017 da 218642.

73) Administrative Court ruling on September 29, 2016: 2015 Guhap 8459.

등이다.[71)]

3. 입증책임

누구에게 입증책임이 있는가에 따라서 소송의 유불리가 나누어진다. 일반적으로 입증책임은 이를 주장하는 측에서 지게 된다. 그러나 공정대표의무의 입증책임에 대해 대법원은 "교섭대표노동조합이나 사용자가 교섭창구 단일화 절차에 참여한 다른 노동조합 또는 그 조합원을 차별한 것으로 인정되는 경우, 그와 같은 차별에 합리적인 이유가 있다는 점은 교섭대표노동조합이나 사용자에게 그 주장-증명책임이 있다."고 판시하고 있다.[72)] 이는 노조법 제29조의4에 따라서 교섭대표노조와 사용자가 소수노조에 지는 공정대표의무를 법규정으로 명시하고 있기 때문에 입증책임은 교섭대표노조와 사용자에게 있다고 판단하였다.[73)]

Ⅴ. 복수노조 허용에 따른 법적 문제

1. 사업 또는 사업장 판단

교섭창구를 단일화해야 하는 단위는 "사업 또는 사업장"이다. 사업이란 장소와 관계없이 경영상의 일체를 이루면서 유기적으로 운영되는지 여부에 따라 판단하여야 한다. 경영주체인 법인체는 하나이므로 그 법인 내에 있는 모든 사업장 및 사업부서 전체를 하나의 교섭단위로 본다. 다만, 하나의 법인체라 하더라도 각 사업장 또는 사업부문별로 근로조건의 결정권이 있고, 인사 노무관리 회계 등이 독립적으로 운영되는 등 독립성이 인정되는 경우에는 예외적으로 개별 사업장 또는 사업부분을 하나의 교섭단위로 본다.

---

71) 이경우, "공정대표의무 대상과 판단 기준", 노동법률 12월호, 2018, 중앙경제사
72) 대법원 2018.8.30. 선고 2017다218642 판결
73) 행정법원 2016.9.29. 선고 2015구합8459 판결

or each business department has authority to determine its working conditions, and if its personnel, labor management, and accounting have been separately operated, exception shall be made, and such individual workplace or business department shall be regarded as an independent bargaining unit.

2. Joining two labor unions (dual membership)

Joining two or more labor unions is an exercise of "the employee's freedom to choose a labor union," since the employee is free to organize or join such union(s). In cases where an identified person has joined two or more labor unions, calculation of the number of members in each union shall be determined as those who pay union fees.[74)]

3. Collective withdrawal from a labor union and division of its property

Should a single member or multiple members withdraw from a labor union, in principle, the labor union's basic property and debts, and the collective agreement, are not transferred to the newly joined or organized labor union. Therefore, as a union member withdrawing from the labor union would lose any rights to the previous labor union's property, and he/she cannot request any division of the property unless there exists a stipulated right to divide its property.

4. Effect of the phrase, sole bargaining body

The phrase, sole bargaining body, refers to the part of a collective agreement that states: "The Company shall acknowledge no other labor organizations, except for a particular labor union, as the exclusive body with the right to bargain for the sake of its union members." This article is null and void as it violates Article 33(1) of the Constitution and Article 5 of the Trade Union Act by depriving other labor unions the right to negotiate with the consent of two exclusive parties.

5. Effect of agreement on union shop

Union shop refers to the part of a collective agreement that stipulates that the employee

---

74) Article 14-7 of the Enforcement Decree of the Trade Union Act.

2. 두 개 이상의 노동조합 가입(이중가입)

노동조합을 조직하거나 가입하는 것은 근로자의 자유의사에 따라 선택할 수 있는 것이므로, 2개 이상의 노동조합에 가입하는 것도 '단결선택의 자유'에 포함된다. 동일인이 2개 이상의 노동조합에 가입하는 경우에는 이중가입 조합원에 대한 조합원수 산정방법은 조합비 납부여부를 가지고 판단한다.[74)]

3. 조합원의 집단적 탈퇴와 노동조합의 재산 분할

기존 노동조합에서 개별 또는 집단적으로 탈퇴하더라도 기본 노동조합의 채권 채무나 단체협약은 새로이 가입하거나 설립된 노동조합에 승계되지 않는 것이 원칙이다. 따라서 노동조합에서 탈퇴한 조합원은 기존 노동조합의 재산에 대한 일체의 권리를 상실하는 것으로 재산분할에 관한 합의 등 별도의 법률행위가 존재하지 않는 이상 재산분할을 요구할 수 없다.

4. 유일교섭단체 조항의 효력

유일교섭단체 조항이란 통상 '사용자는 특정 노동조합이 해당 기업의 근로자를 대표하여 근로조건 등에 관하여 교섭하는 유일한 노동단체임을 인정하고 다른 어떠한 제2의 노동단체도 인정하지 않는다'는 취지의 단체협약 조항을 말한다. 이러한 조항은 당사자 간의 합의를 통해 다른 노동조합의 단체교섭권을 근본적으로 박탈하는 것으로 헌법 제33조 제1항 및 노조법 제5조에 위배되어 무효이다.

5. 유니온 숍 협정의 효력

유니온 숍(Union shop)이란 근로자를 채용할 때에 특정 노동조합의 조합원이 될 것을 고용조건으로 하는 단체협약으로 근로자들의 단결을 강제하는 대표적

74) 노조법 시행령 제14조의7.

is hired on condition that he/she becomes a member of the labor union, which is the most typical means to force union membership on employees. In this case, when a new employee refuses to join the labor union within a certain period of time or chooses to withdraw his/her membership, the labor union can request that the company dismiss that employee and the company shall comply with the union's request. However, starting July 1, 2011, when permission for multiple unions comes into effect, the company shall not put the employee in any disadvantageous position in terms of status, on the grounds that the employee has withdrawn from the labor union to organize a new one or join another existing union.[75]

Ⅵ. Criteria for Determining Whether a Unified Bargaining Channel Can Be Separated

1. Concept

With the introduction of multiple unions in one business or workplace from July 1, 2011, the system for unifying collective bargaining channels was implemented to reduce the adverse effects of multiple unions. The single bargaining channel system is required to create a practical guarantee of collective bargaining rights - namely the implementation of proper working conditions on the principle of equal power in labor-management decision-making.[76] Allowing two or more labor unions to negotiate individually with the employer at one workplace is expected to result in conflicts between labor unions and increase the employer's bargaining costs.[77] To this effect, current law requires negotiation be done by a designated representative union if there are two or more labor unions in an organization in one business or one workplace(Article 29-2 of the Trade Union Act). Nevertheless, if there are significant differences in working conditions, employment patterns, and negotiation practices in one business or workplace, separate bargaining units may resolve conflicts

75) Article 81 (2) of the Trade Union Act.

76) The Constitutional Court confirmed constitutionality of the law on Apr. 24, 2012, hunjae 2011 hunma 338.

77) Lim, Jongyul, 「Labor Law」, 18th ed., Park Young Sa, 2020, p. 124; Lee, Sungwook, Content and Issues of the Bargaining Union Separation System Labor Review, Korea Labor Institute, June 2011, p. 8.

인 수단의 하나이다. 이 경우 노동조합은 신규 근로자가 일정한 기간 내에 노동조합에 가입하지 않거나, 노동조합을 자진 탈퇴한 경우 사용자에게 해고할 것을 요구할 수 있고, 사용자는 이에 응할 의무를 부담한다. 그러나 복수노조가 허용되는 2011.7.1부터는 노동조합을 탈퇴하여 새로 노동조합을 조직하거나 다른 노동조합에 가입하는 것을 이유로는 신분상 불이익한 행위를 할 수 없도록 하였다.[75]

Ⅵ. 교섭단위 분리결정

1. 교섭단위 분리의 의의

하나의 사업 또는 사업장에 복수노조가 2011년 7월 1일부터 도입되면서 복수노조의 부작용을 줄이기 위해 단체교섭 창구 단일화 제도가 시행되었다. 교섭창구 단일화 제도는 노사대등의 원리 위에서 적정한 근로조건의 구현이라는 단체교섭권의 실질적인 보장을 위해 요구되는 불가피한 제도이다.[76] 하나의 사업장에 2개 이상의 노동조합을 각각 사용자와 개별적으로 교섭하도록 허용하면 노동조합 사이에 갈등과 사용자의 교섭비가 증가하는 부작용이 예상되기 때문이다.[77] 이러한 취지에서 현행법은 하나의 사업 또는 사업장에 조직형태를 같이 하는 노동조합이 2개 이상인 경우에는 그 대표교섭 노동조합을 정하여 교섭을 요구하여야 한다(노조법 제29조의2)고 규정함으로써 1사 1교섭대표노조 원칙을 취하고 있다. 그럼에도 불구하고 하나의 사업 또는 사업장에서 현저한 근로조건의 차이, 고용형태, 교섭 관행 등이 있는 경우에는 단위를 분리하여 교섭하는 것이 노동조합 간의 갈등을 해결하고 근로자의 근로조건 향상을 기할 수 있다. 이러한 취지로 교섭단위를 분리할 필요가 있다고 인정되는 경우에는 노동위원회의 승인을 얻어 교섭단위를 분리할 수 있다(법 제29조의3).

---

75) 노조법 제81조 제2호.

76) 헌법재판소 합헌 결정: 2012.4.24, 헌재2011헌마 338.

77) 임종률, 「노동법」 제18판, 박영사, 2020. 124면; 이승욱, "교섭단위 분리제도의 내용과 쟁점," 노동리뷰, 노동연구원, 2011.6, 8면.

between labor unions and improve working conditions for workers. Where it is deemed necessary to separate the bargaining unit to this effect, this may be done with approval of the Labor Relations Commission(LRC)(Article 29-3 of the Act). Separating bargaining units can weaken the bargaining power of labor unions, as unity and numbers in collective bargaining help to protect the power advantage with the employer. Therefore, the Trade Union Act allows unions to unify their collective bargaining channels and only recognizes the decision to separate them in exceptional circumstances.[78)]

2. Procedure for separating the bargaining unit

(1) Applicants

A company or a labor union party to labor relations may unilaterally file for separation of bargaining units(Article 29-3(2) of the Act). Labor unions that have not participated in the process of unifying bargaining channels may also apply, as may branches or unit unions under the umbrella of industrial unions(Article 14, Paragraph 1, 2 of the Enforcement Decree to the Act).

(2) At the time of application

① The labor union or employer may apply for a decision on the separation of bargaining units(Paragraph 1 of the above law) before the employer gives notice of the request and ② after the date on which the representative labor union is determined. Therefore, it is possible to apply for a separate bargaining unit decision at any time except for the period during which the negotiation channel unification process is carried out.

(3) Effect of application

The LRC shall, upon receipt of an application for separation of bargaining units, notify all labor unions and the employer of the business concerned and require them to submit their opinions. The LRC shall make a decision on separation within 30 days from the date of receipt of the application. Once an application for separation of bargaining units is made, the process of unifying the bargaining channel shall cease(paragraphs 1 through 5).

---

78) Supreme Court ruling on Sept. 13, 2018: 2015 doo 39361.

노동조합이 단체교섭을 통해 사용자의 관계에서 힘의 우위를 지키기 위해서는 더 많은 조합원으로 구성된 단결된 힘이 필요하기 때문에 오히려 교섭단위 분리는 노동조합의 협상력을 약화시킬 수 있다. 따라서 노동조합법은 노동조합의 단체교섭 창구 단일화를 원칙으로 하고, 교섭단위 분리 결정을 예외적인 상황에서만 인정하고 있다.[78)]

2. 교섭단위 분리절차

(1) 신청권자

교섭단위 분리는 노동관계 당사자인 회사와 노동조합이 같이 할 수 있고, 노동조합이나 회사가 일방적 신청도 가능하다(법 제29조의3 제2항). 교섭창구 단일화 절차에 참여하지 않은 노동조합도 교섭단위 분리를 신청할 수 있고, 산별노조 산하의 지회나 분회가 교섭단위 분리를 신청할 수도 있다(법 시행령 제14조의 11 제1항 제2호).

(2) 신청시기

노동조합 또는 사용자는 ① 사용자가 교섭요구 사실을 공고하기 전과 ② 사용자가 교섭요구 사실을 공고한 경우에는 교섭대표노동조합이 결정된 날 이후에 교섭단위 분리의 결정을 신청할 수 있다(위 동법 제1호). 따라서 교섭창구 단일화 절차가 진행되는 기간을 제외하고 언제든지 교섭단위 분리결정 신청을 할 수 있다.

(3) 신청효과

노동위원회는 교섭단위 분리신청을 받은 경우에는 해당 사업 또는 사업장의 모든 노동조합과 사용자에게 그 내용을 통지하고, 그 의견의 제출을 요구한다. 그리고 노동위원회는 신청을 받은 날로부터 30일 이내에 교섭단위 분리에 관한 결정을 하여야 한다. 교섭단위 분리 신청이 된 경우에는 교섭창구 단일화 절차의 진행이 중단된다(위 동법 제1항 내지 제5항).

---

78) 대법원 2018.9.13, 2015두39361.

(4) Upon decision

If the LRC decides to split the bargaining unit, the labor union may ask the employer for collective bargaining. In such a case, the employers required to engage in collective bargaining shall resume the process of unifying the bargaining channels for each separate bargaining unit from the beginning. However, if there is an existing collective agreement, collective bargaining may be requested from the date three months before expiration of that collective agreement(paragraph 3).

(5) Procedures and standards for appeal

The provisions of Article 29-3 and 69 of the Act apply to the procedures for non-compliance with the LRC's decision to separate the bargaining units. Thus, an objection may be raised with the National Labor Relations Commission within 10 days if it is felt that the LRC's decision is illegal or it is overstepping its authority. The Supreme Court has stated, The arbitration award may be appealed only if the procedure is illegal or its contents are illegal due to violation of the Labor Standards Act, or if the arbitration is beyond the scope of the dispute between the parties without justifiable reason, on the grounds that it is illegal or overstepped. Appeals made simply because the arbitration is unfavorable to either party will not be accepted."[79]

3. Requirements for separation of bargaining units

The court or LRC determines the need for separate bargaining units based on four criteria: ① there shall be differences in working conditions, ② there shall be differences in form of employment, ③ there shall be differences in the negotiating practice, and ④ these together shall require separation of the bargaining unit. The LRC decides after a comprehensive look at the higher value of benefit between maintenance of procedures for unifying negotiation channels and separation of bargaining units.[80]

---

79) Supreme Court ruling on Aug. 20, 2009: 2008 doo 8024.

80) Shim, Yo-seop, "Legislative Issues in the Separation of Negotiation Units," Labor Law Forum (23), Labor Law Theory Working-level Study Society, pp. 290-291.

(4) 결정효과

노동위원회가 교섭단위 분리 결정을 하면, 노동조합은 사용자에게 단체교섭을 요구할 수 있다. 이 경우 단체교섭을 요구받은 사용자는 분리된 교섭단위별로 각각 교섭창구 단일화 절차를 처음부터 다시 개시해야 한다. 다만, 기존의 단체협약이 있는 경우에는 그 단체협약의 유효기간 만료일 이전 3개월이 되는 날부터 단체교섭을 요구할 수 있다(위 동법 제3항).

(5) 불복 절차 및 기준

노동위원회의 교섭단위 분리 결정에 대한 불복 절차에 대해 중재재정의 불복절차에 관한 규정을 준용하고 있다(법 제29조의 3, 제69조). 따라서 노동위원회의 교섭단위 분리 여부 결정이 위법이나 월권인 경우에 한해 중앙노동위원회에 10일 이내에 이의를 제기할 수 있다.

대법원은 "중재재정은 그 절차가 위법하거나 그 내용이 근로기준법 위반 등으로 위법한 경우 또는 당사자 사이에 분쟁의 대상이 되지 않는 사항이나 정당한 이유 없이 당사자의 분쟁범위를 벗어나는 부분에 대하여 월권으로 중재재정을 한 경우와 같이 위법이거나 월권에 의한 것임을 이유로 하는 때에 한하여 불복할 수 있다. 중재재정이 단순히 어느 일방에 불리한 내용이라는 사유만으로는 불복이 허용되지 않는다."라고 판시하고 있다.[79)]

3. 교섭단위 분리 요건

교섭 단위의 분리 필요성을 판단할 때, 판례나 노동위원회는 4가지를 기준으로 판단하고 있다. 하나의 사업 또는 사업장에서 ① 현격한 근로조건의 차이, ② 고용형태, ③ 교섭관행을 차례대로 판단한 후, ④ 교섭단위를 분리할 필요가 인정되어야 한다. 노동위원회는 '교섭창구 단일화 절차 유지'와 '교섭단위 분리' 사이의 이익 형량을 통해 교섭단위 분리의 필요성 유무를 종합적으로 고려해 결정한다.[80)]

79) 대법원 2009.8.20, 2008두8024.
80) 심요섭, "교섭단위 분리 제도의 법적 쟁점," 노동법포럼(제23호), 노동법이론실무학회, 2018.2 290~291면.

(1) Significant differences in working conditions

Differences in working conditions need to be those where it would be considered reasonable for collective bargaining to be conducted separately, not as a difference in the individual nature of the workers. Thus, differences in personal attributes(such as proficiency, experience, educational background, years of service, etc.) do not constitute objective differences.[81)]

(2) Employment types

There should be a difference in employment patterns objectively, beyond simply whether a worker is temporary, contract, or part-time, to include things such as whether a specific job is designed for part-time workers after retirement, so it is desirable to elect a separate representative union to conduct collective bargaining independently.[82)]

(3) Negotiating practices

Negotiating practices are not considered based on negotiations in formally separated units, but on the basis of the need to negotiate in separate units. In other words, the separation of bargaining units is not always justified by having collective bargaining practices that are different from the majority labor union of one company due to reasons such as occupation, merger or business establishment.[83)]

(4) Necessity to separate bargaining units

The LRC shall elect a separate negotiation representative union to determine whether the essential basis of labor-management relations is different to the extent that each union needs to engage in independent collective bargaining. The LRC shall make a decision in consideration of the actual status of labor-management relations in the business or workplace, such as the distribution and number of members, negotiation requirements, the details and nature of labor relations, and the degree of independence in personnel management.[84)]

---

81) National Labor Relations Commission, decision on Nov. 21, 2012: Central 2012 Unit 8 (The Only One Company labor case).

82) Labor Relations Commission, decision on Sept. 11, 2013: Seoul 2013 Unit 42 (Korean Air case).

83) Labor Relations Commission, decision on July 27, 2011: Seoul 2011 Unit 1 (Road Traffic Corporation case).

84) Park, Dong-gook, "The Issue on Deciding to Separate Bargaining Units," Labor Law, Central Economy, Jan. 2015.

(1) 현격한 근로조건의 차이

현격한 근로조건의 차이는 근로자의 개인적 속성에 의한 차이가 아니라 객관적인 차이로 단체교섭을 별도로 행하는 것이 합리적이라고 볼 수 있는 근로조건이어야 한다. 이에 근로자의 개인적 속성(숙련도, 경력, 학력, 근속연수 등)의 차이는 객관적인 사유에 의한 차이로 보지 않는다.[81)]

(2) 고용형태

고용형태의 경우 단순히 임시직, 계약직, 시간제 근로자 등으로 비교할 것이 아니라, 타 직종과 달리 정년 이후 촉탁직 등으로 재고용 하도록 규정된 경우처럼 객관적으로 고용형태의 차이가 존재하여 교섭대표노조를 별도로 선출해 단체교섭을 독자적으로 진행하는 것이 실익이 있어야 한다.[82)]

(3) 교섭관행

교섭관행은 형식적으로 분리된 단위로 교섭했던 것을 기준으로 하는 것이 아니라 실질적으로 분리해 교섭할 필요성을 기준으로 판단한다. 즉, 직종별, 합병, 사업장별 등의 사유로 인해 1사 다수 노조 사업장으로 별개의 단체교섭 관행이 있다고 하여 항상 교섭단위 분리가 정당화되는 것은 아니다.[83)]

(4) 교섭단위 분리의 필요성

교섭단위 분리 필요성에 대해 노동위원회는 별도의 교섭대표노조를 선출해 각각 독자적인 단체교섭을 해야 할 정도로 노사관계의 본질적인 기초를 달리하고 있는지 여부를 판단한다. 노동위원회는 조합원의 분포, 조합원 수, 교섭요구사항, 근로관계의 내용과 성격, 인사노무 관리의 독립성 정도 등 해당 사업 또는 사업장의 노사관계 실태를 고려하여 판단한다.[84)]

---

81) 중앙노동위원회, 2012.11.21, 중앙2012단위8, ㈜온리원 교섭단위사건 재심신청 사건.
82) 노동위원회, 서울2013단위42, 2013.9.11. ㈜ 대한항공 교섭단위 분리 결정신청 사건.
83) 노동위원회, 서울2011단위1, 2011.7.27. 도로교통공단 교섭단위 분리신청 사건.
84) 박동국, "교섭단위 분리 결정에 관한 쟁점," 노동법률, 중앙경제, 2015.1.

4. Decisions on separation of bargaining units Cases of acceptance

(1) Entrusted and directly operated workers[85)]

One company has a general labor union and a postal delivery service union. The company's general labor union engages in collective bargaining with the bargaining representative union. The new postal delivery union applied for separation of bargaining units on the grounds that the working conditions and employment types were different because they were postal delivery service providers with qualifications as individual business operators, not full-time employees of the company. The LRC acknowledged that it was necessary to separate the bargaining representative union into separate bargaining units for effective negotiations between labor and management, as there were wide differences in working conditions and types of employment for general employees and entrusted postal delivery service workers, and uniformity in working conditions was not reasonably achievable.

(2) Separation of bargaining units for broadcasting personnel[86)]

Broadcasters have the right to call for collective bargaining because they are workers under the Trade Union Act. Therefore, the Labor Standards Act recognizes the validity of their application for separation of bargaining units due to their different working conditions.

(3) Non-fixed-term contract workers and full-time employees[87)]

Fifty-nine non-fixed-term workers in a certain corporation were responsible for office assistance, parking, driving, facilities and counseling, while 137 persons were full-time employees in general, technical or functional positions. The corporation recognized a labor union composed of full-time workers as the representative labor union and engaged in negotiations with it. Non-fixed-term workers were not permitted into the full-time union.

---

85) Labor Relations Commission, decision on Aug. 16, 2018: Seoul 2018 Unit 11 (Postal Logistic Agency case).

86) Supreme Court ruling on Oct. 12, 2018: 2015 doo 38092 (KBS).

87) Supreme Court ruling on Sept. 13, 2018 (Goyang-si City Management Corporation).

4. 교섭단위 분리결정 사례

(1) 위탁 근로자와 직영근로자의 경우[85)]

회사의 노동조합은 일반직 노동조합과 위탁 택배배달원 노동조합으로 구성하고 있다. 회사의 일반직 노동조합은 교섭대표 노조를 중심으로 단체교섭을 실시하고 있다. 신생 택배노조는 회사의 정규직 근로자가 아닌 개인사업자 자격의 택배 배달원이므로 근로조건과 고용형태가 다르다는 이유로 교섭단위 분리신청을 하였다.

노동위원회는 일반직원과 위탁 택배원의 근로조건, 고용형태에서 현격한 차이가 있고, 근로조건의 통일성을 기하기 어려우므로 노사 간 효율적인 교섭을 위하여 택배 직종을 별도의 교섭단위로 분리할 필요성이 있다고 인정하였다.

(2) 방송연기자의 교섭단위 분리[86)]

방송연기자들은 노동조합법상의 근로자에 해당되므로 단체교섭을 요구할 권리가 있다. 따라서 KBS의 근로기준법상 근로자와 다른 근로조건을 가지고 있으므로 교섭단위 분리 신청에 타당성을 인정하였다.

(3) 무기계약직(상용직)과 정규직의 경우[87)]

상용직 근로자 59명은 사무보조나 주차, 운전, 시설, 상담 업무를 담당하였고, 공사의 정규직 근로자 137명은 일반직이나 기술직, 기능직으로 구성돼 있다. 공사는 정규직 근로자로 구성된 노동조합을 교섭대표 노조로 인정하여 교섭을 진행하고 있다. 정규직 노동조합은 상용직의 노동조합 가입을 배제하고 있다.

대법원은 임금수준의 차이, 상용직에 대해 별도의 관리규정이 적용되고, 고용형태도 상용직과 정규직으로 구분되어 있다. 교섭관행도 정규직의 단체협약은 상용직에 적용되지 않고 있다. 따라서 대법원은 교섭단위 분리를 인정하지

---

85) 노동위원회, 서울2018단위11, 2018.8.16(우체국물류지원단).

86) 대법원 2018.10.12, 2015두38092(한국방송공사).

87) 대법원 2018.9.13, 2015두39361(고양시도시관리공사).

The Supreme Court has separate management regulations for wage levels and employment types are divided into non-fixed-term and regular jobs. Negotiating practices also do not apply to regular workers' collective agreements. Therefore, the Supreme Court recognizes the separation of bargaining units as negative to stable labor-management relations as it can cause more conflict between labor and management.

(4) Different workplaces[88)]

In one business, several divisions were divided into separate factories, there were wide differences in working conditions, and individual bargaining was carried out according to practice. The labor union in a relatively superior position applied for the bargaining unit to be separated.

The LRC agreed to separate, recognizing the interests of the labor unions involved, as each business unit had different working conditions and negotiated individually.

5. Decisions on separation of bargaining units Cases of rejection

(1) Office workers and field workers in one workplace[89)]

A union of office workers was recently established in a company in charge of post office logistics. Previously, three labor unions(about 1,300 union members in total) were formed around the site and had been negotiating through the bargaining representative union. After the office workers' union reported its establishment with 110 general office workers, the office workers applied for a separation of bargaining units on the grounds of a wide gap in working conditions.However, the LRC judged that there were no significant differences in working conditions or employment patterns between office workers and other workers. It rejected the request for separation in accordance with the principle of unifying negotiating channels, in the interest of unified labor conditions and stability in labor-management relations.

---

88) National Labor Relations Commission ruling Apr. 2, 2018: NLRC 2018 unit 3.

89) LRC decision on Mar. 12, 2020: Seoul 2020 union 8 (POLA).

않는 것은 노-노간의 갈등을 유발하여 안정적 노사관계에 부정적이라고 판단하여 교섭분리를 인정하였다.

(4) 서로 다른 사업장의 경우[88)]

하나의 사업에서 여러 개의 사업부가 별도의 공장으로 구분되어 있고, 현격한 근로조건의 차이가 있고, 관행에 따라 개별교섭을 해온 경우에는 상대적으로 우월한 지위에 있던 노동조합이 교섭단위 분리를 신청하였다.

노동위원회는 사업부 별로 별도의 사업장에서 근무하며 근로조건이 다르고 개별적으로 교섭을 해온 관례가 있기 때문에 개별교섭을 인정하는 게 노동조합의 이익을 균형 있게 반영할 수 있도록 인정하여 교섭단위 분리를 인정하였다.

5. 교섭단위 분리신청 기각 사례

(1) 사업장 내의 관리직과 현장직 근로자[89)]

우체국 물류를 담당하는 회사에 사무직 노조가 최근에 설립되었다. 기존에 현장을 중심으로 노동조합 3개(조합원 1300여명)가 구성되어 교섭대표 노조를 통해 교섭해오고 있다. 사무직 노조는 일반 사무직 110명으로 노동조합 설립신고를 하고, 현장직 직원과 사무직 직원은 근로조건이 현격히 차이가 난 다는 이유로 교섭단위 분리신청을 하였다.

노동위원회는 사무직과 그 외 직종 사이에 교섭단위를 분리할 만큼의 근로조건이나 고용형태에 현격한 차이가 있다고 보기 어렵다고 판단하였다. 이에 노동위원회는 사무직의 근로조건 개선을 위하여 교섭대표노동조합에 공정대표의무 이행을 요구할 수 있다는 점을 등을 고려하면 근로조건의 통일적 형성과 이를 통한 노사관계의 안정이라는 교섭창구 단일화의 취지에 따라 교섭단위 분리청구를 기각하였다.

---

88) 중앙노동위원회 중앙2018단위3, 2018.4.2.

89) 노동위원회, 서울2020단위8, 2020.3.12(우체국물류지원단)

(2) Street cleaners and other public service workers[90)]

Street cleaners in Jeju City applied for separation of bargaining unit. However, there is not much difference in working conditions between regularly-employed street cleaners and non-fixed-term workers. In terms of employment status, retirement age is guaranteed as they are considered non-fixed-term contract workers, similar to civil servants. However, there was a negotiation practice in which individual negotiations had been held even before the single negotiation channel was taken. In response, the LRC rejected the request for separation of bargaining units in accordance with the principle to maintain a single bargaining channel for multiple labor unions.

(3) Non-fixed-term contract workers and fixed-term workers in the restaurant industry, and full-time workers[91)]

A newly hired non-fixed-term contract worker and a fixed-term worker in charge of restaurant affairs, both working for the same restaurant, applied for separation of bargaining units into one for non-fixed-term workers and one for regular workers. In application of remarkable working conditions, the LRC found that there was no difference in working conditions as regular and non-fixed-term contract workers had the same salary system, as did part-time workers. The types of employment given were that nutritionists and chefs with the necessary qualifications were considered full time, while the rest of the staff were hired on contract. There had been no practice of separate negotiations. Therefore, it was deemed reasonable to keep the bargaining channel unified to protect the labor-management relations that would not be so stable if separate negotiations were to occur.

---

90) Seoul Hight Court ruling on Oct. 19, 2016: 2016 noo 48234 (Jeju City).

91) NLRC June 4, 2018: Joongang 2018 unit 5.

(2) 환경미화원과 다른 공무직 근로자[90)]

제주시는 공무직으로 환경미화원과 다양한 업종의 공무직 근로자들이 있다. 환경미화원만 별도로 교섭단위 분리 결정을 신청하였지만 이에 대해 환경미화원과 공무직 근로자들은 같은 취업규칙을 적용받으므로 근로조건의 차이가 많지 않다. 고용형태에서도 공무직과 같이 모두 무기계약직으로 정년이 보장되어 있다. 다만 교섭창구 단일화 이전부터 개별교섭을 해온 교섭관행이 있었다. 이에 대해 노동위원회는 복수노조의 교섭창구단일화 조치가 원칙임을 이유로 교섭단위 분리신청을 기각하였다.

(3) 식당업무 담당 무기계약직과 기간제 근로자와 정규직 근로자[91)]

식당업무 담당 무기계약직과 기간제 근로자와 정규직 근로자 사이에서 새로이 신설된 무기계약직과 기간제 근로자가 교섭단위 분리결정을 신청하였다. 이에 대해 노동위원회는 현격한 근로조건 적용에 있어 정규직과 무기계약직은 호봉제, 기간제 근로자는 월급제를 시행하고 있으나 근로조건에는 차이가 없다. 고용형태는 식당에서 필요한 자격을 갖춘 영양사나 요리사의 경우 정규직으로 하고, 나머지 직원들은 무기계약직으로 하고 있다. 또한, 이전 교섭에서도 분리교섭한 사례가 없었다. 따라서 분리교섭을 할 경우에 통일적인 근로조건 형성이나 노사관계 안정을 기대할 수 없어 분리교섭보다는 교섭창구를 일원화하는 것이 타당하다고 보았다.

---

90) 서울고등법원 2016누48234, 2016.10.19(제주도특별자치도).

91) 중앙노동위원회 중앙2018단위5, 2018.6.4.

Section 3: Understanding Collective Agreements

Ⅰ. Concept

1. Concept of collective agreement

A collective agreement is an agreed set of rules between the labor union and the employer concerning wage, working hours, and other issues. Even though it is an agreement on working conditions between the two parties, this agreement has normative effects on labor relations.

2. Contracting procedures for collective agreements

Article 31 (Drawing up of collective agreements)

① collective agreements shall be in writing, and both parties concerned shall sign their names or affix their seals thereto.

② The parties to collective agreements shall report the conclusion of collective agreements to the Administrative Authorities within fifteen days of the date of such conclusion.

③ If any provision of a collective agreement is determined to be unlawful, the Administrative Authorities may, upon resolution of the Labor Relations Commission, order amendment of that collective agreement.

A collective agreement that was not prepared in the method stipulated in Article 31(1) of the Trade Union Act is null and void. Article 31(1) of this Act stipulates that a collective agreement shall be prepared in writing and both parties shall affix their signatures and seals thereto. The purpose of the procedure is to clarify the details of the collective agreement, to prevent any future disputes surrounding those details, and to confirm the final positions of both parties to ensure truthfulness in the collective bargaining process. Therefore, if collective bargaining does not follow this procedure, any agreement cannot remain effective.

제3절 단체협약의 이해

Ⅰ. 단체협약 의의와 체결방식

1. 단체협약의 의의

단체협약은 노동조합과 사용자가 임금·근로시간 기타의 사항에 대하여 단체교섭과정을 거쳐 합의한 사항을 말하는 것으로서 근로조건 등에 대한 노사간 합의사항이지만 그것에 규범적 효력이 인정되어 노사관계에 미치는 영향이 대단히 크다.

2. 단체협약의 체결방식

노조법 제31조【단체협약의 작성】
① 단체협약은 서면으로 작성하여 당사자 쌍방이 서명 또는 날인하여야 한다. ② 단체협약의 당사자는 단체협약의 체결일부터 15일 이내에 이를 행정관청에 신고하여야 한다. ③ 행정관청은 단체협약중 위법한 내용이 있는 경우에는 노동위원회의 의결을 얻어 그 시정을 명할 수 있다.

노조법 제31조 제1항이 단체협약은 서면으로 작성하여 당사자 쌍방이 서명·날인하여야 한다고 규정하고 있는 취지는 단체협약의 내용을 명확히 함으로써 장래 그 내용을 둘러싼 분쟁을 방지하고 아울러 체결당사자 및 그의 최종적 의사를 확인함으로써 단체협약의 진정성을 확보하기 위한 것이므로, 그 방식을 갖추지 아니하는 경우 단체협약은 효력을 가질 수 없다.

(1) The agreement shall be written

A collective agreement may be a general agreement on labor relations, but the contents shall be in writing.

(2) The agreement shall be effective only if it is signed and sealed

The representative of the labor union or union chairman shall sign or seal, and the business owner shall do the same on the company's behalf.

(3) The agreement shall be reported

The parties to the collective agreement shall make a report of the collective agreement to administrative agencies within fifteen days from the date of its conclusion. However, this report of the collective agreement is not a formal approval; therefore, it is unrelated to the effect of the collective agreement.

Ⅱ. Valid Term of Collective Agreements

Article 32 (Valid Term of collective agreements)

① No collective agreement shall have a term of validity exceeding three years(revised on Dec 10, 2020).

② In cases where a collective agreement does not specify a term of validity or has a term exceeding the period stipulated in paragraph (1), it shall automatically be deemed to be three years.

③ Unless otherwise provided in a separate agreement, if no new collective agreement is concluded by the expiry date of the existing agreement even though the parties have continuously engaged in collective bargaining before and after the expiry date, the existing collective agreement shall remain effective for up to three months after its expiry date. If no conclusion is made on a new collective agreement after expiration of the extended effective term, the existing agreement shall be applicable only if the existing agreement specifically provides that it shall remain in effect until a new collective agreement is concluded, provided, however, that any one party concerned may terminate the collective agreement by giving notice to the other party six months in advance.

(1) 서면으로 작성하여야 한다.

단체협약은 노사관계에 관한 총괄적인 협정인 경우도 있는데, 그 내용이 어떠한 것이든 이를 불문하고 서면으로 작성하지 않으면 아니 된다.

(2) 서명·날인하여야 효력이 발생한다.

단체협약은 이를 문서화한 후에 양 당사자의 서명 또는 날인을 하여야 하는데 노동조합은 그 대표자, 즉 노동조합의 위원장이 서명 · 날인하여야 하고, 사용자측은 법인기업인 경우 대표이사가, 개인기업인 경우 사업주가 서명 · 날인하여야 한다.

(3) 단체협약을 신고하여야 한다.

단체협약을 체결한 당사는 단체협약 체결일로부터 15일 이내에 쌍방이 연명으로 이를 고용노동부 장관 또는 관할 지방노동관서의 장에게 신고하여야 한다. 그러나 이와 같은 단체협약의 신고는 고용노동부 장관(지방노동관서의 장)의 인가를 얻기 위한 요식행위가 아니기 때문에 단체협약의 효력 발생과는 아무런 관계가 없다.

Ⅱ. 단체협약의 유효기간

제32조【단체협약의 유효기간】

① 단체협약에는 3년을 초과하는 유효기간을 정할 수 없다(2020.12.10 변경).

② 단체협약에 그 유효기간을 정하지 아니한 경우 또는 제1항의 기간을 초과하는 유효기간을 정한 경우에 그 유효기간은 3년으로 한다.

③ 단체협약의 유효기간이 만료되는 때를 전후하여 당사자 쌍방이 새로운 단체협약을 체결하고자 단체교섭을 계속하였음에도 불구하고 새로운 단체협약이 체결되지 아니한 경우에는 별도의 약정이 있는 경우를 제외하고는 종전의 단체협약은 그 효력만료일부터 3월까지 계속 효력을 갖는다. 다만, 단체협약에 그 유효기간이 경과한 후에도 새로운 단체협약이 체결되지 아니한 때는 새로운 단체협약이 체결될 때까지 종전 단체협약의 효력을 존속시킨다는 취지의 별도의 약정이 있는 경우에는 그에 따르되, 당사자 일방은 해지하고자 하는 날의 6월전까지 상대방에게 통고함으로써 종전의 단체협약을 해지할 수 있다.

1) No collective agreement may be effective for longer than 3 years. The effects of a collective agreement are lost when its term of validity is exhausted, but the parts concerning employee working conditions(normative section) shall remain effective as being part of the contract of employment(Article 32).

2) If the employer and the union have yet to reach a collective agreement despite their good-faith commitment to working out a new agreement to replace the existing one, the existing collective agreement shall remain valid for 3 more months from the date of its termination.

3) If there is an additional agreement within the document that the existing collective agreement shall remain valid after its effective duration expires and until a new agreement is concluded, the existing agreement shall be applicable in that way. However, either party may terminate the existing collective agreement by giving notice to the other party 6 months before the date the party wants the agreement to be terminated.

The purpose of an upper limit for the effective period of a collective agreement
If a collective agreement were allowed to remain effective for an excessively long period of time, it would probably serve as an unnecessary restriction to both parties. Furthermore, it would be contradictory to the fundamental purpose of the collective agreement, which is to maintain or improve working conditions and stabilize labor relations. Accordingly, in order to keep a collective agreement relevant, it is necessary to put an upper limit on the effective term.[92)]

Ⅲ. Details and Effects of a Collective Agreement

A collective agreement is made up of two different parts: one concerning working conditions and treatment of employees(normative section), and one concerning the rights and obligations of the employer(contractual section). Any part of the work rules or an individual employment contract which contradicts the normative part of the collective agreement is invalid and is replaced by the corresponding provisions of the collective agreement.[93)]

---

92) Supreme Court ruling on Feb.9.1993, 92Da27120

93) Article 33 of the Trade Union Act.

1) 단체협약의 유효기간은 3년을 초과할 수 없다. 유효기간이 종료되면 단체협약의 효력이 상실되나, 근로조건 기타 근로자의 대우에 관한 부분 (규범적 부분)은 근로계약의 내용으로 효력이 유지된다.

2) 노사가 성실하게 단체협약의 갱신을 위하여 교섭하고 있음에도 불구하고 새로운 단체협약이 체결되지 아니한 경우에는 유효기간 종료일로부터 3월간은 기존 단체협약의 효력이 유지된다.

3) 단체협약에 그 유효기간이 경과한 후에도 새로운 단체협약의 체결 시까지 종전 단체협약의 효력을 존속시킨다는 취지의 별도 약정이 있는 경우에는 유효기간이 경과한 후에도 단체협약의 효력은 유지된다. 그러나 당사자 일방이 해지하고자 하는 날의 6월 전까지 상대방에게 통고하면 종전의 단체협약을 해지할 수 있다.

단체협약의 유효기간을 제한하는 규정을 둔 취지

단체협약의 유효기간을 제한하는 규정을 둔 것은 이를 너무 길게 하면 변동하는 산업사회의 사회적, 경제적 여건의 변화에 적응하지 못하여 당사자를 부당하게 구속하는 결과가 되고 그렇게 되면 단체협약에 의하여 적절한 근로조건을 유지하고 노사관계의 안정을 도모하고자 하는 목적에도 어긋나게 되므로 그 유효기간을 일정한 범위로 제한하여 단체협약의 내용을 시의에 맞고 구체적이며 타당성 있게 조정해 나가도록 하자는 데 있다.[92)]

Ⅲ. 단체협약의 내용과 효력

단체협약은 크게 근로조건 기타 근로자의 대우에 관한 부분(규범적 부분)과 노동조합과 사용자 간의 권리·의무에 관한 부분(채무적 부분)으로 구분된다. 단체협약에서 정한 규범적 부분에 위배되는 취업규칙이나 개별 근로계약의 해당부분은 무효이며, 단체협약상의 기준이 적용된다.[93)]

---

92) 대법원 1993.2.9, 92다27102.

93) 노조법 제33조.

1. Normative section

The Trade Union Act: Article 33 (Validity of Standards)

① Any part of the rules of employment or a labor contract that violate standards concerning working conditions and other matters concerning the treatment of workers as prescribed in the collective agreement shall be null and void.

Article 92 (Penal Provisions) A person to whom any of the following subparagraphs apply shall be punished by a fine not exceeding ten million won:

1. A person who violates the matters falling under any of the following items from among the contents of a collective agreement concluded pursuant to Article 31 (1):
   (a) Matters regarding wage, welfare costs and retirement allowances;
   (b) Matters regarding working and resting hours, holidays and vacations;
   (c) Matters regarding causes for discipline and dismissals and important procedures;
   (d) Matters regarding safety, health and disaster relief;
   (e) Matters regarding provision of facilities and conveniences and participation in meetings during on-duty hours; and
   (f) Matters regarding industrial action.

The normative section of the collective agreement regards matters concerning working conditions and other matters concerning the treatment of workers. The normative section contains amount of wages, method of wage calculation, working hours, paid off-days, paid leaves, bonuses, agreements on welfare, kinds and calculations of industrial accidents, agreements on progressive severance pay, retirement age, etc.

Normative effects of the collective agreement include compulsory and direct effects.[94)]

1) Compulsory effect is nullification of any part of the rules of employment or a labor contract that violates standards of working conditions and other matters concerning the treatment of workers as prescribed in the collective agreement.

2) Direct effect refers to matters not covered in a labor contract. Any part which is made null and void by compulsory effect shall be governed by those standards of the collective agreement.

(1) Effect after expiration of the collective agreement.[95)]

Although the effective period of the collective agreement expires or the collective agreement

94) Article 33 of the Trade Union Act.

95) MOEL Guidelines: Nosa Relations Team-1049, on Apr. 14, 2006.

1. 규범적 부분

노조법 제33조【기준의 효력】

① 단체협약에 정한 근로조건 기타 근로자의 대우에 관한 기준에 위반하는 취업규칙 또는 근로계약의 부분은 무효로 한다.

제92조【벌 칙】 다음 각호의 1에 해당하는 자는 1천만원이하의 벌금에 처한다.

1. 제31조 제1항의 규정에 의하여 체결된 단체협약의 내용중 다음 각목의 1에 해당하는 사항을 위반한 자가. 임금·복리후생비, 퇴직금에 관한 사항

 나. 근로 및 휴게시간, 휴일, 휴가에 관한 사항

 다. 징계 및 해고의 사유와 중요한 절차에 관한 사항

 라. 안전보건 및 재해부조에 관한 사항

 마. 시설·편의제공 및 근무시간중 회의참석에 관한 사항

 바. 쟁의행위에 관한 사항

단체협약의 규범적 부분은 '근로조건 기타 근로자의 대우'에 관한 사항이다. 임금액, 임금지급 방법, 근로시간, 유급휴일, 유급휴가, 상여금 지급, 복지에 관한 협정, 재해보상의 종류 및 산정, 누진퇴직금 지급협정, 정년제에 관한 협정 등은 규범적 부문에 속한다.

단체협약의 규범적 부분은 강행적 효력과 직접적 효력을 갖는다.[94)]

1) 강행적 효력이라 함은 단체협약의 근로조건 기타 근로자의 대우에 관한 기준에 위반하는 취업규칙 또는 근로계약의 부분을 무효로 하는 효력이다.

2) 직접적 효력이라 함은 강행적 효력에 의하여 무효가 된 경우에, 그 부효로 된 부분은 단체협약에 정한 기준에 의하고 또한, 근로계약에 규정되지 않은 사항에 관하여는 단체협약의 기준에 의한다는 효력을 말한다.

(1) 단체협약 만료 또는 해지후의 효력[95)]

단체협약의 유효기간이 만료되거나 동 협약의 자동연장 기간 중 당사자 일방의 해지통보로 인하여 단체협약이 실효되었다 하더라도 당해 협약의 내용 중

---

94) 노조법 제33조.

95) 행정해석: 노사관계법제팀-1049, 2006.4.14.

becomes invalid due to one party's notice of cancellation of the agreement during the autonomous extension period, standards concerning working conditions and other matters concerning the treatment of employees(namely, the normative section) as prescribed in the collective agreement would be transformed to the working conditions of individual employees and remain effective in their labor contracts. If the employer wants to revise the normative section, he shall conclude a new collective agreement in accordance with legitimate procedures, or revise the rules of employment and obtain the collective consent of the employees concerned.

On the other hand, the term working conditions means standards concerning the treatment of employees under the labor contract between the employer and those employees. Concrete contents refer to items stipulated in Article 96 of the Labor Standards Act(Rules of Employment) as well as wages, working hours, welfare, and dismissal procedures stipulated in that Act. Regulations in the collective agreement concerning disciplinary procedures such as composition of the disciplinary action committee falls under matters pertaining to awards and punishment pursuant to Article 96(10) of the same Act. So, this item shall be working conditions and be included under the normative section.[96)]

(2) Although a newly concluded collective agreement was less favorable than the previous collective agreement, the new collective agreement will apply.[97)]

(3) Concluding a collective agreement that is unfavorable to employees is still effective.[98)]

According to the principle of freedom to contract, when a labor union concludes a collective agreement with a company, it may revise it for more or less favorable working conditions. In cases where the collective agreement was revised with unfavorable working conditions, such an agreement is not null and void, with the exception of a special situation where the revision was concluded so disadvantageously that it goes beyond the purpose of the labor union. The labor union does not have to obtain advance individual agreement or authority from employees in relation to such an agreement. Whether the collective agreement is lacking such remarkable rationality or not shall be estimated by various situations, considering the contents of the collective agreement, its concluding procedures, business conditions for the employer, etc.

---

96) Supreme Court ruling on Feb. 23, 1996, 94Nu9177.

97) MOEL Guidelines: Union 01254-623, on May 30, 1995.

98) Supreme Court ruling on Sept. 29, 2000, 99Da67536.

'근로조건 등 기타 근로자의 대우에 관한 사항'(이른바 규범적 부분)은 개별근로자의 근로계약으로 전환되어 계속 효력을 유지한다. 사용자가 이를 변경하고자 하는 경우에는 적법절차에 따라 새로운 단체협약을 체결하거나, 취업규칙의 변경 또는 근로자의 동의를 얻어야 한다. 한편, 근로조건이라 함은 사용자와 근로자 사이의 근로계약 관계에 있어서 근로자의 대우에 관하여 정한 조건을 말하는 것이고, 구체적으로는 근로기준법에 정하여진 임금·근로시간· 후생·해고뿐만 아니라 동법 제96조 소정의 취업규칙으로 정하여야 할 사항이 포함된다. "징계위원회 구성 등 징계절차"에 관한 단체협약의 규정은 동법 제96조 제10호 소정의 "표창과 제재에 관한 사항"에 속하는 것으로서 근로조건에 해당되어 규범적 부분에 포함된다.[96)]

(2) 단체협약의 갱신으로 인하여 새롭게 체결된 단체협약이 구 단체협약 보다 불리한 경우라 하더라도 질서원칙에 따라 새로운 단체협약이 적용된다.[97)]

(3) 근로자에게 불리한 단체협약의 체결은 유효하다.[98)]

협약자치의 원칙상 노동조합은 사용자와 사이에 근로조건을 유리하게 변경하는 내용의 단체협약뿐만 아니라 근로조건을 불리하게 변경하는 내용의 단체협약을 체결할 수 있으므로, 근로조건을 불리하게 변경하는 내용의 단체협약이 현저히 합리성을 결하여 노동조합의 목적을 벗어난 것으로 볼 수 있는 경우와 같은 특별한 사정이 없는 한 그러한 노사 간의 합의를 무효라고 볼 수는 없다. 노동조합으로서는 그러한 합의를 위하여 사전에 근로자들로부터 개별적인 동의나 수권을 받을 필요가 없으며, 단체협약이 현저히 합리성을 결하였는지 여부는 단체협약의 내용과 그 체결경위, 당시 사용자 측의 경영상태 등 여러 사정에 비추어 판단해야 한다.

---

96) 대법원 1996.2.23, 94누9177.
97) 행정해석: 노조 01254-623, 1995.5.30.
98) 대법원 2000.9.29, 99다67536.

(4) In cases where a new collective agreement has not been concluded after one year from the expiration date of the previous agreement and the employees had been governed, with regard to their wages, by the previous agreement in the meantime, such application of the previous agreement is still effective.

Even when a collective agreement has ceased to be effective due to expiration of its term of validity, such provisions about wages, retirement pay, and other individual working conditions are still incorporated in the contract of employment of individual employees unless a new collective agreement or new rules of employment that prescribe otherwise is adopted or individual employees give their consent to extermination of those provisions in the previous agreement. Accordingly, even if the previous agreement had applied to the employees for more than one year due to belated conclusion of a new agreement, such application is deemed to be valid and is not against Article 35 of the former Trade Union Act that limits the effective term of a collective agreement on wages to one year.[99)]

(5) Even though a collective agreement provides for less favorable conditions than the rules of employment, such provision is effective.

When a collective agreement is devised or revised to include less favorable conditions than the existing rules of employment set forth for the same subject, the new or revised agreement implies that both parties have agreed to exclude application of the rules of employment for the subject. In the case in question, it is deemed that the revised collective agreement excludes application of the rules of employment with regard to dismissal criteria.[100)]

(6) Even if a collective agreement includes a clause on individual employees waiving claims regarding their wages, such agreement is not valid.

As individual employees already have the right to wages, retirement pay or bonuses, such things are at the disposal of the employees. Therefore, a labor union, unless with the consent or a mandate from individual employees to do so, cannot waive or delay the right to wages, etc., simply by means of a collective agreement with the employer.[101)]

---

99) Supreme Court ruling on June 9, 2000, 98Da13747.

100) Supreme Court ruling on Dec. 27, 2002, 2002Du9063.

101) Supreme Court ruling on Sept. 29, 2000, 99Da67536.

(4) 단체협약이 실효되었으나 새로운 단체협약이 늦게 체결됨에 따라 근로자가 기존 단체협약의 임금에 관한 부분을 1년 넘게 적용받아 온 경우, 그 부분은 유효하다.

단체협약이 실효되었다고 하더라도 임금, 퇴직금 등 개별적인 노동조건에 관한 부분은 그것을 변경하는 새로운 단체협약, 취업규칙이 체결, 작성되거나 개별적인 근로자의 동의를 얻지 아니하는 한 개별적인 근로자의 근로계약의 내용으로서 여전히 남아 있어 사용자와 근로자를 규율한다. 새로운 단체협약이 늦게 체결됨에 따라 근로자가 기존 단체협약의 임금에 관한 부분은 1년 넘게 적용받게 되더라도 임금에 관한 단체협약의 유효기간을 1년으로 정하고 있는 구 노조법 제35조에 위반되지 않는다.[99)]

(5) 취업규칙보다 불리한 내용을 담은 단체협약은 유효하다.

동일한 내용의 취업규칙이 그대로 적용된다면 단체협약의 개정은 그 목적을 달성할 수 없으므로 개정된 단체협약에는 당연히 취업규칙상의 유리한 조건의 적용을 배제하고 개정된 단체협약이 우선적으로 적용된다는 내용의 합의가 포함된 것이기 때문에 개정된 후의 단체협약에 의하여 취업규칙상의 면직기준에 관한 규정의 적용은 배제된다.[100)]

(6) 조합원 개인의 임금채권을 포기하는 단체협약을 체결한 경우에는 그 효력이 없다.

이미 구체적으로 그 지급청구권이 발생한 임금 또는 상여금, 퇴직금은 근로자의 개인 재산이므로 그 처분도 근로자에게 맡겨진 것이기 때문에 노동조합이 근로자들로부터 개별적인 동의나 수권을 받지 않는 이상, 사용자와 사이의 단체협약만으로 이에 대한 포기나 지급유예와 같은 처분행위를 할 수는 없다.[101)]

---

99) 대법원 2000.6.9, 98다13747.

100) 대법원 2002.12.27, 2002두9063.

101) 대법원 2000.9.29, 99다67536.

(7) If a labor union concludes a collective agreement including working conditions less favorable to employees, the agreement is valid.

A labor union and an employer may conclude a collective agreement that provides for better or poorer working conditions. Unless the working conditions included are too poor to be reasonable or to be in compliance with the purpose of a labor union, a collective agreement may not be deemed as ineffective just because it includes poorer working conditions. In order to determine whether a collective agreement is reasonable or not, all surrounding conditions, such as the general contents of the agreement, the developments leading to conclusion of the agreement, and the employer's financial situation, should be thoroughly examined.[102)]

(8) Upon expiration of a collective agreement, the provisions on the employment relationship, such as working hours or wages, continue to be valid.

When a collective agreement is concluded, its provisions on working conditions and other standards for employee treatment are incorporated into the employment relationship of individual employees. Therefore, even after expiration of the collective agreement, the normative provisions on working conditions, etc., will remain effective. In addition, as the provisions on personnel management and dismissal are also included in the normative section of the collective agreement, those provisions also continue to be effective, even after termination of the agreement and until a new collective agreement takes effect.[103)]

(9) Effect of a collective agreement restricting managerial dismissal

Should a company plan to restructure, it is the employer's right to do so through managerial dismissals, mergers or abolition of an organization, and should not be part of collective bargaining. However, despite items in the collective bargaining that may affect the managerial rights of the employer, the labor union and the employer can conclude a collective agreement, and this collective agreement would be valid as long as those items do not violate the mandatory rules or disturb public order. Accordingly, if the employer agreed to provisions that restrict managerial dismissals in the collective agreement with the labor union, that collective agreement would not violate law or

---

102) Supreme Court ruling on Sept. 29, 2000, 99Da67536.

103) Supreme Court ruling on Jan. 14, 1994, 93Da968.

(7) 노동조합이 사용자와 근로조건을 불리하게 변경하는 내용의 단체협약을 체결한 경우, 그 합의는 유효하다.

협약자치의 원칙상 노동조합은 사용자와 사이에 근로조건을 유리하게 변경하는 내용의 단체협약뿐만 아니라 근로조건을 불리하게 변경하는 내용의 단체협약을 체결할 수 있으므로, 근로조건을 불리하게 변경하는 내용의 단체협약이 현저히 합리성을 결하여 노동조합의 목적을 벗어난 것으로 볼 수 있는 경우와 같은 특별한 사정이 없는 한 그러한 노사 간의 합의를 무효라고 볼 수 없다. 단체협약이 현저히 합리성을 결하였는지 여부는 단체협약의 내용과 그 체결경위, 당시 사용자 측의 경영상태 등 여러 사정에 비추어 판단해야 한다.[102)]

(8) 단체협약이 종료되더라도 근로시간, 임금 등에 관한 근로관계의 내용은 효력이 계속 유지된다.

단체협약의 근로조건 기타 근로자의 대우에 관한 부분인 규범적 부분은 협약의 성립과 함께 개별적 근로관계의 내용이 되는 것이므로 협약이 실효되더라도 개별적 근로관계의 내용으로 된 부분은 그대로 존속한다. 또한, 조합원에 대한 인사 및 해고에 관한 규정도 규범적 효력을 지니는 부분이므로 협약이 만료되더라도 새로운 협약이 체결될 때까지는 그 효력이 지속된다.[103)]

(9) 경영해고를 제한하는 단체협약의 효력

정리해고나 사업조직의 통폐합 등 기업의 구조조정의 실시 여부는 경영주체에 의한 고도의 경영상 결단에 속하는 사항으로서 원칙적으로 단체교섭의 대상이 될 수 없다. 그러나 사용자의 경영권에 속하는 사항이라 하더라도 노사는 임의로 단체교섭을 진행하여 단체협약을 체결할 수 있고, 그 내용이 강행법규나 사회질서에 위배되지 않는 이상 단체협약으로서의 효력이 인정된다. 따라서 사용자가 노동조합과의 협상에 따라 정리해고를 제한하기로 하는 내용의 단체협약을 체결하였다면 특별한 사정이 없는 한 단체협약이 강행법규나 사회질서에

102) 대법원 2000.9.29, 99다67536

103) 대법원 1994.1.14, 93다968.

upset social order unless special circumstances apply. Furthermore, as any collective agreement deals with standards for working conditions and other treatment of employees, any managerial dismissal in opposition to this provision is not justifiable. However, in cases where the company's situation has seriously changed from the time the collective agreement was concluded, and in cases where the company would suffer gravely negative outcomes(objectively determined) if it were forced to follow the collective agreement in this way, the employer can ignore these restrictions in the collective agreement and use managerial dismissal as needed.[104)]

2. Contractual section

The contractual section refers to the rules in a collective agreement regulating rights and duties between the two parties concerned in that collective agreement. The contractual section affects the labor union and the employer, but not the union members. Generally it contains articles of peace, solitary bargaining groups, union activities, shop, strikes, etc.

The contractual section has a liability effect in which one party binds the other party to some duty. The concrete items are as follows:

① Both parties to the agreement shall observe their duties in respect to their contractual sections(obligation to observe the agreement).

② Neither party shall induce an industrial action to change the contents of the agreement during the effective period of the agreement, which is usually the union's duty(duty to maintain peace).

③ The labor union shall execute a duty of peace, as the employer shall be responsible for implementing the contents of the agreement(duty to implement).

(1) Normative and contractual sections[105)]

The 'normative sections' in the collective agreement mean the standards concerning working conditions and other matters concerning the treatment of employees, such as wages and their payment, working hours, paid holidays, severance pay, etc. The contractual sections refer to the rules regulating rights and duties between the two parties

---

104) Supreme Court ruling on Mar. 27, 2014, 2011doo20406.

105) MOEL Guidelines: Nojo 01254-605, on May 26, 1993.

위배된다고 볼 수 없다. 나아가 이는 근로조건 기타 근로자에 대한 대우에 관하여 정한 것으로서 그에 반하여 이루어지는 정리해고는 원칙적으로 정당한 해고라고 볼 수 없다. 다만 정리해고의 실시를 제한하는 단체협약을 두고 있더라도, 단체협약을 체결할 당시의 사정이 현저하게 변경되어 사용자에게 단체협약의 이행을 강요한다면 객관적으로 명백하게 부당한 결과에 이르는 경우에는 사용자가 단체협약에 의한 제한에서 벗어나 정리해고를 할 수 있다.[104)]

2. 채무적 부문

채무적 부문은 단체협약 당사자 상호간의 권리·의무를 규율하는 단체협약상의 규정을 의미한다. 채무적 부문은 노동조합과 사용자에게만 그 구속력이 있고 노동조합의 조합원에게는 효력이 미치지 않는다. 일반적으로 평화조항, 유일교섭단체조항, 조합활동조항, shop조항, 쟁의조항 등이 이에 속한다.

채무적 부문은 단체협약의 당사자가 상대방에 대하여 어떤 의무를 부담 지우는 채권법적 효력을 가지며, 구체적으로 다음과 같다.

① 채무적 부분에 대하여는 협약당사자 쌍방이 이를 준수하여야 한다(협약준수의무).

② 협약기간 중에는 그 협약사항의 변경을 위한 쟁의행위를 하여서는 아니된다. 이는 주로 노동조합 측의 의무이다(평화의무).

③ 노동조합이 평화의무를 지는 반면, 사용자는 협약준수의 구체적 의무로서 협약내용의 실행의무를 진다(실행의무).

(1) 규범적 부분과 채무적 부분[105)]

단체협약의 내용 중 '규범적 부분'이라 함은 근로조건 기타 근로자의 대우에 관한 부분, 즉 임금액, 임금 지급방법, 근로시간, 유급휴일, 퇴직금 지급협정 등을 말하며, '채무적 부분'이라 함은 협약당사자 상호간의 권리·의무에 관한

104) 대법원 2014.3.27, 2011두20406.
105) 행정해석: 노조 01254-605, 1993.5.26.

in the collective agreement, such as articles of peace, solitary bargaining groups, shop, strikes, etc.

(2) If the collective agreement becomes ineffective, standards concerning working conditions and other matters concerning the treatment of employees will be transformed to working conditions of individual employees and continue to remain effective, but the obligation section, such as pay to a full-time union officer, will cease to have effect.[106)]

Principally, the collective agreement ceases to have effect when its term of validity expires. However, according to Article 32(3) of the Trade Union Act, even though both parties continue to engage in collective bargaining to make a new collective agreement before or after expiration of the effective term of an existing agreement, the parties fail to make a new collective agreement, the existing collective agreement shall remain valid for three more months after its expiration. However, if the collective agreement contains a separate provision to the effect that when a new collective agreement is not made in spite of the expiration of the term of an existing collective agreement, the said existing collective agreement shall remain effective until a new collective agreement is made, such a separate provision shall be observed. Any party to the agreement may, however, terminate the existing collective agreement by notifying the other party of such termination six months in advance of the date the party intends to terminate it. If the collective agreement becomes ineffective, standards concerning working conditions and other matters concerning the treatment of employees(namely, the normative section) will be transformed to working conditions of individual employees and remain effective continuously, but the obligation section, such as pay to a full-time union officer, will cease to have effect.

(3) Industrial action in violation of a duty to maintain peace and its justification[107)]

The duty to maintain peace is the obligation that neither party shall revise or abolish the agreed upon matters unilaterally, nor request new conditions during the effective period

---

106) MOEL Guidelines: Nojo 68107-1065, on Nov. 16, 2000.

107) Supreme Court ruling on Sept. 11, 1992, 92Nu7733.

규정으로서 평화조항, 유일교섭 단체조항, 숍(shop)조항, 쟁의조항 등을 말한다.

(2) 단체협약의 효력이 상실된 경우 근로조건 기타 근로자의 대우에 관한 기준은 행정해석

노사 간 별도의 합의가 없는 한 개별근로자의 근로조건으로 계속 효력을 유지하는 것이나, 전임자의 급여지급 등 채무적 부분은 그 효력을 상실하게 된다.[106)]

단체협약은 그 유효기간이 만료되면 효력이 상실되는 것이 원칙이나, '노조법' 제32조 제3항의 규정에 의거 단체협약의 유효기간이 만료되는 때를 전후하여 당사자 쌍방이 새로운 단체협약을 체결하고자 단체교섭을 계속하였음에도 불구하고 새로운 단체협약이 체결되지 아니한 경우에는 종전의 단체협약은 그 효력만료일로부터 3월까지 계속 효력을 갖게 되고, 단체협약에 그 유효기간이 경과한 후에도 새로운 단체협약이 체결되지 아니한 때는 새로운 단체협약이 체결될 때까지 종전 단체협약의 효력을 존속시킨다는 취지의 별도의 약정이 있는 경우에는 유효기간이 만료된 이후에도 단체협약의 효력은 계속 유지된다. 그러나 당사자 일방은 해지하고자 하는 날의 6월 전까지 상대방에게 통고함으로써 종전의 단체협약을 해지할 수 있다. 또한, 단체협약의 효력이 상실된 경우 그 내용 중 근로조건 기타 근로자의 대우에 관한 기준(이른바 규범적 부분)은 노사 간 별도의 합의가 없는 한 개별근로자의 근로조건으로 계속 효력을 유지하는 것이나, 전임자의 급여지급 등 채무적 부분은 그 효력을 상실한다.

(3) 평화의무 위반의 쟁의행위와 그 정당성[107)]

평화의무란 단체협약의 유효기간 중에는 협약사항의 개정 또는 폐지나 새로운 요구를 하지 않을 의무를 말하며, 단체협약에 명문으로 규정하지 않더라도 단체협약의 평화유지 기능에 내재하는 본래의 의무라 할 것이며, 평화의무가

---

106) 행정해석: 노조 68107-1065, 2000.11.16.
107) 대법원 1992.9.11, 92누7733.

of the collective agreement. Although there is no regulation stipulated in the collective agreement, such an agreement contains the intrinsic obligation inherent in its function of maintaining peace. Since the duty to maintain peace is very important to peaceful labor relations and preservation of order, industrial actions taken during the effective period of the collective agreement are not justifiable as part of the purpose of the labor union.

Ⅳ. Extended Coverage of Collective Agreements

In principle, a collective agreement is binding to the signatories(the labor union, its member employees and the employer) to the agreement. In exceptional cases, however, the effect of a collective agreement is extended to general employees so long as certain requirements are met.

1. General binding force at company level

If a majority of comparable regular employees at a business or workplace are bound to the same collective agreement, the remaining comparable regular employees at the business or workplace shall also be covered by the collective agreement.[108)]

(1) By general binding force, collective bargaining is applicable to all employees including non-union members.[109)]

According to the principle of freedom to contract, when a labor union concludes a collective agreement with a company, it does not have to only revise it to include better working conditions, but can also include less favorable conditions. In cases where the collective agreement is concluded with less favorable working conditions, such agreement cannot be null and void, with the exception of special situations where the revision is so disadvantageous as to go beyond the purpose of the labor union.[110)] In a case where both parties concluded a collective agreement in which employees would receive reduced wages temporarily for six months starting June 1, 2006, in an extraordinary

108) Article 35 of the Trade Union Act.

109) MOEL Guidelines: Nosa Relations Team 776, on Mar. 22, 2006.

110) Supreme Court ruling on Dec. 26, 2002, 2001Da36504.

노사관계의 안정과 단체협약의 질서 형성적 기능을 담보하는 것인 점에 비추어 볼 때, 보충협약이라는 명분으로 평화의무의 기본정신에 위배되는 쟁의행위를 하는 것은 노동조합으로서의 정당성을 결여한 것이다.

Ⅳ. 단체협약의 효력 확장

원칙적으로 단체협약은 유효기간 동안 당해 노동조합과 조합원, 사용자에 대하여 적용된다. 그러나 일정한 요건이 충족될 경우 예외적으로 일반 근로자에게까지 단체협약의 효력이 확장된다. 효력확장의 경우 비조합원에게 채무적 부분을 적용할 수 없기 때문에 적용되는 단체협약의 내용은 규범적 부분에 한한다.

1. 사업장 단위의 일반적 구속력

하나의 사업 또는 사업장에 상시 사용되는 동종의 근로자의 반수 이상이 하나의 단체협약의 적용을 받게 된 때는 당해 사업 또는 사업장에 사용되는 다른 동종 근로자에 대하여도 당해 단체협약이 적용된다.[108]

(1) 단체협약이 일반적 구속력에 의거 비조합원 등 모든 직원에게 확장 적용되는지 여부[109]

협약자치의 원칙상 노동조합은 사용자와 사이에 근로조건을 유리하게 변경하는 내용의 단체협약뿐만 아니라 근로조건을 불리하게 변경하는 내용의 단체협약을 체결할 수 있으므로, 근로조건을 불리하게 변경하는 내용의 단체협약이 현저히 합리성을 결하여 노동조합의 목적을 벗어난 것으로 볼 수 있는 경우와 같은 특별한 사정이 없는 한 그러한 노사 간의 합의를 무효라 볼 수 없다.[110] 경영악화로 인한 파산 위기에 처한 회사를 살리기 위하여 노사 당사자가 노동조

108) 노조법 제35조.

109) 행정해석: 노사관계법제팀-776, 2006.3.22.

110) 대법원 2002.11.26, 2001다36504.

general assembly to save the nearly bankrupt company due to business deterioration, the collective agreement is effective unless there are special conditions that would make it ineffective.

On the other hand, a collective agreement concluded by mutual agreement between the company and the union is basically applicable to the two parties concerned: the employer and the labor union and its union members. However, in accordance with Article 35 of the Trade Union Act, when a collective agreement is made with a majority of employees with the same kind of job employed under ordinary circumstances in a business or workplace, the normative sections concerning working conditions and other matters concerning the treatment of employees as prescribed in the collective agreement shall apply to the other employees with the same kind of job employed in the same business or workplace. Accordingly, if a majority of employees with the same kind of job fall under the general binding force of the collective agreement, non-labor union members in the same kind of job shall fall under the normative sections of the collective agreement, such as wages of the corresponding collective agreement, unless there are special conditions not to do so.

(2) In principle, the collective agreement concluded shall be definitely applicable to the parties concerned: the employer and the labor union's members, except if general binding force applies.[111)]

The representative of a labor union shall have the authority to bargain for working conditions and other conditions with the employer for the labor union and its members. In principle, the collective agreement concluded shall be definitely applicable to the parties concerned, the employer and the labor union's members, except if general binding force applies, according to Article 35 of the Trade Union Act. Even though the company fits in the application of general binding force by the Trade Union Act and so its working conditions become applicable to non-union members by the enlarged effect of the collective agreement, the enlarged effect of the collective agreement cannot be applicable to the employer and those who cannot have union membership according to the union's bylaws.

---

111) MOEL Guidelines: Nojo 01254-27, Jan. 11, 1999.

합의 임시총회 결의에 따라 2006. 6.1.부터 6개월 동안 한시적으로 근로자 임금을 일정액 삭감한다는 취지의 단체협약을 체결한 경우라면, 달리 볼 사정이 없는 한 그 효력을 부인하기 어렵다.

한편, 노사가 합의하여 체결한 단체협약은 원칙적으로 체결 당사자인 사용자와 노동조합 그리고 소속 조합원에게 그 효력이 미친다고 할 것이나, 노조법 제35조에 의하여 하나의 사업 또는 사업장에 상시 사용되는 동종의 근로자 반수 이상이 하나의 단체협약을 적용받게 된 때는 당해 사업 또는 사업장에 사용되는 다른 동종의 근로자에 대하여도 당해 단체협약의 내용 중 근로조건 기타 근로자의 대우에 관한 사항을 정한 규범적 부분이 확장 적용된다. 따라서 귀 사업(장)이 동법 제35조 소정의 일반적 구속력이 적용되는 사업장인 경우에는 특별한 사정이 없는 한 비조합원인 근로자에 대하여도 당해 단체협약의 임금 등 규범적 부분이 적용된다.

(2) 교섭결과 체결된 단체협약도 일반적 구속력의 요건에 해당되는 경우를 제외하고는 그 당사자인 사용자와 노동조합의 조합원에 한정 적용된다.[111)]

노동조합의 대표자는 소속 조합원을 대표하여 사용자와 근로조건 기타의 사항에 관하여 교섭할 권한을 가지는 것이며, 교섭결과 체결된 단체협약도 '노조법' 제35조 소정의 일반적 구속력의 요건에 해당되는 경우를 제외하고는 그 당사자인 사용자와 노동조합의 조합원에 한정 적용되는 것이 원칙이다. 또한, 법 소정의 일반적 구속력의 요건에 해당되이 단체협약의 효력이 확장 적용되는 경우라도 법 소정의 사용자나 노조규약 상 조직대상에 해당되지 아니하여 동 협약의 적용이 예상되지 아니하는 자에게까지 동 협약의 효력이 확장 적용되는 것은 아니다.

---

111) 행정해석: 노소 01254-27, 1999.1.11.

(3) In cases where the collective agreement of a company does not specify the scope of its membership and therefore applies to all kinds of jobs, all employees of the company are deemed as employees with the same kind of job because of the enlarged effect of general binding force.[112)]

In principle, the effective scope of the collective agreement is confined to the two parties concerned: the employer and the labor union's members, but in accordance with Article 35(General Binding Force) of the Trade Union Act, when a collective agreement is made with a majority of employees with the same kind of job employed under ordinary circumstances in a business or workplace, it shall apply to other employees with the same kind of job employed in the same business or workplace. In this case, employees with the same kind of job employed under ordinary circumstances means all employees with the same kind of job as a matter of fact in the company regardless of the employee position and type, fixed or unfixed employment period, or the name of the labor contract. In cases where the collective agreement does not specify the scope of its membership and so applies to all kinds of common occupations, all employees of the company are deemed as employees with the same kind of job because of the enlarged effect of general binding force. However, in cases where the collective agreement specifies a scope of membership for the type of job and excludes a certain group of employees from application of the collective agreement, it is hard to regard that certain group of employees as having the same kind of job under which the enlarged effects of the collective agreement are applied in terms of general binding force.

(4) The scope of working conditions in the collective agreement for technical (blue-collar) employees cannot be enlarged and applied to other white-collar or managerial employees.[113)]

If the members of a labor union, party to the collective agreement, consist of only technical(blue-collar) employees, and if working conditions are not the same between the technical employees(union members) and the white-collar or managerial employees(non-union members), the collective agreement is not applicable to white-collar or managerial employees in terms of the purpose of Article 35 of the Trade Union Act concerning

112) MOEL Guidelines: Nojo 01254-869, Dec. 24, 1998.

113) MOEL Guidelines: Nojo 01254-218, Mar. 10, 1992.

(3) 단체협약의 직종별 적용범위가 특정되지 아니하여 단체협약이 모든 직종에 공통적으로 적용되는 경우에는 직종의 구분 없이 사업장 내의 모든 근로자가 동종의 근로자에 해당된다.[112)]

단체협약의 효력이 미치는 범위는 그 당사자인 사용자와 노동조합의 조합원에 한정되는 것이 원칙이나, 노조법 제35조의 규정에 의하여 하나의 공장, 사업장 기타 직장에 상시 사용되는 동종 근로자의 반수 이상이 하나의 단체협약의 적용을 받게 된 때는 다른 동종 근로자에 대하여도 당해 단체협약의 효력이 미치게 된다. 이 경우 "상시 사용되는 동종의 근로자"라 함은 근로자의 지위나 종류, 고용기간의 정함의 유무 또는 근로계약상의 명칭에 구애됨이 없이 사업장에서 사실상 계속적으로 사용되고 있는 동종의 근로자 전부를 의미하는 것으로서 체결된 단체협약의 직종별 적용범위가 특정되지 아니하여 단체협약이 모든 직종에 공통적으로 적용되는 경우에는 직종의 구분 없이 사업장 내의 모든 근로자가 동종의 근로자에 해당된다. 그러나 단체협약에 직종별 적용범위가 특정되어 있거나 그 단체협약의 적용이 예상되지 않는 근로자의 경우에는 단체협약의 내용이 확장 적용되는 동종의 근로자로 보기 어렵다.

(4) 기능직 사원의 단체협약은 근무조건이 다른 사무 · 관리직 사원에 확장 적용될 수 없다.[113)]

단체협약 당사자인 노동조합의 조합원이 기능직 사원으로만 구성되어 있으며, 기능직 사원과 비조합원인 사무·관리직 사원의 근무조건 등이 동일하지 아니하다면 단체협약의 효력확장에 관한 노조법 제37(35)조의 취지를 감안하여 볼 때 사무·관리직 사원에게 단체협약을 확장하여 적용하기 어렵다.

2. 지역적 단위의 일반적 구속력

하나의 지역에 있어서 종업하는 동종의 근로자 3분의 2이상이 하나의 단체협

---

112) 행정해석: 노조 01254-869, 1998.12.24.
113) 행정해석: 노조 01254-218, 1992.3.10.

enlarged application of the collective agreement.

2. General binding force at regional level

If two-thirds or more of comparable regular employees in a region are bound to the same collective agreement, it can be determined that the remaining comparable regular employees and their employers in the region shall also be subject to the collective agreement. For such extension of the coverage of a collective agreement, the competent authority, at the request of either party or both parties or on its own, shall bring the case before the Labor Relations Commission for resolution.[114)]

Ⅴ. Termination of Collective Agreements

A collective agreement is terminated in any of the following cases:

- Expiration of the term of validity;
- Withdrawal or termination of the collective agreement;
- Dissolution of a party to the agreement; or
- Unilateral termination of the automatic extension contract.

1) The effective period of the collective agreement expires or the collective agreement becomes invalid by one party cancelling the agreement during the autonomous extension period.

2) Unless otherwise provided in a separate agreement, if no new collective agreement is concluded by the expiry date of the existing agreement even though the parties have continuously engaged in collective bargaining before and after the expiry date, the existing collective agreement shall remain effective for up to three months after its expiry date.[115)]

3) If no new collective agreement is concluded after expiration of the extended effective term, the existing agreement shall be applicable only if the existing agreement specifically provides that it shall remain in effect until a new collective agreement is concluded. Provided, however, that any one party concerned may terminate the collective agreement by giving notice to the other party six months in advance.[116)]

---

114) Article 36 of the Trade Union Act.

115) Article 32 of the Trade Union Act.

116) Article 32 of the Trade Union Act.

약의 적용을 받게 된 때는 당해 지역에서 종업하는 다른 동종의 근로자와 사용자에 대하여도 당해 단체협약을 적용하는 결정을 할 수 있다. 이를 위해서는 행정관청이 당해 단체협약의 당사자의 쌍방 또는 일방의 신청에 의하거나 그 직권으로 노동위원회의 의결을 얻어야 한다.[114)]

Ⅴ. 단체협약의 소멸

단체협약은 다음의 경우 소멸하게 된다.

- 유효기간의 만료
- 단체협약의 취소 또는 해지
- 협약당사자의 해산 등에 의한 소멸
- 자동연장협정의 일방해지

1) 단체협약의 유효기간이 만료되거나 동 협약의 자동연장 기간 중 당사자의 일방 해지통보로 인해 단체협약이 해지된다.

2) 단체협약의 유효기간이 만료되는 때를 전후하여 당사자 쌍방이 새로운 단체협약을 체결하고자 단체교섭을 계속하였음에도 불구하고 새로운 단체협약이 체결되지 아니한 경우에는 별도의 약정이 있는 경우를 제외하고는 종전의 단체협약은 그 효력만료일부터 3월까지 계속 효력을 갖는다.[115)]

3) 다만, 단체협약에 그 유효기간이 경과한 후에도 새로운 단체협약이 체결되지 아니한 때는 새로운 단체협약이 체결될 때까지 종전 단체협약의 효력을 존속시킨다는 취지의 별도의 약정이 있는 경우에는 그에 따르되, 당사자 일방은 해지하고자 하는 날의 6월전까지 상대방에게 통고함으로써 종전의 단체협약을 해지할 수 있다.[116)]

---

114) 노조법 제36조.
115) 노조법 제32조 3항의 전단.
116) 노조법 제32조 3항의 후단.

Chapter 15

Industrial Actions

Section 1: Industrial Disputes and Industrial Action

Ⅰ. Industrial Disputes

The term industrial dispute refers to any controversy or difference arising from disagreements between a labor union and an employer or employers' association concerning the conditions of employment such as wages, working hours, welfare, dismissal.[117)]

1. Disputes arising from disagreements

Disagreements between the two parties are not always considered industrial disputes. However, if the two parties engage in collective bargaining but fail to reach an agreement, then their conflict is considered an industrial dispute.

2. State of disputes

Industrial disputes signify a state of dispute. Accordingly, it is a different concept from an industrial action under Article 2, subparagraph 6, of the Trade Union Act, which is an actual practice of collective power. However, in actual practice it is difficult to differentiate between the occurrence of industrial disputes and the occurrence of industrial action. In general, industrial actions are taken for a certain period of time after the parties of the Trade Union Act apply for mediation of an industrial dispute.

---

117) Article 2, subparagraph 5, of the Trade Union Act.

Chapter 15

쟁의행위

제1절 노동쟁의와 쟁의행위

Ⅰ. 노동쟁의

노동쟁의라 함은 노동조합과 사용자 또는 사용자단체 간에 임금·근로시간 · 복지·해고 기타 대우 등 근로조건의 결정에 관한 주장의 불일치로 인하여 발생한 이익분쟁 상태를 말한다.[117)]

1. 주장의 불일치로 인하여 발생한 분쟁

노사 간의 주장이 불일치한다 하여 그것이 바로 이 노동쟁의라고 할 수 있는 분쟁상태가 되는 것은 아니며, 단체교섭을 진행하여 보아도 그 주장의 내용이 일치되지 아니하여 당사자 서로가 반목의 상태에 놓이게 되어야 노동쟁의에 해당된다고 볼 수 있다.

2. 분쟁의 상태

노동쟁의는 분쟁의 상태를 나타낸다. 따라서 노동쟁의는 노조법 제2조 제6호의 쟁의행위가 실력을 행사하는 행동을 나타내는 것과 구별되는 개념이다. 그러나 실제에 있어서 노동쟁의의 발생과 이로 인한 쟁의행위의 발생 간에 반드시 명확한 선이 그어지지 아니하나 노조법상 당사자는 노동쟁의의 조정신청을 한 후 일정기간(조정기간)이 경과하여야 쟁의행위를 할 수 있다는 점에서 시기적으로 구별된다.

117) 노조법 제2조 제5호.

Ⅱ. Types of Industrial Actions

Labor rights are among the basic rights guaranteed by the Constitution of the Republic of Korea for citizens. In the event an employer suffers damage due to a collective action of a labor union, it cannot claim compensation from the union or its workers (Article 3 of the *Trade Union and Labor Relations Adjustment Act,* hereinafter the *"TULRAA"*). Collective actions by labor unions aiming to improve working conditions are not subject to criminal punishment under Article 20 of the *Criminal Act* (Article 4 of the *TULRAA*). However, if a labor union's actions during a dispute are unlawful, those unlawful actions become subject to civil and criminal liabilities, as well as disciplinary action by the employer. For such actions to be considered legitimate labor actions, the justifiably established union, purpose, procedures, and means and methods must all be justifiable. In other words, for a workers' dispute to be deemed justified, it must meet these four criteria: ① The independent union must be an entity eligible to negotiate collectively; ② The purpose should involve fostering autonomous negotiations between labor and management for the improvement of working conditions; ③ It must commence only if the employer refuses collective bargaining on specific demands for improving working conditions and should follow the legal procedures, including obtaining the prior consent of union members, unless there are special circumstances otherwise; ④ The means and methods must be in harmony with the employer's property rights and should not involve or condone any acts of violence.[118)]

Labor union actions during disputes involve collective refusal to provide labor, which can be divided into general strikes (full strikes) and partial strikes. Secondary actions such as slowdown strikes, work-to-rule, workplace occupations, and picketing lines accompany these dispute actions. Regarding the methods and means of these labor actions, labor union laws have various restrictions: ① Labor actions are prohibited if they violate laws or societal order (Article 37 of the *TULRAA*); ② Acts that disrupt the entry of individuals unrelated to the dispute or those seeking to provide labor and acts that interfere with operations or that disrupt regular work processes while soliciting or persuading participation in dispute actions through violence or coercion are prohibited (Article 38, Paragraph 1); ③ Labor actions must not hinder the regular performance of tasks aimed at preventing damage to workplace facilities, spoilage of materials, or products (Article 38, Paragraph 2); ④ Acts of violence, destruction, or occupation of facilities as designated by presidential decree that are related to production facilities or other major operations are

118) Supreme Court ruling 99do4837, Unanimous Decision by Full Bench, October 25, 2001.

Ⅱ. 쟁의행위

노동3권은 헌법이 보장된 국민의 기본권에 해당이 된다. 사용자가 노동조합의 쟁의행위로 인하여 손해를 입은 경우에 노동조합과 근로자에게 배상을 청구할 수 없다(노조법 제3조). 노동조합이 근로조건의 향상을 위한 집단적 행동은 형법 제20조에 의한 정당행위로 행사처벌을 할 수 없다(노조법 제4조). 그러나 노동조합의 쟁위행위가 위법한 경우에는 민형사상 책임과 사용자의 징계책임의 대상이 된다. 이러한 정당한 쟁의행위가 되기 위해서는 주체, 목적, 절차, 그리고 수단과 방법이 정당해야 한다. 즉, 근로자의 쟁의행위가 정당하기 위해서는 ① 그 주체가 단체교섭의 주체로 될 수 있는 자이어야 하고, ② 그 목적이 근로조건의 향상을 위한 노사 간의 자치적 교섭을 조성하는 데에 있어야 하며, ③ 사용자가 근로자의 근로조건 개선에 관한 구체적인 요구에 대하여 단체교섭을 거부하였을 때 개시하되 특별한 사정이 없는 한 조합원의 찬성결정 등 법령이 규정한 절차를 거쳐야 하고, ④ 그 수단과 방법이 사용자의 재산권과 조화를 이루어야 하고, 폭력의 행사에 해당되지 아니하여야 한다는 4가지 조건을 모두 구비하여야 한다.[118)]

그러면 노동조합의 쟁의행위는 집단적으로 근로제공을 거부하는 것으로 전면파업과 부분파업이 있으며, 쟁의행위에 수반되는 수단이나 방법으로 태업, 준법투쟁, 직장점거, 피켓팅의 행동이 부가적으로 이루어진다. 이러한 쟁의행위 수단과 방법과 관련하여 노동조합법은 여러가지 제한하는 내용을 가지고 있다. 그 내용은 다음과 같다. ① 쟁위행위는 '법령 기타 사회질서에 위반'의 금지(노조법 제37조), ② 쟁위행위는'쟁의행위와 관계없는 자 또는 근로를 제공하고자 하는 자의 출입, 조업 기타 정상적인 업무를 방해하는 방법으로 행하여져서는 아니되며, 쟁의행위의 참가를 호소하거나 설득하는 행위로서 폭행, 협박을 사용'하는 것을 금지(노조법 제38조 제1항), ③ 쟁위행위는 '작업시설의 손상이나 원료, 제품의 변질 또는 부패를 방지하기 위한 작업'의 정상적인 수행(노조법 제38조 제2항), ④ 쟁의행위는 '폭력이나 파괴행위 또는 생산시설 기타 주요업무에 관련되는 시설과 이에 준하는 시설로서 대통령령이 정하는 시설을 점거하는 형태'의 금지(제42조 제1

118) 내법원 2001.10.25. 선고 99도4837 전원합의체 판결

prohibited (Article 42, Paragraph 1);[119] ⑤ Actions that suspend, abolish, or interfere with the normal maintenance and operation of safety facilities are prohibited (Article 42, Paragraph 2); ⑥ Actions that impede the legitimate maintenance and operation of essential duties are prohibited (Article 42, Paragraph 3).

These fundamental principles of legislation on labor actions explain how they specifically apply in actual strike-supportive measures like secondary actions such as slowdown strikes, work-to-rule, workplace occupations, and picketing.

A. Slowdown Strikes

1. Concept

Work slowdowns or deliberate reductions in work efficiency by labor unions, where employees formally provide labor but intentionally perform tasks slowly, incompletely, or in a sloppy manner to reduce productivity, are termed "slowdowns" (태업). Slowdowns differ from full strikes (파업) in that they involve partial non-fulfillment or incomplete fulfillment of labor, rather than a complete refusal to provide labor.

2. Criteria for validity of slowdown strikes

Unlike strikes, slowdowns occur within the workplace where employees only partially follow the employer's instructions. Therefore, they should, in principle, abide by the employer's managerial rights regarding labor instructions. Refusal to perform tasks not covered by slowdown intentions, contrary to the union's intentions, might result in violation of Article 37, Paragraph 2 of the *TULRAA*, leading to disciplinary action as per employment regulations.

1) Case #1: Implementation of lawful operations following resolutions by the union's operating committee resulted in hindering the normal functioning of the company's operations, seemingly to advocate for the workers' demands. This could be seen as a form of dispute, but it failed to comply with such requirements as the union membership

---

119) Facilities where occupation is prohibited include electrical, computer, or communication facilities, railway vehicles or tracks, places storing hazardous materials, among others. Occupation of these facilities could result in the suspension or cessation of production and other major operations or areas of business (Article 21 of the *Enforcement Decree to the TULRAA*).

항)[119], ⑤ 쟁의행위는 '안전보호시설에 대하여 정상적인 유지, 운영을 정지, 폐지 또는 방해하는 행위'의 금지(노조법 제42조 제2항), ⑥ '필수유지업무의 정당한 유지, 운영을 저지, 폐지 또는 방해하는 행위'의 금지 (노조법 제42조 제3항)을 들 수 있다. 이러한 쟁의행위에 관한 법령의 기본원칙이 실제 파업의 보조 수단인 (A) 태업, (B)준법투쟁, (C)직장폐쇄, (D)피케팅에서 어떻게 구체적으로 적용되는지 살펴보고자 한다.

A. 태업

1. 의의

노동조합이 형식적으로는 노동력을 제공하지만 고의적으로 불성실하게 근무함으로써 실제적으로는 작업을 하지 않거나 필요 이상의 완만한 작업 또는 조잡한 작업을 하여 작업능률을 저하시키는 행위를 태업이라고 한다. 태업은 노무제공의 부분적 불이행 또는 불완전한 이행이라는 점에서 노무제공의 전면 불이행인 파업과 구분된다.

2. 태업의 정당성 판단기준

태업은 파업과 달리 사업장에 체류하면서 사용자의 지휘명령에 따르되 이를 부분적으로 배제하는 것이므로, 원칙적으로 사용자의 노무지휘권에 따라야 한다. 노동조합의 의사에 반하여 태업의 대상이 아닌 업무를 거부하는 경우에는 노동조합법 제37조제2항 위반, 취업규칙 등에 의한 징계책임이 따를 수 있다.

① **사례#1:** 노조 운영위원회의 결의를 거쳐 시행한 준법 운행은 근로자가 그 주장을 관철할 목적으로 회사의 업무의 정상적인 운영을 저해한 행위로서, 노동조합법이 규정하고 있는 일종의 쟁의행위(태업 또는 부분파업)라고 보아야 할 것이고, 위 쟁의행위는 쟁의행위 찬반투표, 냉각기간(조정절차), 노동쟁의 신고 등의

---

119) 점거가 금지되는 시설로는 전기, 전산 또는 통신시설, 철도의 차량 또는 선로, 유독물질을 보관 저장하는 장소 등이다. 기타 점거될 경우 생산 기타 주요업무의 정지 또는 폐지를 가져오는 시설(동법 시행령 제21조).

needing to vote on whether to take such action and regulations on cooling-off periods (conciliation procedures) and reporting the labor dispute, making it an illegal act.[120)]

2) Case #2: Setting a daily income cap of KRW 50,000 for a taxi driver and intentionally controlling it to cause substantial financial losses for the company is disruptive. Additionally, influencing operations to match the income cap, like operating sparsely populated coastal routes or engaging in gambling during work stoppages, seems to align with a form of dispute (slowdown strikes or partial strikes). These actions appear to violate regulations outlined in the *TULRAA*.[121)]

3. Slowdowns and wage reductions

Even during slowdowns, the principle of "no work, no pay" naturally applies, allowing for wage reductions. The extent of such wage reductions can be based on the proportion of work refused as per the usual workload specified in the employment contract or other agreements. Calculating the proportion of work refused requires comprehensive consideration of the details of the work, type of tasks involved, and other relevant factors. According to Article 44, Paragraph 1 of the *TULRAA*, the employer is not obligated to pay wages to employees for times while they participate in labor actions and do not provide labor accordingly. Slowdowns involve partially withholding the labor agreed upon in the employment contract, enabling wage reductions for the corresponding portion on the part of the employer. In determining the level of reduction, factors such as how much labor was withheld, how much output was reduced, and the company's wage calculation method should be considered if not stipulated in the related collective agreement or employment rules.[122)]

4. Slowdowns and workplace closures

When a labor union withholds some labor as part of a slowdown, the employer can rightfully refuse to accept any labor through workplace closures and thereby be relieved

---

120) Supreme Court ruling on May 15, 1990, 90do357.

121) Supreme Court ruling on December 10, 1991, 91nu636.

122) Labor Administrative Guidelines: Nojo 68110-40, February 4, 2003.

제 규정을 지키지 아니한 불법적인 행위이다.[120]

② **사례#2:** 1일 수입금까지 1일 50,000원 이하로 할 것을 정하여 놓고 위 금액을 초과하지 못하도록 통제를 하여 회사로 하여금 영업수익 면에서 큰 손해를 보게 하였다. 또한 위 수입금액에 맞추기 위하여 인적이 드문 해안도로를 공차로 운행하거나 운행을 정지하고 도박을 하는 등의 파행적인 운행을 하게 하는 결과까지 낳게 하였다. 이는 근로자가 그 주장을 관철할 목적으로 회사의 업무의 정상적인 운영을 저해하는 행위로서 일종의 쟁의행위(태업 또는 부분파업)에 해당되며, 노동조합법의 제 규정을 지키지 아니한 불법적인 행위에 해당한다.[121]

3. 태업과 임금삭감

태업의 경우에도 당연히 무노동무임금 원칙이 적용되므로 임금을 삭감할 수 있다. 이때 임금의 삭감범위는 근로계약 등에 의하여 평상시 행할 노무중 거부업무의 비중 등 '노무를 제공하지 않은 비율'에 따라 임금을 삭감할 수 있다. 노무를 제공하지 않은 비율에 대해서는 근무내용, 작업형태 등을 종합적으로 고려하여 개별적·구체적으로 산정하여야 한다. 노동조합법 제44조제1항의 규정에 의하면 사용자는 쟁의행위에 참가하여 근로를 제공하지 아니한 근로자에 대하여는 그 기간 중의 임금을 지급할 의무가 없다. 태업은 쟁의행위 수단 중 하나로 근로계약으로 약정된 노무를 불완전하게 제공한 것이므로 그 부분만큼의 임금을 지급하지 않을 수 있으며, 감액수준을 결정함에 있어 단체협약 및 취업규칙에 정한 바가 없다면 근로제공의 불완전 정도, 생산량 감소정도 및 당해 사업장의 임금 계산방법 등을 종합적으로 고려하여 결정할 수 있다.[122]

4. 태업과 직장폐쇄

사용자는 노동조합이 태업으로 불완전한 노무를 제공하는 경우 직장폐쇄를 통하여 정당하게 노무수령을 거부하고 임금지급 의무를 면할수 있다. 이때 태

---

120) 대법원 1990.5.15. 선고 90도357 판결

121) 대법원 1991.12.10. 선고 91누636 판결

122) 행정해석: 노조 68110-40, 2003.2.4.

of the obligation to pay wages. The legitimacy of workplace closures due to slowdowns is determined after considering specific circumstances such as reasonableness, attitudes during negotiations and progress between labor and management, the nature and duration of the slowdowns, and impact of the slowdown on the employer.

B. Work-to-Rule

1. Concept

Work-to-rule refers to the collective actions of labor unions or groups of workers within a workplace, aimed at supporting their demands by strictly adhering to laws, collective agreements, or regulations that are not usually strictly followed. This behavior involves exercising the rights granted to workers collectively, thereby disrupting the normal functioning of business operations. In essence, it involves intentional, exaggerated adherence to laws, collective agreements, or employment rules to decrease work efficiency or performance, pressuring the employer to concede to their demands. Generally, work-to-rule operates similarly to strikes or slowdowns. It commonly manifests as strict adherence to regular working hours, refusal to do overtime or work on holidays, collective use of vacation days, strict and literal compliance with safety and health regulations in all situations, and other similar actions.

For instance, compelling union members to collectively take vacation days during negotiations on renewing a collective agreement aims to secure a favorable position, constituting a form of confrontational legal advocacy. Similarly, nurses, particularly those required to wear specific attire for identification and hygiene reasons, not adhering to the prescribed attire collectively, disrupts normal hospital operations and also falls under this category of confrontational work-to-rule.[123)]

Additionally, if workers, to support their demands, collectively refuse customary holiday work which they have traditionally performed, this constitutes disruptive behavior affecting normal company operations, qualifying as a form of labor action.[124)]

---

123) Supreme Court ruling on June 14, 1994, 93da 2916.

124) Supreme Court ruling on December 26, 1997, 95nu8427.

업에 대한 직장폐쇄의 정당성 여부는 노사간의 교섭태도 및 경과, 태업의 형태 및 기간, 그로 인하여 사용자측이 받는 타격의 정도 등 구체적 사정에 비추어 형평의 견지에서 정당성을 판단한다.

B. 준법투쟁

1. 의 의

준법투쟁이란 노동조합 또는 근로자집단이 자신의 주장을 관철하기 위하여 사업장에서 평소 잘 지키지 않는 법률 또는 단체협약 등의 규범을 엄격히 지키거나 근로자들에게 보장된 권리를 일제히 행사하여 업무의 운영을 저해하는 행위이다. 즉, 노동조합이 의도적으로 법령이나 단체협약, 취업규칙 등의 내용을 필요이상으로 엄격히 준수함으로써 업무의 능률이나 실적을 떨어뜨려 자신의 주장을 받아들이도록 사용자에게 압력을 가하는 집단행동을 의미한다. 일반적으로 준법투쟁은 법령·단체협약 등에 따라 엄격하게 노동력을 제공하거나 그 제공을 거부함으로써 파업·태업 등의 쟁의행위와 같은 효과를 발휘하게 된다. 정시 출·퇴근 등 근무시간 준수, 시간외·휴일근로 집단 거부, 연·월차휴가 집단사용, 안전·보건수칙 준수 등의 형태로 나타난다.

사용자와의 단체협약갱신협상에서 유리한 지위를 차지하기 위하여 조합원들로 하여금 집단으로 월차휴가를 실시하게 한 것은 이른바 쟁의적 준법투쟁으로서 쟁의행위에 해당하고, 위생문제에 특히 주의해야 하고 신분을 표시할 필요가 있는 간호사들이 집단으로 규정된 복장을 하지 않는 것은 병원업무의 정상적인 운영을 저해하는 것으로서 역시 쟁의행위에 해당한다.[123]

근로자들이 주장을 관철시킬 목적으로 종래 통상적으로 실시해 오던 휴일 근무를 집단적으로 거부하였다면, 이는 회사업무의 정상적인 운영을 저해하는 것으로서 쟁의행위에 해당한다.[124]

---

123) 대법원 1994.6.14. 선고 93다2916 판결
124) 대법원 1997.12.26. 신고95누8427 판결

2. Legal nature of work-to-rule

For work-to-rule actions to be considered legitimate labor actions, the following must be evident:

① Purposeful Intent: It should aim to support the labor demands in question; ② Collective Action: It must be a collective effort; and ③ Disruption of Normal Operations: It should result in "disruption of normal business operations." Here, "normal operations" do not refer strictly to "lawful operations" but rather to activities that are practically or customarily carried out. Thus, any action that disrupts these practical or customary operations is considered a form of labor action. However, when specific labor-management practices are established, while the parties should generally comply, if these practices blatantly violate mandatory regulations, adherence cannot be enforced. Actions demanding correction in line with legal regulations due to established practices blatantly violating these regulations are not deemed labor actions. The legitimacy of work-to-rule as a form of labor action is judged based on general criteria for assessing the legitimacy of labor actions.

For example, refusing overtime work typically conducted according to collective agreements, employment rules, labor contracts, or customary practices is considered disruptive to normal business operations and qualifies as a form of labor action. However, if the actual practice of overtime work blatantly violates legal regulations stipulated in labor standards, demanding corrective actions in compliance with the law doesn't constitute a labor action. In such cases, the labor beyond legally mandated overtime hours does not need to be provided.[125)]

3. Types of work-to-rule

(1) Refusal to work overtime or on holidays

Workers collectively refusing, in support of their labor claims, to work overtime or on holidays as normally done in alignment with collective agreements, employment rules, labor contracts, or customary practices, which in turn has the potential to disrupt normal business operations, qualifies as a form of labor action.

1) Case #1: Refusal to engage in customary practices

Even if overtime work is typically agreed upon by the parties involved, if workers

125) Labor Administrative Guidelines, Hyup-Lyuk 68140-208, May 29, 1997.

2. 준법투쟁의 법적성격

준법투쟁이 쟁의행위에 해당되기 위해서는 ① 자신의 주장을 관철할 목적을 가지고 ② 집단적으로 ③ 「업무의 정상적인 운영을 저해」하는 결과를 초래하여야 한다. 「업무의 정상적인 운영」이란 엄격한 의미에서의 "적법한 운영"을 의미하는 것이 아니라 사실상 또는 관행상 행해지고 있는 "평상의 운영"을 의미한다. 따라서 사실상 또는 관행에 기초하여 이루어지는 "평상의 운영"을 저해하는 경우에는 쟁의행위에 해당한다. 다만, 특정한 노사관행이 형성된 경우 근로계약 당사자는 이를 준수하여야 하나, 노사관행이 강행법규를 명백히 위반한 경우에 이의 준수를 강요할 수 없으므로 사실상 행해지고 있는 노사관행이 강행법규를 명백히 위반하고 있을 때 이를 법에 따라 시정토록 요구하는 행위의 경우에는 쟁의행위로 볼 수 없다. 준법투쟁이 쟁의행위에 해당할 경우 그 정당성은 일반적인 쟁의행위의 정당성 판단기준에 따라 판단한다.

예를들면, 단체협약, 취업규칙, 근로계약 및 사실상 관행에 의하여 통상 이루어지고 있는 연장근로의 거부는 업무의 정상적인 운영을 저해하는 것으로써 쟁의행위에 해당된다. 다만, 사실상 행해지고 있는 연장근로가 근로기준법상의 강행규정을 명백히 위반하고 있을 때 이를 법에 따라 시정토록 요구하는 행위의 경우에는 쟁의행위로 볼 수 없으며, 이 경우 법상 연장근무시간을 초과하는 근로는 제공하지 않을 수 있다.[125)]

3. 준법투쟁의 유형

(1) 연장근로·휴일근로 거부 등

단체협약·취업규칙·근로계약 및 사실상 관행으로 이루어지고 있는 연장근로·휴일근로 등을 그 주장의 관철을 위해 집단적으로 거부하여 업무의 정상적인 운영을 저해하는 것은 쟁의행위에 해당한다.

1) 사례#1: 사실상의 관행을 거부하는 경우

연장근로가 당사자 합의에 의하여 이루어지는 것이라고 하더라도 근로자들을

125) 행정해석: 협력 68140-208, 1997.5.29.

are instigated to collectively refuse overtime they have traditionally performed, thereby impeding normal business operations, this is considered a form of labor action.[126)]

2) Case #2: Refusing to work overtime

Despite a collective agreement allowing for holiday work due to unavoidable work circumstances or production disruptions, workers collectively refuse to work on holidays without valid reasons, despite the customary nature of the company's directive to work on holidays. This refusal disrupts normal business operations and qualifies as a labor action.[127)]

3) Case #3: Strict adherence to stipulated working hours

For instance, if a collective agreement mandates that employees start work at 9:00 AM, but the union instructs its members to all arrive precisely at 9:00 AM, causing delays in operations such as repairs due to a sudden influx of employees at that hour, this disrupts normal business operations. This collective action, intended to support workers' labor claims, obstructs the company's usual operations and qualifies as a labor action.[128)]

(2) Collective use of annual leave and similar actions

Collective utilization of annual leave by a labor union to advocate for its claims, obstructing normal business operations, qualifies as a form of dispute action. Although it might formally appear as individual workers exercising their holiday rights, the collective need for holiday usage becomes unlikely, and could be viewed as an infringement on the employer's right to adjust the timing of employee holidays.

Instances that qualify as labor actions are those where collective annual leave is used with the intent to disrupt normal business operations. Using collective leave solely to interfere with work is not considered a legitimate action.

---

126) Supreme Court ruling on October 22, 2001, 91do600; Supreme Court ruling on February 27, 1996, 95do2970.

127) Supreme Court ruling on July 9, 1991, 91do1051.

128) Supreme Court ruling on May 10, 1996, 96do419.

선동하여 근로자들이 통상적으로 해 오던 연장근로를 집단적으로 거부하도록 함으로써 회사업무의 정상운영을 저해하였다면 이는 쟁의행위로 보아야 한다.[126)]

2) 사례#2: 사규 하여 사유 발생 시마다 실시해 온 연장근로 · 휴일근로를 거부한 경우

노사간에 체결된 단체협약에 작업상 부득이한 사정이 있거나 생산계획상 차질이 있는 등 업무상 필요가 있을 때에는 사용자인 회사가 휴일근로를 시킬 수 있도록 정하여져 있어서 회사가 이에 따라 관행적으로 휴일근로를 시켜 왔음에도 불구하고 근로자들이 자신들의 주장을 관철할 목적으로 정당한 이유도 없이 집단적으로 회사가 지시한 휴일근로를 거부한 것은 회사업무의 정상적인 운영을 저해하는 것으로서 쟁의행위에 해당한다.[127)]

3) 사례#3: 단체협약에 규정된 출 · 퇴근시간을 필요 이상으로 엄격히 준수하는 경우

단체협약에 따른 사장의 지시로 09:00 이전에 출근하여 업무준비를 한 후 09:00부터 근무를 하도록 되어 있음에도 조합원들로 하여금 집단으로 09:00 정각에 출근하도록 지시를 하여 수천명의 조합원들이 집단적으로 09:00 정각에 출근함으로써 전화고장 수리가 지연되는 등으로 업무수행에 지장을 초래하였다. 이는 실질적으로 회사의 정상적인 업무수행을 저해함으로써 그들의 주장을 관철시키기 위하여 한 쟁의행위이다.[128)]

(2) 연차휴가 등의 집단사용

노동조합이 그 주장을 관철시킬 목적으로 집단적으로 연차휴가를 일제히 사용하는 것은 업무의 정상적인 운영을 방해하는 것으로 쟁의행위에 해당한다. 집단적인 연차휴가 사용의 경우 형식적으로는 개별 근로자의 휴가권의 행사로 보이나, 실질적으로는 집단적으로 휴가를 사용하여야 할 필요성이 발생하는 것은 예상하기 어려우며, 사용자의 휴가시기 변경권의 침해로 볼 수도 있다.

---

126) 대법원 1991.10.22. 선고 91도600 판결;대법원 1996.2.27. 선고 95도2970 판결 등
127) 대법원 1991.7.9. 선고 91도1051 판결
128) 대법원 1996.5.10. 선고 96도419 판결

1) Case #1: Misuse of monthly paid leave

If a worker, without having a genuine purpose to take leave, exploits the monthly paid leave for other motives, this is not considered legitimate use of holiday entitlements.[129)]

2) Case #2: Collective use of annual leave to gain advantage in negotiations

Failing to follow proper procedures when utilizing collective annual leave during contract negotiations to cause the employer severe financial loss and undermine the company's normal operations towards increasing the workers' negotiation strength constitutes an illegitimate labor action.[130)]

(3) Work-to-rule in safety and health regulations

Safety and health work-to-rule entails adhering strictly to safety regulations and general rules to ensure safety, indirectly impacting operations. If such stringent adherence disrupts work to advocate for workers' claims, it can be deemed a form of labor action. Whether strict compliance with safety rules constitutes a labor action depends on whether it genuinely aims at improving safety or merely serves as a means to disrupt work. If the strict adherence to safety rules surpasses what is objectively necessary for safety or aims solely at hindering work operations, it is considered a form of labor action.

---

129) Supreme Court ruling on March 13, 1992, 91nu10473.

130) Supreme Court ruling on April 23, 1993, 92da34940.

쟁의행위에 해당하는 사례는 회사의 정상적인 업무수행을 방해할 의도로 이루어지는 집단적 연차휴가 사용은 쟁의행위에 해당한다. 오로지 업무방해를 목적으로 실시하는 집단적인 휴가사용은 정당하다고 할 수 없다.

① **사례#1**: 근로기준법 제60조제2항은 "사용자는 1월에 대하여 1일의 유급휴가를 주어야 한다"고 규정하고 있을 뿐 이에 관한 특별한 제한을 두고 있지 아니하므로, 특별한 사정이 없는 한 근로자는 1월에 1일의 월차휴가권을 행사할 수 있다고 할 것이나, 휴가 자체가 목적이 아니라 다른 목적을 위하여 월차휴가를 빙자한 것이라면 이는 정당한 휴가권의 행사라 할 수 없다.[129)]

② **사례#2**: 단체협약 갱신협상에서 유리한 지위를 차지하기 위하여 실시한 집단월차휴가는 그 목적으로 보아 근로기준법상의 정당한 월차휴가라기보다는 회사의 정상적인 운영을 저해함으로써 그 주장을 관철하기 위한 쟁의행위로서, 그 절차를 거치지 않은 점과 회사의 업무가 마비되어 피보험자에게 막대한 손해를 끼친 점 등을 감안하면, 정당하지 아니한 쟁의행위에 해당한다.[130)]

(3) 안전·보건 투쟁

안전·보건투쟁이란 안전·보건을 담보하기 위한 법령 등 제반규칙을 더욱 엄격하게 규정대로 준수함으로써 간접적으로 조업에 영향을 미쳐 업무를 저해하는 것을 의미한다. 안전·보건투쟁은 근로자들이 그 주장을 관철하기 위한 압력수단으로써 안전·보건규정을 필요 이상으로 철저히 준수하는 것은 근로의무의 불성실한 이행에 해당하므로 쟁의행위(태업)에 해당될 수 있다. 안전·보건수칙 준수가 쟁의행위에 해당되는지 여부는 관련된 수칙을 필요 이상으로 엄격하게 준수하는 목적이 진정으로 당해 규정이 의도 하는 안전의 확보나 운행의 정상성의 회복을 목적으로 하는지, 단순히 업무저해를 위한 수단인지 여부에 따라 판단한다. 안전·보건수칙의 취지상 객관적으로 요구하는 한도를 넘어서까지 그 규정의 준수를 고집하는 경우에는 쟁의행위에 해당된다.

---

129) 대법원 1992.3.13. 선고 91누10473 판결
130) 대법원 1993.4.23. 선고 92나34940 판결

C. Workplace Occupations

1. Concept

Workplace occupation refers to a form of labor action where workers remain in the workplace facilities, engaging in continuous rallies or demonstrations to increase the effectiveness of primary labor actions like strikes. Occupying workplace facilities is an active form of labor action. When the occupation involves only a portion of the workplace facilities and does not block the employer from accessing, controlling or supervising the work facilities, it can be considered a legitimate labor action. However, if the occupation completely and exclusively blocks access to non-union individuals or prevents the employer from managing, leading to work disruptions or chaos, it surpasses the limits of legitimacy. [131)]

When union members occupy the main entrance of a factory and the corridors leading to the factory manager's office, making it nearly impossible for outsiders to enter the main building and causing significant disruption to the company's normal operations during lunchtime or at night by chanting slogans or singing, such actions by union members are considered illegal labor actions.[132)]

2. Justification of workplace occupations

During labor disputes, strikes often accompany sit-ins at workplaces as a means to secure and strengthen the efficiency of work stoppage. Sit-ins themselves cannot be deemed illegal. If the occupation does not completely block the employer from entering or exiting the facilities and does not interfere with company operations but remains a partial and coexisting occupation, it is recognized as justified.[133)]

However, occupying the employer's business facilities entirely and exclusively over an extended period infringes upon the employer's facility management rights and cannot be

131) Supreme Court ruling on June 1, 1991, 91do383.

132) Supreme Court ruling on January 15, 1991, 90snu6620.

133) Supreme Court ruling on July 14, 1992, 91da43800.

C. 직장점거

1. 의의

직장점거란 쟁의행위 중에 근로자가 사업장시설에 머물면서 집회나 시위를 계속하면서 파업과 같은 주된 쟁의행위의 실효성을 확보하기 위하여 사업장시설을 점거하는 쟁위행위이다. 사업장 시설의 점거는 적극적인 쟁의행위의 한 가지 형태로서 그 점거의 범위가 사업장 시설의 일부분이고 사용자 측의 출입이나 관리지배를 배제하지 않는 일부 점거에 지나지 않을 때에는 정당한 쟁의행위로 볼 수 있다. 그러나 이와 달리 직장 또는 사업장 시설을 전면적, 배타적으로 점거하여 조합원 이외의 자의 출입을 제지하거나 사용자 측의 관리지배를 배제하여 업무의 중단 또는 혼란을 야기케 하는 것과 같은 행위는 이미 정당성의 한계를 벗어난 것이라고 볼 수 있다.[131)]

노동조합원들이 공장본관의 현관과 여기에서 공장장실 등으로 통하는 복도를 점거하여 점거기간중 점심시간이나 야간에는 구호를 외치고 노래를 부르는 등 농성을 함으로 인하여 외부인의 본관 건물에의 출입이 거의 불가능하게 되고 사용자 회사의 정상적인 업무수행에 큰 지장을 초래하였다면 조합원들의 위 점거농성은 쟁의행위에 해당된다.[132)]

2. 직장점거의 정당성 판단

쟁의행위 중 파업은 그 노무정지의 효율성을 확보, 강화하기 위하여 그 보조수단으로 직장에 체류하여 농성하는 직장점거를 동반하기도 하는 것으로서 그 자체는 위법하다고 할 수 없으나, 이러한 직장점거는 사용자측의 점유를 완전히 배제하지 아니하고 그 조업도 방해하지 않는 부분적, 병존적 점거일 경우에 정당성이 인정된다.[133)]

쟁의행위 중 직장점거는 사용자측의 점유를 완전히 배제하지 아니하고 그 조업도 방해하지 않는 부분적·병존적 점거일 경우에 한하여 정당성이 인정되고, 이를

131) 대법원 1991.6.11. 선고 91도383 판결
132) 대법원 1991.1.15. 선고 90누6620 판결
133) 대법원 1992.7.14. 선고 91다43800 판결

justified.[134)]

1) Case #1: SsangYong Motor's labor union occupied the workplace from May 26, 2009, to August 6, 2009, utilizing violence and occupying the factory completely and exclusively. Due to this overstepping of legitimate action, the defendant had the obligation to compensate the plaintiff for its losses.[135)]

2) Case #2: The defendant conspired with around 70 other labor union members to physically occupy the company's factory gate, securing it with locks they had acquired on their own, partially or completely controlling the access of transport vehicles utilized by the company or its branch managers. Even if these actions were taken by the labor union to counter the company's attempts to neutralize their declared strike, their methods involved active interference with work, not merely passive disruption. Thus, it surpassed the justified limits of labor actions.[136)]

3. Facilities where workplace occupations are never justified

Article 42, Paragraph 1 of the *TULRAA* prohibits the occupation of "facilities related to production, other major tasks, and facilities equivalent to them as designated by presidential decree." Presidential decrees outline specific facilities where occupations are prohibited, including electrical, computing or telecommunication facilities, railway vehicles or tracks, and places storing hazardous substances. Other facilities subject to prohibition include those whose occupation could lead to the suspension or termination of production or other major tasks (Article 21 of the *Enforcement Decree to the TULRAA*).

However, if an employer hires individuals unrelated to the affected business to carry out tasks disrupted by the labor dispute, striking workers may occupy key facilities needed exclusively by the substitute workers. In this scenario, if an employer violates the prohibition against substitute labor stipulated in Article 43, Paragraph 1 of the *TULRAA*, worker occupation of facilities to prevent substitute labor is considered a justified act under the Article 20 of the *Criminal Act* (Justifiable Acts) concerning criminal liability related to obstruction of business.[137)]

---

134) Supreme Court ruling on July 14, 1992, 91da43800.

135) Supreme Court ruling on June 15, 2023, 1019da38543.

136) Supreme Court ruling on July 9, 1991, 91do1051.

137) Jang Seung-hyuk, "Permissible Scope and Criminal Liability of Collective Actions by Workplace Occupation," *Labor Law Research*, Vol. 48, First Half of 2020, Seoul National University Labor Law Research Society, pp. 198-199.

넘어 사용자의 기업시설을 장기간에 걸쳐 전면적·배타적으로 점유하는 것은 사용자의 시설관리권능에 대한 침해로서 정당화될 수 없다.[134]

① **사례#1:** 쌍용자동차 노동조합이 2009.5.26.부터 2009.8.6.까지 원고의 본사 공장에서 진행한 직장 점거 파업은 폭력적인 방법을 동원하여 위 공장을 전면적·배타적으로 점거하는 방식으로 이루어지는 등으로 그 정당성의 한계를 벗어났으므로, 피고는 그로 인한 원고의 손해를 배상할 의무가 있다.[135]

② **사례#2:** 피고인이 노동조합원 70여명과 공모하여 회사 공장의 정문을 실력으로 점거하고 미리 준비한 자물쇠를 채워 봉쇄한 채 회사측 또는 회사의 대리점경영자들이 동원한 수송용 차량의 출입을 부분적으로 또는 전면적으로 통제하거나 막음으로써, 회사나 대리점경영자들의 제품수송업무를 방해하였다면, 그와 같은 행동이 노동조합측이 결정한 파업을 무력화시키려는 회사측의 기도를 통제하기 위한 조치였다고 하더라도, 그 수단이나 방법이 소극적으로 업무의 정상적인 운영을 저해하는 데에 그친 것이 아니라, 다중의 위력이나 물리적 강제력으로써 적극적으로 업무를 방해한 것이어서, 쟁의행위로서의 정당한 한계를 벗어난 것이다.[136]

3. 직장점거가 제한되는 시설

노동조합법 제42조 제1항은 '생산시설 기타 주요업무에 관련되는 시설과 이에 준하는 시설로서 대통령령이 정하는 시설을 점거하는 형태'의 금지하고 있다. 대통령령이 정하는 점거가 금지되는 시설로는 전기, 전산 또는 통신시설, 철도의 차량 또는 선로, 유독물질을 보관 저장하는 장소다. 기타 점거될 경우 생산 기타 주요 업무의 정지 또는 폐지를 가져오는 시설이다.(노조법 시행령 제21조).

다만, 사용자가 쟁의행위로 중단된 업무의 수행을 위하여 당해 사업과 관계없는 자를 채용하여 투입하는 경우에 파업근로자들은 주요시설에 대한 직장점거로 대체근로를 저지할 수 있다. 이 경우 사용자가 노동조합법상 대체근로금지 조항(제43조의 제1항)에 위반하였기 때문에 업무방해죄와 같은 형사책임과 관련해서는 대체근로 방지의 직장점거는 형법상 정당행위(제20조)에 해당하여 위법성이 조각된다.[137]

---

134) 대법원 1992.7.14. 선고 91다43800 판결

135) 대법원 2023.6.15. 선고 2019다38543 판결

136) 대법원 1991.7.9. 선고 91도1051 판결

137) 장승혁, "직장점거에 의한 쟁의행위의 허용 범위와 형사책임", 노동법연구, 2020 상반기 제48호, 서울대노동법연구회, 198-199면.

D. Picketing

1. Concept

Picketing refers to the act where a labor union obstructs the entry of non-union members or others to the workplace and calls for support for a strike. Essentially, it involves encouraging workers to participate in the strike while gaining public support for the union's demands, aiming to economically impact the employer more effectively. Picketing itself is not an independent form of labor action but primarily serves as a supplementary means carried out to enhance the effect of strikes or boycotts.

Picketing entails appealing to non-striking workers or third parties to support the strike and align with it. Therefore, it usually takes the form of an appeal or surveillance but can manifest in various ways based on specific needs. Commonly, methods involve installing placards at the workplace entrance, using loudspeakers, or distributing printouts to persuade and encourage alignment.

Picketing involves urging those not participating in the strike to cooperate with it or prevent actions that obstruct the strike. It is employed by labor unions as an auxiliary method to effectively execute their labor actions. Typically, it involves union members hanging placards at the company entrance or holding signs with slogans or demands while stationed at the entrance and voicing their demands.

Strikes, as part of labor action, may be accompanied by picketing as a supportive measure or simultaneous occupation of the workplace for rallies and protests, and picketing itself cannot be considered illegal. However, in such cases, picketing should ideally involve peaceful persuasion within the realm of verbal and written communication to persuade those who continue to work to instead join the strike. Resorting to physical force, threats, or coercion is not justified.[138)]

138) Supreme Court ruling on July 14, 1992, 91da43800.

D. 피케팅

1. 의의

피케팅은 노동조합이 쟁의행위를 효과적으로 수행하기 위하여 비조합원 등의 사업장 출입을 저지하고 파업에 동조하도록 호소하는 행위를 의미한다. 즉, 근로를 희망하는 근로자에게 파업에 참가할 것을 권유하고 노동조합의 요구에 대한 공중의 이해를 얻음으로써 사용자에게 경제적인 타격을 보다 효과적으로 가하려는 것이므로 피케팅 자체는 독립된 쟁의행위가 아니고 주로 파업, 보이콧 등의 효과를 높이기 위하여 부수적으로 행하여지는 보조적 수단이다.

피케팅은 파업불참자 또는 제3자에게 파업에 참여할 것을 호소하여 동조할 것을 요구하는 것이므로 호소 또는 감시 등의 형태를 취하는 것이 보통이나 구체적인 필요에 의하여 여러 가지 형태로 나타날 수 있다. 일반적으로 사업장 입구에 플래카드를 설치하거나 확성기를 이용하거나 유인물을 배포하여 동조를 권유·설득하는 방법이 사용된다.

피케팅은 파업에 참가한 근로자들이 파업에 동조하지 않고 조업을 하려는 자에게 파업에 협조하도록 하거나 파업의 방해 행위를 방지하도록 하는 쟁의행위이다. 피케팅은 노동조합의 쟁의행위를 효과적으로 수행하기 위하여 사용하는 보조수단으로서 통상적으로 사업장의 출입문에 플래카드를 걸어둔다거나 조합원들이 구호나 요구사항을 쓴 나무판자 등을 들고 사업장의 출입문에 서성거리거나 열을 지어 서서 구호를 외치는 방법을 많이 사용한다.

쟁의행위 중 파업은 그 노무정지의 효율성을 확보·강화하기 위하여 그 보조수단으로 소위 '피케팅'을 동반하거나, 직장에 체류하여 연좌, 농성하는 직장점거를 동반하기도 하는 것으로서 그 자체는 위법하다고 할 수 없으나, 이 경우 '피케팅'은 파업에 가담하지 않고 조업을 계속하려는 자에 대하여 평화적 설득, 구두와 문서에 의한 언어적 설득의 범위 내에서 정당성이 인정되는 것이 원칙이고, 폭행 협박 또는 위력에 의한 실력적 저지나 물리적 강제는 정당화될 수 없다.[138)]

---

138) 대법원 1992.7.14 선고 91다43800 판결

2. Criteria for determining the legitimacy of picketing

(1) Picketing is considered legitimate only when peaceful persuasion methods, such as verbal and written communication, are employed toward workers who refuse to participate in a strike and wish to continue working.

During labor actions, strikes sometimes accompany picketing as a supportive measure to enhance the effectiveness of work stoppages. While picketing itself cannot be considered illegal, when it comes to those who do not join the strike and wish to continue working, legitimacy is acknowledged within the bounds of peaceful persuasion and verbal and written communication. Resorting to physical violence, threats, or coercion is not justifiable.[139)]

(2) According to Article 38, Paragraph 1 of the TULRAA, actions obstructing the normal entry, work, or operation of prospective workers at the workplace are unjustifiable.

In a situation where the plaintiff obstructed the access of employees attempting to enter the company's premises for about a month, using force to block the entrance, it disrupts the company's operations. Hence, such strike action cannot be considered socially justified due to its method or means, hence qualifying as an illegal action.[140)]

1) Case #1: Assaulting, threatening, pressuring or otherwise harassing employees who wish to continue working to stop working:

The labor union occupied various branch offices of an insurance company during working hours or very close to them, involving 16 to 160 union members who chanted slogans, sang labor songs, verbally abused the CEO, physically restrained employees, and chased them away. These actions, even if considered labor actions, went beyond the acceptable limits of law, infringing on property rights through comprehensive and exclusive facility occupation or by employing threats (grabbing by the neck and making intimidating statements) and violence, which fall outside the boundaries of legitimate labor

---

139) Supreme Court ruling on October 12, 1990, 90do1431.

140) Supreme Court ruling on September 30, 1994, 94da4042.

2. 피케팅의 정당성 판단기준

(1) 피케팅은 파업에 가담하지 않고 조업을 계속하려는 근로자에 대하여 구두와 문서 등 평화적 설득의 방법에 의한 경우에만 정당하다.

쟁의행위 중 파업은 그 노무정지의 효율성을 확보, 강화하기 위하여 그 보조수단으로 소위 피케팅을 동반하기도 하는 것으로서 그 자체는 위법하다고 할 수 없으나, 이 경우 파업에 가담하지 않고 조업을 계속하려는 자에 대하여 평화적 설득, 구두와 문서에 의한 언어적 설득의 범위 내에서 정당성이 인정되는 것이 원칙이고, 폭행·협박 또는 위력에 의한 실력적 저지나 물리적 강제는 정당화될 수 없다.[139)]

(2) 노동조합법 제38조제1항의 규정에 따라 근로희망자 등의 사업장 출입·조업 기타 정상적인 업무를 방해하는 것은 정당하지 않다.

원고가 1개월 정도 위력을 사용하여 회사의 출입문 등을 봉쇄하여 출근하려는 사원 등의 출입을 방해하여 회사의 업무를 방해한 사실을 인정하고 있으므로 이러한 파업행위는 쟁의행위의 방법이나 수단면에서 사회적 상당성을 갖추었다고 볼 수 없어 불법파업이다.[140)]

1) 사례#1: 근로희망자 등에 대하여 폭행, 협박, 압력 등으로 조업을 중지시키거나 폭언, 인신비방 등으로 조업을 방해하는 경우

노동조합은 ○○보험조합의 각 지부사무실 등을 근무시간 중이나 이와 아주 근접한 시간에 무단으로 점거하고, 적게는 16명, 많게는 160명의 노조원들을 동원하여 구호와 노동가 등을 제창하고 대표이사에게 욕설을 하거나 멱살을 잡고 직원들을 밀치거나 쫓아내는 등의 방법으로 위력을 행사하여 업무를 방해한 사실이 인정되는 바, 이를 쟁의행위로서 한 것이라고 하더라도 법률상 허용될 수 없는 전면적·배타적 시설점거와 같은 재산권 침해행위나, 협박(멱살을 잡고 "신나를 뿌리고 너죽고 나죽자"라고 하고 "부당징계 철회"라고 쓴 혈서를 얼굴에 들이대고 "이놈의 새끼 피냄새를 맡아봐라"고 말하여 생명신체에 위해를 가할 듯한 태도를 보여 협박)에

139) 대법원 1990.10.12. 선고 90도1431 판결
140) 대법원 1994.9.30. 선고 94다4042 판결

actions.[141)]

2) Case #2: Obstructing workplace entry, such as closing the main gate:

The labor union, in collusion with its members, forcibly occupied the entrance of the company's factory by locking it with their own locks, preventing access by the company's security personnel, controlling the entry and exit of transportation vehicles used by the company and the managing agents of the company's, thereby disrupting the product transport operations of the company or its agents. This kind of action, which actively disrupted work through various forms of coercion or physical force, exceeded the legitimate boundaries of labor actions.[142)]

3) Case #3: Using force or threats to participate in a strike:

The labor union occupied parts of an office, engaging in night vigils with groups of around 10 members taking turns and making noise, shouting slogans or singing songs, playing musical instruments, causing disturbances, verbally attacking and threatening employees who were not participating in the strike, actively urging them to join, and damaging the functioning of the equipment on-site. These actions, extending beyond the boundaries of legitimacy in terms of methods and means used during labor actions, were unjustifiable.[143)]

4) Case #4: Actively obstructing the work of other workers or third parties:

The picketing of workers participating in a strike was directed at those who continued working. While such actions are viewed as part of alliance strikes to achieve effective labor actions, obstructing the mailing operations of notifications to everyone by hiding and confiscating all notifications at the worksite cannot be justified even as a form of supportive picketing during a strike.[144)]

---

141) Supreme Court ruling on November 10, 1992, 92do1315.

142) Supreme Court ruling on July 9, 1991, 91do1051.

143) Supreme Court ruling on May 8, 1992, 91do3051.

144) Supreme Court ruling on July 14, 1992, 91da43800.

의한 폭력행위 등을 한 것은 쟁의행위의 정당성의 범위를 벗어난 것이다.[141)]

2) 사례#1: 정문 폐쇄 등 사업장 출입을 방해하는 경우

노동조합이 조합원들과 공모하여 회사 공장의 정문을 실력으로 점거하고 미리 준비한 자물쇠를 채워 봉쇄한 다음, 회사측 경비원들의 접근을 제지하고 회사측에서 동원한 수송용 차량의 출입을 통제하거나, 회사의 대리점을 경영하는 자들이 동원한 차량의 출입을 막음으로써, 회사나 대리점 경영자들의 제품수송 업무를 방해한 것은 그 수단이나 방법이 소극적으로 업무의 정상적인 운영을 저해하는 데에 그친 것이 아니라, 다중의 위력이나 물리적 강제력으로써 적극적으로 업무를 방해한 것이어서, 쟁의행위로서의 정당한 한계를 벗어난 것이다.[142)]

3) 사례#3: 파업참여를 호소하면서 위력을 행사하거나 협박하는 경우

노동조합이 사무실 일부를 점거하여 야간에는 10여명씩 조를 짜서 교대로 철야농성을 하고 주간에는 다 함께 모여 농성을 하면서 구호를 외치거나 노래를 부르고 북, 장구, 징, 꽹과리를 두드리며 소란행위를 계속하고, 농성에 가담하지 아니하고 근무하는 직원들에게 "노조원들과 적이 되려 하느냐"는 등의 야유와 협박을 하며 농성가담을 적극 권유하고, 그 곳에 있는 테렉스 기기에 들어가는 테렉스 용지를 찢거나 그 작동을 중단시키는 등의 행위는 그 방법이나 수단에 있어서 쟁의행위의 정당성의 한계를 벗어난 것이다.[143)]

4) 사례#4: 다른 근로자 또는 제3자의 업무를 적극적으로 저지하는 경우

파업에 참가한 근로자들이 파업에 동조하지 아니하고 조업을 하는 사람들에게 "피케팅"을 하는 것은 동맹파업 등 근로자들에 의한 쟁의행위가 실효를 거둘 수 있도록 하기 위하여 허용된다고 보아야 할 것이나, 그렇다고 하더라도 모든 사람에 의한 고지서 발송작업을 전면적으로 저지하기 위하여 그 작업현장에 있던 고지서를 전부 탈취하여 은닉한 행위는 파업의 보조적 쟁의수단인 "피케팅"으로서도 정당화 될 수 없다.[144)]

---

141) 대법원 1992.11.10. 선고 92도1315 판결
142) 대법원 1991.7.9. 선고 91도1051 판결
143) 대법원 1992.5.8. 선고 91도3051 판결
144) 대법원 1992.7.14. 선고 91다 43800 판결

5) Case #5: Individuals in a third-party position picketing in specialized areas:

Considering the airport's significance in prioritizing the safety and order of domestic and foreign individuals, the prohibition of unauthorized occupation of airport facilities under the former *Aviation Act*, and the control and supervision of airport facilities' security and safety by the airport corporation under supervision of the Minister of Land, Infrastructure, and Transport, picketing actions carried out by the defendant and others as part of the union's activities at the airport, despite being asked to discontinue the protest and vacate the facilities, persisted, and continued to be regarded as unlawful acts in the contractual relationship between the subcontractor, the airport corporation, and the workers' positions as third parties.[145)]

Ⅲ. Lockout due to Union Strikes

1. Concept

Lockout is a situation in which the employer refuses to receive employees' labor as a counteraction to their industrial action and to prevent their entry onto the work premises. The lockout sustains the balance of power between labor and management. Case law states that a lockout must be conducted in a confrontational and defensive manner in response to a labor union strike.

If a lockout is deemed a reasonable defensive measure against an industrial action by the union, it can be recognized as a legitimate industrial action by the employer, which would then mean the employer has no obligation to pay wages to the affected workers during the period of the lockout.[146)] However, even if initiation of the lockout itself is justified given the specific circumstances of the workers' industrial action, if at some point the workers cease their industrial action and express a genuine intention to return to work, yet the employer continues the lockout, the lockout then moves from being a

145) Supreme Court ruling on November 12, 2020, 1016do8627.

146) Supreme Court ruling on May 26, 2000, Case No. 98da34331.

5) 사례#5: 제3자 지위이면서 특수한 장소에서 피케팅을 하는 경우

○○공항은 이용개인 내·외국인들의 안전과 질서가 무엇보다 중시되는 장소인 점, 구 항공법에 의하여 공항시설의 무단점유 등이 금지되어 있고(제106조의2), ○○공항을 관리하는 ○○공사는 공항시설의 보안과 안전에 관한 사항에 관하여 국토교통부장관의 지도·감독을 받는 점, 이사건 공소사실 기재 행위의 방법·규모·피고인 등이 들고 있던 피켓에 적힌 문구의 내용 등에 비추어 ○○공항의 이용객들에게 위압감과 불안감을 주었을 것으로 보이는 점 및 ○○공항공사는 피고인 등과 직접적인 근로계약관계나 근로자파견관계에 있다고 보기 어려워 원칙적으로 제3자의 지위에 있다는 점 등 그 판시와 같은 사정을 들어 노동조합의 조합활동으로 이루어진 피고인 등의 이 사건 피켓시위 및 ○○공항공사 시위 중단·퇴거 요구에 불응한 채 계속해서 시위를 지속한 것은 도급인인 ○○공항공사에 대한 관계에서 위법한 행위라고 판단하였다.[145]

Ⅲ. 직장폐쇄 – 사용자의 쟁의행위

1. 개념

직장폐쇄는 사용자가 근로자들의 쟁의행위에 맞서 근로자들의 근로를 받아들이지 않고, 회사에 출입하지 못하게 하는 것을 말한다. 근로자들의 쟁의행위에 대하여 사용자에게도 그 대항수단을 허용함으로써 노사관계의 균형을 유지하려는 것이다. 판례는 직장폐쇄는 노동조합의 파업에 대한 대항적이고 방어적으로 해야 한다고 판시하고 있다.

사용자의 직장폐쇄가 근로자의 쟁의행위에 대한 방어수단으로서 상당성이 있으면 사용자의 정당한 쟁의행위로 인정될 수 있고, 그 경우 사용자는 직장폐쇄 기간 동안 대상 근로자에 대한 임금지불의무를 면한다.[146] 그러나 근로자의 쟁의행위 등 구체적인 사정에 비추어 직장폐쇄의 개시 자체는 정당하더라도 어느 시점 이후에 근로자가 쟁의행위를 중단하고 진정으로 업무에 복귀할 의사를 표시하였음에도 사용자가 직장폐쇄를 계속 유지함으로써 근로자의 쟁의행위에

145) 대법원 2020.11.12. 선고 2016도8627 판결
146) 대법원 2000.5.26. 선고 98다34331 판결

defensive measure to an aggressive one, thereby losing its legitimacy from that point onwards. In such cases, the employer is not free from the obligation to pay wages, from that point on.[147)]

2. Requirement (defensive lockout)

The employer usually implements a defensive lockout after inception of an industrial action.[148)] Therefore, the employer may only implement a lockout after the labor union takes a justifying industrial action. In principle, the law prohibits preemptive lockouts or any measures that exceed the scope and method of an industrial action to a considerable degree.[149)]

As a related case, even before the labor union of a bus company held a "strike rally," the company closed its main gate and initiated a lockout. Despite the clear expression of willingness to work by only three union members, the company refused to assign them to buses and, the following day, filed a report of partial lockout limited only to a few vehicles operated by union members in a certain city. The company continued its operations by assigning vehicles only to non-union members. This indicates that the lockout went beyond a defensive action against a labor union's industrial actions and became a preemptive, aggressive lockout aimed at actively weakening the organizational strength of the labor union. Such a lockout has no legitimacy.[150)]

3. Method

(1) Practical measures

A lockout is not legitimate if the labor union is notified only once it has begun. Other actions must be taken before refusing employees' work. Employers must announce their intention to initiate a lockout by posting notices detailing the timing and the subjects of the lockout before it is implemented, ensuring that workers are aware of the possibility.

---

147) Court ruling on May 24, 2016, Case No. 2012da85335.

148) Ministry of Employment and Labor (MOEL) Guidelines, June 24, 1998, Labor-Management No. 32281-1703.

149) Daejeon District Court ruling on Feb. 9, 1995, Case No. 93gahap566.

150) Supreme Court ruling on June 13, 2003, Case No. 2003du1097.

대한 방어적인 목적에서 벗어나 공격적 직장폐쇄로 성격이 변질되었다고 볼 수 있는 경우에는 그 이후의 직장폐쇄는 정당성을 상실하게 된다. 이 경우 사용자는 그 기간 동안의 임금에 대해서는 지불의무를 면할 수 없다.[147)]

2. 요건 (대항적, 방어적 조치)

직장폐쇄는 사용자가 행하는 쟁의행위이며 근로자들의 노무수령을 집단적으로 거부하는 것으로서 노동조합이 쟁의행위를 개시한 이후에만 대항 또는 방어적인 수단으로서 행사해야 한다.[148)] 따라서 직장폐쇄는 근로자의 쟁의행위에 대하여 방어적으로 행해져야 하고, 공격적으로 행해지는 것은 그 정당성을 피할 수 없다. 원칙적으로 근로자측에서 쟁의상태에 이르기 이전에 선행적으로 직장폐쇄를 실행하여서는 아니되고, 근로자측이 이미 쟁의상태에 들어간 이후에도 그 규모, 방법에 대응하는 상당한 정도를 초과하여 직장폐쇄를 실행하는 것은 허용되지 않는다.[149)]

관련 사례로, 버스 회사의 노동조합이'파업출정식'을 하기도 전에 회사는 정문을 폐쇄하고 직장폐쇄를 하였다. 조합원 3인이 승무할 의사가 있음을 분명히 표시하였음에도 배차를 거부한 채 다음날에 △△시에 조합원들이 운행하는 소수의 차량에 한하여 부분직장폐쇄 신고를 하였고, 비조합원들에게만 차량을 배차하여 사업을 계속 영위 하였다. 이는 회사의 직장폐쇄는 노동조합의 쟁의행위에 대한 방어적인 목적을 벗어나 적극적으로 노동조합의 조직력을 약화시키기 위한 목적 등을 갖는 선제적이고 공격적인 직장폐쇄에 해당하므로 그 정당성이 인정될 수 없다.[150)]

3. 방법

(1) 사실상의 조치

직장폐쇄는 노동조합에 통보하는 것만으로는 안 되고, 근로자들의 근로를 받아들이지 않겠다는 사실상의 조치가 있어야 한다. 직장폐쇄는 사용자가 근로자의 쟁의행위에 대항하여 노무수령을 거부하는 행위이므로 노무수령을 거부하

147) 대법원 2016.5.24. 선고 2012다85335 판결
148) 행정해석1998.6.24. 노사32281-1703
149) 대전지법판례 1995.02.09. 93가합566
150) 대법원 2003.6.13. 선고 2003두1097 판결

The notice must be posted in a place accessible to workers prior to the start date of the lockout. If there is a practice of communication between labor and management occurring online, announcing through the company intranet or website, or sending individual emails to the workers subject to the lockout is also possible.

(2) Applicable to any industrial action

A lockout can be implemented in response to all forms of industrial action. This includes slow-downs and work-to-rule actions, where workers are technically performing their duties.[151)] If a labor union aims to maximize the effect of a strike or strategically conducts industrial actions for certain hours each day, the employer can counter this by implementing a defensive lockout. As long as the lockout is deemed a reasonable action against the labor union's repeated industrial actions, there is no need to repeatedly start and end the lockout in response to each action. Therefore, unless the labor union expresses an intention to withdraw its industrial actions, the employer can maintain the lockout throughout the period of industrial action, including times when no industrial actions are taking place.[152)]

(3) Partial and total lockouts

An industrial action refers to acts such as strikes, work slowdowns, and lockouts, which are undertaken by parties in labor relations to assert their demands, and the actions taken in response to them. Similarly to how a labor union can conduct either a general or partial strike as part of its industrial action toolkit, employers can also counteract with either a total or partial lockout.[153)] A partial lockout means closing down certain operations (departments) or locking out certain personnel while continuing operations elsewhere, whereas a total lockout means halting operations across the entire workplace, similar in appearance to a suspension of business.

In principle, a partial strike should be met with a partial lockout. However, if a partial strike leads to the stoppage or closure of the entire workplace's operations, then a total lockout may be implemented.

151) MOEL Guidelines, Oct. 26, 1995, Cooperation 68107-333.

152) MOEL Guidelines, Nov. 7, 2008, Labor Law Division-1019.

153) MOEL Guidelines, Aug. 31, 1998, Cooperation 68140-327.

고 임금지급의무를 이행하지 않겠다는 사용자의 의사표시를 분명히 해야 한다. 사용자는 직장폐쇄 실시 전에 직장폐쇄 일시와 대상 등을 게재한 내용의 공고문 게시하여 근로자가 직장폐쇄 사실을 알 수 있도록 조치를 하여야 한다. 이때 공고문 게시는 근로자가 알 수 있는 장소에 하여야 하며, 최소한 직장폐쇄 개시일 이전에 게시하여야 한다. 노사 간 의사소통이 온라인을 통해 이루어져 온 관행이 있는 경우라면 사내전산망 또는 홈페이지를 통해 공고하거나 직장폐쇄 대상이 된 근로자에게 개별 메일을 전송하는 방법도 가능하다.

(2) 모든 쟁의행위에 적용

직장폐쇄는 모든 쟁의행위에 대하여 행할 수 있다. 특히 태업, 준법투쟁에 대하여도 근로자가 근로에 임하고 있다고 할지라도 직장폐쇄를 할 수 있다.[151] 노동조합이 파업 효과를 극대화할 목적이거나 전략적으로 매일 일부시간을 반복하여 쟁의행위를 하는 경우 이에 대항하여 사용자가 직장폐쇄를 함에 있어 대항적으로 방어수단으로서 상당성이 부인되지 않는 한, 계속 반복되는 노동조합의 쟁의행위에 따라 직장폐쇄의 유지와 철회를 반복할 필요는 없다. 따라서 노동조합이 쟁의행위 철회 의사를 표명하지 않는 한 이러한 쟁의행위 기간 동안 쟁의행위를 하지 않는 시간에 대해서도 직장폐쇄를 계속 유지할 수 있다.[152]

(3) 부분 직장폐쇄와 전체 직장폐쇄

쟁의행위란 파업, 태업, 직장폐쇄 기타 노동관계 당사자가 주장을 관철할 목적으로 행하는 행위와 이에 대항하는 행위로 노동조합이 쟁의행위의 일환으로 전면또는 부분파업을 할 수 있는 것과 마찬가지로 사용자도 이에 대항하여 전면 또는 부분 직장폐쇄를 할 수 있다.[153] 분직장폐쇄는 일부 업무(부서)나 일부 인원에 대하여 직장폐쇄를 하고 조업을 계속하는 경우를 의미하고 전면직장폐쇄는 전 사업장의 조업을 중단하는 상황을 의미하는 것으로 외형상 휴업 조치와 유사하다.

부분파업이 발생한 경우 원칙적으로 부분직장폐쇄로 대응하는 것이 노동조합의 쟁의행위에 대한 대항수단이라는 할 수 있다. 다만, 부분파업이 전체 사업장 업무의 정지·폐지를 가져오는 경우에는 전면적인 직장폐쇄를 하는 것도 가능하다.

151) 행정해석 1995. 10. 26. 협력 68107-333
152) 행정해석 2008. 11. 7. 노사관계법제과-1019
153) 행정해석 1998.8.31, 협력 68140-327

The subjects of a lockout, in principle, can include both union and non-union members, depending on the form of the industrial action. That is, the targets can be limited to strike participants, all union members, or all workers, depending on whether some union members fully refuse to provide labor, or all union members are providing incomplete labor, such as in work slowdowns or intermittent strikes.

In a partial lockout, employers have the freedom to continue operations by accepting labor from workers not participating in the industrial action, so assigning non-striking non-union members to operate vehicles previously operated by striking union members does not constitute a violation of the prohibition against replacement labor during a strike.[154)]

Generally, a partial strike achieves a similar effect as a total strike while minimizing the risk of wage loss. Even if employers accept labor from these workers, practically combining this labor force is challenging, leading to the dual burdens of operation stoppages and wage payments. In such cases, employers can implement a total lockout against the union, even if the union has only conducted a partial strike.[155)]

As a related case, even if the labor union of a bus company declared a partial strike and conducted industrial actions for 1-2 days, such as operating only once as per the predetermined number of trips or refusing to drive, the substantial impact of such erratic operations and the unpredictability of their duration mean that the mere refusal of employers to assign work to the participating union members does not constitute an unfair labor practice.[156)]

4. Effect

(1) Employer exempt from obligation to receive labor services and pay wages

An employer has the right to refuse to receive labor services from employees during a lockout. In addition, the employer is not obligated to pay wages to employees who do not provide labor services due to a lockout, since wages are remuneration for work. This applies not only to union members subject to lockout, but also to all other non-union employees. However, if an employee who is not subject to the lockout provides regular

154) MOEL Guidelines, Sept. 14, 1999, Cooperation 68140-14.

155) Supreme Court ruling on Mar. 9, 2001, Case No. 2000da63813.

156) Supreme Court ruling on Sept. 29, 2003, Case No. 2003du5792.

직장폐쇄의 대상은 원칙적으로 조합원·비조합원을 불문하며 쟁의행위의 형태에 따라 그 대상자를 정할 수 있다. 즉, 일부 조합원이 노무제공을 전면 거부하는 경우, 전체 조합원이 태업과 파상파업 등 불완전한 노무를 제공하는 경우 등 쟁의행위의 형태에 따라, 파업참가자에 한정하거나 전체 조합원 또는 모든 근로자를 대상으로 할 수도 있다.

부분적 직장폐쇄의 경우에는 사용자가 쟁의행위에 참가하지 아니한 근로자의 근로 제공을 수령하여 조업을 계속할 수 있는 조업계속의 자유를 갖고 있으므로 파업에 참가한 조합원이 운행하던 차량에 대하여 사용자가 파업불참 비조합원으로 하여금 대체승무 운행토록 하는 행위는 파업 중 대체근로금지에 해당되지 않는다.[154]

일반적으로 부분파업은 전면파업에 비하여 임금상실의 위험을 최소화 시키면서도 실질적으로는 전면파업과 유사한 효과를 올리게 된다. 사용자가 이들의 노무제공을 수령 하더라도 실질적으로 이들 노동력을 결합시키기가 곤란하므로 조업중단과 임금지급이라는 이중 부담을 안게 된다. 이러한 경우 사용자는 비록 노조가 부분파업을 하였다 하더라도 노조에 대한 전면적인 직장폐쇄를 할 수 있다.[155]

관련 사례로, 버스회사의 노동조합이 부분파업을 선언하고 정해진 운행횟수 등 1회만을 운행하거나 승무를 거부하는 등의 쟁의행위를 1~2일간 하였더라도 이러한 파행운행으로 인한 타격이 클 뿐 아니라 파행운행이 언제까지 지속 될지 예측할 수 없었던 점 등과 같은 상황에서 사용자가 쟁의행위 참가 조합원에 대한 배차를 거부하였다는 것만으로 부당노동행위가 성립한다고 할 수 없다.[156]

4. 효과

(1) 노무수령의무 및 임금지급의무의 면제

직장폐쇄 대상인 근로자에 대하여 직장폐쇄 기간 중에 사용자의 노무수령거부가 합법적으로 인정된다. 임금은 사용자가 근로의 대상으로 근로자에게 지급하는 금품을 말하는 것이므로 직장폐쇄로 인해 근로자가 근로를 제공하지 않은데 대한 사용자의 임금지급 의무는 없으며, 이는 직장폐쇄 대상에 속하는 조합원 이외의 여타 근로자에 대하여도 같다. 다만, 직장폐쇄 대상이 아닌 자가 회사업무수행을

154) 행정해석 1999.9.14, 협력 68140-14,
155) 대법원 2001.3.9. 선고 2000다63813 판결
156) 대법원 2003.9.29. 선고 2003두5792 판결

work for the company, contractual wages shall be paid for the services provided.[157)]

(2) Holidays and leave

As an employer can legitimately refuse to receive labor services from the employees subject to the lockout, there is no longer any obligation for the employer to honor the statutory holiday and leave stipulations outlined in the *Labor Standards Act*.[158)]

(3) Premises off-limits to employees

A lockout allows the employer to prevent employees from entering the workplace, by closing the company entrance gates or withdrawing employees from production facilities and precluding their provision of labor service. Accordingly, employee refusal to leave the workplace during a legitimate lockout may be subjected to criminal charges such as failure to comply with a deportation order. Provided that, a lockout shall be limited to production facilities or office facilities as “lockout” refers to prohibiting employees from production and service. Nevertheless, the employer may allow union members entry to certain facilities necessary for union activities or welfare under a reasonable scope, such as the union office, dormitory, canteen, and other facilities not related to production or work.[159)]

Despite the employees’ legitimate occupancy of a workplace before a lockout is declared, once a lockout has been declared, the employer has full control of the workplace and may order all employees to leave the work facilities during that lockout. Sustained occupancy at this time is illegal and persons engaging in such actions will be subject to punishment under the law for failure to comply with a deportation order.[160)]

(4) The possibility of partial operations

Even during a lockout, it is not mandatory to completely halt operations. It is merely necessary to restrict the entry of striking workers; non-striking workers may be allowed to continue operations.[161)] The freedom to operate is guaranteed independently of industrial

157) MOEL Guidelines, Nov. 21, 1994, Nosa 68107-338.

158) MOEL Guidelines, Nov. 10, 1994, Kungi 68040-1769.

159) MOEL Guidelines, Oct. 30, 1998, Cooperation 68140-409.

160) Supreme Court ruling on Jan. 27, 2004, Case No. 2003do6026; Supreme Court ruling June 9, 2005, Case No. 2004do7218.

161) MOEL Guidelines, Sept. 9, 1997, Cooperation 68140-368.

위해 정상근로를 제공하였다면 그에 따른 소정의 임금은 지급되어야 한다.[157]

(2) 휴일, 휴가의 문제

직장폐쇄 대상인 근로자에 대하여는 직장폐쇄 기간중에는 사용자의 노무수령거부가 합법적으로 인정되므로 근로기준법상 휴일·휴가의 문제는 발생하지 않는다.[158]

(3) 근로자의 출입제한

직장폐쇄는 사실상의 노무수령 거부행위로 사업장의 출입문을 폐쇄하거나 근로자들을 생산시설로부터 배제하여 노무제공을 차단하는 조치를 포함한다. 직장폐쇄 시에는 근로자들의 사업장 출입을 저지할 수 있다. 따라서 정당한 직장폐쇄 후 근로자들에게 퇴거명령을 하였음에도 이에 불응하는 경우에는 형법상 퇴거불응에 해당된다. 다만, 직장폐쇄가 미치는 범위는 생산시설 내지 업무시설에 한정되나, 생산이나 업무와 관계없는 시설로서 노조사무실, 기숙사, 식당 등 조합활동 또는 후생복리를 위한 시설에 대해서도 노조원의 출입을 합리적인 범위내에서 일부 제한할 수 있다.[159]

근로자들의 직장점거가 개시 당시 적법한 것이었다 하더라도 사용자가 이에 대응하여 적법하게 직장폐쇄를 하게 되면, 사용자의 사업장에 대한 물권적 지배권이 전면적으로 회복되는 결과 사용자는 점거중인 근로자들에 대하여 정당하게 사업장으로부터의 퇴거를 요구할 수 있다. 점거중인 근로자들이 퇴거를 요구받은 이후의 직장점거는 위법하게 되므로, 사용자의 퇴거 요구를 받고도 불응한 채 직장점거를 계속한 행위는 퇴거불응죄에 해당된다.[160]

(4) 부분조업의 가능

직장폐쇄 중이라도 완전히 조업을 중단해야 하는 것은 아니며, 단지 파업참가 근로자의 출입을 제한하는 것이므로 파업에 참가하지 않는 근로자로 하여금 조업을 계속해도 된다.[161] 조업의 자유는 쟁의행위와는 별개로 보장되는 것으

157) 행정해석 1994.11.21, 노사 68107-338
158) 행정해석 1994.11.10, 근기 68040-1769
159) 행정해석 1998.10.30, 협력 68140-409
160) 대법원 2004.1.27. 선고 2003도6026; 대법원 2005.6.9. 선고 2004도 7218 판결
161) 행정해석 1997.9.9, 협력 68140-368

actions, meaning that employers can continue operations during a lockout using non-union workers or those not targeted by the lockout.

Case #1: In a partial lockout, employers have the freedom to continue operations by accepting labor from workers not participating in the industrial action. It cannot be considered a violation of the replacement prohibition rules for an employer to have non-union members who did not participate in the strike perform the duties of striking union members who were drivers.[162)]

Case #2: The prohibition of replacement labor during industrial actions is a rule that restricts hiring or replacing workers unrelated to the business for the performance of work halted by the union's actions. Therefore, using non-union workers from within the same business, including headquarters and technical departments, for replacement labor in operations halted due to industrial actions is permitted.[163)]

(5) Effects of an unlawful lockout

If an employer's lockout is unjustifiable, workers entering the workplace where they are usually allowed does not constitute trespassing, unless there are special circumstances otherwise.[164)] Additionally, while an employer is not obligated to pay wages if the workplace is legally closed in response to union industrial actions (such as strikes or work slowdowns), if a preemptive or aggressive lockout is taken to suspend work, the employer must pay wages (suspension allowance).[165)]

Case #1: A lockout initiated abruptly after three days of legal action is not a passive or defensive measure taken out of necessity. Therefore, the company's lockout lacks justification, and the employer is not exempt from the obligation to pay wages during the lockout period.[166)]

Case #2: If an employer's lockout is not recognized as a legitimate industrial action, workers who refuse to vacate the parts of the workplace they have occupied as part of a lawful industrial action, even if the employer has initiated a lockout, are not committing

---

162) MOEL Guidelines, Sept. 14, 1999, Cooperation 68140-14.

163) MOEL Guidelines, May 13, 2010, LaborDept-383.

164) Supreme Court ruling on Sep. 24, 2002, Case No. 2002do2243.

165) MOEL Guidelines, Oct. 30, 1969 Kijoon 1455.9-11349.

166) Supreme Court ruling on May 26, 2000, Case No. 98da34331.

로, 사용자는 직장폐쇄 기간 중에도 비조합원 등 직장폐쇄 대상이 아닌 근로자를 이용하여 조업을 계속할 수 있다.

사례 #1: 부분적 직장폐쇄의 경우에는 사용자가 쟁의행위에 참가하지 아니한 근로자의 근로 제공을 수령하여 조업을 계속할 수 있는 조업계속의 자유를 갖고 있다. 파업에 참가한 조합원이 운행하던 차량에 대하여 사용자가 파업불참 비조합원으로 하여금 대체승무 운행토록 하는 행위가 대체금지 규정에 위반된다고 볼 수는 없다.[162)]

사례 #2: 쟁의행위 중 대체근로 금지 규정은 노동조합의 중단된 업무의 수행을 위해 당해 사업과 관계없는 근로자의 채용 또는 대체를 제한하는 규정이다. 따라서 쟁의행위로 중단된 업무에 당해 사업내의 본사 및 각 기술단의 비조합원 근로자를 대상으로 한 대체근로는 허용된다.[163)]

(5) 위법한 직장폐쇄의 효과

사용자의 직장폐쇄가 정당하지 못하다면 다른 특별한 사정이 없는 한 근로자가 평소 출입이 허용되던 사업장 안에 들어가는 것이 주거침입죄에 해당되지 않는다.[164)] 또한 노조의 쟁의행위(파업·태업)에 대항하여 적법하게 직장을 폐쇄한 경우에는 사용자는 임금지불의 의무가 없으나 선제적·공격적 직장폐쇄시에는 휴업으로 보아 사용자는 임금(휴업수당)을 지급하여야 한다.[165)]

사례#1: 준법투쟁 3일만에 전격적으로 단행한 직장폐쇄는 수동적·방어적인 수단으로서 부득이하게 개시된 것이라고 보기 어려우므로, 결국 회사의 직장폐쇄는 정당성을 결여하였다 할 것이고, 따라서 직장폐쇄기간 동안의 임금지급 의무를 면할 수 없다.[166)]

사례#2: 사용자의 직장폐쇄가 정당한 쟁의행위로 인정되지 아니한 때에는 적법한 쟁의행위로서 사업장을 점거중인 근로자들이 직장폐쇄를 단행한 사용자로부터 퇴거요구를 받고도 이에 불응한 채 직장 점거를 계속하더라도 퇴거불응

162) 행정해석 1999.9.14. 협력 68140-14
163) 행정해석 2010.5.13. 노사관계법제과-836
164) 대법판례 2002.9.24, 2002도2243
165) 행정해석 1969.10.30, 기준 1455.9-11349
166) 대법원 2000.5.26. 선고 98다34331 판결

any crime in refusing to vacate those premises.[167)]

Case #3: Even when an employer's lockout is considered a legitimate industrial action, access to facilities necessary for normal union activities within the workplace, such as union offices, and basic living facilities like dormitories, shall be allowed. However, considering the nature of the dispute, lockout, and subsequent developments, if the union uses the union office itself as a location for dispute, or if the office and production facilities are inseparably located or structured such that the union's access and potential occupation of production facilities are reasonably foreseeable, and the employer provides an alternative location for the union office that is recognized as a reasonable alternative for normal union activities as the original location, it is permissible to restrict access to the union office within reasonable limits.[168)]

5. Reporting

When conducting a lockout, employers must report in advance to the administrative authorities and the Labor Commission. However, the reporting of a lockout is not a requirement for its validity but a procedural requirement, demanded by administrative necessity. Therefore, failure to report does not invalidate the lockout.

Employers are required to report the lockout to both the competent administrative authorities and the Labor Commission. The competent administrative authority is the administrative agency that handles union establishment reports, i.e., it is the same as the entity that has jurisdiction over the main office of the labor union. The Labor Commission refers to the branch of the Labor Commission with jurisdiction over the area where the lockout occurs. If the report of a lockout is filed with the competent administrative authority, a local government entity, this local government must send a copy of the lockout report to the local employment and labor office that oversees the jurisdiction of the main office of the labor union involved in the lockout. Administrative authorities, upon a lockout being conducted without prior reporting, must immediately order corrective actions and may impose a fine for non-compliance.[169)]

167) Supreme Court ruling on Dec. 28, 2007, Case No. 2007du5204; Supreme Court ruling on Mar. 29, 2007, Case No. 2006du9307.

168) Supreme Court ruling on June 10, 2010, Case No. 2009do12180.

169) Enforcement Decree to the TULRAA, Article 12-3; TULRAA Article 96 (Penalty fine).

죄가 성립하지 아니한다.[167)]

사례#3: 사용자의 직장폐쇄가 정당한 쟁의행위로 평가받는 경우에도 사업장 내의 노조사무실 등 정상적인 노조활동에 필요한 시설, 기숙사 등 기본적인 생활근거지에 대한 출입은 허용되어야 한다. 다만 쟁의 및 직장폐쇄와 그 후의 상황전개에 비추어 노조가 노조사무실 자체를 쟁의장소로 활용하는 하거나, 사무실과 생산시설이 장소적, 구조적으로 분리될 수 없는 관계에 있어 생산 시설에 대한 노조의 접근 및 점거가능성이 합리적으로 예상되고, 사용자가 노조의 생산시설에 대한 접근, 점거 등의 우려에서 노조사무실 대체 장소를 제공하고 그것이 원래 장소에서의 정상적인 노조활동과 견주어 합리적 대안으로 인정된다면, 합리적인 범위 내에서 노조사무실의 출입을 제한할 수 있다.[168)]

5. 신고

사용자는 직장폐쇄를 할 경우에는 행정관청과 노동위원회에 미리 신고해야 한다. 그러나 직장폐쇄에 있어서 그 신고는 효력요건이 아니라 절차적 요건이므로 행정상의 필요에 의해 요구된 것이라 할 수 있다. 따라서 그 신고를 하지 않았다고 하여 직장폐쇄가 효력이 없는 것은 아니다.

사용자는 직장폐쇄를 할 경우 관할 행정관청 및 노동위원회에 각각 그 사실을 신고해야 한다. 관할 행정관청은 노조설립신고를 처리하는 행정기관 즉, 노동조합의 주된 사무소 소재지 관할과 동일하며 노동위원회는 직장폐쇄 발생지에 소재한 노동위원회를 의미한다. 지방자치 단체인 관할 행정관청에 직장폐쇄 신고가 접수된 경우 지방자치단체는 직장폐쇄 신고서 사본을 직장폐쇄 당사자인 노동조합의 주된 사무소 소재지를 관할하는 지방고용노동지청에 송부하여야 한다. 행정관청은 사전신고 없이 직장 폐쇄를 한 경우 즉시 시정토록 지시하고 이행하지 않을 시 과태료 부과한다.[169)]

167) 대법원 2007.12.28. 선고 2007도5204; 대법원 2007.3.29. 선고 2006도9307 판결

168) 대법원 2010.6.10. 선고 2009도12180 판결

169) 노조법 시행규칙 제12조의3, 노조법 제96조(과태료)

6. Lifting the Lockout

When a labor union withdraws its strike, the employer must lift the lockout. If the labor union stops its ongoing industrial actions and clearly expresses its intention to return to work, the employer must withdraw the lockout. If workers genuinely express their intention to return to work but the employer continues the lockout, the lockout loses its justification. In this case, the employer will not be exempt from the obligation to pay wages for period after the related strike is lifted.[170)]

Since the labor union's industrial action is both a condition for initiating and maintaining a lockout, if the union's intention to return to work is genuine and there is objectively no urgency to continue the lockout, the employer must stop the lockout. However, if there is a high likelihood of the labor union resuming industrial actions and the intention to return to work isn't considered genuine, maintaining the lockout is not deemed unlawful.[171)]

Case #1: After a temporary strike ended, the labor union immediately expressed its intention to return to normal duties. Despite reaching an agreement on the dispute's issues right after the lockout, the employer continued the lockout and sent individual withdrawal forms to union members. In this case, the lockout lacked urgency, necessity, and reasonableness, and seemed more aggressive than defensive against the labor union's industrial actions.[172)]

Case #2: If workers cease their industrial actions and genuinely express their intention to return to work, but the employer continues the lockout, the lockout transitions from being a defensive measure to an aggressive one aimed at weakening the labor union's organizational strength. In such cases, the lockout loses justification, and the employer is obligated to pay wages for the period beginning immediately upon the lockout losing its justification.[173)]

---

170) Supreme Court ruling on May 24, 2016, Case No. 2012da85335.

171) MOEL Guidelines, Oct. 30, 1998, Cooperation 68140-409.

172) Daejeon High Court ruling on Dec. 19, 1995, Case No. 95na1697.

173) Supreme Court ruling on May 24, 2016, Case No. 2012da85335.

6. 해제

사용자는 노동조합이 파업을 철회하면 사용자도 직장폐쇄를 해제하여야 한다. 노동조합이 진행 중인 쟁의행위를 중단하고 조업복귀 의사를 명백히 한 경우에는 사용자는 직장폐쇄를 철회하여야 한다. 근로자가 진정으로 업무 복귀 의사를 표시하였음에도 사용자가 직장폐쇄를 지속하면 그 직장폐쇄는 정당성을 상실한다. 이 경우 사용자는 그 기간 동안의 임금지불의무를 면할 수 없다.[170)]

노동조합의 쟁의행위는 직장폐쇄의 개시요건임과 동시에 존속요건이므로 노조의 직장복귀의사가 명백한 진의이고, 달리 직장폐쇄를 지속할 긴급성이 없음이 객관적으로 인정될 경우에는 사용자는 직장폐쇄를 중단하여야 한다. 그러나 노동조합이 쟁의행위를 재개할 가능성이 크고, 직장복귀 의사가 진정한 의사라고 볼 수 없을 때에 사용자가 직장폐쇄를 지속하더라도 위법한 직장폐쇄라고 할 수 없다.[171)]

사례#1: 노동조합이 시한부 파업종료 후 곧바로 정상업무로 복귀하겠다고 의사를 표시하였다. 직장폐쇄 이후 곧바로 쟁의행위의 쟁점에 관한 합의가 있었음에도 사용자는 직장폐쇄를 계속하였고 노동조합의 조합원들에게 개별적으로 조합탈퇴를 위한 탈퇴서를 송부하였다. 이 경우, 위 직장폐쇄는 노동조합의 쟁의행위에 대항하여 방어적으로 이루어진 것이라기보다는 오히려 공격적인 것으로서 직장폐쇄로서의 긴급성과 필요성 및 상당성이 결여되었다.[172)]

사례#2: 근로자가 쟁의행위를 중단하고 진정으로 업무에 복귀할 의사를 표시하였음에도 사용자가 직장 폐쇄를 계속 유지한다면, 근로자의 쟁의행위에 대한 방어적인 목적에서 벗어나 적극적으로 노동 조합의 조직력을 약화시키기 위한 목적 등을 갖는 공격적 직장폐쇄의 성격으로 변질된 것이다. 이 경우에는 직장폐쇄는 정당성을 상실된 것이고 사용자는 그 기간 동안의 임금지불의무를 면할 수 없다.[173)]

---

170) 대법원 2016.5.24. 선고 2012다 85335 판결
171) 행정해석: 1998.10.30, 협력 68140-409
172) 대전고등법원 1995.12.19. 선고 95나1697 판결
173) 대법원 2016.5.24. 선고 2012다85335 판결

Section 2: Protection of Industrial Actions

Ⅰ. Justification for Industrial Action

A labor union may take industrial action as the means of gaining a strong position at the bargaining table, and shall be exempt from any civil or criminal liability if it is taken in a legitimate manner. The requirements for legitimacy of an industrial action are: it shall be taken by a legitimate labor union; its purpose shall be to maintain or improve working conditions of the employees and promote their social and economic status; and it shall follow the procedures stipulated in law.

> An employee can be exempt from penalties only when the industrial actions are legal. Legal requirements for such exemption from penalties shall be the following: Firstly, the subject shall be the person who is subject to collective bargaining. Secondly, the purpose of the action must be to cultivate negotiations between labor and management in order to improve working conditions. Thirdly, industrial actions must be taken only when the employer rejects collective bargaining requests to resolve employee demands for improved working conditions. In these cases, as preceding conditions, the labor union shall engage in a yes/no voting process and report the occurrence of any industrial action unless there is a special reason not to do so. And fourthly, the ways and methods shall be in harmony with the employer's property rights and shall not involve any violent behavior.[174)]

1. Substantial requirements

(1) Justification of subjects

The parties engaged in industrial action shall be the parties to collective bargaining. Thus, a legitimate labor union shall represent the employee side. Industrial actions are legitimate only when they are taken by the labor union as a whole. That is, if some union members begin an industrial action, regardless of the position of the union, such industrial action will not be regarded as legitimate. A branch or chapter of a labor union is a lower organization of a labor union and therefore, cannot serve as a counterpart to management in collective bargaining or agreement, or industrial action within the range of authorities

174) Supreme Court ruling on May 24, 1991 91Do324

제2절 쟁의행위의 보호

Ⅰ. 쟁의행위 정당성

노동조합은 단체교섭을 유리하게 진행하여 그 주장을 관철시키기 위한 수단으로 쟁의행위를 할 수 있으며, 정당하게 수행할 경우 그로 인한 형사상·민사상 책임을 면제받을 수 있다. 쟁의행위는 첫째, 적법한 노동조합이 수행하여야 하고, 둘째, 목적이 근로조건의 유지·개선 기타 근로자의 경제적·사회적 지위의 향상을 도모하는 것이어야 하며, 셋째, 법에 정하여진 절차를 거쳐야 정당성을 인정받을 수 있다.

> 근로자의 쟁의행위는 그것이 정당할 때에 한하여 형법상 위법성이 부정되어 처벌되지 아니한다. 쟁의행위의 정당성은 첫째, 그 주체가 단체교섭의 주체로 될 수 있는 자이어야 하고 둘째, 그 목적이 근로조건의 향상을 위한 노사 간의 자치적 교섭을 조성하는 데에 있어야 하며 셋째, 사용자가 근로자의 근로조건 개선에 관한 구체적인 요구에 대하여 단체교섭을 거부하였을 때 개시하되 특별한 사정이 없는 한 조합원의 찬성결정 및 노동쟁의 발생신고를 거쳐야 하는 한편 넷째, 그 수단과 방법이 사용자의 재산권과 조화를 이루어야 할 것은 물론 폭력의 행사에 해당하지 아니하여야 한다는 여러 조건을 모두 구비하여야 비로소 인정될 수 있다.[174)]

1. 쟁의행위 정당성의 실질적 요건

(1) 주체의 정당성

쟁의행위의 당사자는 단체교섭의 당사자가 될 수 있어야 한다. 따라서 근로자 측 으로는 적법한 노동조합이 당사자가 된다. 쟁의행위는 노동조합의 의사에 의하여 행하여져야 하며 조합원의 일부가 노동조합의 의사와 관계없이 독자적으로 행하는 쟁의행위는 정당성을 확보할 수 없다. 노동조합의 지부, 분회 등은 노동조합의 하부조직에 불과하므로 단체교섭 및 쟁의행위의 주체가 될 수 없다. 다만, 노동조합 규약 등에 의하여 위임된 권한 범위 내에서 쟁의행위의

---

174) 대법원 1991.5.24, 91도324.

commissioned to them by the labor union rules.

1) Those engaged in industrial actions shall be those persons who are capable of conducting collective bargaining and signing collective bargaining agreements.[175)]

2) Industrial actions are legal only when they are authorized by an established labor union in accordance with the regulations of the Trade Union Act. However, industrial actions are not legal if they are conducted by a group of employees not yet established as a labor union. Industrial actions are designed to accomplish their claims concerning working conditions by executing collective bargaining agreements. Industrial actions by persons not subject to collective bargaining(e.g., a temporary body for industrial actions) cannot be engaged in order to provide assistance in the settlement of industrial disputes. Accordingly, it is necessary to prevent any irresponsible industrial actions by such groups.[176)]

3) Strikes conducted by a small group of labor union members without the labor union's approval or against the majority of union members, which is designated a wildcat strike, will not be considered legal because the strike was taken by persons not subject to collective bargaining(e.g., a temporary body for industrial actions).[177)]

4) An individual employee or a temporary body for industrial actions cannot be a party to the collective agreement. An industrial action is a last resort on which a union can rely in order to ensure favorable working conditions in negotiating a collective agreement. Accordingly, an industrial action is permitted only when it is aimed at a matter that is subject to collective bargaining and is taken by a party to collective bargaining and agreement.[178)]

5) It is not justifiable for some union members to begin an industrial action without the approval of the union or against its instructions. At least under the labor laws currently in force, an industrial action is justifiable and its participants immune to criminal liability only when the action is taken by a labor union that is entitled to conduct collective bargaining or reach a collective agreement. If some union members begin an industrial

---

175) Supreme Court ruling on June 25, 1999, 99Da8377.

176) Supreme Court ruling on June 25, 1999, 99Da8377.

177) Supreme Court ruling on Apr. 22, 1997, 95Do748.

178) Constitution Court ruling on Jan. 15, 1990, 89HeonGa103.

주체가 될 수 있다.

1) 그 주체가 단체교섭이나 단체협약체결능력이 있는 자이어야 한다.[175)]

2) 쟁의행위는 적어도 노조법의 규정에 따른 노동조합으로서 실질적 요건을 갖춘 '노동조합'이 주체일 경우에 한하여 정당하고 그러한 노동조합이 아닌 근로자집단에 의한 쟁의행위는 정당성이 인정되지 않는다. 쟁의행위는 궁극적으로 단체교섭을 통한 단체협약을 체결함에 있어서 근로조건에 관한 주장을 관철하기 위한 것이므로 단체교섭이나 단체협약을 체결할 능력이 없는 자 (예: 일시적인 쟁의집단)의 쟁의행위는 노동쟁의의 해결에 도움을 주지 않고, 따라서 그러한 자들에 의한 무책임한 쟁의행위의 남용을 방지할 필요가 있기 때문이다.[176)]

3) 노동조합의 일부 조합원이 조합의 승인 없이 또는 조합원 전체의 의사에 반하여 행하는 파업[흔히 '살쾡이파업(wildcat strike)'이라 부른다] 역시 일시적인 쟁의단의 쟁의행위와 마찬가지로 단체교섭 또는 단체협약의 체결능력이 없는 자들에 의한 파업이므로 정당성을 인정받을 수 없다.[177)]

4) 단체협약의 당사자로서 쟁의단, 근로자 개인 등은 당사자가 될 수 없다. 쟁의행위는 노동관계 당사자가 임금 및 근로조건 등을 정하는 단체협약을 체결함에 있어 보다 유리한 결과를 자신에게 가져오게 하기 위하여 행사하는 최후의 강제수단이다. 따라서 쟁의행위는 주로 단체협약의 대상이 될 수 있는 사항을 목적으로 하는 경우에만 허용되는 것이고, 단체협약의 당사자가 될 수 있는 자에 의하여서만 이루어져야 하는 것이다[178)]

5) 일부 조합원 집단이 노동조합의 승인 없이 또는 그 지시에 반하여 쟁의행위를 하는 것은 정당하지 않다. 현행법상 적어도 노동조합이 결성된 사업장에 있어서의 쟁의행위가 형사상 책임이 면제되는 정당행위가 되기 위하여서는 반드시 그 쟁의행위의 주체가 단체교섭이나 단체협약을 체결할 능력이 있는 노동조합일 것이 요구되고, 일부 조합원의 집단이 노동조합의 승인 없이 또는 그 지

175) 대법원1999.6.25, 99다8377.

176) 대법원 1999.6.25, 99다8377.

177) 대법원 1997.4.22, 95도748.

178) 헌법재판소 1990.1.15, 89헌가103.

action without the approval of the union or against its instructions, the action is neither justifiable nor immune to criminal liabilities.[179)]

(2) Justification of purpose

Industrial actions are behaviors through which the parties involved in the labor relationship intend to accomplish their means(Article 2, subparagraph 6, of the Trade Union Act), concerning employment conditions such as wages, working hours, welfare, dismissal, and other issues(Article 2, subparagraph 5, of the same Act). In general, political strikes or sympathy strikes are not legitimate.

1) The purpose of industrial actions shall be to cultivate autonomous negotiations between labor and management to improve working conditions. That is, the labor union's demand shall be a matter pertaining to a collective agreement that it expects to accomplish through the industrial actions.[180)]

2) Industrial actions shall be undertaken to cultivate autonomous negotiations between labor and management. Industrial actions are actions designed to accomplish a party's claims when there is disagreement between two parties with respect to working conditions and the claims of parties described here shall include any matters pertaining to individual and collective labor relations. They shall not only include claims described in the collective agreement or labor agreement but will include claims for the establishment of additional rules and/or amendments to those agreements. Accordingly, they shall include all claims with respect to the determination of conditions of employment such as wages, working hours, welfare, dismissal, and other issues, but shall not be limited to wages or improving and maintaining workers' economic status.[181)]

3) If an industrial action is taken for several reasons, some of which are unjustified, the main purpose of the industrial action shall be examined in order to determine whether the action is justified or not. If it is estimated that the labor union would not risk taking industrial action if the unfair demand was absent from its purposes, the entire industrial action cannot be justified.[182)]

---

179) Supreme Court ruling on Oct. 12, 1995, 95Do1016.

180) Supreme Court ruling on June 25,1999, 99Da8377.

181) Supreme Court ruling on Mar. 25, 1994, 93Da30342.

182) Supreme Court ruling on Jan. 21, 1992, 91Nu5204.

시에 반하여 쟁의행위를 하는 경우에는 형사상 책임이 면제될 수 없어 일부 조합원의 집단은 쟁의행위 주체가 될 수 없다.[179)]

(2) 목적의 정당성

쟁의행위는 노조법 제2조 제6호의 규정에 따라 노동관계 당사자가 자기의 주장을 관철할 목적으로 행하는 행위인데, 이 주장은 같은 법 제2조 제5호의 규정에 따라 임금·근로시간·복지·기타 근로조건의 결정에 관한 주장인 것이다. 정치파업과 동정파업은 일반적으로 정당성이 인정되지 않는다.

1) 그 목적이 근로조건의 향상을 위한 노사 간의 자치적 교섭을 조성하기 위한 것, 즉 그 쟁의행위에 의하여 달성하려는 요구사항이 단체교섭 사항이 될 수 있는 것이어야 한다.[180)]

2) 쟁의행위는 노사의 자치적 교섭을 조성하기 위한 목적에 적합하여야 한다. 쟁의행위는 근로조건에 관한 노동관계 당사자 간의 주장의 불일치가 있을 때, 그 주장을 관철하기 위한 목적으로 행하는 행위이고, 여기서 말하는 노사관계 당사자의 주장은 개별적 노동관계와 집단적 노동관계의 어느 것에 관한 주장이라도 포함되는 것이고, 단체협약이나 근로계약상 권리의 주장뿐만 아니라 그것들에 관한 새로운 합의의 형성을 꾀하기 위한 주장도 포함되며, 따라서 노조법 제2조 제5호 소정의 임금, 근로시간, 후생, 해고 기타 대우 등 근로조건에 관한 주장 모두를 포괄하고, 반드시 임금 등 근로자의 경제적 지위의 유지, 향상에 국한되는 것은 아니다.[181)]

3) 하나의 쟁의행위에서 추구하는 목적이 여러 가지이고 그중 일부가 정당하지 못한 경우에는 '주된 목적' 내지 '진정한 목적'의 당부에 의하여 그 쟁의행위의 정당성 여부를 판단하여야 하고, 부당한 요구사항을 뺐더라면 쟁의행위를 하지 않았을 것이라고 인정되는 경우에는 그 쟁의행위 전체가 정당성을 갖지 못한다.[182)]

---

179) 대법원 1995.10.12, 95도1016.
180) 대법원 1999.6.25, 99다8377.
181) 대법원 1994.3.25, 93나30242.
182) 대법원 1992.1.21, 91누5204.

4) As long as the reason for the industrial action is not justifiable, even though the labor union has engaged in the prescribed mediation process required by the Trade Union Act before the industrial action commenced and/or there have been no legal violations in the ways and methods of the action, the action cannot be considered justifiable actions.[183)]

5) It is not justifiable to begin industrial action in protest of dismissals(massive lay-offs) for managerial reasons or integration or abolition of business departments as part of a restructuring process. A decision to dismiss employees for managerial reasons or remove or reduce business departments for restructuring purposes is exclusively up to the employer and, in principle, such decisions are not subject to collective bargaining. Unless the employer intends to carry out the restructuring process for an unfair reason(other than urgent business purposes, etc.), no industrial action taken by the union to protest the restructuring is justifiable, even though the action is aimed at improving working conditions and the status of the employees.[184)]

6) When an industrial action is taken to protest dismissal for managerial reasons, such action cannot be justified. A certain industrial action was begun to block a restructuring process, including massive lay-offs to be done for economic reasons. This was a clear infringement on the employer's prerogatives in business management. There was no evidence that the restructuring was being carried out for unjustifiable reasons. Given this, the industrial action was not justifiable.[185)]

7) It is not justifiable to begin industrial action in order to get compensation for something, even when the compensation is not one of the issues subject to collective bargaining. In a certain case, a business transfer was the result of the employer's decision to change the structure of the business. In addition, as the proceeds from the transfer did not come from business activities, the decisions on use of the proceeds may not be negotiated at a bargaining table. Nevertheless, the union, under the leadership of some union officials, demanded compensation and resorted to industrial actions with a view to having its demand met. When all things were considered, the industrial actions were not

---

183) Supreme Court ruling on Apr. 24, 2001, 99Do4893.

184) Supreme Court ruling on Feb. 26, 2002, 99Do5380.

185) Supreme Court ruling on Feb. 11, 2003, 2000Do4169.

4) 쟁의행위의 목적이 정당하지 않은 이상 설사 쟁의행위에 이르기 전에 노조법의 소정의 조정절차를 거쳤다거나 쟁의행위 수단과 방법에 있어 어떠한 위법이 없었다 하더라도 그것만으로 이 사건 쟁의행위가 정당하게 되는 것은 아니므로, 이에 관하여 더 나아가 살펴볼 필요 없이 이 사건 쟁의행위는 정당성 없는 위법한 행위임을 면하지 못한다 할 것이다.[183)]

5) 정리해고나 사업조직의 통폐합 등 기업의 구조조정 실시 자체에 반대하는 쟁의행위는 정당하지 않다.

정리해고나 사업조직의 통폐합 등 기업의 구조조정의 실시 여부는 경영주체에 의한 고도의 경영상 결단에 속하는 사항으로서 이는 원칙적으로 단체교섭의 대상이 될 수 없고, 그것이 긴박한 경영상의 필요나 합리적인 이유 없이 불순한 의도로 추진되는 등의 특별한 사정이 없는 한, 노동조합이 실질적으로 그 실시 자체를 반대하기 위하여 쟁의행위를 행하여 근로자들의 지위나 근로조건의 변경이 필연적으로 수반된다 하더라도 그 쟁의행위는 목적의 정당성을 인정할 수 없다 할 것이다.[184)]

6) 정리해고 자체를 반대하는 쟁의행위는 쟁의행위로서 정당하지 않다. 쟁의행위가 정리해고 등 구조조정의 실시 자체를 저지하기 위한 것으로서 사용자의 경영권을 본질적으로 침해하는 내용에 해당함을 알 수 있고, 정리해고 등 구조조정 방침이 긴박한 경영상의 필요나 합리적 이유 없이 결정되었다고 볼 만한 아무런 자료도 없으므로, 특별한 사정이 없는 한 쟁의행위는 그 목적의 정당성을 인정할 수 없다.[185)]

7) 단체교섭 사항이 아닌 보상금 지급을 관철시킬 목적의 쟁의행위는 정당하지 않다. 영업양도는 회사의 구조조정을 위해 취해진 조치로서 경영 주체의 경영의사 결정에 의한 경영조직 변경에 해당하고 그 양도대금 또한 영업활동을 통한 수익으로 볼 수 없어 그 귀속 내지 사용에 관한 결정 자체는 단체교섭 사항이 될 수 없다. 따라서 노동조합이 피고인들의 주도하에 단체교섭 사항이 될 수 없는 보상금 지급을 요구하며 이를 관철시킬 목적으로 쟁의행위를 한 것으

183) 대법원 2001.4.24, 99도4893.
184) 대법원 2002.2.26, 99도5380.
185) 대법원 2003.2.11, 2000도4169.

justifiable.[186)]

(3) Justification of methods

According to Article 4 of the Trade Union Act, a labor union's collective bargaining or other collective activities are admitted as industrial actions that are exempt from criminal liability, but it also regulates that acts of violence or destruction shall not be construed as justifiable for any reason. Article 42 of the Act also states that industrial actions shall not be conducted with violence or destruction.

Any industrial action which suspends, closes, or hampers normal functioning of safety facilities(emergency rooms and intensive care units of hospitals, gas explosion prevention facilities, etc.) shall be deemed illegitimate. Therefore, a labor union shall ensure that a minimal number of employees required for normal functioning of those safety facilities are at work, even while the union is in the course of industrial action.

1) Industrial actions shall be to partially or totally prevent the provision of labor services by negative methods to damage the employer's business. Industrial actions shall be implemented fairly through a principle of faith and sincerity, be in harmony with the employer's property rights regarding the corporate facilities, and shall not be accompanied by violence or destruction.[187)]

2) In a certain case, the plaintiff held a labor union meeting during working hours without the employer's approval and conducted union activities using a high performance megaphone inside company facilities. He led the labor union to collectively refuse to provide labor services, which was characteristic of an industrial action, without appropriate procedures such as holding a union assembly or engaging in an adjustment process for labor disputes. He blocked the entrance gate, which disturbed the company's normal operations. Furthermore, he used force to occupy the president's office for a considerable period of time and, in this process, used violence toward managerial employees. He humiliated the company's labor managers and distributed printed handouts containing defamatory untruths them. Even though the plaintiff insisted that the purpose of the union activities was to ensure the health and safety of the union members, such

---

186) Supreme Court ruling on May 8, 2001, 99Do4659.

187) Supreme Court ruling on June 25, 1999, 99Da8377.

로 이는 목적에 있어 정당하지 않다.[186)]

(3) 수단의 정당성

노조법 제4조에서 노동조합의 단체교섭 기타의 단체행동을 형사상 책임을 면할 수 있는 정당행위로서 인정하되 그것은 "정당한 행위에 대하여 적용되고 어떠한 경우에도 폭력이나 파괴행위는 정당한 행위로 해석되어서는 아니 된다"라고 규정하고 있으며, 같은 법 제42조에서는 "쟁의행위는 폭력이나 파괴행위로써 이를 행할 수 없다"라고 규정하고 있는 것도 이러한 취지를 명시한 것이다.

안전보호시설(병원응급실·중환자실, 가스폭발방지시설 등)의 정상적인 유지·운영을 정지·폐지 또는 방해하는 행위는 정당성이 인정되지 않는다. 따라서 노동조합은 쟁의행위에 돌입하더라도 안전보호시설의 정상적인 운영에 필요한 인원은 작업에 종사시켜야 한다.

1) 그 방법은 소극적으로 노무의 제공을 전면적 또는 부분적으로 정지하여 사용자에게 타격을 주는 것이어야 하며, 노사관계의 신의성실의 원칙에 비추어 공정하게 이루어져야 하고, 사용자의 기업시설에 대한 소유권 기타의 재산권과 조화를 이루어야 함은 물론 폭력이나 파괴행위를 수반하여서는 안 된다.[187)]

2) 원고가 사용자의 승낙 등이 없이 근무시간 중에 노동조합의 회의를 개최하거나 사내에서 고성능 확성기를 사용한 집회를 하는 등 조합활동을 하였고, 총회나 조정절차 등 적법한 절차를 따를 수 없는 이해할 만한 사정이 없는 상태에서 이를 서치시 아니한 채 쟁의행위의 성격을 띠는 집단 노무제공 거부를 주도한 행위나 출입로를 봉쇄하는 등의 방법으로 참가인 회사의 업무를 방해하였으며, 더 나아가 강제로 참가인 회사의 사장실을 상당기간 무단 점거하였고, 그 과정에서 다른 노조지부의 간부들과 함께 참가인 회사의 관리직원들을 폭행하는 등 폭력이나 파괴행위를 수반하였으며, 참가인 회사의 노무관리담당인 등을 모욕하고 허위의 사실로 명예를 훼손하는 내용의 유인물을 배포한 이상, 원고가 수행한 위와 같은 조합활동의 목적이 원고의 주장대로 조합원의 건강과 작업장의 안전보건을 확보하기 위한 것이었다고 하더라도 이러한 형태의 조합

---

186) 대법원 2001.5.8, 99도4659.
187) 대법원 1999.6.25, 99다8377.

types of union activities cannot be seen as justifiable union activities or industrial actions and so they were considered illegal.[188)]

3) When a dismissed employee occupies a building of the company he once worked for, such action is not justifiable.

A dismissed employee, along with 570 other striking employees, stormed into the main building of the company he had worked for and, in doing so, forcefully pushed away about 400 employees who were trying to stop the striking employees from coming into the building. It does not seem that such an act of occupation was legitimate. Furthermore, the building occupation prevented about 600 employees from engaging in their work, which is not an unavoidable result of the strike. All considered, the dismissed employee committed the offenses of unlawful entry and obstruction of business.[189)]

(4) Justification of timing

Industrial actions are designed to make one party yield to the other's demands. Thus, if such demands are included in the contents of the existing collective agreement, it is not justifiable to make demands during the effective period of that agreement. If the labor union, while the collective agreement is still in effect, attempts industrial action by obstructing the normal operation of business, this violates the duty to maintain peace and shall not be justifiable unless the employer willingly accepts the union's demand to negotiate at that time.

The peace obligation is inherent in the collective agreement, whether or not it is explicitly included in that agreement. Under the peace obligation, neither party to the collective agreement may demand revision or repeal of the existing provisions in that agreement, or insertion of new provisions, while the agreement remains effective. Considering that the peace obligation is to ensure stability in the labor relationship and maintain the effectiveness of the collective agreement, any industrial actions which a union engages in to invalidate a collective agreement without providing a justifiable reason constitute a violation of the peace obligation and cannot be justified.[190)]

---

188) Seoul District Court ruling on Aug. 11, 2005, 2005Guhap9392.

189) Supreme Court ruling on June 12, 1990, 90Do672.

190) Supreme Court ruling on Sept. 1, 1992, 92Nu7733.

활동은 사회통념에 비추어 볼 때 그 행위의 성질상 정당한 노동조합의 활동 또는 쟁의행위의 일환으로 행해진 것으로 볼 수 없어 불법행위에 해당한다 할 것이다.[188)]

3) 해고근로자가 회사의 건물을 점거하는 행위는 정당하지 않다.

해고되어 회사의 근로자도 아닌 피고인이 시위 근로자 570명과 함께 회사건물 본관 앞까지 이동한 다음 무단점거를 저지하려는 관리직 사원 등 400여명을 힘으로 밀어붙이고 동 건물을 점거하였는데 이러한 집단행위가 적법한 쟁의행위도 아니었으며, 또한, 쟁의행위에 당연히 수반되는 행위라고는 할 수 없는 관리직 사원 600여명의 업무영역에 관하여 방해를 한 경우에 있어서 위 피고인의 행위는 건조물 침입죄 및 업무방해죄가 된다.[189)]

(4) 시기의 정당성

쟁의행위는 단체교섭에서 노사 간에 대립된 주장을 상대방이 수락하도록 하기 위한 목적에서 행하는 것이다. 따라서 이미 그러한 내용에 대하여 단체협약으로 정하여져 있는 경우에는 그 협약의 유효기간 동안은 그러한 주장을 하는 것도 부당하지만 그것을 평화적인 방법에 의하여 사용자가 받아들이는 것은 별개의 문제이고 그것을 받아들이도록 하기 위하여 업무의 정상적인 운영까지 저해하는 쟁의행위를 하는 것은 평화의무를 위반한 것으로서 정당하지 않은 것이다.

평화의무란 단체협약의 유효기간 중에는 협약사항의 개정 또는 폐시나 새로운 요구를 하지 않을 의무를 말하며, 단체협약에 명분으로 규정하지 않았다고 하더라도 단체협약의 평화유지기능에 내재하는 본래의 의무라 할 것이며, 평화의무가 노사관계의 안정과 단체협약의 질서 형성적 기능을 담보하는 것인 점에 비추어 볼 때, 보충협약이라는 명분으로 평화의무의 기본정신에 위배되는 쟁의행위를 하는 것은 노동조합 활동으로서의 정당성을 결여한 것이다.[190)]

188) 행정법원 2005.8.11, 2005구합9392.

189) 대법원 1990.6.12, 90도672.

190) 대법원 1992.9.1, 92누7733.

2. Procedural requirements

Industrial actions are legal only if they are in accordance with the timing requirements and procedures under the law. However, the purpose of the timing requirements and procedures for industrial action are to provide opportunities to avoid industrial actions by allowing preventive measures to be taken by the parties, to predict when industrial actions will be taken, and to allow them to take place.[191)]

Industrial actions must start after the employer refuses the labor union's attempts at reaching a collective agreement on substantial demands related to improving working conditions or when the employer rejects such demands during collective bargaining. As long as there are no special cases, industrial actions shall follow the appropriate procedures in accordance with the Trade Union Act: decision-making process by workers' secret and unsigned vote,[192)] preceding adjustment procedures,[193)] and reporting of the occurrence of an industrial action.[194) 195)]

(1) Voting by union members

Before the labor union conducts industrial action, it shall undertake a democratic decision-making process within the union. Thus, the labor union shall not conduct industrial actions unless decided on by a majority of union members by direct, secret, and unsigned ballot.[196)]

The legal provision requiring that an industrial action shall be brought to a vote by the union membership is intended to promote independent and democratic operation of the union and to ensure that the union is prudent enough in making any decision that might bring disadvantages to the union members involved. No industrial action that was taken without the requirement of voting being fulfilled can be justified, unless it is objectively established that there was an unavoidable reason to omit the required procedure.[197)]

---

191) Supreme Court ruling on Dec. 8, 1992, 92Do1645.

192) Article 41 (1).

193) Article 45 (2), Article 54, and Article 63.

194) Article 45 (1).

195) Supreme Court ruling on June 25, 1999, 99Da8377.

196) Article 41 ① of the Trade Union Act.

197) Supreme Court ruling on Oct. 25, 2001, 99Do4837 en banc.

2. 쟁의행위 정당성의 절차적 요건

쟁의행위는 원칙적으로 그 시기나 절차가 법령의 규정에 따라야만 정당하다고 할 수 있다. 그러나 쟁의행위의 시기나 절차에 관한 법령의 규정의 취지가 분쟁을 사전 조정하여 쟁의발생을 회피하는 기회를 주고, 또 쟁의발생을 사전 예고하게 하여 손해방지조치의 기회를 주려는 데에 있으며 쟁의행위 자체를 적극적으로 금지하려는 것이 아니다.[191)]

쟁의행위의 시기는 사용자가 근로자의 근로조건 개선에 관한 구체적인 요구에 대하여 단체교섭을 거부하거나 단체교섭의 자리에서 그러한 요구를 거부하는 회답을 했을 때 개시하되, 특별한 사정이 없는 한 그 '절차'가 법령의 규정에 따라 조합원의 비밀, 무기명투표에 의한 찬성결정[192)] 조정 전치[193)] 및 노동쟁의 발생통보[194)] 등을 거쳐야 한다.[195)]

(1) 조합원의 찬반투표

쟁의행위는 조합원의 민주적 의사결정을 거쳐야 한다. 즉, 조합원의 직접·비밀·무기명투표에 의한 조합원의 과반수의 찬성으로 결정하지 아니하면 쟁의행위를 할 수 없다.[196)]

조합원의 직접·비밀·무기명투표에 의한 찬성 결정이라는 절차를 거쳐야 한다는 법규정은 노동조합의 자주적이고 민주적인 운영을 도모함과 아울러 쟁의행위에 참가한 근로자들이 사후에 그 쟁의행위의 정당성 유무와 관련하여 어떠한 불이익을 당하지 않도록 그 개시에 관한 조합의사의 결정에 보다 신중을 기하기 위하여 마련된 규정이므로 위의 절차를 위반한 쟁의행위는 그 절차를 따를 수 없는 객관적인 사정이 인정되지 아니하는 한 정당성을 인정받을 수 없다.[197)]

---

191) 대법원 1992.12.8, 92도1645.
192) 노조법 제41조 제1항.
193) 노조법 제45조 제2항, 제54조, 제63조.
194) 노조법 제45조 제1항.
195) 대법원 1999.6.25, 99다8377.
196) 노조법 제41조 제1항.
197) 대법원 2001.10.25, 99도4837 전원합의체 판결.

(2) Adjustment of labor disputes[198]

Adjustment of labor disputes refers to a process intended to help resolve disagreements between the parties to collective bargaining. Mediation means that a mediator, who is a third party, gives a proposal to solve the labor dispute, which the parties to the labor dispute concerned shall review. However, the parties are not bound to accept the proposal. Arbitration means that an arbitrator, who is also a third party, gives a proposal to solve the labor dispute, which the parties to the dispute concerned shall accept to reach an agreement.

1) Mediation

Upon initiating a labor dispute, one party to the dispute shall notify the other party of it in writing. No industrial action shall be permitted without completing adjustment procedures of mediation. This shall not apply in cases where adjustment procedures are not completed within an established period of time, or where arbitration is not made within an established period of time.

According to Article 54 of the Trade Union Act, mediation shall be completed within ten days for general businesses, or within fifteen days for public services, after a request for mediation. The period of mediation may be extended up to no more than ten days for general businesses, and no more than fifteen days for public services.

The mediation committee within the competent Labor Relations Commission shall mediate the labor dispute brought before it. The mediation committee is made up of three commissioners of the Commission: one representing the employer, one the labor force, and one the public interest. The mediation committee or the single mediator shall hear the opinions of both parties to the labor dispute and make fact-finding investigations to map out a mediator's proposal, and shall recommend that both parties to accept it.

If the mediator's proposal is accepted by both parties, it shall have the same effect as a collective agreement. If the mediator's proposal is not accepted by both parties, the mediation committee shall notify the parties that the mediation procedure is ended. Then, arbitration shall commence if the parties have agreed on that. If there is no such agreement, the parties may take industrial action.

---

198) Refer to Chapter 17: The Labor Relations Commission for more information.

(2) 노동쟁의의 조정[198)]

노동쟁의의 조정(adjustment)이란 당사자 간의 단체교섭상의 주장의 불일치를 해결하도록 도와주는 것이다. 조정(mediation)은 제3자인 조정자가 분쟁의 당사자인 노사 양측에게 분쟁에 대한 해결안을 제시하고 당사자가 이를 검토하여 합의에 이르게 하는 것을 말하나, 당사자는 반드시 해결안에 구속될 필요는 없다. 중재(arbitration)는 중재인이 양 당사자의 분쟁에 대한 중재안을 제시하고 당사는 이 중재안에 구속되어 합의에 이르러야 하는 것을 말한다.

1) 조정(Mediation)

노동관계 당사자는 노동쟁의가 발생한 때는 어느 일방이 이를 상대방에게 서면으로 통보하여야 하며 쟁의행위는 조정 또는 중재절차를 거치지 아니하면 이를 행할 수 없다. 다만, 조정기간 내에 조정이 종료되지 아니하거나 중재 시의 쟁의행위 금지기간 내에 중재재정이 이루어지지 아니한 경우에는 그러하지 아니하다.

노조법 제54조에 의하면 조정은 조정의 신청이 있는 날부터 일반 사업에 있어서 10일, 공익사업에 있어서는 15일 이내에 종료하여야 하며 당사자 간의 합의로 일반사업에 있어서는 10일, 공익사업에 있어서는 15일 이내에서 연장할 수 있으며 조정기간은 노동위원회에 조정신청이 있는 날부터 기산한다.

관할 노동위원회에 설치된 조정위원회가 노동분쟁의 조정을 담당하며, 노동위원회의 위원 중에서 각각 사용자를 대표하는 자, 근로자를 대표하는 자, 공익을 대표하는 자 등 3인의 조정위원으로 구성된다. 조정위원회 또는 단독조정인은 노사 당사자의 의견 청취 및 조사 후 조정안을 작성하여 양 당사자에게 수락을 권고한다.

쌍방에 의해 수락된 조정안은 단체협약과 동일한 효력을 갖게 된다. 조정안이 수락되지 않는 경우에는 조정위원회는 조정의 종료를 쌍방에게 통보하고, 노사 당사자는 중재하기로 합의된 경우에는 중재절차를 개시하고, 이러한 합의가 없는 경우에는 노동조합은 쟁의행위를 할 수 있다.

---

198) 자세한 내용은 "제17장 노동위원회" 참조.

2) Arbitration

Industrial action shall not be implemented for fifteen days from the date when a labor dispute is referred to arbitration. It shall begin:

① When both parties concerned request arbitration; or

② When either party requests arbitration in accordance with the provisions of the collective agreement.

An arbitrator, who is also a third party, gives a proposal to solve the labor dispute, which the parties to the dispute concerned shall accept to reach an agreement. Arbitration is carried out by the arbitration committee within the Labor Relations Commission. A finalized arbitration award shall have the same effect as a collective agreement.

(3) Suspension of industrial actions during emergency adjustment

The Minister of Employment and Labor may decide to conduct an emergency adjustment of any industrial action, in cases that are related to public services or are likely to impair the national economy or endanger the welfare of the general public owing to the vast extent and unique characteristics of its effects. If the Minister of Employment and Labor decides to conduct an emergency adjustment, he shall first hear the opinion of the chairman of the National Labor Relations Commission.

When the decision to conduct an emergency adjustment is publicly announced, the parties concerned shall immediately suspend any industrial action, and no industrial action shall resume until thirty days have passed from the announcement date of the decision.

Ⅱ. Protections for Justifiable Industrial Actions

1. Immunity from civil and criminal claims from justifiable industrial action

When an employer has suffered damages due to collective bargaining or industrial action under this Act, he/she shall not claim damages against the labor union or workers. Article 20 of the Criminal Act states that actions, which by law, etc., do not violate other regulations shall not be punished(Article 3 and 4 of the Trade Union Act).

Although an industrial action, as it usually leads to impediment of the business, seems

2) 중재(Arbitration)

노동쟁의의 중재는 다음의 경우에 개시되며 노동쟁의가 중재에 회부된 경우에는 그날로부터 15일간은 쟁의행위를 할 수 없다.

① 관계 당사자의 쌍방이 함께 중재의 신청을 한 때

② 관계 당사자의 일방이 단체협약에 의하여 중재신청을 한 때

제3자의 중재인이 양 당사자의 분쟁에 대한 중재안을 제시하고 당사자는 이 중재안에 구속되어 합의에 이르러야 하는 것을 말한다. 중재는 관할 노동 위원회에 설치된 중재위원회에서 담당한다. 확정된 중재재정의 내용은 단체협약과 동일한 효력을 가진다.

(3) 긴급조정 시의 쟁의행위 금지

쟁의행위가 공익사업이거나 그 규모가 크거나 또는 그 성질이 특별한 것으로서 현저히 국민경제를 해하거나 국민의 일상생활을 위태롭게 할 위험이 현존하는 때는 고용노동부 장관은 중앙노동위원회 위원장의 의견을 들어 긴급조정의 결정을 할 수 있다.

긴급조정의 결정이 공표된 때는 관계 당사자는 즉시 쟁의행위를 중지 하여야 하며, 공표일로부터 30일이 경과하지 아니하면 쟁의행위를 재개할 수 없다.

Ⅱ. 정당한 쟁의행위에 대한 보호조치

1. 정당한 쟁의행위의 민·형사상 면책

노조법 제3조에서는 "사용자는 이 법에 의한 단체교섭 또는 쟁의행위로 인하여 손해를 입은 경우에 노동조합 또는 근로자에 대하여 그 배상을 청구할 수 없다"라고 규정하고 있다. 형법 제20조는 "법령에 의한 행위 또는 업무로 인한 행위 기타 사회상규에 위배되지 아니하는 행위는 벌하지 아니한다"고 규정하고 있다.

쟁의행위는 업무의 저해라는 속성상 그 자체로서 시민형법상의 여러 가지 범죄의 구성요건에 해당될 수 있음에도 불구하고 그것이 정당성을 가지는 경우에

likely to constitute several offenses under the law, participants are immune to civil or criminal liability as long as the action can be justified.[199)]

2. Restriction on employer's hiring others or replacing striking employees[200)]

An employer shall not hire or bring in any person not related to the relevant business as a substitute during the period of industrial action in order to continue work which has been interrupted by the industrial action. Moreover, the employer may not contract out or subcontract the work discontinued by an industrial action while the industrial action is in process.[201)]

However, the employer of an essential public service is allowed to replace striking employees with external employees who have no relation with the business, or to outsource or subcontract the work, so long as the external employees account for 50% or fewer of the strikers. Since replacement work is available only during the period of industrial actions, the employer may not use replacement work on a permanent basis because of the strike.

3. Restriction on detention of workers

With the exception of a criminal caught in the act, workers shall not be detained for any violation of this Act during the period of industrial action.[202)]

Ⅲ. Civil or Criminal Claims for Illegal Industrial Actions

1. Civil claims

Acts(which result in damage to the company) excluded from liability for civil compensation according to Article 3 of the Trade Union Act, are restricted to justifiable industrial actions. For unjustifiable industrial action that consists of illegal acts resulting in damage to the employer, that employer can demand compensation for such damage from the labor union and the employees concerned.[203)]

---

199) Constitutional Court ruling on July 16, 1998, 97Heonba23.

200) Detailed explanations are provided in "Section 3: Restrictions on Replacing Workers on Strike"

201) Article 43 of the Trade Union Act.

202) Article 39 of the Trade Union Act.

203) Supreme Court ruling on Mar. 25, 1994, 93da32828, 32835【Compensation for Damages】.

는 형사책임이 면제되며, 민사상 손해배상 책임도 발생하지 않는다.[199)]

2. 쟁의행위기간 중의 사용자의 채용·대체 금지[200)]

사용자는 쟁의행위기간 중 그 쟁의행위로 중단된 업무의 수행을 위하여 당해 사업과 관계없는 자를 채용 또는 대체할 수 없다. 또한, 사용자는 쟁의행위기간 중 그 쟁의행위로 중단된 업무를 도급 또는 하도급을 줄 수 없다. 다만, 2008년 1월 1일부터 필수공익사업에 한하여 대체근로가 허용된다.[201)]

필수공익사업의 사용자는 파업참가자의 50% 범위 내에서 당해 사업과 관계없는 자를 채용 또는 대체하거나 그 업무를 도급 또는 하도급 줄 수 있다. 대체근로는 쟁의행위 기간 중에 한하여 가능하므로 파업을 이유로 한 영구적 대체근로는 허용되지 않는다.

3. 근로자의 구속 제한

근로자는 쟁의기간 중에는 현행범 외에는 이 법 위반을 이유로 구속되지 아니한다.[202)]

Ⅲ. 불법쟁의행위의 민·형사상 책임

1. 민사상 책임

노조법 제3조에 의하여 민사상 배상책임이 면제되는 손해는 정당한 쟁의행위로 인한 손해에 국한된다고 풀이하여야 할 것이고, 정당성이 없는 쟁의행위는 불법행위를 구성하고 이로 말미암아 손해를 입은 사용자는 노동조합이나 근로자에 대하여 그 손해배상을 청구할 수 있다.[203)]

---

199) 헌법재판소 1998.7.16, 97헌바23.
200) "제3절 쟁의행위기간 중 대체근로금지" 에서 구체적 내용 설명함.
201) 노조법 제43조.
202) 노조법 제39조.
203) 대법원 1994.3.25, 93다32828, 32835【손해배상】.

(1) Claims for default

When employees refuse to work on account of industrial actions, such as an illegal strike, etc. claims for default can be filed for violation of duty to work.[204)]

In cases where the debtor cannot carry out repayment of the debt, the creditor can claim compensation for damage. However, in cases where the debtor unintentionally(and not due to negligence) does not carry out repayment, the creditor cannot claim compensation.

(2) Claims for illegal acts

For picketing by force or obstruction of business by occupying working place, etc., claims for illegal acts of violence or obstruction of business can be filed.[205)]

"Anyone who harms another person by an illegal act, intentionally or by negligence, shall be responsible for the damage and resulting compensation.

2. Criminal claims

Criminal claims on account of industrial actions are not justifiable actions under the Labor Union Act, but are distinguished under the Criminal Act.

The criminal claims most often filed in relation to labor disputes or industrial actions are as follow:

(1) Crimes against a person[206)]

"Anyone who damages another person's body shall be imprisoned up to seven years, suspended for his/her civil rights up to 10 years, or fined up to 10 million won."

(2) Crimes of violence[207)]

"Anyone who does violence to another person's body shall be imprisoned up to two years, fined up to 5 million won, or punished by detention or a fine.

---

204) Article 390 of the Civil Act (Claims for default).

205) Article 750 of the Civil Act (Claims for illegal acts).

206) Article 257 of the Criminal Act.

207) Article 260 of the Civil Act.

(1) 채무불이행책임

정당성이 없는 파업 등 쟁의행위로 인하여 노무의 제공을 거부한 경우 노무제공의무 위반으로 인한 채무불이행책임이 발생한다.[204)]

– 민법 제390조(채무불이행과 손해배상 책임)

"채무자가 채무의 내용에 좇은 이행을 하지 아니한 때는 채권자는 손해배상을 청구할 수 있다. 그러나 채무자의 고의나 과실 없이 이행할 수 없게 된 때는 그러하지 아니하다."

(2) 불법행위책임

폭력에 의한 피케팅 또는 직장점거로 인한 업무방해 등의 경우 폭행 또는 업무방해에 의한 불법행위책임이 발생한다.[205)]

"고의 또는 과실로 인한 위법행위로 타인에게 손해를 가한 자는 그 손해를 배상할 책임이 있다."

2. 형사상 책임

쟁의행위로 인하여 형벌을 받아야 하는 형사책임이 발생하려면 그 쟁의행위가 노동법상 정당성을 인정받을 수 없고 그 행위가 형법상의 구성요건에 해당되어야 한다.

노사분규 또는 쟁의행위와 관련하여 가장 많이 적용되는 형사상의 범죄는 다음과 같다.

(1) 상해죄[206)]

"사람의 신체를 상해한 자는 7년 이하의 징역, 10년 이하의 자격정지 또는 1천만원 이하의 벌금에 처한다."

(2) 폭행죄[207)]

"사람의 신체에 대하여 폭행을 가한 자는 2년 이하의 징역, 500만원 이하의 벌금, 구류 또는 과료에 처한다."

---

204) 민법 제390조(채무불이행과 손해배상 책임).

205) 민법 제750조(불법행위와 손해배상 책임).

206) 형법 제257조.

207) 형법 제260조.

(3) Obstruction of implementation of rights by violence[208)]

"Anyone who obstructs another person's implementation of rights by violence or intimidation or forces another person to do something which is not compulsory for the other person to do shall be imprisoned up to five years."

(4) Obstruction of business[209)]

"Anyone who obstructs another person's business by the method detailed in Article 313(damage of trust) or by force, shall be imprisoned up to five years or fined up to 15 million won.

(5) Breaking-and-entering[210)] or crimes of special breaking-and-entering[211)]

"Breaking-and-entering: Anyone who breaks and enters another person's house, premise, ship or airplane, or room occupied by another person shall be imprisoned up to three years or fined up to five million won.

"Special breaking-and-entering: Anyone who breaks and enters another person's house, premise, ship or airplane, or room occupied by another person in a group or by collective intimidation or by carrying dangerous goods shall be imprisoned up to five years."

(6) Destruction of property[212)]

"Anyone who harms utility by damaging or concealing another person's property, documents or special recordings, such as electronic recordings, etc., shall be imprisoned up to three years or fined up to 7 million won."

3. Responsibility for disciplinary action

The employer shall take disciplinary measures to maintain company order as a result of employees violating the labor contract, the rules of employment, or other management rules.

---

208) Article 324 of the Civil Act.

209) Article 314 of the Civil Act.

210) Article 319 of the Civil Act.

211) Article 320 of the Civil Act.

212) Article 366 of the Civil Act.

(3) 폭력에 의한 권리행사 방해죄 : 강요죄[208)]

“폭행 또는 협박으로 사람의 권리행사를 방해하거나 의무없는 일을 하게 한 자는 5년 이하의 징역에 처한다.”

(4) 업무방해죄[209)]

“제313조(신용훼손)의 방법 또는 위력으로써 사람의 업무를 방해한 자는 5년 이하의 징역 또는 1천500만원 이하의 벌금에 처한다.”

(5) 주거침입죄[210)] 및 특수 주거침입죄[211)]

“주거침입: 사람의 주거, 관리하는 건조물, 선박이나 항공기 또는 점유하는 방실에 침입한 자는 3년 이하의 징역 또는 500만원 이하의 벌금에 처한다.”

“특수주거침입: 단체 또는 다중의 위력을 보이거나 위험한 물건을 휴대하여 전조의 죄를 범한 때는 5년 이하의 징역에 처한다.”

(6) 손괴죄[212)]

“타인의 재물, 문서 또는 전자기록등 특수매체기록을 손괴 또는 은닉 기타 방법으로 기 효용을 해한 자는 3년 이하의 징역 또는 700만원 이하의 벌금에 처한다.”

3. 징계책임

불법쟁의행위로 인하여 근로계약을 위반하거나 취업규칙 등 경영규범을 위반하게 되면 기업의 질서유지를 위하여 기업 내부적으로 징계처분을 하게 된다. 징계의 내용으로는 가장 강한 ‘해고’부터 가벼운 ‘경고’ 등 기업의 취업규칙 등

---

208) 형법 324조.
209) 형법 제314조.
210) 형법 제319조.
211) 형법 제320조.
212) 형법 제366조.

Details of disciplinary punishment are stipulated in the rules of employment with respect to the degree of punishment, dismissal being the strongest and a warning being the weakest.

If an employee engages in unjustified industrial actions, his/her behavior is subject to disciplinary dismissal under the collective agreement or rules of employment such as severe misbehavior or intentional disobedience of a justifiable order[213)]

4. Related judicial rulings

(1) Calculation of damages for business discontinuance resulting from an unlawful industrial action

1) From the viewpoint of jurisprudence, an employer may demand compensation for damages suffered in terms of the loss of product sales income that would have been earned if the business had not been discontinued by the industrial action, and for the loss of fixed costs(e.g., rents, taxes, utilities, depreciation expenses, insurance premiums, etc.) that he/she had to pay while the business was interrupted.[214)]

2) The scope of compensation that a labor union and the employees involved would be responsible for shall be all damages with considerable causal relationship to illegal industrial actions. The damages suffered by an employer engaged in delivering medical services due to illegal industrial actions by a labor union and employees shall consist of revenue whose loss has a considerable causal relationship to those illegal industrial actions. This lost revenue shall be calculated by considering the related revenue during the same period of the previous year, or by considering the related revenue during the previous month, and then deducting all related profit costs from the calculated lost revenue.[215)]

(2) Agreement on immunity to liability

If an employer has agreed not to hold the strike participants responsible for damage done during the strike, the agreement covers not only the acts done during the strike but also the acts done to prepare for or induce the strike.[216)]

---

213) Supreme Court 91da4137.

214) Supreme Court ruling on Dec. 10, 1993, 93Da24735.

215) Supreme Court ruling on Mar. 25, 1994, 93da32828, 32835【Compensation for damages】.

216) Supreme Court ruling on Jan. 28, 1994, 93Da49284.

의 규정에 따라 그 정도가 정하여 진다.

근로자가 정당성이 없는 쟁의행위를 하였다면, 이는 단체협약 또는 취업규칙 상의 징계해고 사유 중 "중대한 비행 또는 정당한 명령에 대한 고의적인 불복종"에 해당한다.[213)]

4. 관련 판례

(1) 불법휴무로 인하여 회사 측이 입은 손해배상의 범위

1) 법리상 제조업체에 있어서 불법휴무로 인해 조업을 하지 못함으로써 기업이 입는 손해로는 조업중단으로 제품생산을 못해 생산제품의 판매로 얻을 수 있는 매출이익을 올리지 못한 손해와 조업중단 여부와 관계없이 고정적으로 지출되는 비용(차임, 제세공과금, 감가상각비, 보험료 등)을 무용하게 지출해 입은 손해를 들 수 있다.[214)]

2) 불법쟁의행위로 인하여 노동조합이나 근로자가 그 배상책임을 지는 배상액의 범위는 불법쟁의행위와 상당인과관계에 있는 모든 손해이다. 노동조합이나 근로자의 불법쟁의행위로 인하여 의료업무를 수행하는 사용자가 그 영업상의 손실에 해당하는 진료수입의 감소로 입은 손해는 일실이익으로서 불법쟁의행위와 상당인과관계가 있는 손해이다. 그 일실이익의 산정방법은 구체적 사정에 따라 다를 것이나 우선 불법쟁의행위가 없었던 전년도의 같은 기간에 대응하는 진료수입과 대비한 감소분이나 불법쟁의행위가 없었던 전월의 같은 기간에 대응하는 진료수입과 대비한 감소분을 산출한 다음 그 수입을 얻기 위하여 소요되는 제 비용을 공제하는 방법으로도 산정할 수 있다.[215)]

(2) 노동조합원들에 대하여 책임을 묻지 않기로 노사 간에 합의한 면책 합의의 범위

농성기간 중 노동조합원들에 대하여 일체의 책임을 묻지 않기로 노사 간에 합의한 경우 그 취지는 농성기간 중의 행위뿐만 아니라 농성과 일체성을 가지는 그 준비행위, 유발행위까지도 포함된다.[216)]

---

213) 대법원 91다4137.

214) 대법원 1993.12.10, 93다24735.

215) 대법원 1994.3.25, 93다32828, 32835【손해배상】.

216) 대법원 1994.1.28, 93다49284.

(3) Should union executives play a leading role in an illegal industrial action by planning the industrial action and instructing or guiding the participants, it is possible to hold individual officials responsible for the illegal action.

Given that union executives did what they did on behalf of the union, the union is liable to pay damages to the employer for losses caused by the illegal industrial action. In addition, the union executives are responsible, as individuals, for the leading role they played in planning, instructing and guiding.[217)]

Ⅳ. Prohibition against Demand for Payment of Wages during Periods of Industrial Action

When an employee participates in an industrial action and does not provide work for a period of time, his/her employer is not obligated to pay wages to the employee for the time he/she did not work. A labor union may not initiate an industrial action in order to demand and secure payment of wages for a period of industrial action(Article 44 of the Trade Union Act). The Supreme Court has ruled,[218)] in conjunction with the principle of no work, no payment, that the employee's right to a wage request, which is equivalent to a right of work provision, does not occur during a period of industrial actions.

> h he/she did not provide work because he/she participated in an industrial action.
> During a period of industrial action, a participating employee has his/her obligation to provide work under the contract of employment suspended, and his/her right to wage, which is given in return for the obligation to provide work, is also suspended for the period, unless otherwise prescribed in the collective agreement, the rules of employment or another agreement between the employer and employees.[219)]

217) Supreme Court ruling on Mar. 25, 1994, 93Da32828.

218) Supreme Court ruling on Dec. 21, 1995, 94Da26721.

219) Supreme Court ruling on Oct. 25, 1996, 96Da5346.

(3) 노동조합의 간부들이 불법쟁의행위를 기획·지시·지도하는 등으로 주도한 경우에 노동조합 간부에게도 책임을 물을 수 있다.

간부들의 행위는 조합의 집행기관으로서의 행위라 할 것이므로 노동조합은 그 불법쟁의행위로 인하여 사용자가 입은 손해를 배상할 책임이 있고, 한편 조합간부들의 행위는 노동조합 단체로서의 행위라고 할 수 있는 외에 개인의 행위라는 측면도 아울러 지니고 있고, 일반적으로 쟁의행위가 개개 근로자의 노무정지를 조직하고 집단화하여 이루어지는 집단적 투쟁행위라는 그 본질적 특징을 고려하여 볼 때 노동조합의 책임 외에 불법쟁의행위를 기획·지시·지도하는 등으로 주도한 조합의 간부들 개인에 대하여도 책임을 지우는 것이 당연하다.[217)]

Ⅳ. 쟁의행위기간 중의 임금지급 요구

사용자는 쟁의행위에 참가하여 근로를 제공하지 아니한 근로자에 대하여는 그 기간에 대한 임금을 지급할 의무가 없다. 노동조합은 쟁의행위 기간에 대한 임금의 지급을 요구하여 이를 관철할 목적으로 쟁의행위를 할 수 없다(노조법 제44조). 대법원도 "쟁의행위기간 동안에는 근로제공의무와 대가관계에 있는 근로자의 주된 권리로서 임금청구권이 발생치 않는다.[218)]" 면서 무노동 무임금 원칙을 적용하고 있다.

근로자가 근로를 제공하지 아니한 쟁의행위기간 동안에 대하여 임금을 청구할 수 없다. 쟁의행위시의 임금지급에 관하여 단체협약이나 취업규칙 등에서 이를 규정하거나 그 지급에 관한 당사자 사이의 약정이나 관행이 있다고 인정되지 아니하는 한, 근로자의 근로제공의무 등의 주된 권리·의무가 정지되어 근로자가 근로제공을 하지 아니한 쟁의행위기간 동안에는 근로제공의무와 대가관계에 있는 근로자의 주된 권리로서의 임금청구권은 발생하지 않는다.[219)]

217) 대법원 1994.3.25, 93다32828.
218) 대법원 1995.12.21, 94다26721 전원합의체 판결.
219) 대법원 1996.10.25, 96다5346.

Section 3: Restrictions on Replacing Workers on Strike

Ⅰ. Concept

Article 33 of the Constitution guarantees three basic rights of labor to enhance working conditions, and the Trade Union & Labor Relations Adjustment Act(hereinafter referred to as the Trade Union Act) was established towards guaranteeing those rights in practical terms. Labor unions and employees are free from civil and criminal liability for justifiable industrial action and shall not be treated unfavorably in personnel management.

Labor unions can acquire better working conditions through collective agreements, and while engaging in collective bargaining with the employer, they can request better wages, working hours, and welfare, etc. At the beginning of collective bargaining, employers often reject union demands because labor costs directly affect overall production costs. Labor unions then collectively refuse to provide labor service in order to achieve their demands, and obstruct normal business operations. The employer counteracts this with the no pay, no work principle, which deprives the employees participating in strikes from receiving their wages. This confrontation between labor union and company then leads to conclusion of an adjusted agreement, called the collective agreement.

Here, if the employer is allowed to hire persons unrelated to business operations or use replacements during a period of industrial action - if contracting or subcontracting out is allowed - so as to continue work which has been stopped by that industrial action, a strike will not affect an employer as much as planned and the labor union will be discouraged from going on strike and therefore more easily agree to employer proposals. In order to prevent practical infringement of this right to take industrial action, it is stipulated in the Trade Union Act that hiring new employees or outsourcing jobs which have been interrupted by industrial action is not permitted. Therefore, provisions restricting replacement of workers during strikes are protections designed to maintain the balance of power between the labor union and the employer.

Here, I would like to concretely review the concept and content of these restrictions on the replacement of workers involved in strikes, and essential public services where this replacement is allowed.

제3절 쟁의행위기간 중 대체근로금지

Ⅰ. 의 의

헌법 제33조는 근로자에게 근로조건의 향상을 위한 노동3권을 보장하고 있으며 이를 실질적으로 보장하기 위해 노조법이 제정되었다. 노동조합과 근로자는 정당한 쟁의행위에 대해 민·형사상 면책조항의 적용을 받고 인사상 불이익 취급도 받지 않는다.

노동조합은 근로조건의 향상을 단체협약 체결을 통해서 확보하게 되는데, 이 과정에서 사용자와 단체교섭으로 임금, 근로시간, 복지 등 더 나은 근로조건을 요구한다. 이에 사용자는 인건비가 회사제품의 원가인상과 직결되기 때문에 노동조합의 요구를 거부하게 된다. 노동조합은 그 요구를 관철하기 위해 집단적으로 노무제공을 거부하여 업무의 정상적인 운영을 저해하는 파업을 하게 된다. 이에 맞서 사용자는 무노동 무임금으로 대응하여 파업에 참가한 근로자를 지치게 한다. 노사 간의 힘의 대결을 통해 절충된 합의문이 작성되고, 이것이 단체협약이 된다.

여기서 만약 사용자가 노동조합의 쟁의행위로 중단된 업무의 수행을 위하여 당해 사업과 관계없는 자를 채용 또는 대체하거나, 도급 또는 하도급을 줄 수 있게 된다면 노동조합의 파업 효과는 현저히 줄어들어 더 이상 파업을 계속할 수 없게 되어 사용자에게 굴복하게 된다. 이러한 단체행동권의 침해를 방지하기 위해 쟁의행위 기간 중 쟁의행위로 중단된 업무의 수행을 위해 신규로 근로자를 채용하거나 외주를 줄 수 없다고 노조법은 명시하고 있다. 따라서 쟁의행위 중 대체근로금지는 노사 간 힘의 균형을 유지하여 단체협약을 자율적으로 체결하도록 도와주기 위한 보호법규이다.

이와 관련, 대체근로금지의 의의와 내용 및 대체근로가 허용된 필수공익사업의 범위 등에 대해 구체적으로 살펴보고자 한다.

Ⅱ. Concept behind Restrictions on Employee Replacement

Article 43 of the Trade Union Act regulates that no employer shall hire persons unrelated to their business operations, or use replacements during a period of industrial action so as to continue work which has been stopped by that industrial action. This includes contracting or subcontracting work out(Paragraph(1) and(2)). Penal provisions are implemented in the event of violations. Article 16 of the Act on the Protection, etc. of Dispatched Workers(Employee Dispatch Act) also regulates that a sending employer shall not dispatch an employee to a workplace where industrial action is underway to perform the work stopped due to such industrial action.

The purpose for restricting employee replacement during a period of industrial action is to protect the employee right to strike according to the Constitution, in practical terms. Restrictions on employee replacement are institutional mechanisms designed to guarantee effectiveness of industrial action by a labor union, and are also unavoidable in realizing the principle of equality in collective bargaining. If an employer is allowed to take unrestricted counteraction against a labor union's industrial actions, those industrial actions lose all effectiveness as a tool for the union to achieve its goals.[220)]

Ⅲ. Scope of Restrictions on Employee Replacement

1. The meaning of persons unrelated to business operations

Judicial rulings on the concept of business generally explain that business refers to an independent company organization operating continuously and organically in one managerial body such as an individual business or corporate entity.[221)] Subsidiaries within a larger company are considered different businesses. However, a particular company with headquarters in one city and plants or branch offices located in other areas is regarded as

---

220) Kim, Heesung, A study of the restrictions on employee replacement during a period of industrial action, 「Labor Law Studies」, Korean Labor Law Studies Association, June 2010, p. 229.

221) Supreme Court ruling on Aug. 20, 1998: 98Da18365.

Ⅱ. 대체근로금지의 의의

노조법 제43조(사용자의 채용제한)는 「사용자는 쟁의행위 기간 중 그 쟁의행위로 중단된 업무의 수행을 위하여 당해 사업과 관계없는 자를 채용 또는 대체할 수 없으며, 도급 또는 하도급을 줄 수 없다(제1항, 제2항)」고 규정하고, 이를 위반할 경우 처벌규정을 두고 있다. 이외에도 파견 근로자보호 등에 관한 법률(파견법) 제16조(근로자 파견의 제한)에서 「파견사업주는 쟁의행위 중인 사업장에 그 쟁의행위로 중단된 업무의 수행을 위하여 근로자를 파견하여서는 아니된다」고 규정하고 있다.

쟁의행위기간 중의 대체근로제한규정의 취지는 헌법상 근로자의 쟁의권을 실질적으로 보장하기 위한 것이다. 사용자의 대체근로의 제한은 노동조합의 단체행동권의 실효성을 담보하기 위해 취한 제도적 장치이자 무기대등의 원칙을 실현하기 위하여 마련된 불가피한 조치라는 것이다. 노동조합의 쟁의행위에 대해 사용자의 대항행위가 제한 없이 허용되는 경우에는 노동조합의 쟁의행위가 아무런 실효성을 거두지 못할 것이고, 이것은 노동조합의 단체행동권 행사의 본질적인 내용을 침해할 수 있기 때문에 쟁의행위 중에 당해 사업과 관계없는 자를 대체할 수 없도록 정한 것이다.[220]

Ⅲ. 대체근로 제한의 범위

1. 당해 사업과 관계없는 자의 의미

사업의 개념에 대해 판례는 「사업」이라 함은 개인사업체 또는 독립된 법인격을 갖춘 회사 등과 같이 경영상의 일체를 이루면서 계속적, 유기적으로 운영되고 전체로서의 독립성을 갖춘 하나의 기업조직을 뜻한다고 일반적으로 해석하고 있다.[221] 이에 대하여 대기업의 경우, 계열사 간에는 서로 다른 사업으로 인정된다. 그러나 특정 기업이 본사를 서울에 두고 공장이나 지점을 여러 곳에 둔

220) 김희성, 쟁의행위기간 중 대체근로제한에 관한 연구, 「노동법학」, 한국노동법학회, 2010.6, 229면.

221) 대법원 1998.8.20, 98다18365.

one business.

The restriction on the use of persons unrelated to business operations means that persons who are related to business operations can be used as replacements during a period of industrial action. This makes it possible to continue the work stopped during industrial action, with union members not participating in the strike, non-union members, and other employees who are related to the company's business operations.

2. Restrictions against hiring new employees

Article 43(1) regulates that no employer shall hire persons who are not related to that employer's business operations, or use replacements during a period of industrial action so as to continue work which has been stopped by that industrial action. In this case, there are two representative judicial rulings.

1) An employer hired new persons before a period of industrial action, with the intent of continuing to perform the work of strikers during the period of industrial action. This case violated Article 43 of the Trade Union Act.[222)]

2) An employer hired new persons gradually to fill vacated positions. Even though these persons were used to continue the work stopped by later industrial action, this replacement was justifiable exercise of the employer's personnel management rights as they were not hired specifically to replace the workers taking industrial action.[223)]

3. Conditions for justification of counteractions by a labor union

Judicial rulings on the conditions for justification of labor union counteractions against replacement by an employer during a period of industrial action can be divided into justifiable replacement and illegal replacement.

1) The court determined obstruction of business as a violation in cases where the labor union members entirely and exclusively occupied company premises to block the employer's justifiable replacement of workers to perform work stopped due to industrial action.[224)]

---

222) Supreme Court ruling on Nov. 28, 2001: 99Do317.

223) Supreme Court ruling on Nov. 13, 2008: 2008Do4831.

224) Supreme Court Ruling on Oct. 7, 2005: 2005Do5351.

경우에 하나의 사업으로 본다.

당해 사업과 관계있는 자에 대해서는 쟁의행위기간 중 업무의 대체가 가능하다는 뜻이다. 즉, 파업에 참가하지 않은 조합원, 비조합원, 당해 사업과 관계가 있는 다른 사업장에 근무하는 근로자는 업무대체가 가능하다고 본다.

2. 신규채용의 제한

노조법 제43조 제1항은 사용자는 쟁의행위 기간 중 그 쟁의행위로 중단된 업무의 수행을 위하여 당해 사업과 관계없는 자를 채용할 수 없다.라고 규정하고 있다. 이 경우 판례에서 문제가 되는 경우로서 다음의 2가지가 있다.

1) 쟁의행위기간 중 쟁의행위 참가자들의 업무를 수행시킬 의도로 쟁의행위 기간 전에 근로자들을 신규 채용한 경우이다. 이 경우 사용자의 의도가 쟁의행위 기간 중에 쟁의행위로 중단된 업무에 대해 대체할 대체인력이므로 이는 노조법 제43조를 위반한 것으로 판단하였다.[222)]

2) 자연 감소인원을 보충하기 위해 신규 채용한 경우이다. 자연감소 인원을 충원하였고, 이러한 인원이 차후 노동쟁의로 중단된 업무에 대체인력으로 투입되었다고 하더라도 이는 사용자의 대체인력을 목적으로 한 것이 아니기 때문에 정당한 인사권 행사로 판단하였다.[223)]

3. 대항행위의 정당성 요건

쟁의행위기간 중의 대체근로에 있어 노동조합의 대항행위가 정당성 요건을 갖추었는지 여부에 대하여 판례들은 적법한 대체근로인 경우와 위법한 대체근로로 나누어 판단하고 있다.

1) 사용자의 적법한 대체근로에 대해서 노동조합이 대체근로의 저지를 위한 파업참가근로자들의 전면적·배타적 직장점거가 정당하지 않다는 이유로 법원은 업무방해죄를 인정하고 있다.[224)]

---

222) 대법원 2001.11.28, 99도317.

223) 대법원 2008.11.13, 2008도4831.

224) 대법원 2005.10.7, 2005도5351.

2) As long as strikers did not use violence or destruction or threatening actions to block an employer's illegal replacement of workers to continue work stopped due to industrial action, the court ruled that considerable counteractions are acceptable.[225)]

4. Applicability to illegal industrial action

The provision placing restrictions on replacement may be applicable to justifiable industrial action only. Since there are provisions protecting labor union members from civil and criminal liability during industrial action according to the Trade Union Act, the employer can continue business operations by using replacements to do the work stopped due to illegal industrial action. That is, an employer can hire new persons or use employee replacements to prevent damage caused by a labor union's illegal industrial actions.[226)]

However, in reality there are many cases where determining whether industrial action is justifiable or not is complicated and cannot easily be determined outside of a courtroom. In cases where an employer hires new persons or uses as replacements those unrelated to business operations on the assumption that a strike is illegal, this can infringe on a labor union's right to take industrial action. Therefore, employee replacement should be prohibited in principle in cases where the justification for industrial action is unclear, but used in cases where the industrial action clearly has no justification.[227)]

5. Prohibition against contracting or subcontracting work out during periods of industrial action

Article 43(2) of the Trade Union Act makes it very clear that no employer shall, during a period of industrial action, contract or subcontract out work which has been suspended because of that industrial action. Provided, in cases where a subcontractor company's labor union takes industrial action and the subcontractor company cannot carry out the duties assigned under the service contract with the contractor company, the contractor

---

225) Supreme Court Ruling on July 14, 1992: 91Da43800.

226) Lim, Jongryul, 「Labor Law」, 13th ed., 2015, Parkyoungsa, p. 32.

227) Kim, Heesung, ibid., p. 247.

2) 쟁의행위기간 중 사용자의 위법한 대체근로저지를 위해 파업참가 근로자들은 폭력이나 파괴·협박행위를 수반하지 않는 한, 상당한 정도의 실력을 행사하는 것이 가능하다고 판단하고 있다.[225)]

4. 불법 쟁의행위에 대한 적용

대체근로 제한규정은 정당한 쟁의행위에 대해서만 해당된다고 본다. 노조법상 쟁의행위 시 민형사상의 면책 규정은 정당한 쟁의행위를 전제로 하므로, 정당성이 없는 쟁의행위에 대해서는 사용자가 대체근로를 이용하여 업무수행을 계속할 수 있다. 즉, 노동조합의 불법쟁의행위에 대해 사용자는 손실을 방지하기 위해 신규채용이나 대체근로를 할 수 있다.[226)]

그러나, 현실적으로 쟁의행위가 불법파업에 해당하는지 여부는 법원의 판단을 받기 전에는 단정하기 어려운 경우가 많다. 사용자가 일방적으로 노동조합의 파업을 불법 쟁의행위로 판단하여 쟁의행위로 중단된 업무에 대해 당해 사업과 관계없는 자를 채용하거나 대체하여 투입하는 경우에 이는 노동조합의 단체행동권을 무력화 할 수 있다. 그러므로 쟁의행위의 정당성이 불분명한 경우에 대체근로는 원칙적으로 금지되어야 함이 원칙이고, 명백히 정당성이 없는 쟁의행위에 한해서 대체근로를 허용하도록 하여야 할 것이다.[227)]

5. 도급 또는 하도급 금지

노조법 제43조 제2항은 사용자는 쟁의행위 기간 중 그 쟁의행위로 중단된 업무를 도급 또는 하도급 줄 수 없다고 규정하고 있다. 이에 대해 사용자가 쟁의행위 기간 중에 그 쟁의행위로 중단된 업무를 도급 또는 하도급을 줄 수 없다는 것에 대해서는 문제가 없다. 다만, 도급업체와 하도급 업체 사이의 관계에서 하도급 회사의 노동조합이 쟁의행위를 할 경우에 도급업체와의 도급계약 상

225) 대법원 1992.7.14, 91다43800.

226) 임종률, 『노동법』, 제20판, 2020, 박영사, 32면.

227) 김희성, 쟁의행위기간 중 대체근로제한에 관한 연구, 247면.

company can terminate the service contract or continue the interrupted work with its own direct employees, and hire new employees or make a subcontract agreement with other companies. There are no related judicial rulings,[228] but Ministry of Employment and Labor Guidelines interpret that such replacement actions are not in violation of the provision to prohibit employee replacement.

In a related case, a district(gu) office and a cleaning company entered into a service contract for the cleaning company to collect household trash in that district. When the cleaning company's labor union took industrial action and stopped work, the gu office was allowed to collect the trash using its own employees and have other cleaning companies carry out this duty. This was determined as not in violation of the Trade Union Act's related provision because the gu office was not the employer of the subcontract workers involved.[229]

6. Prohibition against employee dispatch

Article 16 of the Employee Dispatch Act regulates that a sending employer shall not dispatch an employee to a workplace where industrial action is underway to perform the work stopped due to such industrial action. If employee dispatch is allowed, it has the same effect as replacing the workers engaged in industrial action with persons unrelated to business operations. This kind of replacement is prohibited, whether by the using employer or the sending employer. Provided, this provision was designed to prohibit new employees from being used to replace striking workers during a period of industrial action, but using dispatched employees who are currently dispatched at the workplace to carry out work stopped at the same workplace by industrial action is permitted.

---

228) Kim, Dongwoo, Content and coverage of the prohibition against employee replacement during a period of industrial action, 「Labor Law」, Sept. 2015, Joongang Economy.

229) MOEL Guideline: Hyupryeok 68140-173, issued on May 6, 1997.

의무를 이행하지 못할 경우, 도급업체가 도급계약을 해지하거나 도급업체 자신의 근로자를 이용하여 중단된 업무를 대체할 수 있고, 다른 근로자를 채용하거나 다른 하도급 업체와 계약을 맺을 수 있다. 이와 관련된 판례는 아직 없지만[228] 행정해석은 도급업체의 행위는 대체근로금지 규정에 위반되지 않는 것으로 해석하고 있다.

관련된 사례로, 구청과 청소용역업체 간에 생활쓰레기 수거사업 도급계약을 체결하였으나 청소용역업체 노조의 쟁의행위로 인해 업무가 중단된 경우 자치구가 생활쓰레기 처리업무를 직접 수행하거나 다른 용역업체를 지정할 수 있다. 구청과의 용역계약 관계에 있는 용역업체 노사 간의 쟁의행위로 인하여 중단된 업무를 구청이 직접 수행하거나 다른 용역업체로 하여금 수행토록 하는 것은 구청이 쟁의행위의 당사자인 사용자의 지위에 있지 아니하므로 동법 규정에 저촉되지 아니한다.[229]

6. 근로자파견의 금지

파견법 제16조(근로자 파견의 제한)에서 파견사업주는 쟁의행위 중인 사업장에 그 쟁의행위로 중단된 업무의 수행을 위하여 근로자를 파견하여서는 아니된다고 규정하고 있다. 근로자파견이 허용되면 당해 사업에 관계없는 자를 대체근로 시키는 것과 다를 바 없으므로 사용사업주뿐만 아니라 파견사업주에 대하여도 이를 금지시키고자 하는 것이다. 다만, 이 규정은 쟁의행위기간에 신규 근로자를 파견하는 것을 금지시킨 것이고 사용사업주가 이미 파견 받아 당해 사업에 사용 중인 근로자로 하여금 중단된 업무를 수행하게 하는 것은 허용된다.

---

228) 김동욱, 쟁의행위 기간 중 대체근로금지의 내용과 적용범위, 「노동법률」, 2015.9. 중앙경제
229) 행정해석: 협력 68140-173, 1997.5.6.

Chapter 16

Mediation of Industrial Disputes

Section 1: Understanding the Labor Relations Commission's Mediation Committee[230]

Ⅰ. Concept

The Mediation Committee refers to a committee set up to facilitate public mediation that both parties shall go through before the labor union takes industrial action. The term labor disputes in the Trade Union Act means any controversy or difference arising from disagreement between the employer and the labor union concerning the determination of terms and conditions of employment such as wages, working hours, welfare, dismissal, or other treatment, etc. Accordingly, the Mediation Committee in the Labor Relations Commission shall deal with disputes concerning each party's interests, but disputes related to each party's rights shall not be subject to bargaining or mediation procedures.

Ⅱ. Composition of the Mediation Committee

The Mediation Committee shall be composed of three members(an employer representative, employee representative, and a public interest representative). The Mediation Committee members shall be designated by the Chairperson of the Labor Relations Commission from among members of the Labor Relations Commission concerned so that employers, workers, and the public interest are represented. The employee representative shall be chosen from a list

230) Jung Bongsoo, 「Labor Union Manual」, KangNam Labor Law Firm, 2019, pp. 155-176; Korea Employers Federation "A Practical Guidelines to the Labor Relations Commission". printed on May 2012.

노동쟁의의 조정

제1절 노동쟁의 조정의 이해[230)]

Ⅰ. 조정제도의 의의

노동위원회의 조정위원회는 노동조합의 쟁의행위를 개시하기 전에 반드시 거쳐야 하는 공적 조정제도를 말한다. 노조법 제45조에서 노동쟁의의 조정전치를 명문화하여 노동조합이 쟁의행위를 개시하기 전에 반드시 조정회의를 거쳐야 한다고 명시되어 있다. 노동쟁의는 노조법에 '노동조합과 사용자 사이에 임금, 근로시간, 복지, 해고 기타 근로조건의 결정에 관한 주장의 불일치로 발생한 분쟁상태를 말한다.' 따라서 이는 노동위원회의 조정내용은 이익분쟁에 한해서 조정을 하는 것이고 권리 분쟁에 대해서는 쟁의행위의 대상이 되기 않기 때문에 조정의 대상이 되지 않는다고 판단하고 있다.

Ⅱ. 구성방식

조정위원회 조정위원은 당해 위원 중에서 노, 사, 공익위원(전체 3인)으로 구성한다. 조정위원은 당해 노동위원회의 위원 중에서 사용자를 대표하는 자, 근로자를 대표하는 자 및 공익을 대표하는 자 각 1인을 그 노동위원회의 위원장이 지명하되, 근로자를 대표하는 조정위원은 사용자가, 사용자를 대표하는 조

---

230) 정봉수, 「노동조합 매뉴얼 」, 2019, 강남노무법인, 155~176면.: "노동위원회 실무참고 자료집", 한국경영자총협회, 2012.

recommended by the employer, and the employer representative shall be chosen from a list recommended by the labor union. However, in cases where a list of recommended Mediation Committee members is not submitted within three days prior to a meeting of the Mediation Committee, the Chairperson may designate the members him/herself. The Chairperson of the Mediation Committee shall be the public interest representative. Special Mediation Committees shall be composed of three public interest representatives.

Ⅲ. Procedures for Mediation

1. Mediation activities

The Mediation Committee or a single mediator, as the case may be, shall specify a date for the parties concerned to appear so as to verify the main points of their respective claims. The Chairperson of the Mediation Committee may restrict attendance at the hearing to the parties concerned and witnesses. The Mediation Committee shall prepare a proposal to be presented to the parties concerned, with recommendation for their acceptance. If the Mediation Committee determines that further proceedings are not warranted due to the parties' refusal to accept the proposal, it shall terminate mediation and notify the parties concerned.[231] If an application for mediation is determined as unsuitable for mediation or arbitration, the Labor Relations Commission shall inform the applicant of the reasons for rejection of the application and other possible courses of action(Administrative Order).

2. Interpretation and implementation of the Mediation Committee proposal

If the parties concerned, after accepting the Mediation Committee proposal, do not agree on its interpretation or implementation, they shall request the Mediation Committee to provide clarity. Upon receiving such a request, the Mediation Committee shall clarify the measures within seven days of the date of receipt of such request. None of the parties concerned shall conduct industrial action on issues for which clarity on interpretation or implementation has been requested, until such clarity is rendered by the Mediation Committee.

231) Article 60 (2) of the Trade Union Act.

정위원은 노동조합이 각각 추천하는 노동위원회의 위원 중에서 지명해야 한다. 다만, 조정위원회의 회의 3일전까지 관계 당사자가 추천하는 위원의 명단제출이 없을 때는 당해 위원을 위원장이 따로 지명할 수 있다. 조정위원회의 위원장은 지명된 노, 사, 공익위원 중에서 공익위원이 맡게 되는데, 공익위원은 노동조합과 사용자의 관여 없이 노동위원회 위원장이 된다. 공익사업의 경우 공익위원 3인으로 특별조정위원회를 구성한다.

Ⅲ. 운영절차

1. 조정활동

조정위원회(단독조정인)는 기일을 정하여 관계 당사자 쌍방을 출석하게 하여 주장의 요점을 확인해야 한다. 조정위원회의 위원장은 관계 당사자와 참고인 외의 자의 출석을 금할 수 있다. 조정위원회는 조정안을 작성하여 이를 관계 당사자에게 제시하고 그 수락을 권고한다.

조정위원회는 관계 당사자가 수락을 거부하여 더 이상 조정이 이루어질 여지가 없다고 판단되는 경우에는 조정의 종료를 결정하고 이를 관계 당사자 쌍방에 통보해야 한다.[231] 노동쟁의의 조정신청이 조정 또는 중재의 대상이 아니라고 인정되는 경우에는 그 사유와 다른 해결방법을 알려주어야 한다(행정지도의 결정).

2. 조정안의 해석·이행

조정안이 관계 당사자의 쌍방에 의하여 수락된 후 그 해석 또는 이행방법에 관하여 관계 당사자간에 의견의 불일치가 있는 때는 관계 당사자는 서면으로 당해 조정위원회에 그 해석 또는 이행방법에 관한 명확한 견해의 제시를 요청해야 한다. 조정위원회는 견해제시의 요청을 받은 날부터 7일 이내에 명확한 견해를 제시해야 한다. 해석 또는 이행방법에 관한 견해가 제시될 때 까지 관계 당사자는 당해 조정안의 해석 또는 이행에 관하여 쟁의행위를 할 수 없다.

231) 노조법 제60조 2항.

3. Effect of Mediation Committee proposal

If the parties accept the Mediation Committee proposal, all members of the Mediation Committee shall prepare the mediated agreement in writing, and sign or seal it together with the parties concerned. The labor disputes shall be considered resolved, and the mediated agreement shall have the same effect as a collective agreement. Clarity on the interpretation and implementation measures rendered by the Mediation Committee shall have the same effect as an arbitration ruling.

<Procedures for Mediation>

Labor Union | Failure to reach agreement | Employer

↓

1. Application for mediation (by either party)

↓

2. Advance Investigation (by inspector)

↓

3. Mediation Committee set up

Mediation Committee (for general purposes)

1 employer representative,
1 employee representative, 1 public interest representative
※ The employer representative and the employee representative are cross-recommended.

Special Mediation Committee (public services, essential public services)

Made up of 3 public interest representatives in charge of mediation
※ To be chosen by the Chairman among the 4~6 public interest representatives not excluded by either employer or labor union

↓

4. Mediation draft prepared (by investigator)

↓

5. Advance mediation

- o Interview with both parties : labor and management (Listening to both parties' views)
- o Interviewswitheachpartyseparately

↓

6. Mediation Committee meeting (all committee members participate)

- o Meeting opened, participants confirmed, and committee members introduced
- o Investigator:summaryofmajordispute(s)
- o VoicingofopinionsfrombothpartiesandCommitteeQ&Asession

① Mediator's proposal

Takes effect upon acceptance by both parties.

② Discontinuance of mediation

If the employer and the union are divided greatly on the issue, the process ends with no proposal being made.

③ Administrative guidance

For mediation that concerns a matter not subject to mediation.

3. 조정의 효력

조정안이 관계 당사자에 의하여 수락된 때는 조정위원 전원은 조정서를 작성하고 관계 당사자와 함께 서명 또는 날인해야 한다. 노사 당사자가 조정안을 수락한 경우에는 노동쟁의가 해결되게 되며, 수락한 조정안은 단체협약과 동일한 효력을 가진다. 조정위원회가 제시한 해석 또는 이행방법에 관한 견해는 중재재정과 동일한 효력을 가진다.

〈노동쟁의 조정(調停) 절차도〉

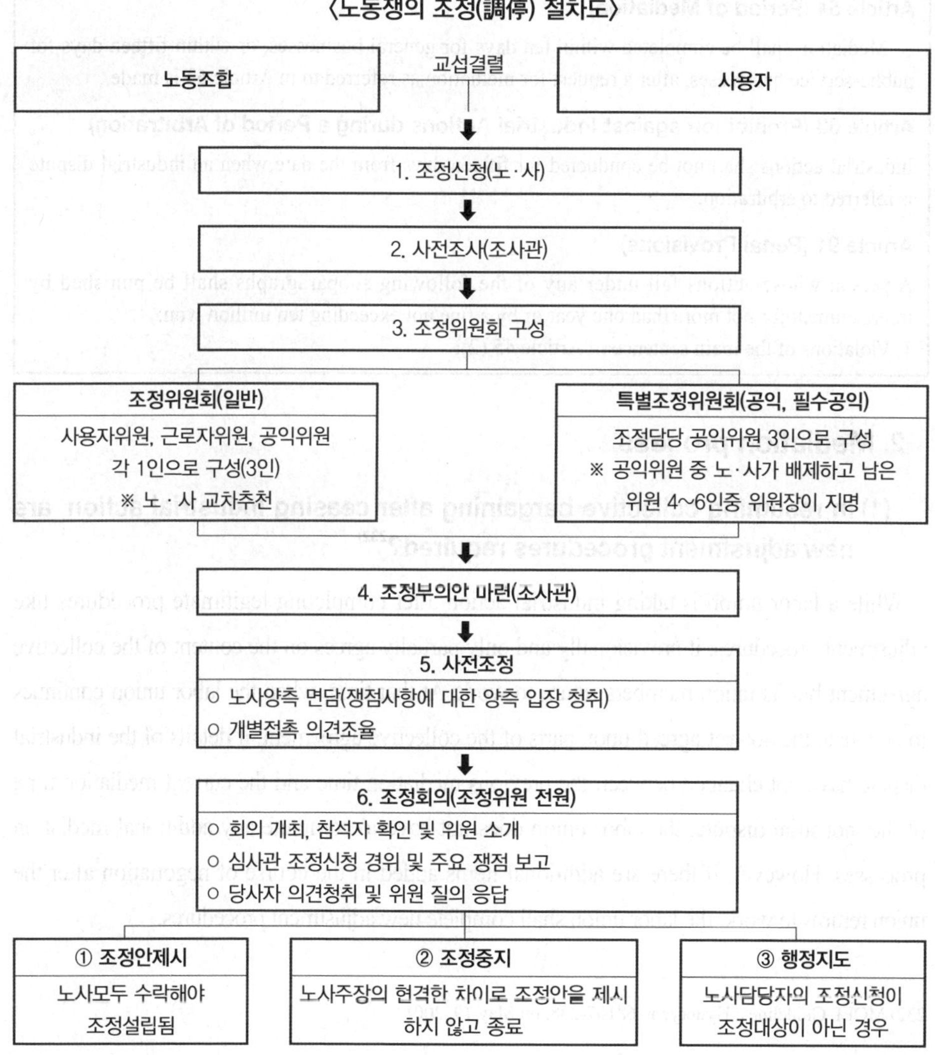

Ⅳ. System Preceding Adjustment (Cooling-off Period)

1. Related articles

Article 45 (System Preceding Adjustment)

② No industrial action shall be conducted without completing adjustment procedures as referred to in Sections 2 through 4 of Chapter 5; Provided that this shall not apply in cases where adjustment procedures are not completed within the period as provided for in Article 54 or where an arbitration award is not made within the period as provided for in Article 63.

Article 54 (Period of Mediation)

① Mediation shall be completed within ten days for general businesses, or within fifteen days for public-service businesses, after a request for mediation as referred to in Article 53 is made.

Article 63 (Prohibition against Industrial Actions during a Period of Arbitration)

Industrial actions shall not be conducted for fifteen days from the date when an industrial dispute is referred to arbitration.

Article 91 (Penal Provisions)

A person whose actions fall under any of the following subparagraphs shall be punished by imprisonment for not more than one year or by a fine not exceeding ten million won:

1. Violations of the main sentence of Article 45 (2);

2. Mediation process

(1) In resuming collective bargaining after ceasing industrial action, are new adjustment procedures required?[232]

While a labor union is taking industrial action after completing legitimate procedures like adjustment procedures, it provisionally and only partially agrees on the content of the collective agreement but its union members return to work. At that time, when the labor union continues to negotiate the not-yet-agreed-upon parts of the collective agreement, if details of the industrial dispute have not changed between the previous mediation time and the current mediation time of the industrial dispute, the labor union does not have to complete any additional mediation processes. However, if there are additional items added in the course of negotiation after the union returns to work, the labor union shall complete new adjustment procedures.

232) MOEL Guidelines: Hyupryeok 68107-238, on May 19, 2001.

Ⅳ. 조정전치주의 (냉각기간)

1. 관련 법규

제45조【조정의 전치】
② 쟁의행위는 제5장제2절 내지 제4절의 규정에 의한 조정절차를 거치지 아니하면 이를 행할 수 없다. 다만, 제54조의 규정에 의한 기간내에 조정이 종료되지 아니하거나 제63조의 규정에 의한 기간내에 중재재정이 이루어 지지 아니한 경우에는 그러하지 아니하다.

제54조【조정기간】
① 조정은 제53조의 규정에 의한 조정의 신청이 있은 날부터 일반사업에 있어서는 10일, 공익사업에 있어서는 15일 이내에 종료하여야 한다.

제63조【중재시의 쟁의행위의 금지】
노동쟁의가 중재에 회부된 때는 그 날부터15일간은 쟁의행위를 할 수 없다.

제91조【벌칙】
다음 각호의 1에 해당하는 자는 1년 이하의 징역 또는 1천만원 이하의 벌금에 처한다.
1. 제45조 제2항 본문의 규정에 위반한 자

2. 조정의 절차

(1) 쟁의행위 중단 후 재교섭 시 새로이 조정절차를 거쳐야 하는지 여부[232)]

노동조합에서 조정전치 등의 적법절차를 거쳐 쟁의행위를 행하다가 일부 단체협약 사항에 대하여만 잠정 합의한 후, 업무에 복귀하였다. 복귀 후 기존 합의사항 이외의 내용에 대하여 교섭을 계속한 경우에 있어서 조정신청 여부는 최초 조정신청 당시와 재차 쟁의행위 돌입 사이에 노동쟁의 상태의 동일성이 인정된다면 별도의 조정절차를 거칠 필요가 없다고 판단된다. 그러나 업무복귀 후 교섭과정에서 새로운 쟁점이 추가되는 경우에는 별도의 조정절차를 거쳐야 할 것이다.

---

232) 행정해석: 협력 68107-238, 2001.5.19.

(2) In cases where the labor union put forth a new demand and took industrial action, it had to complete adjustment procedures again in advance.[233)]

When a certain labor union resumed a strike, collective bargaining for wage that the labor union proposed was not included in the first application for mediation for industrial disputes in October 1997. Accordingly, as the two cases are hard to regard as identical in industrial disputes, the two parties shall negotiate new disputes sufficiently first, and then, if there is no agreement, complete adjustment procedures for industrial disputes.

(3) When the labor union requested adjustment procedures, proposed items were not acknowledged as objects of adjustment. In this case, industrial action cannot be justifiable if it is conducted without completing adjustment procedures.[234)]

The Mediation Committee shall commence mediation without delay when any one of the parties concerned submits a request for adjustment of an industrial dispute. However, if the items submitted for adjustment were not acknowledged as objects of adjustment, the Mediation Committee shall inform the concerned parties of the reason for rejection and other problem-solving methods in accordance with Article 24(2) of the Enforcement Decree of the Trade Union Act. If the Mediation Committee reviews whether or not the case belongs to industrial disputes, finds the case cannot be an object for adjustment, and informs the parties of other problem-solving methods, such as independent bargaining procedures for both parties, the labor union shall be viewed as not having completed adjustment procedures, in accordance with Article 45(2) of the Trade Union Act.

(4) If a mediation proposal was suggested but not accepted by both parties, the labor union can begin industrial action. In this case, it is regarded that the adjustment procedures have been completed.[235)]

One party applied for adjustment concerning implementation of a monthly pay system and the Mediation Committee suggested a mediation proposal. However, when the two parties could not reach agreement during the mediation period, adjustment procedures are regarded as having been completed.

---

233) MOEL Guidelines: Hyupryeok 68140-359, on Sept.25,1998.

234) MOEL Guidelines: Hyupryeok 68140-87, on Mar.12, 1998.

235) MOEL Guidelines: Kungi 68140-458, on Dec. 5, 1998.

(2) 노조가 새로운 요구사항을 추가 제시하면서 쟁의행위를 재개한 경우 별도의 조정절차를 거쳐야한다[233)]

노조가 쟁의행위를 재개할 당시 쟁의행위의 전제로서 내세우고 있는 임금협약 체결문제는 1997.10 최초 조정신청 시에는 포함되지 않았던 새로운 쟁점이었다. 따라서 양자는 동일한 분쟁(노동쟁의) 상태로 보기 어려우므로 새로운 쟁점에 대한 충분한 교섭을 실시한 후 새로운 노동쟁의 상태의 발생을 이유로 한 조정절차를 밟아야 할 것으로 사료된다.

(3) 조정을 신청한 노동조합이 조정대상이 아닌 것으로 인정되었음에도 향후 별도의 조정절차를 거치지 않고 바로 쟁의행위에 돌입하였다면 정당하지 못하다[234)]

노동위원회는 노동관계 당사자 일방의 조정신청이 있으면 지체 없이 조정을 개시하여야 하나 신청내용이 조정대상이 아니라고 인정한 때는 노조법 시행령 제24조 제2항 규정에 따라 그 사유와 다른 해결방법을 알려주어야 하는 바, 노동위원회가 동법 제2조 제5호에 의한 노동쟁의에 해당되는지의 여부를 검토하고 조정대상이 아니라고 인정하여 당사자에게 자주적 교섭진행을 권고하는 등 다른 해결방법을 알려주었다면 이는 동법 제45조 제2항에 규정된 조정절차를 거쳤다고 할 수 없다.

(4) 노동위원회에서 조정안을 제시하였으나 당사자의 수락거부로 조정불성립되자 노조가 쟁의행위에 돌입한 경우 조정절차를 이행한 것으로 본다.[235)]

월급제시행과 관련하여 당사자 일방이 조정신청을 하여 노동위원회에서 조정안이 제시되었으나, 당사자 쌍방 또는 일방이 이를 거부하여 조정 불성립으로 종료되었다면, 이는 조정절차를 거친 것으로 보아야 할 것으로 판단된다.

---

233) 행정해석: 협력 68140-359, 1998.9.25.
234) 행정해석: 협력 68140-87, 1998.3.12.
235) 행정해석: 근기 68140-458, 1998.12.5.

(5) In cases where a strike was stopped but later resumed, shall the labor union complete adjustment procedures?[236)]

The goal of an industrial action at the time of application for mediation was not yet achieved. If there is no objective reason to deny the identity of the industrial actions between the first strike and the later strike, the labor union does not have to complete adjustment procedures and take a vote of the union members again.

(6) In cases where the labor union returned to work after a strike and then resumed the strike without completing additional adjustment procedures, is this legally acceptable?[237)]

A labor union went on strike from February 28 to June 1, 2001, then returned to work and continued collective bargaining. When the two sides could not reach agreement, the labor union resumed the strike on August 20, 2001, without completing additional adjustment procedures. Whether the union completed additional adjustment procedures or not shall be determined based upon recognition of legitimacy for industrial actions between the time of its first application for mediation and the time of the resumed industrial action.

<Types of Labor Committee Mediations>

<table>
<tr><td rowspan="2">Suggested mediation proposal</td><td colspan="2">① Accepted by both parties</td><td>Mediated agreement (Yes)</td><td>Mediation done</td></tr>
<tr><td colspan="2">② Rejected by one party or both</td><td>Mediated agreement (No)</td><td>Industrial action possible, Review for arbitration (essential public services)</td></tr>
<tr><td rowspan="7">No mediation proposal</td><td>① Accepting guidance</td><td>Agreement by guidance and withdrawal of application</td><td>Collective Agreement (Yes)</td><td>No need for industrial action</td></tr>
<tr><td>② Mediation stopped</td><td>Apparent disagreement</td><td>Collective Agreement (No)</td><td>Industrial action possible</td></tr>
<tr><td rowspan="5">③ Administrative guidance: no mediated agreement (return)</td><td>No eligible party</td><td>Return</td><td>Industrial action impossible</td></tr>
<tr><td rowspan="2">No subject of industrial action</td><td>Return</td><td rowspan="2">Industrial action impossible</td></tr>
<tr><td>Guiding compromise (e.g. reinstatement of dismissed employee)</td></tr>
<tr><td rowspan="2">Lack of bargaining (not due to disagreement)</td><td>Employer side reason</td><td>Industrial action possible</td></tr>
<tr><td>Employee side reason</td><td>Industrial action impossible</td></tr>
</table>

236) MOEL Guidelines: Hyupryeok 68107-168, on May10,2002.

237) MOEL Guidelines: Hyupryeok 68107-427, on Aug.23,2001.

(5) 파업을 중지하였다가 다시 쟁의행위를 할 경우 조정절차 등을 다시 거쳐야 하는지 여부[236)]

조정신청 당시의 쟁의상태가 해소되었다고 볼 수 없고, 새로운 쟁점이 추가되어 교섭을 실시하는 등 두 시점 사이에 노동쟁의 상태의 동일성을 인정하기 어려운 객관적인 사정이 없다면 조정절차, 조합원 찬반 투표 등을 거치지 아니하여도 무방할 것으로 판단된다.

(6) 파업 후 업무에 복귀하였다가 별도의 조정절차를 거치지 않고 재파업을 하였을 경우의 정당성 여부[237)]

2001.2.28부터 6.1까지 파업하다가 업무복귀 후 교섭을 계속하였으나 합의에 이르지 못하자, 별도의 조정절차를 거치지 아니하고 같은 해 8.20 파업을 재개한 경우에 있어서 그 정당성(조정전치 이행 여부)은 최초 조정신청 당시와 쟁의행위를 재개한 시점 사이에 노동쟁의 상태의 동일성이 인정되는지 여부에 따라 판단하여야 한다.

〈노동위원회 조정유형〉

<table>
<tr><td rowspan="2">가. 조정안 제시</td><td colspan="2">① 쌍방수락</td><td>조정서 작성
(○)</td><td>조정 완료</td></tr>
<tr><td colspan="2">② 일방 또는 쌍방의 거부</td><td>조정서 작성
(×)</td><td>쟁의행위 가능, 중재검토
(필수공익사업)</td></tr>
<tr><td rowspan="7">나. 조정안 미제시</td><td>① 지도합의</td><td>지도에 따라
합의하고 신청 취하</td><td>단체협약
(○)</td><td>쟁의행위 불필요</td></tr>
<tr><td>② 조정중지</td><td>현저한 불일치</td><td>단체협약
(×)</td><td>쟁의행위 가능</td></tr>
<tr><td rowspan="5">③ 행정지도
- 조정안 제시 불가
(반려)</td><td>당사자 부적격</td><td>반 려</td><td>쟁의행위 불가</td></tr>
<tr><td rowspan="2">쟁의대상 아님</td><td>반 려</td><td rowspan="2">쟁의행위 불가</td></tr>
<tr><td>별도 합의유도
(예: 해고자 복직 등)</td></tr>
<tr><td rowspan="2">교섭미진</td><td>사용자 측 귀책사유</td><td>쟁의행위 가능</td></tr>
<tr><td>근로자 측 귀책사유</td><td>쟁의행위 불가</td></tr>
</table>

236) 행정해석: 협력 68107-168, 2002.5.10.
237) 행정해석: 협력 68107-427, 2001.8.23.

3. Administrative guidance

(1) Items subject to adjustment procedures for industrial disputes[238)]

1) According to Article 2(5) of the Trade Union Act, "the term 'industrial dispute' means any controversy or difference arising from disagreements between a labor union and an employer or employers' association with respect to the determination of conditions of employment, such as wage, working hours, welfare, dismissal, and other issues. In this case, the disagreements refer to situations in which the parties to labor relations are no longer likely to reach an agreement by means of voluntary bargaining even if they continue to make such an attempt."

2) Whether an individual item is subject to adjustment procedures or not shall be determined in accordance with concrete actual practices, such as practical bargaining situations. If one party has requested collective bargaining for wage but there has not been any negotiation between the parties and no bargaining proposal has been suggested, this case cannot be seen as a disagreement(namely, an industrial dispute) between the labor union and the employer with respect to the determination of conditions of employment. It is therefore hard to consider this request as subject to adjustment procedures.

(2) Since an application for mediation was submitted in a situation where there had been no sufficient negotiation between the labor union and the employer, adjustment procedures could not be completed because there had been no identical industrial disputes arising from disagreements. In this case, the mediation procedures cannot satisfy the criteria for justification.[239)]

The "disagreements" applicable to mediation for industrial actions under the Trade Union Act refer to "situations in which the parties to labor relations are no longer likely to reach an agreement by means of voluntary bargaining even if they continue to make such an attempt." This clear definition is designed to ensure sufficient bargaining before completing adjustment procedures. As the labor union requested adjustment for its proposal to collective bargaining without there having been mutual efforts to

---

238) MOEL Guidelines: Hyupryeok 68140-85, on Mar.8,1999.

239) MOEL Guidelines: Hyupryeok 68140-314, on Aug.6.1997.

3. 행정지도

(1) 노동쟁의 조정대상 여부[238)]

1) "노동쟁의"라 함은 노조법 제2조 제5호에 규정한 바와 같이, "노동조합과 사용자 또는 사용자단체 간에 임금·근로시간·복지·해고 기타 대우 등 근로조건의 결정에 관한 주장의 불일치로 인하여 발생한 분쟁상태"로서 "근로조건의 결정"에 관하여 노사 당사자 간에 합의를 위한 노력을 계속하여도 더 이상 자주적 교섭에 의한 합의의 여지가 없는 주장의 불일치 상태를 말한다.

2) 개별사안이 노동쟁의 조정대상이 되느냐 여부는 실질적 교섭상황 등 구체적인 사실관계에 따라 판단하여야 할 것이나, 당사자 일방이 임금협상을 요구하였음에도 노사 간에 단 한 번도 교섭을 한 사실이 없고 교섭안도 제시된 적이 없는 등 실질적인 교섭이 이루어지지 아니하여 "근로조건의 결정"에 관한 노사 간 주장의 불일치 상태(즉, 노동쟁의)로 볼 사정이 없다면 조정대상에 해당된다고 보기 어려울 것이다.

(2) 노사 당사자 간에 충분한 교섭이 이루어지지 아니한 상태에서 행한 조정신청은 주장의 불일치로 인한 노동쟁의 상태라 할 수 없고 이 경우 소정의 절차를 거친다 하더라도 그 정당성을 갖출 수 없다.[239)]

노조법에서는 노동쟁의의 조정을 신청할 수 있는 "주장의 불일치"의 개념을 "당사자 간에 합의를 위한 노력을 계속하여도 더 이상 자주적 교섭에 의한 합의의 여지가 없는 경우"로 명확히 하여 노사 간 충분한 교섭 이후에 조정을 신청할 수 있도록 하고 있으므로(노조법 제2조 제5호) 노동관계 당사자 간에 이러한 합의의 노력도 없이 단협개정안만 제시된 상태에서 조정 신청한 때는 주장의 불일치로 인한 노동쟁의 상태라 할 수 없고, 이 경우 쟁의행위 찬반투표 등 소정의 절차를 거친다 하더라도 동법에서 정하는 노동쟁의 및 쟁의행위의 정당한 요건을 갖출 수 없다고 판단된다.

---

238) 행정해석: 협력68140-85, 1999.3.8.
239) 행정해석: 협력 68140-314, 1997.8.6.

reach agreement, this situation cannot be regarded as an industrial dispute coming from disagreement. In this case, although the labor union has followed required procedures, such as a yes/no vote of its members, it cannot satisfy requirements for deeming industrial disputes and industrial actions justifiable.

(3) Procedural justification for an industrial action after administrative guidance from the Mediation Committee[240)]

If the Mediation Committee acknowledges that bargaining items cannot be objects for mediation in the adjustment of industrial disputes but the labor union began industrial action without additional adjustment procedures, this is a violation of Article 45(2) of the Trade Union Act(system proceeding adjustment).

(4) An industrial action is not illegal after administrative guidance from the Mediation Committee in relation to 'system proceeding adjustment'.[241)]

It is not illegal to begin a strike right after completion of a mediation period when the labor union applied for adjustment for industrial disputes but mediation was not accepted or terminated.

(5) Handling an application for mediation when it was requested without sufficient bargaining between the parties.[242)]

Article 2 of the Trade Union Act regulates that the term "industrial disputes" means situations in which the parties to labor relations are no longer likely to reach an agreement by means of voluntary bargaining even if they continue to make such attempts. Accordingly, if both parties to labor relations have not conducted sufficient negotiations, it is hard to regard the situation as an industrial dispute. In cases where there is application for mediation according to Article 53 of the Trade Union Act, the Labor Committee shall hear the opinions of the two parties. If the situation cannot be acknowledged as an industrial dispute, the Labor Committee shall suggest another problem-solving method, like recommending independent negotiation in accordance with Article 24(2) of the

240) MOEL Guidelines: Hyupryeok 68140-132, on Apr. 10, 2000.

241) Supreme Court ruling on June 26, 2001, 2000Do2871.

242) MOEL Guidelines: Hyupryeok 68140-220, June 4, 1997.

(3) 노동위원회의 행정지도 이후 쟁의행위의 절차적 정당성 여부[240)]

노동위원회가 조합의 노동쟁의조정신청 사건에 대하여 조정대상이 아닌 것으로 인정하였음에도 불구하고 노동조합이 별도의 조정절차를 거치지 않고 바로 쟁의행위에 돌입하였다면 이는 동법 제45조 제2항(조정전치) 위반이라 할 것이다.

(4) '조정전치제도' 관련 중노위의 행정지도 후 파업은 불법이 아니다[241)]

노조가 노동위원회에 노동쟁의 조정신청을 하고 조정절차를 마치거나 조정이 종료되지 않은 채 조정기간이 끝나면 노동조합은 쟁의행위를 할 수 있다.

(5) 당사자 간 충분한 교섭이 이루어지지 아니한 조정신청에 대한 처리[242)]

"노동쟁의"라 함은 노조법 제2조에서 규정한 바와 같이 노동관계 당사자 간에 임금 등 근로조건의 결정에 관하여 합의를 위한 노력에도 불구하고 더 이상 자주적인 교섭을 통한 합의가 불가능한 상태이므로 노동관계 당사자 간의 충분한 논의가 이루어지지 아니한 경우에는 노동쟁의 상태라 할 수 없을 것이므로 동법 제53조에 의한 조정신청이 있는 경우 노동관계 당사자의 의견을 청취한 후 노동쟁의 상태가 아니라고 판단되는 경우에는 동법 시행령 제24조 제2항에 의거 당사자 간의 자주적인 교섭진행을 권고하는 등 다른 해결방법을 알려 주어야 할 것이다.

---

240) 행정해석: 협력 68140-132, 2000.4.10.
241) 대법원 2001.6.26, 2000도2871.
242) 행정해석: 협력 68140-220, 1997.6.4.

Enforcement Decree of the Trade Union Act.

(6) After the Labor Committee determined a termination of adjustment due to the absence of the parties at a mediation meeting, an industrial action taken without completing additional adjustment procedures is in violation of Article 45(2) of the Trade Union Act.[243)]

According to Article 45(2) of the Trade Union Act, industrial action shall be taken only after completing adjustment procedures. Also, Article 53 and 58 of the Act regulate that the parties related shall participate in adjustment procedures in good faith, attend mediation meetings, and confirm their opinions. In cases where the Labor Committee determined "a termination of mediation process" due to the absence of the parties at a mediation meeting, adjustment procedures were not completed. Accordingly, industrial action taken without completing adjustment procedures is in violation of Article 45(2) of the Trade Union Act.

243) MOEL Guidelines: Hyupryeok 68140-97, Mar. 25, 1998.

(6) 노동위원회가 조정절차 불참에 따른 조정중지 결정 이후에 별도의 조정절차 없이 행한 쟁의행위는 법 제45조 제2항에 위반되는 쟁의행위이다.[243)]

노조법 제45조 제2항은 조정절차를 거친 이후에만 쟁의행위를 할 수 있도록 하고 있고, 또한, 동법 제53조 및 제58조는 관계 당사자의 조정절차에의 성실 참여와 조정위원회의 출석 및 주장을 확인토록 규정하고 있는바, 노동위원회가 관계 당사자의 조정절차 불참으로 "조정중지"를 결정하는 경우에는 조정절차를 거친 것으로 볼 수 없다. 따라서 노동위원회가 조정절차 불참에 따른 조정중지 결정 이후에 별도의 조정절차 없이 쟁의행위는 법 제45조 제2항에 위반되는 쟁의행위이다.

---

243) 행정해석: 협력 68140-97, 1998.3.25.

Section 2: Essential Public Service and Minimum Services to be Maintained

Article 71 (Scope of Public Services, etc.)

① "Public service" under this Act means a service described in any of the following subparagraphs, which is indispensable to the daily lives of the general public or has great influence on the national economy:

1. Regular line public transportation services;
2. Water, electricity, gas supply, oil refinery and supply services;
3. Public health and medical services and blood supply services;
4. Banking and mint services;
5. Broadcasting and telecommunication services.

② "Essential public service" under this Act means any service described in the following subparagraphs, which falls within the category of public services under paragraph (1) and whose stoppage and discontinuance may endanger the daily lives of the general public, or may undermine the national economy considerably, and whose replacement presents a grave hardship:

1. Railroad services, inter-city railroad services, and aviation services;
2. Water, electricity, gas supply, oil refinery and supply services;
3. Hospital and blood supply services;
4. The Bank of Korea;
5. Telecommunication services.

Article 42-2 (Restrictions on Industrial Action in Minimum Services to Be Maintained)

① The term "minimum services to be maintained" in this Act refers to those services among essential public services prescribed in Article 71 (2), which, if suspended or discontinued, could remarkably endanger the lives, health, physical safety or daily lives of the public and are prescribed by Presidential Decree.

② No act of stopping, discontinuing or obstructing the proper maintenance and operation of the minimum services to be maintained shall be carried out as legitimate industrial action.

Ⅰ. Essential Public Services and Minimum Services to be Maintained

Article 71(2) of the Trade Union Act refers to essential public services as meaning any service described in the following subparagraphs, which fall within the category of public service under paragraph(1) and whose stoppage and discontinuance may endanger the daily lives of the general public, or may considerably undermine the national economy, and whose replacement presents an undue hardship:

제2절 필수공익사업과 필수유지업무

제71조【공익사업의 범위등】
① 이 법에서 "공익사업"이라 함은 공중의 일상생활과 밀접한 관련이 있거나 국민경제에 미치는 영향이 큰 사업으로서 다음 각호의 사업을 말한다.
1. 정기노선 여객운수사업 및 항공운수사업
2. 수도사업, 전기사업, 가스사업, 석유정제사업 및 석유공급사업
3. 공중위생사업, 의료사업 및 혈액공급사업
4. 은행 및 조폐사업
5. 방송 및 통신사업
② 이 법에서 "필수공익사업"이라 함은 제1항의 공익사업으로서 그 업무의 정지 또는 폐지가 공중의 일상생활을 현저히 위태롭게 하거나 국민경제를 현저히 저해하고 그 업무의 대체가 용이하지 아니한 다음 각호의 사업을 말한다.
1. 철도사업, 도시철도사업 및 항공운수사업
2. 수도사업, 전기사업, 가스사업, 석유정제사업 및 석유공급사업
3. 병원사업 및 혈액공급사업
4. 한국은행사업
5. 통신사업

제42조의2【필수유지업무에 대한 쟁의행위의 제한】
① 이 법에서 "필수유지업무"라 함은 제71조 제2항의 규정에 따른 필수공익사업의 업무 중 그 업부가 정지되거나 폐지되는 경우 공중의 생명·건강 또는 신체의 안전이나 공중의 일상생활을 현저히 위태롭게 하는 업무로서 대통령령이 정하는 업무를 말한다.
② 필수유지업무의 정당한 유지·운영을 정지·폐지 또는 방해하는 행위는 쟁의행위로서 이를 행할 수 없다.

Ⅰ. 의 의

노조법 제71조 제2항은 "필수공익사업"이라 함은 제1항의 공익사업으로서 그 업무의 정지 또는 폐지가 공중의 일상생활을 현저히 위태롭게 하거나 국민경제를 현저히 저해하고 그 업무의 대체가 용이하지 않은 다음 가호의 사업을

① Railroad services, inter-city railroad services, and aviation services; ② Water, electricity, gas supply, oil refinery and supply services; ③ Hospital and blood supply services; ④ The Bank of Korea; ⑤ Telecommunication services.

Prior to 2008, in a case involving an essential public service, the right to strike was totally limited through arbitration by a special labor commission. As a complementary measure, the Trade Union Act introduced on January 1, 2008 abolished the arbitration system for mandatory public services and instead introduced a mandatory maintenance service system for essential public services.[244)]

The Trade Union Act stipulates that the term minimum services to be maintained in the Act refers to those essential public services prescribed in Article 71(2), which, if suspended or discontinued, could remarkably endanger the life, health, physical safety or daily lives of the public and are prescribed by Presidential Decree(Article 42-2, paragraph 1). Furthermore, stopping, discontinuing or obstructing the proper maintenance and operation of the minimum services to be maintained shall not be carried out as a legitimate industrial action(Article 42-2, paragraph 2). Those in violation of this shall be subject to imprisonment for up to 3 years or a penalty of up to KRW 30 million(Article 89, paragraph 1). The parties to labor relations shall conclude an agreement in writing that stipulates the levels of minimum services to be maintained and provided, the specific work designated as minimum service, the necessary number of workers, etc., in order to ensure the proper maintenance and operation of minimum services during a period of industrial action. In this case, both parties shall sign or seal an agreement on minimum services to be maintained(Article 42-3). Therefore, unions will be held liable for illegal disputes in cases where they do not engage in agreement on minimum services to be maintained.[245)]

Ⅱ. Criteria for Classification of a Business as Providing an Essential Public Service[246)]

In order for a specific business to be an essential public service in the interpretation of the provisions related to the Trade Union Act, ① the public service pursuant to Article 71(1) of the Act shall meet the formal requirements under the provisions of Article 71(2); ② the suspension or

244) Ministry of Employment and Labor, Explanation of Operations for Minimum Services to be Maintained Nov. 2007.

245) Moon, Moo-gi, The scope of minimum services to be maintained during strikes, Labor Review 26, Korea Labor Institute, Jan. 2007, p. 38.

246) Ministry of Employment and Labor, Explanation of Operations for the Minimum Services to be Maintained Nov. 2007, p. 7-9.

말한다. ① 철도사업, 도시철도사업 및 항공운수사업, ② 수도사업, 전기사업, 가스사업, 석유정제사업 및 석유공급사업, ③ 병원사업 및 혈액공급 사업, ④ 한국은행사업, ⑤ 통신사업.

2008년 이전에는 필수공익사업의 경우 특별노동위원회의 직권중재를 통해 파업권이 전면적으로 제한되었다. 이에 대해 보완책으로 2008.1.1. 부터 시행된 노조법은 필수공익사업에 대한 직권중재제도를 폐지하면서 필수공익 사업에 필수유지업무제도를 도입하였다.[244]

노조법은 필수공익사업의 업무 중 그 업무가 정지되거나 폐지되는 경우 공중의 생명, 건강 또는 신체의 안전이나 공중의 일상생활을 현저히 위태롭게 하는 업무를 '필수유지업무'로 규정하고 그 구체적인 내용은 시행령에서 정하고 있다(제42조의2 제1항). 더욱이 필수유지업무의 정당한 유지, 운영을 정지, 폐지 또는 방해하는 행위를 금지하고 있으며(제42조의2 제2항), 위반 시 3년이하의 징역 또는 3천만원 이하 벌금형을 처한다(제89조 제1호). 노동관계 당사자는 쟁의행위 기간 동안 필수유지업무의 정당한 유지·운영을 위하여 필요 최소한의 유지·운영 수준, 대상직무 및 필요인원 등을 정한 필수유지업무협정을 서면으로 체결하여야 한다(제42조의3). 따라서 노동조합은 필수유지업무협정이 체결되지 않은 상황에서 쟁의행위를 할 경우에는 불법쟁의행위의 책임을 지게 된다.[245]

Ⅱ. 필수공익사업의 해당 여부 구분기준[246]

노조법 관련 규정의 해석상 특정 사업이 필수공익사업에 해당되기 위해서는 ① 법 제71조 제1항의 규정에 의한 공익사업으로, 법 제71조 제2항 각호의 규정에 의한 사업이라는 형식적 요건을 충족하여야 하며, ② 업무의 정지 또는 폐지가 공중의 일상생활을 현저히 위태롭게 하거나 국민경제를 현저히 저해하고 그 업무의 대체가 용이하지 않은 실질적 요건을 구비하여야 한다.

244) 노동부, "필수유지업제도 운영 해설", 2007.11.
245) 문무기, "파업시 유지되는 필수업무의 범위", 「노동리뷰」 26, 한국노동연구원, 2007.2, 38면.
246) 행정해석, 노동조합과-1393, 2008.6.23. 7~9면.

abolishment of the work shall have substantial repercussions that significantly jeopardize the daily lives of the public or that significantly impede the national economy and are not easily replaceable.

Formal requirements are in accordance with Annex 1 of the Enforcement Decree to the Trade Union Act: Each minimum service to be maintained per essential public service. Substantive requirements are: ① to become an essential public service, the suspension or abolishment of work due to industrial action must seriously endanger the daily lives of the public or hinder the national economy; ② since the suspension or abolishment of such service should concern a business having a large effect on the daily lives of the public or the national economy, the service, the production scale of the goods, and the service supply target should be targeted to the general public; ③ the substitution of workers should not be easy, so that it is difficult to substitute other similar companies in consideration of production and service scale. In other words, if a substitute can easily be accomplished through canceling an outsourcing contract, it should be considered that there is a possibility for substitution.

Therefore, whether the service is an essential public service or not is decided with the following condition: it should meet both of the formal and substantial requirements mentioned above.

Ⅲ. Employee Replacement for Essential Public Services

Article 43 (Restriction on Hiring by Employer)

① No employer shall hire persons who are not related to their business operations, or use replacements during a period of industrial action so as to continue works which have been stopped by industrial actions.

② No employer shall, during a period of industrial action, contract or subcontract out work which has been suspended because of the industrial action concerned.

③ The provisions of paragraphs (1) and (2) shall not apply to the employer of essential public services who hires persons unrelated to the business concerned or use replacements, or contract or subcontract out the work only during a period of industrial action.

④ In the case of paragraph (3), an employer may hire or use replacements or contract or subcontract out the work as long as the proportion of the replacement workers do not exceed 50/100 of strike participants of the business or workplace concerned. In this case, method to calculate the number of strike participants, etc., shall be prescribed in the Presidential Decree.

1. Concept

Article 43(3 and 4) of the Trade Union Act regulates that the provisions of paragraphs(1) and(2) shall not apply to an employer of essential public services who hires persons

필수공익사업에 해당되기 위한 형식적 요건은 노조법 시행령 별표1 “필수공익사업별 필수유지업무”에 따른다. 필수공익사업의 실질적 요건은 ① 쟁의행위로 인한 업무의 정지나 폐지가 공중의 일상생활을 현저히 위태롭게 하거나 국민경제를 저해하여야 한다. 또한, ② 사업의 정지나 폐지가 공중의 일상생활 및 국민경제에 미치는 파급효과가 큰 사업이어야 하므로 서비스, 재화의 생산규모 및 서비스 공급대상이 일반 공중을 대상으로 하여야 하고, ③ 그 업무의 대체가 용이하지 아니하여야 하므로 생산, 서비스 규모 등을 감안할 때 다른 동종 업체가 대체하는 것이 곤란할 정도이어야 한다. 즉, 도급, 위탁 등을 통해 외부업체가 수행하는 사업으로서 외주계약 취소를 통하여 용이하게 대체수행이 가능한 경우라면 대체 가능성이 있다고 보아야 한다.

그 사업이 필수공익사업인지 여부는 앞서 언급한 형식적 요건과 실질적 요건을 모두 갖추어야 필수공익사업이라고 할 수 있다.

Ⅲ. 필수공익사업의 대체근로

제43조【사용자의 채용제한】
① 사용자는 쟁의행위 기간중 그 쟁의행위로 중단된 업무의 수행을 위하여 당해 사업과 관계없는 자를 채용 또는 대체할 수 없다.
② 사용자는 쟁의행위기간중 그 쟁의행위로 중단된 업무를 도급 또는 하도급 줄 수 없다.
③ 제1항 및 제2항의 규정은 필수공익사업의 사용자가 쟁의행위 기간 중에 한하여 당해 사업과 관계 없는 자를 채용 또는 대체하거나 그 업무를 도급 또는 하도급 주는 경우에는 적용하지 아니한다.
④ 제3항의 경우 사용자는 당해 사업 또는 사업장 파업참가자의 100분의 50을 초과하지 않는 범위 안에서 채용 또는 대체하거나 도급 또는 하도급 줄 수 있다. 이 경우 파업참가자 수의 산정 방법 등은 대통령령으로 정한다.

1. 의 의

노조법 제43조 제3항과 제4항은 필수공익사업의 사용자가 쟁의행위 기간 중에 한하여 당해 사업과 관계없는 자를 채용 또는 대체하거나 그 업무를 도급 또

unrelated to the business concerned or uses replacements, or contracts or subcontracts out the work only during a period of industrial action. In this case, the employer may hire or use replacements or contract or subcontract out the work as long as the proportion of the replacement workers does not exceed 50/100 of the strike participants of the business or workplace concerned(implemented January 1, 2008).

2. Requirements

Essential public services are those public services where stoppages and discontinuance may endanger the lives of members of the general public, or considerably undermine the national economy, and whose replacement presents undue hardship: ① Railroad services; ② Water, electricity, gas supply, oil refinery and supply services; ③ Hospital services; ④ The Bank of Korea; and ⑤ Telecommunication services.

Since compulsory mediation for essential public services has been abolished, all personnel filling jobs in essential public services(besides the minimum to be maintained) are entirely permitted to take industrial action. However, in order to protect the public interest, partial employee replacement is permitted as long as the number of replacement workers(who can be new hires, existing workers, or workers used by a company receiving a contract or subcontract for the work) does not exceed 50/100 of the strike participants of the business or workplace concerned.

3. Effect

In cases where industrial action is taken in essential public services, employee replacement is permitted on a limited basis to positively minimize the risk to the general public or the national economy. These exceptions, such as the minimum services to be maintained and permitting employee replacement, were introduced in return for abolishment of the mandatory mediation system and as a way to provide a balance between labor protections and the public interest.[247)]

---

247) Kim, Hyungbae, & Park, Jisoon, 「Lectures on Labor Laws」, 4th ed., 2015, Shinjosa, p. 567.

는 하도급 주는 경우에는 동법 동조 제1, 2항의 규정을 적용하지 아니하고, 그 경우 사용자는 당해 사업 또는 사업장 파업 참가자의 100분의 50을 초과하지 않는 범위 안에서 채용 또는 대체하거나 도급 또는 하도급 줄 수 있다.고 규정하고 있다(2008.1.1 시행).

2. 요 건

공익사업 중 그 업무의 정지 또는 폐지가 공중의 일상생활을 현저히 위태롭게 하거나 국민경제를 현저히 저해하고, 그 업무의 대체가 용이하지 아니한 철도 운송사업, 수도·전기·가스·석유정제 및 석유공급사업, 병원사업, 한국은행, 통신사업 등을 필수공익사업이라 한다. 이러한 필수공익사업에 대한 직권중재가 폐지됨에 따라, 필수유지업무 외의 업무에 대해서는 쟁의행위가 전면적으로 허용됐으며 공익을 보호하기 위해 필수공익사업에서는 대체근로를 일부 허용하게 됐다. 필수공익사업의 경우에는 파업참가자의 100분의 50을 초과하지 않는 범위 안에서, 쟁의행위로 중단된 업무의 수행을 위한 채용, 대체 또는 도급, 하도급이 허용된다.

3. 효 과

이 규정들은 필수공익사업에서 쟁의행위가 일어난 경우에 공중의 일상생활 또는 국민경제에 대한 현저한 위해를 최소화하기 위하여 제한된 범위에서 대체근로를 할 수 있도록 허용한 것이다. 즉 직권중재제도를 대신하여 필수공익사업의 쟁의행위를 규율하기 위하여 필수 유지업무제도와 대체근로 허용제도가 채택된 것으로 국민의 일상생활의 유지를 위한 필수적 서비스를 담당하는 필수공익사업에 대한 직권중재의 폐지에 대하여 한편으로는 필수 유지업무제도를 도입하고 다른 한편으로 대체근로를 허용함으로써 공익 보호와의 균형을 추구하고 있다.[247]

---

247) 김형배·박지순, 『노동법강의』, 제8판, 2019, 신소사, 567면.

Chapter 17

Unfair Labor Practice

Section 1: Understanding Unfair Labor Practice

Ⅰ. Concept

Article 33 Paragraph 1 of the Constitution stipulates that workers have the right to independent association, collective bargaining and collective action in order to improve their working conditions. These three labor rights are basic rights of the people guaranteed by the Constitution. The Trade Union and Labor Relations Adjustment Act (hereafter, the Labor Union Act) mentions these three labor rights and provisions on unfair labor practices. It describes in detail what amounts to violation of each of the three labor rights, stipulates the procedure for applications for remedy against unfair labor practices through the Labor Relations Commission, and allows criminal punishment for unfair labor practices through the Labor Office. According to the courts, a system to deal with unfair labor practice was specifically established by the Labor Union Act to quickly normalize labor relations by securing the three rights of labor, and preventing and stopping the actions of employers that destroy the order of collective labor relations.[248)]

Unfair labor practices can be said to infringe on the three labor rights, and are divided into five types of actions (as described in Article 81 of the Labor Union Act) by the employer and any person in a position equivalent to employer that disadvantage the union or its members.

---

248) Supreme Court ruling May 8, 1998: 97nu7448.

Chapter 17

부당노동행위

제1절 부당노동행위 이해

Ⅰ. 부당노동행위의 의의

헌법 제33조 제1항은 “근로자는 근로조건의 향상을 위하여 자주적인 단결권, 단체교섭권과 단체행동권을 가진다.” 라고 명시하고 있다. 노동3권은 헌법에서 보장된 국민의 기본권이다. 노동조합법은 위의 노동3권과 부당노동행위에 대한 규정을 두고 있다. 노동3권의 침해행위를 구체적으로 기술하고, 이에 대한 노동위원회를 통해 부당노동행위 구제신청의 절차를 규정하고 있으며, 노동관청을 통한 부당노동행위에 대한 형사처벌을 할 수 있도록 하고 있다. 판례에 따르면, 부당노동행위제도는 집단적 노사관계의 질서를 파괴하는 사용자의 행위를 사전에 예방, 제거함으로써 노동3권을 확보하여 노사관계의 질서를 신속하게 정상화하기 위하여 노동조합법에서 특별히 규정하고 있다고 한다.[248)]

부당노동행위는 노동3권을 침해하는 행위이다. 그 내용은 사용자와 사용자의 지위에 있는 자가 노동조합법 제81조의 기술된 5가지의 부당노동행위를 통하여 노동조합이나 조합원들에게 불이익을 주는 행위이기 때문이다.

---

248) 대법원 1998.5.8. 선고 97누7448 판결.

Ⅱ. Criteria for Judging Labor Practices as Unfair

There are three elements that must be present for a labor practice to be deemed unfair: it should include actions by the employer, at least one of the five items described in Article 81 of the Labor Union Act should exist, and the employer must intend to engage in the unfair labor practice.

1. Actions by the employer

Unfair labor practices are a result of actions of an employer. In the Labor Union Act, an employer is excluded from membership in a labor union, is someone in charge of managing the business, someone acting on behalf of the employer in matters relating to the employed workers, or someone always acting specifically in the employer's interest (Articles 2 and 4). Here, the acts by "someone acting on behalf of the employer in matters relating to the employed workers" refer to matters such as determining the working conditions of workers, managing personnel, salaries, welfare, and labor, or giving orders or supervising work—a person who has been given certain powers and responsibilities by the employer. "Someone always acting specifically in the employer's interest" refers to ① those directly participating in labor relations decisions such as personnel management, salary, disciplinary action, auditing, and labor management of workers, or ② those working to implement the employer's plans and policies for employment relations, and has the authority to handle confidential matters.[249)]

Even if a worker who does not fall within the scope of employer follows the employer's instructions or acts specifically under the tacit approval of the employer, acts that obstruct the organization or operation of the union must be regarded as an employer's acts.[250)] However, if an ordinary worker personally engages in unfair labor practices that infringe on the three labor rights, it cannot be regarded as an unfair labor practice by the employer.

---

249) Supreme Court ruling on Sep. 8, 2011: 2008doo13873.

250) Lim, Jong Ryul, 「Labor」 18th ed, Parkyoungsa, 2020, p. 283.

Ⅱ. 부당노동행위의 판단기준

부당노동행위를 구성하는 3가지 요소는 다음과 같다.

첫째, 사용자의 행위여야 하고 둘째, 사용자의 행위가 노동조합법 제81조에 기술된 5가지의 내용 중 하나에 해당되어야 하며 셋째, 사용자의 부당노동행위 의사가 있어야 한다.

1. 사용자의 행위

부당노동행위는 사용자의 행위에 의해 이루어진다. 노동조합법에서 사용자는 노동조합의 가입대상에 제외되는 사업주, 사업의 경영담당자, 그 사업의 근로자에 관한 사항에 대하여 사업주를 위하여 행동하는 자 그리고 사용자의 이익을 대표하여 행동하는 자를 말한다(노조법 제2조제2호, 제4호). 여기서 '그 사업의 근로자에 관한 사항에 대하여 사업주를 위하여 행동하는 자'라 함은 근로자의 인사, 급여, 후생, 노무관리 등 근로조건의 결정 또는 업무상의 명령이나 지휘 감독을 하는 등의 사항에 대하여 사업주로부터 일정한 권한과 책임을 부여받은 자를 말한다. 그리고 '항상 사용자의 이익을 대표하여 행동하는 자'라 함은 ①근로자에 대한 인사, 급여, 징계, 감사, 노무관리 등 근로관계 결정에 직접 참여하거나 ②사용자의 근로관계에 대한 계획과 방침에 관한 기밀사항 업무를 취급할 권한이 있는 자를 말한다.[249)]

사용자 범위에 속하지 않는 근로자라 하더라도 사용자의 지시에 따르거나 사용자의 묵시적 승인 아래 노동조합의 조직이나 운영을 방해하는 행위를 한 경우, 사용자의 행위로 보아야 한다.[250)] 그러나 일반 근로자가 개인적으로 노동3권을 침해하는 부당노동행위를 한 경우에는 이를 부당노동행위로 볼 수 없다.

---

249) 대법원 2011.9.8. 선고 2008두13873 판결

250) 임종률, 「노동법」 18판, 박영사, 2020, 283면.

2. Five types of unfair labor practice

① Disadvantageous treatment due to labor union activity: Dismissal or unfavorable treatment of a worker on the grounds that he/she has joined or intends to join a labor union, or has attempted to organize a labor union, or has performed any other lawful act for operation of a labor union (Infringement of the right to organize);

② Anti-union contract: Dismissal or unfavorable treatment of a worker is written into the contract for joining or intending to join a labor union, or attempting to organize a labor union, or performing any other lawful act for operation of a labor union (Violation of the right to organize);

③ Refusing or neglecting to engage in collective bargaining: Refusing or delaying execution of a collective agreement or other collective bargaining with the representative or other person authorized by the labor union, without justifiable reason (Infringement of the right to collectively bargain);

④ Domination of, interference in, or subsidizing operating expenses for labor union activities: Dominating or interfering in the organization or operation of a labor union by workers, and paying wages to full-time officers of a labor union or financially supporting labor union operations (Violation of the right to organize);

⑤ Disadvantageous treatment for reporting on collective actions or unfair labor practices: Dismissal of workers or acts against their interest on the grounds that they have participated in justifiable collective activities, or that they reported to or testified before the Labor Relations Commission the fact that the employer has violated the provisions of this Article, or that they have presented other evidence to the relevant administrative agencies (Violation of the right to take industrial action);

3. Intention to engage in unfair labor practice

In order to judge a labor practice as unfair, it must be done with a clear intention by the employer to engage in what he/she knows is unfair, such as an employer intentionally disadvantaging a worker for his/her legitimate union activities. According to a related court ruling, "Whether an employer's conduct falls under the unfair labor practices stipulated in the Labor Union Act is determined after comprehensively reviewing all circumstances that can infer whether the employer intends to engage in unfair labor practice."[251)]

---

251) Supreme Court ruling on Nov. 15, 2007: 2005 doo 4120.

2. 부당노동행위의 5가지 유형

① 노동조합 활동을 한 것을 이유로 하는 불이익 처분: 근로자가 노동조합에 가입 또는 가입하려고 하였거나 노동조합을 조직하려고 하였거나 기타 노동조합의 업무를 위한 정당한 행위를 한 것을 이유로 그 근로자를 해고하거나 그 근로자에게 불이익을 주는 행위 (단결권 침해)

② 반조합계약 작성: 근로자가 어느 노동조합에 가입하지 아니할 것 또는 탈퇴할 것을 고용조건으로 하거나 특정한 노동조합의 조합원이 될 것을 고용조건으로 하는 행위 (단결권 침해)

③ 단체교섭을 거부하거나 해태: 노동조합의 대표자 또는 노동조합으로부터 위임을 받은 자와의 단체협약체결 및 기타 단체교섭을 정당한 이유없이 거부하거나 해태하는 행위 (단체교섭권 침해)

④ 노동조합 활동에 대한 지배 및 개입이나 운영비 원조: 근로자가 노동조합을 조직 또는 운영하는 것을 지배하거나 이에 개입하는 행위와 근로시간 면제한도를 초과하여 급여를 지급하거나 노동조합의 운영비를 원조하는 행위 (단결권 침해)

⑤ 단체행동이나 부당노동행위에 대한 신고를 한 것을 이유로 하는 불이익 처분: 근로자가 정당한 단체행위에 참가한 것을 이유로 하거나 또는 노동위원회에 대하여 사용자의 부당노동행위를 신고하거나 그에 관한 증언을 하거나 기타 행정관청에 증거를 제출한 것을 이유로 그 근로자를 해고하거나 그 근로자에게 불이익을 주는 행위 (단체행동권 침해)

3. 부당노동행위의 의사

부당노동행위를 판단하기 위해서는 사용자의 부당노동행위에 대한 분명한 의사를 가지고 행하여야 한다. 근로자의 정당한 조합활동을 이유로 한 의도적인 불이익처분이 있어야 하다. 관련 판례에 따르면, “사용자의 행위가 노동조합 및 노동관계조정법에서 정한 부당노동행위 여부는 사용자의 부당노동행위 의사의 존재 여부를 추정할 수 있는 모든 사정을 전체적으로 심리 검토하여 종합적으로 판단하여야 한다.”고 판시하고 있다.[251)]

---

251) 대법원 2007.11.15. 선고 2005두4120 판결

Ⅲ. Types of Unfair Labor Practice

1. Unfair treatment

Article 81 (Unfair Labor Practices)

1. Dismissal or unfavorable treatment of a worker on grounds that he has joined or intends to join a labor union, or has attempted to organize a labor union, or has performed any other lawful act for the operation of a labor union; and
2. Dismissal of workers or acting against their interests on the grounds that they participated in justifiable collective activities or that they reported to or testified before the Labor Relations Commission regarding the employer violating provisions of this Article, or that they presented other evidence to relevant administrative agencies.

Dismissal or unfavorable treatment of a worker on grounds that he/she has joined or intends to join a labor union, or has attempted to organize a labor union, or has performed any other lawful act for the operation of a labor union is unfair treatment.

<Cases Not Deemed Unfair Treatment>

① Disciplinary punishment of a labor union's key officers, who have led or agitated the refusal of extended or night work that was already determined by the labor-management council, on account of activities of the union establishment
② Dismissal of an employee who has led a labor union establishment in foreign embassies where Korean labor laws are not applicable
③ Dismissal of a temporary or short-term employee whose contract has expired
④ Dismissal of an employee who has been expelled from the union for leading an illegal strike without justifiable procedures
⑤ Dismissal of an employee related to establishing and operating a social club, not related to labor union activities
⑥ Dismissal of an employee who has violated managerial orders on account of feigning career history, etc.
⑦ Dismissal of a union's full-time officer who has been dismissed from the labor union for refusing to work at the department he/she belongs to
⑧ Dismissal of an employee who has been sentenced as a criminal for an incident not related to union activities
⑨ Disciplinary punishment of a nurse who has violated the rules of employment by wearing union clothes instead of a nurse's uniform

Ⅲ. 부당노동행위의 유형

1. 불이익취급

노조법 제81조【부당노동행위】

1. 근로자가 노동조합에 가입 또는 가입하려고 하였거나 노동조합을 조직하려고 하였거나 기타 노동조합의 업무를 위한 정당한 행위를 한 것을 이유로 그 근로자를 해고하거나 그 근로자에게 불이익을 주는 행위
2. 근로자가 정당한 단체행위에 참가한 것을 이유로 하거나 또는 노동위원회에 대하여 사용자가 이 조의 규정에 위반한 것을 신고하거나 그에 관한 증언을 하였거나 기타 행정관청에 증거를 제출한 것을 이유로 그 근로자를 해고하거나 그 근로자에게 불이익을 주는 행위

사용자는 근로자가 노동조합에 가입 또는 가입하려고 하였거나, 노동조합을 조직하려고 하였거나 기타 노동조합의 업무를 위한 정당한 행위를 한 것을 이유로 그 근로자에게 불이익을 주는 행위를 말한다.

〈불이익취급이 아닌 사례〉

① 노조설립 활동을 구실로 노사협의회에서 결정한 연장, 야간근로거부 및 선동을 주도한 노조간부 징계
② 우리 노동법이 적용되지 않는 외국공관에서 노조설립 주동을 이유로 해고
③ 임시적 또는 기한부로 고용된 자의 작업종료에 따른 해고조치
④ 정당한 절차 없이 쟁의행위 주동으로 조합에서 쫓겨난 자를 감원시킨 경우
⑤ 조합활동과 무관한 진복단체조식, 운영을 이유로 해고된 경우
⑥ 경력사칭 등을 이유로 경영질서가 침해되어 해고된 경우
⑦ 노조에서 직위해제 된 노조 전임자가 변형된 소속부서로의 출근거부로 해고된 경우
⑧ 조합활동과 무관한 사건으로 유죄판결을 받음에 따라 해고한 경우
⑨ 간호사가 노조활동을 이유로 간호복 대신 노조 업무복을 입는 등 복무규정을 위반한 이유로 징계

(1) Is it unfair labor practice to promote a union officer to a position which does not allow him to belong to a labor union?

Whether a personnel order to a certain union member is an unfair labor practice or not shall be determined collectively in consideration of all factors, such as relations between the timing of the order and union activities, job necessity, eligibility and the rationale for the personnel selection, and the relations between the company and the labor union. Consideration will also be given to whether a personnel order is an attempt to violate the employees' three rights. However, when a personnel order to a union member is implemented as a regular personnel order because of job necessity or general standards, such a personnel order shall not be deemed unfair labor practice.[252)]

(2) In cases where an employer fires an employee who staged a sit-in without the union's resolution or instruction, this is not unfair labor practice.

An employee staged a sit-in and, in doing so, obstructed the business. Furthermore, the sit-in was not due to a union resolution or instruction but was simply on the employee's own initiative. The employer's decision to dismiss the employee on the grounds of the unauthorized sit-in does not constitute an act of unfair labor practice.[253)]

(3) If an employer promotes an employee who is entitled to join the union to a higher position which prevents him/her from joining the union, is this an act of unfair labor practice?

In order to determine whether such job promotion constitutes an act of unfair labor practice, it is necessary to consider the timing of the promotion, its impact on union activities, necessity of the promotion for business purposes, the employee's job skills, reasonable nature of the promotion, etc. If the employer's decision to promote the employee to a higher post was based on reasonable criteria for personnel management and the principle of equitability, the promotion is not an unfair labor practice, given that the employee had refused to accept the promotion.[254)]

---

252) MOEL Guidelines: Nojo 10254-68, on Jan.22,2001.

253) Supreme Court ruling on Nov. 13, 1990, 89Nu5102.

254) Supreme Court ruling on Oct. 27, 1992, 92Nu9418.

(1) 노조 임원을 승진 발령하는 것이 부당노동행위에 해당하는지 여부

특정 조합원에 대한 인사조치가 부당노동행위에 해당하는지 여부는 당해 인사조치의 시기와 조합활동과의 관련성, 업무상의 필요성, 능력의 적격성과 인선의 합리성 등 유무, 회사와 노동조합과의 관계 등 제반 사정을 종합적으로 고려하여 당해 인사조치가 노동 3권을 침해하려는 의도로 이루어졌는지 여부에 따라 판단하여야 할 것이나, 조합원에 대한 인사조치가 업무상의 필요성 또는 일반적인 기준에 따른 정기적인 인사조치의 일환으로 이루어진 것이라면 법 소정의 부당노동행위에 해당한다고 보기 어려울 것이다.[252)]

(2) 노동조합 결의나 지시가 없는 농성행위를 한 근로자를 해고하는 것이 부당노동행위는 아니다.

농성에 의한 업무방해행위가 노동조합의 결의를 거쳤다거나 조합의사에 따른 것이 아닌 조합원으로서의 자발적인 활동에 불과한 것이며, 이에 따라 해고한 것은 단체행동에 대한 불이익처분에 해당하는 부당노동행위가 아니다.[253)]

(3) 노동조합 가입대상 근로자를 가입대상이 아닌 지위로 승진시키는 것에 대한 부당노동행위 여부

근로자의 승진이 사용자의 부당노동행위 의사에 의하여 이루어진 것인지의 여부는 승진의 시기와 조합활동과의 관련성, 업무상 필요성, 능력의 적격성과 인신의 합리성 등의 유무와 당해 근로자의 승진이 조합활동에 미치는 영향 등 제반 사정을 고려하여 판단하여야 할 것인 바, 근로자가 승진거부의 의사를 표명하였음에도 불구하고 그 근로자에 대한 승진조치는 회사가 정기 승진인사의 일환으로 승진 대상자에 대한 합리적 사정을 거쳐 회사의 인사질서와 입사동기생 간의 형평을 고려하여 행해졌다면 부당노동행위가 아니다.[254)]

---

252) 행정해석: 노조 10254-68, 2001.1.22.

253) 대법원 1990.11.13, 89누5102.

254) 대법원 1992.10.27, 92누9418.

(4) If an employer, with a view to interfering with union activities, transfers a union member to another location of work where it is not easy to perform union work, this is an act of unfair labor practice.

The employee in question played a leading role in expanding union membership and worked more than 20 years in the production department. He was first transferred to a job in the public affairs department, for which he had no experience, and was then removed to a remote office where he was not entitled to several employee benefits and could hardly do any union work as there were only three or four employees working. Unless the employer proves the necessity of such job transfer for business purposes, the transfer constitutes an unfair labor practice.[255)]

(5) If an employer transfers employees to a different location of work in order to prevent them from joining the union and doing union work, the employee transfer is an act of unfair labor practice.

The reason given by the employer for such employee transfer was to fill vacancies at the location to which they were transferred. The real reason, however, was to prevent them from joining the union and engaging in union activities. Therefore, the transfer amounts to an act of unfair labor practice. Furthermore, the dismissal of those employees because they failed to follow the transfer instructions also constitutes unfair dismissal.[256)]

2. Conditional contracts (yellow dog contract)

Article 81 (Unfair Labor Practices)

2. Employment of a worker on the condition that he should not join or should withdraw from a labor union, or on the condition that he should join a particular labor union, provided that in cases where the labor union represents two-thirds or more of the workers working in the workplace concerned, a collective agreement under which a person, who is employed on condition that he should join the labor union, shall be allowed as an exception. In such cases, no employer shall act against a worker on the grounds that the worker is excluded from the labor union concerned;

A yellow dog contract provides employment to a worker on the condition that he/she should not join or should withdraw from a particular union. The condition also guarantees

255) Supreme Court ruling on Dec. 10, 1991, 91Nu3789.

256) Supreme Court ruling on Nov. 13, 1992, 92Nu9425.

(4) 노동조합활동을 방해할 목적으로 조합활동을 하기 힘든 곳으로 전보 발령한 것은 부당노동행위에 해당한다.

노동조합 가입추진 등의 활동을 주도적으로 하고 있으며, 20년 이상 생산과에 근무해 온 근로자를 전혀 생소한 업무분야인 공무과에 전보발령하고, 곧이어 본사에서 멀리 떨어진 출장소에 전근발령을 하여 각종 수당을 지급받지 못하게 되고, 출장소는 파견직원 3~4명만이 근무하는 외진 곳이어서 노동조합활동을 계속 수행하기가 곤란한 데다가 특별히 전근 발령하여야 할 경영상의 필요성이 없다면, 전근발령은 부당노동행위에 해당한다.[255)]

(5) 노동조합의 가입과 활동을 사전 봉쇄하려는 의도에서 행한 전보발령이 부당노동행위에 해당한다.

근로자에 대한 전보발령이 표면적인 사유는 결원충원의 필요이나, 근로자의 노동조합 가입 및 활동을 사전에 봉쇄하려는 의도에서 행한 것이므로 부당노동행위에 해당하고, 위 전보발령에 응하지 아니한 행위를 징계사유로 삼아 이루어진 해고조치 역시 부당노동행위로서 부당해고에 해당한다.[256)]

2. 조건부 계약 (황견계약)

노조법 제81조【부당노동행위】

2. 근로자가 어느 노동조합에 가입하지 아니할 것 또는 탈퇴할 것을 고용조건으로 하거나 특정한 노동조합의 조합원이 될 것을 고용조건으로 하는 행위. 다만, 노동조합이 당해 사업장에 종사하는 근로자의 2/3 이상을 대표하고 있을 때는 근로자가 그 노동조합의 조합원이 될 것을 고용조건으로 하는 단체협약의 체결은 예외로 하며, 이 경우 사용자는 근로자가 당해 노동조합에서 제명된 것을 이유로 신분상 불이익한 행위를 할 수 없다.

황견계약(yellow dog contract) 또는 비열계약이란 고용계약 체결의 조건으로 특정조합에 가입 또는 불가입할 것을 제시하는 것인데, 이는 채용뿐만 아니라

---

255) 대법원 1991.12.10, 91누3789.
256) 대법원 1992.11.13, 92누9425.

continuous employment.

(1) It is illegal to strictly control admission to the labor union in the union shop contract.

The labor union is not allowed to refuse an eligible employee membership in the union. In cases where all employees join the labor union in accordance with the union shop provision in the collective agreement, the employer shall dismiss employees who withdraw from union membership upon the labor union's request, despite the collective agreement being silent on the issue. Accordingly, when the labor union refuses admission of an employee, this will directly lead to a condition where the employer shall dismiss the employee because the employee does not hold union membership. Unless there is a special reason(e.g., he was expelled from the union) applicable to the union member, the union cannot reject/her his application for membership. It is illegal and unfair to have restrictions for membership. The restrictions typically found are that the employee must receive prior approval from the labor union in order to join the labor union or the employees who withdraw from union membership should receive a concurrent vote of a two-thirds majority of the members present in the representatives meeting or the general meeting if he wants to join the labor union after withdrawing. Accordingly, under no special condition, enforcing such restrictions is an abuse by the labor union in a good-faith principle.[257)]

(2) The scope of employees engaged in the workplace under the union shop contract.

According to the proviso of Article 81(2) of the Trade Union Act, in cases where a labor union represents at least a two-thirds majority of employees in the workplace concerned, a collective agreement, where every employee is hired on condition that he/she join the labor union, which is called a union shop contract, can be allowed as an exception. In these cases, the scope of employees engaged in the workplace means employees who are eligible for union membership among all employees by Article 2(1) of the Act, excluding an employer or other persons who always act in the interest of the employer according to Article 2(4) of the Act.[258)]

257) Supreme Court ruling on Oct. 29, 1996, 96Da25599.

258) MOEL Guidelines: Nojo 68107-450, on May 22, 2002.

고용계속의 조건으로 제시되는 경우도 포함된다.

(1) 유니온 숍 상태에서 조합가입을 엄격히 통제하는 것은 위법이다.

조합이 조합원의 자격을 갖추고 있는 근로자의 조합 가입을 함부로 거부하는 것은 허용되지 아니하고, 특히 유니언숍 협정에 의한 가입강제가 있는 경우에는 단체협약에 명문 규정이 없더라도 노동조합의 요구가 있으면 사용자는 노동조합에서 탈퇴한 근로자를 해고할 수 있기 때문에 조합 측에서 근로자의 조합 가입을 거부하게 되면 이는 곧바로 해고로 직결될 수 있으므로 조합은 노조가입 신청인에게 제명에 해당하는 사유가 있다는 등의 특별한 사정이 없는 한 그 가입에 대하여 승인을 거부할 수 없고, 따라서 조합 가입에 조합원의 사전 동의를 받아야 한다거나 탈퇴 조합원이 재가입하려면 대의원대회와 조합원총회에서 각 3분의 2 이상의 찬성을 얻어야만 된다는 조합 가입에 관한 제약은 그 자체가 위법 부당하므로, 특별한 사정이 없는 경우에까지 그와 같은 제약을 가하는 것은 기존 조합원으로서의 권리남용 내지 신의칙 위반에 해당된다.[257]

(2) 유니언숍 협정 체결의 요건이 되는 당해 사업장에 종사하는 근로자의 범위

노조법 제81조 제2호 단서의 규정에 의거 노동조합이 당해 사업장에 종사하는 근로자의 2/3 이상을 대표하고 있을 때는 근로자가 그 노동조합의 조합원이 될 것을 고용조건으로 하는 단체협약(이른바 유니언숍 협정)을 체결할 수 있으며, 이 경우 당해 사업장에 종사하는 근로자라 함은 동법 제2조 제1호의 근로자 중 동법 제2조 제4호 가목의 규정에 의한 사용자 또는 항상 그의 이익을 대표하여 행동하는 자로써 노조에 가입할 수 없는 근로자를 제외한 노조조직 가능 근로자를 의미한다고 보아야 할 것이다.[258]

257) 대법원 1996.10.29, 96다28899.
258) 행정해석: 2002.5.22, 노조 68107-450.

(3) If a collective agreement provides for a union shop system in which every employee is a member of the union, should the employer dismiss an employee who has departed from the union?

Under the union shop system, which is intended to strengthen the bond among the union members, a precondition for employment is to join the representative union. If a collective agreement includes a clause on union shop, the employer is obliged to dismiss an employee who has walked out of the union, even if there is no additional clause. However, the employer's obligation to dismiss an employee departing from the union is simply his/her obligation under the collective agreement. It cannot always be said that the employer's non-compliance with the obligation constitutes his/her unfair intervention in or domination over the union, which is an act of unfair labor practice.[259)]

3. Refusal of the right to collective bargaining

Article 81 (Unfair Labor Practices)

3. Refusal or delay in the execution of a collective agreement or other collective bargaining arrangement, without justifiable reason, with the representative of a labor union or with a person authorized by the labor union;

Refusal or delay of the execution of a collective agreement or other collective bargaining without justifiable reason with the representative of a labor union or person authorized by the labor union is considered unfair labor practice.

---

259) Supreme Court ruling on Mar. 24, 1998, 96Nu16070.

(3) 단체협약에 유니언 숍 협정에 따라 근로자는 노동조합의 조합원이어야만 된다는 규정이 있는 경우에 사용자는 노동조합에서 탈퇴한 근로자를 해고할 의무가 있는가?

단체협약에 유니언 숍 협정에 따라 근로자는 노동조합의 조합원이어야만 된다는 규정이 있는 경우에는 다른 명문의 규정이 없더라도 사용자는 노동조합에서 탈퇴한 근로자를 해고할 의무가 원칙적으로 있다. 그러나 단체협약상의 유니언숍 협정에 의하여 사용자가 노동조합을 탈퇴한 근로자를 해고할 의무는 단체협약상의 채무일 뿐이고, 이러한 채무의 불이행 자체가 노동조합에 대한 지배·개입의 부당노동행위에 해당한다고 단정할 수 없다.[259)]

3. 단체교섭의 거부

노조법 제81조【부당노동행위】

3. 노동조합의 대표자 또는 노동조합으로부터 위임을 받은 자와의 단체협약체결 기타의 단체교섭을 정당한 이유없이 거부하거나 해태하는 행위

사용자는 노동조합의 대표자 또는 노동조합으로부터 위임받은 자와의 단체협약 체결 기타의 단체교섭을 정당한 이유 없이 거부하거나 해태하는 행위를 할 수 없다(법 제81조 제3호).

---

259) 대법원 1998.3.24, 96누16070.

< Refusal to Engage in Collective Bargaining>

	Justifiable reasons	Unfair labor practice
1. Party-related	① Absence of employer (Busan cargo union: ice-storage agents' association) ② The union requests a multi-group bargaining before settlement of the system ③ Requesting a temporary strike group or a dismissed employees' group ④ When demanding that the union become a qualified party, which delays negotiations ⑤ Adjustment for right of negotiation is not made between the unit union and associated union ⑥ The party to negotiation does not have authority ⑦ The union's negotiation committees do not have control over multi-group negotiation ⑧ The union's bargaining representatives do not have authority to make an agreement ⑨ When requesting the union's chairman for his/her right to make agreement	① The bargaining representative from the company does not have the authority to make agreement, but has to wait for directions from the company ② The employer rejects negotiation with the other union on the basis of the bargaining party article ③ The employer makes a labor contract with an individual employee, while disregarding negotiations with the union
2. Bargaining item-related	① Non-compulsory negotiation items: Items for which the employer does not have disposal authority, or which are unrelated to work. ② Personnel and management items (Matters which are directly related to working conditions become bargaining items, but when the union's demand violates the right of personnel management, the employer can request their exclusion.)	① The employer insists that the labor union's request is a non-compulsory negotiation item ② Excessive union demands (they can be adjusted in the bargaining process, but the employer cannot reject them)
3. Bargaining time, procedures, and methods	① Disagreements over bargaining time, place, etc. (follow collective agreement and habitual practice, or reach mutual agreement) ② When fatigue sets in after long-term bargaining ③ The union demands a bargaining place that can cause the employer difficulties due to concerns that his/her house may be entered without permission, or bargaining will be more likely to take place late at night, etc. ④ The union's attitude or reaction seems absurd in an objective sense ⑤ The union suggests or threatens violence ⑥ There are too many bargaining representatives to conduct normal negotiations	① The employer refuses to negotiate any renewal of a collective agreement when due for renewal ② Through bargaining, the employer continues to oppose the union's demands without suggesting alternatives. ③ The employer refuses to sign and seal the collective agreement after the items for bargaining have been agreed ④ The employer refuses to negotiate on account of ongoing industrial action

〈단체교섭 거부의 관련사례〉

항 목	정당한 사유	부당노동행위
1. 당사자의 자격 관련	① 사용자가아님 (부산항운노조사건: 냉동창고중개인협회) ② 노사간 체제가 정비되어 있지 아니한데 통일교섭, 집단교섭을 요구하는 경우 ③ 일시적 쟁의단, 해고자 단체의 교섭요구 ④ 조합측에 대해 교섭 당사자 자격확정을 요구하고 확정시까지 교섭을 연기하는 경우 ⑤ 단위노조와 상급단체의 교섭권에 대한 조정이 이루어지지 않아 이중교섭의 우려가 있는 경우 ⑥ 교섭당사자가 교섭권한이 없는 경우 ⑦ 조합측 교섭위원간에 통일적 교섭을 위한 통제가 없는 경우 ⑧ 타결·협약체결의 단계에 조합측 교섭담당자에게타결권한·협약체결 권한이 없는 경우 ⑨ 노조대표자에게 협약체결권확보를 요구하는 경우	① 교섭권한이 없는 자가 사용자측 위원으로 나와, 상부의 지시에만 따르겠다는 자세 ② 유일교섭단체조항을 이유로 한 제2노조와의 교섭 거부 ③ 노조의 교섭신청은 무시하고 개별 근로자와 근로계약을 체결
2. 교섭 대상 관련	① 의무적 교섭사항이 아닌 것, 사용자에게 처분권한이 없거나 근로조건 개선에 관계없는 사항 ② 인사경영사항 (근로조건에 직접 영향을 미치는 경우 해당 부분은 교섭대상이 되나, 그 범위를 넘어서서 인사·경영권의 본질을 침해하는 요구사항은 사용자가 교섭대상에서 배제토록 요청할 수 있음)	① 의무적 교섭사항을 아닌 것으로 주장 ② 노조측의 과대한 요구 (교섭과정에서 조정할 문제이지 일률적으로 거부할 수 없음)
3. 교섭 시기 · 절차 · 방법 관련	① 교섭시기, 장소 등에 대하여 노사간 의견이 대립되는 경우 (협약·관행이 있으면 그에 따르고, 없는 경우에는 노사가 합의해야 함) ② 장시간의 협의로 심신이 피로하여 더 이상 정상적 협의를 기대할 수 없는 경우 ③ 사용자의 사택침입, 심야교섭 등 사용자에게 불안을 줄 수 있는 장소에서의 교섭요구 ④ 조합측의 교섭태도나 대응에 현저한 불합리성이 있는 경우 ⑤ 조합측의 폭력, 위협적인 언동사용 ⑥ 교섭담당자 수가 지나치게 많아 원활한 교섭을 기대하기 어려운 경우	① 갱신체결을 위해 합리적인 시기의 교섭요구를 거부 ② 교섭은 하되 노조의 유구에 대해 대안을 제시하지 아니하고 무조건 반대만 하는 경우 ③ 교섭사항에 관해 의견의 일치를 보았음에도 단체협약에 서명·날인을 거부하는 행위 ④ 쟁의행위 중이라는 이유로 교섭에 불응

(1) Is it an unfair labor practice for the employer to refuse to engage in collective bargaining when the labor union has violated the collective agreement's prohibition regarding non-delegation to a third party?

If the collective agreement contains an article that stipulates both labor and management shall not delegate their negotiation rights to a third party, both parties must follow this. In cases where the labor union violates the above article and delegates its bargaining rights to a third party(e.g., an umbrella labor union), the employer can request direct negotiations with its counterpart labor union. If this has caused a delay in collective bargaining, it is hard to deem it an unfair labor practice by the employer under the Act.[260)]

(2) Criteria for evaluating justifiable causes to refuse to engage in collective bargaining

In deciding whether there is a justifiable reason to refuse collective bargaining, consideration shall be given to the labor union's positions, including the requested time and place, items and attitude, and shall be evaluated by the standards of whether the employer can implement such collective bargaining requests generally.[261)]

(3) Is it an unfair labor practice for the employer to refuse the labor union's request for collective bargaining because of a structural change within the labor union and despite the current collective agreement still being effective?

In cases where the company-level labor union has been restructured to a branch union or a unit union of the industrial union association, the branch union or unit union still maintains organizational identity as the existing company-level labor union. This means the current collective agreement will continue to remain effective during this period. Therefore, labor and management shall not demand change or abolition of the current collective agreement during its term of validity.[262)]

(4) Is it justifiable for the labor union to demand collective bargaining over an objection to the reappointment of a university's president or the resignation of its chief director?

The Trade Union Act does not stipulate clear rules regarding the object of collective

---

260) MOEL Guidelines: Nojo 01254-477, on May 28, 1997.

261) Supreme Court ruling on May 22, 1998, 97Nu8076.

262) MOEL Guidelines: Nojo 68107-508, on Apr. 28, 2001.

(1) 교섭위임 금지조항에 위반한 교섭요구를 거부하는 것이 부당행위에 해당 여부

단체협약상 '노사 양측은 교섭당사자로서 제3자에게 교섭을 위임하지 아니한다'라고 규정하고 있다면 이에 따라야 할 것이므로, 노동조합이 동 규정을 위반하여 상급단체 등 '제3자'에게 교섭권을 위임하는 경우 사용자는 당해 노동조합과의 직접 교섭을 요구할 수 있을 것이며 이로 인해 교섭이 지연된다 하더라도 이를 법 소정의 부당노동행위에 해당한다고 보기 어려울 것이다.[260)]

(2) 정당한 교섭거부 사유의 판단기준

단체교섭거부의 정당한 이유가 있는지 여부는 노사양측의 교섭권자, 노동조합 측이 요구하는 교섭시간, 교섭장소, 교섭사항 및 교섭태도 등을 종합하여 사회통념상 사용자에게 단체교섭 의무의 이행을 기대하는 것이 어렵다고 인정되는지 여부에 따라 판단하여야 할 것이다.[261)]

(3) 노조조직형태 변경을 이유로 한 노조의 교섭요구를 거부하는 것이 부당노동행위에 해당하는지 여부

기업별 노동조합이 산업별 노동조합의 지부, 분회로 조직형태를 변경하는 경우 다른 사정이 없는 한 동 지부, 분회는 기존 기업별 노동조합과의 조직적 동일성을 그대로 유지하고 있는 것이므로 단체협약은 그 유효기간동안 계속 효력을 유지한다고 보아야 할 것이며, 또한, 단체협약의 유효기간 중에 노사 당사자는 동 단체협약의 변경, 폐지를 요구할 수 없는 것이 원칙이다.[262)]

(4) 총장 연임 반대, 이사장 퇴직요구에 대한 교섭 요구가 정당한지 여부

노조법상 단체교섭의 대상에 대하여는 명시적인 규정을 두고 있지 아니하나 단체교섭은 근로조건의 결정에 관한 사항에 대하여 교섭하는 것이므로 단체교

---

260) 행정해석: 노조 01254-477, 1997.5.28.

261) 대법원 1998.5.22, 97누8076.

262) 행정해석: 노조 68107-508, 2001.4.28.

bargaining, but its purpose is to negotiate conditions of employment. Therefore, the objective of collective bargaining shall be to negotiate matters within the employer's range of authority, be related to the determination of conditions of employment, and be of a collective characteristic. Matters belonging to the employer's personnel and management rights shall not be objects of collective bargaining in principle, but such matters which are closely related to working conditions can be the object of collective bargaining within a certain limit. Even in this case, such demands intrinsically infringing on the employer's right of determination cannot justifiably be allowed.[263)]

(5) In cases where the labor union requests collective bargaining during the term of the current agreement regarding matters not addressed in the previous collective bargaining process, can the employer reject such a demand?

A collective agreement concluded legitimately by labor and management is a standard order regulating labor and management relations and shall be implemented in good faith by both labor and management during its effective period. It is a principle that both sides shall not demand change or abolition during the agreement's effective period, unless there is a substantial change required.

Where the labor union requests renegotiation only because some matters were not addressed in the existing collective agreement, this demand violates the duty to maintain peace inherent in the collective agreement. In this case, although the employer rejects the labor union's demand, this is a justifiable refusal.[264)]

(6) In cases where a person whose dismissal was legally confirmed demands collective bargaining with the assistance of a labor union representative, is it an unfair labor practice if the employer rejects his request for collective bargaining?

According to the proviso of subparagraph(D), Article 2(4) of the Trade Union Act, a dismissed employee who has applied to the Labor Relations Commission for remedy for unfair labor practices shall not be regarded as a non-employee until a review decision has been made by the National Labor Relations Commission. According to this question,

---

263) MOEL Guidelines: 68107-672. on June 9, 2001.

264) MOEL Guidelines: Nojo 68107-166. on Feb. 22, 2002.

섭 대상은 사용자의 처분 권한 범위내의 사항으로서 근로조건의 결정과 관련되며 집단적인 성격을 띠어야 할 것이다. 또한, 사용자의 고유한 인사, 경영권에 속하는 사항은 단체교섭 대상이 되지 않는 것이 원칙이나, 근로조건과 밀접하게 관련이 있는 경우에는 그 한도 내에서 교섭대상이 된다고 보아야 할 것이며, 이 경우에도 사용자의 결정권을 본질적으로 침해하는 요구는 그 정당성을 인정받기 어려울 것이다.[263)]

(5) 단체협약에 누락된 사항에 대하여 그 유효기간 중에 단체교섭을 요구하는 경우 이를 거부할 수 있는지 여부

노사 당사자가 합의에 의해 적법하게 체결된 단체협약은 기업 내 노사관계를 규율하는 질서규범이므로 그 유효기간 동안 노사 공히 이를 성실히 이행하여야 하는 것이며, 중대한 사정변경이 없는 한 노사 당사자는 동 유효기간 중에 이의 변경, 폐지를 요구할 수 없는 것이 원칙이다.

노동조합이 재교섭을 요구하게 된 배경이 단순히 협약에 누락되었다는 사실만으로 누락된 사항에 대해 재교섭을 요구하는 것은 단체협약에 내재된 평화의무에 위배된다 할 것이며, 이러한 노사 일방의 요구에 타방이 교섭을 거부하는 것은 정당한 교섭거부 사유에 해당된다 할 것이다.[264)]

(6) 해고가 확정된 자가 노동조합의 대표자 자격으로 단체교섭을 요구할 경우 사용자가 이를 거부하면 부당노동행위에 해당되는지 여부

노조법 제2조 제4호 라목 단서의 규정에 의하면 해고된 자가 노동위원회에 '부당노동행위 구제신청'을 한 경우에는 중앙노동위회의 재심판정이 있을 때까지 근로자의 자격을 인정하고 있다. 귀 질의내용과 같이 노동조합의 대표자가 해고되고 이에 대해 노동위원회에 부당노동행위 구제신청을 하였으나 중앙노동위원회의 재심판정 결과 기각되었다면 동 재심판정 이후부터 해고된 노동조합의 대표자는 동법상의 근로자로 볼 수 없다 할 것이며 동법 제23조의 규정에

263) 행정해석: 노조 68107-672, 2001.6.

264) 행정해서: 노조 68107-166, 2002.2.22.

the labor union representative was dismissed and then applied to the Labor Relations Commission for remedy for unfair labor practices. If his application to the National Labor Relations Commission for a review decision is rejected, the dismissed labor union representative cannot be deemed an employee under the Trade Union Act from the time of the review decision and loses qualification as a labor union representative under Article 23 of the Trade Union Act. Even though qualification for labor union membership(according to the Constitution) is still maintained despite the provisions of the Trade Union Act, his dismissal shall not be interpreted differently.[265)]

(7) In the collective bargaining process for the renewal of a wage issue under the collective agreement, is it justifiable to demand collective bargaining about personnel matters already stipulated in the existing collective agreement?

The present Trade Union Act only regulates that the effective term for the collective agreement cannot exceed two years, but there are no other regulations regarding how to classify the issues for collective bargaining and how to negotiate each collective agreement. Accordingly, the parties to labor relations can engage in collective bargaining regarding wages and other issues, and separately conclude wage and other general agreements respectively stipulating different effective terms for each one. In these cases, both parties shall observe the contents of the collective agreements during each effective term, unless there are special circumstances that merit otherwise.

Because the effective term of the current collective agreement regarding general matters(other than wages) will remain for a considerable period, it is not justifiable for the labor union to request collective bargaining about other matters besides wages in the negotiating process to renew the wage agreement. Even if the employer insists on negotiating only wages from the labor union's additional demands, it is not justifiable to consider this an unfair labor practice.[266)]

(8) When does an employer's refusal or neglect to conduct collective negotiations amount to unfair labor practice?

An employer commits an unfair labor practice when he/she rejects or neglects to

---

265) MOEL Guidelines: Nojo 68107-551. on Oct. 22, 2003.

266) MOEL Guidelines: Nojo 68107-599. on Nov. 24, 2003.

의거 노동조합 대표자 자격도 상실한다. 이는 노동조합의 규약에서 조합원 자격 등을 상기 법 규정과 상이하게 규정하였다 하여 달리 해석할 수는 없다 할 것이다.[265)]

(7) 임금협약 갱신을 위한 단체교섭 과정에서 기존의 단체협약에 규정된 인사사항에 대하여 교섭을 요구하는 것이 정당한지 여부

현행 노조법에는 단체협약의 유효기간이 2년을 초과할 수 없도록 규정하고 있을 뿐 교섭대상을 유형별로 구분하여 단체협약을 체결할 수 있는지에 대하여 별도 규정을 두고 있지 아니하므로, 노동관계 당사자는 임금에 관한 사항과 그 외의 사항을 구분하여 교섭하고 그 결과 임금협약과 그 외의 사항에 관한 단체협약을 각각 체결하면서 각 협약의 유효기간을 달리 정할 수 있다. 이 경우 달리 볼 특별한 사정이 없는 한, 양 당사자는 각 협약의 유효기간 내에는 동 협약 내용을 성실히 준수하여야 할 것이다.

임금 외의 사항에 관한 단체협약의 유효기간이 상당기간 남아 있음에도 불구하고 노동조합이 임금협약을 갱신 체결하기 위한 교섭과정에서 임금 외의 사항에 교섭을 요구하는 것은 정당하다 할 수 없으며, 이와 같은 노동조합의 교섭요구에 대하여 사용자가 임금에 관한 교섭만을 주장하였다 하여 이를 부당노동행위로 보기는 어려울 것이다.[266)]

(8) 단체교섭 거부·해태로 인한 부당노동행위 성립요건

부당노동행위는 사용자가 아무런 이유 없이 단체교섭을 거부 또는 해태하는 경우는 물론이고, 사용자가 단체교섭을 거부할 정당한 이유가 있다거나 단체교섭에 성실히 응하였다고 믿었다 하더라도, 객관적으로 정당한 이유가 없고 불성실한 단체교섭으로 판정되는 경우에도 성립한다고 할 것이고, 한편 정당한 이유인지의 여부는 노동조합 측의 교섭권자, 노동조합 측이 요구하는 교섭시간, 교섭장소, 교섭사항 및 그의 교섭태도 등을 종합하여 사회통념상 사용자

---

265) 행정해석: 노조 68107-551, 2003.10.22.
266) 행정해석: 노조 68107-599, 2003.11.24.

conduct collective negotiations without objective, justifiable reasons. Meanwhile, in order to determine whether the reasons are justifiable or not, it is necessary to take into consideration all relevant factors, such as the union negotiators, the time and place demanded by the union for negotiations, the issues subject to bargaining, and the employer's behavior towards collective bargaining. If the result is that, from circumstantial evidence, it is not possible to expect him/her to sit at a negotiating table, the reason given by the employer will be regarded as justifiable.[267)]

4. Domination, interference, or support of operational expenses

Article 81 (Unfair Labor Practices)

4. Domination of or interference in the organization or operation of a labor union of workers, and the payment exceeding the limit of paid time off or financial support for union operations; Provided, that it may be justified when the employer allows workers to consult or bargain with him during working hours, and it shall be allowed as an exception that the employer contributes funds for the welfare of workers, or for the prevention and relief of economic or other misfortune, or that the employer provides a labor union with an office of minimum size.

<Types of Domination and Interference by the Employer>

① The employer refuses to allow a labor union to be established
② The employer recommends and seeks to persuade employees to join a company-controlled union
③ The employer establishes a subcontractor company and pushes the union members into the subcontractor company in an attempt to break up the union
④ The employer establishes an anti-union organization such as a non-union members' organization
⑤ The employer pretends to shut down the company
⑥ The employer disturbs or monitors union members at union meetings
⑦ The employer orders a full-time officer of the union to return to a previous job
⑧ The employer attempts to bribe the union officers
⑨ The employer makes comments or opens a lecture with anti-union related content
⑩ The employer intentionally fails to deduct the union fees that have normally been deducted
⑪ The employer surveys the union members on union operations
⑫ The employer dismisses an employee upon request from a union officer

267) Supreme Court ruling on May 22, 1998, 97Nu8076.

에게 단체교섭 의무의 이행을 기대하는 것이 어렵다고 인정되는지 여부에 따라 판단한다.[267)]

4. 지배·개입 및 경비원조

노조법 제81조【부당노동행위】
4. 근로자가 노동조합을 조직 또는 운영하는 것을 지배하거나 이에 개입하는 행위와 근로시간 면제한도를 초과하여 급여를 지급하거나 노동조합의 운영비를 원조하는 행위. 다만, 근로자가 근로시간중에 사용자와 협의 또는 교섭하는 것을 사용자가 허용하는 것은 무방하며, 또한 근로자의 후생자금 또는 경제상의 불행 기타 재액의 방지와 구제 등을 위한 기부와 최소한의 규모의 노동조합사무소의 제공은 예외로 한다.

〈사용자의 지배·개입의 형태〉

① 노조결성을 인정하지 않겠다는 발언을 하는 경우
② 어용노조에의 가입을 권유, 설득하는 경우
③ 하도급업체를 만들어 조합원을 동업체 유인·흡수함으로써 조합은 해산하게 하는 경우
④ 비노조원의 조직 등 노동조합의 대항단체 결성·비호
⑤ 위장폐업하는 경우 등
⑥ 조합대회에의 출석을 방해 또는 감시하는 행위
⑦ 조합전임자에 대한 원직복귀명령
⑧ 조합간부 매수
⑨ 반조합적 내용의 강연 또는 강좌의 실시
⑩ 공제해 오던 조합비의 불공제
⑪ 조합운영에 대해 조합원을 상대로 설문조사
⑫ 노조간부의 요청에 따른 근로자 해고

267) 대법원 1998.5.22, 97누8076.

(1) Can the employer's personal speeches be considered domination of or interference with the organization or operation of a labor union?

Domination or interference as an unfair labor practice under Article 81(4) of the Trade Union Act means the employer's behavior infringes on the labor union's independence in union activities. Whether the employer's behavior is considered an unfair labor practice or not shall be decided based on a consideration of the situation and place where the behavior occurred, the contents and method, and influences on the labor union's operation or activities, and whether the behavior was performed with the intent to dominate or interfere with the labor union's organization or operation.[268)]

On the other hand, the employer himself/herself has freedom of speech to express his/her own opinion through speeches, letters, etc. according to Article 21 of the Constitution. Therefore, appropriate harmony is required to adjust the interests of the two opposing articles. Domination or interference is found in cases where the employer's behavior(e.g., through speeches and letters) in relation to justifiable union establishment and operation are generally seen to infringe on the independence of the labor union through compulsion or coercion, suggestive or influencing behavior, etc. However, it is hard to treat it as unfair labor practice that the employer simply brings forth counter arguments to indicate or criticize its faults, and expresses his/her own opinions about the company's conditions and progress of the collective bargaining process.[269)]

(2) Is it an unfair labor practice to unilaterally stop paying a full-time union officer's wage?

Subparagraph(E) of Article 92(1) of the Trade Union Act stipulates that an employer who violates the part of a collective agreement to provide facilities and convenience will be fined 10 million won or less. Providing convenience in the above article refers to every behavior of the employer who promised to provide things necessary for union activities, and so the above article for payment of a full-time union officer's wage shall be seen as one method of providing convenience to the labor union. Accordingly, if the employer does not implement

---

268) Supreme Court ruling on May 22, 1998, 97Nu8076.

269) MOEL Guidelines: Nojo 68107-745. on June 30, 2001.

(1) 사용자의 언론행위가 지배, 개입에 해당하는지 여부

노조법 제81조 제4호의 부당노동행위로서 지배, 개입이라 함은 노동조합의 단결활동의 자주성을 저해하는 사용자의 행위를 의미하는 것으로 부당노동행위(지배, 개입)에 해당하는지 여부는 그것이 행하여진 상황, 장소, 그 내용, 방법, 노동조합의 운영이나 활동에 미친 영향 등을 종합하여 노동조합의 조직이나 운영을 지배하거나 이에 개입하는 의사가 인정되는지 여부에 따라 판단하여야 할 것이다.[268)]

한편, 사용자도 헌법 제21조의 규정에 의해 연설, 서한 등을 통해 자신의 의견을 표명할 수 있는 언론의 자유를 가지고 있다. 따라서 양자의 법익간에는 적절한 조화가 필요한바, 정당한 노조결성 및 운영과 관련하여 사용자의 연설, 서한 등 언론행위가 강제 또는 위압 내지 반대급부의 명시, 암시를 내포하는 등 노동조합의 자주성을 저해하는 것으로 통상 볼 수 있는 경우에는 지배, 개입에 해당한다 할 것이나, 단순히 노조의 주장에 대한 반론 제기나 그 잘못을 지적, 비판하는 행위, 회사의 사정 및 단체협약 진행상황 등에 관한 입장표명은 부당노동행위로 보기 어려울 것으로 사료된다.[269)]

(2) 노조 전임자 급여의 일방적인 지급 중단이 부당노동행위에 해당하는지 여부

노조법 제92조 제1호 마목은 단체협약의 내용 중 시설, 편의제공에 해당하는 사항을 위반한 자에 대해 1천만원 이하의 벌금에 처하도록 규정하고 있는바, 동 조항의 편의제공이라 함은 노동조합 활동을 위해 필요한 사항에 대해 사용자가 배려하기로 한 일체의 행위라고 봄이 타당할 것이므로 노조 전임자 급여지급 조항은 동 조항의 편의제공의 하나라고 보아야 할 것이며, 따라서 단체협약상 노조 전임자 급여지급 규정에도 불구하고 이를 이행하지 않는 것은 동법 제92조 제1호 마목의 규정에 해당한다고 보아야 할 것이다.

한편, 부당노동행위라 함은 노동조합을 혐오하거나 노동조합의 단결력을 저

268) 대법원 1998.5.22, 97누8076.

269) 행정해석: 노조 68107-745, 2001.6.30,

it, despite the collective agreement stipulating provision of a full-time union officer's wage, this is an unfair labor practice under subparagraph(E) of Article 92(1) of the Act.

On the other hand, an unfair labor practice means a behavior of the employer showing disregard for the union and which intends to obstruct union unity. If the employer has paid the full-time union officer's wage according to the collective agreement but suddenly stops with the explicit and implied intension of weakening the activities of and unity within the labor union, then it is an unfair labor practice(domination and interference) under Article 81(4) of the Act. However, if the wage are stopped because of an unavoidable situation going on with the company, such as financial problems, but without the intent to engage in an unfair labor practice, then this violation can be considered non-fulfillment of the collective agreement, but not an unfair labor practice.[270)]

(3) When company executives induced the union members to oppose the work-to-rule action of the union, such an act is an unfair labor practice.

The president and managing director of the company in question had separate meetings with some union members to persuade them to work as usual instead of resorting to work-to-rule. The consequence was that some union members opposed the proposed work-to-rule and decided to work in the same way as usual. The company executives committed an unfair act of interference with the union operations.[271)]

(4) If an employer makes a speech before the employees in order to weaken union activities, this constitutes unfair labor practice.

The company president in question gave an address at the closing of the business year, saying that the union should not have come into being; that, in light of the organizational structure of the company, there were limitations on union activities; that he hoped the union would not be a further source of tension and dispute; and that he did not want to have to have every employee resign from the company and fill the vacancies with new employees. It was quite clear that his address was intended to confirm his opposition to the union and weaken it. Making such an address is an act of unfair labor practice.[272)]

---

270) MOEL Guidelines: Nojo 68107-870, on Aug. 1, 2001.

271) Supreme Court ruling on Dec. 10, 1991, 91Nu636.

272) Supreme Court ruling on May 22, 1998, 97Nu8076.

해할 목적으로 행하는 사용자의 행위를 의미한다 할 것이므로 단체협약의 규정에 의해 노조 전임자에 대해 급여를 지원하여 오다가 그 급여지원을 중단하는 행위가 노동조합의 활동을 약화시키고 단결을 저하시킬 명시적, 묵시적 의사를 가지고 행하여 진 것이라면 동법 제81조 제4호의 부당노동행위(지배, 개입)에 해당한다고 보아야 할 것이나, 회사의 재정사정 등 부득이한 사정에 의한 경우로서 부당노동행위 의사와 무관하게 이루어진 것이라면 단체협약 불이행은 될 수 있어도 부당노동행위라고 할 수는 없을 것이다.[270)]

(3) 회사가 노동조합의 준법투쟁을 반대하는 조합원의 결의를 유도한 행위는 부당노동행위에 해당된다.

회사의 대표이사나 전무가 노동조합의 일부 조합원들을 개별적으로 만나거나 모아서, 준법운행에 반대하여 종전과 같은 방식으로 근무할 것을 종용하는 등의 행위를 하여 조합원들 중의 일부가 준법운행을 반대하고 종전과 같은 방식으로 근무할 것을 결의하는 등의 행위를 하게 되었다면, 회사가 조합의 준법운행에 대항하여 한 행위는 부당노동행위에 해당한다.[271)]

(4) 사용자가 노동조합의 활동을 위축시킬 의도로 연설을 한 경우는 부당노동행위에 해당된다.

회사대표가 종무식장에서 전 직원을 상대로 생기지 말아야 할 노동조합이 생겼으며, 자신을 포함한 우리 모두가 노동자인 것이고, 회사 조직의 성격상 노동조합활동에는 한계가 있다고 보며, 계속하여 분쟁이 야기되어 전 직원으로부터 사표를 받고 공개채용으로 다시 충원해야 하는 일이 없길 바란다는 취지로 발언한 것은, 노동조합을 부인하는 태도를 명백히 함과 동시에 조합활동을 위축시킴으로써 조합의 조직과 활동에 영향을 미치고자 하는 의도임이 충분히 인정되므로, 연설행위는 부당노동행위에 해당된다.[272)]

---

270) 행정해석: 노조 68107- 870, 2001.8.1.
271) 대법원 1991.12.10, 91누636.
272) 대법원 1998.5.22, 97누8076.

(5) When, as a result of strong demands and actions by the union, full-time union officials and union executives have come to receive wage from the employer, such wage payment by the employer is not an act of unfair labor practice.

Unless there is a high likelihood that such wage payment will jeopardize independence of the union, simply paying wage to full-time union officials is not an unfair labor practice. In addition, considering that such wage payment is a result of the union's strong demands and actions, it does not seem a likely threat to the union's independence and autonomy.[273)]

(6) Perpetrator of unfair labor practice[274)]

In cases where a person supervises and manages the employees substantially regarding basic working conditions, just like their real employer having authority over and responsibility for the employees he/she has hired, if such person dominates or intervenes in the labor union's organization or operations in a way that falls under Paragraph 4 of Article 81 of the Trade Union Act, that person shall be deemed the employer who must follow any order for correction of such actions, and shall be considered to have an equivalent position to an employer. Accordingly, if a primary contractor supervises subcontractor employees or determines their basic working conditions through a separate employment contract, and if that primary contractor cancels the contract with the subcontractor company to discourage or infringe upon the activities of the subcontractor's labor union, said contractor would be deemed the perpetrator of unfair labor practice and would need to carry out any correction order according to Paragraph 4 of Article 81 of the Trade Union Act.

---

273) Supreme Court ruling on May 22, 1990, 90Nu639.

274) Supreme Court ruling of Mar. 25, 2010, 2007doo8881【Unfair labor practice】

(5) 노동조합의 적극적인 요구 또는 투쟁결과로 노조 전임자나 노조간부가 사용자로부터 급여를 지급받는 것이 부당노동행위에 해당되지 않는다.

부당노동행위의 성립 여부는 형식적으로만 볼 것은 아니고, 급여지급으로 인하여 조합의 자주성을 잃을 위험성이 현저하게 없는 한 부당노동행위가 성립되지 않는다고 봄이 상당하고, 특히 그 급여지급이 조합의 적극적인 요구 내지는 투쟁 결과로 얻어진 것이라면 급여지급으로 인하여 조합의 자주성이 저해될 위험은 거의 없다고 보아야 할 것이므로 이는 부당노동행위에 해당하지 않는다고 보아야 할 것이다.[273)]

(6) 부당노동행위 주체[274)]

근로자의 기본적인 노동조건 등에 관하여 그 근로자를 고용한 사업주로서의 권한과 책임을 일정 부분 담당하고 있다고 볼 정도로 실질적이고 구체적으로 지배·결정할 수 있는 지위에 있는 자가, 노동조합을 조직 또는 운영하는 것을 지배하거나 이에 개입하는 등으로 노조법 제81조 제4호에서 정한 행위를 하였다면, 그 시정을 명하는 구제명령을 이행하여야 할 사용자에 해당한다. 따라서 원청회사가 개별도급계약을 통하여 사내 하청업체 근로자들의 기본적인 노동조건 등에 관하여 고용사업주인 사내 하청업체의 권한과 책임을 일정 부분 담당하고 있다고 볼 정도로 실질적이면서 구체적으로 지배·결정할 수 있는 지위에 있다. 원청회사가 사내 하청업체의 사업폐지를 유도하는 행위와 그로 인하여 사내 하청업체 노동조합의 활동을 위축시키거나 침해하는 지배·개입 행위를 하였다면, 원청회사는 노조법 제81조 제4호에서 정한 부당노동 행위의 시정을 명하는 구제명령을 이행할 주체로서의 사용자에 해당한다.

---

273) 대법원 1991.5.28, 90누639.

274) 대법원 2010.3.25, 2007두8881【부당노동행위】.

Section 2: Remedy Procedures for Unfair Labor Practice

If an employer dismisses, lays off, suspends, or transfers a worker, or reduces wage, or takes other punitive actions against a worker without justifiable reason, the worker may apply to the Labor Relations Commission for remedy. In addition, any labor union whose rights have been infringed by unfair labor practices may also do so (Article 28 of the Labor Standards Act, Article 28 of the Union Act). As these labor disputes are dynamic, continuous, and collective, administrative agencies or courts cannot always be expected to handle them fairly, promptly, and reasonably, due to the inflexibility of bureaucracy and lack of experience of some agencies. The Labor Relations Commission is an independent administrative agency that has the authority and the ability to resolve labor disputes fairly, promptly, and in a way that is appropriate to the professional situation at hand.[275)]

Here, I would like to review the quasi-judicial functions within the Labor Relations Commission.

The Labor Relations Commission has an organizational structure in response to local administration. The National Labor Relations Commission covers the entire country, while 13 district Labor Relations Commissions cover the capital, metropolitan cities and the provinces. The National Labor Relations Commission can approve, cancel, or change the decisions of district Labor Relations Commissions. The judicial arm of the Labor Relations Commission is composed of three public interest committee members(including a chairperson or one standing commissioner) and one worker and one employer committee member.[276)]

1. Procedures for the judicial functions

The Labor Relations Commission reviews applications and admits, rejects or cancels labor cases, determines eligibility of the parties involved, investigates, conducts

275) Lee, Byungtae, Labor Law (7th ed.), pp. 487.

276) National Labor Relations Commission, A Manual on Judgment Function (July 2018); Kim, Hongyoung, A study on improving the dispute-resolution system, Korea Labor Institute, 2009, pp. 90~110.

제2절 부당노동행위의 구제절차

근로자는 사용자가 정당한 이유 없이 해고, 휴직, 정직, 전직, 감봉, 그 밖의 징벌을 한 경우에 노동위원회에 구제신청을 할 수 있고, 근로자 또는 노동조합은 사용자가 노동조합 활동과 관련하여 부당노동행위를 하여 노동3권을 침해당한 경우에도 노동위원회에 구제신청을 할 수 있다(근로기준법 제28조, 노동조합법 제82조). 노동관계의 분쟁은 유동적이고 계속적이고 집단적인 성격을 가지고 있어 그 해결을 일반 행정기관이나 사법기관에서 처리할 경우, 관료주의성, 경직성, 비전문성 등으로 인해 공정하고 신속하며 합리적인 해결을 기대하기 어려운 측면이 있다. 이러한 이유로 인해 독립된 행정기구로 설치된 노동위원회를 통하여 노동분쟁을 신속 · 공정하고 합리적으로 처리하고 있다.[275]

아래에서는 노동위원회의 주요 기능인 심판회의의 구성, 처리 절차 내지 운영 방법, 그리고 그 결과물의 처리에 대해 구체적으로 살펴보고자 한다.

노동위원회는 지방행정과 대응하는 조직체계를 갖추고 있다. 전국을 단위로 하는 중앙노동위원회와 서울특별시·광역시와 도를 단위로 하는 13개 지방노동위원회로 구성된다. 그리고 노동위원회는 고용노동부 장관이 관리하도록 되어 있다. 중앙노동위원회는 지방노동위원회의 처분을 재심하며 이를 승인, 취소 또는 변경할 수 있다. 노동위원회의 심판위원회는 위원장 또는 상임위원을 포함한 공익위원 3명과 근로자위원과 사용자 위원 각 1인으로 구성하고 있다.[276]

1. 노동위원회 심판회의의 업무 처리 절차

노동위원회는 구제신청서가 접수된 날로부터 60일 이내에 신청요건(당사자 적합 여부 등), 사실조사를 거친 후 당사자 및 증인에 대한 심문을 다루는 심문

275) 이병태, 노동법(제7판), p.487.

276) 중앙노동위원회, '심판업무 처리요령' 참조 (2018.7); 김홍영, 노동위원회와 분쟁해결시스템 개선방안 연구, 노동연구원, 2009, pp.90~110 요약

interviews and holds judgment hearings within 60 days after the initial application date.

(1) Applications for remedy

If an employer dismisses or treats a worker unfairly, the worker may apply to the Labor Relations Commission for remedy. This application for remedy shall be made within three months from the date on which the unfair dismissal and/or related actions took place(or from the date of termination in cases where such activities continue). The worker must apply for remedy with the Labor Relations Commission nearest his/her workplace regarding unfair dismissal or unfair labor practice.

(2) Investigation

The Labor Relations Commission shall, without delay, conduct necessary investigations and inquiry of the parties concerned, upon receipt of an application for remedy. The Labor Relations Commission shall ① designate an investigator responsible for the process of investigation, ② demand the applicant submit evidence of the reason(s) for the application, ③ deliver a copy of the application for remedy or statement of reasons to the employer, and give opportunity for rebuttal and associated evidence to explain the employer's actions, and, ④ if necessary, order the parties, witnesses or other related persons to attend a hearing and give their testimonies. Further investigation will then be carried out as deemed necessary.[277)]

(3) Hearing

The Labor Relations Commission shall hold a hearing within 60 days from the date the application was received. This hearing is to review documented evidence both parties have submitted, and information gathered during investigation, and then decide whether unfair dismissal or unfair labor practice actually took place. The committee members(public-interest, worker and employer representative members) assigned to the case shall attend the hearing, have both parties verify their claims, and interview witnesses and other related persons. At the judgment hearing right after the hearing, the public interest committee members shall decide whether unfair dismissal or unfair labor practice took place. The worker and employer committee members may also interview the parties to the

---

277) Article 45 and 46 of the Enforcement Decree of the LRC Act.

회의와 판정회의를 거쳐 사건의 인정과 기각, 각하 여부를 결정한다.

(1) 신 청

부당해고 판정 내지 부당노동행위 판정과 관련한 심판은 근로자가 관할 지방노동위원회에 구제를 신청함으로써 개시된다. 근로자의 신청은 사용자의 부당해고 또는 부당노동행위가 행해진 날(그러한 행위가 계속될 경우 그 종료일)부터 3개월 이내에 행해져야 한다. 관할 지방노동위원회는 부당해고 또는 부당노동행위가 발생한 사업장의 소재지를 관할하는 지방노동위원회를 말한다.

(2) 조 사

노동위원회는 구제가 신청된 사건에 대해 지체 없이 필요한 조사와 관계 당사자에 대한 심문을 한다. 조사의 과정으로 ① 노동위원회가 담당 조사관을 지정하고, ② 신청인에게 신청 이유를 소명하기 위한 증거 제출을 요구하고, ③ 피신청인에게 구제신청서 및 이유서의 부본을 송부하여 그에 대한 답변서 및 그 이유의 소명을 위한 증거의 제출을 요구하고, ④ 필요한 경우 당사자, 증인 또는 참고인의 출석을 요구하여 진술을 듣고 사실조사를 하는 과정이 진행된다.[277)]

(3) 심 문

노동위원회는 구제신청이 이루어진 사건 접수일로부터 60일 이내에 심문회의를 열어 부당해고 또는 부당노동행위의 성립 여부를 판단하기 위해 사건에 대한 심문을 진행하게 된다. 심문회의는 당사자가 제출하는 증거서류와 조사절차 중에 수집된 증거 자료에 대해 심사를 하여 부당해고 또는 부당노동행위의 성립여부를 판단하기 위한 사전 절차이다. 사건을 배정받은 공익위원 및 노사위원이 출석하여, 당사자의 쌍방에게 자신의 주장을 입증하게 하고, 증인과 참고인을 심문하기도 한다. 공익위원은 심문회의에서 심문을 한 후 판정회의에서 부당해고 또는 부당노동행위의 성립 여부를 판단하여 의결한다. 심문회의에 참석한 근로자위원과 사용자위원은 당사자나 증인을 심문할 수 있고, 판정회의

277) 노동위원회규칙 제45조 및 제46조.

case and witnesses, and give their opinions before the public interest committee members give their decision during the judgment hearing.

〈Burden of Proof〉

1) Regarding decisions disadvantageous to certain personnel such as dismissal, the first burden of proof is on the employer to verify whether the worker committed a particular action, whether such action violated the rules of employment, and whether the disciplinary action, severity and suitability of punishment is justified. Regarding unfair labor practice, the first burden of proof is on the worker and the labor union to verify the employer's intention to commit the unfair labor practice, unfair treatment, and/or the existence of domination and interference.[278)]
2) However, regarding an employer's statements of reasons for decisions disadvantageous to certain personnel such as dismissal, the burden of proof then falls on the worker to verify that he/she did not commit a particular action, that he/she did not violate the rules of employment, and/or that the punishment was too severe or unsuitable to the violation. Regarding unfair labor practices, the employer also has a burden of proof to verify that he/she did not intend to commit an unfair labor practice, or give disadvantageous treatment to the company personnel due to their union activities, or obstruct those union activities, or cause deterioration to the union organization.[279)]

(4) Settlement

Labor cases filed for remedy at the Labor Relations Commission are often resolved between the two parties peacefully before going to the judgment stage of the Commission's activities. Such settlement not only helps to restore labor-management stability, but also aids implementation of the employer's agreement more effectively than a remedy order from the Labor Relations Commission. The Labor Relations Commission can always recommend or arrange a draft of settlement for both parties in the process of investigation and interview. Once settlement is established, the statement of settlement is composed, which has the same effect as settlement decided by a court.[280)]

(5) Judgment

The judgment hearing is for the purpose of determining whether unfair dismissal or unfair labor practice has occurred, and takes place after the hearing. The judgment hearing is held with all three public interest committee members, and resolutions pass

278) Supreme Court ruling on Aug 14, 1992, 91da29811
279) Supreme Court ruling on Sep 10, 1996, 95nu16738
280) Article 16-3 of the Labor Relations Commission Act

에서 공익위원이 판정을 의결하기 전에 자신의 의견을 개진할 수 있다.

〈입증책임〉

1) 해고 등 불이익한 인사조치의 정당성에 관하여 근로자의 특정한 행위의 존재, 그 행위가 취업규칙 등 징계사유에 해당하는 사실, 징계절차의 정당성, 징계양정 및 형평의 적정성 등에 관한 1차적인 입증책임은 사용자에게 있고, 부당노동행위 성립에 관하여 부당노동행위의 의사, 불이익 처분, 지배개입행위의 존재 등에 대한 1차적인 입증책임은 근로자·노동조합에 있음.[278]
2) 그러나 해고 등 불이익한 인사조치에 있어서 사용자의 정당성 주장에 대하여 근로자가 특정행위의 부존재, 취업규칙 등의 징계사유에 해당하지 않는 점, 징계절차 및 양정상의 하자 등을 주장하는 경우에 그 입증책임은 근로자에게 있고, 부당노동행위에 있어서 사용자가 부당노동행위 의사의 부존재, 인사조치가 조합활동에 대한 불이익처분이 아니며 인사조치로 인하여 조합활동의 장애, 조직력의 약화가 없었던 점 등을 주장하는 경우에 그 입증책임은 사용자에게 있는 것임.[279]

(4) 화 해

노동위원회에 구제가 신청된 사건 중에는 노동위원회로부터 판정이 내려지지 않고 당사자 간 화해로 당해 사건을 해결하는 경우가 많다. 화해는 노사 당사자 간 대립된 입장을 해소시켜 이후의 원활한 노사관계를 회복시켜 줄 수 있으며, 또한, 사용자가 임의로 합의한 바는 자발적으로 이행되므로 노동위원회가 구제명령으로 강제하는 것보다 그 이행이 담보되는 면도 있다. 노동위원회는 조사 및 심문 과정에서 언제든지 당사자에게 화해안을 제시하고 화해를 권고하거나 주선할 수 있다. 화해가 성립하면 화해조서(和解調書)를 작성하는데, 이 화해조서는 재판상 화해와 동일한 효력을 가진다.[280]

(5) 판 정

노동위원회의 심판회의는 심문을 종료하면 판정회의를 개최하여 부당해고 또는 부당노동행위의 성립 여부를 판정한다. 판정회의는 공익위원 3인의 전원 출석으로 개의하고 위원 3인 중 과반수인 2인이 찬성하여야 성립한다. 부당해고 또는 부당노동행위가 성립한다고 판정한 때는 사용자에게 구제명령을 내리며,

278) 대법원 1992.8.14, 91다29811.
279) 대법원 1996.9.10, 95누16738.
280) 노동위원회법 제16조의3.

with approval from at least two of the three committee members. The Labor Relations Commission issues an order for remedy to the employer when it is deemed that unfair dismissal or unfair labor practice has occurred, or cancels the application for remedy if it is deemed that they have not. The Labor Relations Commission shall deliver a letter of the verdict to the employer and workers concerned within 30 days of the date of judgment.

(6) Details in orders for remedy

The Labor Commission, upon arrival of the application for remedy, shall carry out an investigation into factual aspects of the case and conduct an inquiry of the parties concerned and, based on the outcome of the investigation and the inquiry, may issue an order for a remedial action by the employer or decide to dismiss or return the application for remedy when the case is found not to be subject to unfair labor practice.[281)]

※ The application may be dismissed or returned in any of following cases:

- When the applicant union is not a union organization recognized under the Trade Union Act;
- When the filing is made after 3 months from occurrence of the alleged unfair labor practice;
- When it is clear that the action in question is not an act of unfair labor practice; or
- When the remedy is neither beneficial to the employee nor possible to achieve.

1) Dismissal cases

① Rehabilitation

If a new labor contract is drawn in the form of re-employment, it is violating the purpose of rehabilitation, so the employer shall reinstate the dismissed employee to his/her pre-dismissal position or equivalent position.

② Back pay(Retroactive pay)

The employer shall pay the amount of wage the employee could not receive during the dismissal period. However, if the employee has earned any income from post-employment, the amount of back pay shall be adjusted according to the income earned.

2) Conditional contract (Yellow-dog contract)

The contract shall be nullified.

3) Refusal of collective bargaining

Order for Initiation of collective bargaining or collective agreement shall be given.

4) Domination or interference

Remedy is almost impossible, but such behaviors shall be at least stopped or prevented from reoccurrence.

281) Article 84 of the Trade Union Act.

성립되지 않는다고 판정한 때는 그 구제신청을 기각하는 결정을 한다. 노동위원회는 판정회의가 있은 후 30일 이내에 판정서를 당해 사용자와 신청인에게 각각 교부한다.

(6) 구제명령의 내용

노동위원회는 부당노동행위 신청에 대한 사실조사를 통하여 부당노동행위가 성립한다고 판정한 때는 사용자에게 구제명령을 하며, 부당노동행위가 성립되지 아니한다고 판정한 때는 구제신청을 기각 또는 각하의 판정을 하게 된다.[281)]

※ 각하 사유

- 신청한 노동조합이 노조법상의 노동조합이 아닌 경우
- 제척기간인 발생일 이후 3개월이 지난 경우
- 부당노동행위가 아닌 것이 명백한 경우
- 구제의 실익이 없거나 불가능한 경우 등

1) 해고의 경우

① 원직복귀

재고용이라는 형식으로 근로계약을 체결하는 것은 원상회복 취지에 어긋나며 해고 전의 직무 또는 그에 상당한 직에 복직시켜야 한다.

② 임금의 소급지불(back pay)

해고기간 중 받지 못한 임금 상당액을 지급하여야 한다. 그러나 해고된 후 다른 곳에 취업하여 얻은 수입이 있을 경우 원상회복에 의해 그 수입부분은 공제할 수 있다.

2) 조건부계약(황견계약)의 경우

계약서를 파기한다.

3) 단체교섭 거부의 경우

단체교섭 개시명령이나 단체협약 체결명령을 내린다.

4) 지배·개입의 경우

이에 대한 구제는 대단히 곤란한 것으로 원상회복이 불가능한 경우가 많으나 그 행위의 중지 또는 재발방지를 명한다.

281) 노조법 제84조.

Part Ⅳ Additional Sections (노동법의 그 밖의 부문)

Chapter 18

Labor-Management Council

Ⅰ. Concept

The purpose of this Act is to maintain order in industry, and contribute to development of the national economy by promoting the common interests of labor and management through joint participation and cooperation. This Act concerning the Promotion of Worker Participation and Cooperation(hereby, called the Worker Participation Act) provides for a consulting organization, known as the labor-management council(hereinafter also referred to as the Council).

All businesses that ordinarily hire more than 30 persons shall establish a Council. The number of employees hired ordinarily shall meet the standards of Article Article 2 of the Labor Standards Act of the Labor Standards Act, with the exception of the business owner, business representative, and all who are working in favor of the employer.

The unit for its establishment shall be a unit of business or a workplace that is given the authority to outline working conditions. For two different working places for one company, a separate workplace can be established for each. The Council of the Worker Participation Act shall not affect collective bargaining of the labor union, or other union activities.

1. Employers who have 30 employees or more shall establish a labor-management council in the main office and are permitted to establish a labor-management council in the workplace.[1)]

According to the Labor-Management Council Act(hereinafter the LMC Act), a labor-management council shall be established in a unit of the business or workplace where there are at least 30 normal employees, so that the employer shall promote employee welfare and healthy development of a business and workplace. The number of employees related to the establishment of the labor-management council shall be estimated on the basis of each

1) MOEL Guidelines Hyupryeok 68210-409, on Nov. 20, 2003.

Chapter 18

노사협의회 설치 · 운영

Ⅰ. 노사협의회 제도의 의의

회사와 근로자 쌍방이 참여와 협력을 통하여 상호 공동 이익을 증진함으로써 산업평화를 도모할 목적으로 '근로자참여 및 협력증진에 관한 법률'(이하 '근참법')에 의거하여 구성하는 협의 기구를 노사협의회라고 한다.

상시 근로자가 30인 이상인 사업장은 반드시 노사협의회를 설치해야 한다. 상시근로자 수는 근로기준법 근로기준법 제2조(근로자의 정의)의 근로자 총인원에서 사업주, 경영담당자, 사용자를 위하여 행위하는 자를 제외하여 산정한다.

설치 단위는 근로조건 결정권이 있는 사업 또는 사업장 단위로 설치하되, 하나의 사업에 지역을 달리하는 사업장이 있을 경우에는 해당 사업장 단위로 설치할 수 있다. 노사협의회가 설치되어 있더라도 노동조합의 단체교섭, 기타 모든 활동은 이 법에 의하여 영향을 받지 않는다.

1. 전체 근로자 수가 30인 이상일 경우 그 주된 사무소에 노사협의회를 설치하여야 하고 그 사업장에 대하여도 노사협의회를 설치할 수 있다[1)]

현행 근참법 상의 노사협의회는 근로조건이 있는 상시 30인 이상의 근로자를 사용하는 사업 또는 사업장 단위로 설치하여 당해 사업 또는 사업장의 근로자 복지증진과 기업의 건전한 발전을 도모하는 협의기구로 노사협의회의 설치와 관련된 근로자 수는 노사협의회 설치 단위인 각 사업 또는 사업장별로 판단되어야 할 것인 바, 사업장의 근로자 수가 30인 미만인 경우 해당 사업장에 노사

1) 행정해석: 협력 68210-409, 2003.11.20.

business or workplace. In cases where there are fewer than 30 employees in one workplace, the employer does not have to establish a labor-management council. In accordance with Article 4(2) of the LMC Act and Article 2(2) of the Enforcement Decree, where the total number of workers engaged in one business is 30 or more, even if the workers in one business are dispersed in different regions, a labor-management council shall be established at the principal office, and each workplace can also establish a labor-management council.

2. Non-profit businesses or workplaces are not exempt from the duty to establish a labor-management council.[2)]

A labor-management council shall be established in each business or workplace ordinarily employing 30 employees or more, which is vested with the right to decide working conditions. A non-profit business or workplace is not exempt from the duty to establish a labor-management council.

3. In cases where one business consists of several workplaces in different regions, the employer shall establish an overall labor-management council combining several workplaces.[3)]

In cases where one business consists of several workplaces in different regions, the employer shall establish an overall labor-management council combining several workplaces(including the headquarters). Accordingly, in cases where workplaces are in Seoul, Jinju, and Daegu, the employer shall establish and operate an overall labor-management council combining the three workplaces. The representative director shall attend the combined labor-management council meetings and the employee members shall be composed of members representing each of the three workplaces. On the other hand, the employer does not have to establish and operate a labor-management council in each workplace, but, if possible, it is recommended. In this case, the labor-management council in each workplace can be held with the attendance of the top-level managers(plant manager, etc.) and employee members from that workplace.

---

2) MOEL Guidelines: Nosa 68107-151, on June 18, 1997.

3) MOEL Guidelines: Nosa 32271-1633, on Feb. 3, 1987.

협의회 설치 의무가 없다고 할 것이다. 근참법 제4조 제2항 및 동법 시행령 제2조 제2항에 따라 하나의 사업에 당해 근로자가 지역별로 분산되어 있더라도 전체 근로자 수가 30인 이상일 경우에는 그 주된 사무소에 노사협의회를 설치하여야 하고, 그 사업장에 대하여도 노사협의회를 설치할 수 있다.

2. 영리를 목적으로 하지 않는 사업 또는 사업장이라 해서 노사협의회 설치대상에서 제외되는 것은 아니다[2)]

노사협의회는 근로조건 결정권이 있는 상시 30인 이상 근로자를 사용하는 모든 사업 또는 사업장에 설치하도록 되어 있으며 영리를 목적으로 하지 않는 사업 또는 사업장이라 해서 설치대상에서 제외되지는 않는다.

3. 하나의 사업이 지역을 달리하는 여러 개의 사업장으로 구성되어 있는 경우 각 사업장을 통합하는 통합 노사협의회는 반드시 설치되어야 한다[3)]

하나의 사업이 지역을 달리하는 여러 개의 사업장으로 구성되어 있는 경우 각 사업장(본사 포함)을 통합하는 통합 노사협의회는 반드시 설치되어야 한다. 따라서 서울과 진주, 대구에 사업장이 있는 경우 3곳을 통합한 통합 노사협의회가 설치·운영되어야 하며, 통합 노사협의회 회의 시 대표이사는 반드시 참석하여야 하며, 근로자위원도 3개 사업장을 대표하는 위원으로 구성되어야 함. 반면에 각 사업장단위로 노사협의회를 설치·운영하여야 하는 것은 아니나 가급적 설치·운영토록 권장하고 있다. 이 경우 당해 사업장의 최고책임자(공장장 등)와 당해 사업장 근로자위원이 사업장 노사협의회에 참석하면 된다.

---

2) 행정해석: 노사 68107-151, 997.6.18.

3) 행정해석: 노사 32271-1633, 1987.2.3.

4. In cases where the company has been divided into two entities, a labor-management council shall be established and operated for each.[4)]

According to the LMC Act, the labor-management council is different from a labor union. A labor union is organized for the purpose of maintaining and improving working conditions and enhancing economic and social status. However, the labor-management council is a consulting organization for the promotion of employee welfare and healthy development of the workplace, and shall be established in each business or workplace ordinarily employing at least 30 employees, which is vested with the right to decide working conditions.

Ⅱ. Composition of the Council

The Council shall be made up of an equal number of members representing the employer and the employees, the number of which shall be at least three but fewer than ten.

While members representing employees shall be elected by the employees, labor union representatives or those recommended by a labor union shall be the employee representative in cases where the labor union is formed by a majority of employees. Employee members of a business or workplace where such a labor union consisting of a majority of employees fails to organize shall be elected by direct and secret vote. If this is deemed impossible due to certain characteristics of the business or workplace, employees may elect their representatives in proportion to the number of employees in different departments. Then, the representative shall be elected by direct and secret vote with majority participation of the voters. However, members representing employers shall be representatives of the business or workplace concerned or the persons designated by such representatives.

The tenure of membership shall be three years until renewal. A representative shall continue to perform his duties until a successor is elected even if the term of office has expired. Members shall not work exclusively for the Council, but shall be compensated for their services to the Council, which exists to maintain the neutrality of members' status and to make certain of work efficiency and impartiality. However, the time spent by the members to attend meetings of the Council shall be regarded as hours devoted to work. The employer shall not take disadvantageous action against the

---

4) MOEL Guidelines: Nosa Hyupryeok Team-3072, on Dec. 2, 2004.

4. 회사가 2개의 법인으로 분할된 경우에 별도의 노사협의회 설치·운영하여야 한다[4]

'근로자참여 및 협력증진에 관한 법률'(이하 '근참법')상 노사협의회는 근로조건 유지·개선 및 근로자의 사회적·경제적 지위향상을 목적으로 하는 노동조합과는 달리 근로자와 사용자가 참여와 협력을 통해 근로자 복지증진과 기업의 건전한 발전을 도모하는 협의기구로 근로조건 결정권이 있는 상시 30인 이상 근로자를 사용하는 사업 또는 사업장 단위로 설치하여야 한다.

Ⅱ. 노사협의회의 구성

노사협의회는 근로자와 사용자를 대표하는 동수의 위원으로 구성하되, 위원 수는 각 3인 이상 10인 이내로 한다.

근로자의 과반수로 조직된 노동조합이 있는 경우 근로자를 대표하는 위원 즉 근로자위원은 노동조합의 대표자가 당연직으로 참가하게 되고, 기타 위원은 노동조합에서 위촉하는 자로 한다. 그 외의 경우 근로자위원은 근로자의 직접·비밀·무기명투표로 선출함이 원칙이나, 사업(장)의 특수성으로 부득이할 때는 작업부서별로 근로자 수에 비례하여 선거인단을 선출하여 이들 과반수의 직접·비밀·무기명투표로 근로자위원을 선출할 수도 있다. 한편, 사용자위원은 당해 사업장의 대표자가 당연직이 되고 기타 위원은 그 대표자가 위촉한다. 위원의 임기는 3년으로 하되 연임할 수 있도록 하고, 임기가 만료되더라도 후임자가 선출될 때까지는 계속 그 직무를 담당하도록 하여 협의회 운영의 연속성을 꾀하고 있다. 위원의 신분상 중립과 업무수행상의 효율과 공정성을 확보하기 위해 협의회 위원은 비상임·무보수로 하되, 협의회 출석에 소요되는 시간에 대하여는 이를 근로한 것으로 본다. 그리고 사용자는 협의회 위원으로서의 직무수행과 관련해서 근로자위원을 불이익처분을 해서는 아니 된다.

---

4) 행정해석: 노사협력복지과-3072, 2004.12.2.

members' interests in relation to the performance of their duties as members of the Council.

1. The members of the labor-management council representing employees in a unit of a plant where there is no labor union or employee representative shall be elected in a direct and secret vote by the employees.[5)]

Article 6 of the LMC Act stipulates that, while members representing employees shall be elected by employees, labor union representatives or those recommended by a labor union shall be the employee members in cases where the labor union is formed by a majority of employees. The employee members shall be employees in the corresponding business or workplace and the majority of employees shall be estimated in a unit of the corresponding business or workplace. Accordingly, in establishing a labor-management council in a unit of the workplace, the employee members shall be recommended by the labor union in cases where the labor union is formed by a majority of employees. If the union is formed by less than a majority of employees, the employee members shall be elected by direct and secret vote by the employees.

2. Employer behavior that may affect the election of employee members directly or indirectly shall be prohibited.[6)]

1) According to Article 6(2) of the LMC Act and Article 3 of its Enforcement Decree, the employee members shall be elected by a free choice of all employees in cases where there is no labor union representing a majority of employees. This means that employees shall voluntarily compose an election administration commission that can implement the registration of candidates and manage the election.

In this regard, Article 10(1) of the LMC Act stipulates that, No employer shall intervene in or interfere with an election of the employee members. This means that the employer shall not take any action directly or indirectly to influence the result of the election.

The employer shall not only be prohibited from actions designed to influence winning or losing of election for a particular candidate, but shall also not influence decision-making about general matters related to the election of an employee commission, like the establishment or activities of an election administration commission. Article 11 of the

5) MOEL Guidelines: Nosa Hyupryeok Team-102, on Feb. 6, 2004.

6) MOEL Guidelines: Nosa Team-239, on Jan. 30, 2004.

1. 노동조합(지부) 또는 근로자대표가 없는 공장 단위의 행정해석[5)]

노사협의회 근로자위원은 근로자들의 직접·비밀·무기명 투표에 의해 선출하여야한다

근참법 제6조에 의하면 노사협의회 근로자위원은 '근로자가 선출하되, 근로자의 과반수로 조직된 노동조합(과반수 노조)이 있는 경우에는 노동조합의 대표자와 그 노동조합이 위촉하는 자로 한다.'고 규정하고 있는바, 이때 근로자위원은 당해 사업 또는 사업장 소속 근로자이어야 하고 과반수 노조여부는 당해 사업 또는 사업장 단위로 판단되어야 할 것이다. 따라서 사업장 단위 노사협의회 설치 시 당해 사업장에 소속 근로자의 과반수로 조직된 노동조합이 있는 경우에는 당해 노동조합에서 근로자위원을 위촉할 수 있으나 그렇지 않은 경우에는 근로자들의 직접·비밀·무기명 투표에 의해 근로자위원을 선출하여야 할 것이다.

2. 근로자위원 선출에 직·간접적으로 영향을 미칠 수 있는 일체의 사용자 행위는 금지된다[6)]

1) 현행 '근로자참여 및 협력증진에 관한 법률'(이하 '근참법') 제6조 제2항 및 동법 시행령 제3조에 따라 근로자의 과반수로 구성된 노동조합이 존재하지 않는 경우 노사협의회 근로자위원은 전체 근로자의 자유의사에 의하여 선출되어야 할 것으로 근로자들에 의해 자주적으로 구성된 선거관리위원회 등의 주관하에 후보자등록 및 투표실시 등이 이루어져야 할 것이다. 이와 관련하여 근참법 제10조 제1항은 "사용자는 근로자위원의 선출에 개입하거나 방해해서는 안된다"고 규정함으로써 근로자위원 선출결과 등에 직·간접적으로 영향을 미칠 수 있는 일체의 사용자 행위를 금지하고 있는바, 입후보 방해·제한 등 특정 근로자의 당선 내지 낙선을 목적으로 하는 행위뿐만 아니라 선거관리위원회의 구성·활동 등 근로자위원 선출절차에 관련한 제반사항에 대한 의사결정에 영향

5) 행정해석: 노사협력과-102, 2004.2.6.

6) 행정해석: 노사협력과-239, 2004.1.30.

LMC Act stipulates an order of correction for these violations.

2) The employer of the LMC Act is the identical employer stipulated in Article 2 of the Labor Standards Act in accordance with Article 3(3) of the LMC Act: The employer means a business owner, or a person responsible for management of a business or a person who acts on behalf of a business owner with respect to matters relating to workers. The term, a person who acts on behalf of a business owner with respect to matters relating to workers means a person given by the employer a certain range of responsibilities and authority for the determination of working conditions like personnel, wages, welfare, and labor management, and command and supervision for implementation of labor service. This shall not be estimated by a formal job title, such as Section Manager or Senior Manager, but shall be estimated in an individual and concrete manner on the basis of job characteristics and actual work performance.

3. Although the representative of a labor union was dismissed and filed a dismissal case, he cannot maintain his status as employee member because he is not an employee under the Labor Standards Act due to his dismissal.[7)]

The term Employee in Article 2 of the LMC Act is defined in accordance with the Labor Standards Act. A representative in a labor union that was formed by a majority of employees can become an employee member under Article 6 of the Act and he/she must become an employee under the Labor Standards Act. Accordingly, although a representative of a labor union was dismissed and filed a dismissal case, he/she cannot maintain his status as employee member because he/she is not an employee under the Labor Standards Act due to his/her dismissal.

4. A union officer of an upper level labor union cannot become an employee member of the labor-management council.[8)]

The labor-management council is a conversational organization between labor and management, involving only employees and employers in the corresponding workplace. This does not only apply to a compulsory labor-management council under Article 4(1)

---

7) MOEL Guidelines: Nosa 68107-5, on Jan. 6, 1998.

8) MOEL Guidelines: Nosa 68107-277, on Oct. 22, 1997.

을 미치는 행위까지도 금지된다 할 것으로 근참법 제11조는 이러한 행위에 대한 시정명령을 규정하고 있다.

2) 근참법상 사용자는 근참법 제3조 제3호 규정에 의거 근로기준법 제2조의 규정에 의한 사용자로 "사업주 또는 사업경영담당자 기타 근로자에 관한 사항에 대하여 사업주를 위하여 행위하는 자"를 의미한다. 이때 '기타 근로자에 관한 사항에 대하여 사업주를 위하여 행위하는 자'라 함은 인사·급여·후생·노무관리 등 근로조건의 결정 또는 근로의 실시에 관한 지휘명령 내지 감독과 관련한 일정한 책임과 권한이 사업주에 의하여 주어진 자를 말하는 바, 과장·부장 등의 형식적인 직명에 의거 판단할 것이 아니라 여타 근로자에 대한 지휘감독권(업무지시권), 징계·인사권, 복무·근태관리 등 업무성격과 근무실태 등을 토대로 개별·구체적으로 판단되어야 할 것이다.

3. 노조대표자가 해고의 효력을 다투고 있다 하더라도 해고로 인하여 근로기준법상 근로자로서 인정이 되지 않는다면 근로자위원의 자격을 유지한다고 볼 수 없다[7)]

'근로자참여 및 협력증진에 관한 법률' 제2조의 「근로자」는 근로기준법에 의한 근로자로 정의되어 있는바, 같은 법 제6조의 근로자위원이 될 수 있는 근로자 과반수로 조직된 노동조합의 대표자 역시 근로기준법상 근로자라야 할 것이다. 따라서 당해 노조대표자가 해고된 경우에는 부당노동행위로 인한 해고의 효력을 다투고 있다 하더라도 근로기준법상 근로자로서 인정이 되지 않는다면 근로자위원의 자격을 유지한다고는 볼 수 없을 것이다.

4. 본조 간부는 사업장별 행정해석: 노사협의회의 근로자위원이 될 수 없다[8)]

노사협의회는 당해 사업장의 노사 간 대화기구로서 당해 사업장의 근로자와

7) 행정해석: 노사 68107-5, 1998.1.6.
8) 행정해석: 노사 68107-277, 1997.10.22.

of the LMC Act, but also to an arbitrary labor-management council under Article 4(2) of the LMC Act. Accordingly, the employee members in the labor-management council established per workplace shall consist of only employees engaged in that workplace, so a union officer of an upper level labor union cannot become a member.

Ⅲ. Operation of the Council

1. Council bylaws

A Council shall establish bylaws governing its organization and operations and shall submit a report on them to the Minister of Employment and Labor within fifteen days from the date of establishment. Any amendment thereto shall also be submitted to the Minister of Employment and Labor within fifteen days(Article 18 of the LMC Act).

Where the bylaws of the Council are made or modified, they shall be passed by decision of the Council. The bylaws of the Council shall contain such matters as listed in the following:

① Number of members;

② Matters relating to the procedures for election of employee members and registration of candidates;

③ Matters relating to the qualification of employer members;

④ Matters concerning hours regarded as hours worked by Council members;

⑤ Matters concerning the calling of meetings, sessions and operation, etc. of the Council;

⑥ Matters relating to the method of and procedures for voluntary arbitration; and

⑦ Matters relating to the number of grievance-handling members and to the handling of grievances, etc.

2. Meetings

In general, the Council shall hold meetings once every three months, but it can hold additional meetings if deemed necessary. The chairman shall call for and preside over the meetings of the Council. If the representative of either labor or management requests a meeting to be held, specifying the purpose of the meeting in writing, the chairman shall call for a meeting of the Council. The chairman shall notify each member of the date,

사용자만이 그 주체가 될 수 있으며, 이는 '근로자참여 및 협력증진에 관한 법률' 제4조 제1항에 의한 의무설치 노사협의회 뿐 아니라 같은 법 제4조 제2항에 의한 임의설치 노사협의회에도 적용된다 할 것이다. 따라서 사업장별로 설치된 노사협의회의 근로자위원은 그 사업장 소속 근로자들만으로 구성되어야 하므로 본조 간부는 근로자위원이 될 수 없다 할 것이다.

Ⅲ. 노사협의회의 운영

1. 노사협의회 규정

노사협의회는 그 조직과 운영에 관한 규정을 제정하고 이를 협의회의 설치일로부터 15일 이내에 고용노동부 장관에게 제출하여야 하며, 이 규정을 변경한 때에도 15일 이내에 고용노동부 장관에게 제출해야 한다(근참법 제18조).

협의회 규정은 노사협의회의 운영을 위한 자치규범으로 그 제정이나 변경은 노사협의회의 의결을 거쳐야 한다. 협의회 규정에는 다음과 같은 필요적 기재사항이 포함되어야 한다.

① 노사협의회의 위원 수
② 근로자위원의 선출절차 및 후보등록에 관한 사항
③ 사용자위원의 자격에 관한 사항
④ 협의회 위원이 근로한 것으로 보는 시간에 관한 사항
⑤ 협의회의 회의 소집, 회기(會期), 그밖에 협의회의 운영에 관한 사항
⑥ 임의중재의 방법·절차 등에 관한 사항
⑦ 고충처리위원 수 및 고충처리에 관한 사항

2. 회 의

노사협의회는 3개월마다 정기적으로 회의를 개최하여야 하고 필요할 때는 임시회의를 개최한다. 회의는 의장이 소집하거나 노사 어느 한 쪽의 대표자가 회의의 목직사항을 문서로 명시하여 회의의 소십을 요구함으로써 개최된다. 의장

time, place, agenda, etc. of the meeting seven days prior to the meeting.

Meetings shall open in the presence of a majority of employee members and employer members respectively, and a resolution shall be passed by a vote of more than two-thirds of all members present. Council meetings shall be open to the public; however, they may be closed to the public upon resolution of the Council.

The minutes shall include the signatures and seals of all attending members and shall be preserved for three years from the date drawn.

Ⅳ. Council Functions

The function of the Council is to promote employee interests and contribute to managerial rationalizations by consulting about specific items between labor and management.

1. Matters subject to consultation

Matters subject to consultation are mainly focused on production and personnel & labor management, and those matters discussed at the meetings of the Council are as follows:

① Productivity improvement and gain sharing

② Recruitment, placement, education and training of workers

③ Handling of worker grievances

④ Improvement of occupational safety and health and other aspects of the work environment and promotion of worker health

⑤ Improvement of personnel and labor management systems

⑥ General rules for employment adjustment, such as assignment and transfer, retraining and dismissal of workers for managerial or technological reasons, etc.

⑦ Administration of working hours and recess hours

⑧ Improvement of wage payment methods, wage structure, wage system, etc.

⑨ Introduction of new machines and technologies or improvement of work processes

⑩ Establishment or revision of rules of employment

⑪ Establishment of employee stock ownership plans and other support for the creation

은 회의개최 7일 전에 회의일시·장소·의제 등을 각 위원에게 통보해야 한다.

회의는 근로자위원과 사용자위원의 각 과반수의 출석으로 개최하고 출석위원 3분의 2 이상의 찬성으로 의결한다. 협의회의 회의는 협의회 의결로 공개하지 않는 경우를 제외하고는 공개회의를 원칙으로 한다.

노사협의회는 회의의 결과를 기록하여 출석위원 전원이 서명·날인한 회의록을 사업장에 비치하여야 하며, 이를 3년간 보존하여야 한다.

Ⅳ. 노사협의회의 임무

노사협의회의 임무는 노사 간에 일정한 사항을 협의함으로써 근로자의 이익을 증진시키는 한편 경영의 합리화를 꾀하는 데 있다고 하겠다.

1. 협의사항

협의사항은 대개 생산이나 인사·노무관리에 관한 사항이다. 노사협의회에서의 협의사항은 다음과 같다.

① 생산성 향상과 성과 배분
② 근로자의 채용·배치 및 교육훈련
③ 근로자의 고충처리
④ 안전, 보건, 그 밖의 작업환경 개선과 근로자의 건강증진
⑤ 인사·노무관리의 제도 개선
⑥ 경영상 또는 기술상의 사정으로 인한 인력의 배치전환·재훈련·해고 등 고용조정의 일반원칙
⑦ 작업과 휴게 시간의 운용
⑧ 임금의 지불방법·체계·구조 등의 제도 개선
⑨ 신기계·기술의 도입 또는 작업 공정의 개선
⑩ 작업 수칙의 제정 또는 개정
⑪ 종업원지주제(從業員持株制)와 그밖에 근로자의 재산형성에 관한 지원

of worker wealth

⑫ Matters concerning rewards given to workers for their work-related inventions, etc.

⑬ Promotion of worker welfare

⑭ Installation of employee surveillance equipment within a workplace; and

⑮ Matters concerning the maternity protection of female workers and support for reconciliation between work and family life.

⑯ Other matters concerning labor-management cooperation

2. Matters subject to Council resolution

The employer shall seek a resolution from the Council on each of the following

① Establishment of basic plans for the education and training and skills development of workers

② Setting up and management of welfare facilities

③ Establishment of an employee welfare fund

④ Matters not resolved by the grievance handling committee

⑤ Establishment of various labor-management cooperative committees.

Matters subject to Council resolution are regulated under the LMC Act to promote the common interests of labor and management through participation and cooperation to prevent the employer from implementing them on the basis of his/her sole judgment.

Meetings shall open in the presence of a majority of worker members and employer members, and resolutions shall be passed by a vote of at least two-thirds of all members present. The matters decided by the Council shall be publicized immediately through company broadcasting, bulletin boards, posting notices and other pertinent methods. The two parties shall be equally responsible for implementing them.

3. Matters to be reported

The employer shall report and explain in good faith at a regular meeting the following:

① Matters concerning overall management plans and results

② Matters concerning quarterly production plans and results

③ Matters concerning manpower plans; and

④ Economic and financial conditions of the enterprise.

⑫ 직무 발명 등과 관련하여 해당 근로자에 대한 보상에 관한 사항
⑬ 근로자의 복지증진
⑭ 사업장 내 근로자 감시 설비의 설치
⑮ 여성 근로자의 모성보호 및 일과 가정생활의 양립을 지원하기 위한 사항
⑯ 그 밖의 노사협조에 관한 사항

2. 의결사항

사용자가 노사협의회의 의결을 거쳐야 하는 사항은 다음과 같다.
① 근로자의 교육훈련 및 능력개발 기본계획의 수립
② 복지시설의 설치와 관리
③ 사내근로복지기금의 설치
④ 고충처리위원회에서 의결되지 아니한 사항
⑤ 각종 노사공동위원회의 설치

이처럼 의결사항을 법정화한 것은 사용자가 일방적으로 시행할 수 없도록 하여 근로자의 참여와 협력을 증진시키려는 취지이다.

의결은 근로자위원과 사용자위원 각 과반수의 출석으로 개최한 회의에서 출석위원 3분의 2 이상의 찬성이 있어야 가능하다. 노사협의회에서 의결된 사항은 사내방송·사내보·게시 기타 적절한 방법으로 신속하게 전체 근로자에게 공지시키도록 하는 한편, 의결된 사항을 성실하게 이행할 의무를 노사 모두에게 부과하고 있다.

3. 보고사항

사용자는 다음 사항을 노사협의회에 성실하게 보고하고 설명하여야 한다.
① 경영계획 전반 및 실적에 관한 사항
② 분기별 생산계획과 실적에 관한 사항
③ 인력계획에 관한 사항
④ 기업의 경제적·재정적 상황

If the employer regularly reports and explains the above matters, a mutual trust in information sharing builds easily between labor and management. Thus, the employer shall report and explain matters faithfully and formally. In cases where the employer fails to give reports or an explanation, employee members may request relevant documents, and the employer shall respond in good faith to such requests. If the employer does not submit the appropriate data, he/she may be liable under penalty clauses.

(1) The concrete realm of matters subject to consultation and matters subject to the Council's resolutions[9)]

Matters subject to consultation in accordance with Article 19 of the LMC Act are items to promote the common interests of labor and management, which shall be suggested by one or both parties for consultation and be dealt with by the Council. The concrete realm of matters subject to consultations shall be determined by voluntary discretion of labor and management on the basis of general principles and criteria. Accordingly, the employer shall not have a duty to go through prior consultation with the Council for individual items, such as employment of specific individuals, nor need to issue the council's resolutions(in accordance with Article 20 of the LMC Act), even though some items for consultation were suggested by either labor, management, or both. The realm of employee training and skill development plans among the matters subject to Council resolution shall be standard plans for yearly training hours, major training items, etc. in general job training, cultural education, and other training related to the employee's skills training, but does not have to include concrete implementation plans.

(2) The concrete realm of matters subject to consultation shall be determined voluntarily by labor and management. The consultation does not require a precondition for agreement and industrial actions are not allowed in the event of non-agreement.[10)]

According to the LMC Act, the concrete realm of matters subject to consultation shall be determined voluntarily by labor and management, but consultation from the Council does not mean its agreement is a precondition and industrial actions are not allowed if there is no agreement from the Council. In cases where Council agreement has been reached(and a resolution passed to that effect) on matters subject to consultation in accordance with Article

9) MOEL Guidelines: Nosa 68107-41, on Feb. 14, 1998.

10) MOEL Guidelines: Hyupryeok 68210-303, on Aug. 2, 2003.

사용자는 이러한 사항에 대하여 정기적으로 보고하고 설명한다면 정보공유에 의해 노사 간에 신뢰가 형성될 것인데, 여기서 사용자가 보고사항을 진지하고 성실한 자세로 보고·설명하는 것이 매우 중요하다. 사용자가 보고·설명을 행하지 아니하는 경우에는 근로자위원은 자료의 제출을 요구할 수 있고, 사용자는 이에 성실히 응하여야 한다. 정당한 이유 없이 자료제출의무를 이행하지 않을 경우 벌칙이 부과된다.

(1) 행정해석: 노사협의회 협의사항 및 의결사항의 구체적 범위[9)]

'근로자참여 및 협력증진에 관한 법률' 제19조에 의한 협의사항은 노사공동이익의 증진을 위하여 노사협의회에서 협의해야 할 사항으로서 노사일방 또는 쌍방이 협의안건을 제시함으로써 협의회의 협의의제로 다루어지게 되는 것이므로 각 협의사항의 구체적인 범위는 일반적인 원칙·기준 등을 중심으로 노사가 자율적으로 결정할 사항인 것이다. 따라서 개별근로자 채용과 같은 개별사안에 대하여 사용자가 반드시 노사협의회의 사전협의를 거쳐야 할 의무를 지는 것은 아니며 노사일방 또는 쌍방의 협의안건 제시에 의해 협의하는 경우에도 동법 제20조에 의한 의결사항과는 달리 반드시 의결을 얻어야만 사용자가 이를 시행할 수 있는 것은 아니다. '근로자참여 및 협력증진에 관한 법률' 제20조에 의한 의결사항 중 "근로자의 교육훈련 및 능력개발 기본계획"의 범위는 사용자가 행하는 직업훈련, 교양교육, 기타 근로자의 능력개발을 위한 일체의 교육훈련으로 연간 교육훈련시간, 주요 교육훈련내용 등 "기본계획"이며, 구체적인 실시계획까지는 포함되지 않는다.

(2) 협의사항의 구체적인 협의범위는 노사에 의해 자율적으로 결정되고, 협의는 합의를 전제하지 않으며, 합의되지 않음을 이유로 한 쟁의행위는 허용되지 않는다[10)]

근참법상 협의사항의 구체적인 협의범위는 노사에 의해 자율적으로 결정되어진다 할 것이나 근참법상 협의회의 협의는 합의를 전제하지 않으며, 합의되지

9) 행정해석: 노사 68107-41, 1998.2.14.
10) 행정해석: 협력 68210-303, 2003.8.2.

19(2) of the LMC Act, both employees and employer shall enforce these matters in good faith in accordance with Article 23 of the LMC Act. If the employer does not implement matters determined by the Council, he/she may be punished under Article 30 of the LMC Act.

(3) On matters subject to consultation, it is enough for labor and management to consult sincerely. The employer does not have to reach agreement with labor or follow the decisions made.[11)]

According to Article 19 of the LMC Act, on matters subject to consultation, it is enough for labor and management to consult sincerely. The employer does not have to reach agreement with labor or follow the decisions made. Accordingly, if matters concerning institutional improvement for personnel management are consulted on sincerely, this is enough even though the employer does not follow Council resolutions or agreements.

(4) Whether Council resolutions concerning working condition are as effective as that of the collective bargaining agreement[12)]

The purpose of the LMC Act is to promote the common interests of labor and management through their joint participation and cooperation. The LMC Act shall also require establishment of a labor-management council to be able to consult or determine matters concerning personnel and management, excluding matters concerning wages and working conditions subject to collective bargaining. Accordingly, it is taken for granted that matters concerning wages and working conditions shall be determined through collective bargaining. However, if both parties agreed on wages and working conditions in a labor-management council in order to conclude a collective agreement, the Council meeting shall be regarded as part of collective bargaining.

(5) Consultation regarding the number of full-time union officers in a labor-management council is not among the 'matters subject to consultation with the labor-management council'.[13)]

Article 19 of the LMC Act regulates matters to be consulted on by the labor-management council. As paragraph 14(other matters as to cooperation between workers and employers) of Article 19 includes consultable matters other than those stated, the realm of matters shall be

11) MOEL Guidelines: Nosa 68010-235, on July 9, 2001.

12) MOEL Guidelines: Nosa 68107-356, on Dec. 1, 1998.

13) MOEL Guidelines: Nosa-1401, on June 29, 2004.

않음을 이유로 한 쟁의행위가 허용되지 않는다는 점에서 쟁의행위가 인정되는 노동조합의 임금협상과는 차이가 존재한다 할 것이다. 또한, 근참법 제19조 제2항에 의거 협의사항을 의결한 경우 같은 법 제23조에 따라 근로자와 사용자는 의결된 사항을 성실히 이행하여야 하며, 정당한 사유 없이 이행하지 않는 경우 법 제30조에 의한 벌칙이 부과된다 할 것이다.

(3) 협의사항은 노사가 성실히 협의하는 것으로 충분하며, 반드시 노사합의 또는 결정에 이르러야 하는 것은 아니다[11]

'근로자참여 및 협력증진에 관한 법률' 제19조에서 정한 협의사항은 노사가 성실히 협의하는 것으로 충분하며, 반드시 노사합의 또는 결정에 이르러야 함을 강제하고 있지는 않다. 따라서 "인사·노무관리의 제도개선"에 관한 사항을 노사협의회에 상정하여 성실히 협의하였다면, 그에 대한 의결 또는 합의 유무와 상관없이 그 효력을 동법에 의해 부인할 수 없을 것으로 사료된다.

(4) 근로조건에 대한 노사협의회 합의사항이 단체협약과 동일한 효력을 갖는지 여부[12]

'근로자참여 및 협력증진에 관한 법률'(이하 '법') 제정취지는 노사 쌍방의 참여와 협력을 통해 노사공동의 이익을 증진하고자 하는 것이며 법에 노사협의회라는 기구를 두어 단체교섭 대상사항인 임금 등 근로조건을 제외한 인사·경영에 관한 근로조건에 관한 사항은 당연히 단체협약을 통해 결정되어야 할 것이며 노사 간 단체협약을 체결할 목적으로 노사협의회에서 임금 등 근로조건에 관하여 합의를 하였다면 단체교섭으로 보아야 할 것이다.

(5) 노조 전임자의 수에 대해 행정해석: 노사협의회에서 협의하는 것은 '행정해석: 노사협의회에서 협의할 사항'으로 볼 수 없다[13]

근참법 제19조는 노사협의회에서 협의하여야 할 사항을 규정하고 있는바, 동조 제1항 제14호의 '기타 노사협조에 관한 사항'은 본조에 적시된 사항들 외에

---

11) 행정해석: 노사 68010-235, 2001.7.9.
12) 행정해석: 노사 68107-356, 1998.12.1.
13) 행정해석: 협력-1401, 2004.6.29.

estimated individually and concretely, but shall be limited to matters within the purpose and intent of the LMC Act. Accordingly, in accordance with Article 24 of the Trade Union Act, matters related to full-time union officers are matters concerning labor union activities, and consulting on the number of full-time union officers in the labor-management council is not among the 'matters subject to consultation with the labor-management council' and does not correspond to the purpose and intent of the LMC Act.

(6) In establishing employee training plans and skill development, seeking a resolution from the labor-management council is required, but this does not mean that a Council resolution is necessary whenever the company implements training and education.[14)]

Article 19 and Article 20 of the LMC Act stipulates matters subject to consultation and matters subject to Council resolutions. The matters subject to Council resolutions shall be items that the employer shall consult and determine in the labor-management council in advance, which is distinct from matters subject to consultation not necessarily requiring resolution. Article 20 of the LMC Act requires the employer to seek labor-management council resolution in establishing employee training plans and skill development, but this does not mean that it is necessary to seek Council resolution whenever the company implements training and education. The employer shall sincerely implement the items decided by the Council or else will be fined 10 million won or less. However, there is no penal provision in the LMC Act when the company does not take issue on matters subject to a Council resolution.

(7) Although a matter concerning wages was agreed on by a labor-management council, the decision cannot be effective in accordance with the LMC Act. However, if the matter was concluded as part of a collective bargaining process, it is effective as a collective agreement.[15)]

In estimating the content of the Council's meeting minutes, a certain meeting did not deal with matters subject to consultation stipulated by Article 20 of the LMC Act, but rather dealt with collective bargaining items. Accordingly, the items agreed upon are not effective according to LMC Act. However, if the agreement was concluded as a collective agreement relating to wages, it is effective as a collective agreement.

---

14) MOEL Guidelines: Nosa 68010-222, on June 23, 2001.

15) MOEL Guidelines: Nosa 32271-6506, on Apr. 17, 1986.

도 필요한 사항을 협의할 수 있음을 규정한 것으로 그 범위는 사안에 따라 개별·구체적으로 판단되어야 할 것이나 기본적으로 근참법의 목적과 취지에 벗어나지 않은 사항으로 한정된다고 할 것이다. 따라서 '노동조합 및 노동관계조정법' 제24조에 의거 노조 전임자는 노동조합 활동에 관한 사항으로 노조 전임자의 수에 대해 노사협의회에서 협의하는 것은 근참법의 목적과 취지에 부합하지 않는 것으로 '노사협의회에서 협의할 사항'으로 볼 수 없다 할 것이다.

(6) 근로자의 교육훈련 및 능력개발 기본계획의 수립 시 노사협의회의 의결을 거치도록 하는 것이지 교육이나 훈련을 실시할 때마다 의결을 거쳐야 하는 것은 아니다[14)]

'근로자참여 및 협력증진에 관한 법률' 제19조 및 제20조는 노사협의회에의 협의사항 및 의결사항을 규정하고 있는바, 의결사항이라 함은 사용자가 사전에 노사협의회에서 의논하여 결정해야 하는 사항으로서 반드시 의결을 필요로 하지 않는 협의사항과 구별된다. '근로자참여 및 협력증진에 관한 법률' 제20조는 근로자의 교육훈련 및 능력개발 기본계획을 수립할 경우에 노사협의회의 의결을 거치도록 하는 것이지 교육이나 훈련을 실시하는 그때마다 의결을 거쳐야 하는 것은 아니다. 협의회에서 의결된 사항은 성실히 이행되어야 하며 그렇지 아니한 경우에는 1,000만원 이하의 벌금이 부과될 수가 있으며, 의결사항에 대해 의결을 거치지 아니하는 것에 대한 제재규정은 마련되어 있지 않다.

(7) 임금에 관련된 사항을 행정해석: 노사협의회에서 합의하였더라도 행정해석: 노사협의회법상 효력이 인정되지 않으나 임금협약으로 체결되었다면 단체협약으로서의 효력을 갖는다[15)]

노사협의회 회의록으로 판단컨대 노사협의회는 노사협의회법 제20조에 명시되어 있는 협의사항이 아닌 단체교섭 사항을 다루었으므로 이 노사협의회에서 합의된 사항이 노사협의회법상의 효력을 발생한다고는 볼 수 없으나, 임금협약이 체결되었다면 노동조합법상 단체협약으로서의 효력을 갖는다고 볼 것이다.

---

14) 행정해석: 노사 68010-222, 2001.6.23.
15) 행정해석: 1986.4.17, 노사 32271-6506.

(8) Employee members of the Council do not have authority to agree to unfavorable changes to working conditions on behalf of other employees.[16)]

The labor-management council system is designed to maintain order in the industry by promoting the common interests of labor and management through joint participation and cooperation, which is distinct in purpose from a labor union. Although the company stipulates matters concerning working conditions in the matters subject to consultation, employee members of the Council who were elected by the employees do not have authority to agree to unfavorable changes to working conditions on behalf of other employees.

(9) It is null and void for a labor-management council to agree that the service period for overseas assignments will be exempted from calculation of the total service period.[17)]

The consecutive service period to calculate severance pay shall be a period from the first service date to the last day of service. Through mutual agreement in a Council, the service years of employees assigned overseas is regarded as a period included in calculations for interim severance pay and their severance pay will be calculated from the time after the adjustment period of severance pay. Even though the agreement is as effective as a collective agreement, the agreement violates lawthe Labor Standards Actand is therefore null and void.

Ⅴ. Grievance Handling

Grievances refer to individual complaints or difficulties concerning employees' working environment or working conditions. A grievance is a complaint from an individual employee, which is different from industrial disputes related to collective complaints. Compulsory procedures are established to prevent individual employee complaints from enlarging into collective complaints. They also contribute to building mutual reliability in the process of handling such grievances.

---

16) Seoul Administrative Court ruling on Dec. 13, 2002 Guhap12519.

17) Supreme Court ruling on July 25, 1997, 96Da22174.

(8) 노사협의회의 근로자위원들에게 근로조건 불이익 변경에 관해 근로자를 대신해 동의할 권한이 있지 않다[16)]

노사협의회는 근로자와 사용자 쌍방이 이해와 협조를 통하여 노사공동의 이익을 증진함으로써 산업평화를 도모할 것을 목적으로 하는 제도로서 노동조합과 그 제도의 취지가 다르므로 비록 회사가 근로조건에 관한 사항을 그 협의사항으로 규정하고 있다 하더라도 근로자들이 노사협의회를 구성하는 근로자위원들을 선출함에 있어 그들에게 근로조건을 불이익하게 변경함에 있어서 근로자들을 대신하여 동의를 할 권한까지 포괄적으로 위임한 것으로 볼 수 없다.

(9) 해외파견 근로자들에 대하여 근속기간의 통산에 따른 이익을 사전에 포기하도록 하는 내용의 노사협의회 합의는 무효이다[17)]

퇴직금 산정의 기초가 되는 계속근로연수는 최초 입사일 부터 최종 퇴직일까지 통산하여야 할 것인 바, 만일 중간퇴직이 무효로 인정된다면, 노사협의회에 따른 합의에 의하여 해외파견 근로자들의 퇴직금중간정산의 효력을 인정하고 최종 퇴직 시에는 중간퇴직금정산일 이후의 기간에 대해서만 퇴직금을 계산하기로 한 것은, 결국 최종 퇴직 시 발생하는 퇴직금 청구권의 일부를 사전에 포기하게 하는 것으로서 그와 같은 합의사항이 단체협약과 동일한 효력이 있다고 하더라도 강행법규인 근로기준법에 위반되어 무효이다.

Ⅴ. 고충처리

고충이라 함은 근로자의 근로환경이나 근로조건에 관한 개별적인 불만이나 애로를 가리킨다. 고충은 개별 근로자가 가지는 불만이라는 점에서 집단성을 띠는 노동쟁의와 구별된다. 이처럼 고충처리절차의 설치를 의무화한 취지는 근로자 개인의 고충이라 하더라도 불만이 누적되면 분쟁화 될 가능성이 있으므로 이것을 미연에 방지하고, 또한, 고충처리 과정에서 노사 간의 신뢰가 조성되기를 기대하는 것이라 할 수 있다.

---

16) 행정법원 2002.12.13, 2002구합12519.

17) 대법원 1997.7.25, 96다22174.

1. Grievance handling representatives

All businesses or workplaces that ordinarily hire 30 employees or more shall have a grievance handling representatives to hear and handle workers' grievances. There shall be a maximum of three grievance handling representatives, representing labor and management, who shall be elected from the Council members by the Council in a business or a workplace where a Council is established, and shall be appointed by the employer in a business or a workplace where no Council is established. Tenure, status and treatment of grievance handling representatives are the same as those of the labor-management council.

2. Procedures for grievance handling

If a worker has a grievance, he/she may report it to a grievance handling representative verbally or in writing. In this case, the grievance handling representative who receives such a report shall handle it without delay. When a worker takes a grievance to the grievance handling representative, he/she shall be informed of the measures taken and results thereof within ten days by the grievance handling representative. The grievance handling representative shall draw up and keep a ledger relating to the receipt and handling of grievances and keep it for one year.

Ⅵ. Labor-Management Councils and the Labor Union

A labor-management council shall be established in each business or workplace that ordinarily employs 30 employees or more and is vested with the right to decide the working conditions, in accordance with the LMC Act. It refers to the consulting organization designed to promote the welfare of employees and healthy development of the company through joint participation and cooperation. This labor-management council is distinct from a labor union, as a labor union means an organization(or associated organization) of workers, which is formed in a voluntary and collective manner upon worker initiative for the purpose of maintaining and improving their working conditions and enhancing their economic and social status. A labor union can be organized by voluntary decision of the employees in accordance with Article 5 of the Trade Union Act. Also, Article 5 of the LMC Act regulates that collective bargaining of

1. 고충처리위원

상시 30인 이상의 근로자를 사용하는 모든 사업(장)에는 고충처리위원을 두도록 하고 있는데, 이들은 근로자의 고충을 청취하고 이를 처리하는 기능을 한다. 위원의 수는 3인 이내로 하되, 노사협의회 설치 사업장에서는 협의회가 그 위원 가운데 고충처리위원을 선임하고, 노사협의회가 없는 사업장인 경우에는 사용자가 고충처리위원을 위촉토록 한다. 고충처리위원의 임기·신분·처우는 노사협의회 위원에 관한 것과 동일하다.

2. 고충처리절차

고충처리는 근로자가 고충을 고충처리위원에게 구두 또는 서면으로 신고함으로써 개시된다. 고충을 청취한 고충처리위원은 지체 없이 이를 처리하여야 하고, 접수한 날로부터 10일 이내에 조치사항 기타 처리결과를 당해 근로자에게 통보하여야 한다. 고충처리위원은 고충사항의 접수 및 그 처리에 관한 대장을 작성·비치하고 이를 1년간 보존하여야 한다.

Ⅵ. 노사협의회와 노동조합 비교

노사협의회는 근참법에 의하여 근로조건 결정권이 있는 상시 30인 이상의 근로자를 사용하는 사업 또는 사업장 단위로 설치하는 것으로 "근로자와 사용자가 참여와 협력을 통해 근로자 복지증진과 기업의 건전한 발전을 도모함을 목적으로 구성하는 협의기구"를 말한다. 이러한 노사협의회는 '근로자가 주체가 되어 자주적으로 단결하여 근로조건의 유지·개선 및 근로자의 사회적·경제적 지위향상을 목적으로 조직하는 (연합)단체'인 노동조합과는 그 제도적 취지를 달리하는 것으로 노동조합의 경우 '노동조합 및 노동관계조정법' 제5조에 의거 근로자가 자유로이 조직하거나 이에 가입할 수 있다. 아울러, 근참법 제5조는 노동조합의 단체교섭 기타 모든 활동은 이 법에 의하여 영향을 받지 아니한다

the labor union and other activities will not be affected by the LMC Act.[18)]

	Labor-Management Council	Labor Union
Purpose	Mutual understanding and cooperation; promoting mutual interests; contributing to industrial peace	Basic rights under the constitution, maintaining and improving working conditions, promoting employee welfare, improving employees' economic and social status
Labor relations	Cooperative relations	Competing relations
Items for consultation	Mutual interest, improving productivity and promoting employee welfare - matters on preventing labor disputes - matters on handling grievances and training - matters on safety & health, improvement of the working environment	Matters about competing interests - wages - maintaining and improving working conditions - promoting employee welfare - matters about employees' economic and social status
Bargaining party	Employee and employer representatives (3~10 persons) → Delegation prohibited	Union representative and employer (no limit to number) → delegation possible
Bargaining method	Conversation, consultation - no background for industrial action (cooperative, non-compulsory) - no relation to union organization	Collective bargaining, collective actions, adjustment system
Penalty	Fine of up to 10 million won	Fine of up 10 million won
Establishment	Compulsory establishment	Voluntary establishment
Result	Establishment of Council resolutions (enacted in 1997)	Collective agreement

18) MOEL Guidelines: Nosa-1212, on June 8, 2004.

고 규정하고 있다.[18)]

<table>
<tr><th>구 분</th><th>노사협의회</th><th>노동조합</th></tr>
<tr><td>목 적</td><td>노사 쌍방의 이해, 협조
노사공동의 이해 증진
산업평화 도모</td><td>헌법보장 기본권
근로조건 유지·개선
근로자 복지 증진
근로자의 경제적·사회적 지위향상</td></tr>
<tr><td>노사관계 개념</td><td>협력 관계</td><td>대립 관계</td></tr>
<tr><td>협의 내용</td><td>노사공동의 이익사항
– 생산성 향상 및 근로자 복지증진
– 노사분규 예방에 관한 사항
– 고충처리 및 교육훈련 사항
– 안전보건, 작업환경 개선사항</td><td>노사 대립적 이해사항
– 임금
– 근로조건 유지개선
– 근로자 복지증진
– 근로자의 경제적·사회적 지위 향상에 관련된 사항</td></tr>
<tr><td>협의 당사자</td><td>종업원 대표와 사용자
(각 3~10인) → 위임 금지</td><td>노동조합대표와 사용자
(인원제한 없음) → 위임 가능</td></tr>
<tr><td>협의방법
(수단·배경)</td><td>대화·협의
– 쟁의행위라는 배경 없음(합의적, 비강제적)
– 노동조합 조직 여부와 무관</td><td>단체교섭, 단체행동, 조정제도</td></tr>
<tr><td>합의사항 불이행시 벌칙</td><td>벌금 1천만원 이하</td><td>벌금 1천만원 이하</td></tr>
<tr><td>설치에 대한 구속력</td><td>강제 설치</td><td>자주적 설치</td></tr>
<tr><td>결 과</td><td>의결사항 신설(1997 제정)</td><td>단체협약 체결</td></tr>
</table>

18) 행성해석: 노사협력복지과-1212, 2004.6.8.

Chapter 19

The Four Types of Social Insurances

The four statutory insurances of Korea are employment insurance, industrial accident compensation insurance, national pension, and national health insurance. 1) Employment insurance, started in 1995, is to provide income in case of unemployment, to promote employment, and to help develop vocational skills of employees. 2) Industrial accident compensation insurance, which took effect in 1964, is aimed at supporting employees and their families with costs associated with occupational injury, disease, disability, or death. 3) The national pension plan, which began in 1988, is to provide a pension for people during retirement, invalidity, or death of a spouse. 4) The national health insurance plan, which began in 1977, aims at preventing, diagnosing, and treating people's injuries and illnesses.

Section 1: Employment Insurance

Ⅰ. Employment Insurance System

Employment insurance includes the traditional social security insurance that provides unemployment benefits to unemployed employees, in addition to employment security insurance, which promotes re-employment through government vocational guidance, which exists to improve employee job security, the employment structure, employee vocational skills development, etc.

Employment insurance premiums are classified into unemployment benefits and premiums for employment stability and vocational skills development projects.

4대 사회보험 업무

4대 법정보험으로는 고용보험, 산재보험, 의료보험, 국민연금 등이 있다. 1) 고용보험제도는 실업 예방, 고용 촉진 및 근로자의 직업능력 개발 등을 목적으로 1995년부터 시행. 2) 산재보험제도는 업무상 부상, 질병, 신체장애 또는 사망 등 재해의 구제 등을 목적으로 1964년부터 시행. 3) 국민연금제도는 국민의 노령, 폐질 또는 사망에 따른 연금 지원 등을 목적으로 1988년부터 시행. 4) 건강보험제도는 질병, 부상에 대한 예방, 진단, 치료 등을 목적으로 1977년부터 시행되고 있다.

제1절 고용보험

Ⅰ. 고용보험제도의 의의

고용보험이란 실직근로자에게 실업급여를 지급하는 전통적 의미의 실업보험사업 외에 취업알선을 통한 재취업의 촉진과 근로자의 직업안정 및 고용구조 개선을 위한 고용안정사업, 근로자의 능력개발사업 등을 상호 연계하여 시행하는 사회보험제도이다.

고용보험 보험료는 실업급여와 고용안정·직업능력개발사업의 보험료로 구분하여 부과되는데, 실업급여 보험료는 근로자와 사용자가 각 1/2씩 부담하고,

Unemployment benefit premiums are borne by both workers and employers, while employers are responsible for employment security and vocational skills development projects(Article 6 of the Employment Insurance Act, hereafter, the EIA).[19] Unemployment benefits are payable only when a worker is involuntarily unemployed and seeking work.[20]

Ⅱ. Operational Structure of the Employment Insurance System

1. Scope of application

(1) Applicable businesses

In principle, employment insurance shall be applicable to any business or workplace that ordinarily hires an employee, but the following businesses shall be restricted based upon the size of the business. Even if the business is not eligible for employment insurance, the business owner can independently apply for insurance with the consent of the majority of employees and the approval of the Minister of Employment and Labor.

Businesses ineligible for employment insurance are as follows:

① Businesses engaged in farming, forestry, fishing and hunting, which ordinarily hire 4 workers or fewer;

② Housekeeping businesses; and

③ Construction projects estimated to cost less than the amount prescribed annually by the Minister of Labor.

※ Prescribed amount in 2025: Less than 20 million won, provided that the total size of the building construction is 100㎡ or less; or the total size of the repair construction is 200㎡ or less, done by non-housing companies under the Housing Construction Promotion Act or non-construction companies under the Construction Industry Standards Act.

---

19) Korea Labor Welfare Corporation, Working Guide for Industrial Accident Compensation Insurance and Employment Insurance in 2024, pp. 7-46.

20) Employment Insurance Act. Article 40 (Eligibility Requirements for Job-Seeking Benefits) ① The unit period of insurance under Article 41 during the 18-month period (hereinafter referred to as base period) prior to the date of separation shall not be less than 180 days in total;
② Despite his/her willingness and ability to work, he/she shall be out of employment (including cases where he/she operates a business for the purpose of making profit; hereinafter the same shall apply in this Chapter and Chapter 5);
③ The reasons for separation shall not be any of the reasons for restricting eligibility for benefits under Article 58;
④ He/she shall be actively seeking reemployment;

고용안정·직업능력개발사업 비용은 사용자가 부담한다(고보법 제6조).[19] 실업급여의 수급자격을 갖춘 상태에서 비자발적으로 실업이 되고 구직노력을 하여야 지급된다.[20]

Ⅱ. 고용보험제도의 운영체계

1. 적용대상

(1) 적용 사업장

고용보험은 모든 사업 또는 사업장에 적용되는 것을 원칙으로 하되 사업의 규모를 고려하여 다음의 사업에 대하여는 적용되지 않는다. 고용보험이 당연히 적용되는 사업장이 아니라 하더라도 근로자 과반수의 동의를 얻어 고용노동부 장관의 승인을 받은 때는 임의적용 사업장으로 고용보험에 가입할 수 있다.

고용보험에 적용되지 않는 사업은 다음과 같다.

① 농업·임업·어업 및 수렵업 중 상시 5인 미만의 근로자를 사용하는 사업
② 가사서비스업
③ 총 공사금액이 매년 고용노동부 장관이 고시하는 금액 미만인 공사

※ 2025년 고시금액: 2천만원 미만. 다만, 총 공사금액의 산정이 곤란한 주택건설촉진법에 의한 주택건설사업자 또는 '건설산업기본법'에 의한 건설업자가 아닌 자가 시공하는 건축물의 건축은 100제곱미터 이하 또는 대수신에 관한 공사는 연 면적 200제곱미터 이하로 한다.

---

19) 근로복지공단, "2024년 산재·고용보험 가입 및 부과업무 실무편람", 7~46면.

20) 고용보험법 제40조【구직급여의 수급 요건】① 이직일 이전 18개월간(기준기간) 피보험단위기간이 통산하여 180일 이상일 것
② 근로의 의사와 능력이 있음에도 불구하고 취업(영리를 목적으로 사업을 영위하는 경우 포함)하지 못한 상태에 있을 것
③ 재취업을 위한 노력을 적극적으로 할 것
④ 이직사유가 비자발적인 사유일 것 (이직 사유가 법 제 58조에 따른 수급자격의 제한사유에 해당하지 아니할 것)

(2) Applicable employees

Employment insurance shall be applicable to all employees in principle, but the following employees shall be excluded:

① Those who are employed beyond 65 years old

② Daily workers whose contractual working hours are fewer than 60 hours per month(15 hours per week)

③ Government employees under the State Public Officials Act and the Local Public Officials Act

④ Those subject to the Private School Teachers Pension Act

⑤ Special post office staff who are referred to in the Special Post Office Act

⑥ Seamen under the Seamen Act; and

⑦ Foreign workers without residence permits(foreign workers who have residence permits may be insured independently).

2. Report of establishment/termination of insurance relationship

The business owner shall report to the Minister of Employment and Labor within fourteen days from the establishment date of the employment insurance, and within fourteen days from the date of discontinuation/suspension of the business.

3. Report on acquisition or loss of insurance qualification

The business owner shall inform the Employment Security Office with jurisdiction over the business concerned within 14 days of the acquisition or loss of their employment insurance qualifications.

(2) 적용 근로자

고용보험은 모든 근로자에게 적용하는 것이 원칙으로 하되 다음에 해당하는 사람에게는 적용치 않는다.

① 65세 이후에 고용된 자

② 1월간의 소정근로시간이 60시간(1주간 15시간) 미만인 자

③ 국가공무원법 및 지방공무원법에 의한 공무원

④ 사립학교교원연금법의 적용을 받는 자

⑤ 별정우체국법에 의한 별정우체국 직원

⑥ 선원법에 의한 선원

⑦ 거주 자격이 없는 외국인 근로자(체류자격을 가진 외국인은 임의가입 가능)

2. 회사의 보험가입 및 소멸신고

고용보험 적용 사업주는 사업의 소재지를 관할하는 근로복지공단 지사에 고용보험의 적용을 받게 된 날부터 14일 이내에 '고용보험 관계성립신고서'를, 폐지 또는 종료일로부터 14일 이내에 '고용보험 관계소멸신고서'를 제출하여야 한다.

3. 종업원에 대한 피보험자 신고

사업주는 고용보험을 적용을 받는 근로자에 대하여 취득사유가 발생한 날이 속하는 달의 다음 달 15일까지 '피보험자격취득신고서'를, 피보험자격을 취득한 자가 이직 등으로 피보험자격을 상실하는 경우에는 상실사유가 발생한 날이 속하는 달의 다음 달 15일까지 '피보험자격상실신고서'를 각각 사업자의 소재지 관할 지방노동관서 고용안정센터에 신고하여야 한다.

Ⅲ. Premium Rate

1. Principle of premium charge

Premiums are charged according to the unemployment benefits premium rate and the employment security & vocational ability development premium rate. The unemployment benefits premium is shared equally between employee and employer, whereas the employment security and vocational skills development premiums are charged only to the employer.

2. Premium rate

<Premium Rate, as of 2025>

Projects	Premium rate	Paid by
Unemployment benefits	1.8%	0.9% equally by both parties
Employment Security & Vocational skill development	• Fewer than 150: 0.25% • More than 150 or preferred companies: 0.45% • More than 150, but not preferred companies: 0.65% • More than 1,000: 0.85%	Employer

* Preferred Companies: ① Mining industry: 300 employees or fewer, ② manufacturing industry: 500 employees or fewer, ③ construction industry: 300 employees or fewer or ④ transportation, storage and communication: 300 employees or few

3. Calculation and payment of premiums

The premium is calculated by multiplying the employee's total annual income by the premium rate of the employer. The business owner must pay the premium plus the amount the employee is being charged; unemployment benefit premiums charged to the employee shall be withheld from monthly pay.

The Employer shall report each individual employee's total income data for all employees for the previous year to the branch office of the Labor Welfare Corporation by the end of February every year. Then, the Labor Welfare Corporation calculates and determines the employment insurance premium and the National Health Insurance Corporation levies its premium invoice along with other social security insurance premiums to each company.

Ⅲ. 고용보험 비용 부담

1. 부담원칙

고용보험 비용은 실업급여 보험료와 고용안정·직업능력개발사업의 보험료로 구분·부과되는데, 실업급여 보험료는 근로자와 사용자가 각 1/2씩 부담하고 고용안정·직업능력개발사업 비용은 사용자가 부담한다.

2. 부담수준

〈사업별 보험요율, 2025년 기준〉

사업명	보험요율	부담주체
실업급여	1.8%	노·사 각 0.9%
고용안정·직업능력 개발사업	· 150인 미만 기업 0.25% · 150인이상이나우선지원대상기업 0.45% · 150인 이상이며 우선지원대상 기업이 아닌 기업 0.65% · 1,000인 이상 기업 0.85%	사업주

* 참고: 우선지원 대상기업 ① 광업: 300인 이하, ② 제조업: 500인 이하, ③ 건설업: 300인 이하, ④ 운수, 창고 및 통신업: 300인 이하

3. 보험료의 산정납부

보험료는 근로자의 연간 보수총액에 해당 보험사업의 보험료율을 곱하여 산정한다. 사업주는 근로자 부담 분까지 포함하여 보험료 납부의무가 있으며 근로자가 부담하여야 할 실업급여보험료는 매월 임금을 지급할 때 원천 공제한다.

사업주는 매년 2월 말까지 전년도 전체 근로자에 대한 개인별 보수총액 자료를 사업장의 소재지 관할 근로복지공단 지사에 신고하고, 근로복지공단에서 고용보험료를 산정·부과하고 이를 국민건강보험공단에서 다른 사회보험료와 함께 사업장에 고지한다.

Ⅳ. Projects Promoted through Employment Insurance

Employment insurance projects are divided into unemployment benefits, employment security, and vocational skills development projects.

1. Unemployment benefits

(1) Employees eligible for unemployment benefits

Employment benefits are paid to unemployed persons who satisfy the following two criteria: employees who had to leave a job involuntarily for reasons such as dismissal for managerial reasons, expiration of contract period, etc. after having worked at least 180 days during the last 18month period, and unemployed people who are actively seeking to become reemployed. However, unemployment benefits shall not be given in cases where an employee has left his/her job to start another job or become self-employed or in cases where the employee is separated from employment following the advice of the employer or dismissed due to reasons attributable to him/herself.

※ Cases dismissed due to critical reasons attributable to employee

① The employee is sentenced to imprisonment (without being assigned prison labor or more severe punishment) for violating the Criminal Act or laws relating to employment;

② The employee has, on purpose, caused a considerable hindrance to the business or inflicted any damage to property due to embezzlement, disclosure of corporate secrets, damage to property, etc.; and

③ The employee has been absent from work for a long time without due notice or justifiable reasons.

* If an employee to whom any of the above items apply resigns voluntarily at the employer's advice, he/she shall not be eligible to receive unemployment benefits.

Unemployment benefits are paid to an unemployed person when he/she reports unemployment and is recognized as an eligible recipient, and when he/she begins seeking reemployment. Therefore, this beneficiary process requires the recognition of unemployment status and evidence to prove the applicant is actively seeking reemployment for a unit period of three to four weeks. Therefore, in principle, a reemployed employee is not eligible for unemployment benefits. If an eligible recipient is employed in a job that is deemed certain to keep him/her employed for at least six months, or if an eligible recipient is deemed certain to run his/her own business for six months or more, then the reemployed person can get a certain portion(1/3 ~ 2/3) of the benefit still left as an early reemployment incentive.

Ⅳ. 고용보험이 행하는 사업

고용보험사업은 실업급여사업, 고용안정사업, 직업능력개발사업으로 구분된다.

1. 실업급여

(1) 실업급여의 지급대상

실업급여는 고용보험 가입사업장에서 퇴직 전 18개월 중 180일 이상 피보험자로 근무하다가 경영상 해고, 계약기간만료 등 비자발적으로 사유로 이직한 근로자가 근로의 의사와 능력을 가지고 적극적으로 재취업 활동을 하는 경우에 한하여 지급되고 있다. 다만, 전직, 자영업을 위하여 스스로 직장을 그만두었거나 본인의 중대한 귀책사유로 권고사직하거나 해고된 경우에는 실업급여를 받을 수 없다.

※ 중대한 귀책사유로 해고된 경우란

① 형법 또는 직무와 관련된 법률을 위반하여 금고이상의 형을 선고받고 해고된 경우

② 공금횡령, 회사기밀누설, 기물파괴 등 고의적으로 회사에 막대한 지장 또는 재산상의 손해를 끼쳐 해고된 경우

③ 정당한 사유 없이 장기간 무단결근하여 해고된 경우 등

* 위 3가지 중대한 귀책사유에 해당하는 자가 해고되지 아니하고 권고사직으로 이직하더라도 구직급여 수급대상으로 인정하지 않는다.

실업급여는 실업을 신고하고 수급자격을 인정받은 수급자격자가 실업상태에서 적극적으로 재취업활동을 하여 실업인정(1주~4주 단위)을 받은 경우 지급되므로 재취업을 하게 되면 원칙적으로 실업급여를 받을 수 없다. 다만, 수급자격자가 구직급여를 받는 기간 중에 6개월 이상 고용될 것이 확실한 직장에 재취업하거나 또는 6개월 이상 자영업을 하는 것이 확실한 경우에는 재취업시점에 따라 미지급 금액의 일부(1/3~2/3)를 조기 재취업수당으로 받을 수 있다.

전직, 자영업을 위해 사표를 쓰거나 학업 등 개인적인 사유로 사표를 쓰는 등의 자발적 이직의 경우에는 원칙적으로 구직급여를 받을 수 없다. 다만, 다음의 사유로 이직한 경우에는 예외적으로 실업급여를 받을 수 있다.

In cases where an employee resigns from a company voluntarily by submitting a resignation letter or changing occupation, becoming self-employed, or going back to school, unemployment benefits shall, in principle, not be given. However, the employee can receive unemployment benefits under the following special circumstances:

◈ Reasons for unemployment benefit acceptable for eligible beneficiary
(Employment Insurance Decree Regulation (Article 101(1)-Table 2, 2022.6.30.)

1. If any of the following happens within a period of two months or more within one year prior to the date of unemployment:
   (1) The actual working conditions are lower than the working conditions presented at the time of hiring or the working conditions generally applied after hiring;
   (2) The payment of wages is delayed;
   (3) If the wage paid for prescribed work falls below the minimum wage under the Minimum Wage Act;
   (4) If the restrictions on extended work in Article 53 of the Labor Standards Act are violated;
   (5) Due to workplace closures, less than 70 percent of average wage is paid.
2. If the employee received unreasonable discrimination on the grounds of religion, sex, physical disability, union activities, etc. at the workplace;
3. If the employee was unwillingly subjected to sexual harassment, sexual assault, or other sexual bullying in the workplace;

3-2. In case of workplace harassment pursuant to Article 76-2 of the「Labor Standards Act」

4. The business is certain to go bankrupt or close, or large-scale layoffs are planned;
5. If the employee is advised to terminate employment by the employer due to any of the following conditions, or if he or she leaves the job due to the recruitment of early retirement applicants pursuant to an employment adjustment plan caused by the inevitability of staff reductions:
   (1) Transfer, acquisition, merger of business;
   (2) Partial business abolition or business conversion;
   (3) Abolition and reduction of organization by reorganization;
   (4) Changes in work patterns due to the introduction of new technologies and technological innovations;
   (5) Deterioration of management, congestion of human resources or other similar reasons.
6. If the employee experiences difficulties in commuting due to any of the following reasons (at least three hours are required to get to the workplace and back by ordinary means of transportation):
   (1) Relocation of business;
   (2) Transfer to another business location;
   (3) Transfer of residence for the purpose of cohabiting with a spouse or relatives in need of support;
   (4) Other unavoidable reasons for the difficulty.
7. Due to the circumstances of the company, the employee could not take vacation or temporary leave and terminated employment during the period of more than 30 days of supporting his or her parents or cohabitating relatives for sickness or injury;
8. The employee works at a workplace where, despite a "serious accident" occurring in accordance with Article 2, Item 2 of the Occupational Safety and Health Act, and a correction order received from the Minister of Employment and Labor, the company has taken no corrective actions within the given period and employees are exposed to the same danger;
9. Termination of the employee's employment is objectively recognized based on the opinion of a doctor or the employer, etc., due to an insured worker being unable to perform given task(s) due to a lack of physical strength, physical or mental disability, illness, injury, loss of sight, hearing or tactile sense (job transfers and temporary leaves are also allowed if they are due to company circumstances);
10. The insured worker is unable to continue work due to pregnancy, childbirth, childcare of a child under the age of 8 or up to second grade in elementary school (including an adopted child), or the employer cannot allow vacation or temporary leave for the employee to fulfill his obligatory service under the Military Service Act;
11. If the details of the business of the employer become illegal due to enactment or amendment of laws and ordinances or produces or sells goods or services not illegal at the time of employment, but now prohibited by laws or regulations;
12. The employee reaches retirement age or the employee's contract expires;
13. In addition, it is objectively recognized that other workers in the workplace under the circumstances of the insured person may have resigned.

◈ 수급자격이 제한되지 아니하는 이직사유
(고용보험법 시행규칙 제101조 제1항 별표2, 개정 2022.6.30.)

1. 다음 어느 하나에 해당하는 사유가 이직일 전 1년 이내에 2개월 이상 발생한 경우
   (1) 실제 근로조건이 채용 시 제시된 근로조건이나 채용 후 일반적으로 적용받던 근로조건보다 낮아지게 된 경우
   (2) 임금체불이 있는 경우
   (3) 소정근로에 대하여 지급받은 임금이 「최저임금법」에 따른 최저임금에 미달하게 된 경우
   (4) 「근로기준법」 제53조에 따른 연장 근로의 제한을 위반한 경우
   (5) 사업장의 휴업으로 휴업 전 평균임금의 70퍼센트 미만을 지급받은 경우
2. 사업장에서 종교, 성별, 신체장애, 노조활동 등을 이유로 불합리한 차별대우를 받은 경우
3. 사업장에서 본인의 의사에 반하여 성희롱, 성폭력, 그 밖의 성적인 괴롭힘을 당한 경우

3의2. 「근로기준법」 제76조의2에 따른 직장 내 괴롭힘을 당한 경우

4. 사업장의 도산·폐업이 확실하거나 대량의 감원이 예정되어 있는 경우
5. 다음 어느 하나에 해당하는 사정으로 사업주로부터 퇴직을 권고받거나, 인원 감축이 불가피하여 고용조정계획에 따라 실시하는 퇴직 희망자의 모집으로 이직하는 경우
   (1) 사업의 양도·인수·합병
   (2) 일부 사업의 폐지나 업종전환
   (3) 직제개편에 따른 조직의 폐지·축소
   (4) 신기술의 도입, 기술혁신 등에 따른 작업형태의 변경
   (5) 경영의 악화, 인사 적체, 그 밖에 이에 준하는 사유가 발생한 경우
6. 다음 어느 하나에 해당하는 사유로 통근이 곤란(통근 시 이용할 수 있는 통상의 교통수단으로는 사업장으로의 왕복에 드는 시간이 3시간 이상인 경우를 말한다)하게 된 경우
   (1) 사업장의 이전
   (2) 지역을 달리하는 사업장으로의 전근
   (3) 배우자나 부양하여야 할 친족과의 동거를 위한 거소 이전
   (4) 그 밖에 피할 수 없는 사유로 통근이 곤란한 경우
7. 부모나 동거 친족의 질병·부상 등으로 30일 이상 본인이 간호해야 하는 기간에 기업의 사정상 휴가나 휴직이 허용되지 않아 이직한 경우
8. 「산업안전보건법」 제2조제2호에 따른 "중대재해"가 발생한 사업장으로서 그 재해와 관련된 고용노동부장관의 안전보건상의 시정명령을 받고도 시정기간까지 시정하지 아니하여 같은 재해 위험에 노출된 경우
9. 체력의 부족, 심신장애, 질병, 부상, 시력·청력·촉각의 감퇴 등으로 피보험자가 주어진 업무를 수행하는 것이 곤란하고, 기업의 사정상 업무종류의 전환이나 휴직이 허용되지 않아 이직한 것이 의사의 소견서, 사업주 의견 등에 근거하여 객관적으로 인정되는 경우
10. 임신, 출산, 만 8세 이하 또는 초등학교 2학년 이하의 자녀(입양한 자녀를 포함한다)의 육아, 「병역법」에 따른 의무복무 등으로 업무를 계속적으로 수행하기 어려운 경우로서 사업주가 휴가나 휴직을 허용하지 않아 이직한 경우
11. 사업주의 사업 내용이 법령의 제정·개정으로 위법하게 되거나 취업 당시와는 달리 법령에서 금지하는 재화 또는 용역을 제조하거나 판매하게 된 경우
12. 정년의 도래나 계약기간의 만료로 회사를 계속 다닐 수 없게 된 경우
13. 그 밖에 피보험자와 사업장 등의 사정에 비추어 그러한 여건에서는 통상의 다른 근로자도 이직했을 것이라는 사실이 객관적으로 인정되는 경우

(2) Amount of unemployment benefit

The unemployment benefit is 60% of the average wage prior to separation within the range of 100 to 270 days in accordance with the age and insured period as of separation time.

⇨ Maximum amount: 66,000 won per day(As of 2025)

⇨ Minimum amount: daily contractual working hours x 80% of daily minimum wage; However, if the lowest amount calculated(based upon 80% of the minimum wage) is less than 64,192 won, the amount is 64,192 won.

⇨ Number of days unemployment benefits can be received

Insured period / Age	Less than 1 year	1 year~less than 3 years	3 years~less than 5 years	5 years~less than 10 years	10 years or more
Younger than 50	120 days	150 days	180 days	210 days	240 days
50 or older, or disabled	120 days	180 days	210 days	240 days	270 days

Even though an unemployed person is eligible for unemployment benefits, he/she cannot receive them if 12 months have passed from the initial date of unemployment. These 12 months are called the period of benefit payment. As unemployment benefits cannot be paid if the period of benefit payment expires, an unemployed person shall apply for benefits with the Employment Support Center without delay right after termination of employment.

※ Reasons for extension of payment period (maximum extension is 4 years)

- Injury or illness of the recipient (excluding injuries or illnesses for which injury and disease benefits are being paid);
- Injury or illness of the recipient's spouse or lineal ascendants or descendants;
- Mandatory military service under the Military Service Act;
- Detention or execution of sentence on criminal charges; and
- Pregnancy, childbirth, and childcare (limited to within 3 years after the birth of a child).

(3) Payment procedures for unemployment benefits

To receive unemployment benefits, immediately upon termination of employment, the unemployed person shall visit the Employment Support Center in his/her location with identification documents, such as a residence card or driver's license, and report unemployment. The report of unemployment shall include an application for work and an application for the recognition of eligibility for benefit. The head of the Employment Security Office shall then notify the applicant of its decision within 14 days.

(2) 실업급여지급액

구직급여는 퇴직 당시 연령과 고용보험 가입기간에 따라 120~270일의 범위 내에서 퇴직 전 평균임금의 60% 지급된다.

⇨ 최고액 : 1일 66,000원 (2025년 기준)

⇨ 최저액 : 1일 소정근로시간 × 최저임금법상 시간급 최저임금의 80%

단, 계산된 하한액(최저임금의 80%)이 64,192원 보다 낮은 경우 64,192원

⇨ 구직급여지급일수(소정급여일수)

피보험기간 / 연 령	1년 미만	1년 이상 3년 미만	3년 이상 5년 미만	5년 이상 10년 미만	10년 이상
50세 미만	120일	150일	180일	210일	240일
50세 이상 및 장애인	120일	180일	210일	240일	270일

구직급여는 수급자격이 있다 하더라도 퇴직한 다음 날부터 12개월이 경과하면 지급받을 수 없으며, 이 12개월을 '수급기간'이라고 한다. 수급기간이 경과하면 원칙적으로 구직급여가 지급되지 않기 때문에, 퇴직 후 지체없이 거주지 관할 고용지원센터에 수급자격 신청을 하여야 한다.

* 수급기간 연장사유(최대연장기간 4년)
- 본인의 질병 부상(상병급여를 지급받은 경우는 제외)
- 배우자 또는 직계존비속의 질병, 부상
- 병역법에 의한 의무복무
- 구속 또는 형의 집행
- 임신, 출산, 육아(육아의 경우 생후 3년 미만의 영아에 한함)

(3) 실업급여의 지급절차

실업급여를 지급받으려면 실직 즉시 주민등록증이나 운전면허증 등 본인임을 증명할 수 있는 신분증을 가지고 거주지 관할 고용지원센터에 방문하여 실업의 신고를 하여야 한다. 실업의 신고는 고용지원센터에 구직신청 및 수급자격 인정신청서를 작성하여 제출하면 되고, 직업안정기관의 장은 원칙적으로 접수 후 14일 이내에 수급자격인정여부를 결정하여 통지한다.

1) Recognition of unemployment

Recognition of unemployment means that the head of an Employment Security Office recognizes that the applicant has become unemployed and is actively seeking reemployment during a certain recognition period of unemployment, and is eligible for unemployment benefits. An eligible recipient shall present him/herself on the date of recognition of unemployment designated by the head of the Employment Security Office over the course of one to four weeks from the date the unemployment was reported, and shall report the efforts he/she has made to become reemployed, and the head of the Employment Security Office shall recognize his/her unemployment based upon the details of the report. Eligible recipients cannot receive unemployment benefits if they were not recognized as being unemployed because of a failure to report to the Employment Security Office on the day(s) required.

2) Actively seeking to become reemployed

Eligible recipients shall actively seek to become reemployed(i.e., get another job) in accordance with the reemployment action plan completed on the first day of unemployment so that they can be recognized as being unemployed. Here, "actively seeking to become reemployed" means the unemployed person has taken action such as submitting job applications or participating in job interviews, and/or made efforts to become self-employed. Job-seeking activities also include submission of job applications by mail, fax or email, participation in job interviews with recruiters at a job fair, or attending occupation guidance programs conducted by the Employment Security Office.

(4) Fraudulent receipt of unemployment benefits

Unemployment benefits are payable when an applicant is recognized as an unemployed person by the head of an Employment Security Office and actively seeks to become reemployed during the recognition period of unemployment. It is illegal to receive unemployment benefits through false or fraudulent methods.

※ The most common cases of illegally receiving benefits involve a person not reporting reemployment during the recognition period of unemployment or reporting it using fraudulent information, or making a false report regarding his/her wages while employed or the reason(s) for termination.

If it is found that a person has received unemployment benefits through illegal methods, he/she shall refund the benefit received and, as a penalty, pay an additional, identical

1) 실업의 인정

실업인정이란 퇴직근로자가 구직급여를 받을 수 있는 수급자격인정을 받은 경우, 실업인정대상기간 중에 실업상태에서 적극적으로 재취업활동을 하고 있다는 것을 직업안정기관의 장이 인정하는 것을 말한다. 수급자격자는 최초 실업인정일 이후에는 1주~4주 범위 내에서 직업안정기관의 장이 지정한 날에 직접 고용지원센터에 출석하여 지난 해당 실업 인정기간 동안 실업상태에서 적극적으로 재취업 활동을 한 사실을 신고하여야 하며, 직업안정기관의 장은 수급자격자의 신고 내용을 토대로 실업인정을 하고 구직급여를 지급하게 된다. 수급자격자가 출석하지 않아 실업인정을 받지 못하면 원칙적으로 구직급여를 지급받을 수 없다.

2) 적극적 구직활동

수급자격자가 실업인정을 받기 위해서는 최초 실업인정일에 작성한 재취업 활동 계획서에 따라 적극적으로 재취업 활동(구직활동)을 하여야 하는데, 재취업 활동이란 입사원서 제출, 면접 참가 등 재취업활동과 자영업을 준비하는 활동을 말한다. 우편이나 팩스, 전자메일을 이용하여 구인처에 입사 원서를 제출하거나 채용박람회 등에 참석하여 구인자와 면접을 본 경우, 직업안정기관에서 행하는 직업지도 프로그램에 참가하는 경우에도 적극적 구직활동으로 인정된다.

(4) 부정수급

실업급여는 퇴직근로자가 직업안정기관의 장으로부터 수급자격을 인정받고 실업인정 대상기간 중에 실업상태에서 재취업 활동을 하는 경우 받을 수 있는데 거짓 그 밖의 부정한 방법으로 실업급여를 받았거나 받고자 하는 경우에는 부정수급에 해당된다.

※ 대표적인 부정수급사례로는 실업인정대상기간 중 재취업사실을 신고하지 않거나 허위로 신고한 경우, 이직사유 또는 임금 등을 허위로 신고하는 경우 등을 들 수 있다.

부정한 방법으로 실업급여를 지급받은 사실이 적발된 경우에는 부정수급액의 반환은 물론 부정수급액 만큼의 추가징수, 부정수급한 날 이후의 구직급여지급

amount equivalent to the illegally received benefit. Further, his/her unemployment benefits will stop and the person concerned could face criminal prosecution. If a company manager was involved in perpetuating the illegality, the employer shall also share joint responsibility with the person.

1) A small illegal benefit can be forgiven only once.

2) Criminal punishment can be pursued when a person violates the law twice, where two people or more collaborate and receive benefits illegally, and in cases where a person rejects the requests to repay the illegally received benefits despite repeated demands from the Employment Security Office.

3) In cases where illegal benefits were paid due to a falsified description on the company's confirmation of severance, an additional fine(2~3 million won) will be levied against the company.

2. Employment security project

It is important for the employer to be familiar with the contents and prepare in advance to receive these subsidies.

These subsidies are available to the employers who, instead of cutting their workforce, retain jobs or recruit unemployed people, so as to increase job security for incumbent employees while promoting employment of disadvantaged persons.

(1) Subsidy for employment adjustment

When the employer adjusts employment through suspension of business, reduction of working hours, training, suspension of work, and personnel rearrangement, the Ministry of Employment and Labor provides a subsidy to the employer if he/she maintains employment of the employees concerned(Article 21 of the EIA).

(2) Subsidy for employment creation

The Minister of Employment and Labor may provide support to employers who have expanded employment opportunities by improving employment environments, changing work arrangements, etc(Article 20 of the EIA).

(3) Subsidy for employment promotion

① Subsidy for employment promotion: older workers, those with disabilities, young

중지, 사법처리 등 가혹한 불이익 처분을 받는다. 회사의 관계자가 부정행위에 개입한 경우에는 사업주도 연대하여 책임을 묻게 된다.

1) 경미한 부정수급의 경우라도 1회만 정상 참작이 될 뿐이다.

2) 2회 이상 부정수급을 한 경우, 2인 이상이 공모하여 부정수급을 한 경우, 부정수급액의 반환독촉을 받고도 이행하지 않은 경우에는 형사처벌 될 수도 있다.

3) 이직확인서 허위 기재 신고로 부정수급이 발생한 경우에는 사업주에게 별도의 과태료(200~300만원)가 부과된다.

2. 고용안정사업

사업주를 지원하는 고용안정사업은 사업주가 미리 지원내용을 알고 준비하지 않으면 지원을 받을 수 없다.

근로자를 감원하지 않고 고용을 유지하거나 실직자를 채용하여 고용을 늘리는 사업주를 지원하여 근로자의 고용안정 및 취업 취약계층의 고용 촉진을 지원한다.

(1) 고용조정지원

매출액 및 생산량 감소 등 경영상의 이유로 고용조정이 불가피하게 되어 휴업, 근로시간 단축, 훈련, 휴직, 인력 재배치의 고용유지 조치를 실시하여 근로자의 고용을 유지하는 사업주에게 지원한다(고용보험법 제21조).

(2) 고용창출지원

고용노동부 장관은 고용환경 개선, 근무형태 변경 등으로 고용의 기회를 확대한 사업주에게 필요한 지원을 할 수 있다(고용보험법 제20조).

(3) 고용촉진지원

① 신규고용촉진장려금: 고령자, 장애인, 청년, 여성가장, 출산여성, 장기구직자, ② 고령자: 다수고령자, 정년연상, 정년퇴식자 계속고용, ③ 육아유식 상

people, female heads of households, women who have just given birth, long-term unemployed, ② Older workers: employing many older people, extending retirement age, continuing employment after retirement, ③ Subsidy to promote childcare leave and subsidy for hiring replacement personnel, ④ Subsidy for reducing working hours during childcare period, ⑤ Nursery, ⑥ Maintaining allowance for the wage peak system, ⑦ Subsidy for continuous employment after childbirth, ⑧ Employment for construction workers

3. Vocational skills development project

Financial backing is offered to employers who give vocational training to their employees and employees who take up training for the purpose of self-development.

(1) Support for the employer

① Support for vocational skills development training, ② Support for paid-leave training

③ Support, etc., for vocational skills development training facilities, ④ Support for vocational skills development of construction workers

(2) Support for the employee

① Support for tuition, ② Loan for tuition, ③ Re-employment training for the unemployed, ④ Support for government-commissioned training expenses

려금 및 대체인력 채용장려금, ④ 육아기 근로시간 단축장려금, ⑤ 보육시설, ⑥ 임금피크제 보전수당, ⑦ 출산후 계속고용지원금, ⑧ 건설근로자 고용안정

3. 직업능력 개발사업

사업주가 근로자에게 직업훈련을 실시하거나 근로자가 자기개발을 위해 훈련을 받을 경우 사업주·근로자에게 일정 비용을 지원한다.

(1) 사업주에 대한 지원

① 직업능력개발훈련 지원, ② 유급휴가훈련 지원, ③ 직업능력개발 훈련시설·장비설치비용 대부, ④ 건설근로자 직업능력개발 지원

(2) 근로자에 대한 지원

① 근로자 수강지원금 지원, ② 근로자학자금 대부, ③ 능력개발비용(훈련비) 대부, ④ 실업자 재취직훈련비용 지원

Section 2: Industrial Accident Compensation Insurance

Ⅰ. Concept

Industrial accident compensation insurance(hereinafter, the IACI) is a social insurance system in which the government provides occupationally ill and injured employees with compensation to be paid by his/her employer under the Labor Standards Act. Under this system, individual employers are obligated to make a given rate of contribution to the insurance fund and, in return, are exempted from paying compensation for occupationally ill or injured employees. The government uses this fund to compensate employees for work-related injuries and illnesses.

IACI premiums are fully paid by the employer, and are calculated by multiplying the total income of all workers in the workplace by the insurance rate announced by the government according to the business' risk level. In applying the industrial accident insurance premium rate for the same business, if the premium benefits to workers exceed 85% or less than 75% of the previous three years of premium payments, the premium rate applied to the business is determined up to 50% higher or lower for the next business year.[21] As a result, industrial accident insurance premiums may increase the following year if a lot has been paid out in IACI benefits, which will affect the company's intention to apply to IACI as it can expect higher premiums.[22]

Insurance benefits shall be paid at the worker's(or survivor's) request if a worker at a workplace covered by IACI has an injury, illness or accident requiring at least four days of medical care. Types of insurance benefits include nursing care, leave of absence, sick compensation pensions, disability, survivor, nursing care, funeral expenses, and vocational rehabilitation.

---

21) Lee, Sang-Kook, The Industrial Accident Compensation Insurance Act (I), 9th Ed., Daemyung Publisher, 2020, p. 554.

22) Jeon, Kwang-seok, Park, Ji-soon and Kim, Bok-ki, The Social Security Act, 4th Ed., Shinjosa, 2017, p. 188.

제2절 산업재해보상보험

Ⅰ. 산업재해보상 보험제도의 의의

산업재해보상보험제도는 근로자가 업무상 사유로 부상을 당하거나 질병에 걸리는 경우 근로기준법상 사업주가 부담해야 할 보상책임을 국가가 대신하여 수행하는 사회보험제도이다. 따라서 산재보험 적용대상 사업주는 일정한 보험료를 납부함으로써 근로자에 대한 개별보상책임을 면제받게 되며, 국가는 사업주가 납부한 보험료를 재원으로 근로자에게 직접 보상을 실시하게 된다.

산재보험료는 사업주가 전액부담하며, 산재보험료율은 사업업종의 위험여부에 따라 정부에서 고시하는 보험료율을 사업장의 보수총액을 곱하여 계산된 보험금을 납부한다. 동일사업의 산재보험료율을 적용함에 있어서 과거 3년간의 보험급여 금액의 85%를 넘거나 75% 이하인 경우 그 사업에 적용되는 보험료율을 50% 범위 안에서 결정해서 인상 또는 인하하여 그 사업에 대한 다음 사업연도의 산재보험료율로 적용한다.[21] 따라서 산재보험 수급으로 인해 다음연도의 산재보험료가 높아지게 될 수 있기 때문에 기업체에서는 가급적 산재보험처리를 기피하게 된다.[22]

보험급여는 산재보험 적용대상 사업장의 근로자가 업무상 사유로 4일 이상의 요양을 요하는 부상, 질병을 얻거나 사망한 경우 당해 근로자(또는 유족)의 신청에 따라 지급한다. 보험급여의 종류에는 요양급여, 휴업급여, 상병보상연금, 장해급여, 유족급여, 간병급여, 장례비, 직업재활급여가 있다.

21) 이상국, 「산재보험법(I)」, 제9판, 대명출판사, 2020.1. 554면.
22) 전광석·박지순·김복기 「사회보장법」, 제4판, 신조사, 2017, 188면

Ⅱ. Application

1. Working places

This Act shall be applicable to all businesses or workplaces, with the exception of those prescribed by Presidential Decree, in regards to the risk ratio, scale, place, etc. of the business.

The employer of a non-compulsory business may also choose to take out or terminate insurance with approval from the Korea Labor Welfare Corporation.

	Details
Businesses excluded from the application of Act	· Household affairs services industry · Businesses in agriculture, forestry, fishing, hunting, that ordinarily hire fewer than 5 permanent workers

2. Separate insurance for overseas dispatch employees

For an overseas dispatch employee(excluding a short-term visitor), the employer shall take out insurance separately with the Labor Welfare Corporation. Even if the employee concerned is subject to the four social security insurances and income tax in Korea, he/she will not be eligible for the industrial accident compensation if he/she is not additionally insured for IACI.

Ⅲ. Covering an Accident through Industrial Accident Compensation Insurance

Industrial accident compensation is commissioned to and handled by the Employee Welfare Corporation under the Ministry of Employment and Labor. The ill or injured employee shall apply to the district office of the Employee Welfare Corporation for the benefits by filling out the form, Application for Medical Care Benefits and receiving the employer's confirmation signature on the form. In cases where a serious industrial accident has occurred, the employer shall report to the Ministry of Employment and Labor immediately, while for minor industrial accidents, the employer shall submit an Occupational Accident Report Form to the district Labor Office within one month from the date the accident occurred. For accidents that are very clearly occupational only two or three weeks are necessary to receive confirmation as an industrial accident and

Ⅱ. 재해보상의 적용범위

1. 적용 사업장

산업재해보상보험법은 근로자를 사용하는 모든 사업 또는 사업장에서 적용되는 것이 원칙으로 하면서, 사업의 위험률, 규모 및 사업장소 등을 참작하여 대통령령으로 정한 사업은 예외적으로 적용치 않을 수 있도록 규정하고 있다.

산업재해보상보험법에 의한 당연가입사업이 아니라 하더라도 근로복지공단의 승인을 얻어 보험에 가입 및 해지가 가능하다.

구 분	내 용
적용제외 대상	• 가사서비스업 • 농업, 임업, 어업, 수렵업 중 상시 5인 미만의 근로자를 사용하는 사업

2. 해외파견자의 별도 가입

해외파견자(단기출장자 제외)가 있는 회사에서는 별도로 근로복지공단에 신청하여 산재보험을 가입하여야 하며, 회사에서 4대 보험, 갑근세를 모두 적용하더라도 별도로 산재보험에 가입을 하지 않으면 업무상 재해라도 보상을 받지 못함을 유의해야 한다.

Ⅲ. 산재처리 방법

산업재해보상업무는 고용노동부로부터 위임 받아 근로복지공단이 처리하고 있다. 재해를 당한 근로자는 관할 근로복지공단지사에 「요양신청서」를 작성하여 회사와 연명으로 날인하여 신청하여야 한다. 회사는 중대재해인 경우에는 노동부에 지체 없이 신고를 하여야 하지만, 일반적인 업무상 사고인 경우에는 사고발생일로부터 1개월 이내에 관할 노동청에 산업재해조사표를 작성하여 제출해야 한다. 재해사건의 사실관계가 명확한 경우에는 2~3주 내에 산재승인과 함께 관련된 보상이 이루어지지만, 업무상 질병인 경우에는 산재신청 처리에 최소 2개월의 시간이 소요된다. 그 절차는 요양신청서 접수, 상병상태확인,

related compensation. However, for occupational illnesses, it will take a minimum of two months for confirmation as an industrial illness. The procedures for determining whether an accident or illness is occupational are: Application for medical care benefits ? Confirmation of illness details ? Analysis of relationship between working environment and illness ? Confirmation of advisory medical doctor's opinion ? Approval or rejection by the Occupational Illness Deliberation Committee.

Ⅳ. Criteria for Determining an Incident as an Industrial Accident

1. General criteria

1) Accident compensation is rendered in case of injury, disease, handicap, death, etc. caused by a work-related accident.

2) Article 37 of the Presidential Decree to the Industrial Accident Compensation Insurance Act(IACI Act) stipulates that a work-related accident shall reveal causality between the work and the accident.

3) The accident shall not be caused by the employee's intentions, self-injury, criminal behaviors, etc. However, if an employee who has received mental treatment due to work stress or whose normal abilities to recognize, select, or control themselves has been affected by work(as determined by medical diagnosis) commits suicide, it shall be admitted as a work-related accident.

2. Considerations for work-related accidents

In general, a work-related accident is distinguished between those caused by work and those related to work. In practicality neither one can be overemphasized nor excluded. Accordingly, an accident is recognized as an industrial accident if it has work-related causes.

(1) Related to work

If an accident occurs when preparing for work, at work, or after work under the employer's supervision or management, then it can be said to have been caused by a reason related to work performance.

재해 상황과 상병상태 관계 확인, 자문의사 확인, 질병판정위원회를 통한 최종 승인·불승인 결정 순서로 이루어진다.

Ⅳ. 재해인정기준

1. 일반적 기준

1) 재해보상은 부상·질병·장해·사망 등의 재해가 '업무상'의 사유에 의하여 발생한 경우에만 지급된다. 업무상 재해란 업무상의 사유에 의한 근로자의 부상·질병·신체장해 또는 사망을 말한다.

2) 업무상 재해인지 여부를 판단하기 위한 근거를 제시하고 있는 산업재해보상보험법 제37조는 업무와 사고 사이의 인과관계가 있고 재해와 근로자의 사상과 인과관계가 있는 때는 업무와 재해 사이에 상당한 인과관계가 있는 것으로 보고 있다.

3) 근로자의 고의·자해행위나 범죄행위 또는 그것이 원인이 되어 발생한 사상이 아니어야 한다. 다만, 업무상 스트레스로 인하여 정신과 치료를 받았거나 업무상 재해로 인하여 요양 중인 자가 정신장해로 인하여 정상적인 인식능력이나 행위선택능력 또는 정신적 억제력이 현저히 저하된 상태에서 자살행위로 인하여 사상한 경우는 인정 된다(의학적 소견이 있을 것).

2. 업무상 재해의 성립요건

업무상 재해의 판단기준으로는 일반적으로 업무기인성과 업무수행성을 들 수 있다. 업무기인성과 업무수행성의 관계에 대해서는 많은 논란이 있어 왔으나 현실적으로 업무수행성과 업무기인성을 구분하는 것이 쉽지 않고 어느 한쪽에 중요성을 두거나 다른 한쪽을 배제하는 것 또한 타당치 않으므로 업무상 상당인과 관계가 있으면 업무상 재해가 인정된다고 본다.

(1) 업무수행성

사업주의 지배·관리 아래서 근로자가 작업준비 중, 작업 중, 작업종료 전후에 업무와 관련하여 발생한 재해는 업무상 재해로 인정한다.

(2) Caused by work

If there is considerable causality between the employee's work and the accident that occurred, it is recognized as an industrial accident. The causality shall be verified by the plaintiff. The cause and effect shall not only be verified in terms of medical or physical science, but also by considering all given facts such as the employee's health at the time of employment, materials at the work place, working hours, contact with other workers, etc. If the employee has not been engaged in the work concerned, it shall be admitted that the accident has not been caused by work. However, if the employee has been engaged in the work concerned, the accident may have been caused by work.

3. Work-related accidents

The following suggests concrete criteria:

① When the accident takes place while the employee performs contractual duties under supervisory control and management of the employer, or when the accident occurs due to defects in facilities or management;

② An accident which happens while the worker is commuting to and from work;

③ An accident that happens while the worker is participating in or preparing an event organized by the employer or an event following the directions of the employer;

④ An accident which happens during recess hours due to an act that can be seen as under the control of the employer; and

⑤ Other accidents which happen in relation to work.

4. Work-related diseases

The following suggests concrete criteria:

① An illness which occurs due to the handling of, or exposure to, elements, including physical agents, chemical substances, dust, pathogens, and physically straining work, which could harm a worker's health while he/she is performing his/her duties;

② An illness which occurs as a result of a work-related injury; and

③ Other illnesses which occur in relation to work.

(2) 업무기인성

근로자가 담당하는 업무와 재해발생 사이에 상당한 인과관계가 있으면 업무상 재해로 인정된다. 인과관계성은 이를 주장하는 측에서 입증하여야 한다. 인과관계는 반드시 의학적·자연과학적으로 명백하여야 하는 것은 아니며 근로자의 취업 당시 건강상태, 작업장에 발병물질이 있는지와 그러한 사업장에서의 근무시간, 다른 근로자에 대한 이환 여부 등을 종합적으로 고려하여 판단한다.

해당 업무에 종사하지 않았다면 재해가 발생하지 않았을 것이라고 인정되거나, 해당 업무에 종사하면 그러한 재해가 발생할 수 있다고 인정되면 업무기인성이 있다고 볼 수 있다.

3. 업무상 사고

구체적인 기준을 제시하면 다음과 같다.

① 근로자가 근로계약에 의한 업무를 사업주의 지배·관리하에 수행하는 상태에서 사고가 발생하거나 사업주가 관리하고 있는 시설물의 결함 또는 관리상의 하자로 인하여 사고가 발생하여 사상하였을 것
② 출퇴근 중 발생한 사고
③ 사업주가 주관하거나 사업주의 지시에 따라 참여한 행사나 행사준비 중에 발생한 사고
④ 휴게시간 중 사업주의 지배관리하에 있다고 볼 수 있는 행위로 발생한 사고
⑤ 그밖에 업무와 관련하여 발생한 사고

4. 업무상 질병

구체적인 기준을 제시하면 다음과 같다.

① 업무수행 과정에서 물리적 인자(因子), 화학물질, 분진, 병원체, 신체에 부담을 주는 업무 등 근로자의 건강에 장해를 일으킬 수 있는 요인을 취급하거나 그에 노출되어 발생한 질병
② 업무상 부상이 원인이 되어 발생한 질병
③ 그밖에 업무와 관련하여 발생한 질병

According to Article 5(1) of the IACI Act, occupational accident includes any illness caused by his/her duties, with verifiable causality between the employee's work and the illness. Although there is no direct relation between the main cause of the illness and work performance, if occupational fatigue or stress at least overlaps with the main causes of the illness, causing or deteriorating it, it is assumed that there is causality between them. The cause and effect shall not only be verified in terms of medical or physical science. If it is assumed that there is considerable causality between the work and the illness in considering all given facts, this shall be regarded as verification. In cases where the basic and potential illness that is no problem carrying out normal work duty has become suddenly deteriorated faster than natural speed of deterioration due to heavy workload, it is also regarded that there was verification. Whether there is causality between the work and a death shall be estimated not by the health and physical conditions of the employee concerned, but of an average employee.[23)]

Ⅴ. Insurance Benefits

When an employee of the employer covered by IACI suffers an occupational injury or illness which requires 4 days or more of medical treatment, or dies from a work-related cause, the IACI benefit shall be paid at the request of the employee(or his/her surviving family member). IACI benefits include medical care benefit, suspension benefit, injury-disease compensation annuity, disability benefit, survivors' benefit, nursing benefit, funeral expense benefit, vocational rehabilitation benefit(newly created on July 1, 2008). If an employee is given the industrial accident compensation insurance benefit due to an industrial accident, the employer responsible for compensating the employees for the damage incurred by the accidents under the Labor Standards Act. The employer is also excused from civil liabilities within the range of the insurance benefit.

1. Medical care benefits

Medical care benefits shall provide for the total medical care expenses and be available at any medical institution insured by the Corporation, or at any institution designated by the Corporation, provided that, in cases of great disadvantage, expenses spent for medical treatment may be paid in lieu of the actual medical care.

---

23) Supreme Court ruling on Mar. 9, 2006: 2005 doo 13841.

산업재해보상보험법 제5조 제1호에 정한 업무상 재해라 함은 근로자의 업무수행 중 그 업무에 기인하여 발생한 질병을 의미하는 것이므로 업무와 사망의 원인이 된 질병 사이에 인과관계가 있어야 한다. 그러나 질병의 주된 발생 원인이 업무수행과 직접적인 관계가 없더라도 적어도 업무상의 과로나 스트레스가 질병의 주된 발생원인에 겹쳐서 질병을 유발 또는 악화시켰다면 그사이에 인과관계가 있다고 보아야 한다. 그리고 이러한 인과관계는 반드시 의학적, 자연과학적으로 명백히 입증하여야 하는 것은 아니고 여러 사정을 고려할 때 업무와 질병 사이에 상당인과관계가 있다고 추정되는 경우에는 그 입증이 있다고 보아야 하며, 또한, 평소에 정상적인 근무가 가능한 기초질병이나 기존질병이 직무의 과중 등이 원인이 되어 자연적인 진행속도 이상으로 급격하게 악화된 때는 그 입증이 있는 경우에 포함되는 것이고, 업무와 사망과의 인과관계의 유무는 보통 평균인이 아니라 당해 근로자의 건강과 신체조건을 기준으로 판단하여야 한다.[23)]

Ⅴ. 보험급여

산재보험 적용대상 사업장의 근로자가 업무상의 사유로 4일 이상의 요양을 요하는 부상, 질병을 얻거나 사망한 경우 당해 근로자(또는 유족)의 신청에 따라 보험급여를 지급한다. 보험급여의 종류에는 요양급여, 휴업급여, 상병보상연금, 장해급여, 유족급여, 간병급여, 장례비, 직업재활급여(2008.7.1 신설)가 있다. 근로자가 업무상의 재해로 인해 산재보험 급여를 지급받는 경우, 사업주의 근로기준법상 재해보상 책임이 면제되며, 해당 재해관련 손해배상책임도 보험급여의 범위 내에서 면제된다.

1. 요양급여

산업재해보상법에 있어서의 요양급여는 요양비의 전액으로 하며, 근로복지공단이 설치한 보험시설 또는 지정된 의료기관에서 요양을 하게 한다. 다만, 부득이한 경우에는 요양에 갈음하여 요양비를 지급할 수 있다.

23) 대법원 2006.3.9, 2005두13841.

2. Suspension benefits

Suspension benefits shall be provided for the period in which an employee is unable to work due to medical care needed from injury at work or contracting an occupational illness. The amount to be paid for a day shall be limited to 70% of the average wage. If the period of medical leave is three days or less, no payment shall be given.

3. Disability benefits

If a worker still remains handicapped upon completion of treatment received for an occupational injury or illness, the employer shall provide the handicapped worker, according to the level of disability, compensation equivalent to the sum of average wages multiplied by the number of days provided in the table(Attachment to the IACI).

4. Survivors' benefits

Survivors' benefits shall be paid to the surviving family of the worker who has died from a work-related cause. The benefits are 1,300 days of average wage, which can be rendered in either of the following two methods: ① 50% paid in a lump sum and 50% in pension; or ② 100% paid in pension.

5. Funeral expenses

Funeral expenses shall be paid for a deceased worker killed by a work-related accident. An additional payment equivalent to 120 days' worth of the worker's average wage shall be provided to the entity performing the funeral service.

6. Nursing benefits

Nursing benefits shall be paid to those who receive medical care benefits pursuant to Article 61 as 1st or 2nd degree seriously disabled persons and to those who receive actual nursing services for constant or frequent nursing needs after treatment.

7. Lump sum compensation

If a worker who receives medical care benefits is also paid an injury-disease compensation

2. 휴업급여

휴업급여는 요양으로 인하여 취업하지 못한 기간 중 1일에 대하여 평균임금의 100분의 70에 상당하는 금액으로 한다. 다만, 취업하지 못한 기간이 3일 이내인 때는 휴업급여를 지급하지 아니한다.

3. 장해급여

근로자가 업무상 부상 또는 질병에 걸려 완치 후 신체에 장해가 있는 경우에는 사용자는 장해 정도에 따라 평균임금에 그 등급표에 정한 일수를 곱하여 얻은 금액의 장해급여를 지급하여야 한다.

4. 유족급여

근로자가 업무상 사망한 경우에는 근로복지공단은 그 유족에 대해 평균임금의 1,300일분의 유족급여를 ① 1/2 일시금, 1/2 연금, ② 전액 연금 중 택일토록 하여 지급한다.

5. 장례비

근로자가 업무상 사망한 경우 사용자는 평균임금의 120일분의 장례비를 지급하여야 한다.

6. 간병급여

치료 종결 후에도 의학적으로 상시 또는 수시로 간병이 필요하여 실제로 간병을 받는 장해 1, 2급의 중증장해자에게는 산재법 제61조에 의해 간병급여를 지급한다.

7. 일시보상

산재법 제80조 제4항에서는 요양급여를 받는 근로자가 요양개시 후 3년이

annuity after three years of receiving medical care, then the employer may terminate the worker's service upon the fourth year as prescribed in Article 84 of the Labor Standards Act, in accordance with the provisions of the proviso of Article 23 ② of the LSA(Article 80 of the IACI).

8. Injury-Disease compensation annuity

If a worker who has received medical care benefits continues to be in a state that meets all the requirements described in the following subparagraphs, after two years have passed since the start of the medical care, he/she shall be paid an injury-disease compensation annuity instead of wage replacement benefits(Article 66 of the IACI). Such a state includes.

① The injury or illness remains uncured;

② The degree of invalidity caused by the injury or illness meets the standards for invalidity grades prescribed by Presidential Decree;

③ The worker has not been employed because of the need for medical care.

9. Vocational rehabilitation benefit (newly created July 1, 2008)

For a worker who receives disability benefits or needs vocational training to be employed, expenses required for the training and vocational training allowance are subsidized.

Ⅵ. Premium Rates

1. Premiums

Premium rates are directly related to the insured's premium. To ensure fairness of the premium, every June 30, the rates are determined(according to the category of business) under the potential rate of accidents based upon the ratio of the total insurance benefits to the total wages for the past three years.

The premium rate applies as follows:

- A single premium rate shall be applied in the same workplace.
- In a workplace that operates at least two businesses with different rates, the principal business shall be determined as follows:

경과한 날 이후에 상병보상연금을 받고 있는 경우에는 근로기준법 제23조 제2항 단서의 규정에 의해 해고를 허용하고 있다.

8. 상병보상연금

요양급여를 받는 근로자가 요양을 시작한 지 2년이 지난 날 이후에 다음 각 호의 요건 모두에 해당하는 상태가 계속되면 휴업급여 대신 상병보상연금을 그 근로자에게 지급한다(산재법 제66조).

① 그 부상이나 질병이 치유되지 아니한 상태일 것
② 그 부상이나 질병에 따른 폐질(廢疾)의 정도가 대통령령으로 정하는 폐질등급 기준에 해당할 것
③ 요양으로 인하여 취업하지 못하였을 것

9. 직업재활급여

장해급여를 받은 자 중 취업을 위하여 직업훈련이 필요한 자에 대하여 실시하는 직업훈련에 드는 비용 및 직업훈련수당을 지급한다.

Ⅵ. 산재보험요율

1. 일반적인 산재보험요율

산재보험요율은 보험가입자의 보험료부담과 직결되는 것으로서, 보험료부담의 공평성 확보를 위하여 매년 6월 30일 현재 과거 3년간의 보수총액에 대한 보험급여 총액의 비율을 기초로 재해발생의 위험성에 따라 분류된 사업집단별(업종별)로 보험요율을 세분화하여(보통 매년 12월 31일경 고시) 적용한다.

보험요율을 적용함에 있어,

- 하나의 적용사업장에 대하여는 하나의 보험요율을 적용한다.
- 하나의 사업장에서 보험요율이 다른 2종 이상의 사업이 행하여지는 경우 다음 순서에 따라 주된 사업을 결정하여 적용한다.

① The business with the larger number of workers;
② If there is an equal number of workers, or the number of workers cannot be determined, the business with the higher total wages; and
③ If it is impossible to determine the principal business by the 1) or 2) above, the business with the higher sales of manufactured products or services.

2. Adjustment of premiums in exceptional cases

Applying the same rate for identical industries is designed to create a balance between employers taking significant steps to avoid occupational accidents and employers who do not. In cases where the insurance benefits paid during the previous three years exceeds 85%, or is less than 75%, of the premiums for the same years, the applicable rate for that industry shall be adjusted up or down by 20% up to a maximum of 50%. This new rate will be applied at the beginning of the following year.

(1) Application of premiums

This special premium rate applies to companies that hire 30 employees or more, excluding those in construction or logging. However, as of July 30, which is the period when the premiums for individual companies are calculated, if the type of industry to which the premiums apply has changed within the previous three years, this special premium application shall not be reflected.

(2) Method of calculation

① Ratio of benefits vs. premiums = total insurance benefits paid during the previous three years / total premiums paid during the previous three years 100
② The insurance benefits paid for unavoidable reasons due to occupational accidents by a third party, natural disasters, power outages, etc. shall be excluded in calculation.

Ⅶ. Compensation Procedures and Relation to other Compensation

1. Compensation procedures under the IACI Act

As with a relief application for remedy against unfair dismissal, in the event that the application is not accepted at a branch office of the Labor Welfare Corporation, the

① 근로자 수가 많은 사업
② 근로자 수가 동일하거나 그 수를 파악할 수 없는 경우는 임금 총액이 많은 사업
③ 상기 방법에 의하여 주된 사업을 결정할 수 없는 경우에는 매출액이 많은 사업을 주된 사업으로 결정

2. 산재보험료율 적용의 특례

동일사업의 보험료율을 적용함에 있어서 재해방지를 위해 노력한 사업주와 그렇지 못한 사업주간에 형평의 원칙을 실현하기 위해 과거3년간의 보험급여 금액의 85%를 넘거나 75%이하인 경우 그 사업에 적용되는 보험료율을 50% 범위 안에서 사업의 규모와 무관하게 최대 20%까지 인상 또는 인하하여 그 사업에 대한 다음 사업연도의 산재보험료율로 적용한다.

(1) 보험료율 적용

건설업 및 벌목업을 제외한 사업으로서 상시 근로자 수가 30인 이상인 사업에 적용한다. 개별실적요율의 기준보험연도의 6월 30일 이전 3년의 기간 중에 산재보험료율 적용사업 종류가 변경된 경우 개별실적요율 적용 제외한다.

(2) 산정방법

① 수지율 = 3년간의 보험급여총액 / 3년간의 보험료총액×100
② 제3자의 행위에 의한 재해나 천재지변·정전 등 불가항력적인 사유로 지급된 보험 급여액은 보험급여액에서 제외한다.

Ⅶ. 산재법상 보상절차 및 다른 보상과의 관계

1. 산재법상 보상절차

부당해고구제신청과 마찬가지로 행정소송법 개정으로 근로복지공단 지사에

employee may bring an administrative suit without requesting an examination to the headquarters of the Corporation or a review by the IACI Examination Committee. In general, the request for an examination and request for review are processed rapidly and economically, but the initial applications are usually denied, whereas administrative suits are more commonly accepted, though they take much longer and cost more.

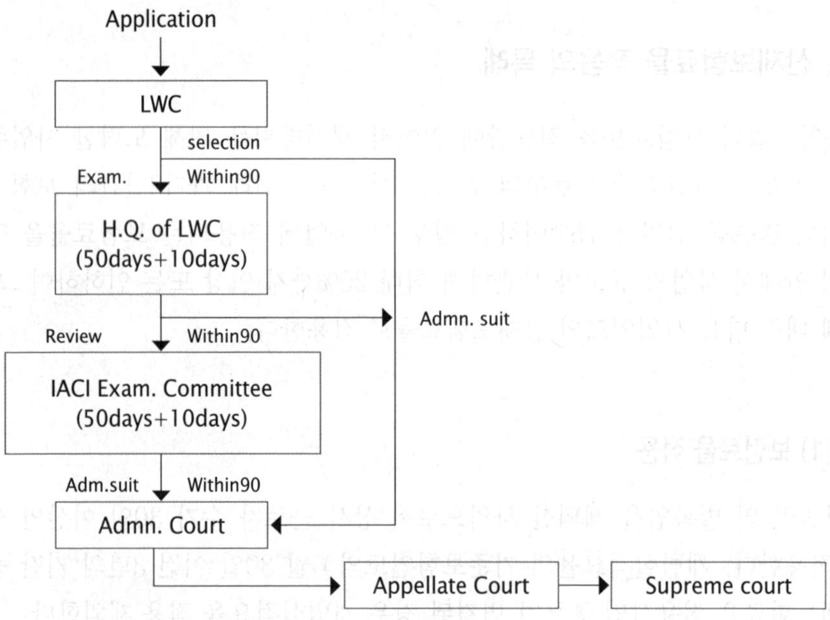

2. Labor Standards Act

If the employee concerned receives insurance benefits from the IACI, the employer may be excused from his/her responsibilities to the Labor Standards Act. With the exception of such accidents requiring less than a 4-day treatment at a hospital not covered by the IACI, the employee shall not receive compensation according to the Labor Standards Act until the payment status for the insurance benefits is determined. An employer shall not dismiss any employee during the period of medical leave for an occupational injury or illness, nor 30 days thereafter.

However, if an employee who has received medical care benefits for the last three years, receives the injury-disease compensation annuity, the employer concerned may terminate his/her service upon the fourth year as prescribed in Article 84 of the Labor Standards Act(Article 80(4) of the IACI

서 부지급이 결정되면, 심사청구(근로복지공단 본사)나 재심사청구(산업재해보상보험심사위원회)를 거치지 않고 곧바로 행정법원에 행정소송을 제기할 수 있다(택일). 심사청구, 재심사청구는 신속하고 소송 경제적인 반면 취소율이 높고, 행정소송은 승소율은 높으나 시간과 비용이 많이 든다.

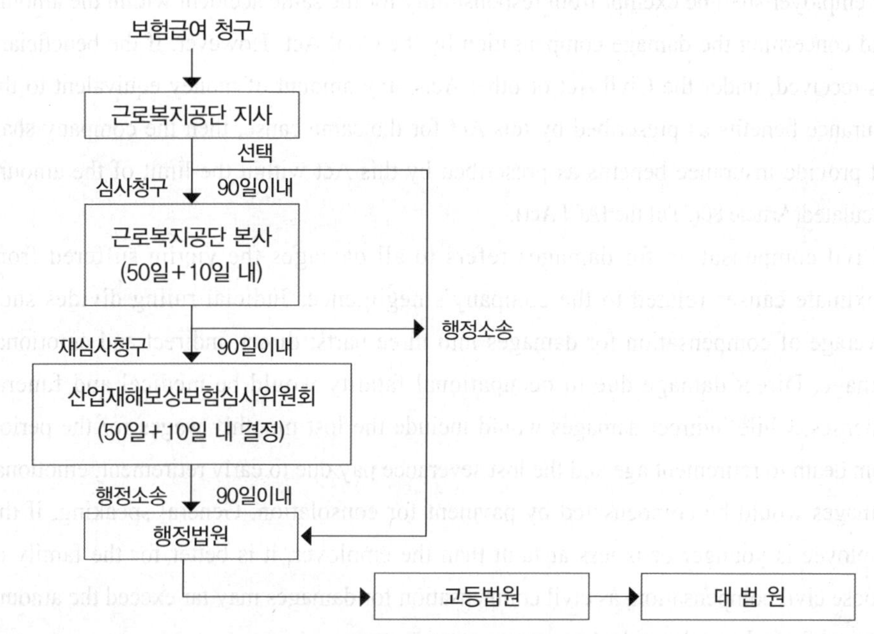

2. 근로기준법과의 관계

재해근로자가 산업재해보상보험으로 보험급여를 받을 수 있는 경우에는 근로기준법상 면책이 된다. 따라서 산업재해보상 보험법에 의해 산업재해 보험급여가 지급되지 않는 '4일 미만의 요양을 요하는 재해'를 제외하고는, 보험급여 미지급이 확정되기 전까지는 사용자에게 직접 근로기준법에 의한 재해보상책임을 물을 수 없다. 업무상 재해로 인하여 근로자가 요양 중인 경우 회사는 요양기간과 그 후 30일간 근로관계를 일방적으로 단절시킬 수 없다.

그러나 요양급여를 받는 근로자가 요양을 개시한 후 3년이 경과한 날 이후에 상병보상 연금을 지급받고 있는 경우에는 3년이 경과한 날 이후에 근로기준법

Act). In this case, the period of treatment of 3 years shall be calculated into the severance pay.

3. Damage compensation according to the Civil Act

If a beneficiary has received benefits under the Labor Standards Act or the IACI Act, the employer shall be exempt from responsibility for the same accident within the amount paid concerning the damage compensation by the Civil Act. However, if the beneficiary has received, under the Civil Act or other Acts, any amount of money equivalent to the insurance benefits as prescribed by this Act for the same cause, then the company shall not provide insurance benefits as prescribed by this Act within the limit of the amount calculated(Article 80(3) of the IACI Act).

Civil compensation for damages refers to all damages the victim suffered from proximate causes related to the company's negligence. Judicial ruling divides such coverage of compensation for damages into three parts: direct, indirect and emotional damage. Direct damage due to occupational fatality would be medical and funeral expenses, while indirect damages would include the lost monthly wages for the period from death to retirement age and the lost severance pay due to early retirement; emotional damages would be compensated by payment for consolation. General speaking, if the employee is younger or is less at fault than the employer, it is better for the family to choose civil compensation, as civil compensation for damages may far exceed the amount claimed for industrial accident insurance compensation.

<Relation with Other Compensations>

	Civil Laws	Labor Standards Act	Industrial Accident Compensation Insurance Act
Object	Damage compensation for illegal actions or default on fulfillment	Industrial accident compensation	Industrial accident compensation
Principle	Duty for fault	Employer's duty for non-fault	Employer's duty for non-fault
Typeof benefits	Direct compensation	Direct compensation	Social security type (indirect compensation)
Requir-ement	Illegal actions or default on fulfillment	Employee's work related injury, disease, physical handicap, death	Employee's work-related injury, disease, physical handicap, death

제84조에 규정한 일시보상을 지급한 것으로 간주하기 때문에 해고할 수 있다(산재법 제80조 제4항). 이때 퇴직금을 산정하기 위한 근속기간은 요양 개시 후 3년이 경과한 날까지 포함해야 한다.

3. 민법상 손해배상

재해근로자가 근로기준법 또는 산업재해보상보험법상 보상을 받는 경우, 사용자는 근로자에 대한 민사상 손해배상과 관련하여 동일한 사유의 손해에 대해 지급한 보험급여 금액의 한도 내에서 책임을 면한다. 반면에 재해근로자가 동일한 사유로 민법, 기타 법령에 의해 재해보상에 상당한 금품을 받은 경우에는 그 가액의 한도 내에서 산업재해보상 보험의 보험급여는 받지 못한다(산재법 제80조 제3항).

민사상 손해배상의 범위는 회사의 과실과 상당인과관계에 있는 재해자의 모든 손해를 말하며, 판례에서 인정하는 손해배상의 범위는 적극적 손해, 소극적 손해, 정신적 손해로 구분하고 있다. 일반적으로 근로자가 사망한 경우, 그 범위는 소극적 손해로 일실수입(사망한 시점에서 퇴직시점까지의 잃게 된 수입금)과 일실퇴직금(조기퇴직으로 인해 발생하는 퇴직금 손해액), 적극적 손해로서 장의비, 그리고 정신적 손해로서 위자료로 구성되고 있다. 통상 재해사고를 입은 근로자의 나이가 적거나 본인 과실이 적은 경우에는 민사상 손해배상액이 산재보상금액을 훨씬 초과하여 발생한다.

〈산재보상과 다른 보상의 관계〉

	민 법	근로기준법	산업재해보상보험법
대 상	불법행위 또는 채무불이행 손해배상	산업재해보상	산업재해보상
원 칙	과실책임주의	사용자의 무과실책임주의	사용자의 무과실책임주의
보상 방식	직접보상방식	직접보상방식	사회보험방식(간접보상방식)
요 건	불법행위 또는 채무불이행	근로자의 업무상의 부상·질병·신체장해·사망	근로자의 업무상의 부상·질병·신체장해·사망

	Civil Laws	Labor Standards Act	Industrial Accident Compensation Insurance Act
Remedy Contents	Damage compensation	Fixed rate compensation Typical compensation (lump sum payment): five types ① Medical treatment ② Compensation for suspension of work (60% of average wage) ③ Compensation for the handicapped (Maximum 1st grade: 1, 340days; Minimum 14th grade: 50 days) ④ Compensation for survivors (1,000 days) ⑤ Funeral expenses(90days) ※ Lump sum compensation(1,340 days)	Fixed rate compensation Typical compensation: six types ① Medical treatment ② Benefits for suspension of work(70% of average wage) ③ Benefits for the handicapped (Maximum 1st grade: 1,474days; Minimum 14th grade: 55 days) - Injury/illnesscompensation annuity or lump sum payment(1~14th grade) - Special disability benefits(1st~3rd grade) Treatment of 3 days or less is not covered. ④ Survivors' benefits(1,300 days) - Survivors' compensation annuity - Special survivors' benefits ⑤ Funeral expenses(120 days) ⑥ Injury/disease compensation annuity (1st~3rd grade) ⑦ Vocational rehabilitation benefit
Benefits relations		※ Compensation is available while under employment. Medical treatment and compensation for suspension of work can be terminated by a lump sum compensation after two years.	※ Benefits are available after the termination of employment. Medical treatment is available until full recovery. Continued treatment after two years is available through injury/illness compensation annuity. It is considered as lump sump benefits if the workers receives injury/illness compensation annuity after 3 years.
Respon-sibility	Individual responsibility	Individual responsibility (employerthe injured employee)	Social responsibility(nation-the injured employee)
Remedy process	Judicial court	Minister of Labor's reappraisal and arbitration → Labor Relations Commission's reappraisal and arbitration	First examination of Labor Welfare Corp. Review of the IACI Examination Committee

4. Industrial accident compensation and claims for criminal damage compensation

If there exists a direct offender and victim relationship in an occupational fatality, the surviving family can seek compensation for criminal behavior against the individual offender.

	민 법	근로기준법	산업재해보상보험법
구제 내용	손해배상	정률보상방식 정형화된 보상(일시금): 5가지 ① 요양보상 ② 휴업보상(평균임금 60%) ③ 장해보상(최대 1급: 1,340일분 최소 14급:50일분) ④ 유족보상(1,000일분) ⑤ 장례비(90일분) ※ 일시보상(1,340일분)	정률보상방식 정형화된 보상: 8가지 ① 요양급여 ② 휴업급여(평균임금 70%) ③ 장해급여(최대 1급: 1,474일분, 최소 14급: 55일분) – 장해보상연금(일시금과 택일) 1~14등급 – 장해특별급여(1~3등급)단, 3일 이내에 치유되는 경우 요양·휴업급여 배제 ④ 유족급여(1,300일분) – 유족보상연금 – 유족특별급여⑤ 장례비 (120일분) ⑥ 상병보상연금 (1급~3급) ⑦ 직업재활급여
보상 관계		※ 근로관계 유지시만 보상. 요양보상, 휴업보상은 2년 후 일시보상으로 보상관계 종료 가능	※ 근로관계 종료 후에도 계속 요양급여는 완치 시까지 계속 2年후 계속요양은 상병보상연금지급. 요양 3년 후 상병보상연금 받고 있으면 일시보상으로 간주
책임 귀속	개별책임	개별책임 (사용자 – 피재근로자)	사회책임 (국가 – 피재근로자)
권리 구제 절차	법 원	고용노동부장관 심사·중재 → 지방노동위원회 심사·중재	근로복지공단의 1차 심사 산업재해보상보험심사위원회의 재심사

4. 산재보상과 형사상 책임

산재 사망사고에 대해 직접적 가해자와 피해자 관계가 발생한다면 피해자의 유족이 가해자 개인을 상대로 과실치사로 형사고소가 가능하다. 중대재해 발생 사업장에 대해 「산업안전보건법」에 따른 산업안전 준수여부에 대해 근로감독관

The company may be the target of an intensive audit by the labor inspector for compliance with occupational safety rules according to the Occupational Safety and Health Act, if the workplace had a serious industrial accident. If, during this audit, the company is found to have violated any of the safety rules, it would have criminal charges filed against it.

> **Article 167 (Penal Provisions) of the Occupational Safety and Health Act: A person who has caused the death of a worker in violation of Article 38 (Safety Measures)** (1) through (3), or Article 24 (Health Measures) (1) shall be punished by imprisonment for not more than seven years or a fine not exceeding 100 million won.

5. National pension

Even if an employee is compensated for an industrial accident through the Industrial Accident Compensation Insurance or the Labor Standards Act, he/she can also demand a survivors' pension or disability pension. If the beneficiary for the survivors' pension or disability pension, according to the Article 113 of the National Pension Act, has already received payment under other laws, then only 50% of the survivor's pension(Article 68) and disability pension(Article 74) shall be granted.

6. Automobile insurance

If an employee is injured in a traffic accident while working, he/she can receive compensation from either Industrial Accident Compensation Insurance or the automobile insurance. Accordingly, the employee can select the more favorable insurance after considering the cause of the accident. Generally, if the employee is elderly or holds the greater fault, it is better to choose Industrial Accident Compensation Insurance, given that automobile insurance deducts payment according to the degree of fault.

7. Other insurances

Other insurance benefits such as survivors' pension, unemployment benefits, etc. from life insurance, damage insurance, fire insurance, or mutual aid insurance are remunerations for the deposits paid in advance. Given that additional benefits are provided for other reasons by a separate contract, benefits from the Industrial Accident Compensation Insurance Act shall not be deducted.

점검을 받게 되고, 여기서 산업안전 준수사항에 대해 위반여부가 있는 경우에 사업주는 형사처벌을 받게 된다.

산업안전보건법 제167조【벌칙】제38조【안전조치】 제1항부터 제3항까지 또는 제24조(보건조치) 제1항을 위반하여 근로자를 사망에 이르게 한 자는 7년 이하의 징역 또는 1억원 이하의 벌금에 처한다.

5. 국민연금

업무상 재해로 인하여 산재보상 또는 근로기준법에 의한 보상을 받았더라도 국민연금공단에 국민연금법에 의한 장해연금 또는 유족연금을 청구할 수 있다. 국민연금법 제63조에 의거하여 장해연금 또는 유족연금의 수급권자가 동일한 사유로 다른 법률의 규정에 의해 급여를 받는 경우, 국민연금법 제68조에 의한 장해연금액 또는 제74조에 의한 유족연금액은 2분의 1에 해당하는 금액을 지급한다.

6. 일반 자동차보험

업무수행 중 교통사고로 인해 부상을 입은 경우에 근로자는 산업재해보상보험법 또는 자동차보험으로 보상받을 수 있다. 따라서 재해발생 경위를 고려하여 근로자의 자유의사에 따라 보상받을 보험의 종류를 선택하도록 한다. 일반적으로 재해사고를 입은 근로자의 나이가 많거나 본인 과실이 큰 경우에는 자동차보험은 과실상계를 하므로 산업재해보상 보험을 청구하는 것이 좋다.

7. 일반 보험

피해를 입은 근로자가 가입한 생명보험, 손해보험, 화재보험, 공제조합법에 의한 유족연금, 실업보험금 등의 급여는 이미 불입한 보험료에 대한 대가의 성질을 가지며, 이익이 보험계약이라는 별도의 원인에서 생기는 것이기 때문에 산업재해보상 보험법에 의한 보상을 해도 이를 공제하지 않는다.

Section 3: National Pension Plan

Ⅰ. Nation Pension System

The National Pension Scheme is a system that pays old-age pensions to citizens who reach a certain age, or pays the pension to the citizen's family if the pensioner is disabled or dies(Article 1 of the National Pension Act, or NPA). The National Pension Scheme was enacted on January 1, 1988, when the NPA came into effect. Initially, it applied only to workplaces hiring 10 or more workers, but then gradually expanded to every company(Article 6). However, civil servants, soldiers, and private school workers subject to the Civil Service Pension Act, the Military Pension Act, and the Private School Pension Act, respectively, are excluded from membership. The National Pension Plan is divided into workplace subscribers and regional subscribers, and it is mandatory for workplaces that use one or more workers at all times to be subscribed. Excluded from workplace subscribers are the self-employed who do not employ workers, daily workers employed for less than one month, non-employed workers, or part-time workers who work less than 60 hours a month. Premiums are in proportion to income, with 50% borne by the worker and 50% by the employer.[24)] The types of benefits under the NPA include old-age pension, survivor's pension, disability pension, and lump-sum refund.[25)]

Ⅱ. Application of National Pension and Premiums

1. Scope of application

All persons residing in the country who are between the ages 18 and 60 are eligible for national pension. However, civil servants, soldiers, employees of private schools, or other

24) As of 2025, the National Pension premium is charged 9% of standard monthly income, which is each distributed to 4.5% respectively to the employer and the worker.

25) National Pension Service, "A Practical Guide to National Pension Workplaces 2024," 2024, pp. 32-36.

제3절 국민연금

Ⅰ. 국민연금제도의 의의

국민연금제도는 국민이 납부한 연금재원을 가지고, 해당 국민이 일정한 연령에 이르렀을 때 노령연금을 지급하거나, 연금가입자가 장애나 사망한 경우 그 가족의 생계를 위해 연금을 지급하는 제도이다(국연법 제1조). 국민연금은 1988년 1월 1일 국민연금법 시행으로 시행되어 초기에는 10인 이상 사업장만 적용하다가 그 후 점차적으로 확대하여 국내에 거주하는 18세 이상 60세 미만의 국민은 국민연금의 가입대상이 된다(동법 제6조). 다만, 공무원연금법, 군인연금법 및 사립학교연금법의 적용을 받는 공무원·군인 및 사립학교 직원은 가입대상에서 제외된다. 국민연금 가입대상자는 사업장가입자와 지역가입자로 구분되는데, 상시 1인 이상의 근로자를 사용하는 사업장은 당연적용사업장이 된다. 사업장 가입자에서 적용제외 되는 자는 근로자를 채용하지 않은 자영업자, 1월 미만의 기간 동안 고용되는 일용근로자, 비상근근로자 또는 1개월간의 소정근로시간이 60시간 미만인 시간제 근로자 등이다. 연금보험료는 소득에 비례하여 근로자와 사용자가 각각 50%씩 부담한다.[24] 국민연금법에 따른 급여의 종류는 노령연금, 유족연금, 장애연금, 반환일시금이 있다.[25]

Ⅱ. 국민연금 대상 및 보험료

1. 가입대상

국내에 거주하는 18세 이상 60세 미만의 국민은 국민연금의 가입대상이 된

24) 2025년 기준보험료는 기준소득 월액의 9%로 사용자가 4.5%와 근로자가 4.5% 각각 부담한다.
25) 국민연금, "2024년 알기 쉬운 국민연금 사업장 실무안내", 2024, 32~36면.

employees described in the Presidential Decree are ineligible for the pension, under the Civil Servants' Pension Act, the Veteran's Pension Act, or the Private School Teachers Pension Act.

The scope of application is divided between the company and individual. For companies ordinarily hiring one or more workers, application for national pension is mandatory.

2. Premium rate

The National Health Insurance Corporation collects from each company a total premium of 9% each month as private and company burden, collecting 4.5% of the standard wage from the employee and the employer each.

Ⅲ. Benefits of the National Pension

National pension benefits are calculated in respect to basic pension and additional pension, and rendered by the National Pension Corporation at the request of the beneficiary.

Kinds		Requirements	Benefits
Old age pen-sion	Old age pension	Insured for 10 years or more and aged 60(If the employee did not have any income until 65 years old.)	· Basic pension+pension for dependents (5% annual increase per year after paying into it for 20years)
	Incumbent old age pension	In case the recipient of the old age pension was engaged in earning income before 65 years of age (Between ages 60 – 65)	· 50% of the basic pension + 10% added gradually per year): 50% for 60 years; 60% for 61 years; 70% for 62 years, 80% for 63 years; 90% for 64 years)
	Early old age pension	Insured for 10 years or more, and expecting to claim pension between ages 55 – 60	· 70% of basic pension + 6% added per year) : 70% at 55 years; 76% at 56 years; 82% at 57 years; 88% at 58 years; 94% at 59 years)
	Partition pension	Married for 5 years or more during the insured period	· Spouse's old age pension (excluding additional pension), 1/12 of pension divided by the period of marriage
Disability pension		Insured for more than one year, illness or accidents(if the treatment is not completed within two years, on the day exceeding 1.5 years, the degree of disability will be decided)	· 100% of basic pension (for 1st grade; 80% for 2nd grade; 60% for 3rd grade)+additional pension · 225% compensation in lump sum for 4th grade

다. 다만, 공무원연금법, 군인연금법 및 사립학교교원연금법의 적용을 받는 공무원·군인 및 사립학교 직원 기타 대통령령이 정하는 자는 제외된다.

국민연금 가입 대상자는 사업장가입자와 지역가입으로 구분되는데 사업장과 관련하여서는 상시 1인 이상의 근로자를 사용하는 사업장은 당연적용 사업장이 된다.

2. 연금보험료의 부담

사업장 가입의 경우 기금부담은 가입자 및 사용자로부터의 매월 개인기여금, 연금보험료로서 각각 표준소득월액의 1,000분의 45씩, 전체로는 1,000분의 90에 해당하는 금액이 되며 국민건강보험공단에서 일괄적으로 매월 징수한다.

Ⅲ. 국민연금의 지급

연금액은 그 지급사유에 따라 기본연금액과 가급연금액을 기초로 하여 산정하며 수급권자의 청구에 의해 국민연금관리공단이 지급한다.

종류		요건	급여액
노령연금	노령연금	가입기간 10년 이상, 60세에 달한 자(65세 이전까지는 소득이 없는 경우에 한함)	• 기본연금액 + 부양가족연금액(20년 초과 1년당 기본연금액 5%증액)
	재직자 노령연금	노령연금수급권자가 65세 이전에 소득이 있는 업무에 종사하는 경우(60~65세)	• 기본연금액의 50% + 매년 10%: 60세 50%, 61세 60%, 62세 70%, 63세 80%, 64세 90%
	조기노령 연금	10년 이상 가입, 55세 이상 자가 60세 전에 연금수급을 원할 때	• 기본연금액의 70% + 매년 6%: 55세 70%, 56세 76%, 57세 82%, 58세 88%, 59세 94%.
	분할연금	가입기간 중 혼인 기간이 5년 이상인 자	• 배우자의 노령연금액 중 혼인기간에 해당하는 연금액을 1/2 금액
장애연금		1년 이상 가입자로서 질병 · 사고(1년 6개월 이상 경과하여도 완치되지 않으면 1년 6개월이 경과되는 날을 기준으로 장해정도 결정)	• 기본연금액 100%(1급 기준,2급은 80%, 3급은 60%) + 가급연금액 • 4급은 기본연금액의 225% 일시 보상

Kinds	Requirements	Benefits
Survivors' pension	Beneficiary for old age pension; more than 10 years insured; among the insured (insured for less than 10 years, but died of illness, etc. during the insured period) death of a recipient to 2nd degree of disability	· 60% of basic pension (for more than 20 years insured, 50% for 10~20 years, 40% for less than 10 years)+additional pension
Return lump sum	Insured less than 10 years by the age of 60; death during the insured period of a worker with insurance history; loss of nationality or immigration; when subject to the Civil Service Act, etc.	· Pension premium+interest rate (based on holding for 3years before payout) + additional amount from the payment day (interest rate based on holding for one year before payout)

[Expected National Pension Benefits (old age pension)]

Standard monthly income	Pension premium(9%)	Monthly expected benefits (by insured period)			
		15 years	20 years	30 years	40 years
1,210,000	108,900	262,610	343,980	506,720	669,460
2,190,000	197,100	341,690	447,560	659,290	871,030
2,280,000	205,200	348,950	457,070	673,310	889,540
3,600,000	324,000	455,460	596,580	878,810	1,161,050

(Data : National Pension Service Nov 2008; Currency: Won(₩))

Ⅳ. Eligible Age Extended for Old Age Pension

The eligible age to receive old age pension is currently 60(55 for early old age pension). However, the age of eligibility will is being extended every five years between 2013 and 2033. This is designed to maintain financial stability of the pension scheme as Korean society ages.

[Age of Eligibility for Old Age Pension]

Year of birth	Old age pension	Year of birth	Early Old age pension
Up to 1952	60 years old	Up to 1957	55 years old
1953-56	61 years old	1958-61	56 years old
1957-60	62 years old	1962-65	57 years old
1961-64	63 years old	1966-69	58 years old
1965-68	64 years old	1970-73	59 years old
1969~	65 years old	1974~	60 years old

종 류	요 건	급 여 액
유족연금	노령연금 수급권자, 가입기간이 10년 이상인 가입자였던 자, 가입중인 자(10년 미만자는 가입 중 발생할 질병 등으로 사망한 자) 장해등급이 2급 이상의 장해연금 수급권자 등의 사망	• 기본연금액 60%(가입기간20년 이상 기준, 10~20년은 50%, 10년 미만은 40%) + 가급연금액
반환일시금	10년 미만 가입자로 60세 도달 시, 가입중인 자 또는 가입하였던 자 사망, 국적상실 · 국외이주, 공무원법 등의 적용을 받게 된 때	• 연금보험료+가입기간 동안의 이자(3년만기 정기예금 기준)+지급사유 발생일까지의 가산금(1년만기 정기예금 기준)

〈국민(노령)연금 예상 연금액〉

표준 월 소득액	연금 보험료 (9%)	월 예상 연금액 (가입기간기준)			
		15년	20년	30년	40년
1,210,000	108,900	262,610	343,980	506,720	669,460
2,190,000	197,100	341,690	447,560	659,290	871,030
2,280,000	205,200	348,950	457,070	673,310	889,540
3,600,000	324,000	455,460	596,580	878,810	1,161,050

(자료: 국민연금관리공단, 2016.1)

Ⅳ. 노령연금 수급개시 연령 연장

노령연금을 받을 수 있는 연령은 현재 60세(조기노령연금은 55세)이나 2013년부터 5년마다 단계적으로 1세씩 연장하여 2033년 이후에는 65세(조기노령연금은 60세)가 된다. 평균수명이 연장되고 노령화가 지속적으로 심화되는 사회에서 연금재정의 건전화를 위한 것이다.

〈노령연금 등 생년별 수급개시 연령〉

출생연수	노령연금	출생연수	조기노령연금
~1952년생	60세 부터	~1957년생	55세부터
1953~1956년생	61세 부터	1958~1961년생	56세부터
1957~1960년생	62세 부터	1962~1965년생	57세부터
1961~1964년생	63세 부터	1966~1969년생	58세부터
1965~1968년생	64세 부터	1970~1973년생	59세부터
1969년생~	65세 부터	1974년생~	60세부터

Section 4: National Health Insurance

Ⅰ. Concept

1. Purpose

National Health Insurance aims to improve public health and social security by providing insurance benefits for the prevention, diagnosis, treatment, and rehabilitation of injured and ill people, as well as assist with costs of childbirth and death, and promote health(Article 1 of the National Health Insurance Act, or NHIA). National Health Insurance is a compulsory insurance that is divided into workplace and regional insurers. Currently, it covers about 97% of all citizens, with other medical services covered under the Medical Benefits Act, which is a form of public assistance for beneficiaries of the Basic Livelihood Subsidy.[26)] The self-employed who do not employ workers, daily workers employed for less than one month, and part-time workers who work less than 60 hours a month are not required to subscribe.[27)]

2. Scope of application for working places

The National Health Insurance Plan is applicable to workers at all companies.

3. Workers excluded from corporate insurance coverage

- Daily workers who are hired for less than one month
- Workers or employees working at seasonal or temporary work places
- Irregular workers or part-timers(whose working hours are less than 60 hours per month) who do not attend the work place regularly.

---

26) Roh, Ho-chang et al, Social Security of Foreigners, Immigration Law, p. 468.

27) National Health Insurance, National Health Insurance Operational Guide in 2024, pp. 33-36.

제4절 국민건강보험

Ⅰ. 건강보험의 의의

1. 목 적

국민건강보험은 국민의 질병이나 부상에 대한 예방, 진단, 치료, 재활과 출산, 사망 그리고 건강증진에 대하여 보험급여를 실시함으로써 국민보건을 향상시키고 사회보장을 증진하기 위함을 목적으로 한다(건보법 제1조). 국민건강보험은 직장가입자와 지역가입자로 구분되는 의무보험으로, 현재 전체국민의 약 97%가 국민건강보험에 적용되고, 그 외에는 기초생활보장수급자 등에 속하는 공공부조에 해당하는 의료급여법에 의하여 의료서비스를 제공받고 있다.[26] 직장가입자에서 제외되는 자는 근로자를 채용하지 않은 자영업자, 1월 미만 기간 동안 고용되는 일용근로자, 비상근 근로자 또는 1개월간의 소정근로시간이 60시간 미만인 시간제 근로자 등이다.[27]

2. 사업장의 적용범위

모든 사업장에 적용된다.

3. 직장가입자에서 제외되는 자 (지역 가입자에 해당)

- 1월 미만의 기간 동안 고용되는 일용근로자
- 소재지가 일정하지 아니한 사업장 또는 계절적·임시적 사업장의 근로자 및 사용자
- 비상근 또는 시간제근로자(월 근로시간이 60시간 미만인 자) 등 사업장에서 상시근로에 종사할 목적으로 사용된 자가 아닌 자

26) 노호창외, “외국인의 사회보장”, 「이민법」, 468면.
27) 국민건강보험, “2024 사업장 업무편람”, 33~36면.

4. Employer's major duties

① Application report of workplace

Within 14 days after it becomes mandatory for the company to apply

② Report any changes at the workplace

When there is a change in the employer, category of business, name, location, telephone number, etc.

③ Acquisition(change) and loss report of the insured or his/her dependents

④ Retrieval and return of health insurance card when no longer eligible(retirement or severance)

⑤ Report wages and change of standard monthly wage for the insured

- Report total wages paid last year by the end of February each year
- Report total wages of an employee with whom the employment relationship has ended
- Report any changes in the standard monthly wage

⑥ Deduction and payment of the premium

- Premiums are deducted from the wages of the insured
- Payment on the 10th of the following month for the present month

⑦ Measures necessary to check health for the insured and his/her dependents, and report the medical analysis results from the health examination center

⑧ Keep documents concerning health insurance for 3 years for each employee; health checkup reports for 5 years

Ⅱ. Insurance Premiums

1. Premium rate

The insurance premiums for subscribing workers are an amount calculated by multiplying the standard monthly salary by the premium rate, with 50% of the premiums borne by workers and 50% by employers(Article 69). Therefore, the premiums are paid

4. 적용사업장 사용자의 주요업무

① 사업장 적용 신고
당해 사업장이 건강보험 당연 가입대상이 된 때로부터 14일 이내

② 사업장 변경사항의 신고
사용자, 사업종류, 명칭, 소재지, 전화번호 등 변경이 있을 때

③ 가입자 및 피부양자의 자격취득(변동), 상실 신고

④ 가입자 자격상실자(퇴직, 퇴사자)에 대한 건강보험증 회수 및 반납

⑤ 가입자 보수의 신고 및 표준보수월액 변경 신고
- 매년 2월 말까지 전년도 지급한 보수의 총액 등 신고
- 퇴직·퇴사한 자 등에 대하여 지급한 보수총액 신고
- 보수가 인상·인하되었을 때 표준보수월액의 변경 신고

⑥ 보험료의 공제 및 납부
- 가입자가 부담하여야 하는 그달의 보험료액을 그 보수에서 공제
- 해당 월의 보험료를 그 다음 달 10일까지 납부

⑦ 가입자·피부양자가 건강검진을 받을 수 있도록 필요한 조치와 공단 또는 검진기관으로부터 통보받은 건강검진 결과를 가입자에게 통보

⑧ 건강보험에 관련 서류의 보존은 작성된 날로부터 3년, 건강검진에 관한 서류는 5년

Ⅱ. 건강보험료

1. 보험료

직장가입자의 보험료는 표준보수월액에 보험료율을 곱한 금액이 되며, 여기서 산출된 금액에 근로자와 사용자가 각각 50%씩 부담한다(건보법 제69조). 따

according to the individual's standard monthly salary.[28] The standard monthly wage refers to the total monthly wage that the insured receives at the workplace each month. Monthly wage is graded within a range of a given amount, and the standard amount of each grade is then used to calculate the premium by multiplying the premium rate.

2. Premium calculation

The standard monthly wage of the current year calculated based upon the previous year's premium adjustment serves as the basic data for the premium charge. Thus, the actual standard monthly wage of the current year must be calculated after the end of the fiscal year to determine the premium for the next year.

Ⅲ. Insurance Benefits

1. Medical treatment benefits

Medical treatment benefits include prevention, diagnosis, treatment and rehabilitation for the insured and his/her dependents, childbirth, and death, and direct medical service(material or cash benefits) for health examinations.

2. Medical treatment expenses

(1) Childbirth expenses

If the insured(or dependent) gives birth at a place other than a medical institute(in cases of stillbirth, 16-week pregnancy), an estimated amount of medical expenses shall be paid.

28) National health insurance premiums as of 2025 are 7.09% of monthly income, with the employer and employee each paying 3.545%. Long-term care insurance (total 12.95%) is covered by an additional 6.475% of the national health insurance premiums, paid by both employer and worker.

라서 개인의 표준보수월액에 따라 차등 납부가 된다.[28] 표준보수월액이란 직장가입자가 당해사업장에서 받은 매월의 보수총액을 보수월액이라 하는데, 보험료를 산정할 때는 보수월액을 그대로 적용하는 것이 아니라 보수월액의 일정액별로 등급을 매기고 각 등급별로 표준이 되는 금액을 정하여 이를 보험료율과 곱하여 보험료를 산정한다.

2. 보험료의 정산

보험료 부과의 기초가 되는 당해 연도 표준보수월액은 사실상 전년도 보험료 정산 결과에 따라 산출된 것이므로 당해 연도 표준보수월액은 결국 회계연도가 종료되어야 알 수 있기 때문에 반드시 정산이 필요하다.

Ⅲ. 보험급여

1. 요양급여

가입자 및 피부양자의 질병·부상에 대한 예방·진단·치료·재활과 출산·사망 및 건강검진에 대하여 직접 의료서비스(현물·현금급여)를 받는 것을 말한다.

2. 요양비

(1) 출산비

가입자(피부양자)가 요양기관 이외의 장소에서 출산(사산의 경우에는 임신 16주 이상)을 한 경우 요양급여에 상당하는 금액을 지급한다.

28) 국민건강보험료는 2025년 기준 7.09%로 사용자 3.545%와 근로자 3.545%를 납부한다. 여기에 추가되는 노인장기요양보험료는 사용자와 근로자가 각자의 보험건강보험료율에 각각 6.475%를 곱한 금액 (총 12.95%)을 납부한다.

(2) Medical expenses

If the insured(or dependent) is unable to use a certified medical center and instead uses a facility under operational suspension or an unverified medical institute, an estimated amount of the medical expenses shall be paid regardless.

3. Health examination

At least one health examination every two years shall be given to diagnose disease at its premature stage(for non-office workers, once a year).

4. Support with private charges

If the insured(or dependent) pays more than 2 million won per 6 month-period for medical treatment at a medical center, the corporation shall bear the exceeded amount, to help reduce the personal financial burden of the heavy medical expenses.

5. Assistive devices for the handicapped

If the insured(or dependent) who is registered as a disabled person under Article 32 of the Disabled Welfare Act and purchases an assistive device, then a partial reimbursement of the purchase shall be provided. If the price is under the criteria amount for the help-aid device, 80% of the actual expenses(including VAT) shall be reimbursed.

6. Refund of individual burden

If the insured(or dependent) receives treatment and pays over the amount of his/her legal individual burden, the exceeded amount shall be reimbursed.

(2) 요양비

가입자(피부양자)가 긴급 기타 부득이한 사유로 인하여 요양기관을 이용할 수 없어 업무정지처분 기간 중인 요양기관이나 요양기관에서 제외되는 의료기관에서 요양을 받은 경우, 그 요양급여에 상당하는 금액을 지급한다.

3. 건강검진

가입자 및 피부양자에 대한 질병의 조기발견을 위해 2년마다 1회 이상 건강검진을 실시한다(사무직 종사자가 아닌 가입자는 1년에 1회 실시).

4. 본인부담액 보상금

진료비 지출로 인한 가계의 재정부담을 경감시켜 주기 위해 건강보험 가입자(피부양자 포함)가 요양기관에서 요양급여를 받고 납부한 본인 부담액이 6월간 200만원을 초과한 경우에 지급하되 그 초과한 금액을 공단이 부담한다.

5. 장애인 보장구 급여비

장애인복지법 제32조에 의하여 등록한 장애인인 가입자 및 피부양자가 장애인 보장구를 구입한 경우 구입금액의 일부를 현금급여비로 지급한다. 보장구 구입금액(부가가치세 포함)이 보장구 유형별 기준액 이내의 경우에는 실구입가(부가가치세 포함)의 80%에 해당하는 금액을 지급한다.

6. 본인부담금 환급금

건강보험 가입자 및 피부양자가 진료를 받고 납부한 본인 부담금이 법정본인부담금보다 과다하게 납부되었을 경우 과다 납부한 금액을 되돌려 주는 제도이다.

Ⅳ. Long-term Care Insurance

1. Concept

Long-term care insurance is a social insurance system separate from National Health Insurance. It was introduced in July 2008 due to aging of the population and the necessity to care for the elderly. It provides essential care services such as face washing, bathing, meals, assistance with using the toilet, and nursing care for elderly persons unable to move alone due to age-related diseases such as dementia and stroke.[29)]

2. Categories of long-term care

- Category 1: Incapable of activities for daily living and getting in and out of bed; requires full assistance in all daily activities; those who show problem behavior almost every day with reduced judgment. Examples would be those who stay in bed almost all day, or who cannot eat without assistance.
- Category 2: Requires considerable assistance with basic activities such as eating and dressing; those who frequently exhibit problematic behavior with reduced judgment. Examples would be those who can sit or move within their rooms without assistance.
- Category 3: Requires partial assistance for eating, dressing and bathing. Examples would be those who can move only short distance with a walker.

3. Contribution for Long-term Care Insurance

A contribution for long-term care insurance(12.95%) will be added to the premium for National Health Insurance.

Contribution for long-term care insurance = premium for National Health Insurance × Rate of contribution for long-term care insurance (12.95%).
(Employer and employee shall each pay half.)

29) Article 2 (Definition) of the Long-Term Care Insurance Act. 1. "Elderly people," etc. are those aged 65 years or older or those under 65 who have age-related diseases such as dementia or cerebrovascular disease. 2. Long-term care benefits means services such as assistance with physical activities, household support or care, or cash to pay for such assistance for those who are deemed to have been unable to carry out daily necessary activities on their own for the previous six months.

Ⅳ. 노인장기요양보험

1. 노인장기 요양보험의 의의

노인장기요양보험은 인구의 고령화와 노인요양의 필요성으로 인해 2008년 7월부터 국민건강보험에서 별도로 도입된 사회보험제도이다. 고령이나 치매·중풍 등의 노인성 질병으로 혼자서는 거동이 불편한 노인에게 세수, 목욕, 식사 배변처리, 간호 등 필요한 요양서비스를 제공하는 제도이다.[29)]

2. 장기요양등급

장기요양등급 1~3등급을 인정받아야 장기요양서비스를 받을 수 있다.

- 1등급: 혼자서는 거의 움직이지 못하거나 이상행동이 거의 매일 나타나는 상태(예: 하루에 대부분을 누워 지내며, 식사 등을 혼자 할 수 없는 분)
- 2등급: 일상생활의 기본 행동에 다른 사람의 상당한 도움이 필요하거나 이상행동이 자주 나타나는 상태(예: 혼자 앉을 수 있고 방 안에서 이동할 수 있는 분)
- 3등급: 일상생활의 기본 행동에 다른 사람의 부분적인 도움이 필요한 상태 (예: 보행기를 이용해서 가까운 거리를 어렵게 이동할 수 있는 분)

3. 장기요양보험료

건강보험료에 장기요양보험료율(12.95%)을 곱한 금액을 건강보험료와 함께 납부하면 된다.

장기요양보험료 = 건강보험료 × 12.95%

(직장가입자의 경우 가입자와 사용자가 각각 50%씩 부담)

---

29) 노인장기요양보험법 제2조【정의】1. "노인등"이란 65세 이상의 노인 또는 65세 미만의 자로서 치매, 뇌혈관성질환 등 노인성 질병을 가진 자를 말한다. 2. "장기요양급여"란 6개월 이상 동안 혼자서 일상생활을 수행하기 어렵다고 인정되는 자에게 신체활동, 가사활동의 지원 또는 간병 등의 서비스나 이에 갈음하여 지급하는 현금 등을 말한다.

<Summary of statutory social insurances (2021)>

		Employment insurance	Industrial accident compensation insurance	National pension	Health insurance
Employees covered		Those below age 65	All employees	Employees aged 18 or older but younger than 60	All employees
Those excluded		Employers, foreigners	Employers	Employees who have worked less than 1 month	Employees who have worked less than 1 month
Coverage for foreigners		Employee's option	Shall be covered	In principle, they shall be covered, depending on their nationalty.	Shall be covered
Insurance contribution	Employee	Employment benefit: Total wage × 0.90%	None	Standard monthly income × 4.5%	Health insurance = Standard monthly income × 3.545% Long-term care insurance = Health insurance × 6.475%
	Employer	-Unemployment benefit: total wage × 0.90% - Employment security/Vocational ability development program: total wage x 0.25~0.85%	Total wage × 0.73~18.63% (varies depending on industrial sector)	Standard monthly income × 4.5%	Health insurance = Standard monthly income × 3.545% Long-term care insurance = Health insurance × 6.475%
Benefits guaranteed		Unemployment benefit/ employment security program/ vocational skills development program	Medical care, suspended work, disability, and survivor benefits, funeral expenses, injury/disease compensation annuity, nursing, vocational rehabilitation	Old-age pension, disability pension, survivor pension	Medical care, expenses, medical checkups, funeral expenses
Governing body		Ministry of Labor (Korea Labor Welfare Corporation, Job Center)		Ministry of Health and Welfare (National Pension Corporation)	Ministry of Health and Welfare(National Health Insurance Corporation)

〈4대 법정보험제도 (2021)〉

구 분		고용보험	산재보험	국민연금	건강보험
가입 대상		65세 미만자	모든 근로자	18세 이상 60세 미만자	모든 근로자
가입 제외		사업주, 외국인	사업주 (예외적 가입 가능)	1월 미만 근무자	1월 미만 근무자
외국인 가입 여부		가입을 희망할 경우에 가입 가능	가입대상	원칙적 가입대상 ※ 국가별 차등 적용	가입대상
보 험 료	근 로 자	실업급여: 임금총액×0.90%	없 음	표준보수월액×4.5%	건강보험 = 표준소득월액×3.545% 장기요양 = 건강보험×6.475%
	사 용 자	실업급여: 임금총액×0.90% 고용안정·직업능력개발 사업: 0.25~0.85% (사업규모별 차이)	임금총액× 0.73~18.63% (업종별 차이)	표준보수월액×4.5%	건강보험 = 표준소득월액×3.545% 장기요양 = 건강보험×6.475%
보장 내용		실업급여 고용안정· 직업능력개발사업	요양급여 휴업급여 장해급여 유족급여 장의비 상병보상연금 간병급여 직업재활급여	노령연금 장애연금 유족연금	요양비 건강검진 장제비
주관 (수행)		노동부 (고용지원센터, 근로복지공단)		보건복지부 (국민연금관리공단)	보건복지부 (건강보험공단)

Index

A

B

색 인

C

D

E

ㄴ

ㄷ

ㅅ

J

L

ㅇ

R

S

저자 약력 (Author's Career)

정 봉 수(鄭奉守)

Bongsoo Jung

Ph.D in Law (Labor Law) / Labor Attorney 법학박사 / 공인노무사
Immigration Attorney / Certified Translator 일반행정사 / 번역행정사

KangNam Labor Law Firm 강남노무법인
Tel. 02-539-0098
Website: www.k-labor.com,
Email: bongsoo@k-labor.com
Mobile App: Korean Labor Law (노동법)

About the Author

- Managing Attorney at KangNam Labor Law Firm	강남노무법인 대표노무사
- Committee Member in HR Services, Korean Agency for Technology & Standards	국가기술표준원 인적자원서비스 전문위원
- (Former) Outside Director of Korea Postal Logistics Agency	(전) 우체국물류지원단 사외이사
- (Former) Regular Advisor to Seoul Global Center (15 years)	(전) 서울글로벌센터 위촉 노무사
- (Former) Personnel Team Manager at Robert Bosch Korea	(전) 보쉬코리아 인사팀장
- Ph.D. in Law (Labor Law), Ajou University	아주대학교 법학박사 – 노동법
- M.A. in Labor Law, Korea University	고려대학교 노동대학원 법학석사
- AA. in Business, University of Maryland University College	미국 메릴랜드 대학교 대학 경영학과
- BA. in Law, Korea National Open University	한국방송통신대학교 법학과
- BA in Safety and Health, Korea National Open University	한국방송통신대학교 보건환경안전학과
- BA. In English, Hannam University	한남대학교 영문학과

Dr. Jung has Authored

500 Labor Cases	주제별 노동판례 500선 / 강남노무법인
Practical HR & Labor Management	인사노무실무 / 시간여행
Korean Labor Law: Disputes & Resolutions	노사문제 사례별 대응방안 / ㈜중앙경제
A Bilingual Code of Korean Labor Law	영한 노동법전 발행인 / ㈜중앙경제
Labor Law Practical Manuals Series:	**노동법 실무 매뉴얼 시리즈 / 강남노무법인**
(1) Work Force Restructuring	(1) 구조조정
(2) Foreign Employment and Immigration	(2) 외국인 고용과 비자
(3) Lawful Dismissal	(3) 해고
(4) Labor Union Manual	(4) 노동조합
(5) Wage Manual	(5) 임금
(6) Working Hours, Holidays and Leave	(6) 근로시간, 휴일, 휴가
(7) Irregular Employment and	(7) 비정규직과 근로자성 판단
(8) Employment Contract	(8) 근로계약
(9) Industrial Accident Compensation	(9) 산재보상
(10) Workplace & Sexual Harassment	(10) 괴롭힘과 성희롱 예방
(11) Labor Inspection	(11) 근로감독
(12) Rules of Employment	(12) 취업규칙
(13) Labor Auditing	(13) 노무감사